The Handbook of
Language Variation and Change

Blackwell Handbooks in Linguistics

This outstanding multi-volume series covers all the major subdisciplines within linguistics today and, when complete, will offer a comprehensive survey of linguistics as a whole.

Already published:

The Handbook of Child Language
Edited by PAUL FLETCHER and BRIAN MACWHINNEY

The Handbook of Phonological Theory
Edited by JOHN A. GOLDSMITH

The Handbook of Contemporary Semantic Theory
Edited by SHALOM LAPPIN

The Handbook of Sociolinguistics
Edited by FLORIAN COULMAS

The Handbook of Phonetic Sciences
Edited by WILLIAM J. HARDCASTLE and JOHN LAVER

The Handbook of Morphology
Edited by ANDREW SPENCER and ARNOLD ZWICKY

The Handbook of Japanese Linguistics
Edited by NATSUKO TSUJIMURA

The Handbook of Linguistics
Edited by MARK ARONOFF and JANIE REES-MILLER

The Handbook of Contemporary Syntactic Theory
Edited by MARK BALTIN and CHRIS COLLINS

The Handbook of Discourse Analysis
Edited by DEBORAH SCHIFFRIN, DEBORAH TANNEN, and HEIDI E. HAMILTON

The Handbook of Language Variation and Change
Edited by J. K. CHAMBERS, PETER TRUDGILL, and NATALIE SCHILLING-ESTES

The Handbook of Historical Linguistics
Edited by BRIAN D. JOSEPH and RICHARD D. JANDA

The Handbook of Language and Gender
Edited by JANET HOLMES and MIRIAM MEYERHOFF

The Handbook of Second Language Acquisition
Edited by CATHERINE DOUGHTY and MICHAEL H. LONG

The Handbook of Bilingualism
Edited by TEJ K. BHATIA and WILLIAM C. RITCHIE

The Handbook of Pragmatics
Edited by LAURENCE R. HORN and GREGORY WARD

The Handbook of Applied Linguistics
Edited by ALAN DAVIES and CATHERINE ELDER

The Handbook of Language Variation and Change

Edited by

J. K. Chambers,
Peter Trudgill,
and Natalie Schilling-Estes

© 2002, 2004 by Blackwell Publishing Ltd

BLACKWELL PUBLISHING
350 Main Street, Malden, MA 02148-5020, USA
9600 Garsington Road, Oxford OX4 2DQ, UK
550 Swanston Street, Carlton, Victoria 3053, Australia

First published 2002 by Blackwell Publishing Ltd
First published in paperback 2004

3   2006

Library of Congress Cataloging-in-Publication Data

The handbook of language variation and change / edited by J. K. Chambers, Peter Trudgill, and Natalie Schilling-Estes.
    p. cm. — (Blackwell handbooks in linguistics)
  Includes bibliographical references and index.
  ISBN 0-631-21803-3 (hbk. : alk. paper) — ISBN 1-4051-1692-7 (pbk. : alk. paper)
    1. Language and languages—Variation. 2. Linguistic change.
3. Sociolinguistics. I. Chambers, J. K. II. Trudgill, Peter. III. Schilling-Estes, Natalie. IV. Series.
P120.V37 H365 2001
417.7—dc21

2001037548

ISBN-13: 978-0-631-21803-6 (hbk. : alk. paper) — ISBN-13: 978-1-4051-1692-3 (pbk. : alk. paper)

A catalogue record for this title is available from the British Library.

Set in 10/12 pt Palatino
by Graphicraft Ltd, Hong Kong
Printed and bound in the United Kingdom
by TJ International Ltd, Padstow, Cornwall

The publisher's policy is to use permanent paper from mills that operate a sustainable forestry policy, and which has been manufactured from pulp processed using acid-free and elementary chlorine-free practices. Furthermore, the publisher ensures that the text paper and cover board used have met acceptable environmental accreditation standards.

For further information on
Blackwell Publishing, visit our website:
www.blackwellpublishing.com

For William Labov

whose work is referred to in every chapter
and whose ideas imbue every page

"*The Handbook of Language Variation and Change* is a convenient, hand-held repository of the essential knowledge about the study of language variation and change. This *Handbook* allows the next generation of academics to perpetuate all of these fields of study and explore them with the kind of depth unimaginable to their predecessors."

Folia Linguistica

"Languages do not exist but in space and time. Their variability is what allows them to function as means of communication and social interaction. The present *Handbook* presents an up-to-date and in-depth account of how to study this aspect of language which is at the interface of historical linguistics, dialectology, and sociolinguistics. The editors and contributing authors are among the most prolific scholars in the field. Their collective effort shows us how the versatility of 'real' situated speech can be made an object of rigorous scientific investigation and what can be learned from it about language and society."

Florian Coulmas, Gerhard Mercator University

"At last we have an authoritative place to go to discover the impressive accomplishments of the research on linguistic variation and change over the past forty years and to get a glimpse of the future. The editors of this *Handbook* have put together an excellent survey of what variationists do, produced by an admirable combination of scholars who helped found the field along with linguists from the next generation. This is an excellent volume. Buy it!"

Ralph Fasold, Georgetown University

Contents

Contributors

Arto Anttila
New York University, USA
arto.anttila@nyu.edu

Sharon Ash
University of Pennsylvania, USA
ash@babel.ling.upenn.edu

Guy Bailey
University of Texas at San Antonio, USA
gbailey@utsa.edu

Laurie Bauer
Victoria University of Wellington, NZ
laurie.bauer@vuw.ac.nz

Robert Bayley
University of Texas at San Antonio, USA
rbayley@lonestar.utsa.edu

David Britain
Essex University, England
dbritain@essex.ac.uk

J. K. Chambers
University of Toronto, Canada
jack.chambers@utoronto.ca

Jenny Cheshire
Queen Mary and Westfield College, University of London, England
j.l.cheshire@qmw.ac.uk

Crawford Feagin
University of Zurich, Switzerland
feagin@erols.com

Carmen Fought
Pitzer College, USA
carmen_fought@pitzer.edu

Matthew J. Gordon
University of Missouri at Columbia, USA
gordonmj@missouri.edu

Kirk Hazen
West Virginia University, USA
khazen2@wvu.edu

Alison Henry
Queen's University, Belfast, Northern Ireland
AM.Henry@ulst.ac.uk

Paul Kerswill
Reading University, England
p.e.kerswill@reading.ac.uk

Ronald Macaulay
Pitzer College, USA
rmacaulay@compuserve.com

Norma Mendoza-Denton
University of Arizona, USA
nmd@u.arizona.edu

Miriam Meyerhoff
University of Edinburgh, Scotland
miriam.meyerhoff@ed.ac.uk

Lesley Milroy
University of Michigan, USA
amilroy@umich.edu

Peter L. Patrick
Essex University, England
patrickp@essex.ac.uk

Dennis R. Preston
Michigan State University, USA
preston@pilot.msu.edu

John R. Rickford
Stanford University, USA
rickford@csli.stanford.edu

Julie Roberts
University of Vermont, USA
jroberts@polyglot.uvm.edu

Gillian Sankoff
University of Pennsylvania, USA
gillian@central.cis.upenn.edu

Natalie Schilling-Estes
Georgetown University, USA
ns3@georgetown.edu

Edgar W. Schneider
University of Regensburg, Germany
edgar.schneider@sprachlit.uni-regensburg.de

Sali Tagliamonte
University of Toronto, Canada, and
University of York, England
sali.tagliamonte@utoronto.ca

Erik R. Thomas
North Carolina State University, USA
ethomas@social.chass.ncsu.edu

Peter Trudgill
University of Fribourg, Switzerland
peter.trudgill@unifr.ch

Walt Wolfram
North Carolina State University, USA
wolfram@social.chass.ncsu.edu

Introduction

J. K. CHAMBERS, PETER TRUDGILL, AND
NATALIE SCHILLING-ESTES

The study of language variation and change, the core of the sociolinguistic enterprise, has a relatively short history, but it is a burgeoning history, as might be expected of an idea whose time had truly come or, indeed, was overdue. This *Handbook* reflects the vitality and growth, representing the discipline in its multifaceted pursuits. The chapters that follow are not retrospective, apart from Chambers' "informal epistemology," which immediately follows. Instead, we have invited the authors of the chapters to discuss the ideas – hypotheses, axioms, lemmata, premises, probabilities – that drive their branch of the discipline, and to illustrate them with empirical studies, their own or others, that not only demonstrate their applications but also their shortcomings and strengths. The historical sequence will be implicit, we trust, if and when it has a bearing on the ideas.

Our emphasis on empirical issues and applications is intended to make the *Handbook* serviceable to the third generation of sociolinguists, now being trained, and beyond. The contributors to the *Handbook* have been chosen partly to strike a balance between the first two academic generations, the founders, so to speak, and their intellectual offspring. The topics we enlisted them to write about are likewise balanced between the relatively mature and the relatively recent. Within each topic, the ideas naturally find a balance between the tried-and-probably-true and the potentially productive. We expect that the next generation will perpetuate all of these fields of study and, indeed, explore them with the kind of depth unimaginable to their predecessors.

Thinking about the contributors as members of one or another academic generation makes sense in terms of the symbolic genealogy of one-time mentors and their sometime students, but realistically there has been and continues to be a sense of community without any noticeable generation gap. This was almost certainly brought about by the novelty of sociolinguistics. The first professors and their first graduate students were united by the fact that they all, in effect, had everything to learn. They were inventing their discipline, and doing it together. Important ideas issued from dissertations and conference presentations as well as from professorial publications, and their provenance was less important than their potential.

Until sometime in the 1980s, it was possible for an enterprising graduate student facing comprehensive examinations to read virtually everything in the field of sociolinguistics. That is no longer true, of course, because of the cumulative growth of research from one generation to the next, the spread of variationist methods into neighboring subject areas or brand-new ones, and the international spread of the discipline, first through the emigration of trained sociolinguists to virgin territories and then through the rise of native sociolinguists in those countries.

This exponential growth in the discipline gives the *Handbook* a kind of utility that was previously not needed. We see it as a convenient, hand-held repository of the essential knowledge about the study of language variation and change. Although it cannot cover everything in the field, as might have been possible twenty years ago, it can aspire to being a resource for readers to turn to for garnering basic information about any of the subfields and for getting directions on where to go to learn more.

We have partitioned the *Handbook* into five major parts. Each part begins with its own introduction by the editors, setting out the boundaries of the field and putting each of the chapters into perspective. Part I examines the methodologies employed by linguists working in the field of linguistic variation and change, both in terms of the forms of fieldwork and data collection that characterize our science, and in terms of the various types of data analysis employed by our colleagues. Part II deals with the levels of linguistic structure that have been the main foci of work in linguistic variation and change studies: phonology, syntax, and discourse. In Part III we present views of linguistic variation in the diverse contexts that give it meaning and significance, across the generations and the social strata and the domains of interaction. Part IV covers variation through geographical space, and language and dialect contact from a variationist perspective; while Part V is concerned with the implications that research in different types of societies may have for work in our field.

The contributors of the chapters make a distinguished international roster. Our invitations went to scholars with recognized expertise, either established or potential, with no thought to anything but expertise. The final reckoning gives an accidental profile of the culture in which sociolinguistics has developed and keeps growing. Thirty chapters by 29 linguists, 12 women and 17 men, from eight nations – these numbers are striking, but the reality is even more striking, because more than one-third of the contributors live and work in countries far removed from their native lands. Good ideas are irrepressible, and it takes people to spread them. This book is about those good ideas. In bringing them together in one book, as many of them as we could accommodate, it is our hope that they will spread even further in settings where they will continue to be keenly tested and critically refined.

Studying Language Variation: An Informal Epistemology

J. K. CHAMBERS

Sociolinguistics is the study of the social uses of language, and the most productive studies in the four decades of sociolinguistic research have emanated from determining the social evaluation of linguistic variants. These are also the areas most susceptible to scientific methods such as hypothesis-formulation, logical inference, and statistical testing. Studying language variation proceeds mainly by observing language use in natural social settings and categorizing the linguistic variants according to their social distribution.

In this chapter, I sketch an informal epistemology of sociolinguistics by outlining its development as a social science (see section 2), its place among the linguistic sciences (section 3) and its basis in cognition (section 4). I begin by showing that the social evaluation of linguistically equivalent variants belongs to the common experience of all of us. Notwithstanding the pervasive effects of the social milieu on the accents and dialects which are its medium of communication, the study of socially-conditioned variation in language is relatively recent.

1 The Social Basis for Linguistic Variation

The foundations of variationist sociolinguistics come from the rudimentary observation that the variants that occur in everyday speech are linguistically insignificant but socially significant. The linguistic equivalence of the variants of a linguistic variable is evident in a comparison of any paired variants, as, for instance:

> Adonis saw himself in the mirror.
> Adonis seen hisself in the mirror.

These utterances differ with respect to two morphological variables: (1) the verb *see* is represented in the first sentence by *saw*, the strong form of the past tense, and in the second by *seen*, and (2) the reflexive pronoun takes the form *himself* in the first and *hisself* in the second. Notwithstanding these differences, the two sentences convey exactly the same grammatical meaning and everyone who speaks English with even minimal competence recognizes their semantic identity.

The sentences do, however, convey very different social meanings as a direct result of their morphological variants. That is, they carry *socio*linguistic significance. The first, with its standard forms, is emblematic of middle-class, educated, or relatively formal speech, while the second is emblematic of working-class, uneducated, or highly colloquial (vernacular) speech. These differences will also be readily recognized by virtually every speaker of the language.

The social evaluations associated with these two sentences are conventional, and they appear to have no deeper sources than other types of social conventions, such as the convention in western nations that women precede men when they enter a room together on formal occasions, or that people clasp one another's right hands on being introduced to one another. In fact, the analogy with etiquette can be taken further, because standard speech as exemplified by the first sentence is associated with 'good manners' in many settings, such as schools, white-collar work environments, and cultural institutions, whereas the second sentence conveys 'bad manners' in those same settings. Someone uttering the second sentence in response to a teacher's question might be regarded as boorish, as would a man preceding his female partner into a banquet hall. Someone uttering the second sentence at the intermission of a play might be regarded as rough and unschooled, as would a man who failed to extend his right hand on being introduced to another man.

These evaluations are evoked without any regard for the linguistic content of the sentences. In answer to the teacher's question, the second sentence is correct if the first one is. As an observation about on-stage action, the second sentence would be no less true than the first one. From this, it follows that the variants come into being and are sustained not for their linguistic content but for their social function.

So deeply ingrained are these evaluations that there exists a venerable history of attempts to put them on some kind of rational ground. Language arbiters have promulgated claims that vernaculars are illogical, inconsistent, sloppy, and inferior in other ways. In most cultures, the arbiters are self-appointed, typically teachers, parents, editors, and other authority figures (Milroy and Milroy 1985). In several continental European nations, they are government appointees and members of prestigious academies. The arbiters wield authority, and so it often comes as a surprise when sociolinguists and others point out that their pronouncements have no linguistic basis but are merely arbitrary social conventions.

Recognizing the pronouncements as arbitrary and conventional does not entail that they are superficial. On the contrary, people whose speech is judged adversely can suffer socially, occupationally and educationally (as discussed by Preston in this volume). All developed societies seem to tolerate social judgments of linguistic performance, and typically promote those judgments as part of the institutional mandate of schools, government offices, and professional societies. So pervasive are they in social behavior that they must be embedded in human nature, perhaps as an irrepressible adjunct of human communicative competence (as in §4 below). They have been documented from the beginning of the written record. Thus Sirach, the Old Testament moralist, declared: "When a sieve is shaken, the rubbish is left behind; so too the defects of a person appear in speech. As the kiln tests the work of the potter, so the test of a person is conversation" (Ecclesiasticus 27: 4–5). And Cicero, in 55 BC, enjoins his readers to "learn to avoid not only the asperity of rustic pronunciation but the strangeness of outlandish pronunciation" (*De Oratore* III, 12).

With such a continuous and intimate relation to the human condition, it would be natural to expect a fairly long history of human inquiry into the sources, functions, and significations of language in its social context, but, as we shall see, the history is relatively recent.

2   Sociolinguistics as a Discipline

Leaving aside a few maverick precursors, variationist sociolinguistics had its effective beginnings only in 1963, the year in which William Labov presented the first sociolinguistic research report at the annual meeting of the Linguistic Society of America and also the year in which he published "The social motivation of a sound change" (Labov 1963). Those events mark the inception of linguistic studies imbued by the identification of linguistic variants correlated with social factors, by the incorporation of style as an independent variable, and by the apparent-time apprehension of linguistic changes in progress – all hallmarks of the sociolinguistic enterprise to this day (as discussed below, especially in the chapters by Ash, Schilling-Estes and Bailey).

The time was ripe for these initiatives. Labov recalls feeling some trepidation as he prepared to present his results in public for the first time. "In those days . . . , you practically addressed the entire profession when you advanced to the podium," he recalled (in 1997). "I had imagined a long and bitter struggle for my ideas, where I would push the social conditioning of language against hopeless odds, and finally win belated recognition as my hair was turning gray. But my romantic imagination was cut short. They ate it up!" The easy reception may have obscured the revolutionary turn that sociolinguistics represents in the history of language study, as discussed in §3.

The term sociolinguistics had been coined a decade before Labov's inaugural presentation, in 1952, by one Haver C. Currie, in a programmatic commentary on the notion that "social functions and significations of speech factors offer a prolific field for research." With baptismal zeal, Currie (1952: 28) proclaimed, "This field is here designated *socio-linguistics*."

Before that, of course, there existed the long tradition of dialectology, with its studies of regional speech variation, dating from 1876 and thus antedating modern linguistics, let alone sociolinguistics. The relationship between traditional dialectology and sociolinguistics is oblique rather than direct, but both are in the broadest sense dialectologies (studies of language variation). In terms of intellectual history it is plausible to view sociolinguistics as a refocusing of traditional dialectology in response to cataclysmic technological and social changes that required (and facilitated) freer data-gathering methods using larger and more representative population samples (Chambers 2002). Traditional dialect studies with genuine sociolinguistic bearings are not nonexistent (for example, Gauchat 1905, McDavid 1948), nor are neighboring social science studies with authentic sociolinguistic insights (for example, Fischer 1958), but they are rare. The emergence of an international movement for socially perspicacious linguistic studies belongs incontrovertibly to the last 40 years.

3   Studying Language as a Social Phenomenon

The brevity of this history appears paradoxical in view of the obvious social role of language. Perhaps its social role is too obvious, or perhaps it is so integral in language as to escape notice. The classical Greeks missed it entirely. Plato and Aristotle were mainly concerned with categorizing linguistic forms, that is, with grammar in the sense discussed in the next section. Neither of them noticed linguistic variation of any kind, and their overwhelming influence on Western thought undoubtedly contributed to the antisocial bias of Western linguistic tradition. The Sanskrit grammarian Pāṇini (ca. 600 BC) did recognize systematic variability, which he called *anyatarasyām*, but his distinction was trivialized by his successors as meaning 'marginal' or 'unacceptable', for which Pāṇini had actually used different terms (Kiparsky 1979). Pāṇini's followers missed the distinction, and as a result Pāṇini's insight had no impact on tradition.

The classical scholar with the best claim as patriarch of sociolinguistics is the Roman polymath Varro (116–27 BC), who not only recognized linguistic variation (*anomalia*) but also linked it to vernacular language use (*consuetudo*; see Taylor 1975). Varro observed, among other things, that "the usage of speech is always shifting its position: this is why words of the better sort [i.e. morphologically regular forms] are wont to become worse, and worse words better; words spoken wrongly by some of the old-timers are . . . now spoken correctly, and some that were then spoken according to logical theory are now spoken wrongly" (IX, 17; Kent 1938: 453). Varro's maxim – *consuetudo loquendi est in motu* – could be emblazoned as the motto of sociolinguistics: "the vernacular is always in motion." Unfortunately, Varro's linguistic treatise, which survives only as a fragment, gave rise to no school of thought. He remains an isolated figure in the history of language study.

Enlightenment authors presupposed the social basis of language. Locke, in *An Essay Concerning Human Understanding* (1690: 101), wrote: "God, having designed man for a sociable creature, made him not only with an inclination, and under a necessity to have fellowship with those of his kind, but furnished him also with language, which was to be the great instrument and common tie of society." But the social uses of the instrument, under the presumption that it was God-given, were apparently deemed to be beyond human scrutiny. Similarly, modern linguists dutifully enshrined the social function in their definitions. "Language is defined as the learned system of arbitrary vocal symbols by means of which human beings, as members of a society, interact and communicate in terms of their culture," according to one introductory textbook (Trager 1972: 7). Bloomfield (1933: 42) said, "All the so-called higher activities of man – our specifically human activities – spring from the close adjustment among individuals which we call society, and this adjustment, in turn, is based upon language; the speech-community, therefore, is the most important kind of social group." Firth (1937: 153) said, "speech is social 'magic'. You learn your languages in stages as conditions of gradual incorporation into your social organization. . . . The approach to speech must consequently be sociological."

Yet neither Bloomfield nor Firth nor any of the linguists who shared their structuralist concepts directly studied the social uses of language. Until the advent of sociolinguistics in the broadest sense, including studies of discourse, pragmatics, interaction rituals, and subjective evaluation tests which sprang into being around the same time, there were no concentrated attempts at discovering the social significance of linguistic variation. That may be partly explicable in terms of intellectual history. All the social sciences are relatively young. Psychology, sociology, economics, and anthropology had their effective beginnings around the turn of the twentieth century, whereas subject areas less intimately involved with the human condition such as algebra, physics, and zoology have ancient origins. Sociolinguistics, as the social science branch of linguistics (along with developmental psycholinguistics), is a newcomer compared to the branch known as theoretical linguistics, which descends from more venerable studies of grammar, rhetoric, and philology.

Nor was the shunting aside of the social significance of language an oversight or an accident. Saussure, the founder of modern linguistics, noted that "speech has both an individual and a social side, and we cannot conceive of one without the other" (1916: 8). Inconceivable it may have been, but he nevertheless advocated the study of the former without the latter. His famous distinction between *langue*, the grammatical system, and *parole*, the social uses of language, came into being expressly to demarcate what he considered the proper domain of linguistic study:

> But what is *langue*? It is not to be confused with human speech [*parole*], of which it is only a definite part, though certainly an essential one. It [*parole*] is both a social product of the faculty of speech and a collection of necessary conventions

that have been adopted by a social body to permit individuals to exercise that faculty. Taken as a whole, speech is many-sided and heterogeneous; straddling several areas simultaneously – physical, physiological, and psychological – it belongs to both the individual and to society; we cannot put it into any category of human facts, for we cannot discover its unity.

Language [*langue*], on the contrary, is a self-contained whole and a principle of classification. As soon as we give language first place among the facts of speech, we introduce a natural order into a mass that lends itself to no other classification. (1916: 9)

Saussure's doubts about a possible science of *parole* seem curmudgeonly, with hindsight, but he was not alone. Before him, Humboldt had made a similar distinction between a formless *ergon* and a well-formed *energeia*, the former "divided up into an infinity as the sole language in one and the same nation," that is, speech (or *parole*), and the latter language in the abstract sense (or *langue*), with "these many variants . . . united into one language having a definite character" (1836: 129). After Saussure, Chomsky made a similar distinction between competence, "the speaker-hearer's knowledge of his language," and performance, "the actual use of language in concrete situations," and he went on to say that "observed use of language . . . surely cannot constitute the actual subject matter of linguistics, if this is to be a serious discipline" (1965: 4).

Humboldt, Saussure, and Chomsky were obviously right in pointing out that speech, *parole*, is heterogeneous, but they have been proven wrong in dismissing heterogeneity as a possible object of study. From the beginning, the challenge facing sociolinguistics, the science of *parole*, has been to arrive at an understanding of language as, in Weinreich, Labov, and Herzog's phrase, "an object possessing orderly heterogeneity" (1968: 100).

4   Communicative Competence

Studying language as *langue* (or *energeia* or competence), as distinct from *parole* (or *ergon* or performance), requires abstracting linguistic data from the real-world variability in which it naturally occurs. Grammarians impose a hypothetical filter on natural language data to make it invariant, discrete, and qualitative. The filter, called the axiom of categoricity (Chambers 1995: 26–7), has been described in numerous ways. Here is Hjelmslev: "Linguistics must attempt to grasp language, not as a conglomerate of non-linguistic (e.g. physical, physiological, psychological, logical, sociological) phenomena, but as a self-sufficient totality, a structure *sui generis*" (1961: 5–6; for comparable statements by Humboldt, Saussure, Joos, and Chomsky, see Chambers 1995: 25–33). By contrast, sociolinguists attempt to grasp language as it is used in social situations, which is to say variant, continuous, and quantitative.

Langue and *parole* remain useful distinctions today for a reason that Saussure would undoubtedly have found unimaginable, because they now help to define the different objects of inquiry of theoretical linguistics and sociolinguistics. They are separable in theory as natural partitions of the language faculty, or what might plausibly be considered distinct cognitive modules.

Chomsky has argued for the language faculty as comprised of interacting systems conceived as "'mental organs' analogous to the heart or the visual system or the system of motor coordination and planning" (1980: 39). Theoretical linguists who adopt the axiom of categoricity are primarily interested in discovering the properties of one of those systems of the language faculty, called GRAMMAR, conceived as a language-specific bioprogram (to use Bickerton's incisive but apparently unloved term: 1984). The GRAMMAR is made up of, in Chomsky's terms (1980: 55), "a system of 'computational' rules and representations." Attempts at discovering its innate computational properties have led Chomsky and his followers into minute examinations of surface-structure puzzles involving linguistic coreference, scope, and other structural intricacies. They have produced insights into the grammatical processor as "structure-dependent" rather than strictly linear (cf. Crain and Nakayama 1987) and, crucially for Chomsky's tenacious but disputed stance on the grammatical component's language-specificity, not reducible to other, independently motivated, non-language-processing cognitive systems.

The GRAMMAR is presumably the module in the language faculty that accounts for the uniquely human attributes of creativity in language production and comprehension, and for the rapidity of language acquisition in infancy. However, it is obviously not autonomous. Linguistic production and comprehension require real-world orientation to express meanings, and the acquisition device requires the stimulus of social interaction to activate learning. Chomsky, of course, recognizes its interdependence with other systems, and he has isolated two of them as follows: "A fuller account of knowledge of language will consider the interactions of grammar and other systems, specifically the system of conceptual structures and pragmatic competence, and perhaps others" (1980: 92). The real-world orientation has its source in what Chomsky calls the CONCEPTUAL SYSTEM, and the social stimulus has its source in what Chomsky calls "pragmatic competence" but is generally called COMMUNICATIVE COMPETENCE.

By the CONCEPTUAL SYSTEM, Chomsky means "the system of object-reference and also such relations as 'agent', 'goal', 'instrument' and the like; what are sometimes called 'thematic relations'" (1980: 54). It also includes vocabulary items, the most obvious intermediaries between grammar and the world. The conceptual system has received little attention from linguists of any stripe, but it too reveals uniquely human properties most easily discerned in acquisition. Children master fine semantic distinctions of the sort found in verbs such as *follow* and *chase* relatively early, certainly long before they can consciously define what they mean. They universally develop lexical distinctions in number and color categorization that are unmatched by, say, olfactory categories (Strozer 1994: 40–5). These fine vocabulary distinctions recur in all natural languages. One way of explaining this mastery, Chomsky (1988: 31) says, is by postulating that words "enter into systematic structures based on certain elementary re-current notions and principles of combination." More generally, he says, "The rate of vocabulary acquisition is so high at certain stages of life, and the precision and delicacy of the concepts acquired so remarkable, that it seems necessary to conclude that in some manner the conceptual system with which lexical items are connected is already substantially in place" (1980: 139). These are stimulating ideas that invite empirical research.

Chomsky's third cognitive module, "pragmatic competence," takes in, in his words, "knowledge of conditions and manner of appropriate use, in conformity with various purposes. . . . We might say that pragmatic competence places language in the institutional setting of its use, relating intentions and purposes to the linguistic means at hand" (1980: 224–5). This notion has a familiar ring to sociolinguists. It was influentially described by Hymes as "sociolinguistic competence" or COMMUNICATIVE COMPETENCE, as follows:

> Within the social matrix in which [a child] acquires a system of grammar, a child acquires also a system of its use, regarding persons, places, purposes, other modes of communication, etc. – all the components of communicative events, together with attitudes and beliefs regarding them. There also develop patterns of the sequential use of language in conversation, address, standard routines, and the like. In such acquisition resides the child's sociolinguistic competence (or, more broadly, communicative competence), its ability to participate in its society as not only a speaking, but also a communicating member.   (1974: 75)

Hymes adds, "What children so acquire, an integrated theory of sociolinguistic description must be able to describe."

Like the other organs of the language faculty, COMMUNICATIVE COMPETENCE develops early and rapidly in normal children with little or no tutoring. Since most of the conventions governing communicative events are beneath consciousness, explicit teaching is impossible in any case. Evidence for COMMUNICATIVE COMPETENCE as an entity independent of GRAMMATICAL COMPETENCE (and presumably the other organs of the language faculty) can be found in extreme social situations and in clinical settings in which people are forced to function with one in the absence of the other.

East Sutherland in the Scottish Highlands provides a striking case known from research by Nancy Dorian. Her subjects included bilingual Gaelic-English fisherfolk, younger English-speaking monolinguals, and a middle group of English speakers described as "low-proficiency semi-speakers of East Sutherland Gaelic and . . . near-passive bilinguals" (1982: 27). This third group, despite their lack of grammatical competence in Gaelic, interacted freely and comfortably with their Gaelic neighbors. They were fully integrated in the bilingual community, and their integration depended largely or perhaps solely upon their communicative competence. "They knew when it was appropriate to speak and when not," Dorian says (1982: 29), "when a question would show interest and when it would constitute an interruption; when an offer of food or drink was mere verbal routine and was meant to be refused, and when it was meant in earnest and should be accepted; how much verbal response was appropriate to express sympathy in response to a narrative of ill health or ill luck; and so forth."

Their communicative competence was so perfectly attuned, in fact, that neither the fluent bilinguals nor the semi-speakers themselves were aware of the extent of their grammatical shortcomings. In one instance, Dorian inadvertently exposed those shortcomings by testing the language proficiency of one of the semi-speakers in the presence of her bilingual friends, to the considerable embarrassment of everyone, including Dorian. In the East Sutherland speech community, they were all peers by dint not of their shared language but rather of their shared communicative competence.

The independence (or modularity) of COMMUNICATIVE COMPETENCE is also revealed by the fact that it can be disturbed and disrupted in neurological disorders. People suffering from what is called "semantic-pragmatic disorder" tend to interrupt the conversational flow with inappropriate or ill-timed assertions, fail to follow topics, introduce what appear to be digressions or non-sequiturs, and speak out of turn (Bishop and Adams 1989, Mogford-Bevan and Sadler 1991). Typically, their speech is phonologically and grammatically well-formed, and not infrequently their speech is remarkably fluent.

Clinical researchers usually rely on standardized tests as diagnostic tools, but people with semantic-pragmatic disorder tend to score within normal ranges on such tests. As a result, descriptions of semantic-pragmatic disorder in the psycholinguistic literature often appear to be cursory and vague. As a sociolinguistic disorder, it would undoubtedly benefit from sociolinguistic observation and analysis for its description. In any event, what malfunctions in the people who are afflicted with it is their communicative competence. Just as myxedema proves the existence of the thyroid gland in the endocrine system (if proof were needed), so semantic-pragmatic disorders prove the existence of communicative competence in the language faculty.

5   Communicative Competence in Performance

It must have been obvious since time began that normal human beings have unbounded capabilities for social intercourse, conversational interaction, repartee, self-expression, and communal expression, all governed by intricate sets of conventions normally beneath consciousness. For social interaction to work, both the content of speech and its form must be appropriate to the speakers and their interlocutors in the particular social context. Sociolinguistic analysis has revealed that our main resources come from modulating linguistic elements in subtle (and clearly unteachable) ways, selecting, so to speak, a particular vowel variant with a certain frequency in a particular situation or a past tense variant or other structural variant in various contexts.

Our repertoire of variants usually has a linguistic basis, as when a form like *hisself* arises to compete with the historically established form *himself* (Lightfoot 1999: 14–16), apparently because it is paradigmatically regular, formed with the possessive pronoun *his-* as its first element, as are *myself*, *yourself*, and *herself*. There is no linguistic principle, however, that can explain the recognition of one of the variants as standard and the other as nonstandard. It defies 'logic' or any conscious rationalization when it is the paradigmatically regular form, *hisself*, the one that Varro would have called "words of the better sort," that is the socially stigmatized form. There is also no linguistic principle behind their distribution in the speech of different social groups in the community, or the relative frequency of their use from one generation to the next.

It is these aspects that underlie the age-old mystery of language change, which is irrepressible and inexorable in spite of the fact that it is, from a purely linguistic viewpoint, dysfunctional, in so far as it impedes communication in the long run, and otiose, in so far as it does not demonstrably improve or degrade the language. The root causes seem to be nothing more profound than fashion. As Hall (1964: 298) says: "Every human language . . . has been re-made in accordance with our whims since the confusion of the Tower of Babel . . . and since [humankind] is a most unstable and variable being, language cannot be long-lasting or stable; but like other human things, such as customs and dress, it has to vary in space or time."

Four decades of sociolinguistic research show that the "whims" are socially motivated, though pinpointing the motivations and giving them empirical substance remains perhaps our greatest challenge. We are gaining an understanding of human communicative competence. Every chapter of this book provides evidence, in its own way, of how people respond to social evaluations of their speech, which are always shifting, usually tediously but sometimes rapidly, and almost always tacitly. *Consuetudo loquendi est in motu.*

The wonder of it is that it took place with virtually no conscious investigation for centuries and indeed millennia – much longer, for instance, than metaphysical speculations about free will or grammatical taxonomies of verb conjugations. It is surely a measure of how deeply ingrained our communicative competence is in all our activities that it could lay hidden so long from consciousness, and a measure as well of how deeply embedded it is in our human nature.

REFERENCES

Bickerton, Derek (1984). The language bioprogram hypothesis. *The Behavioral and Brain Sciences* 7: 173–87.

Bishop, Dorothy V. M. and C. Adams (1989). Conversational characteristics of children with semantic-pragmatic disorder. *British Journal of Disorders of Communication* 24: 241–63.

Bloomfield, Leonard (1933). *Language*. New York: Holt, Rinehart and Winston.

Chambers, J. K. (1995). *Sociolinguistic Theory: Linguistic Variation and Its Social Significance*. Oxford: Blackwell.

Chambers, J. K. (2002). *Dialectology*. In Neil J. Smelser and Paul B. Baltes (eds.), *International Encyclopedia of the Social and Behavioral Sciences*. Amsterdam: Elsevier Science.

Chomsky, Noam (1965). *Aspects of the Theory of Syntax*. Cambridge, MA: MIT Press.

Chomsky, Noam (1980). *Rules and Representations*. New York: Columbia University Press.

Chomsky, Noam (1988). *Language and Problems of Knowledge: The Managua Lectures*. Cambridge, MA: MIT Press.

Crain, Stephen, and Mineharu Nakayama (1987). Structure dependence in grammar formation. *Language* 63: 522–43.

Currie, Haver C. (1952). A projection of socio-linguistics: the relationship of speech and its social status. *The Southern Speech Journal* 18: 28–37.

Dorian, Nancy C. (1982). Defining the speech community to include its working margins. In Suzanne Romaine (ed.), *Sociolinguistic Variation in Speech Communities*. London: Edward Arnold. 25–33.

Firth, J. R. (1937). *The Tongues of Men*. London: Watts.

Fischer, John L. (1958). Social influences on the choice of a linguistic variant. *Word* 14: 47–56.

Gauchat, Louis (1905). L'unité phonetique dans le patois d'une commune. *Festschrift Heinreich Morf: Aus Romanischen Sprachen und Literaturen*. Halle: M. Niemeyer. 175–232.

Hall, Robert A. (1964). *Introductory Linguistics*. Philadelphia: Chilton Books.

Hjelmslev, Louis (1961). *Prolegomena to a Theory of Language*, trans. Francis J. Whitfield. Madison: University of Wisconsin Press.

Humboldt, Wilhelm von (1836). *Linguistic Variability and Intellectual Development*, trans. George C. Buck and Frithjof A. Raven. Philadelphia: University of Pennsylvania Press. 1972.

Hymes, Dell (1974). *Foundations in Sociolinguistics: An ethnographic approach*. Philadelphia: University of Pennsylvania Press.

Kent, Roland G. (1938). *Varro on the Latin Language with an English Translation*, vol. 2. London: William Heinemann; Cambridge, MA: Harvard University Press.

Kiparsky, Paul (1979). *Pāṇini as a Variationist*. Cambridge, MA: MIT Press.

Labov, William (1963). The social motivation of a sound change. *Word* 19: 273–309.

Labov, William (1997). How I got into linguistics, and what I got out of it. Undergraduate address 1987, revised. http://www.ling.upenn.edu/~labov/Papers.

Lightfoot, David (1999). *The Development of Language: Acquisition, Change, and Evolution*. Oxford: Blackwell.

Locke, John (1690). *An Essay Concerning Human Understanding*. New York: Dolphin Books.

McDavid, Raven I. (1948). Postvocalic /-r/ in South Carolina: a social analysis. *American Speech* 23: 194–204.

Milroy, James and Lesley Milroy (1985). *Authority in Language: Investigating Language Prescription and Standardisation*. London: Routledge and Kegan Paul.

Mogford-Bevan, K. and J. Sadler (1991). *Child Language Disability*, vol. II: *Semantic and Pragmatic Difficulties*. Clevedon and Philadelphia: Multilingual Matters.

Saussure, Ferdinand de (1916). *Course in General Linguistics*, ed. Charles Bally and trans. Albert Sechehaye, Wade Baskin. New York and Toronto: McGraw-Hill.

Strozer, Judith R. (1994). *Language Acquisition After Puberty*. Washington, DC: Georgetown University Press.

Taylor, Daniel J. (1975). *Declinatio: A Study of the Linguistic Theory of Marcus Terentius Varro*. Amsterdam: John Benjamins.

Trager, George L. (1972). *Language and Languages*. San Francisco, CA: Chandler.

Weinreich, Uriel, William Labov and Marvin I. Herzog (1968). Empirical foundations for a theory of language change. In Winfred P. Lehmann and Yakov Malkiel (eds.), *Directions for Historical Linguistics: A Symposium*. Austin TX: University of Texas Press. 95–188.

Part I
Methodologies

Field Methods

In an early discussion of linguistic methodology, William Labov classified the different subfields of linguistics according to whether their practitioners were primarily to be found working in "the library, the bush, the closet, the laboratory . . . [or] the street" (Labov 1972: 99). The library was the provenance of the historical linguist, the remote and sparsely populated bush the venue of the anthropological linguist, the laboratory the home of the psycholinguist, and the closet the circumscribed space of theoretical linguists speculating about their own linguistic usages. Sociolinguists, on the other hand, boldly stepped beyond the bounds of their research institutions out into the street, to gather data on language as the people around them actually used it in everyday life. The heavily populated city street was, and continues to be, especially important to variationist sociolinguists, since their concern has always been with uncovering and seeking to explicate patterns of variation and change – patterns that emerge only when sufficient quantities of data have been obtained from a substantial number of speakers.

It seems fitting that the first section of this *Handbook* opens with a chapter on how to get out into the street in the first place. In "Entering the Community: Fieldwork," Crawford Feagin provides a practical, hands-on guide to planning and executing the type of community study that has been at the heart of variation analysis since its inception. Students new to sociolinguistic research will benefit from Feagin's discussion of such potentially daunting matters as selecting informants, choosing recording equipment, and designing and conducting the sociolinguistic interview, while novices and experts alike will appreciate her discussion of such persistent issues as how to gain acceptance into the community, how to compensate subjects, and whether it is ethical to downplay one's research interests in the service of obtaining unselfconscious speech. Feagin's liberal use of anecdotes from her own and others' field efforts, including cases where things went awry, lends an empathetic tone that will be appreciated by all who have ever felt the self-doubt that arises when you try to match your clear-cut fieldwork goals with the messy realities of working with real people with goals of their own.

Despite the importance of naturalistic data on language in daily use, they sometimes need to be supplemented with data on what people think about their own and others' language uses. In "Language with an Attitude," Dennis R. Preston discusses sociolinguistic investigations of non-linguists' attitudes toward various languages, language varieties, and specific features of these varieties. Understanding language attitudes is important for both scientific and humanistic reasons: not only does such understanding provide insight into such central linguistic issues as the relationship between perception and production and the role of saliency in language variation and change, but it also allows for fuller understanding of how and why people's attitudes toward language varieties are often translated into attitudes toward, and discrimination against, speakers who use particular varieties. So far, linguists have had little success in changing the folk attitudes that underlie accent discrimination (for example, the belief that nonstandard varieties are "bad" or "sloppy" or "lazy"); perhaps we will have better luck when we have a greater understanding of the belief systems we are seeking to replace – in other words, when we have developed a full-fledged "folk theory of language" to supplement our linguistic understandings.

Given their interest in language change, variationists also often have to supplement taped records of spoken language with written records from previous time periods. In "Investigating Variation and Change in Written Documents," Edgar W. Schneider discusses the numerous troublesome issues that arise when the researcher must rely on written evidence as reflective of once-spoken language. Most important is validity – that is, the extent to which the written document represents the variety it supposedly depicts. Schneider points out that some text types tend to be more faithful to spoken forms than others. For example, transcripts of interviews (whether tape-recorded or not) tend to be more faithful to spoken language than literary works, whose authors tend to overuse stereotypical features and reduce variability. It is necessary to assess the validity of any text type by evaluating the conditions under which the document was produced (such as whether it was written during or after the event it depicts), checking it for internal consistency, and comparing one's results with those of other studies. The issues that arise in working with written documents are by no means unique to this type of data. As Schneider points out, tape recordings and transcriptions are also removed from the "reality" of speech performance, albeit to a lesser degree than most written historical records. With careful handling, written records can indeed serve as a valuable source of data in the quantitative investigation of language variation and change.

In the final chapter in this section, "Inferring Variation and Change from Public Corpora," Laurie Bauer discusses another type of data sample that is not usually gathered directly by the linguistic investigator – the public corpus. Although the term "corpus" technically may be used to refer to any body of data, recent decades have seen the compilation of several large collections of naturally occurring (or naturalistic) language data that have been made available to the scientific community and the general public. Often, these collections are computerized and computer-searchable, rendering them even more accessible and useful. They are especially useful for variationists, since they are usually quite large in size, and since there exist samples of various regional and national varieties, as well as samples from different time periods. However, caution must be exercised in comparing corpora to infer variation and change, since different collections may be comprised of slightly different types of data (e.g. data from a different range of registers). In addition, public corpora are limited in that not all of them provide social information on speakers (or writers). Despite these difficulties, public corpora have proven to be a valuable source of data for variationists, and technological advances promise to make them even more so in the near future. Hence, variationists are now supplementing their work in the street, the laboratory and the library with research in a new location, only vaguely anticipated in the early 1960s – cyberspace.

REFERENCE

Labov, William (1972). Some principles of linguistic methodology. *Language in Society* 1: 97–120.

NATALIE SCHILLING-ESTES

1 Entering the Community: Fieldwork

CRAWFORD FEAGIN

While the ultimate goal of sociolinguistic research is to resolve questions of linguistic importance, such as how language change comes about, nothing of that sort can be accomplished without first entering a community in order to collect data which will help provide the basis for any such answers. The central problem in collecting sociolinguistic data has been described by Labov as the Observer's Paradox: "our goal is to observe the way people use language when they are not being observed" (1972a: 61). Sociolinguistic fieldwork of all kinds, whether tape-recorded interviews, participant observations or street-corner quizzes, must be geared to overcome this problem. In this chapter, I consider several well-established methods. I begin with a section on "Planning the Project", dealing with preliminary considerations for a survey. The heart of the chapter, as indeed of field research, is the second section on the "Socio-linguistic Interview", the Labovian protocol for selecting informants and eliciting different styles of speech. I then consider some other elicitation methods used in sociolinguistics: participant observation, rapid and anonymous observations, and telephone surveys.

1 Planning the Project

Although the methods involved are presented here as if they were sequential, in practice the various phases of fieldwork and other aspects of research are cyclical, or perhaps spiral. Investigation in one area will influence what can be done in another. An interview might provide insights about the community that can be incorporated into the protocol and produce a much better interview with subsequent informants. For instance, in my work in Anniston, Alabama (Feagin 1979), one teenager mentioned a recent snowstorm, an unexpected and exciting phenomenon in that part of the world, so in later interviews I asked the rest of the teenagers about it. As a result, I came away with excited accounts of sledding on garbage-can tops and cookie sheets, wearing improvised boots made from plastic bags, and skidding dangerously over slippery roads. My interview protocol for the older people already included questions about a tornado that had hit Anniston 20 years before; the snowstorm provided similarly dramatic stories from an incident in the living memories of the teenagers.

Similarly, sometimes in the course of an interview, investigators might discover an unexpected grammatical form or phonological realization. They must be attentive and flexible in order to pursue the newly discovered linguistic feature for that community.

As an aid to planning, a small-scale pilot project along the general lines of the main research will indicate more precisely what might be feasible goals and procedures. A larger consideration is that collecting data is only an intermediate goal. The ultimate goal is linguistic.

The hypothesis that motivates the project will influence how to go about collecting the data. Again, I can illustrate this from my field research in Anniston. I hypothesized that over the three-and-a-half centuries of close contact, African-American speech would have influenced European-American grammar in the South. I therefore set out to elicit data from the white community that was parallel to Labov's African-American data from Harlem (Labov et al. 1968; Labov 1972b). Even though it turned out in large part that my hypothesis was not correct, nonetheless it was important to try to get parallel data so that a comparison would be possible.

An important guideline for fieldworkers at the planning stage is that a close analysis of a small amount of data is better than an unfinished grandiose project. With that in mind, I concentrated on the extreme generations (teenagers and grandparents) and extreme social classes (local working class and upper class), and the older rural working class (with no younger counterpart). More than that I could not handle, though ideally I would have liked to include the middle class and the middle aged, not to mention the local African-American community. However, examining only the two urban classes plus the older rural working class, using adolescents and grandparents in the city and elderly people from the country, keeping the genders even, I was able to see change progressing through the community.

A rule of thumb in disciplines that require fieldwork is that one third of the project time will be spent in fieldwork, one third in analysis, and the final third in writing up the work. Though far from scientific, this rule provides an effective reminder of the point that time required for analysis and writing increases in a ratio of about 2:1 for each hour of data elicitation.

Competent fieldworkers have included a wide range of personality types. Because fieldwork requires face-to-face interaction, it is usually assumed that gregarious persons do best, and it seems likely that they would have an advantage, at least in getting started. Shy people might find this sort of work excruciating, especially in the beginning. However, shy people have sometimes proven highly successful in conducting interviews and obtaining data, for the simple reason that people often open up when talking to quiet people, perhaps because they find them unthreatening and perhaps because the lack of interruptions encourages them to speak at length. Also, in certain types of communities, reserved people, who build social relations slowly, might be more accepted than gregarious people who rush in too quickly (Schilling-Estes, personal communication).

1.1   *Library research*

Once the community has been selected for research, the next step is to get a perspective on the community itself – linguistic, demographic, and historical. Information on local speech, major industries, labor, religious institutions, communications, movement of peoples, and the historical development of the area can aid in understanding local society.

A survey of previous linguistic work must be carried out, both on the linguistic aspects you intend to study and on any previous research concerning the local language variety. Earlier work on the local variety, regardless of its quality, can be useful for time depth or for pinpointing interesting problems.

First-hand accounts of fieldwork can be found in Labov (1966), Feagin (1979), Milroy (1980), Dayton (1996), and Eckert (2000) for linguistics, and in Whyte (1955; 1984) and Liebow (1967) for ethnography. Such personal accounts are rarely published, but dissertations often include them in a chapter on methodology. More general discussions may be found in Labov (1972a, 1984), Wolfram and Fasold (1974), Milroy (1987), Romaine (1980) and Baugh (1993). For sociolinguistic fieldwork in non-Western societies where the investigator is clearly an outsider, see Albó (1970), Harvey (1992), and Wald (1973). Obviously, a different set of problems arises when the fieldworker is a foreigner, of different ethnicity, and not a native speaker of the language. While addressed to researchers doing basic linguistic fieldwork (rather than sociolinguistic research) in non-Western languages (frequently in remote areas), Samarin (1967) provides an overview of linguistic fieldwork, though now somewhat dated.

1.2   *Ethnography*

Along with gathering linguistic data, it is important to study the community itself in situ. While material collected from library research must not be overlooked if it is available, the researcher in the field must begin by observing the physical layout of the place, who lives where, who associates with whom, and in what situations particular people associate with each other. While this type of research can be seen in Fischer (1958) and more elaborately in Labov (1963), subsequent studies have become more sophisticated and more detailed, culminating in Eckert's intricate study of a suburban Detroit high school (Eckert 2000). It is through an understanding of both the structure and dynamics of the local community that the structure and dynamics of the speech community

can be understood. While some linguists have criticized sociocultural investigations as outside the competence of linguists who are not specialists in sociology or anthropology (C.-J. Bailey 1996), the only way some aspects of language
behavior can be understood and analyzed is through such an undertaking.
This type of study will guide the selection of speakers as well as contributing
to the analysis of the resulting data. See Mendoza-Denton, Hazen, Meyerhoff,
Milroy, and Patrick, in this volume, for discussion of topics related to this issue.

It was through such a study that Labov was able to show that younger people
on the island of Martha's Vineyard who had decided to remain on the island
after their high school years were picking up the fishermen's pronunciation of
(ay) and (aw), regardless of their social class, while those who had decided to
leave the island for further education and employment were shifting toward
mainland speech norms (Labov 1963). Similarly, Eckert (2000) was able to
show that the social division between "jocks" (middle class) and "burnouts"
(working class) in suburban high schools played a role in transmitting urban
Detroit features into suburban teenage speech. See Eckert (2000: chapter 3) for
a valuable account of the process of studying the ethnography of a community.

1.3   *Linguistic variables*

In a quantitative study of linguistic variation, acquaintance with previous work
and perhaps a pilot study should help to narrow the focus of the project. In
practical terms, however, this does not always take place right at the beginning.
What needs to be isolated before analysis can begin, and preferably before
data-gathering begins, is a selection of linguistic variables to be studied.

The linguistic variable, a concept originating with Labov (1963, 1966), is a
linguistic entity which varies according to social parameters (age, sex, social
class, ethnicity), stylistic parameters (casual, careful, formal), and/or linguistic
parameters (segmental, suprasegmental). Usually the social and stylistic variation will be coordinated in some way, so that the casual speech of an account-
ant will be similar to the formal speech of a plumber – though that remains to
be seen in the course of the investigation.

The linguistic variable can be found at all linguistic levels: most common are
phonological, such as, for example, (r) might be realized as [ɹ] or as Ø in a
community which has been r-less and is becoming r-ful; morphophonological
as in (ing), the English present participle marker which has two common pronunciations, standard [ɪŋ] and casual [ən]; morphological as in the realization of
the past tense form of *dive* either as *dived* or as *dove*; syntactic as in the realization
of negated *be* variously as *ain't, isn't, 's not, is not*; or lexical as in the use of
either *hero* or *grinder* as the word to designate a particular kind of sandwich.
The most frequently studied variables are phonological and morphological.

The main criterion for determining the set of variants of a single variable is
that the referential meaning must be unchanged regardless of which variant
occurs. (This can present a problem when dealing with grammar, as pointed

out by Lavandera (1978) and Romaine (1981).) The selection of one variant from the set will generally be motivated by either social or stylistic considerations. See Wolfram (1993) and Guy (1993) for discussions of some of the problems connected to settling on the variable(s) to be investigated.

1.4   Equipment

To name particular types of equipment would not be useful, because technology changes so rapidly. However, some types of equipment have abiding advantages. The lavaliere microphone improves the quality of the sound and minimizes the speaker's attention to the recording mechanism. Fieldworkers have been known to develop fixations on the equipment in their kit after long and reliable use in numerous settings. In years past, it was not unheard of for a fieldworker to use the same piece of equipment for 30 years, and Samarin (1967) even recommended that fieldworkers should learn how to repair their machinery themselves. With technology changing as rapidly as it has in the decades since Samarin wrote, it seems unlikely that anyone will want to stick to equipment more than a decade old, and the development of solid-state technology makes recording equipment much more durable (and, incidentally, less repairable). Solid-state technology also makes equipment much lighter, a great blessing for fieldworkers. Thirty years ago, most fieldworkers used Uher reel-to-reel tape recorders. They weighed about 22 pounds, but every fieldworker who ever carried one knew that their weight seemed to increase dramatically every 500 meters or so.

The main point is to get the best equipment possible given the practical constraint of expense. Recording fidelity is the primary consideration, and after that come ease of use, flexibility, weight, and other factors. Field recordings can be useful for many years, for purposes unplanned. In my case, tape recordings intended only for a study of grammar have since been used for work on phonology, both using impressionistic phonetic transcription and computer-assisted vowel analysis.

1.5   Self-presentation of the fieldworker

Having selected the community and investigated the locale, culture, and speech, the investigator finally has to actually go there and find people to talk to. This is a rather stressful position to be in, from all accounts. Eckert (2000) describes the nightmares she had before beginning her work in the Detroit suburbs. Entering any community carries with it certain responsibilities for respecting the privacy and customs of local people. Most often, this is not a great problem because researchers tend to investigate cultures with which they have some personal familiarity. It is a much greater problem, obviously, in a culture and language that is not native to the investigator. In these situations, Samarin

(1967: 19) recommends that the researcher undertake meticulous planning to deal with the pressures, being aware of the problems that might arise and arranging for breaks in order to get away from the locale from time to time.

Often, cultural alienation is not a factor. My own fieldwork, for instance, took place in my home town, where I had lived until I was 15, and where both my mother and grandfather had grown up. My role there, while conducting fieldwork between 1969 and 1973 and again in 1990 and 1991, was both as a visitor in the town, staying with my grandparents, and as a researcher working on my dissertation, carrying out interviews. On my side of town I was known to the people I interviewed as a friend's granddaughter or cousin, but on the other side of town I was a complete stranger doing research. I told people that I was working on a book on growing up in the town, and how it was changing over time, especially for the teenagers. I said I wanted to record speech in the interests of accuracy, so I would get the dialog right. As a former resident with kinship ties in the town, I attended church with my family, visited friends, and took my grandmother to her club meetings. I also attended revival meetings and visited a church on the other side of town, which helped me learn about the life and culture outside of my own experience and to meet older people who were members of the church I visited.

I was careful to dress suitably according to local custom, always wearing a skirt and stockings to interview older people and to attend classes at the high school, but sometimes wearing blue jeans and sitting on the floor when interviewing teenagers, explaining that I needed to watch the level on the tape recorder while we were talking. In this way I was showing respect to my elders and solidarity with the younger group. With teenagers, I generally took along sodas and chips, which helped make the recording less formal, though the crunch of potato chips sometimes is noticeable on the tape.

In reporting on his research in a small town in North Carolina, Hazen (2000a) explains that before beginning his fieldwork he had married a woman from the community, which gave him entree. However, as a native of suburban Detroit, he was not as well-acquainted with the culture as he might have liked, though this also allowed him to assume the role of a student of that culture and ask questions that only an outsider could ask.

Albó (1970) describes in detail his entry into rural communities in Andean Bolivia where his identity as a priest proved advantageous. He was sometimes asked to bless houses, which gave him an opportunity to observe the living standards of the families. This contributed to his understanding of the degree of modernization of the household, giving insight into the relationship between the borrowing of linguistic forms and of material culture. It also gave him opportunities to line up interviews. Similarly, Harvey (1992), whose research was in Southern Peru after it became a dangerous area for outsiders, was considered the adopted daughter of a local family, which gave her a place in the community, allowing her to observe both language and culture.

Both Whyte (1955) and Liebow (1967) emphasize that it is never possible to completely fit in, nor is it necessary or even advisable. As white middle-class men carrying out ethnographic research among working-class men, one group white and the other black, they report that they were able to lower the barriers between their subjects and themselves but not to remove them. Liebow uses the image of the chain-link fence: you can see through it, but it remains a barrier. The researcher can become a friend, and even find a role in the community, but skin color, class affiliation, speech, or education may all set the investigator apart, which can also serve as a protection in some situations.

While I fit in on my own side of town in Anniston to a certain degree, I often heard expressions of polite amazement from the more traditional citizens that I had driven from Washington to Alabama "all by myself," and there was some not-so-polite gossip that I had left my husband, which accounted for my long visits to my grandparents.

2   The Sociolinguistic Interview

The classic method of sociolinguistic research is the one-on-one tape-recorded conversational interview (Labov 1972a, 1984; Wolfram and Fasold 1974). Tape-recording has the obvious advantage of permanency, so that it is possible to return to the recording again and again, either for clarification or for further research. A second major advantage is that the tape-recording permits the researcher to fulfill the Principle of Accountability (Labov 1972c: 72), so that all occurrences as well as non-occurrences of the variable can be identified and accounted for. In this way statistical manipulations of the data can show whether the occurrence of a variable is happenstance or patterned, and, if patterned, to what degree in contrast to the occurrence in the speech of others of varying social characteristics – age, sex, social class, ethnicity. This, then, is the primary method of quantitative sociolinguistics.

Variations on this approach include interviewing two or more speakers together (Feagin 1979). Labov used group interviews in his work with Harlem street gangs (Labov et al. 1968, Labov 1972b), with one lavaliere microphone per person, and a multitrack recorder. These variations on the one-on-one interview are intended to reduce the formality of the interview, turning it into a more natural social event.

However, the sociolinguistic interview – regardless of the variations on it – does carry some disadvantages. The interview as a speech event is a special genre (Wolfson 1976), so the naturalness and certainly the informality of the recorded speech can be called into question, regardless of efforts to make the speaker feel comfortable with the situation. The use of lavaliere microphones may remove the microphone from view, but the tape recorder is always there.

The interview method works best for frequently occurring variables, especially phonological and morphological, and certain syntactic forms, such as negation. But many syntactic structures, including interrogatives, double modals, and special auxiliaries such as perfective *done*, do not occur frequently enough in interviews to provide sufficient data for analysis. Moreover, the interview is problematical for discourse studies and ethnomethodology (Briggs 1986).

2.1   Selecting speakers

The earliest community-based research in sociolinguistics, Labov's work in Martha's Vineyard (1963), used a judgment sample, selecting subjects to fill pre-selected social categories, all locally born and raised adults and teenagers. His categories crisscrossed geographic area, profession, and ethnicity. It is interesting that in this early study gender was not considered a separate social variable, though only men were used for acoustic analysis. In his New York study a few years later, Labov was able to base his subject selection on a previous random survey by the Mobilization for Youth, a project of the School of Social Work at Columbia University, which had conducted a random-sample survey of the Lower East Side. Labov used their demographic data to select natives of the area or people who had arrived by age five. This was, then, a stratified random sample in that it selected a stratified sample from what had originally been a random sample. In his third major project (Labov et al. 1968, Labov 1972b), Labov worked with teenage boys who were members of street gangs. This represents an early – possibly the earliest – study of language variation through social networks.

Trudgill (1974: 20–30), who followed soon after with a study of Norwich, England, relied on a quasi-random sample taken from four ward voter registration lists. The names from the voter lists were chosen randomly, but the wards were not random but were selected "so that they had, between them, social and economic characteristics that were, on average, the same as those of the city as a whole" (1974: 22).

My own work in Anniston, Alabama, was based on a judgment sample, filling pre-selected cells on a number of criteria. First, speakers were chosen because they were native-born or had arrived by age five. Second, preference was given to those whose parents were from the area. Though I did not know of the literature on networks at the time, I often selected subjects who were "a friend of a friend," using the resources of my family and their acquaintances for contacts. I began with friends of a younger cousin, then moved on to friends of my grandparents. Later, when I wanted to work in another section of town, I began with a home economics teacher who turned out to be an acquaintance and an admirer of my grandfather. She welcomed me into her classes where I was able to observe, and in some cases (with permission) to record the students and make appointments with them for interviews. Twenty years later, in 1990, I followed the same procedures to find teenaged subjects on both sides of town. Luckily enough, the new home economics teacher said that if the earlier one, who had been her own teacher, had let me visit her class, it was all right with her. The now-retired home economics teacher was still in touch with the students I had interviewed 20 years before, and through her I was able to find those students again, most of whom still lived in the area.

When the Milroys were selecting informants in Belfast (1980), they were forced to rely on the "friend of a friend" method for contacts because of the sectarian problems in the city, and especially in the working-class neighborhoods where they intended to work. Their methods auspiciously introduced the concept of the network to sociolinguists. (See Milroy in this volume, on social networks.)

Generally, researchers must use common sense to select subjects not by some pre-ordained "social-science" formula but according to the prevailing conditions of the setting they are working in. Thus a recent study of speech on the Outer Banks, a group of islands in the Atlantic off the coast of North Carolina, selected ancestral islanders because the purpose of the study was to recover, as far as possible, traditional speech (Wolfram et al. 1999). Eckert (2000) selected high school students of opposing ideologies and styles, known as Burnouts and Jocks, basically working-class and upper-middle-class adolescents, because she was studying the dynamics of adolescent speech and culture in the school setting.

One danger with selecting informants by pre-selected categories is that the result can be self-fulfilling or circular. For a more general community study, Horvath (1985) gathered speech data from a stratified judgment sample in Sydney, Australia, and analyzed it using principal components analysis so that the analysis incorporated no assumptions about class membership or sex. The principal components analysis put speakers into clusters according to their linguistic similarities, and in that way revealed what the sociolinguistic groupings of Sydney were, based entirely on speech.

Except for studies that take a special interest in the language of children (as Roberts in this volume), it is better to avoid speakers younger than adolescents, since there is the possibility of confounding phonological or grammatical development with local variation.

The two genders must be kept fairly even numerically in order to prevent a confounding of gender differences with the other distinctions. Many studies have demonstrated gender differences in language, beginning with Fischer's (1958) study of (ing) which showed that boys in a small New England town were more likely to use the [ən] variant than girls.

Attention must be given to social class in regard to informants (as in Ash, this volume). The older members of any class usually have the most conservative phonology; teenage working-class boys and girls are often the leaders in innovation, with certain items being more characteristic of one gender than the other. Eckert (2000) elaborates a striking example of highly innovative teenagers with gender differentiation in that innovation. In regard to grammar, the higher classes will use a local variety of the standard; the older members of the working class will maintain older forms which have become nonstandard and which may be obsolete in other places, while the younger speakers may still use those forms, but may also show innovative forms. For example, an older working-class woman in Anniston used *clim* as the past participle of *climb*, a form which existed in seventeenth- and eighteenth-century English but which since has become obsolete.

Ethnicity often provides a striking correlate with linguistic variation. Wolfram et al. (1999) and Rickford (1985) have shown that African-Americans and European-Americans living together on isolated islands, of the same socioeconomic background, education and age, show consistent differences in their speech, both in phonology (on the Outer Banks) and in grammar (Sea Islands and Outer Banks).

2.2 Sample size

The next question to be resolved is how many speakers are needed. The question depends most directly on the number of independent variables. If you are interested in comparing the speech of working-class men and women of the same age, say, 30 years old, then you have subjects in only two cells: 30-year-old women and 30-year-old men. If you expand the study to include men and women of 60 as well, the number of cells doubles to four. If you expand to include both working-class and middle-class subjects, it doubles again to eight cells. Obviously, each cell must be filled with enough subjects to provide confident generalizations about the social group.

How many subjects should fill each cell? The simple answer is: the more the better. In practice, sociolinguistic analysis requires isolating and classifying dozens and sometimes hundreds of tokens from each subject. It bears no resemblance to the sampling carried out in many kinds of social sciences for the purposes of opinion polls or voter preferences. As a rule of thumb, five persons per cell is often adequate, assuming the cells are well-defined in terms of local social categories (Guy 1980). I followed this rule in my Anniston study, where cells consisted of the independent variables of age/sex/social class/locale (urban/rural); so, for instance, I had to locate and interview at least five older rural working-class male informants.

2.3 Interview protocols and questionnaires

There are two main types of sociolinguistic interviews. The most influential one, modeled on Labov's work, uses a set of questions to elicit as much free conversation as possible, with some reading tasks designed to elicit a range of styles. Another way of going about it is simply to let the conversation flow (Briggs 1986, Hazen 2000a). This more open-ended type of interviewing is intended to reduce the distance between interviewer and subject, making the interaction more natural.

For the more structured interview, protocols may be found in appendices of several reports (Labov 1966, Feagin 1979, Labov 1984, Horvath 1985, Wolfram et al. 1999, to name a few). The goal is to sample a range of styles, from formal to casual. Some researchers, however, have considered the conceptualization of style as a unidimensional "formal–informal" continuum to be problematic (see Schilling-Estes, this volume).

These interviews usually begin by asking subjects about themselves – year and place of birth, parents' birthplace, schooling (speaker's and parents'), occupation (their own or their parents or spouse). Questions like these elicit a relatively formal or selfconscious speaking style, known as Interview Style, as will discussion of school or the workplace (see Sankoff and Laberge 1978). Such questions invite selfconscious responses by asking the subjects to reflect on their histories and their accomplishments. Under other circumstances, asking about school activities may elicit informal and spontaneous speech, if directed to subjects deeply and personally involved in those activities. Thus Eckert's teenaged subjects become very animated when talking about activities, groups, and characters in their school, as did mine (Eckert 2000, Feagin 1979). This distinction is crucial in planning the interview protocol. The least selfconscious speech comes from topics in which the subjects are intimately involved, and the most selfconscious speech comes from asking people to talk about their credentials.

In the opening section on demographics, asking the subjects to list the houses they have lived in can lead to a discussion of the neighborhood where the speakers grew up, and that can lead to discussing childhood friends and describing rules for various games, jump-rope rhymes, and so on. Here the speaker will probably switch to a less formal, more conversational style. It is difficult to monitor one's speech when recalling and reciting such rhymes as "Fatty, fatty two-by-four, can't get through the bathroom door."

Asking the subjects about their first dates or how they met their spouses sometimes elicits a flood of speech, at least in the European-American context. Labov's best known question has to do with the danger of death: "Have you ever been in a situation where you nearly lost your life? Where you thought This is *it*!" While sometimes this elicits an outstanding narrative, it seems to work better in New York City than anywhere else. My speakers in Alabama, asked the same question, generally responded, after a pause, "No." In a sociolinguistic survey in Toronto, Chambers (1980) originally included Labov's famous question in his interview protocol, but soon deleted it after one older man replied, with furrowed brow, that he had attended a funeral a couple of weeks before. Trudgill (1974) also had no success with the "danger of death" question in Norwich, England. Milroy (1980) found that in Belfast, where danger of death is quite common, it did not trigger emotional narratives.

In Anniston, after the danger-of-death question proved unsuccessful, I discovered that the question "Have you ever heard of anybody seeing a ghost around here?" often elicited long elaborate narratives of local mayhem and murder from older working-class speakers. Similarly, with his Canadian subjects in Toronto, Chambers discovered he could elicit passionate speech by saying, "People keep saying we're getting more and more American. Do you think that's true?"

The interview, obviously, must be adjusted for local conditions. Familiarity with local customs helps develop questions such as "When did you get your first gun?" in the Southern United States, or "What you were doing when that tornado hit back in 1954?" There is no simple formula for eliciting relatively unmonitored, casual styles. The best advice is for researchers to know their regions, especially the tensions in the community, when planning the interview protocol.

2.4   More formal styles: Reading passages, word lists, minimal pairs

The use of written materials in the interview protocol depends on the focus of the research. Presenting subjects with a reading passage, word list, and minimal pair list can certainly be useful for research oriented toward phonology, because the researcher can ensure that the same words, involving phonological contrasts or variables, are recorded for every subject. In studying syntax, having the speaker read sentences while being recorded can produce valuable results, if they are used to elicit judgments on grammaticality or acceptability. The speakers can be asked who would use such a sentence, even if they themselves would not. If reading is a problem, as it often is for the oldest rural subjects either through poor eyesight or through illiteracy, having subjects repeat sentences read by the interviewer can also be a source of information. Wolfram and Fasold (1974) discuss repetition tasks and some of the information they can yield. In my own work, I started out using word lists and sentences, but dropped them, since I was concentrating on grammar alone. However, judgments on sentences proved to be useful, as ancillary evidence. Now that I am using the same tapes to work on phonology, I am very much aware that it would have been helpful to have kept the word list to observe style shifting, and to get an idea of what might be considered more selfconscious speech.

Word lists and reading passages that have been used successfully may be found in the appendix to Labov (1966), Trudgill (1974), and elsewhere. See also Labov (1984) for a description of various field experiments and references to their use. Each community and each set of variables requires its own materials, but looking at previous models can be helpful.

2.5   During the interview

Keeping the attention and interest of the speaker during the interview is obviously important, and that makes it hard for the researcher to limit backchannelling. It is natural to respond to what the speaker says, to offer your own opinions and to bring up parallel experiences. As Milroy (1987) notes, the interview is an exchange in which the interviewer has to contribute to get quality conversation back. Breaking my self-imposed silence in a second interview with one of my subjects, comparing notes with the speaker on some experiences we shared, I discovered that the speaker's phonology and grammar altered at that point, with more local vowels – more breaking and shifting – and nonstandard grammar where there had been little or none before.

Still, it is important not to waste time and not to tape record one's own voice. Perhaps the most embarrassing moment for novice fieldworkers is the discovery, on listening to interviews they have made, that their own contributions limited what the subject might have offered by interjecting friendly asides or interrupting the flow of the subject's conversation. The interview tapes sometimes preserve hard evidence of misguided sociability.

While controlling the inclination to take the floor, the interviewer nevertheless must maintain eye contact (if appropriate in the culture) and all the other outward signs of involvement, at the same time keeping a watchful eye on the recording equipment and a dutiful ear on the production of the desired variables.

2.6   After the interview

Whether or not to pay informants is subject to debate (as in Whyte 1984: 361–5). While I have never paid speakers for interviews, others have and do. This may be a community-specific issue. Researchers are often graduate students working on doctoral dissertations – unpaid or poorly paid themselves, so what most of them rely on is an exchange of services, such as giving rides, if the researcher has a car, or helping with schoolwork, or writing letters, as did Dayton (1996). As Whyte points out (1984) paying speakers can change the nature of the enterprise, even compromising the possibility of further research by making it much too expensive for others following after.

Before leaving the speaker, an important legal matter must still be addressed: the person interviewed must sign a release to allow the interview to be used for scholarly purposes. The wording should be in conformity with university or funding agency rules.

2.7   Ethics

Surreptitious recordings, made by planting a recording device where it will capture ambient conversations without the knowledge or consent of the participants, are considered unethical, illegal, and pointless. In their favor, of course, is the elimination of the Observer's Paradox, but in purely practical terms, apart from ethics, sound quality is usually so poor that it is a waste of time, and discovery by the community can lead to serious repercussions. However, the legal aspects of surreptitious tapings have been discussed and defended by Larmouth et al. (1992). They review state and federal laws of the United States, and illustrate their points with examples of real or possible situations and their legal outcomes.

Harvey (1992) made covert recordings of drunken speech because it was central to her research, and she states that, while she found it distasteful, she would do it again (1992: 80). She considers surreptitious recordings as no more culpable than researchers not being entirely open about their research agenda with speakers, as in my telling speakers that I was interested in what it was like growing up in Anniston, Alabama, rather than saying outright that I was interested in their grammar.

Most researchers consider that surreptitious taping violates the privacy of the subjects. Even in open recording, it is usually necessary to respect the privacy of subjects by disguising their identities. Some researchers use alphanumeric codes for speakers, but a better system is to use pseudonyms that preserve their ethnicity and other essential traits, so that someone with a German name would be given a German pseudonym, and the same style of naming. This results in a much more readable text. Taped discussions of illegal activities or private matters should be treated as confidential, regardless of the informant's attitude toward such things at the time.

3 Participant Observation

Because the effect of recording on the interview can never be completely eradicated and because interviews are entirely unsuitable for obtaining certain kinds of data, participant observation has come into being as a complementary method of data collection. This entails living and participating in the community in some function other than as a linguist, but observing and noting particular types of linguistic data. Such observations are frequently used to supplement material collected from interviews, as by Labov et al. (1968) and Feagin (1979), but they can also be used as the primary source of data, as in Rickford (1975), Mishoe and Montgomery (1994), and Dayton (1996).

Participant observation is especially useful for studying infrequent grammatical items such as questions, modals, and particles, where tape-recorded interviews will not capture these forms. Either the discourse constraints are such that the question/answer format or the extended narrative of the interview do not allow the forms, or the forms are too rare to make an interview worthwhile. For such variables, participant observation becomes necessary. The researcher must become a member of the community.

The best discussion of the rationale for using participant observation as well as the most complete description of this method is found in Dayton (1996: chapter 2). Here Dayton relates how she, a white woman, became a member of an African-American working-class community in Philadelphia. She first lived in that neighborhood for two years simply as a graduate student, not participating in the life there. Then she lived as a participant observer for four and half more years, becoming a block chairman, organizing clean-ups, volleyball games, and generally entering into the local African-American life in that block.

The participant observer, instead of tape-recording data, writes it down as soon as possible. Dayton managed to write down most of the data for her study within an hour of hearing it. She seldom attempted to store and remember more than three items at a time. Mishoe and Montgomery (1994) who collected their corpus of double modals through participant observation, report that they wrote items down within a minute of hearing them.

This technique has certain advantages over the tape-recorded interview in that the researcher becomes an insider, and can in this way overcome the Observer's Paradox. In order to do this the researcher must reach the point of understanding the communicative and interactional norms of the speech community and participating in the informal social ties and exchange relationships that hold the community together (Dayton 1996: 71).

In the course of her study, Dayton collected 3,610 tokens of African-American tense/mood/aspect markers (Dayton 1996: 55), probably the largest corpus of these grammatical forms. Her observations also included the more general social context as well as the linguistic context of the use of these markers.

The drawback of participant observation is that researchers cannot write down all the tokens of the variable they might hear. There is an inevitable selectivity in the linguistic record. The selectivity means that the data cannot be quantified, so that it is impossible to provide information on the relative frequency of the variable. In addition, there is no permanent record of the speakers, so that it is not possible to return to the evidence. Here the question of accuracy and reliability naturally arises. Counterbalancing that, it permits the study of rare forms, otherwise undocumentable. And the perceptual saliency of the items can abet the accuracy of the observations. In another context, Wolfram suggests that socially marked items are the most transparent differences, and as such they rank high on a "continuum of linguistic trustworthiness" (Wolfram 1990: 125; similarly Dayton 1996: 68–80).

4   Rapid and Anonymous Observations

While participant observation is a very time-consuming and labor-intensive way to overcome the Observer's Paradox, another, faster technique is "rapid and anonymous observation," first described by Labov (1966, 1972c). By this method, the variable under study is embedded in the answer to a question that can be posed to strangers. Labov, in a famous example, asked sales clerks in department stores, "Where can I find Women's shoes?" The respondents replied, "The fourth floor." What Labov was interested in was the pronunciation of (r) in the words *fourth* and *floor*. Labov selected a range of stores, from luxury (Saks Fifth Avenue) to bargain basement (Kleins), and was able to confirm that sales clerks tend to speak in a manner that reflect the clientele. The clerks at Saks were r-ful as are upper-middle-class New Yorkers, while those at Kleins were r-less, like working-class New Yorkers. Labov was able to capture 528 tokens of *fourth floor* from 264 subjects in approximately 6.5 hours.

The simplicity of this study has encouraged replications of it in New York and many other places, either studying (r) or other variables. For example, in some communities, the question "Excuse me. Could you tell me what time it is?" (at the right time of day) will produce many tokens of *five* or *four*. This type of study obviously sacrifices knowledge of the background of the speaker in favor of the naturalness of the speech.

5 Telephone Surveys

In addition to the sociolinguistic interview and participant observation, a third method of obtaining data is over the telephone. Labov included telephone interviews in his survey of the Lower East Side (1966: 118–20), when he called people who had refused to be interviewed, or could not be interviewed because of schedule conflicts or the like. The purpose was to get information on their phonology in order to ascertain whether it was similar to those who were interviewed. The first part of the telephone conversation was designed to elicit the variables being studied, and the second part was to elicit natural conversational speech (Labov 1966: 457–8). Later, as part of his Philadelphia study, Labov incorporated a random sample telephone survey to supplement the neighborhood studies (Labov 1984).

The obvious advantage of the telephone is its efficiency in covering a large territory. As part of a study of low back vowel merger in Pennsylvania, Herold (1990) carried out a state-wide telephone survey. She describes in detail how she selected the locale and the individual by searching for uncommon names in the telephone book with multiple entries (ten or more) on the assumption that those families would be well-established in the area. Father and son entries allowed the inference that the son had probably grown up in the town. By these means, Herold located a sample that was local, defined as someone "who had lived within a 30-mile radius of the county seat (or largest city) from the age of three or younger, until the age of 16" (1990: 23), The interviews were recorded (with permission), using a questionnaire designed to elicit near-minimal pairs (1990: Appendix).

Bailey and Bernstein devised the Phonological Survey of Texas as one component of a random sample tape-recorded survey of the entire state of Texas (Bailey and Bernstein 1989, Bailey and Dyer 1992). They carried it out by "piggybacking" on the Texas Poll of January and November 1989, a large-scale service sponsored by Texas A&M University that conducts quarterly telephone surveys of 1,000 adult Texans selected by random sampling. The Poll mounts surveys for business, public policy agencies, and academic researchers. The January poll included questions to elicit data on phonological features undergoing change in Texas, and the November poll included questions designed to elicit lexical, grammatical, and language policy data. Both polls provided some longer passages of discourse as well as a wide range of phonological variables. The results provided a broad-based and almost instantaneous picture of the spread of linguistic changes in Texas.

Labov's Telsur project (Telephone Survey of North America) is completely telephone-based, independent of any other survey, and his sole data source for the *Atlas of North American English* (Labov 2000, Labov et al. forthcoming). Labov became convinced of the feasibility of a large-scale telephone survey when he made a pilot survey in the late 1960s (Labov 1991: 31–2, 42). That survey elicited certain key words from long-distance operators across the United States in order to check contrasts in the low back vowels (*cot/caught*). From that start, Labov and his team have carried out a broader telephone survey of the United States and English-speaking Canada.

The sample consists of almost 700 speakers, selected to represent all urban areas. Interviews have been undertaken with speakers from 161 urbanized areas, most with a population of over 200,000, but including a few smaller cities in sparsely populated areas (Ash 2000). The speakers were chosen to represent the dominant national ancestry groups of each area, with names selected from telephone books based on national ancestry figures from the 1990 census.

The telephone interview itself is carefully scripted to elicit phonological contrasts or vowel shifts, resulting in up to an hour of recorded speech. The subject then receives a word list by mail, and reads the list in a follow-up telephone call. All interviews are impressionistically coded for all variables elicited on mergers and near-mergers, as well as syntactic and lexical variables. The resulting phonological data are then analyzed acoustically and plotted on feature maps. The grid is broad, usually with only two speakers in each city, but the methodology provides an efficient phonological overview of a vast region.

6   Life after Fieldwork

Whatever methods the researcher uses, when the fieldwork is finally completed, any sense of relief evaporates rapidly as the reality of analysis of all that data dawns. Analysis, of course, moves the sociolinguist onto an entirely different level, with its own problems and its own rewards (as the following chapters make clear). The crucial first step, the fieldwork, becomes subordinated to finding, expressing and disseminating the substantive results of the project. It is undoubtedly true that the more successful the fieldwork, the less noticeable it is in the final analysis. Fieldwork draws attention to itself mainly when the researcher has to concede that there are gaps in the data or flawed elicitations or results that require caution in the interpretation. It is inconspicuous when it has yielded a well-formed database for making generalizations and testing hypotheses. The sociolinguist's prowess as fieldworker is often a private source of professional pride that only occasionally seeps into the public domain when sociolinguists gather informally at conferences and meetings. Inconspicuous it may be, but it is the bedrock of the sociolinguistic enterprise.

REFERENCES

Albó, Xavier (1970). Social constraints on Cochabamba Quechua. Ph.D. dissertation, Cornell University.

Ash, Sharon (2000). Sampling strategy for the Telsur/Atlas Project. http://www.ling.upenn.edu/ phonoatlas/sampling

Bailey, Charles-James N. (1996). *Essays on Timed-based Linguistic Analysis.* Oxford: Oxford University Press.

Bailey, Guy and Cynthia Bernstein (1989). Methodology of a phonological survey of Texas. *Journal of English Linguistics* 22: 6–16.

Bailey, Guy and Margie Dyer (1992). An approach to sampling in dialectology. *American Speech* 67: 3–20.

Baugh, John (1993). Adapting dialectology: The conduct of community language studies. In Dennis R. Preston (ed.), *American Dialect Research.* Amsterdam and Philadlephia: John Benjamins. 167–91.

Briggs, Charles L. (1986). *Learning How to Ask: A Sociolinguistic Appraisal of the Role of the Interview in Social Science Research.* Cambridge: Cambridge University Press.

Chambers, J. K. (1980). Linguistic variation and Chomsky's "homogeneous speech community." In Murray Kinloch and A. B. House (eds.), *Papers from the Fourth Annual Meeting of the Atlantic Provinces Linguistic Association.* Fredericton: University of New Brunswick. 1–32.

Dayton, Elizabeth (1996). Grammatical Categories of the Verb in African-American Vernacular English. Ph.D. dissertation, University of Pennsylvania.

Eckert, Penelope (2000). *Linguistic Variation as Social Practice: The Linguistic Construction of Social Identity in Belten High.* Oxford: Blackwell.

Feagin, Crawford (1979). *Variation and Change in Alabama English: A Sociolinguistic Study of the White Community.* Washington, DC: Georgetown University Press.

Fischer, John L. (1958). Social influences on the choice of a linguistic variant. *Word* 14: 47–56.

Guy, Gregory R. (1980). Variation in the group and in the individual. In William Labov (ed.), *Locating Language in Time and Space.* New York: Academic Press. 1–36.

Guy, Gregory R. (1993). The quantitative analysis of linguistic variation. In Dennis Preston (ed.), *American Dialect Research.* Philadelphia: John Benjamins. 223–49.

Harvey, Penelope (1992). Bilingualism in the Peruvian Andes. In Deborah Cameron, Elizabeth Frazer, Penelope Harvey, M. B. H. Rampton and Kay Richardson (eds.), *Researching Language: Issues of Power and Method.* London: Routledge. 65–89.

Hazen, Kirk (2000a). *Identity and Ethnicity in the Rural South: A Sociolinguistic View through Past and Present* be. Publication of the American Dialect Society 83. Durham, NC: Duke University Press.

Hazen, Kirk (2000b). The role of researcher identity in conducting sociolinguistic research: A reflective case study. *Southern Journal of Linguistics* 24: 103–20.

Herold, Ruth (1990). The implementation and distribution of the low back merger in eastern Pennsylvania. Ph.D. dissertation, University of Pennsylvania.

Horvath, Barbara (1985). *Variation in Australian English: The Sociolects of Sydney* Cambridge: Cambridge University Press.

Labov, William (1963). The social motivation of a sound change. *Word* 19: 273–309.

Labov, William (1966). *The Social Stratification of English in New York City.* Washington, DC: Center for Applied Linguistics.

Labov, William (1971). Methodology. In William Orr Dingwall (ed.), *A Survey of Linguistic Science.* Linguistics Program, University of Maryland. 413–97.

Labov, William (1972a). Some principles of linguistic methodology. *Language in Society* 1: 97–120.

Labov, William (1972b). *Language in the Inner City.* Philadelphia: University of Pennsylvania Press.

Labov, William (1972c). *Sociolinguistic Patterns.* Philadelphia: University of Pennsylvania Press.

Labov, William (1984). Field methods of the project on linguistic change and variation. In John Baugh and Joel Sherzer (eds.), *Language in Use.* Englewood Cliffs, NJ: Prentice-Hall. 28–53.

Labov, William (1991). The three dialects of English. In Penelope Eckert (ed.), *New Ways of Analyzing Sound Change.* San Diego, CA: Academic Press. 1–44.

Labov, William (2000). The Telsur Project at the Linguistics Laboratory, University Pennsylvania. http://www.ling.upenn.edu/phonoatlas

Labov, William, Paul Cohen, Clarence Robins and John Lewis (1968). A study of the Non-Standard English of Negro and Puerto Rican speakers in New York City. Cooperative Research Project No. 3288. Office of Education, US Department of Health, Education, and Welfare.

Labov, William, Sharon Ash, and Charles Boberg (forthcoming). *Atlas of North American English: Phonetics, Phonology, and Sound Change.* Berlin: Mouton de Gruyter.

Larmouth, Donald W., Thomas E. Murray and Carin Ross Murray (1992). *Legal and Ethical Issues in Surreptitious Recording.* Publication of the American Dialect Society, 76. Tuscaloosa: University of Alabama Press.

Lavandera, Beatriz (1978). Where does the sociolinguistic variable stop? *Language in Society* 7: 171–83.

Liebow, Elliot (1967). *Talley's Corner: A Study of Negro Streetcorner Men.* Boston, MA: Little, Brown.

Milroy, Lesley (1987). *Observing and Analyzing Natural Language.* Oxford: Blackwell Publishers.

Milroy, Lesley (1980). *Language and Social Networks.* Oxford: Basil Blackwell.

Mishoe, Margaret and Michael Montgomery (1994). The pragmatics of multiple modal variation in North and South Carolina. *American Speech* 69: 3–29.

Rickford, John (1975). Carrying the new wave into syntax: The case of Black English BIN. In Ralph W. Fasold and Roger W. Shuy (eds.), *Analyzing Variation in English.* Washington, DC: Georgetown University Press. 162–83.

Rickford, John (1985). Ethnicity as a sociolinguistic boundary. *American Speech* 60: 99–125.

Romaine, Suzanne (1980). A critical overview of the methodology of urban British sociolinguistics. *English World-Wide* 1: 163–98.

Romaine, Suzanne (1981). On the problem of syntactic variation: A reply to Beatriz Lavandera and William Labov. *Working Papers in Sociolinguistics 82*. Austin, TX: Southwest Educational Development Laboratory.

Samarin, William (1967). *Field Linguistics: A Guide to Linguistic Field work*. New York: Holt, Rinehart and Winston.

Sankoff, David and Suzanne Laberge (1978). The linguistic market and the statistical explanation of variability. In David Sankoff (ed.), *Linguistic Variation: Models and Methods*. New York: Academic Press. 239–50.

Trudgill, Peter (1974). *The Social Differentiation of English in Norwich*. Cambridge: Cambridge University Press.

Wald, Benji (1973). Variation in the system of tense markers of Mombasa Swahili. Ph.D. dissertation, Columbia University.

Whyte, William F. (1943/1955/1993). *Street Corner Society: Structure of an Italian slum*. 4th edn. Appendix A: On the Evolution of Street Corner Society. Chicago: University of Chicago Press.

Whyte, William F. (1984). *Learning from the Field: A Guide from Experience*. Beverly Hills, CA: Sage Publications.

Wolfram, Walt (1990). Review article: Re-examining Vernacular Black English. *Language* 66: 121–33.

Wolfram, Walt (1993). Identifying and interpreting variables. In Dennis R. Preston (ed.), *American Dialect Research*. Amsterdam: John Benjamins. 193–221.

Wolfram, Walt and Ralph Fasold (1974). *The Study of Social Dialects in American English*. Englewood Cliffs, NJ: Prentice Hall.

Wolfram, Walt, Kirk Hazen and Natalie Schilling-Estes (1999). *Dialect Change and Maintenance on the Outer Banks*. Publication of the American Dialect Society 81. Tuscaloosa: University of Alabama Press.

Wolfson, Nessa (1976). Speech events and natural speech. *Language in Society* 5: 189–209.

2 Language with an Attitude

DENNIS R. PRESTON

Language attitude study has focused largely on the clues that language use provides a listener to a speaker's group membership and the triggering of the listener's beliefs about the group. Although classic work in the social psychology of language supports this general picture, elaborating on the substructure of those beliefs through various techniques, it is also clear that language has a life of its own and that our understanding of folk belief about various aspects of language itself also plays an important role in understanding the foundations for language attitudes.

In other words, although stereotypes are strong in attitudinal responses, they must be interpreted through the template of folk theories of language as well as of groups, and the results of both folk and attitudinal studies are tied here to a more linguistically-oriented interpretation, one which tries to develop a connection among performance, attitudes, perceptions, acquisition, and (almost needless to say) variation.

1 Language and People

It is perhaps the least surprising thing imaginable to find that attitudes towards languages and their varieties seem to be tied to attitudes towards groups of people. Some groups are believed to be decent, hard-working, and intelligent (and so is their language or variety); some groups are believed to be laid-back, romantic, and devil-may-care (and so is their language or variety); some groups are believed to be lazy, insolent, and procrastinating (and so is their language or variety); some groups are believed to be hard-nosed, aloof, and unsympathetic (and so is their language or variety), and so on. For the folk mind, such correlations are obvious, reaching down even into the linguistic details of the language or variety itself. Germans are harsh; just listen to their harsh, gutteral consonants. US Southerners are laid-back and lazy; just listen to their lazy, drawled vowels. Lower-status speakers are unintelligent; they don't even understand that two negatives make a positive, and so on. Edwards summarizes this correlation for many social psychologists when he notes that "people's reactions to language varieties reveal much of their perception of the speakers of these varieties" (1982: 20).

Of course, none of this correlation of stereotypes to linguistic facts will do for linguists, who find the structure of language everywhere complex and fully articulated, reflecting, as most present-day linguists would have it, the universal and species-specific human capacity for language. Where consonants are made, how vowel length is distributed, and what morphological, lexical, syntactic, semantic, and pragmatic strategies are employed to express negation are all reflexes of the complex interaction of the underlying components of the organizing system which allows human language.[1] Nevertheless, an understanding of this correlation between group stereotypes and linguistic facts, no matter how scientifically suspect at the linguistic end, appears to be particularly important in the more scientific calculation of the social identities we maintain and respond to. The apparent difficulty in establishing language-and-people connections was, at first, a great concern to social psychologists. The person-in-the-street might not be so willing to own up to racist, sexist, classist, regionalist, or other prejudicial attitudes. Questionnaires, interviews, and scaling techniques (which asked about such characteristics directly) were suspect data-gathering methods since they allowed respondents to disguise their true feelings, either to project a different self-image and/or to give responses they thought the interviewer might most approve of.

An early method used to circumvent such suspected manipulation of attitudes by respondents was the "semantic differential" technique (developed by the psycholinguist Charles Osgood at the University of Illinois, e.g. Osgood et al. 1957) set within a "matched-guise" stimulus presentation. The Canadian social psychologist Wallace Lambert and his colleagues played recordings of the same speaker (to avoid voice quality interference in judgments) in two "guises" (in the earliest case, in French and English to determine attitudinal responses to these two languages in French-speaking Canada, e.g. Lambert et al. 1960). Judges marked scales of opposites such as "fast–slow," "heavy–light," and so on (which did not appear to directly assess language characteristics), and the statistical treatment and interpretation of these ratings set off a frenzy of language attitude studies (most fully developed in the work of Howard Giles and his various associates and provided with both examples and theoretical foundations in Giles and Powesland 1975). Although this work was not without criticism (for its artificiality and other drawbacks, e.g. Agheyisi and Fishman 1970), it set the standard for such studies for quite some time and managed to provide the first important generalization in language attitude studies – that of the "three factor groups." Analyses of large amounts of data seemed to group together paired opposites which pointed to *competence*, *personal integrity*, and *social attractiveness* constructs in the evaluation of speaker voices (summarized in Lambert 1967). A great deal of subsequent research in this mode confirmed that these constructs were very often at work, and, more interestingly, that standard (or "admired accent") speakers were most often judged highest on the *competence* dimension while nonstandard (or regionally and/or ethically distinct speakers) were rated higher for the *integrity* and *attractiveness* dimensions. Subsequent work has often conflated the two latter categories into one, usually referred to as *solidarity* (e.g. Edwards 1982).

Even early on, however, it became clear that the path from stimulus to group identification to the triggering of attitudes towards the group so identified was not a trouble-free one. In perhaps the earliest study of attitudes towards regional and ethnic varieties in the US, Tucker and Lambert (1969) note that neither northern nor southern European-American judges identified the ethnicity of educated African-American speakers better than chance (scores ranging from 47 percent to 54 percent). If judges misidentify the group membership of the stimulus voice, how can consistent or even valid attitude judgments be collected? Milroy and McClenaghan (1977) note an interesting consistency of ratings of Scottish, Southern Irish, Ulster, and RP (i.e. "Received Pronunciation," the superposed British-English standard pronunciation) varieties even when judges misidentified accents. They comment on this finding as follows:

> It has been widely assumed that an accent acts as a cue identifying a speaker's group membership. Perhaps this identification takes place below the level of conscious awareness. . . . Presumably by hearing similar accents very frequently [one] has learnt to associate them with their reference groups. In other words, accents with which people are familiar may *directly* evoke stereotyped responses without the listener first consciously assigning the speaker to a particular reference group.   (1977: 8–9; italics in original)

Irvine (1996) has more recently commented on this transfer of linguistic features to social facts which apparently make the unconscious reactions Milroy and McClenaghan note possible:

> *Iconicity* is a semiotic process that transforms the sign relationship between linguistic features and the social images to which they are linked. Linguistic differences appear to be *iconic* representations of the social contrasts they *index* – as if a linguistic feature somehow depicted or displayed a social group's inherent nature or essence.   (1996: 17; italics in original)

In other words, the presumed social attributes of a group are transferred to the linguistic features associated with it (as Irvine notes), and an occurrence of those features may directly trigger recognition of those attributes without being filtered through (conscious) identification of the group (as Milroy and McClenaghan note). Extremes of such iconicity in American English might include "ain't" and multiple negation, both of which apparently trigger negative evaluations with no need for any (specific) group association.

Although this program of social psychological research into language atti-tudes has been productive, I believe it has left much to be done. If Irvine is correct, there are at last two very large areas left relatively unexplored.

1   What linguistic features play the biggest role in triggering attitudes?
2   What beliefs (theories, folk explanations) do people have about language variety, structure, acquisition, and distribution which underlie and support their attitudinal responses and how might we go about finding them out and using them to supplement and even guide future language attitude research?

2   The Linguistic Detail

Perhaps not surprisingly, the study of the relative importance of various specific linguistic features has not been prominent in the work conducted by social psychologists. They have typically used such global stimuli as "languages" or "dialects" (the latter in the broad sense to include class-, gender-, and even age-related varieties), but they have not asked which of the lower-level features of those varieties were most important to the triggering of an attitudinal reaction. Sociolinguists, on the other hand, armed with the knowledge of the delicate variability in performance, have sought to find out whether or not that variation is mirrored in judgments.

Aware of the low regard in which their variety is held, New Yorkers have, as a rule, severe "linguistic insecurity." But Labov's work in the 1960s (1966) shows that they are also very sensitive to some specific linguistic features which they most strongly associate with their "bad" speech. As is well-known, the pronunciation of "r" (after vowels) in New York City (NYC) is the "pres-tige" or "correct" form. Higher-status speakers (and all speakers when they are more careful of their speech) are more likely to pronounce such words as "car," "here," and "door" with a final "r."

Labov designed perhaps the first linguistically-sensitive attitude research experiment in which he asked NYC judges to listen to passages which con-tained such sentences as "He *darted* out about *four* feet *before* a *car* and got hit *hard*" and "We didn't have the *heart* to play ball *or cards* all *morning*." He got the same female respondents to read these passages several times and obtained samples in which they always used "r" and others in which they deleted "r" only once (one in the word *hard* in the first passage and another in *cards* in the second). He called these "r" passages the "consistent r" and "inconsistent r" samples. He then played both samples of each woman's performances inter-spersed with other voice samples and asked NYC judges from several differ-ent social status groups to pretend that they were personnel managers who were to rate the voice samples they heard for "occupational suitability" along a seven-point scale (Labov 1966: 411):

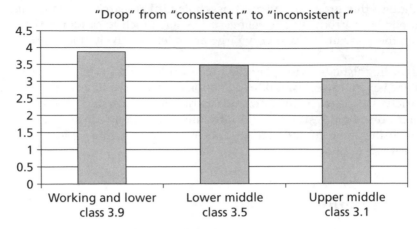

Figure 2.1 Three social status group judgments of lower "occupational suitability" of "inconsistent r" production
Source: Labov (1972)

    TV personality
    Executive secretary
    Receptionist
    Switchboard operator
    Salesgirl
    Factory worker
    None of these

The judges in every social status group rated the "inconsistent r" performances lower on the occupational suitability scale by dramatic margins. Figure 2.1 shows the average drop in ratings along the occupational suitability scale between the "consistent r" and "inconsistent r" performances. For example, if a lower- or working-class judge said that a "consistent r" performance was that of an "executive secretary," then he or she was likely to rate the "inconsistent r" presentation as that of a "factory worker" (four steps down the scale). It's interesting to note that upper-middle-class judges rated the two performances less dramatically different (only three steps down the scale for the "inconsistent r" performance), and such differences allowed Labov to consider at the same time the differential rates of "r" production according to status and the different judgments of variable "r" production by the same groups.

New Yorkers are, as these ratings show, extremely sensitive to even "mild" use of "r"-deletion, rating speakers three to four full categories down on the seven-point occupational scale when they fail to realize only one out of four or five instances of this feature. I have no doubt that such tests can be developed for a large range of linguistic features. Of course, they should test the sensitivity of out-group as well as in-group respondents (expecting that different features and different degrees of sensitivity might emerge).

Table 2.1   Confusion matrix and summary statistics by dialect

Responses	Stimuli									Row	
		AAVE			ChE			SAE		Total	
AAVE	a	923	(15%)	b	280	(5%)	c	196	(3%)	1,399	(23%)
ChE	d	235	(4%)	e	1,607	(27%)	f	41	(1%)	1,883	(31%)
SAE	g	842	(14%)	h	113	(2%)	i	1,763	(29%)	2,718	(45%)

$\chi^2 = 4{,}510$; $df = 4$; $p < 0.001$; AI = 0.72; percentages = percent of total for that cell.
Source: Purnell et al. (1999)

Since Labov played New York voices for New Yorkers, one might still ask what role linguistic detail plays in the recognition (and, presumably, subsequent evaluation) of a greater variety of voices, particularly when evaluation may be done along scales tuned to discover more than occupational suitability. In a recent study, Purnell et al. (1999) recorded three versions of the same speaker saying "hello" in Chicano-English (ChE), African-American Vernacular English (AAVE), and Standard American English (SAE).

As table 2.1 shows, even though they were exposed to only one word, the respondents identified ethnicity far better than chance (at an "Accuracy Index" level of .72, indicating that better than 70 percent of the tokens were correctly identified). The diagonal cells (*a*, *e*, and *i*) should be approximately 33 percent each if the respondents had been 100 percent accurate, and two of the cells (*e* and *i*, at 27 and 29 percent, respectively) are very close to that ideal. Only cell *a* is low (at 15 percent), and cell *g* shows why: 14 percent of the AAE voices were incorrectly recognized as SAE.

Although this one discrepant cell is difficult to account for, the acoustic factors which allowed identification appear to be straightforward. In an analysis of the tokens of "hello" which were presented for identification, it was found that the first vowel (/ɛ/) was significantly fronter (determined by extracting its F2 value) in the AAVE and ChE guises. Additionally, pitch peak was higher for the /hɛ/ syllable in the AAVE guise token only (as was syllable duration). With these minimal acoustic cues, therefore, AAVE and ChE could be distinguished from SAE (on the basis of a fronter or tenser /ɛ/ vowel), and AAVE could be distinguished from ChE (and further from SAE) on the basis of pitch peak and syllable duration. Purnell et al. (1999) also show how dialect identification allows the realization of attitudinal factors in specific action, for the three varieties used in the acoustic experiment were also used in telephone calls to prospective landlords (each of which began with the sentence "Hello, I'm calling about the apartment you have advertised in the paper"). The two non-SAE varieties fared considerably worse in securing appointments; for example, in the Woodside (CA) area; the SAE speaker guise was given an appointment to see housing at roughly the 70 percent level; both AAVE and ChE guises were given appointments only about 30 percent of the time.

It may not be the case, however, that all linguistic markers of social identity have the same force. In an older study, Graff et al. (1983) altered only the formant characteristics of the onset of the /aʊ/ diphthong in an otherwise typically AAVE speaker from Philadelphia (so that the diphthong was altered to /æʊ/. When the sample was played for both African-American and European-American judges in Philadelphia, both groups agreed that the speaker was European-American. Apparently, the realization of this diphthong as /æʊ/ is so strongly associated with European-American speakers that it was able to "overwhelm" any other evidence of ethnicity in the sample.

So far these approaches to linguistic detail in attitude study (or to the background information respondents use in making judgments which reflect attitude) have not assumed any level of awareness of the feature in question by the respondents themselves. In fact, Labov reports that "few of the respondents consciously perceived the values of the variables which caused their reactions" (1966: 455). In other work, however, a more direct appeal to respondent consciousness of variation has been made. Modifying a "Self-Evaluation Test" developed in Labov (1966), Trudgill (1972) measured the difference between performance and obviously conscious self-report for a number of variables in Norwich English. A respondent was acquainted with a local variable and asked to make a self-report of his or her use of it. For example, the vowel of "ear" has a prestigious form [ɪə] and a nonprestigious (local) form [ɛː]. Trudgill classified his respondents as speakers of the prestige form if they used more than 50 percent of that form in the casual speech portion of their interviews. He then classified as "over-reporters" those respondents who claimed to use [ɪə] but, in fact, preferred [ɛː] in their casual speech. Likewise, he classified as "under-reporters" those who claimed to use [ɛː] but in fact preferred the prestige form in their casual speech. The remaining respondents were classified as "accurate." His results are shown in table 2.2.

These data show that men say they use a great deal more of the local (nonprestigious) form than they actually do (and that women say they use more of the prestigious one). From this, Trudgill suggested that some variables have a "covert prestige," an attraction based on working-class, local, non

Table 2.2   Percentage over- and under-reporters for the "ear" vowel in Norwich

	Total	Male	Female
Over-r	18	12	25
Under-r	36	54	18
Accurate	45	34	57

Source: Trudgill (1972:187)

"school-oriented" norms and that such norms were particularly appealing to men. Women, he suggested, were more oriented, perhaps because of power differentials in society, to norms which reflect the "overt prestige" of the wider society. Although his conclusions are far-reaching for general sociolinguistic work and work on gender in particular, here it is simply important to note that his respondents provided interesting attitudinal information based on specific linguistic features and that those responses were made at a conscious level.

Consciousness, however, may mislead assessment of others' performances as well as our own. Niedzielski (1999) studied the local (Detroit) awareness of "Canadian raising" (in which the onsets of the /aʊ/ and /aɪ/ diphthongs are raised before voiceless consonants). She played a Detroit female speaker's pronunciation of the word "house" in which the onset of /aʊ/ was considerably raised (see figure 2.2). Although Detroiters associate this pronunciation with Canadians (even caricaturing it with a /hus/ imitation), they quite regularly perform it themselves, as this speaker obviously does. She asked Detroit

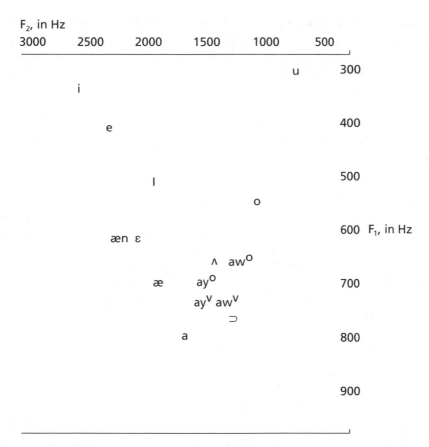

Figure 2.2　Vowel space of the Detroit female speaker on the test tape
Source: Niedzielski (1999)

Table 2.3   Influence of nationality labels on token selection (for "house")

token label	#2 ultra- low	#3 canonical /a/	#4 actual token	Total
CANADIAN	15%	25%	60%	
n =	6	10	24	40
MICHIGAN	38%	51%	11%	
n =	15	20	4	39

$\chi^2 = 23.48$; $p < 0.001$
Source: Niedzielski (1999)

respondents to match this vowel with one of three others (synthesized tokens, which they had heard several times). The first (#2 in table 2.3) is called "ultra-low" since it represented an onset considerably below the norm (for F1) for /a/ in local speech. The second is called "canonical" /a/ and represented the height of /a/ as given in Peterson and Barney (1952), an acoustic study of "General American" vowels. The third token to which the sample was to be matched is called "actual," and was the same token used in the sample itself, one in which the onset was considerably raised (as seen in figure 2.2). Respondents heard these tokens mixed with others, but the presentation was significantly different for two groups of respondents. Although the same token of "house" was played for both, one received an answer sheet which had the word "CANADIAN" prominently printed (in red) at the top of the page; the second group received an answer sheet with the word "MICHIGAN" at the top. Any difference in token-matching by the two groups, therefore, can be attributed to that apparent "identification."

As table 2.3 shows, the labeling had a strong effect: 60 percent of the 40 respondents who had the word "CANADIAN" printed on their response sheets matched the token presented with the "actual" one (i.e. accurately) in contrast to only 11 percent of the 39 who had sheets with "MICHIGAN" on them. Fully 51 percent of the "MICHIGAN" respondents heard the token as "canonical /a/" and 38 percent even heard it as "ultra-low." It is obvious that the exterior identification of the home site of the sample voice exerted an enormous effect on the sound which was "heard" by the respondents.[2]

In Labov (1966) another appeal was made to the conscious level in the evaluation of specific linguistic variables in the construction of a "Index of Linguistic Insecurity." Labov asked respondents in his New York City study which of two variants (e.g. [kætʃ] versus [kɛtʃ]) of a number of variables was correct and which they typically used themselves. Each time they noted that one was correct but that they used the other, he added a point to their "insecurity

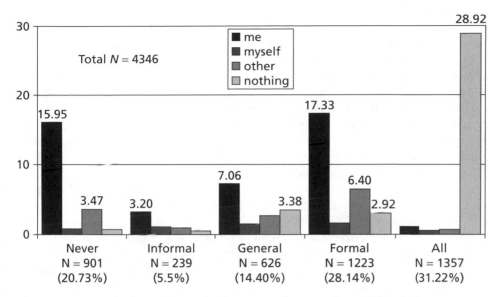

Figure 2.3 Results for ratings of "They gave the award to Bill and I"
Source: Al-Banyan and Preston (1998)

index." Although he was able to show from this that the most insecure group was the lower-middle class (paralleling a distinct linguistic insecurity he had shown earlier in their hypercorrect behavior in performance, see Schilling-Estes, this volume), he did not show the degrees of insecurity associated with the specific variables he presented.

In a modification of this approach, Al-Banyan and Preston (1998) presented a number of traditionally nonstandard morphosyntactic and syntactic constructions to undergraduate students at a large, Midwestern US university. In each case, the respondents were asked if they would (1) always use the construction given, (2) use it only formally, (3) use it in ordinary, "on-the-street" interaction, (4) use it only very casually, or (5) never use it. For example, they were asked to evaluate the sentence "The award was given to Bill and I," illustrating the hypercorrect (but historically well-precedented) substitution of the nominative for oblique case in conjoined noun phrases in object position. They supplied the form they would use in the variety of situations presented them if they did not choose the form given. Their responses were coded according to whether they chose "me," "myself," or "other" as the alternative. Figure 2.3 shows the results for this one grammatical item.

Of the only 21 percent of the respondents who indicated that they would never use this form, the majority (16 percent) indicated that they would use the prescriptively sanctioned "me"; but 28 percent found it the form they would use for "formal" situations, indicating that they would use "me" in less formal contexts. Thirty-one percent (the highest percentage) indicated that it was, for them, the form appropriate for all contexts. If attitudes to "standard" usage are to be measured, such studies as these reveal that a modern standard (for these university students, reflected in the combined "formal" and "always" categories at a level of 59 percent) rather than one which even liberally-minded linguists might agree on needs to be taken into consideration.

Such studies make it clear that language attitudes can be related very specifically to individual linguistic features, but it is equally clear that that relationship is not a simple one. In some cases, precise acoustic features appear to trigger accurate identification (e.g. the frontness or tenseness of the vowel and pitch prominence on the first syllable of "hello" as shown in Purnell, et al. 1999); in others, an acoustic feature appears to be so strongly identified with a group that it can overcome all other surrounding evidence (e.g. the [æ] onset to the /aU/ diphthong as a marker of European-American identity in Philadelphia as shown in Graff 1983); in others, the frequency of one variant or another has a powerful effect on social judgments (e.g. r-deletion in New York City as shown in Labov 1966); in still others, there may be a great deal of inaccuracy in both self-report of the use of a specific feature (e.g. for the vowel of "war" as shown in Trudgill 1972) or in the identification of the vowel quality of a specific feature (e.g. for the presence of "Canadian Raising" as shown in Niedzielski 1999).

This variety of identification and attitude potential for precise linguistic features will come as no shock to sociolinguists, who have found for some time now just such careful tuning in the factors which govern production, reaching from Fischer's (1958) account of how gender and status guided children's production of the velar and alveolar variants of "-ing" to Schilling-Estes' (1998) account of how membership in a male poker-playing network predicted the use of a classically "local" variant of /ay/ on Ocracoke Island, North Carolina.

It is hardly surprising, therefore, to find that finely-tuned choices among linguistic features, reflecting the social forces and groups which surround them, play as complex a role in attitudinal formation and perception as they do in language variation itself. In fact, it seems to me that perception, evaluation, and production are intimately connected in language variation and change and that much that might go by the name "sociolinguistics" could as well be known as "language attitude study."

Perhaps some of these differential responses to a variety of linguistic details may operate along a continuum (or several continua) of consciousness or "awareness" (just as language use involves degrees of "monitoring" or "attention to form," e.g. Labov 1972: 208). In Preston (1996a) I review a number of these possibilities for "folk linguistics," suggesting that folk-linguistic facts (i.e. linguistic objects as viewed by nonlinguists) may be subdivided for "awareness" along the following clines.

1   *Availability*:   Folk respondents range in their attention to linguistic features from complete disregard for to frequent discussion of and even preoccupation with them.

2 *Accuracy*: Folk respondents may accurately, partially accurately, or completely inaccurately represent linguistic facts (and their distribution).
3 *Detail*: Folk respondents' characterizations may range from *global* (reflecting, for example, only a general awareness of a variety) to *detailed* (in which respondents cite specific details).
4 *Control*: Folk respondents may have complete, partial or no "imitative" control over linguistic features.

An important fact about these several clines is their relative independence. For example, a respondent who claims only a general awareness of a "foreign accent" may be capable of a completely faithful imitation of some of its characteristics and a completely inaccurate imitation of others. On the other hand, a respondent who is preoccupied with a variety might have no overt information about its linguistic make-up but be capable of performing a native-like imitation of it.

Perhaps the range of so-called language attitude effects ought to be treated in a similar way. That is, attitudinal responses which are based on the respondents' association of a sample voice with a particular social group may be different from ones based on reactions to linguistic caricatures such as *ain't*. Responses which may be based on some sort of cline (e.g. masculine–feminine, degree of "accent") may be different from those based on the recognition of "categorical" features (e.g. correct–incorrect).

3 Attitudes and Folk Perceptions

Since linguists know, however, that linguistic details have no value of their own (in spite of the "life" they seem to achieve by virtue of their social associations), it will be important to return to the second of the questions suggested above: what underlying beliefs, presuppositions, stereotypes, and the like lie behind and support the existence of language attitudes? Ultimately, it seems to me, this will require us to give something like an account of a folk theory of language, and in what remains I will try to offer some thoughts in that direction.

In doing language attitude research, perhaps it is important to first determine which varieties of a language are thought to be distinct. For example, where do people believe linguistically distinct places are? That is, what mental maps of regional speech areas do they have? In Preston (1989) I complained that language attitude research did not determine where respondents thought regional voices were from and, worse, did not know if respondents even had a mental construct of a "place" where a voice could be from; that is, their mental maps of regional speech areas might not include one with which a sample voice could be identified.

For example, if one submitted a voice from New England to California judges and the judges agreed that the speaker was "intelligent," "cold," "fast,"

Figure 2.4 A Michigan respondent's hand-drawn map

and so on, researchers could reasonably conclude that Californians judged that voice sample in that way. They should not conclude, however, that that is what Californians believe about New England voices, for a majority of the judges might not have agreed that the voice was from New England. (Perhaps they would have called it a "New York" voice.) More generally, Californians may not even have a concept of "New England" speech. Perhaps the most detailed mental map of regional US speech available to them is one which simply identifies the "Northeast" (whatever their folk name for that region might be).

How can we devise research which avoids this problem? Following the lead of cultural geographers (e.g. Gould and White 1974), we might simply ask respondents to draw maps of where they believe varieties are different. Figures 2.4 and 2.5 are typical examples of such hand-drawn maps from Michiganders.

Although we may profit from an investigation of these individual maps (by, for example, looking at the labels assigned to various regions, as in, e.g. Hartley and Preston 1999), their usefulness for general language attitude studies depends on the degree to which generalizations may be drawn from large numbers of such maps. This may be done by drawing an (approximate) boundary for each salient region from the first map and then "overlaying" each subsequent respondent's map and drawing the "perceptual isoglosses" for each region. A more sophisticated version of this procedure makes use of a digitizing pad which feeds the outlined area of each salient region into a

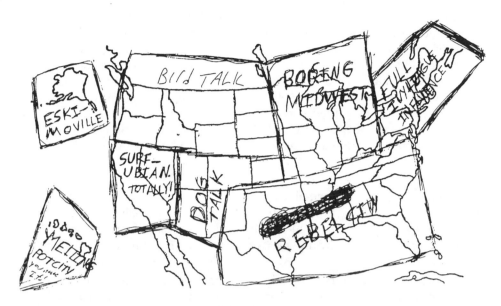

Figure 2.5   Another Michigan hand-drawn map

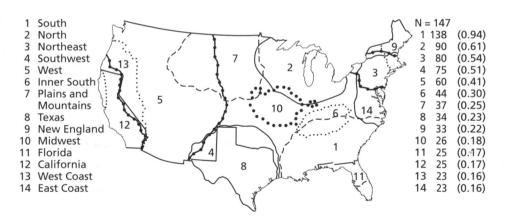

		N = 147	
1	South	1	138 (0.94)
2	North	2	90 (0.61)
3	Northeast	3	80 (0.54)
4	Southwest	4	75 (0.51)
5	West	5	60 (0.41)
6	Inner South	6	44 (0.30)
7	Plains and	7	37 (0.25)
	Mountains		
8	Texas	8	34 (0.23)
9	New England	9	33 (0.22)
10	Midwest	10	26 (0.18)
11	Florida	11	25 (0.17)
12	California	12	25 (0.17)
13	West Coast	13	23 (0.16)
14	East Coast	14	23 (0.16)

Figure 2.6   Computer-assisted generalizations of hand-drawn maps showing where southeastern Michigan respondents believe speech regions exist in the USA

computer so that a more precise numeric determination can be made of the "boundary" of each hand-drawn region (Preston and Howe 1987). Figure 2.6 shows a computer-determined map for the mental map of US regional speech areas derived from the hand-drawn maps of 147 southeastern Michigan respondents (from a variety of status and age groups, male and female).

Armed with this "cognitively real" map of the dialect areas of the USA (as seen by Michiganders), we might now approach the study of attitudes towards these regions in a classically social psychological manner. What characteristics would be relevant to an investigation of attitudes to these speech areas? Again, the best method is to go to the respondents themselves. Characteristics for judging were elicited by showing a large number of Michigan respondents a simplified version of figure 2.6 and asking them to mention any characteristics of the speech of those regions which came to mind. The most frequently mentioned items were selected and arranged into the following pairs.

slow–fast	formal–casual	educated–uneducated
smart–dumb	polite–rude	snobbish–down-to-earth
nasal–not nasal	normal–abnormal	friendly–unfriendly
drawl–no drawl	twang–no twang	bad English–good English

It was important, of course, that the Michigan map was shown to Michigan respondents and that the characteristics elicited were to be used by Michigan judges. Respondents from other areas have different mental maps and might list other characteristics.

The judges (85 young, European-American lifelong southern Michigan residents who were undergraduate students at Michigan State University) were shown a simplified version of figure 2.6 and given the following instructions:

> This map shows where many people from southern Michigan believe speech differences are in the USA. We will give you a list of descriptive words which local people have told us could be used to describe the speech of these various regions. Please think about twelve of these regions, and check off how each pair of words applies to the speech there.

> For example, imagine that we gave you the pair "ugly" and "beautiful"

$$\text{ugly} \underline{\quad} \quad \underline{\quad} \quad \underline{\quad} \quad \underline{\quad} \quad \underline{\quad} \quad \underline{\quad} \text{ beautiful}$$
$$\quad\quad\quad a \quad\quad b \quad\quad c \quad\quad d \quad\quad e \quad\quad f$$

> You would use the scale as follows:

> If you very strongly agree that the speech of a region is "ugly," select "a."
> If you strongly agree that the speech of a region is "ugly," select "b."
> If you agree that the speech of a region is "ugly," select "c."
> If you agree that the speech of a region is "beautiful," select "d."
> If you strongly agree that the speech of a region is "beautiful," select "e."
> If you very strongly agree that the speech of a region is "beautiful," select "f."

The next step in this research is to determine whether or not the number of paired items used in evaluating the regional dialects can be reduced, a procedure normally carried out by means of a factor analysis (which groups together

Table 2.4   The two factor groups from the ratings of all areas

Factor group no. 1		Factor group no. 2	
Smart	0.76	Polite	0.74
Educated	0.75	Friendly	0.74
Normal	0.65	Down-to-earth	0.62
Good English	0.63	(Normal)	(0.27)
No drawl	0.62	(Casual)	(0.27)
No twang	0.57		
Casual [formal]	−0.49		
Fast	0.43		
Down-to-earth [snobbish]	−0.32		

Parenthesized factors indicate items which are within the 0.25 to 0.29 range; "−" prefixes indicate negative loadings and should be interpreted as loadings of the opposite value (given in brackets).

the paired opposites). The results of such an analysis for all areas rated are shown in table 2.4.[3]

Two groups emerged from this statistical procedure. The first (which I will call "Standard") contains those characteristics which we associate with education and the formal attributes of the society. Note, however, that the last three items in this group ("Formal," "Fast," and "Snobbish") are not necessarily positive traits. Group no. 2 (which I will call "Friendly") contains very different sorts of characteristics (including two which are negative in Group no. 1 but positive here – "Down-to-earth" and "Casual").

These two groups will not surprise those who have looked at any previous studies of language attitudes. As already noted, many researchers have found that the two main dimensions of evaluation for language varieties are most often those of *social status* ("Educated" above) and *group solidarity* ("Friendly" above).

A full analysis of these data would go on to consider how each of the regions rated fared with regard to these two groups, but I believe a sample of two particularly important areas (for these respondents and doubtless others) will provide a good insight into the mechanisms at work here.

I have chosen to look at the respondent ratings of areas 1 and 2 from figure 2.6. The reasons are straightforward. Region 1 is the US "South," and figure 2.6 shows that it was outlined by 94 percent (138) of the 147 respondents who drew hand-drawn maps. For these southeastern Michigan respondents, it is clearly the most important regional speech area in the USA. The second most frequently rated region (by 90 out of 147 respondents or 61 percent) is the local one, called "North" in figure 2.6, but perhaps more accurately "North Central" or "Great Lakes." At first, one might be tempted to assert that the local area is always important, but a closer look at figure 2.4 will show that these southeastern Michigan raters may have something else in mind when they single out their home area; this respondent was not unique among Michigan respondents in identifying Michigan, and only Michigan, as the uniquely "normal" or "correct" speech area in the country.

Table 2.5 shows the means scores for the individual attributes for the North and South. Perhaps the most notable fact is that the rank orders are nearly opposites. "Casual" is lowest-rated for the North but highest for the South. "Drawl" is lowest-rated (meaning "speaks with a drawl") for the South but highest rated (meaning "speaks without a drawl") for the North. In factor group terms, the scores for Group no. 2 (and "–1" loadings, where the opposite value was strongly loaded into a factor group) are the lowest-ranked ones for the North; these same characteristics ("Casual," "Friendly," "Down-to-earth," and "Polite") are the highest-ranked for the South. Similarly, Group no. 1 characteristics are all low-ranked for the South; the same attributes are all highest-ranked for the North.

These scores are not just ordered differently. A series of statistical tests showed that there is a significant difference between the attribute ratings for the North and the South, except for "Nasal" and "Polite." For those attributes in Group no. 1 ("No Drawl," "No Twang," "Fast," "Educated," "Good English," "Smart," and "Normal"), the means scores are all higher for the North. In other words, these Michigan raters consider themselves superior to the South for every attribute of the "Standard" factor group. This is not very surprising, considering well-known folk and popular culture attitudes.

For those attributes in Group no. 2 (or –1), the means score is higher for the South for "Casual," "Friendly," and "Down-to-earth." There is no significant difference for "Polite" (as noted above), and the North leads the South in Group no. 2 attributes only for "Normal," but it is important to note that "Normal" is to be found in both groups. These data suggest that, at least for these 85 young Michiganders, the "Friendly" attributes (excepting only "Polite") are more highly associated with southern speech than with speech from the local area.

A few other statistical facts confirm and add to the results reported so far. Note (in table 2.5) that no attribute rating for the North falls below 3.5 (the median value of the six-point scale), while all of the Group no. 1 ("Standard") attributes are rated below that score for the South. Perhaps even more dramatically, statistical tests of the means scores for North and South independently show that there is no significant break between any two adjacent means scores for ratings of the attributes for the North. On the other hand, there *is* such a significant difference for the South between the Group no. 2 (and –1) attributes and the Group no. 1 attributes, as shown by the "*" in table 2.5. In other words, there is a continuum of relatively positive scores for the North and a sharp break between the two groups for the South.

Since many of the hand-drawn maps of US dialect areas by Michigan respondents label the local area "standard," "normal" (as in figure 2.4), "correct," and "good English," there is obviously no dissatisfaction with the local variety as a representative of "correct English." What is the source of the

Table 2.5 Means scores of both factor groups for ratings of the "North" and "South"

	Means scores (ordered) South			Means scores (ordered) North			
Factor	Mean	Attribute	Rank	Rank	Factor	Mean	Attribute
−1 & 2	4.66	Casual	1	12.0	−1 & 2	3.53	Casual
2	4.58	Friendly	2	9.5	2	4.00	Friendly
2 & −1	4.54	Down-to-earth	3	6	2 & −1	4.19	Down-to-earth
2	4.20	Polite	4	9.5	2	4.00	Polite
ø	4.09	Not nasal	5	11	ø	3.94	Not nasal
	*						
1 & 2	‡3.22	Normal [abnormal]	6	3	1 & 2	4.94	Normal
1	‡3.04	Smart [dumb]	7	4	1	4.53	Smart
1	‡2.96	No twang [twang]	8	2	1	5.07	No twang
1	‡2.86	Good English [bad English]	9	5	1	4.41	Good English
1	‡2.72	Educated [uneducated]	10	8	1	4.09	Educated
1	‡2.42	Fast [slow]	11	7	1	4.12	Fast
1	‡2.22	No drawl [drawl]	12	1	1	5.11	No drawl

* Only significant (0.05) break between any two adjacent means scores; "‡" marks values below 3.5 (which may be interpreted as the opposite polarity – shown in brackets here and in Table 2.4)

preference for the southern varieties along the "friendly" dimensions? Perhaps a group has a tendency to use up what might be called the "symbolic linguistic capital" of its variety in one way or the other (but not both). Speakers of majority varieties have a tendency to spend the symbolic capital of their variety on a "Standard" dimension. Speakers of minority varieties usually spend their symbolic capital on the "Friendly" dimension.

Perhaps many northerners (here, southeastern Michiganders) have spent all their symbolic linguistic capital on the standardness of local English. As such, it has come to represent the norms of schools, media, and public interaction and has, therefore, become less suitable for interpersonal value. These young Michiganders, therefore, assign an alternate kind of prestige to a variety which they imagine would have more value than theirs for interpersonal and casual interaction, precisely the sorts of dimensions associated with Group no. 2.

Already armed with the information that respondents tend to evaluate language variety along these two dimensions, I took an even more direct approach to eliciting judgments about such variety, again with no recourse to actual voice samples. I asked southeastern Michigan respondents to rate the 50 states (and Washington, DC and New York City) for "correctness." The results are shown in figure 2.7.

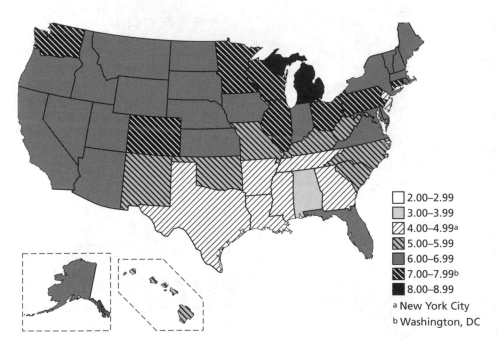

☐	2.00–2.99
▦	3.00–3.99
▨	4.00–4.99a
▧	5.00–5.99
▓	6.00–6.99
◪	7.00–7.99b
■	8.00–8.99

a New York City
b Washington, DC

Figure 2.7   Means of ratings for language "correctness" by Michigan respondents for US English (on a scale of 1–10, where 1 = least, and 10 = most correct)

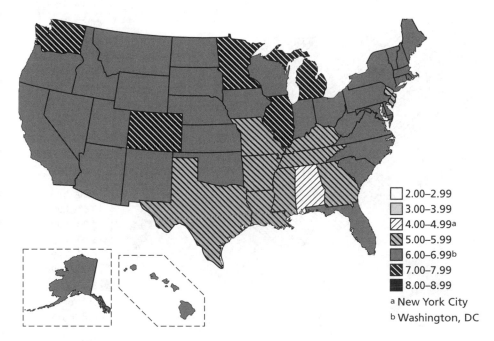

Figure 2.8 Means of ratings for language "pleasantness" by Michigan respondents for US English (on a scale of 1–10, where 1 = least, and 10 = most pleasant)

Again, it is clear that the South fares worst. On a one–ten scale (with one being "least correct"), Alabama is the only state which reaches a mean score in the 3.00–3.99 range, and, with the exception of New York City and New Jersey, the surrounding southern states (Texas, Arkansas, Louisiana, Mississippi, Tennessee, and Georgia) are the only other areas rated in the 4.00–4.99 range. In short, the importance of southern speech would appear to lie in its distinctiveness along one particular dimension – it is incorrect English. It is only Michigan which scores in the heady 8.00–8.99 means score range for language "correctness."

What parallel can we find in such work as this to the scores for the attributes in Factor Group no. 2 ("Friendly") already reported? Figure 2.8 shows what Michigan raters have done in a direct assessment of the notion "pleasant" (as was shown above in figure 2.7 for "correctness"). As figure 2.8 shows, the South fares very badly again. Alabama (actually tied here by New York City) is the worst-rated area in the USA, and the surrounding southern states are also at the bottom of this ten-point rating scale. One may note, however, that the ratings for the "pleasantness" of the English of southern states are one degree less harsh than those for "correctness." Similarly, there is no "outstanding" (8.00–8.99) rating as there was for "correctness," making Michigan no

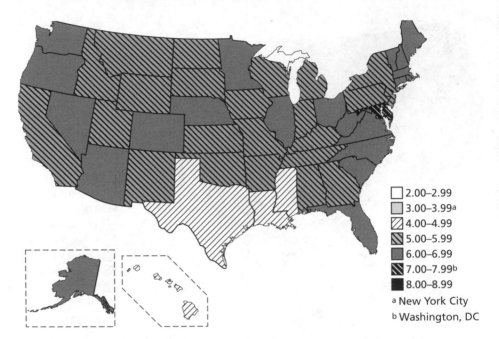

2.00–2.99
3.00–3.99a
4.00–4.99
5.00–5.99
6.00–6.99
7.00–7.99b
8.00–8.99

a New York City
b Washington, DC

Figure 2.9 Means of ratings for language "correctness" by Alabama respondents for US English (on a scale of 1–10, where 1 = least, and 10 = most correct)

longer the uniquely best-thought-of area (since it is joined here by Minnesota, Illinois, Colorado, and Washington). In previous work (e.g. Preston 1996b), I have taken this to indicate that northern speakers have made symbolic use of their variety as a vehicle for "standardness," "education," and widely-accepted or "mainstream" values.

Then what about US southerners? If northerners (i.e. Michiganders) are committed to their "correctness" but only half-heartedly to the "pleasantness," will southerners (e.g. Alabamians) show an interestingly different pattern of responses? Unfortunately, I have no factor analytic study based on the cognitive maps of southerners, but I can show you how they have responded to the "correct" and "pleasant" tasks already discussed for Michiganders.

Just as one might have suspected, as figure 2.9 shows, Alabamians are much less invested in language "correctness" (and well they should not be since they are constantly reminded in popular culture and even personal encounters that their language is lacking in this dimension). Imagine the horror of a Michigander in seeing figure 2.9. Their own "correct" English speaking state scores no better than the fair-to-middling "5" which Alabamians assign to

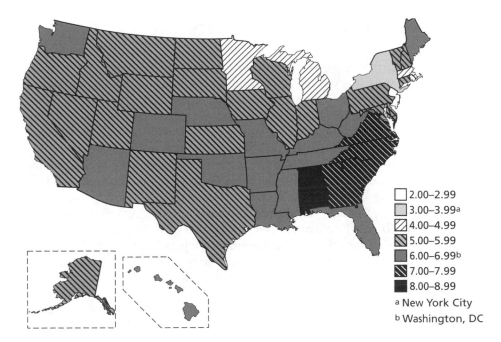

Figure 2.10 Means of ratings for language "pleasantness" by Alabama respondents for US English (on a scale of 1–10, where 1 = least, and 10 = most pleasant)

many areas, including their own (showing no break in correctness on a trip from Alabama all the way north to Michigan!).

If figure 2.10 reminds you of figure 2.7, you will surely conclude that Alabamians are invested in something, just as Michiganders are, but it is clearly "pleasantness," not "correctness." In this simple task, therefore, I believe to have shown very straightforwardly the sort of differential investment in local varieties discussed above. In one sense, of course, such studies are "language attitude" studies; in another sense, however, they form important background understandings for the study of attitudes among different social and regional groups. How can we study more detailed aspects language attitudes unless we know that a group is "correctness" investing or "solidarity" investing? And, of course, as I hope to have shown in this entire section, how can we measure language attitudes unless we know something of the cognitive arrangements our respondents have made of the terrain we want to explore? Although part of the game belongs to us (the linguistic detail), the real territory (as perhaps in any linguistic work) lies within the cognitive maps (whether of geographic or social facts) of those we study.

4   Toward a General Folk Theory

What of the larger promise? How can we go about fashioning a more general folk theory of language, one which surely underlies all attitudinal responses? I believe much of the attitudinal data outlined above, including the mental maps of and attitudinal responses to regional varieties of US English, is dominated by the notions of "correctness" (the more powerful) and "pleasantness." I also believe a great deal of folk belief and language ideology stems from these facts. Speakers of "correct" dialects do not believe they speak dialects, and educational and even legal repercussions arise from personal and institutional devaluing of "incorrect" varieties. On the other hand, speakers of prejudiced-against varieties (like prejudiced groups in general) derive solidarity from their distinct cultural behaviors, in this case, linguistic ones.

In a more direct attempt to get at this underlying fact, although the research tradition is not as long or as active, particularly in the USA, some attitude researchers have collected and analyzed overt folk comment about language (e.g. Labov 1966). When asked how New Yorkers speak, for example, a southern Indiana respondent replied with a little folk poetry (showing that sensitivity to NYC "r" is not an exclusively in-group phenomenon):

> T'ree little boids, sitting on a coib
> Eating doity woims and saying doity woids.

Some comment is more detailed and revealing. The following Michiganders assure the fieldworker (H) that they (just like national newscasters) are speakers of "standard" English:

H: Northern English is standard English?
D: Yeah, yeah.
G: That's right. What you hear around here.
S: Yeah, standard.
D: Because that's what you hear on the TV. If you listen to the newscast of the national news, they sound like we do; they sound sort of Midwestern, like we do.

And, not surprisingly, Michiganders know where English which is not so standard is spoken:

G: Because of TV though I think there's kind of a standard English that's evolving.
D: Yeah.
G: And the kind of thing you hear on TV is something that's broadcast across the country, so most people are aware of that, but there are definite accents in the South.

There are more complex (and rewarding) conversations about social and regional varieties of US English which may be analyzed to show not only relatively static folk belief and attitudes but also how these beliefs and attitudes are used in argument and persuasion. Such investigations are particularly important in showing what deep-seated presuppositions about language are held (e.g. Preston 1994). Many of these conversations (and their parallels and contrasts to professional opinion) are given Niedzielski and Preston (1999). I will provide only one here which I think supports the claim that correctness dominates in US folk perceptions of language but which also allows a slightly deeper look at what sort of theory might allow that domination. H (the fieldworker) has asked D and G (his respondents) if there is any difference in meaning between the words "gift" and "present" (Niedzielski and Preston 1999).[4]

D: Oftentimes a gift is something like you you go to a Tupperware party and
     they're going to give you a gift, it's – I think it's more impersonal, – than a=
                                          [
H: Uh huh.
D: =present.

                                                [
G: No, there's no difference.
     [
D: No? There's real – yeah there's really no difference.
                                               [
G: There is no difference.
D: That's true. Maybe the way we use it is though.
U: Maybe we could look it up and see what "gift" means.
                                            [
D: I mean technically there's no difference.
((They then look up *gift* and *present* in the dictionary.))

Although there are several interesting folk linguistic (and of course discoursal) facts about this short excerpt, the shock for linguists comes in D's remark that there is no difference in the meaning except in "the way we use it." Of course, what other difference could there be? I believe this remark (and many others I have seen in the course of surveying "folk linguistic conversations") points to a folk theory of language in which language itself is somehow external to human cognitive embedding – somewhere "out there." Figure 2.11 illustrates what I have come to believe the essential difference between folk and professional theories to be.

In the linguistic theory, one moves up (and away from) the concrete reality of language as a cognitively embedded fact in the capacities of individual speakers to the social constructions of language similarity. These higher-level constructs are socially real but considerably more abstract than the "real" language, embedded in individual speakers.

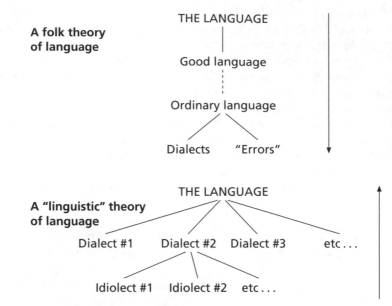

Figure 2.11   Folk and "linguistic" theories of language

In the folk theory, just the opposite is true. A Platonic, extra-cognitive reality is the "real" language, such a thing as English or German or Chinese. Speakers who are directly connected to it speak a fully correct form (the only rule-governed variety), although one may deviate from it comfortably not to sound too "prissy." Go too far, however, and error, dialect, or, quite simply, bad language arises. Since this connection to the rule-governed, exterior "real" language seems a natural (and even easy) one, many folk find it difficult to understand why nonstandard speakers, for example, persist in their errors (and often find them simply lazy or recalcitrant).

It is such a theory, I believe, which lies at the root of most evaluations and discriminations of language variety. It is the overwhelming fact against which all language attitude study (at least in US English) must be measured. In short, attitude study, within a linguistic setting, should proceed along both lines of enquiry: what are the linguistic facts of identification and reaction, and what are the underlying constructs which promote and support them? In "correct-ness," I believe, we have at least some of the answer.

NOTES

1   This does not mean that linguists themselves have no "language attitudes." First, there will be some viscerally, intellectually uncontrollable responses to language variety which maintain

themselves from the scientist's pre-scientific period. Second, what attitudinal responses linguists might have to languages and varieties after they are trained as linguists is an empirical question, one little investigated – but see Preston (1975) for, at least, grammaticality and acceptability judgment differences between linguists and non-linguists.

2   This study is an acoustic corollary to such interesting global studies (in which linguistic detail is not explored) as Williams et al. (1971). They showed, for example, that standard English-speaking children's voice samples were downgraded (for such traits as "industriousness" and "competence") if they were played so that the judges thought a minority child (Mexican-American or African-American) was actually speaking.

3   Although the paired opposites were presented to the respondents with "negative" and "positive" sides randomly distributed, the "positive" poles were all moved to the high (i.e. "6") end of the scale for all the quantitative analyses reported below. I realized after I did this that there might be cultural misunderstandings of what I consider to be the "positive" end. They are "Fast," "Polite," "Down-to-earth," "Educated," "Normal," "Smart," "Casual," "Good English," "Not nasal," "Friendly," "Speaks without a drawl," and "Speaks without a twang." I apologize to readers who disagree with my assignments. That should not detract from the contents of the paper.

4   Since H is not a native speaker, such a question seemed "reasonable."

REFERENCES

Agheyisi, R. and Joshua A. Fishman (1970). Language attitude studies: A review and proposal. *Anthropological Linguistics* 12: 131–57.

Al-Banyan, Ahmed and Dennis R. Preston (1998). What is Standard American English? *Studia Anglica Posnaniensia* 33: 29–46 (Festschrift for Kari Sajavaara).

Edwards, John R. (1982). Language attitudes and their implications among English speakers. In Ellen Bouchard Ryan and Howard Giles (eds.), *Attitudes towards Language Variation*. London: Edward Arnold. 20–33.

Fischer, J. L. (1958). Social influence in the choice of a linguistic variant. *Word* 14: 47–56.

Giles, Howard and P. F. Powesland (1975). *Speech Style and Social Evaluation*. London: Academic.

Gould, Peter and Rodney White (1974). *Mental Maps*. Harmondsworth, Middx: Penguin.

Graff, David, William Labov and Wendell Harris (1983). Testing listeners' reactions to phonological markers of ethnic identity: A new method for sociolinguistic research. In David Sankoff (ed.), *Diversity and Diachrony*. Amsterdam/ Philadelphia: John Benjamins. 45–58.

Hartley, Laura and Dennis R. Preston (1999). The names of US English: Valley girl, cowboy, Yankee, normal, nasal, and ignorant. In T. Bex and R. J. Watts (eds.), *Standard English*. London: Routledge. 207–38.

Irvine, Judith T. (1996). "Style" as distinctiveness: The culture and ideology of linguistic differentiation. Paper presented to the NSF

Workshop on "Style," Stanford University, February.

Labov, William (1966). *The Social Stratification of English in New York City*. Arlington, VA: Center for Applied Linguistics.

Labov, William (1972). *Sociolinguistic Patterns*. Philadelphia: The University of Pennsylvania Press.

Lambert, Wallace E. (1967). A social psychology of bilingualism. *Journal of Social Issues* 23: 91–109.

Lambert, Wallace E., R. Hodgson, R. C. Gardner and S. Fillenbaum (1960). Evaluational reactions to spoken languages. *Journal of Abnormal and Social Psychology* 60: 44–51.

Milroy, Lesley and Paul McClenaghan (1977). Stereotyped reactions to four educated accents in Ulster. *Belfast Working Papers in Language and Linguistics* 2: 1–11.

Niedzielski, Nancy (1999). The effect of social information on the perception of sociolinguistic variables. *Journal of Language and Social Psychology* (Lesley Milroy and Dennis R. Preston, guest eds, Special Issue: Attitudes, Perception, and Linguistic Features) 18 (March).

Niedzielski, Nancy and Dennis R. Preston (1999). *Folk Linguistics*. Berlin: Mouton de Gruyter.

Osgood, Charles H., G. J. Suci and P. Tannenbaum. (1957). *The Measurement of Meaning*. Urbana: University of Illinois Press.

Peterson, G. and H. Barney (1952). Control methods used in a study of the vowels. *Journal of the Acoustical Society of America* 24: 2175–84.

Preston, Dennis R. (1975). Linguists versus non-linguists and native speakers versus non-native speakers. *Biuletyn Fonograficzny* 16: 5–18.

Preston, Dennis R. (1989). *Perceptual Dialectology*. Dordrecht: foris.

Preston, Dennis R. (1994). Content-oriented discourse analysis and folk linguistics. *Language Sciences* 16, 2: 285–331.

Preston, Dennis R. (1996a). Whaddayaknow: The modes of folk linguistic awareness. *Language Awareness* 5, 1: 40–74.

Preston, Dennis R. (1996b). Where the worst English is spoken. In Edgar Schneider (ed.), *Focus on the USA*. Amsterdam: John Benjamins 297–360.

Preston, Dennis R. and George M. Howe (1987). Computerized generalizations of mental dialect maps. In Keith Denning et al. (eds.), *Variation in Language: NWAV-XV at Stanford*, Stanford, CA: Department of Linguistics, Stanford University. 361–78.

Purnell, Thomas, William Idsardi, and John Baugh (1999). Perceptual and phonetic experiments on American English dialect identification. *Journal of Language and Social Psychology* (Lesley Milroy and Dennis R. Preston, guest eds, Special Issue: Attitudes, Perception, and Linguistic Features) 18 (March). 189–209.

Schilling-Estes, Natalie (1998). Investigating "self-conscious" speech: The performance register in Ocracoke English. *Language in Society* 27: 53–83.

Tucker, G. Richard and Wallace E. Lambert (1969). White and Negro listeners' reactions to various American-English dialects. *Social Forces* 47: 463–8.

Trudgill, Peter (1972). Sex, covert prestige and linguistic change in the urban British English of Norwich. *Language in Society* 1(2): 179–95.

Williams, Frederick, Jack L. Whitehead and Leslie M. Miller (1971). Ethnic stereotyping and judgments of children's speech. *Speech Monographs* 38: 166–70.

3 Investigating Variation and Change in Written Documents

EDGAR W. SCHNEIDER

1 Introduction: How to Listen without Hearing

Language, Saussure taught us, is first and foremost a spoken system – writing is a secondary coding, but speech is primary (1916, repr. 1967: 45, cf. Milroy 1992: 45). In a default setting, the study of language variation and change starts out from performance data and thus employs methodological tools appropriate to the study of spoken records – sociolinguistic interviews, tape recordings, acoustic analysis, etc. However, there are areas of study for which spoken records are simply not available. In many cases we are interested in long-term developments, such as the evolution of vernaculars; and these periods of interest to linguists extend considerably beyond the time when tape recorders, or, more generally, audio recordings of speech were first available as a by-product of technological developments. It is prototypically in such instances that variation and change has to be studied on the basis of written documents only.

Normally, as variationist linguists we are not directly interested in the written record as such, not being concerned with the evolution of writing or spelling systems, questions of literacy, etc. – its function is predominantly to serve as a clue, a pathway to the variation and change of the language system in itself. More directly, most written records of interest in this context represent a speech act: either a genuine, historical one that took place at a specific time and place, recorded but indirectly in writing, or a perhaps fictional but necessarily characteristic one, rendering speech forms that a typical member of a given speech community might have uttered with some degree of likelihood, representative of the everyday communication in this community. In such cases, the written record functions as a filter, as it were: it provides us with a representation of a speech act that we would have liked to have listened to and recorded acoustically and that without the written record would have been lost altogether; but at the same time the rendering of the speech event is only indirect and imperfect, affected by the nature of the recording context in certain ways. The crucial question is to what extent the effects of the recording contexts are predictable, or recoverable. It is essential for us to know, or to reasonably assess, what effect this filter had, how accurately the original speech event is represented. The level of accuracy may vary from a fairly faithful rendering to a gross distortion, and for the analyst it is essential to determine where on this continuum of faithfulness any given record is positioned, and what consequences this may have. In other words, whether explicitly or indirectly, a variationist linguist analyzing written records is likely to observe what I call a *Principle of Filter Removal*: a written record of a speech event stands like a filter between the words as spoken and the analyst. As the linguist is interested in the speech event itself (and, ultimately, the principles of language variation and change behind it), a primary task will be to "remove the filter" as far as possible, i.e. to assess the nature of the recording process in all possible and relevant ways and to evaluate and take into account its likely impact on the relationship between the speech event and the record, to reconstruct the speech event itself, as accurately as possible.

This chapter sets out to survey and discuss some possibilities and problems associated with this approach, and some necessary considerations and steps in the process of "filter removal". I will begin by briefly pointing out other sub-disciplines and approaches in linguistics that have faced similar problems; obviously, variationists are neither the first nor the only group of linguists wishing to study speech through writing, and we should learn from related efforts. Subsequently, I will discuss some characteristics of the major text types available, considering their consequences for our purposes. Finally, the general methodological and theoretical problems that need to be addressed and solved as far as possible will be pointed out.

2   Charting the Territory: Precursors and Neighbors

Obviously, many of the questions addressed here are closely related to those historical linguists have faced for over 200 years: *historical linguistics* is also concerned with recovering earlier stages of a language (sound laws and systems, morphological categories, syntactic patterns) solely on the basis of written records that have come down to us through the centuries (cf. Cable 1990). Thus, historical linguists are also interested in collecting reliable data, evaluating sources, assessing style levels, and the role of editing (for which the philological tradition has provided principles and guidelines); in many cases they also wish to approximate speech as closely as possible (Kytö 1991: 30 lists some relevant references), and of course they face the same fundamental problem of having to cope with substantial gaps in the historical record (Thomason 1993). However, there are also differences in approaches and research interests. One concerns the application of comparative and internal reconstruction (cf. Campbell 1998: 108–48, 201–19), methods which are essential in historical linguistics but of no concern for variation studies because they assume language uniformity – "there is nothing built into the comparative method which would allow it to address variation directly" (Campbell 1998: 146). Also, there is a difference in the time depth of investigations and in ultimate goals. In historical linguistics, the documentation of earlier stages of a language is seen as a goal in itself; traditionally, documentation and analysis have covered extended periods back to earliest records, way over a thousand years, and typically the orientation has been either strictly diachronic (i.e. describing changes of one subsystem in the course of time) or synchronic (i.e. existing forms at a given point in time). Conversely, the variationist paradigm has transcended Saussure's claim of a separation of synchrony and diachrony (Polomé 1990: 7–8) and has typically investigated diachrony-in-synchrony, ongoing changes as reflected in social, stylistic, or linguistic distributional patterns. While variationist work can be and has been carried out as applied to early periods such as Old or Middle English, in practice the requirement of a dense documentation of vernacular speakers and styles has resulted in research activities being focused upon relatively recent periods (say, texts characteristic of nineteenth-century speech of some kind[1]); and while historical linguistics has had to work with poetic and formal styles to a great extent, the study of variation and change requires a focus on vernacular styles.[2]

Traditional dialectology provides us with large data sets that were mostly collected many decades ago and even then focused upon older speakers, so from a present-day perspective these records become increasingly valuable as historical data (cf. Klemola, this volume). For instance, this applies to the *English Dialect Dictionary* (Wright 1898–1906), based upon nineteenth-century collections, or to the *Linguistic Atlas of the Middle and South Atlantic States* in the USA, to which Kretzschmar and Schneider (1996: 32) explicitly ascribe a "historical orientation" and which Bailey (1997a) used in a reconstruction of variation and change in early southern English.

Another discipline that has pursued very similar goals is *historical sociolinguistics* (cf. Milroy 1992, Raumolin-Brunberg 1996, Romaine 1982), although scholars working within this framework have tended to emphasize the broader sociopolitical context of language evolution rather than detailed descriptive documentations of individual forms of a language – perhaps for want of reliable data. Milroy (1992) argues for a "variationist view of language change" (1992: 123),[3] and rejects tendencies to limit historical language study to the study of the history of the standard language only and to regard variability "as an obstacle rather than a resource" (1992: 132). However, although he looks into some exemplary data (for instance on *h*-dropping) of Middle English, most of the evidence in his book is derived from his modern analyses of Belfast English – essentially his proposal is programmatic only. In recent years the analysis of electronic text corpora stemming from the Helsinki school (see below) has partially redressed the balance. The most notable strictly sociolinguistic historical project to date, a remarkably successful correlation of sociohistorical class stratifications with linguistic variation, is the work done on the "Corpus of Early English Correspondence" (Nevalainen and Raumolin-Brunberg 1996).

Building a bridge between historical linguistics proper and sociolinguistics, historical *corpus linguistics* has adopted many of the incentives of the variationist paradigm (cf. Bauer, this volume). The Helsinki Corpus of historical English texts, widely used in recent years, was inspired to a considerable extent by a post-Labovian line of thinking and explicitly designed to facilitate cross-stylistic quantitative studies. Analyzing computerized samples of historical texts has turned out to be a particularly promising line of pursuit: historical records, being available in written form, lend themselves easily to computerization, and electronic corpora permit easy access to large numbers of instances of any form in context. The Helsinki school has deliberately adopted a variationist framework in their historical-linguistic analyses, as is suggested by their project title "English in transition: Change through variation," and the fact that special attention is paid "to the role played by textual and discourse factors across the centuries" (Rissanen et al. 1997a: v, 1997b: v; cf. the papers in these volumes as well as in Hickey et al. 1997 or Nevalainen and Kahlas-Tarkka 1997) as reflected in genre and register categories. Operating within the same methodological framework, Kytö's work on early American English (1991, on the development of modals; 1993 on third-person verbal inflection) also sees itself in a variationist tradition (1991: 83–5).

Since the 1980s the field of *pidgin and creole linguistics* has increasingly been concerned with unearthing written records as evidence of early stages of creoles. While frequently motivated by questions on the genesis of creoles, such studies have contributed significantly to our understanding of the historical evolution and the variability of these languages. Rickford (1987), for instance, uses early written texts to reconstruct the recent history of Guyanese Creole, while at the same time paying considerable attention to its internal variation. Several other creoles and pidgins, including Sranan, Negerhollands, Jamaican, Trinidadian, Bajan, Kittitian, and West African Pidgin English have received important historical documentation and analysis, mostly in book-length studies (e.g. Arends 1995, Baker and Bruyn 1999, D'Costa and Lalla 1989, Huber 1999, Rickford and Handler 1994). Theoretically and methodologically, these studies operate in a slightly different but clearly related paradigm, pursuing the same goals by means of similar approaches.

3   Assessing the Sources: Text Types and their Relative Proximity to Speech

Written records that are of interest in the present context typically share certain properties and have originated in characteristic contexts. Thus, I will first consider basic requirements for texts to be acceptable for variationist analyses, then categorize them by text types, and finally discuss some characteristics of the most important text types in the light of their usefulness for variationist purposes.

3.1 Some basic requirements for texts to be useful for a variationist analysis

Only a relatively small fraction of all the historical texts that have come down to us lend themselves to a variationist analysis. Obviously, the usefulness of texts varies also individually, from one text to another, but can be broadly generalized for certain text types which share relevant discourse characteristics. Some requirements need to be fulfilled:

1   Texts should be as close to speech, and especially vernacular styles, as possible (Montgomery 1997a: 227). This condition largely excludes formal and literary writing – such texts may be of marginal interest, but, being shaped by prescriptive traditions and conventions, they normally display categorical, invariant usage and fail to reflect natural speech behavior and associated processes. Notably, this is at odds with the esteem attributed to texts in related disciplines; typically, we want "documents often of no particular interest to scholars in any field but linguistics" (Montgomery 1997a: 227), so there is but limited support available, and not infrequently do variationist linguists use unedited, even manuscript sources, which may cause readability problems.

    Example 1: In compiling an electronic corpus of overseers' letters from the pre-Civil War ("antebellum") American South (Schneider and Montgomery, 1999), Montgomery consulted with local historians and autograph experts to eliminate undecipherable passages as far as possible.

2   To facilitate correlations with extralinguistic parameters, the texts should be of different origins, i.e. stem from several authors from different social classes, possibly also age groups, and both sexes, and should represent varying stylistic levels.
3   Texts must display variability of the phenomenon under investigation, i.e. the use of functionally equivalent variants of a linguistic variable.
4   With quantification being the staple methodology of variationism, texts must fulfill certain size requirements. There is no figure specifying any precise minimum number of words required – but usable texts must provide reasonably large token frequencies of individual variants, and they should (though need not) allow quantitative analyses of several phenomena, i.e. display variation in a wider range of linguistic phenomena.

3.2 Categorization of text types

While there is always some individual variation in style and expression, essentially texts come in text types, determined by their respective discourse parameters, which, in turn, condition their proximity to speech. Thus, it will be useful to categorize text types along these lines and then to consider their individual properties in the light of their usefulness for the study of variation and change. A variety of communicative determinants of the context of situation will play a role here – whether or not texts are speech-based, whether the relationships between the participants in a discourse is close or distant, whether a communication situation is private or public, etc. (cf. Kytö 1991: 37–44). Given the requirements spelled out earlier, however, in what follows I will concentrate upon text types which bear some relatively direct relationship to speech events and ignore others, which lead us into the fuzzy boundaries between variationist and historical-linguistic analyses proper.[4] Adopting the Principle of Filter Removal and admitting that the "filter" may consist of a varying number of "layers," I am proposing five text categories which represent a continuum of increasing distance between an original speech event and its written record,[5] based upon the following criteria:

- the reality of a speech event portrayed: a written record may be a rendition of a real and unique speech event that took place at a given time and location, or it may represent a hypothetical utterance – one that a typical member of a speech community could have made, or one that an individual would have wanted to make but was forced to make through an indirect, written channel;
- the relationship between the speaker and the person who wrote the utterance down, who may or may not have been identical; and
- the temporal distance between the speech event itself and the time of the recording (which may or may not have been simultaneous).

Table 3.1 summarizes these points and the resulting categorization. I posit the following five broad categories of the relationship between a speech event and its written record:

1 *Recorded*: A direct record of a singular speech event, whether written down on location and simultaneously (as in the case of trial records) or transcribed later from a mechanical recording (as in the case of Hyatt's Hoodoo interviews).
2 *Recalled*: A record of a singular speech event, although written down some time after the utterance itself, presumably from notes and/or memory. The writer intends to take note of what was said verbatim and faithfully, but allowance must be made for factors such as lapses of memory or limitations of understanding. Examples: WPA ex-slave narratives, travelers' records.
3 *Imagined*: A writer records potential, conceived utterances by himself which, for lack of the presence of the addressee, need to be written down rather than said; but he remains in a near-speech mode. Clearly, the boundary to genuine writing is fuzzy here, but prototypically this state of affairs characterizes writers with limited proficiency and practice in writing, who simply

Table 3.1 Categorization of text types according to their proximity to speech

Category	Reality of speech event	speaker – writer identity	temporal distance speech – record	Characteristic text types
Recorded	real, unique	different	immediate	interview transcripts, trial records
Recalled	real, unique	different	later	ex-slave narratives
Imagined	hypothetic, unique	identical	immediate	letters, diaries
Observed	usu. real, unique	different	later	commentaries
Invented	hypothetic, unspecified	n. a.	unspecified	literary dialect

need to put their thoughts onto paper for some reason. Thus, letters by semi-literate writers belong here, but also some questionnaire responses (e.g. the *Tennessee Civil War Veterans Questionnaires*).

4 *Observed*: A writer cites samples of typical utterances by others that he regards as characteristic of their speech and has overheard repeatedly. Typically, such contemporaries' statements are prescriptively motivated. This is similar to category 2, except that the speech events recorded here are not unique but typical ones, and thus one step more indirect as a record of speech, filtered not only by the perception but also by the evaluation of the author.

5 *Invented*: This is hypothetical, imagined speech, usually thought to be uttered by others than the writer but by speakers with whose real-life models he is familiar; there is no association with a real-life speech event, but the fictitious utterance is intended to be characteristic of its – frequently also fictitious – speaker.

3.3   Transcripts (Category 1: Recorded)

Direct transcripts are clearly the most reliable and potentially the most interesting amongst all these text types – provided that they are faithful to the spoken word and the speech thus recorded represents the vernacular. Interestingly, indirect transcripts – those based upon an audio-recording of the speech event itself, can be expected to be even more accurate than direct, simultaneously

written ones, as in these cases the scribe presumably had more time to bridge
the gap between speaking and writing speeds and thus to record every turn
of the utterance, if desired. This is not unlike the situation of a modern
sociolinguist, who has typically collected tape recordings but frequently
works from transcripts of these – and the process of transcription necessarily
involves some difficult decisions and some degree of subjective interpretation.
Thus, transcripts of all kinds are more reliable than other types of written
records, but even modern transcripts of sociolinguistic interviews are not
simple representations of "reality" either, as one might think. Typically, the
transcriber is the only person to have access to the audio-recording itself, so it
is unusual for disagreements on transcription details to really surface in the
research community[6] – but the problem itself clearly deserves more awareness
(cf. Miethaner 2000).

It is actually not as uncommon as it may appear at first sight that a researcher
has access to a written transcript of an audio-recording but not to the oral source
itself. Not infrequently are transcripts of interviews but not the interviews
themselves published (see example 2). In addition, there is also the more interesting (because it is diachronically relevant) case that early audio-recordings
were lost but their transcripts have survived (see example 3).

Example 2: Loman (1967) is a collection of AAVE texts that can be read but
not audited, and Patrick et al. (1996) used it as a database for a variationist
analysis. Rickford (1987) contains several fieldwork transcripts, systematically
put together to cover several parameters of speaker variability. In Bailey
et al. (1991; cf. fn. 6) the entire transcripts of interviews with former slaves
are published; the recordings themselves, however, are unpublished, available only through personal contacts.

Example 3: Another most promising source of earlier AAVE are the
"Hoodoo"-transcripts by Harry Middleton Hyatt, used in dissertations by
Ewers (1996) and – together with other sources – Kautzsch (2000a). In the
1930s, 1940s and 1970s Hyatt conducted over 1600 interviews with black
practitioners of witchcraft and rootwork in 13 states. The early ones were
recorded by an Ediphone with a speaking-tube, the later ones with an
Ediphone and a microphone. All interviews were transcribed exactly, and the
transcripts have been preserved and published, while the audio-recordings
(originally on aluminium discs) were destroyed.

Direct written records of speech have been used as parts of electronic corpora
and in the wake of the Helsinki school. Trial proceedings, court and meeting
records, witness accounts, transcripts of sermons, and so on are "speech-based
registers" (Biber and Finegan 1997: 253) which typically provide verbatim
renderings of actual speech, though frequently in speech events marked by a
rather formal atmosphere (Kytö 1991: 29, cf. Culpeper and Kytö 1999). Rissanen
(1997) discussed the Salem witchcraft trials as linguistic evidence, in which

"particular attention was paid to every word and turn of phrase uttered by the suspects" (1997: 185).

3.4 Recall protocols (Category 2: Recalled)

These are renderings of specific speech events not taken down on the spot but at some later time from memory, possibly supported by notes. We may assume that a writer wanted to produce a transcript as faithful as possible, but perfect accuracy cannot be expected due to unavoidable distortions caused by lapses of memory and other "noise" factors, such as misperception. Psycholinguists have carried out research on what is memorized in "free recall protocolls" (Hildyard and Olson 1982: 19), frequently of stories. In general, the results suggest that to some extent "surface structure features of the sentences" (1982: 19) are remembered, though a listener's mind focuses more upon the meaning of the message than upon "the actual words, syntax and intonation," these being rather ephemeral (1982: 20).

> **Example 4:** The so-called WPA ex-slave narratives, a large-scale systematic collection of interviews with very old African Americans compiled in the 1930s (Rawick 1972/1977/1979) and analysed amongst others by Brewer (1974) and Schneider (1989), are an important source of earlier AAVE, belonging to this category. Reacting to publications which questioned their validity (see below), Schneider (1997) considered the consequences of the recording procedures in detail, and concluded that the narratives are composed of four layers of text, decreasing in their trustworthiness:
> - verbatim notes;
> - statements remembered accurately;
> - rephrasings of the speaker's words by the writer; and
> - invented words.
> Given that three of these four layers are (more or less accurate) renditions of a specific and unique speech event, and that additional evidence can be adduced for comparison and validation (like contemporary socio-linguistic analyses, or studies of other earlier records; cf. ex. 14), he believes there is no "cause for too much pessimism" (1997: 37) and classifies the narratives as "note-supported mental protocols" (1997: 44), texts composed of written notes enhanced by memory.

3.5 Private letters by semi-literate writers (Category 3: Imagined)

Clearly, letters do not represent spoken utterances; but when persons who have had but limited experience in writing and exposure to the norms of written expression are forced to write nevertheless, their writing reflects many features of their speech fairly accurately: what they do is put their own "imagined" words onto paper, if only with difficulty. Thus, what we are most interested in are letters by semi-literate writers, a type of resource discovered, analyzed and evaluated most authoritatively in several publications by Michael Montgomery (1995, 1997a, 1997b, 1999, Montgomery et al. 1993).

> **Example 5:** Montgomery (1995, 1997a, 1997b) uses Irish emigrant letters to establish transatlantic linguistic connections; he calls emigrant letters "the best resource for reconstructing early stages of American English" (1995: 5). In a very important contribution based upon letters written by African-Americans after the Civil War, Montgomery et al. (1993) document significant parallels between nineteenth-century AAVE and white dialects with respect to constraints on 3rd person plural –*s* use. Montgomery (1999) and Kautzsch (2000b) use letters by African-American repatriates, from Sierra Leone and Liberia, respectively, to reconstruct features of earlier AAVE.

However useful, such letters are often products of the "vagaries and accidents of history (such as which family chose to preserve letters, whether letters survived decay)" (Montgomery 1997a: 227). One of their advantages is that they are "usually datable without ambiguity" (Montgomery 1999: 21) and "more often than not localizable to a specific place" (1999: 22; cf. Montgomery et al. 1993: 342–3). Letters "do not reflect everyday speech habits in a straightforward way [because] . . . literacy . . . always affects a person's writing habits to some degree" (Montgomery 1995: 7), but even if they are not transcripts "with care and judgement we can separate out the evidence for speech" (1995: 5). Approximation to speech is signalled by "the lack of punctuation and other formal conventions like paragraphing" (1995: 6), unpredictable capitalization, or phonetic spellings (1995: 7).

Montgomery (1999) presents a strong principled argument in favor of the use of documents by semi-literate authors in variation studies, based on an adequate assessment of the difficulties involved. He identifies and addresses four possible problem areas:

1 *Authorship*: It is necessary to ask "on a case-by-case basis" (1992: 22), often in collaboration with archivists and historians, whether letters are indeed autographs (hand-written personally) or were possibly written by an amanuensis (a helper writing from dictation).
2 *Use of models*: The presence of opening and closing formulae and other rhetorical conventions cast doubt upon the naturalness of the speech in letters, but Montgomery argues convincingly that spelling, punctuation and other features indicate clearly that the writers do not copy from a written guide but rely on oral models, having heard letters read out aloud before. (1999: 24; cf. Montgomery 1995: 6)

3 *Difficulties in manipulating the written code*: While obviously even the very
   act of writing was difficult for many writers and many features of the
   letters appear "erratic and unsystematic" (1999: 24), the "conformity of
   many misspellings to pronunciation and the systematic patterning of grammatical features according to known constraints [show the documents to
   be] far from random and haphazard" (1999: 24).

4 *Representativeness*: Were those who could read or write not set apart from a
   vernacular community and its speech norms by this very ability? This is an
   objection which cannot be discarded but also should not be taken too seriously, Montgomery argues; in most cases the writers were not members of
   an elite or a distinct social group (1999: 25).

However, Kautzsch (2000a) shows that literacy results in reduced rates of
vernacular forms (2000a: 189; 207) and thus keeps the Liberian letters distinct
from transcript sources (which would represent categories 1 and 2 in my
scheme). He suggests that certain salient nonstandard forms, including contractions, *ain't*, negative concord, zero copula (e.g. *he old*), and the nonstandard
relativizers *what* and subject zero (e.g. *a man what helped me; it's the devil [Ø]
makes folks do bad*), fail to surface in writing, with speakers being aware of their
stigmatization (2000a: 222).

Other uses of semi-skilled letters include Bailey et al. (1989), who document
the presence of the subject type constraint on plural verb-*s*[7] in Early Modern
English, and Filppula (1999), who confirms that "private correspondence provided the most fruitful source for vernacular features" (1999: 43; cf. 43–6) in
early Hiberno-English. A machine-readable corpus of antebellum overseers'
letters, the compilation of which has just been completed, promises interesting
insights into the nature and variability of early nineteenth-century southern
US dialect (Schneider and Montgomery 1999).

A particularly interesting research strategy is suggested by Meurman-Solin
(1999) in her work on early Scots. She finds an exceptionally high frequency
of phonetic spellings in women's autograph letters (1999: 305), thus documenting a most interesting, culturally-based gender difference (because women had
more limited access to schooling), and continues with an observation which
I find remarkable: "phonetic spellings previously labeled as 'nonstandard' or
'irregular' are in fact evidence of an early adoption of later widely diffused
variants. A finding of this kind may lead to a reassessment of the role of
inexperienced writers as informants in the reconstruction of phonological developments" (1999: 306). This, I believe, holds great promise. It is well-known
that the chronology of historical sound changes is particularly difficult to determine and tends to be fixed at the time of its completion, with little interest
shown in and evidence available for the earlier stages of a change (cf. Milroy
1992: 46). If it turned out that letters allow us to detect "embryonic variants,"
early traces of future changes (Gordon and Trudgill 1999), that could be an
important advancement in our understanding of the mechanisms of sound change.

3.6   *Other autograph records (Category 3: Imagined)*

To the extent that semi-skilled writers wrote anything other than letters (and such writings have been preserved), such texts will be equally interesting for variationist analyses: "The unselfconscious wording scribbled down in appeals, answers and witness depositions filed to courts by untutored writers, offer unique instances of lively language . . . [and] of current colloquial usage" (Kytö 1991: 31). Such writings are rare, however, simply for lack of motivation and circumstances. Diaries may be an interesting type of text; some were used by Kytö (1991, 1993). On the other hand, the very habit of writing a diary is untypical of semi-literate writers; not surprisingly, Filppula (1999: 43) states that diaries "were disappointing in that all were written in standard language."

There is one collection of texts that falls into this category and has been used for analyses of variation and change in early southern English, if only rarely so far: *The Tennessee Civil War Veterans Questionnaires* (Elliott and Moxley 1985). These are "first-hand reports of war-stories and attitudes of Civil War veterans" (Maynor 1993: 180), systematically collected between 1915 and 1922 in the state of Tennessee by two historians interested in writing history from below (i.e. as experienced by the common people), "a true history of the Old South" (ibid.). The questionnaire consisted of 46 questions on antebellum lifestyle, wartime experiences, etc. Some 1,650 autograph responses were submitted in response, including a wide variety of nonstandard language forms, as many of the writers were barely literate (but still willing to share their views and experiences); and they were published "exactly as written by the veterans" (ibid.). This is a very promising source, "one of very few reliable sources of data on the language of ordinary people in the nineteenth century" (Maynor 1993: 184–5), although the nature of the data, which consist largely of brief responses (except for some narrations on battles, etc.), also imposes limitations (for instance, there are many past tense verb forms, some repeating those of the questions, but no interrogatives). Little use has been made of this source so far (see Bailey 1997a and Maynor 1993 for references), but Bailey (1997a: 256) shows how data from this source can be combined with linguistic atlas records and sociolinguistic survey samples in documenting long-term change, based upon the apparent time construct.

An equally unusual but remarkable source from this category was analyzed by Bailey and Ross (1988), namely ship logs from the sixteenth through eighteenth centuries as evidence for the "Ship English" spoken by British sailors, which was the contemporary superstrate input to creolization in the New World. They faced similar problems (brevity and semantic similarity of responses; questionable representativeness because of the widespread illiteracy amongst sailors), but did find some interesting documentation of nonstandard uses, including variable constraints.

3.7   Contemporary commentaries (Category 4: Observed)

This category comprises statements on (and citations representative of) some-one else's perceived, typical speech patterns, without rendering a specific speech event (in contrast with travelers' observations). Such testimony, as a mani-festation of a " 'negative approach' to grammar and usage [which] has a long tradition in England" (Sundby et al. 1991: 1), was typically motivated by pre-scriptive attitudes: observers quoted "vulgarisms" which they believed were to be avoided (but which, to turn the argument around, they perceived as being in common use around them). In historical linguistics, such evaluations have been relatively important sources of dialectal forms banned from and invisible in the written standard (cf. Tiecken-Boon van Ostade 1997). A note-worthy source, underused so far, is Sundby et al. (1991), a fairly comprehen-sive and systematic inventory of such statements on "vulgar" usage in England in the eighteenth century. Of course, there are also difficulties involved: such forms may have been misconceived; the representation may be distorting; usually we get isolated forms out of any context, and have little extralinguistic information on users and contexts of use – so both representativeness and validity of these examples need to be assessed with care and reluctance. Still, they do indicate earlier variation and change.

> **Example 6:** Gordon (1998) provides an interesting use and evaluation of such sources in tracing the earliest stages of New Zealand English. She systematically collected comments on pronunciation in letters to news-papers and – "very valuably" (1998: 64), she says – school inspectors' reports (in which some concern on local pronunciations was voiced). Interestingly enough, the availability of archival recordings of speakers from the same period allowed her to compare and thus evaluate these comments. She finds that the written records are "reasonably reliable in certain respects" (1998: 81; e.g. with respect to *h*-dropping and the rendering of diphthongs and the centralization of /ɪ/) but fail to record some other developments altogether, fail to comment on degrees of variability, and do not indicate earliest uses; apparently it takes a time lag for innovations to be commented on.

3.8   Literary sources (Category 5: Invented)

Literary dialect constitutes a topic in its own right – Ives (1950) is a widely-known classic, which points out its characteristics and suggests it should be assessed in comparison with modern dialect data. But it is also familiar as a source of information on variation and change (cf. several contributions in Taavitsainen et al. 1999), despite some limitations. Literary attestations have been used "routinely, but uncritically, in attempts to document and reconstruct AA[V]E" (Montgomery 1999: 21); on the other hand, many scholars have pointed out the limitations of this approach: literary sources tend to overuse stereotypical markers but reduce variability, and they "tend to be relatively brief and open to serious questions of authenticity" (Rickford 1998: 159; cf. Maynor 1988: 110–11, Schneider 1989: 46–7). Cooley (1997) is a case in point: She shows that the speech of an African-American character in a successful eighteenth-century play is actually "based upon Caribbean varieties" (1997: 52), but nevertheless "constituted a prototype for other early African-American literary representations regardless of provenance" (1997: 53) and "became part of early American popular culture" (1997: 56). Lakoff (1982) provides a principled explanation of some of the difficulties involved. She states that the transfer of spoken discourse to fiction writing is problematic due to the different discourse requirements of the two channels (1982: 244–5) because devices of spontaneous speech function differently in written texts while, conversely, "transcripts do not feel to readers like 'real' conversation" (1982: 245).

Despite these reservations, literary dialect can be and has been used successfully for linguistic purposes. For instance, Mille (1997) investigates a literary representation of Gullah "as a resource to study Gullah's history" (1997: 98), finds it helpful, and cites assessments and comparative studies that categorize it as remarkably accurate (1997: 99). Trudgill (1999) uses literary dialect to identify different degrees of salience of certain features of Norfolk dialect to Norfolk dialect writers, paying close attention to variants of nonstandard dialect orthography and their phonetic interpretation. He deduces a principle that appears generally valid for dialect orthography: "only phonological features which are currently undergoing dedialectalisation [i.e. disappearing in a dialect] are systematically represented by nonstandard dialect orthography as written by native speakers" (1999: 326).

> **Example 7:** Ellis (1994) is a careful analysis of some features of Southern dialect in writings by authors from the three decades before the Civil War. Amongst other things, he documents the familiar "subject type constraint" on a broad basis, thus suggesting that "authors were using an authentic and regionally distinctive feature of early and mid-nineteenth-century Southern dialects" (1994: 135). He warns against taking literary representations at face value (1994: 128), but even after a consideration of some methodological pitfalls and limitations he argues that literary dialect should be exploited appropriately.

In using written documents for an analysis of language variation and change, it is clear that the idiosyncratic properties of each category and each individual text, resulting from its recording conditions, have to be assessed as accurately as possible to weigh its effects upon the results. In practice, however, the scarcity of useful sources recommends a broad strategy of analysing and comparing as many different sources of a single variety as possible, with results from different text categories supplementing each other and contributing to a mutual evaluation.

> **Example 8:** Though predating the variationist paradigm, Eliason (1956) is an impressive model case of an investigation of written records (in a dialectological and historical perspective). He states that after 1750 there are "plentiful" records which "reflect colloquial usage" (1956: 27) in North Carolina, and in his chapter 2 he surveys a wide range of archival manuscript sources screened for traces of vernacular language, including legal papers, bills and occupational records, plantation books and overseers' reports, church records, children's and students' writings, diaries, etc.

All of the above-mentioned text categories suffer from shortcomings; and the following section will look more closely into some of the problems which they have in common. Still, despite unavoidable limitations many of the studies cited above are suggestive of the fundamental insights that can be gained from a proper analysis of such texts, and encourage researchers to go back to archives and libraries, look for appropriate texts, and investigate these in a variationist perspective – a research strategy which holds promises of substantial advances in the recovery of variation and change in earlier periods.

4   Problems

4.1   *Representativeness*

Variationists wish to understand certain principles of language organization in a speech community in general; thus, individual informants and text or tape samples are of interest only in so far as they reflect a global distribution, i.e. can be interpreted as samples drawn from and representative of a population. Representativeness is defined as the fit between a sample and the population it stands for: are we justified in assuming that the speakers and samples under investigation display the same behavior as the entire speech community? There is a crucial difference between the situations of a sociolinguist planning a present-day survey and a researcher working with historical and written data in so far as the modern sociolinguist can define a sample and select interviewees accordingly, while historical work will typically be constrained by the availability of records. Thus, assessing the representativeness of one's sample is by necessity a crucial, unavoidable problem in working with written documents. Rather than selecting a sample from a population, the researcher typically faces the reverse situation: "The issue is not whether one has a 'representative sample' but to profile the sample at hand to see what inferences may reasonably be drawn from it" (Montgomery 1999: 26).

Example 9: In terms of sample size (1,650 respondents), the *Tennessee Civil War Veterans Questionnaires* leave nothing to be desired, and the fact that these individuals represent a broad range of social status parameters suggests there should be no problem of representativeness. However, this applies only as long as one restricts one's interests to white males, as all respondents are men, and most of them are white.

Still, many sources are voluminous enough to allow or require a selection from all the texts available. In such cases, certain simple rules should be applied to avoid any additional bias:

- Measure and constrain quality: check whether there are internal differences in validity. If so, devise a way of measuring them, and select only (from) the best sources available.
- Avoid circularity: in measuring the quality of the texts, do not use phenomena that will be the subject of the investigation proper, to avoid skewing the results.
- Diversify and stratify the sample: other considerations notwithstanding, select a diversified variety of texts (or text producers), to avoid the effects of unwanted correlations or idiolectal bias.
- All other things being equal, select a random sample: for instance, select every n-th text, with n roughly equaling the number of texts available divided by the number of texts to be sampled.

Example 10: In compiling a corpus of Ulster emigrant letters, Montgomery (1995) adopted only two simple selection criteria: all writers had to be from Ulster, and their letters had to attest a minimum of one nonstandard grammatical form (1995: 9). It would have been desirable to apply further criteria, but the scarcity of records did not allow any other limitations. In contrast, Schneider (1989) was lucky to be able to select a working corpus from thousands of ex-slave narratives; for these, representativeness is not a problem (though validity is). He applied a fairly elaborate procedure involving several stages and independent considerations, in line with the above recommendations (cf. 1989: 53–61).

With respect to autograph documents, there is a natural mismatch between our desire for representativeness and the quest for vernacular speech, illustrated, for example, by the fact that their sample is "skewed toward StE" in the Ship English study of Bailey and Ross (1988): most sailors were unable to write, so those who did write the ship logs were possibly not representative. This is a general problem which Montgomery identifies as a genre-specific variant of the well-known "observer's paradox" and which he calls the "researcher's paradox" (1997b: 125): "that individuals of lower social status whose speech intruded more directly into their writing usually wrote infrequently and were less likely to have their writing preserved" (Montgomery 1999: 26). To overcome this difficulty, Montgomery suggests an ingenious procedure, clearly related to the role of emotional questions in overcoming the observer's paradox:

the researcher must identify persons of little education who had a compelling reason to write – preferably with some frequency, to a government official or an estate, for example – and thus who had a chance to have their letters preserved in other collections of papers. . . . there are at least three types of such individuals. These may be called lonelyhearts, desperadoes, and functionaries. If we can identify those individuals who were separated from loved ones, were in desperate straits and needed help, or were required by their occupation to submit periodic reports, we may be on the path to locating the letters of greatest interest. These three situations cut sharply across much of the social spectrum, as people of different social stations face loneliness, deprivation, or the requirement to inform others of their work, so the prospect of finding letters of less-educated persons fitting these descriptions is realistic. More important, these situations are compelling enough to motivate individuals to write for themselves, to do their best in putting words to paper regardless of their levels of literacy. In other words, someone pleading for mercy or relief may well pay little attention to the form (spelling, capitalization, grammar, etc.) of his or her writing, being more concerned with getting an unambiguous message across. The written version of the observer's paradox is accordingly overcome – as much as is possible to do.   (Montgomery 1999: 229)

It is clear that especially with small, unchangeable sample sizes representativeness can become a crucial limitation. In such cases, all that can be done is to assess the representativeness of one's sample as well as possible, and to be reluctant in interpreting the data.

Example 11: Montgomery (1997b: 137) points out that the study of verbal suffixation in Early Modern English by Bailey et al. (1989) suffers from an error of representativeness: They "argue that fifteenth-century London English, represented by letters from the Cely merchant family, exhibited plural verbal –s. However, a close analysis of the data reveals that only one member of the family, Richard Cely the Younger, used the suffix regularly in nonexistential sentences; since he was reared in Yorkshire, his language most likely followed the Northern British pattern."

Still, we should not be overly pessimistic about the limitations of written sources based on the representativeness issue – when the samples are large enough, all kinds of parameters can be investigated. Kautzsch (2000b) shows that an impressive level of sophistication can be achieved: compiling a unified corpus drawn from several independent sources, he is able to carry out apparent-time analyses of change in Earlier AAVE, with speakers' birth years extending between the 1830s and the early twentieth century.

4.2 Validity

Validity relates to the quality of a record, its relationship to the target of investigation. If the record relates to a unique speech event (text type categories

1, 2, and 3, possibly also 4), a valid record matches what was uttered faithfully; with the other text categories, it reflects the everyday speech habits of the target community in a more global, indirect fashion. Unavoidably, the very process of writing speech down reduces validity, either because certain components of speech cannot be rendered in writing or because a writer expresses himself differently than a speaker. In autograph records, "the process of putting words into a written code operates in ways that linguists do not understand, filtering out some nonstandard forms completely, lessening the frequency of others while sometimes producing hypercorrections" (Montgomery 1999: 6). The validity of written texts for speech analyses largely depends upon the writer: his or her willingness to render speech forms, and his or her ability to do so. In addition, the recording conditions, and hence the text categories, which are shaped by these, are influential, and there is a tendency for validity to vary by text type. Thus, the validity of any individual document has to be assessed on a cline from most to least accurate. For example, in the case of travelers' reports the validity of an observation depends on the writer's familiarity with the variety in question, his physical proximity to the speech act itself, the temporal distance between the hearing and the taking note of an utterance, and also the discourse-pragmatic function of the written text itself. Similar considerations obtain for narratives, literary dialect, and other direct records. For example, Rissanen (1997) observes a "scale of closeness to spoken expression in the Salem documents" (1997: 185). For some text types (especially published sources), the potentially distorting influence of editing has to be considered (Maynor 1988), although that is the exception rather than the rule in the types of documents (frequently manuscripts) variationists are most interested in. Essentially, we need transcriptions which "adhere strictly to the spelling and punctuation in the original manuscript as much as possible in transcribing text to typewritten copy" (Montgomery et al. 1993: 341).

It is important and also instructive to see how an awareness of this issue has grown in the field; however, this concerns not only work with written documents but is equally valid for the assessment of other kinds of sources. Bailey (1997b) regards "evaluating data" as one of the central concerns of the discipline in the future and points out that this applies equally to written as well as spoken sources (1997b: 27–8). We are used to accepting sociolinguistic interviews and tape recordings as direct evidence, but in practice what is published and what many sociolinguists commonly work with is transcripts, and transcribing is anything but objective and unambiguous (Bailey 1997b: 28, Miethaner 2000).

Example 12: A growing awareness of the need to address the validity issue has become palpable in dealing with the ex-slave narratives (cf. ex. 4). Dillard (1972) was the first linguist to use selections based upon these records as illustrative examples – but he used not originals but texts from an edited selection (with linguistic modifications admitted by its editor, B. Botkin; cf. Schneider 1989: 50), and he cited these examples as representative of current, not historical, AAE. Fasold (1976) uses the same source, Botkin's edition, as evidence for the dialect's diachrony, and briefly considers its validity (1976: 80). Brewer (1974) used the original typescripts of the narratives rather than Botkin's edition as diachronic evidence, but did not question their validity or select individual samples from the overall collection in a principled manner. Schneider (1989: 53–62) addressed these issues and thus, before selecting his sample for the analysis proper, carried out a linguistic "pre-test", a preliminary study of a feature analysed in Brewer's earlier research (copula concord, as in *I am* vs. *I is*) with the sole aim of finding out which interviewers could be assumed to have produced reliable records. Maynor (1988) compared the published versions of some of these typescripts with earlier versions in local archives and detected severe editing interference, casting doubt upon the value of these texts. In reaction, Schneider (1997) argued that the narratives combine text passages that individually can be assigned to four layers of validity (see example 4), and that these texts remain useful, within limitations (cf. Brewer 1997: 74). Kautzsch (2000a: 17–24) restricted his selection from the narrative collection to the earlier typescript versions from two states only and also regarded the interviewers as the decisive criterion for selection, admitting only texts by interviewers whose work was marked as particularly reliable by extralinguistic evidence (explicit statements on their interview practice, African-American ethnicity).

What is needed, therefore, is some means of *assessing the validity* of individual texts or collections. In what follows I propose four hierarchically ordered sets of criteria, with the higher levels indicating a higher level of validity, respectively. Each of these categories is fuzzy in itself, building upon several indicators of varying degrees of strengths; so overall a rating process will end somewhere on a continuum between relatively dubious and quite reliable validity.

1 *Nature of texts*: just like linguistic intuitions unavoidably influence our analyses, the surface appearance of a text, including criteria like the presence and frequency of dialectal forms, the presence of variation, and the overall impression of authenticity, plays a role in assessing a text. In practice, this is mostly a negative criterion: texts like letters, narratives, and so on will have to be excluded from further analysis if they are too close to or entirely written in the standard.

2 *Recording conditions*: this criterion relates to the notion of "filter removal" and the classification of text types discussed earlier: the more the recording situation is removed from the original utterance temporally, locally, and personally (from the writer's perspective), the "thicker" the filter, the less valid the rendering of text. Temporal and local distance and the degree of personal involvement are usually deducible from a text. In addition, sometimes we have explicit external evidence on the quality of a record, such as statements on interviewing and recording policy.

Example 13: Kautzsch (2000a) builds upon evidence of this kind when he admits texts by an interviewer whose work can be assumed to be exceptionally good, having moved into a community and acted as a participant observer. In contrast, Gordon (1998: 68) cites an interesting example of an idiosyncratic, almost haphazard limitation to the validity of early pronunciation reports in various localities across Australia and New Zealand, viz. the case of a traveler who recorded a particular pronunciation detail only after it had been explicitly pointed out to him, but subsequently he noted it in all localities – a distribution which is most unlikely to reflect real-life facts.

3   *Internal consistency*: in relatively large corpora, especially if they derive from several primary sources (e.g. independent sub-corpora, records by different fieldworkers, writers, or authors), it is possible to check for internal consistency. If variable features are consistently portrayed in a similar fashion, if there is a "momentum of overall consensus across fieldworkers and regions" (Schneider 1997: 37), then we can rightly assume that this reflects external reality. Similarities in constraints hierarchies and frequencies, i.e. in largely subconscious structural patterns, across independent writers and sources cannot be explained in any other reasonable way (cf. Ellis 1994: 136).

4   *External fit*: similarly, if the results of an investigation concur with results of other studies and familiar linguistic distributions, such as "conformity of misspellings to known phonological tendencies" (Montgomery 1999: 28), this proves the results to be trustworthy, and thus increases our overall trust in the respective source – again, it is hard to see what other cause apart from both analyses describing the same reality could explain such conformity.

Example 14: Maynor (1988: 115–16) admits that some of Brewer's (1974) results match data of her own from taped interviews from the same period. In the context of the controversy over the genesis of AAVE mentioned earlier, Schneider (1983) claimed that Earlier AAVE was rich in verbal endings in all grammatical persons, a proposal which at that time was in stark contrast to conventional wisdom, which assumed an earlier creole stage of AAVE marked by a lack of inflectional endings as observed in creoles. However, his claim was supported by various observations: internal consistency of the data stemming from 104 speakers and some 40 writers (1983: 103), a regionally systematic patterning across nine states (with adjacent states showing identical inflectional systems; 1983: 105), some socially interpretable variation (1983: 106), and similarities with other descriptive statements relating to that period (1983: 103–4) as well as present-day AAVE (1983: 101) and with phonological and lexical constraints in present-day investigations (Schneider 1989: 66–71, 80–81). Schneider (1997: 41–43) shows that the written ex-slave narratives display the same rank ordering of verbal –s frequencies across grammatical persons (despite significant differences in the quantities themselves) and also fairly similar frequency figures of past tense and noun plural marking as do tape recordings of socially comparable speakers. (Bailey et al. 1991)

4.3 Analyzing different levels of language organization

It is intuitively clear that the validity of speech representation will also correlate with the nature of the linguistic phenomenon under investigation: certain structural types, or, more broadly, levels of language organization are represented fairly accurately while the representation of others will be more difficult, open to doubt, or even impossible (like some phonetic details without grapheme correspondences: voicing in certain fricatives, for example). Whether or to what extent a given linguistic pattern will be represented in written encoding depends upon the following factors:

1 *Heaviness*: it is difficult to provide an accurate definition of the concepts of "heaviness" or "weight" (cf. Wasow 1997). For the present purpose, it is sufficient to state that heaviness correlates with length and sonority (i.e. roughly, the intensity and loudness of a given sound, measurable as its sound pressure level in air and correlating with its perceptive audibility; cf. Crystal 1991: 321–2): the longer a form is, the more phonological and morphological material is employed in its encoding, and the more sonority its phonemes have, the heavier it is, and the more likely it is to be noticed, memorized, and written down (Schneider 1997: 38). By implication, this correlates with language levels, with syntactic forms being more likely to be rendered accurately than morphological ones and, in turn, than phonological details. For example, a plural form *book-dem* is more likely to be noticed and recorded than the suffix in *books*; the same goes for a pattern like *Ain't nobody told me* as against the dental suffix in *told/tol'*, and for a past tense form *clum* as against *climbed*. Montgomery agrees that "letters offer evidence for pronunciation [but] are most amenable for the investigation of grammatical features" (1995: 7). It is worth noting that the heaviness hierarchy just sketched out applies independent of specific languages and is likely to operate universally.

2 *Salience*: in contrast, salience (roughly, greater awarenes associated with a linguistic marker in a community, but essentially this is also a concept which is difficult to grasp; cf. Trudgill 1986) is variety-specific, but has the same effect. Features which are known to be characteristic of or socially diagnostic in a speech community are also likely to be recorded more frequently than actual usage would justify. Gordon notes this effect in observers' commentaries (1998: 68), and it is also known to occur regularly in literary dialect; in general we can expect it when a writer feels a need "to

improve the apparent authenticity of the narrative" (Schneider 1997: 38). Thus, high frequencies of occurrences of such markers in certain text types will have to be interpreted reluctantly. In contrast, inconspicuous forms, indicators which operate below the level of consciousness, are unlikely to be exaggerated or artificially inserted by a writer, and are thus more likely to be authentic when recorded. On the other hand, Kautzsch (2000a: 222) suggests that certain overtly stigmatized forms totally or largely fail to surface in writing; in his materials he finds this to be true for *ain't* (to some extent) negative concord, zero copula, and the nonstandard relativizers *what* and subject zero.

3 *Pragmatic and semantic conditions*: which linguistic elements are used or fail to show up in a text also depend upon its topic and pragmatic function. Most obviously this concerns the vocabulary of a text, which is frequently constrained by a narrow range of topics. However, grammatical patterns may be similarly restricted.

Example 15: In ship logs Bailey and Ross (1988) find "little data on indirect and direct questions, relative clauses, and modal verbs; ... [as well as] little evidence on aspectual markers or the possible deletion of auxiliary verbs" (1988: 197–8). The extremely rare use of double modals (like *might could*) in written documents neatly illustrates the role of pragmatics: they "cluster in certain types of interactions (subtle give-and-take negotiations and sensitive face-saving situations in which highly conditional and indirect speech takes place) that are rarely found in the written record of the language" (Montgomery 1998: 96). Montgomery hypothesizes that similar restrictions might hold for double negatives, the negator *ain't* and perfective *done*.   (1998: 120)

4.4   *Analyzing phonetics with written records*

This is what variationists are often interested in, but what is also most difficult, given the impact of heaviness just discussed. Again, we need to find some reasonable middle ground. On the one hand, as Gordon (1998: 67–8) shows in some detail, there are some pronunciation features which orthography simply cannot render, as well as some spellings for which it is not clear what they indicate phonetically. On the other hand, "variable scribal usage is likely to be functional in some way, ... and the most immediately obvious function of an alphabetic writing system is to relate writing to speech-forms, however complicated this relationship may be" (Milroy 1992: 142), and in a similar vein, based on his experience, Montgomery (1999: 25) confirms that "unconventional spellings almost always turn out ... to be phonetically based in whole or in part." After all, even if the orthography of English is fairly inconsistent, there are well-established sets of grapheme-phoneme-correspondences which can be employed in writing (cf. Eliason 1956: 191–231, Miethaner 2000).

Example 16: Montgomery (1995: 7) discusses the phonetic interpretation of some spelling variants. He distinguishes linguistically trivial misspellings, such as a lack of double letters (*stoped*), a lack of silent letters, or spellings reflecting common pronunciation (*cuntry, sitty*), from meaningful spellings, such as *injoying* (suggesting the presence of the prenasalic e/i-merger) or *Prevealed* "prevailed", *Beaker* "baker", which implies that to the writer the spelling <ea> suggests a historically older and unraised, /e:/-like pronunciation, resulting in homophony between *reason* and *raisin*.

4.5 Choosing between qualitative and quantitative approaches

Essentially, the variationist paradigm builds upon quantitative methodology, aiming at correlations between linguistic variants and internal or external context factors. This is also the goal of analyses of written documents, but it requires a certain breadth of coverage of variants and extralinguistic parameters of variation. Given the sampling difficulties sometimes involved in work with written documents, such frequency requirements are not always met, so quantification may not be possible or justified. Still, that does not render smaller corpora useless, but forces the analyst to resort to a more elementary level of description: if it is not possible to ask and analyse how often a variant occurs, frequently it still makes sense to ask if it occurs at all, which variants are found, and, possibly, who its users are. Two simple levels of analysis are possible underneath the level of quantification: a strictly inventorial, token-based approach (cf. Bailey and Ross 1988: 198) which limits itself to documenting which forms are found, and a slightly broader idiolect-based mode of analysis which looks both at which forms occur and which are the social characteristics of their users (ideally hoping for some pattern to emerge). A qualitative investigation is usually less sophisticated but more robust than a quantitative one, because some potentially distorting effects (such as overuse of a salient form) skew frequencies of occurrence but not necessarily the qualitative inventory of forms in a variety (cf. Schneider 1997: 43–4). It is possible that a written corpus allows reasonable (but isolated) observations, though not broader generalizations (cf. Montgomery 1995: 9).

4.6 Determining extralinguistic context parameters

Finally, in working with semi-vernacular texts it may be difficult to adequately categorize and manipulate the extralinguistic context parameters of interest, especially style and class. Frequently an assessment of these parameters requires culture-specific knowledge that may be hard to obtain. Familiar categories derived from present-day investigations may prove of little value in earlier times and other contexts. For example, Nevalainen (1996: 58–61) discusses the social hierarchy in Tudor England with the aim of establishing a model of "social class" distinctions appropriate for early England, and she arrives at a class stratification that looks alien to a modern sociolinguist, comprising strata like "nobility", "lower gentry", "upper clergy", "merchants", etc. In some cases very little may be known at all: according to Montgomery (1999: 21), "lack of personal information about the writers" is characteristic in the case of documents by semi-literate writers", because "less-educated people didn't usually write to strangers" (1997a: 228). Estimating the stylistic level of some documents may be equally difficult. The only solution to this problem is to collect as much relevant factual information as possible from expert sources, to arrive at a maximally appropriate ranking of styles, status levels, and the like.

5   Conclusion: Pitfalls and Advantages

As is conveniently summarized by Montgomery et al. (1993: 345), analyses of written documents hold specific "potential pitfalls for linguists. Assessing the degree of their vernacularity is a crucial issue that must always be addressed, though it is very often slighted by linguists. Written documents inevitably conceal some, perhaps many, of the speech patterns of their authors and can never be taken at face value as the equivalent of transcripts, especially for phonological purposes." It is necessary to assess the characteristics of text types and individual texts in the light of their historical and culture-specific settings; it is necessary to judge the representativeness of one's sample as well as the validity of a group of texts or a single source, and it is necessary to consider the possible effects of these factors upon the representation of a given linguistic level or feature with care, judgment, and reluctance: it is to be expected that these vary greatly from one source to another, from one goal of analysis to another. Mostly the nature of the sources available will determine, sometimes limit, what can be achieved with them.

But that is not to say that analysing written sources is a second-best solution by necessity. It is important to understand that essentially the same considerations and sometimes also limitations hold, *mutatis mutandis*, for tape-recorded surveys as well, so perhaps the above considerations also serve to sharpen our eye for essentially similar requirements in working with all kinds of real-life language, a need for the qualification, assessment and interpretation of one's sources (cf. Bailey 1997b: 27–8). Perhaps written documents are one further step removed from the "reality" of speech performance than tape recordings. However, tape recordings are also not the direct road to "truth" without further considerations: transcriptions are anything but objective, as Miethaner (2000) shows convincingly, and the need to deal with parameters of cultural context, class, and style (including, for instance, the observer's paradox), arises in much the same way. Working with written data requires somewhat more judgment and assessment than an analysis of audio recordings, but the difference is a matter of degree: essentially, with both approaches the goal is the same, and the pathways to reach it are very similar.

NOTES

1 A case in point is the history of African American Vernacular English (AAVE): this dialect has been of particular importance to variationists because of the sociopolitical and linguistic interest in it and because its origins have been contested, with proposals ranging between a largely creole-derived and African-influenced genesis and a predominantly British-dialectal and archaic character. Thus, many of the examples to be discussed below reflect efforts to uncover the early history or the nineteenth-century character of AAVE.

2 Obviously, the boundary between the two approaches is notoriously and unavoidably fuzzy. There is some degree of overlap in the fundamental interest in documenting systematic patterns of change, in the search for precise conditions of and constraints on the use of functionally similar alternatives, and in an emphasis on taking various style levels into account – studies marked by these three features are clearly of interest in both paradigms. As an example, take Ball (1994), an investigation of *it*-clefting based upon "treatises, essays and fiction, representing, it was hoped, a continuum from learned to more colloquial prose" (1994: 184; cf. Ball 1996 on relative pronoun choice). An emphasis on ordered variability with a strong theoretical interest and the uses of quantitative methods are relatively more characteristic of the "variation and change" paradigm than of a traditional historical-linguistic framework. For

thoughts on the distinction between "traditional" and "variational" historical approaches, see also Kytö (1991, e.g. 70–1).

3 With respect to the study of Middle English, he states: "One of the advantages of studying Middle English is that its written forms are highly variable. . . . not only is there considerable divergence *between* different texts, there is also normally great variability (particularly in spelling and inflexional forms) *within* the texts. Thus, ME language states, being so variable, should in principle be suited to the same kind of analysis that we use in present-day social dialectology, and by using variationist methods we should be able to explore at least some of the constraints on variation that might have existed in ME. . . . in ME we must locate these constraints initially through the writing system" (Milroy 1992: 131).

4 Such marginally relevant text types comprise what Kytö (1993: 117) calls "scripts", "texts written to be spoken", including sermons, for instance.

5 A comparable categorization of early dialogue texts is proposed by Culpeper and Kytö (1999), who distinguish the following three types: "(1) *Recorded* – texts produced from notes taken down by an individual, such as a clerk, present at a particular speech event; (2) *Reconstructed* – texts which purport to present dialogue which actually took place at some point in the past (usually, the

narrator was present at the speech event in question); and (3) *Constructed* – texts which contain constructed imaginary dialogue" (1999: 173).

6   A case in point is the variant readings of the ex-slave tapes whose transcripts are published and interpreted in Bailey et al. (1991), a well-known and widely discussed resource for earlier AAVE. The authors explicitly describe the process of composing the transcripts, which went through five separate auditings and still left some points of disagreement marked (1991: 14–17). Nevertheless, Rickford (1991) challenged some interpretations of these recordings, claiming that the transcript is unreliable and potentially biased. Most recently, Sutcliffe (2001) has built far-reaching assumptions on the origin of AAVE on the presumed presence of weak, admittedly doubtful and almost inaudible forms on these tapes that everybody but he, he claims, has failed to hear so far.

7   This is a tendency, documented in some dialects of English, for a third person plural predicate verb to be marked with a suffix –s after a full noun phrase subject but to have no such suffix after a pronoun subject, i.e. a preference for forms like *the dogs barks* but *they bark*.

REFERENCES

Arends, Jacques (ed.) (1995). *The Early Stages of Creolization*. Amsterdam, PA: John Benjamins.

Bailey, Guy (1997a). When did Southern English begin? In Edgar W. Schneider (ed.), *Englishes around the World 1: General Studies, British Isles, North America*. Amsterdam: John Benjamins. 255–75.

Bailey, Guy (1997b). Southern American English: a prospective. In C. Bernstein, Th. Nunnally and R. Sabino (eds.), *Language Variety in the South Revisited*. Tuscaloosa and London: University of Alabama Press. 21–31.

Bailey, Guy, Natalie Maynor, and Patricia Cukor-Avila (1989). Variation in subject-verb concord in Early Modern English. *Language Variation and Change* 1: 285–300.

Bailey, Guy, Natalie Maynor and Patricia Cukor-Avila (1991). *The Emergence of Black English: Text and Commentary*. Amsterdam: John Benjamins.

Bailey, Guy and Garry Ross (1988). The shape of the superstrate: Morphosyntactic features of Ship English. *English World-Wide* 9: 193–212.

Baker, Philip and Adrienne Bruyn (eds.) (1999). *St. Kitts and the Atlantic Creoles: The Texts of Samuel Augustus Mathews in Perspective*. London: University of Westminster Press.

Ball, Catherine N. (1994). Relative pronouns in it-clefts: The last seven centuries. *Language Variation and Change* 6: 179–200.

Ball, Catherine N. (1996). A diachronic study of relative markers in spoken and written English. *Language Variation and Change* 8: 227–58.

Bernstein, Cynthia, Thomas Nunnally and Robin Sabino (eds.) (1997). *Language Variety in the South Revisited*. Tuscaloosa and London: University of Alabama Press.

Biber, Douglas and Edward Finegan (1997). Diachronic relations among

speech-based and written registers
in English. In T. Nevalainen and
L. Kahlas-Tarkka (eds.), *To Explain
the Present. Studies in the Changing
English Language in Honour of Matti
Rissanen*. Helsinki: Société
Néophilologique. 253–76.

Brewer, Jeutonne P. (1974). The verb be
in Early Black English: A study
based on the WPA ex-slave
narratives. Ph.D. dissertation,
University of North Carolina at
Chapel Hill.

Brewer, Jeutonne P. (1997). Challenges
and problems of recorded
interviews. In C. Bernstein,
Th. Nunnally and R. Sabino
(eds.), *Language Variety in the South
Revisited*. Tuscaloosa: University
of Alabama Press. 59–75.

Cable, Thomas (1990). Philology:
Analysis of written records. In
E. Polomé (ed.), *Research Guide in
Language Change*. Berlin and New
York: Mouton de Gruyter. 97–106.

Campbell, Lyle (1998). *Historical
Linguistics: An Introduction*.
Edinburgh: Edinburgh
University Press.

Cooley, Marianne (1997). An early
representation of African-
American English. In C. Bernstein,
Th. Nunnally and R. Sabino
(eds.), *Language Variety in the South
Revisited*. Tuscaloosa and London:
University of Alabama Press. 51–8.

Crystal, David (1991). *A Dictionary of
Linguistics and Phonetics*. 3rd edn.
Oxford: Blackwell.

Culpeper, Jonathan and Merja Kytö
(1999). Investigating nonstandard
language in a corpus of Early
Modern English dialogues:
Methodological considerations
and problems. In I. Taavitsainen,
G. Melchers and P. Pahta (eds.),
Writing in Nonstandard English.
Amsterdam: John Benjamins.
171–87.

D'Costa, Jean and Barbara Lalla (eds.)
(1989). *Voices in Exile: Jamaican
Texts of the 18th and 19th Centuries*.
Tuscaloosa: University of Alabama
Press.

Dillard, Joey L. (1972). *Black English:
Its History and Usage in the United
States*. New York: Random House.

Eliason, Norman E. (1956). *Tarheel Talk:
An Historical Study of the English
Language in North Carolina to 1860*.
Chapel Hill: University of North
Carolina Press.

Ellis, Michael (1994). Literary dialect as
linguistic evidence: subject–verb
concord in nineteenth-century
southern literature. *American
Speech* 69: 128–44.

Ewers, Traute (1996). *The Origin of
American Black English: Be-forms
in the HOODOO texts*. Berlin and
New York: Mouton de Gruyter.

Fasold, Ralph (1976). One hundred
years from syntax to phonology.
In Sanford B. Steever, Carol A.
Walker and Salikoko S. Mufwene
(eds.), *Papers from the Parasession
on Diachronic Syntax*. Chicago:
Chicago Linguistic Society.
79–87.

Filppula, Markku (1999). *The Grammar of
Irish English: Language in Hibernian
Style*. London: Routledge.

Gordon, Elizabeth (1998). The origins
of New Zealand speech: The limits
of recovering historical information
from written records. *English
World-Wide* 19: 61–85.

Gordon, Elizabeth and Peter Trudgill
(1999). Shades of things to come:
Embryonic variants in New
Zealand English sound changes.
English World-Wide 20: 111–24.

Hickey, Raymond, Merja Kytö, Ian
Lancashire and Matti Rissanen
(eds.) (1997). *Tracing the Trail of
Time. Proceedings from the Second
Diachronic Corpora Workshop*.
Amsterdam and Atlanta: Rodopi.

Hildyard, Angela and David R. Olson (1982). On the comprehension of oral vs. written discourse. In D. Tannen (ed.), *Spoken and Written Language: Exploring Orality and Literacy*. Norwood, NJ: Ablex. 19–33.

Huber, Magnus (1999). *Ghanaian Pidgin English in its West African Context. A Sociohistorical and Structural Analysis*. Amsterdam and Philadelphia: John Benjamins.

Ives, Sumner (1950). A theory of literary dialect. *Tulane Studies in English* 2: 137–82.

Kautzsch, Alexander (2000a). The historical evolution of earlier African American English: A comparison of written sources. Ph.D. dissertation, University of Regensburg.

Kautzsch, Alexander (2000b). Liberian letters and Virginian narratives: Negation patterns in two new sources of earlier AAE. *American Speech* 75: 34–53.

Kretzschmar, William A. Jr and Edgar W. Schneider (1996). *Introduction to Quantitative Analysis of Linguistic Survey Data: An Atlas by the Numbers*. Thousand Oaks, CA: Sage.

Kytö, Merja (1991). *Variation and Diachrony, with Early American English in Focus*. Frankfurt: Peter Lang.

Kytö, Merja (1993). Third-person present singular verb inflection in early British and American English. *Language Variation and Change* 5: 113–39.

Lakoff, Robin Tollmach (1982). Some of my favorite writers are literate: The mingling of oral and literate strategies in written communication. In D. Tannen (ed.), *Spoken and Written Language: Exploring Orality and Literacy*. Norwood, NJ: Ablex. 239–60.

Loman, Bengt (1967). *Conversations in a Negro American Dialect*. Washington, DC: Center for Applied Linguistics.

Maynor, Natalie (1988). Written records of spoken language: How reliable are they? In A. R. Thomas (ed.), *Methods in Dialectology*. Clevedon, PA: Multilingual Matters. 109–20.

Maynor, Natalie (1993). Reconstructing nineteenth-century Southern White English: more evidence from *The Tennessee Civil War Veterans' Questionnaires*. In W. Viereck (ed.), *Historical Dialectology and Linguistic Change: Proceedings of the International Congress of Dialectologists, Bamberg*, vol. 2. Stuttgart: Steiner. 180–90.

Meurman-Solin, Anneli (1999). Letters as a source of data for reconstructing early spoken Scots. In I. Taavatsainen, G. Melchers and P. Pahta (eds.), *Writing in Nonstandard English*. Amsterdam: John Benjamins. 305–22.

Miethaner, Ulrich (2000). Orthographic transcriptions of nonstandard varieties: the case of earlier African American English. *Journal of Sociolinguistics* 4: 534–60.

Mille, Katherine Wyly (1997). Ambrose Gonzales's Gullah: What it may tell us about variation. In C. Bernstein, Th. Nunnally and R. Sabino (eds.), *Language Variety in the South Revisited*. Tuscaloosa: University of Alabama Press. 98–112.

Milroy, James (1992). *Linguistic Variation and Change: On the Historical Sociolinguistics of English*. Oxford and Cambridge, MA: Blackwell.

Montgomery, Michael (1995). The linguistic value of Ulster emigrant letters. *Ulster Folklife* 41: 1–16.

Montgomery, Michael (1997a). A tale of two Georges: The language of Irish Indian traders in colonial North America. In Jeffrey Kallen (ed.), *Focus on Ireland*. Amsterdam: John Benjamins. 227–54.

Montgomery, Michael (1997b). Making transatlantic connections between varieties of English: The case of plural verbal –s. *Journal of English Linguistics* 25: 122–41.

Montgomery, Michael (1998). Multiple modals in LAGS and LAMSAS. In M. Montgomery and Th. Nunnally (eds.), *From the Gulf States and Beyond: The Legacy of Lee Pederson and LAGS*. Tuscaloosa: University of Alabama Press. 90–122.

Montgomery, Michael (1999). Eighteenth-century Sierra Leone English: Another exported variety of African American English. *English World-Wide* 20: 1–34.

Montgomery, Michael, Janet M. Fuller and Sharon DeMarse (1993). "The black men has wives and Sweet harts [and third person plural –s] Jest like the white men": Evidence for verbal –s from written documents on 19th-century African American speech. *Language Variation and Change* 5: 335–57.

Nevalainen, Terttu and Leena Kahlas-Tarkka (eds.) (1997). *To Explain the Present: Studies in the Changing English Language in Honour of Matti Rissanen*. Helsinki: Société Néophilologique.

Nevalainen, Terttu and Helena Raumolin-Brunberg (eds.) (1996). *Sociolinguistics and Language History: Studies Based on the Corpus of Early English Correspondence*. Amsterdam: Rodopi.

Patrick, Peter et al. (1996). 100 years of (TD)-deletion in African American English. Paper given at NWAVE25, Las Vegas.

Polomé, Edgar C. (1990). Language change and the Saussurean dichotomy: Diachrony versus synchrony. In E. Polomé (ed.), *Research Guide in Language Change*. Berlin and New York: Mouton de Gruyter. 3–9.

Raumolin-Brunberg, Helena (1996). Historical sociolinguistics. In T. Nevalainen and H. Raumolin-Brunberg (eds.), *Sociolinguistics and Language History: Studies Based on the Corpus of Early English Correspondence*. Amsterdam: Rodopi. 11–37.

Rawick, George P. (ed.) (1972/1977/1979). *The American Slave: A Composite Autobiography*, 19 vols.; Supplement Series 1, 12 vols.; Supplement Series 2, 10 vols. Westport, CT: Greenwood.

Rickford, John R. (1987). *Dimensions of a Creole Continuum: History, Texts & Linguistic Analysis of Guyanese Creole*. Stanford, CA: Stanford University Press.

Rickford, John R. (1991). Representativeness and reliability of the ex-slave materials, with special reference to Wallace Quarterman's recording and transcript. In G. Bailey, N. Maynor and P. Cukor-Avila (eds.), *The Emergence of Black English: Text and Commentary*. Amsterdam: Benjamins. 191–212.

Rickford, John R. (1998). The creole origins of African-American Vernacular English: evidence from copula absence. In Salikoko S. Mufwene, John R. Rickford, Guy Bailey and John Baugh (eds.), *African-American English: Structure, History and Use*. London: Routledge. 154–200.

Rickford, John R. and Jerome Handler (1994). Textual evidence on the nature of early Barbadian speech, 1676–1835. *Journal of Pidgin and Creole Languages* 9: 221–55.

Rissanen, Matti (1997). "Candy no witch, Barbados": Salem witchcraft trials as evidence of Early American English. In Heinrich Ramisch and Kenneth Wynne (eds.), *Language in Time and Space*. Stuttgart: Steiner. 183–93.

Rissanen, Matti, Merja Kytö, and Kirsi Heikkonen (eds.) (1997a). *English in Transition: Corpus-Based Studies in Linguistic Variation and Genre Styles*.

Berlin and New York: Mouton de Gruyter.

Rissanen, Matti, Merja Kytö and Kirsi Heikkonen (eds.) (1997b). *Grammaticalization at Work: Studies of Long-Term Developments in English.* Berlin and New York: Mouton de Gruyter.

Saussure, Ferdinand de. (1916, repr. 1967). *Cours de linguistique générale.* Paris: Payot.

Schneider, Edgar W. (1983). The origin of the verbal –s in Black English. *American Speech* 58: 99–113.

Schneider, Edgar W. (1989). *American Earlier Black English: Morphological and syntactic variables.* Tuscaloosa: University of Alabama Press.

Schneider, Edgar W. (1997). Earlier Black English revisited. In C. Bernstein, Th. Nunnally and R. Sabino (eds.), *Language Variety in the South Revisited.* Tuscaloosa: University of Alabama Press. 35–50.

Schneider, Edgar W. and Michael Montgomery (1999). On the trail of early nonstandard grammar: An electronic corpus of Southern US antebellum overseers' letters. Paper given at NWAVE28, Toronto.

Sundby, Bertil, Anne Kari Bjørge and Kari E. Haugland (1991). *A Dictionary of English Normative Grammar, 1700–1800.* Amsterdam: Benjamins.

Sutcliffe, David (2001). The voice of the ancestors: new evidence on 19th-century precursors to 20th-century African American English. In S. Lanehart (ed.), *Sociohistorical and Cultural Contexts of African-American English.* Amsterdam: Benjamins.

Taavitsainen, Irma, Gunnel Melchers and Päivi Pahta (eds.) (1999). *Writing in Nonstandard English.* Amsterdam: Benjamins.

Thomason, Sarah Grey (1993). Coping with partial information in historical linguistics. In H. Aertsen and R. J. Jeffers (eds.), *Historical Linguistics 1989.* Amsterdam: Benjamins. 485–96.

Tiecken-Boon van Ostade, Ingrid (1997). Lowth's corpus of prescriptivism. In T. Nevalainen and L. Kahlas-Tarkka (eds.), *To Explain the Present: Studies in the Changing English Language in Honour of Matti Rissanen.* Helsinki: Société Néophilologique. 451–63.

Trudgill, Peter (1986). *Dialects in Contact.* Oxford and New York: Blackwell.

Trudgill, Peter (1999). Dedialectalisation and Norfolk dialect orthography. In I. Taavatsainen, G. Melchers and P. Pahta (eds.), *Writing in Nonstandard English.* Amsterdam: Benjamins. 323–9.

Wasow, Thomas (1997). Remarks on grammatical weight. *Language Variation and Change* 9: 81–105.

Winter, Werner (1990). Linguistic reconstruction: The scope of historical and comparative linguistics. In E. Polomé (ed.), *Research Guide in Language Change.* Berlin and New York: Mouton de Gruyter. 11–21.

Wright, Joseph (1898–1906). *The English Dialect Dictionary,* 6 vols. London: Oxford University Press.

4 Inferring Variation and Change from Public Corpora

LAURIE BAUER

When Lass (1987: 21) presents three versions of the same biblical passage to illustrate the differences between Old English, Middle English, and Early Modern English, he is using a technique which is well-established in the tradition of introducing historical variation to beginners. These three texts, he notes, are all called English, yet they are visibly different and in lectures they might also be shown to be audibly different. We infer change to the language in the periods between the times when these three translations appeared by considering an easily available sample of comparable material produced at three periods. These samples provide a small corpus of publicly available (and thus confirmable) data on the basis of which we infer language change. In this sense the whole philological tradition is based on the study of public corpora, and the study of language change that derives from this tradition is a corpus-based study.

Traditional dialectology takes this notion one step further by creating corpora rather than using pre-existing corpora. When Edmond Edmont cycled around France noting answers to the questions on his questionnaire, he was collecting a corpus, which became public with the publication of the *Atlas linguistique de la France* (Gilliéron, 1902–10). At that point, the corpus could be exploited by Gilliéron and other researchers to illustrate linguistic variation within the "Gallo-Roman" area, and to consider mechanisms of linguistic change.

Today, with the rapid improvements in computerized type-setting and scanning technology, with the decreasing cost and increasing efficiency of computer memory, we tend to interpret the word "corpus" rather more narrowly to mean "electronically searchable text database." This rather new usage means that we need to be explicit in defining our notion of a corpus. We also need to consider what exactly it means for a corpus to be "public."

1   The Notion of Public Corpus

1.1   *What is a public corpus?*

Kennedy (1998: 1) defines a corpus as "a body of written text or transcribed speech which can serve as a basis for linguistic analysis and description." Even this wide definition may seem in some respects too narrow. For example, it excludes a body of sound recordings which can serve as a basis for linguistic analysis and description, although sound recordings (not necessarily transcribed in any sense whatsoever) might be the best basis for providing a linguistic analysis of the phonology of a particular variety. By focusing on "text," Kennedy's definition might be taken to exclude word-lists and the like, which might nevertheless be an appropriate basis for the description of things like word formation patterns in a particular variety. Accordingly, I would prefer to modify Kennedy's definition to read "a body of language data which can serve as a basis for linguistic analysis and description." This definition is (intentionally) inclusive, possibly excessively so, since it would even allow a set of sentences invented by so-called "arm-chair" linguists to prove a particular grammatical point as a corpus. We might wish to modify the definition further to guarantee that the language data are naturally occurring language data (although that might be hard to define strictly), or at least language whose original purpose was not to explain or justify some linguistic analysis.

"Public" is defined (in the relevant sense) by *The Macquarie Dictionary* (Delbridge 1997) as "open to the view or knowledge of all." In principle this looks clear-cut: Edmond Edmont's transcriptions noting the answers he received to the questions on his questionnaire were his own personal research notes and were not "open . . . to all," while the *Atlas linguistique de la France*, by virtue of being published, is open to all because it is in the public domain. In practice there are many intermediate stages. Let us consider just two.

In 1946 the New Zealand Broadcasting Service established a Mobile Disc Recording Unit which traveled round various parts of provincial New Zealand recording pioneer reminiscences for posterity. Unfortunately not all areas of New Zealand were covered, since a change of government curtailed finances for the project. Mainly elderly people were interviewed, although some middle-aged speakers were included. Their dates of birth range from approximately 1850 to 1900. This material was made available to the Origins of New Zealand English (ONZE) project under the direction of Elizabeth Gordon and Lyle Campbell at the University of Canterbury, New Zealand in 1989 (Lewis 1996). Some of this material has been transcribed orthographically and some has been subjected to detailed phonetic analysis, both auditory and acoustic by members of the ONZE team. Various results from the project have been published (see, e.g., Gordon 1994, 1998, Trudgill et al. 1998). This material was collected by a public company, was intended for broadcast, and can be regarded as a kind of archive to which later broadcasters might have access. This seems "public" in the relevant sense. The corpus is available in two research libraries in New Zealand, and this too seems "public" in the relevant sense. Yet it is public in a very restricted way because it is hard for most researchers to get to the libraries, and the associated speaker data collected later by the ONZE team is not part of the library record. A release of material on CD is foreseen, but currently the corpus is only marginally "public," and the original intention behind the data collection is a poor guide to the current status of the corpus.

In order to create a corpus for tracking the progress of grammatical change in twentieth-century English, I used leading articles from *The Times* newspaper of London (Bauer 1994: 50). The first ten leading articles, excluding Sunday leaders in later years, were chosen from the March editions of the newspaper (the month was chosen at random) for the years 1900, 1905, 1910, 1915 . . . 1985. Given that information, it should be possible for other researchers to recreate precisely the database that I was working with without making any direct application to me. *The Times* can be consulted on microfilm in many good libraries all round the world, and is clearly public domain material. The collected material remains in my own research notes, and is not public material, but anyone can recreate the same files that I had to look at. This seems to me to be a slightly marginal case, but basically to be a public corpus. It is marginal because any other linguist wishing to check my findings would have to go to considerable effort to replicate the material I used; it cannot simply be purchased/downloaded as a body of material. Now that newspapers are producing back-copies in annual form on CD-ROM, patterns of what is possible may be changing here (Minugh 1997). Had the material been spoken instead of written, the case might have been different. This is the situation with Van de Velde's (1996) study of Dutch pronunciation on the basis of tapes from Dutch and Belgian radio. The original broadcasts were public, but it is extremely difficult for other linguists to reconstruct Van de Velde's data for themselves, since they would have to apply to all the original radio stations, or to Van de Velde himself. This corpus thus seems not to be a public one, and the implication is that a public corpus of spoken data for phonetic analysis will be extremely difficult to find, although CD-technology means that it is becoming more possible. The recently-published CD of Survey of English Dialects material (SED 1999) is an as yet rare example.

We have thus defined a public corpus as a body of data which can serve as the basis for linguistic analysis and description and which is available to linguists in general either as an identifiable whole or from easily accessible materials. We shall now go on to consider the types of such corpora which are available.

1.2   Types of corpus

We can distinguish several types of public corpus, in a multidimensional matrix. First, we must distinguish between corpora which are individual linguists' ad hoc collections of available materials (such as the one described for Bauer 1994 above) and those which are created as deliberately structured corpora, and which are made available as such. There are benefits to each type. The corpora which are created as such are more likely to have texts carefully chosen to be representative in some way – for instance the texts for the Brown corpus of written American English from 1961[1] were specifically "selected by a method that makes it reasonably representative of current printed American English" (Kučera and Francis 1967: xvii). On the other hand, such corpora may not be suitable for answering all questions of linguistic description. However representative the Brown corpus is of written American English in 1961, it could not hope to answer the questions of diachronic development for which I developed my own ad hoc corpus of material from *The Times*, already mentioned above, because that was not what it was constructed to do.

Next we must distinguish between corpora collected in paper form and those which are collected in electronic form, and thus allow electronic searches with any one of the large number of software packages now available for the purpose, e.g. The Oxford Concordance Program, TACT, WordCruncher or WordSmith to name but a few (for a review of these and others, see Hofland 1991, Kennedy 1998: 259–67, McEnery and Wilson 1996: 189–91). On the whole, this is a question of the age of the corpus and whether the corpus is being created for a particular project or being seen as something that can be exploited for multiple purposes. It was some time after the appearance of the Brown corpus in 1964 that its full value could be exploited by linguists all round the world, because in 1964 computing was still seen as something for the sciences rather than the humanities and as being very esoteric. Even today, the collection of a corpus is not a trivial matter and for many purposes it remains as easy to search a corpus by eye (or by hand) as to search it electronically (consider, for example, corpora of data from young children or second-language learners, where the same lexical item may appear in more forms than it could have in the standard language, and where the computer may not be able to predict the full range of relevant forms). On the whole, paper-based corpora do not get the same kind of wide distribution that electronic corpora get, but it must be recalled that corpora such as the Bible, the complete works of Shakespeare or *The Oxford English Dictionary* have been in use for many years, and some of the London-Lund Corpus of Spoken British English is available as a book as well as in electronic form (Svartvik and Quirk 1980).

Next we need to distinguish between corpora of written and spoken language. Corpora of spoken language may simply provide an orthographic transcription (e.g. The Wellington Corpus of Spoken New Zealand English (WCSNZE)), or they may provide a more or less detailed phonetic transcription (e.g. The London-Lund corpus which is marked up for prosodic categories such as stress and intonation). In principle, even the orthographic transcription is not necessary if the sound recordings are available.

Next we need to distinguish between simple and comparative corpora. The labels are mine, but the idea is to distinguish been corpora which represent the language/variety to be described at one synchronic moment in time versus those which present diachronic data; to distinguish between those which represent a single variety as opposed to those which represent two or more varieties, and so on. A corpus such as Brown is a simple corpus, in these terms, describing written American English in 1961, but may nevertheless be used comparatively alongside the Lancaster-Oslo-Bergen (LOB) corpus which is closely modeled on Brown, but presents written British English in 1961. Although this division may seem a clear-cut one, it is not. Following the publication of the Brown corpus, a number of 1-million word corpora were developed which were modeled on it and which, like Brown, contain a number of thematic sections, such as press reportage, government documents, and scientific writing. It is a repeated research finding (and not at all a surprising one) that these different sections differ from each other linguistically, perhaps especially in terms of style (Biber 1988, Sigley 1997a, 1997b, 1997c). Thus it might be claimed that corpora which contain stylistically differentiated sub-components are implicitly comparative rather than simple. Taken to extremes this would mean that no corpus was ever simple, since even a single work can have passages which are stylistically distinct within it. This dichotomy has thus to be applied in a fairly uncritical manner.

Finally we need to distinguish between corpora which are made up of textual material and those which are made up of word-lists. Among the former are all the major electronic corpora that have been discussed so far, among the latter are dictionaries, thesauruses, vocabularies, and the like. Although most electronic corpora are made up of texts, these word-lists deserve the title of "corpora" (1) functionally, in that they allow comparisons of language types along several different dimensions and (2) formally since they are bodies of data created for one purpose which may nevertheless be exploited for other purposes "for linguistic analysis and description." Table 4.1 provides a classification of several public corpora according to these distinctions.

An appendix in Aijmer and Altenberg (1991) provides a short description of the electronic corpora discussed in that volume, along with some bibliographical references. McEnery and Wilson (1996: 181–7) provide brief characterizations of the electronic corpora they discuss in their text, with addresses (electronic and snail-mail) for further information. Kennedy (1998: 23–57) provides a detailed survey of most of the major electronic corpora available for English. Rissanen (2000) provides a useful overview of historical corpora of English in electronic form, including e-mail addresses or URLs for getting details on availability, etc.

Table 4.1 Classification of some public corpora

Corpora	Classification and comments
Brown, LOB, Kolhapur, ACE, WCWNZE, Frown, FLOB	Structured, electronic, written language, simple, textual. Since these corpora are all constructed on the same basic model, any two or more of them may be used comparatively.
ICE	Structured, electronic, both written and spoken language, comparative (in that written and spoken are both extensively covered, but also in that the various national sections of ICE can be compared), textual.
Jones, *English Pronouncing Dictionary* (Jones, 1917–)	Structured (in its attempt at exhaustivity), paper, spoken language, simple, word-list. The various editions together can be used as a comparative (diachronic variation) corpus, as in Bauer (1994).
The Bible	Ad hoc, paper (now also available electronically), written language, simple (although various editions can provide comparative diachronic data), textual.
Helsinki	Structured, electronic, written language, comparative, textual.
The Bank of English	Ad hoc (its representativeness arises through its sheer size rather than through the careful selection of texts), electronic, written, simple, textual.

2   Benefits and Problems Provided by Public Corpora

The main benefit accruing from the use of a public corpus is replicability. Sigley (1997c: 218) reports that *whose* and *of which* are more or less evenly divided in nonrestrictive relative clauses with inanimate antecedents – i.e. sentences such as *These menus present . . . alternate choices, whose selection/selection of which leads to further menus . . .* – in New Zealand English (55.6 percent and 44.4 percent respectively). If subsequent researchers find this distribution unexpected, they can check the results for themselves in the relevant corpus. While there may be some slight variability caused by experimental method (e.g. in the case in point, the definition of nonrestrictive or inanimate), we would not expect any gross deviations without contrasting theoretical presuppositions (e.g. a presuppositions that some of the tokens of *of which* belong to some completely separate grammatical structure). Replicability of this type is a sign of good science.

The other major benefit of corpora, the possibility of treating such phenomena numerically, accrues to all corpus studies, not just to studies based on public corpora.

There are also a number of problems which corpora give rise to. Again, these problems are not specific to public corpora, but to all corpus studies. Some of these are discussed, in no particular order, below.

First, by allowing numerical treatment, corpus studies allow an appearance of precision which may be totally spurious. The researcher needs to ask how far the corpus reflects anything but the collection of texts/words which make up the corpus. Does the 55.6 percent figure for *whose* in nonrestrictive relative clauses with inanimate antecedents really tell us about New Zealand English, or just about the Wellington Corpus of Written New Zealand English (WCWNZE, reflecting language in 1986)? Even if the Brown corpus was deliberately constructed to reflect printed American English in 1961, is there any guarantee that a different sample of actual texts built on the same framework for the same variety of English and in the same year would give the same results for any (let alone all) of the linguistic variables? We do not know what the margin of error is in linguistic corpora of these types.

Correspondingly, there are problems when comparing two or more corpora. The Freiburg versions of Brown and LOB (Frown and FLOB), with texts from 1991 and 1992 rather than 1961, are specifically designed to be comparable with their earlier congeners. Yet where a difference is discovered between the language of the two, it is not necessarily clear that it can be entirely attributed to the 30-year gap between the two corpora. Mair (1998: 148) reports that an increase in progressives between Brown and Frown (and also between LOB and FLOB) is due to the more frequent choice of an informal option rather than a non-progressive formal option in places where either is possible. While this might be a language change, it might equally be viewed as a societal change in perception of formality or as no change at all, just a different exploitation of precisely the same system. Moreover, that exploitational difference might reflect text-selection rather than any change in norms. Similarly, WCWNZE was based firmly on LOB, and is intended to be comparable with LOB. Yet at least one major difference between the two is drawn attention to in the manual which accompanies WCWNZE: the fact that because of different publishing traditions, mass-market fiction is not often published in New Zealand, and what is published in New Zealand is "more consciously literary" (Bauer 1993: 2). The fiction categories of the two corpora are thus different, and so the differences between the two corpora as wholes might reflect differences in style as much as differences in geographical origin or diachronic differences. Problems of this type are soluble only in terms of consistency of findings. Where research based on different corpora shows comparability of results in terms of varietal or temporal differences, we can be relatively sure that these represent genuine differences of variety. The more such results we have, the more we can trust results from corpora which have in other ways shown themselves to be representative.

Next, corpus size provides a problem. It is not necessarily clear in advance of testing whether a corpus is large enough to provide an answer or not. Yet too large a corpus means that the experimenter is left analyzing unnecessary data. In Bauer (1994: 50–1) I referred to this as Murphy's Law applied to corpora. The corpus I used from *The Times*, and another from the *New York Times*, were too small to provide particularly clear results on the subject of whether there is a change in comparative and superlative marking in English from a synthetic form like *remoter* to an analytic form like *more remote*. Work using the larger British National Corpus (BNC) (Kytö and Romaine 1997; Leech and Culpepper 1997) provides rather more definite results (although even those results are not entirely clear). Corpora used to investigate lexical matters generally have to be extremely large (hence the involvement of so many dictionary-publishers in the construction of the BNC); some grammatical phenomena are also so rare in texts as to require very large corpora if reasonable amounts of data are to be found: the use of *whose* and *whom* in modern English are phenomena in point.

It was implicit in what was said above that corpora are not consistent in their style level across all the texts they include. Some corpora, such as WCSNZE, the Helsinki corpus of historical English, and the various corpora involved in the International Corpus of English (ICE) project, with parallel 1-million word corpora planned from some 20 countries, include biographical details (including age, gender, ethnicity, educational achievement) of all the speakers/writers whose output is represented. This makes it possible to look for linguistic differences between the various social groupings for which the corpus is marked up. In most written corpora, this information is at best indirectly derivable and at worst unavailable: corpora of press materials, especially reportage, rarely mark authors' gender, for example, for the simple reason that it is usually unknown, in that most such items are not signed/by-lined; indeed, a single news item may have been edited so many times that it no longer has "an author" of identifiable gender. This does not mean that differences correlated with gender (or, a fortiori, the other social categories) are not present in the text; it just means that they cannot be isolated. Accordingly, the entire corpus will be undetectably biased for any relevant factors by the language of the social group which provided the majority of the texts. In practical terms, this should probably be interpreted as implying that marginally significant differences in linguistic behavior measured in corpora cannot be trusted, and that statistical significance has to be treated with great care.

We can summarize the general point here by saying that different corpora assume different degrees of idealization about the speech community they attempt to represent: Brown assumes homogeneity across the community, the WCSNZE assumes homogeneity only within the categories it identifies (gender groups with certain educational backgrounds, etc.). In principle, these differences lead to incommensurability between corpora; in practice, as long as the statistics are dealt with carefully, they need not prevent similarities and differences from being discovered.

3   Using Corpora to Infer Variation and Change

Although there may be difficulties in interpreting results from corpus-based comparisons, as we have just seen, discovering variation or change from public corpora would seem to be relatively straightforward. Find a corpus or corpora which allow comparison on the required dimension (e.g. corpora from different historical periods, corpora of different national varieties, corpora containing written and spoken material, corpora containing utterances from both males and females who are identified as such, etc.). Comparability is a problem, but has been dealt with above. Assuming a two-way comparison, with two varieties we can call A and B, measure the linguistic behavior in variety A in the corpus, and measure the linguistic behavior of variety B in exactly the same way with respect to some potential linguistic variable V. If V is indistinguishable in A and B, assume no variation/lack of change. If V is measurably and significantly different in the two cases, postulate variation/change.

Consider the following example from Hundt (1998: 32). Hundt counts the number of regular and irregular past tense forms of various verbs in the WCWNZE and in FLOB, with the results shown in table 4.2 (taken from Hundt's 1998: 32 Table 3.4). The difference between FLOB and WCWNZE, she says, "proved significant at the 1 percent level" using a chi-square test, and we have a case for variation between these two varieties. She also comments that in the Brown corpus 96.7 percent of the relevant verb-forms are regular, so that there is a difference between American English, British English and New Zealand English on this measure, with New Zealand English being more like British than like American English, but different from both.

This example is of interest not only because it illustrates a canonical instance of the argument showing regional variation in English, but also because this result feeds in to Hundt's final conclusion, namely that "synchronic 'snapshots' focusing on regional differences can be interpreted as stages in the (regional) diffusion of change" (Hundt 1998: 134) and that what we have seen operating in table 4.2 is regional variation, but regional variation originating from different speeds of diffusion of grammatical change. Such a conclusion would not be possible on the basis of a simple two-way comparison, such as is presented in table 4.2, but emerges because of the range of material Hundt is able to sample. In other words, we have to be careful in interpreting the results of any such experiments: there may be more (or less!) to them than superficially appears.

The problems of interpretation become greater when less canonical forms of the argument are used. A cautionary tale is provided by my own study of relativization strategies in English (Bauer 1994: 66–83). Although I had created my own diachronic corpus, it was not always sufficient, and I also tried to make comparisons with other linguists' corpora. In particular, I compared the percentage of various relativization strategies (the use of a *wh*-word, the use of *that*, or the lack of any complementizer) across various corpora. Among a

Table 4.2   Irregular and regular past tense forms of various verbs

	WCWNZE	FLOB
burned	13	16
burnt	28	11
dreamed	9	5
dreamt	4	5
leaned	26	25
leant	4	13
leaped	0	3
leapt	6	7
learned	69	81
learnt	37	22
smelled	7	6
smelt	5	4
spelled	0	4
spelt	3	2
spilled	3	5
spilt	2	5
spoiled	0	4
spoilt	9	2
-ed	127 (56.4%)	149 (68.7%)
-t	98 (43.6%)	68 (31.3%)
Total	225 (100%)	217 (100%)

Source: Hundt (1998: 32)

number of linguists who reported the use of *that* as a relativizer in 15–20 percent of restrictive relative clauses, one stood out as reporting *that* use in 54 percent of cases (Biesenbach-Lucas 1987). Because the proportion was so different, I concluded that "Biesenbach-Lucas (1987) does not seem to be counting the same thing as I am, when we talk about restrictive relatives" (Bauer 1994: 80). This seemed the only way to explain the large discrepancy, particularly given that terms like "restrictive" are well-known to be hazardous. I thus made what seemed like a conservative decision that, despite appearances to the contrary, our corpora were not comparable because we were not measuring the same thing. This is a genuine problem in interpreting others' results, but in this particular case, I was wrong. In a considerably more sophisticated analysis,

Sigley (1997a: 467–73) shows that there *is* a difference between American English and other varieties on this point. Sigley's analysis shows that the difference between American English and other varieties is significant only in press usage (Biesenbach-Lucas studies the language of *The Washington Post*). He attributes the difference to overt prescription in American English for *that*-usage in restrictive relative clauses, e.g. in *The Chicago Manual of Style* (anon. 1993: §5.42). My caution in interpreting corpus results made me miss one of the most important markers of regional variation in this part of the grammar.

One point to note in all of this is that using electronic corpora limits the types of phenomena that can practicably be studied, while making it easier to study those which can be retrieved. While it is relatively simple to consider the differences in use between *which* and *that* using electronic corpora, it is extremely hard to study the use of the zero relative (as in *the man Ø I met yesterday*) because there is no form to search for. Although Sigley (1997a) managed to do a lot of searching by finding relevant environments, in the end a manual pass through the text is required. In principle, tagged corpora solve this problem, because they mark relative clauses as such, and all relative clauses can then be pulled out automatically. In practice, unless the corpus has been manually tagged, reliance on tagging is dangerous, since it is likely to miss particular types of data in a systematic manner. Since manual tagging is so time-consuming, most tagged corpora have the tags determined by computer program. While the best of these claim an accuracy of approximately 95 percent, the errors tend to congregate in particular categories, with the tag for singular noun, in particular, being over-assigned (DeRose 1991: 11; Kennedy 1998: 220). In any case, many tagged corpora do not get beyond part-of-speech tagging, and it is not possible to find relative clauses using such tagging. A notable exception is the ICE-GB corpus, which allows syntactic trees to be matched and retrieved from the corpus. It is not yet possible to assign such trees automatically, so that this extremely useful outcome is the result of a huge amount of preparation of the corpus.

4   Results

Kennedy (1998: 180–203) provides an excellent summary of the major findings concerning English that are discussed in the literature. A brief recapitulation of some of these is provided below.

4.1   *Dialectal variation*

On the whole corpora have been built for national varieties of English rather than for regional dialects within one country. Thus we do not have public electronic corpora that would allow us to investigate differences in the syntax of

Newfoundland and Vancouver Englishes, or of Cornish and Tyneside dialects. The presupposition is that such comparisons would either be meaningless (in that it is not clear that comparing the syntax or vocabulary of Cornish and Tyneside would be any more meaningful than comparing the syntax and vocabulary of two distinct languages), or vacuous (in that no distinctions are expected – e.g. Newfoundland vs. Vancouver). Certainly, a number of studies based on the Brown and LOB corpora found very few significant differences between American and British English grammar except for the wider use of *that* in restrictive relative clauses in American English, the greater use of regular forms of certain verbs already mentioned above, and the use of the minor construction *this prevented me from leaving* in British but not American English (Mair 1998). Studies of Australian and New Zealand Englishes have also found differences in the weighting of different strategies, but very few absolute grammatical distinctions such that one variety uses a particular construction and another invariably uses a contrasting construction (or has no equivalent construction) in the same environments. Those that have been suggested (the transitive use of *farewell*, the mediopassive use of *screen* in New Zealand English – Hundt 1998) are very much at the lexical end of grammar. However, the extent to which particular grammatical structures are used by speakers/writers may be an entirely different matter, and here Biber (1987) shows that American English uses more nominalizations, more passives and more *it*-clefts than British English, while British English uses more place and time adverbials and more subordinator deletion than American English.

That there are lexical differences between the major international varieties of English is not something about which there is any doubt, and here the best corpora are perhaps the dictionaries (although dictionaries do not give information about extent of usage, which may give a rather different picture of what is really going on; see Kennedy and Yamazaki 1999, Kennedy 2001). There are probably also differences in interactional styles. Tottie (1991) finds that American speakers provide three times as many backchannel agreement markers as their British counterparts.

4.2   *Written and spoken language*

The most important work in considering the differences between written and spoken English is clearly Biber (1988). Biber argues that the differences between different text types within written or spoken English are sometimes greater than the differences between written and spoken. This observation, of course, is based on treating both written and spoken language as text, and ignores the phonetic nature of spoken language completely. Others have commented on differences of vocabulary in the two media. Kennedy (1998: 184) points out that *pretty* is mainly used as a descriptive adjective in writing (the LOB corpus), and mainly used as an intensifier in speech (the London-Lund corpus).

4.3   Style

Questions of grammatical determinants of style have been considered particularly by Biber (1988) and Sigley (1997b). In particular Biber points out that syntactic complexity and lexical complexity may not (as is often assumed) go together.

4.4   Language change

Studies of language change have always, in some sense, been corpus-based (see above). The interesting discussions on the basis of modern corpora are thus not those which simply report or date a change (although some of those can provide surprising results, e.g. Peitsara 1993), but those which show a pattern to the change, which re-examine change in the light of modern sociolinguistic theory. An example is Nevalainen (2000), where, on the basis of the Corpus of Early English Correspondence developed at the University of Helsinki, women are shown to lead the introduction of verbal -(e)s (replacing -th) in Early Modern English and the use of *you* in subject position, but men are shown to lead in the move to single negation instead of double negation. The development of Frown and FLOB at Freiburg also means that we can expect to see more studies emerging of the progress of change in twentieth-century English.

4.5   Sociolinguistic variation

All variationist studies are corpus-based, but most of the corpora have not been public ones, and the results are thus not strictly germane to this survey. What we can say, perhaps, is that the use of public corpora has not led to radically different conclusions in areas such as the correlations between ethnicity, gender, or geographical origin and linguistic usage from those provided by the private corpora which preceded them. This is just what we would expect. The classic variationist studies also dealt exclusively with phonetic/ phonological variation, while the rise in the use of public corpora is increasing the range of phenomena that can be studied within this framework. Morphological and syntactic phenomena, it turns out, can often be considered in precisely the same ways when sufficient searchable text is available. Nevalainen's study mentioned above is a simple example. Sigley (1997a) considers variation in relative clause construction from speakers/writers of different genders, and educational levels, and finds some significant (but numerically not very important) differences. Holmes (1998a, 1998b) illustrates the fact that corpus studies can be used to go beyond the study of forms into functions and interactional choices.

4.6   *Variation in word-list corpora*

The discussions above have been largely based on results obtained from public electronic corpora. Since the kind of use to which word-list corpora can be put is perhaps less obvious, it is worth devoting some space considering the kind of results that can be obtained from them.

Bauer (1994) illustrates the use of pronouncing dictionaries to show variation in particular phonological phenomena synchronically, but also, by using a number of editions of the same works, to show change in these phenomena. Specifically, stress in polysyllabic words and /j/-dropping following coronal consonants are studied, with the latter being considered in different national varieties. Bauer (1994) also uses the *Supplement to the Oxford English Dictionary* (Burchfield 1972–86) to illustrate the change in sources of borrowed words in English over a 100-year period. Dictionaries are now being widely used by morphologists as evidence for changing patterns of productivity in particular patterns of word-formation (Anshen and Aronoff 1997, Bolozky 1999, Bauer 2001).

5   Descriptive Use

A quick glance at many of the collections of papers on corpus linguistics may make it look as though the main interests which corpora present to the linguist are the problems of constructing them in the first place and the problem of parsing them once they are constructed. Both are matters of extreme complexity, and I do not wish to underestimate their importance or difficulty. In the present context, however, what is more important is the descriptive use that can be made of corpora. At one level, corpora can be used to make sure our descriptive facts are correct, and to improve the quality of grammatical descriptions and lexicological descriptions (consider, for example, the extensive use of corpora made by some of the major dictionaries aimed at non-native learners of English, such as COBUILD – Sinclair 1987). As long as care is taken, this descriptive basis can be extended fairly readily to a consideration of variation and change. While the study of variation and change is made easier by the existence of electronic corpora which are deliberately created for this purpose (the ICE corpus, the various parallels to the Brown corpus, the Helsinki corpus), variation (which may indicate change in progress) can also be discovered in simple corpora, because the set of texts used in a corpus can never be stylistically completely homogeneous.

Whereas in the past, corpora tended to be collected by individuals for their own use, the availability of corpora has increased enormously in the last 30 years or so as computers have become more readily accessible, computer memory has become cheaper, and scanning techniques have improved, and, correspondingly, the amount of work on language variation and change that uses them has also increased. It is now easier for individual scholars to make their databases generally available than ever before. While there are often legal and ethical problems involved in doing so, it is to be hoped that this will continue to happen in the foreseeable future, because the greater the amount of genuine data that is available in this way, the better the descriptions that will be possible and the surer linguists will be of the replicability of their findings. The main point about public corpora as opposed to private ones is that their representativeness can be openly considered, and that they provide a large and readily-available body of agreed-upon data against which hypotheses can be tested. Corpora, even public corpora, are not new; the widespread use of them derives from the fact that they have become so valuable and so available. We are now almost reaching the stage where corpus studies based on public corpora are the default way of providing robust descriptions.

Appendix: List of Electronic Corpora Cited

Corpus	Abbreviation	Variety of English	Written/ spoken	Sample date	Corpus family	Size in words
Australian Corpus of English	ACE	Australian	written	1986	Brown	1m
Bank of English		mainly British	mainly written	1960–		300m+
British National Corpus	BNC	British	written and spoken	1960–		100m
Brown		American	written	1961	Brown	1m
Corpus of Early English Correspondence	CEEC		written			2.7m
Freiburg Brown	Frown	American	written	1991	Brown	1m
Freiburg LOB	FLOB	British	written	1992	Brown	1m
Helsinki		Historical	written	b. 850–1720		1.6m
International Corpus of English	ICE	Various	written and spoken	c. 1990		1m for each country
Kolhapur		Indian	written	1978	Brown	1m
Lancaster–Oslo– Bergen	LOB	British	written	1961	Brown	1m
London–Lund		British	spoken	1975–81		
Wellington Corpus of Spoken New Zealand English	WCSNZE	New Zealand	spoken	1986		1m
Wellington Corpus of Written New Zealand English	WCWNZE	New Zealand	written	1986	Brown	1m

ACKNOWLEDGMENTS

* I should like to thank Janet Holmes and Tom Lavelle for their perceptive comments on an earlier draft, which have led to many improvements. They are of course not to blame for what I have included.

NOTE

1   See Appendix for a list of the electronic corpora mentioned in the text.

REFERENCES

Aijmer, Karin and Bengt Altenberg (eds.) (1991). *English Corpus Linguistics: Studies in Honour of Jan Svartvik*. London and New York: Longman.

anon. (1993). *The Chicago Manual of Style*, 14th edn. Chicago and London: Chicago University Press.

Anshen, Frank and Mark Aronoff (1997). Morphology in real time. In Geert Booij and Jaap van Marle (eds.), *Yearbook of Morphology, 1996*. Dordrecht: Kluwer. 9–12.

Bauer, Laurie (1993). *Manual of Information to Accompany the Wellington Corpus of Written New Zealand English*. Wellington: Victoria University, Department of Linguistics.

Bauer, Laurie (1994). *Watching English Change*. London and New York: Longman.

Bauer, Laurie (2001). *Morphological Productivity*. Cambridge: Cambridge University Press.

Biber, Douglas (1987). A textual comparison of British and American writing. *American Speech* 62: 99–119.

Biber, Douglas (1988). *Variation Across Speech and Writing*. Cambridge: Cambridge University Press.

Biesenbach-Lucas, Sigrun (1987). The use of relative markers in modern American English. In Keith M. Denning, Sharon Inkelas, Faye C. McNair-Knox and John R. Rickford (eds.), *Variation in Language: NWAV-XV at Stanford*. Stanford, CA: Department of Linguistics, Stanford University. 13–21.

Bolozky, Shmuel (1999). *Measuring Productivity in Word Formation*. Leiden: Brill.

Burchfield, R. W. (ed.) (1972–86). *A Supplement to the Oxford English Dictionary*. Oxford: Clarendon Press.

Delbridge, A. (ed.) (1997). *The Macquarie Dictionary*. Sydney: Macquarie Library.

DeRose, Steven J. (1991). An analysis of probabilistic grammatical tagging. In Stig Johansson and Anna-Brita Stenström (eds.), *English Computer Corpora*. Berlin and New York: Mouton de Gruyter. 9–13.

Gilliéron, Jules (1902–10). *Atlas linguistique de la France*, 13 vols. [Paris]: Champion.

Gordon, Elizabeth (1994). Reconstructing the past: written and spoken evidence of early New Zealand speech. *New Zealand English Newsletter* 8: 5–10.

Gordon, Elizabeth (1998). The origins of New Zealand speech: the limits of recovering historical information from written records. *English World-Wide* 19: 61–85.

Hofland, Knut (1991). Concordance programs for personal computers. In Stig Johansson and Anna-Brita Stenström (eds.), *English Computer Corpora*. Berlin and New York: Mouton de Gruyter. 283–306.

Holmes, Janet (1998a). Generic pronouns in the Wellington corpus of spoken New Zealand English. *Kotare* 1: 32–40.

Holmes, Janet (1998b). Narrative structure: some contrasts between Maori and Pakeha story-telling. *Multilingua* 17: 25–57.

Hundt, Marianne (1998). *New Zealand English Grammar, Fact or Fiction? A Corpus-Based Study in Morphosyntactic Variation.* Amsterdam and Philadelphia: Benjamins.

Jones, Daniel (1917–). *English Pronouncing Dictionary.* London and Melbourne: J.M. Dent. 2nd edn, 1924; 3rd edn, 1926; 4th edn, 1937; 5th edn, 1940; 6th edn, 1944; 7th edn, 1945; 8th edn, 1947; 9th edn, 1948; 10th edn, 1949; 11th edn, 1956; 12th edn, 1963; 13th edn, 1967; 14th edn, 1977.

Kennedy, Graeme (1998). *An Introduction to Corpus Linguistics.* London and New York: Longman.

Kennedy, Graeme (2001). Lexical borrowing from Maori in New Zealand English. In Bruce Moore (ed.), *Who's Centric Now? The Present State of Post-Colonial Englishes.* Melbourne: Oxford University Press. 59–81.

Kennedy, Graeme and S. Yamazaki (1999). The influence of Maori in the New Zealand English lexicon. In

J. Kirk (ed.), *Corpora Galore: Analyses and Techniques in Describing English.* Amsterdam: Rodopi. 33–44.

Kučera, Henry and W. Nelson Francis (1967). *Computational Analysis of Present-day American English.* Providence, RI: Brown University Press.

Kytö, Merja and Suzanne Romaine (1997). Competing forms of adjective comparison in Modern English: what could be *more quicker* and *easier* and *more effective*? In T. Nevalainen and L. Kahlas-Tarkka (eds.), *To Explain the Present: Studies in the Changing English Language in Honour of Matti Rissanen.* Helsinki: Société Néophilologique. 329–52.

Lass, Roger (1987). *The Shape of English: Structure and History.* London and Melbourne: J.M. Dent.

Leech, Geoffrey and Jonathan Culpepper (1997). The comparison of adjectives in recent British English. In T. Nevalainen and L. Kahlas-Tarkka (eds.), *To Explain the Present: Studies in the Changing English Language in honour of Matti Rissanen.* Helsinki: Société Néophilologique. 353–73.

Lewis, Gillian (1996). The origins of New Zealand English: a report on work in progress. *New Zealand English Journal* 10: 25–30.

Mair, Christian (1998). Corpora and the study of the major varieties of English: issues and results. In Hans Lindquist, Staffan Klintborg, Magnus Levin and Maria Estling (eds.), *The Major Varieties of English.* Acta Vexionensia Humaniora 1. Växjö: Växjö University. 139–57.

McEnery, Tony and Andrew Wilson (1996). *Corpus Linguistics.* Edinburgh: Edinburgh University Press.

Minugh, David (1997). All the language that's fit to print: using British and American newspaper CD-ROMs as corpora. In Anne Wichmann, Steven Fligelstone, Tony McEnery and

Gerry Knowles (eds.), *Teaching and Language Corpora*. London: Longman.

Nevalainen, Terttu (2000). Gender differences in the evolution of standard English. *Journal of English Linguistics* 28: 38–59.

Peitsara, Kirsti (1993). On the development of the *by*-agent in English. In Matti Rissanen, Merja Kytö and Minna Palander-Collin (eds.), *Early English in the Computer Age*. Berlin and New York: Mouton de Gruyter. 219–33.

Rissanen, Matti (2000). The world of English historical corpora. From Cædmon to the computer age. *Journal of English Linguistics* 28: 7–20.

SED (1999). *The Survey of English Dialects on CD-ROM*. London and New York: Routledge.

Sigley, Robert J. (1997a). Choosing your relatives: relative clauses in New Zealand English. Unpublished Ph.D. thesis, Victoria University of Wellington.

Sigley, Robert (1997b). Text categories and where you can stick them: a crude formality index. *International Journal of Corpus Linguistics* 2: 199–237.

Sigley, Robert (1997c). The influence of formality and channel on relative pronoun choice in New Zealand English. *English Language and Linguistics* 1: 207–32.

Sinclair, John (ed.) (1987). *Collins COBUILD English Language Dictionary*. London and Glasgow: Collins.

Svartvik, Jan and Randolph Quirk (eds.) (1980). *A Corpus of English Conversation*. Lund: Lund University Press.

Tottie, Gunnel (1991). Conversational style in British and American English: the case of backchannels. In K. Aijmer and B. Altenberg (eds.), *English Corpus Linguistics: studies in honour of Jan Svartvik*. London: Longman. 254–71.

Trudgill, Peter, Elizabeth, Gordon and Gillian Lewis (1998). New dialect formation and southern hemisphere English: the New Zealand short front vowels. *Journal of Sociolinguistics* 2: 35–51.

Velde, Hans van de (1996). *Variatie en verandering in het gesproken Standaard-Nederlands (1935–1993)*. Nijmegen: Katholieke Universiteit Nijmegen.

Evaluation

Sociolinguists collect the speech they study from people engaged in ordinary activities, as we have seen in the previous section. The people may be reading aloud or writing, but they are more likely to be selling cars or discussing politics or gossiping. In a discipline that sets out to study language in its social uses, there really is no substitute for observing and recording ordinary speech.

Ordinary speech makes uncommon demands when it comes to analysis. For one thing, the tokens that carry social significance in speech events occur with wildly varying frequencies. A particular vowel phoneme may occur two or three times in every recorded minute, but a passive verb form may turn up only once or twice in an hour. For another thing, the social significance of these forms is very often an attribute not of their presence or absence in a person's speech but of their frequency in that speech compared to someone else's speech. For yet another, the differences that give speech its social significance are often minuscule. This is true not only of phonetic differences, in which it can be important to recognize that a vowel is slightly raised on one occurrence compared to another, or slightly more open. It is also true of grammatical differences, which are often carried by unstressed clitics that fade very quickly in the stream of speech.

Sociolinguists, like professional researchers in all empirical disciplines, develop refined sets of research skills that allow them to cope with the demands of their data. Most sociolinguists are exceptionally good at hearing vowel and consonant nuances in the speech stream, possibly because it is their aptitude for audio discrimination that attracts them to the work in the first place, but undoubtedly because they get exposed early and often to such nuances.

However, even the best ear can go no further in the analysis than assigning tokens to types. Much more than that is required, of course, and the study of actual speech has fostered a battery of analytic tools.

Observations involving social significance start with observations of frequencies, and frequencies require counting variants and correlating them with contextual features. Robert Bayley, in "The Quantitative Paradigm," discusses the principles that govern counting and correlating. He looks closely at VARBRUL, the logistic regression program expressly devised for handling variable data with distributional imbalances of the kind that inevitably accrue in real (as opposed to artificial) situations. VARBRUL has been developed over some 30 years for sociolinguistic purposes, and along with it have come other quantitative methods for supplementing it and in some cases replacing it. Bayley discusses these too, and also some syntheses that are developing.

Variable frequencies are also at the heart of John R. Rickford's chapter on "Implicational Scales." The systematic nature of sociolinguistic data often reveals itself in robust implicational relationships between speech features, defined schematically by the formula "If X, then Y but not vice-versa." So, in Rickford's focal case study, Jamaican Creole speakers who use *no ben* for "didn't" inevitably use *pikni* for "child", but there are other speakers who use *pikni* and never use *no ben*. Implicational relationships like these constrain the range of variation that actually occurs in a dialect continuum, and reveal the structure in variability.

Erik R. Thomas in "Instrumental Phonetics" discusses the identification of sociolinguistic tokens through the use of acoustic technology of several kinds. He reviews the application of instrumental methods in vowel variation, a fairly well-developed area, but advocates and explores additional acoustic applications that could be imported into sociolinguistics or implemented more extensively. Although some sociolinguists have exploited the rapid developments that have taken place in instrumental analysis, the possible uses, as Thomas points out, are considerably broader, and the potential gains in accountability and accuracy are inestimable.

J. K. CHAMBERS

5 The Quantitative Paradigm

ROBERT BAYLEY

The quantitative paradigm in sociolinguistics originated in the studies conducted by William Labov in New York and Philadelphia in the 1960s and 1970s (Labov 1966, 1969a, 1972a, 1972b). This approach to the study of language was subsequently extended to a wide variety of language communities around the world, including Panama (Cedergren 1973), Norwich, England (Trudgill 1974), Anniston, Alabama (Feagin 1979), Guyana (Rickford 1987), and Rio de Janeiro (Guy 1981), to name just a few. The central ideas of this approach are that an understanding of language requires an understanding of variable as well as categorical processes and that the variation that we witness at all levels of language is not random. Rather, linguistic variation is characterized by orderly or "structured heterogeneity" (Weinreich et al. 1968: 99–100). That is, speakers' choices between variable linguistic forms are systematically constrained by multiple linguistic and social factors that reflect underlying grammatical systems and that both reflect and partially constitute the social organization of the communities to which users of the language belong. In addition, synchronic variation is often a reflection of diachronic change (Labov 1994).

In this chapter, I outline the assumptions underlying this approach to the study of language variation and change. I then focus on methods of quantitative analysis, with an emphasis on variable rule, or VARBRUL, analysis, the most common method of multivariate analysis in quantitative sociolinguistics. The next section considers alternative methods that have been recently proposed to overcome some of the limitations of VARBRUL. Finally, I examine recent work that synthesizes traditional approaches to the study of linguistic variation and ethnography.

1 Theoretical Principles of the Quantitative Paradigm

Several key principles underlie the quantitative study of linguistic variation. Among the more important are the "principle of quantitative modeling" and the "principle of multiple causes" (Young and Bayley 1996: 253). The "principle of quantitative modeling" means that we can examine closely the forms that a linguistic variable takes, and note what features of the context co-occur with these forms. By context is meant the surrounding linguistic environment and the social phenomena that co-occur with a given variable form. With a large enough set of data, we are able to make statements about the likelihood of co-occurrence of a variable form and any one of the contextual features in which we are interested.

These statements express in quantitative terms the strength of association between a contextual feature and the linguistic variable. For example, Bayley and Pease-Alvarez (1997), in a study of Mexican immigrant and Chicano Spanish, were interested in the relationship between the degree of discourse connectedness, operationalized as continuity of subject, tense, and mood with the preceding tensed verb, and the likelihood that Mexican-born and Chicano children would use an overt pronoun rather than a null subject in sentences such as (1) and (2):

(1)   *una noche cerca de navidad ella/Ø nos dijo que se sentía muy mal . . .*
      one night near Christmas she told us that she felt very bad . . .

(2)   *entonces él/Ø tuvo que cerrar la ventana.*
      then he had to close the window.

After conducting a VARBRUL analysis, Bayley and Pease-Alvarez reported that in cases where there was continuity of subject, tense, and mood, the weight of the factor was .293. On the other hand, in cases with there was a change in discourse topic, the likelihood of an overt pronoun was .653. Factor weights favor the variant when they exceed .50 and otherwise disfavor it (as discussed in more detail below). This means that an overt pronoun is highly unlikely to occur when continuity of subject, tense, and mood is preserved. However, overt pronouns are quite likely to occur when the discourse topic changes. Moreover, as shown in table 5.1, in the narrative discourse that Bayley and Pease-Alvarez investigated, the likelihood of an overt pronoun increases as the degree of discourse connectedness decreases. To the extent that these results are representative of other Mexican-born and Chicano children, we may expect that the use of overt pronouns in the speech of these children will pattern in the same way.

The second principle, the "principle of multiple causes," means that it is unlikely that any single contextual factor can explain the variability observed in natural language data. For example, in Bayley and Pease-Alvarez's study, the degree of discourse connectedness with the preceding tensed verb was not the only significant constraint on variation between null and overt pronouns. Person and number, verb type (present; preterit; imperfect, conditional, or subjunctive), immigrant generation, and speaker gender also proved to have statistically significant effects.

Table 5.1 Degree of discourse connectedness and overt pronoun use in Mexican immigrant and Chicano children's Spanish

Degree of discourse connectedness	% overt pronoun	VARBRUL weight
First degree: continuity of subject, tense, and mood	12	.293
Second degree: continuity of subject, different tense and/or mood	20	.405
Third degree: subject continuity interrupted by one or more intervening clauses	21	.490
Fourth degree: last occurrence of subject in another syntactic function	35	.607
Fifth degree: change in narrative section or discourse topic	32	.653
Total/input probability	24	.198

Source: Bayley and Pease-Alvarez (1997: 360)

The great majority of studies of linguistic variation has shown that the variables that have been closely examined, like null pronoun variation in Spanish, are subject to not one, but many contextual conditioning factors. For example, studies of a variety of English dialects have shown that final consonant cluster reduction, or -t,d deletion, is subject to a wide range of linguistic factors that exhibit remarkable cross-dialectal consistency (see e.g. Bayley 1994a, Guy 1980, 1991, 1997, Labov 1989, 1997, Labov et al. 1968, Roberts 1997, Santa Ana 1992, Wolfram 1969, Wolfram and Fasold 1974). In most dialects in which this variable has been studied, -t,d is far more likely to be deleted if it is part of a monomorpheme, as in *mist*, than if it is a past tense marker, as in *missed*. Deletion is also subject to phonological constraints. Final -t,d is more likely to be deleted if the following segment is a consonant than if it is a vowel. Other linguistic factors also influence the likelihood of -t,d deletion. The complexity of the multiple factors is succinctly illustrated by Labov's summary of the pan-English pattern, using variable rule notation (1989: 92):[1]

/-t,d/ → <∅>/<str.> <C> <−cont. +cons.> <cat.> _ <features>

$$<\alpha \text{ voi}> \qquad\qquad <\alpha \text{ voi}>$$

a   b   c   d   e

f   f

a   *syllable stress* (unstressed > stressed)
b   *cluster length* (CCC > CC)

c   the phonetic features of the *preceding consonant*, yielding the segmental order /s/ > stops > nasals > other fricatives > liquids

d   the *grammatical status* of the final /-t,d/, with the order: part of *-n't* morpheme > part of stem > derivational suffix > past tense or past participial suffix

e   the phonetic features of the *following segment*, yielding the order: obstruents > liquids > glides > vowels > pauses

f   *agreement in voicing* of the segments preceding and following the /-t,d/ (homovoiced > heterovoiced)

Not only is deletion constrained by the grammatical status of final -t,d and the features of the following segment, it is also constrained by syllable stress, with -t,d in unstressed syllables more liable to deletion than -t,d in stressed syllables, and by cluster length, with triclusters more liable to reduction than biclusters. In addition, -t,d deletion is affected by the phonetic features of the preceding segment and by voicing agreement of the segments preceding and following the variable.

In addition to the principles of quantitative modeling and multiple causes, two other principles are critical to the variationist paradigm. These are summarized by Guy (1991):

- Individual speakers may differ in their basic rate of use of a variable rule, that is, in their input probability for the rule.
- Individuals should be similar or identical in the factor values assigned to linguistic constraints on the rule. (This assumption is usually qualified to apply just to people who belong to the same speech community.)

The first of these principles offers a way to understand how groups of speakers who use a particular variant at very different rates may be regarded as members of the same speech community. For example, Wolfram found that Detroit African-Americans deleted -t,d at very different rates, depending on the social class to which they belonged, as well as on a number of linguistic factors. Table 5.2 shows his results for social class, grammatical function, and following phonological environment, expressed in percentages. Figure 5.1 presents the same information graphically.

In these results, we can see that the rate of -t,d deletion by these speakers is affected by all three of the factors examined. When -t,d is a past tense morpheme and is followed by a vowel, the deletion rate for upper-middle-class (UM) speakers is only 7 percent. In contrast, lower-working-class (LW) speakers delete -t,d in the same environment at a 34 percent rate. When -t,d is not a past tense morpheme and the following segment is a consonant, the rate of deletion increases to 79 percent for upper-middle-class speakers and to a near categorical 97 percent for lower-working-class speakers. Note, however, that the linguistic factors have the same effect on speakers of all social classes, despite differences in the overall percentages of deletion. Regardless of social class, the order of environments for final -t,d deletion is: –past, +cons > –past,

Table 5.2 Percentages of -t,d deletion in Detroit African-American English by linguistic environment and social class

Environments	Social class			
	Upper-middle	Lower-middle	Upper-working	Lower-working
Following vowel:				
-t,d is past morpheme (e.g. "missed in")	7	13	24	34
-t,d is not past morpheme (e.g. "mist in")	28	43	65	72
Following consonant:				
-t,d is past morpheme (e.g. "missed by")	49	62	73	76
-t,d is not past morpheme (e.g. "mist by")	79	87	94	97

Source: Wolfram and Fasold (1974: 132)

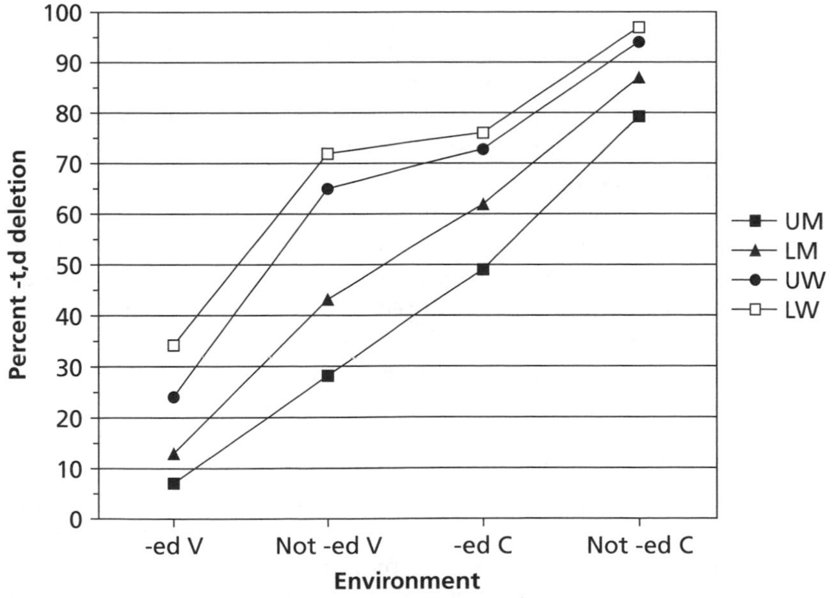

Figure 5.1 -t,d deletion in Detroit African-American English by linguistic environment and social class

Source: Wolfram & Fasold, 1974: 132

+vowel > +past, +cons > +past, +vowel. With respect to this aspect of the grammar, then, members of different social classes can be said to belong to the same speech community, even though they differ considerably in their over-all rate of -t,d deletion. The speakers Wolfram studied thus provide a clear example of Labov's definition of a speech community:

> The speech community is not defined by any marked agreement in the use of language elements, so much as by participation in a set of shared norms: these norms may be observed in overt types of evaluative behavior, and by the uni-formity of abstract patterns of variation which are invariant in respect to particu-lar levels of usage.   (Labov 1972b: 120–1)

Thus far, the discussion has concerned social groups rather than individuals. However, it is conceivable that the percentages in studies such as Wolfram's might be arrived at by averaging speakers who happened to belong to the same social group but who exhibited very different behavior with respect to particular linguistic variables. For example, the -t,d deletion rate of 43 percent by lower-middle-class speakers when the -t,d is not a past tense morpheme and the following segment is a vowel might be arrived at by combining tokens from speakers who delete -t,d at a rate of 86 percent with an equal number of tokens from speakers who never delete -t,d in this environment. In practice, however, this does not happen. Guy (1980), for example, examined -t,d deletion in a sample of New Yorkers and Philadelphians. His results showed that, as long as a sufficient number of tokens was available (approximately 20 per cell), results for individuals closely matched the group pattern. Later studies, including my own work on the role of grammatical aspect in the acquisition of past-tense marking by Chinese learners of English (Bayley 1994b), have confirmed Guy's finding concerning the relationship between group and indi-vidual patterns of variation.

To summarize, research in the quantitative paradigm has demonstrated the systematic nature of much of the linguistic variation that was previously thought to be random. Moreover, research has shown in fine detail that variable lin-guistic forms are constrained by multiple internal and external factors. And, research has shown that, at least with respect to major linguistic constraints, given sufficient data, individual patterns do in fact match group patterns. These insights have been gained by adopting certain methods of analysis. Perhaps most obvious of these is the focus on actual language as produced by speakers in communities rather than on linguistic intuitions, or grammaticality judgments, as has been the practice in formal linguistics. The data gathered through sociolinguistic interviews of the type pioneered by Labov (1963, 1966), the social network approach developed by James and Leslie Milroy in Belfast (Milroy 1987), or the intense participant observation exemplified by Eckert's (2000) study of a Detroit area high school have been subject to a variety of interpretations based on different theoretical principles. In its concentration on language as used by members of the communities under study, however, research in the quantitative paradigm has remained resolutely "secular," to use Labov's term. That is, regardless of the theoretical predisposition of the researcher, work in the quantitative tradition has tended to preserve the principle of accountability (Sankoff 1990), which involves dealing with the full range of variability present in the (relatively) informal interactions of language users. Given the multitude of factors, both linguistic and social, that can potentially influence a language user's choice of one or another variable form, adherence to the principle of accountability necessitates multivariate analysis.

2 Quantitative Analysis

The quantitative modeling of the correlations between language variation and the multiple contextual factors that promote or inhibit use of a particular variant is no easy matter. In studies that relate variation to a single contextual factor, a simple statistical procedure such as a comparison of two means with the help of a t-test has been used (e.g. by Beebe 1977). However, such a model is inadequate when multiple influences are likely to be involved. Analysis of variance is another technique that has been used (e.g. Tarone 1985) to relate variation to a single independent variable with multiple levels. In principle, it is possible to extend an analysis of variance to additional variables, but with the kind of data usually collected in studies of linguistic variation, this is hardly ever practicable. An example should help make clear why this is the case. In a study of -t,d deletion in Tejano/Chicano English (Bayley 1994a), I originally hypothesized that the variation would be influenced by eleven separate independent variables, each of which had theoretical and empirical support from previous studies. The eleven independent variables were all nominal (that is to say they could be further subdivided into two or more categories) and were as follows:

> Morphological class: monomorpheme, semiweak verb (e.g. *left*), past tense or past participle, *-n't*;
> Phonetic features of the preceding segment: /s/, nasal, stop, fricative, /r/, /l/;
> Phonetic features of the following segment: consonant, /l/, /r/, glide, vowel, pause;
> Syllable stress: unstressed, stressed;
> Voicing agreement of the preceding and following segments: homovoicing, heterovoicing;
> Cluster length: CCC, CC;
> Speech style: conversation, reading continuous passage, word list;
> Reported first language: English, Spanish;
> Current home language: English, English and Spanish, Spanish;
> Gender: male, female.
> Age: 14–24, over 25.

In this model there are 11 separate factor groups (independent variables) comprising a total of 34 separate factors (categories). The number of possible combinations of factors (also known as cells) is 82,944. This is an extremely large number of cells for a multiple ANOVA to handle. In addition, most cells are empty, although nearly 5,000 tokens of the dependent variable – final consonant clusters – were collected for the study. This is because many combinations are linguistically impossible or highly unlikely, leaving more than 80,000 cells with missing data. Moreover, the majority of the filled cells represent only one token of the dependent variable, presence or absence of final -t,d. Algorithms for calculating ANOVA normally require equal numbers of tokens in each cell and are clearly inapplicable to such a case. Even algorithms for calculating unbalanced ANOVAs will fail when faced with such extreme distributional imbalances. ANOVA is a statistical procedure designed to deal with the kind of balanced data that emerge from controlled experiments. It is inadequate to handle the kind of naturally occurring data that are collected in studies of sociolinguistic variation.

3   Multivariate Analysis with VARBRUL

Modeling linguistic variation can be carried out by a number of commercial statistical software packages, usually under the name of logistic regression (e.g. Norušis and SPSS 1996, SAS Institute 1996). However, the programs known as VARBRUL have been used most extensively in sociolinguistics because they have been deliberately designed to handle the kind of data obtained in studies of variation. They also provide heuristic tools that allow the investigator to modify hypotheses and reanalyze the data easily. The statistical bases for the VARBRUL programs are set out in Sankoff (1988), and the procedures for using the software are explained in detail in Young and Bayley (1996) and in the documentation that accompanies the programs. The two most widely available versions are GoldVarb for the Macintosh (Rand and Sankoff 1991) and VARBRUL for the PC (Pintzuk 1988).[2]

A full explanation of the steps involved in carrying out a multivariate analysis with VARBRUL is beyond the scope of this chapter. Here, the discussion will be limited to addressing several questions that arise in any study, including defining the envelope of variation, testing for significance, interpreting the results, and dealing with the limitations inherent in the program. Readers who wish to pursue the topic in greater depth should consult the extensive literature on variable rule analysis and use of the VARBRUL programs (e.g. Cedergren and Sankoff 1974, Guy 1980, 1988, 1993, Rousseau 1989, Rousseau and Sankoff 1978, Sankoff 1988, Sankoff and Labov 1979, Young and Bayley 1996).

The first steps in conducting a VARBRUL analysis are to define the variable and the envelope of variation. That is, what forms count as instances of the variable? Are the forms that vary indeed two ways of saying the same thing?

In many studies, particularly studies of phonological variation, defining the envelope of variation is not a problem. For example, *fishing* and *fishin'* clearly have the same referential meaning, as do *west side* and *wes' side*. However, it becomes less obvious that variable forms meet the criterion of being two ways of saying the same thing at higher levels of linguistic structure. VARBRUL has been used to analyze variation in syntax, discourse, and code-switching (e.g. Poplack 1980, Poplack and Budzhak-Jones 1998, Schiffrin 1982, Weiner and Labov 1983). However, the use of VARBRUL analysis for modeling variation in syntax in particular has given rise to considerable controversy (see e.g. Labov 1978, Lavendera 1978). In fact, the problem of defining what counts as an instance of the variable may affect the study of even such frequently examined variables as copula deletion in African American Vernacular English (AAVE), which has been referred to as a "showcase variable of American dialectology and quantitative sociolinguistics" (Rickford et al. 1991: 104).

Rickford et al. (1991) examined the quantitative consequences of different decisions about defining the envelope of variation for this often studied variable, as well as underlying models, i.e. whether variable AAVE copula absence results from a deletion or an insertion rule[3] and whether *is* and *are* should be analyzed separately or combined. Rickford et al. (1991) performed nine separate multivariate analyses of 1,424 tokens extracted from interviews and peer group sessions with approximately 30 speakers in East Palo Alto, California. Their results for *is* and *are* showed that these two variants could best be accounted for within a single model that included a person-number factor group to account for the different forms. However, to perform the analyses, they found it necessary to exclude approximately 2,000 tokens in addition to nonfinite and past tense forms of *be*. Although Rickford et al. (1991) recognized that excluded tokens were relevant to the question of whether AAVE has an underlying copula, it was nevertheless necessary to exclude them from the quantitative analyses because they showed invariant copula presence (e.g. *am* was present in contracted form nearly 100 percent of the time) or because it was impossible to determine whether the copula was present or not (e.g. cases of contracted *is* followed by a sibilant) (1991: 107).

The second issue that arises early in a study concerns specifying the factors that may potentially influence the choice of a variant. In general, it is best to be liberal at this stage, although each factor group should be based on a well-motivated hypothesis. Lucas (1995), for example, investigated the potential effects of eight separate factor groups on the choice of a variant of the sign DEAF in American Sign Language. As it turned out, most of these groups proved not to be statistically significant. However, the labor of coding for many factors was not expended in vain. The study demonstrated that Liddell and Johnson's (1989) claim that variation in the form of DEAF is influenced primarily by the location of the preceding sign, a phonological constraint, is at best incomplete. Lucas also demonstrated the previously unsuspected influence on the choice of variant of the grammatical category to which DEAF belongs, a finding that was later confirmed in a larger study based on a representative sample of the Deaf community in the United States (Bayley et al. 2000).

Once coding is complete and the data are entered into the program, VARBRUL estimates the factor values (or probabilities) for each contextual factor specified (e.g. the phonetic features of the following environment or the social class to which a speaker belongs). This is done by combining the input probability (p_0, the likelihood that the "rule" will apply regardless of the presence or absence of any other factor in the environment) with the applicable factor weights from each of the factors in the model ($p_1, p_2, \ldots, p_n$), according to the formula:

$$p = \frac{p_0 \times \ldots \times p_n}{[p_0 \times \ldots \times p_n] + [(1 - p_0) \times \ldots \times (1 - p_n)]}$$

The program provides a numerical measure of the strength or influence of each factor, relative to other factors in the same group, on the occurrence of the linguistic variable under investigation. Values range between 0 and 1.00. A value, or weight, between .50 and 1.00 indicates that the factor favors use of a variant relative to other factors in the same group. For example, Baugh (1983) examined -t,d deletion in AAVE, among other variables. Among the factor groups for which he coded were the grammatical function of the word containing the -t,d cluster and the type of speech event from which the data were extracted. The factors in the grammatical function group were monomorphemes, e.g. *mist*, *past*, semiweak verbs, e.g. *kept*, *lost*, and past tense forms, e.g. *missed*, *passed*. Baugh divided the speech events into four types, depending on the speakers' familiarity with one another and the extent to which they participated in African-American vernacular culture. He hypothesized that participants in Type 1 events, characterized by familiarity of the speakers and shared participation in African-American vernacular culture, would favor use of vernacular forms, in this case, -t,d deletion. Conversely, he hypothesized that vernacular forms would be less likely to occur in Type 4 events, where the speakers were not well-acquainted and where AAVE was not common to all. Results for these two factor groups are shown in table 5.3.

Baugh reported that the results for the grammatical function group were significant. Like speakers of other English dialects, speakers of AAVE are more likely to delete final -t,d when it does not carry any grammatical meaning, as is the case in monomorphemic words. They are less likely to delete -t,d when it functions as a past tense ending. Semi-weak, or ambiguous, verbs, which are characterized by an internal vowel change and affixation of -t,d, have an intermediate value. The type of speech event, however, failed to reach significance. The values for all four types of speech events hover around .5. Contrary to Baugh's hypothesis, -t,d deletion was *not* affected by this factor.

In addition to calculating values or weights for each factor, VARBRUL also calculates the input probability, which, as noted above, is the overall likelihood that speakers will choose the variant selected as the application value (the value

Table 5.3 -t,d deletion by grammatical function and speech event type in African-American Vernacular English

Factor group	Factor	VARBRUL weight
Grammatical function	No grammatical function, e.g. *past*	0.683
	Ambiguous function, e.g. *lost*	0.523
	Past tense function, e.g. *passed*	0.353
Speech event type	**Type 1**: Familiar participants, all of whom are natives of African-American vernacular culture	0.482
	Type 2: Participants are not well acquainted, but all are members of African-American vernacular culture	0.523
	Type 3: Participants are well acquainted, but do not share AAVE	0.499
	Type 4: Participants are not well acquainted and AAVE is not common to all	0.496

Source: Baugh (1983: 98)

that counts as an application of the "rule" being investigated). In my own study of -t,d deletion in Tejano English, for example, the input probability was .469, indicating that -t,d would be likely to be deleted nearly half the time regardless of the presence or absence of any other factor in the environment.

The program also provides several measures of goodness of fit between the model and the data. These include the total chi-square, the chi-square per cell, and the log likelihood. The total chi-square measures the degree of interaction among factors from different factor groups. An acceptable value for the total chi-square is derived by looking at a table of the chi-square distribution at the desired probability level (say $p < .05$) and the appropriate number of degrees of freedom in the model. The degrees of freedom in any VARBRUL model are calculated by subtracting the number of factor groups from the total number of factors. For example, in the case of a model with 6 factors distributed among 3 binary factor groups, the number of degrees of freedom is 3. From a chi-square table, we can see that the total chi-square should be less than 7.815 for us to accept that our model has less than 1 chance in 20 of being right by chance ($p < .05$).

The chi-square per cell figure is simply calculated by dividing the total chi-square by the number of cells. The lower the chi-square per cell figure, the less likely there is interaction among factors. As a general rule, a chi-square per cell figure greater than 1.5 suggests that there may be an interaction between two or more factor groups, e.g. ethnicity and social class. In such cases, it may be necessary to recode the data to remove the interaction. For example, rather than have separate factor groups for ethnicity and social class, it may be better to combine them. Thus two binary factor groups for African-American and Euro-American and for working and middle class speakers might be combined to form a single factor group consisting of African-American working class, African-American middle class, Euro-American working class, and Euro-American middle class.[4] Finally, VARBRUL provides the log likelihood statistic, also a measure of goodness-of-fit. Figures closer to zero represent better models than log likelihoods further removed from zero (see Young and Bayley 1996: 272–3).

The factor values and input probability reported in a VARBRUL run provide useful information. They are not sufficient, however, to confirm or disconfirm the hypotheses that led to the inclusion of the factors in the original model of variation. Our goal in VARBRUL analysis, as in any scientific endeavor, is to develop the most parsimonious model that still accounts for the data. To achieve this goal, we need to test whether the results are statistically significant or whether there is a good likelihood that they might be due to chance. In VARBRUL analysis, achieving the most parsimonious model involves testing whether entire factor groups significantly contribute to the overall goodness-of-fit of the model and testing whether factors within groups differ significantly from one another. Naturally, factors should only be combined where there is linguistic or social justification for doing so. Guy (1980), for example, in a study of -t,d deletion, found that the VARBRUL weights for regular past tense verbs and past participles did not differ significantly from one another. As discussed in more detail below, he combined these forms on the basis of their common underlying morphological structure. It would have made little sense, however, to combine following consonants and vowels, for example, which not only contrast phonologically but have been found in other studies to differ significantly in their effect on deletion.

3.1   Significance testing with VARBRUL

VARBRUL provides a means of testing whether a particular factor group contributes significantly to the model of variation by means of *step-up/step-down analysis*. This involves performing a run with only one factor group and then adding each of the other factor groups to the analysis, one at a time, until all factor groups are included. When the full model with all factor groups is reached, VARBRUL then removes one factor group at a time until only one remains. During each individual run, the factor weights and the log-likelihood are calculated. At the end of the analysis, the program outputs a file with the details of each run and an indication of the best stepping-up run and the best stepping-down run. The factor groups included in the best stepping-up and stepping-down runs should be the same. These are the factor groups that are significant at or above the $p < .05$ level. Factor groups that are not included in these runs do not contribute significantly to the variation. The factor weights calculated during these runs are used to report the results of the study.

In addition to testing the significance of factor groups, it is also necessary to test whether individual factors within groups differ significantly from one another. This calculation is done by comparing the log likelihoods of two VARBRUL runs, one with the factor coded as is, and one with a recode in which the factor is eliminated or collapsed with another factor. The following test is used in order to determine whether the difference between the VARBRUL weights is significant:

$$\chi^2_{v\alpha} \approx -2 \, (\text{log likelihood}_1 - \text{log likelihood}_2)$$

That is, twice the difference in the log likelihoods of the separate analyses performed (1) with and (2) without the factor in question asymptotically approximates a chi-square distribution where v is the number of degrees of freedom and α is the probability that the effect attributed to the factor in question is greater than would be expected by chance. The degrees of freedom used in calculating the above chi-square statistic are the difference between the degrees of freedom in the two runs. If only one factor is eliminated, there will only be a single degree of freedom used in testing for the significance of that factor.

3.2 Interpreting the results of VARBRUL analysis

VARBRUL enables us to give precise and replicable measures of the strength of a wide range of contextual influences on the choice among variable linguistic forms. However, simply reporting results is not sufficient. Rather, our goal is to understand why we achieve the results that we do. Take the effect of grammatical category on the likelihood of -t,d deletion as an example.

A number of explanations have been proposed for the pattern for grammatical function seen in Wolfram (1969), Guy (1980), Baugh (1983), and numerous other studies. At first glance, it appears that the functional load carried by final -t,d might provide an adequate explanation. Nothing is lost if a speaker says *jus' me* instead of *just me*, but it is not so easy to determine whether *I miss/Ø/ my friend* refers to a missed past appointment or to an ongoing emotional state. As we have seen, however, Guy (1980), showed that the rate of -t,d deletion from past participles, e.g. *she was miss/Ø/ by all*, did not differ significantly from the rate of deletion from past tense forms, despite the fact that past participles carry a lighter functional load.

Guy's (1980) finding that -t,d is deleted from past participles and past tense verbs at the same rate suggests that we must look beyond functionalism for an explanation of the ordering of grammatical constraints. A number of possible explanations have been proposed. Guy (1993), for example, observed that the grammatical categories that are subject to -t,d deletion are characterized by different internal morphological boundaries, and that regular past tense forms and past participles have the same internal structure. The results for grammatical category can thus be explained by a boundary constraint on -t,d deletion. A deletion rule applies freely when no internal boundary is present, as is the case with monomorphemes such as *past*. Deletion is inhibited somewhat by the formative boundary in semi-weak verbs, and strongly inhibited by the inflectional boundary in regular past tense verbs and past participles.

Other explanations have also been advanced (see Labov 1997 for a full account). Guy (1991) proposed an exponential model of constraints to explain the relationships observed in the grammatical category factor group, which related the retention of past tense, semi-weak, and monomorphemic clusters in the ratio of $x: x^2: x^3$. He explained this ratio as a consequence of the multilevel architecture of lexical phonology (Kiparsky 1985), whereby the three types of clusters are subject to one, two, or three passes of a deletion rule. Two subsequent studies (Bayley 1997, Santa Ana 1992) confirmed the predictions of the exponential model. More recently, Kiparsky (1994) suggested that the exponential relationship pointed out by Guy could be explained by an exploded optimality constraint.

The purpose here is not to argue which of these explanations is correct. The point is to demonstrate that the results achieved by the use of VARBRUL – or any other statistical program – do not in and of themselves provide explanations about linguistic structure or the meaning of the social distribution of linguistic variants. Rather, explanations must be sought in linguistic theory and in our understanding of the history and social structure of the communities we study.

3.3   Limitations of VARBRUL

VARBRUL has proven to be an extremely productive tool for the study of linguistic variation. However, it does suffer from a number of limitations. First, GoldVarb, the Macintosh version of the program dates from 1991, and a multinomial version has not been implemented for the Macintosh operating system. Also, until very recently, PC users had to resort to Susan Pintzuk's DOS version dating from 1988. Recently, however, Sali Tagliamonte, Pintzuk, and other researchers at the University of York have begun to develop a Windows version of the program, scheduled for release in 2001.[5] Second, because the use of the program has generally been restricted to research in sociolinguistics and second language acquisition (by researchers who have also been trained in sociolinguistics), VARBRUL users often find themselves without support. As Young and Yandell (1999) note, statistical consultants at most universities are not aware of VARBRUL. Third, as noted in the previous section, VARBRUL does not provide a convenient way to test for interactions among factor groups. As Sankoff (1988) observed, in the case of properly defined linguistic factors, interaction is not normally a problem. To return to the example of -t,d deletion in English, clearly there is no a priori reason to suspect that grammatical function and the following segment, or syllable stress and the preceding segment, will interact. However, as noted above, non-linguistic factors such as social class, gender, and ethnicity often interact. It is possible – and sometimes desirable – to control such interactions within VARBRUL by recoding. Alternately, one might consider each participant in the study as a separate factor and, assuming that the variable under investigation has social significance, use the VARBRUL weights to group individuals into relevant social categories.[6] Whether such procedures are desirable, however, depends on the goals of the study. If potential interactions among various social factors are a major interest of the investigation, VARBRUL is not the most suitable tool.

4   General Logistic Regression Models

In recent years, a number of researchers have used the logistic regression modules in commercially available statistical packages to overcome some of the limitations of VARBRUL.[7] Berdan (1996), for example, used the logistic regression module in SPSS to reanalyze Schumann's (1978) longitudinal data on the acquisition of English negation by "Alberto," a Costa Rican immigrant to the United States. Schumann's original study, which has been influential in second language acquisition research, provided the basis for his acculturation model and for the concept of fossilization. According to Schumann, Alberto showed very little progress in the acquisition of negation. He concluded that during the course of the study, which lasted a year, his subject "remained in the first [no + V] stage" (1978: 65).

In his reanalysis, Berdan was able to show that Alberto did in fact make progress toward the target language. Although he used *no + V* to express negation throughout the year, this most basic structure alternated with the more target-like unanalyzed *dont*, which became more frequent over time. Berdan used a general logistic regression model rather than VARBRUL for two main reasons. First, the general model enables the researcher to represent independent variables as continuous, "[a] procedure [that] allows for an intuitive representation of time – the variable that is integral to the modeling of learning or language acquisition" (Berdan 1996: 212). Second, the logistic regression model allows the researcher to calculate the main effects for independent variables (factors in VARBRUL) as well as to calculate interactions among them. Since the interaction of linguistic variables with time and with style was a main focus of Berdan's study, the general logistic model proved the more useful tool.

Young and Yandell (1999) provide an example of a direct comparison of results from a general logistic regression model and from VARBRUL. The comparison was undertaken in response to Saito's (1999) critique of Young's

(1991) original VARBRUL analysis of -s plural variation in the interlanguage of Chinese learners of English. Saito criticized Young's study for grouping speakers together by proficiency level rather than considering them individually and for failing to consider possible interactions between proficiency and the preceding segment effect. The first criticism is not germane to the choice between general logistic regression models and VARBRUL because it is a simple matter to include individuals as factors, regardless of the statistical package used. The second criticism is perhaps more relevant because, as we have seen, VARBRUL does not provide an easy way to deal with interactions. In the original study, Young (1991) found that proficiency level was statistically significant when all of the data were run together, with high proficiency learners more likely to mark -s plurals than low proficiency learners. He subsequently ran two separate analyses by proficiency level and found that the preceding segment, animacy, and definiteness affected high and low proficiency learners differently.

Young and Yandell used the GENMOD procedure in the SAS/STAT software package (SAS Institute 1996) to reanalyze the original data. As shown in table 5.4, the results are comparable to the original analysis. Both the original VARBRUL analysis and the GENMOD analysis showed that proficiency, noun position, syntactic function, preceding and following segments, and redundancy significantly affected speakers' use of plural -s. In addition, the GENMOD analysis showed significant interactions between proficiency and definiteness, animacy, and the preceding segment.

As we see in table 5.4, for example, both VARBRUL and GENMOD show that redundant plural marking in the NP favors -s plural marking for speakers at all levels of English proficiency, as do prenominal modifiers. When all speakers are included in the analysis, following vowels favor -s plural marking. However, this is a rather weak constraint, as indicated by the fact that it failed to reach statistical significance when separate analyses were run by proficiency level. Table 5.4 also allows us to compare the interactions found in the GENMOD analysis with the results of the separate VARBRUL analyses by proficiency level. For example, in the GENMOD analysis, proficiency by animacy is significant because, as revealed in the VARBRUL analyses by proficiency level, the animacy of the NP affects high and low proficiency speakers differently. For high proficiency speakers, animate NPs favor -s plural marking. For low proficiency speakers, animate NPs disfavor plural marking.

5   Multivariate Analysis: Summary and Conclusions

Numerous examples from studies of linguistic variation conducted around the world have shown that multivariate analysis is necessary if we are to understand the complex array of factors that may potentially influence the choice of

Table 5.4 Comparison of VARBRUL and GENMOD results for the analysis of -s plural marking in Chinese-English interlanguage

Factor	VARBRUL: all speakers	VARBRUL: low proficiency	VARBRUL: high proficiency	GENMOD
Proficiency	High proficiency favors	na	na	na
Individual speaker	na	na	na	significant
Redundant plural marking in NP	Redundant marking favors	Redundant marking favors	Redundant marking favors	Redundant marking favors
Syntactic function of NP	Adverbial favors	Adverbial favors	Adverbial favors	Adverbial favors
Position of noun within NP	Prenominal modifier favors	Prenominal modifier favors	Prenominal modifier favors	Prenominal modifier favors
Preceding segment	Vowels, stops, and non-sibilant fricatives favor	Vowels and stops favor	ns	Factor order is fricative > stop > vowel > nasal > sibilant > lateral
Following segment	Vowels favor	ns	*ns*	Vowels favor
Animacy	ns	disfavors	favors	ns
Definiteness	ns	ns	disfavors	ns
Proficiency x definiteness	na	na	na	significant
Proficiency x animacy	na	na	na	significant
Proficiency x preceding segment	na	na	na	significant

na = not applicable, either because the factor group was not included in the model (e.g. the interaction factor groups in the VARBRUL analyses) or because the factors in the group were dealt with elsewhere in the model (e.g. when speakers were coded as individual factors, the proficiency factor group was no longer relevant). ns = not significant at $p < 0.05$.
Sources: Young (1991: 144–5), Young and Yandell (1999)

one or another linguistic variant and the systematicity that often underlies variable language production. The choice then, is not whether to do multivariate analysis, but which particular model to use. Within the quantitative tradition, VARBRUL has generally been the preferred tool. As Berdan notes, "VARBRUL has . . . proven to be a powerful analytic device for identifying significant linguistic, social, and interactional factors that differentiate or condition probabilities associated with linguistic variables" (1996: 209). Nevertheless, although VARBRUL can serve effectively to model variation among linguistic factors, it is not appropriate where interaction, either among non-linguistic factors, or between non-linguistic and linguistic factors, is a main focus of the study. In that case, a more general logistic regression model is preferable. Finally, there is the question of audience. Most researchers trained in quantitative sociolinguistics are familiar with VARBRUL, at least to the extent of being able to interpret the results presented in variationist studies. However, the program and the terminology associated with it are unfamiliar to readers outside the field of quantitative sociolinguistics. For this reason, Young and Yandell (1999) recommend the use of widely available programs such as the GENMOD procedure in SAS/STAT for the analysis of interlanguage variation, where the audience is drawn from many disciplines.

6   Future Directions: Variationist Ethnography

Books by Chambers (1995) and Wolfram and Schilling-Estes (1998) review in detail many of the achievements of more than three and a half decades of research within the quantitative paradigm. It is now beyond dispute that much of the variation in language that was previously thought to be random is indeed systematic, and that eloquence, logic, and clarity of expression are not the particular properties of standard languages. Moreover, although public attitudes have been slow to change, work on socially stigmatized varieties, particularly the varieties used by ethnic minorities and members of the working class, has served as important evidence to combat popular misperceptions of such varieties as being illogical and their speakers as incapable of mastering national or regional standard varieties. On the contrary, sociolinguistic analysis has revealed beyond any doubt that these varieties are orderly, complex, and complete linguistic systems. In this respect, Labov's (1969b) seminal essay, "The logic of nonstandard English," has proven particularly important. The work of Geneva Smitherman, Labov, and other scholars in establishing the linguistic rights of African-American school children (Labov 1982), at least in one area of the United States, provides an example of the influence of sociolinguistics in the judicial arena. More recently, Baugh (2000), Rickford (1999), and many others in the field have sought to resolve some of the public confusion and to combat the racist stereotypes surrounding the Oakland, California school board's attempt to use AAVE to teach standard English. Finally, it is well-established that synchronic variation provides a key to understanding language change (Milroy 1992).

Despite these substantial achievements, work in the quantitative paradigm has focused less on exploring the meaning of linguistic variation to the members of the communities studied than on demonstrating the systematic nature of variability at an abstract level and establishing correlations among linguistic variables and traditional social categories such as age and class. Studies are beginning to appear, however, that not only demonstrate the correlations between the use of linguistic variables and social categories, but also show how speakers deploy their linguistic resources, along with other symbolic resources, to construct and reinforce the social categories to which they belong. Eckert's (1989, 2000) work on Euro-American high school students in the Detroit area and Mendoza-Denton's (1997) study of Chicana and Mexican immigrant adolescents in California are two important examples of this direction in research within the quantitative paradigm.

Traditionally, variationist studies have grouped participants according to pre-determined social categories such as class, ethnicity, gender, and age,[8] and examined possible correlations between these non-linguistic factors and use of socially salient linguistic variables. Rather than grouping participants by pre-determined social categories, Eckert and Mendoza-Denton, through intensive ethnographic investigation, sought to discover the social categories that participants themselves found meaningful. At times, these categories overlapped with the categories usually considered in variationist studies, but at other times they differed considerably. For example, Mendoza-Denton found six distinct groups among the Mexican immigrant and Chicana students in a California high school, ranging from immigrant *piporras* ("country girls"), who tended to preserve traditional rural Mexican values, to the mostly non-immigrant "Latina jocks," who participated in the school culture, especially sports, and tended to accept the values of the larger society that the school represented. Moreover, different group affiliation was associated with differing patterns of language use, including different VARBRUL weights for raising and lowering of /ɪ/, the variable Mendoza-Denton examined in detail. Clearly, much would have been lost by simply grouping speakers according to ethnicity or immigrant generation.

Although ethnographically oriented studies of variation such as Eckert (2000) and Mendoza-Denton (1997) have been relatively unusual, they are certainly not unprecedented. As Eckert points out, the concern with local identity and participants' views of that identity was a central focus of one of the earliest studies in the quantitative tradition, Labov's (1963) examination of centralization of (ay) and (aw) by residents of Martha's Vineyard in Massachusetts. In this sense, then, some of the more interesting recent work within the quantitative paradigm represents a return to the roots of the discipline.

In summary, quantitative analysis has enabled us to obtain numerous insights into linguistic structure, the social meaning of linguistic variation, and the nature of language change. From a social perspective, the methods of multivariate analysis developed in sociolinguistics have been particularly important in demonstrating the systematic nature of stigmatized language varieties, including AAVE, Montreal French, popular Puerto Rican and US Spanish, as well as many others. Current work, in which quantitative analysis is informed by ethnographic fieldwork, promises further insights into the ways in which language users employ variation to construct social identities. Finally, thanks to the widespread availability of powerful statistical software packages, sociolinguists now have many options at their disposal. As the field becomes more experienced in quantitative methods, and particularly in the range of available multivariate applications, new creative possibilities for quantitative analysis will doubtless open up.

ACKNOWLEDGMENTS

Work on this chapter was supported by a University of Texas at San Antonio Faculty Research Award. Many of the ideas expressed here have been developed over the years through conversations with Gregory Guy and Dennis Preston, and through collaboration with Richard Young, with whom I co-authored a guide to VARBRUL analysis (Young and Bayley, 1996) and conducted a number of workshops on quantitative methods. The chapter also benefited from Jack Chambers' careful editing and numerous helpful suggestions. Faults that remain, of course, are my own.

NOTES

1   A number of researchers, including Berdan (1996), Fasold (1991), Guy (1993), and Sankoff (1988), have pointed out that much of the work done as "variable rule analysis" does not involve rules of the type illustrated here. As Sankoff (1988) observed, however, the statistical analysis does not depend on the origin of the variation in the data.

2   GoldVarb 2.1 and a brief manual may be downloaded from David Sankoff's web page: www.crm.umontreal.ca/~sankoff/GoldVarb_Eng.html. VARBRUL for MS-DOS is available by anonymous ftp at the University of Pennsylvania by setting your web browser to: ftp://ftp.cis.upenn.edu/pub/ldc/misc_sw/varbrul.tar.Z.

3   The issue of whether copula absence represents a deletion or an insertion rule is important to debates about the origin of AAVE. Evidence that copula absence is the result of an insertion rule would support a creolist position on the origin of AAVE. On the other hand, evidence for a deletion rule, whereby copula deletion follows copula contraction, as Labov (1969a) proposed, would support the position that AAVE is essentially similar to other dialects of English.

4   Guy (1988) discusses the issue of dealing with interactions in detail. See also Bayley et al. (2000) for one solution to the problem of interaction.

5 For up-to-date information on VARBRUL for Windows, contact Dr. Sali Tagliamonte at sali.tagliamonte@utoronto.ca.

6 When more than one linguistic variable is involved, and the researcher wishes to investigate the relationship between individual use of a number of potentially related linguistic variables (e.g. -t,d deletion, alveolization of /ŋ/, and negative concord) and social distinctions, principal components analysis is an effective method. See Horvath and Sankoff's (1987) study of the Sydney speech community for an example of the use of this method.

7 See Reitveld and van Hout (1993) for information on the use and interpretation of general logistic regression models.

8 There are, of course, important exceptions to this traditional practice, including Labov's (1972a) work with the Jets and the Cobras in New York. In addition, Gillian Sankoff (1980, 1989) has long combined ethnographic and variationist approaches in her work in Montreal and New Guinea. The social network approach developed by James and Lesley Milroy represents another exception.

REFERENCES

Baugh, John (1983). *Black Street Speech: Its History, Structure, and Survival*. Austin, TX: University of Texas Press.

- Baugh, John (2000). *Beyond Ebonics: Linguistic Pride and Racial Prejudice*. New York: Oxford University Press.

Bayley, Robert (1994a). Consonant cluster reduction in Tejano English. *Language Variation and Change* 6: 303–26.

Bayley, Robert (1994b). Interlanguage variation and the quantitative paradigm. In Elaine Tarone, Susan M. Gass and Andrew Cohen (eds.), *Research Methodology in Second-language Acquisition*. Hillsdale, NJ: Lawrence Erlbaum. 157–81.

Bayley, Robert (1997). Variation in Tejano English: Evidence for variable lexical phonology. In Cynthia Bernstein, Thomas Nunnally and Robin Sabino (eds.), *Language Variety in the South*

Revisited. Tuscaloosa: University of Alabama Press. 197–209.

Bayley, Robert, Ceil Lucas and Mary Rose (2000). Variation in American Sign Language: The case of DEAF. *Journal of Sociolinguistics* 4: 81–107.

Bayley, Robert and Lucinda Pease-Alvarez (1997). Null pronoun variation in Mexican-descent children's narrative discourse. *Language Variation and Change* 9: 349–71.

Beebe, Leslie M. (1977). The influence of the listener on code-switching. *Language Learning* 27: 331–9.

Berdan, Robert (1996). Disentangling language acquisition from language variation. In Robert Bayley and Dennis R. Preston (eds.), *Second Language Acquisition and Linguistic Variation*. Amsterdam: John Benjamins. 203–44.

Cedergren, Henrietta (1973). The interplay of social and linguistic factors in Panama. Ph.D. dissertation, Cornell University.

Cedergren, Henrietta and David Sankoff (1974). Variable rules: Performance as a statistical reflection of competence. *Language* 50: 233–55.

Chambers, J. K. (1995). *Sociolinguistic Theory: Linguistic Variation and its Social Significance*. Oxford: Blackwell.

Eckert, Penelope (1989). *Jocks and Burnouts: Social Categories and Identity in the High School*. New York: Teachers' College Press.

Eckert, Penelope (2000). *Linguistic Variation as Social Practice: The Linguistic Construction of Identity in Belten High*. Oxford: Blackwell.

Fasold, Ralph (1991). The quiet demise of variable rules. *American Speech* 66: 3–21.

Feagin, Crawford (1979). *Variation and Change in Alabama English: A Sociolinguistic Study of the White Community*. Washington, DC: Georgetown University Press.

Guy, Gregory R. (1980). Variation in the group and in the individual: The case of final stop deletion. In William Labov (ed.), *Locating Language in Time and Space*. New York: Academic. 1–36.

Guy, Gregory R. (1981). Linguistic variation in Brazilian Portuguese: Aspects of the phonology, syntax, and language history. Ph.D. dissertation, University of Pennsylvania.

Guy, Gregory R. (1988). Advanced VARBRUL analysis. In Kathleen Ferrara, Becky Brown, Keith Walters and John Baugh. (eds.), *Linguistic Contact and Change: Proceedings of the Sixteenth Annual Conference on New Ways of Analyzing Variation*. Austin, TX: University of Texas Department of Linguistics. 124–36.

Guy, Gregory R. (1991). Explanation in variable phonology. *Language Variation and Change* 3: 1–22.

Guy, Gregory R. (1993). Quantitative analysis. In Dennis R. Preston (ed.), *American Dialect Research*. Amsterdam: John Benjamins. 223–49.

Guy, Gregory R. (1997). The grammar of variation. In Frans Hinskens, Roeland van Hout and W. Leo Wetzels (eds.), *Variation, Change and Phonological Theory*. Amsterdam: John Benjamins. 125–43.

Horvath, Barbara and David Sankoff (1987). Delimiting the Sydney speech community. *Language in Society* 16: 179–204.

Kiparsky, Paul (1985). Some consequences of lexical phonology. In Colin McEwen and James Anderson (eds.), *Phonology Yearbook 2*. Cambridge: Cambridge University Press. 85–138.

Kiparsky, Paul (1994). An optimality-theoretic perspective on variable rules. Paper presented at NWAVE 23, Stanford University, California.

Labov, William (1963). The social motivation of a sound change. *Word* 19: 273–307.

Labov, William (1966). *The Social Stratification of English in New York City*. Washington, DC: Center for Applied Linguistics.

Labov, William (1969a). Contraction, deletion, and inherent variability of the English copula. *Language* 45: 715–62.

Labov, William (1969b). The logic of nonstandard English. *Georgetown Monographs in Languages and Linguistics* 22: 1–44.

Labov, William (1972a). *Language in the Inner City: Studies in the Black English Vernacular*. Philadelphia: University of Pennsylvania Press.

Labov, William (1972b). *Sociolinguistic Patterns*. Philadelphia: University of Pennsylvania Press.

Labov, William (1978) Where does the sociolinguistic variable stop? A reply to B. Lavendera. *Texas Working Papers in Sociolinguistics* 44. Austin, TX: SW Educational Development Laboratory.

Labov, William (1982). Objectivity and commitment in linguistic science: The case of the Black English trial in Ann Arbor. *Language in Society* 11: 165–201.

Labov, William (1989). The child as linguistic historian. *Language Variation and Change* 1: 85–97.

Labov, William (1994). *Principles of Linguistic Change*, vol. 1: *Internal factors*. Oxford: Blackwell.

Labov, William (1997). Resyllabification. In Frans Hinskens, Roeland van Hout and W. Leo Wetzels (eds.), *Variation, Change and Phonological Theory*. Amsterdam: John Benjamins. 145–79.

Labov, William, Paul Cohen, Clarence Robins and John Lewis, (1968). *A Study of the Non-standard English of Negro and Puerto Rican Speakers in New York City*. Philadelphia: US Regional Survey.

Lavendera, Beatrice (1978). Where does the sociolinguistic variable stop? *Language in Society* 7: 171–82.

Liddell, Scott K. and Robert E. Johnson (1989). American Sign Language: The phonological base. *Sign Language Studies* 64: 195–278.

Lucas, Ceil (1995). Sociolinguistic variation in ASL: The case of DEAF. In Ceil Lucas (ed.), *Sociolinguistics in Deaf Communities*, vol. 1. Washington, DC: Gallaudet University Press. 3–25.

Mendoza-Denton, Norma (1997). Chicana/Mexican identity and linguistic variation: An ethnographic and sociolinguistic study of gang affiliation in an urban high school. Ph.D. dissertation, Stanford University, California.

Milroy, James (1992). *Linguistic Variation and Change*. Oxford: Blackwell.

Milroy, Lesley (1987). *Language and Social Networks*, 2nd edn. Oxford: Blackwell.

Norušis, Marija J. and SPSS Inc. (1996). *SPSS Advanced Statistics 6.1*. Chicago: SPSS Inc.

Pintzuk, Susan (1988). VARBRUL programs for MS-DOS [computer software]. Philadelphia: University of Pennsylvania Department of Linguistics.

Poplack, Shana (1980). "Sometimes I'll begin a sentence in Spanish and *termino in español*": Towards a typology of code-switching. *Linguistics* 18: 581–618.

Poplack, Shana and Svitlana Budzhak-Jones (1998). The visible loanword: Processes of integration seen in bare English-origin nouns in Ukrainian. In Vera Regan (ed.), *Contemporary Approaches to Second Language Acquisition in Social Context*. Dublin: University College Dublin Press. 137–67.

Rand, David and David Sankoff (1991). *GoldVarb: A Variable Rule Application for the Macintosh* (version 2.1) [computer program]. Montreal: Centre de recherches mathématiques, Université de Montréal.

Reitveld, Toni and Roeland van Hout (1993). *Statistical Techniques in the Study of Language and Language Behavior*. Berlin: de Gruyter.

Rickford, John R. (1987). *Dimensions of a Creole Continuum: History, Texts, and Linguistic Analysis of Guyanese Creole*. Stanford, CA: Stanford University Press.

Rickford, John R. (1999). The Ebonics controversy in my backyard: A sociolinguist's experiences and reflections. *Journal of Sociolinguistics* 3: 267–75.

Rickford, John R. Arnetha Ball, Renée Blake, Raina Jackson and Naomi Martin (1991). Rappin on the copula coffin: Theoretical and methodological issues in the analysis of copula variation in African-American Vernacular English. *Language Variation and Change* 3: 103–32.

Roberts, Julie (1997). Acquisition of variable rules: A study of (-t,d) deletion in preschool children. *Journal of Child Language* 24: 351–72.

Rousseau, Pascale (1989). A versatile program for the analysis of sociolinguistic data. In Ralph W. Fasold and Deborah Schiffrin (eds.), *Language Change and Variation*. Amsterdam: John Benjamins. 395–409.

Rousseau, Pascale and David Sankoff (1978). Advances in variable rule methodology. In David Sankoff (ed.), *Linguistic Variation: Models and Methods*. New York: Academic. 57–69.

Saito, Hidetoshi (1999). Dependence and interaction in frequency data analysis in SLA research. *Studies in Second Language Acquisition* 21: 453–75.

Sankoff, David (1988). Variable rules. In Ulrich Ammon, Norbert Dittmar and Klaus J. Mattheier (eds.), *Sociolinguistics: An International Handbook of the Science of Language and Society*, vol. 2. Berlin: de Gruyter. 984–97.

Sankoff, David and William Labov (1979). On the uses of variable rules. *Language in Society* 9: 189–222.

Sankoff, Gillian (1980). *The Social Life of Language*. Philadelphia: University of Pennsylvania Press.

Sankoff, Gillian (1989). A quantitative paradigm for the study of communicative competence. In Richard Bauman and Joel Sherzer (eds.), *Explorations in the Ethnography of Speaking*, 2nd edn. Cambridge: Cambridge University Press. 18–49.

Sankoff, Gillian (1990). The grammaticalization of tense and aspect in Tok Pisin and Sranan. *Language Variation and Change* 2: 295–312.

Santa Ana A., Otto (1992). Chicano English evidence for the exponential hypothesis: A variable rule pervades lexical phonology. *Language Variation and Change* 4: 275–89.

SAS Institute Inc. (1996). *SAS/STAT Software: Changes and Enhancements through Release 6.11*. Cary, NC: SAS Institute Inc.

Schiffrin, Deborah (1982). Tense variation in narrative. *Language* 57: 45–62.

Schumann, John H. (1978). *The Pidginization Process: A model for Second Language Acquisition*. Rowley, MA: Newbury House.

Tarone, Elaine (1985). Variability in interlanguage use: A study of style-shifting in morphology and syntax. *Language Learning* 35: 373–404.

Trudgill, Peter (1974). *The Social Differentiation of English in Norwich*. Cambridge: Cambridge University Press.

Weiner, E. Judith and William Labov (1983). Constraints on the agentless passive. *Journal of Linguistics* 19: 29–58.

Weinreich, Uriel, William Labov and Marvin Herzog (1968). Empirical foundations for a theory of language change. In Winfred P. Lehmann and Yakov Malkiel (eds.), *Directions for Historical Linguistics: A Symposium*. Austin, TX: University of Texas Press. 95–188.

Wolfram, Walt (1969). *A Sociolinguistic Description of Detroit Negro Speech*. Washington, DC: Center for Applied Linguistics.

Wolfram, Walt and Ralph W. Fasold (1974). *The Study of Social Dialects in* the United States. Englewood Cliffs, NJ: Prentice-Hall.

Wolfram, Walt and Natalie Schilling-Estes (1998). *American English: Dialects and Variation*. Oxford: Blackwell.

Young, Richard (1991). *Variation in Interlanguage Morphology*. New York: Peter Lang.

Young, Richard and Robert Bayley (1996). VARBRUL analysis for second language acquisition research. In Robert Bayley and Dennis R. Preston (eds.), *Second Language Acquisition and Linguistic Variation*. Amsterdam: John Benjamins. 253–306.

Young, Richard and Brian Yandell (1999). Top-down versus bottom-up analyses of interlanguage data: A reply to Saito. *Studies in Second Language Acquisition* 21: 477–88.

6 Implicational Scales

JOHN R. RICKFORD

Implicational scales represent an important device for revealing structure in variability, and for demonstrating that what some linguists might dismiss as random or free variation is significantly constrained.[1] Introduced to linguistics in 1968 by David DeCamp for the analysis of the Jamaican Creole continuum, they have since been used for studying sociolinguistic variation and change in a wide spectrum of language varieties (including American sign language), for understanding linguistic intuitions, and for modeling second language acquisition (SLA).

In recent years, it is primarily variationists engaged in the study of SLA who have continued to make active use of implicational scales – for instance, Pienemann and Mackey (1993), Nagy et al. (1996), and Bayley (1999). But because of their potential utility, all students of linguistic variation and change should know how to interpret and use them. Variationists should also be familiar with some of the theoretical and descriptive issues involved in the use of implicational scales in the literature, including the role that scaling and its associated "dynamic" paradigm played in the development of variation theory.

The use of implicational scales in sociolinguistics has declined after an auspicious start. At the 29th annual conference on New Ways of Analyzing Variation (NWAV 29) in October, 2000, the only significant references to implicational scales occurred in a workshop on multidimensional scaling and correspondence analysis. By contrast, at the very first NWAV conference in October, 1972 (Bailey and Shuy 1973), there were at least ten papers that referred to implicational scales. One such paper was Derek Bickerton's "Quantitative versus dynamic paradigms: the case of Montreal *que*" (1973a) whose very title drew attention to differences between the quantitative and implicationalist or dynamic approaches. Sankoff (1973) and Labov (1973), leaders of the quantitative paradigm, included implicational scales as models of the facts of Montreal French and the possible relations between dialects, respectively. Anshen (1973), Fasold (1973) and Robson (1973) discussed problems with assumptions or methods of the implicationalist approach, while DeCamp (1973) attempted to provide solutions to two earlier critiques of implicational scales. The syntactic squishes of Albury (1973), Sag (1973) and Ross (1973), though far removed from the "dynamic" approach that C. J. Bailey and Derek Bickerton were advocating for implicational patterns, all used implicational arrays to demonstrate that their synchronic syntactic "dialects" were well-ordered. Clearly, then, implicational scales were a central element in the early days of variation theory.

What are implicational scales? In linguistics – this qualification is necessary because similar scales are widely used in the social sciences for the measurement of attitudes and other constructs (see Gorden 1977) – implicational scales depict hierarchical co-occurrence patterns in the acquisition or use of linguistic variables by individuals or groups, such that x implies y but not the reverse. When linguistic variables are distributed in implicational patterns, the scope of variability is significantly constrained. For instance, suppose that dialects in a community differ with respect to whether they have or do not have each of three rules, A, B, and C. If the variation is random, there are a total of *eight* possible dialect patterns (2^3, or in general, k to the n, where k = the number of values or variants of each variable, and n = the number of variables). But if the variation forms a perfect implicational pattern, there are only *four* possible dialect patterns or scale types ($n + 1$, for a binary variable), for instance, those shown in table 6.1a. The four excluded patterns are shown in table 6.1b. Because the data form a linear, unidimensional scale, we are able to reduce

Table 6.1a Implicational scale of four lects in relation to use of three hypothetical rules

Scale types or lects	Rule A	Rule B	Rule C
1	+	+	+
2	+	+	−
3	+	−	−
4	−	−	−

Table 6.1b Patterns or lects excluded by the scale model underlying table 6.1a

Excluded patterns	Rule A	Rule B	Rule C
5	−	+	−
6	−	+	+
7	−	−	+
8	+	−	+

the number of possible patterns by half, and to make very precise predictions. If a dialect has only one of these rules, for instance, we can predict that the rule in question is A (not B or C); if it has only two, that the second rule is B (not C), and so on. As the number of items increases, the constraining effect and predictive power of scaling are even more dramatic. For example, with nine binary variables – and several scales in the variation literature have at least this many – there are 512 (or 2^9) possible arrangements of + and −, but only 10 (or 9 + 1) scale types actually occur.

1   In the Beginning: DeCamp's Scale for the Jamaican Creole Continuum

As noted above, David DeCamp is credited with introducing implicational scales to linguistics, in a paper presented at a 1968 creole conference in Jamaica whose proceedings (Hymes 1971) were highly influential both in pidgin-creole studies and variation theory.[2] This credit is fully deserved, but there are three curious things about it from a history of science perspective. First of all, the scaling technique itself had been invented earlier by Guttman (1944) for the measurement of social attitudes, and it is known among statisticians and social scientists as Guttman scaling or scalogram analysis (see for instance, Torgerson 1958, Dunn-Rankin 1983). As DeCamp later noted (1971: 369), he did not realize he had been "anticipated" by Guttman until after the 1968 Jamaica conference; he had independently developed the scaling technique in 1959 and had been presenting it at professional meetings and in public lectures as his own innovation. Second, although DeCamp used them in a somewhat different way, it was Greenberg (1963: 73), studying language universals and typology, who first discovered the existence of implicational relationships in language (see Politzer 1976: 123): given x in a language, we always find y. Thirdly, while DeCamp (1971: 355–7) outlined a method for constructing an implicational scale based on the usage of six features and seven Jamaican speakers, and told us what the resultant orderings would be, he did not actually present the completed scale.

The only tabular array DeCamp provided in relation to his six features and seven speakers is the unordered array shown as table 6.2a, but since this is closer to the point at which the work of the variation analyst actually begins, it is excellent for pedagogical purposes. Most statistical packages (SPSS, SYSTAT, and so on) include programs for Guttman or scalogram analysis, but it is helpful to know how to construct one by hand. I do not recommend following the procedure DeCamp himself outlined (1971: 356) – which does not result in anything looking like a conventional implicational scale. What I will present instead is a modified version of the procedure outlined in McIver and Carmines (1981: 44–6).

Table 6.2a   The unordered array of Jamaican speakers and features in DeCamp (1971: 355)

Speakers	Features A	B	C	D	E	F
1	+	+	+	−	+	+
2	−	+	−	−	+	+
3	−	+	−	−	−	−
4	−	−	−	−	−	−
5	+	+	+	+	+	+
6	+	⊦	−	−	+	+
7	−	+	−	−	+	−

Key:

A	B	C	D	E	F
+ = child	+ = eat	+ = /th~t/	+ = /dh~d/	+ = granny	+ = didn't
− = pikni	− = nyam	− = /t/	− = /d/	− = nana	− = no ben

Table 6.2b   Reordering or "translating" the columns of table 6.2a in terms of number of plusses

Speakers	Features B	E	F	A	C	D
1	+	+	+	+	+	−
2	+	+	+	−	−	−
3	+	−	−	−	−	−
4	−	−	−	−	−	−
5	+	+	+	+	+	+
6	+	+	+	+	−	−
7	+	+	−	−	−	−
Plusses:	6	5	4	3	2	1

Beginning with unordered data, you first compute the number of plusses for each column, and then reorder or "translate" the columns (McIver and Carmines 1981: 45) in descending order from left to right with respect to the number of plusses they contain, as in table 6.2b. You then compute the number of plusses per row, and reorder those so that they form a descending series from top to bottom, as in table 6.2c. Alternatively, you could reorder the rows first and then the columns, but in each case the output of the first operation

Table 6.2c Reordering or "translating" the rows of table 6.2b to yield a perfect implicational scale

Speakers	B	E	F	Features A	C	D	plusses
5	+	+	+	+	+	+	6
1	+	+	+	+	+	–	5
6	+	+	+	+	–	–	4
2	+	+	+	–	–	–	3
7	+	+	–	–	–	–	2
3	+	–	–	–	–	–	1
4	–	–	–	–	–	–	0

Key:

B	E	F	A	C	D
+ = eat	+ = granny	+ = didn't	+ = child	+ = /th~t/	+ = /dh~d/
– = nyam	– = nana	– = no ben	– = pikni	– = /t/	– = /d/

serves as input to the second. The cumulative result of both operations is the perfect scale shown in table 6.2c, which we can now use to make several observations about implicational scales, their interpretation and use, and their significance in variation theory.[3]

1.1   *Interpreting the scales*

Table 6.2c provides an implicational ordering both horizontally (from left to right), in terms of linguistic features, and vertically (up and down), in terms of speaker outputs. The *horizontal* implicational relations – the ones to which variationists usually give pride of place – can be stated as follows: a plus anywhere in the matrix implies plusses to the left; a minus anywhere implies minuses to the right. Minuses in this scale represent Creole features, and plusses represent English features,[4] or in the case of columns C and D, variable use of English features. To translate the abstract implicational pattern into linguistic reality, let us focus on just one feature, A. Speakers (like 5, 1, and 6) who have a plus for feature A (saying *child* instead of *pikni*) will also have plusses for features F, E, and B (using *didn't* instead of *no ben*, *granny* instead of *nana*, and *eat* instead of *nyam*). By contrast, speakers (like 2, 7, 3, and 4) who have a minus for feature A (saying *pikni*), will have minuses for features C and D as well (using voiceless and voiced stops instead of interdental fricatives).

Scaling, as Gorden (1977: 1) reminds us, is a means of measuring a common underlying property, and an implicational scale, as Pavone (1980: 64–5) observes, is a sophisticated ordinal scale, simultaneously ordering subjects and items with respect to that underlying property. In the case of table 6.2c, and most creole continuum scales, the property is relative ordering on a Creole-to-English continuum, which we could conceptualize as relative "Creoleness." What the horizontal ordering of features in this table reveals is that while *nyam, nana, no ben* and so on are all Creole variants, some are more markedly Creole than others; *nyam*, for instance, is the most markedly Creole variant, and using it predicts use of Creole variants for each of the other features. To the extent that one thinks of table 6.2c as depicting a continuum produced by a diachronic process of decreolization – a point on which we will elaborate below – it is in this most marked environment (note the plethora of plusses for column B) that the process would be assumed to have begun. Alternatively, one could conceptualize the underlying property that table 6.2c measures as "Englishness" – treating the variable use of the voiced interdental fricative as the most marked feature, the one that predicts use of English variants (or decreolization) in every other linguistic category. Regardless of how we conceptualize it (in terms of the plus values, or relative "Englishness," or in terms of the minus values, or relative "Creoleness"), table 6.2c represents one underlying dimension (as is usually the case with implicational scales), not two.[5]

Vertically, a plus anywhere in table 6.2c implies plusses above, and a minus anywhere implies minuses below. It is not clear what the vertical ordering in any one column means, at the level of individual cognition and use. Presumably speakers like 1 who use a plus for feature E might be aware that there are more speakers like them who have plus values for this feature than there are who have plus values for feature C, but this has never really been considered or investigated. In terms of the overall ordering of speaker outputs or lects, defined by Bailey (1973a: 11) as "a completely noncommital term for any bundling together of linguistic phenomena,"[6] lect 5 is the acrolect (most English or least Creole variety), and lect 4 the basilect (least English or most Creole). The intervening varieties are mesolects, or intermediate varieties, illustrating DeCamp's more general point that the Jamaican Creole continuum does not simply consist of two discrete varieties. At the same time, recognition of a continuum does not open the door to chaos; for a six-variable (n) two-valued (k) scale like this one, scaling limits the number of possible lects or scale types to seven ($n + 1$) instead of 64 (k^n).

More importantly, once speakers' outputs are ordered on purely linguistic grounds, they can be given social interpretations. DeCamp notes, for instance, that

> informant 5, at one end . . . , is a young and well-educated proprietor of a successful radio and appliance shop in Montego Bay; that informant 4, at the other end . . . , is an elderly and illiterate peasant farmer in an isolated mountain village; and that the social and economic facts on the other informants are roughly (not exactly) proportional to these informants' positions on the continuum. (DeCamp 1971: 358)

DeCamp (1971) and Bickerton (1971, 1973a: 40) both emphasized the importance of ordering individuals on the basis of their linguistic usage and then looking at their social characteristics in terms of socioeconomic class, network and the like, and they were critical of the quantitativists for beginning with social categories and presenting group means that might obscure or distort individual patterns. In this respect, they were followed by variationists such as LePage and Tabouret-Keller (1985: 137ff), who although using statistical clustering techniques instead of implicational scales, also began by clustering their speakers in terms of common linguistic behavior rather than in terms of social categories. Quantitativists never followed the implicationalists in this regard – Sankoff (1974) explicitly defended the practice of beginning with social categories in order to have results that "correspond to socially or culturally meaningful categories." However, as a result of the implicationalist critique, they began making more of an effort to show that individuals exemplified the constraint patterning postulated on the basis of group averages, and they began to address the relation of individual to group grammars as a theoretical and empirical issue (Guy 1980).

1.2   *Scales, rules, and style-shifting*

DeCamp suggested that the scalar ordering of features and varieties could be used to facilitate the writing of linguistic rules for the entire community:

> it would be unnecessary to specify within each rule the entire list of speech varieties (i.e. points on the continuum) which activate or block that rule. It would be sufficient to identify the point on the continuum beyond which the rule does or does not operate.   (DeCamp 1971: 353)

For instance, for the hypothetical data set in table 6.1a, one could add to rule A the notation [≤3], to show that it applies to lect 3, and to all lower numbered lects (2, 1). As DeCamp observed (1971: 353), "this approach thus provides a very economical and meaningful way of incorporating many linguistic varieties into one grammatical description." DeCamp's useful suggestion was never really taken up by subsequent researchers. This was partly perhaps because of practical difficulties (the number and composition of possible lects could vary from one area of the grammar to another, even from one set of constraints on a single rule to another), and partly perhaps because of theoretical or conceptual ones (a declining interest in community-wide "grammars," and in the mechanics of rule-writing itself).[7]

DeCamp also suggested that the lects of an implicational scale could be used for the study of style shifting, since individuals would not shift randomly, but only to implicationally ordered patterns already present in the community. That is, that socially or geographically defined "dialects" could also be alternative "stylelects" within the range of an individual speaker's repertoire. This proposal was endorsed by Stolz and Bills (1968: 21) and Bickerton (1973b), and it has intriguing parallels with the subsequent proposal of Bell (1984) that intra-speaker variation is in general later than and to some extent parasitic on inter-speaker variation.

There are several ways in which subsequent implicational scales in the literature differed from DeCamp's pioneering scale. For one thing, DeCamp's scale, like Stolz and Bill's (1968) scale for Central Texas English, covered a disparate set of linguistic features (phonological, lexical, and morpho-syntactic), but subsequent researchers preferred to scale closely related items in a single area of the phonology or grammar, or related environments of a single rule. Second, while the scales of both of these pioneering studies were restricted to binary values (+ and −), and arbitrary thresholds were sometimes set up to classify speakers' variable usage as belonging to one categorical extreme or another (see Stolz and Bills 1968: 13–14), subsequent researchers allowed for greater variation within each lect. In the simplest case, scales became three-valued, allowing for variable use of a feature or variable application in an environment (marked by "x" in table 6.3, for instance); in the most complicated case, they included frequencies themselves, permitting a level of precision in terms of implicational orderings which was initially considered to be difficult (cf. DeCamp 1973: 147) or to be excluded by the implicational paradigm (Fasold 1970). Third, subsequent scales based on speaker outputs often included a "scalability" measure of the goodness-of-fit between the actual data and the predictions of the scale model. Although table 6.2c was a perfect scale, in the sense that it included no cells deviating from the ideal scale pattern, DeCamp himself told James Pavone (see Pavone 1980: 120, 178) that the actual data were not error-free, and this was the experience of all later researchers. Finally, DeCamp offered no diachronic interpretations for the implicational patterns in his data, but Bailey (1971, 1973a, 1973b) and Bickerton (1971, 1973a, 1973b) linked such patterns to the effects of ongoing or completed change, leading to the characterization of the implicational approach as the "dynamic" paradigm. We will touch on these issues (and others) as we review the scales of other researchers below.

2 Dynamicizing and Elaborating the Model: Bailey and Bickerton

C. J. Bailey, in a series of papers (1969, 1970, 1973b) and an integrative book (1973a), built on DeCamp's "important paper of 1968" (Bailey 1970: 3) to construct a dynamic model of variation in which synchronic implicational patterns are seen as reflections of linguistic changes spreading in waves through linguistic and geographical/social space. Derek Bickerton, in a series of papers from the same period (1971, 1973a, 1973b, 1973c), articulated, exemplified, and extended Bailey's principles and the method of implicational scaling, primarily with data from the highly variable Guyanese Creole-English continuum. He also launched the most trenchant critiques of the quantitative, variable rule paradigm,[8] and the fact that these attacks were published in leading linguistics journals (*Language, Journal of Linguistics*) increased their impact.

Probably the clearest and most succinct statement of Bailey's dynamic interpretation of synchronic implicational patterns comes from Bickerton:

> implicational phenomena ... arise as a result of waves of change spreading through a speech community (therefore moving in time as well as space) so that at any given time a particular change will not have 'passed' certain speakers but will not yet have 'reached' others, while those who it has 'passed' will also (anomalies apart) have experienced the change waves that preceded it. ... In other words, a wave model, collapsing the synchronic–diachronic distinction, had dimensions of both space and time, and implicational relationships come about only because an original change, while it is being diffused through (in this case, social) space, is also being generalized through time in the place where it

Table 6.3 Schematized illustration of the change that raises the vowel nucleus of words like *ham* to that of *hem* in the different environments shown[a]

Following consonants:	m n	f θ s	d	b	ʃ	g	v z	p t k	l
Locales/lects	(a)	(b)	(c)	(d)	(e)	(f)	(g)	(h)	(i)
0 *	−	−	−	−	−	−	−	−	−
1 *	×	−	−	−	−	−	−	−	−
2 Birdsboro	+	×	−	−	−	−	−	−	−
3 Philadelphia	+	+	×	−	−	−	−	−	−
4 Mammouth Junction	+	+	+	×	−	−	−	−	−
5 Ringoes	+	+	+	+	×	−	−	−	−
6 Jackson	+	+	+	+	+	×	−	−	−
7 New York City	+	+	+	+	+	+	×	−	−
8 *	+	+	+	+	+	+	+	×	−
9 *	+	+	+	+	+	+	+	+	×
10 Buffalo	+	+	+	+	+	+	+	+	+

[a] "A minus denotes the categorical nonoperation of the rule for the change; x denotes the variable operation of the rule; a plus sign denotes its categorical operation. An asterisk denotes a thus far unattested, but presumably discoverable pattern. The change is presumed to originate in locale 10, where it is complete in the vernacular style of speaking – the style illustrated in this table" (Bailey 1973b: 158).

originated (i.e. it spreads to more and more environments until it is completely unconditioned). (Bickerton 1971: 476–81)

We can use this general statement and Bailey's principle 20 – "What is quantitatively less is slower and later; what is more is earlier and faster" (1973a: 82) – to interpret the implicational scale in table 6.2c as depicting a general process of decreolization. It is most advanced in lect 5 (the one with the most plusses), and at the other extreme, has not yet begun to affect lect 4 (which has no plusses). Again, from the more/less evidence of the columns, we might assume that, in terms of these six features at least, decreolization began with feature B and spread in waves to features E, F, A, C, and D. Of course, this depends on whether one believes in decreolization as a qualitative phenomenon, involving the progressive loss of basilectal features (see Mufwene 1999: 158ff) and whether one has independent evidence (from real or apparent time) that it has taken place or is taking place.[9] But the implicational scale, interpreted according to dynamic principles, provides a clear set of diachronic predictions which can be empirically investigated.

Table 6.3, described by Bailey as as "an idealization of [the] data" in Labov (1971: 427), illustrates two more of Bailey's dynamic principles: that linguistic change begins in a very restricted or marked environment (principle 8a in Bailey 1973a: 55–6) and spreads from there to less marked or more general environments; and that it begins variably before becoming categorical. The scale as a whole depicts the raising of /æ/ in a range of following phonological environments and geographic locales; a plus (categorical application) anywhere implies plusses to the right and below, and a minus (categorical nonapplication) implies minuses to the right and above. The scale is three-valued, with a single *x* (optional or variable usage) intervening between minuses and plusses. Following Bailey's principle 20, we would once more infer that the change originated in lect 10 (Buffalo) and before non-velar nasals, and spread outwards in linguistic and social space as depicted in table 6.3. Figure 6.1 (from Bailey 1973b: 159, 1973a: 68) is another way of representing the diachronic interpretation of table 6.3, in terms of the kinds of varieties (with respect to the tensing rule) that exist at each locale at successive time periods.

That Bailey was not averse to the incorporation of frequencies in models of the change process is clear from Figure 6.2, which depicts hypothetical frequencies for a linguistic change at a particular point in time. The synchronic implicational pattern – any frequency of rule application implies equivalent or higher frequencies to the left (and below) – is taken to be a reflection of the diachronic spread of the change in waves from the locale and environment at the lower left hand corner of the table (environment a, locale 0) outward and upward. If the change continues to completion, all the cells will eventually reach 100 percent.

Although his 1971 paper is better known for its "no holds barred" attack on the quantitative paradigm, Bickerton's (1973c) paper, dealing with three variables in the Guyanese Creole continuum, better exemplifies the substantive

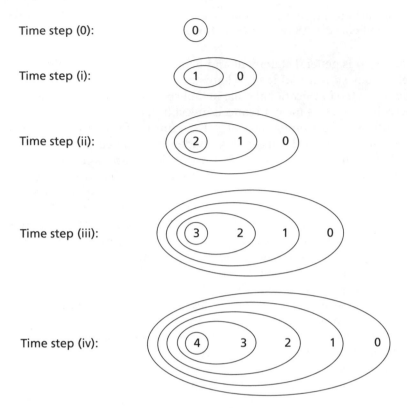

Time step (0):

Time step (i):

Time step (ii):

Time step (iii):

Time step (iv):

Figure 6.1   Wavelike propagation of the change shown in table 6.3. The arabic numerals represent the same varieties of the language here as in table 6.3. The time steps are defined by the changes themselves

Source: Bailey (1973b: 231)

Environment d	20%	10%	0	0
Environment c	80%	20%	10%	
Environment b	90%	80%	20%	10%
Environment a	100%	90%	80%	20%
Locales	0	1	2	3

Figure 6.2   Hypothetical frequencies, at one point in time, for a change spreading in waves to different locales and linguistic environments (point of origin: locale 0, environment a)

Source: Adapted from Bailey (1973a: 79)

Table 6.4 *Tu/fu* variation in the Guyanese Creole Continuum

Speaker	After non-inceptive, non-desiderative verbs (e.g. kom_)	After desiderative and "psychological" verbs (e.g. waan_)	After inceptive and modal verbs (e.g. staat_)
3	1	–	–
6	1	–	–
9	1	1	1
12	1	–	1
20	1	–	–
21	1	–	–
22	1	–	–
24	1	–	1
7	1	–	2
13	1	1	2
16	1	–	2
26	1	1	2
28	1	–	2
11	1	12	2
25	1	12	2
8	1	2	2
2	12	–	(1)
5	12	2	–
14	12	2	2
15	12	–	2
17	12	–	2
27	12	(1)	(1)2
1	2	2	2
4	2	–	2
10	2	–	–
19	2	2	2

1 = fu; 2 = tu. A dash indicates empty cells/no data; parentheses enclose deviant cells, ones which do not confirm to implicational patterning.

Source: Bickerton (1973c: 647) Scalability = 94.64 percent

contributions he made to the implicational scaling paradigm. Table 6.4 shows the implicational scale for variation between *fu* and *tu* as infinitival complementizers (as in *staat fu/tu go* 'start to go') which it contains (1973c: 647).[10] The scale is three-valued, allowing for alternation between basilectal and acrolectal variants (12) as well as categorical use of the basilectal (1) and acrolectal (2) variants, and the linguistic categories are three types of predicates in which these infinitival complementizers arise: I = after modal and inceptive verbs (e.g. staat 'start'), II = desiderative and other psychological verbs (e.g. waan 'want'), III = after verbs not in categories I or II (e.g. kom 'come'). The implicational relations are more complex than in previous scales in the literature, stated by Bickerton as follows:

> deviances apart, the presence of a basilectal index ALONE in a given column implies the presence of similar indices in all columns to the left; while the presence of a non-basilectal index, alone or otherwise, implies the presence of similar indices, alone or otherwise, in all columns to the right.   (Bickerton 1973c: 646)

Deviations from this implicational prediction are enclosed in parentheses, and the scale is accompanied by a "scalability" figure of 94.64 percent, which represents the proportion of non-deviant cells (53) out of the total of filled cells (56). This is somewhat similar to Guttman's Index of Reproducibility (IR), which is:

$$\text{IR} = 1 - \frac{\text{Total number of errors}}{\text{Total number of opportunities for error}} = 1 - \frac{\text{Total number of errors}}{\text{No. cols.} \times \text{No. rows}}$$

except that Guttman's IR presumes completely filled cells, and almost one-third of the cells in table 6.4 are missing, a point to which we will return below.

Bickerton (1973c) also contains substantive implicational analyses of variation in the Guyanese copula system and the singular pronouns, and includes panlectal grids, showing the totality of possible isolects for each subsystem, (e.g. Table 6, 1973c: 664) whether attested or not. Such grids also allowed him to show the distribution of all his speakers on the continuum (e.g. in Figure 2, 1973c: 665), a useful innovation. Finally, in addition to providing information on the social correlates of individuals' placement on the continuum, Bickerton attempted to correlate the relative positions that individuals in one village occupied on implicational scales for the copula and the singular pronouns. He found such correlations weak, casting doubt on the value of seeking implicational relations across different areas of the grammar, as DeCamp (1971) had done. Bickerton also expressed the conviction that inter-subsystem correspondences would be found, "given time, patience, and knowledge of the principles on which they are based" (1973c: 666), but to date, there has been no progress on this front.

3   Other Uses of Implicational Scales

Given their initial use by DeCamp and Bickerton with creole data, it is no surprise that implicational scales have been popular in studies of variation and change in pidgin and creole continua. They have been exploited in the description of Tok Pisin (Woolford 1975), Providence Island Creole (Washabaugh 1977), Belizean Creole (Escure 1982), Hawaiian pidgin and creole (Day 1973, Bickerton and Odo 1976), Jamaica Creole (Akers 1981) and Guyanese Creole (Rickford 1979, 1987b), among others. Interestingly, most of these studies dealt with grammatical variables. By contrast with the quantitative model, which was originally applied to variation in phonology and only later extended to syntax and semantics, the implicational model received its early applications in syntax and the lexicon, and it was only later extended to the analysis of phonological problems (Bailey 1973a, Fasold 1975, Akers 1981).

Implicational scales have also been used for the analysis of linguistic intuitions with regard to syntactic phenomena (e.g. Elliot et al. 1969, Rickford 1975, Hindle and Sag 1975 in addition to the studies by Albury 1973, Ross 1973, and Day 1973 cited earlier). They have also been used to model variation in American sign-language (e.g. by Battison et al. 1975, Woodward 1975), and in a variety of North American and European language situations (Bickerton 1973a, Bailey 1973a, Napoli 1977). Gal's (1979) use of scaling to model the kinds of interlocutors to whom speakers in Oberwart, Austria, used either German or Hungarian, was particularly innovative. "God" was the context in which Hungarian was most highly favored, followed by "grandparents and their generation." At the other extreme, one's "doctor" was the interlocutor to whom German was reported to be most commonly used, followed by "grandchildren and their generation." The differential use of German and Hungarian was evidence of an evolving language shift from Hungarian to German.

However, since the mid-1970s and continuing to today, the subfield of variation studies that has been most favorable to the use of implicational scales, is, as noted above, the study of second language acquisition. Politzer (1976) used scaling to model mastery of the rules for five grammatical contrasts in French and English by San Francisco Bay Area students enroled in bilingual schools. Andersen (1978) used it to study the acquisition of 13 grammatical morphemes in English by Spanish-speaking students at the University of Puerto Rico. Trudgill (1986: 25), drawing on data in Nordenstam (1970), used it to model the order in which Swedes living in Norway acquire Norwegian pronouns. Implicational scales have also been used by Pienemann and Mackey (1993) to depict the acquisition of various English structures by child learners from a variety of language backgrounds; by Nagy et al. (1996) to illustrate the ordered acquisition of /l/-deletion in Montreal French by anglophone speakers, and by Bayley (1999) to model the use of the preterit and imperfect tense by aspectual class in Mexican-origin children's narratives. Using the implicational scale shown in table 6.5, Pienemann (1998: 178, drawing on work by M. Johnston) depicts the acquisition of twelve English grammatical structures in Australia by 16 adult immigrants from Polish and Vietnamese backgrounds. Speaking of this table, Pienemann notes that:

Table 6.5   Acquisition of English grammatical rules by 16 Vietnamese and Polish adult immigrants to Australia

| | Stages | | | | | | | | | | | |
| | 6 | 5 | | 4 | | 3 | | | | 2 | | 1 |
Structures	A	B	C	D	E	F	G	H	I	J	K	L
phuc	−	+	+	+	/	+	+	+	+	+	+	/
dung	−	+	+	+	/	+	+	+	+	+	+	/
ja	−	−	+	/	+	+	+	+	+	+	+	/
ij	−	−	+	/	+	+	+	+	+	+	+	/
es	−	−	−	+	+	+	+	+	+	+	+	/
ka	−	−	−	+	+	+	+	+	+	+	+	/
bb	−	−	−	+	+	+	+	+	+	+	+	/
sang	−	−	−	+	/	+	+	+	+	+	+	/
jr	−	−	−	−	+	+	+	+	+	+	+	/
vinh	−	−	−	−	+	+	+	+	+	+	+	/
long	−	−	−	−	+	+	/	+	+	+	+	/
tam	−	−	−	−	+	+	+	+	+	+	+	/
ks	−	−	−	−	−	+	+	+	+	+	+	/
my	−	−	−	−	−	−	+	+	+	+	+	/
IS	−	−	−	−	−	−	−	−	−	+	+	/
van	−	−	−	−	−	−	−	−	−	−	−	+

Key:
+ = acquired; − = not acquired; / = no context for an obligatory rule, or no tokens for an optional rule. A = Cancel inversion; B = Aux2nd/Do2nd; C = 3sg. –s; D = Y/N inversion; E = PS Inversion; F = Neg+V; G = Do Front.; H = Topi.; I = ADV; J = SVO; K = Plural; J = single words

Source: modified from Pienemann (1998: 178)

The scalability . . . is 100 per cent. This means that there is not a single piece of evidence to contradict the hypothesized implicational pattern, and this means that Johnston's study strongly supports the English processability hierarchy.

There are several factors which add to the strength of this support. First of all, five of the six levels of processability are documented . . . there is at least one speaker for whom the given level is the highest.

The second contributing factor is the richness of the database. This is evident in the small number of slashes [= empty cells]. . . . Leaving aside one-constituent words [= the rightmost column], such gaps occur in merely 3.125 per cent of Johnson's corpus. In other words, in this corpus it hardly ever happens that it provides neither evidence for nor against the hypothesized hierarchy.

(Pienemann 1998: 178)

4 Three Caveats about the Use of Implicational Scales

Useful though implicational scales have proven to be as an heuristic and data-ordering device, I must mention three caveats about their use.

4.1 *Avoid empty cells and weak goodness-of-fit measures*

The power of scaling lies in its ability to predict that data in the area of grammar under consideration will occur in highly constrained, non-random implicational patterns. In general, we want to make the strongest predictions consistent with the scaling model, but empty cells and sloppy tests of the goodness-of-fit between the scaling model and the actual data militate against the validity of the results.

Some of the earliest scales in the variationist literature are less than ideal in this regard (for instance, Bickerton's (1973c) *tu/fu* scale, in which 28.2 percent of the cells are empty – see table 6.4), and some of the most recent are equally wanting (for instance, the ESL scale in Pienemann and Mackey 1993, in which 24 percent of the cells have no data). Referring to the gaps in the latter scale, Pienemann (1998: 181) claims that "this in no way disqualifies the hypothesis it highlights," but this is disputable. Ignoring empty cells in a table, and computing scalability figures only on the basis of filled cells, amounts to a leap of faith that if the empty cells were to be filled, they would pattern in accord with the implicational predictions of the scale model. This is clearly not a valid procedure. To avoid it, we simply have to continue collecting data until our scales contain no empty cells, or devise procedures for filling the empty cells by other means, for instance, reproducing the proportions of attested deviations (see Pavone 1980: 111–19).

Second, the statistically accepted rate for scalability or the Index of Reproducibility (IR) is 90 percent, not the 85 percent figure that has been accepted in a number of linguistic studies. As Dunn-Rankin (1983: 107) notes, Guttman has stated that a scale with an IR less than 90 percent "cannot be considered an adequate approximation to a perfect scale," and an IR of .93 approximates the .05 level of significance. To be sure of the validity of our findings we should probably accept 93 percent as the minimum "scalability" figure.

Third, as observed and exemplified by Pavone (1980) – the most statistically sophisticated study of linguistic scaling available – there are more demanding tests of the goodness-of-fit between scale models and actual data than IR, the one which virtually all linguists use. For instance, Pavone's implementation of Jackson's (1949) "Plus Percentage Ratio" and Green's (1956) "Index of Consistency," results in the rejection of several classic scales in the variationist literature that would otherwise pass muster with IR.[11]

4.2   Attempt frequency-valued (instead of binary) scales where possible

In the early literature on implicational scales, binary (+, –) or at best, trinary (+, –, x) scales were the norm. To the extent that one's data came in that format (as, for instance, where informants either accepted, rejected, or were uncertain about the grammaticality of a sentence), this made perfect sense. Sometimes data could scale only when converted from frequencies to plusses and minuses, although such conversions invariably involved arbitrary procedures and the resultant order could conceal vast extremes of variability. A case in point is Day's (1973: 98) copula scale, whose application symbol (x) covered frequencies from 2.1 percent to 100 percent and virtually everything in between, as shown by his subsequent percentage use array for the same variable (1973: 106). As Pavone (1980: 146–7) points out, the real problem with this is that Day goes on to write variable rules for his data, which make unmotivated predictions about speakers' knowledge of more or less relations between the relevant environments when only either/or relations are justified.

Of course, implicationalists like Bickerton (e.g. in 1973a: 24–5) explicitly eschewed the incorporation of frequencies in implicational scales, and the use of variable rules, on the grounds that they require unorthodox and overly strong assumptions about the cognitive linguistic capacity of human beings. However, as quantitativists have often emphasized, it is not the statistics, but the relationships between environments they represent which humans are assumed to have as part of human competence. And, as Fasold (1970: 558) shows convincingly, attention to frequency relationships leads to the discovery of linguistic patterning where implicational analysis with only binary- or trinary-valued scales does not.

Although a number of researchers have incorporated frequencies into their implicational scales, they are usually hypothetical (e.g. the frequencies in figure 6.2 above, from Bailey 1973a), or based on the data of social classes rather than individuals (e.g. Tables 5 and 6 in Fasold 1970, based on Wolfram's Detroit data). Aggregated social class data limit the number of outputs which have to be scaled and so provide a weaker test of the model than scales that use the data of individual speakers.

I know of only three frequency-valued scales in the literature that pass the IR: Fasold's (1975: 53) scale of Sankoff's que-deletion data from Quebec,[12] Andersen's (1978: 226) scale for the acquisition of four grammatical features, and my own (Rickford 1979: 261) scale for vowel-laxing by pronoun form, shown as table 6.6. Note that in my case, the frequency-valued scale replaced an earlier binary scale (Rickford 1979: 255, 1991: 234), based on the same data. In both cases, the scales have an acceptably high IR,[13] but the frequency-valued scale makes a finer discrimination of the pronoun forms into four groups rather than two, and this discrimination is better supported on independent

Table 6.6 Frequency-valued scale for vowel laxing by pronoun form in Guyana

Lects	Speaker	Speaker	ju	de, shi	mi	wi
A	4	Reefer	1.00	0.89	0.84	0.08
	10	Ajah	1.00	0.89	0.80	0.00
B	12	Nani	0.96	0.94	0.76	0.00
	11	Darling	0.96	0.94	0.76	0.00
	2	James	0.96	0.88	0.76	0.00
	24	Granny	0.96	0.92	0.68	0.32
	6	Raj	(0.88)	0.89	0.80	0.00
	1	Derek	0.96	0.94	0.62	0.12
	5	Sultan	0.96	0.84	0.72	0.24
	7	Irene	0.96	0.84	0.72	0.00
	8	Rose	0.96	0.81	0.76	0.00
	9	Sari	0.96	0.85	0.72	0.12
	13	Mark	0.96	0.80	0.76	0.04
	3	Florine	0.92	0.90	0.60	0.04
C	17	Sheik	0.88	(0.68)	0.68	0.04
	20	Claire	0.88	(0.68)	0.68	0.04
	14	Magda	0.84	0.72	0.60	0.24
	19	Radika	0.84	0.63	0.52	0.00
D	18	Seymour	0.72	0.56	0.40	0.04
	16	Kishore	0.64	0.57	0.52	0.00
	23	Oxford	0.68	0.48	0.36	0.32
	15	Katherine	0.70	0.51	0.20	0.00
	22	Ustad	0.56	0.38	0.36	0.08
	21	Bonnette	0.76	0.60	0.20	0.00

Implicational pattern: Frequencies are higher in cells to the left, lower in cells to the right. Deviations parenthesized. IR = 96.9 percent (1–3/96). The solid step-like line running from lower left to upper right separates cells with 80 percent or more rule application from those with less; lects – demarcated by dotted lines – differ from each other in the number of pronoun forms they have with 80 percent or more rule application.

Source: adapted from Rickford (1979: 261)

linguistic (see below) and quantitative grounds.[14] The moral is that we should *not* be content with binary or trinary scales just because they scale successfully. To the extent that our data permit it, we should go for frequency-valued or more discriminatory scales, and the stronger predictions and alternative patternings they afford us.

4.3   *Seek explanations for the implicational patterns*

To my mind, a major flaw in the literature on linguistic variation is the tendency to be satisfied with the data orderings provided by our heuristic tools (frequencies, variable rule programs, implicational scales), without seeking to explain them in linguistic (or social) terms. Bickerton (1971) showed the danger of this with his spurious constraints on *tu/fu* variability which satisfied the constraints of the quantitative paradigm. But the problem afflicts implicationalists as well.

For instance, for all the vaunted regularity of the alpha scale in the implicationalist framework – DeCamp's (1971) scale of six features in the Jamaican Creole continuum – neither DeCamp nor anyone else ventured an explanation as to why *nyam* and *nanny* were the most marked creole features and earliest to decreolize, and why the nonstandard stop pronunciations for English interdental fricatives were the least marked. But as I have suggested elsewhere (1991: 238), it is because direct African loans like *nyam* and *nanny* (which unlike loan translations tend to be more obviously non-English in form or function) are for historical and sociological reasons (see Alleyne 1971: 181, Smith 1962: 41) particularly stigmatized in Caribbean societies, while nonstandard phonological variants like *t* and *d* are considerably less so. The fact that phonological features tend to be more gradient, and to function less frequently as ethnic and class barriers (see Rickford 1985) may also be related.

In the case of vowel-laxing by pro-form in the Guyanese continuum (table 6.6), justification for the more stringent frequency-valued ordering derives from the fact that an independent variable rule analysis of the data produces exactly the same ordering of the forms (with feature weights of .84 for *ju*, .68 for *de* and *shi*, .48 for *mi*, and .04 for *wi*), while Allsopp's (1958) study orders the forms similarly (*ju* .80, *de* .67, *shi* .59, *mi* .56, *wi* .32). Moreover, the independently established consonantal strength hierarchy (Hooper 1973, Jakobson and Halle 1956) provides a powerful explanation for this ordering. The generalization is that the stronger the preceding consonant (in this hierarchy), the greater the likelihood of vowel laxing: the /w/ in *wi* ranks lowest on this scale; nasals, as in *mi*, are ranked 3; and voiced stops and voiceless continuant, as in *de/shi* are ranked 5. The form *ju*, with a weak initial glide, should be ranked least with respect to vowel laxing, like *wi*. But it is the most recoverable by syntactic rules and therefore the most reducible and loseable of all.[15]

Whether our scales are for the variable use of linguistic features, for intuitions, or for patterns of language acquisition, we should not be satisfied to locate descriptive regularities without attempting to explain them.

The corollary of the injunction that implicational scales require interpretation is that they provide descriptions and orderings of data that invite interpretation. Clearly, attempts at arranging variable data as implicational scales can reveal regularities in that data hitherto hidden from the investigator's eye, and it is those regularities that may – indeed, should – invite the investigator to search

further for explanations. The relative neglect of implicational scales by sociolinguists in recent years has removed one of the methods for organizing data
from our active tool kit. I hope I have demonstrated in this chapter that the
neglect did not follow from any inherent shortcomings of the method. Certainly
we do not have so many methods that we can afford to neglect any of them.
Implicational scales have served variationists well in the past, and should
continue to do so in the future.

NOTES

1   This chapter incorporates some
    material from Rickford (1991).
2   Because of the widespread linguistic
    variability which they display,
    pidgin and creole speech
    communities have often been of
    interest to variationists, and creolists
    have often been contributors to and
    pioneers in the study of linguistic
    variation. See LePage and Tabouret-
    Keller (1985) and Rickford (1987a)
    for more discussion.
3   It is very important to note that the
    feature letters (A–F) and speaker
    numbers (1–7) in table 6.2c (and of
    course 6.2a and 6.2b) correspond
    exactly to those originally used
    by DeCamp (1971) and *not* to
    alternative versions of table 6.2c in
    Fasold (1970: 552), Pavone (1980: 32),
    or Rickford (1991: 227). In the latter
    works, the feature columns are
    relettered and the speaker rows
    renumbered so that they themselves
    form a neat series matching the
    ordering produced by the
    implicational scale. By contrast, I
    have chosen in this article to retain
    DeCamp's original designations
    even if the resultant orderings are
    messier (BEFACD, 5162734). I did
    so to permit easier comparison
    with DeCamp's original article,
    and to make the point that one does
    not start with a perfectly ordered
    implicational scale (or something

    close to it), but gets to it by
    reordering the rows and columns
    in which one's raw data come.
4   To avoid any implication that
    speaking Creole is a "minus"
    and English a "plus," one could
    represent the varieties respectively
    as *x* and *y* or 1 and 2, but I have
    chosen to follow DeCamp's
    designations in this as in other
    matters, and trust that readers
    will not attach any unintended
    sociopolitical interpretations to it.
5   Variationists (e.g. Bickerton 1973b:
    20, LePage 1980: 127) sometimes use
    the term "bidimensional" for creole
    continua and the implicational scales
    used to describe them, when they
    clearly mean "unidimensional." The
    confusion perhaps arises because
    creole continua are bipolar, with
    the two poles English and creole,
    or acrolect and basilect.
6   The lects of table 6.2c and similar
    implicational scales actually
    represent *isolects*, "varieties of a
    language that differ only in a
    minimal way" (Bailey 1973a). Bailey
    did not seem to mind speaking of
    idiolects (individual speaker patterns,
    at least with respect to particular
    features or restricted sets of
    features), but he was chary about
    the utility of the notion of *dialects*,
    "mutually intelligible forms of a
    language delimited by isoglossic

bundles," on the grounds that "such dialects are rarely found" (Bailey 1973b: 161).

7   Witness the parallel decline in the writing of variable rules by quantitativists (see Fasold 1991, "The quiet demise of variable rules").

8   Bickerton (1971: 461) openly mocked the quantitativist tendency to focus on group means, using an absurd thought-experiment: "since the group figure is the crucial one . . . each individual must – if that group figure is to be maintained – keep track, not merely of his own environments and percentages, but also of those produced by all other members of his group; in other words, speaker B must continually be saying to himself things like: 'Good Lord! A's percentage of contractions in the environment +V __ + __ NP has fallen to 77! I'll have to step up mine to – let's see: A's production of this environment-type stands to mine in the ratio 65:35 over the last 100 token-occurrences, so I'd better compensate by shooting up to /// what? About 86 percent?' And, to crown it all, he must not only be able to perform all these highly sophisticated calculations – he must also . . . somehow continue to do so EVEN IN THE PHYSICAL ABSENCE OF ALL OTHER GROUP-MEMBERS!"

9   See Fasold (1973) for other critiques of Bailey's more = earlier/less = later assumptions, as likely to lead to wrong results in cases of rule acceleration, rule stagnation, and rule inhibition, and Bailey's response (1973a: 82–6).

10 Like his precursor DeCamp (1971), Bickerton had described this scale but not actually provided it in his (1971) article.

11 Attempting to explain these complex measures of goodness-of-fit would take us far afield. The reader is referred to Pavone (1980), Dunn-Rankin (1983), and Chilton (1969) for further discussion.

12 Fasold's scale barely passes (or fails), with an IR of 89.6 percent; Andersen's has an IR of 94 percent.

13 In earlier versions of table 6.6, the IR was reported as 99 percent instead of 96.9 percent, because the two occurrences of .68 in the *de/shi* columns for Sheik and Claire – equivalent to the .68 values to their immediate right – were not counted as deviations. However, requiring frequencies to the left to be everywhere higher (rather than higher or equivalent) than frequencies to the right is more in keeping with the predictions of a true frequency-valued scale. The one exception might be at the extreme categorical values of 0 or 100 percent where equivalence might be considered non-deviant (as in Andersen 1978: 226 – see Rickford 1991: 236–7).

14 The reason for selecting 80 percent as the basis for dividing the outputs in table 6.6 into lects is that this represents the final inflection point of Bailey's (1973a: 77) S-curve model of change and its associated principle 17: "A given change begins quite gradually; after reaching a certain point (say, 20 percent) it picks up momentum and proceeds at a much faster rate; and finally [around 80 percent as indicated in his S-curve] tails off slowly before reaching completion. The result is an S curve." To see the validity of this prediction in the data of Table 6.6, note that there are only 38 cells in the broad middle range of frequencies between .21 and .70, but there are more (58) in the

narrower .00–20 and .81–1.00 ranges, showing that individuals really do go through the middle range of frequencies more quickly than the extremes.

15 See Rickford (1979: 221–4) for details, and note that this discussion is related to unstressed syllables, and not to stressed syllables, which are categorically tense.

REFERENCES

Akers, Glenn (1981). *Phonological Variation in the Jamaican Continuum*. Ann Arbor, MI: Karoma.

Albury, Donald H. (1973). The clause-internal sentence squish. In C. J. Bailey and R. W. Shuy (eds.), *New Ways of Analyzing Variation in English*. Washington, DC: Georgetown University Press. 69–82.

Alleyne, Mervyn (1971). Acculturation and the cultural matrix of creolization. In Dell Hymes (ed.), *Pidginization and Creolization of Languages*. Cambridge: Cambridge University Press. 169–86.

Allsopp, Richard (1958). Pronominal forms in the dialect of English used in Georgetown (British Guiana) and its environs by persons engaged in non-clerical occupations. MA thesis, London University, vol. II.

Andersen, Roger W. (1978). An implicational model for second language research. *Language Learning* 28: 221–82.

Anshen, Frank (1973). Some data which do not fit some models. In C. J. Bailey and R. W. Shuy (eds.), *New Ways of Analyzing Variation in English*. Washington, DC: Georgetown University Press. 62–8.

Bailey, Charles-James N. (1969). Implicational scales in diachronic linguistics and dialectology. *Working Papers in Linguistics* 1.8, University of Hawaii, Honolulu.

Bailey, Charles-James N. (1970). The integration of linguistic theory: Internal reconstruction and the comparative method. *Working Papers in Linguistics* 2. Honolulu: University of Hawaii.

Bailey, Charles-James N. (1971). Trying to talk in the new paradigm. *Papers in Linguistics* 4: 312–38.

Bailey, Charles-James N. (1973a). *Variation and Linguistic Theory*. Arlington, VA: Center for Applied Linguistics.

Bailey, Charles-James, N. (1973b). The patterning of linguistic variation. In R. Bailey and J. Robinson (eds.), *Varieties of Present-Day English*. New York: Macmillan. 156–87.

Bailey, Charles-James N. and Roger W. Shuy (eds.) (1973). *New Ways of Analyzing Variation in English*. Washington, DC: Georgetown University Press.

Battison, Robbin, Harry Marcowicz, and James Woodard (1975). A good rule of thumb: variable phonology in American sign language. In R. W. Fasold and R. W. Shuy (eds.), *Analyzing Variation in Language*. Washington, DC: Georgetown University Press. 291–302.

Bayley, Robert (1999). The primacy of aspect hypothesis revisited: Evidence from language shift. *Southwest Journal of Linguistics* 18, 2: 1–22.

Bickerton, Derek (1971). Inherent variability and variable rules. *Foundations of Language* 7, 4: 457–92.

Bickerton, Derek (1973a). Quantitative versus dynamic paradigms: The case of Montreal *que*. In C.-J. N. Bailey and R. W. Shuy (eds.), *New Ways of Analyzing Variation in English*. Washington, DC: Georgetown University Press. 23–43.

Bickerton, Derek (1973b). The structure of polylectal grammars. In Roger W. Shuy (ed.), *Report of the Twenty-Third Annual Round Table Meeting on Linguistics and Language Studies*. Washington, DC: Georgetown University Press. 17–42.

Bickerton, Derek (1973c). The nature of a creole continuum. *Language* 49, 3: 640–69.

Bickerton, Derek and Carol Odo (1976). *Change and Variation in Hawaiian English*, vol. I. Honolulu: Social Sciences and Linguistics Institute, University of Hawaii.

Chilton, Ronald J. (1969). A review and comparison of simple statistic tests for scalogram analysis. *American Sociological Review* 34: 238–45.

Day, Richard R. (1973). Patterns of variation in copula and tense in the Hawaiian post-creole continuum. *Working Papers in Linguistics* 5.2, University of Hawaii, Honolulu. Reprint of 1972 University of Hawaii dissertation.

DeCamp, David (1971). Toward a generative analysis of a post-creole speech continuum. In Dell Hymes (ed.), *Pidginization and Creolization of Languages*. Cambridge: Cambridge University Press. 349–70.

DeCamp, David (1973). What do implicational scales imply? In C.-J. N. Bailey and R. W. Shuy (eds.), *New Ways of Analyzing Variation in English*. Washington, DC: Georgtown University Press. 141–8.

Dunn-Rankin, Peter (1983). *Scaling Methods*. Hillsdale, NJ: Lawrence Erlbaum.

Elliot, D., S. Legum and S. A. Thompson (1969). Syntactic variation as linguistic data. In R. Binnick et al. (eds.), *Papers from the Fifth Regional Meeting of the Chicago Linguistic Society*. Chicago: University of Chicago Press. 52–9.

Escure, Genevieve (1982). Contrastive patterns of intragroup and intergroup interaction in the creole continuum of Belize. *Language in Society* 11: 239–64.

Fasold, Ralph W. (1970). Two models of socially significant linguistic variation. *Language* 46: 551–63.

Fasold, Ralph W. (1973). The concept of "earlier–later": More or less correct. In C.-J. N. Bailey and R. W. Shuy (eds.), *New Ways of Analyzing Variation in English*. Washington, DC: Georgetown University Press. 183–97.

Fasold, Ralph W. (1975). The Bailey wave model: A dynamic quantitative paradigm. In Ralph W. Fasold and Roger W. Shuy (eds.), *Analyzing Variation in Language*. Washington, DC: Georgetown University Press. 27–58.

Fasold, Ralph (1991). The quiet demise of variable rules. *American Speech* 66: 3–21.

Fasold, Ralph W. and Roger W. Shuy (eds.) (1975). *Analyzing Variation in Language*. Washington, DC: Georgetown University Press.

Gal, Susan (1979). *Language Shift: Social Determinants of Linguistic Change in Bilingual Austria*. New York: Academic Press.

Gorden, Raymond L. (1977). *Unidimensional Scaling of Social Variables: Concepts and Procedures*. New York: The Free Press.

Green, Bert F. (1956). A method of scalogram analysis using summary statistics. *Psychometrika* 21: 79–88.

Greenberg, Joseph H. (1963). Some universals of grammar with particular reference to the order of meaningful elements. In Joseph H. Greenberg (ed.), *Universals of Language*. Cambridge, MA: MIT Press. 73–113.

Guttman, Louis (1944). A basis for scaling qualitative data. *American Sociological Review* 9: 139–50.

Guy, Gregory (1980). Variation in the group and the individual: the case of final stop deletion. In William Labov (ed.), *Locating Language in Time and Space*. New York: Academic Press. 1–36.

Hindle, Don and Ivan Sag (1975). Some more on *anymore*. In R. W. Fasold and R. W. Shuy (eds.), *Analyzing Variation in Language*. Washington, DC: Georgetown University Press. 89–110.

Hooper, J. B. (1973). Aspects of natural generative phonology. Ph.D. dissertation, Department of Linguistics, University of California, Los Angeles.

Hymes, Dell (ed.) (1971). *Pidginization and Creolization of Languages*. Cambridge: Cambridge University Press.

Jackson, J. M. (1949). A simple and more rigorous technique for scale analysis. In *A Manual of Scale Analysis*, part II. MS, Montreal: McGill University.

Jakobson, Roman and Morris Halle (1956). *Fundamentals of Language*. The Hague: Mouton.

Labov, William (1971). Methodology. In William O. Dingwall (ed.), *A Survey of Linguistic Science*. College Park, MD: Linguistics Program, University of Maryland. 412–91.

Labov, William (1973). The boundaries of words and their meanings. In C.-J. N. Bailey and R. W. Shuy (eds.), *New Ways of Analyzing Variation in English*. Washington, DC: Georgetown University Press. 340–73.

Le Page, Robert B. (1980). Hugo Schuchardt's creole studies and the problem of linguistic continua. In K. Lichem and H. J. Simon (eds.), *Hugo Schuchardt: Symposium, 1977 in Graz*. 114–45.

Le Page, Robert B. and Andrée Tabouret-Keller (1985). *Acts of Identity: Creole-Based Approaches to Language and Identity*. Cambridge: Cambridge University Press.

McIver, John and Edward G. Carmines (1981). *Unidimensional Scaling*. Beverly Hills, CA: Sage.

Mufwene, Salikoko S. (1999). Accountability in descriptions of creoles. In John R. Rickford and Suzanne Romaine (eds.), *Creole Genesis, Attitudes and Discourse: Studies Celebrating Charlene J. Sato*. Amsterdam and Philadelphia: John Benjamins. 157–85.

Nagy, Naomi, Christine Moisset, and Gillian Sankoff (1996). On the acquisition of variable phonology in L2. University of Pennsylvania Working Papers in Linguistics 3.1: 111–26.

Napoli, Donna Jo (1977). Variations on relative clauses in Italian. In R. W. Fasold and R. W. Shuy (eds.), *Analyzing Variation in Language*. Washington, DC: Georgetown University Press. 37–50.

Nordenstam, K. (1970). *Svenskan i Norge*. Gothenberg: University Press.

Pavone, James (1980). Implicational scales and English dialectology. Ph.D. dissertation, Department of English, Indiana University. (Available from University Microfilms International, Ann Arbor, Michigan, dissertation no. 8020249.)

Pienemann, Manfred (1998). *Language Processing and Second Language Development: Processability Theory*. Amsterdam and Philadelphia: John Benjamins.

Pienemann, Manfred and A. Mackey (1993). An empirical study of children's ESL development and rapid profile. In P. McKay (ed.), *ESL Development: Language and Literacy in Schools*, vol. 2. Commonwealth of Australia and National Languages and Literacy Institute of Australia. 115–259.

Politzer, Robert L. (1976). The implicational relation paradigm in language acquisition. In Alphonse Juilland (ed.), *Linguistic Studies Offered to Joseph Greenberg*. Saratoga, CA: Anma Libri. 123–35.

Rickford, John R. (1975). Carrying the new wave into syntax: the case of Black English BIN. In R. W. Fasold and R. W. Shuy (eds.), *Analyzing Variation in Language*. Washington, DC: Georgetown University Press. 162–183.

Rickford, John R. (1979). Variation in a creole continuum: Quantitative and implicational approaches. Ph.D. dissertation, University of Pennsylvania.

Rickford, John R. (1985). Ethnicity as a sociolinguistic boundary. *American Speech* 60, 2: 99–125.

Rickford, John R. (ed.) (1987a). Sociolinguistics and Pidgin–Creole studies. *International Journal of the Sociology of Language* 71. The Hague: Mouton.

Rickford, John R. (1987b). The haves and have nots: Sociolinguistic surveys and the assessment of speaker competence. *Language in Society* 16: 149–77.

Rickford, John R. (1991). Variation theory: Implicational scaling and critical age limits in models of linguistic variation, acquisition and change. In Thom Huebner and Charles A. Ferguson (eds.), *Crosscurrents in Second Language Acquisition and Linguistic Theories.*

Amsterdam and Philadelphia: John Benjamins. 225–46.

Robson, Barbara (1973). Pan-lectal grammars and adult language change. In C.-J. N. Bailey and R. W. Shuy (eds.), *New Ways of Analyzing Variation in English*. Washington, DC: Georgetown University Press. 164–170.

Ross, John Robert (1973). A fake NP squish. In C.-J. N. Bailey and R. W. Shuy (eds.), *New Ways of Analyzing Variation in English*. Washington, DC: Georgetown University Press. 96–140.

Sag, Ivan (1973). On the state of progress on progressives and statives. In C.-J. N. Bailey and R. W. Shuy (eds.), *New Ways of Analyzing Variation in English*. Washington, DC: Georgetown University Press. 83–95.

Sankoff, Gillian (1973). Above and beyond phonology in variable rules. In C.-J. N. Bailey and R. W. Shuy (eds.), *New Ways of Analyzing Variation in English*. Washington, DC: Georgetown University Press. 44–61.

Sankoff, Gillian (1974). A quantitative paradigm for the study of competitive competence. In Richard Bouman and Joel Sherzer (eds.), *Explorations in the Ethnography of Speaking*. Cambridge: Cambridge University Press. 18–49.

Smith, Raymond T. (1962). *British Guiana*. London: Oxford University Press.

Stolz, Walter and G. Bills (1968). *An Investigation of the Standard–Nonstandard Dimension of Central Texan English*. Austin, TX: University of Texas Child Development Evaluation and Research Center.

Torgerson, Warren S. (1958). *Theory and Methods of Scaling*. New York: John Wiley and Sons.

Trudgill, Peter (1986). *Dialects in Contact*. Oxford: Basil Blackwell.

Washabaugh, William (1977).
Constraining variation in
decreolization. *Language* 53, 2:
329–52.

Woodward, James C. (1975). Variation in
American sign-language syntax:
agent–beneficiary directionality. In
R. W. Fasold and R. W. Shuy (eds.),
Analyzing Variation in Language.

Washington, DC: Georgetown
University Press. 303–11.

Woolford, Ellen (1975). Variation and
change in the *i* "predicate marker"
of New Guinea Tok Pisin. Paper
presented at the International
Conference on Pidgins and
Creoles, Honolulu, Hawaii.

7 Instrumental Phonetics

ERIK R. THOMAS

1 Instrumental Phonetic Studies in Sociolinguistics

Since the appearance of Labov, Yaeger, and Steiner's *A Quantitative Study of Sound Change in Progress* (1972), instrumental phonetic studies have gradually taken up a larger and larger portion of the quantitative sociolinguistic research on phonetic variation. This growth is encouraging to acousticians. Sociolinguistics is far ahead of phonology, another theoretical discipline that deals with pronunciation, in incorporating instrumental methods. However, much remains to be done. Most instrumental sociolinguistic work has been restricted to a few research issues and methods. It has been concentrated on variation in vowels; variation in consonants, prosody, and voice quality has received little acoustic analysis. In addition, much of the instrumental inquiry has focused on investigating the phonetic or phonological motivations for sound change. Instrumental methods could be applied more widely to a variety of other issues, ranging from ethnic relations to phonetic variation as an indicator of the mental representation of sounds. The greater part of the corpus of instrumental studies of phonetic variation presently consists of studies of speech production. Perceptual studies still represent a largely untapped potential, though they are becoming more common.

Certainly, then, instrumental analysis could be applied much more extensively than it has been thus far. It is not, of course, practical for all studies of phonetic variation. Some variables, such as *r*-lessness (e.g. production of *four* and *here* as [foə] and [hiə]), are more easily approached impressionistically. Lindblom (1980) reminds his readers that acoustic measurements are useful only in so far as they reflect linguistically relevant factors, and for *r*-lessness, it can be argued that what is important is whether listeners perceive [ɹ] or [ə]. In any case, the phonetic attributes of *r*-fulness and *r*-lessness – the threshold and rate of the fall in F_3 (the third formant) necessary for perception as [ɹ], the effect of the phonetic context, the effect of duration, etc. – are complicated and have yet to be worked out (though they would make for fascinating perception experiments).

1.1 Measuring the effects of phonetic context

However, there are many issues for which instrumental techniques are more appropriate than other methods. One example is measurement of the effect of consonantal context on vowel realizations. This issue has been important in studies of vowel change because vowel shifts are often conditioned by particular contexts. Experimental studies have demonstrated that perceptual processing of vowels normalizes the effects of consonantal context (Lindblom and Studdert-Kennedy 1967, Ohala 1981a: 179 ff., especially 181, where he cites other studies; Ohala and Feder 1994, Nábělek and Ovchinnikov 1997). Ohala (1981a) terms this process "corrective rules." For example, a given vowel will ordinarily have a lower F_2 (second formant) in the context of labial consonants than in the context of coronal consonants, but listeners will hear the two variants as "the same." Phonetic training does not enable scribes to escape the effects of context entirely (Nairn and Hurford 1995). For that reason, impressionistic transcriptions of vowels in different contexts do not reflect the actual production of the vowel by a speaker as much as they reflect the scribe's perception. In most studies of the role of consonantal context in sound change, however, the ostensible focus is on production, not on perception (and especially not on scribal perception). Instrumental measurement, naturally, is not affected by "corrective rules." Thus impressionistic transcription is poorly suited for examinations of contextual effects, while instrumental measurement is well suited for it. Nevertheless, impressionistic transcription has often been used for contextual studies, in large part because it produces the discrete data necessary for the popular VARBRUL statistical analysis package while acoustic measurements produce data that are continuous and also require inter-speaker normalization.

1.2 Ethnic identification

Another example for which instrumental techniques are more appropriate than other methods involves the perception of a speaker's ethnicity. Speech synthesizers allow researchers to investigate what cues listeners use for ethnic identifications. Without synthesis, researchers are limited to using recordings of speakers, either of natural speech or, following Lambert's (1967) matched-guise experiment, of some sort of performance speech. A number of studies have demonstrated with stimuli that were not synthetically modified that American listeners are able to distinguish African-American voices from white voices (Roberts 1966, Tucker and Lambert 1969, Lass et al. 1979, Bailey and Maynor 1989, Haley 1990, Trent 1995, Baugh 1996). These studies were incapable of determining which features listeners used for their identifications, though Roberts (1966) asked her subjects for subjective guesses about the features they used.

One method of ascertaining what features are utilized for ethnic identifications was employed by Walton and Orlikoff (1994), who took careful measurements of voice quality features in their stimuli and correlated them with the accuracy of ethnic identifications of the stimuli by listeners. However, speech synthesizers allow researchers to conduct perception experiments in which the different phonetic attributes are varied. Although a talented impersonator might be able to produce passable manipulations of particular phonetic attributes, it would be impossible to calibrate the manipulations precisely and the impersonator might unintentionally modify other features, too. Synthetic manipulation can be calibrated exactly and without affecting other features. Graff et al. (1986) used synthetic manipulation to show that Philadelphians could base their identifications of a speaker's ethnicity on whether the nuclei of /o/ and /au/ were fronted (for whites) or not (for African Americans). Hawkins (1993) used both natural and synthetically modified voices. After finding that listeners could identify the ethnicity of unmodified voices most of the time, even after hearing only isolated vowels, she synthetically altered the F_0 (fundamental frequency) of voices and found that listeners tended to identify voices with lower F_0 as African-American and those with higher F_0 as white. Because the correlation was not the same across listener groups, she speculated that stereotype, not physiology, was the cause. (In contrast, Walton and Orlikoff 1994 suggested that physiological differences might account for the voice quality differences that they found.) Lass et al. (1978) found that playing signals backward and compressing the time adversely affected ethnic identifications. In a follow-up study, Lass et al. (1980) found that listeners could identify the ethnicity of lowpass-filtered voices, suggesting that intonation was an important cue. Foreman (1999) conducted a similar experiment involving lowpass-filtered samples of read speech. She found that listeners with extensive exposure to speakers from both ethnicities identified the voices better than those with extensive exposure to only one group and that stimuli exhibiting prosodic contours and pitch ranges typical of only one of the ethnic groups were most accurately identified.

2   Instrumental Studies of Variation in Production

Labov et al. (1972), the study that popularized the use of instrumental techniques in sociolinguistics, focused on vowel shifting in dialects of English as evidenced by patterns of the first two formants (F_1 and F_2). Although they included a few small-scale perception experiments designed to investigate near-mergers and cross-dialectal misperception, they concentrated on speakers' production. Most other sociolinguistic researchers have followed their lead, so, not surprisingly, the largest share of instrumental sociolinguistic work since then has involved the study of vowel shifting in production, based on F_1 and F_2 patterns. Instrumental analyses of consonantal variation (Docherty and Foulkes 1999), prosodic variation (see, e.g., Britain 1992: 102–4, Jun and Foreman 1996, Yaeger-Dror 1997), and variation in voice quality (Walton and Orlikoff 1994) are scarce. Consonants, prosody, and voice quality remain, for the most part, in the realm of impressionistic phonetics. The vocalic inquiry has been centered on the study of stressed vowel nuclei; unstressed vowels and the glides and structure of diphthongs have received much less attention. Furthermore, the focus on diachronic shifts has overshadowed other issues for which instrumental analysis would be useful.

2.1   Studies of vowel variation and change in production

Labov et al. (1972) and Labov's subsequent works on the topic of vowel shifting (particularly Labov, 1991, 1994) discussed acoustic analyses of vowel configurations in several dialects in the United States and the British Isles. Their most often cited result was that they found two shifting patterns associated with particular dialects: the "Northern Cities Shift" in the Great Lakes region of the United States and the "Southern Shift" in the American South. Both of these shifts are described below. Comparing their results with a survey of shifts reported in the historical linguistics literature from a variety of languages, they discovered four recurring patterns of vowel shifting. From these recurring patterns, they derived several principles, e.g. in chain shifts, tense nuclei rise along a peripheral track; lax nuclei fall along a nonperipheral track; tense vowels move to the front along peripheral paths; low nonperipheral vowels become peripheral; etc. (Labov 1994: 176, 200, 280). Further testing of the universality of these principles is warranted (see Cox 1999).

   Labov (1991, 1994) treats tenseness as a phonological abstraction and prefers to account for his descriptions of vowel shifting patterns in terms of peripherality, which, he observes, usually but not always corresponds with tenseness. He seems less interested in the phonetic correlates of tenseness other than relative peripherality in F_1/F_2 space and length. However, in order to explain the diachronic shifting patterns exhibited by vowels, it is necessary to examine all the phonetic attributes closely. Labov does offer a plausible articulatory explanation for the fronting of tense back vowels (Labov 1994: 261–4), though it is not the only possible explanation (see Ohala 1981b). He also offers perceptual explanations for some vowel shifts (e.g. Labov 1994: 332). Even so, the phonetic explanations for many of the shifting patterns remain unclear. Why, for example, should peripheral vowels tend to rise? Additional instrumental investigation would shed light on this issue. Tenseness is manifested as a bundle of phonetic attributes, as Labov et al. (1972: 41) acknowledge. Tense vowels are generally breathier than lax vowels, more diphthongal, produced with the tongue body higher, and produced with advancement of the tongue root, as well as being more peripheral in F_1/F_2 space and longer (Lindau 1978, Kingston et al. 1997). Raising of the tongue body and advancement of the tongue root both contribute to lengthening the pharyngeal cavity, which lowers F_1, thus effecting the raising of tense vowels. Viewing one phonetic attribute, e.g. peripherality, in isolation from the others may obscure some of the answers. Investigations of why the different phonetic attributes of tenseness co-occur and how consistently they do so could go further to explain why vowel shifting follows certain patterns. For example, why do pharyngeal cavity lengthening and breathiness develop when a vowel becomes durationally lengthened, how general is this process across dialects, and is lengthening of duration the first step?

2.2   Instrumental studies of vowel variation in individual dialects

Since the appearance of Labov et al. (1972), acoustic inquiry into vowel variation and change has grown at a healthy pace. As Docherty and Foulkes (1999) note, however, virtually all of this inquiry has focused on comparisons of F_1 and F_2 values. Other components of vowels have received almost no instrumental attention from sociolinguists. Di Paolo and Faber (1990), Di Paolo (1992), Faber (1992), and Faber and Di Paolo (1995) found that phonation could be used to preserve vowel distinctions in Utah English that were no longer maintained by differences in formant values. A few other studies have examined vocalic duration. Feagin (1987) and Wetzell (2000) discussed the "Southern drawl," the lengthening of stressed vowels associated with the American South. In Thomas (1995), I correlated durational variation with truncation of the /ai/ diphthong, as in *tide*. Scobbie et al. (1999) examined the effects of the "Scottish vowel length rule." Nevertheless, F_1 and F_2 remain the primary focus of instrumental vowel analysis. The following paragraphs survey this research; I have limited the survey to studies of English, though F_1/F_2 studies of other languages exist (e.g. Sabino 1996, Yaeger-Dror 1996).

The description of the Northern Cities Shift is one of the most important results of Labov's instrumental research. The Northern Cities Shift consists of a chain of vowel shifts. /æ/, as in *cat*, is raised to [ɛə~eə~iə]. /ɑ/, as in *cot*, is fronted to [a], perhaps approaching [æ]. /ɔ/, as in *caught*, is lowered and often unrounded to [ɑ]. /ʌ/, as in *cut*, is backed and may be rounded to [ɔ]. /ɛ/, as in *bed*, may be lowered toward [æ] or backed toward [ɜ ~ʌ]. Finally, /ɪ/, as in *bid*, tends to be somewhat lowered or, more often, centralized (though centralization of /ɪ/ is actually rather widespread in American English: see Thomas 2001). Analyses of the Northern Cities Shift based on acoustic measurements are found in Labov et al. (1972) and Labov (1991, 1994), as well as in Veatch (1991) and Labov et al. (2001). Ito and Preston (1998) and Ito (1999) used acoustic analysis to examine the spread of the Northern Cities Shift on a more local scale, in small towns in Michigan. Acoustic analysis of Northern Cities Shift vowels is also found in Hillenbrand et al. (1995), albeit not by the authors' intention.

Labov's Southern Shift consists of several developments. One set involves diphthongs. /oi/, as in *boy*, is raised to something approaching [ui]; /ai/, as in *by*, may be backed to [ɑi~ɒi] or monophthongized to [aː]; /e/, as in *bay*, may be widened to [ɛi~ɜi~æi~ai]; and /i/, as in *bee*, may be widened to [ei~əi]. In England, these shifts – except for monophthongization of /ai/ – have been termed the "Diphthong Shift" (Wells 1982). In a similar fashion, /o/, as in *coat*, may be widened to, e.g., [ɐu], and /u/, as in *coot*, may be widened to [əu] or something similar. Other components of the Southern Shift are the fronting of /ɪ/ and /ɛ/ to positions peripheral in the vowel envelope, roughly [i] and [e], respectively, and shifting of /ɔ/ by either raising to [o] or diphthongization to [ɔo~ɑo]. Besides the general discussion of the Southern Shift in Labov et al. (1972) and Labov (1991, 1994), other acoustic analyses are found in Habick (1980, 1993), Feagin (1986), Veatch (1991), Labov and Ash (1997), Fridland (1998, 2000), and Thomas (2001). Schilling-Estes (1996), Schilling-Estes and Wolfram (1997), Wolfram et al. (1999), and Wolfram et al. (2000) included some acoustic analyses of the vowels of speakers from Smith Island, Maryland, and the Pamlico Sound region of North Carolina. In these areas, /ai/ shifts to [ɑi~ɒi] and /ɔ/ to [o], unlike other parts of the South, where /ai/ is monophthongized in some or all contexts and /ɔ/ is diphthongized.

Other dialects have been studied using spectrographic analyses of vowel formants, too. Labov et al. (fc.) is a continent-wide dialect survey based on acoustic analyses of telephone interviews that charts the geographical distribution of numerous vowel variables. Thomas (2001) is a continent-wide and cross-ethnic acoustic survey of vowel variation. Hindle (1980), Kroch (1996), Labov (1980), and Roberts (1997) examined various aspects of the Philadelphia vowel configuration. Herold (1990) included some acoustic analysis in her study of the merger of /ɑ/ and /ɔ/ in the Scranton/Wilkes-Barre region of Pennsylvania. Additional instrumental studies include Habick (1980, 1993) and Thomas (1996) on communities in central Illinois and central Ohio, respectively; Ash's (1996) study of the fronting of /u/ in the Great Lakes region; two studies of Texas English, Thomas and Bailey (1992) and Thomas (1997); and studies of the dialect of Vancouver, British Columbia, by Esling (1991) and Esling and Warkentyne (1993). Thomas (1991, 1995) and Niedzielski (1996) examined "Canadian raising," which involves raising of the nuclei of /ai/ (as in *sight*) and /au/ (as in *out*) before voiceless consonants, in the Great Lakes area. Instrumental dialectal analyses from other parts of the English-speaking world are not numerous, though see the formant plots from the British Isles in Labov et al. (1972) as well as those from New Zealand in Maclagan (1982), from Scotland in McClure (1995), and from Australia in Cox (1999).

Minority dialects have recently begun to attract some instrumental analysis. Acoustic analyses of the vowel formants of African Americans have appeared in Graff et al. (1986), Denning (1989), Deser (1990), Bailey and Thomas (1998), Thomas and Bailey (1998), and Wolfram et al. (2000). Acoustic analyses of the vowels of Jamaican creole appear in Veatch (1991) and Patrick (1996). Analyses of the vowels of Mexican Americans are found in Godinez (1984), Godinez and Maddieson (1985), Thomas (1993, 2000), Fought (1997). Anderson (1999) analyzed the diphthongs of North Carolina Cherokees. Thomas (2001) includes analyses and discussion of the vowels of African Americans, Mexican Americans, and a few Native Americans. Other minority groups, particularly Asian Americans and non-Chicano Hispanics, have been neglected.

2.3   Vowel normalization

A problem faced by many of the above-mentioned acoustic studies of vowel production is that speakers' mouth sizes differ, which results in differing formant values for "the same" vowel uttered by different speakers. As a result, quantitative comparison of vowel formant measurements from different speakers requires normalization. Disner (1980) states that normalization should reduce interspeaker variance but should preserve linguistic (and by implication, dialectal) differences. Other goals of normalization include keeping separate the contrasting vowels of a language or dialect and perhaps reflecting how human vowel perception operates. Numerous formulas for vowel normalization have been developed; all require F_1 and F_2 measurements, many require F_3 and/or F_0, and a few require other data, such as formant bandwidths, formant amplitudes, or F_4. Reviews of some of these methods can be found in, e.g., Hindle (1978), Disner (1980), and Syrdal and Gopal (1986). The fact that male and female formants are not scaled in exactly the same way (see, e.g., Fant 1966, Yang 1992) complicates normalization. All normalization techniques have drawbacks; choosing one is a matter of deciding which drawbacks are tolerable for the study at hand.

   Labov (1994: 54–72) used a method developed by Nearey (1978) for his studies of vocalic change in Philadelphia. This method involves computation of a scaling factor for F_1 and one for F_2 based on the entire range of F_1 and F_2 values – or at least part of the range – produced by a given speaker. It reduces interspeaker differences effectively and discriminates contrasting vowels of a dialect, so it is suitable for comparisons of speakers of the same dialect, as Labov used it. However, because differing vowel configurations skew the scaling factors, it does not preserve linguistic and dialectal differences well. That is, for a dialect in which /o/, /ʊ/, and /u/ are fronted, the scaling factor for F_2 would be skewed toward higher F_2 values, while for a dialect with backed /o/, /ʊ/, and /u/ it would be skewed toward lower F_2 values, and the two dialects would not be comparable. Thus, it is inappropriate for cross-dialectal comparisons. Another disadvantage of this method is that it does not reflect human speech perception, since listeners are capable of normalizing a single vowel without hearing another vowel by the same speaker; even hearing point vowels has little effect on identification (Verbrugge et al. 1976). In Thomas (1996, 1997), I used a normalization formula developed by Iri (1959) that uses F_1, F_2, and F_3 and can normalize based on a single vowel. Iri's method has its own weaknesses, e.g. it is highly sensitive to perturbations of F_3 and the normalized values of the three formants are not mathematically independent of each other.

Syrdal and Gopal (1986) model human vowel perception by computing the F_1–F_0 distance (in Bark units) and the F_3–F_2 distance (in Barks) and suggest that this method could be used for vowel normalization. A third measure that they discuss, the F_2–F_1 distance (also in Barks), could be added or substituted to resolve differences that the other two measures do not (e.g. [e] vs. [ɪ] or [i] vs. [ü]). Variations in F_0, such as from intonation, individual voice quality differences, and aging, can disrupt the height (F_1–F_0) dimension, but this problem can be circumvented by using the F_3–F_1 distance in place of the F_1–F_0 distance. Syrdal and Gopal's method appears to fulfill all of the goals of normalization listed above.[1] Figure 7.1 shows the mean measured F_1 and F_2 values of the vowels of a married couple, both lifelong residents of Johnstown, Ohio, and both born in 1959. Figure 7.2 shows their vowels normalized by the Syrdal and Gopal method (using F_2–F_1 instead of F_3–F_2), demonstrating that this method indeed reduces interspeaker differences.

2.4   *The mental representation of sounds*

Most of the studies of dialectal variation cited above are concerned with linguistic variation and change. In fact, one issue – the forms and causes of sound change – is a focus of the majority of them; discerning why language change has always been a mainstay issue of sociolinguistics. Some of those studies used instrumental techniques to address other issues, of course. Several investigated how identity with social groups is manifested in vowel production (e.g. Habick 1980, Fought 1997, Schilling-Estes 1996). The role of gender variation is intertwined with the issue of what causes diachronic shifts (Fridland 1998, Schilling-Estes 1996). Several of the studies that investigated ethnic dialects used instrumental analysis to investigate ethnic identity (e.g. Anderson 1999, Fought 1997, Wolfram et al. 2000). Stylistic variation is addressed as well (e.g. Hindle 1980, Schilling-Estes 1996). Language variationists could employ instrumental methods far more extensively on these matters. However, the causes of change and variation represent only one group of issues that variationists could address using instrumental techniques. As noted in the opening paragraph, another important group of issues that variationists could address – even though they have largely conceded it to phonologists and phoneticians in recent years – is that of the mental organization of sounds.

Research on the relationship between phonetics and phonology has indicated that the mental representation of sounds is far more complex than simply contrasts and phonological features (e.g. Keating 1990, Ohala 1981a). This fact,

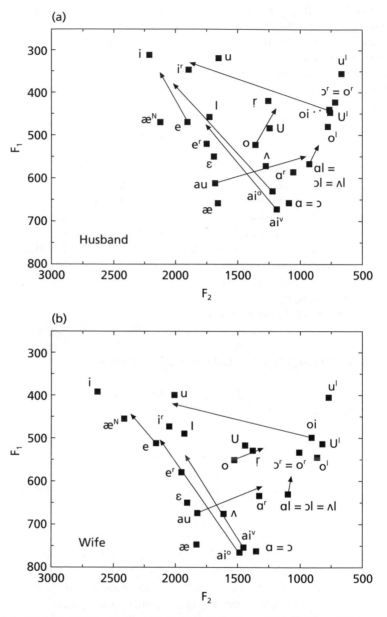

Figure 7.1 Vowel formant plots for (a) the husband and (b) the wife, both born in 1959, from Johnstown, Ohio

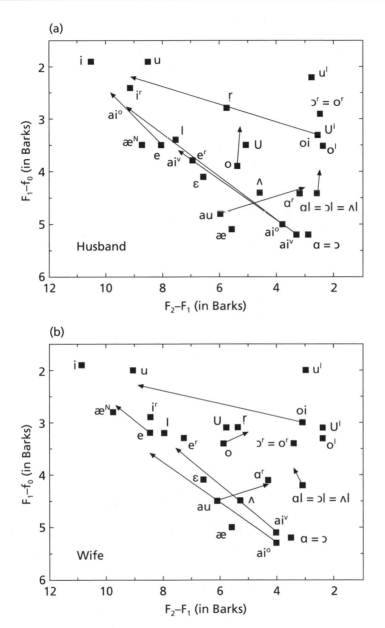

Figure 7.2 Vowels of (a) the husband and (b) the wife from Johnstown, Ohio, normalized with the method described in Syrdal and Gopal (1986)

of course, lay behind the notion of "variable rules" (see Fasold 1991). Recent phonetic work has discussed the degree to which different phonetic processes are automatic phonetic effects or are learned. Lectal variation can shed light on this issue simply because processes that show such variation cannot be automatic phonetic effects, but must be learned and therefore must be represented mentally. In fact, because lectal variation is such a valuable clue as to whether a process is automatic or not, variationists may be in a better position to study these processes than experimental phoneticians are. In the following paragraphs, I discuss four types of phonetic processes for which variationist approaches would illuminate the extent of mental representation.

The first type of phonetic process involves the means by which contrasts are made. The various phonetic cues used for the tense/lax vowel distinction were discussed previously. The realization of these cues differs from dialect to dialect. It is well-known that tense vowels are more diphthongal than lax vowels in many dialects of English, but not in all lects, e.g. those of parts of Ireland and Scotland and for many speakers in northern and western England or in Minnesota and adjacent states. Diphthongization is often viewed as a phonological process, but could as easily be viewed as a phonetic correlate of certain contrasts. Another example is the finding of Di Paolo and Faber (1990), Faber (1992), and Faber and Di Paolo (1995) that phonation may remain as a cue when formant values no longer differentiate tense and lax vowels. Sociolinguistic studies could say a great deal about how much the realization of the tense/lax contrast varies.

Perhaps the most extensively researched example in the phonetics literature is that of how the voicing of stops is distinguished. Lisker (1986), for example, lists 16 phonetic cues that may distinguish medial /p/ and /b/ in trochees, such as the duration of the closure, the duration of the preceding vowel, and the contours of F_0 and F_1 before and after the closure. Other phonetic cues occur in initial and final positions. Kingston and Diehl (1994) discuss the cues used to differentiate "voiced" and "voiceless" stops in several languages and find that the sole cue used by all the languages was that F_0 was lower after "voiced" stops than after "voiceless" stops. The fact that such differences occur among languages implies that they could also occur among dialects and individuals and perhaps among speaking styles. One of the cues that Lisker mentioned, the duration of the preceding vowel, has attracted an especially large amount of attention from phoneticians (e.g. House and Fairbanks 1953, Denes 1955, Peterson and Lehiste 1960, Chen 1970, Waldrip-Fruin 1982). Generally, vowels are longer before phonologically voiced obstruents than before phonologically voiceless obstruents. Keating (1985: 120–4), drawing on various studies, reports that some languages realize this difference to a greater degree than others. Laeufer (1992), comparing French and English, suggests, however, that the reported cross-linguistic discrepancies may be artifacts of the various designs of the studies. Davis and Summers (1989) find that the situation is more complicated in that the difference is realized in stressed syllables but perhaps not in unstressed syllables. Certainly, variationist studies could enable researchers to make sense of the contradictory evidence about vowel length before voiced and voiceless stops (see Scobbie et al. 1999).

A cue used to discriminate the voicing of final stops, and one that is not contrastive by itself, is the release burst. Many speakers are inconsistent in their production of releases; furthermore, dialects differ in their rates of production. In Thomas (2000), I find that white Anglos from central Ohio and Mexican Americans from southern Texas differ considerably in their rates of production of /t/ and /d/ releases. Not only do they differ in their overall rates – the Ohioans produce them much less often – but they also differ in whether /t/ or /d/ was released more often, with the Ohioans releasing /d/ more often and the Texans /t/. These results suggest not only that the production of releases is learned, but also that the importance that phoneticians often place on releases as a perceptual cue should be reevaluated.

The second type of phonetic process is duration-dependent reduction (Lindblom 1963). Vowels tend to become more schwa-like or to show more coarticulatory assimilation with neighboring sounds at short durations than at long durations. Lindblom proposed that phonetic vowel reduction, which he termed "undershoot," was entirely due to differences in the duration of vowels. In subsequent years, researchers have discovered that undershoot also varies according to the stress level of the vowel (Delattre 1969, Engstrand 1988, Harris 1978, Nord 1986, van Son and Pols 1990), the particular phoneme (Flege 1988), the individual speaker (Flege 1988, Kuehn and Moll 1976), the speaking style (Lindblom 1990), or the particular language (Delattre 1969). Individual and stylistic differences, as well as cross-dialectal differences (implied by the cross-linguistic differences that Delattre, 1969, reported) fall within the realm of sociolinguistics. For that reason, undershoot could serve as a useful variable for sociolinguistic studies. Beyond that fact, however, sociolinguists are well-suited for determining the extent to which undershoot is a learned process. In Thomas (1995), I examined duration-dependent truncation of the onset of the /ai/ diphthong, a process closely related to undershoot. When the duration of /ai/ is short, the onset of the diphthong is truncated and, as a result, the nucleus becomes more like the [i] glide in quality. Figure 7.3 shows plots of the data for F_2 of the /ai/ nucleus, plotted against the duration ot the diphthong, for four sixth-grade girls from Johnstown, Ohio, who were included in the study. All four plots show data for the girls' readings of the same words from a story and minimal pairs. The *y*-axis is scaled so that the lowest value is the mean value of /ul/, as in *pool*, and the highest value is the mean value of /i/, as in *eat*. Although all four speakers show similar forms of /ai/ when its duration is long, each one shows a different regression slope, indicating that they are affected to different degrees by the truncation process. These differences may represent projections of individual identity, but they also appeared to be part of a shift in progress in Johnstown.

The third type of process concerns the relative timing of articulatory gestures. Fourakis and Port (1986) compared epenthesis of [t] in words such as *dense* in Midwestern American English and South African English. The Americans

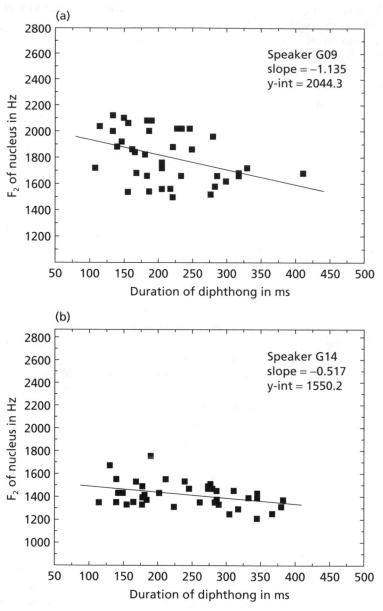

Figure 7.3 F_2 values of /ai/ nuclei plotted against diphthong duration for sixth-grade girls from Johnstown, Ohio

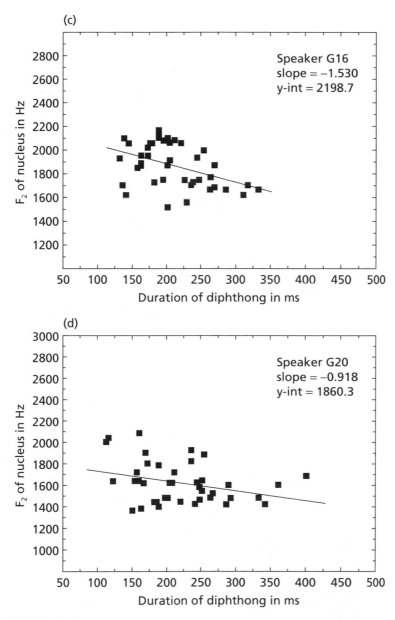

Figure 7.3   (*cont'd*)

generally produced an epenthetic [t], e.g. *dense* [dɛnts], whereas the South Africans did not. Fourakis and Port attributed this dialectal discrepancy to a difference in the phasing of gestures: the Americans ceased vocal fold vibration before commencing frication, while the South Africans did not. They suggested the term *phase rule* for such processes. There are undoubtedly many other dialectal variations involving differential phase rules. For example, I have observed that some speakers seem to begin unrounding before fronting for the /oi/ diphthong (indicated by a rise and subsequent fall of F_1), while other speakers show the opposite sequence. Additional examples of differences in phasing of gestures are discussed in Browman and Goldstein (1991).

The last type of lect-specific phonetic process to be discussed here is the steady-state pattern of diphthongs. Diphthongs necessarily show transitions in which formants move. However, they may also show steady states, in which the formants are relatively level. Steady states may appear at the beginning or end of a diphthong, or in the center of a triphthong. Lehiste and Peterson (1961) examined the diphthongs of American English. They found that /e/ typically showed one steady state – at the end – while /o/ showed a single steady state at the beginning. They stated that /ai/, /au/, and /oi/ showed steady states at both the beginning and end. Other important papers on steady-state patterns of diphthongs include Gay's (1968) study of American English, Peeters' (1991) perceptual comparison of British English with other Germanic languages, Manrique's (1979) study of Spanish, and Jha's (1985) study of Maithili. However, steady-state patterns have received little attention from either variationists or phoneticians. They exhibit more variation, both allophonic and dialectal, than the above studies suggest. For example, /ai/ may indeed show two steady states when its duration is long. In many American dialects, though, when /ai/ shows only one steady state, it is at the beginning before a voiced consonant, as in *tide*, and at the end before a voiced consonant, as in *tight*. Figure 7.4 shows spectrograms of the minimal pair *tide . . . tight* uttered by four speakers: two from central Ohio, where "Canadian raising" is not prevalent, and one speaker each from northern Ohio and Newfoundland, where

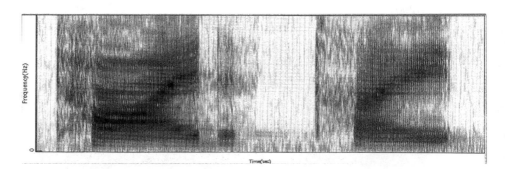

Figure 7.4(a) Spectrogram of the minimal pair *tide . . . tight* uttered by a sixth-grade girl from Johnstown, Ohio

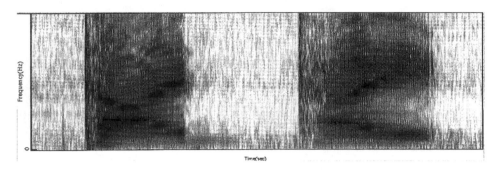

Figure 7.4(b) Spectrogram of minimal *tide . . . tight* uttered by a sixth-grade boy from Johnstown, Ohio

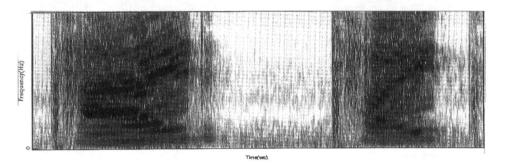

Figure 7.4(c) Spectrogram of *tide . . . tight* uttered by a woman from Euclid, Ohio (a suburb of Cleveland)

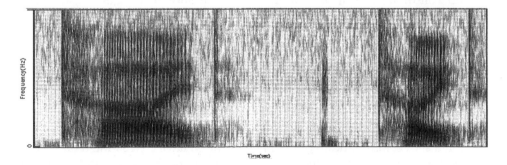

Figure 7.4(d) Spectrogram of *tide . . . tight* uttered by a man from St. John's, Newfoundland

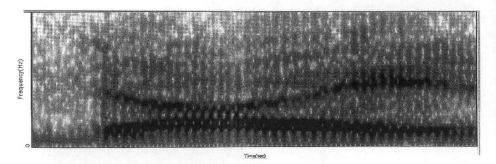

Figure 7.5(a)   Spectrogram of *died* uttered by a man, born 1860, from North Truro, Massachusetts

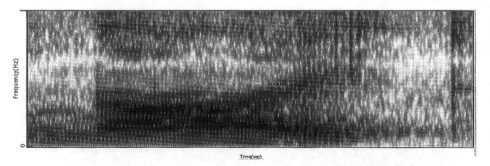

Figure 7.5(b)   Spectrogram of *night* uttered by a woman from Swan Quarter, North Carolina

"Canadian raising" predominates. All four speakers show this steady-state pattern, which may be a causal factor for certain mutations of /ai/, including "Canadian raising." Not all dialects show this pattern, as figure 7.5 shows. Some very old Northerners consistently showed offset steady states before voiced consonants, as in the utterance of *died* shown in figure 7.5a. Many Southerners show only an onset steady state before voiceless consonants, as in the utterance of *night* shown in figure 7.5b.

3   Instrumental Studies of Variation in Perception

As noted above, most studies of phonetic variation have concentrated on speech production. Speech perception is equally important, however, and although socio-perceptual experiments are now firmly part of sociolinguistics, much more work is needed. Those studies conducted thus far have focused mainly on a few issues, which the following discussion describes. The emphasis here is on studies that involve instrumental modification of the signal, such as with a speech synthesizer or the use of gating, but perceptual studies using unmodified signals are also included because perception experiments themselves can be considered instruments. Speech synthesis is an invaluable tool for examining perception; even though it can be difficult to ensure that the stimuli sound naturalistic, synthetic modification of signals permits researchers to address certain issues that no other method allows. Sociolinguists could contribute to the understanding of perceptual problems beyond traditional sociolinguistic concerns. For example, the differences between perception in optimal and "normal" listening conditions have hardly been addressed by phoneticians (Kewly-Port and Zheng 1999), but sociolinguistics, for whom attaining "normal" conditions for speech has always been a prime concern, could apply their expertise to that issue.

3.1 Sociolinguistic reactions to linguistic differences

A group of socio-perceptual studies has investigated the sociolinguistic reactions of listeners to recordings of voices. One procedure involves testing listeners' ability to identify the dialect of a speaker. Some of these studies, such as Preston (1993), Wolfram et al. (1999: 129–31), and several of the ethnic identification studies mentioned earlier, involve unmodified recordings. Others involve manipulation of the signals in order to test what features listeners utilize for their identifications. Bush (1967) used stimuli with different filterings to determine how listeners distinguished speakers of American, British, and Indian English. Some ethnic identification studies, such as Graff et al. (1986), Hawkins (1993), and Foreman (1999), have modified different aspects of the acoustic signals. Gooskens (1997) used stimuli that were either unmodified, lowpass filtered to eliminate segmental information, or monotonized to eliminate intonation in order to determine whether listeners relied more on segmental variation or intonation to identify dialects. She found that intonation was more important for identification of English dialects than for identification of Dutch dialects.

Another group of studies has investigated the intelligibility of dialects. These studies, naturally, have involved stimuli that were spliced but otherwise unmodified. Labov et al. (1972: 135–44) and Labov and Ash (1997) tested cross-dialectal perception of vowels in American English. The latter study involved gating the test words, playing them to subjects with minimal, moderate, and extensive amounts of context. Van Bezooijen and van den Berg (fc.) investigated the intelligibility of words in Dutch dialects by asking subjects to identify a word that they heard, with the frame printed for them.

A number of studies have examined listeners' perceptions of the personalities of speakers. Many such studies, such as those using matched-guise technique developed by Lambert (1967), have used unmodified voices (see Brown and

Bradshaw 1985, and Giles and Powesland 1975, for selective reviews; see also Brown et al. 1985). However, a few have employed synthetically manipulated stimuli. Brown et al. (1972, 1973, 1974), Smith et al. (1975), and Apple et al. (1979) variously modified the rate of speech, the mean F_0, and the variance of F_0. Listeners rated the stimuli on personality scales. Van Bezooijen (1988) conducted a similar experiment involving stimuli that were unmodified, lowpass filtered, randomly spliced, or written. Listeners judged the stimuli on personality scales and their judgments were compared with voice quality ratings.

Linguistic stereotypes can also be studied with perception experiments. Niedzielski (1999) examined stereotyping of "Canadian raising" of /au/, as in *house*, in Detroit. Detroit natives listened to a tape of another Detroiter, but half were told that she was a Canadian and the other half that she was a Detroiter. The listeners then matched the /au/ variants on the tape with synthesized tokens. Those told that the speaker was a Canadian tended to identify her /au/ nuclei as higher than those told that she was a Detroiter. Strand (1999) investigated how gender stereotypes are manifested through the "McGurk effect" (McGurk and MacDonald 1976). In the McGurk effect, visual stimuli override auditory stimuli in subjects' perception of speech sounds. Strand, using synthetic stimuli, found that subjects shifted their perceptual boundary between /s/ and /ʃ/ depending on whether they saw a video of a male or a female face producing such a sound. This method could be useful for studying a wide variety of other stereotypes.

3.2   Perception and sound change

Perception experiments can be applied to the issue of what causes sound change. One approach is that of John J. Ohala, who argues that sound change can be modeled in laboratories by finding parallels with results of instrumental perception experiments and production studies. In a number of papers, he has compared historically known shifts with evidence from perception and production (Hombert et al. 1979; Ohala, 1974, 1975, 1981b, 1983, 1985, 1986, 1987, 1989, 1990, and 1993). Foulkes (1997) also takes that approach. Ohala considers misperception, specifically by language learners (Ohala 1989: 186, 1993: 246–7) to be the *most* important factor in sound change (e.g. Ohala 1985). He also argues that sound change is non-teleological, i.e. it does not serve a purpose such as ease of articulation or making speech clearer for listeners. Lindblom et al. (1995) contest those points, citing Lindblom's (1990) model that speakers articulate carefully or sloppily depending on listeners' needs; they assert that speakers deliberately select the resulting variants and that this selection leads to sound change. Much sociolinguistic thought on the spread of changes is also based on the notion that speakers select variants, generally as projections of identity. Browman and Goldstein (1991) take an intermediate stance, agreeing with Lindblom et al. that production, not perception, is primary but with Ohala that change is accidental, not deliberate.

Ohala (e.g. 1993: 238) states that he is attempting to explain only the origin of shifts, not their spread, while Lindblom et al. (1995) attempt to explain both. However, Ohala's model of accidental misperception could be applied to the spread of shifts for two reasons. First, the origin and spread of sound changes may not be distinct: if phonetic conditions are right, many people may independently develop the same innovation at about the same time (Thomas 1995).[2] Second, the spread of changes, as among adolescents, does not have to occur by deliberate imitation. It is conceivable that listeners, exposed to variants in the speech of their friends or others whom they emulate, misperceive those variants as their own and subsequently begin to produce them – a "garbage in, garbage out" means of propagation. Such a process fits with Labov's outline of the mechanism of internally-motivated sound changes as "changes from below," which are "below the level of social awareness" (Labov 1972b: 178). Yet the model of deliberate selection espoused by Lindblom et al. (1995) mirrors the widespread view that speakers manipulate variants as signals of identity. Labov, of course, considers conscious selection to be the major factor in the spread of externally-motivated changes, but what about those that show internal motivation? It would appear that a major empirical issue to be resolved is whether sound changes that are not due to overt prestige occur through deliberate selection of variants, through misperception, or through both. The resolution of this issue will depend on examinations of young sound changes, not just on studies of the more stratified or stereotyped variables on which sociolinguists often focus. More significantly, however, perception experiments will necessarily play a role in the resolution.

One example of the role of perception in sound change that is relevant to many sociolinguistic studies is the perception of word-final stops. Several phonetic studies, e.g. Browman and Goldstein (1990, 1991) and Surprenant and Goldstein (1998), have found that the articulatory gesture for a word-final stop may not produce an audible signal if the following word begins with a consonant, and that coronal stops are more susceptible to this effect than other stops. The effect is due partly to the fact that the stop may be unreleased in this context. It is especially strong when the final stop is part of a cluster, as with the /t/ in *perfect memory*. This perceptual result explains the oft-reported tendency toward consonant cluster simplification, especially when the cluster is followed by another consonant (e.g. Wolfram 1969, Labov 1972a, Fasold 1972, Guy 1980). It also suggests that many tokens that have been classified as instances of stop deletion are cases of imperceptibility, not of deletion in production.

Other approaches to sound change involving perception experiments include following perceptual changes in shifting sounds and examining how contrasts are maintained perceptually. Janson (1979, 1983, 1986), using synthetic stimuli representing phonetic continua, found that vowel shifts in Stockholm Swedish were reflected in perceptual shifts in the boundaries between phonemes. His work raises the question of whether production shifts or perceptual shifts are primary (in time and/or importance), but other researchers have not followed up on his work. Studies of perceptual boundaries between sounds will have to incorporate the fact that misperceptions between sounds are often asymmetrical (Ohala 1985: 462–7) – e.g. [ü] is misperceived as [i] more often than vice versa.

There are a number of dialectal perception studies on how contrasts may be maintained, especially where sound changes have created unusual variants in some dialects or have eliminated some cues used for distinctions. Commutation tests – in which listeners identify words uttered by themselves or by other speakers of their own dialect – involve unmodified speech. Several examples are described in Labov (1994); others appear in Costa and Mattingly (1981), Di Paolo and Faber (1990), and Labov and Ash (1997). Janson and Schulman (1983) took a different approach. They created synthetic stimuli representing a continuum in order to investigate the merger of Swedish short /ε/ and short /e/. Subjects were instructed to label each stimulus as a particular Swedish word. The experiment suggested that speakers of a dialect in which the distinction was maintained were unable to perceive it, and Janson and Schulman (like Costa and Mattingly 1981) concluded that distinctions could be lost in perception but maintained in production. However, Labov et al. (1991) argued that Janson and Schulman's experiment was flawed because the task involved labeling of isolated stimuli instead of discrimination in conversations. Using non-synthetic stimuli, they constructed a task in which the interpretation of a narrative rested on listeners' ability to distinguish, in one particular word, vowels that were nearly merged by Philadelphians. The results showed that Philadelphia natives were usually able to perceive the distinction, but that their ability to do so was impaired.

3.3   Perception and mental processing of sounds

Socio-perceptual studies can address issues regarding the mental processing of sounds as well, though few have. The cross-linguistic and cross-dialectal perceptual study of diphthong steady-state patterns by Peeters (1991), mentioned earlier, showed that there is considerable variation in which patterns listeners rate as most realistic. This result suggests that steady-state patterns are language- and dialect-specific and thus part of a person's phonetic knowledge. In Thomas (2000), I found that non-Hispanic whites from Ohio and Mexican Americans from Texas differ in how they perceive /ai/ glides. The Ohioans associated glides closely approaching [i] in quality with a following voiceless stop and those closer in quality to [ε] with a following voiced stop. The Texans did so to a lesser extent and confused that distinction with the presence or absence of the final stop. The likely reason was that the Texans may have placed more perceptual weight on the presence of a stop release than the Ohioans and the stimuli, which represented a continuum from *tight*-like to *tide*-like forms, lacked final stop releases.

Sociolinguists could also contribute to the resolution of perceptual issues related to mental processing that are currently debated by phoneticians. For example, Kuhl (1991) proposed the "perceptual magnet effect," i.e. that listeners discriminate formant differences more poorly around a vowel target than away from it. Lotto et al. (1998) contested that notion, arguing that what Kuhl found was simply the effect of the perceptual boundaries between phonemes. A study comparing the perceptual discrimination abilities of, say, speakers of a dialect in which /u/ is fronted and speakers of a dialect in which it remains back could shed light on which theory is correct. That is, are formant differences within "unused" vowel space less apparent if that space is closer to a target? Comparisons of discrimination abilities by speakers who have been exposed to many dialects and those who have not may yield other significant findings about the nature of speech perception.

4   Toward Sociophonetics

Melding of sociolinguistics and phonetics is sometimes referred to as *sociophonetics*, e.g. by Esling (1991). This essay has advocated a greater melding of the two. Integration of sociolinguistics with other disciplines is beneficial, as Docherty et al. (1997) note in their discussion of the links between sociolinguistics and phonology. Experimental phonetics, however, shares a special attribute with sociolinguistics: as Chambers (1995: 26–8) notes, neither adopts the "axiom of categoricity" that linguistic competence is best studied "at some remove from its real-life performance" (1995: 26). Both subfields are focused primarily on observing linguistic behavior directly. Thus, there would seem to be natural links between them.

Each discipline has weaknesses that the other can address. Experimental phoneticians seldom use naturalistic data. They often use small samples of speakers and usually examine subjects' behavior in laboratories. As sociolinguists know well, subjects' linguistic behavior in a formal setting like a laboratory is not always representative of their ordinary linguistic behavior. Phoneticians could benefit from greater sociolinguistic awareness. In addition, more extensive cross-lectal comparisons can shed light on issues that phoneticians usually study. Foulkes and Docherty (1999: 22) point out that many (but not all) phoneticians have been "treating variation as a nuisance" even though it could be a useful tool.

At the same time, sociolinguists too often do not examine closely the phonetic details of the variables they study. For example, a sociolinguistic study of /ai/ in the South may code tokens simply as diphthongal or monophthongal, perhaps categorizing the tokens according to what sort of consonant follows /ai/ or a few other factors, and then move on to the sociological aspects of the inquiry. Glide weakening of /ai/ is actually a gradient process that depends on factors such as duration and steady-state structure that require instrumental measurement. Avoiding instrumental analysis can sometimes lead to erroneous phonetic descriptions and also undoubtedly causes sociolinguists to miss many important variables.

Sociolinguists, furthermore, should avoid becoming too parochial in the phonetic issues that they study. The manifestation of vowel shifting in production has preoccupied sociophonetic inquiry for a generation. Sociolinguists should now nurture other types of phonetic analyses just as much. More instrumental studies of consonantal, prosodic, and voice quality variation are needed. Instrumental analysis can yield greater insights into traditional sociolinguistic constructs such as ethnic or social group identity. Cross-dialectal studies can allow sociolinguists to address issues, particularly those concerning the mental processing of sounds, that they have barely touched in recent years. Perhaps most importantly, the still-nascent field of socio-perceptual inquiry needs to expand and mature. Sociolinguists have already made significant strides in instrumental phonetic analysis. However, for sociolinguistics to remain viable, many more strides into the areas discussed here will be necessary as the twenty-first century progresses.

ACKNOWLEDGMENT

Part of the research for this paper was supported by NSF Grant # 9809385.

NOTES

1   This method reflects human vowel perception in that it requires only a single vowel for normalization. However, it is linked to the assumption by Syrdal and Gopal (1986) that listeners normalize vowels based on steady-state values. Other researchers have argued that listeners identify vowels from formant movements; see, e.g., Strange (1989) and Hillenbrand and Nearey (1999). The issue is still controversial (Pitermann 2000). The F_3–F_1 distance metric can be skewed by contexts with an adjacent /r/. These contexts should be examined separately. One of the original reasons for using the F_1–F_0 value is that high vowels tend to show higher F_0 values than low vowels, thereby minimizing the F_1/F_0 distance for high vowels and maximizing it for low vowels, but this effect is so small that little is lost in not using the F_1/F_0 distance.

2   I do not mean this in the same sense as Weinreich et al. (1968). Weinreich et al. asserted that the origin and propagation of a change are the same because a change is not a change if it involves a single person, but only when it begins to spread (for a critique of this notion, see Romaine 1982: 244f). In contrast, I assume that a change could theoretically involve only one person, but that in real life many people independently and simultaneously show the same innovation. Thus a change has "spread" at the same time that it originates.

REFERENCES

Anderson, Bridget L. (1999). Source-language transfer and vowel accommodation in the patterning of Cherokee English /ai/ and /oi/. *American Speech* 74: 339–68.

Apple, William, Lynn A. Streeter and Robert M. Krauss (1979). Effects of pitch and speech rate on personal attributions. *Journal of Personality and Social Psychology* 37: 715–27.

Ash, Sharon (1996). Freedom of movement: /uw/-fronting in the Midwest. In J. Arnold, R. Blake, B. Davidson, S. Schwenter and J. Solomon (eds.), *Sociolinguistic Variation: Data, Theory, and Analysis. Selected Papers from NWAV 23 at Stanford*. Stanford, CA: CSLI Publications. 3–25.

Bailey, Guy and Natalie Maynor (1989). The divergence controversy. *American Speech* 64: 12–39.

Bailey, Guy and Erik Thomas (1998). Some aspects of African-American Vernacular English phonology. In S. S. Mufwene, J. Rickford, J. Baugh and G. Bailey (eds.), *African American English*. London: Routledge. 85–109.

Baugh, John (1996). Perceptions within a variable paradigm: Black and white racial detection and identification based on speech. In E. W. Schneider (ed.), *Focus on the USA*. Varieties of English around the World, General Series, vol. 16. Amsterdam: John Benjamins. 169–82.

Bezooijen, Renée van (1988). The relative importance of pronunciation, prosody, and voice quality for the attribution of social status and personality characteristics. In R. van Hout and U. Knops (eds.), *Language Attitudes in the Dutch Language Area*. Dordrecht: Foris. 85–103.

Bezooijen, Renée van and Rob van den Berg (forthcoming). Word

intelligibility of language varieties in the Netherlands and Flanders under minimal conditions. In R. Kager and R. van Bezooijen (eds.), *Linguistics in the Netherlands* 16. Amsterdam: John Benjamins.

Britain, David (1992). Linguistic change in intonation: The use of high rising terminals in New Zealand English. *Language Variation and Change* 4: 77–104.

Browman, Catherine P. and Louis Goldstein (1990). Tiers in articulatory phonology, with some implications for casual speech. In J. Kingston and M. Beckman (eds.), *Papers in Laboratory Phonology I: Beyond the grammar and Physics of Speech*. Cambridge: Cambridge University Press. 341–76.

Browman, Catherine P. and Louis Goldstein (1991). Gestural structures: Distinctiveness, phonological processes, and historical change. In I. G. Mattingly and M. Studdert-Kennedy (eds.), *Modularity and the Motor Theory of Speech Perception*. Hillsdale, NJ: Lawrence Erlbaum. 313–38.

Brown, Bruce L. and Jeffrey M. Bradshaw (1985). Towards a social psychology of voice variations. In H. Giles and R. N. St. Clair (eds.), *Recent Advances in Language, Communication, and Social Psychology*. London: Lawrence Erlbaum. 144–81.

Brown, Bruce L., William J. Strong and Alvin C. Rencher (1972). Acoustic determinants of perceptions of personality from speech. *International Journal of the Sociology of Language* 6: 11–32.

Brown, Bruce L., William J. Strong and Alvin C. Rencher (1973). Perceptions of personality from speech: Effects of manipulations of acoustical parameters. *Journal of the Acoustical Society of America* 54: 29–35.

Brown, Bruce L., William J. Strong and Alvin C. Rencher (1974). Fifty-four voices from two: Rate, mean fundamental frequency and variance of fundamental frequency on ratings of personality from speech. *Journal of the Acoustical Society of America* 55: 313–18.

Brown, Bruce L., Howard Giles and Jitendra N. Thakerar (1985). Speaker evaluations as a function of speech rate, accent, and context. *Language and Communication* 5: 207–20.

Bush, Clara N. (1967). Some acoustic parameters of speech and their relationships to the perception of dialect differences. *TESOL Quarterly* 1, 3: 20–30.

Chambers, J. K. (1995). *Sociolingusitic Theory: Linguistic Variation and its Social Significance*. Language in Society, vol. 22. Oxford: Blackwell.

Chen, Matthew (1970). Vowel length as a function of the voicing of the consonant environment. *Phonetica* 22: 129–59.

Costa, Paul and Ignatius G. Mattingly (1981). Production and perception of phonetic contrast during phonetic change. *Journal of the Acoustic Society of America* 69: S67.

Cox, Felicity (1999). Vowel change in Australian English. *Phonetica* 56: 1–27.

Davis, Stuart and W. Van Summers (1989). Vowel length and closure duration in word-medial VC sequences. *Journal of Phonetics* 17: 339–53.

Delattre, Pierre (1969). An acoustic and articulatory study of vowel reduction in four languages. *International Review of Applied Linguistics in Language Teaching* 7: 295–325.

Denes, Peter B. (1955). Effect of duration of the perception of voicing. *Journal of the Acoustical Society of America* 27: 761–4.

Denning, Keith (1989). Convergence with divergence: A sound change in vernacular Black English. *Language Variation and Change* 1: 145–67.

Deser, Toni (1990). Dialect transmission and variation: An acoustic analysis of vowels in six urban Detroit families. Ph.D. dissertation, Boston University.

Di Paolo, Marianna (1992). Hypercorrection in response to the apparent merger of (ɔe) and (ɑ) in Utah English. *Language and Communication* 12: 267–92.

Di Paolo, Marianna and Alice Faber (1990). Phonation differences and the phonetic content of the tense-lax contrast in Utah English. *Language Variation and Change* 2: 155–204.

Disner, Sandra Ferrari (1980). Evaluation of vowel normalization procedures. *Journal of the Acoustical Society of America* 67: 253–61.

Docherty, Gerard J. and Paul Foulkes (1999). Derby and Newcastle: Instrumental phonetics and variationist studies. In P. Foulkes and G. J. Docherty (eds.), *Urban Voices*. London: Arnold. 47–71.

Docherty, Gerard J., Paul Foulkes, James Milroy, Lesley Milroy and David Walshaw (1997). Descriptive adequacy in phonology: A variationist perspective. *Journal of Linguistics* 33: 275–310.

Engstrand, Olle (1988). Articulatory correlates of stress and speaking rate in Swedish VCV utterances. *Journal of the Acoustical Society of America* 83: 1863–75.

Esling, John H. (1991). Sociophonetic variation in Vancouver. In J. Cheshire (ed.), *English Around the World: Sociolinguistic Perspectives*.

Cambridge: Cambridge University Press. 123–33.

Esling, John H. and Henry J. Warkentyne (1993). Retracting of /æ/ in Vancouver English. In S. Clarke (ed.), *Focus on Canada*. Varieties of English around the world, general series, vol. 11. Amsterdam: John Benjamins. 229–46.

Faber, Alice (1992). Articulatory variability, categorical perception, and the inevitability of sound change. In G. W. Davis and G. K. Iverson (eds.), *Explanation in Historical Linguistics*. Amsterdam: John Benjamins. 59–75.

Faber, Alice and Di Paolo, Marianna (1995). The discriminability of nearly merged sounds. *Language Variation and Change* 7: 35–78.

Fant, Gunnar (1966). A note on vocal tract size factors and non-uniform F-pattern scalings. *Speech Transmission Laboratory – Quarterly Progress and Status Report (STL-QPSR) 4/1966*. Stockholm: Royal Institute of Technology. 22–30.

Fasold, Ralph W. (1972). *Tense Marking in Black English: A Linguistic and Social Analysis*. Washington, DC: Center for Applied Linguistics.

Fasold, Ralph W. (1991). The quiet demise of variable rules. *American Speech* 66: 3–21.

Feagin, Crawford (1986). More evidence for major vowel change in the South. In D. Sankoff (ed.), *Diversity and Diachrony*. Amsterdam studies in the theory and history of linguistic science, series IV: Current issues in linguistic theory, vol. 53. Amsterdam: John Benjamins. 83–95.

Feagin, Crawford (1987). A closer look at the Southern drawl: Variation taken to extremes. In K. M. Denning, S. Inkelas, F. C. McNair-Knox and J. Rickford (eds.), *Variation in Language: NWAV-XV at Stanford. Proceedings of the Fifteenth Annual Conference on New Ways of Analyzing Variation*. Stanford, CA: Dept. of Linguistics, Stanford University. 137–50.

Flege, James Emil (1988). Effects of the speaking rate on tongue position and velocity of movement in vowel production. *Journal of the Acoustical Society of America* 84: 901–16.

Foreman, Christina Gayle (1999). The identification of African-American English from prosodic cues. Paper presented at the seventh annual meeting of the Symposium About Language and Society – Austin, Austin, TX, 9 April.

Fought, Carmen (1997). A majority sound change in a minority community. *University of Pennsylvania Working Papers in Linguistics* 4: 39–56.

Foulkes, Paul (1997). Historical laboratory phonology – investigating /p/>/f/>/h/ changes. *Language and Speech* 40: 249–76.

Foulkes, Paul and Gerard J. Docherty (eds.) (1999). *Urban voices: Accent studies in the British Isles*. London: Arnold.

Foulkes, Paul and Gerard J. Docherty (1999). Urban Voices – overview. In P. Foulkes and G. J. Docherty (eds.), *Urban Voices*. London: Arnold. 1–24.

Fourakis, Marios and Robert Port (1986). Stop epenthesis in English. *Journal of Phonetics* 14: 197–221.

Fridland, Valerie (1998). The Southern vowel shift: linguistic and social factors. Ph.D. dissertation, Michigan State University.

Fridland, Valerie (2000). The Southern Shift in Memphis, Tennessee. *Language Variation and Change* 11: 267–85.

Gay, Thomas (1968). Effect of speaking rate on diphthong formant movements. *Journal of the Acoustical Society of America* 44: 1570–73.

Giles, Howard and Peter F. Powesland (1975). *Speech Style and Social Evaluation*. London: Academic Press.

Godinez, Manuel, Jr. (1984). Chicano English phonology: Norms vs. interference phenomena. In J. Ornstein-Galicia (ed.), *Form and Function in Chicano English*. Rowley, MA: Newberry. 42–48.

Godinez, Manuel, Jr. and Ian Maddieson (1985). Vowel differences between Chicano and general Californian English? *International Journal of the Sociology of Language* 53: 43–58.

Gooskens, Charlotte Stenkilde (1997). On the role of prosodic and verbal information in the perception of Dutch and English language varieties. Ph.D. dissertation, Katholieke Universiteit Nijmegen.

Graff, David, William Labov and Wendell A. Harris (1986). Testing listeners' reactions to phonological markers of ethnic identity: A new method for sociolinguistic research. In D. Sankoff (ed.), *Diversity and Diachrony*. Amsterdam studies in the theory and history of linguistic science, vol. 53. Amsterdam: John Benjamins. 45–58.

Guy, Gregory R. (1980). Variation in the group and the individual: The case of final stop deletion. In W. Labov (ed.), *Locating Language in Time and Space*. Orlando, FL: Academic Press. 1–36.

Habick, Timothy (1980). Sound change in Farmer City: A sociolinguistic study based on acoustic data. Ph.D. dissertation, University of Illinois at Urbana-Champaign.

Habick, Timothy (1993). Farmer City, Illinois: Sound systems shifting south. In T. C. Frazer (ed.), *"Heartland" English: Variation and Transition in the American Midwest*. Tuscaloosa, AL: University of Alabama Press. 97–124.

Haley, Kenneth (1990). Some complexities in speech identification. *The SECOL Review* 14: 101–13.

Harris, Katherine S. (1978). Vowel duration change and its underlying physiological mechanisms. *Language and Speech* 21: 354–61.

Hawkins, Francine Dove (1993). Speaker Ethnic Identification: The roles of speech sample, fundamental frequency, speaker and listener variations. Ph.D. dissertation, University of Maryland at College Park.

Herold, Ruth (1990). Mechanisms of merger: The implementation and distribution of the low back merger in eastern Pennsylvania. Ph.D. dissertation, University of Pennsylvania.

Hillenbrand, James M. and Terrance M. Nearey (1999). Identification of resynthesized /hVd/ utterances: Effects of formant contour. *Journal of the Acoustical Society of America* 105: 3509–23.

Hillenbrand, James, Laura A. Getty, Michael J. Clark and Kimberlee Wheeler (1995). Acoustic characteristics of American English vowels. *Journal of the Acoustical Society of America* 97: 3099–111.

Hindle, Donald (1978). Approaches to vowel normalization in the study of natural speech. In David Sankoff (ed.), *Linguistic Variation: Models and Methods*. New York: Academic Press. 161–71.

Hindle, Donald (1980). The social and structural conditioning of vowel variation. Ph.D. dissertation, University of Pennsylvania.

Hombert, Jean-Marie, John J. Ohala and William G. Ewan (1979). Phonetic explanations for the development of tones. *Language* 55: 37–58.

House, Arthur M. and Grant Fairbanks (1953). The influence of consonant environment upon the secondary acoustical characteristics of vowels. *Journal of Speech and Hearing Research* 5: 38–58.

Iri, Masao (1959). A mathematical method in phonetics with a special reference to the acoustical structure of Japanese vowels. *Gengo Kenkyu* 35: 23–30.

Ito, Rika (1999). Diffusion of urban sound change in rural Michigan: A case of Northern Cities Shift. Ph.D. dissertation, Michigan State University.

Ito, Rika and Dennis R. Preston (1998). Identity, discourse, and language variation. *Journal of Language and Social Psychology* 17: 465–83.

Janson, Tore (1979). Vowel duration, vowel quality, and perceptual compensation. *Journal of Phonetics* 7: 93–103.

Janson, Tore (1983). Sound change in perception and production. *Language* 59: 18–34.

Janson, Tore (1986). Sound change in perception: An experiment. In J. J. Ohala and J. J. Jaeger (eds.), *Experimental Phonology*. Orlando, FL: Academic Press. 253–60.

Janson, Tore and Richard Schulman (1983). Non-distinctive features and their use. *Journal of Linguistics* 19: 321–36.

Jha, Sunil Kumar (1985). Acoustic analysis of Maithili diphthongs. *Journal of Phonetics* 13: 107–15.

Jun, Sun-Ah and Christina Foreman (1996). Boundary tones and focus realization in African-American English intonations. *Journal of the Acoustical Society of America* 100: 2826.

Keating, Patricia A. (1985). Universal phonetics and the organization of grammars. In V. A. Fromkin (ed.), *Phonetic Linguistics: Essays in Honor of Peter Ladefoged*. Orlando, FL: Academic Press. 115–32.

Keating, Patricia A. (1990). Phonetic representations in a generative grammar. *Journal of Phonetics* 18: 321–34.

Kewly-Port, Diane and Yijian Zheng (1999). Vowel formant discrimination: Towards more ordinary listening conditions. *Journal of the Acoustical Society of America* 106: 2945–58.

Kingston, John and Randy L. Diehl (1994). Phonetic knowledge. *Language* 70: 419–54.

Kingston, John, Neil A. Macmillan, Laura Walsh Dickey, Rachel Thornburn and Christine Bartels (1997). Integrality in the perception of tongue root position and voice quality in vowels. *Journal of the Acoustical Society of America* 101: 1696–709.

Kroch, Anthony (1996). Dialect and style in the speech of upper class Philadelphia. In G. R. Guy, C. Feagin, D. Schiffrin and J. Baugh (eds.), *Towards a Social Science of Language: Papers in Honor of William Labov*. Amsterdam studies in the theory and history of linguistic science. Series IV: Current issues in linguistic theory 127. Amsterdam: John Benjamins. 23–45.

Kuehn, D. P. and K. L. Moll (1976). A cineradiographic study of VC and CV articulatory velocities. *Journal of Phonetics* 4: 303–20.

Kuhl, Patricia K. (1991). Human adults and human infants show a "perceptual magnet effect" for the prototypes of speech categories, monkeys do not. *Perception and Psychophysics* 50: 93–107.

Labov, William (1972a). *Language in the Inner City: The Black English Vernacular*. Philadelphia: University of Pennsylvania Press.

Labov, William (1972b). *Sociolinguistic Patterns*, vol. 4: *Conduct and*

Communication. Philadelphia: University of Pennsylvania Press.

Labov, William (1980). The social origins of sound change. In W. Labov (ed.), *Locating Language in Time and Space*. Orlando, FL: Academic Press. 251–65.

Labov, William (1991). The three dialects of English. In P. Eckert (ed.), *New Ways of Analyzing Sound Change*, vol. 5: *Quantitative Analyses of Linguistic Structure*. Orlando, FL: Academic Press. 1–44.

Labov, William (1994). *Principles of Linguistic Change*, vol. 1: *Internal Factors*. Language in Society, vol. 20. Oxford: Blackwell.

Labov, William and Sharon Ash (1997). Understanding Birmingham. In C. Bernstein, T. Nunnaly and R. Sabino (eds.), *Language Variety in the South Revisited*. Tuscaloosa, AL: University of Alabama Press. 508–73.

Labov, William, Mark Karen and Corey Miller (1991). Near-mergers and the suspension of phonemic contrast. *Language Variation and Change* 3: 33–74.

Labov, William, Malcah Yaeger, and Richard Steiner (1972). *A Quantitative Study of Sound Change in Progress*. Philadelphia: US Regional Survey.

Labov, William, Sharon Ash and Charles Boberg (2001). *Phonological Atlas of North American English*. Berlin: Mouton de Gruyter.

Laeufer, Christiane (1992). Patterns of voicing-conditioned vowel duration in French and English. *Journal of Phonetics* 20: 411–40.

Lambert, Wallace E. (1967). A social psychology of bilingualism. *Journal of Social Issues* 23: 91–109.

Lass, Norman J., Pamela J. Mertz and Karen L. Kimmel (1978). The effect of temporal speech alterations on speaker race and sex identifications. *Language and Speech* 21: 279–90.

Lass, Norman J., John E. Tecca, Robert A. Mancuso and Wanda I. Black (1979). The effect of phonetic complexity on speaker race and sex identifications. *Journal of Phonetics* 7: 105–18.

Lass, Norman J., Celest A. Almerino, Laurie F. Jordan and Jayne M. Walsh (1980). The effect of filtered speech on speaker race and sex identifications. *Journal of Phonetics* 8: 101–12.

Lehiste, Ilse and Gordon E. Peterson (1961). Transitions, glides, and diphthongs. *Journal of the Acoustical Society of America* 33: 268–77.

Lindau, Mona (1978). Vowel features. *Language* 54: 541–63.

Lindblom, Björn (1963). Spectrographic study of vowel reduction. *Journal of the Acoustical Society of America* 35: 1773–81.

Lindblom, Björn (1980). The goal of phonetics, its unification and application. *Phonetica* 37: 7–26.

Lindblom, Björn. (1990). Explaining phonetic variation: A sketch of the H&H theory. In W. J. Hardcastle and A. Marchal (eds.), *Speech Production and Speech Modelling*. Dordrecht: Kluwer. 403–39.

Lindblom, Björn E. F. and Michael Studdert-Kennedy (1967). On the role of formant transitions in vowel recognition. *Journal of the Acoustical Society of America* 42: 830–43.

Lindblom, Björn, Susan Guion, Susan Hura, Seung-Jae Moon and Raquel Willerman (1995). Is sound change adaptive? *Rivista di Linguistica* 7: 5–37.

Lisker, Leigh (1986). "Voicing" in English: A catalogue of acoustic features signaling /b/ vs. /p/ in trochees. *Language and Speech* 29: 3–11.

Lotto, Andrew J., Keith R. Kluender and Lori L. Holt (1998). Depolarizing the perceptual magnet effect. *Journal of the Acoustical Society of America* 103: 3648–55.

Maclagan, Margaret A. (1982). An acoustic study of New Zealand English vowels. *New Zealand Speech Therapists' Journal* 37: 20–6.

Manrique, Ana Maria Borzone de (1979). Acoustic analysis of the Spanish diphthongs. *Phonetica* 36: 194–206.

McClure, J. Derrick (1995). The vowels of Scottish English – formants and features. In J. W. Lewis (ed.), *Studies in General and English Phonetics: Essays in Honour of Professor J. D. O'Connor.* London: Routledge. 367–78.

McGurk, Harry and John MacDonald (1976). Hearing lips and seeing voices. *Nature* 264: 746–8.

Nábělek, Anna K. and Alexandra Ovchinnikov (1997). Perception of nonlinear and linear formant trajectories. *Journal of the Acoustical Society of America* 101: 488–97.

Nairn, Moray J. and James R. Hurford (1995). The effect of context on the transcription of vowel quality. In J. W. Lewis (ed.), *Studies in General and English Phonetics: Essays in Honour of Professor J. D. O'Connor.* London: Routledge. 96–120.

Nearey, Terrance Michael (1978). Phonetic feature systems for vowels. Ph.D. dissertation, University of Alberta.

Niedzielski, Nancy (1996). Acoustic analysis and language attitudes in Detroit. *University of Pennsylvania Working Papers in Linguistics* 3: 73–85.

Niedzielski, Nancy (1999). The effect of social information on the perception of sociolinguistic variables. *Journal of Language and Social Psychology* 18: 62–85.

Nord, Lennart (1986). Acoustic studies of vowel reduction in Swedish. *Papers from the Institute of Linguistics, University of Stockholm (STL-QPSR)* 4: 19–36.

Ohala, John J. (1974). Experimental historical phonology. In J. M. Anderson and C. Jones (eds.), *Historical Linguistics*, vol. II *Theory and Description in Phonology. Proceedings of the First International Conference on Historical Linguistics, Edinburgh 2nd–7th September 1973.* Amsterdam: North-Holland. 353–89.

Ohala, John J. (1975). Phonetic explanations for nasal sound patterns. In C. A. Ferguson and L. M. Hyman (eds.), *Nasalfest: Papers from a Symposium on nasals and Nasalization.* Stanford, CA: Language Universals Project. 289–316.

Ohala, John J. (1981a). Articulatory constraints on the cognitive representation of speech. In Terry Myers, John Laver and John Anderson (eds.), *The Cognitive Representation of Speech.* Amsterdam: North-Holland. 111–22.

Ohala, John J. (1981b). The listener as a source of sound change. In C. S. Masek, R. A. Hendrick and M. F. Miller (eds.), *Papers from the Parasession on Language and Behavior, Chicago Linguistic Society, May 1–2, 1981.* Chicago: Chicago Linguistic Society, University of Chicago. 178–203.

Ohala, John J. (1983). The direction of sound change. In A. Cohen and M. P. R. van den Broecke (eds.), *Abstracts of the Tenth International Congress of Phonetic Sciences.* Dordrecht: Foris Publications. 253–58.

Ohala, John J. (1985). Linguistics and automatic processing of speech. In R. De Mori and C. Y. Suen (eds.), *New Systems and Architectures for Automatic Speech Recognition and Synthesis.* Berlin: Springer-Verlag. 447–75.

Ohala, John J. (1986). Phonological evidence for top-down processing in speech perception. In J. S. Perkell and D. H. Klatt (eds.), *Invariance and Variability in Speech Processes*. Hillsdale, NJ: Lawrence Erlbaum. 386–97.

Ohala, John J. (1987). Experimental phonology. *Proceedings of the Annual Meeting, Berkeley Linguistic Society* 13: 207–22.

Ohala, John J. (1989). Sound change is drawn from a pool of synchronic variation. In L. E. Breivik and E. H. Jahr (eds.), *Language Change: Contributions to the Study of its Causes*. Berlin: Mouton de Gruyter. 173–98.

Ohala, John J. (1990). The phonetics and phonology of aspects of assimilation. In J. Kingston and M. Beckman (eds.), *Papers in Laboratory Phonology I: Between the Grammar and Physics of Speech*. Cambridge: Cambridge University Press. 258–75.

Ohala, John J. (1993). The phonetics of sound change. In C. Jones (ed.), *Historical Linguistics: Problems and Perspectives*. London: Longman. 237–78.

Ohala, John J. and Deborah Feder (1994). Listeners' normalization of vowel quality is influenced by "restored" consonantal context. *Phonetica* 51: 111–18.

Patrick, Peter (1996). The urbanization of creole phonology: Variation and change in Jamaican. In G. R. Guy, C. Feagin, D. Schiffrin and J. Baugh (eds.), *Towards a Social Science of Language: Papers in Honor of William Labov*. Amsterdam studies in the theory and history of linguistic science. Series IV: Current issues in linguistic theory 127. Amsterdam: John Benjamins. 329–55.

Peeters, Wilhelmus Johannes Maria (1991). Diphthong dynamics: A cross-linguistic perceptual analysis of temporal patterns in Dutch, English, and German. Ph.D. dissertation, Rijksuniversiteit te Utrecht.

Peterson, Gordon E. and Ilse Lehiste (1960). Duration of syllable nuclei in English. *Journal of the Acoustical Society of America* 32: 693–703.

Pitermann, Michel (2000). Effect of speaking rate and contrastive stress on formant dynamics and vowel perception. *Journal of the Acoustical Society of America* 107: 3425–37.

Preston, Dennis R. (1993). Two heartland perceptions of language variety. In T. C. Frazer (ed.), *"Heartland" English: Variation and Transition in the American Midwest*. Tuscaloosa: University of Alabama Press. 23–47.

Roberts, Julie. (1997). Hitting a moving target: Acquisition of sound change in progress by Philadelphia children. *Language Variation and Change* 9: 249–66.

Roberts, Margaret M. (1966). The pronunciation of vowels in Negro speech. Ph.D. dissertation, Ohio State University.

Romaine, Suzanne (1982). *Sociohistorical Linguistics: Its Status and Methodology*. Cambridge: Cambridge University Press.

Sabino, Robin (1996). A peak at death: Assessing continuity and change in an undocumented language. *Language Variation and Change* 8: 41–61.

Schilling-Estes, Natalie (1996). The linguistic and sociolinguistic status of /ay/ in Outer Banks English. Ph.D. dissertation, University of North Carolina at Chapel Hill.

Schilling-Estes, Natalie and Walt Wolfram (1997). Symbolic identity and language change: A comparative analysis of post-insular /ay/ and /aw/. *University of Pennsylvania Working Papers in Linguistics* 4: 83–104.

Scobbie, James M., Nigel Hewlett, and Alice Turk (1999). Standard English in Edinburgh and Glasgow: The Scottish Vowel Length Rule revisited. In P. Foulkes and G. J. Docherty (eds.), *Urban Voices*: London: Arnold. 230–45.

Smith, Bruce L., Bruce L. Brown, William J. Strong and Alvin C. Rencher (1975). Effects of speech rate on personality perception. *Language and Speech* 18: 145–52.

Son, R. J. J. H. van and Louis C. W. Pols (1990). Formant structure of Dutch vowels in a text, read at normal and fast rate. *Journal of the Acoustical Society of America* 88: 1683–93.

Strand, Elizabeth A. (1999). Uncovering the role of gender stereotypes in speech perception. *Journal of Language and Social Psychology* 18: 86–100.

Strange, Winifred (1989). Evolving theories of vowel perception. *Journal of the Acoustical Society of America* 85: 2081–87.

Surprenant, Aimée M. and Louis Goldstein (1998). The perception of speech gestures. *Journal of the Acoustical Society of America* 104: 518–29.

Syrdal, Ann K. and H. S. Gopal (1986). A perceptual model of vowel recognition based on the auditory representation of American English vowels. *Journal of the Acoustical Society of America* 79: 1086–100.

Thomas, Erik R. (1991). The origin of Canadian raising in Ontario. *The Canadian Journal of Linguistics/La Revue canadienne de Linguistique* 36: 147–70.

Thomas, Erik R. (1993). Why we need descriptive studies: Phonological variables in Hispanic English. In R. Queen and R. Barrett (eds.), *SALSA I (Proceedings of the First Annual Symposium about Language and Society – Austin)*. Texas Lingusitic Forum,

vol. 33. Austin: Dept. of Linguistics, University of Texas. 42–9.

Thomas, Erik R. (1995). Phonetic factors and perceptual reanalysis in sound change. Ph.D. dissertation, University of Texas at Austin.

Thomas, Erik R. (1996). A comparison of variation patterns of variables among sixth-graders in an Ohio community. In E. W. Schneider (ed.), *Focus on the USA*. Varieties of English around the World, general series, vol. 16. Amsterdam: John Benjamins. 149–68.

Thomas, Erik R. (1997). A rural/metropolitan split in the speech of Texas Anglos. *Language Variation and Change* 9: 309–32.

Thomas, Erik R. (2000). Spectral differences in /ai/ offsets conditioned by the voicing of the following consonant. *Journal of Phonetics* 28: 1–25.

Thomas, Erik R. (2001). An acoustic analysis of vowel variation in New World English. *Publication of the American Dialect Society* 85.

Thomas, Erik R. and Guy Bailey (1992). A case of competing mergers and their resolution. *The SECOL Review* 16: 179–200.

Thomas, Erik R. and Guy Bailey (1998). Parallels between vowel subsystems of African American Vernacular English and Caribbean Anglophone creoles. *Journal of Pidgin and Creole Languages* 13: 267–96.

Trent, Sonja A. (1995). Voice quality: Listener identification of African-American versus Caucasian speakers. *Journal of the Acoustical Society of America* 98: 2936.

Tucker, G. Richard and Wallace E. Lambert (1969). White and Negro listeners' reactions to various American-English dialects. *Social Forces* 47: 463–68.

Veatch, Thomas Clark (1991). English vowels: Their surface phonology and phonetic implementation in vernacular dialects. Ph.D. dissertation, University of Pennsylvania.

Verbrugge, Robert R., Winifred Strange, Donald P. Shankweiler and Thomas R. Edman (1976). What information enables a listener to map a talker's vowel space? *Journal of the Acoustical Society of America* 60: 198–212.

Waldrip-Fruin, Carolyn (1982). On the status of temporal cues to phonetic categories: Preceding vowel duration as a cue to voicing in final stop consonants. *Journal of the Acoustical Society of America* 71: 187–95.

Walton, Julie H. and Robert F. Orlikoff (1994). Speaker race identification from acoustic cues in the vocal signal. *Journal of Speech and Hearing Research* 37: 738–45.

Weinreich, Uriel, William Labov, and Marvin I. Herzog (1968). Empirical foundations for a theory of language change. In W. P. Lehmann and Y. Malkiel (eds.), *Directions for Historical Linguistics: A Symposium*. Austin: University of Texas Press. 95–188.

Wells, J. C. (1982). *Accents of English*, 3 vols. Cambridge: Cambridge University Press.

Wetzell, W. Brett. (2000). Rhythm, dialects, and the Southern drawl. MA thesis, North Carolina State University.

Wolfram, Walter A. (1969). *A Sociolinguistic Description of Detroit Negro Speech*. Washington, DC: Center for Applied Linguistics.

Wolfram, Walt, Kirk Hazen and Natalie Schilling-Estes (1999). Dialect change and maintenance on the Outer Banks. *Publication of the American Dialect Society* 81: 1–209.

Wolfram, Walt, Erik R. Thomas and Elaine W. Green (2000). The regional context of earlier African-American speech: Evidence for reconstructing the development of AAVE. *Language in Society* 29: 315–55.

Yaeger-Dror, Malcah (1996). Phonetic evidence for the evolution of lexical classes: The case of a Montreal French vowel shift. In G. R. Guy, C. Feagin, D. Schiffrin and J. Baugh (eds.), *Towards a Social Science of Language: Papers in Honor of William Labov*. Amsterdam studies in the theory and history of linguistic science. Series IV: Current issues in linguistic theory 127. Amsterdam: John Benjamins. 263–87.

Yaeger-Dror, Malcah (1997). Contraction of negatives as evidence of variance in register-specific interactive rules. *Language Variation and Change* 9: 1–36.

Yang, Byunggon (1992). An acoustical study of Korean monophthongs produced by male and female speakers. *Journal of the Acoustical Society of America* 91: 2280–83.

Part II
Linguistic Structure

Linguistic Structure

Of all the subfields of sociolinguistics, the study of linguistic variation is perhaps the one with the strongest emphasis on the "linguistic" side of "sociolinguistics." While variationists are indeed concerned with understanding social structures and forces, as well as with helping to effect social change, they are also vitally interested in furthering the scientific understanding of language. Unlike theoretical linguists, who typically rely on idealized versions of homogeneous languages in their search for underlying structure, variationists maintain that any valid linguistic theory must give central place to the variation and change that pervade all human languages. Unfortunately, it has proven difficult to incorporate variation into linguistic theory or theoretical linguistic models into variation study. However, as the chapters in this section amply demonstrate, the effort has not been abandoned, and important inroads are being made.

In "Variation and phonological theory," Arto Anttila demonstrates that, despite the failure of early attempts to modify phonological rules to incorporate variation, current efforts at reconciling phonological theory and variable data have proven more successful. In large part, this is because of the dramatic transformation of phonological theory, as it has moved from early rule-based approaches to Optimality Theory, which is based on constraints on the well-formedness of output strings rather than on inviolable rules. Constraints are universal but violable, and differences between different languages are the result of different orderings of constraints among different groups of speakers. It is a small step to extend this notion to dialect differentiation. Using data from English and Finnish, Anttila takes us through step-by-step analyses that demonstrate that Optimality Theory can account quite well for observed patterns of intra-language variation, especially if the theory is modified slightly to allow for multiple constraint orderings (multiple grammars) within the individual speaker. Anttila further demonstrates that certain types of multiple-grammar models can account not only for the qualitative fact of variation but for observed quantitative patterns. Hence, Optimality Theory is a promising direction indeed as researchers work to bridge the gap between phonological theory and variation study.

Although it has been difficult to incorporate variation into theories of synchronic linguistic structure, variationists have been more successful in informing the study of language change. In "Investigating Chain Shifts and Mergers," Matthew J. Gordon discusses variationist investigations of two important types of language change and demonstrates how these studies have led us to rethink traditional notions regarding how and even why such changes take place. Investigations of vowel mergers have called into question the traditional functionalist notion that speakers make distinctions between sounds in order to make meaning distinctions, since researchers have uncovered cases in which speakers produce distinctions between vowel sounds but cannot perceive them – that is, cannot use them to distinguish meanings. Similarly, the variationist investigation of chain-shifting, the related movement of a series of vowels through phonetic space, also raises questions for long-established views on language change. Data on chain shifts currently in progress (especially the Northern Cities Shift in the USA) provide evidence against the functionalist notion that the motivation underlying chain shifting is the need to preserve phonological distinctions – that is, to avoid merger when one vowel encroaches on the phonetic space of another. It is only through investigating vowel changes in progress rather than "after the fact" that we gain understanding of not only the linguistic but also the social forces that drive language change.

Variation analysis has had little impact on syntactic theory over the decades. In "Variation and Syntactic Theory," Alison Henry discusses reasons for this, as well as reasons why syntactic theory should incorporate variable data – and why variation study should take better account of theoretical considerations. Although syntacticians have traditionally abstracted away from the variation they find, the fact remains that variation is pervasive and linguistic theories rest on shaky foundations indeed when we attempt to base them on invariant data. A central tenet of the Minimalist Program is that movement only occurs when it is forced; hence, variable movement is impossible. However, the observed facts of syntactic change seem difficult to reconcile with the notion that each speaker's individual grammar is, at heart, invariable. It may be possible to account for syntactic change in general by positing that speakers have several competing grammars, each of which is invariant, and that change results when one competitor wins out, but this view does not seem to allow for stable variation between old and new forms over long periods of time, a phenomenon that is by no means rare. Just as variable data can inform syntactic theory, so too can theory inform the study of language variation and change. For example, theoretical syntactic considerations can lead to a fuller understanding of the types of conditioning factors that are likely to affect variation, as well as the types of features (e.g. marked vs. unmarked) that are likely to be affected by change. Despite the longstanding gap between variation study and theoretical syntax, Henry notes that valuable contributions are currently being made toward bridging this chasm, to the mutual benefit of both fields.

In the final chapter in this section, "Discourse Variation," Ronald Macaulay investigates how variation study relates to discourse structure. Macaulay notes that there are many problems associated with conducting quantitative analyses in this area. It is difficult to establish the "envelope of variation" for discourse-level features (for example, discourse markers, tag questions), since it is nearly impossible to identify all and only the locations where such features could occur. In addition, it is difficult to establish variants of a particular variable (that is, different ways of saying the same thing), since the meanings associated with discourse features tend to be multifaceted and quite context-specific. However, variationists have conducted both quantitative and qualitative analyses of discourse-level features with fruitful results. Macaulay outlines a number of these studies, ranging from Labov's classic studies of narrative structure to investigations of the discourse patterns of women vs. men, to studies of discourse-level differences across social class groups, including Macaulay's own work in Scotland. Such studies are not without their limitations, and Macaulay urges caution as variationists proceed with their work in discourse. For example, sociolinguistic interviews may be quite different from naturally occurring conversations at the discourse level, since the interviewee usually does most of the talking. However, Macaulay stresses that even in the most one-sided interactions, talk is never simply an individual effort but always a joint production; hence variationists must pay attention to the contributions of *all* participants, no matter how seemingly unimportant.

NATALIE SCHILLING-ESTES

8 Variation and Phonological Theory

ARTO ANTTILA

In recent years, there have been several attempts to understand language variation from the perspective of Optimality Theory (Prince and Smolensky 1993).[1] This chapter has three main goals: (1) to point out why variation matters to the theoretical phonologist; (2) to list some central questions that any phonological theory of variation should address; (3) to give a brief introduction to the use of Optimality Theory in language variation, including concrete examples. Since the discussion will necessarily be selective, the reader will find it useful to follow up on the cited work for a fuller picture.

1 Internal Factors in Variation

Phonological variation is often studied from a sociolinguistic point of view, i.e. by examining the use of variants as a function of EXTERNAL FACTORS, such as sex, age, style, register, and social class. The fact that variation is also conditioned by INTERNAL FACTORS, such as phonology, morphology, syntax, and the lexicon, is what makes it interesting for the theoretical phonologist. We start with two concrete examples of internal conditioning. The purpose of these examples is to illustrate the sorts of phonological, morphological, and lexical facts that any grammatical theory of variation should explain.

In many dialects of English, word-final consonant clusters are variably simplified by deleting a coronal stop, e.g. *cost me~cos' me*. This is a well-studied phenomenon with interesting phonological and morphological structure (see e.g. Labov et al. 1968, Wolfram 1969, Fasold 1972, Guy 1980, Neu 1980, Guy and Boyd 1990, Guy 1991a, 1991b, Kiparsky 1993b, Reynolds 1994, Guy 1994, Guy and Boberg 1997, Labov 1997, among others). The examples in (1) illustrate two well-known generalizations: *t,d*-deletion rate depends on the quality of the following segment and the morphological status of the segment subject to deletion.

(1)   a.
   t,d-deletion rate: the following segment effect. Celeste S., Philadelphia, word-final clusters only. Figures from Labov 1997.

Following segment		Following segment	
stop	78%	/l/	40%
/w/	68%	pause	17%
fricative	65%	vowel	6%
nasal	57%	/r/	7%
/h/	45%	/y/	5%

   b.
   t,d-deletion rate: the morphological effect. Figures from Guy 1994.

Morphology	Guy 1991b	Santa Ana 1992
Monomorphemes (*cost*)	38.1%	57.9%
Irregular past (*lost*)	33.9%	40.7%
Regular past (*tossed*)	16.0%	25.7%

Various explanations for these effects have been offered. The following segment effect has been commonly attributed to syllable structure. Specifically, it has been proposed that the final coronal consonant tends to be retained if it can be resyllabified as a part of the following onset. This is the case before vowels, e.g. in *lost.Anna~los.tAnna*, but not before /l/, e.g. *lost:Larry* (*los.tLarry*) because *tl* is not a possible onset in English. The resyllabification hypothesis thus predicts that there should be more deletion before /l/ than before /r/ because *tr* is a possible onset in English. This is confirmed by the data (Guy 1994: 143–4, Labov 1997: 165).

As for the morphological generalization, at least two different explanations have been put forward. Kiparsky (1982) proposed that deletion is less frequent in the regular past tense (*tossed*) because it would make past and present tenses identical. The explanation would thus be homonymy avoidance, a principle with an obvious functional appeal (but see Labov 1994: ch. 19). A very different structural explanation was put forward by Guy (1991b) who posited a variable rule of *t,d*-deletion which applies inside out in the morphological structure: first to roots (*cost*), then to stems (*cost, los+t*) and finally to words (*cost, los+t, toss#ed*), subjecting roots to deletion three times, stems twice and words only once. This hypothesis makes the specific quantitative prediction that the retention rates in the three groups should be related exponentially, in the ratios of x, x^2 and x^3. This appears to be confirmed by the data (Guy 1991b).

As a second example, consider variable vowel coalescence in Colloquial Helsinki Finnish (Kiparsky 1993a, Paunonen 1995, Anttila to appear a). Vowel coalescence turns heterosyllabic vowel sequences into long vowels as follows:

(2)   Colloquial Helsinki Finnish vowel coalescence
   a.   má.ke.a~má.kee "sweet"
   b.   lá.si.-a~lá.sii "glass-PAR(TITIVE)"

Rule: $V_1.V_2 \to V_1$: where V_1, V_2 are unstressed and V_2 is [+low]

Vowel coalescence is variable within an individual. The following dialogue fragment comes from an electronic corpus of spoken Helsinki Finnish (Paunonen 1995).[2] The same speaker sometimes does, sometimes does not coalesce, apparently unpredictably. The last line shows that both variants may occur within the same noun phrase (for more examples, see Paunonen 1995: 106–7).

(3) OH: Milla**sii** ihmi**sii** siel käy jud**oo**massa?
/millas-i-a/, /ihmis-i-ä/, /judoa-ma-ssa/
What sort of people practise judo there?

JS: Siel käy iha, nuo**ria** ja vanhojaki.
/nuor-i-a/
Some are really young, but there are old people too.

OH: Miehi**ä** nai**sia**?
/mieh-i-ä/, /nais-i-a/
Men? Women?

JS: Joo miehii ja nai**sia**.
/mieh-i-ä/, /nais-i-a/
Yes, men and women.

While the variation may initially seem random, vowel coalescence turns out to be subject to the following phonological and morphological conditions:

(4) a. Coalescence is favored in mid-low sequences (/ea/, /oa/, /öä/) and disfavored in high-low sequences (/ia/, /ua/, /yä/) (Paunonen 1995).
   b. Coalescence is favored in derived environments and disfavored in roots (Anttila to appear a).
   c. Coalescence is favored in adjectives and disfavored in nouns (Anttila to appear a).

Example (5) shows how these regularities emerge in Paunonen's corpus based on the phonological and morphological tagging carried out by the present author. The sample is based on 126 speakers and contains approximately 13,000 coalescence environments. The factors favoring coalescence are boldfaced. There were no examples of derived /ea/-final adjectives in this corpus.

(5) Vowel coalescence rate by environment

		/ea/	/ia/	*Examples*
a.	Noun & Root	14.8%	0%	hopea, rasia
	Noun & **Derived**	41.0%	20.0%	suome-a, lasi-a
	Adjective & Root	72.4%	0%	makea, kauhia
	Adjective & **Derived**	–	30.2%	–, uus-i-a

		Derived	Root	
b.	Noun & /ia/	20.0%	0%	lasi-a, rasia
	Noun & /ea/	41.0%	14.8%	suome-a, hopea
	Adjective & /ia/	30.2%	0%	uus-i-a, kauhia
	Adjective & /ea/	–	72.4%	–, makea

		Adjective	Noun	
c.	Root & /ia/	0%	0%	kauhia, rasia
	Root & /ea/	72.4%	14.8%	makea, hopea
	Derived & /ia/	30.2%	20.0%	uus-i-a, lasi-a
	Derived & /ea/	–	41.0%	–, suome-a

Glosses: *hopea* "silver", *rasia* "box", *makea* "sweet", *kauhia* "terrible", *suome-a* "Finnish-PAR", *lasi-a* "glass-PAR", *uus-i-a* "new-PL-PAR".

The regularities in (4) sometimes yield categorical, sometimes quantitative effects. For example, as (5a) shows, changing /ea/ to /ia/ in nouns results in categorical blocking in roots, but only in a quantitative dispreference in derived environments. If we divide the speakers into groups by sex (2 groups), age (3 groups), social class (3 groups), and neighborhood (2 groups), the same regularities continue to hold in each subgroup.

In addition to phonological and morphological conditions, both cases of variation show lexical conditions as well. Myers and Guy (1997) report that *t,d*-deletion frequency is higher in high-frequency words than low-frequency words, but intriguingly, only in monomorphemes. Thus, the deletion rate is higher in *past* (high-frequency) than *priest* (low-frequency), whereas regularly inflected past tense forms, such as *passed* (high-frequency) and *kissed* (low-frequency) are not significantly different. As for Finnish, native noun roots like *hopea* "silver" coalesce variably, whereas otherwise identical recent borrowings like *idea* "idea" never coalesce.

These two examples illustrate internal conditioning: the distribution of variant pronunciations is conditioned by phonology, morphology, and the lexicon. It is evident that phonological, morphological, and lexical regularities sometimes yield obligatory and categorical effects (i.e. "rules"), sometimes variable and quantitative effects (i.e. "tendencies"). Note that in neither case can the variability and quantitative effects be reduced to phonetics: both *t,d*-deletion and vowel coalescence are morphophonemic alternations, witness the presence of morphological and lexical conditions.

One possibility would be to assume that phonological theory should only explain categorical, but not quantitative regularities. However, while it is perfectly acceptable to simplify the object of study, it is hard to see why one would want to seriously commit oneself to such a position. It would be like declaring a priori that phonological theory should only explain alternations, but not static phonotactic regularities, or that it should only explain allophonic, but not morphophonemic alternations. There seems to be no reason to limit the scope of phonological theory in such ways. The question is how exactly phonological theory should address facts of this sort; for a general discussion of various options, see Pierrehumbert (1994). The work reviewed in this chapter takes the view that both categorical and quantitative regularities derive from the same grammatical principles, which need to be identified, and that the differences in realization strength (invariant vs. variable, categorical vs. quantitative) can be explained by referring to the ways these principles interact.

Finally, a brief note on the definition of variation is due. One possibility is to regard variation as a form-meaning relation of a special kind. It has been suggested that the form-meaning relation in natural languages is ideally one-to-one and that this is a principle that languages strive to satisfy (Anttila 1989). The two possible types of deviations from this ideal state are illustrated in (6): one meaning (M_1) corresponds to several forms (F_1, F_2) i.e. we have VARIATION; one form (F_1) corresponds to several meanings (M_1, M_2), i.e. we have AMBIGUITY.

(6)   Variation and ambiguity

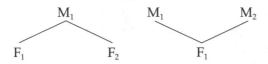

While the existence of ambiguity is usually accepted as a mundane fact, the existence of intra-individual variation is sometimes questioned. For example, it has been suggested that apparent variation results from lumping together individuals with different, but invariant dialects (Bickerton 1971). However, well-documented cases of intra-individual variation clearly exist, among them our two examples. Another common observation is that putative free variants sometimes have subtly different meanings, suggesting that genuine variation may be hard to find. We will return to this point in section 3.3. In any case, the issue is less important than it might first seem. What makes phenomena like *t,d*-deletion and vowel coalescence interesting for the phonologist is that they reflect the workings of phonology, morphology, and the lexicon, sometimes categorically, sometimes quantitatively, and these facts call for an explanation, no matter whether the phenomena are instances of "genuine" variation or not.

2   The Goals of a Phonological Theory of Variation

The following is an open-ended list of questions that any phonological theory of variation should address. The discussion draws upon Liberman (1994) where many of the questions were originally stated.

2.1   The locus of variation

Why does variation occur in some environments, but not in others? While it is of some interest to study those isolated cases of variation that we happen to notice, it would be more interesting to know why just these cases of variation exist instead of the many other conceivable ones that do not. For example, *t,d*-deletion in e.g. *cos(t) me* has been attributed to cluster simplification due to ease of articulation, itself presumably a functional universal (Chambers 1995: 235–7). But why is the deleted segment /t/, instead of /s/ or /m/, even though deleting any of the three would yield a simpler cluster? Why are only coronal stops deleted instead of all obstruents or all consonants? Why only final clusters, but not initial as well (*stress* → **sress*)? Why consonant deletion instead of vowel epenthesis (**cost[ə]me*) which would also serve to break up the cluster? At this point, the functional explanation is no longer very helpful. Moreover, in some languages we find the reverse of the English pattern. In Lardil, only coronals fail to be deleted in the coda (Wilkinson 1988, Kiparsky 1993b). In Finnish, we find variable initial cluster simplification in loanword nativization, e.g. *stress* becomes *stressi~tressi~ressi*, depending on the speaker. While articulatory economy may be a driving force behind *t,d*-deletion, it leaves us puzzled about the details. The conclusion is inevitable: if we want to explain what varies and how in each language, we need a good understanding of the language-specific phonologies. One commonsense intuition is that optionality/variation arises in environments where the regularities of the language are somehow "relaxed" or where they "conflict." What exactly this means in any given language is a question that can only be answered through phonological analysis.

2.2   The degrees of variation

Why are phonological alternations sometimes obligatory, but sometimes only optional? Within the latter group, how can we explain frequency effects that reflect internal factors such as syllable structure, segment quality, vowel height, morphological constituency and part of speech? If the same grammatical principles are responsible for both categorical and quantitative effects, what determines the realization strength in a particular case? One grammatical constraint that has been studied cross-linguistically from this point of view is the Obligatory Contour Principle (Leben 1973, Goldsmith 1976): "Adjacent identical elements are prohibited." For example, Guy and Boberg 1997 argue that *t,d*-deletion is more likely the more similar the preceding segment is to *t,d*. Thus, *wrist* shows a higher deletion rate than *rift* because /s/ and /t/ share two features, [+cor] and [−son], whereas /f/ and /t/ share only one, [−son]. For other quantitative OCP-effects, see McCarthy (1986, 1988, 1994), Frisch et al. (1997, Arabic), Berkley (1994, English), Anttila (to appear b, Finnish), Kang (1996, Korean) and Liberman (1994, Latin).

2.3   Markedness

How are the loci and degrees of variation related to the cross-linguistic issues of naturalness or markedness? For example, are new variants which are initially optional/variable always easier to articulate, either easier universally (cf. cluster simplification as a result of articulatory economy) or easier in some language-particular relativized sense? Does variation arise in situations where there are two equally marked alternatives available and obligatory patterns in situations where there is one clearly least marked alternative available? Does the quantitative distribution of variants reflect markedness, i.e. are the common variants less marked than the less common variants in some independently definable sense?

2.4   Interfaces

How do phonological, morphological, and lexical factors interact in variation? How should phonological theory explain cases where variation shows a phonological pattern, perhaps even a universal tendency, yet at the same time different word classes and individual lexical items show their own characteristic patterns of behavior, perhaps by being totally or partially exempt from variation or by showing a different quantitative pattern? The interaction between phonology, morphology, and the lexicon is a central problem in synchronic phonological theory; see e.g. Hargus (1993) and Mohanan (1995) for recent overviews. On the diachronic side, the problem is related to the long-standing controversy between neogrammarians and lexical diffusionists (Wang 1969, Labov 1994, Kiparsky 1995): is sound change mechanical and phonetically conditioned or does it proceed word by word? Variation is a unique source of evidence as it often reveals subtle implicational and quantitative relations among phonological, morphological, and lexical factors.

2.5   External factors

How do internal factors interface with external factors in variation? While it is not the business of grammatical theory to explain the effects of sex, age, style, register and social class, one would like to have at least a plausible scenario of where such facts fit. There would seem to be two possibilities: (1) The modular view: internal and external factors are of a fundamentally different nature: grammars are structural objects built out of (innate) universal principles; external factors reflect the ways in which these structural objects are used. This implies that external factors can be reduced to choices among grammars; (2) The anti-modular view: there is no important theoretical difference between internal and external factors, which interact with each other fairly directly. This seems to be the position assumed in a good part of the Variable Rule literature where internal and external constraints are freely mixed in the context conditions of variable rules.

2.6 Language change

Change presupposes a period of variation although variation need not produce change. Why do some cases of variation linger for centuries without very much change, while others move, quickly or slowly, towards a categorical resolution? (Liberman 1994: 1)

In the current state of theoretical phonology, the immediate problem facing anyone who wants to work on variation is to find a formal framework that is capable of at least describing variable phenomena, including their quantitative aspects. As we will see, several proposals have been put forward. These proposals can be evaluated in terms of descriptive adequacy, e.g. how accurate the resulting quantitative predictions are. The next step is to evaluate them in terms of their restrictiveness, i.e. whether they exclude anything, and if they do, whether they exclude the linguistically bizarre and hence systematically unattested types of variation and allow the linguistically plausible and, in particular, the actually attested types of variation. Finally, one can evaluate the proposals in terms of whether they generalize in the right way beyond the variation problem. For example, does a particular approach shed light on the interaction of phonology and morphology more generally? Does a theory that is developed for intra-individual variation lend itself to explaining cross-linguistic variation as well? Are the proposed classes of grammars learnable?

3 Standard Optimality Theory

Classical generative phonology outlined in Chomsky and Halle's (1968) *The Sound Pattern of English* (SPE) recognized the existence of optionality in phonology and provided two devices for describing it: optional rules and allomorphy. Going beyond optionality, Labov (1969) and Cedergren and Sankoff (1974) proposed a statistical technique for estimating the relative weight of different internal and external factors based on corpus frequencies. They further proposed to associate the resulting weights with the structural descriptions of SPE-style phonological rules. This well-known Variable Rule model has been highly influential in variationist phonology for over three decades.

Meanwhile, phonological theory has moved on. In particular, there has been a gradual shift away from rule-based theories to constraint-based theories which leave little if any role for rules and derivations. Consequently, the notion "variable rule" is not easy to interpret in the context of current phonological theory. At the same time, work on phonological variation has continued largely independently of phonological theory, often consciously emphasizing its empirical character. While variationist phonological analyses make heavy use of the quantitative analysis tools developed in connection with the Variable Rule model, this is often done with no particular commitment to the theoretical notion "variable rule" itself (Fasold 1991).

One constraint-based framework that emerged in the early 1990s and soon became very influential, especially in phonology, is Optimality Theory (OT) (Prince and Smolensky 1993). Among other things, Optimality Theory opened up new ways of thinking about variation. In the rest of this chapter, we will examine some of these recent approaches, emphasizing their similarities and differences, and, where possible, evaluate their merits and shortcomings. Some of the papers discussed here are available at the Rutgers Optimality Archive (http://roa.rutgers.edu).

3.1   A synopsis of Optimality Theory

In this section, we give a brief synopsis of Optimality Theory. (For thorough textbook discussions, see e.g. Archangeli and Langendoen 1997 and Kager 1999.) An optimality-theoretic grammar consists of the following components:

(7)   a.   LEXICON: A set of inputs (underlying forms).
      b.   GENERATOR (GEN): A function that takes an input and returns a set of output candidates. GEN is maximally permissive: any output candidate is permitted for any input within very general limits of structural well-formedness. Thus, for the input /kæt/ "cat" GEN would yield {[kʰæt], [kæt], [kæ], [ba], . . . }.
      c.   EVALUATOR (EVAL) which consists of two parts: (1) A universal constraint set CON which contains two principal types of constraints: faithfulness constraints that prefer the output that most closely resembles the input and markedness constraints that prefer the phonologically least marked output; (2) A language-particular RANKING of the universal constraints. Ranking selects the least offensive candidate from among the output candidates and calls it optimal. This is the actual output.

We now turn to a concrete example. Assume the following three constraints. For more discussion and exemplification, see Kager (1999: ch. 3).

(8)   ONSET   Onsets are required. (markedness)
      *CxCOD   No coda clusters. (markedness)
      MAX(C)   No consonant deletion. (faithfulness)

One of the central hypotheses of Optimality Theory is that constraints are universal. This means that variation among languages should be reducible to differences in ranking. Let us assume that the three constraints in (8) are ranked as in (9) in a particular dialect of English. Ranking is indicated by ">>".

(9) ONSET >> *CxCOD >> MAX(C)

We now work out the pronunciation this grammar assigns to the input /mɪst/ using the TABLEAU in (10). For the purposes of this illustration, we only consider two output candidates: [mɪst] and [mɪs].

(10)

INPUT: /mɪst/	ONSET	*CxCOD	MAX(C)
1a. [mɪst]		*!	
1b. ⇒ [mɪs]			*

Both candidates have exactly one syllable which has an onset ([m]). Thus, both satisfy ONSET. The candidates differ with respect to the last two constraints. Candidate (1a) [mɪst] is perfectly faithful: it realizes all the input segments and only those. However, it contains a coda cluster [st] in violation of *CxCOD. A constraint violation is marked by "*". Candidate (1b) [mɪs] does not violate *CxCOD because [t] has been deleted, but the deletion amounts to a violation of MAX(C). Thus, both (1a) and (1b) incur exactly one constraint violation. The decisive factor is that in this dialect *CxCOD is ranked higher than MAX(C). This makes the *CxCOD violation fatal for (1a). A fatal violation is marked by "!". As a consequence, (1a) loses and (1b) wins. Since we now have a winner, the remaining constraint columns are irrelevant, which is indicated by shading. More generally, given two candidates, we can find the winner by checking the highest constraint on which the two candidates differ (here *CxCOD): the winner is the candidate that better satisfies this constraint. The candidate that beats all its competitors is called the OPTIMAL candidate and marked by the arrow. Note that the optimal candidate need not be perfect: it is just better than any of its competitors.

The dialect described here is a *t,d*-deletion dialect of a slightly odd type: the final *t* is invariably deleted under the pressure to avoid coda clusters created by the ranking *CxCOD >> MAX(C). The reverse ranking MAX(C) >> *CxCOD yields a dialect where *t* is invariably retained. Since most dialects are variable, the question arises how variation can be accommodated in standard Optimality Theory. It turns out that there are at least two ways of getting at variation without modifying any of the assumptions laid out so far. We will now examine these two approaches in turn.

3.2 Tied violations

In *tied violations*, two or more candidates incur exactly the same violations with respect to all the constraints in the grammar. As an example, consider variable stress in Walmatjari, spoken by fewer than a thousand people in the

Kimberley division of Western Australia (Hudson and Richards 1969). The analysis is based on Hammond (1994); the data come from Hudson and Richards (1969: 183–5). The basic generalization goes as follows: (1) in all two-syllable words, main stress falls on the first syllable; (2) in words with three syllables, main stress may fall on the first or second syllable, with most words showing variable pronunciation; (3) in words with four syllables, main stress may fall on the first or second syllable, with some words showing variable pronunciation.[3]

(11)   a.   yápa   "child"
           pálma   "creek"
       b.   mánalu~manálu   "we (pl. excl.)-him"
           yútanti~yutánti   "sit"
       c.   páljmanàna~paljmánana   "touching"
           ṭúnmanàna~ṭunmánana   "burying"

The question is what determines the locus of variation: why does stress vary between the first and second syllable, instead of, say, the first and the last syllable? And why only in words longer than two syllables? Let us assume that stress in Walmatjari is assigned by grouping syllables into binary feet where the strong syllable is on the left. The resulting trochaic stress pattern is cross-linguistically very common. Variability now follows from the fact that it is sometimes possible to group syllables into feet in more than one way. Following the ideas in Hammond (1994), we propose the constraints in (12). For a textbook discussion of stress in Optimality Theory, see Kager (1999: ch. 4).

(12)   a.   TROCH   Feet are left-headed (trochaic).
       b.   FTBIN   Feet are binary.
       c.   *LAPSE   No sequences of two unfooted syllables.

We now display the tableaux. Example (13) shows that stress is correctly predicted to fall on the first syllable in disyllables, with no variation. Note also that ranking does not matter. The same winners would emerge under any ranking.

(13)   Disyllables: No variation

	/yapa/	TROCH	FTBIN	*LAPSE
a.	yapa			*!
b. ⇒	(yápa)			
c.	ya(pá)		*!	
d.	(yá)(pá)		*!*	
e.	(yapá)	*!		

Leaving the word completely unfooted (13a) fatally violates *LAPSE; forming monosyllabic feet (13c–d) fatally violates FTBIN; forming a right-headed (iambic) foot (13e) fatally violates TROCH.

We now come to the interesting part: the variable cases.

(14) Trisyllables: Variation

	/yutanti/	TROCH	FTBIN	*LAPSE
a.	yutanti			*!*
b. ⇒	(yútan)ti			
c. ⇒	yu(tánti)			
d.	yutan(tí)		*!	*
e.	(yú)(tánti)		*!	
f.	(yú)tan(tí)		*!*	
g.	yu(tán)(tí)		*!*	
h.	(yú)(tán)(tí)		*!**	
i.	yu(tantí)	*!		

As (14) shows, the grammar correctly predicts that stress varies between the first and second syllables in three-syllable words. This is because there are two (and only two) acceptable ways of grouping syllables into feet. The constraints cannot tell the two candidates apart and both slip through, hence variation. As the reader can easily verify, the same variation pattern is also predicted in four-syllable words. The upshot is that the grammar correctly predicts the locus of variation.

Despite this success, the tied violations approach has two inherent limitations. First, truly identical violation profiles seem extremely difficult to achieve given two common assumptions: (1) all constraints are universal and thus present in all grammars; (2) constraints are sufficiently fine-grained to distinguish any two non-identical candidates. Thus, there will always be some low-ranking constraint that will distinguish between the purported optional variants, blocking variation. The above analysis works only because we have failed to include all the members of the universal constraint set in our tableau. Second, the approach provides no way of modeling degrees of variation, but reduces variation to optionality. Nevertheless, there is an interesting insight: the approach claims that variation involves candidates that are equally good in terms of some subset of high-ranking constraints. This idea reappears in subsequent work, as we will see shortly.

3.3   *Pseudo-optionality*

Another approach to variation is to attribute it to free choice between alternative inputs. Following Müller (1999), we call this approach PSEUDO-OPTIONALITY. Thus, in the case of *t,d*-deletion, we could posit two underlying forms: /cost/ and /cos/ which both mean "cost". The fact that a variant sometimes conveys information about the context of utterance, linguistic or otherwise, might be taken as an argument for pseudo-optionality. For example, in Colloquial Helsinki Finnish, we might posit two distinct lexical items with slightly different meanings:

(15)   a.   /makea/ "sweet"
      b.   /makee/ "sweet, colloquial, most typically uttered by a young working-class female"

The "uncoalesced" (15a) and the "coalesced" (15b) would thus be distinct inputs. We could now set up the grammar in such a way that the two variants would be the unique winners in their respective competitions, e.g. by ranking faithfulness reasonably high. The two variants would thus not compete in phonology at all, but at the point where lexical items are introduced into syntax. Interestingly, this seems to be the favored solution to optionality in optimality-theoretic syntax. Müller (1999) notes that proponents of pseudo-optionality often try to argue for subtle differences in meaning (i.e. different inputs) in cases like *A review of this article came out yesterday* and *A review came out yesterday of this article* (for criticism, see Newmeyer 2000). The reasoning is analogous.

The pseudo-optionality approach to variation is attractive because of its austerity: it proposes to derive variation from the unavoidable assumption that the speaker can select from among different inputs. However, as a general model of phonological variation it has a number of weaknesses. Essentially, pseudo-optionality proposes to reduce all apparent variation to linguistic free will, manifested for example in lexical alternations like *thirsty* vs. *hungry* in the frame *I'm ___* where the choice is clearly unpredictable from grammar-internal factors and for all intents and purposes also from grammar-external factors. As we have seen, this is not generally true of phonological variation: phonological (morphological, lexical, . . .) factors do emerge in variation, sometimes categorically, sometimes quantitatively. But if variation is independent of phonology and reducible to optionality at the point of lexical insertion, then it is not clear how such phonological effects can be modeled, or even how they are possible in the first place.

The argument from putative meaning differences is not convincing either. While it is true that in Colloquial Helsinki Finnish *makea* and *makee* have different connotations, so do hundreds of other word pairs, and in exactly the same way: the coalesced variant is always "more colloquial." Thus, the additional shade of meaning is clearly not a property of a specific lexical item, but rather, coalescence itself. In other words, the young working-class females have a "colloquial" phonology rather than a "colloquial" vocabulary.

We have now reviewed two optimality-theoretic approaches to variation. These approaches are attractive because they do not modify the standard assumptions of Optimality Theory in any way. At the same time, both have conceptual and empirical weaknesses. We will now turn to approaches that have given up one or more of the basic assumptions in order to account for variation, in particular its quantitative aspects.

4   The Multiple Grammars Model

The multiple grammars model proposes that variation arises from the competition of distinct grammatical systems within an individual. This view has been defended by e.g. Kiparsky (1993b) for phonology and Kroch (1989, 1994, 2001) for morphosyntax. That an individual can simultaneously possess several grammars is uncontroversial in the case of multilingualism. The question is whether multilingualism, multidialectalism, an individual's ability to switch among styles and registers, and ultimately, an individual's ability to involve in free variation are all fundamentally similar phenomena.

In optimality-theoretic terms, the multiple grammars model implies that a single individual commands a set of distinct total rankings of constraints, or tableaux for short. For example, an individual grammar might consist of the three tableaux in (16). As the reader can easily verify, grammar (16a) deletes the final *t* in /mɪst/, whereas both (16b) and (16c) retain it.

(16)   Input   Tableau   Output
    a.   /mɪst/   Onset >> *CxCod >> Max(C)   [mɪs]
    b.   /mɪst/   Onset >> Max(C) >> *CxCod   [mɪst]
    c.   /mɪst/   Max(C) >> Onset >> *CxCod   [mɪst]

The simplest interpretation of the multiple grammars model is that any set of tableaux is a possible system for an individual. On each occasion of use, defined as e.g. word, utterance, etc., the speaker would reach into the grammar pool and select a tableau. In the absence of good reasons to think otherwise, it would be natural to assume that each tableau has the same probability of being selected. This does not imply that variation is free: the grammar pool available to the speaker may be biased in various ways. For example, in (16) the number of *t*-retention grammars is greater than the number of *t*-deletion grammars. Specifically, one might expect this speaker to delete *t* in *mist* approximately 33 percent of the time. We might even propose an explicit QUANTITATIVE INTERPRETATION of the multiple grammars model along these lines:

(17)   *A quantitative interpretation of multiple grammars.* The number of grammars that generate a particular output is proportional to the relative frequency of this output.

There are two common objections to the multiple grammars model. First, it has been suggested that the number of grammars per individual becomes implausibly large (Reynolds 1994, Guy 1997b). Three grammars may not sound too bad, but how about an individual with 120 or 40,320 grammars? While initially persuasive, this objection is difficult to evaluate unless we have some way of determining how many grammars are too many. Second, the model seems unconstrained. If any combination of grammars is possible for an individual speaker, we run the risk that any kind of variation, including any kind of frequencies, can be modeled. This would imply that the theory does not exclude anything and is thus vacuous (Liberman 1994). For example, the *t*-retention bias in (16) follows from nothing in particular. In fact, we could have chosen any tableaux, with consequently different results. However, biases like (16) may have a principled basis. As we will see shortly, phonological and morphological constraints themselves introduce inherent biases into the system, setting firm limits on how many and what kinds of grammars can be constructed in the first place. In addition, external factors like sex, age, style, register and social class may be responsible for systematic differences among individuals. For example, old and young speakers may have systematically different grammar pools, although they may be overlapping.

We now exemplify the multiple grammars model by outlining the beginnings of an optimality-theoretic analysis of English *t,d*-deletion based on the fuller analysis in Kiparsky (1993b). The model predicts that certain types of variable dialects are possible, others impossible, and that certain types of statistical distributions of variants are possible, others impossible. Our goal is to show that the multiple grammars model is a serious hypothesis concerning variation, although not without problems.

Following the approach in Liberman (1994), let us first define a grammar as a set of input/output pairs where for every input there is some fixed output. We start by assuming a particularly simple grammar that does not impose any constraints on the possible input/output mappings, but accepts them all. While such a grammar is unlikely to do anything linguistically interesting, it will give us a baseline: any analysis that we may come up with should do better, and certainly not worse, than this linguistically naive grammar.

Next, we define the possible inputs and possible outputs in the domain of interest, which is *t,d*-deletion. Here we will only consider two inputs and three outputs. On the input side, *t* can occur either before a vowel or before a consonant. On the output side, we consider three options: *t* in the syllable coda, *t* resyllabified as part of the following onset and *t*-deletion.

(18)   Inputs: /cost##V/, /cost##C/
        Outputs: [cost.X], [cos.tX], [cos.X]

Next, we ask what are the possible input/output mappings, i.e. grammars. Since there are two inputs and three outputs, we have $3^2 = 9$ distinct grammars, shown in (19).

(19) The nine possible grammars (the naive model)

	/cost##V/	/cost##C/	
1	cost.V	cost.C	complex coda, complex coda
2	cost.V	cos.tC	complex coda, resyllabification
3	cost.V	cos.C	complex coda, *t*-deletion
4	cos.tV	cost.C	resyllabification, complex coda
5	cos.tV	cos.tC	resyllabification, resyllabification
6	cos.tV	cos.C	resyllabification, *t*-deletion
7	cos.V	cost.C	*t*-deletion, complex coda
8	cos.V	cos.tC	*t*-deletion, resyllabification
9	cos.V	cos.C	*t*-deletion, *t*-deletion

It is immediately obvious that some of these grammars are linguistically natural, others are not. For example, grammar 6 yields resyllabification pre-vocalically (*cos.tAnna*) and deletion pre-consonantally (*cos.me*), which seems plausible. On the other hand, grammar 8 yields the reverse pattern (*cos.Anna, cos.tme*) which is unheard of. In addition, given the multiple grammars model, we predict a speaker who combines grammars 4 and 6. Such an individual shows invariant resyllabification pre-vocalically (*cos.tAnna*) and optional deletion pre-consonantally (*cost.me~cos.me*), which is again plausible. On the other hand, a combination of 8 and 9 gives a dialect with invariant deletion pre-vocalically (*cos.Anna*) and variable deletion pre-consonantally (*cos.tme~cos.me*), which seems extremely odd. What we clearly need is a phonological theory that rules out the unnatural grammars and keeps the natural ones.

Following Kiparsky (1993b), let us now enrich our linguistically naive model by adopting some basic optimality-theoretic constraints on syllable structure. Three of these constraints have already been introduced. To simplify discussion, we substitute MAX(t) for the more general MAX(C).

(20) *CxCOD No coda clusters.
       *CxONS No onset clusters.
       ONSET   Onsets are required.
       MAX(t)   No *t*-deletion.
       ALIGN   Morpheme and syllable boundaries coincide.

We now ask the following question: given these five constraints, Optimality Theory and the multiple grammars model, what patterns are predicted? The answer could be one of the following:

(21) 1   We continue to predict all the nine logically possible patterns. This would show that our constraints and Optimality Theory serve no useful purpose at all.

       2   Some of the nine logically possible patterns are excluded. Now the question is: which patterns? The best scenario is that our model rules out all the linguistically unnatural and hence unattested

patterns, and keeps all the natural patterns, including the attested ones. A worse scenario is that the resulting pattern is more or less random in which case we would not be doing any better than the naive model. The worst scenario is that our system rules out all the right patterns and keeps all the wrong ones.

In order to see what is being predicted, we must take all the possible tableaux and apply them to all the possible inputs. Five constraints can be ranked in $5! = 5 \times 4 \times 3 \times 2 \times 1 = 120$ possible ways. This so-called FACTORIAL TYPOLOGY exhausts the space of grammatical possibilities. Recall that there are two inputs: /cost##V/ (the pre-vocalic environment) and /cost##C/ (the pre-consonantal environment). This means we will have to check 240 tableaux in all. To get started, we select one tableau at random and apply it to both inputs.

(22)   A sample tableau. . = syllable boundary, | = morpheme boundary

	/cost##V/	*CxOns	*CxCod	Onset	Align	Max(t)
1a.	cost |.V		*!	*		
1b.	cos |.V			*!		*
1c. ⇒	cos.t |V				*	
	/cost##C/					
2a.	cost |.C		*!			
2b. ⇒	cos |.C					*
2c.	cos.t |C	*!			*	

This grammar resyllabifies *t* before a vowel (*cos.tAnna*) and deletes it before a consonant (*cos.me*). Looking back to (19), we see that this is a type 6 grammar, one of the linguistically plausible types. This is a good start, but since we are testing the limits of the model, we still need to check what happens under the remaining 119 rankings. This can be done either by brute force, i.e. by working through the tableaux one by one, either by hand or by computer (as has been done here), or by ingenious reasoning. The results are shown in (23).

(23)   The five possible grammars (Optimality Theory)

	/cost##V/	/cost##C/	
1	cost.V	cost.C	complex coda, complex coda
4	cos.tV	cost.C	resyllabification, complex coda
5	cos.tV	cos.tC	resyllabification, resyllabification
6	cos.tV	cos.C	resyllabification, *t*-deletion
9	cos.V	cos.C	*t*-deletion, *t*-deletion

Instead of the logically possible nine output patterns, we only get five. This means that there is no way of ranking the five constraints such that we would get patterns 2, 3, 7 and 8. These patterns are thus excluded as impossible.[4] Taking a closer look at (23), we can see that all three outputs (complex coda, resyllabification, *t*-deletion) are predicted to be possible both pre-vocalically and pre-consonantally. However, the environments show clear preferences. Resyllabification is favored pre-vocalically, whereas complex coda and *t*-deletion are favored pre-consonantally. This is an example of an inherent bias introduced by the constraints. A more accurate picture is shown in (24) which sums up the number of tableaux predicting each output in each environment, both in actual numbers and percentages (out of 120 tableaux).

(24)   The number of tableaux predicting each output

	V	C	V%	C%
resyllabification	70	20	58%	17%
complex coda	25	50	21%	42%
t-deletion	25	50	21%	42%

Assuming the quantitative interpretation in (17), we can take the percentages in (24) to represent the quantitative output of a speaker who possesses all the 120 grammars. This hypothetical speaker exhibits the well-documented vowel/consonant asymmetry, deleting *t,d* approximately 21 percent of the time before vowels and about 42 percent of the time before consonants. Different percentages can be obtained by throwing out grammars from the pool. For example, by throwing out all grammars except types 6 and 9 we get a dialect where *t*-deletion is categorical in the pre-consonantal environment, but optional in the pre-vocalic environment (50 percent resyllabification, 50 percent *t*-deletion), another dialect with a vowel/consonant asymmetry of the right kind.

A very important question is what kinds of dialects are excluded. Recall the bizarre dialects predicted by the naive model, for example dialect 8 with pre-vocalic deletion (*cos.Anna*) and pre-consonantal resyllabification (*cos.tme*). This dialect is now excluded, a good result. Also excluded is the dialect with invariant pre-vocalic deletion (*cos.Anna*) and variable pre-consonantal deletion (*cos.me~cost.me* or *cos.me~cos.tme*). To see why this should be, note that to get invariant pre-vocalic deletion we are limited to tableaux of type 9. But this means that we will also get invariant pre-consonantal deletion. Yet another excluded dialect is one where deletion is more frequent pre-vocalically than pre-consonantally. In conclusion, a very simple analysis that assumes five phonological constraints, Optimality Theory, and the multiple grammars model excludes several unattested *t,d*-deletion patterns, among them unattested quantitative patterns. This is a promising initial result.

However, some odd predictions persist. For example, the model predicts variable dialects without a consonant/vowel asymmetry. Such a dialect can be obtained by combining tableaux of types 1, 5 and 9, and those only. Such a speaker will vary between resyllabification, complex coda and *t*-deletion, but show no quantitative differences between the vowel and consonant environments. Dialects of this kind do not seem to exist. There are at least three possible diagnoses: (1) not all relevant constraints have been included in the analysis; (2) the phonology of English contains rankings that are responsible for the robust vowel/consonant asymmetry; (3) the multiple grammars model is false. Here it suffices to note that there are clearly many constraints that matter to *t*-deletion and that have not been included, for example constraints referring to segment quality. In addition, the phonology of English is likely to have at least some partial rankings (see sections 5.2 and 5.3) that restrict the pool of available grammars. Thus, concluding (3) is clearly premature.

Finally, the question arises how to incorporate morphological effects in the analysis. Kiparsky's (1993b) solution is to posit morphologically specialized phonological constraints that check syllable well-formedness separately for roots, stems and words. This puts *cost*, *los+t* and *toss#ed* in unequal positions as the schematic tableau (25) shows.

(25)

		*CxCOD$_{root}$	*CxCOD$_{stem}$	*CxCOD$_{word}$
1a.	cost	*	*	*
1b.	cos			
2a.	los+t		*	*
2b.	los			
3a.	toss#t			*
3b.	toss			

The regularly inflected *tossed* only violates the word-level constraint, the semiregular *lost* violates both stem-level and word-level constraints, and the monomorphemic *cost* violates all three. Interspersed among the five constraints discussed so far, these new constraints will bias the output pattern in a particular way. The overall effect is easy to see even without working out the tableaux: all else being equal, there will be more tableaux that delete *t* in *cost* than in *lost*, and more tableaux that delete *t* in *lost* than in *tossed*, the desired result.

In sum, we have presented a multiple grammars approach to variation within Optimality Theory and exemplified it by outlining a possible analysis of *t,d*-deletion along the lines of Kiparsky (1993b). We have seen that the model yields falsifiable, and mostly reasonable, predictions both in the categorical and quantitative domains. Certain types of variable dialects are predicted to be possible, others impossible; certain types of statistical distributions of variants are predicted to be possible, others impossible. The limits of the model can be explored further by applying it to specific *t,d*-deletion dialects. Empirically the model needs to be augmented to cover the effects of segment quality, the

Obligatory Contour Principle, and the pause environment (for the treatment of pause, see Kiparsky 1993b), both in their categorical and quantitative manifestations. All this seems straightforward in principle, but detailed analyses may prove otherwise.

An interesting general aspect of the model is that it explicitly identifies cross-linguistic variation and intra-individual variation: both reduce to differences in constraint ranking. In this particular sense, intra-individual variation is cross-linguistic variation within an individual. One would thus expect to find the same regularities in both domains. Thus, for example, cross-linguistic variation in syllable structure parameters should emerge intra-individually in the relevant types of variation, perhaps in a statistical form. This is indeed what seems to happen in the case of *t,d*-deletion.

To refute the multiple grammars model, one can proceed in two ways:

(26) a. Show that the model is too powerful. This would involve a demonstration that the model predicts systematically unattested types of variation, i.e. the model overgenerates and a more restrictive theory is needed. Alternatively, one could adopt a less powerful model (see e.g. section 5.3) and show that it is sufficient for all the attested cases of variation.

   b. Show that the model is too weak. This would involve documenting cases of variation that cannot be captured in the multiple grammars model under reasonable linguistic assumptions, i.e. the model undergenerates and something more powerful is needed.

Since most optimality-theoretic work on variation has so far concentrated on getting the descriptive facts right, one way or the other, very little attention has been paid to general theory comparison issues such as (26a) and (26b). However, both kinds of arguments are already on record. In the rest of this chapter, we will review two analyses of the same corpus of data: 28,000 tokens of variable genitive plurals in Finnish. The first analysis (Anttila 1997a) adopts multiple tableaux, but places a particular restriction on their possible combinations. The second analysis (Boersma and Hayes 2001) introduces numerical ranking in order to better capture quantitative distinctions in the data.

5   Alternatives to Multiple Grammars

5.1   *The data*

The Finnish genitive plural can be formed in two principal ways which we will here call the WEAK ENDING /-ien/ (also /-jen/) and the STRONG ENDING /-iden/. We will now examine the distribution of the two types of endings in vowel-final stems. (Consonant-final stems are systematically different and will not be discussed.)

(27)   Genitive plural inflection in Finnish

	Stem	Variants	Gloss
a.	/puu/	pu-iden	"tree-PL-GEN"
	/maa/	ma-iden	"land-PL-GEN"
b.	/lasi/	las-ien	"glass-PL-GEN"
	/margariini/	margariin-ien	"margarine-PL-GEN"
	/sosialisti/	sosialist-ien	"socialist-PL-GEN"
c.	/naapuri/	naapure-iden~naapur-ien	"neighbor-PL-GEN"
	/ministeri/	ministere-iden~minister-ien	"minister-PL-GEN"
	/aleksanteri/	aleksantere-iden~aleksanter-ien	"Alexander-PL-GEN"

The stems in (27a) choose the strong variant, the stems in (27b) the weak variant, and the stems in (27c) are variable. This raises the locus of variation problem: why does variation only occur in the last group? An important observation is that the first group contains all the monosyllabic stems, the second group all the disyllabic stems (as well as certain longer stems, e.g. /margariini/ "margarine" and /sosialisti/ "socialist") and the variable stems may have any number of syllables greater than two. This shows that word length in syllables is somehow involved, reminding us of the Walmatjari pattern (section 3.2).

In addition, variable stems are variable to different degrees. Native speakers often report that one variant sounds better than the other, although both are possible. These subtle differences in judgments are reflected in corpus frequencies: the better-sounding variant tends to be more common. The following numbers are based on the 1987 issues of the *Suomen Kuvalehti* weekly (approximately 28,000 genitive plurals).[5]

(28)		Stem type	Strong	Weak
	a.	/ka.me.ra/	ka.me.roi.den (99.4%)	?ka.me.ro.jen (0.6%)
	b.	/sai.raa.la/	sai.raa.loi.den (50.5%)	sai.raa.lo.jen (49.5%)
	c.	/naa.pu.ri/	naa.pu.rei.den (37.2%)	naa.pu.ri.en (62.8%)
	d.	/po.lii.si/	?po.lii.sei.den (1.4%)	po.lii.si.en (98.6%)

Glosses: *kamera* "camera", *sairaala* "hospital", *naapuri* "neighbor", *poliisi* "police"

Two phonological generalizations emerge: (1) stems ending in an underlyingly [+low] vowel /a/ prefer the strong variant; stems ending in an underlyingly [+high] vowel /i/ prefer the weak variant (Anttila 1997a); (2) Stems with a light penultimate syllable (CV) prefer the strong variant; stems with a heavy penultimate syllable (CVV) prefer the weak variant (Itkonen 1957).[6] These tendencies have a cumulative effect: /ka.me.ra/ (final /a/, light penult) favors the strong variant almost categorically, and /po.lii.si/ (final /i/, heavy penult) favors the weak variant almost categorically. The mixed cases /sai.raa.la/ and /naa.pu.ri/ fall in between.

To summarize, the locus of variation depends on the number of syllables in the stem; the degree of variation depends on the height of the final vowel and the weight of the penultimate syllable of the stem. The question is: why would such things matter? We suggest that they do because the shapes of the variants are different: the strong variant /-iden/ makes the preceding syllable heavy, e.g. *naa.pu.***rei**.*den* whereas the weak variant /-ien/ makes the preceding syllable light, e.g. *naa.pu.***ri**.*en*. While this may seem to be yet another puzzling observation, this is the crucial phonological fact that makes everything fall into place.

5.2   The constraints

We now introduce the constraints. For a more detailed discussion, see Anttila (1997a). First, heavy syllables tend to be stressed and stressed syllables tend to be heavy universally (see e.g. Kager 1999: 155, 268). This is expressed as the constraint hierarchy in (29). The constraints are stated negatively, e.g. *ʹL means "Avoid a stressed light syllable."

(29)   The Weight-Stress Principle
       {*H, *ʹL} >> {*ʹH, *L}
       "Unstressed heavies and stressed lights are worse than stressed heavies and unstressed lights."

Second, we propose that stress, syllable weight and vowel height are preferably combined as stated in (30)–(31):

(30)   The Weight-Sonority Principles
       a.   *H/I >> *H/O >> *H/A
       b.   *L/A >> *L/O >> *L/I
       "A heavy syllable with a high nucleus is worse than a heavy syllable with a mid nucleus, which is worse than a heavy syllable with a low nucleus. The reverse holds for light syllables."

(31)   The Stress-Sonority Principles
       a.   *ʹI >> *ʹO >> *ʹA
       b.   *A >> *O >> *I
       "A stressed syllable with a high nucleus is worse than a stressed syllable with a mid nucleus, which is worse than a stressed syllable with a low nucleus. The reverse holds for unstressed syllables."

Finally, we propose the following rhythmic principles:

(32)   The Rhythmic Principles
       a.   *ʹX.ʹX   "No adjacent stressed syllables."
            *X.X   "No adjacent unstressed syllables."
       b.   *H.H   "No adjacent heavy syllables."
            *L.L   "No adjacent light syllables."

5.3   Analysis 1: Stratified grammar

First, we address the locus of variation problem. There are two separate questions here: (1) Why do monosyllabic and disyllabic stems choose different variants? (2) Why does variation require a minimum of three syllables? We start by noting that in Finnish words the first syllable is always stressed, the second always unstressed. This follows from two undominated constraints: INITIALSTRESS (not mentioned in the tableaux) and *'X.'X "No adjacent stressed syllables". The correct distribution of variants now follows by ranking the Weight-Stress constraints *H and *'L as in (33). Note that these two constraints need not be ranked with respect to each other: both rankings (TABLEAU 1, TABLEAU 2) yield the same winner.

(33)   /maa/ "land"

TABLEAU 1		*X́.X́	*Ĺ	*H	...
a.	⇒ mái.den			*	
b.	*má.jen		*!	*	
TABLEAU 2		*X́.X́	*H	*Ĺ	...
a.	⇒ mái.den		*		
b.	*má.jen		*	*!	

Since the first syllable is always stressed, and stressed syllables are preferably heavy, the strong variant with the heavy penult invariably wins. In disyllables the reverse situation obtains, as shown in (34): since the second syllable is always unstressed and unstressed syllables are preferably light, the weak variant with the light penult invariably wins.

(34)   /lasi/ "glass"

TABLEAU 1		*X́.X́	*Ĺ	*H	...
a.	*lá.sei.den		*	**!	
b.	⇒ lá.si.en		*	*	
TABLEAU 2		*X́.X́	*H	*Ĺ	...
a.	*lá.sei.den		**!	*	
b.	⇒ lá.si.en		*	*	

We are here making the idealizing assumption that the final syllable is never stressed, implying an undominated constraint *FINALSTRESS. In fact, final syllables may be optionally stressed if heavy (cf. Hanson and Kiparsky 1996). Here we abstract away from this additional variable pattern.

We now understand why monosyllabic and disyllabic stems show no variation: this is an effect of the invariant initial stress. However, nothing has been said about stress beyond the second syllable. This has the consequence in (35):

(35) /naapuri/ "neighbor"

TABLEAU 1		*X́.X́	*Ĺ	*H	…
a.	⇒ náa.pu.rèi.den			*	
b.	⇒ náa.pu.ri.en			*	
TABLEAU 2		*X́.X́	*H	*Ĺ	…
a.	⇒ náa.pu.rèi.den		*		
b.	⇒ náa.pu.ri.en		*		

As (35) shows, the third syllable may be stressed, in which case we get the strong variant, or it may be unstressed, in which case we get the weak variant.[7] This explains why variation requires a minimum of three syllables: after the second syllable stress is essentially optional. However, not all long words show variation. As the reader can easily verify, the analysis predicts variation in /mi.nis.te.ri/ "minister" (*minister-ien~ministere-iden*) and /a.lek.san.te.ri/ "Alexander" (*aleksanter-ien~aleksantere-iden*), but not in the very similar /mar.ga.rii.ni/ "margarine" (*margariin-ien/*margariine-iden*) and /so.si.a.lis.ti/ "socialist" (*sosialist-ien/*sosialiste-iden*), which is correct.

The remaining question is how to predict degrees of variation in cases like /naapuri/ "neighbor". For this purpose, we place another set of constraints below the three constraints discussed so far. This is shown in (36). Note that the universal rankings proposed in section 5.2 are respected; we are simply adding rankings.

(36) A grammar for Finnish: augmented version
      *'X. 'X >> {*H, *'L} >> {*L.L, *H/I, *'I}

The new set contains three mutually unranked constraints. They can be spelled out as the six tableaux in (37). However, unlike (33)–(35), where different rankings produce the same winner, here different rankings produce different winners:

(37) /naapuri/ "neighbor"

Tableau 1		…	*H/I	*Í	*L.L
a.	náa.pu.rèi.den		*!	*	
b.	⇒ náa.pu.ri.en				*
Tableau 2		…	*H/I	*L.L	*Í
a.	náa.pu.rèi.den		*!		*
b.	⇒ náa.pu.ri.en			*	
Tableau 3		…	*Í	*L.L	*H/I
a.	náa.pu.rèi.den		*!		*
b.	⇒ náa.pu.ri.en			*	
Tableau 4		…	*Í	*H/I	*L.L
a.	náa.pu.rèi.den		*!	*	
b.	⇒ náa.pu.ri.en				*
Tableau 5		…	*L.L	*H/I	*Í
a.	⇒ náa.pu.rèi.den			*	*
b.	náa.pu.ri.en		*!		
Tableau 6		…	*L.L	*Í	*H/I
a.	⇒ náa.pu.rèi.den			*	*
b.	náa.pu.ri.en		*!		

The candidate *naapur-ien* wins in four tableaux, the candidate *naapure-iden* in two tableaux. Assuming the quantitative interpretation in (17), the predicted frequencies are 2/3 and 1/3, respectively. This is reasonably close to the actually observed frequencies 62.8 percent and 37.2 percent.

The grammar in (36) consists of internally unranked strata of constraints which are strictly ranked with respect to each other. Following the terminology of Tesar and Smolensky (1995) and Boersma (2001), we call such grammars STRATIFIED GRAMMARS. The complete stratified grammar needed to account for the Finnish facts is given in (38). The quantitative results will be displayed in section 5.5.

(38) A grammar for Finnish: final version

{*'X. 'X} >>	Stratum 1
{*H, *'L} >>	Stratum 2
{*L.L, *H/I, *'I} >>	Stratum 3
{*L/A, *H/O, *'O, *H.H, *X.X, *'H}	Stratum 4

A stratified grammar like (38) can be viewed from two angles. If we look at (38) as a relation, i.e. as a set of ordered pairs of constraints, we have a single grammar, not multiple grammars. Alternatively, if we spell out all the possible linearizations of the constraints in (38), we have multiple tableaux. From the second perspective it is clear that a stratified grammar is a special case of the multiple grammars model. Thus, all stratified grammars are instances of the multiple grammars model, but the converse does not hold: there are instances of the multiple grammars model that are not stratified grammars. For example, the tableaux in (39) constitute a perfectly well-formed grammar in the multiple grammars model, but not a stratified grammar.

(39) *'X.'X >> *H >> *'L
       *'L >> *H >> *'X.'X

Other special cases of the multiple grammars model we have not discussed for reasons of space include FLOATING CONSTRAINTS (Reynolds 1994, Nagy and Reynolds 1997) and PARTIALLY ORDERED GRAMMARS (Anttila and Cho 1998, Anttila to appear a, Anttila to appear b). The latter subsume stratified grammars as a special case, as pointed out by Boersma (2001).

It is not clear which of these approaches is correct, if any. It may turn out that some restricted version of the multiple grammars model (e.g. stratified grammars) is sufficient. It may also be that the full power of multiple grammars is necessary. Finally, it is possible that something quite different is needed. This claim has been made by proponents of CONTINUOUS RANKING which generalizes Optimality Theory itself by introducing numerical ranking.

5.4 Analysis 2: Continuous ranking

In standard Optimality Theory, the ranking A >> B >> C means that A dominates B which dominates C. There is no sense in which A and B could lie "closer together" than B and C. In the continuous ranking model (Zubritskaya 1997, Hayes 2000, Hayes and MacEachern 1998, Boersma 1998 and especially Boersma and Hayes 2001 which we will follow here) such a statement is meaningful. This model generalizes standard Optimality Theory by adopting a CONTINUOUS RANKING SCALE. Each constraint has a fixed RANKING VALUE along a real-number scale where higher values correspond to higher-ranked constraints. For example, the ranking values of A, B, and C could be 125, 93.75, and 31.25, respectively, as shown in (40). How ranking values are determined will be discussed shortly.

(40)   Ranking values

In order to describe variation, the model introduces STOCHASTIC CANDIDATE EVALUATION. Boersma and Hayes (2001) propose that, at evaluation time (i.e. the moment of speaking), a random positive or negative value is temporarily added to the ranking value of each constraint. The resulting actual ranking value is called the SELECTION POINT. As the selection points will vary around the fixed ranking value from evaluation to evaluation, the constraints begin to act as if they were associated with ranges of values, instead of points. This means that constraint ranges may overlap to different degrees. Consider the hypothetical examples in (41) and (42). A, B, and C are constraints with ranking values 125, 93.75, and 31.25, respectively, and *a*, *b*, and *c* are their respective selection points in a particular evaluation.

(41)   Evaluation 1: common result

(42)   Evaluation 2: rare result

In evaluation (41), the selection points happen to fall roughly in the middle of each constraint which results in the ranking *a* >> *b* >> *c*. In evaluation (42), *a* happens to be chosen very near the bottom of A and *b* very near the top of B which results in the ranking *b* >> *a* >> *c*. In the continuous ranking model, such differences between evaluations are responsible for variation. Boersma and Hayes (2001) explicitly assume that selection points are distributed normally around the ranking value, which means that they tend to cluster near the center of the constraint, but will occasionally fall near the edges. They also assume that every constraint has the same standard deviation, or equal "breadth." The degree of variation will depend on how close the fixed ranking values are to each other. Thus, the ranking $a \gg b$ will be common, $b \gg a$ rare, and C is too far away for c to ever rise above either a or b, i.e. the ranking is categorical.[8]

An advantage that continuous ranking currently enjoys over various other models is that there exists an algorithm, the GRADUAL LEARNING ALGORITHM, that is able to learn continuously ranked grammars, including variation.[9] The algorithm has been implemented as a computer program and it seems to perform well in empirical tests. This is also good news for stratified grammars: as Boersma (2001) notes, stratified grammars are a special case of continuously ranking grammars. The algorithm works roughly as follows (for a more detailed description, see Boersma and Hayes 2001). The algorithm starts out with a set of constraints with arbitrary (e.g. identical) ranking values. It reads a learning datum that consists of a surface form and its corresponding underlying form and checks whether the grammar is able to generate this surface form from the given underlying form. If not, the ranking must be incorrect, and the algorithm responds by promoting and demoting constraints by small amounts along the continuous ranking scale in a way that is likely to improve the situation. Given the adjusted grammar and further learning data, the algorithm will keep repeating these steps. If the algorithm behaves as desired, the end result is a ranking that correctly describes the data, including the quantitative preferences observed during learning.

To test the performance of continuous ranking and the Gradual Learning Algorithm, Boersma and Hayes replicated Anttila's (1997a) study of the Finnish genitive plural based on the same 28,000-token corpus. In this experiment, each variant was presented to the algorithm in the relative frequency in which it occurs in the corpus. In a representative run, the following ranking values emerged:

(43)

*H	288.000	*O	196.754
*'I	207.892	*X.X	188.726
*L.L	206.428	*'O	3.246
*A	199.864	*'A	0.136
*H.H	199.274	*I	−7.892

5.5 A comparison of results

The tables in (44)–(47), reproduced from Boersma and Hayes (2001), contrast the performance of the two models. SG stands for stratified grammar, CRG for continuously ranking grammar.

(44) 2-syllable stems

Example	Candidates	Obs.%	SG	CRG	Tokens
kala	ká.lo.jen	100	100	100	500
'fish'	ká.loi.den	0	0	0	0
lasi	lá.si.en	100	100	100	500
'glass'	lá.sei.den	0	0	0	0

(45)   3-syllable stems

Example	Candidates	Obs.%	SG	CRG	Tokens
kamera	ká.me.ro.jen	0	0	0.52	0
'camera'	ká.me.ròi.den	100	100	99.48	720
hetero	hé.te.ro.jen	0.5	0	0.57	2
'hetero'	hé.te.ròi.den	99.5	100	99.43	89
naapuri	náa.pu.ri.en	63.1	67	69.51	368
'neighbor'	náa.pu.rèi.den	36.9	33	30.49	215
maailma	máa.il.mo.jen	49.5	50	42.03	45
'world'	máa.il.mòi.den	50.5	50	57.97	46
korjaamo	kór.jaa.mo.jen	82.2	80	81.61	350
'repair shop'	kór.jaa.mòi.den	17.8	20	18.39	76
poliisi	pó.lii.si.en	98.4	100	100	806
'police'	pó.lii.sèi.den	1.6	0	0	13

(46)   4-syllable stems

Example	Candidates	Obs.%	SG	CRG	Tokens
taiteilija	tái.tei.li.jo.jen	0	0	0.52	0
'artist'	tái.tei.li.jòi.den	100	100	99.48	276
luettelo	lú.et.te.lo.jen	0	0	0.56	0
'catalogue'	lú.et.te.lòi.den	100	100	99.44	25
ministeri	mí.nis.te.ri.en	85.7	67	69.49	234
'minister'	mí.nis.te.rèi.den	14.3	33	30.51	39
luon.neh.din.ta	lúon.neh.dìn.to.jen	100	100	100	1
'charaterization'	lúon.neh.dìn.noi.den	0	0	0	0
edustusto	é.dus.tùs.to.jen	100	100	100	84
'representation'	é.dus.tùs.toi.den	0	0	0	0
margariini	már.ga.rìi.ni.en	100	100	100	736
'margarine'	már.ga.rìi.nei.den	0	0	0	0

(47)   5-syllable stems

Example	Candidates	Obs.%	SG	CRG	Tokens
ajattelija	á.jat.te.li.jo.jen	0	0	0.52	0
'thinker'	á.jat.te.li.jòi.den	100	100	99.48	101
televisio	té.le.vi.si.o.jen	0	0	0.57	0
'television'	té.le.vi.si.òi.den	100	100	99.43	41
Aleksanteri	á.lek.sàn.te.ri.en	88.2	67	69.51	15
'Alexander'	á.lek.sàn.te.rèi.den	11.8	33	30.49	2
evankelista	é.van.ke.lìs.to.jen	100	100	100	2
'evangelist'	é.van.ke.lìs.toi.den	0	0	0	0
italiaano	í.ta.li.àa.no.jen	100	100	100	1
'Italian'	í.ta.li.àa.noi.den	0	0	0	0
sosialisti	só.si.a.lìs.ti.en	100	100	100	99
'socialist'	só.si.a.lìs.tei.den	0	0	0	0

(48)   6-syllable stems

Example	Candidates	Obs.%	SG	CRG	Tokens
koordinaatisto	kóor.di.nàa.tis.to.jen	80	80	81.61	8
'coordinate grid'	kóor.di.nàa.tis.tòi.den	20	20	18.39	2
avantgardisti	á.vant.gàr.dis.ti.en	100	100	100	2
'avant-gardist'	á.vant.gàr.dis.tèi.den	0	0	0	0

Boersma and Hayes conclude that both models predict the empirical frequencies fairly well. The mean absolute error for the percentage predictions is 2.2 percent for the stratified grammar and 2.53 percent for the machine-learned continuously ranking grammar, averaged over 100 runs. Since stratified grammars are less powerful than continuously ranking grammars, the result is very encouraging for stratified grammars. However, more case studies are needed to evaluate the empirical adequacy of the two models in different domains. The question whether standard Optimality Theory needs to be replaced by numerical ranking still remains open.

6   Conclusion

In this chapter, I have discussed the following optimality-theoretic approaches to variation:

1. Tied violations
2. Pseudo-optionality
3. Multiple grammars (the generic model)
4. Stratified grammars
5. Continuously ranking grammars

Tied violations and pseudo-optionality are theoretically the most conservative approaches: they do not assume anything beyond standard Optimality Theory. However, neither seems capable of accommodating the kinds of data variationist linguists are used to seeing in their daily work. The multiple grammars model goes further. In particular, there are obvious ways of extending this model to quantitative regularities. Here the problem takes on the opposite character: unless constrained in principled ways, the multiple grammars model may be able to accommodate any kind of variation, linguistically natural or unnatural, a theoretically bad result. Approaches like stratified grammars address this concern by proposing restrictions on possible ranking relations. Not enough work has been done to determine how well motivated the proposed restrictions are empirically and whether they make the right kinds of predictions beyond the particular analyses at hand. Finally, the continuous ranking hypothesis challenges one of the basic assumptions of Optimality Theory itself by adopting real-number weighting. While this added power is a descriptive advantage, it remains to be seen whether it is necessary and whether it has undesirable consequences in other domains.

All the approaches, except pseudo-optionality, take essentially the same view on LOCUS OF VARIATION and the role of MARKEDNESS: variation occurs in environments where the constraints are unable to distinguish between candidates that are almost equally good in terms of markedness and faithfulness. It is important to see that, even in the absence of quantitative predictions, an analysis that correctly predicts the locus of variation has made a major contribution. This step is usually taken for granted in quantitative analyses of variation.

The proposals differ in how they approach DEGREES OF VARIATION. Tied violations and pseudo-optionality do not address the problem at all. The multiple grammars model and its derivatives (e.g. stratified grammars) usually rely on some version of grammar-counting, although this is not a necessary feature of the approach, and there are many conceivable ways of linking abstract grammatical structure with concrete corpus frequencies and/or gradient well-formedness judgments. As always, it is not obvious how to cross the competence/performance divide. Finally, continuous ranking is clearly motivated by the desire to enhance the power of Optimality Theory in the quantitative direction. This is also a domain where the competing proposals seem fairly easy to compare in concrete terms.

Less work has been done on the problem of INTERFACES: how do phonological, morphological, and lexical information interact in variation? In addition to morphologically specialized phonological constraints, such as *CxCoD$_{\text{ROOT}}$, *CxCoD$_{\text{STEM}}$, and *CxCoD$_{\text{WORD}}$, there is the possibility that different morphological and lexical categories subscribe to (slightly) different rankings; for general discussion, see e.g. Itô and Mester (1995a, 1995b, 1998), Orgun (1996), Inkelas (1998, 1999), Anttila (to appear a, to appear b), Kiparsky (to appear). The morphological and lexical aspects of variation are an interesting general challenge for all these models and are likely to be useful in distinguishing them empirically. Relatively little work has been done on the interface of grammar and EXTERNAL FACTORS; however, see Oostendorp (1997) and Morris (1998) for analyses of stylistic variation. There is a steadily growing literature on Optimality Theory and LANGUAGE CHANGE, often explicitly related to variation. A useful starting point is the bibliography compiled by Gess (2000).

While the work reviewed here is still in its beginnings, it seems fair to conclude that Optimality Theory has opened up a new perspective for the study of phonological variation. A number of technical proposals have been put forward, some initial results have been obtained, and a concrete research agenda is taking shape. The proposed models remain to be evaluated both formally, i.e. by working out the genuine (as opposed to notational) similarities and differences between the models, and empirically, i.e. by investigating many more cases of variation in many more languages, with the specific goal of finding evidence that would decide between the models. The initial empirical success of Optimality Theory gives one hope that generative phonology is beginning to answer some of the empirical questions raised by variationist linguists. It should also encourage theoretical phonologists to pay close attention to variable (including quantitative) data since such data are likely to have implications beyond variation.

Appendix

OT analyses of phonological variation

Anttila (1997a), Anttila (1997b), Anttila (to appear a, to appear b), Anttila and Cho (1998), Anttila and Revithiadou (2000), Auger (2000), Boersma (1997, 1998), Boersma and Hayes (2001), Borowsky and Horvath (1997), Demuth (1997), Hammond (1994), Hayes (2000), Hayes and MacEachern (1998), Hinskens et al. (1997), Holt (1997), Itô and Mester (1997), Iverson and Lee (1994), Kager (1996), Kang (1996), Kiparsky (1993b, to appear), Liberman (1994), Morris (1998), Nagy and Reynolds (1997), Oostendorp (1997), Reynolds (1994), Ringen and Heinämäki (1999), Rose (1997), Zubritskaya (1997).

Of related interest

Bailey (1973), Berkley (1994), Cedergren and Sankoff (1974), Frisch (1996), Frisch et al. (1997), Guy (1991a, 1991b, 1997a, 1997b), Guy and Boberg (1997), Labov (1969, 1972, 1994), Müller (1999), Myers (1995), Myers and Guy (1997), Paolillo (2000), Pierrehumbert (1994), Vennemann (1988), Weinreich et al. (1968).

NOTES

1 This paper was written while I was a Faculty of Arts and Social Sciences Postdoctoral Fellow at the Department of English Language and Literature, National University of Singapore. I thank Jack Chambers, Vivienne Fong and Natalie Schilling-Estes for valuable comments.

2 The corpus is available on the University of Helsinki Language Corpus Server at http:// www.ling.helsinki.fi/uhlcs/.

3 For reasons of space, we will not consider the following additional facts: (1) besides variable stress, four-syllable words show two fixed stress patterns: initial stress (*tjí.ni.njà.ɽa* "midday"), a pattern limited to monomorphemic words, and second syllable stress (*tja: ḷá.na.na* "dispersing"); (2) five-syllable and six-syllable words also show variation, but only in secondary stress placement. See Hammond (1994) for an analysis.

4 As always, we need to add the caveat "all else being equal." By adding a linguistically ill-motivated constraint into the system, this prediction might no longer hold.

5 The corpus is available on the University of Helsinki

Language Corpus Server at
http://www.ling.helsinki.fi/uhlcs/.
6   In Finnish (C)VV and (C)VC count as
heavy syllables for the purposes of
stress assignment, whereas (C)V
counts as light.
7   The system predicts that secondary
stresses only occur on heavy
syllables. It must be duly noted that
secondary stresses on light syllables
have been reported, see e.g. Hanson
and Kiparsky (1996), Elenbaas (1999),

Elenbaas and Kager (1999). Thus, the
present analysis only captures a
subset of actual secondary stresses.
The fact that these light syllable
secondary stresses do not play a role
in allomorph selection may imply
that they have a postlexical origin.
8   This statement is not exactly true,
but it is close enough. See Boersma
and Hayes (2001) for discussion.
9   See http://www.fon.hum.uva.nl/
praat/.

REFERENCES

Anttila, Arto (1997a). Deriving variation
from grammar. In Frans Hinskens,
Roeland van Hout and Leo Wetzels
(eds.), *Variation, Change and
Phonological Theory*, Amsterdam/
Philadelphia: John Benjamins
Publishing Company. 35–68. Also:
http://www.roa.rutgers.edu, ROA-63.

Anttila, Arto (1997b). *Variation in Finnish
phonology and morphology*. Doctoral
dissertation, Stanford University,
Stanford, California.

Anttila, Arto (to appear a). Derived
environment effects in Colloquial
Helsinki Finnish. Stanford,
California: CSLI Publications. Also
http://www.roa.rutgers.edu, ROA-
406-08100.

Anttila, Arto (to appear b).
Morphologically conditioned
phonological alternations. *Natural
Language and Linguistic Theory*. Also
http://www.roa.rutgers.edu, ROA-
425-10100.

Anttila, Arto and Young-mee Cho.
(1998). Variation and change in
Optimality Theory. *Lingua* 104:
31–56. Special issue on Optimality
Theory.

Anttila, Arto and Anthi Revithiadou
(2000). Variation in Allomorph
Selection. *Proceedings of NELS 30*.

Anttila, Raimo (1989) *Historical and
Comparative Linguistics*.
Amsterdam/Philadelphia: John
Benjamins Publishing
Company.

Archangeli, Diana and D. Terence
Langendoen (eds.) (1997). *Optimality
Theory: An Overview*. Oxford:
Blackwell.

Auger, Julie (2000). Phonological
Variation and Optimality Theory:
Evidence from word-initial vowel
epenthesis in Picard. In Julie
Auger and Andrea Word-Allbritton
(eds.), *The CVC of Sociolinguistics:
Contact, Variation, and Culture*.
Indiana University Working Papers
in Linguistics, vol. 2, pp. 1–20.

Bailey, Charles-James N. (1973). *Variation
and Linguistic Theory*. Arlington,
Virginia: Center for Applied
Linguistics.

Berkley, Deborah Milam (1994).
Variability in obligatory contour
principle effects. In Beals et al.
(eds.), *CLS 30, Volume 2: Parasession
on Variation in Linguistic Theory*,
Chicago: CLS. 1–12.

Bickerton, Derek (1971). Inherent
variability and variable rules.
Foundations of Language 7:
457–92.

Boersma, Paul (1997). How we learn variation, optionality, and probability. *Proceedings of the Institute of Phonetic Sciences of the University of Amsterdam* 21. 43–58. Also http://roa.rutgers.edu, ROA-221-1097.

Boersma, Paul (1998). Functional phonology. Doctoral dissertation, University of Amsterdam. The Hague: Holland Academic Graphics. Also: http://uvafon.hum.uva.nl/paul/.

Boersma, Paul (2001). Review of Arto Anttila (1997): Variation in Finnish Phonology and Morphology. *Glot International*. 5(1): 33–40. Also http://uvafon.hum.uva.nl/paul/.

Boersma, Paul and Bruce Hayes (2001). Empirical tests of the gradual learning algorithm. *Linguistic Inquiry* 32(1): 45–86. Also http://www.roa.rutgers.edu, ROA-348-1099.

Borowsky, Toni and Barbara Horvath (1997). L-vocalization in Australian English. In Frans Hinskens, Roeland van Hout and Leo Wetzels (eds.), *Variation, Change and Phonological Theory*. Amsterdam/Philadelphia: John Benjamins Publishing Company. 101–23.

Cedergren, Henrietta J. and David Sankoff (1974). Variable rules: Performance as a statistical reflection of competence. *Language* 50: 333–55.

Chambers, J. K. (1995). *Sociolinguistic Theory*. Oxford, UK, and Cambridge, USA: Blackwell.

Chomsky, Noam and Morris Halle (1968). *The Sound Pattern of English*. Cambridge, Massachusetts: MIT Press.

Demuth, Katherine (1997). Multiple optimal outputs in acquisition. In Viola Miglio and Bruce Morén (eds.), *University of Maryland Working Papers in Linguistics* 5, College Park, MD: Linguistics Department, University of Maryland. 53–71.

Elenbaas, Nine (1999). *Foot typology and ternary stress systems*. Doctoral dissertation, Utrecht Institute of Linguistics, OTS. The Hague: Holland Academic Graphics. Also: http://www.roa.rutgers.edu, ROA-397-06100.

Elenbaas, Nine and René Kager (1999). Ternary rhythm and the lapse constraint. *Phonology* 16(3): 273–329.

Fasold, Ralph (1972). *Tense Marking in Black English*. Arlington, Va.: Center for Applied Linguistics.

Fasold, Ralph (1991). The quiet demise of variable rules. *American Speech* 66: 3–21.

Frisch, Stefan (1996). *Similarity and frequency in phonology*. Doctoral dissertation, Northwestern University. http://www.roa.rutgers.edu, ROA 198-0597.

Frisch, Stefan, Michael Broe and Janet Pierrehumbert (1997). Similarity and phonotactics in Arabic. http://www.roa.rutgers.edu, ROA 223–1097.

Gess, Randall (2000). Bibliography: Optimality Theory and Language Change. http://www.roa.rutgers.edu, ROA-359-1199.

Goldsmith, John (1976). *Autosegmental phonology*. Doctoral dissertation, Massachusetts Institute of Technology, Cambridge, Massachusetts.

Guy, Gregory and Sally Boyd (1990). The development of a morphological class. *Language Variation and Change* 2: 1–18.

Guy, Gregory R. (1980). Variation in the group and the individual: The case of final stop deletion. In William Labov (ed.), *Locating Language in Time and Space*, New York: Academic Press. 1–36.

Guy, Gregory R. (1991a). Contextual conditioning in variable lexical phonology. *Language Variation and Change* 3: 223–39.

Guy, Gregory R. (1991b). Explanation in variable phonology. *Language Variation and Change* 3: 1–22.

Guy, Gregory R. (1994). The phonology of variation. In Beals et al. (eds.), *CLS 30, Volume 2: The Parasession on Variation in Linguistic Theory*, Chicago: CLS. 133–49.

Guy, Gregory (1997a). Competence, performance, and the generative grammar of variation. In Frans Hinskens, Roeland van Hout and Leo Wetzels (eds.), *Variation, Change and Phonological Theory*, Amsterdam/Philadelphia: John Benjamins Publishing Company. 125–43.

Guy, Gregory (1997b). Violable is variable: Optimality theory and linguistic variation. *Language Variation and Change* 9: 333–47.

Guy, Gregory and Charles Boberg (1997). Inherent variability and the Obligatory Contour Principle. *Language Variation and Change* 9: 149–64.

Hammond, Michael (1994). An OT account of variability in Walmatjari stress. http://www.roa.rutgers.edu, ROA-20-0794.

Hanson, Kristin and Paul Kiparsky (1996). A parametric theory of poetic meter. *Language* 72: 287–335.

Hargus, Sharon (1993). Modeling the phonology–morphology interface. In Sharon Hargus and Ellen Kaisse (eds.), *Phonetics and Phonology, Volume 4: Studies in Lexical Phonology*, San Diego, California: Academic Press. 45–74.

Hayes, Bruce (2000). Gradient well-formedness in Optimality Theory. In Joost Dekkers, Frank van der Leeuw and Jeroen van de Weijer (eds.) *Optimality Theory: Phonology, Syntax and Acquisition*. Oxford: Oxford University Press. 88–120. Also: http://www.linguistics.ucla.edu/people/hayes/gradient.htm.

Hayes, Bruce and Margaret MacEachern (1998). Quatrain form in English folk verse. *Language* 74: 473–507. Also: http://www.linguistics.ucla.edu/people/hayes/metrics.htm.

Hinskens, Frans, Roeland van Hout and Leo Wetzels (eds.) (1997). *Variation, Change and Phonological Theory*. Amsterdam/Philadelphia: John Benjamins Publishing Company.

Holt, David Eric (1997). The role of the listener in the historical phonology of Spanish and Portuguese: An optimality-theoretic account. Doctoral dissertation, Georgetown University. Also: http://www.roa.rutgers.edu, ROA-278-0898.

Hudson, J. and E. Richards (1969). The Phonology of Walmatjari. *Oceanic Linguistics* 8: 171–88.

Inkelas, Sharon (1998). The theoretical status of morphologically conditioned phonology: a case study of dominance effects. In Geert Booij and Jaap van Marle (eds.), *Yearbook of Morphology 1997*, Dordrecht: Kluwer Academic Publishers. 121–55.

Inkelas, Sharon (1999). Exceptional stress-attracting suffixes in Turkish: representations versus the grammar. In René Kager, Harry van der Hulst and Wim Zonneveld (eds.), *The Prosody–Morphology Interface*, Cambridge: Cambridge University Press. 134–87.

Itkonen, Terho (1957). Mellakoihin vai mellakkoihin? Yleiskielemme eräiden taivutushorjuvuuksien taustaa. *Virittäjä*. 259–86. (Abstract: Des raisons de certaines hésitations dans les déclinaisons du finnois littéraire).

Itô, Junko and Armin Mester (1995a). The core-periphery structure in the lexicon and constraints on re-ranking. In Jill N. Beckman, Laura Walsh Dickey and Suzanne Urbanczyk (eds.), *Papers in Optimality Theory*, University of Massachusetts, Amherst: GLSA. 181–210.

Itô, Junko and Armin Mester (1995b). Japanese phonology. In John A. Goldsmith (ed.), *The Handbook of Phonological Theory*, Oxford: Blackwell. 817–38.

Itô, Junko and Armin Mester (1997). Correspondence and compositionality: The Ga-gyō variation in Japanese phonology. In Iggy Roca (ed.), *Derivations and Constraints in Phonology*, Oxford University Press. 419–62. Also: http://www.roa.rutgers.edu, ROA-145-0996.

Itô, Junko and Armin Mester (1998). The phonological lexicon. In Natsuko Tsujimura (ed.), *A Handbook of Japanese Linguistics*. Oxford: Blackwell. 62–100.

Iverson, Gregory K. and Shinsook Lee (1994). Variation as optimality in Korean cluster reduction. Paper presented at ESCOL 94, University of South Carolina.

Kager, René (1996). On affix allomorphy and syllable counting. In U. Kleinhenz (ed.), *Interfaces in Phonology*, *Studia Grammatica* 41, Berlin: Akademie Verlag. 155–71. Also: http://www.roa.rutgers.edu, ROA-88.

Kager, René (1999). *Optimality Theory*. Cambridge: Cambridge University Press.

Kang, Hyeon-Seok (1996). The deletion of *w* in Seoul Korean and its implications. In David Dowty, Rebecca Herman, Elizabeth Hume and Panayiotis A. Pappas (eds.), *Working Papers in Linguistics No. 48*, The Ohio State University, Department of Linguistics. 56–76.

Kiparsky, Paul (1982). *Explanation in Phonology*. Dordrecht, Holland: Foris Publications.

Kiparsky, Paul (1989). Phonological change. In Frederick Newmeyer (ed.), *Linguistics: The Cambridge Survey*, Cambridge: Cambridge University Press. 363–415.

Kiparsky, Paul (1993a). Blocking in nonderived environments. In Sharon Hargus and Ellen Kaisse (eds.), *Phonetics and Phonology, Volume 4: Studies in Lexical Phonology*, San Diego, California: Academic Press. 277–313.

Kiparsky, Paul (1993b).Variable rules. Handout distributed at the Rutgers Optimality Workshop (ROW1).

Kiparsky, Paul (1995). The phonological basis of sound change. In John A. Goldsmith (ed.), *The Handbook of Phonological Theory*, Oxford: Blackwell. 640–70.

Kiparsky, Paul (to appear). *Paradigm Effects and Opacity*. Stanford, CA: CSLI Publications.

Kroch, Anthony (1994). Morphosyntactic variation. In Beals et al. (eds.), *CLS 30, Volume 2: The Parasession on Variation in Linguistic Theory*, Chicago: CLS. 180–201.

Kroch, Anthony S. (1989). Reflexes of grammar in patterns of language change. *Journal of Language Variation and Change* 1(3): 199–244.

Kroch, Anthony (2001). Syntactic change. In Mark Baltin and Chris Collins (eds.) *The Handbook of Contemporary Syntactic Theory*. Oxford: Blackwell. 699–729.

Labov, William (1969). Contraction, deletion and inherent variability of the English copula. *Language* 45: 715–62.

Labov, William (ed.) (1972). *Sociolinguistic Patterns*. Philadelphia: University of Pennsylvania Press.

Labov, William (1994). *Principles of Linguistic Change: Internal Factors*.

Oxford, UK, and Cambridge, USA: Blackwell.

Labov, William (1997). Resyllabification. In Frans Hinskens, Roeland van Hout and Leo Wetzels (eds.), *Variation, Change and Phonological Theory*, Amsterdam/Philadelphia: John Benjamins Publishing Company. 145–79.

Labov, William, Paul Cohen, Clarence Robins and John Lewis (1968). *A Study of the Nonstandard English of Negro and Puerto Rican Speakers of New York City*. Cooperative Research Report 3288, Vols I and II, Philadelphia: U.S. Regional Survey.

Leben, William R. (1973). *Suprasegmental phonology*. Doctoral dissertation, Massachusetts Institute of Technology, Cambridge, Massachusetts.

Liberman, Mark (1994). Optionality and optimality. Fragment of a draft, Department of Linguistics, University of Pennsylvania.

McCarthy, John (1986). OCP Effects: Gemination and Antigemination. *Linguistic Inquiry* 17(2): 207–63.

McCarthy, John (1988). Feature geometry and dependency: A review. *Phonetica* 43: 84–108.

McCarthy, John (1994). The phonetics and phonology of Semitic pharyngeals. In Patricia Keating (ed.), *Papers in Laboratory Phonology III*, Cambridge: Cambridge University Press. 191–283.

Mohanan, K. P. (1995). The organization of the grammar. In John A. Goldsmith (ed.), *The Handbook of Phonological Theory*, Oxford: Blackwell. 24–69.

Morris, Richard E. (1998). *Stylistic variation in Spanish phonology*. Doctoral dissertation, Ohio State University. http://www.roa.rutgers.edu, ROA-292-0199.

Müller, Gereon (1999). Optionality in optimality-theoretic syntax. *Glot International* 4(5).

Myers, James (1995). The categorical and gradient phonology of variable *t*-deletion in English. MS., York University.

Myers, James and Gregory R. Guy (1997). Frequency effects in variable lexical phonology. In Charles Boberg, Miriam Meyerhoff, Stephanie Strassel, and the PWPL series editors (eds.), *University of Pennsylvania Working Papers in Linguistics*, 4(1): 215–27.

Nagy, Naomi and William Reynolds (1997). Optimality theory and variable word-final deletion in Faetar. *Language Variation and Change* 9(1): 37–55.

Neu, Helene (1980). Ranking of Constraints on /t,d/ Deletion in American English: A Statistical Analysis. In William Labov (ed.), *Locating Language in Time and Space*, New York: Academic Press. 37–54.

Newmeyer, Frederick J. (2000). Optimality and functionality: Some critical remarks on OT syntax. http://www.roa.rutgers.edu, ROA-402-08100.

Oostendorp, Marc van (1997). Style registers in conflict resolution. In Frans Hinskens, Roeland van Hout and Leo Wetzels (eds.), *Variation, Change and Phonological Theory*. Amsterdam/Philadelphia: John Benjamins Publishing Company. 207–29.

Orgun, Cemil Orhan (1996). Sign-based morphology and phonology with special attention to optimality theory. Doctoral dissertation, Department of Linguistics, University of California, Berkeley. http://www.roa.rutgers.edu, ROA-171.

Paolillo, John (2000). A probabilistic model for Optimality Theory. In

Julie Auger and Andrea Word-Allbritton (eds.), *The CVC of Sociolinguistics: Contact, Variation, and Culture*. Indiana Working Papers in Linguistics, vol. 2, pp. 89–107.

Paolillo, John (forthcoming). *Analyzing Linguistic Variation: Statistical Models and Methods*. Stanford, CA: CSLI Publications.

Paunonen, Heikki (1995). *Suomen kieli Helsingissä. Huomioita Helsingin puhekielen historiallisesta taustasta ja nykyvariaatiosta* (The Finnish language in Helsinki. Observations on the historical background of and current variation in spoken Helsinki Finnish). Helsinki: Helsingin yliopiston suomen kielen laitos.

Pierrehumbert, Janet (1994). Knowledge of variation. In Beals et al. (eds.), *CLS 30, Volume 2: Parasession on Variation in Linguistic Theory*, Chicago: CLS. 232–56.

Prince, Alan and Paul Smolensky (1993). *Optimality Theory: Constraint Interaction in Generative Grammar*. Rutgers University, New Brunswick, and University of Colorado, Boulder.

Reynolds, William Thomas (1994). *Variation and phonological theory*. Doctoral dissertation, University of Pennsylvania.

Ringen, Catherine O. and Orvokki Heinämäki (1999). Variation in Finnish vowel harmony. *Natural Language and Linguistic Theory* 17: 303–37.

Rose, Sharon (1997). Featural morphology and dialect variation. In Frans Hinskens, Roeland van Hout and Leo Wetzels (eds.), *Variation, Change and Phonological Theory*, Amsterdam/Philadelphia: John Benjamins Publishing Company. 231–66.

Santa Ana, Otto (1992). Locating the linguistic cycle in vernacular speech: Chicano English and the Exponential Hypothesis. In J. M. Denton, G. P. Chan and C. P. Canakis (eds.), *CLS 28: Papers from the 28th Regional Meeting of the Chicago Linguistic Society, Vol. 2: The cycle in linguistic theory*, Chicago: CLS. 277–87.

Tesar, Bruce and Paul Smolensky (1995). The learnability of Optimality Theory. In Raul Aranovich, William Byrne, Susanne Preuss and Martha Senturia (eds.), *The Proceedings of the Thirteenth West Coast Conference on Formal Linguistics (WCCFL XIII)*, Stanford, California: Stanford Linguistics Association/CSLI. 122–37.

Vennemann, Theo (1988). *Preference Laws for Syllable Structure and the Explanation of Sound Change*. Amsterdam: Mouton de Gruyter.

Wang, William S.-Y. (1969). Competing changes as a cause of residue. *Language* 45: 9–25. Reprinted in Philip Baldi and Ronald N. Werth (eds.), (1978). *Readings in Historical Phonology*. University Park and London: The Pennsylvania State University Press.

Weinreich, Uriel, William Labov and Marvin I. Herzog (1968). Empirical foundations for a theory of language change. In W. P. Lehmann and Yakov Malkiel (eds.), *Directions for Historical Linguistics: A Symposium*, Austin: University of Texas Press. 95–195.

Wilkinson, Karina (1988). Prosodic Structure and Lardil Phonology. *Linguistic Inquiry* 19: 325–34.

Wolfram, Walter A. (1969). *A Sociolinguistic Description of Detroit Negro Speech*. Washington, DC: Center for Applied Linguistics.

Zubritskaya, Katya (1997). Mechanism of sound change in OT. *Language Variation and Change* 9(1): 121–48.

9 Investigating Chain Shifts and Mergers

MATTHEW J. GORDON

For students of language change, the most challenging questions begin with *why*. Why did pattern A change to pattern B? Why did the change happen when it did? Why did the change occur in one variety and not in others? Trying to explain language change has occupied generations of diachronically minded linguists and remains the most important task facing the field today. One perspective on this issue focuses on the basic roles in communication and weighs the relative needs of speakers with those of hearers. Such an approach is reflected in Martinet's view that "Linguistic evolution may be regarded as governed by the permanent conflict between man's communicative needs and his tendency to reduce to a minimum his mental and physical activity" (1964: 167). This functionalist approach to language change is by no means shared by all, perhaps not even by most, linguists (see, e.g., Lass 1978). Nevertheless, it does provide essential groundwork for the subject matter of this chapter, MERGERS and CHAIN SHIFTS, and offers insight into why these two types of sound change are discussed together.

1 Chain Shifts and Mergers as Alternatives

Chain shifts and mergers can be seen as alternative outcomes of a change situation. Both involve the encroachment of one phoneme into the phonological space of another. If the second phoneme changes so that the distinction between the two is maintained, then the result is a chain shift. If, however, the second phoneme does not change, the distinction is lost, and a merger occurs. From a functionalist perspective, the former case illustrates the power of "communicative needs," and the latter the power of "articulatory and mental inertia" (Martinet 1964: 169).

Long the domain of historical linguists, chain shifts and mergers have more recently drawn increasing attention from variationist sociolinguists. Particularly influential in this area (as in many others) has been the work of William Labov (see, e.g., Labov et al. 1972, Labov 1994). The variationist approach pioneered by Labov rejects the traditional belief that linguistic changes can only be observed after the fact. Indeed, decades of research into this paradigm have shown the value of studying language change in progress, and the benefits of this approach are perhaps nowhere more evident than in the re-examination of traditional concepts like chain shifts and mergers.

Some of the most intriguing questions posed by mergers and chain shifts relate to the underlying mechanisms and motivations that drive them, and such issues are the subject of ongoing debate in the field. The discussion here attempts to remain more or less neutral on these issues and focuses on empirical matters. I describe various approaches and suggest several methodologies for investigating such changes. I look first at mergers and explore some of the complications involved in the crucial notion of losing phonological contrasts. Then I turn to chain shifting and discuss how the fundamental elements of this process can be identified. Most of the variationist research on mergers and chain shifts has dealt with vocalic changes, and the discussion here reflects this bias in the examples and in some of the procedures described. Still, the core issues will also apply to the study of consonantal changes, and many of the techniques can be utilized with some modification. The ultimate goal here is to paint a picture of this fascinating area of study that will stimulate further research leading the field in new directions.

2   The Study of Mergers

Traditional approaches to sound change have treated merger as an essentially structural phenomenon. Comparing the phonological structure of a language at two points in time, it is observed that a distinction in the earlier structure is lost in the later structure; where there were two sounds, now there is one. Actually, the structural possibilities are much more varied. Several patterns of change involving merger are detailed by Hoenigswald (1960). For our purposes, it will suffice to distinguish cases of "unconditional merger," in which the phonemic contrast is lost in all phonological environments and a single phoneme remains, from cases of "conditioned merger" in which the merger appears only in more limited contexts. In the latter case, separate phonemes are retained in the inventory, but they are no longer contrastive in certain environments. Two changes active in American English today illustrate these types. The contrast between /ɑ/ and /ɔ/ is lost completely in the case of the unconditional "*cot/caught* merger" whereas in the case of the conditioned "*pin/pen* merger," the distinction between /ɪ/ and /ɛ/ is maintained except preceding nasal consonants (see, e.g., Wolfram and Schilling-Estes 1998).

In discussions of historical phonology, mergers are often represented abstractly as they are in Hoenigswald's (1960) mathematical grid diagrams. This approach makes clear the connections between different stages in a language's history, but it does not provide any insight into how the transition between the stages progressed, how the changes were actually achieved. This short-coming is no doubt a consequence of the post hoc perspective on the changes. Evidence of intermediate stages is not always available when dealing with changes that took place centuries or even millennia earlier. Related to this problem is the mechanistic view of the change process that this focus on language system can produce. From this perspective, language change is governed by internal structural factors and the role of speakers is irrelevant.

In contrast to the approach in historical linguistics, variationist work on sound change has tended to focus on active changes in progress. For the study of mergers, this perspective has proven very illuminating. Opening access to the process of change while it is still ongoing has added a new dimension that complements well the traditional approach to mergers. Research on active mergers has aided our understanding of how such changes operate, from both the perspective of the linguistic system and the perspective of the speaker.

2.1   What does "merged" mean?

The central question at issue in the study of any putative merger is whether a distinction is lost. From a traditional structuralist perspective, the investigation of this question is a fairly straightforward matter. The answer lies in the phonological system of the language and can be determined by examining the distributions of the relevant sounds following the procedures taught in most introductory linguistics classes. When we consider language in its communicative context, however, we find the question is more complicated.

Ordinarily, language users are both speakers and hearers, and it is important to examine both roles in the study of mergers. Losing a distinction between two sounds involves losing the ability to produce it as well as to perceive it. In most cases we expect production and perception to go together. Thus, in a change situation involving merger, conservative speakers will consistently pronounce the sounds differently and will be able to judge which sound is which in the speech of other conservative speakers. Conversely, speakers who have the merger are expected not to show a consistent difference in their pronunciation and not to distinguish the sounds in others' speech. They may be able to learn to hear a distinction, but it is not one to which they normally attend.

Various techniques have been developed to investigate active mergers. Labov (1994: ch. 12) describes two tests designed to examine both the production and perception aspects of a merger. The first is a minimal pair test, which can be used to investigate directly speakers' intuitions about their own pronunciation. The procedure is fairly simple. The investigator compiles a list of potential minimal pairs involving the relevant sounds; that is, items that are minimal pairs for speakers who make a distinction. Pronunciations of the desired words are elicited from the subjects using a written list, pictures, or some other method. The investigator records these pronunciations, preferably on tape, but possibly in written transcription. Then, after producing each pair of words, the subject is asked whether the words sound the same or different. In this way, the test measures each subject's production of the sounds as well as perception of any contrast and provides for an easy means of comparing these two aspects.

While minimal pair tests can be a convenient means of exploring the status of a merger, some caution is advised in using such tests. This technique is not appropriate for all speech communities nor all speakers. The elicitation part of the task draws maximal attention to the features under investigation and, therefore, produces the speakers' most careful pronunciations. This usage may differ significantly from the patterns of more casual speech. Since we are interested in native speakers' ability to produce and perceive a contrast, this result is appropriate; however, it will be important to compare this usage with speech in less guarded contexts. Evidence of style shifting along such lines can provide important information about the sociolinguistic status of a merger. For example, Labov (1994: 354–5) notes that many New York City speakers consistently distinguish *god* and *guard* in minimal pair tests even though the words are nearly identical in their casual speech due to the /r/-less pronunciation of the latter item. This pattern reflects the stigma associated with /r/-lessness in this speech community.[1] More extreme cases are found in areas like Belfast (Milroy 1992) where the vernacular coexists with the standard dialect, and speakers have access to both codes. In such communities, formal speech events, such as a minimal pair test, condition the use of standard pronunciations, and most speakers resist producing vernacular forms in such situations.

Similar caveats pertain to the perception part of the minimal pair test. This task relies on subjects' metalinguistic judgments. In making these judgments, subjects may rely on more than a simple auditory perception of their own speech. For example, the potential influence of spelling is an obvious concern when dealing with literate subjects. Homophonous forms that are spelled differently may be judged as sounding different because subjects believe orthography reflects pronunciation. To identify influence of this type, it can be helpful to ask subjects who judge words as sounding different for clarification. For example, researching the merger of the voiced and voiceless glides in English, /w/ and /ʍ/, I have found subjects who noted a difference in the pair *witch* and *which*. As they explained, however, the distinction was that *witch* "had more of a 't' in it." Although that study did not measure production, this is likely a case in which spelling led these subjects to believe they had distinctions where none existed. In any event, the follow-up explanation made clear that the subjects did not have the distinction under investigation.

A second test discussed by Labov (1994: 356–7) addresses some of these problems inherent in the minimal pair test. To insure that speakers rely only on the speech signal in making their perceptual judgments, a commutation test can be used. For this test, a speaker suspected of having a merger is recorded pronouncing several randomized tokens of each word in a relevant minimal pair. The words can be presented in a written list or using picture cards if orthography is likely to influence production or the subject is illiterate. The recording is played back to the speaker, and he/she is asked to identify each word.[2] It is crucial, of course, that during the playback the subject not be able to rely on the original order in which the words were pronounced. The surest way to prevent this is to edit the recording to randomize the tokens again. In the field, it may suffice to begin the playback of the tape at a point unknown to the subject.

The results of a commutation test indicate the strength of a phonemic contrast based on its "primary function" – to convey meaning (Labov 1994: 356). If the words can be identified with 100 percent accuracy, the distinction is clearly maintained. Results closer to random chance (i.e. 50 percent) reveal a merger has occurred. Crucially, the information gained here about the perceived difference between the sounds comes from a simple listening task. As a result, the kind of metalinguistic judgments about whether there "should" be a distinction (based on spelling, sociolinguistic norms, etc.) that are a concern with minimal pair tests seem less likely to play a role here. Nevertheless, the task is still relatively artificial. As Labov (1994: 402) notes, many open questions remain about the connection between the ability to label categories in a commutation or minimal pair test and the process of interpreting actual utterances in context.

In addition to these two tests, a variety of other techniques have been developed for investigating active mergers. For example, Labov (1994: 403–6) discusses the ingenious "coach" test which involves subjects' listening to a narrative that contains a crucial minimal pair. Following the narrative, the subjects are questioned about what happened, and their responses indicate how they interpreted the crucial sequence. The test virtually eliminates the intervention of metalinguistic judgments by making the task a more natural one of semantic interpretation.

A rather different approach is seen in the self-categorization experiment Di Paolo (1988) employed in her study of the contrast between tense and lax vowel pairs (/i ~ ɪ/; /u ~ ʊ/; /e ~ ɛ/) in Utah English. In this test, subjects were asked to categorize words according to the vowel they contained. They did this by writing the words in the appropriate place in a table in which each cell contained sample words illustrating a particular vowel phoneme. This task is useful only in cases of conditioned merger. The merger Di Paolo was investigating only appears before /l/. For this reason, she chose sample words for the table that did not contain this environment and had subjects categorize words that did. An obvious deficiency of written tasks like this test is that they do not provide information about the phonetic quality of the sounds examined. They are best used in conjunction with other techniques as they were by Di Paolo (1988) and Di Paolo and Faber (1990). In fact, given the complexity of the issues involved, a variety of approaches should be explored in any case of suspected merger.

2.2   When is a merger not a merger?

As noted above, phonemic contrast involves perception as well as production, though the normal expectation is for these two aspects to pattern together. People who maintain the contrast will consistently produce and perceive it; those who have lost the contrast will do neither. A minimal pair test may find some subjects who identify words as distinct even though their actual pronunciation belies this claim (as can be demonstrated with a commutation test), but such cases can often be explained as evidence of the influence of orthography. Much more challenging to our usual understanding are cases of the opposite pattern: people who consistently distinguish sounds in their production, but do not perceive a contrast between these sounds. In a minimal pair test, such speakers would identify the two words as "the same" despite a regular difference in their pronunciation. The scenario strikes many linguists as impossible. How can someone consistently produce a difference they don't perceive as being there? The proposal has met with substantial resistance from various corners of the linguistics world, as Labov (1994: ch. 12) details. Nevertheless, the evidence for such cases, which are called "near" or "apparent" mergers, continues to accumulate.

Consider, for example, the case first reported by Labov et al. (1972: 236–42) of Dan Jones. Jones was a teenager from Albuquerque, New Mexico, whom Labov and his colleagues interviewed for their investigation of the reported merger of /ul/ and /ʊl/, the same merger studied by Di Paolo and Faber (1990). In a minimal pair test, Jones labeled *fool* and *full* as well as *pool* and *pull* as the same. A commutation test using Jones' readings of *fool* and *full* and judged by two of his peers showed mixed results: 82.5 percent of the tokens were correctly identified, but the judges struggled with their decisions about which words they were hearing. Acoustic analysis of the tokens from the commutation test was performed to search for some aspect of the speech signal on which the judges might have relied. When analyzing vowels instrumentally, it is common to interpret the frequencies of the first and second formants (F1 and F2) as acoustic correlates of vowel height and backness respectively. The analysis in this case revealed a fairly clear separation of the vowels in acoustic space, specifically a slight difference (in the range of 50 Hz) in terms of F2 (see Labov 1994: 361). In his production, therefore, Jones maintained a distinction between words that he considered to have the same pronunciation. Acoustically the difference is very minor, but crucially it was consistent.

A similar effect was found with a pair of teenagers, David and Keith, from Norwich, England (Labov et al. 1972: 242–6; Labov 1994: 364–6). For these boys, words like *too* and *toe* have vowels that are very close in acoustic space; i.e. in terms of F1 and F2. However, the vowels involve a consistent difference in terms of the direction of gliding (see Labov 1994: fig. 12.4). Despite this phonetic distinction, Keith was unable to identify reliably David's pronunciation of *too* and *toe* in a commutation test. Like Dan Jones, then, Keith is an example of someone who produces a distinction that he seems not to hear.

The notion of a near merger is intriguing, but it is difficult to assess the significance of this situation on the basis of isolated cases. From Labov's early discussion of near mergers, the phenomenon seems to be almost an idiosyncrasy of a few speakers. Clearly, what is needed are broader community surveys to determine how common near mergers are and what their role in the change process is.

The series of experiments on the (near) merger of /ɛr/ and /ʌr/ (e.g. *ferry* ~ *furry*) in Philadelphia described by Labov (1994: ch. 14) have helped to address this need. Also important in this regard is the research on the tense/lax vowel distinction in Salt Lake City (Di Paolo 1988, Di Paolo and Faber 1990). As discussed briefly above, Utah (like other areas of the USA) is apparently undergoing a merger of certain tense/lax pairs (/i ~ ɪ/; /u ~ ʊ/; /e ~ ɛ/) in the phonological environment of following /l/. Thus, the *fool* ~ *full* pattern in Albuquerque is part of a larger trend. The Intermountain Language Survey investigated this trend by sampling the speech of dozens of speakers across three generations (Di Paolo 1988). Results from the self-categorization experiment described earlier suggested a merger was in progress, and impressionistic transcriptions of subjects' pronunciation generally agreed with this interpretation. Both indicators of merger (i.e. how subjects categorize the sounds and their actual production) were found to increase across the generations in the usual pattern of language change in progress (Di Paolo 1988). The phonetic details of this change situation were examined by Di Paolo and Faber (1990) who studied both the formant structure of the vowels (F1 and F2 frequencies) and their phonation patterns. The latter involves differences of voice quality like breathiness or creakiness. They found that, contrary to the suggestions of a merger, speakers maintain a distinction at the phonetic level. Interestingly, the nature of the distinction between tense and lax vowels varied. Many speakers demonstrated differences in formant frequencies like those found in the Albuquerque and Norwich cases, but the acoustic analysis revealed that even when the F1/F2 contrast is lost, speakers avoid complete merger through phonation differences. A perception experiment similar to a commutation test confirmed the persistence of the distinctions. Compared with earlier reports, the Utah studies (Di Paolo 1988, Di Paolo and Faber 1990) offer a broader perspective on the phenomenon of the near merger by considering a wide range of speakers across a large community. The phonetic analysis also makes clear the importance of looking beyond F1 and F2 when investigating reported mergers.

Demonstrating that a near merger can be more widespread in a community lends credence to this notion and expands its explanatory value. One of the most exciting applications of the near-merger concept has been with certain problematic cases in the history of English, such as "the *meat*/*mate* problem" in Early Modern English (Labov 1994, Milroy and Harris 1980). This case involves the apparent merger of the vowel class of *meat* (Middle English /ɛ:/)

with that of *mate* (Middle English /aː/) during the Early Modern period. The difficulty stems from the fact that this merger, it appears, was later undone, and the *meat* class eventually merged with the class of *meet* (Middle English /eː/), a scenario that is deemed impossible by linguists who believe that mergers are irreversible. What, then, should be made of the evidence that suggested the first merger? As Labov (1994) explains, the concept of the near merger offers a solution to this problem if we view the original evidence as reflecting the perception of a merger that had not actually occurred in production. According to this proposal, the distinction between the *meat* and *mate* classes was never lost, and, thus, there is no need to propose a reversal of a merger.

Other approaches to this problem challenge the claim that mergers are irreversible. Scholars such as Wyld (1936) accept the existence of the merger of *meat* and *mate* and have explained the later unmerging as a product of dialect mixing. Explanations of this type often meet with criticism from traditional historical linguists, but variationist work in vernacular speech communities has lent support to this scenario. For example, in their approach to the *meat*/*mate* problem, Milroy and Harris (1980) examine the situation in Hiberno-English, a variety in which the merger was reportedly never undone. Nevertheless, the vernacular variety coexists with more standard varieties, and "speakers appear to have access to two systems here, one in which *meat* merges with *mate* and one in which *meat* merges with *meet*" (Milroy 1992: 157). The *meat* class, thus, maintains a kind of distinctiveness from the other two classes by virtue of its ability to alternate between [eː] and [iː]. In this way, the proposal of an "alternating class" provides a solution to the problem of unmerging suggested by the Early Modern English evidence. The earlier merger of *meat* and *mate* was not reversed, rather the system in which it existed was supplanted by a different one in which the vowels were distinct (Milroy 1992).

The contrasting solutions to the *meat*/*mate* problem outlined by Labov (1994) and Milroy (1992) help focus our attention on fundamental issues of interpretation. The near merger concept was developed to account for an unexpected result from a minimal pair test: subjects who produce a distinction they do not perceive. Much of the literature on near mergers has been concerned with establishing the existence of such cases and identifying the phonetic differences involved. An important consequence of this research for the study of mergers (both real and apparent) is an expanded understanding of perception, which now must be seen as including a subconscious dimension. Speakers appear to be able somehow to hear subtle phonetic differences well enough to reproduce them but without enough conscious attention to know that they are actually hearing them.[3] Substantial empirical questions about this scenario remain, but if we assume that it is possible, we must ask how it comes about. What leads speakers to contradict their perception by their production?

In addressing this question, it can be helpful to recall Milroy's (1992) description of the Hiberno-English situation. Those speakers have access to two phonological systems, and presumably also have the ability to choose between them. If the analogy to the *meat/mate* problem in Early Modern English is correct, then historically such a choice was made, discarding the system in which *meat* was merged with *mate* for one in which *meat* was merged (or was free to merge later) with *meet*. Describing this process in terms of "choices" may seem to place too much faith in speakers' decision-making abilities, but the process of choosing need not involve any conscious determination. Essentially what is involved in this situation, as with all linguistic changes, are speakers effecting and responding to a shift in sociolinguistic norms.

Applying this idea to the case of a near merger, we might treat it as a situation in which speakers accept an incoming norm in stages. They first accept the idea that two sounds should be merged, and only later does their production catch up and actually reflect that belief. Labov offers some support for this idea in his description of the "Bill Peters effect" (1994: 363–4, Labov et al. 1972: 235–6), a phenomenon named for an older, rural man from central Pennsylvania who had a clear distinction between /ɔ/ and /ɑ/ in his spontaneous speech, but who reduced that distinction in the more formal context of a minimal pair test and identified pairs like *caught ~ cot* and *dawn ~ Don* as sounding the same. Such style shifting can be an important indicator of speakers' norms; suggesting in this case that Peters "had unconsciously adopted the incoming merged norm as a guide in the minimal pair test, but not for speech" (Labov 1994: 363). Considering that Peters was 80 years old when he was interviewed, his case also makes clear that with this two-step acceptance of new norms, the second step may never come; that is, a complete merger in production may never take place. In this way, near mergers need not be seen as transitional situations preceding complete mergers.

These suggestions regarding differential responses to changing norms reinforce a point made earlier about the need to utilize a variety of methods in the study of reported mergers. Minimal pair tests allow access to a subject's relatively conscious sense of the status of a contrast. The consciousness involved may lead to discrepancies. As was discussed in the previous section, factors like spelling may affect subjects' judgments, causing them to claim differences that they do not produce. Conversely, the influence of community norms may cause speakers to deny differences that they do produce. The information provided by such disagreements between perception and production is useful, but researchers must explore these situations with a range of investigative tools to begin to answer some of the many questions they pose.

The central lesson to be taken from this discussion is the need for investigators to be attentive to the complexity inherent in the perception of phonological contrasts. The process of perception involves more than a straightforward interpretation of the speech signal; it is subject to influence of various types. While we are just beginning to appreciate the challenges presented by phenomena like the near merger, their "discovery" nevertheless testifies to the power of variationist approaches to the topic of mergers. Research in this paradigm has expanded our understanding of the issues, even if it has sometimes generated as many questions as it has answered.

3   The Study of Chain Shifting

Variationist approaches have also been fruitfully applied to the study of chain shifting, a process that represents a kind of structural alternative to merger.[4] Like mergers, chain shifts affect two sounds from the same phonological neighborhood, but unlike mergers, chain shifts maintain the distinction between the sounds. It is common to distinguish two main types of chain shifts based on the ordering of the stages involved. Some chains begin as the movement of one sound brings it into the space occupied by another sound which in turn moves so that the distance between the two is maintained. This case is referred to as a "push" chain. The opposite ordering is found in a "drag" chain. In this case, the movement of one sound creates an opening which another sound moves to occupy. With either type, the chain may continue beyond these initial events to involve more sounds.

The concept of chain shifting has generated substantial debate among historical linguists (see Hock 1991). At the center of the controversy is the teleology implied by the chain shift model, particularly the push chain scenario. For Martinet, chain shifts demonstrated the power of "communicative needs" because they were motivated by "the preservation of useful phonemic opposition" (1952: 126). Critics may question the importance of avoiding merger by pointing to the evidence which indicates that mergers are, in general, much more common than chain shifts. Also troubling for traditional historical linguists is the role that speakers are presumed to play in a functionalist account like Martinet's. Roger Lass, for example, rejects the suggestion that people "can make comparisons between the present state of their language and some as yet unrealized one, and opt for one or the other" (1978: 266). More recently, in his extensive treatment of the subject, Labov (1994) offers an intriguing compromise that seems to reconcile some of these differences. He accepts Martinet's basic notions of how chain shifts operate (see, e.g., his formulation of "The Chain-Shifting Principle" (1994: 184)) but rejects Martinet's teleological account of their motivations, describing instead how they result from a purely mechanical process inherent in auditory perception (1994: ch. 20). Labov (1994) also presents a typology of chain shifts and a series of general principles governing the process based on his analysis of several historical and ongoing shifts.[5]

Questions about mechanisms and motivations are central to any treatment of chain shifting. Nevertheless, in the following discussion, these issues are examined rather indirectly by taking an empirical approach to the problem of chain shifting. In keeping with the focus of this chapter, the discussion here will address the seemingly basic question: How can an ongoing chain shift be identified and studied? Put more plainly, how do we know a chain shift when we see one up close? While similar methodological questions have been central to the study of merger, surprisingly this is an issue that has not been much discussed or even considered in the literature on chain shifts. To address these issues, the presentation below considers the two main definitional criteria related to chain shifting. First is the requirement that distinctions between sounds be preserved, and second is the fact that the sound changes involved in the putative chain be interrelated. Several suggestions for examining these criteria are made, and the general points are illustrated with examples from research on the Northern Cities Shift, a pattern of change that has been much discussed in variationist work on chain shifting (e.g. Labov 1994).

3.1   *What does it mean to preserve distinctions?*

Fundamental to the definition of chain shifting is the end result that although the phonetic values associated with the affected phonemes are altered, no phonemic distinctions are lost. This observation has led to the interpretation that chain shifts are driven by an avoidance of merger (see, e.g., Martinet 1952). Still, one need not accept a functionalist view of the process to recognize the basic principle that chain shifts result, by whatever means, in the preservation of contrasts. With the understanding, therefore, that preserving contrasts is central to how chain shifts work, the discussion here examines ways of observing this aspect of the process in a series of ongoing changes.

In a sense, determining whether contrasts are maintained is a straightforward matter, one that we have already covered in the discussion of mergers. The techniques developed to examine potential mergers in terms of production and perception can also be applied in the study of chain shift situations. If subjects demonstrate the ability to distinguish the sounds involved in a chain shift, then this criterion may be interpreted as fulfilled. However, simply establishing that distinctions are maintained is not enough; this observation must be tied to the changes taking place. Preservation of contrast is not an inadvertent consequence of a chain shift, but rather an integral part of the process. Whether we believe that chain shifting is driven by functional concerns or by more mechanical processes, we should expect to find evidence of contrasts being preserved in the operation of a putative chain shift.

To clarify this point we may consider an example of series of changes that are commonly interpreted as participating in a chain shift. The changes are known as the Northern Cities Shift (NCS). This pattern of change is heard across a wide section of the northern USA and is particularly associated with the urban centers of the Great Lakes region (e.g., Chicago, Detroit, Buffalo). The NCS involves changes in six vowels and is commonly represented as in figure 9.1.

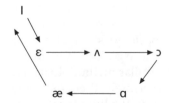

Figure 9.1 A view of the Northern Cities Shift
Source: based on Labov (1994: 191)

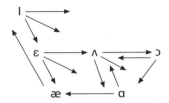

Figure 9.2   A different view of the Northern Cities Shift
Source: based on Gordon (2001)

When changes are represented as in figure 9.1, the process of contrast preservation seems obvious. The changes appear joined together in a loop where
each vowel moves to maintain its distance from its neighbors. This picture,
however, represents an extreme abstraction from phonetic reality. The actual
variation associated with these vowels suggests a much more complicated
picture, something more like the view in figure 9.2.

As this diagram reveals, almost all the vowels shift along multiple trajectories. Certainly some of the variants represented here are more common than
others, but all have been documented with several speakers (Gordon 2001).
When this fuller picture is considered, contrast preservation seems less a guiding force in the construction of the NCS. The alternative trajectories may still
take the vowel out of the space of one of its neighbors, but they often bring it
closer to another neighbor. Thus, the shift appears to work to preserve some
distinctions while endangering others. Consider, for example, the low back
corner of vowel space where the alternative paths taken by /ɔ/ and /ɑ/
(fronting and raising, respectively) appear to lead them directly into the path
of /ʌ/ as it is backed or lowered.

Of course, even though figure 9.2 presents a more complete view of the
variation found with the NCS, it too is an abstraction. A useful complement
to such depictions can be sought in acoustic analysis. In the previous discussion of mergers, we saw the utility of acoustic analysis as a tool for investigating questions of contrast preservation. For the NCS case, the acoustic
evidence tends to confirm the messiness of the picture in figure 9.2. In formant
frequency plots (F1 × F2) such as those presented by Labov (1994), the ranges
associated with the shifting vowels are seen not only to approach each other
but in many cases to overlap.[6] To be sure, F1 and F2 measurements offer a
very limited picture of the phonetic information available in the speech
signal,[7] and for this reason, it would be premature to interpret this evidence
as indicating that mergers are occurring or even that distinctions are necessarily being compromised. Nevertheless, if we accept the premise offered
earlier that indications of contrasts being preserved should be evident in the
operation of a chain shift, then these findings challenge the usual interpretation of the NCS. If maintaining contrasts were a principal concern influencing

the NCS changes, it seems unlikely that a pattern like that of figure 9.2 would result.

The NCS example raises important questions of interpretation that researchers will face with any putative chain shift. How can we determine whether contrast preservation plays a role in a given change? Should we expect all links in a chain to reflect the influence of contrast preservation? Is it appropriate to rely on the spatial perspective provided by auditory impressions and/or acoustic measurements of the shifting vowels in our search for evidence of contrast preservation? Such issues have not yet been raised in the literature on chain shifting, a fact that is, unfortunately, in keeping with the general absence of methodological considerations by scholars working in this area.

To further the present break with scholarly tradition, we might consider an example of an alternative approach to exploring the issue of contrast preservation, one that examines patterns of phonological conditioning. If we think about maintenance of contrast in terms of homophony avoidance, we can see the potential significance of context-sensitive effects. In a chain shift, the vowels often shift at differential rates according to phonological context; some environments seem to favor the change, and others disfavor it. The vocalic distinctions will best be preserved if the shifting elements respond similarly to their contexts. Returning to the Northern Cities Shift example, if the changes affecting both /ɔ/ and /ɑ/ are favored when the vowels appear before a /t/, then *caught* can be pronounced with an [ɑ] without being confused with *cot* since the vowel in *cot* has a quality closer to [æ]. Even if /ɑ/ words involving other contexts retain their [ɑ] pronunciation, the contrast between /ɔ/ and /ɑ/ is not threatened provided that the /ɔ/ items involving those same contexts maintain their [ɔ] value. In this way, phonemes can have overlapping allophonic distributions without necessarily losing the contrast between them, a fact that may help us understand the messy picture of the NCS described earlier. On the other hand, conflicting responses to phonological conditioning can endanger vocalic contrasts. In the NCS case, if the environment of following /t/ favors shifting of /ɔ/ but disfavors shifting of /ɑ/, then the potential for homophony between *caught* and *cot* is greater.

A test of this approach to contrast preservation using the NCS case produced mixed results. The details are discussed in Gordon (2001), but we can consider the findings for /æ/, /ɑ/ and /ɔ/ as a representative sampling of the overall picture. The conditioning patterns for /æ/ and /ɑ/ showed a relatively high degree of consistency. Both of these changes are favored by preceding voiceless obstruents (e.g. in *fad*, *pad*, and *fox*, *pod*), following interdentals (e.g. *math* and *father*), and following /l/ (e.g. *pal* and *college*), and both are disfavored by preceding /r/ (e.g. *rap* and *rob*) and following palatal consonants (e.g. *match* and *Josh*). However, the responses of these vowels differ in the context of preceding palatals, which disfavor shifting of /æ/ but favor shifting of /ɑ/. This discrepancy is important to the topic at hand since it suggests that the contrast is reduced in this environment as /ɑ/ shifts forward while /æ/ remains in place (e.g. *shock* comes to sound like *shack*). A similar potential threat to vocalic contrast is found in the data for /ɑ/ and /ɔ/. The context of preceding /r/ favors the lowering and fronting of /ɔ/, a movement that brings it well into the range of /ɑ/, whose shifting is disfavored in this same context. The vowels also show different tendencies in the context of preceding nasals, but in this case the contrast is not threatened because the environment serves to promote /ɑ/ fronting while disfavoring /ɔ/ shifting (e.g. *knotty* shifts forward but *naughty* remains back and rounded). The other links in the NCS chain reveal a similar variety of results.

As the examples discussed here suggest, evidence related to the preservation of phonemic contrasts can lead to questions about the status of a putative chain shift. The notion that chain shifts operate to preserve phonemic distinctions is central to the definition of this process, yet this matter is rarely examined directly. The objective in this section (and in the one that follows) has been not only to raise the issues but to offer some suggestions for how researchers may approach them.

3.2 What does it mean for changes to be interrelated?

A second fundamental aspect of the definition of chain shifting holds that the changes involved be interrelated. This criterion stems from the assumption that a causal relationship obtains between individual changes in a chain shift. While scholars may disagree about the nature of the causal connection (e.g. whether it is functionally motivated), some sort of causation is essential to the chain shift model. The interrelatedness question is examined here from various directions. We will discuss ways of exploring connections among putatively related changes in the spatial dimension as well as in the usage patterns of individual speakers. We begin, however, by considering relatedness in the temporal dimension. As before, the general points are illustrated with examples related to the Northern Cities Shift.

3.2.1 Temporal connections

As an initial approach to the issue of interrelatedness, we consider how changes involved in a chain shift are connected in time. The causal relations that are presumed to hold between changes in a chain shift rely crucially on sequential ordering. Determining that Change A occurred prior to Change B is a necessary (but, of course, not sufficient) component of any claim that A caused B. The methods available for making such determinations in the case of a chain shift are largely the same used in attempts to date any linguistic change. For researchers engaged in the study of changes in progress, these methods include the examination of "real-time" evidence, such as earlier dialectological or orthoepic research, as well as the collection of "apparent-time" evidence in the form of data from speakers representing a broad age-range. Because thorough descriptions of general methods for gathering and interpreting real- and apparent-time evidence in variationist research are available elsewhere (see, e.g., Guy Bailey's contribution to this volume), the present discussion is framed as more of a case study highlighting how such evidence might be brought to bear on the more specific question of temporal ordering in a chain shift situation. The case that is studied here is the NCS, and the presentation summarizes aspects of the discussion from Gordon (2001: ch. 6).

In his account of the NCS, Labov (1994: 195) proposes a chronology of the changes based on the following scenario and represented in figure 9.1. The first element to shift was /æ/, whose raising and fronting created a void that /ɑ/ then fronted to fill. The shifting of /ɑ/, in turn, led /ɔ/ to lower and front. The next element to be affected was /ɛ/ which was lowered, inspiring a drag chain that also pulled down /ɪ/. Later, /ɛ/ changed its course and came to be backed which produced a push chain with /ʌ/ also backing to avoid encroachment by /ɛ/. Thus, the order of the changes from first to last is: /æ/ > /ɑ/ > /ɔ/ > /ɛ/ > /ɪ/ > /ʌ/.

Labov notes that this chronology is based on "apparent-time data and the limited evidence from real-time differences" (1994: 195), and some support for his proposal can be seen by comparing the vowel systems of speakers surveyed by Labov et al. (1972). For example, the oldest speakers in that study show apparent fronting and raising of /æ/ while /ɑ/ and /ɔ/ appear to be more conservative. Still, the ordering of some other elements is not so clear from this evidence. Some middle-aged speakers with fairly conservative positioning of /ɑ/ and /ɔ/ show lowering and/or centralization of /ɛ/ and /ɪ/, while some younger speakers with innovative positioning of /ɑ/ and /ɔ/ show no movement of /ɛ/ and /ɪ/.[8] Much of the difficulty in verifying the proposed chronology stems from the limitations presented by the evidence offered. The vowel systems of the speakers are represented using raw formant frequency data (F1 × F2), which, as discussed below, allow only for impressionistic comparisons across the systems of different speakers.

A more quantifiable approach is possible using data from index scores. An index score is a measure of a speaker's usage of a given variable. With vocalic variables, they are constructed by assigning numbers to variants on a scale from conservative to innovative. The number of points on the scale will vary depending on the sound change being measured and the ability of the researcher to reliably distinguish variants (see, e.g., Labov 1966). For each speaker, several tokens of the variable are coded (0, 1, 2, etc.) as to which variant was produced and an average is calculated from these codes. This average is the index score and it, thus, provides a combined measure of how far and how frequently a vowel is shifted by a given speaker. Index scores from several speakers can be averaged to provide an overall measure of the degree of shifting of a given vowel, and these measures, in turn, can be used as a kind of apparent-time evidence. Higher mean scores demonstrate greater shifting of the vowel and, thus, indicate an older, more established change, while lower scores suggest the reverse. Some caution is advised, however, in comparing the values for different

Table 9.1 Mean index scores for the NCS vowels (*n* = 32)

Variable	/ɔ/	/æ/	/ɑ/	/ɛ/	/ɪ/	/ʌ/
Mean index	.815	.521	.469	.181	.075	.055

variables in this way. Even when the same basic coding scheme is applied for all the variables investigated and the codes attempt to mark equal distances in vowel space, it is not a given that the codes represent equivalent measures for each vowel in terms of perceptibility, the consequences for the system, etc.

With this caveat in mind, the ordering of the NCS elements can be examined through the data in table 9.1. Listed here are the mean index scores for the six NCS variables from a study of 32 speakers (Gordon 2001).

These scores suggest a chronology of the NCS changes very much in line with Labov's proposal. Certainly, the data for the upper half of the shift (/ɛ/, /ɪ/, and /ʌ/) are consistent with the suggestion that movement of /ɛ/ spurred movement of /ɪ/ then of /ʌ/. For the lower half of the NCS, the only inconsistency with Labov's chronology relates to /ɔ/ which was found to have the highest mean score. It should be noted, however, that the comparability problem mentioned above may be of particular concern in the case of /ɔ/ given that the change affecting this vowel and the coding system used to measure it involve not only tongue movement (fronting and lowering) but also reduced lip-rounding. For this reason, we might question the deduction that the high mean index score for /ɔ/ is an accurate reflection of its time depth.

On the other hand, examination of the real-time evidence related to the NCS changes tends to complicate matters. For example, DeCamp (1940) describes lowered and unrounded pronunciations of /ɔ/ as well as fronted pronunciations of /ɑ/ in his study of Scranton, PA. A similar tendency for /ɔ/ to be lowered and have reduced rounding was documented by Marckwardt (1941, 1942) for a broad section of the Northern dialect region. To my knowledge, the earliest report describing /æ/-raising like that heard in the NCS comes from Thomas' (1935–7) study of upstate New York. Thomas, however, sampled the usage of college students, most of whom were presumably born around 1915, whereas Marckwardt studied much older speakers who were born around or before 1870. Thus, the limited real-time evidence tends to agree with the index data suggesting /ɔ/ is the earliest piece in the NCS puzzle. Of course, under this scenario, we must reexamine the ordering of /æ/ and /ɑ/ indicated by the index data if we want to claim that the NCS is indeed a chain shift. Still, given that the difference between /æ/ and /ɑ/ in terms of their mean index scores is fairly slight, it is not unreasonable to suggest that the shifting affected /ɑ/ before /æ/. As will be discussed below, the data from many of the individual speakers support this possibility in that they show relatively high levels of shifting of /ɑ/ with less enthusiastic shifting of /æ/. The real-time evidence of DeCamp (1940) also supports the ordering of /ɑ/ before /æ/ as do other reports of /ɑ/-fronting in the Northern region including Thomas (1958) and Kurath and McDavid (1961).

While the discussion here has raised questions about the chronology of the NCS, there are, I hope, more general lessons to be learned. The case of the NCS is offered as an example of some of the challenges facing the researcher investigating the temporal ordering of elements in a chain shift. It illustrates the necessity and the value of considering a range of evidence and of remaining open to alternative interpretations.

3.2.2   Spatial connections

Clarifying the temporal relationships among changes is essential to establishing a chronology for a putative chain shift. Nevertheless, even the strongest chronological evidence cannot by itself prove a causal connection between changes. Other types of evidence must be sought. This section outlines some of the questions involved in the investigation of spatial connections among sound changes.

To approach this issue, it is useful to consider space in geographical as well as linguistic terms. The geographical requirement seems fairly obvious; for changes to constitute a chain shift, they must be found in the same dialect. The reasoning is clear when we are dealing with regional dialects, but the requirement should also apply in the case of social dialects. It is possible for a change in one variety to contribute somehow to a change in another variety, but these changes would not qualify as a chain shift as it is usually understood. By this same reasoning, if changes are indeed related through chain shifting, we should expect them to co-occur in the same varieties. If Change A is causally linked to Change B, then every variety that has one of the changes should also have the other.

Another approach to the issue of spatial connectedness focuses on the linguistic system. The changes in a chain shift involve related sounds. Relatedness in this sense might be examined phonologically or phonetically. Sounds might be counted as phonologically related if they belong to the same subclass. For example, in the case of the NCS, most of the vowels are related as members of the category of short (or lax) vowels. This class is distinguished from that of long (or tense) vowels by phonetic characteristics (e.g. the absence of accompanying upglides) as well as by distributional characteristics (e.g. they never appear word finally). Such classificatory distinctions are clearly relevant to the question of contrast preservation. The threat to vocalic contrast is greater when a vowel encroaches on another vowel of the same subclass than when it encroaches on a vowel of a different class since it has more in common (phonetically and distributionally) with the former.

Vowel space, defined in articulatory and acoustic terms, offers another arena in which relatedness between sounds can be examined. Changes involved in a chain shift affect vowels that are contiguous in this two-dimensional space, and the connection between the changes should be clearly represented by one vowel entering the space previously occupied by another. Whether any reasonably complete representation of the variation found with an ongoing shift would ever actually show these relationships among the shifting elements remains to be seen. As discussed above, this certainly has not been the case with the NCS evidence. If we re-examine figure 9.2, we see the causal links are often far from obvious. Consider, for example, the shifting of /ɪ/. According to the usual chronology of the NCS changes (as will be discussed below), the change to /ɪ/ is a drag-chain response to earlier lowering of /ɛ/. While this might account for /ɪ/'s lowering tendency, it is hard to relate it to the backing also seen with this vowel. Similarly, the backing of /ʌ/ makes some sense as a push-chain reaction to the backing of /ɛ/, but the other trajectories taken by /ʌ/ are harder to connect with changes to /ɛ/ or any other vowel.[9] In short, describing changes in terms of their relations within vowel space can be a useful approach to the question of spatial connectedness, but the resulting picture is often more complicated than expected, and investigators must keep in mind that the usual two-dimensional view offers a rather limited perspective on phonetic reality.

3.2.3   *Connections within the speech of individuals*

If we accept that changes linked in a chain shift must co-occur in space, a logical extension of that premise is that they also must co-occur in the vowel systems of individual speakers. While speaker-based approaches may draw criticism within traditional historical linguistics (e.g. Lass 1978), standard accounts of the functioning of chain shifts suggest that individuals do have a role to play. Such a role is evident in Martinet's conception of the process as motivated by "the basic necessity of securing mutual understanding" (1952: 126). Even the antifunctionalist account proposed by Labov (1994) seems to rely on the interactions of individual speaker/hearers. For this reason, therefore, when we look for causal connections among elements in a chain shift, we should also consider the speech patterns of individuals.

As a way of investigating such connections, we can compare the effects that various changes have on the speech of individuals. If two changes are related, then we expect their effects on a given speaker's system to be similar. We also expect the relative usage of such changes to be mostly consistent across speakers; we do not expect to find one speaker using a lot of Change A and very little of Change B, while another speaker uses a lot of Change B and very little of Change A.

The kind of acoustic data (F1 × F2) that are commonly used to represent relations among vowels offer one way of approaching these questions. Such representations usually describe the vowel systems of individual speakers because of the difficulties in normalizing the data in order to compare individuals in a single plot. Connections among shifting vowels can be examined by comparing the relative influence of the changes on the systems of several speakers plotted individually. In an early example of this approach, Labov et al. (1972: 118) traced the relations among /ɔ/, /ɑ/, and /æ/ in the NCS by comparing

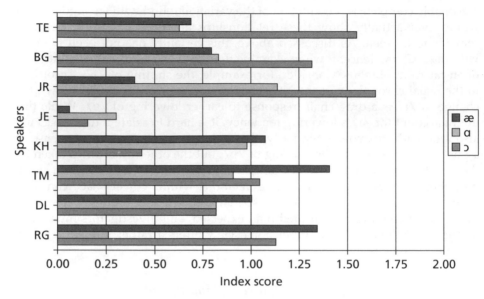

Figure 9.3 Index scores from adult females showing shifting of NCS vowels
Source: Gordon (2001)

formant frequency plots from three generations of speakers from Buffalo, NY. When the acoustic picture is fairly clear, this approach can be quite useful. However, when the pictures are more ambiguous, this technique has its limitations. Comparing vowel systems in this way is necessarily impressionistic. A researcher can see the relative positions of vowels in a speaker's system and compare those positions with the situation in another speaker's system, but the characterization of any differences or similarities between the systems can only be done in terms of "more" or "less," because the frequency measurements from one speaker cannot be directly compared to another.[10]

Direct comparisons among speakers can be much easier when the data from index scores are used. The index scores from different speakers can readily be compared because they come from auditorially coded data, for which the ear does the normalization. Still, as noted earlier, comparison across variables is in some ways more questionable. We should recall this caveat, therefore, as we consider the following illustration of how index data may represent connections among elements in a chain shift.

In Gordon (2001), I compare index scores for all six of the NCS vowels from a survey of 32 Michigan speakers. A sampling of those data is presented in figures 9.3 and 9.4, which graph the scores for the vowels /æ/, /ɑ/, and /ɔ/ from female speakers representing two generations. According to the chronology of the NCS proposed by Labov (1994: 195), the first element to change was /æ/, whose fronting and raising created a drag chain leading to the fronting of /ɑ/ which in turn led to the lowering and fronting of /ɔ/. If this scenario is

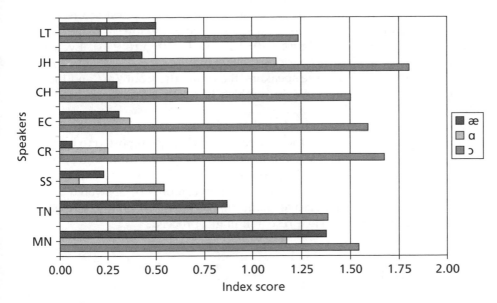

Figure 9.4 Index scores from adolescent females showing shifting of NCS vowels
Source: Gordon (2001)

correct, we might expect speakers to show the highest rates of shifting for the /æ/ variable, somewhat less shifting for /ɑ/, and even less for /ɔ/. In areas where the NCS has run its course and is more fully implemented, we might find speakers showing very high usage of all three of these elements. We should not, however, find speakers with high rates of shifting for /ɑ/ but not for /æ/ or for /ɔ/ but not for /ɑ/.

The evidence presented in these graphs offers mixed results for the usual interpretation of the NCS changes. The fact that at least some usage of each variable was found with each of these speakers confirms the regular co-occurrence of the changes. Moreover, we see hints of a correlation among the changes in speakers with consistently high or consistently low scores for all the variables. Consider, for example, TM (figure 9.3) and MN (figure 9.4) who actively shift all three vowels and JE (figure 9.3) and SS (figure 9.4) who do not shift any of the vowels very commonly; these cases suggest the changes come as a kind of package deal. With regard to the temporal ordering of the changes, support for all three stages in Labov's chronology is seen in some speakers' patterns (viz. KH and DL (figure 9.3)). If we examine just the relationship between /æ/ and /ɑ/, many more speakers seem to conform to expectations (viz. TE, TM, and RG (figure 9.3); LT, SS, TN, and MN (figure 9.4)). There are, however, several speakers who shift /ɑ/ at a higher rate than /æ/, a pattern that contradicts Labov's proposal (see, e.g., JR (figure 9.3) and JH and CH (figure 9.4)). Furthermore, the evidence regarding the relationship between

/ɑ/ and /ɔ/ rarely patterns as expected. Some of the highest scores for /ɔ/ shifting are found with speakers who show some of the lowest scores for /ɑ/ shifting (e.g. TE and RG (figure 9.3); LT and CR (figure 9.4)). Even more bizarre for the drag-chain scenario is the fact that RG and LT also shift /æ/ at relatively high rates. For these speakers, therefore, the front /æ/ and the back /ɔ/ are shifting, but somehow /ɑ/, which lies between them, is left largely unaffected.

Once again, an examination of evidence from the NCS has shown some of the difficulties in establishing the relatedness of changes reported to be a chain shift. As before, we must ask ourselves whether these difficulties indicate problems with the NCS case in particular or whether we are expecting too much of the methods. Ultimately, this question can only be answered through further research on other putative chain shifts. The approaches described here offer suggestions for how such research might proceed.

4   Conclusion

Chain shifts and mergers illustrate the advantages as well as the difficulties of studying language change in progress. Having access to communities in which these sound changes are active allows investigators a wealth of evidence that is simply not available in the case of historical changes. This evidence not only illuminates the facts of a given situation but may also suggest new possibilities for understanding the processes in general (e.g. "near mergers," a scenario previously unimagined). As some of the above examples have indicated, however, evidence from in-depth studies of ongoing changes does not always point clearly in a single direction, and researchers must be prepared to wade carefully through the often muddy waters of linguistic variability. Still, as scientists, we welcome the new data and the new methods for mining it.

Generations of historical linguists and more recently sociolinguists have been fascinated by mergers and chain shifts. These changes raise fundamental issues about the forces shaping language structure. Understanding more about the processes that underlie mergers and chain shifts can offer important insight for the study of language change in general. Variationist research of the type described here has opened new avenues of investigation, but clearly much work remains to be done.

NOTES

1   Labov (1994: 343–5) observes that mergers seem not to draw the social awareness found with many other types of sound change. As he admits, however, research directly addressing this issue has been

lacking. If future research shows this to be indeed the case, it raises interesting questions of why mergers should escape social evaluation.

2 It is also possible to use different subjects as judges as was done by Labov et al. (1972) and by Di Paolo and Faber (1990). Labov cautions, however, that "if there is variation within the community, the experimenter does not know whether the rate of success is due to the ability of one speaker to produce the distinction or the ability of the other speaker to discriminate the tokens produced" (1994: 356).

3 Certainly, allophonic differences operate in this way, but in these cases the differences are typically conditioned by distinct phonetic environments.

4 Many of the ideas and examples presented here are discussed more fully in Gordon (2001).

5 For a discussion and critique of some of Labov's proposals see Gordon (2001) and Stockwell and Minkova (1997).

6 See, e.g., Labov's figure 6.13 (1994: 187) which presents acoustic data from an adolescent Chicagoan. For this speaker, the range of /ɛ/ is almost completely included within the range of /ɑ/ and both these vowels overlap with /æ/ and /ɪ/.

7 For a critique of the common (over)reliance on formant frequency data by sociolinguists see Watt (1998).

8 See the data for Dulsey Hankey, aged 64 (Labov et al. 1972: figure 14) and Joyce Norton, aged 16 (Labov et al. 1972: figure 20).

9 Actually, in Gordon (2001), I suggest that the alternative trajectories associated with /ʌ/, /ɛ/, and /ɪ/ are connected through a kind of parallelism.

10 Frequency data from multiple speakers can be compared if they are subjected to normalization. Various formulae have been developed for this purpose and there is no general agreement among phoneticians as to which routine is most accurate.

REFERENCES

DeCamp, L. Sprague (1940). Scranton pronunciation. *American Speech* 15: 368–71.

Di Paolo, Marianna (1988). Pronunciation and categorization in sound change. In K. Ferrara et al. (eds.), *Linguistic Change and Contact: NWAV-XVI.* Austin: Department of Linguistics, University of Texas. 84–92.

Di Paolo, Marianna and Alice Faber (1990). Phonation differences and the phonetic content of the tense–lax contrast in Utah English. *Language Variation and Change* 2: 155–204.

Gordon, Matthew J. (2001). *Small-Town Values, Big-City Vowels: A Study of the Northern Cities Shift in Michigan* (Publications of the American Dialect Society 84), Durham, NC: Duke University Press.

Hock, Hans Heinrich (1991). *Principles of Historical Linguistics*, 2nd edn. Berlin: Mouton de Gruyter.

Hoenigswald, Henry M. (1960). *Language Change and Linguistic Reconstruction*. Chicago: University of Chicago Press.

Kurath, Hans and Raven I. McDavid, Jr. (1961). *The Pronunciation of English in the Atlantic States*. Ann Arbor: University of Michigan Press.

Labov, William (1966). *The Social Stratification of English in New York City*. Washington, DC: Center for Applied Linguistics.

Labov, William (1994). *Principles of Linguistic Change*, vol. 1: *Internal Factors*. Oxford: Blackwell.

Labov, William, Malcah Yaeger and Richard Steiner (1972). *A Quantitative Study of Sound Change in Progress*. Philadelphia: US Regional Survey.

Lass, Roger (1978). Mapping constraints in phonological reconstruction: on climbing down trees without falling out of them. In Jacek Fisiak (ed.), *Recent Developments in Historical Phonology*. The Hague: Mouton. 245–86.

Marckwardt, Albert H. (1941). Middle English *o* in American English of the Great Lakes area. *Papers of the Michigan Academy of Science Arts and Letters* 26: 561–71.

Marckwardt, Albert H. (1942). Middle English *wa* in the speech of the Great Lakes region. *American Speech* 17: 226–34.

Martinet, Andre (1952). Function, structure and sound change. *Word*, 8: 1–32. Reprinted in P. Baldi and R. Werth (eds.), (1978). *Readings in Historical Phonology*. University Park:

The Pennsylvania State University Press. 121–59.

Martinet, Andre (1964). *Elements of General Linguistics*, trans. by E. Palmer. Chicago: University of Chicago Press.

Milroy, James (1992). *Linguistic Variation and Change*. Oxford: Blackwell.

Milroy, James and John Harris (1980). When is a merger not a merger? The MEAT/MATE problem in a present-day English vernacular. *English World Wide* 1: 199–210.

Stockwell, Robert and Donka Minkova (1997). On Drifts and Shifts. *Studia Anglica Posnaniensia* 31: 283–303.

Thomas, Charles K. (1935–7). Pronunciation in Upstate New York. *American Speech* X (1935): 107–12, 208–12, 292–97; XI (1936): 68–77, 142–44, 307–13; XII (1937): 122–7.

Thomas, Charles K. (1958). *An Introduction to the Phonetics of American English*. 2nd edn. New York: Ronald Press.

Watt, Dominic J. L. (1998). Variation and change in the vowel system of Tyneside English. Unpublished Ph.D. dissertation, University of Newcastle.

Wolfram, Walt and Natalie Schilling-Estes (1998). *American English*. Oxford: Blackwell.

Wyld, Henry Cecil (1936). *A History of Modern Colloquial English*. 3rd edn. Oxford: Basil Blackwell.

10 Variation and Syntactic Theory

ALISON HENRY

This chapter investigates the relationship of variation to (Chomskyan) syntactic theory. In contrast to sociolinguistics, where variation has been central, the study of variation has made much less impact, if any, on the development of syntactic theory. This chapter considers the reasons for this, suggests that variation needs to be integrated into syntactic theory, and proposes some means by which this might be achieved.

The central goal of syntactic theory has been to develop a theory of the representation of language in the mind/brain of individual speakers, whereas the goal of work on language variation within sociolinguistics has mainly been concerned with the understanding of how language operates in society. The data of syntactic theory have relied on the intuitions of native speakers, whereas sociolinguistic approaches study language as actually used. It is perhaps not surprising therefore that rather different perspectives have developed about the nature, and indeed the very existence, of variation.

In sociolinguistics, language is seen as inherently variable, and much work has been concerned with identifying the conditioning factors – both linguistic and social – that determine that variation. One might say that if language was not variable, there would be no sociolinguistics.

By contrast, the study of variation has generally been explicitly or implicitly excluded from work on syntactic theory. Chomsky (1965) proposed that the subject of study should be "the ideal speaker-hearer in a homogeneous speech community," arguing that this idealization was justifiable unless it was the case that such a speaker could not learn language. Of course, idealization may be necessary in scientific endeavor, but it is important that such idealization should not fundamentally alter the nature of the object under study. If syntax is inherently variable, then studying it as if it were not will not advance understanding.

As Hudson (1997) notes of work on variation:

> most of this work has fallen clearly within the sphere of sociolinguistics, with its special focus on the relationships between linguistic and social structures; very

little could be described as the study of language structure as such, and even less has had any influence on (synchronic) theories of language structure. Indeed, it is hard to think of a single example (until very recently) where statistical data on inherent variability has been used as evidence in discussion on language structure.   (Hudson 1997: 73)

A number of aspects of work on syntactic theory and morphosyntax have indeed been contingent upon *lack* of variation. For example, Chomsky (1995) proposed an economy principle under which movement occurs only when it is forced to do so. Such a grammar explicitly excludes optionality. If something moves only if forced, it will be impossible in principle for there to be an internalized grammar in which any movement operation is optional. If the option not to move exists, movement will not take place, since it will not be forced to do so.

It is perhaps surprising that the body of work on language variation has not had more impact than it has on work on syntactic theory. One of the reasons that syntactic theory has not been confronted with the data of variation is that these data in general are collected in rather different ways, and with different goals, from those of syntactic theory. This, as we shall see in the next section, has meant that there has sometimes been a quite different understanding of what the facts are, with the research methods within syntactic theory tending not to lead to findings of variation.

1   The Nature of the Data

Work on syntactic theory and on language variation has on occasion been based on quite different raw data, with work on syntactic theory finding no variation, while that in sociolinguistics has found a considerable amount of variability. This is no doubt because the nature of the data collection mechanism can lead to quite different data being gathered. A clear example of this is in relation to agreement patterns in sentences with expletive *there*.

The study of such sentences has been central to the development of syntactic theory. In particular, syntacticians have sought to explain why, in sentences such as (1), the verb agrees with the Noun Phrase which follows it:

(1)   There are three books on the table

A major proposal of Minimalist Syntax – that there is a numeration, a list of words selected from the lexicon prior to the generation of a sentence – has its roots in the nature of expletive structures, and a proposal by Chomsky (1998) that feature movement does not imply movement of the overt Noun Phrase, is again closely tied to the nature of expletives, which require long-distance agreement between the verb and post-verbal subject. Thus, these structures have been very central in the development of the theory.

One striking feature of work on English expletive structures within syntactic theory has been that it has assumed the standard English structure, with agreement, to be the only possible one in English. Chomsky (1995: ch. 4) does note in a footnote that some speakers can say:

(2)   There's three books on the table

as an alternative to

(3)   There are three books on the table

but argues that *There's* is a low-level substitution for *There are* and that the construction without agreement is not productive, since, he claims, it does not occur in uncontracted form, in the past tense or in questions:

(4)   *There is three books on the table
(5)   *There was three books on the table
(6)   *Is there three books on the table

Thus, the possibility of lack of agreement here has been largely excluded from consideration of these structures within syntactic theory.

While it may be the case for some speakers that, as Chomsky (1995) claims, the verb must agree with the post-verbal associate, studies from a variationist perspective on agreement in expletive structures have consistently shown that there is variation in agreement patterns, and indeed that the pattern without agreement is more common, even among standard speakers. Thus, Tagliamonte (1998), in a study of speakers in York, shows that non-agreement is almost categorical for her subjects in existentials. Indeed Sobin (1997) goes so far as to argue that the standard form with agreement is unnatural, an overlay on the natural non-agreeing form of a learned alternative which he calls a "virus."

What is clear is that agreement is obligatory for few speakers, yet much work on syntactic theory has been based on it being so, and none, as far as I am aware, on the need to account for variable agreement existing within the grammars of individual speakers, even though, if sociolinguistic work on expletive structures is representative of the general case, this is the dominant position in the population of English speakers at large. Thus, the question for syntacticians should be, not how there is agreement with a post-verbal noun-phrase, but how there is optional agreement.

Another central aspect of syntactic theory has been the null subject parameter (see, for example, Jaeggli and Safir 1989). Thus, it is generally claimed that English is a non-null subject language, with a requirement to have an overt subject in finite clauses, so that a sentence like (7) is ungrammatical (except where ellipsis is permitted, as an answer to a question such as "What does he do on Saturdays?"). This contrasts with languages like Spanish which allow apparently subjectless sentences, as the Spanish equivalent in (8) shows.

(7)   *Goes to the theatre
(8)   Va al teatro

However, study of spontaneous speech has led to the realization that English can at least under certain circumstances permit null subjects. Thus Cote's (1996) study of telephone conversations showed widespread use of null subjects, which were almost as frequent as overt pronouns in subject position.

It thus seems to be the case that English, at least under certain conditions, permits null subjects, something that has not really entered into the analysis of null arguments. Rizzi (1994), noting the existence of these null arguments, argues that they never occur in subordinate clauses, but spoken data show that this does occur, though less frequently than in matrix clauses.

While it is not surprising that different areas of linguistics have focused on different aspects of the constructions – one might not expect theoretical syntacticians to be particularly interested in how social factors impinge on the choice of forms with and without agreement or the possibility of a null subject – it is perhaps a matter of concern that the nature of the raw data is in question on such central issues. This seems to be a confirmation that the use purely of intuitions as linguistic data do not necessarily reflect what speakers do. There are perhaps two aspects to this. The first is that the use of intuitions in practice often means the intuitions of the linguists themselves, colleagues and students in higher education, which means that there is a strong bias towards the standard language. Second, the reported judgments of speakers are undoubtedly influenced by what they have been taught about grammar, and by considerations of the supposed "correctness" of standard forms. This is particularly likely to be the case because, in practice, sentences are most often presented in written form, on a blackboard or printed sheet, and the standard is used more or less exclusively in writing. Moreover, the technique does not work very well when working on non-standard varieties, whose speakers generally err on the side of the standard when giving judgments (for discussion of this, see Henry 1992, 1995). Criticism of the use of intuitions as linguistic data has a long history within linguistics (see Labov 1998 for an outline and discussion of this), with an extended treatment in Schütze's (1996) book. This is not to say that such intuitions do not have their uses, especially as the sparseness of data on the syntax of many constructions in spoken data, and the need to establish what cannot be said, as well as what can, mean that intuitions are a useful shortcut. But they can clearly indicate ungrammaticality of aspects of the language that are in fact wholly grammatical. And this has undoubtedly masked the variability present in language, and meant that it has not been a core issue in the development of syntactic theory.

However, why have findings of variation in sociolinguistic studies not impacted on syntactic theory? As we note in Wilson and Henry (1998), work on variation and on syntax has essentially gone on in parallel, undertaken by different practitioners, with different outlets for disseminating their results. There is no doubt a further reason, however. Syntactic theory has as its goal the representation of language in the mind/brain of a speaker-hearer. This has not on the whole been the aim of variationist studies. Thus, there have not been clear findings presented that individual grammars – as distinct from "community" grammars – contain variability. However, the need to encompass variation within the theory has become clear in the study of historical linguistics, as we shall see in the next section.

2   Variation in a Historical Context

It is not surprising that when "production data" are considered, the existence of variation becomes clear. This has particularly occurred in looking at syntactic change, where in an historical context, the absence of native speakers means it is necessary to look at textual data. In periods of language change, the general picture is of alternating forms persisting over a period, followed by the use of the new form, rather than abrupt adoption of a new form.

This might have led to the conclusion that variability is present in individual grammars, even if unstable historically. However, this has not been the case. The period of alternation, however, is in general viewed, not as a period of variation, but as one of competing grammars, bidialectalism, or internal diglossia. It is suggested, then, that speakers do not have grammars including variability, but rather alternate between different grammars.

An important contributor to work in this area, Kroch (1994) considers the rise of the use of periphrastic *do* in English, resulting in the use of constructions like (10), (12), and (14), as distinct from (9), (11), and (13).

(9)   How great tribulations suffered the Holy Apostle?
(10) How great tribulations did the Holy Apostle suffer?

(11) . . . which he perceiueth not
(12) . . . which he does not perceive

(13) . . . Queen Ester looked never with swich and eye.
(14) . . . Queen Ester never looked with such an eye.

He argues that the change is explained by the loss of raising of the verb from the verb phrase into I. According to syntactic theory, based on the work of Pollock (1988), languages differ according to whether or not the verb can move out of the verb phrase into I (the position normally occupied by auxiliaries) when no auxiliary is present, and this accounts for a number of differences between languages in relation to negation, inversion, and adverb placement.

Kroch shows that over a period, there is a shift towards the use of *do* instead of verb raising, with the frequency of use gradually increasing in various sentence types. The data are shown in table 10.1.

Table 10.1   Frequency of *do* by sentence type

Time		Negatives				Affirmative questions					
Dates	years	declarative		question		transitive		intransitive		wh-object	
		%	N	%	N	%	N	%	N	%	N
1400–1425	25	0.0	177	11.7	17	0.0	3	0.0	7	0.0	1
1426–1475	50	1.2	903	8.0	25	10.7	56	0.0	86	0.0	27
1476–1500	25	4.8	693	11.1	27	13.5	74	0.0	68	2.0	51
1501–1525	25	7.8	605	59.0	78	24.2	91	21.1	90	11.3	62
1526–1535	10	13.7	651	60.7	56	69.2	26	19.7	76	9.5	63
1536–1550	15	27.9	735	75.0	84	61.5	91	31.9	116	11.0	73

Source: Kroch (1994)

Kroch proposes that there is a "constant rate effect", by which he means that the frequency of *do* changes at the same rate across different constructions, and argues that this is because the underlying mechanism – loss of verb movement to I – is the same.

There is a problem with this however. If there is a change in a parameter – the loss of V movement to I – then one would expect the frequency of use of the new structure to be the same across all sentence types. But that is clearly not the case, with the frequency differing between, for example, negative declaratives and negative questions, and between affirmative questions with transitive and intransitive verbs. While one might argue for there being an explanation for a difference between negatives and questions – with the latter involving verb movement beyond I to C – there is no reason whatever why the transitivity of the verb should have any effect on movement of the verb to I, according to syntactic theory. The latter would in fact predict an instantaneous shift for individual speakers, or if there was "grammar competition" at the individual level, similar frequencies across all constructions which depended on the setting of this parameter.

Kroch emphasizes that the change was not instantaneous, but rather involved the alternation of old and new forms over a considerable period of time. However he does not grasp the nettle and allow that variable grammars must be possible. Rather, he argues that there are two grammars in operation, in competition with one another (Kroch 1994):

> The options in question . . . are not alternating realisations within a single grammar, like extraposed versus non-extraposed constituents. Rather they seem always to involve opposed grammatical choices not consistent with the postulation of a single unitary analysis. In the present case, for example, contemporary accounts of verb-movement to INFL all agree that it is forced by the morphosyntactic contents of functional heads and cannot be optional. Because the variants in

syntactic changes we have studied are not susceptible of integration into a single grammatical analysis, the variation does not stabilize and join the ranks of a language's syntactic alternations. Instead, the languages evolve further in such a way that one or the other variant becomes extinct.   (Kroch 1994: 183)

At least in relation to morphological doublets, Kroch argues that the child can only learn a single form in the course of language acquisition. He says, "Speakers can learn one or the other form in the course of language acquisition, but not both" (1994: 185). According to Kroch another form may be acquired later as a borrowing, but in a different way from the core acquisition of the language. Thus, variation is seen as something that occurs at certain periods, but is not part of the true nature of syntax as such.

Note that there is a considerable difference between a person having two grammars, and a single grammar which admits optionality. There is, further, a difference between optionality which results from lexical choices, and optionality which offers the speaker a real choice in terms of syntactic operations. If we return to expletives, we can see that the possibilities of saying

(15)   There are three books on the table

Or

(16)   There's three books on the table

could be attributed to there being two different *theres*. *There* (1) would not check all the properties of are, leaving these to be checked by the associate *three books*; *there* (2) would check all the properties, so that the associate *three books* would have no role in agreement. On the contrary, there might be a single *there* with true optionality in agreement.

A problem with Kroch's competition analysis is that it does not allow for stable variation across long periods of time. In his discussion of Kroch's paper, Hudson (1997) argues that there are cases where variation has continued for a considerable period in the language. For example, he cites the case of word order in Greek, where the alternation between SVO and SOV found in Homeric Greek continues into the language of the present day. Similar variability appears to have existed in relation to agreement in expletives over an extended period.

Thus Kroch's analysis faces syntactic theory with variation data, but does not conclude that there can be true optionality, preferring instead an analysis where there are competing grammars. A problem of the "grammar competition" model as a model of synchronic variability in syntax is that variability is not in general restricted at any one time to a single construction, but rather occurs in a range of structures. Thus in Henry (1995), I show that within Belfast English, there is variability in relation to agreement patterns, word order in imperatives, inversion in embedded questions, and the use of the relative pronoun in subject contact relative clauses. By no means every speaker has variation in all of these, so that there is a range of possible grammars with and without variation for a range of structures; if there is grammar competition, then it is between a wide range of grammars, not just two, and a better characterization seems to be that individual structures/parameter settings are variable, rather than that there are actually separate grammars.

3   Frequency and Syntactic Theory

A key feature of variation is its statistical property: it is not just the case that there are two or more alternative forms, but each occurs with a particular frequency. It is certainly the case that while syntactic theory has sometimes been amenable to encompassing optionality, it has never incorporated statistical properties of those alternations. Before we go on to look at those properties, and how and if they might be encompassed in a grammar, it will be useful to look at the historical development of syntactic theory, which has alternated between highly restrictive versions where it is difficult to see how optionality would be incorporated, and more flexible theories where it would be possible to envisage optionality.

Syntactic theory has, during its development, been, fortuitously, alternately more and less amenable to accommodating variation within the theory. Thus, the first syntactic frameworks (Chomsky 1957, 1965) viewed linguistic theory as for the most part a matter of prescribing rule formats. Language structure consisted of rules, consisting of a structural description and a structural change. The fact that more or less any rule was possible if it could be expressed in a given format, and that it was possible to envisage rules having some percentage of likelihood of applying, meant that it was particularly amenable to incorporation of variation, and indeed this was the period when this rule format was adopted and incorporated as "variable rules" into sociolinguistics.

After this, it became apparent that this format was not restrictive enough to make significant claims about natural language, and, with Government and Binding Theory (Chomsky 1981), came the claim that there was only a single rule – Move α – under which anything could in principle be moved anywhere. Its operation was constrained by a number of principles, such as subjacency, which restricted the distance that an element could move, and the empty category principle, which required that any element, including a trace left by movement, had to be properly governed. Clearly, under such a theory, there can be optionality: an element may move somewhere, but need not, as long as in both cases the principles of the theory are not violated. It is, however, more difficult to see where variability would attach, the principles being absolute and the single rule of Move α not being what is variable, but rather some of its individual manifestations.

Parameter theory developed out of Government and Binding Theory, and envisaged that languages differed from one another along certain fixed parameters, perhaps with binary values. As we point out in Wilson and Henry

(1998), parameter theory is in itself an acknowledgment of variation; though of highly constrained variation, and the question arises as to whether it is possible to analyze the wide variety of dialects and indeed idiolects in a system which seems more adapted to characterizing differences between "languages."

Within the parameter-setting framework, studies began to be undertaken to a greater extent on non-standard dialects. Thus work by Benincà (1989), Brandi and Cordin (1989), Abraham and Bayer (1993) and Penner (1995) among others considered how the syntax of a range of dialects could be encompassed within the framework, that is whether the theory which had been developed to account for contrasts between different languages, could account for differences between dialects. But, with some exceptions, this work did not seek to encompass variation, but rather account for the structure of "dialects" that were considered homogeneous. Henry (1995), a study of Belfast English, does consider variability, at least in that variant realizations of the same construction are considered, and the implications for the theory of syntax dealt with. For example, there is optional fronting of the verb to C, the complementizer position, in imperatives.

(17) You read that!
(18) Read you that!

With both forms coexisting in the grammar of speakers, it is proposed therefore that there must be optionality available in the syntax, and that therefore C must be optionally strong – strength of features of a head determining whether an element is moved to that position – contrary to the general view in the theory that such optionality is not possible, movement only occurring if forced.

The Minimalist approach to syntax (Chomsky 1995) began with a recognition that the number of parameters was becoming so large as to be almost meaningless. It sought to reduce syntax back to basics and to establish how far the characteristics of human language were in accordance with the minimal requirements of a system linking sound and meaning. One can immediately see that the possibility of variation is further reduced – we have gone from a system emphasizing the differences between language varieties to one focusing on the highly constrained possibilities available. There has recently been a suggestion that certain rules can operate at a post-syntactic level, rather than in the syntax proper, and here there may be scope for variation to be included. However, it should be noted that variation is not seen only in peripheral stylistic aspects of language. Rather, it also appears in those core aspects that differentiate between languages.

We have seen that there has been considerable work on dialect variation, and some work taking into account optionality, but within core syntactic theory there has been little attempt to take frequency of variants into account. Where there are variants of a structure in use, it is often the case that they are used with different frequencies. An example is the use of non-agreement in existentials, mentioned above. Studies have consistently found that in spoken

English, the forms without agreement are more common than those with. While most of these studies have been done at a group, rather than an individual, level, it is clear that when it is found for example that one variant occurs 28 percent of the time, and the other 72 percent, this is not merely because 28 percent of the speakers use it all the time, and 72 percent never use it. Rather, we must assume that individual speakers have variable usage, and that part of their knowledge of language is that certain variants are more frequent than others.

The question arises as to whether this is a core part of linguistic competence, or something which is separate from the knowledge of grammar as such. While it is clear that it must be possible for a grammar to include variant realizations of different forms, it could be the case that the grammar allows these, but some other faculty determines their percentage use. On the other hand, it may be that such frequency is at the very core of the grammar.

What is clear is that frequency seems to be important in explaining language change, as seen in the work of Kroch and others. It has often been found that where there are two alternants, one gradually declines in frequency, until there is a stage where it is no longer used. Moreover, if change proceeds gradually as Kroch suggests, then a variable grammar must be able to be transmitted across generations in language acquisition. If this is the case, then grammars must be able to include "variable rules," and the acquisition mechanism must be able to acquire them, including the statistical properties. If acquisition is relatively constrained – involving the setting of a small number of parametric options – then this suggests that the mechanism is as Valian (1990) suggests – the learning mechanism knows what the alternatives are, and evidence is weighted in favour of each alternative. Valian envisages that one alternative falls out of use, but if variation theory is correct, then in fact both variants may remain in use if each is used frequently enough, with the frequencies attached representing the amount of evidence the learner has had for each alternative.

4   The Implications of Syntactic Theory for Studying Variation

We have thus far concentrated on considering why syntactic theory needs to incorporate variation; but does variation need syntactic theory? That is, are we saying that syntax is variation, and that "anything goes" as far as syntactic structures are concerned? Do we need a syntactic theory? We argue in Wilson and Henry (1998) that the answer is yes. In particular, in order to understand how language changes, we need to be able to look at the interaction of the general structure of language, and the possible structures of human languages, with the variability that occurs when change is taking place. Thus, we argue that the use of inverted imperatives is disappearing, and that this is because of a conjunction of two factors – low frequency of use in the input data to language acquisition – a "variation" factor – and the fact that raising of the verb in one particular structural type – imperatives – when verbs do not in general raise in English – makes the structure marked in terms of Universal Grammar. Low frequency in itself is not, as we shall see below, enough to predict change: rather there must be an interplay of frequency with linguistic factors.

Moreover, we need to understand the factors which can predispose the choice of variant in syntax. The factors predisposing the choice of one variant over another are, according to variation studies, many and varied. If these are to occur in grammars, and are to be learnable, one would expect them to be "natural kinds" in syntax. Thus one would not expect to find factors such as the phonological shape of words conditioning the occurrence of particular syntactic variants.

Within variationist studies, however, there has been little discussion of what type of factors can affect choice of variants, or of how the particular factors are chosen for analysis in any given case. Typically the factors chosen for entry into VARBRUL analysis appear without extensive discussion, and it is not clear how, apart from the intuitions of the researcher, these are arrived at, or whether there are any constraints on what can be a factor here. In acquisition, this makes the child's search space extremely large, and ideally one would want to develop a theory of how language can vary. It might be found that it varies largely along the lines syntactic theory would predict, with variation between "parameter settings"; or it may be that it is restricted to this and some kind of syntactic natural classes.

There are some cases where the conditioning factors can be related to difference in the syntax predicted by syntactic theory. Let us look at the example of singular concord (Henry 1995, Montgomery 1997). In some varieties of English including Belfast English, the verb can apparently be singular while the subject is plural

(19)   The kids is out late
(20)   The kids are out late

Sociolinguistic work on this, primarily undertaken by Montgomery (1994, 1995) has shown that one major factor which influences use of the singular form is what he calls the "Subject type constraint"; in other words, the verb generally agrees with a pronominal subject, but not necessarily with other types of subjects. In sociolinguistic work, there does not appear to be a theory of what can be a conditioning factor. Thus, it would appear that, for example, "occurs after a word ending in –t" or "refers to a colour term," or, perhaps more realistically, "occurs after a full noun phrase" could equally well be a conditioning factor as "pronominal" – nothing leads us to expect that there is anything special about pronouns. On the contrary, work in linguistic theory has shown that pronouns are more likely to trigger agreement, and be subject to particular constraints, cross-linguistically than full noun phrases; for example Koopman (1990) argues that pronouns must appear in a specifier position. Thus, the explanation of what can vary, and how, needs to look at work on syntactic theory.

5   Evidence for Variability in Core Syntax

If grammars are naturally variable, we would expect variation to appear in the early stages of children's grammars. On the other hand, if grammars were in some sense naturally invariant, then we would expect children to perhaps acquire a single grammar, only later adding another variant for stylistic or sociolinguistic reasons.

In a recent study of the acquisition of English in Belfast, we discovered that children not only acquired variable forms at an early stage, but also reflected the proportion in which the variants occurred in the input to which they were exposed. The following data are from (Henry et al. 1998).

As noted above, in Belfast English, there is a process known as "singular concord" (Henry 1995: ch. 2), under which subject-verb agreement is optional where the subject is a full noun phrase (rather than a pronoun); where there is no agreement, the verb shows up in the default third person singular form. Thus, there is alternation between forms like these:

(21)   The books goes on the shelf
(22)   The book go on the shelf

The adult pattern is generally to have singular concord occur less frequently than agreement, and the child adopts this in their grammar, as seen in table 10.2. The table shows, for all plural non-pronominal subjects, whether agreement occurred in the output of 2–4 year old children and their caregivers. An example of (–agr) is (23) and of (+agr) is (24):

Table 10.2   Agreement between children and caregivers: non-pronominal subjects

| | Child | | Caregivers | |
	−agr	+agr	−agr	+agr
Stuart	3	33	2	17
Barbara	4	16	2	40
Conor	15	36	20	51
Michelle	0	25	2	22
Courtney	2	12	21	12
David	0	2	4	34
Rachel	0	4	3	37
Johnny	0	3	1	5
Total-	24	131	55	218
agreement	15%		20%	

Table 10.3   Agreement between children and caregivers: expletive *there*

| | Child | | Caregivers | |
	−agr	+agr	−agr	+agr
Stuart	23	2	18	1
Barbara	14	0	24	4
Conor	30	0	29	0
Michelle	18	0	17	2
Courtney	33	3	25	1
David	5	0	32	0
Rachel	12	0	37	9
Johnny	2	1	2	0
Total-	137	6	184	17
agreement	96%		92%	

(23)   The toys is there
(24)   The toys are there

Although the occurrence of these structures is rather sparse, it is clear that the children can acquire variable use of the structure and use it in frequencies similar to those occurring in the input.

The pattern in "singular concord" sentences contrasts with agreement with the associate in sentences with expletive *there*, shown in table 10.3. An example of a sentence which is (−agr) is (25) and (+agr) is (26):

(25)   There was some flowers in the window
(26)   There were some flowers in the window

Here, we see a strong difference in pattern from the case with agreement with plurals in subject position. Agreement is much less frequent than non-agreement in the adult language. Again, this is the pattern the children also adopt. The children have learned the statistical distribution of forms at an early stage, apparently indicating that it is possible to acquire the statistical properties of syntactic structures as part of the acquisition process.

A similar pattern emerges with negative concord. Belfast English has variable use of negative concord: negative elements such as *no one, nothing no more* may or may not be licenced by a negative element *not* or *-n't*. Again, all children showed use of the more frequent form, and the frequency of use was similar to that in adult input, with negative concord occurring much less frequently than non-concord. Table 10.4 shows whether, in contexts where negative

Table 10.4   Use of negative concord by children and caregivers

| | Child | | Caregivers | |
	+NC	–NC	+NC	–NC
Stuart	1	33	1	22
Barbara	9	11	8	39
Conor	3	37	21	58
Misha	1	27	5	68
Courtney	3	28	0	23
David	0	6	7	51
Rachel	0	4	0	28
Johnny	1	3	2	8
Total	18	149	44	297
%NC use	11%		13%	

concord is permitted, it occurred or did not occur. Thus a (+NC) sentence would be (27) and a (–NC) example would be (28):

(27)   He didn't do nothing
(28)   He did nothing

Note that the children appear capable of acquiring alternants with rather low frequencies. Thus the acquisition device, and the syntax acquired, must be frequency-sensitive in the way that studies of variability would lead us to expect.

6   Syntax, Variation, and Learnability

We have seen that the existence of variation, as commonly understood – that is, systematic variability between different ways of saying the same thing within the competence of a single speaker – has considerable implications for syntactic theory. However, these implications have scarcely been taken into account in the development of that theory, or in studies of language acquisition based on that theoretical model.

Minimalist syntax seeks to establish how good a fit the design features of natural language are for the minimal requirements of a system linking sound and meaning. The question arises as to why such a system should have variation – this simply seems to add complications, both in terms of the syntax itself, and of the learnability of the syntax. Thus, a learner will have to acquire more than one form for some structures, and also learn to use each of the forms with a particular frequency. To see why this is in fact a good design feature, however, we must think about the actual circumstances of language acquisition. A child is generally acquiring a grammar from the output of a number of different speakers, whose grammars are probably not identical; in order to do this, the child's acquisition device must be able to incorporate variation. Thus, imagine that the child is faced with two grammars, one of which generates (29) and the other (30):

(29) There are three books on the table
(30) There is three books on the table

To function as a member of a community, a child must be able to acquire a grammar which generates both (see Henry 1998). And to ensure that the child's grammar is not altered by very rare occurrences, which may be speech errors or the language of outsiders who are occasional visitors, the acquisition device must be frequency-sensitive. Thus, the community grammar provides input to the child, and the child acquires a "community grammar." Perhaps this is a design specification for a grammatical system, and acquisition device, which enables the child not only to acquire a language, but to operate as a member of the community.

REFERENCES

Abraham, W. and J. Bayer (eds.) (1993). *Dialectsyntax*. Opladen: Westdeutscher Verlag.

Beninca, P. (1989). *Dialect Variation and the Theory of Grammar*. Dordrecht: Foris.

Brandi, P. and P. Cordin (1989). Two Italian dialects and the Null Subject Parameter. In O. Jaeggli and K. Safir (eds.), *The Null subject parameter*. Dordrecht: Kluwer.

Chomsky, N. (1957). *Syntactic Structures*. The Hague: Mouton.

Chomsky, N. (1965). *Aspects of the Theory of Syntax*. Cambridge, MA: MIT Press.

Chomsky, N. (1981). *Lectures on Government and Binding*. Dordrecht: Foris.

Chomsky, N. (1995). *The Minimalist Program*. Cambridge, MA: MIT Press.

Chomsky, N. (1998). Minimalist inquiries: The framework. *MIT Occasional Papers in Linguistics* 15.

Cote, S. A. (1996). Grammatical and discourse properties of null arguments in English. Ph.D. dissertation, University of Pennsylvania.

Henry, A. (1992). Infinitives in a *for-to* dialect. *Natural Language and Linguistic Theory* 10: 279–301.

Henry, A. (1995). *Belfast English and Standard English: Dialect Variation and Parameter Setting*. New York: Oxford University Press.

Henry, A. (1998). Dialect variation, optionality and the learnability guarantee. *Linguistica Atlantica* 21: 41–78.

Henry, A., J. Wilson, C. Finlay and S. Harrington (1998). *Language Acquisition in Conditions of Variable Input*. Report to Economic and Social Research Council.

Hudson, R. (1997). Inherent variability and linguistic theory. *Cognitive Linguistics* 8: 73–108.

Jaeggli, O. and K. Safir (eds.) (1989). *The Null Subject Parameter*. Dordrecht: Kluwer.

Koopman, H. (1990). The syntax of the verb-particle construction. MS UCLA.

Kroch, A. (1994). Morphosyntactic variation. In K. Beals, J. Denton, R. Knippen, L. Melnar, H. Suzuki and E. Zeinfeld (eds.), *Papers from the 30th Regional Meeting of the Chicago Linguistic Society Vol 2: The Parasession on Variation in Linguistic Theory*.

Labov, W. (1996). When intuitions fail. *CLS 32: Papers from the Parasession on Theory and Data in Linguistics* 32: 76–106.

Labov, W. (1998). When intuitions fail. Paper presented at the Parasession on Theory and Data in Linguistics, Chicago, Chicago Linguistics Society.

Montgomery, M. (1994). The evolution of verb concord in Scots. In A. Fenton and D. Macdonald (eds.), *Studies in Scots and Gaelic: Proceedings of the Third International Conference on the Languages of Scotland (81–95)*. Edinburgh: Cannongate Academic.

Montgomery, M. (1995). The linguistic value of Ulster Emigrant Letters. *Ulster Folklife* 41: 26–41.

Montgomery, M. (1997). A Tale of Two Georges. In J. Kallen (ed.), *Focus on Ireland*. Amsterdam: Benjamins.

Penner, Z. (1995). *Topics in Swiss German Syntax*. Bern: Peter Lang.

Pollock, J. Y. (1988). Verb movement, UG and the structure of IP. *Linguistic Inquiry* 20: 365–424.

Rizzi, L. (1994). Early null subjects and root null subjects. In T. Hoekstra and B. Schwartz (eds.), *Language Acquisition Studies in Generative Grammar: papers in honour of Kenneth Wexler from the 1991 GLOW Workshops*. Amsterdam: Benjamins.

Schütze, Carson T. (1996). *The Empirical Base of Linguistics: Grammaticality Judgments and Linguistic Methodology*. Chicago: University of Chicago Press.

Sobin, N. (1997). Agreement, default rules and grammatical viruses. *Linguistic Inquiry* 28: 318–43.

Tagliamonte, S. (1998). *Was/were* variation across the generations: View from the city of York. *Language Variation and Change* 10: 153–91.

Valian, V. (1990). Null Subjects: a problem for parameter setting models of language acquisition. *Cognition* 35: 105–22.

Wilson, J. and A. Henry (1998). Parameter setting in a socially realistic linguistics. *Language in Society* 27: 1–21.

11   Discourse Variation

RONALD MACAULAY

Mais le discours sied mal à qui cherche du sang

Cyrano de Bergerac

Linguists have generally been suspicious of the notion of discourse. Chomsky influentially declared that the proper study of linguistics was sentences and that studies of language use were irrelevant (Chomsky 1986), and so it is perhaps ironical that the literature on discourse analysis should begin with the work of Chomsky's mentor Zellig Harris (1952, 1963) whose work starts from the principle that language consists of small units that are combined into larger ones: phonemes are combined to make morphemes, morphemes are combined to make words and phrases, and so on. Harris was attempting to find "some global structure characterizing the whole discourse" by identifying "a pattern of occurrence (i.e. a recurrence) of segments of the discourse relative to each other" (Harris 1963: 7). Harris believed that "such relative occurrence of parts is the only type of structure that can be investigated by inspection of the discourse without bringing into account other types of data, such as relations of meanings throughout the discourse" (Harris 1963: 7). However, Harris found that he could not avoid "judgment of the meanings of morphemes" (1963: 72) but "we try to apply [this operation] sparingly, in a way that leads to fewest applications" (1963: 65). In practice, Harris was principally concerned with what Halliday and Hasan (1976) call *cohesion*, represented in an abstract schema.

Harris's definition of discourse was "any connected linear material . . . which contains more than one elementary sentence" (1963: 7), echoed by Stubbs, in his textbook as "the organization of language above the sentence or above the clause" (1983: 1). This reflects what Linell (1982) calls "the written bias in linguistics," since the appropriateness of the term "sentence" in describing spoken language has still to be demonstrated (O'Connell 1988: 258–9; Macaulay 1997: 140). A range of definitions of discourse is examined by Schiffrin (1994:

20–43), distinguishing between structural (formalist) and functional approaches. Since the purpose of this chapter is not to examine discourse analysis per se, but the results of studies that show discourse variation, it is not necessary to define the term narrowly. People use language, both spoken and written, for a variety of purposes and all these uses can be examined under the heading of discourse. The study of discourse variation is the attempt to find patterns of language use that characterize the spoken language of a definable group in a specific setting. In this chapter I will not deal with written discourse.

However, that does not eliminate all problems. One of the most common functions of discourse is to communicate something, but the proper study of linguistics is not communication. (In this case, I agree with Chomsky.) Linguists are concerned with the use of language in communication, but that is a very different thing. To take an obvious example, conversation analysts (e.g. C. Goodwin 1981, Sacks 1992, Schegloff 1992) and psychologists (e.g. O'Connell 1988) have shown the significance of pauses and silence in communicating. However, there can be no *linguistic* analysis of silence, though pauses may be a guide to linguistic units. Similarly, the use of gestures and facial expressions can be crucial to communication (Kendon 1990, McNeill 1992, McNeill and Levy 1993), but they form part of a different system than that of verbal communication.

Investigating variation in discourse presents different problems from those in examining variation in other aspects of language. Ever since Labov's pioneering work on Martha's Vineyard (Labov 1963) quantitative methods have been used in sociolinguistic investigation. Usually the items counted have been phonological or morphological, following Labov's view that the most appropriate candidates to be treated as linguistic variables are those that occur frequently and are less liable to conscious manipulation (Labov 1966). For this purpose, relatively small samples of speech may be adequate, and even such unnatural speech acts as reading out a list of words may provide useful information on differences between speakers. The investigation of spoken discourse, however, requires evidence collected in settings where the nature of the speech event is clear and the roles of the participants can be established. The study of discourse also usually requires larger samples of language use. It also requires many methodological decisions that are not crucial in studying other kinds of variation.

It is also fair to say that the study of discourse variation is at an elementary stage. There is no general agreement on methods of collecting or analyzing data, on what features are suitable for investigation, on how to identify possible discourse features, and what significance to attach to the use of a particular feature (Tannen 1994). Even when a feature is relatively easy to identify formally (e.g. tag questions) it may be less easy to determine what functions the feature performs. Moreover, unlike phonological and morphological variables, for discourse features there is seldom a context in which one variant or another must occur. Instead, the most important aspect of a discourse may be the frequency with which some feature occurs. Since samples are often of unequal size, it is essential for comparative purposes that the raw count of occurrences be converted to a frequency of, say, number of occurrences per thousand words. Where samples of equal length have been analyzed this is not necessary for internal comparisons but has to be calculated for comparison with other studies.

1   Two Approaches to Discourse Studies

Much of this chapter will be taken up with examining individual studies, not only for what their results show but also to find out what lessons can be learned from the approach employed. This emphasis will be most evident in the section on quantitative methods. Since the field is so broad, it would be impossible to provide a comprehensive survey of all the work that has been done. Instead, I will try to provide examples of different kinds of investigations and the methods involved. Since this is obviously not a complete review, no inferences should be drawn from the failure to mention any individual work. Finally, there are many works on discourse analysis that are not cited because they do not deal with *variation* in discourse.

The two approaches to the study of discourse that I will be concerned with are the ethnographer's observation of communicative practices and the sociolinguist's examination of language use, principally from a variationist perspective. The first approach requires that the investigator spends time in the community, observing behavior, identifying speech events in all the complexity set out by Hymes (1974). Sociolinguists, on the other hand, have concentrated more on the characteristics of texts, either written materials or transcripts of recorded speech. Some investigators have combined both approaches. I will not be directly concerned with the Foucauldian notion of discourse as "grouping of utterances or sentences, statements which are enacted within a social context, which are determined by that social context and which contribute to the way that social context continues its existence" (Mills 1997: 11) or what Gee (1999: 7) calls "Big D Discourses . . . to enact specific activities and identities," though any discourse variation will have social consequences. I will also not attempt to cover the field of discourse analysis as a whole but only deal with studies where there is variation in language use that can be identified with membership in a socially determined group.

There is a further problem, however, in limiting the scope of a chapter on "discourse variation" since almost all variation will be in "discourse," but phonetic, phonological, syntactic, etc., variation are examined elsewhere in this volume. In a sense, therefore, "discourse variation" refers to the messy bits that most other contributors steer clear of. Researchers have investigated a wide range of features under the label "discourse," though I will not attempt to deal with all of these. Moreover, much of the variation in discourse involves categories such as social class, gender, and age, etc., that are also dealt with in other chapters, but the kind of variation examined here is different from that in the other chapters. Finally, some studies of variation in discourse compare differences in language use between different groups or subgroups, while others present accounts of language use in particular societies without making explicit comparisons.

2   Ethnographic Studies

The ethnographic study of discourse is exemplified in the pioneering work of Malinowski (1923, 1935) in his aim to link up "ethnographic descriptions with linguistic analysis which provides language with its cultural context and culture with its linguistic interpretation" (1935: 73). Also influential was the collection of articles edited by Bloch (1975) dealing with political language and oratory. More recent collections on similar topics are Brenneis and Myers (1984) on political language in Oceania, Watson-Gegeo and White (1990) on conflict resolution in Pacific societies, and Hill and Irvine (1993) on the notions of agency, responsibility, and evidence in a range of societies. Duranti (1994) describes the political use of language in a Samoan village. Hanks (1990) examines spatial reference and deixis in a Mayan community. Urban (1991) describes myths and ceremonial rituals in South America. Besnier (1995) deals with emerging literacy on the small Polynesian island of Nukilaelae. Other investigators have reported on characteristic styles of speech: Errington (1988) on Javanese; Katriel (1986) on *dugri* speech in Israel; and Tannen (1984) on New Yorkers' dinner conversation. Moerman (1988) provides a rare example of conversation analysis in a non-western society, Thailand. Studies such as these provide illustrations of language use that can be used for comparative purposes and also provide models for examining discourse in other societies.

One area in which ethnographic studies have been particularly influential has been the investigation of the situations under which children's language development takes place. Ochs' (1988) work on language socialization in Samoa and Schieffelin's (1990) on the Kaluli show that caregivers' behavior towards young children may be very different from that of mainstream American parents. Ward (1971) and Heath (1983) had already shown that ethnic and social class factors also affect child-rearing practices in the USA. These studies show that the pattern of attentive caregivers using child directed speech and making every attempt to understand the young child's initial tentative utterances (e.g. Snow and Ferguson 1977) is far from universal.

Ethnographic studies have also been influential in reporting gender differences in discourse. The most influential has been Robin Lakoff's work (1973, 1975) in which she reported on her own intuitions and as a participant observer of the behavior of middle-class women in the USA and listed a number of features that she claimed were characteristic of "women's language." Lakoff's work stimulated numerous empirical studies of these features in attempts to support or refute her claims. In particular, there has been strong resistance to her suggestion that women's language "submerges a woman's personal identity, by denying her the means of expressing herself strongly, on the one hand, and encouraging expressions that suggest triviality in subject-matter and uncertainty about it" (Lakoff 1973: 48). Some of these studies will be discussed below.

Keenan Ochs (1974) reports that in a Malagasay community on Madagascar it is the women and not the men who are more outspoken and do not mitigate their speech in expressing criticism or anger. Irvine (1973) shows that among the rural Wolof in Senegal it is the lower caste griots who use the more elaborated speech style while the higher caste nobles take pride in a kind of linguistic incompetence. Basso (1990) observes that the Western Apache prefer silence to speech in encounters where they are unsure about their interlocutor. Bauman (1983) describes the distinctive ways of speaking among Quakers in seventeenth-century England. Studies such as these are a valuable corrective to universalistic claims about speech behavior that are ethnocentrically based.

Ethnographic studies depend directly on the accuracy of the investigator's observations and interpretations, and these will be affected by the role played by the investigator in an interactive context (Duranti and Goodwin 1992). Until another investigator visits a similar Malagasay or Kaluli community, the observations by Keenan Ochs and Schieffelin are likely to remain unchallenged. If challenges do arise at some future time, then a verdict on who is right will depend largely upon the credibility of the researchers. In the case of Lakoff's claims about women's language in the USA, those who were unconvinced usually did not resort simply to counter-claims, based on their own experience. Instead, they attempted to test those claims against empirical evidence collected systematically for the purpose.

3   Sociolinguistic Studies

The most commonly used method for collecting information on language variation has been "the sociolinguistic interview" (Labov 1966, 1981). Wolfson (1976) and Milroy and Milroy (1977) adversely criticize the quality of speech recorded in interviews. I argued against this negative view (Macaulay 1984, 1991) by showing that useful samples of speech could be recorded under these circumstances. Schiffrin (1987) also shows that important discourse features can be studied on the basis of interview data.

Despite the adverse criticism, sociolinguistic interviews can provide valuable evidence of more than phonetic or phonological features, particularly where the same interviewer conducts all the interviews so that there is some consistency in the approach to the interviewee. The role of the interviewer, however, is heavily biased in favor of being a receptive listener rather than an equal partner in the conversation between "intimate strangers" (Gregersen and Pedersen 1991: 54). In an ideal sociolinguistic interview the interviewee is essentially a monologuist, telling stories, reminiscing, offering opinions, and so on. Clearly, individuals differ in the ways in which they take advantage of this opportunity (Macaulay 1984, 1991, 1999), and one of the important factors will be how the interviewee perceives and reacts to the interviewer (Dubois and Horvath 1993, Eisikovits 1989, Laforest 1993, Macaulay 1991, Schilling-Estes 1998). This is not simply a matter of "audience design" (Bell 1984) since the contribution of both participants is critical and the interviewer's interest in and rapport with the interviewee can have an important effect on the quality of speech recorded (Macaulay 1990, 1991, 2001). Such factors will affect any findings on the use of discourse features.

One alternative is to set up group interviews (Eckert 1990, Gregersen and Pedersen 1991, Labov 1972, Labov et al. 1968). In group sessions, however, there is a much greater chance of extraneous noise and unless each speaker is recorded on a separate track from an individual microphone there is always a risk that it may be difficult to separate out the contribution of each speaker unless their voices are clearly distinct. It is also difficult to arrange a systematic set of group interviews by speakers chosen on the basis of their membership in a particular social category and the results may be disappointing because of the unnaturalness of the speech event (Gregersen and Pedersen 1991: 56). This makes it difficult to obtain comparable samples of speech.

There is a form of data-collecting that lies between the monologues of individual interviews and the polyphony of group sessions. This is to set up a situation in which two speakers, who know each other and who are from the same kind of background, talk to each other in unstructured conversations in optimal recording conditions. This avoids the danger of accommodation (Giles and Powlesland 1975) to the speech of an interviewer, perhaps from outside of the community (Douglas-Cowie 1978) or from a different sector of the community (Rickford and McNair-Knox 1993). Naturally, speakers may react differently to the artificiality of the situation but the method permits the systematic collection of extended samples of speech from a selected sample of the population. The resulting data set will provide materials for comparison between categories of speakers recorded under similar conditions and therefore appropriate for an analysis of any differences that may emerge.

These methods require the cooperation of the speakers and there is always the indeterminate effect of the recording situation. Moreover, many aspects of language use are unlikely to arise in these settings. For some features, it is possible to count their occurrence in a given situation through participant observation. For example, it is possible to observe compliments or apologies (Holmes 1990) and to make a note of the sex of the participants and make an estimate of their age. However, the frequency with which these will occur in the observer's presence will be affected by the sex and age of the observer and the situations that can be observed. It is also possible to obtain information on language use by means of self-report questionnaires.

4   Qualitative Sociolinguistic Studies of Discourse

Labov's earliest work on discourse was his analysis of oral narratives of personal experience (Labov and Waletzky 1967), a work that continues to dominate the field, as a volume celebrating the 30th anniversary of the paper's publication shows (Bamberg 1997). Most of the more than 50 celebrants testify to the usefulness of Labov and Waletzky's model but few have much to offer in the way of additions or improvements.

Labov's (1972) next venture into discourse analysis was to demonstrate that there was no evidence that the kinds of characteristics Basil Bernstein (1962) found in his *elaborated code* represented "a subtle and sophisticated mode of planning utterances" (Labov 1972: 222) and that we need to discover "how much of middle-class style is a matter of fashion and how much actually helps us express ideas clearly" (Labov 1972: 222). The challenge is one that has not so far been met.

The first major work showing variation in narrative following Labov is Barbara Johnstone's (1990) study, based on 68 stories collected by Johnstone's students in Fort Wayne, Indiana 1981–85. One of Johnstone's (1990) main findings is that there are gender differences and these are worth quoting at length:

> While women's stories are about social reality, men's stories are about individual reality. [66] . . . women's stories tend to be "other oriented," underplaying the protagonists' personal roles and emphasizing social community and mutual dependence. [66] Fort Wayne men tell stories which make statements about their own character and abilities. Men's stories are about events in which their skill, courage, honor, or sense of humor was called upon and successfully displayed: hunting and fishing, fights, successfully solved problems on the road or in the military, clever pranks and clever reactions in awkward moments. [66–7] Men's stories are about skill rather than luck. [67] Though women do on occasion tell stories about their personal exploits – getting the better of authority or pulling off a prank – their skill is always abetted by luck, and more often their stories are about experiences that were embarrassing or frightening or taught them a lesson. [67] When a woman is not the protagonist of her story, the protagonist is either male or female; while men do not tell stories about women's skill, women do tell stories about men's. [67] When men act alone in their stories, they are almost always successful; when women act alone, the outcome is usually negative. [67] Women use more personal names in their stories than do men, even when their audiences are unfamiliar with the names. Men provide more details about objects. [68] The result of these differential discourse choices is that women's stories typically create a storyworld populated with specific, named people engaged in interaction, while the storyworld created in men's stories is more often silent, and the characters are more often nameless.   (Johnstone 1990: 66–8)

Holmes (1997a) drew similar conclusions based on a sample of 30 same-sex conversations recorded as part of the Wellington Corpus of Spoken New Zealand

English. Holmes found that the stories reflected the different daily preoccupations of men and women (1997a: 286): "The women focus on relationships and people, affirm the importance of their family roles, family connections and friendships. The men focus on work and sport, events, activities and things, and affirm the importance of being in control, even when they don't achieve it."

Neither Johnstone nor Holmes gives numbers to support their claims. Kipers (1987) recorded 470 conversations in the faculty room of a middle school in New Jersey. Although Kipers does not give information on the amount of speech recorded, she does provide figures on the distribution of topics. She found that in female-only conversations the most frequent topics were on house and family (28 percent), social issues (21 percent), work (14 percent), and personal and family finance (12 percent). For male-only conversations the most frequent topics were work (39 percent), recreation (28 percent), and miscellaneous (11 percent). (The latter category consisted of "telling jokes," "the weather," "book read by the conversants," and "quitting smoking.") In mixed-sex conversations the most frequent conversations were work (25 percent), home and family (22 percent), and social issues (15 percent). This suggests that the men adapted more to the presence of women than the other way around. The greatest differences in individual topics are that their own children take up 9 percent of the women's conversations, 5 percent of the mixed-sex conversations, but less than 1 percent of the men's. In contrast, spectator sports occupy 13 percent of the men's conversations, 4 percent of the mixed-sex conversations, but none of the women's conversations.

Coates (1996) gives a detailed account of women's talk, showing the features used and drawing inferences as to the significance of this kind of speech. Although Coates also collected equal numbers of men's conversations she does not present any information on it in this work for comparative purposes. Nor does she give quantitative information that would allow comparison with other studies. In a short article (Coates 1997: 126), she discusses one comparative aspect of men's and women's speech: "the research I have carried out focusing on single-sex friendship groups shows that all-female groups of friends typically choose to organize talk using a collaborative floor, while all-male groups typically choose a one-at-a-time floor." With roughly equal samples of speech, to devote over 300 pages to women's talk and just over 20 pages to men's talk does seem to be redressing the male bias in research with a vengeance.

While Coates (1996) is an illuminating examination of language use, the concentration on the speech of one gender may have the effect of creating or reinforcing stereotypes. To claim that a certain feature is characteristic of one gender may seem to imply that it is not characteristic of the other, but unless both genders have been investigated under the same conditions, there is no evidence that it is not characteristic of both. This is an endemic problem with gender studies and may lead to misinterpreting or misrepresenting the data, as happened with claims about girls' precocity in language development (Macaulay 1978).

Even in a comparative study such as Holmes (1997a) there can be a problem, such as that of distinguishing between minimal responses as providing positive feedback or as neutral, non-committal responses. As Holmes (1997a: 290) admits, "any interpretation will be subjective," though there may be prosodic or paralinguistic evidence to support the interpretation. The more the investigator approaches the data with preconceptions about gender differences the greater the risk of biasing the subjective interpretation in one direction or the other.

Even Holmes' valuable *Women, Men and Politeness* (1995) in which she presents evidence to show that "in general, women are more polite than men, and that in particular they are more positively polite or linguistically supportive in interaction" (1995: 29) is not immune from this criticism. Holmes is careful to make it clear that her evidence comes from middle-class speakers in New Zealand and that the results may not generalize elsewhere, but that is not where the problem lies. For example, Holmes refers to the interviews collected for the Wellington Social Dialect Survey and she explains (1995: 34): "As far as we were concerned, the more talk the better. Being polite in this context meant being prepared to answer questions fully and at length. It soon became apparent that the least cooperative and polite participants were the young Pakeha males (i.e. those of European origin)." This statement attributes a motive to the young Pakeha males that may not be justified. There are many possible explanations for a respondent's reticence, including his/her perception of the task, the topics raised, the attitude of the interviewer, etc. Even the same interviewer can be either more or less successful in getting a respondent to speak at length (Dubois and Horvath 1993, Laforest 1993, Macaulay 1984, 1991, 1996). To treat all interviews as equivalent speech events is to ignore the complexity of the situation (Macaulay 2001).

Holmes (1995: 36–7) cites two other studies using artificial tasks in which "the women interviewees were more cooperative and polite, contributing substantially more talk overall than the men" (1995: 37). On the other hand, Holmes observes that "when talk offers the possibility of enhancing the speaker's status, men tend to talk most" (1995: 37). The point is not whether Holmes is correct in her interpretation but rather to note that there is a leap between the data and the interpretation. This caveat is important when evaluating studies of this type and even more so in quantitative studies.

Ochs and Taylor (1995) examined 100 past-time narratives told by seven two-parent families. They define a "story" as "a problem-centered past-time narrative" (1995: 100). They found what they construe as "a commonplace scenario of narrative activity at family dinners":

> First, mothers introduce narratives (about themselves and their children) that set up fathers as primary recipients and implicitly sanction them, as evaluators of others' actions, conditions, thoughts, and feelings. Second, fathers turn such opportunities into forums for problematizing, with mothers themselves as their chief targets, very often on grounds of incompetence. And third, mothers

respond in defense of themselves and their children via the counterproblematizing of fathers' evaluative, judgmental comments.   (Ochs and Taylor 1995: 116)

They conclude this gloomy report with the comment:

"Father knows best" – a gender ideology with a deeply rooted politics of asymmetry that has been contested in recent years – is still in reverberating evidence at the two-parent family dinner table, jointly constituted and re-created through everyday narrative practices.   (Ochs and Taylor 1995: 117)

If Ochs and Taylor's findings are generalizable, it would appear that Victorian "family values" continue to thrive in the present-day USA.

Blum-Kulka (1997) also studied dinner table conversation, comparing Jewish American families, American Israeli families, and Israeli families. Although her primary interest was in socialization and sociability, she points out a cross-cultural difference in choice of topic (1997: 55): "The American preoccupation with health (i.e., sports, physical fitness, health foods) is absent from the Israeli conversations. Israelis, on the other hand, tend to topicalize food and language more than Jewish Americans do." Blum-Kulka also found gender differences: "only in the Israeli families did we find men actually engaged in talk about shopping and preparing food" (1997: 88). There was a difference interpreted as dominance: "We have seen that in the Jewish American families the fathers raise more topics and talk more than the mothers and that this gender balance is reversed in the two groups of Israeli families" (1997: 90).

Findings such as these reinforce the warning given by Cameron et al. (1989): "It needs to be borne in mind generally that 'women' do not form a homogeneous group" (1989: 91). Freed and Greenwood (1996), in a small-scale study of same-sex dyadic conversations, report (1996: 21): "Our findings on the distribution of *you know* and the use of questions in same-sex friendly dyadic conversation show that it is the specific requirements associated with the talk situation that are responsible for eliciting or suppressing specific discourse forms, not the sex or gender of the speakers, or some abstract notion about the relationship of the speakers, or their group membership." This observation, though limited to only two features in the speech of a small number of speakers, should be kept in mind when strong claims are made about group differences in discourse. James and Clarke (1993) and James and Drakich (1993), in their critical reviews of research on interruptions and on amount of talk, found no significant differences between the sexes despite the many claims to the contrary.

Eggins and Slade (1997) examined three hours of casual conversation collected during coffee breaks in three different workplaces. They found that "the most frequently occurring stretch of talk in the all-male group was teasing or sending up (friendly ridicule)" (1997: 267). They did not gossip and tended to talk about work or sports rather than personal details. In the all-female group there was a predominance of gossip ("broadly defined as talk which involves pejorative judgment of an absent other" 1997: 278) and storytelling. There was no teasing. They discussed "quite personal details including boyfriends, weddings, marriages, children, and relatives" (1997: 268). In the mixed group of men and women "amusing or surprising stories dominated the conversation" (1997: 268), there was some joke-telling and some teasing. This is a small sample on which to base strong claims, but the results are interesting, so it is to be hoped that Eggins and Slade will explore this area further.

Schilling-Estes (forthcoming) points out the problems that can arise because one speaker's voice may be "fraught with echoes of the voices of others," not only in quoted dialogue (Macaulay 1987a) but in other subtle ways: "If people are continually uttering the words of others, then how are variationists to know which utterances they should count as a speaker's own and which they should not, especially given that bits of prior text are uttered in voices that may have been obviously altered to reflect source voices and sometimes not?"

Coates (1999) also looked at changes with age in the discourse of teenage girls, based on transcriptions of conversations among four white middle-class girls in London, recorded by themselves from the age of 12–15. This is a remarkable data set, judging from the examples Coates cites in her paper, as the girls range over a wide spectrum of topics, which do not vary greatly as they grow older, with one exception. In later conversations the girls provide "information of a highly personal nature" (1999: 126), which makes them more vulnerable, and "the ludic aspect of their talk decreases" (1999: 137). Coates reports that she was amazed at how much the 12-year-olds' talk differed from that of her female friends, and also how much the girls' talk changed over the years. As Coates remarks, "there is a dearth of research in this area" (1999: 142), which seems surprising, given the interest in all aspects of gender differences. This is an excellent example of small-scale research carried out with imagination, energy, and good will.

Another investigator to make use of resources close at hand is Morgan (1989, 1991, 1999), who recorded members of her own family. Morgan points out that most accounts of African-American English have been based on the speech of adolescent males who participate in the street culture. Morgan provides intergenerational information on how "as African-American girls grow into women, their everyday conversations often involve the expression and defense of social face" (1999: 37). Morgan (1991) also shows how indirectness is used and evaluated differently by African-American women than would be the case in mainstream society. Morgan's work, like Coates's, provides an insider's perspective on language use that would be hard to match by survey methods. Given the problems of obtaining valid samples of speech, this is an approach that would be even more valuable if the researchers would make more of the raw data available for comparative purposes.

Of course, all such samples are biased. As Mitchell-Kernan (1972) comments on her choice of informants from the mothers of children in pre-school playgroups in Oakland, "a sample which selects on the basis of the presence or absence of pre-school children is, of course, age biased" (1972: 13–14). Yet Mitchell-Kernan's description of "signifying," "loud talking," and "marking" remains one of the best accounts of speech behavior among African-American women. In discourse studies, the quality of the interaction recorded or reported is more important than any objectivity gained by random sampling methods.

Efforts using questionnaires to gain information about the use of features that are hard to record have not been noticeably successful. De Klerk (1992, 1997) used questionnaires to gain information on the use of taboo words and expletives by teenagers, but the results of self-report studies of this kind tend to be unsatisfying because one would like to know from actual examples who says what when. Hughes (1992) observed her speakers as well as administering a questionnaire and found that "their use of taboo or swearwords is an integral part of their language" (1992: 297) as anyone who had encountered them in their daily activities would know. But Hughes also found through her questionnaire that the women were more cautious about potentially blasphemous words such as *Jesus*, *Christ*, and *God*. This is the kind of information that can only be obtained through direct questioning.

Bates and Benigni (1975) used a questionnaire to investigate pronoun use in Italy, following up the original study by Brown and Gilman (1960). Their most interesting finding was that the lower-class speakers reported that they were more likely to use the formal terms (*Lei* and *voi*) than the upper-class speakers. Bates and Benigni offer an interesting explanation of this finding in social and political terms. This is a good example of the use of questionnaire methods not least because Bates and Benigni administered the questionnaires in a way that allowed respondents to explain and comment on their choices.

5   Quantitative Studies of Discourse Features

One of the first quantitative studies of a single discourse feature was Dubois and Crouch's investigation of the use of tag questions during the discussion sessions after papers at a small academic workshop. Contrary to Lakoff's claim (1973: 53–5) that women are more likely to use question tags than men, they found that all 33 tags in the sessions were produced by men (Dubois and Crouch 1975: 293). Interestingly, these results are sometimes reported (Cameron et al. 1989: 77, Holmes 1995: 84) as that men used *more* tags than women, not that *only* the men used tags.

Holmes (1984, 1995), using a balanced sample of men's and women's speech in New Zealand, found that women used more tags (51) than men (36). Cameron et al. (1989), examining examples from 25 speakers recorded as part of the Survey of English Usage (Svartvik and Quirk 1980), found that the men used almost twice as many tag questions (60) as the women (36). They give as a possible explanation that two of the men had known that they were being recorded, so perhaps "their speech reflected a concern to elicit as much talk as possible from other participants" (Cameron et al. 1989: 85) and increased their use of tag questions. This illustrates the problem of using surreptitious recording, when one of the participants knows about it. It also is part of a general problem of using "confederates" in interactional research (Duncan and Fiske 1985). More importantly, it illustrates a search for an explanation when the results are not what the investigators expected. This is legitimate but it draws attention to a fundamental problem in quantitative research of discourse features. To what extent can we trust the figures? In many cases, there will be no additional information available to the investigators that might help to explain apparent anomalies, but that does not mean that there may not be factors that skew the results. The most reliable way to check on unknown factors would be to carry out similar studies on equivalent populations, but few scholars are interested in replicating what they themselves or others have done.

Holmes (1984) introduced a refinement by classifying tag questions as either (1) epistemic modal (focusing on information); (2) challenging; (3) facilitative (encouraging the listener to speak); and (4) softening. She showed that women were more than twice as likely to use facilitative tags as men. Cameron et al. (1989) found that the proportion of facilitative tags was greater for women than for men but the total number of facilitative tags was greater for men (perhaps for the reason given above). Cameron et al. also report that the task of classifying the tag questions "was not unproblematic" (1989: 83), partly because most utterances are multifunctional. They also did not find intonation an infallible guide to the different categories of tag questions. They found that Holmes's framework "compelled us to make a somewhat artificial choice" (Cameron et al. 1989: 84) between categories. This point underlines one of the problems with replicating another investigator's method. While the method may appear straightforward when originally reported, attempts to repeat the procedures often raise questions about how to deal with borderline cases.

Erman (1993) reports on an examination of the speech of 22 speakers in the London-Lund corpus (Svartvik and Quirk 1980) for the use of what she calls "pragmatic expressions." The pragmatic expressions she tabulates are the phrases *you know, you see*, and *I mean*. She found that almost twice as many of these expressions occurred in same-sex sessions compared with mixed-sex sessions (Erman 1992: 228). She also found that the men used considerably more of these expressions than the women. She also found a functional difference in that "the women tended to use pragmatic expressions between complete propositions to connect consecutive arguments, whereas the men preferred to use them either as attention-drawing devices or to signal repair work" (1992: 217). Erman's conclusion is "that pragmatic expressions, although sometimes nearly depleted of semantic meaning, serve a number of communicative functions; they facilitate the speaker's encoding of the message as well as the addressee's decoding of it and serve interpersonal as well as textual ends" (1992: 233). Erman's work shows that it is not necessary to attribute specific meanings to discourse features in order to provide an enlightening analysis of their use.

Studies of discourse variation in terms of social class are comparatively rare, perhaps because in language studies in the USA social class is almost a taboo subject (despite Labov 1966), though not in Europe. The earliest quantitative study of social class differences in discourse is probably Bernstein (1962), based on small samples (about 2,000 words) taken from group discussions on the topic of the abolition of capital punishment. The subjects were males aged 15–18 in groups identified (on the basis of education) as either working-class or middle-class. Bernstein found that the working-class speakers "used a considerably longer phrase length (3.8 more words to the phrase) and spent much less time pausing (0.06 seconds) than the middle-class group" (Bernstein 1971: 87). He also found that the middle-class speakers used a high proportion of subordination, complex verbal stems, passive voice, uncommon adjectives, adverbs, and conjunctions, and the personal pronoun *I*. The working-class speakers used more personal pronouns (especially *you* and *they*) and what Bernstein called "sympathetic circularity sequences," tag questions and discourse markers, such as *you know* and *I mean* (1971: 115–16). Bernstein's pioneering efforts in discourse analysis have perhaps received less recognition because of the controversy that arose over the implications of his interpretation of his findings into restricted and elaborated codes (Rosen 1972, Trudgill 1975).

Dines (1980) examined the use of terminal tags (*and things like that, and that, or something*, etc.) in interviews with 18 middle-class and working-class women in Australia. She found that the working-class women used more than three times as many of these tags (58) as the middle-class women (18). Dines does not give any indication of the length of the interviews and we have to assume that they were roughly equal. It would have been helpful, however, if she had given relative frequencies (see below). Dines had earlier discovered that such tags were stigmatized. In looking at the use of the tags in relation to Bernstein's sociolinguistic codes, Dines found "that there is nothing to suggest that the occurrence of set-marking tags marks 'vague and inexplicit speech'" (1980: 30).

Dubois (1993) reports on a careful examination of similar features that she calls "extension particles" in the 1971 Sankoff and Cedergren corpus (Sankoff and Sankoff 1973) and the Montréal corpus of 1984 (Thibault and Vincent 1990).[1] Dubois found that in the overall use of these extension particles "there was no class difference discernible and no difference between the 1971 and 1981 interviews" (Dubois 1993: 185). Younger speakers used the most particles, and only in the 1971 data did women use more particles than men. There were, however, some significant differences in the kinds of extension particles used, showing the effects of time, gender, and class.

Vincent (1993), also using the 1971 and 1984 Montréal corpora, found gender, schooling, and occupational differences in the use of "exemplification particles" (e.g. *par exemple, comme, genre, disons*, etc.). Like Dubois, she found an age difference: "young speakers clearly produce more exemplifying utterances than do older speakers" (Vincent 1993: 160) but the decrease was not gradual over time. Instead, for both corpora, there is a break between those under 48 and older speakers. The similarity of these findings with Dubois' suggests that it might be worth looking to see whether there are qualitative differences between the interviews with younger and older respondents that might explain the differences in the frequencies with which these features are used. That this is likely follows from the conclusions of Vincent and Sankoff (1993) summarized below.

Vincent and Sankoff (1993) analyzed 13 interviews from the Sankoff-Cedergren corpus for the frequency of what they call "punctors." Punctors are assimilated prosodically to the preceding phrase, almost never preceded by a pause, show a high degree of phonological reduction, and have lost their original meaning or function (1993: 205–6). The punctors include *la* "there," *tu sais, vous savez* "you know," *n'est-ce pas* "isn't it so," and others. The number of punctors used by the 12 speakers ranges from 54 to 551. Vincent and Sankoff also give the frequency of punctors per line of transcription, showing that "the rate of punctor use increases with the length of the interview, that is, with loquacity or fluency of speech" (1993: 212). They also show that "punctors are not frequent in simple answers or when utterances are short, objective, and without much speaker involvement" (Vincent and Sankoff 1993: 212). They claim that the use of punctors is linked to fluency and expressivity. They conclude that the distribution of punctors "is conditioned by factors such as prosodic rupture [i.e. a break in the melody of the sentence], context, and genre of discourse; only the choice of individual punctors seems to be conditioned by social class" (1993: 214). This short article is a model for future analysis of discourse variation, not least because it does not depend upon interpretative judgments of variants.

In a small study of social class differences in discourse, Horvath (1987) found that the working-class speakers told almost all of their stories about themselves or members of their families (94.6 percent), whereas in the middle-class, just over half (53.8 percent) told stories about characters that were distant from the story teller, either public figures or strangers (Horvath 1987: 219). It would be interesting to know if this is a general social class difference.

In my own work, I have been interested in social class differences in Scotland (Macaulay 1977), and latterly in social class differences in discourse (Macaulay 1985, 1987b, 1989, 1991, 1995). In Macaulay (1985) I described the narrative skills of a Scottish coal miner, showing his effectiveness as a storyteller, but also providing quantitative information on the use of discourse markers and terminal tags. In Macaulay (1991) this kind of analysis was extended to a sample of 12 speakers with equal numbers of middle-class and lower-class speakers in the town of Ayr in southwest Scotland. I was able to show that the lower-class speakers used more discourse markers and highlighting devices, while the middle-class speakers used more derivative adverbs in *-ly*. This latter point was developed in Macaulay (1995), showing that the middle-class speakers also used more evaluative adjectives.

These works were based on interviews that I carried out myself. A major innovative feature in the study was that I transcribed the interviews in their entirety and thus could present comparisons in terms of the relative frequency of the use of a particular item. This is extremely important when comparing usage because speech samples are rarely identical in length. I have employed the same procedure in analyzing a set of same-sex conversations recorded in connection with a study of language change in Glasgow (Stuart-Smith 1999). Conversations between friends of approximately half an hour were recorded without the investigator being present. There were two age-groups (14-year-olds and adults over 40) and two social class groups (middle-class and working-class). The sessions were transcribed in their entirety and analyzed for age, social class, and gender differences. The results show that the adults talk more than the adolescents, and females talk more than males. The females tell more narratives than the males and use more quoted dialogue. The working-class women use the most quoted dialogue. One of the more notable global differences in topic is that the females talk more about people than the males. In particular, the girls talk about other girls and the women talk about other women. This was the case both quantitatively and qualitatively. As was the case in the Ayr interviews (Macaulay 1991, 1995), the middle-class speakers, both adults and adolescents, use more derivative adverbs in -*ly*. The women, both middle-class and working-class, use *you know* (8.34 per thousand words) almost twice as frequently as the men (4.48); the adolescents (0.86) use *you know* much less frequently than the adults (6.84). There are other features, such as the use of *well*, that show the adolescents do not make the same use of discourse features as the adults.

6   Prospects for Studying Variation in Discourse

As I said at the beginning, the study of discourse variation is still at an elementary stage. It will be obvious from the preceding review that there are many different approaches to the sociolinguistic investigation of discourse, and it would take a braver person than I am to assert with confidence that we have much solid information on gender, age, or social class differences. What we have are a number of intriguing claims that need to be tested again and again, by the same or different methods, in similar or different settings, with similar or different samples (Campbell and Fiske 1959).

Only when there is a convergence of results from numerous studies will it be possible to make confident claims about discourse differences. There are many known (and unknown) variables that may affect samples of speech. Yet we need not despair. One way forward lies in replication. As more studies are carried out, the influence of accidental factors may be easier to detect. Also, methodologies improve as we learn from the successes and failures of our own and others' work. New methods of analysis, such as those illustrated above, lead to more confidence in the results.

We have, however, reached a point where we can see what is needed in order to make progress in future work on discourse variation. Among them surely are these four aspects:

1   We need more data. The extensive use of the London-Lund corpus (Svartvik and Quirk 1980) shows what a valuable resource it has been. Yet it presents a very limited sample of speakers. The Corpus of Spoken American English (Chafe et al. 1991) will no doubt prove equally useful. But we need data from different groups in a variety of settings. Probably more use could be made of evidence from media archives (Dougherty and Strassel 1998, Elliott 2000a, 2000b, Franken 1983 [cited in Holmes 1995: 33–7], Holmes 1997b, Macaulay 1987b).

2   It would help if investigators, regardless of their own particular interest, would report as fully as possible on the frequency in their data of features that other scholars have studied, so that a store of comparative data could be amassed.

3   It is important that the relative frequency of features should be reported in similar terms. My own preference is the frequency per thousand words. Some investigators report frequencies in terms of lines in the transcript but this is less informative because the length of the lines may vary. Since computers provide a word count, it is easy to calculate the frequency per thousand words. It is much less informative to report the proportion of a variant used with no indication of the total sample of speech from which the figures have been derived. If percentages are given, the raw figures should also be provided.

4   As Sinclair (1992) points out, the impact of computers on the study of language is likely to be immense in the next few years. It may not be necessary to follow his guideline – "Analysis should be restricted to what the machine can do without human checking, or intervention" (1992: 381) – but it would be helpful to identify a set of discourse features that can be easily collected by mechanical means.

NOTE

1   The Sankoff–Cedergren corpus consists of 60 interviews with French speakers in Montréal in 1971; in 1984 these speakers were interviewed again, with the addition of 12 younger speakers.

REFERENCES

Bamberg, Michael G. W. (ed.) (1997). *Oral versions of personal experience: Three decades of narrative analysis.* Special issue of *Journal of Narrative and Life History*, 7: 1–4.

Basso, Keith H. (1990). *Western Apache Language and Culture.* Tucson: University of Arizona Press.

Bates, Elizabeth and Laura Benigni (1975). Rules of address in Italy:

A sociological survey. *Language in Society* 4: 271–88.

Bauman, Richard (1983). *Let your words be few: Symbolism of speaking and silence among seventeenth-century Quakers*. Cambridge: Cambridge University Press.

Bell, Allan (1984). Language style as audience design. *Language in Society* 13: 145–204.

Bernstein, Basil (1962). Social class, linguistic codes and grammatical elements. *Language and Speech* 5: 221–40. (Reprinted in Bernstein 1971.)

Bernstein, Basil (1971). *Class, Codes and Control*, Vol. 1. London: Routledge and Kegan Paul.

Besnier, Niko (1995). *Literacy, Emotion, and Authority: Reading and writing on a Polynesian atoll*. Cambridge: Cambridge University Press.

Bloch, Maurice (ed.) (1975). *Politial Language and Oratory in Traditional Society*. New York: Academic Press.

Blum-Kulka, Shoshana (1997). *Dinner Talk: Cultural patterns of sociability and socialization in family discourse*. Mahwah, NJ: Erlbaum.

Brenneis, Donald Lawrence and Fred H. Myers (eds.) (1984). *Dangerous Words: Language and politics in the Pacific*. New York: New York University Press.

Brown, Roger and Albert Gilman (1960). The pronouns of power and solidarity. In Thomas A. Sebeok (ed.), *Style in Language*. Cambridge, MA: MIT Press. 253–76.

Cameron, Deborah, Fiona McAlinden and Kathy O'Leary (1989). Lakoff in context: The social and linguistic functions of tag questions. In Jennifer Coates and Deborah Cameron (eds.), *Women in their Speech Communities*. London: Longman. 74–93.

Campbell, Donald T. and Donald W. Fiske (1959). Convergent and discriminant validation by the multitrait-multimethod matrix. *Psychological Bulletin* 56(2): 81–105.

Chafe, Wallace L., John W. Du Bois and Sandra A. Thompson (1991). Towards a new corpus of spoken American English. In Karin Aijmer and Bengt Altenberg (eds.), *English Corpus Linguistics: Studies in honour of Jan Svartvik*. London: Longman. 64–82.

Chomsky, Noam (1986). *Knowledge of Language: Its nature, origin, and use*. New York: Praeger.

Coates, Jennifer (1996). *Women Talk*. Oxford: Blackwell.

Coates, Jennifer (1997). One at a time: The organization of men's talk. In Sally Johnson and Ulrike Hanna Meinhof (eds.), *Language and Masculinity*. Oxford: Blackwell. 107–29.

Coates, Jennifer (1999). Changing femininities: The talk of teenage girls. In *Reinventing identities: The gendered self in discourse*. In Mary Bucholz, A. C. Liang and Laurel A. Sutton (eds.), New York: Oxford University Press. 123–44.

De Klerk, Vivian (1992). How taboo are taboo words for girls? *Language in Society* 21: 277–89.

De Klerk, Vivian (1997). The role of expletives in the construction of masculinity. In Sally Johnson and Ulrike Hanna Meinhof (eds.), *Language and Masculinity*. Oxford: Blackwell. 144–58.

Dines, Elizabeth R. (1980). Variation in discourse – "and stuff like that." *Language in Society* 9: 13–31.

Dougherty, Kevin A. and Stephanie M. Strassel (1998). A new look at variation in and perception of American English quotatives. Paper given at NWAVE-27, University of Georgia, October 1998.

Douglas-Cowie, Ellen (1978). Linguistic code-switching in a Northern Irish village: social interaction and social ambition. In Peter Trudgill (ed.), *Sociolinguistic Patterns in British English*. London: Arnold. 37–51.

Dubois, Betty Lou and Isabel Crouch (1975). The question of tag questions in women's speech: They don't really use more of them, do they? *Language in Society* 4: 289–94.

Dubois, Sylvie (1993). Extension particles, etc. *Language Variation and Change* 4: 179–203.

Dubois, Sylvie and Barbara Horvath (1993). Interviewer's linguistic production and its effect on speaker's descriptive style. *Language Variation and Change* 4: 125–35.

Duncan, Starkey, Jr. and Donald W. Fiske (1985). *Interaction Structure and Strategy*. Cambridge: Cambridge University Press.

Duranti, Alessandro (1994). *From Grammar to Politics: Linguistic anthropology in a Western Samoan village*. Berkeley: University of California Press.

Duranti, Alessandro and Charles Goodwin (eds.) (1992). *Rethinking Context: Language as an interactive phenomenon*. Cambridge: Cambridge University Press.

Eckert, Penelope (1990). Cooperative competition in adolescent "girl talk." *Discourse Processes* 13: 91–122.

Eggins, Suzanne and Diana Slade (1997). *Analyzing Casual Conversation*. London: Cassell.

Eisikovits, Edina (1989). Girl-talk/boy-talk: Sex differences in adolescent speech. In Peter Collins and David Blair (eds.), *Australian English: The language of a new society*. St. Lucia: University of Queensland Press. 35–54.

Elliott, Nancy C. (2000a). A sociolinguistic study of rhoticity in American film speech from the 1930s to the 1970s. Unpublished Ph.D. dissertation, Indiana University.

Elliott, Nancy (2000b). Rhoticity in 20th century English: A prestige pronunciation change in American film speech. Paper presented at Studies in the History of the English Language 1, University of California Los Angeles, May 26–8.

Erman, Britt (1993). Female and male usage of pragmatic expressions in same-sex and mixed-sex interaction. *Language Variation and Change* 4: 217–34.

Errington, J. Joseph (1988). *Structure and Style in Javanese: A Semiotic View of Linguistic Etiquette*. Philadelphia: University of Pennsylvania Press.

Franken, Margaret (1983). Interviewers' strategies: How questions are modified. Unpublished term paper, Wellington: Victoria University.

Freed, Alice F. and Alice Greenwood (1996). Women, men, and type of talk: What makes the difference? *Language in Society* 25: 1–26.

Gee, James Paul (1999). *An Introduction to Discourse Analysis: Theory and method*. London: Routledge.

Giles, Howard and Peter E. Powesland (1975). *Speech Style and Social Evaluation*. New York: Academic Press.

Goodwin, Charles (1981). *Conversational Organization: Interaction between speakers and hearers*. New York: Academic Press.

Gregersen, Frans and Inge Lise Pedersen (eds.) (1991). *The Copenhagen Study in Urban Sociolinguistics*, 2 vols. Copenhagen: C. A. Reitzels Forlag.

Halliday, M. A. K. and Ruqaiya Hasan (1976). *Cohesion in English*. London: Longman.

Hanks, William F. (1990). *Referential Practice: Language and lived space among the Maya*. Chicago: University of Chicago Press.

Harris, Zellig (1952). Discourse analysis. *Language* 28: 1–30.

Harris, Zellig (1963). *Discourse Analysis Reprints*. The Hague: Mouton.

Heath, Shirley Brice (1983). *Ways with Words: Language, life, and work in communities and classrooms*. Cambridge: Cambridge University Press.

Hill, Jane H. and Judith T. Irvine (eds.) (1993). *Responsibility and Evidence in Oral Discourse*. Cambridge: Cambridge University Press.

Holmes, Janet (1984). Hedging your bets and sitting on the fence: Some evidence for hedges as support structures. *Te Reo* 27: 47–62.

Holmes, Janet (1990). Apologies in New Zealand English. *Language in Society* 19: 155–99.

Holmes, Janet (1995). *Women, Men and Politeness*. London: Longman.

Holmes, Janet (1997a). Story-telling in New Zealand's women's and men's talk. In Ruth Wodack (ed.), *Gender and Discourse*. London: Sage. 245–93.

Holmes, Janet (1997b). Maori and Pakeha English: Some New Zealand social dialect data. *Language in Society* 26: 65–101.

Horvath, Barbara M. (1987). Text in conversation: Variability in story-telling texts. In Keith M. Denning, Sharon Inkelas, Faye C. McNair-Knox and John R. Rickford (eds.), *Variation in Language: NWAV-XV at Stanford*. Stanford: Department of Linguistics. 212–23.

Hughes, Susan E. (1992). Expletives of lower working-class women. *Language in Society* 21: 291–303.

Hymes, Dell (1974). *Foundations in Sociolinguistics: an ethnographic approach*. Philadelphia: University of Pennsylvania Press.

Irvine, Judith T. (1973). Wolof speech styles and social status. *Working Papers in Sociolinguistics* 23. Austin:

Southwest Educational Development Laboratory.

James, Deborah and Sandra Clarke (1993). Women, men, and interruptions: A critical review. In Deborah Tannen (ed.), *Gender and Conversational Interaction*. New York: Oxford University Press. 231–80.

James, Deborah and Janice Drakich (1993). Understanding gender differences in amount of talk: A critical review of research. In Deborah Tannen (ed.), *Gender and Conversational Interaction*. New York: Oxford University Press. 281–312.

Johnstone, Barbara (1990). *Stories, Community and Place: Narratives from Middle America*. Bloomington: Indiana University Press.

Katriel, Tamar (1986). *Talking Straight: Dugri speech in Israeli Sabra culture*. Cambridge: Cambridge University Press.

Keenan (Ochs), Elinor (1974). Norm-makers, norm-breakers: Uses of speech by men and women in a Malagasay community. In Richard Bauman and Joel Sherzer (eds.), *Explorations in the Ethnography of Speaking*, Cambridge: Cambridge University Press. 125–53.

Kendon, Adam (1990). *Conducting Interaction: Patterns of behavior in focused encounters*. Cambridge: Cambridge University Press.

Kipers, Pamela S. (1987). Gender and topic. *Language in Society* 16: 543–57.

Labov, William (1963). The social motivation of a sound change. *Word* 19: 273–309.

Labov, William (1966). *The Social Stratification of English in New York City*. Washington, DC: Center for Applied Linguistics.

Labov, William (1972). *Language in the Inner City*. Philadelphia: University of Pennsylvania Press.

Labov, William (1981). Field methods of the project on linguistic change and variation. *Sociolinguistic Working Paper*, No. 81. Austin: Southwest Educational Development Laboratory.

Labov, William (1982). Speech actions and reactions in personal narrative. In Deborah Tannen (ed.), *Analyzing discourse: Text and talk*. Washington, DC: Georgetown University Press. 219–47.

Labov, William (1984). Intensity. In Deborah Tannen (ed.), *Meaning Form and Use in Context: linguistic applications*. Washington, DC: Georgetown University Press. 43–70.

Labov, William (1986). On not putting two and two together: the shallow interpretation of narrative. Paper given at Pitzer College Forum, March 1986.

Labov, William and Joshua Waletztky (1967). Narrative analysis: Oral versions of personal experience. In June Helm (ed.), *Essays on the Verbal and Visual Arts*. Seattle: University of Washington Press. 12–44.

Labov, William, P. Cohen, C. Robins and J. Lewis (1968). *A Study of the Non-standard English of Negro and Puerto Rican Speakers in New York City*. Cooperative research report 3288. New York: Columbia University.

Laforest, Marty (1993). L'influence de la loquacite de l'informateur sur la production de signaux backchannel par l'intervieweur en situation d'entrevue sociolinguistique. *Language Variation and Change* 4: 163–77.

Lakoff, Robin (1973). Language and woman's place. *Language in Society* 2: 45–80.

Lakoff, Robin (1975). *Language and Woman's Place*. New York: Harper and Row.

Linell, Per (1982). *The Written Language Bias in Linguistics*. Linköping: University of Linköping.

Macaulay, Ronald K. S. (1977). *Language, Social Class, and Education: a Glasgow study*. Edinburgh: Edinburgh University Press.

Macaulay, Ronald K. S. (1978). The myth of female superiority in language. *Journal of Child Language* 5: 353–63.

Macaulay, Ronald K. S. (1984). Chattering, nattering and blethering: informal interviews as speech events. In W. Enninger and L. Haynes (eds.), *Studies in Language Ecology*, Wiesbaden: Franz Steiner Verlag. 51–64.

Macaulay, Ronald K. S. (1985). The narrative skills of a Scottish coal miner. In M. Görlach (ed.), *Focus on: Scotland*. Amsterdam: John Benjamins. 101–24.

Macaulay, Ronald K. S. (1987a). Polyphonic monologues: Quoted speech in oral narratives. *IPRA Papers in Pragmatics* 1/2: 1–34.

Macaulay, Ronald K. S. (1987b). The sociolinguistic significance of Scottish dialect humor. *International Journal of the Sociology of Language* 65: 53–63.

Macaulay, Ronald K. S. (1989). He was some man him: Emphatic pronouns in Scottish English. In Thomas J. Walsh (ed.), *Synchronic and diachronic approaches to linguistic variation and change*. Washington, DC: Georgetown University Press. 179–87.

Macaulay, Ronald K. S. (1990). Conversations as interviews. Paper presented at poster session International Pragmatics Conference, Barcelona July.

Macaulay, Ronald K. S. (1991). *Locating Discourse in Dialect: The language of honest men and bonnie lasses in Ayr*. New York: Oxford University Press.

Macaulay, Ronald K. S. (1995). The adverbs of authority. *English World-Wide*, 16: 37–60. (Reprinted in Macaulay 1997.)

Macaulay, Ronald K. S. (1996). A man can no more invent a new style than he can invent a new language. Paper given at Sociolinguistics Symposium 11, Cardiff, September.

Macaulay, Ronald K. S. (1997). *Standards and Variation in Urban Speech: Some examples from Lowland Scots.* Amsterdam: John Benjamins.

Macaulay, Ronald K. S. (1999). Is sociolinguistics lacking in style? *Cuadernos de Filologia Inglesa* 8: 9–33.

Macaulay, Ronald K. S. (2001). The question of genre. In Penelope Eckert and John R. Rickford (eds.), *Style and Sociolinguistic Variation.* Cambridge: Cambridge University Press.

Malinowski, Brontislaw (1923). The problem of meaning in primitive languages. In C. K. Ogden and I. A. Richards. *The Meaning of Meaning.* London: Kegan Paul. 296–336.

Malinowski, Brontislaw (1935). *Coral Gardens and their Magic.* London: Allen and Unwin.

McNeill, David (1992). *Hand and Mind: What gestures reveal about thought.* Chicago: University of Chicago Press.

McNeill, David and Elena T. Levy (1993). Cohesion and gestures. *Discourse Processes* 16: 363–86.

Mills, Sarah (1997). *Discourse.* London: Routledge.

Milroy, James and Lesley Milroy (1977). Speech and context in an urban setting. *Belfast Working Papers in Language and Linguistics* 2: 1–85.

Mitchell-Kernan, Clandia W. (1972). Signifying and marking. Two Afro-American speech acts. In John J. Gumperz and Dell Hymes (eds.), *Directions in Sociolinguistics: The Ethnography of Communication.* New York: Holt, Rhinehart and Winston. pp. 161–79.

Moerman, Michael (1988). *Talking culture: Ethnography and conversation analysis.*

Philadelphia: University of Pennsylvania Press.

Morgan, Marcyliena (1989). From down South to up South: The language behavior of three generations of Black women residing in Chicago. Unpublished Ph.D. dissertation, University of Pennsylvania.

Morgan, Marcyliena (1991). Indirectness and interpretation in African American women's discourse. *Pragmatics* 4: 421–51.

Morgan, Marcyliena (1999). No woman no cry: Claiming African American women's place. In Mary Bucholz, A. C. Liang and Laurel A. Sutton (eds.), *Reinventing Identities: The gendered self in discourse.* New York: Oxford University Press. 27–45.

Ochs, Elinor (1988). *Culture and Language Development: Language acquisition and language socialization in a Samoan village.* Cambridge: Cambridge University Press.

Ochs, Elinor and Carolyn Taylor (1995). The "Father knows best" dynamic in dinnertime narratives. In Kira Hall and Mary Bucholtz (eds.), *Gender Articulated: Language and the socially constructed self.* New York: Routledge. 97–120.

O'Connell, Daniel (1988). *Critical Essays on Language Use and Psychology.* New York: Springer-Verlag.

Rickford, John R. and Faye McNair-Knox (1993). Addressee- and topic-influenced style shift: A quantitative sociolinguistic study. In Douglas Biber and Edward Finegan (eds.), *Sociolinguistic Perspectives on Register.* New York: Oxford University Press. 235–76.

Rosen, Harold (1972). *Language and Class: A critical look at the theories of Basil Bernstein.* Bristol: Falling Wall Press.

Sacks, Harvey (1992). *Lectures on Conversation,* 2 vols. (ed. Gail Jefferson) Oxford: Blackwell.

Sankoff, David and Gillian Sankoff (1973). Sample survey methods and computer-assisted analysis in the study of grammatical variation. *Canadian Languages in Their Social Context*, ed. Regina Darnell. Edmonton: Linguistic Research Inc., 7–64.

Sankoff, Gillian (forthcoming). Adolescents, young adults, and the critical period: The challenge of the glottal stop in Glasgow. In Carmen Fought (ed.), *Sociolinguistic Methods*.

Schegloff, Emanuel A. (1992). In another context. In Alessandro Duranti and Charles Goodwin (eds.), *Rethinking Context: Language as an interactive phenomenon*. Cambridge: Cambridge University Press. 191–227.

Schieffelin, Bambi B. (1990). *The Give and Take of Everyday Life: Language socialization of Kaluli children*. Cambridge: Cambridge University Press.

Schiffrin, Deborah (1984). How a story says what it means and does. *Text* 4: 313–46.

Schiffrin, Deborah (1987). *Discourse Markers*. Cambridge: Cambridge University Press.

Schiffrin, Deborah (1994). *Approaches to Discourse*. Oxford: Blackwell.

Schilling-Estes, Natalie (1998). Situated ethnicities: Constructing and reconstructing identity in the sociolinguistic interview. Paper presented at NWAVE 27, University of Georgia.

Schilling-Estes, Natalie (forthcoming). Exploring intertextuality in the sociolinguistic interview. In Carmen Fought (ed.), *Sociolinguistic Methods*.

Sinclair, John M. (1992). The automatic analysis of corpora. In Jan Svartvik (ed.), *Directions in Corpus Linguistics*. Berlin: Mouton de Gruyter. 379–97.

Snow, Catherine E. and Charles A. Ferguson (eds.) (1977). *Talking to Children: Language input and acquisition*. Cambridge: Cambridge University Press.

Stuart-Smith, Jane (1999). Glasgow. In Paul Foulkes and Gerry Docherty (eds.), *Urban Voices: Variation and change in British accents*. London: Arnold. pp. 203–22.

Stubbs, Michael (1983). *Discourse Analysis: The sociolinguistic analysis of natural language*. Oxford: Blackwell.

Svartvik, Jan and Randolph Quirk (eds.) (1980). *A Corpus of English conversation*. Lund Studies in English 56. Lund: Gleerup.

Tannen, Deborah (1984). *Conversational Style: Analyzing talk among friends*. Norwood, NJ: Ablex.

Tannen, Deborah (1994). *Gender and Discourse*. New York: Oxford University Press.

Thibault, Pierrette and Diane Vincent (1990). *Un corpus de français parlé*. Québec: Université Laval.

Trudgill, Peter (1975). Review of Bernstein 1971. *Journal of Linguistics* 11: 147–51.

Urban, Greg (1991). *A Discourse-Centered Approach to Culture*. Austin: University of Texas Press.

Vincent, Diane (1993). The sociolinguistics of exemplification in spoken French in Montreal. *Language Variation and Change* 4: 137–62.

Vincent, Diane and David Sankoff (1993). Punctors: A pragmatic variable. *Language Variation and Change* 4: 205–16.

Ward, Martha C. (1971). *Them Children: A Study in Language Learning*. New York: Holt, Rinehart, Winston.

Watson-Gegeo, Karen Ann and Geoffrey M. White (eds.), (1990). *Disentangling: Conflict discourse in Pacific societies*. Stanford: Stanford University Press.

Wolfson, Nessa (1976). Speech events and natural speech: some implications for sociolinguistic methodology. *Language in Society* 5: 189–211.

Part III
Social Factors

Time

One of the distinguishing characteristics of variationist linguistics vis-à-vis areas of language study such as historical and theoretical linguistics has been its insistence that the structure of language in the mind and its patterning in the community cannot be fully understood without paying careful attention to a host of social factors in addition to linguistic considerations. We begin this section by taking a look at one extralinguistic factor that is central to the investigation of language variation and absolutely essential in the study of language change: time. The effects of time on linguistic structure are felt in individuals and at all levels of social organization, ranging from the small village to the "global community." Variationists are interested in change at all levels, as well as in disentangling genuine changes in the course of a language or language variety from age-related changes in the speech of individuals.

Central to the variationist program has been the revelation that language change need not be observed "after the fact" but can be viewed in progress. Sometimes this is accomplished by revisiting the same community at different periods (that is, observing change in real time), but most often it is done through observing change in apparent time – that is, differences across different generations of speakers. In "Real and Apparent Time," Guy Bailey discusses both types of evidence, noting that both must be used cautiously, since neither provides a direct reflection of change in progress. For example, the apparent-time construct is grounded in the assumption that individual vernaculars remain stable after adulthood, but this assumption has yet to be tested in full and most likely is not warranted with features of which speakers are highly aware or with any speakers who have not reached adulthood, even those in late adolescence. In addition, teenagers are very likely to display patterns reflective of age-grading – that is, linguistic usages associated with a particular life stage that are repeated in every generation – rather than genuine change in progress. Although real-time data might seem ideal for investigating language change, Bailey points out that they too must be interpreted with caution, since linguistic differences between two time periods do not necessarily represent authentic changes in a community vernacular but may actually have to do with differences in interview methodology, sampling procedure, or community demographics. However, when judiciously used, both real and apparent time data are indispensable in understanding language change in progress.

Although it may be wise to avoid pre-adult speakers in investigations of community language change in apparent time, Julie Roberts demonstrates in her chapter, "Child Language Variation," that studies of variation in the speech of even preschool children can yield intriguing findings. Roberts notes that the study of child language variation is a relatively new area of study, for both theoretical and methodological reasons. For example, it can take quite a long time to obtain sufficient data from young children for a solid quantitative analysis, and it is difficult to tell whether the variation that is observed is actually socially motivated or merely developmental. Despite the challenges, researchers have been conducting quantitative investigations of child language variation for decades, and interest in this area continues to expand. Roberts provides an overview of such studies and shows that, from the start, results have proven that children actually do exhibit socially significant variation (for example, in terms of social class and gender). In addition, a number of studies, including Roberts' own work with preschool children in Philadelphia, have shown that children from an early age acquire both social and linguistic constraints on variation and even participate in community language changes in progress. Finally, studies indicate that variation in children's speech is modeled closely on that of their caregivers. This strongly suggests that, contrary to mainstream generative linguistic belief, variation in language input is not "noise" that is discarded during the acquisition process but rather an important stage in the development of communicative competence (that is, the ability to use language appropriately in a range of social situations, with a range of interlocutors), rather than mere grammatical competence. Hence, the investigation of variation in child language holds great promise not only for variationists but all linguists interested in how language is structured in the human mind and across social groups.

In the final chapter in this section, "Patterns of Variation, Including Change," J. K. Chambers presents an overview of what he terms the "three overriding social categories in modern industrialized societies": age, social class, and sex, with a special focus on what each of these, especially age, has to tell us about language change. Whereas the stratification of linguistic variants across social class and gender groups is often indicative of stable sociolinguistic variation, stratification by age is often indicative of change. This makes it possible to observe change in progress at a single moment in time (given the cautions discussed in Bailey's chapter). In addition, we can also observe changes in progress by observing language at different time periods, even ones quite distantly removed from one another, since written documents from earlier time periods often display variability between old and new forms, as do recordings of present-day speech. Further, when one is able to examine variable usage levels in detail (as with real and apparent-time data gathered in more recent decades), one will usually find that new variants spread through communities in neat patterns, typically proceeding through a three-stage process in which an initial period of gradual adoption is followed by a period of sudden, rapid change, which in turn is followed by a final period of slow change. In the final section of the chapter, Chambers turns from the examination of *how* change progresses to the larger issue of *why*. Like all variationists, Chambers stands firm in the conviction that although new variants may come into being for linguistic reasons (for example, a marked feature may be altered so that it is unmarked), it is really social forces that drive language change. In particular, linguistic innovations, no matter how linguistically "natural," will not spread unless speakers have the opportunity and motivation to adopt them. In this age of ever-increasing contact among speakers of different languages and varieties, there is more opportunity than ever for dialect and language mixing and hence leveling. It remains to be seen whether speakers have sufficient motivation to relinquish local speech forms, with their strong connection to local identity, in favor of leveled varieties that allow for global communication.

NATALIE SCHILLING-ESTES

12   Real and Apparent Time

GUY BAILEY

The "synchronic approach" to the study of language change, the study of change in progress, forms one of the cornerstones of research in language variation and change. This approach has had an enormous impact both on our knowledge of the mechanisms of change and on our understanding of its motivations. In fact, Chambers believes that the study of change in progress might be "the most striking single accomplishment of contemporary linguistics" (1995: 147)

1   Apparent-time Evidence in Martha's Vineyard

Until the mid-1960s, most linguists concurred with Hockett's assertion (1958: 444–5) that the actual process of language change is unobservable – it can only be detected through its results. Historical linguists, the primary students of language change, simply relied upon the examination of data from different points in history to infer that linguistic changes had occurred and to describe the outcomes of those changes. The historical data provided little insight into how the changes had taken place or into what might have motivated them (except, of course, in the case of language contact). In work on Martha's Vineyard and in New York City in the 1960s, however, William Labov (1963, 1966) developed a set of methodological innovations that allowed linguists to track the progress of linguistic changes as they were taking place and thus established the basis for a synchronic approach to language change. These innovations included methods for quantifying the linguistic variation that is a prerequisite for language change; for examining how variation is embedded in the social and linguistic structures that motivate and constrain change; and for exploring the effect of contextual styles that are a response to the social evaluation of linguistic variants. Perhaps the most important innovation, though, was the apparent-time construct, a surrogate for the real-time examination of data at different points in history.[1]

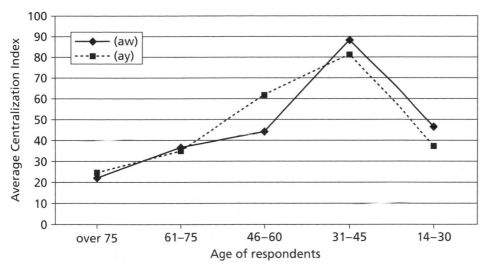

Figure 12.1 Centralization Index by age group for (aw) and (ay) on Martha's Vineyard

Source: Labov (1963)

Labov hypothesized that when social and stylistic factors were held constant, linguistic differences among different generations of a population (apparent-time differences) would mirror actual diachronic developments in the language (real-time linguistic changes). For instance, Labov argued that the increase in the use of centralized onsets of (ay) and (aw) in apparent time, as shown in figure 12.1, mirrored a diachronic increase in the use of these features on Martha's Vineyard. The youngest group does not have the largest index of centralization because, as Labov (1963) points out, the expansion of centralization was a reaction to threats to island identity, such as the need to leave the island to make a living, and these pressures had not yet affected the youngest islanders. Labov's comparison of these apparent-time distributions with real-time evidence collected for the Linguistic Atlas of New England some 30 years earlier corroborated his arguments.

While Labov's work on Martha's Vineyard and in New York City did not provide absolute confirmation of the validity of the apparent-time construct, it did demonstrate the value of the construct as a surrogate for real time in exploring mechanisms of language change. Examining the intersection of apparent-time differences with social and stylistic differences enabled Labov to show how innovations enter the speech of a restricted social group, spread to members of other subgroups, and either expand to the limits of the speech community or give way to retrograde changes. Labov showed, for example, that on Martha's Vineyard, the centralization of (ay) and (aw) began in the speech of Yankee fisherman (those of English descent) whose way of life was threatened by pressures to leave the island; it then spread to other groups as a

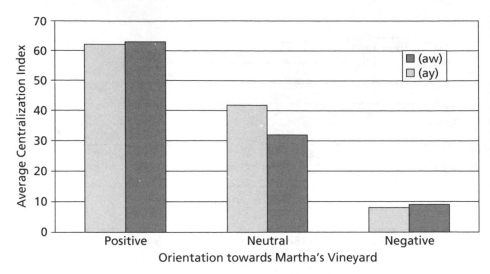

Figure 12.2   Centralization of (aw) and (ay) and orientation towards Martha's Vineyard

Source: Labov (1963)

marker of island identity. As figure 12.2 shows, the use of centralized onsets correlated strongly with a positive orientation toward the island – so strongly that Labov could conclude that the social meaning of this feature was "traditional Vineyarder."

2   The Use of Apparent-time Evidence

Largely as a result of Labov's success in using apparent time to explore the mechanism of language change, over the last 30 years linguists have used the apparent-time construct in a wide range of situations to make inferences about ongoing changes. Nevertheless, the apparent-time data are only a *surrogate* for real-time evidence, and apparent-time data cannot uncritically be assumed to represent diachronic linguistic developments. At least three situations pose potential problems for the apparent-time construct. These include the generality of apparent time (2.1), the stability of individual vernaculars (2.2), and the occurrence of age-graded features (2.3).

2.1   *The generality of apparent time*

While the apparent-time construct has been useful for exploring a wide range of features, how generally apparent-time differences represent ongoing linguistic changes is not entirely clear. To begin assessing the generality of the apparent-

Table 12.1   PST and GRITS features

Target item	Process	Innovative form	Conservative form
lost	merger of /ɔ/ and /ɑ/	[lɑst]	[lɔst]
walk	merger of /ɔ/ and /ɑ/	[wɑk]	[wɔk]
field	merger of /i/ and /ɪ/ before /l/	[fɪɫd]	[fild]
sale	merger of /e/ and /ɛ/ before /l/	[sɛl]	[sel]
school	merger of /u/ and /ʊ/ before /l/	[skʊl]	[skul]
Tuesday	loss of /j/ after alveolars	[tuzdl]	[tjuzdɨ]
Houston	loss of /h/ before /j/	[justn]	[hjustn]
fixin to	use of quasimodal	*fixin to*	—
Washington	intrusive /r/	[waʃɪŋtən]	[waɚʃɪŋtən]
forty-a	merger of /ɑ/ and /ɔ/ before /r/	[fɔɚɾɨ]	[fɑɚɾɨ]
forty-b	unconstricted postvocalic /r/	[fɔɚɾɨ]	[fɔəɾɨ]
thousand	fronted [aʊ] (to [æə])	[θæəzn]	[θaʊzn]
might could	use of double modal combination	*might could*	—
night	monophthongization of /ai/	[naːt]	[naɪt]

time construct, Bailey et al. (1991) compared apparent-time distributions of 14 features of Texas speech in a Phonological Survey of Texas (PST) and a Grammatical Investigation of Texas Speech (GRITS), both of which were completed in 1989, with real-time evidence for those features from the Linguistic Atlas of the Gulf States (LAGS), data for which were gathered some 15–20 years earlier. These features, which are listed in table 12.1, include both phonological and grammatical items. While many of the phonological features occur in other varieties of English, the two grammatical features are largely restricted to Southern American English and African-American Vernacular English. They are the grammaticalized quasimodal *fixin to* (meaning roughly "about to"), as in "I'd be happy to help you but I'm *fixin to* leave," and the multiple modal combination *might could* (meaning roughly "might be able"), as in "I *might could* come early if you need me to."

Of the 14 features, 11 show a straightforward relationship between apparent and real time, as shown in figures 12.3 and 12.4. Figure 12.3 shows the percentages of survey respondents by age cohort who use the innovative form of seven phonological and one innovative grammatical feature.[2] This figure shows a progressively increasing use of innovative forms across the four age groups for all eight variables, with the oldest cohort using the smallest percentage of each innovative form and the youngest using the largest percentage. Middle generations use percentages that are somewhere in between. Since age is statistically significant at the .05 level for each variable (determined by chi square tests) and since other social variables are controlled by the random sampling procedure, which ensures that factors such as social class and ethnicity will be

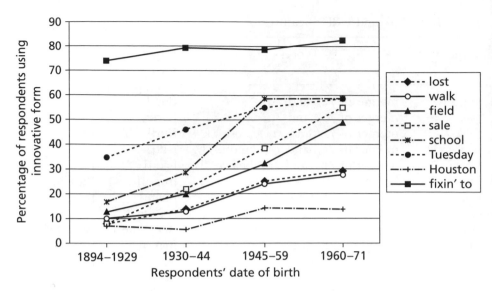

Figure 12.3   Apparent time distributions of innovative features in PST and GRITS
Source: Bailey, Wikle, Tillery, and Sand (1991)

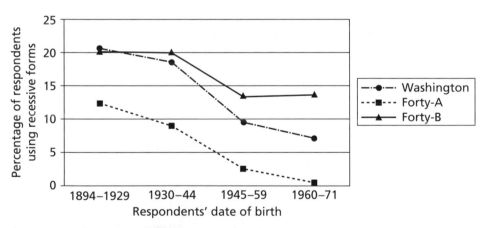

Figure 12.4   Apparent time distributions of recessive features in PST
Source: Bailey, Wikle, Tillery, and Sand (1991)

in proportion to their distribution in the larger population, the apparent-time distributions in figure 12.3 suggest that all eight variables represent diachronic changes that were in progress at the time when the survey was conducted.

The apparent-time distributions in figure 12.4, on the other hand, show a progressively decreasing use of recessive features, with a pattern that forms

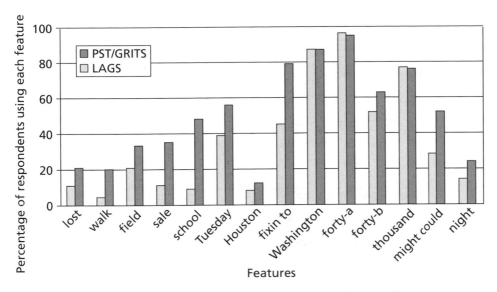

Figure 12.5 Real time comparison of PST/GRITS data with LAGS data

Source: Bailey, Wikle, Tillery and Sand (1991)

a mirror image of figure 12.3. Again, since age is statistically significant, the distributions suggest linguistic change in progress.

Real-time evidence from LAGS confirms the apparent-time distributions in every case, as figure 12.5 shows. For all of the features in figure 12.3, the percentage of PST or GRITS respondents who use the innovative form substantially exceeds the percentage of LAGS informants who do, indicating that these features represent innovations that are accelerating diachronically. For the features in figure 12.4, the percentage of LAGS informants who use the features either exceeds or equals the percentage of PST and GRITS informants who use the forms, confirming that the recessive features are gradually disappearing.

The apparent-time distributions of one of the remaining three features (the use of fronted onsets in *thousand*) suggest that no change is taking place – that the situation is one of "stable variation."[3] The difference in the use of the fronted onsets between the youngest and oldest age cohorts is less than 5 percent, and those differences are not statistically significant. The variation that does exist in the use of fronted onsets of /au/ is primarily a consequence of ethnic differences in the distribution of allophones. Anglos usually have fronted onsets as the result of a linguistic change that began during the last half of the nineteenth century and went to completion by World War II. African Americans and Hispanics, for the most part, did not participate in the process and generally have central onsets (see Bailey 1997). The real-time evidence from LAGS confirms the scenario of stable, ethnically conditioned variation: 77 percent of the LAGS informants have fronted onsets in *thousand*,

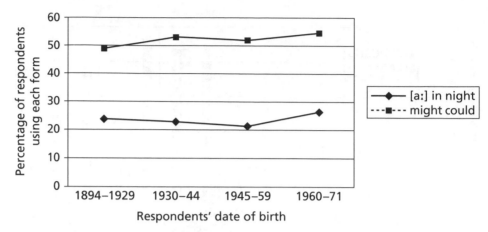

Figure 12.6   Apparent time distributions of *might could* and [aː] in *night* in PST/GRITS

while 76 percent of the respondents in PST do (see figure 12.5). Likewise, in LAGS Anglos are more likely to have fronted onsets, while African American and Hispanics are more likely to have centralized ones.

The distributions of the two remaining features (monophthongal /ai/ in *night* and the use of the double modal *might could*) are more complex. At first glance, their apparent-time distributions suggest situations of stable variation (see figure 12.6).

A comparison with the real-time evidence in LAGS (see figure 12.5) suggests diachronic change, however, with the use of these features increasing over time. In neither case does the real-time evidence actually contradict the apparent-time distributions, though. Rather, the large discrepancy in the occurrence of *might could* in the two surveys reflects methodological differences between them. LAGS generally relied on indirect elicitation to obtain tokens of *might could*, while GRITS relied on informants' self-reports on their use of the form. As Bailey et al. (1996), Bailey and Tillery (1999), and Tillery (2000) point out, the percentage of respondents who acknowledged using *might could* was far greater than the percentage who used the form in response to indirect elicitation, in large part because of the difficulty of framing questions that would actually elicit *might could*.[4] The differences in how the data were elicited for LAGS and GRITS account for most of the variation in the results of the two surveys, and the methodological differences between the surveys in this instance make assessing the status of *might could* impossible.[5]

The discrepancy in the use of monophthongal /ai/ in *night* also reflects methodological differences, but in this case the differences are resolvable since the discrepancy between the real- and apparent-time data reflects differences in the sample populations. The LAGS sample includes only native Texans, while PST and GRITS comprise a random sample of Texas residents that includes

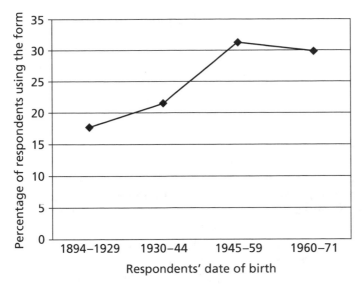

Figure 12.7 Apparent time distribution of [aː] in *night* among native Texan respondents in PST

Source: Bailey, Wikle, Tillery, and Sand (1991)

both natives and non-natives. An analysis of just the native Texans in the PST sample (see figure 12.7) helps clarify the differences between PST and LAGS in regard to /ai/ in *night*.

Figure 12.7 shows that when only native Texans are considered in PST, the data do in fact suggest a change in progress (i.e. monophthongal /ai/ is expanding in words like *night*); the apparent-time data, then, shows exactly what the real-time data lead us to expect.

The comparison of the apparent-time data from PST and GRITS with real-time evidence from LAGS clearly provides strong support for the generality of the apparent-time construct, at least for features of phonology and morphosyntax. In 13 of the 14 cases, the apparent-time distributions were confirmed by the real-time evidence, and in the remaining case methodological differences between the two surveys made the relationship between real and apparent time impossible to assess. In no case did the real-time evidence contradict the apparent-time evidence. Two points, however, should be made with regard to this comparison. First, the apparent-time data come from two random samples of 1,000 Texans each. The generality of the apparent-time construct for the data used here is in large part a function of the size and the representativeness of the samples. Smaller, less representative samples can be expected to produce less general and less valid results.[6] Second, the validity of the apparent-time construct has yet to be shown for lexical, semantic, or pragmatic features. Whether it is useful for exploring ongoing changes for these types of features remains to be seen.

2.2   *The stability of individual vernaculars*

Just as the apparent-time construct relies on the assumption of generality, it also relies on the assumption that in most cases individual vernaculars remain stable throughout the course of an adult lifetime. While many variationists believe that the vernaculars people learn in adolescence remain the basic vernacular that they use throughout their lives, only recently have data become available that bear directly on the subject. That data, of course, can only be acquired through re-interviews with the same informants over an extended period of time – through panel studies in real time. Labov indicates that the extant studies of the stability of phonological systems suggest that while "variables operating at a high level of social awareness are modified throughout a speaker's lifetime, with consistent age-grading throughout the community . . . , the phonological categories that underlie the surface variation remain stable" (1994: 111–12). Labov further notes that the relatively small number of vowel systems that have been investigated instrumentally show "no overall change that would justify a reinterpretation of the apparent-time data as a result of age grading. The most significant shifts are in the reverse direction: they show older speakers influenced slightly by the changes taking place around them" (1994:105).

Cukor-Avila (2000) has examined the stability of individual vernaculars in the rural Texas community of Springville, population 180. (Note that the name "Springville" is a pseudonym, as are all other names used in the project. In a community this small, residents could be identified by the substance of their interviews if the name of the community were known.) To test the assumption that individual vernaculars remain stable over the course of a lifetime, she examined the progress of four well-known features of African-American Vernacular English (AAVE) in the speech of four residents of Springville over a period of nearly a decade. These features include

(1)   zero third person singular, as in
    (a)   let's see how it *look* down there
    (b)   she *work* for the V. A. hospital

(2)   zero copula, as in
    (a)   he jumpin' barrels
    (b)   somebody puttin' the law on them folks

(3)   habitual *be+v+ing*, as in
    (a)   we *be* watchin' a really cute guy come in
    (b)   I *be* doin' those doctors [cleaning the doctors' offices]

(4)   *had*+past used as a simple past
    (a)   when I was workin' at Billups me an' the manager *had became* good friends
    (b)   an' one day I had came over to the store and' tha's when B. *had wanted* to go to work.

The four Springville residents – Wallace (b. 1913), Vanessa (b. 1961), Sheila (b. 1979), and Brandy (b. 1982) – were all first interviewed in 1988 and were frequently reinterviewed for a decade thereafter (see Cukor-Avila 1995, Cukor-Avila and Bailey 1995). Their different social histories provide a range of possible scenarios regarding the stability of individual vernaculars. Wallace was 75 years old and retired by the time of the first interviews in 1988, and while he was formerly quite active selling produce from his garden, his movements and social contacts have become increasingly restricted as he has gotten older. He was 82 at the time of the last interview.

At one time Vanessa spent most of her time in Springville, where she was the clerk at the only store in town, but her social contacts expanded significantly after she got a job as a maid at a nearby university in the early 1990s and began taking classes to help her qualify for her Graduate Equivalency Degree. She was 27 when she was first interviewed and 38 at the time of the most recent interview. Sheila spent most of her early life entirely in Springville, but when she was 12 she began spending summers in Wilson, a nearby city of 100,000. At that time she developed a new set of friends and an orientation away from Springville and toward the city. While in the ninth grade, she dropped out of school and moved to Wilson, although she still spends a great deal of time in Springville. Sheila was nine when she was first interviewed and 20 at the time of the most recent interview. Like Sheila, Brandy began spending most of her summers in Wilson after she turned 12, but unlike Sheila, she remained in school, graduated in May 2000, and is now preparing to attend college. Brandy was 6 at the time of her first interview and 17 at the time of the most recent one.

Figures 12.8–12.11 summarize the real-time data on the four AAVE features (copula absence, verbal -s absence, habitual *be+v+ing*, and *had*+past used as a simple past) for the four Springville residents. As figures 12.8 and 12.9 show, the data for Wallace and Vanessa provide strong confirmation of the stability of individual vernaculars. Like most African-Americans born before World War I, Wallace does not use *had*+past as a simple past and rarely uses habitual *be* (it comprises 0.04 percent of the tokens of the present tense of *be* during 1988–89 and does not occur at all during 1994–95). He does, however, frequently have zero copula and zero third person singular. As figure 12.8 indicates, his use of these features changed only slightly between 1988–89 and 1994–95, and the differences are not significant (as determined by a chi square test). While Vanessa does use both the innovative habitual *be* and the innovative *had*+past, her use of all four AAVE features remains virtually unchanged between 1988 and 1997, as figure 12.9 shows; none of the differences are significant. The stability of Wallace's vernacular is not surprising given his restricted social contacts and movement, but given the changes in her personal history, the stability of Vanessa's vernacular over a ten-year period is remarkable.

By contrast, the data on the vernaculars of the two younger residents, raises a number of questions about the stability of vernaculars of adolescents and teenagers. As figure 12.10 shows, Sheila's vernacular changed substantially between 1988 and 1998. When she was first interviewed, her vernacular was

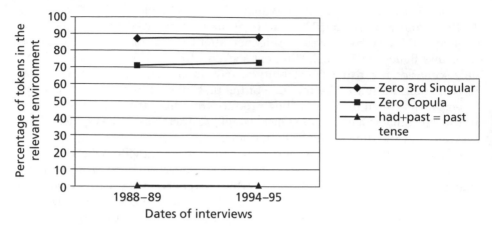

Figure 12.8   Real time distribution of three AAVE features in the speech of an African American male, b.1913

Source: Cukor-Avila (2000)

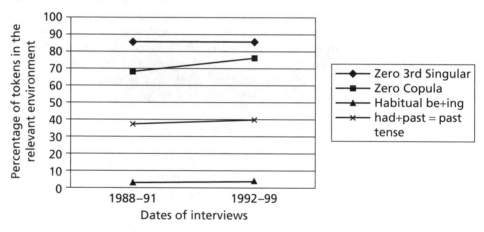

Figure 12.9   Real time distributions of four AAVE features in the speech of an African American female, b.1961

Source: Cukor-Avila (2000)

similar to that of older rural African-Americans. She used habitual *be* rarely (it comprised only 3.1 percent of her present tense of *be* tokens in 1988–89) and had no tokens of *had*+past as a simple past. After she began spending her summers in Wilson in 1990, her use of habitual *be* more than doubled in the 1991–92 interviews, and her use of *had*+past expanded to include nearly three-quarters of all her (morphologically) past perfect tokens (both developments are significant at the .05 level by chi square). Her use of zero copula and zero third singular also increased and continued to do so through 1998. The use of the former increased by more than 10 percent between 1988 and 1998,

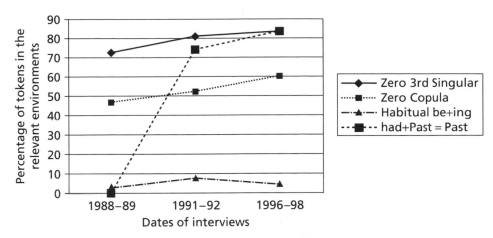

Figure 12.10 Real time distributions of four AAVE features in the speech of an African American female, b.1979

Source: Cukor-Avila (2000)

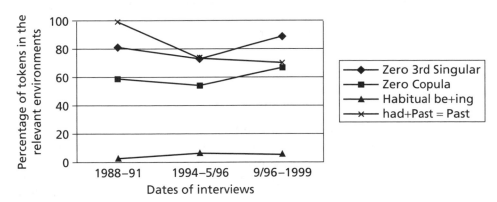

Figure 12.11 Real time distributions of four AAVE features in the speech of an African American female, b.1982

Source: Cukor-Avila (2000)

while the latter increased by some 14 percent during that time (both statistically significant). It seems clear that after 1990 Sheila's vernacular underwent a substantial shift away from the rural norms she grew up with and toward the urban norms she began to encounter in Wilson (cf. Bailey and Maynor 1989). This shift continued throughout Sheila's teenage years and only now as she is reaching adulthood does her vernacular seem to be stabilizing.

The data from the interviews with Brandy provide additional evidence that vernaculars may continue to change throughout even the late teenage years (see figure 12.11). During the 1988–91 period, Brandy's vernacular was generally like that of Sheila's before Sheila began spending summers in Wilson (the high rate of *had*+past use is misleading since there are only two relevant tokens in the data). As she began to spend summers in Wilson, Brandy was clearly affected by her urban peers (note the increased use of habitual *be*), but changes in her vernacular do not represent a straightforward linear development toward urban norms, like Sheila's, but rather the interplay of competing urban and rural norms. For instance, her use of both zero third person singular and zero copula decreased between 1988–91 and 1994–96 and then increased between 1996 and 1999. Her use of habitual *be* and *had*+past as a simple past, on the other hand, declined slightly (but not significantly) after 1994–96. While the full extent of the influence of urban norms on Brandy's vernacular is not yet clear, it is clear that her vernacular had not stabilized by the time she graduated from high school and that it is still developing.

When taken in conjunction, the research discussed in Labov (1994) and the evidence presented in Cukor-Avila (2000) provide strong support for the hypothesis that vernaculars generally remain stable during the adult years. The phrase *adult years* forms an important caveat, however. Cukor-Avila's data clearly demonstrate that in many instances the vernaculars of teenagers, even those of older teenagers, are not yet stable. It is only in the early adult years that we can reasonably assume that a vernacular is relatively stable. Apparent-time data that use teenagers as one of the age cohorts, then, must be viewed with some suspicion.

2.3   *The possibility of age grading*

Changes that are age-graded, that is, correlated with a particular phase in life and repeated in successive generations, have long been recognized as potential problems for the apparent-time construct. Chambers notes that "very few changes of this kind have been reported" (1995: 188). Most of those that have been reported involve the speech of children or adolescents and are thus less relevant to the apparent-time construct than they might otherwise be. More relevant to the construct are the sociolectal adjustments that young adults sometimes make in response to the pressures of the marketplace.

Research in both Canada and the United States suggests that in some cases adults, especially younger adults, may adjust their vernaculars toward the norms of the larger society to better meet the demands of their jobs. Sankoff and Laberge (1978) showed that market pressures were a significant factor in the occurrence of three grammatical variables of Montreal French: auxiliary *avoir* and *être*, complementizer *ce que/ qu'est-ce que*, and indefinite *on/ils*. To some extent, the linguistic changes that New Yorkers make in Labov's (1966) department store survey also seem to represent sociolectal adjustments to the new norm for constricted (r). Labov (1966, 1972) notes that in his New York City department store survey, the youngest Saks employees have the highest rate of r-fulness, but at Macy's it is the oldest group that has the highest rate of r-fulness (see the discussion below). Apparently, Macy's employees do not become aware of the norm for constricted /r/ that is pervasive in much of the United States until later in their careers, when their range of social contacts begins to expand. Responding to this broader social norm, they then make adjustments that Saks employees had made at an earlier age. The study of the effects of the marketplace is not well developed, but it seems clear that for young adults, professional pressures may have linguistic consequences. Age-grading that is driven by the marketplace is much more restricted in scope than is the age-grading that is associated with language acquisition. The relationship between these different kinds of age-grading has yet to be explored, but the possibility of its occurrence must be taken into account in any apparent-time study.

3 The Use of Real-time Evidence

At first glance, real-time evidence would seem to be the ideal mechanism for exploring language change, but real-time evidence actually poses a number of potential problems for researchers. Researchers who want to use real-time evidence for studying language change have only two options: (1) they can compare evidence from a new study to some pre-existing data, or (2) they can re-survey either a community (through a trend survey) or a group of informants (through a panel survey) after a period of time has elapsed. Neither option is without problems, but both can offer valuable insight into language change.

3.1 The use of existing evidence

In many cases, earlier linguistic evidence does not exist, and when it does, it often was not collected or organized in a manner that permits straightforward comparisons. For instance, linguistic atlas data collected between 1930 and 1980 exist for many parts of the United States. Linguistic atlases survey a region to catalog its primary linguistic features, outline the spatial (and to a lesser extent, social) correlates of those features, and provide a historical baseline for reconstructing their linguistic history and measuring their future development.[7] Linguistic atlases record the data they elicit using a fine-grained phonetic alphabet, and because of their historical and spatial orientation, they necessarily have samples that are biased toward older informants and rural areas. Variationists using atlas data to study phonological change may find that the detailed impressionistic phonetic transcriptions used to record atlas data actually provide so much phonetic detail that the transcriptions must be recoded to be comparable to data from other sources. Such recoding requires familiarity with the phonetic norms used by atlas scribes and introduces a potential source of error. Bailey et al. (1991) are able to use LAGS data profitably to test the apparent-time differences in PST mainly because Bailey was both a LAGS scribe (and thus intimately familiar with LAGS phonetic norms) and the principal transcriber of the PST data.

Differences in sampling procedures also pose potential problems. As Bailey et al. (1997b) have shown, relatively small differences in sample populations can have statistically significant effects on results, even when surveys are conducted in the same way. As noted above, differences between the sample populations of LAGS and PST account for the fact that the apparent-time distributions of monophthongal /ai/ in *night* in PST suggest stable variation in the use of this feature, while the differences between LAGS and PST suggest a change in progress. Further, as the discussion of *might could* above shows, differences in the ways that information is elicited can also create significant differences in results (Bailey et al. 1997b).

Although the effects of different elicitation strategies can sometimes be seen even within a single survey (see Bailey and Tillery 1999), apparent time evidence minimizes the variation that might arise from differences in sample populations, in elicitation strategies, and in the recording and presentation of data when evidence from an existing data source is compared to data from a new study. A re-survey of an area can also minimize this kind of variation by explicitly controlling for those factors.

3.2   Re-surveys

Labov notes that "the ideal method for the study of change is diachronic: the description of a series of cross sections in real time" (1982: 218) either through a trend survey (a series of independent random samples) or a panel survey (reinterviewing the same individuals over a period of years). Although re-surveys overcome many of the limitations of existing data, re-surveys are also not without potential problems (see Labov 1994: 73–112). For instance, if we were to re-do PST using the same methods (a random sample telephone survey), the sample populations of the two surveys would not be exactly the same simply because of the rapid, ongoing demographic changes currently taking place in Texas. In 1990, for instance, Hispanics comprised 25.6 percent of the Texas population, while Anglos comprised 60.6 percent and African Americans 11.6 percent. Projections for 2000, however, suggest that Hispanics now make up 29.7 percent of the population of Texas, while the proportion of Anglos has declined to 56.1 percent, and the African-American population remained stable (Murdock et al. 1997). These trends are expected to accelerate over the next few years so that the more distant from 1990 the re-survey is, the more different the sample populations are likely to be.

Because ethnicity correlates with many linguistic features in Texas, the demographic changes that affect the sample populations can be expected to have significant linguistic consequences. Thus a re-survey of Texas in 2000, for example, might find a smaller percentage of the Texas population using *fixin to* (as in "I'd be happy to help you but I'm *fixin to* leave") than our 1989 survey found. The decline in the percentage of *fixin to* users, however, would probably not reflect a change in progress, with a recessive feature disappearing, but rather a change in the demographics of the state. The segment of the population that uses *fixin to* the least, the Hispanics, is expanding rapidly, while the segments that use it the most (Anglos and African-Americans) are either declining or remaining stable. Thus even the apparent-time evidence from a re-survey might also suggest that *fixin to* was disappearing. Since the Hispanic population tends, on average, to be younger than the Anglo population, younger age cohorts in future samples will have higher percentages of Hispanics and, most likely, lower percentages of *fixin to* users.

Researchers conducting trend studies must always be on their guard against confusing demographic change with actual linguistic change within a population. While the evidence from trend studies must be interpreted carefully, they can provide significant insights into language change that either corroborate or lead to the reinterpretation of data from an earlier study, as Johnson (1996) and Fowler (1986) demonstrate. Fowler's precise replication of Labov's department store survey of (r) is particularly useful here since Labov relied heavily on the apparent-time construct in reaching his conclusions about change in New York City speech. In 1962 Labov attempted to gauge the encroachment of constricted /r/, the norm for most of the nation, into New York City, traditionally a bastion of unconstricted /r/. To do this, Labov carried out a rapid, anonymous survey of three Manhattan department stores: Saks Fifth Avenue, a high-end retail store; Klein, a low-end store; and Macy's, a mid-range department store. His basic assumptions were that the linguistic norms of the sales personnel in each store would mirror the linguistic norms of the customers and that, other things being equal, generational differences among personnel would mirror linguistic changes over time. In 1986 Fowler replicated Labov's department store survey by interviewing the same number of informants in the same stores (except that May's had to be substituted for Klein, which had closed) using the same set of questions asked in the same sequence.

Figures 12.12a and 12.12b, which present some of the results of both the 1962 and the 1986 studies, support Labov's hypothesis that the development of a new prestige norm of constricted (r) is leading to linguistic change, but the new data also show that the change is proceeding slowly and in a relatively complex manner. In addition, the re-survey confirms Labov's (1966) identification of a pattern of age-grading, or perhaps "sociolectal adjustment," to use Chambers' term (1995: 181–4), that is superimposed on the pattern of phonological change.[8] In upper-middle-class speech, exemplified by the data from Saks, the new norm is most evident in the speech of the youngest subjects, but in the speech of the lower middle class, exemplified by the data from Macy's, the norms for constricted /r/ are most evident in the oldest informants. Labov (1982) suggests that this pattern reflects the fact that members of the lower middle class only become aware of the new norm as their social contacts and

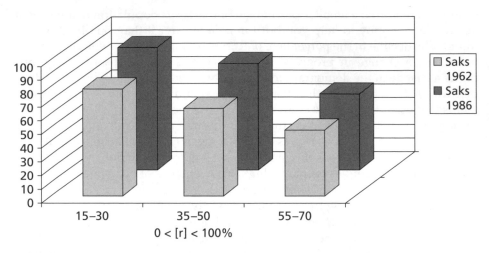

Figure 12.12a   Age stratification of (r) in Saks in 1962 and 1986
Source: Labov (1994)

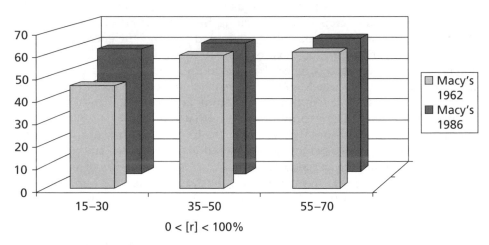

Figure 12.12b   Age stratification of (r) in Macy's in 1962 and 1986
Source: Labov (1994)

social awareness expand as they grow older. Hence they begin to shift toward the new norm at a later age. Labov (1994: 86–94) points out that the re-survey shows the same pattern of age-grading, though the basic rate of r-fulness has increased in the 24-year interval.

Panel surveys are not affected by demographic changes that transform the population of an area, but they present other practical problems. Researchers must find the same informants they originally interviewed and interview them again in the same way. The mobility of many populations makes finding the same informants a difficult task, especially in large-scale surveys. Further, the changing dynamics of communities may make it difficult to re-interview informants in the same way that they were interviewed earlier. Moreover, because it is difficult to re-interview all of the original informants in a panel survey, the sample is likely to be significantly smaller and less representative in the re-survey. Nevertheless, panel surveys are crucial for exploring stability and change in individual vernaculars, as discussed above, and may also offer insight into how linguistic changes diffuse.

The Springville project discussed above represents an attempt to carry out a panel survey on a relatively large scale. The project currently includes interviews with more than 80 residents of the area, half of whom have been interviewed at least twice. About half of these have been re-interviewed on an ongoing basis for more than a decade. The Springville evidence is particularly valuable in documenting the diffusion of features of urban AAVE to the surrounding countryside and in suggesting mechanisms by which this diffusion takes place. The data from Sheila presented above indicate that as late as the mid-1980s, the vernacular which Springville children, 12 years old and under, first acquired was for the most part the older, rural AAVE that had characterized Springville speech for a century or so (Bailey and Maynor 1989). As those children developed urban ties and became more oriented to life in nearby towns and cities as teenagers, they then acquired the urban AAVE that developed in cities after World War II. As these teenagers have reached their 20s, they have maintained the urban vernacular so that if things continue in this fashion, it will supplant rural AAVE as the primary vernacular of the Springville community (for details, see Cukor-Avila and Bailey 1996). In many respects, then, the evolution of Sheila's vernacular is a kind of microcosm of the evolution of AAVE in rural Texas.

4   Progress with Caution

Real-time evidence can clearly provide unique insights into the mechanisms of language change, but it often cannot be used in a straightforward, mechanical way. Real-time evidence introduces issues of comparability, sample design, elicitation strategies, and demographic change in the target population that must be taken into account. Further, the simple difficulty of acquiring real-time evidence often weighs against its use.

Fortunately, the apparent-time construct has proven to be an excellent surrogate for real-time evidence, and the relative ease of collecting apparent-time data means that it will be used most often in research on language change in progress. Like real-time evidence, though, apparent-time evidence often cannot be used in a straightforward, mechanical way. The value of apparent-time data is in large part a function of the size and representativeness of the sample from which it is taken. Moreover, researchers should use only adult cohorts in apparent-time studies, and even then they must be alert to the possible effects of sociolectal adjustments. When researchers heed these cautions, however, apparent time offers a powerful tool for the analysis of language change as it is taking place and forms the basis for a synchronic approach to language change.

In the best of circumstances, of course, researchers will be able to combine apparent-time data with real-time evidence, with the relative strengths of one approach offsetting the weaknesses of the other. It is in these circumstances that researchers will attain the kind of insights that revolutionize our understanding of language change and make the study of change in the progress the apogee not only of sociolinguistics but perhaps, as Chambers (1995: 147) says, of contemporary linguistics.

ACKNOWLEDGMENT

This chapter is based in part on Bailey et al. (1991). I wish to thank Jan Tillery, Tom Wikle and Patricia Cukor-Avila for their assistance.

NOTES

1   As Labov points out, he was not the first to use generational differences to make inferences about diachronic change. Gauchat (1905) had used apparent time to study sound change in the Swiss village of Charmey near the end of the nineteenth century. Hermann's (1929) reinvestigation of the village some 30 years later largely confirmed Gauchat's findings.

2   For a description of PST, see Bailey and Bernstein (1989); both PST and GRITS are discussed in Bailey et al. (1997a) and in Bailey et al. (1997b).

3   It may be that the proportion of the Texas population having fronted onsets will decline over the next three decades as the demographics of the state change, but none of the three ethnic groups shows any evidence of changing its norms for /au/. See Bailey (1997) for further discussion.

4   Internal evidence from LAGS confirms the role of question

strategies in obtaining data on *might could*. The one LAGS fieldworker who relied on self-reports rather than indirect elicitations to obtain the form accounts for more than a third of the LAGS data, even though she conducted fewer than a fifth of the LAGS interviews. See Bailey et al. (1997b).

5   Note, however, that the methodological differences do not affect every feature the same way. The GRITS data on *fixin to* also comes from self-reports, while the LAGS data again come primarily from indirect elicitation. Framing questions that would elicit this feature proved much easier than framing questions for *might could*, and those questions elicited more positive responses in LAGS.

6   Although linguists have sometimes argued that large samples are not as important for linguistic surveys as for

other types of surveys (see Sankoff, 1980: 51–2), there are no empirical studies which actually test the issue of sample size and representativeness in linguistics. Our work on survey methods, however, suggests that even small changes in sample populations can have significant effects on results in linguistic surveys (Bailey et al. 1997b). We are currently exploring the specific issue of sample size and representativeness.

7   See Pederson et al. (1986) for an example of contemporary linguistic atlas methodology.

8   The idea of a "superimposed pattern" represents my interpretation of the New York City data. It may be, however, that the pattern of change is superimposed on the pattern of age-grading since the effects of age-grading are larger than the effects of generational change (see Labov 1994: 86–94).

REFERENCES

Bailey, Guy (1997). When did Southern American English begin? *Englishes Around the World 1: Studies in Honour of Manfred Görlach*, ed. Edgar W. Schneider. Amsterdam: John Benjamins. 255–75.

Bailey, Guy and Cynthia Bernstein (1989). Methodology for a Phonological Survey of Texas. *Journal of English Linguistics* 22: 6–16.

Bailey, Guy and Natalie Maynor (1989). The divergence controversy. *American Speech* 64: 12–39.

Bailey, Guy and Jan Tillery (1999). The Rutledge effect: the impact of interviewers on survey results in linguistics. *American Speech* 74: 389–402.

Bailey, Guy, Jan Tillery and Tom Wikle (1997a). Methodology of a Survey of Oklahoma Dialects. *SECOL Review* 21: 1–30.

Bailey, Guy, Tom Wikle and Jan Tillery (1997b). The effects of methods on results in dialectology. *English World-Wide* 18: 35–63.

Bailey, Guy, Tom Wikle, Jan Tillery and Lori Sand (1991). The apparent time construct. *Language Variation and Change* 3: 241–64.

Chambers, J. K. (1995). *Sociolinguistic Theory: Language Variation and its Social Significance*. Oxford: Basil Blackwell.

Cukor-Avila, Patricia (1995). The evolution of AAVE in a rural Texas community: An ethnolinguistic study. Ph.D. dissertation. Ann Arbor: University of Michigan.

Cukor-Avila, Patricia (2000). The stability of individual vernaculars. University of North Texas MS.

Cukor-Avila, Patricia and Guy Bailey (1995). An approach to sociolinguistic fieldwork. *English World-Wide* 16: 1–36.

Cukor-Avila, Patricia and Guy Bailey (1996). The spread of urban AAVE: a case study. In Jennifer Arnold, et al. (eds.), *Sociolinguistic Variation: Data, Theory, and Analysis*. Stanford: CSLI. 435–51.

Fowler, Joy (1986). The social stratification of (r) in New York City department stores, 24 years after Labov. New York University MS.

Gauchat, Louis (1905). L'unité phonétique dans le patois d'une commune. *Aus Romanischen Sprachen und Literaturen: Festschrift Heinrich Mort*. Halle: Max Niemeyer. 175–232.

Hermann, M. E. (1929).
Lautverändergungen in der
Individualsprache einer Mundart.
*Nachrichten der Gesellschaft der
Wissenschaften zu Göttingen,
Philosophisch-historische Klasse*
11: 195–214.

Hockett, Charles F. (1958). *A Course in
Modern Linguistics*. New York:
Macmillan.

Johnson, Ellen (1996). *Lexical Change and
Variation in the Southeastern United
States, 1930–1990*. Tuscaloosa:
University of Alabama Press.

Labov, William (1963). The social
motivation of a sound change.
Word 19: 273–309.

Labov, William (1966). *The social
stratification of English in New York
City*. Washington: Center for
Applied Linguistics.

Labov, William (1972). *Sociolinguistic
Patterns*. Philadelphia: University of
Pennsylvania Press.

Labov, William (1982). *The Social
Stratification of English in New York
City*. Washington, DC: Center for
Applied Linguistics.

Labov, William (1994). *Principles of
Linguistic Change: Internal Factors*.
Oxford: Basil Blackwell.

Murdock, Steve H. et al. (1997). *The
Texas Challenge: Population Change
and the Future of Texas*. College
Station: Texas A&M University
Press.

Pederson, Lee, Susan Leas McDaniel,
Guy Bailey, and Marvin Bassett
(1986). *Linguistic Atlas of the Gulf
States*, vol. 1: *Handbook*. Athens:
University of Georgia Press.

Sankoff, David and Suzanne Laberge
(1978). The linguistic market and
the statistical explanation of
variability. In David Sankoff (ed.),
*Linguistic Variation: Models and
Methods*. New York: Academic
Press. 239–50.

Sankoff, Gillian (1980). *The Social
Life of Language*. Philadelphia:
University of Pennsylvania Press.

Tillery, Jan (2000). The reliability and
validity of linguistic self-reports.
Southern Journal of Linguistics 24:
55–68.

13 Child Language Variation

JULIE ROBERTS

Child language variation is a relatively new concentration within the field of sociolinguistics. To be sure, children have been included from time to time in studies of variation, beginning with Fischer's groundbreaking examination of (ing) variation among school children in 1958. However, the focus of this work has not been on children before adolescence for both theoretical as well as methodological reasons. The purpose of this chapter will be to review briefly the work leading up to the more recent interest in child language variation, to discuss the possible reasons for the relative neglect of this age group historically, and to examine recent work concentrating on the acquisition of variable features by young children and possible directions for future research.

1 History of Child Language Variation

There are a number of reasons why the early work on language variation and change did not focus on the speech of young children. For one, the field itself is only approximately 40 years old. It appears reasonable in a new field of linguistic study, particularly one building on that of dialectology – a notably adult-focused discipline – that data would be collected first on speakers who were thought to control the particular dialect in question and its variations. Children, on the other hand, were seen primarily as "acquirers" of the vernacular of a speech community, not necessarily as contributors to its maintenance and change. Indeed, Labov (1964) noted that although dialect features are learned during childhood, it is during adolescence that socially significant variation is demonstrated. In addition, with his early work (1963, 1966, for example), Labov initiated the study of language variation and change, including using synchronic data to illuminate past linguistic patterns and changes as well as to predict future change. This practice depends crucially on the assumption that dialect patterns, once attained in adulthood, do not change significantly throughout the life span. Although this assumption continues to be debated within the literature, it is the source of much synchronic work and encourages a focus on the speech of adults, since that of children acquiring a linguistic system would not, in principle, be useful in the study of historical processes.

In addition to adult-focused research, explorations of the speech of adolescents have also been extremely fruitful. The evidence for the robustness of the adolescent peer-group-created vernacular is abundant and will not be disputed in this chapter. Rather, it is suggested that the adolescent does not emerge, dialect intact, from a vacuum (Roberts 1999, Eckert 2000). The foundations for adolescent, and adult, speech patterns are laid down in childhood, during the early language acquisition process, and it would appear useful to look to the dialects of children for answers to some of the questions of linguistic variation and change.

As noted above, some very early variationist work did include children as participants. Most notably, Fischer (1958) found social variation in children, aged 3 to 10, and stylistic variation in a 10-year-old boy. However, he did not separate the children by age in his analysis, so it is impossible to state whether or not the youngest children in his study shared the pattern documented in his overall results.

Others examined variation in young speakers as well, but most frequently concentrated on school age, rather than preschool, children. For example, Romaine (1978) continued the exploration of social and stylistic variation in children by looking at the production of word final /r/ in Scottish English by 6-, 8-, and 10-year-old children and found gender, age, and style variation. Her conclusions were noteworthy not only because they documented the acquisition of social variation in young speakers, but also because she concluded they were participants in linguistic change. That is, the girls were taking part in a change from above the level of consciousness favoring a prestige variant, and the boys were participating in a change from below the level of consciousness favoring a variant with less, or perhaps covert, prestige. Similarly, Reid (1978) examined the production of glottal stop and the alternation of (ing) and found style variation in 11-year-old boys in Edinburgh, Scotland.

Purcell (1984) documented social and style variation operating on several variables produced by 5- to 12-year-old speakers of Hawaiian and "General" American English. She, like Fischer, did not break her findings down by age, making it impossible to determine the contribution of her youngest speakers to her findings. Nevertheless, the results are encouraging in showing the sensitivity to stylistic and social factors in the pre-adolescent years.

One of the first studies to look at variation in preschool children was also one of the first to examine linguistic constraints on variation in children of any age. Kovac and Adamson (1981) studied deletion of finite *be* in African-American and European-American 3-, 5- and 7-year-olds. This is a well-documented feature of African-American English (Wolfram 1969, Labov 1969, 1972, Baugh 1986, Rickford et al. 1991, among others). As has been found to be the case with other dialect features throughout the history of variation studies, *be* is deleted systematically by adult speakers and is much more likely to be deleted in some linguistic and social contexts than in others. For example, Labov (1969) demonstrated the relationship between contraction of *be* in European-American English dialects and deletion of *be* in African-American English. He found that contraction and deletion were favored by the presence of a preceding pronoun over a preceding noun, and by auxiliary *be* over copula *be*, particularly the *be* + *gonna* environment. Preceding phonological environment has also been found to affect contraction and deletion of *be*. By utilizing this variable and following the analysis of Labov (1969) the authors considered a question which continues to be critical in this field – that of developmental versus dialectal variation in child language. They found that for the European American children, absence of finite *be* appeared to be developmental in nature. For the African-American children, however, the results varied by socio-economic class. Working-class African-American children acquired the deletion rule before the middle-class children, whereas contraction preceded deletion for the middle-class children. The constraints on deletion were even more difficult to acquire than the rule itself. Although both grammatical and phonological constraints for contraction had been acquired by both groups of African American children by age 3, the constraints on deletion typical of adult speakers had not been completely acquired by age 7.

Guy and Boyd (1990) examined the grammatical constraints on (-t,d) deletion in their study of its use by speakers aged 4 to 65 in "semi-weak" or "ambiguous" past tense English verbs, such as *lost, told*, and *slept*. Like contraction and deletion of *be*, (-t,d) deletion is a widely studied phenomenon in dialects of English (Labov et al. 1968, Wolfram 1969, Fasold 1972, Guy 1980, Neu 1980). It is a form of consonant cluster reduction involving word-final clusters ending in /t/ or /d/ and is influenced by both the grammatical form of the word in containing the (-t,d) feature as well as phonological constraints, particularly the phonological segment following the cluster, and social features, such as gender, social class, and ethnicity (Guy 1980). Guy and Boyd concluded that acquisition of (-t,d) deletion in semi-weak verbs was potentially a long process, with the youngest speakers not producing the stop segments at all, leading the authors to conclude that they were not present in their underlying representations of the forms. A group of adult speakers deleted (-t,d) in final clusters in semi-weak verbs at an intermediate rate, between monomorphemic words and past tense verbs, demonstrating their analysis as a separate morphological class. A mid-level group, comprising older children and some adults, however, appeared to analyze the semi-weak verbs as essentially the same as monomorphemic words (e.g. *mist, cent*) and deleted the final segment accordingly, demonstrating that the treatment of the semi-weak verbs as a separate morphological class is incomplete even in some adult speakers.

Finally, Labov (1989) studied stylistic and linguistic variation for (-t,d) deletion and (ing) apicalization in a small sample of children and their parents outside Philadelphia. He found that a 7-year-old boy replicated his parents' patterns of stylistic and linguistic variation in (-t,d) deletion with the exception of treating semi-weak verbs identically to monomorphemic words. This child had also mastered both the linguistic and stylistic constraints on the alternation of (ing), a 6-year-old had mastered only the stylistic variation, and a 4-year-old showed no sign of acquiring the constraints on the (ing) alternation at all.

2　Current Issues in Child Language Variation

Early studies that included children in their participant groups suggest that children do acquire socially influenced variable patterns prior to adolescence and may even participate in the process of language change. Methodological challenges, however, make it problematic to answer some of the relevant questions that have emerged. One difficulty is that studies of variation generally require large amounts of data per speaker to be useful – either statistically or in charting vowel systems. In fact, Roberts (1996) reported that approximately 8–14 hours of child interview time was required to collect data on (-t,d) deletion comparable to that collected in a 1- to 2-hour adult interview. This amount of data may be difficult to collect from very young children. The early studies, discussed above, solved this dilemma either by using very small samples (one or two children) or by combining the data from their youngest children with that of older children, particularly as it must be collected in a short period of time to minimize the effect of maturation. Although these methods resulted in clear indications of acquisition of variation, more finely grained analyses are necessary to shed light on the resulting questions.

A second challenge in the exploration of child variation is the difficulty of distinguishing between variation that is socially motivated and that which is developmental in nature. This problem is complicated by the fact that, particularly as children become older, they become far more focused on their peers as primary dialect influences and much less so on their parents and other adult speech community members (Labov 1972, Eckert 2000). Eckert, in particular, notes the importance of emphasizing that the child's sociolinguistic system at any given age is not merely a "manifestation of an effort to develop 'real' language, but a fully mature linguistic form for that stage of language" (2000: 10). Although this child-centered focus on language acquisition is not new to psycholinguistic research (see, for example, Bloom and Lahey 1978), the child variationist, in fact, will receive less help from this field of inquiry than might be expected. One reason for this is that the primary focus of research in child language acquisition has been on categorical features of language. Although individual variation is acknowledged, it is frequently seen as a difference in learning style – with all styles leading to the same endpoint, the acquisition of an adult linguistic system and any remaining differences indicating potential communicative or cognitive disorders (Nelson 1973, 1975). For the most part, child language data have been examined minutely for structural consistencies in the speakers' utterances (Menyuk 1977). At the level of phonology, on which most variation studies, particularly child variation studies, have focused, the emphasis has also been on consistency and categoricity. Intra-speaker variation is characterized in terms of its difference from adult forms. As Ingram (1986: 223) states, "As the child gets away from the peculiarities of his individual 'little language', his speech becomes more regular, and a linguist can in many cases see reasons for his distortions of normal words." More contemporary child language research, following generative linguistic theory, centers on constraints on production, as opposed to rules and processes, but the emphasis continues to be on "emergent systematicity" (Vihman 1996).

Another reason that child language literature is of limited help in tackling the question of socially meaningful variation is related to the methodological challenge posed above. Early child language studies were often diary studies, first with researchers (often also parents) writing down productions of interest, then, later, tape recording them. (See, for example, Bloom 1973, Brown 1973, Labov and Labov 1976.) These studies involved very small subject groups – often only one child. They also tended to be longitudinal in nature, so although the total data pool might be quite large, individual samples at each age were often much smaller. As sociolinguists examine child language samples for the systematic variation located within language itself (as noted by, e.g., Weinreich et al. 1968), the need for larger quantities of data from each speaker becomes obvious. Within the past decade, studies have reflected these concerns by attempting to collect larger quantities of data from younger speakers. An ongoing challenge is that the younger the child, the more such features of child language as limited intelligibility and telegraphic speech greatly increase the time needed to collect a sufficient size data pool. At the same time, the researcher must collect speech samples efficiently to minimize the impact of maturation during the data-gathering period itself. In spite of these concerns, current research has included children at the very early stages of language acquisition as well as older ones. The next section discusses some of this work and its implications on child language and variationist literature.

3   Variable Output: Child Language Production

Whereas most, although not all, of the previously discussed work has included children as the lower end of the age range in a study of speakers of varying ages, more recently the focus of child language variation research has been specifically on these younger speakers. The resultant studies have been characterized, generally, by larger data sets and by child speaker groups broken down into more tightly compressed age ranges. Adults, often the children's parents, have functioned more as comparison data and, in later work, providers of the children's language input, much as they have functioned in studies of first language acquisition.

Labov (1989) noted that as children's language input is variable, as demonstrated by the voluminous research on adult variation, it stands to reason that children's output would be also. This statement, reasonable as it may seem, however, is a long way from demonstrating the connection between language input and a resultant child language system. This very connection has been hotly debated for years by psycholinguists and linguists engaged in the exploration of the nature vs. nuture question in child development. The role of language input in child language variation is discussed in the next section, but, in general, it is not necessary for variationists to enter into the center of this debate in order to discuss the modeling and acquisition of language features that are clearly socially governed and dialect specific. Therefore, the first of these more specific studies took as a working assumption that the early input children receive is indeed variable and examined instead the question of whether or not very young children reproduced these dialect features themselves and at what age.

For example, Roberts (1996, 1997a) examined the much-studied English variable (-t,d) deletion in 3- and 4-year-old Philadelphia children. As discussed above, social, grammatical and phonological constraints have all been found to be operating on the phenomenon of (-t,d) deletion in adult speakers of English. Whereas Guy and Boyd (1990) noted, among other findings, that very young children did not include these word final stops in their lexical representations of semi-weak verb forms, their study was, as noted above, characterized by a rather small sample of children in age groups spanning several years. The purpose of Roberts' study was to examine this same phenomenon with a larger sample of more closely age-matched speakers. Sixteen children served as participants in this study, which comprised 146 hours of audio-taping. Tokens of possible (-t,d) deletion items ranged in number from 44 from an especially quiet child to about 250 from more verbal children. The children were found to be well on their way to acquiring the phonological and morphological constraints on (-t,d) deletion found in many studies of adult speakers. They demonstrated an acquisition of the following segment constraint that was very close to that of adults, including the inhibiting effect of following pause on deletion, found to be typical in Philadelphia but not in New York by Guy (1980). This particular finding suggested strongly that the children were indeed learning socially significant features, not responding to a universal constraint of consonant cluster reduction. Further, the children demonstrated the adult pattern of deleting (-t,d) segments more often in monomorphemic words than in regular past tense verbs. For the semi-weak verbs, however, the similarity with adult speech ended, with the children consistently treating the semi-weak verbs like monomorphemic words (i.e. high probability of deletion, but not categorical deletion as found by Guy and Boyd) and the adults treating them like regular past tense verbs (i.e. low probability of deletion). In addition, examination of the data revealed that as the children produced increased numbers of more sophisticated grammatical forms, such as participles, they demonstrated adult-like deletion with them, suggesting that variation is learned simultaneously with the related grammatical and lexical forms. The resulting argument was that the children were indeed engaging in systematic variation, often quite similar in structure to those of their parents, and they did appear to include the final (-t,d) stops in their underlying representations of semi-weak verbs. The results strongly suggested that the children were formulating rules, not learning patterns in an item-by-item fashion, and they demonstrated adult-like patterns of deletion only when they shared an adult-like structural analysis. Finally, there were indications of early emerging gender differences, as the girls in the study deleted (-t,d) more often than the boys – a finding in contrast to most studies of the same variable in adult speakers. The study explored children's acquisition of stable variation only, however. It did not address children's acquisition of sound change in progress, nor did it explore the question of whether or not children were able to move beyond acquisition and participate in the variation and change patterns of the speech community of which they were a part.

Roberts and Labov (1995) examined these issues in a study of acquisition of the Philadelphia short *a* (as in *cat*) pattern by some of the same preschool children participating in Roberts (1996, 1997a). The vowel pattern in question is a highly complex one and features lexical, phonological, and grammatical conditioning. For example, short *a* preceding /f/, /θ/, /s/, /m/ and /n/ is raised and tensed, whereas in the environment of /p/, /b/, /d/, /k/, etc., the production of short *a* is low and lax. However, there are lexical exceptions to this phonological conditioning in that in the words *mad*, *bad*, and *glad*, in which short *a* would be predicted to be lax, it is, in fact, tense. In spite of the complexity of this pattern, the children demonstrated significant learning of Philadelphia short *a*. Some of the more straightforward and stable constraints, such as tensing before nasals and in *mad*, *bad*, and *glad*, were consistently produced. However, some of these patterns have been demonstrated to be in the process of change, such as the environments before /l/ (e.g. *personality*) and intervocalic /n/ (e.g. *planet*), to the tense short *a* class in adult Philadelphia speakers. Yet, they were still being acquired by the children. Between the ages of 3 and 4, they demonstrated active improvement in their learning of these features. They also showed increased rates of tensing in these environments where change was occurring as compared with adults, which suggested that they were beginning to participate actively in the process of language change. This finding has important implications to the future study of this area as it highlights the possibility that children of this age are interesting to variationists, not only because they are actively acquiring socially-governed features but also because they are influencing changes and may be indicating sites of change that may be accelerated or otherwise modified as the children mature.

Foulkes et al. (1999) also explored the acquisition of variation in preschool children. In their study of glottal variation in 40 children from Newcastle upon Tyne, aged 2 to 4 years, they found that children were able to learn sophisticated variable patterns at quite young ages. Glottalization of /t/ encompasses both the replacement and the reinforcement of /t/ by glottal stop. They pointed out that, unlike traditional phonological researchers, they were not interested in the emergence of phonological contrasts but rather in the range of alternants acquired by the children, and, similar to previous findings on other variables, they concluded that the children were making good progress in mastering the complicated glottal stop pattern. In addition, however, acoustic analysis revealed that high degrees of pre-aspiration of /t/ was found in the children's speech, including that of the 2-year-olds, for (t) in utterance-final position. This finding runs counter to those reported by others, such as Locke (1983, in Foulkes et al. 1999: 17), who claimed children to be "operating under phonological rules of simplification." This pre-aspiration pattern was found to be predominant in the speech of young women in Newcastle upon Tyne, but it was adopted by both the boys and girls in the study. Finally, there are some patterns of glottalization that are lexically restricted, such as the substitution of glottal stop for /t/ in word-final, pre-pausal position, as well as the use of [r] for /t/. Although amounts of this type of data were small in the samples (19 tokens), the children did appear to show sensitivity to this type of lexical conditioning, in that they produced [r] only in words that would tolerate them in adult speech.

The work discussed above demonstrates clearly that children begin their acquisition of variation early – presumably with the acquisition of language. Although the "teasing apart" of social from developmental variation continues to be a challenge in this area, there is evidence in the form of emerging gender differences and some early findings of style differences that socially motivated variation has its beginnings in the earliest phases of language acquisition (Reid 1978, Romaine 1978, Labov 1989, Roberts 1996, 1997a, Eckert 2000). Continued work, with even larger data sets, is necessary to do the type of examinations of social class and other extra-linguistic factors that have been so fruitful in adult language variation studies. In short, however, all of the preceding work underscores the point that children are indeed members of their speech communities from their earliest linguistic interactions and have much to tell us about early variation and change.

4   Variable Input: Child Directed Speech (CDS)

With the existing evidence supporting the hypothesis that children are acquiring variable patterns early along with categorical forms, researchers began to look more closely to the input children were receiving and to their responses to that input. Historically, variation in input has not been seen by the linguistic community as necessarily helpful to a child's acquisition of language. Rather, it has been viewed more frequently as detrimental, or part of the "noise" in the "degenerate quality" of the input data children receive (Chomsky 1965: 58). Even the considerable research on child directed speech (CDS), beginning with Ferguson (1977), is focused on the simplification, exaggeration, and consistency of the input and its effectiveness or, sometimes, lack of effectiveness in language teaching, not on its variety. Closer looks at input have been taken by variationists examining a number of features.

Labov (1990) noted the similarity between children's dialect-specific productions and those of their mothers, and hypothesized that the early child care situation which is often female dominated could lead to a favoring of female-led sound changes and a disfavoring of those led by males. Roberts (1997b) examined this hypothesis again, using the same Philadelphia preschool speakers. It was found that the female-led changes were, in fact, learned most effectively by the children as compared with the one male-led change – the centralization of long (ay), as in *kite*. In addition, even though all of the children in the study were natives of Philadelphia and attended day care with Philadelphia children and teachers, the changes were acquired most effectively by the children who also had parents who were Philadelphia natives. These results support the conclusion that early input is important, at least in the early learning of socially-influenced variables.

Foulkes et al. (1999) also noted the importance of early input. As previously noted, they found that the features of pre-aspiration characterizing the speech of young women were more easily learned by both the boys and girls in their study than features characteristic of adult men in the community. They also made the argument that rather than being dysfunctional to language acquisition, variation in the input to young speakers can actually enhance the movement from the holistic word level of representation to segmental awareness by producing allophonic examples, which "may serve to highlight the location of permutable components of words" (Foulkes et al. 1999: 20).

The movement from the lexical to the segmental level of phonological acquisition is a subject that continues to engage psycholinguists and developmental phonologists. Agreement as to the nature and timing of this process is still elusive. Whereas some researchers have found segmental awareness to occur early in the language acquisition process, others have reported that it continues well into the school years. (See Vihman 1996, for a review of this literature.) In addition to aiding this process in children, as Foulkes et al. propose, it is possible that the presence of socially-governed, allophonic variation in young children, noted by Foulkes et al. and Roberts (1996, 1997a) and others, also supports an argument for early segmental awareness. At the very least, the findings suggest an early beginning to this phenomenon.

This emergence of segmental awareness could also indicate to young children the locations of systematic variation in the input grammar – locations that could be exploited in later years. Some preliminary work on Southern American English, as spoken by mothers to their toddlers and to an interviewer in Memphis, Tennessee suggests that this may be the case (Roberts 1999). Three mothers and toddlers (aged 18 to 19 months) were tape-recorded during play. The variable in question was monothongal long (ay), as in [kaːt] for *kite*, documented both in Alabama speech (Feagin 1979) and in Memphis adults (Fridland 1999). Two of the three children produced both monothongal and diphthongal long (ay), while the third produced only monothongal (ay). As the toddlers

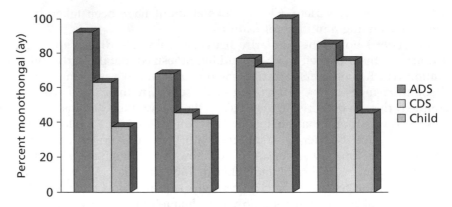

Figure 13.1 Comparison of adult and child directed speech of mothers and their toddlers' speech: monophthongization of long /ay/

were just beginning to acquire diphthongs, the variation in these speakers was most likely developmental, not socially governed. However, observation of two 4-year-old speakers revealed that their long (ay) productions also contained both monothongal and diphthongal tokens. Although further research is needed for documentation, it seems reasonable to hypothesize that in these children, the variation of long (ay) would continue, whereas children speaking dialects in which long (ay) is more consistently diphthongal would move from developmental variation to near-categorically diphthongal productions.

More than the behavior of the children, however, it was the Child Directed Speech (CDS) of their mothers that revealed some clues about the process of early dialect learning. CDS has been frequently studied by psycholinguists as a widespread way of speaking to very young children (Ferguson 1977). (Similar registers have been observed in speech directed to animals, foreigners, intimate acquaintances, etc.) Although the efficacy of this register in stimulating language development continues to be debated, it appears clear that to the extent that variation is present in CDS, it becomes part of the child's linguistic input. In the current study, the mothers were tape-recorded both playing with their toddlers and speaking to an interviewer. Although all three mothers demonstrated variation between diphthongal and monothongal (ay), they all used more diphthongal (ay) when talking to their children than when talking to an interviewer, as shown in figure 13.1. In addition, one of the mothers was especially straightforward in using CDS to instruct her child in the pronunciation of new vocabulary containing long (ay). When introducing a word, particularly a noun, she would produce it with great stress and exaggerate the glide. A likely interpretation of these data would be that the mothers are "instructing" their children in the more standard diphthongal production of (ay). Although this may seem to run counter to the claim that children learn variable patterns very early as they learn invariant ones, an alternative interpretation of the findings suggests that this is not the case. Rather, what the children are, in fact, exposed to is variable production of long (ay). The mothers use quite a bit of monothongal (ay) in both their talk to their children and to the interviewer. In the case of the mother described above, she is actually exposing her daughter to a wide-ranging variable pattern – from no glide at all to an exaggerated, highly stressed glide. The mothers in this study appear to be taking their role as "teachers of language" seriously and utilizing child directed speech to aid them in this process. Variation is present, and sometimes exaggerated, in first language input from very early stages!

Input is also important in the work in second dialect acquisition in children that builds on the work of Payne (1980), who found age and complexity of the feature in relation to the speaker's native dialect to be important factors in the adoption of Philadelphia dialect features by newcomers to the area. Chambers (1992) also found that age of exposure to the second dialect affected the success of its acquisition. That is, the children in his study who were exposed to a new dialect at a later age were far less successful at adopting it than those exposed at an earlier age. Chambers also postulated eight principles of second dialect acquisition to aid in the prediction of the process of dialect feature adoption by new speakers. Whereas some of these, such as the effect of orthographic representation on acquisition, have no relevance to first dialect acquisition, others may be seen as a jumping-off point for future research looking at how preschool and young children acquire dialect forms. For example, Chambers proposes that whether or not a target form is variable in native speech in the dialect being acquired, it is found to be variable in the speech of new speakers. He likens this phenomenon to the process of lexical diffusion in which language change is argued to begin in a few lexical items, then, when it has spread to a critical mass, is generalized into a rule or phonological process.

In a similar vein, Kerswill (1996) examined the dialect in the newly developed town of Milton Keynes. In this and previous work (e.g. Kerswill and Williams 1992), he, too, found that age of dialect exposure greatly affected the process of acquisition. The youngest speakers (aged 4) tended to adopt the features of their parents and, hence, to show more variation in this heterogeneous population than older children, who tended to coalesce toward a common norm. Kerswill also postulates a difficulty hierarchy for second dialect acquisition with vocabulary borrowing as the easiest process, which may be accomplished throughout the life span. The most difficult would be "lexically conditioned phonological rules, which may reflect lexical diffusion nearing completion and which are not sociolinguistically salient" (Kerswill 1996: 200). He hypothesizes that these rules must be learned by age 3 to be fully acquired.

Research on the variability of language input, as can be seen from the above discussion, is an especially new area of research in language variation and change. It can, however, be particularly helpful in looking at such issues as transmission of variation and change across generations. It would also seem to be potentially very useful in examining the genesis of language style in young children, since stylistic range is often accentuated in such registers as child directed speech. Finally, the integration of findings from second dialect acquisition research into that of first dialect acquisition would appear to be fruitful for both areas of study, particularly as some of the more complex dialect features (e.g. short (a) in Philadelphia and the lexically conditioned rules in Milton Keynes) appear to require an intensity of input that may become increasingly rare in more mobile populations or those in which dialect leveling may be occurring.

5   Looking to the Future: Social Practice and Young Children

Eckert (2000) discusses the importance of recognizing dialect variation among children and adolescents as a form of social practice. She notes that although adolescence is a time when vernacular forms accelerate, sociolinguistic competence has been developing for years. By secondary school, the social and educational institutions are such that the speaker's focus is concentrated to a large extent on peers, rather than on adults. Before that time, however, the focus of power and influence is not clear, or, one might say the transition from the full concentration on adults as the source of influence in infancy to the dominance of peer-group influence in adolescence is a gradual process. Such a transitional phase presents a challenge to researchers to sort out the influence of parents and other important adults from that of peers in earlier age groups. Another way of stating this is that determining the point at which children stop primarily imitating the social meaning of adults and begin to utilize language socially themselves is an important goal of child variation research – but an elusive one for the researcher due to the ephemeral nature of the developmental process. Therefore, as Eckert and research reported in the previous discussion show, much of the research on very young children has thus far concentrated on discovering the age(s) at which children acquire particular patterns of variation and their constraints. This work has resulted in important findings that children do, in fact, acquire sometimes complex variable patterns quite early and may begin the social use of variation at the same time. These results continue to be replicated with additional variables in additional dialects and speech communities. It would seem to be a goal of future research to add to these findings an exploration of the emerging social meaning of child variation within the family and peer group interactional settings.

An analogous situation may be seen in earlier psycholinguistic work. Following Chomsky's (1965) work, which had a huge impact not only on linguistics as a whole but also on child language theory and research, much psycholinguistic effort went into syntactic analyses of child language as compared with that of adults. Bloom and Lahey (1978) were among the first to note that child language would be more fruitfully studied if children's utterances were not seen as immature adult sentences and child speakers were not seen as miniature, but flawed, adults rather than fully competent speakers of child language. They make the following argument:

> In the course of development, children are not learning adult "parts of speech," and descriptions of the words that children use in terms of adult parts of speech can be misleading. Instead, children learn whatever forms they hear and see in conjunction with the regular recurring experiences that are represented in memory. Thus, it is only coincidental that in the model of the adult language, "cookie" and "sweater" are *nouns*, "see" and "put" are *verbs*, "there," "more," and "away" are *adverbs*, and "up" is a *preposition*. More important are the ideas, the elements of content that children represent with the words they use.
>
> (Bloom and Lahey 1978: 39)

Bloom and Lahey viewed child language as a viable and vital system in its own right, and one worth studying in all of its complexity. They developed the concept of semantic relations to explore how very young children coded meaning in their spontaneous speech. For example, the relational concept of *non-existence* can be described as an object which does not exist for the child but which the child thinks could exist. A child could express this concept using any of several forms. She could say, for example, "no," "gone," "allgone," or even the object name (e.g. "cookie") with a rising intonation while looking for the cookie. Some of these are adult-like forms, whereas others, such as "allgone," are present only in child language. All, however, serve the function of expressing the meaning of non-existence.

The change from a focus on child language as an imperfect, but emerging, adult system had a large and important impact on the study of child language acquisition. It seems unlikely, or at least of increased difficulty, that such a psycholinguistic advance would have taken place without the previous volume of research on adult language and that comparing emergent child language to an adult model. The same may be true of child language variation study. There is copious evidence of the richness and vitality of variation in adult language and less, but nevertheless increasing, evidence of children's ability to acquire this variation early in their language learning process. It appears to be time to delve more deeply into children's knowledge of variation and their ability to use it to produce social meaning. Again, preliminary results suggest a productive future for this type of work. Preschool children have been found to participate in language change, as shown by their adopting a lexical redistribution of short *a* words at a higher rate than their parents (Roberts and Labov 1995), and to adopt forms in a new dialect not produced by their parents (Roberts 1997b, Kerswill 1996). Gender differences have also been noted (Foulkes et al. 1999, Roberts 1997a). Current work on caretaker input for toddlers and young preschool children has the potential to teach us more about the direct and indirect teaching of language variation as social identity. It remains, however, for in-depth work to be done on the establishment of social practice in children before adolescence. As we look at the future of the study of language variation and change, surely an important aspect of this exploration is the newest speakers of the community as they acquire the dialect patterns of tomorrow.

REFERENCES

Baugh, J. (1986). A re-examination of the Black English copula. In W. Labov (ed.), *Locating Language in Time and Space*. New York: Academic Press. 83–195.

Bloom, L. (1973). *One Word at a Time: The use of single-word utterances before syntax*. The Hague: Mouton.

Bloom, L. and M. Lahey (1978). *Language Development and Language Disorders*. New York: John Wiley and Sons.

Brown, R. (1973). A *First Language, the Early Stages*. Cambridge, MA: Harvard University Press.

Chambers, J. (1992). Dialect acquisition. *Language* 68: 673–705.

Chomsky, N. (1965). *Aspects of the Theory of Syntax*. Cambridge, MA: The MIT Press.

Eckert, P. (2000). *Linguistic Variation as Social Practice*. Oxford: Blackwell.

Fasold, R. (1972). *Tense Marking in Black English*. Arlington, VA: Center for Applied Linguistics.

Feagin, C. (1979). *Variation and Change in Alabama English: A sociolinguistic study of the white community*. Washington, DC: Georgetown University Press.

Ferguson, C. (1977). Babytalk as a simplified register. In C. Snow and C. Ferguson (eds.), *Talking to Children*. Cambridge: Cambridge University Press. 209–35.

Fischer, J. (1958). Social influence of a linguistic variant. *Word* 14: 47–56.

Foulkes, P., G. Docherty and D. Watt (1999). Tracking the emergence of structured variation. *Leeds Working Papers in Linguistics and Phonetics*.

Leeds: University of Leeds. 1–25. (Also accessible on-line, www.leeds.ac.uk/linguistics)

Fridland, V. (1999). The southern shift in Memphis, Tennessee. *Language Variation and Change* 11: 267–86.

Guy, G. (1980). Variation in the group and the individual: The case of final stop deletion. In W. Labov (ed.), *Locating Language in Time and Space*. New York: Academic Press. 1–36.

Guy, G. and S. Boyd (1990). The development of a morphological class. *Language Variation and Change* 2: 1–18.

Ingram, D. (1986). Phonological development: Production. In P. Fletcher and M. Garman (eds.), *Language Acquisition: Studies in first language*. Cambridge: Cambridge University Press. 223–39.

Kerswill, P. (1996). Children, adolescence, and language change. *Language Variation and Change* 8: 177–202.

Kerswill, P. and A. Williams (1992). Some principles of dialect contact: Evidence from the New Town of Milton Keynes. In I. Philippaki-Warburton and R. Ingham (eds.), *Working Papers 1992*. Department of Linguistic Science, University of Reading. 68–90.

Kovac, C. and H. Adamson (1981). Variation theory and first language acquisition. In D. Sankoff and H. Cedergren (eds.), *Variation Omnibus*. Edmonton, Alberta: Linguistic Research. 403–10.

Labov, W. (1963). The social motivation of a sound change. *Word* 19: 273–309.

Labov, W. (1964). Stages in the acquisition of Standard English. In R. Shuy (ed.), *Social Dialects and Language Learning*. Champaign, IL: National Council of Teachers of English. 77–103.

Labov, W. (1966). *The Social Stratification of English in New York City*. Washington, DC: Center for Applied Linguistics.

Labov, W. (1969). Contraction, deletion and inherent variability of the English copula. *Language* 45: 715–62.

Labov, W. (1972). *Language in the Inner City*. Philadelphia: University of Pennsylvania Press.

Labov, W. (1989). The child as linguistic historian. *Language Variation and Change* 1: 85–94.

Labov, W. (1990). The intersection of sex and social class in the course of linguistic change. *Language Variation and Change* 2: 205–54.

Labov, W., P. Cohen, C. Robins and J. Lewis (1968). *A Study of the Non-standard English of Negro and Puerto Rican Speakers in New York City*. Cooperative Research Report 3488. Vols. 1 and 2. Philadelphia: U.S. Regional Survey (Linguistics Laboratory, University of Pennsylvania).

Labov, W. and T. Labov (1976). Learning the syntax of questions. In R. Campbell and P. Smith (eds.), *Recent Advances in the Psychology of Language: formal semantic approaches*. New York: Plenum. 1–44.

Locke, J. (1983). *Phonological Acquisition and Change*. New York: Academic Press.

Menyuk, P. (1977). *Language and Maturation*. Cambridge, MA: MIT Press.

Nelson, K. (1973). Structure and strategy in learning to talk. *Monographs of the Society for Research in Child Development* 38, Serial Number 149.

Nelson, K. (1975). The nominal shift in semantic-syntactic development. *Cognitive Psychology* 7: 461–79.

Neu, H. (1980). Ranking of constraints on /t,d/ deletion in American English: A statistical analysis. In W. Labov (ed.), *Locating Language in Time and Space*. New York: Academic Press. 37–54.

Payne, A. (1980). Factors controlling the acquisition of the Philadelphia dialect by out-of-state children. In W. Labov (ed.), *Locating Language in Time and Space*. New York: Academic Press. 143–78.

Purcell, A. (1984). Code shifting Hawaiian style: Children's accommodation as a decreolizing continuum. *International Journal of the Sociology of Language* 46: 71–86.

Reid, E. (1978). Social and stylistic variation in the speech of children: Some evidence from Edinburgh. In P. Trudgill (ed.), *Sociolinguistic Patterns in British English*. London: Arnold. 158–71.

Rickford, J., A. Ball, R. Blake, R. Jackson and N. Martin (1991). Rappin on the copula coffin: Theoretical and methodological issues in the analysis of copula variation in African-American Vernacular English. *Language Variation and Change* 3: 103–32.

Roberts, J. (1996). *Acquisition of Variable Rules: (-t,d) deletion and (ing) production in preschool children*. Institute for Research in Cognitive Science (IRCS) Report 96–09. Philadelphia: University of Pennsylvania.

Roberts, J. (1997a). Acquisition of variable rules: A study of (-t,d) deletion in preschool children. *Journal of Child Language* 24: 351–72.

Roberts, J. (1997b). Hitting a moving target: Acquisition of sound change in progress by Philadelphia children. *Language Variation and Change* 9: 249–66.

Roberts, J. (1999). Shifting vowels in tiny mouths: Toddlers' acquisition of Southern American English. Paper presented at New Ways of Analyzing Variation (NWAV) Conference, Toronto, October, 1999.

Roberts, J. and W. Labov (1995). Learning to talk Philadelphian. *Language Variation and Change* 7: 101–22.

Romaine, S. (1978). Postvocalic /r/ in Scottish English: Sound change in progress? In P. Trudgill (ed.), *Sociolinguistic Patterns in British English*. Baltimore, MD: University Park Press. 144–57.

Vihman, M. (1996). *Phonological Development: The origins of language in the child*. Oxford: Blackwell.

Weinreich, U., W. Labov and M. Herzog (1968). Empirical foundations for a theory of language change. In W. Lehman and Y. Malkiel (eds.), *Directions for Historical Linguistics*. Austin: University of Texas Press. 95–188.

Wolfram, W. (1969). *A Sociolinguistic Description of Detroit Negro Speech*. Washington, DC: Center for Applied Linguistics.

14 Patterns of Variation including Change

J. K. CHAMBERS

In their third postulate for a theory of language change, Weinreich, Labov and Herzog state: "Not all variability and heterogeneity in language structure involves change, but all change involves variability and heterogeneity" (1968: 188). In this chapter, I demonstrate some of the empirical ramifications of this postulate based on three and a half decades of variationist research. I show that the most salient cases of language variation make partly predictable patterns when plotted against their social correlates. Language change, as the postulate implies, is one type of linguistic variation, with particular social properties.

The demonstration depends upon case studies in terms of social class (section 1), sex and gender (section 2), and age (section 3). For age, the primary social correlate of linguistic change, I distinguish age-grading (section 4) from actual change (section 5), and then I deconstruct a change-in-progress in terms of regional discontinuities (section 6), social gradations (section 7), and, finally, sociocultural motives (section 8).

As illustrations, I have tried to select case studies that are prototypical, that is, as close to "pure" examples as I can find. As befits an empirical discipline, these cases are rooted in times and places, specifically in Detroit (Shuy 1969), Glasgow (Macaulay 1977), and central Canada (Chambers 1998b), but I have tried to emphasize their general properties as far as possible, seeking the broader implications that underlie the cases.

1 Variation and Social Class

The essential function of linguistic variables is to mark group membership. Age is one of the three overriding social categories in modern industrialized societies, along with social class and sex, and it is the social attribute that is the primary correlate of language change, as we shall see. Correlations of linguistic variants with the social class and the sex of speakers are not prototypically associated with language change, though members of one class or one sex may be leaders of the age cohort in the vanguard of the change. Needless to say, sex, class, and age are inextricable elements of individual identity (as Mendoza-Denton discusses in her chapter below), but certain linguistic variants have social value as expressions of one or another attribute, as we will see.

In every community that has been studied so far, sociolinguists have found that phonological variables tend to be distributed throughout the population, regardless of class, but graded so that the higher classes use particular variants infrequently and under more constrained circumstances, usually in casual settings with intimate participants. Grammatical variables are much more likely to be absolute markers of class membership. Syntactic features like multiple negation (as in section 2 below) and morphological variants like *ain't* occur in virtually all English working-class speech varieties but rarely in middle-class speech. They thus tend to be categorical distinguishers rather than graded ones.

A prototypical instance of a diffusely distributed phonological variable is glottal stop [ʔ] as a variant of /t/ in post-tonic position in Scotland and Northern England, in words like *butter, batting, Betty, forty, fitting* and *football* (Milroy et al. 1994). Macaulay notes that in Glasgow the glottal stop is "the most openly stigmatised feature" (1977: 47) and the one "most frequently singled out by teachers as characteristic of a Glasgow accent" (1977: 45). Ironically, the fact that it is the most characteristic feature does not stop people from complaining about it, that is, making it the most stigmatized feature.

Figure 14.1, based on Macaulay's work (1977: 47, table 16), provides empirical support for the teachers' impression of the glottal stop as characteristic of the Glasgow accent by showing that it occurs in the speech of all social classes, including the Middle Middle Class (MMC). Figure 14.1 also shows that it is stable, as indicated by the level lines from the adults to the 15-year-olds in each of the classes. Its use, in plain terms, is neither declining nor increasing in the speech of the young people as compared to their elders but staying about the same.

The gap between the MMC and the two working-class groups, the Upper Working Class (UWC) and the Lower Working Class (LWC), is enormous, about 70 percentage points. Clearly, what differentiates WC speech from MC speech in Glasgow is not the presence or absence of the glottal stop variant but its frequency. There is also a gap between the two WC groups, though a much less dramatic one at about 10 percent. The social classes arrange themselves hierarchically with the frequency of glottal stop variants decreasing up the social scale.

Membership in the Glasgow speech community entails using the glottal stop variant sometimes, regardless of social status, but there is clearly much more to it than that. It also entails a speaker's tacit knowledge of the frequency that is appropriate to one's social status, and this awareness serves both as a regulator of one's own usage and as an evaluator of the usage of others.

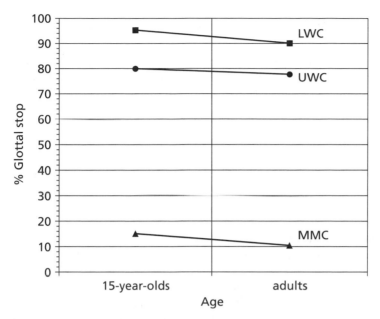

Figure 14.1 Percentage of the glottal stop variant for post-tonic /t/ in adults and 15-year-olds in three social classes in Glasgow
Source: Based on Macaulay (1977: table 16, 47)

Despite the use of the glottal stop across the social spectrum, Glaswegians of all classes share the opinion that the glottal stop is "unattractive" (Macaulay 1977: 112). The fact that it is heard very frequently in working-class speech does not imply approbation: middle-class and working-class subjects are in agreement about its social evaluation. Labov (1972) found a similar situation in New York, leading him to conclude that "the speech community is not defined by any marked agreement in the use of language elements, so much as by participation in a set of shared norms; these norms may be observed in overt types of evaluative behavior, and by the uniformity of abstract patterns of variation which are invariant in respect to certain levels of usage" (1972: 120–1). Put plainly, membership in the speech community is not defined by the simple notion that people speak the same, but by the more abstract notion that they evaluate communal linguistic variation similarly. Groups and individuals reflect the communal norms in complex ways, with subtly different mixes of concord and conflict (Rickford 1986), and the communal evaluation of norms shifts too, making participants "agents in the continual construction and reproduction of the [sociolinguistic] system" (Eckert 2000: 43; also see Patrick below). Membership is determined by consensus about community norms but not by conformity in their use, thus allowing people the latitude to express their diversity within communities.

2   Variation and Sex (and Gender)

Within the class norms, sociolinguistic research has discovered that women use fewer stigmatized and nonstandard variants than do men of the same social group in the same circumstances (as summarized by Eckert 1989, Chambers 1992, 1995a: 102–45). Consequently, speech communities are marked by consistent and, as we shall see, partly predictable linguistic correlations with sex.

An early illustration of what sociolinguists now recognize as a prototypical female/male difference arose in research on inner-city Detroit African-American vernacular. Shuy (1969) investigated, among other features, class-based patterns in the social distribution of sentences with multiple negation:

Standard (single) negation	*Multiple negation*
It isn't anybody's business.	It ain't nobody's business.
Nobody tells us anything.	Nobody don't tell us nothing.

Multiple negation is a grammatical feature, and as such we expect it to be sharply stratified in its social distribution. Figure 14.2 shows that the stratification increases from left to right, down the social hierarchy from Upper Middle Class (UMC) to Lower Working Class (LWC). In many other communities,

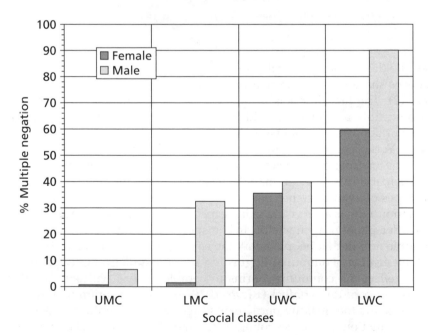

Figure 14.2   Multiple negation by African-American women and men in four social classes in inner-city Detroit

Source: Shuy (1969)

multiple negation is virtually nonexistent in MC dialects, but the communal norms in inner-city Detroit shift the threshold into higher social strata.

Not only is there a systematic class-based pattern in figure 14.2, but there is an equally systematic sex-based pattern as well. In each social class, the men score higher than the women. In the highest class (UMC), the men are the only ones who use multiple negations, and in the other MC group the women score very low (under 2 percent). So, in fact, the women's speech in this respect follows the typical pattern for white MC speech in many communities. The pattern of female/male differentiation carries over into the WC groups as well, though the norms are much higher and females as well as males show dramatic increases. Nevertheless, the pattern holds, with women using significantly fewer multiple negatives than the men in their social class – the men, that is, who are their husbands, brothers, and neighbors.

Wolfram (1969), in a broader study of the same Detroit community, found consistent sex-correlations on three other syntactic variables and four phonological variables, leading him to conclude: "Within each social class it is observed that females generally approximate the standard English norm more than males do" (1969: 215). This result has proven so robust in so many sociocultural settings as to lead sociolinguists to the general conclusion that "women . . . are more sensitive than men to the prestige pattern" (Labov 1972: 243) and that "females are clearly more concerned with the pressure exerted by local norms and asserting their status within the . . . social structure" (Romaine 1978: 156). Holmes (1997: 135) says, "language is an important means by which women assert their authority and position, a form of symbolic capital for women."

Other things being equal, it is the expected result in all comparable situations. For instance, the sociolinguistic setting for Glasgow glottal stop, discussed in the previous section, appears to share certain essential properties of Detroit multiple negation: both are class-based variables, sharply stratified, with the nonstandard variant stigmatized. We should therefore expect to discover that Glasgow glottal stop is sex-correlated within the class divisions. There is also, of course, an important difference in that the Glasgow variable is phonological, not grammatical, and should as a result be distributed more diffusely. But the overriding expectation will be to find that the females in each class score lower than the males.

Figure 14.3 bears out that expectation. The figure is complicated by the need to represent two age groups in each social class, which are then partitioned further into females and males. The Glasgow class stratification observed in figure 14.1 above is here decompressed, so to speak, into its male and female constituents, but it is no less visible in the squat bars for MMC contrasted to the towers for both UWC and LWC.

Within the class stratification, there is also sex stratification. The adult women and men, indicated by the left-hand bars in each social class, exhibit the expected relation exactly as did the adult women and men in inner-city Detroit, with the women in each social class scoring lower than the males. The 15-year-olds in all social classes show the sex-correlation but show it less obviously,

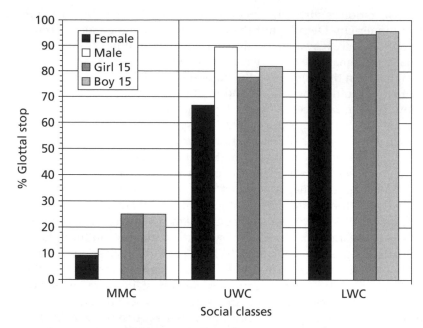

Figure 14.3 Glottal stops by male and female adults and 15-year-olds in three social classes in Glasgow

Source: Macaulay (1977: table 16, 47)

with nearly equal scores for girls and boys in two of the three classes (24.8 to 25 in MMC, 94.1 to 95.6 in LWC), suggesting that adult patterns are still emerging in the mid-teens, but the pattern is discernible because in all three classes the trend in the figures runs exactly as expected.

The female–male discrepancy with respect to nonstandard variants is so firmly established after decades of confirmation that it can serve as a sociolinguistic lemma, in the sense of an empirical expectation that stimulates further investigation into situations that fail to meet it. It is used this way, in effect, by Milroy et al. (1994), for unraveling a phonologically complex pattern of glottal substitution for post-tonic /t/ in northern England, where they ultimately discover that the female–male patterns are mitigated by the fact that females, when they use nonstandard variants, tend to use different ones from the males.

Why the female–male discrepancy exists has been subject to continual investigation and considerable speculation (see, e.g., Trudgill 1972, Deuchar 1988, Eckert 1989, Chambers 1992, Holmes 1997, Gordon and Heath 1998). One plausible explanation comes from the assignment of gender roles, the sociocultural division of labor for males and females. In many working-class enclaves, women tend to be more mobile than men, working outside the community in interactive positions as clerks, tellers, or office cleaners, and women rather than men tend to speak for the family in meetings with teachers, principals, landlords, and bank managers. It is in these communities where the female–male discrepancy is greatest. However, gender role differences can hardly be the whole explanation because the female sociolinguistic advantage also occurs in societies in which there is no clear distinction in gender mobility, as in the middle classes in virtually all modern, industrialized Western societies. Explanations as to why women characteristically use fewer nonstandard variants and a wider range of styles than men of the same social class in the same circumstances remains a challenge (as discussed more fully by Cheshire below).

3   Age and Variation: Change

Language variation can mark stable class differences or stable sex differences in communities, as we have seen in the previous sections, but it can also indicate instability and change. When it marks change, the primary social correlate is age, and the change reveals itself prototypically in a pattern whereby some minor variant in the speech of the oldest generation occurs with greater frequency in the middle generation and with still greater frequency in the youngest generation. If the incoming variant truly represents a linguistic change, as opposed to an ephemeral innovation as for some slang expressions or an age-graded change (section 4 below), it will be marked by increasing frequency down the age scale.

The sociolinguistic representation of linguistic change thus takes the same essential form as representations of class and sex markers, with age instead of class or sex as the independent variable. In the variationist paradigm, linguistic change thus falls out naturally as one particular kind of sociolinguistic variation. Weinreich et al. (1968), in the same article that set out the postulates for change, also claimed that "a model of language which accommodates the facts of variable usage and its social and stylistic determinants not only leads to more adequate descriptions of linguistic competence, but also naturally yields a theory of language change that bypasses the fruitless paradoxes with which historical linguistics has been struggling for half a century" (1968: 99). Their foresight has now been realized in numerous studies and is being refined continuously.

Before the advent of sociolinguistics, observations of linguistic change were traditionally made at two (or more) discrete points on a time line. Structural linguists like Bloomfield and Hockett maintained that that was the only way changes could be observed because apprehending them while they were in progress was theoretically impossible (Bloomfield 1933: 347, Hockett 1958: 444; discussed critically in Labov 1972: 21–3, 1994: 44–5, Chambers 1995a: 185–7). The structuralist position underlies Hoenigswald's assertion that "any historical statement contains, avowedly or otherwise, at least two synchronic statements – one for each of two or more stages" (1960: 3n). That is, the apprehension of change could only be made by comparing two historical moments in the history of the language.

The structuralist position was presumably a carry-over from nineteenth-century philology, which relied on textual evidence. The philologists assumed texts to be static. As we shall see immediately below, they were not actually static because they were not invariant, but the axiom of categoricity required that they be viewed as if they were. (On the axiom of categoricity, see Chambers 1995a: 26–30.) Thus Hoenigswald (1960: 1–2) said, "even if [the speaker] did not say such-and-such at a given time, he could have done so. So long as that is true, the investigator looks upon an idiolect (the corpus of utterances by one speaker) as something static."

Textual material is necessarily fixed but not necessarily static. A simple example (which also serves to introduce variable (wh), which I discuss in sections 5–7) comes from the two texts below, both translations of lines from the Aeneid, Book V, made some 375 years apart. The lines express Aeneas's reaction when his father's ghost appears momentarily and then abruptly disappears. In the Scottish translation by Gavin Douglas, ca. 1515, Aeneas cries out (V, xii, ll. 140–2 [1957: 232]):

> Quhidder bradis thou now sa fast, without abaid?
> Quhidder hastis thou swa? Quhom fleys thou? . . .
> Quhat is the let I may the(e) nocht embrace?

The same passage translated into English verse by Charles Bowen (V, ll. 743–4 [1889: 255]) goes:

> "Whither away?" Æneas replies; "why hurrying so?
> Whom dost dread? What bids thee avoid my loving embrace?"

The most obvious linguistic contrast in the two passages lies in the cognate question-words *quhidder*: *whither*, *quhom*: *whom*, and *quhat*: *what*; elsewhere Douglas also writes *quhy* (I, pro, l. 361) for the word Bowen writes as *why*.

We can infer that these spelling differences encode a phonetic difference, and from other sources we know what the phonetic values are. For most present-day readers, *whither*, *what* and *why* are pronounced with a voiced labiodental approximant [w]; for Bowen and his Oxbridge contemporaries as well as for some present-day readers, they are pronounced [hw] or [ʍ], that is, preaspirated or voiceless; for Gavin Douglas (1457–1522) and his Scottish contemporaries and for the English in the early Middle Ages, they were pronounced [xʷ], as a labialized voiceless velar fricative. So Douglas writes <quh> for [xʷ] where Bowen writes <wh> for [hw]. Douglas's usage preserves the sound in the Germanic language that was the ancestor of English. Before that, in Proto-Indo-European, the ancestor of Germanic, the cognate forms of these words were pronounced *kw, a labialized voiceless velar stop, which became Germanic [xʷ] by Grimm's Law. This historical sequence, still in progress (as we will see in section 5 below), represents a three-millennium lenition, a weakening from stop to fricative to approximant, and from voiceless to voiced, that I believe to be the oldest traceable sound change (Chambers 1998a):

*kw LENITION: PIE *kw > Germanic, Old English, Scots [x^w] > Middle English, modern Scots [hw] > modern English [w]

The historical record for these stages can be recovered from philological sources.

What has become apparent with the sociolinguistic apprehension of sound change is that every step in that history has involved variation and that the variation is discernible even in literary sources. For instance, Douglas normally wrote *quhen*, as we saw, but once he wrote *when* (X, xiii, l. 116: "That he may, when the son schynys aganen . . ." [1839 reprint of Cambridge MS, "presumably the author's personal copy" (Coldwell 1964: 106)]). This spelling variant suggests that even in Douglas's time Scots pronunciations were beginning to weaken from [x^w] to [hw]. The first published edition of Douglas's text tacitly substituted several lenited forms – *whare* (= "where") for *quhare* twice, *what* for *quhat* twice, and *when* for *quhen* once (Coldwell 1964: Glossary). This edition was published in London in 1553, 31 years after Douglas's death, and these variant forms were almost certainly introduced into the text by English editors or perhaps by English typesetters, but the fact that the text retains most of Douglas's *quh-* spellings might suggest that the [x^w] pronunciations had enough currency even in the south of England to preclude wholesale editorial or scribal transliteration.

Today, in the contemporary stages of this long drawn-out sound change, the phonemic contrast between preaspirated /hw/ and plain voiced /w/ survives in Scotland, Ireland, and Northumberland, the northernmost county of England, and in places settled by Scots and their descendants, including Ulster and the southeastern United States. In some places outside these areas, the [hw] variant has been eliminated, but in many communities it survives as variable (wh), heard in upper-class speech or the most careful middle-class styles or occasionally further down the social hierarchy as a kind of relic feature. In all these settings with the possible exception of Scotland, /hw/ is recessive in the sense that it occurs less frequently in the speech of young people than old (Chambers 1998a).

Canada is one of the places where /hw/ has been fairly persistent. Nevertheless, the [hw]-pronunciations have been in decline there for many years, as shown by surveys carried out at different times. Table 14.1 summarizes the results of three such surveys by indicating the percentage of subjects with

Table 14.1 Percentage of Canadians with [w] not [hw] in words like *which* and *whine* in two age groups surveyed about one decade apart

	Older	Younger	Source
ca. 1970	61	67	Scargill and Warkentyne 1972: 71
ca. 1980	63	90	DeWolf 1992: 107
ca. 1990	70	91	Chambers 1998: 25–26

/w/ where the traditional or conservative accent had /hw/, that is, the subjects who pronounce *which* the same as *witch* and *whine* the same as *wine*.

As in most independent surveys, the three surveys represented in table 14.1 are not perfectly comparable, taking in slightly different age groups and different, though partially overlapping, regions. In spite of these disparities, table 14.1 gives a coherent picture of change, with the numbers showing an increase from old to young in each row, and from decade to decade in each column.

The 1970 younger people in table 14.1 would have been about 40 by 1990, old enough that they might have qualified as older subjects for the 1990 survey. The 1970 score for younger people (67 percent) matches fairly closely the score of the 1990 older people (70 percent). By extrapolating across the time interval we might infer that the speech patterns set in late adolescence by the 1970 subjects were maintained in their adult years in 1990. In spite of the fact that this linguistic variable (wh) continued to change in the speech of people who came after them (younger people in 1980, for instance, at 90 percent), the 1970 adolescents evidently did not keep on changing but instead stuck with the variable pattern of their formative years. This rudimentary observation lies at the core of the apparent-time hypothesis, the theoretical construct that underlies many of the breakthroughs in sociolinguistics and contemporary historical linguistics (as discussed by Bailey above). "Apparent time" assumes that people of different ages preserve the speech patterns of their formative years. Speech differences between people of different ages therefore reflect differences in the way people spoke in those years.

Apparent time is the antonym of "real time." In table 14.1, the three surveys were undertaken at real-time intervals of ten years. The results summarized there cover 20 years from the first survey (1970) to the last (1990). Apparent time, in so far as it accurately reflects real time, obviates the need for waiting 20 years (or whatever duration) to gather data. Instead, researchers can interview subjects whose ages differ by 20 years and compare the results. Besides eliminating the waiting interval, apparent-time surveys also permit data-collection in identical settings and circumstances, thereby eliminating the comparability problems that we noticed for table 14.1.

4   Age-grading

That apparent time reflects real time is a hypothesis, not an axiom or a theorem. One sociolinguistic situation that does not conform to the apparent-time hypothesis is age-grading, whereby members of a speech community alter their speech at some juncture in their lives in such a way as to bring it into conformity with adult norms. This retrenchment, so to speak, undoes what might appear, under ordinary circumstances, to be an incipient linguistic change. In the best-documented cases of age-grading (Chambers 1995: 188–93), the linguistic retrenchment occurs in adolescence and has the status of a coming-of-age ritual.

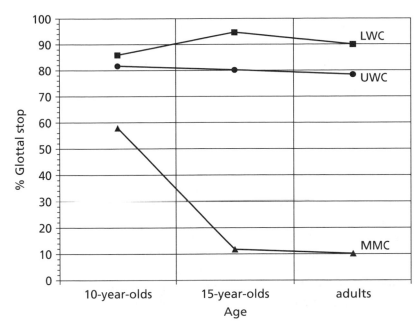

Figure 14.4   Percentage of the glottal stop variant for post-tonic /t/ in adults, 15-year-olds, and 10-year-olds in three social classes in Glasgow
Source: Macaulay (1977: table 16)

One such situation occurs in Glasgow and involves the glottal stop variant which is, as we saw in figure 14.1 above, a stable class marker. Figure 14.4 repeats figure 14.1, but adds another age group, 10-year-olds, to each of the social classes. In the two working-class groups, there is nothing exceptional about the 10-year-olds: they use the glottal stop variant with very similar frequencies to their older siblings and their parents. Their behavior simply reinforces the previous conclusions about the stability of glottal stop in Glasgow and its role in class-marking.

The same is definitely not true for the 10-year-olds in the MMC. They use the glottal variant much more frequently than others in their class and, in fact, show a frequency closer to the WC. Other things being equal, it would not be unreasonable to infer that the 10-year-olds might be leading a change in the direction of the WC norm. But we know that other things are not equal in this situation. For one thing, we know that this variable is stable in the community and, for another thing, we know that it is highly stigmatized. From this perspective, we can see that the sharp downturn from the MC 10-year-olds to the 15-year-olds constitutes a rapid accommodation to the MC norm.

What appears to be happening is that around puberty the MC youngsters begin to curtail their use of the WC marker in their speech, presumably in response to adult pressures. Ideally, we need real-time evidence to corroborate this inference, and we can only presume that real-time evidence would reveal the pattern of "correction" repeating itself in successive cohorts of 10- and 15-year-olds. Until the real-time evidence can be gathered, the weight of evidence from the apparent-time data allows reasonable confidence for this inference on its own.

5   Change in Progress

Unlike age-grading, change in progress shows incremental increases in the use of a particular variant in the speech of younger people. Figure 14.5 illustrates a well-behaved change in progress. It shows a steady rise for the age groups from old to young, with the octogenarians on the left, the teenagers on the right, and subjects in descending ages by decades in between. The line graph plots the use of the innovative or incoming variant as a percentage for each age group: this is variable (wh), introduced above, and the percentages record the proportions of people in each age group who have merged the phonemes /hw/ and /w/ into the latter, the voiced labiovelar approximant.

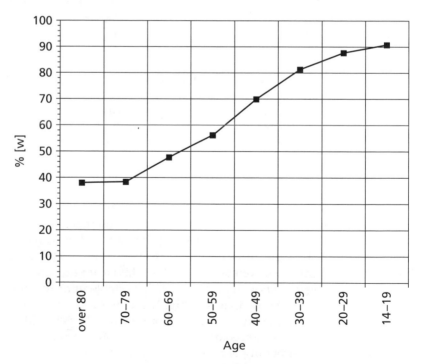

Figure 14.5 Percentage of speakers with [w] not [hw] in words like *which* and *whine* in central Canada by age

The apparent-time span in figure 14.5 happens to have caught the change as it nears completion. The youngest age groups, the teenagers and the 20-year-olds, have all but eliminated the [hw] variant (at 87.6 percent and 90.6 percent). Projecting their trajectory of change into the future suggests (literally, predicts) that none of the people born 30 years after them will use the [hw] variant. Although that projection makes sound scientific sense, we know from numerous other cases that it does not make sound – or at least compelling – linguistic sense. This is because linguistic variants that are well-entrenched in the language, as this one clearly is, tend to linger. They continue to diminish, having lost their social salience except as "quaint" relics. This tailing-off has already begun, and it is visible in figure 14.5 in the flatter trajectory for the two youngest age groups compared to the comparatively steep trajectory for the subjects two or more decades older.

The apparent-time span also captures the starting-point in stasis, with the two oldest groups almost identical (37.7 percent, 38.3 percent). If we project that state of affairs into the past (or retroject it, so to speak), we discover a time when (wh) was stable, and the [hw] variant was the more frequent. That situation was disrupted by the 60-year-olds, whose usage changed the norms of the people older than them, so that, for them, the two variants were about equal. From that point forward, in the speech of people under 60, the [hw] variant was doomed. The trajectory of the change rises steadily, taking in about 10 percent of the population every decade for five decades, bringing it to the tailing-off point in the speech of the youngsters.

Just as the tailing-off period is a recurring pattern in linguistic change, so are the initial stability and the sudden rise. Before a change takes hold, there is a gradual, almost imperceptible, rise in frequency until the new form attains some kind of critical mass. At the earliest stage, the change apparently affects too small a population to serve as a model, but at some point it becomes perceptible, though usually beneath consciousness, and spreads through the community. No one has been able to establish the point of critical mass as an absolute value, and it appears to be different for each change, subject, as are all social developments, to countless possible influences. Once that point is attained, however, the change accelerates relatively rapidly toward the tailing-off point.

The combination of these three stages – initial stasis, rapid rise, and tailing off – gives a characteristic shape in graphic representations that is known as an S-curve. The significance of the S-curve pattern for linguistic change was introduced by Wang and his associates (esp. Wang and Cheng 1970, Chen 1972) as an adjunct of lexical diffusion, a type of change in which lexical items undergo a sound change one at a time, so to speak, and extrapolated in a variationist context by Bailey (1973: 77). The S-curve has since been observed in diffusions of all kinds (Chambers and Trudgill 1998: 162–4), and is now established as a kind of template for change.

Studies of linguistic changes will not necessarily capture all three stages. Available evidence might catch the change near the beginning, when the initial stability shows signs of being disrupted by the first tremors of change, or in the middle when the change is progressing rapidly, or near the end, when it is tailing off toward a new stable state. By accident, figure 14.5 catches all three stages of the change. That means that in the 70-odd years of apparent time covered by this survey, the change took hold, attained critical mass, and rose to near-completion. The graphic display forms an S-curve, albeit a relatively gradual one. Its gradualness is explained by the fact that in the initial stage the amount of variation was already high (roughly, 40/60 for the two variants) so that the acceleration of the change toward completion had only a short distance to go. This in turn is explained by the fact that the period of stable variability was unusually long – indeed, for variable (wh), perhaps the longest on record.

6   Deconstructing the Change

The situation graphed in figure 14.5 is based on evidence from Canadian English, and the figures come from an extensive survey called the Dialect Topography of Canada (Chambers 1994). The subjects whose responses form the S-curve live in four regions with relatively distinctive regional cultures and histories (the Golden Horseshoe, the Ottawa Valley, Montreal and Quebec City). The four regions cover about a thousand kilometers where 11.5 million Canadians live, and the number of sociolinguistic observations underlying figure 14.5 is made up of almost 5,000 tokens of *which/witch* and *whine/wine* from over 2,000 subjects representing both sexes of all ages from all walks of life. This sample is fairly large, similar to public-opinion polls and the like. The sample size actually enhances the observation of change. This follows from the general rule that group results are more revealing than the results for any individual in the group (Guy 1980). The rule holds if the phenomenon under-lying those results has an empirical basis. So, by this AGGREGATE PRINCIPLE, we know that when a trend is real, every additional observation gives it greater substance, and the converse also holds: when the trend is illusory, every addi-tional observation makes it more chaotic. The coherence of figure 14.5 shows that the change it describes, the merger of /hw/ with /w/, is affecting all four regions. The change is not regional but national, taking place in Canadian English generally.

   That does not necessarily mean that the regions are progressing in exactly the same way. In fact, the regional breakdown in figure 14.6 shows that they are not. Close inspection reveals that the uneven trajectories occur mainly in two of the regions, the Ottawa Valley and Quebec City, which appear to take idiosyncratic paths in the middle part of the change. (Quebec City lacks a data-point for the over 80s because of sample size.) Where two of the regions, Montreal and the Golden Horseshoe, trace paths so similar that they are almost inextricable, the other two regions meander through the first decades and then suddenly accelerate so that the people 30 and under in all regions

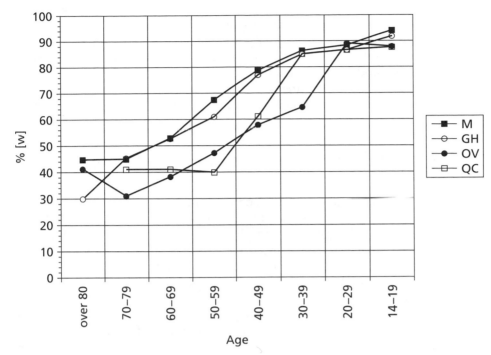

Figure 14.6 Percentage of speakers with [w] not [hw] in words like *which* and *whine* in four Canadian regions: Montreal (M), Golden Horseshoe (GH), Ottawa Valley (OV), Quebec City (QC)

end up at the same point. In Quebec City, the acceleration starts with the 40-year-olds, and in the Ottawa Valley with the 20-year-olds.

Understanding the demographics of the four regions helps to explicate the patterns. The two regions where the change is most regular, the Golden Horseshoe and Montreal, are highly urbanized and densely populated cosmopolitan centers, and the other two regions are less uniform with rural areas and towns as well as cities. Social changes of all kinds generally follow the diffusion route implied here: they take root in large urban areas and then diffuse down the urban hierarchy, from big cities to small cities and from there to towns and smaller settlements (Trudgill 1974, 1983: 52–87, Chambers and Trudgill 1998: 167–85). This pattern refutes traditional assumptions about innovations diffusing like a wave washing across a surface. A better analogy would be a pebble skipping across a pond, where the impact strikes one point and leaps to the next point, sending out ripples from each point of impact. The points of impact are the population centers.

Abrupt changes are rare. The large increases in some decades for Quebec City and the Ottawa Valley in figure 14.6, with 20 percentage points or more, are unusual because changes between contiguous age groups are normally limited (as discussed in the next section). However, the presence of the other two urban regions in figure 14.6, where the change is progressing regularly, provides a context that explains these erratic accelerations. The young people in the Ottawa Valley and Quebec City are engaged in a catching-up process that brings them into line with their age-mates in the other two regions. They were lagging behind in terms of the standard reference points in the larger community. Instead of disrupting the accepted norms, their increases have the effect of bringing their communal norms into line with those around them.

7   Social Embedding of Variation and Change

When sociolinguists began viewing language changes in their social contexts, many of the old mysteries of historical linguistics – "the fruitless paradoxes" that Weinreich et al. (1968) deplored – simply disappeared. For instance, linguists long recognized that rates of change fluctuate, and that periods of relative stability can be followed by periods of considerable flux. In times of flux, if change is viewed from discrete points in time rather than along the whole range, it can take on the appearance of a generation gap or even a communication breakdown. This viewpoint, seeing change as a punctual phenomenon rather than continuous, was the one advocated by Bloomfield, Hoenigswald, and the other structuralists. We now recognize the apparent generation gap as an artifact of the static view.

Canadian English, which has experienced a period of fairly intensive change in the last 60 or 70 years, provides a case study. As it happens, variable (wh), the merger of /hw/ to /w/, is only one among many changes. Table 14.2

Table 14.2   Percentage of incoming variants in the speech of two age cohorts in the Golden Horseshoe, Canada

	1920	1980
[w] in *which*	29	89
[w] in *whine*	31	95
couch replaces *chesterfield*	6	85
napkin replaces (paper) *serviette*	48	85
napkin replaces (cloth) *serviette*	69	97
leisure ryhmes with "seizure" (not "pleasure")	58	99
news has [u] not [ju]	59	91
student has [u] not [ju]	43	89
dove replaces *dived*	59	90
snuck replaces *sneaked*	27	95
Average percentage	42.9	91.5

Source: Chambers (1998b)

takes a sample of these changes and compares the percentages of the incoming variants at two points 60 years apart. These changes are not necessarily the most dramatic, but they serve our purposes here by indicating the extent of the changes that have appeared fairly suddenly in this conservative branch of the English language. They also represent the major structural categories of language: *couch* and *napkin* are lexical changes, replacing the Canadianisms *chesterfield* and *serviette*; *leisure* is a pronunciation change; *which*, *whine*, *news* and *students* are phonological changes; and *dove* and *snuck* are morphological (all described in detail in Chambers 1998b). The purpose in selecting changes from several categories will become evident in the next section.

These extensive changes might suggest a sizable generation gap, especially if they are understood as representative of many more. They show that the speech norms in 1920 are very different from those in 1980. If teenagers spoke only to octogenarians, there might indeed be breakdowns in intelligibility. But such a view presupposes that change is instantaneous. The reductio ad absurdum for instantaneous change, attributed to the late James D. McCawley, imagines a Londoner who slept through the Great Vowel Shift and was bewildered the next day at being served ale when he ordered eel.

The apparent-time hypothesis makes us conscious of the fact that people in both groups in table 14.2 are contemporaries. The speech norms characteristic of people in 1920 and 1980 are mediated by the norms of people in between these groups, and one of the empirical breakthroughs of sociolinguistics, obvious though it seems in retrospect, is the discovery that the intermediate groups are truly intermediaries. Linguistic changes and variations of all kinds occur as gradations rather than discontinuous steps. This gradation is evident in figure 14.5 above, with its graphic representation of a pervasive linguistic change embedded socially as a series of relatively mild increases in contiguous age groups.

Figure 14.7 dramatizes the social embedding by plotting all the changes in table 14.2 against the continuous age scale on the abscissa. Each of the changes, of course, has its own complications. Studying the lines would show, for instance, that *napkin* is coming into use more slowly for a serviette made of paper than it is for a serviette made of cloth, among other nuances. More obviously, each of these changes has its own starting-point and ending-point. In other words, the changes are not synchronous. They are, however, contemporaneous, and after the impression of their differentness vanishes, what leaps out of the aggregated data is the striking diagonal trend that gives a kind of unity to these changes. In effect, the figure smooths out the vagaries in the individual rows of table 14.2. Those differences are represented in figure 14.7, all right, but they are overwhelmed by the larger regularities.

This provides another example of the AGGREGATE PRINCIPLE (defined in the previous section): group results for any empirically-based phenomenon are more revealing than the results for any individual in the group. In this case, the individuals are not subjects but are linguistic changes.

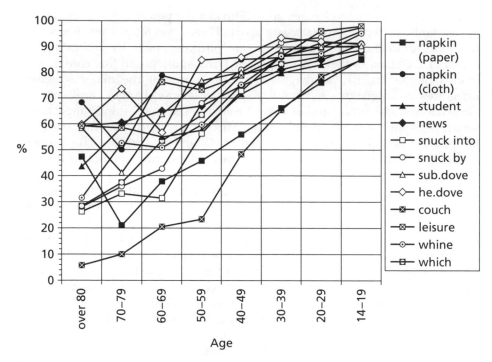

Figure 14.7 Seven changes in progress in Canadian English, illustrated by 12 variants as used by different age groups in the Golden Horseshoe

Source: Chambers (1998b: figure 9, 28)

The diagonal thrust of the changes is not linear but is roughly megaphone-shaped: broad at the left and narrowing rightward. At the broad end, the 80-year-olds have a range of about 65 percent for all the variables but at the narrow end the teenagers have a range of only 15 percent. The speech of older people is clearly more varied and less predictable than the speech of younger people, because more than one variant has fair currency in the speech of older people, but only one is used by most younger people.

Figure 14.7 demonstrates the illuminating effect of viewing sound change as a dynamic process. We recognize that the changes are taking place as an orderly progression, with small – and socially manageable – increments along the age continuum. In all societies, people are in most frequent and intimate daily contact with people in the same age cohort. Spouses, best friends, classmates, team mates, work mates, tennis opponents, bridge partners, club members and business associates tend to be within a decade or so of one another. These are the people who share reciprocal relationships, the kind that carry the most weight both socially and linguistically. The converse also holds. Relationships between people more than a decade apart in age are likely to be non-reciprocal – parents and children, teachers and students, supervisors and workers, managers and clerks. They are likely to be less influential socially – and linguistically.

Figure 14.7 shows that in speech communities people similar to one another in age speak much the same as one another, even with respect to variables that are going through fairly rapid changes. Hence the rarity of abrupt changes. Individual awareness of language change as people go about their mundane activities is mitigated by the insulating effect of these peer-group similarities. The social embedding is structured and cohesive.

8   Social Basis of Change

If we were to consider the changing variables in isolation, it might be possible to conclude that each one was undergoing change for linguistic reasons. Indeed, there is usually, perhaps inevitably, a linguistic aspect in the change. Variable (wh), the merger of /hw/ with /w/, is a case in point. The preaspirated variant [hw] is disappearing for what appear to be cogent structural-functional linguistic reasons. In the English phonemic inventory, it is the only preaspirate, and the only devoiced approximant, and it is defective distributionally because it only occurs initially. These conditions might be construed as sufficient in the sense that they determine the direction of change to be what it is, /hw/ > [w] and not vice versa. Eliminating [hw] rids the system of a highly marked and poorly integrated segment.

However, these linguistic properties have no bearing on the fact that the elimination of [hw] is imminent at this time and in this place. It has, after all, been a highly marked segment for many centuries. It became a preaspirate at the time of the Anglo-Saxon diaspora, and it has been the only preaspirate since approximately the twelfth century, when /hn-/, /hl-/ and /hr-/ dropped out (Lutz 1991: 34–5fn). It has been declining in nearly all varieties of English ever since, but its death throes are only now visible.

The linguistic conditions are sufficient, but it is the social conditions that are necessary. As we have seen, the [hw] variant of variable (wh) is not alone as it nears extinction. It is one of several changes, all of them moving in the same direction, all of them restricting the frequency of one of the variants perhaps ultimately to extinction. Linguistically, these variables have little in common, representing phonology, lexicon, pronunciation, and morphology. Historically, they have widely disparate time lines. *Couch* is replacing *chesterfield*, but *chesterfield* became established in standard Canadian English no earlier than 1900 (Chambers 1995b). *Snuck* is replacing *sneaked*, but the first attestation anywhere of *snuck* only goes back to 1887 (Creswell 1994: 146) and in Canadian English it had very little currency until the 1950s (Chambers 1998b: 22–5). Compared to (wh), these are mere fledglings, and yet all of them are moving in concert in the period covered by figure 14.7.

We can specify that time period with considerable precision by exploiting the apparent-time hypothesis. Closer inspection of figure 14.7 allows very precise inferences about the moment of concentrated change for each variable,

Table 14.3   Formative years for dialect and accent from 8–18 based on birth years

Formative years (8–18)	Birth years (from 1992 survey date)
base	before 1913 (over 80)
1920s	1913–22 (70–79)
1930s	1923–32 (60–69)
1940s	1933–42 (50–59)
1950s	1943–52 (40–49)
1960s	1953–62 (30–39)
1970s	1963–72 (20–29)
1980s	1973–78 (14–19)

determined by the decade when the greatest increase occurred in the use of the incoming variant, which coincides uncannily with the decade in which it became established in majority use. Those increases occur in the speech of 60-year-olds (*leisure, napkin*), or 50-year-olds (*dove, snuck*), or 40-year-olds (*couch, student, which*).

These are subjects who were born between 1930 and 1950. This reckoning is made simply by working back from the survey year, 1992, by the ages of respondents. The formative years for dialect and accent formation are from eight to 18, and the apparent-time hypothesis is predicated upon retention of those dialect and accent features thereafter, other things being equal. This allows closer dating, according to the commonsense calculations shown in table 14.3. For instance, a subject in her 60s (60–69) at the time of the 1992 survey was born in the decade 1923–1932, and so her formative years from eight to 18 were the 1930s.

These formative years appear on the abscissa in figure 14.8, which is a notational variant of figure 14.7. Figure 14.8 is the "first derivative" of figure 14.7, derived by calculating "the rate of change" as the increment of change from one decade to the next in an apparent-time representation like figure 14.7 (Easson 2000). For instance, the difference in the use of the variant *couch* between the 50-year-olds (at 23 percent) and the 40-year-olds (at 49 percent) is 26 (49 − 23 = 26), and the difference between the 40-year-olds and the 30-year-olds (at 65 percent) is 16; the difference is taken as an index of the rate of change (26 for the former, 16 for the latter). As an index score, it has no absolute meaning but is meaningful relative to other scores made from the same database.

Figure 14.8 calculates the rate of change as the average increment for all twelve variants in figure 14.7. It forms a bell, as if plotting normal distribution. This is accidental, but it emphasizes that the research project that gathered these results was fortuitously timed so that it captured virtually the entire

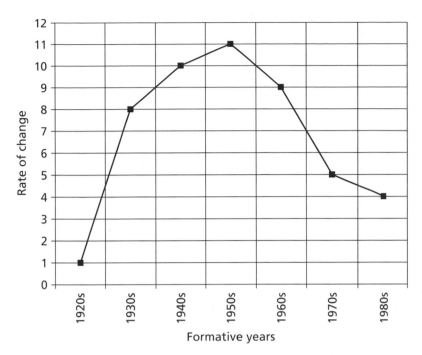

Figure 14.8 Rate of change for the seven changes in progress in the Golden Horseshoe, the first derivative of figure 14.7

Source: Easson (2000)

change cycle from inception to peak to tailing-off (as discussed in section 5 above) in the 70-year span of its apparent-time coverage.

Most important for our purposes here, the representation focuses attention on the social or (in a larger sense) sociocultural basis for the changes. The idea that these linguistically disparate variables trace remarkably similar trajectories was evident from the previous figure, but figure 14.8 makes its temporal regularity even more obvious.

The linguistic changes have sociocultural significance in the Canadian milieu. All of them follow the same pattern: in each, a British English variant diminishes and an indigenous Canadian, or more broadly North American, variant accelerates (Chambers 1998b: esp. 29–30). The chronology of these changes, with their main thrust in the 1940s and 1950s, the apex in figure 14.8, coincides with the time when British influence diminished noticeably in Canada as in other parts of the world, most palpably with the dissolution of the Empire. At the same time, multi-ethnic immigrations diluted and ultimately overwhelmed the Anglo-Celtic hegemony of Canadian ancestry (Chambers forthcoming). The changes were positively reinforced as well. In the second half of the twentieth century, the standard middle-class variety of Canadian English joined certain regional American standard dialects in a continent-wide linguistic movement toward a developing North American standard variety (Chambers 1999). Even that may be too circumscribed: the developing standard may turn out to be not merely continental but global. Some of the features – elimination of /ju/ after coronals and /hw/ in all contexts, *dove* and *snuck* as past tenses, among those shown in table 14.2 – appear to be on the rise in standard English dialects all over the world (Chambers 2000).

Global linguistic changes like these make sense in the light of global social changes. Dialect leveling requires face-to-face interaction among peers, and for several generations interactions have multiplied with advances in geographic mobility, and peers have proliferated with burgeoning social and occupational mobility. From this perspective, the linguistic changes shown in figure 14.7 and echoed in figure 14.8 have merely kept pace with the pervasive sociocultural changes for which they have supplied the constant, and absolutely essential, accompaniment.

Presumably, it has always been so. Language is, after all, one of several sociocultural tools that make human existence possible in the first place, and that empower, enrich, and perpetuate it. Language may be the greatest of those tools and the most palpable effusion of innate human creativity, but it is only a tool nevertheless. Grammars come into being in the service of communication, and both grammar and communication must be enacted through communicative competence. We express who we are with fine nuance and no little grace, selecting linguistic variants contingent upon the setting in which we are speaking and on not only our own class, sex, age, ethnicity, style and much more, but also contingent upon all those things in the people we are speaking to. Human beings have apparently always done so, and it is safe to say they always will.

REFERENCES

Bailey, Charles-James N. (1973). *Variation and Linguistic Theory*. Washington, DC: Center for Applied Linguistics.

Bloomfield, Leonard (1933). *Language*. New York: Holt, Rinehart and Winston.

Bowen, Sir Charles, Right Hon. (1889). *Virgil in English Verse: Eclogues and Æneid I–VI*. 2nd ed. London: John Murray.

Chambers, J. K. (forthcoming). "Canadian Dainty": the rise and decline of Briticisms in Canada. In Raymond Hickey (ed.), *The Legacy of Colonial English: A Study in Transported Dialects*. Cambridge: Cambridge University Press.

Chambers, J. K. (1992). Linguistic correlates of gender and sex. *English World-Wide* 13: 173–218.

Chambers. J. K. (1994). An introduction to Dialect Topography. *English World-Wide* 15: 35–53.

Chambers, J. K. (1995a). *Sociolinguistic Theory: Linguistic Variation and Its Social Significance*. Oxford: Blackwell.

Chambers, J. K. (1995b) The Canada–U.S. border as a vanishing isogloss: the case of Chesterfield. *Journal of English Linguistics* 23: 155–66.

Chambers, J. K. (1998a). Whither withers: last gasp of the oldest sound change. Presented at NWAV 27, University of Georgia.

Chambers, J. K. (1998b). Social embedding of changes in progress. *Journal of English Linguistics* 26: 5–36.

Chambers, J. K. (1999). Converging features in the Englishes of North America. In Juan-Manuel Campoy-Hernández and Juan Camilo Conde-Silvestre (ed.), *Variation and Linguistic Change in English. Cuadernos de Filología Inglesa* 8: 117–27.

Chambers, J. K. (2000). World enough and time: global enclaves of the near future. *American Speech* 75: 285–7.

Chambers, J. K. and Peter Trudgill (1998). *Dialectology*. 2nd edn. Cambridge: Cambridge University Press.

Chen, Matthew (1972). The time dimension: contribution toward a theory of sound change. *Foundations of Language* 8: 457–98.

Coldwell, David F. C. (1964). Glossary. In *Virgil's Aeneid Translated into Scottish Verse by Gavin Douglas*. Vol. I. David F. C. Coldwell (ed.) Scottish Text Society. Edinburgh: William Blackwood & Sons.

Creswell, Thomas J. (1994). Dictionary recognition of developing forms: the case of *snuck*. In Greta D. Little and Michael Montgomery (eds.), *Centennial Usage Studies*. PADS 78. Tuscaloosa: University of Alabama Press. 144–54.

Deuchar, Margaret (1988). A pragmatic account of women's use of standard speech. In Jennifer Coates and Deborah Cameron (eds.), *Women in Their Speech Communities: New Perspectives on Language and Sex*. London and New York: Longman. 27–32.

DeWolf, Gaelan Dodds (1992). *Social and Regional Factors in Canadian English*. Toronto: Scholar's Press.

Douglas, Gavin (1839). *The Aeneid of Virgil Translated into Scottish Verse*. Vol. II. Edinburgh: T. Constable.

Douglas, Gavin (1957). *Virgil's Aeneid Translated into Scottish Verse*. Vol. II. David F. C. Coldwell (ed.) Scottish Text Society. Edinburgh: William Blackwood & Sons.

Easson, Gordon (2000). Variation in optimality theory: the case of yod-dropping. Generals Paper. Department of Linguistics, University of Toronto.

Eckert, Penelope (1989). The whole woman: sex and gender differences in variation. *Language Variation and Change* 1: 245–67.

Eckert, Penelope (2000). *Linguistic Variation as Social Practice*. Oxford: Blackwell.

Gordon, Matthew and Jeffrey Heath (1998). Sex, sound symbolism, and sociolinguistics. *Current Anthropology* 39: 421–49.

Guy, Gregory (1980). Variation in the group and individual; the case of final stop deletion. In William Labov (ed.), *Locating Language in Time and Space*. New York: Academic Press. 1–36.

Hockett, Charles F. (1958). *A Course in Modern Linguistics*. New York: Macmillan.

Hoenigswald, Henry M. (1960). *Language Change and Linguistic Reconstruction*. Chicago: Phoenix Books, University of Chicago Press.

Holmes, Janet (1997). Setting new standards: sound changes and gender in New Zealand English. *English World-Wide* 18: 107–42.

Labov, William (1972). *Sociolinguistic Patterns*. Philadelphia: University of Pennsylvania Press.

Labov, William (1994). *Principles of Linguistic Change: Internal Factors.* Oxford: Blackwell.

Lutz, Angelika (1991). *Phonotaktisch gesteuerte Konsonantenveränderungen in der Geschichte des Englischen.* Tübingen: Max Niemeyer.

Macaulay, R. K. S. (1977). *Language, Social Class and Education: A Glasgow Study.* Edinburgh: Edinburgh University Press.

Milroy, James, Lesley Milroy, Sue Hartley and David Walshaw (1994). Glottal stops and Tyneside glottalization: competing patterns of variation and change in British English. *Language Variation and Change* 3: 327–57.

Rickford, John (1986). Concord and contrast in the characterization of the speech community. In Ralph W. Fasold (ed.), *Proceedings of the Fourteenth Annual Conference on New Ways of Analyzing Variation.* Washington, DC: Georgetown University Press. 215–21.

Romaine, Suzanne (1978). Postvocalic /r/ in Scottish English. In Peter Trudgill (ed.), *Sociolinguistic Patterns in British English.* London: Edward Arnold. 144–56.

Scargill, M. H. and Henry Warkentyne (1972). The survey of Canadian English: a report. *English Quarterly* 5: 47–104.

Shuy, Roger (1969). Sociolinguistic research at the Center for Applied Linguistics: the correlation of language and sex. *Giornata internazionale di sociolinguistica.* Rome: Palazzo Baldassini.

Trudgill, Peter (1972). Sex, covert prestige, and linguistic change in the urban British English of Norwich. *Language in Society* 1: 179–96.

Trudgill, Peter (1974). Linguistic change and diffusion: description and explanation in sociolinguistic dialect geography. *Language in Society* 3: 215–46.

Trudgill, Peter (1983). *On Dialect: Social and Geographical Perspectives.* Oxford: Blackwell.

Wang, William S-Y. and C-C. Cheng (1970). Implementation of phonological change: the Shuang-feng Chinese case. *Chicago Linguistic Society* 6: 552–59.

Weinreich, Uriel, William Labov, and Marvin I. Herzog (1968). Empirical foundations for a theory of language change. In Winfred P. Lehmann and Yakov Malkiel (eds.), *Directions for Historical Linguistics: A Symposium.* Austin, TX: University of Texas Press. 95–188.

Wolfram, Walter A. (1969). *A Sociolinguistic Description of Detroit Negro Speech.* Washington, DC: Center for Applied Linguistics.

Social Differentiation

In the early days of sociolinguistics it was not uncommon to encounter the practice, in studies by workers in other areas of sociolinguistics, of labelling research in the variationist paradigm as "correlational sociolinguistics." Whether deprecation was intended or not – and sometimes it surely was – most of us in the field reacted unfavourably to this designation, and quite rightly too. The implication was that the counting and measuring of linguistic features and the correlating of linguistic variability with different forms of social differentiation was the simple and banal goal of our work. It was as if this was where our research finished. On the contrary, it was and is of course precisely here that our research starts. It was analyses and interpretations of patterns of correlation which enabled us to learn of hitherto unknown relationships – the degree of co-variation between language and speaker-sex was one big surprise, for instance. It was correlation which revealed the degree to which apparently random variation was structured. And it was correlation which gave us insights into the mechanisms involved in the propagation and diffusion of linguistic changes.

The four major forms of social differentiation which have figured in our research from the very beginning are: social context, social class, sex and gender, and ethnicity. Natalie Schilling-Estes' chapter, "Investigating Stylistic Variation," begins with early work on the relationship between language and social context. She deals with variation within rather than between single languages, and within the speech of speakers rather than between speakers or groups of speakers. Schilling-Estes examines shifts in the level of usage of dialect features as well as register variation and variation according to formality, and she also examines the complex notion of genre. In common with the other writers in this section, she gives a more problematized and nuanced treatment to the form of variation she is discussing than was common in much early work in variationist linguistics.

The first major publication in the field of linguistic variation and change was of course William Labov's *The Social Stratification of English in New York City*. Social class has thus from the outset been a pivotal concept in sociolinguistic research, and one which has been particularly insightful for work on linguistic change. Sherry Ash in her chapter, "Social Class", describes the role this concept has played in work in linguistic variation and change, but she also points out that, like sex, ethnic group, and social context, social class has most often been employed by workers in our field as if it were a self-evident and unproblematical notion. It seems we have so far done very well with social class treating it as an intuitive, fairly obvious social division, but doubtless a greater understanding will lead to further progress.

Similarly, sex has been one of the most widely used forms of social differentiation in linguistic variation and change studies. As Jenny Cheshire argues in "Sex and Gender in Variationist Research," this too was formerly regarded as an unproblematical category which sociolinguists took for granted, but has now like social class come to be recognized, following to a certain rather muted extent developments in feminist theory, as more complex than early workers ever realized.

In the same vein, Carmen Fought's chapter, "Ethnicity," argues that the usefulness of "race" as a category to sociolinguistics depends on the understanding that it is communities and societies which *construct* ethnicity. An analysis of the way in which this construction proceeds is in many ways even more fraught with complexities than analyses of the other three forms of social differentiation which are dealt with in this section. Many other branches of sociolinguistics – the social psychology of language, for instance – have benefited from research into ethnicity. Fought's chapter, however, shows that an understanding of this concept has, in particular, been highly informative in the variationist study of linguistic change.

PETER TRUDGILL

15 Investigating Stylistic Variation

NATALIE SCHILLING-ESTES

1 What is "style"?

Roughly speaking, stylistic variation involves variation in the speech of individual speakers (INTRA-SPEAKER VARIATION) rather than across groups of speakers (INTER-SPEAKER VARIATION). Intra-speaker variation encompasses a number of different types of variation, including shifts in usage levels for features associated with particular groups of speakers – i.e. DIALECTS – or with particular situations of use – i.e. REGISTERS (e.g. Crystal 1991: 295, Halliday 1978). As an example of register-based variation, a speaker may show higher usage levels for pronunciation features considered to be "formal" (e.g. [ɪŋ] rather than [ən] in words like *walking* and *swimming*) when talking with a colleague about work-related matters than when talking with a friend about entertainment or family. With regard to dialect variation, a speaker may show higher usage levels for a feature like *r*-lessness (e.g. [fɑːm] "farm"), associated with traditional Southern American speech, when talking with an older Southerner who uses this feature than when talking with a speaker who does not. In addition, intra-speaker variation can involve shifts into and out of language varieties, whether dialects, registers, or GENRES (i.e. highly ritualized, routinized varieties, often associated with performance or artistic display of some kind). For example, a lawyer might switch into a "legalese" register to discuss a case with assistants, a preacher might switch into a "sermon" genre when stepping into the pulpit on Sunday morning, or a white teenager might switch into an approximation of African-American Vernacular English to indicate affiliation with "cool" youth culture (e.g. Bucholtz 1999, Cutler 1999). Switching between different languages rather than varieties of a single language is referred to as CODE SWITCHING and will not be addressed in this chapter. (See Myers-Scotton 1998, whose Markedness Model for code switching in many ways parallels current variationist approaches to stylistic variation, particularly in its emphasis on speakers' active use of stylistic resources to help shape their surroundings and social relations.)

Style shifts – that is, shifts into and out of different language varieties, and shifts in usage levels for features associated with these varieties – may be quite deliberate and involve the self-conscious use of features of which the speaker and audience are very aware, or they may be unconscious, involving features that people do not even realize they are using. In addition, shifts may be quite short-lived, as when a speaker involved in a sociolinguistic interview moment-arily shifts into a more vernacular style during a brief phone conversation; or they may be quite extensive, even part of one's daily routine, as, for example, in the case of a Texas woman who frequently shifts into the "Southern drawl" while at work to improve her sales record (Johnstone 1999). Further, long-standing patterns of stylistic variation can come to characterize a person or group in general, so that we can speak of a person's individual style or of various group styles (e.g. Valley Girl talk, associated with white young women and teens in the San Fernando Valley area of California). Finally, intra-speaker variation may involve any level of language organization, from the phonological and morphosyntactic to the lexical, semantic, pragmatic, and discoursal. Hence, we can talk of a number of different kinds of style, ranging from a "formal style" associated with high usage levels for particular phonological and morphosyntactic features (often, but not always, those associated with a standard variety; see Trudgill 2000: 81–5), to "conversational style" – that is, the broad interactional patterns that characterize entire discourses (e.g. Tannen 1984).

Given the broad range of types of variation employed by individual speak-ers, it is not surprising that variationists have for decades debated exactly what should be subsumed under the notion "stylistic variation," as well as the best way to go about studying this all-encompassing phenomenon. However, it is agreed that intra-speaker variation should hold an important place in variation study. After all, intra-speaker variation is pervasive, perhaps even universal, and we cannot hope to achieve a full understanding of the patterning of variation in language, or of language in general, if we do not understand its patterning within individuals' speech as well as across groups of speakers. Further, since intra-speaker variation lies at the intersection of the individual and the communal, a better understanding of its patterns will lend valuable insight into how the two spheres interrelate – that is, how individuals internal-ize broad-based community language patterns and how these patterns are shaped and re-shaped by individuals in everyday conversational interaction.

2   Approaches to Intra-speaker Variation: An Overview

Traditionally, variationists have considered style shifting to involve shifts in usage levels for phonological and morphosyntactic features, typically arranged along a vernacular-standard continuum, across different speech situations, delimited either according to their relative formality (Labov 1972a) or the composition of the speaker's audience (Bell 1984). In this, studies of intra-speaker variation parallel studies of INTER-SPEAKER VARIATION, in which the patterning of phonological and morphosyntactic variables is investigated across different speaker groups. However, variationist investigations of style shifting are quite different from investigations of speech style conducted in previous decades in other subfields of sociolinguistics. For example, the taxonomic approaches of researchers such as Ervin-Tripp (1964), Halliday (1978), and Hymes (1972) viewed stylistic variation as encompassing a much wider range of types of variation than did early variationists (e.g. variation in address forms, as reported in Ervin-Tripp 1973) and also viewed it as being conditioned by a much broader range of factors, including not only formality of the situation or audience composition but such factors as topic, setting, key (e.g. joking vs. serious), channel (e.g. spoken vs. written), and purpose, to name a few.

In recent years, the variationist study of style shifting has diverged from the tightly focused approaches of early variationists and converged, in at least some ways, with the early broad-based approaches of ethnographers, anthropologists, sociologists, and others. Variationists are no longer as concerned with investigating the patterning of stylistic variation according to just one or a handful of social factors but are considering a full range of factors in their search for influences on intra-speaker variation. In addition, rather than examining variation based on pre-imposed categorizations of the speech situation as "casual," "formal," or "careful," or on pre-imposed social categories like upper middle class/lower middle class, male/female, or black/white, they are conducting extensive ethnographic investigations in order to discover locally salient ways of categorizing language, people, and the world (e.g. Eckert 2000, Kiesling 1996, Mendoza-Denton 1997). Variationist investigations of style shifting are also becoming broader in that they are encompassing more types of features, ranging from the phonological and morphosyntactic to the lexical and pragmatic/interactional (Coupland 2001, Schilling-Estes 1999), to paralinguistic features such as intonation (Arnold et al. 1993), to non-linguistic elements of style such as hair, clothing, makeup, body positioning, and use of space (Eckert 2000, Mendoza-Denton 1997). Further, a greater range of different types of style shifts are being included – not only shifts into and out of more and less formal speech but also shifts in and out of registers, dialects (e.g. Rampton 1999b), and highly performative genres (e.g. Coupland 1985, 2001; Schilling-Estes 1998). Despite their increasingly broad scope, however, variationist studies of intra-speaker variation are not simply converging with taxonomic approaches, since the latter have tended to be qualitative in approach whereas the former retain at least some measure of quantitative analysis, the hallmark of variation study.

At the same time that variationist investigations of stylistic variation are becoming broader, they are also becoming deeper, as variationists increasingly turn toward investigating variation as it patterns in unfolding talk (e.g. Arnold et al. 1993, Bell 1999, in press, Bell and Johnson 1997, Schilling-Estes 1999) rather than relying on aggregate figures compiled from different sections of talk, different speakers, or different speaker groups. With the increasing emphasis on style in action has come increasing focus on two key points: (1) speakers do not shift style merely, or primarily, in reaction to elements of the speech situation (whether formality or audience) but rather are quite active and highly creative in their use of stylistic resources, and (2) not only are speakers *not* bound to elements of the external situation as they shape their speech, but they use their speech to help shape and re-shape the external situation (whether the immediate interactional context or wider societal forces), as well as their interpersonal relationships and, crucially, their personal identities. In their emphasis on speaker creativity, variationists are falling into line with social psychological approaches to stylistic variation, in which speaker agency (as opposed to speaker response to external stimuli) has long been a primary focus (e.g. Giles 1973; see Audience Design, below).

In the sections to follow, I will outline three major approaches to stylistic variation, two of which are more unidimensional (Attention to Speech, Audience Design) and the third more multidimensional (the so-called "Speaker Design" approach). In the final section, I will point to some areas in need of further exploration, as well as suggest some ways in which the insights from various approaches can be integrated as we pursue our investigations of intra-speaker variation.

3   Attention to Speech

The first variationist investigations of stylistic variation were conducted by William Labov (e.g. Labov 1972a). Labov's primary interest in the topic lay in obtaining and identifying data that represented, as closely as possible, people's "casual," "natural" speech rather than speech that has been greatly altered due to the presence of an observer. In order to do this, Labov developed a sociolinguistic interview designed to yield a range of types of speech, from the casual to the highly formal, that could be fairly readily delimited by the analyst. Most of the interview was designed to be conversational and yielded two types of speech: (1) CAREFUL speech, in which the interviewee was somewhat guarded, and (2) CASUAL speech, in which the interviewee spoke in a more "natural" way. Casual speech could be delimited from careful by noting such matters as topic and addressee. For example, speech on such topics as childhood customs and dangerous situations was held to trigger casual speech, as was speech directed to a third party – for example, a spouse or child. In addition, Labov identified five PARALINGUISTIC CHANNEL CUES which seemed to correlate with casual speech: changes in tempo, pitch, volume, and breathing rate, as well as the use of laughter. Further, the interview comprised several tasks designed to elicit speech that was very self-conscious, as well as to yield tokens of phonological variants relevant to the study at hand: (1) a reading passage, (2) a word-list, and (3) a list of minimal pairs, or words that differ by only one phoneme in standard speech but may or may not differ in pronunciation in vernacular varieties (e.g. *source/sauce* is a minimal pair for *r*-pronouncing speakers in New York City but not for more vernacular *r*-less ones).

Underlying the array of styles in Labov's interview was the belief that style shifts are triggered primarily by the amount of attention people pay to their speech itself as they converse – in other words, how self-conscious people are as they speak. When speech is unselfconscious, as for example when an interviewee reprimands a child who has wandered into the interview, it will be more "casual," closer to the "vernacular" – that is, the language variety first acquired by the speaker.[1] When speech is more self-conscious – for example, when reading a list of words that forces the speaker to focus attention on her *r* pronunciations, then it will be more "formal," closer to a more standard variety.

3.1   The patterning of stylistic variation across social groups

The quantitative patterns obtained by Labov and others using his basic interviewing techniques (e.g. Trudgill 1974) reveal that, for the most part, when investigating features that can be arranged along a vernacular-standard continuum, speakers show lower usage levels for vernacular features, and higher levels for their standard counterparts, as they move from casual situations, in which they are relatively unselfconscious, to more formal situations, in which they are carefully monitoring their speech. Figure 15.1 illustrates this patterning for the use of vernacular [t] for [θ] (e.g. [wɪt] for "with", [tɪŋk] for "think") in New York City, based on Labov's (1966) survey.

Figure 15.1 also reveals how closely intertwined stylistic variation is with social class variation: the same variants used in more casual styles are also used with greater frequency in lower social class groups, while those that are used in more formal styles are those associated with higher class groups. In other words, stylistic variation parallels social class variation. It was later observed, by Bell (1984), that not only are the two dimensions parallel, but stylistic variation seems to be derivative of social class variation, since the degree of stylistic variation is almost always less that the degree of differentiation by social group. This notion is encapsulated in Bell's Style Axiom:

> Variation on the style dimension within the speech of a single speaker derives from and echoes the variation which exists between speakers on the "social" dimension.   (Bell 1984: 151)[2]

3.2   Exceptions to the basic pattern

There are several classes of exceptions to this pattern. One involves STATISTICAL HYPERCORRECTION – that is, the use of *higher* rather than *lower* levels of standard variants by middle-status groups (usually the lower middle class) than higher-class groups in more formal styles. When hypercorrection occurs,

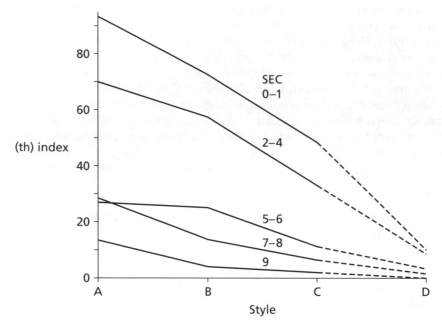

Figure 15.1 Stylistic and social class variation in [t]/[θ] usage in New York City English

Source: From *Sociolinguistic Patterns* by William Labov, copyright © University of Pennsylvania Press 1972; reprinted with permission

Key: Socioeconomic class scale: 0–1, lower class; 2–4, working class; 5–6, 7–8, lower middle class; 9, upper middle class.
  A: casual speech; B: careful speech; C: reading style; D: word lists.

the class exhibiting the hypercorrect behavior usually shows a greater range of variation across speech styles than across social classes, thus violating Bell's Style Axiom. Figure 15.2 illustrates this pattern for the pronunciation of *r* (a prestige feature) in New York City.

The hypercorrect behavior of the lower middle class in such cases has been explained by such factors as the indeterminate (and insecure) position of the lower middle class, as well as the upward mobility that supposedly charac-terizes this group: in their efforts to enter into the higher classes, the lower middle class attempts to speak as "correctly" as possible – more "correctly," in fact, than the higher classes. However, the "cross-over" pattern in figure 15.2 does not seem to hold for all linguistic variables but chiefly those undergoing change (Eckert 2000: 26, Labov 1972a, Preston 1991, Trudgill 1974). In addition, Bell (1984: 154) and Preston (1991: 34) suggest that because hypercorrection usually involves only one social group, it is perhaps best considered a socially motivated phenomenon rather than a stylistic one.

Another class of exceptions to the Style Axiom involves so-called "hyperstyle" variables, or variables that show far more stylistic than social class variation for *all* social groups (Bell 1984: 154–6). For example, Woods (1979) showed

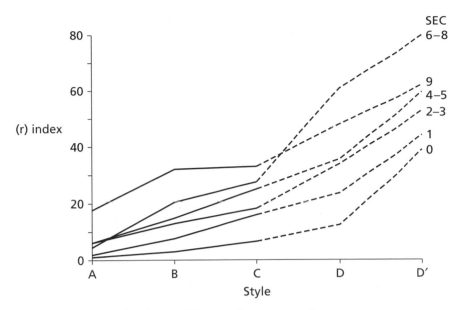

Figure 15.2 Class and style stratification for postvocalic *r*

Source: From *Sociolinguistic Patterns* by William Labov, copyright © University of Pennsylvania Press 1972; reprinted with permission

Key: Socioeconomic scale: 0–1, lower class; 2–3, working class; 4–5, 6–8, lower middle class; 9, upper middle class.
 A: casual speech; B: careful speech; C: reading style; D: word lists; D', minimal pairs

that the envelope of stylistic variation for medial /t/ voicing in Ottawa English is 40 percent, but the range across social groups is only 25 percent; similarly, Modaressi-Tehrani (1978) showed that the range of variation for [æᵉ] raising in Tehran Persian across different speech styles was 94 percent, compared with a social group range of only 17 percent. It may be possible to explain these patterns by considering that, in certain communities, reading may not lie on the same continuum as different types of spoken styles (i.e. speakers may have a specialized "reading style" that is quite different from even their most formal spoken variety; see Milroy 1987: 173–8). In the Persian case, we might also appeal to cultural differences, especially the greater attention to matters of deference in Iranian society vis-à-vis American (Bell 1984: 155–6). Alternatively, we might appeal to relative levels of awareness of different language features, since, as Preston (1991) notes, features of which speakers are highly conscious often show erratic behavior in style shifting, including behavior that leads not only to violations of Bell's Style Axiom, but also Preston's Status Axiom, which holds that:

> Variation on the "status" dimension derives from and echoes the variation which exists within the "linguistic" dimension.   (Preston 1991: 36)

In other words, linguistic stereotypes might show unusual behavior, not only in their social class and stylistic patterning but even in their linguistic patterning.

This observation is borne out, for example, in Schilling-Estes and Wolfram (1999) who note unusual linguistic patterning for stereotypes but not for non-noticeable forms in Ocracoke English, a variety of American English spoken on Ocracoke Island, in the North Carolina Outer Banks, and in Smith Island English, a variety spoken in Maryland's Chesapeake Bay. In addition, Trudgill (1986: 66–78) notes that, in cases of dialect contact, highly noticeable features are often subject to HYPERDIALECTISM, or overgeneralization into environments where they are not linguistically expected.

Despite the exceptions to Bell's Style Axiom, the fact remains that stylistic and social class variation are intimately interconnected, and Labov's early investigations of stylistic variation were instrumental in examining the nature and extent of this interconnection. Labov's studies were also important in that they demonstrated that casual, unmonitored speech seems to be more regular in its patterning than more formal speech, a finding which runs counter to popular notions regarding the "sloppiness" of casual, vernacular speech.

3.3   Limitations of the Attention to Speech approach

Despite the insights offered by the Attention to Speech approach, it has been criticized on a number of grounds. For example, it has been pointed out that it is extremely difficult in practice to separate casual from careful speech in the conversational portion of the sociolinguistic interview. For example, Wolfram (1969: 58–9) noted that "channel cues" are unreliable indicators of casual speech, since, for example, laughter can just as easily be associated with increased nervousness and selfconsciousness rather than increased casualness. In addition, it is quite difficult to quantify attention to speech (Bell 1984), and experiments designed to investigate the effects of differing degrees of attention to speech on variation in usage levels for standard vs. vernacular variants have yielded mixed results (e.g. Bell 1984: 147–50). Further, the approach has been criticized for being too unidimensional, and it has been pointed out that there are certain speech styles that simply do not fit into a continuum based on degree of attention paid to speech, or on formality vs. informality. For example, as noted above, reading styles may not lie on the same plane as spoken styles (e.g. Macaulay 1977, Milroy 1987: 173–8, Romaine 1978, 1980). In addition, level of formality cannot be neatly correlated with attention to speech even in spoken styles, since it is quite possible for speakers to quite consciously shift into vernacular rather than standard speech patterns (e.g. Coupland 1980, Rickford 1979: 230, Wolfram 1981), including exaggerated, highly stylized vernacular "performances" (e.g. Coupland 1985, 2001, Eckert 2000: 79, Schilling-Estes 1998). Further, researchers have noted that the notion of "vernacular" is itself too unidimensional, since speakers exhibit different types of casual, unguarded speech in different casual settings – and even in a single casual setting, depending on such matters as purpose, topic, and participant interrelations (e.g. Hindle 1979). However, Labov himself points out that the Attention to Speech approach was never intended to capture the many different types of speech styles we are likely to find in real life, or their many conditioning factors, but merely to serve as a useful means for identifying "casual" speech in the socio-linguistic interview (Labov 1972a: 97).

One final criticism of the Attention to Speech approach is that it views speakers as passive respondents who alter their speech in response to changes in the external situation rather that crediting them with any agency in their use of stylistic resources. Such a view is perhaps inherent in a sociolinguistic theory that sees language as *reflective* of social structures and interactional norms rather than as a key element in the construction, maintenance, and alteration of these norms and structures. As we shall see, as variationists have become increasingly interested in incorporating social constructionist approaches into their investigations, they have become increasingly dissatisfied with theoretical models (and accompanying methodologies) that force them to view speakers as simply accommodating to given norms, whether of speech situation or social group, rather than taking part in shaping and re-shaping these norms (e.g. Arnold et al. 1993, Bauman and Sherzer 1989, Cameron 1990, Eckert 2000, Rampton 1995, 1999a, 1999b, 1999c, Romaine 1984, Schiffrin 1996).

4 Audience Design

An approach that overcomes some of the limitations of the Attention to Speech model is the Audience Design model, initially proposed by Bell (1984). This model holds that people engage in style shifting, not in response to shifts in amount of attention paid to speech, but in response to audience members. The model has its roots in Speech Accommodation Theory (Giles 1973, Giles and Powesland 1975), a social psychological model which holds that speakers tend to adjust their speech toward that of their addressees, in order to win their approval. Less commonly, speakers may adjust away from addressees' speech, in order to create psychological distance. Speech Accommodation Theory (SAT) is grounded in a number of experiments which show convergence, and sometimes divergence, of speakers to addressees in such matters as speech rate, content, pausing, and "accent" (typically not very precisely defined in SAT). The Audience Design model extends SAT by applying the insights of the theory to the patterning of specific linguistic variables and by going beyond addressee effects to consider the effects of others who might be part of a speaker's audience – namely, AUDITORS, or ratified participants in the interaction who are not being directly addressed, OVERHEARERS, or persons who are not participants but are known to be within hearing distance of the interaction, and EAVESDROPPERS, unratified persons who are not known to be present. Since their original formulations, both SAT and the Audience Design model have been significantly reworked (in fact, SAT is now called Communication

Accommodation Theory, or CAT); some aspects of newer versions of these models are discussed below.

The Audience Design model provides a fuller account of stylistic variation than the Attention to Speech model in several ways. First, it is not limited to speech styles in the sociolinguistic interview but is intended to be applicable to more naturalistic data such as conversational interaction with peers and co-workers. In addition, in attempting to link intra-speaker variation to inter-speaker relations rather than individual psychological factors such as attention to speech, the Audience Design model seeks to provide explanation for the interrelation of intra-speaker and inter-speaker variation, as well as its quant-itative patterning. Bell (1984: 158) notes: "Intraspeaker variation is a *response* to interspeaker variation, chiefly as manifested in one's interlocutors. The fact that style shift falls short of social differentiation . . . reflects the fact that speakers cannot match the speech differences of all their interlocutors – but they can approach them." Finally, the Audience Design model goes part of the way toward introducing an element of speaker agency into stylistic variation. Though the model is essentially RESPONSIVE (in that speakers respond to audi-ence members in shaping their speech), it does include an INITIATIVE dimen-sion, to account for the fact that speakers sometimes engage in style shifts that seem to have nothing to do with the make-up of their present audience.

4.1   The responsive dimension

Bell (1984) presents findings from a number of studies that demonstrate that speakers indeed shape their speech in response to addressees. For example, Bickerton (1980), Douglas-Cowie (1978), Russell (1982), and Thelander (1982) show that speakers use higher levels of vernacular variants when talking with peer groups than with an unfamiliar interviewer. In addition, Trudgill (1981) demonstrates that interviewers as well as interviewees respond to addressees, through analyzing variation in his own speech patterns when conducing inter-views with people of various social class groups in Norwich (Trudgill 1974). Further, Coupland (1980, 1981, 1984) shows that the effects of different ad-dressees on speech style are pervasive in daily interaction, as evidenced in his analysis of the speech of an assistant in a travel agency as she converses with clients, co-workers, and fellow travel agents. Bell also presents evidence from several studies that show that auditor effects are smaller than addressee effects. For example, Bickerton (1980), Thelander (1982), and Douglas-Cowie (1978) show a greater degree of shifting between peer group speech and speech with an interviewer alone than between peer group speech and peer group speech when the interviewer is present as auditor.

Bell also notes that there are factors besides audience members that affect speech style – for example, topic and setting. However, he maintains that the effects of these factors are actually derivative of audience-related concerns: When speakers appear to shift styles based on shifts in topic (e.g. Blom and

Gumperz 1972, Coupland 1981, Douglas-Cowie 1978, Giles and Powesland 1975) or setting (e.g. Hindle 1979), they are actually shifting based on addressees associated with the various topics and settings – in other words, as if talking to these various addressees. If topic- and setting-related effects are indeed derivative of audience effects, then the former should be weaker than the latter (Bell 1984: 178–82). This prediction is borne out in quantitative studies such as Coupland (1981), whose data indicate a greater percentage of shift for certain variables across different audiences than across different topics (see Bell 1984: 179, table 6) and to some extent in Rickford and McNair-Knox (1994), who conducted a thorough quantitative study of usage levels of a number of features associated with African-American Vernacular English in the speech of an African-American teenager, "Foxy," who participates in a series of interviews with an African-American interviewer, as well as a single interview with a white fieldworker. Although Rickford and McNair-Knox show that the amount of style shifting is actually greater across topics within individual interviews than across interviews with different addressees, they maintain that audience effects are actually greater overall, since Foxy generally uses higher frequencies of vernacular variants on *every* topic when talking with the African-American interviewer than with the white fieldworker (1994: 258–62).

4.2 The initiative dimension

Despite their success in identifying the effects of such factors as audience, topic, setting, and even channel (Coupland 1980) on stylistic variation, researchers have determined that there is a great deal of stylistic variation that cannot be accounted by appealing to situational factors, since speakers often creatively initiate style shifts, in order to alter the situation in some way. For example, Blom and Gumperz (1972) noted that, while switches from the local dialect to the standard variety (and vice versa) were indeed often conditioned by changes in the external situation (e.g. a person entering the room during a conversation), switching also frequently took place in the absence of such situational changes. For example, people might suddenly switch to the standard variety during a casual conversation with vernacular-speaking friends in order to clinch an argument. Similarly, Coupland (1980) noted that the travel assistant he studied engaged in style shifting, not only based on who she was talking to or what she was talking about, but also when she changed the purpose of her conversation. For example, she once shifted into more vernacular style when talking with a difficult client in order to indicate increasing desire to be helpful rather than aloof.

In order to account for such shifts, Bell added an initiative component to his essentially responsive model. However, initiative shifts were considered to represent a small part of the Audience Design model, since, Bell maintained, "People do, after all, spend more time responding to others than taking the initiative" (1984: 184). In addition, initiative shifts were seen to be derivative of audience-designed shifts, in that speakers who engage in such shifts are actually responding to non-present audience members (whom Bell calls REFEREES) who are so important to the speaker that they influence speech even when not immediately present (Bell 1984: 186–7). Finally, initiative shifts can be seen as reactive in that, even though speakers rely on styles associated with other situations when engaging in initiative shift, they nonetheless do so in response to the current situation, in order to affect their relations with present audience members. For example, a speaker who switches into a standard dialect in order to win an argument with a vernacular-speaking co-conversationalist does so in order to affect the current interaction, not a distant interaction he once had with a standard-speaking audience (Bell 1984: 184–5).

4.3   *Limitations of the Audience Design model*

Since its inception, the Audience Design model has been well received by variationists, for such reasons as its explanatory power, its applicability to speech events besides the sociolinguistic interview, and for the strong, testable predictions it makes regarding such matters as the ratio of addressee effects to auditor and overhearer effects and the ratio of audience effects to the effects of setting and topic (e.g. Rickford and McNair-Knox 1994: 241). However, the model is not without its limitations.

One limitation is the model's reliance on the responsive dimension of stylistic variation. Since the model was proposed, researchers have increasingly come to realize that speakers engage in initiative shifting far more often than originally conceived. Indeed, Bell himself has noted that the initiative component of his model is "in need of serious rethinking" (Bell 2001), and he has reworked his model considerably in order to give more prominence to initiative shifts. In fact, he now maintains that not only is initiative shift just as pervasive as responsive, but both are always in simultaneous operation in conversation (Bell 1999: 525, 2001). However, Bell still maintains that initiative shifts are essentially reactive, in that they involve utilizing styles normally associated with one group or setting ("responsive" styles) in contexts in which their use is non-normative ("marked"), thereby "infusing the flavour of one setting into a different context" (1999: 524). Although certainly, speech styles do conjure up "flavours" – that is, meanings associated with particular people and situations – this conceptualization may still be in need of some reworking, since it is not clear how to go about identifying marked vs. unmarked styles in all speech situations. In addition, both marked and unmarked styles may be used to infuse meaning into a situation. For example, Kiesling (1998), in his study of fraternity men's speech, shows that the men use both standard and nonstandard variants of the (ing) variable (e.g. *walking* vs. *walkin'*) in formal meetings in order to inject certain meanings (e.g. authoritativeness, hardworkingness) into the meeting (Kiesling and Schilling-Estes 1998). Indeed, researchers in stylistic variation are increasingly taking into consideration the social constructionist view that *all* speech styles play a role in shaping *all* situations (e.g. Arnold et al. 1993, Bauman and Sherzer 1989, Cameron 1990, Eckert 2000, Rampton 1995, 1999a, 1999b, 1999c, Romaine 1984; Schiffrin 1996). Under this view, it is very difficult indeed to correlate styles with situations, since both work together to define (and re-define) one another.

Even if we concede that style shifting is essentially responsive, we are left with the question of exactly what it is about addressees and other audience members that speakers are responding to. As Bell (1984: 167) notes, there are three "increasingly specific" possibilities:

1 Speakers assess the personal characteristics of their addresses, and design their style to suit.
2 Speakers assess the general style level of their addressees' speech, and shift relative to it.
3 Speakers assess their addressees' levels for specific linguistic variables, and shift relative to those levels.

It has been demonstrated that speakers do indeed respond on level 1. For example, in a study of AAVE speakers in Washington, DC, Fasold (1972) notes that informants showed higher usage levels for vernacular variants when talking with *standard*-speaking black interviewers than with white interviewers. However, studies such as this still do not show exactly which personal characteristics of the addressee speakers are responding to – is it ethnicity or some other factor, such as familiarity, age, gender, or even individual personality? In addition, Rickford and McNair-Knox (1994) demonstrated that speakers also respond on level 2, though they do not seem to be capable of level 3. However, given that "the general speech impression of level (2) largely derives from the combined assessment of many individual variables" (Bell 1984: 168), we cannot discount the possibility that, at least at some level, speakers may indeed respond to specific levels for specific variables, as well as more general speech patterns.

A final concern regarding the Audience Design model is that, even though it provides a better model for stylistic variation outside the sociolinguistic interview than the Attention to Speech framework, it too is unidimensional, in that all style shifts, even those seemingly related to non-audience effects, are held to be derivative of audience-related concerns. Hence, it may be inadequate to capture the genuine complexity of stylistic variation in everyday speech. Rickford and McNair-Knox (1994) point out that it is difficult to investigate empirically whether topic effects actually *derive* from audience effects, even if topic effects can be shown to be weaker than audience-related effects. In addition, their data indicate that people do not always behave as if talking to different audience members when talking about different topics. For example, their informant, Foxy, does not talk as if talking *to* her teenage friends when quoting them on the subject of male–female relations; rather, she talks as if she *were* these friends – in other words, she takes on the role of these friends through performing their speech (1994: 258–62).

In more recent formulations of the Audience Design model, the derivative nature of non-audience effects is given much less emphasis, in recognition of the difficulty of empirically demonstrating such derivation. In addition, the model is becoming more multidimensional in that it is taking greater account of factors besides demographic characteristics of audience members in shaping speech style. For example, Bell and Johnson (1997; see also Bell 2001) recently conducted a study in New Zealand in which interviewers and interviewees were paired based on like and unlike gender and ethnicity (Maori and Pakeha [white]). Other demographic and non-demographic factors (e.g. age, familiarity, setting) were kept as constant as possible. Despite these controls, Bell and Johnson found that speakers sometimes used features "against the demographic associations of the feature" (Bell and Johnson 1997: 15). For example, the interviewers used the second highest level of *eh*, a discourse particle associated with Maori men, with the inteviewee who was most distant in terms of demographic associations – the Pakeha woman. Bell and Johnson suggest that the reason for this is not that the interviewers were trying to distance themselves from the interviewee through their linguistic divergence but rather trying bring themselves closer, since *eh* serves as a device for creating solidarity as well as a marker of Maori ethnicity and male gender.

In recognizing that solidarity with one's audience is not always best achieved by using speech features associated with one's addressee, Bell and Johnson bring the Audience Design model closer to newer versions of Communication Accommodation Theory, which hold that there are many communicative strategies for achieving psychological convergence besides linguistic convergence (e.g. Giles et al. 1991). In addition, in recognizing that immediate conversational purpose is just as important as more permanent speaker characteristics in shaping speech style (as well as recognizing the importance of initiative style shift), they are moving the Audience Design framework in the direction of what we might call "speaker design" approaches, following Coupland (1996). Like CAT, "speaker design" approaches also have roots in SAT, in which speaker motivation, both immediate and in terms of more long-range goals, has long been considered of central importance in stylistic variation (e.g. Giles 1973).

5   Speaker Design Approaches

Under speaker design approaches, stylistic variation is viewed not as a reactive phenomenon but as a resource in the active creation, presentation, and re-creation of speaker identity (e.g. Arnold et al. 1993, Campbell-Kibler et al. 2000, Coupland 1985, 2001, Eckert 2000, Kiesling 1996, 1998, Kiesling and Schilling-Estes 1998, Mendoza-Denton 1997, Rose 2000, Schilling-Estes 1999, Traugott and Romaine 1985, Wong and Zhang 2000). Crucially, identity is understood to encompass both personal and interpersonal dimensions, since people necessarily define themselves in relation to others, while engaged in social interaction (e.g. Barth 1969, Coupland, in press, Scollon 1997, Wong and Zhang, in press).

Speaker design models are firmly rooted in social constructionist approaches, in that language and society are viewed as co-constitutive: the linguistic features and patterns speakers use are not mere reflections of static identity, as defined by one's positions in an existent social order (e.g. white middle class male, older Native American female), but rather are resources speakers use to shape and re-shape social structures such as class and gender groups, as well as their positioning with respect to these structures and with respect to one another. In addition, speakers use linguistic resources to position themselves with respect to the talk itself, whether its subject matter or its entire "frame" – that is, the interactants' sense of what sort of speech activity is taking place (e.g. Bateson 1972, Goffman 1974, 1981, Hymes 1974, Tannen 1993). Thus, under speaker design approaches, reified *structures* fade in importance, while *social practice* and speaker agency move to the forefront (e.g. Eckert 2000). Even seemingly reactive linguistic choices (i.e. responsive style shifts) are seen as inevitably involving agency. As Coupland (2001) notes: "From a self-identity perspective, shifts that are "appropriate" [i.e. normative in a given situation] are nevertheless creative in the sense that speakers opt to operate communicatively within normative bounds."

5.1   *Investigating speaker agency*

To achieve some understanding of speaker agency – i.e. *why* people make the stylistic choices they do rather than simply which choices correlate with which situations – researchers are considering a broad range of factors that might influence language choice, including not only factors external to the speaker such as audience, topic, and setting but also speaker-internal factors like purpose, key, and frame. For example, Coupland (1985, 2001) examines how a Cardiff radio announcer uses various stylistic resources to accomplish different purposes and establish different types of joking keys. For example, the announcer uses broad Cardiff dialect to forge connection with Cardiff-related themes and more standard speech to accomplish organizational tasks, such as announcing upcoming events on his show. In addition, he uses Cardiff dialect to poke fun at himself when he stumbles over his words, as well as a fake American accent to parody American radio programs. Similarly, Schilling-Estes (1998) shows how a speaker of Ocracoke English shifts into exaggeratedly broad dialect in order bring to the forefront the fact that what seems to be a casual conversation with a relative stranger is really a sociolinguistic interview – in essence, a "dialect performance."

The study of stylistic variation is also becoming broader in that researchers are increasingly grounding their investigations in long-term, broad-based ethnographic studies, in order to discover how various elements of style are used in the local setting, as well as what these elements actually mean to the people who use them (e.g. Eckert 2000, Kiesling 1996, Mendoza-Denton 1997). In addition, they are looking at a broader range of types of features, not only the phonological and morphosyntactic features associated with classic variationist studies but also lexical, pragmatic, and discourse-level features, as well as paralinguistic features such as intonational contours, and even non-linguistic features. For example, Mendoza-Denton (1997) shows how a group of Latina adolescents (in this case, immigrant Mexicans and Mexican-Americans) use linguistic features such as discourse markers and non-linguistic resources like make-up and clothing style to forge and indicate subtle distinctions in social network and gang affiliation. Similarly, Arnold et al. (1993) show how a California adolescent, "Trendy," uses phonological, lexical, discoursal, and intonational resources in crafting her individual style, as well as that of her "trendy" social group at school.

Examining as many types of features as possible is crucial in any research enterprise concerned with speaker meaning: phonological variants may provide some clue, since they may carry connotations of group belonging, through their association with the groups who use them. However, variants may be associated with more than one group (e.g. Brown and Levinson 1979, Eckert 2000: 114, Schilling-Estes 1999), and in addition, they may carry associations besides group membership. For example, they may be associated with particular *attributes* of a group rather than the group as a whole, with individuals, or with idealizations – whether ideal individuals such as "the ideal man" or ideal qualities such as "honesty" or "toughness" (e.g. Eastman and Stein 1993: 188, quoted in Coupland 2001; Giles et al. 1991: 15–16; Kiesling and Schilling-Estes 1998). In order to discover which attributes and associations are being called forth at any given moment, it is helpful to look beyond variants whose meanings derive solely from their association with groups and individuals to features with inherent semantic meaning. For example, speakers' pronoun choices (e.g. "we" vs. "they") can help indicate whether they are positioning themselves as members of particular groups or not. In addition, we can look to features with pragmatic/interactional to gain information about what sorts of personal and interpersonal meanings are being called forth in interaction. For example, Schilling-Estes (1999) shows how usage patterns for discourse markers indicative of high inter-speaker involvement (e.g. *y'know* and *I mean*; see Schiffrin 1987) help indicate that two interlocutors, an African American and a Native American, sometimes position themselves as good friends whose personal relationship is paramount but at other times as representatives of two distinct, and distant, ethnic groups.

The consideration of pragmatic/interactional features also reminds us that meaning is always situated and that people utilize stylistic resources, not only to indicate relatively longstanding group affiliations and personal attributes but also to make temporary meanings in ongoing interaction – in other words, to accomplish various conversational purposes. Thus, for example, as noted earlier, Bell (2001) and Bell and Johnson (1997) show how the pragmatic marker *eh* sometimes serve as markers of group affiliation but at other times is used in an attempt to "win over" a reticent interviewee. Similarly, Campbell-Kibler et al. (2000) show how a gay activist and lawyer, rather than always using a set "gay" style, constructs a style that is "not too gay" in order to demonstrate professional competence while participating in a radio debate. Given the importance of the discourse contexts in which features occur in shaping their meanings, researchers are increasingly complementing investigations of aggregate levels for features (whether across conversations and speakers or in different sections of a single conversation) with investigations of *where* in discourse stylistic resources are used (e.g. Arnold et al. 1993, Bell in press, Bell and Johnson 1997, Schilling-Estes 1999). For example, Bell and Johnson (1997) note that whereas certain features tend to be fairly evenly distributed in the interviews they analyze (e.g. the discourse marker *y'know*), the pragmatic particle *eh*, which is associated with Maori men, tends to cluster in discussions of Maori-related topics.

Researchers are also concerned with how features co-occur in discourse, whether on a short-term basis, in particular conversations, or on a more long-standing basis, in the creation, maintenance, and re-creation of individual and group styles – for example, the individual style created by "Trendy" (Arnold et al. 1993) or the group styles of school-oriented "jocks" vs. urban-oriented "burnouts" in Detroit-area high schools (Eckert 2000). Individual and group styles can become objectified, or "reified" (Eckert 2000: 42–3), and hence may join the ranks of the various abstractions to which people orient as they engage in conversational interaction. Reified styles may include not only styles associated with relatively small social groups (e.g. the burnouts in suburban Detroit) but also larger groups (e.g. US Southerners or Midwesterners). In addition, they may be associated with particular situations of use (and so termed "registers") or with particular speech events or text types, including performative and artistic ones (so-called "genres"). When speakers engage in conversational interaction, they draw on features, and groups of features, from all these different types of reifications, hence drawing on the meanings associated with each. Thus, for all their emphasis on speaker agency, speaker design approaches do not really maintain that speakers are completely free to invent and re-invent new styles (or new identities) at will. However, speaker agency is still paramount, since it is through combining existing elements in new ways and interjecting these combinations into new contexts that speakers effect change, not only in the current situation but in the meanings of features and styles as well. As noted by the literary theorist Bakhtin, whose ideas figure prominently in speaker design approaches, "Our speech, that is, all our utterances (including creative works), is filled with others' words, varying degrees of otherness or varying degrees of 'our-own-ness', varying degrees of awareness and detachment. These words of others carry with them their own expression, their own evaluative tone, which we assimilate, rework, and re-accentuate" (Bakhtin 1981b: 89 [originally written in 1952–3]).

Central to the creation of new meanings in stylistic variation is the notion of conflict – conflict between the various styles speakers pull together in creating a new style and between this new style and the other styles with which it is juxtaposed (Bakhtin 1981a: 291 [originally written in 1934–5]; Campbell-Kibler et al. 2000, Irvine 2001). For example, Wong and Zhang (2000) show how the meanings of lexical items associated with various discourses (e.g. feminist discourse, Chinese Revolutionary discourse, gay and lesbian discourse in the Western world) are altered when brought into juxtaposition with one another and placed in a new context, a Chinese gay and lesbian magazine, and hence made available for use in the creation of a new non-Western gay and lesbian style. Similarly, Campbell-Kibler et al. (2000) show how a speech style that is designed to contrast with both flamboyantly gay speech and straight speech (i.e. "not too gay" speech) serves as a challenge to the existing social order, which holds that gay and other non-mainstream populations are monolithic. Hence, stylistic variation is a powerful tool for social change. The view that change can be effected through injecting styles from one situation into another echoes recent views of how initiative style shifting operates within the Audience Design framework (Bell 1999). One crucial difference, however, is that under speaker design approaches, styles do not derive their meanings through association to pre-existing situations or groups, nor do speakers simply use pre-existing styles in effecting change. Rather styles play a key role in defining situations and groups, while groups and individuals shape styles as they use them.

5.2   Limitations of speaker design approaches

Although speaker design approaches help address some of the limitations of Attention to Speech- and Audience Design-based approaches to stylistic variation, especially their unidimensionality and their focus on speakers as respondents rather than agents, they also raise new issues. For example, the inclusion of a host of factors that might affect stylistic choices, especially those internal to speakers and hence not readily observable, leads to a loss of the predictive power of unidimensional approaches like Labov's and Bell's (e.g. Rickford and McNair-Knox 1994: 241, 266–7). However, as Bell (1984: 185) notes, "Initiative style shifts [i.e. style shifts that cannot be neatly correlated with changes in the external situation] are not predicable, but they are interpretable." And, as Coupland points out, such shifts are only interpretable when we analyze a wide range of factors, including not only audience-related or attention-related considerations but such matters as "the interplay of message content, status and role relationships among participants, linguistic function and linguistic form" (1980: 11).

A second question raised by speaker design approaches is whether the interpretations gleaned through close-up analysis of individual initiative shifts can be generalized in any way to the larger community. However, it should be pointed out that the micro-level studies of stylistic variation that lie at the heart of speaker design are almost always complemented by macro-level ethnographic and sociolinguistic analyses, since (1) we would be hard pressed to get at speaker meaning without a thorough ethnographic understanding of individual and group meanings in the community under study, and (2) individual stylistic choices are never made in a social vacuum but are always being measured against group styles (and group patterns of stylistic variation), at the same time that groups styles are being shaped by individual language use (Eckert 2000).

Further, despite assertions that it is only through generalizing data from individual speakers that meaningful patterns will emerge (e.g. Bell 1984: 180, Labov 1972a: 101–3, 109, Rickford and McNair-Knox 1994: 258–60), some researchers maintain that such generalization is inappropriate when applied to stylistic variation, which is, after all, chiefly concerned with *intra*-speaker variation – not patterns of variation as they exist across social groups. For example, Coupland (2001) notes, "[W]hen we come to the analysis of style, we see the individual interacting within her/his own space, time and relational contexts. We can of course seek to generalise about 'what most people stylistically do', and the results are informative and important. But this exercise is reductionist in that it rules out any possible interpretation of the *local* intra- and inter-personal processes which are style's domain" (7). The issue of whether intra-speaker variation can ultimately be linked to inter-speaker variation via the aggregation of individual data is an open question; however, the fact remains that the link between the two is inextricable and that learning more about the nature of this link is crucial to continued theory-building in sociolinguistics. Eckert (2000: 69) notes, "The challenge in the study of the social meaning of variation is to find the relation between the local and the global – to find the link between speakers' linguistic ways of negotiating identity and relations in their day-to-day lives, and their place in the social stratification of linguistic variation that transcends local boundaries."

One final concern for speaker design models is that, in their inclusion of features beyond the level of the phonological and morphosyntactic, these approaches move beyond the range of what can comfortably be analyzed using current quantitative variationist techniques. It is relatively unproblematic to investigate usage levels for phonological features, which carry no inherent semantic meaning, as expressed in ratios of actual over potential occurrences of the form. For example, a speaker is said to have 50 percent *r*-lessness if she pronounces *r*'s in half the places where she could potentially either pronounce or drop them. However, it is much more difficult to determine potential environments for the production of features with inherent grammatical, interactional, or referential meaning. One notorious case is that of habitual *be* – that is, the use of uninflected *be* in contexts denoting habitual activity (e.g. *He always be late to school*). In determining where this feature might occur, analysts have wrestled with the question of whether they should count as potential cases all places where standard English *am*, *is*, or *are* could occur or all places where habitual meaning is intended (e.g. Rickford and McNair-Knox 1994: 254–5). Even more problematic is the determination of potential environments for a discourse particle like *eh*: should one assume that it could occur on the end of any declarative sentence, or only in places where the speaker is seeking to draw interlocutors into conversation (Bell and Johnson 1997: 10)? Hence, in attempting to quantify occurrence levels for discoursal, pragmatic, and even some morphosyntactic features, we are often reduced to simple token counts, thereby neglecting the crucial question of whether different levels for particular features in different contexts (e.g. with different audience members or across different topics) genuinely reflect stylistic choices, or simply differing levels of potential environments for their occurrence. (See Rickford and McNair-Knox 1994, and Kiesling 1998, who carefully consider possible internal effects on intra-speaker variation.) Again, this matter is an open question; indeed, it is one that has plagued variationists since the inception of the field (e.g. Lavandera 1978). However, it is important to bear in mind that it is not always frequency levels for features that are of primary importance in considering questions of speaker meaning (and how listeners interpret meaning), since even a single occurrence of a highly salient feature can carry strong social connotations – for example, a single use of a stigmatized feature such as *ain't* (e.g. Trudgill 1986, Rampton 1999c: 423–4).

6   Future Directions for the Study of Stylistic Variation

As variationists continue to approach stylistic variation as a resource in the creation and re-creation of individual and interpersonal identity, it will be necessary to continue to search for answers to the unresolved issues above. For example, in order to increase our understanding of how speakers internalize large-scale patterns in stylistic variation, while at the same time shaping these patterns through their individualized usage in local interaction, it will be necessary to continue to link micro-level analyses with broad-scale ethnographic investigations. In addition, variationist surveys of the patterning of linguistic variation across social groups will be needed as well, in order to provide a backdrop against which to measure individual patterns. However, it remains unclear as to whether data on intra-speaker variation should be aggregated in attempting to link it with data on the inter-speaker patterning of variation.

Another issue for further study is the role of internal linguistic factors in individual and social group variation. Does Preston's (1991: 36) Status Axiom genuinely hold for most communities – that is, is it typically the case that the amount of variation due to internal linguistic factors is greater than the amount of variation by social group, which in turn is greater than the amount of variation by speech style? Or will exceptional cases (e.g. the case of Tehran Persian, as reported in Modaressi-Tehrani 1978) prove to be more widespread than originally thought, especially as researchers glean more information about the patterning of variation in speech communities throughout the world? In addition, what sorts of factors will be shown to underlie exceptional cases, and will these "exceptional" findings prove to be generalizable in any way? For example, will "unusual" patterns turn out to be mostly a matter of cultural difference, as suggested, for example, by Bell (1984: 155–6)? Or will they have more to do with the characteristics of specific features – for example, whether the features serve as indicators, markers, or stereotypes in a given community (e.g. Preston 1991)?

A related question is exactly how different types of features figure in stylistic variation. For example, Rickford and McNair-Knox (1994) suggest that more frequently occurring features may be more likely to be used in stylistic variation than rare ones, while other researchers have suggested such factors as salience, linguistic level (e.g. phonological vs. morphosyntactic), and implication in linguistic systemic considerations as likely to play a role. For example, Eckert (2000) suggests that raised /ai/ figures prominently in individual and group style in Detroit-area high schools because it is not involved in the Northern Cities Chain Shift, a systematic shift in the pronunciations of several vowels in urbanized areas of the Northern USA, in which a change in one vowel affects the pronunciation of others (see Gordon, this volume). On the other hand, negative concord plays a large role because speakers are very aware of it, since it is so highly stigmatized (2000: 170, 216–17). Interestingly, in order to investigate the issue of speaker awareness, it may be that considerations of attention to speech will once again come to the forefront (Rampton 1999c: 423–4). This time, however, the focus would be on the selfconscious speech that variationists once sought to avoid. Further, the investigation of selfconscious speech, even overtly performative speech, seems essential in a research program in which stylistic variation is viewed as a resource for creating and projecting one's persona – that is, with performing an identity. In considering the role of speech performance in stylistic variation, variationists have benefited from the insights offered by anthropological investigations of performative speech events (e.g. Bauman 1975, Bauman and Briggs 1990). More cross-disciplinary research along these lines will likely yield fruitful results.

Given that salience seems to figure so prominently in stylistic variation, a final area for further investigation is that of listener perception: how do listeners determine when style shifting has occurred, and how do they interpret patterns of stylistic variation – and individual instances of particularly noticeable forms? In seeking answers to these questions, it may be useful to pursue a line of inquiry introduced by Coupland (1980), who complemented his own analysis of stylistic variation with a perception test in which listeners were asked to indicate when, in their judgment, style shifts had occurred. In addition, it will be useful to continue to investigate types of features of which listeners are more consciously aware than they typically are of non-stereotypic phonological and morphosyntactic variants – for example, lexical, intonational, and discourse-level features. Finally, it should prove fruitful to continue to pursue the question of how popular notions of "style" relate to variationist conceptualizations of stylistic variation. Non-specialists can readily point to group styles, both linguistic and non-linguistic (e.g. Valley Girl style, punk style), as well as individual styles (e.g. "He's got a certain style"; "She's always so in style"). However, researchers are only just beginning to explore how linguistic and non-linguistic resources are marshaled in the creation of distinctive styles (e.g. Arnold et al. 1993, Campbell-Kibler et al. 2000, Eckert 2000, Mendoza-Denton 1997, Wong and Zhang 2001). In the end, then, we are left with the question with which the exploration of stylistic variation begins: "What is style?"

NOTES

1　This is only one definition of "vernacular," a term which has been plagued by definitional ambiguity since its first uses in sociolinguistics. For example, Milroy (1987: 57–60) points out that the term may be variously used to refer to unmonitored speech, the community lect farthest from the standard, or the variety first acquired. Further discussion of this issue is beyond the scope of this chapter.

2　But cf. Finegan and Biber (1994, 2001), who maintain that social group variation derives from stylistic (actually "register") variation: different social groups have access to different types of registers, characterized by different types of linguistic features, and so show different usage levels for the different types of forms (namely, "economical" vs. "elaborated" forms, such as contractions vs. full forms). Though Finegan and Biber's findings are based on quantitative investigation of the co-occurrence patterns of features across different registers and different social groups, they do not really fit into the "variationist" paradigm, since they do not report on frequency of occurrence, as expressed in the ratio of actual over potential occurrences, but simply present absolute counts of forms (Preston 2001). Further, as Preston (2000) points out, the features they examine are usually ones which carry functional meaning(s) of some sort rather than the features typically examined in variation study (e.g. vowel pronunciations), whose meanings derive solely from their association with social groups. Hence, it is not surprising that Finegan and Biber's findings differ from those of the classic variationist investigations reported in Bell (1984). For in-depth discussion (and critique) of their findings and interpretations, the reader is referred to Preston (1991, 2001) and Rose (2000). See also Chambers (1995: 230–42) on the difficulty of defining linguistic "economy" and of relegating "economical" features to certain social groups.

REFERENCES

Arnold, Jennifer, Renée Blake, Penelope Eckert, Melissa Iwai, Norma

Mendoza-Denton, Carol Morgan, Livia Polanyi, Julie Solomon and

Tom Veatch (1993). Variation and personal/group style. Paper presented at New Ways of Analyzing Variation 22, Ottawa, Ontario.

Bakhtin, M. M. (1981a). Discourse in the novel. In M. M. Bakhtin, *The Dialogic Imagination*, ed. by Michael Holquist; trans. by Caryl Emerson and Michael Holquist. Austin, TX: University of Texas Press. 259–422.

Bakhtin, M. M. (1981b). The problem of speech genres. In M. M. Bakhtin, *Speech Genres and Other Late Essays*, ed. by Caryl Emerson and Michael Holquist; trans. by Vern W. McGee. Austin, TX: University of Texas Press. 60–102.

Barth, Fredrik (1969). Introduction. In Fredrik Barth (ed.), *Ethnic Groups and Boundaries: The Social Organization of Culture Difference*. Oslo: Universitetsforlaget.

Bateson, Gregory (1972). A theory of play and fantasy. Reprinted in *Steps to an Ecology of Mind*. New York: Ballantine Books. 117–93.

Bauman, Richard (1975). Verbal art as performance. *American Anthropologist* 77: 290–311.

Bauman, Richard and Charles L. Briggs (1990). Poetics and performance as critical perspectives on language and social life. *Annual Review of Anthropology* 19: 59–88.

Bauman, Richard and Joel Sherzer (1989). Introduction to the second edition. In Richard Bauman and Joel Sherzer (eds.), *Explorations in the Ethnography of Speaking*, 2nd edn. Cambridge: Cambridge University Press. ix–xxvii.

Bell, Allan (1984). Language style as audience design. *Language in Society* 13: 145–204.

Bell, Allan (1999). Styling the other to define the self: A study in New Zealand identity making. *Journal of Sociolinguistics* 3, 4: 523–41.

Bell, Allan (2001). Back in style: Reworking audience design. In John R. Rickford and Penelope Eckert (eds.), *Style and Variation*. Cambridge/New York: Cambridge University Press. 139–69.

Bell, Allan and Gary Johnson (1997). Towards a sociolinguistics of style. *University of Pennsylvania Working Papers in Linguistics* 4.1: 1–21.

Bickerton, Derek (1980). What happens when we switch? *York Papers in Linguistics* 9: 41–56.

Blom, Jan-Petter and John J. Gumperz (1972). Social meaning in linguistic structure: Code-switching in Norway. In John J. Gumperz and Dell Hymes (eds.), *Directions in Sociolinguistics*. New York: Holt, Rinehart & Winston. 407–34.

Brown, Penelope and Stephen Levinson (1979). Social structure, groups and interaction. In Klaus R. Scherer and Howard Giles (eds.), *Social Markers in Speech*. Cambridge: Cambridge University Press. 291–342.

Bucholtz, Mary (1999). You da man: Narrating the racial other in the production of white masculinity. *Journal of Sociolinguistics* 3, 4: 443–60.

Cameron, Deborah (1990). Demythologizing sociolinguistics: Why language does not reflect society. In John E. Joseph and Talbot J. Taylor (eds.), *Ideologies of Language*. London: Routledge. 79–93.

Campbell-Kibler, Kathryn, Robert J. Podesva and Sarah J. Roberts (2000). Sharing resources and indexing meaning in the production of gay styles. Paper presented at First International Gender and Language Association Conference, Stanford, CA.

Chambers, J. K. (1995). *Sociolinguistic Theory*. Cambridge, MA/Oxford, UK: Blackwell.

Coupland, Nikolas (1980). Style-shifting in a Cardiff work-setting. *Language in Society* 9: 1–12.

Coupland, Nikolas (1981). The social differentiation of functional language use: A sociolinguistic investigation of travel agency talk. Ph.D. dissertation, University of Wales Institute of Science and Technology.

Coupland, Nikolas (1984). Accommodation at work: Some phonological data and their implications. *International Journal of the Sociology of Language* 46: 49–70.

Coupland, Nikolas (1985). "Hark, hark the lark": Social motivations for phonological style-shifting. *Language and Communication* 5, 3: 153–72.

Coupland, Nikolas (1996). Language, situation, and the relational self: Theorising dialect-style in sociolinguistics. Paper presented at Stanford Workshop on Stylistic Variation, Stanford, CA.

Coupland, Nikolas (2001). Language, situation and the relational self: Theorising dialect-style in sociolinguistics. In John R. Rickford and Penelope Eckert (eds.), *Style and Variation*. Cambridge/New York: Cambridge University Press. 185–210.

Crystal, David (1991). *A Dictionary of Linguistics and Phonetics*, 3rd edn. Oxford, UK/Cambridge, MA: Blackwell.

Cutler, Cecilia A. (1999). Yorkville crossing: White teens, hip hop, and African American English. *Journal of Sociolinguistics* 3, 4: 428–42.

Douglas-Cowie. Ellen (1978). Linguistic code-switching in a Northern Irish village: Social interaction and social ambition. In Peter Trudgill (ed.), *Sociolinguistic Patterns in British English*. London: Edward Arnold. 37–51.

Eastman, C. M. and R. F. Stein (1993). Language display: Authenticating claims to social identity. *Journal of Multilingual and Multicultural Development* 14, 3: 187–202.

Eckert, Penelope (2000). *Linguistic Variation as Social Practice*. Malden, MA/Oxford, UK: Blackwell.

Ervin-Tripp, Susan M. (1964). An analysis of the interaction of language, topic an listener. In John Gumperz and Dell Hymes (eds.), *The Ethnography of Communication*. 86–102.

Ervin-Tripp, Susan M. (1973). *Language Acquisition and Communicative Choice*. Stanford, CA: Stanford University Press.

Fasold, Ralph W. (1972). *Tense Marking in Black English: A Linguistic and Social Analysis*. Arlington, VA: Center for Applied Linguistics.

Finegan, Edward and Douglas Biber (1994). Register and social dialect variation: An integrated approach. In Douglas Biber and Edward Finegan (eds.), *Sociolinguistic Perspectives on Register*. New York/Oxford: Oxford University Press. 315–47.

Finegan, Edward and Douglas Biber (2001). Register variation and social dialect variation: Re-examining the connection. In John R. Rickford and Penelope Eckert (eds.), *Style and Variation*. Cambridge/New York: Cambridge University Press. 235–67.

Giles, Howard (1973). Accent mobility: A model and some data. *Anthropological Linguistics* 15: 87–105.

Giles, Howard and Peter F. Powesland (1975). *Speech Style and Social Evaluation*. London: Academic Press.

Giles, Howard, Nikolas Coupland and Justine Coupland (1991). Accommodation theory: Communication, context, and consequence. In Howard Giles, Justine Coupland and Nikolas Coupland (eds.), *Contexts of Accommodation: Developments in Applied Sociolinguistics*. Cambridge: Cambridge University Press. 1–68.

Goffman, Erving (1974). *Frame Analysis*. New York: Harper & Row.

Goffman, Erving (1981). *Forms of Talk*. Philadelphia: University of Pennsylvania Press.

Halliday, M. A. K. (1978). *Language as a Social Semiotic: The Social Interpretation of language and Meaning*. London: Edward Arnold.

Hindle, Donald M. (1979). The social and situational conditioning of phonetic variation. Ph.D. dissertation, University of Pennsylvania.

Hymes, Dell (1972). Models of the interaction of language and social life. In John Gumperz and Dell Hymes (eds.), *Directions in Sociolinguistics*. New York: Holt, Reinhart and Winston. 35–71.

Hymes, Dell (1974). Ways of speaking. In Richard Bauman and Joel Sherzer (eds.), *Explorations in the Ethnography of Speaking*. Cambridge: Cambridge University Press. 433–51.

Irvine, Judith (2001). Style as distinctiveness: The culture and ideology of linguistic differentiation. In John R. Rickford and Penelope Eckert (eds.), *Style and Variation*. Cambridge: Cambridge University Press. 21–43.

Johnstone, Barbara (1999). Uses of Southern-sounding speech by contemporary Texas women. *Journal of Sociolinguistics* 3, 4: 505–22.

Kiesling, Scott Fabius (1996). Language, gender, and power in fraternity men's discourse. Ph.D. dissertation, Georgetown University, Washington.

Kiesling, Scott Fabius (1998). Men's identities and sociolinguistic variation: The case of fraternity men. *Journal of Sociolinguistics* 2, 1: 69–99.

Kiesling, Scott Fabius and Natalie Schilling-Estes (1998). Language style as identity construction: A footing and framing approach. Poster presented at New Ways of Analyzing Variation 27, Athens, GA.

Labov, William (1966). *The Social Stratification of English in New York City*. Washington: Center for Applied Linguistics.

Labov, William (1972a). The isolation of contextual styles. In William Labov, *Sociolinguistic Patterns*. Philadelphia: University of Pennsylvania Press. 70–109.

Labov, William (1972b). The reflection of social processes in linguistic structures. In William Labov, *Sociolinguistic Patterns*. Philadelphia: University of Pennsylvania Press. 110–121.

Lavandera, Beatriz (1978). Where does the sociolinguistic variable stop? *Language in Society* 7: 171–82.

Macaulay, Ronald K. S. (1977). *Language, Social Class and Education: A Glasgow Study*. Edinburgh: University of Edinburgh Press.

Mendoza-Denton, Norma (1997). Chicana/Mexicana identity and linguistic variation: An ethnographic and sociolinguistic study of gang affiliation in an urban high school. Ph.D. dissertation, Stanford University.

Milroy, Lesley (1987). *Observing and Analysing Natural Language*. Oxford, UK/Cambridge, MA: Blackwell.

Modaressi-Tehrani, Y. (1978). A sociolinguistic analysis of modern Persian. Ph.D. dissertation, University of Kansas.

Myers-Scotton, Carol (1998). A theoretical introduction to the markedness model. In Carol Myers-Scotton (ed.), *Codes and Consequences: Choosing Linguistic Varieties*. New York: Oxford University Press. 18–38.

Preston, Dennis R. (1991). Sorting out the variables in sociolinguistic theory. *American Speech* 66, 1: 33–56.

Preston, Dennis R. (2001). Style and the psycholinguistics of sociolinguistics: The logical problem of language variation. In John R. Rickford and Penelope Eckert (eds.), *Style and Variation*. Cambridge/New York: Cambridge University Press. 279–303.

Rampton, Ben (1995). *Crossing: Language and Ethnicity among Adolescents*. London: Longman.

Rampton, Ben (1999a). Deutsch in inner city London and the animation of an instructed foreign language. *Journal of Sociolinguistics* 3, 4: 480–504.

Rampton, Ben (ed.) (1999b). Styling the other. Special issue of *Journal of Sociolinguistics* 3, 4.

Rampton, Ben (1999c). Styling the other: Introduction. *Journal of Sociolinguistics* 3, 4: 421–7.

Rickford, John R. (1979). Variation in a Creole continuum: Quantitative and implicational approaches. Ph.D. dissertation, University of Pennsylvania.

Rickford, John R. and Faye McNair-Knox (1994). Addressee- and Topic-influenced style shift: A quantitative sociolinguistic study. In Douglas Biber and Edward Finegan (eds.), *Sociolinguistic Perspectives on Register*. New York/Oxford: Oxford University Press. 235–76.

Romaine, Suzanne (1978). Post-vocalic /r/ in Scottish English: Sound change in progress. In Peter Trudgill (ed.), *Sociolinguistic Patterns in British English*. London: Edward Arnold. 144–57.

Romaine, Suzanne (1980). A critical overview of the methodology of urban British sociolinguistics. *English World-Wide* 1: 163–98.

Romaine, Suzanne (1984). The status of sociological models and categories in explaining linguistic variation. *Linguistische Berichte* 90: 25–38.

Rose, Mary (2000). Putting aside the curious anecdotes: "Meanings" of nominalization in science writing. MS, Stanford University.

Russell, Joan (1982). Networks and sociolinguistic variation in an African urban setting. In Suzanne Romaine (ed.), *Sociolinguistic Variation in Speech Communities*. London: Edward Arnold. 125–40.

Schiffrin, Deborah (1987). *Discourse Markers*. Cambridge: Cambridge University Press.

Schiffrin, Deborah (1996). Narrative as self-portrait: Sociolinguistic constructions of identity. *Language in Society* 25: 167–203.

Schilling-Estes, Natalie (1998). Investigating "self-conscious" speech: The performance register in Ocracoke English. *Language in Society* 27: 53–83.

Schilling-Estes, Natalie (1999). Situated ethnicities: Constructing and reconstructing identity in the sociolinguistic interview. *University of Pennsylvania Working Papers in Linguistics* 6.2 (Proceedings from NWAVE 27): 137–51.

Schilling-Estes, Natalie and Walt Wolfram (1999). Alternative models of dialect death: Dissipation vs. concentration. *Language* 75, 3: 486–521.

Scollon, Ron (1997). Handbills, tissues and condoms: A site of engagement for the construction of identity in public discourse. *Journal of Sociolinguistics* 1, 1: 39–61.

Tannen, Deborah (1984). *Conversational Style: Analyzing Talk among Friends*. Norwood, NJ: Ablex.

Tannen, Deborah (1993). What's in a frame? Surface evidence for underlying expectations. In Deborah Tannen (ed.), *Framing in Discourse*. Oxford: Oxford University Press. 14–56.

Thelander, Mats (1982). A qualitative approach to the quantitative data of speech variation. In Suzanne Romaine (ed.), *Sociolinguistic Variation in Speech Communities*. London: Edward Arnold. 65–83.

Traugott, Elizabeth Closs and Suzanne Romaine (1985). Some questions for the definition of "style" in sociohistorical linguistics. *Folia Linguistica Historica* 6, 1: 7–39.

Trudgill, Peter (1974). *The Social Differentiation of English in Norwich*. Cambridge: Cambridge University Press.

Trudgill, Peter (1981). Linguistic accommodation: Sociolinguistic observations on a sociopsychological theory. In Carrie S. Masek, Roberta A. Hendrick and Mary Frances Miller (eds.), *Papers from the Parasession on Language and Behavior*. Chicago: Chicago Linguistic Society. 218–37.

Trudgill, Peter (1986). *Dialects in Contact*. Oxford, UK/New York, NY: Blackwell.

Trudgill, Peter (2000). *Sociolinguistics: An Introduction to Language and Society*, 4th edn. London/New York: Penguin.

Wolfram, Walt (1969). *A Sociolinguistic Description of Detroit Negro Speech*. Washington, DC: Center for Applied Linguistics.

Wolfram, Walt (1981). On the orderly relationship of Appalachian dialects. MS.

Wolfram, Walt and Natalie Schilling-Estes (1998). *American English: Dialects and Variation*. Malden, MA/Oxford, UK: Blackwell.

Wong, Andrew and Qing Zhang (2000). The linguistic construction of the *tongzhi* community. *Journal of Linguistic Anthropology* 10, 1–31.

Woods, H. B. (1979). A socio-dialectology survey of the English spoken in Ottawa: A study of sociological and stylistic variation in Canadian English. Ph.D dissertation, University of British Columbia.

16 Social Class

SHARON ASH

Social class is a central concept in sociolinguistic research, one of the small number of social variables by which speech communities are stratified. Trudgill (1974: 32) states that "most members of our society have some kind of idea, intuitive or otherwise, of what social class is," and most people, both specialists and laypeople, would probably agree with this. It is ironic, then, that social class is often defined in an ad hoc way in studies of linguistic variation and change, and linguists do not frequently take advantage of the findings of disciplines that make it their business to examine social class, particularly sociology, to inform their work. Still, social class is uniformly included as a variable in sociolinguistic studies, and individuals are placed in a social hierarchy despite the lack of a consensus as to what concrete, quantifiable independent variables contribute to determining social class. To add to the irony, not only is social class uniformly included as an important variable in studies of linguistic variation, but it regularly produces valuable insights into the nature of linguistic variation and change. Thus, this variable is universally used and extremely productive, although linguists can lay little claim to understanding it. Most sociological definitions include the notion of the "life-chances" of an individual or a class, as does, for example, Michael (1962), the basis of Labov's (1966) study of the Lower East Side of New York City. Here social class is defined as "an individual's life chances stated in terms of his relation to the production and acquisition of goods and services."

1 Sociological Background

The theoretical consideration of the notion of social class in modern times was sparked by the dramatic reorganization of society resulting from the industrial revolution. This overhaul of the social and economic order, which transformed a disseminated, agricultural population into an urbanized one as workers gathered in factory centers, brought about the system of industrial capitalism, beginning in England in the second half of the eighteenth century. It spread to other western countries in the nineteenth century, notably France, Germany, and the United States, and expanded world-wide as the twentieth century progressed.

The term *sociology* was coined in 1838 by Auguste Comte (1798–1857), a French philosopher and social reformer, in his *Cours de philosophie positive* (1830–42). Nearly a century and a half later Wright quoted Stinchcombe as saying that "Sociology has only one independent variable, class" (Wright 1979: 3). This may be an extreme position, but sociologists certainly agree on the centrality of social class to the understanding of social structures, and the sociological literature on class is vast, reflecting the diversity of views on the subject.

Karl Marx (1818–83) is considered by many scholars to be the founder of economic history and sociology, and he developed the first and one of the most influential theories of social class.[1] Marx was a theoretician, but he was an activist as well. Within his larger project of writing the history of all human societies, he took as his object of special study the newly developed system of industrial capitalism. With his theme of the history of society as the history of class struggles, he emphasized the economic aspect of class stratification. His goal was social reform: he believed that the polarization of the owners of the means of production versus the labor force would increase, that revolution would ensue, that the workers would be victorious, private ownership of the means of production would be abolished, and a classless society would be established.

Max Weber (1864–1920) is the second "classical" theorist of social class. While Marx promulgated socialism, Weber supported industrial capitalism and was opposed to socialism. He agreed with Marx that ownership or non-ownership of property is fundamental in determining the life-chances of an individual or a class, but he added the dimensions of power and prestige as interacting factors creating hierarchies. He introduced the concept of social stratification and elaborated a complex, multi-factored social structure.

Two central components of social class, then, are (1) the objective, economic measures of property ownership and the power and control it confers on its possessor, and (2) the subjective measures of prestige, reputation, and status. The most simplistic social classification is based on occupational categories, with non-manual ("white collar") occupations being rated higher than manual ("blue collar") occupations. This factor combines the objective and subjective components, demonstrating that factors other than income are important in the assessment of social status, since skilled tradesmen such as plumbers and carpenters typically earn more income than lower-level white collar workers such as clerks and cashiers. Similarly, a highly trained professional such as an architect may well earn less than the builder who executes his designs. The reliance on occupational categories as a measure of social class is very common in social science research.

The task of the researcher interested in linguistic variation is to find a way to determine, with reliability and validity, the social ranking, social class, or both, of the members of the speech community under investigation. One sociologist who is frequently quoted as a guide is W. Lloyd Warner, although his work is, in practice, not fully utilized by sociolinguists.

Warner and his associates represent the view that status groups form the foundation of social stratification. As a social anthropologist, he set out to study in detail (published in six volumes) contemporary American society by examining a single, self-contained city. The fieldwork in the small New England city of Yankee City, population about 17,000, involved from five to fifteen researchers at any given time. They interviewed 16,785 individuals, most of them repeatedly, over the period from 1930 to 1934. Following the methods of social anthropology, they combined interviewing with observation, gathering a wealth of detailed information that reaches astonishing proportions. In the matter of social class, they followed the indications of their informants, who exhibited a keen sense of the relative social rank of their acquaintances. The researchers quickly learned that neither income nor occupation was the sole predictor of rating on the social scale. The characteristics that were called into play included education, occupation, wealth, income, family, intimate friends, clubs and fraternities, manners, speech, and general outward behavior.

Warner generalized the methods used in Yankee City and in later studies and published a set of procedures for determining social class by two alternative methods: Evaluated Participation and the Index of Status Characteristics (Warner et al. 1960). The explicit purpose of this work was to provide tools for researchers in other fields to use in assessing social class among the populations of their respective interest. The method of Evaluated Participation provides a set of instructions for, in effect, eliciting the types of information that were gathered in the Yankee City study to determine how community members rated each other on the social scale. The Index of Status Characteristics is designed to be simple and inexpensive to use, requiring little skill, little time, and the elicitation of limited, easily obtained information. It was empirically derived and, following testing and refinement, it was validated against the scale of Evaluated Participation which had been calculated for 303 families in a small Midwestern city that had been studied in depth. In these respects Warner's Index of Status Characteristics seems to be eminently suited to use in survey-type studies of speech communities.

The writings of Warner et al. (1960) are firmly grounded in an awareness of the necessity of tailoring any study to the particular characteristics of the community being investigated. They advise against a blanket, unthinking application of their procedures to any social science research project. At the same time, their methods rest on solid research, and they have carefully tested their results and made sensible modifications accordingly. As a tool for judging social class, in a survey study in North America (and, perhaps with adjustments for local conditions, in other industrialized societies), it offers a set of procedures that a linguist could defensibly rely on.

One alternative to Warner's ISC is provided by the occupational prestige ratings and the Socioeconomic Index (SEI) developed by the National Opinion Research Council (NORC). In 1947, the NORC published the North–Hatt scale of occupational prestige, which listed prestige ratings for 90 occupational titles.

In 1950 the US Census Bureau began collecting data on income and education for incumbents of certain occupations, of which 270 were listed that year. To address the need for a ranking of the social status of all occupations, Duncan (1961) calculated a Socioeconomic Index by performing a multiple regression of the NORC prestige ratings on the income and educational levels for those occupations that were common to both the NORC and the Census listings and then extrapolating to occupational titles listed by the Census but not included in the NORC study.

This work has been updated, most recently in 1989. The NORC has reported prestige ratings (Nakao and Treas 1990) for the 503 occupational titles on which the Census Bureau gathered data in 1980, and they also report SEI assignments (Nakao and Treas 1992), using the methods developed by Duncan, with adjustments made for current levels of educational attainment and income. This scale has the advantage of being applicable to speakers on the basis of occupation alone.

2 Treatments of Social Class

To illustrate the variety of treatments of social class and some of the considerations that it raises in studies of linguistic change and variation, we turn now to a review of some of the studies that have included social class as an independent variable.

2.1 The New York City department store survey

This study by Labov (1972) is unique in that three strata defined by prestige were established first, and then subjects were randomly (and as exhaustively as possible) recruited from within each stratum. Stratification was defined by the prestige of the three New York City stores that were studied, Saks Fifth Avenue, Macy's, and Klein's. The relative prestige of the stores was in turn established by a number of independent factors: the location of the store; the amount of advertising in the *New York Times*, with its middle-class readership, and in the *Daily News*, a working-class newspaper; the relative cost of goods in the three stores, the form of prices quoted in advertising copy, and the relative emphasis on prices; the physical plant of the three stores; and information on the regard held by employees for working conditions at the three stores. Thus the social stratification of the three sites was firmly established, while, in this unusual case, the study controlled for occupation: the interviewees were predominantly salespeople, plus a small sample of floorwalkers, cashiers, and stockboys.

2.2   *The Lower East Side*

Labov's study of the Lower East Side of New York City (1966) had the benefit of following in the footsteps of a survey of the same area by the Mobilization for Youth program (MFY), which had been conducted the year before Labov's exploratory interviews. MFY was a publicly funded agency with the mission of attacking the problem of juvenile delinquency. The research design for the MFY study was developed by faculty at the New York School for Social Research at Columbia University, who offered Labov the opportunity to use both the demographic data that had been collected for MFY and the roster of interviewees. Thus, he had access to far more exact information on the prospective speakers than linguistic researchers are normally able to gather on their own.

The MFY approach to social class explicitly chooses to rely on factors of production – that is, on objective factors – rather than on consumption, or status – the expression of choices of lifestyle (Michael 1962). Warner, as we have seen, and also the NYC department store survey, rely instead on factors that reflect status. Persuasive arguments seem to be possible for both sides.

The MFY survey established a 10-point scale of socioeconomic class, based on the occupation, education, and income of the informants. The occupational rank was determined by four categories (Michael 1962: 213):

1   professionals, managers, and officials (salaried and self-employed);
2   clerks and salesmen;
3   craftsmen and foremen; self-employed white and blue-collar workers – including small shopkeepers;
4   operatives, service workers, laborers, and permanently unemployed persons.

The levels for education were as follows (Michael 1962: 214):

1   completed some college or more;
2   finished high school;
3   completed some high school;
4   finished grade school or less.

The MFY staff determined each family's income, and from that they calculated an "adjusted weekly income per equivalent adult" by a procedure that counted children as carrying less weight than adults. The actual income figures are out of date, but the qualitative description can be applied at any time:

1 more than the national median;
2 more than the Lower East Side median but less than the national median;
3 more than the minimum wage but less than the LES median;
4 less than the minimum wage.

The three factors of occupation, education, and income were weighted equally in calculating the index score, which ranged from 0 to 9. The resulting range of index scores was grouped into four categories, when grouping was desired: lower-class, working-class, and middle-class, the last of which was divided into lower middle class and upper middle class when such a division was indicated. It is notable that Labov varied the assignment of index ranges to social classes, depending on what groupings provided the best fit with the data. Thus his approach was to draw on both the possibilities of greater precision offered by the 10-point scale and the possibilities of greater generality offered by the four- or three-class scale, reserving the right to alternate between the two.

2.3 Philadelphia: The neighborhood study

The work of the Language Change and Variation project in Philadelphia in the 1970s, reported by Labov (2001), strives to discover the social location of the innovators of linguistic change and therefore focuses on the embedding of individuals in their neighborhoods. To this end, five neighborhoods were selected to represent the range of community types within the urban area, and one block in each neighborhood was selected as an entry point to the community. They are (1) Wicket Street, in a mill and factory section settled by Irish immigrants in the middle of the nineteenth century; (2) Pitt Street, in a neighborhood settled by the overflow of Irish immigrants from the area of Wicket Street; (3) Clark Street, in an Italian neighborhood of the part of the city which has become the stereotype of working-class Philadelphia; (4) Mallow Street, in a lower middle-class suburb adjoining the city to the west; and (5) Nancy Drive, in a middle- and upper middle-class suburban community.

For purposes of this study, Labov constructed a socioeconomic status index based on education, occupation, and residence value. For each factor, six levels were defined, and an individual's index was calculated as the unweighted sum of the scores for each factor. The categories are as follows:

Education	5	Professional school
	4	College graduate
	3	Some college
	2	High school graduate
	1	Some high school
	0	Grammar school

Occupation	6	Professional, owner-director of large firm
	5	White collar – proprietor, manager
	4	White collar – merchant, foreman, sales
	3	Blue collar – skilled
	2	Blue collar – unskilled
	1	Unemployed

Residence value was ranked in increments of $5,000, with the lowest level being up to $4,900 and the highest being $25,000 and above. Much more than education and occupation, this factor is critically dependent on time and place and must be set separately for each community to be studied.

As attention was also focused on the neighborhoods themselves as units to be studied, Labov seeks to characterize each neighborhood on a socioeconomic scale to judge the adequacy of the sampling of the range of block types in the urban area as a whole. As might be expected, the neighborhoods are most clearly differentiated by house value, although the two Irish neighborhoods, at the lowest levels of the scale, are about equal on this dimension. Occupation shows a similar distribution. The modal value for Wicket and Pitt Streets is unskilled blue collar jobs; Clark Street residents are concentrated in skilled blue collar jobs; Mallow Street is characterized by the lower level of white collar positions; and Nancy Drive is inhabited predominantly by professionals, proprietors, and managers. Interestingly, education does not distinguish the neighborhoods well, since for all neighborhoods, the modal level of educational attainment is high school graduate.

Thus house values rank a neighborhood by social status, but occupation ranks an individual by social status. Education in this case does not contribute to the social stratification of speakers. This is a provocative finding, since it is intuitively understood that education affects an individual's speech. To pursue this issue, linguists might treat education as a separate independent variable, independent of social class.

The Philadelphia study also considered two additional factors in the effort to assess the full character of an individual's social position within the community: house upkeep and social mobility. House upkeep is important to a person's local identity, but it does not apply outside the immediate area. It is judged in relation to local norms of what is expected, and it relates to the inhabitants' age and perceived ability to work on the house. In the five neighborhoods studied, the proportion of houses rated "Improved" as compared to the lower standard "Kept up" increases regularly from the lowest-ranked neighborhood to the lower-middle-class block of Mallow Drive.

Social mobility is judged as a comparison of the head of household's occupation with that of his or her parents, whether higher, equal, or lower. The proportion of upwardly mobile to stable speakers increases regularly across the three working class communities, but the lower-middle-class neighborhood of Mallow Drive had only one upwardly mobile speaker. The upper-middle-class neighborhood had a very high proportion of upward mobility, as is expected at the higher levels in a society where individuals can rise through the ranks on their merits. This distribution suggests that social mobility may *not* be useful as a predictor of linguistic variation, since the two groups that are expected to be most innovative are opposed in their levels of social mobility. But a conclusive result has yet to be obtained.

2.4 *Norwich, England*

For Trudgill's study of Norwich (1974), he set up a social class index based on six parameters: (1) occupation; (2) father's occupation; (3) income; (4) education; (5) locality; and (6) housing. Each parameter was rated on a scale from zero to five, and the scores for all categories were summed without weighting.

The occupational scale presents a familiar ranking:

1 professional workers;
2 employers and managers;
3 other non-manual workers;
4 foremen, skilled manual workers, and own account workers;
5 personal service, semi-skilled, and agricultural workers;
6 unskilled workers.

To obtain information on the sensitive subject of income, Trudgill employed the ingenious technique of showing speakers a card on which salary and wage ranges had been written and asking which range described the income of the person whose occupation was the determinant of occupational status for that speaker (that is, self, husband, or father). With this technique, there were no refusals to give the requested information when it was known to the speaker.

Dividing the educational spectrum into ranges depends in large part on the natural breaking points in the educational system of the place under study. It also has a parallel to the problem of setting up ranges of income in that, since the ideal ranking will maximally differentiate the population under study, it will depend in part on the expected levels of attainment, especially at both ends of the spectrum.

Trudgill's "Locality" is the neighborhood in the city of Norwich where the speaker lives, subjectively ranked for desirability on the basis of the author's native knowledge of the city. Indeed, any researcher who conducts an in-depth study of a speech community ought to be able to judge the relative prestige of neighborhoods within that community.

Trudgill's measure of housing is rather complex, based on three factors: house ownership, age of the house, and building type, with levels selected as measures of the relative prestige of this most conspicuous aspect of a speaker's attainment of lifestyle. Under ownership, he distinguishes council-rented, privately rented, and owner-occupied, with prestige ascending in that order. For the age of the house, he judges a newer house to be more prestigious than an older house, a correlation that would not hold in many communities. The relative prestige of a house as a function of age needs to be assessed with respect to the neighborhoods and communities being studied. For building type, Trudgill distinguishes terraces and flats (rowhouses and apartments), semi-detached, and detached. The three factors are arranged in a grid in which an index of relative prestige is assigned for the joint effect of all three. Of the combinations that actually occur in the sample, the low end of the scale is represented both by council-rented, pre-1939 terraces and flats and by privately rented pre-1914 terraces and flats, and the highest index is assigned to owner-occupied post-war detached houses.

With an index of prestige assigned to each of the six factors, the social class index for each speaker can be calculated. In Trudgill's sample, the actual range of the index is 3–26, out of a possible 0–30. Among the 60 speakers, there are a maximum of eight with any one score, with a concentration of speakers in the lower half of the range, from 6 to 13.

Trudgill observes that with multiple measures contributing to a socio-economic index, it would be possible to examine each one separately and determine which one, or which combination, provides the greatest explanatory power for the study of linguistic variation. This is a tantalizing point; such a study would be invaluable, but, to the best of my knowledge, it has never been done.

With a social class index that takes on such a wide range of values, it is necessary to group the speakers. Trudgill turns to a syntactic variable, the realization of third person singular verb forms with no third person singular marker, to examine the correlation between social class index and linguistic variation. Based on the percentage of markerless forms in formal and casual style for the pooled speakers ranked with each social class index, he is able quite persuasively to divide the spectrum of social class into five groups, which he labels Middle Middle Class, Lower Middle, Upper Working, Middle Working, and Lower Working. Although he declares that occupation is not a critical factor in arriving at this grouping, since its weight is only two-fifths of the index (own occupation and father's occupation), he nevertheless finds that the occupational range of each class is highly systematic. The highest class (MMC) consists mainly of professional people, including teachers, managers, employers, bank clerks, and insurance workers; the next group, the LMC, consists of non-manual workers such as typists, commercial travelers, and office workers; the third (UWC) includes foremen and skilled workers; the fourth (MWC) consists of manual workers; and the fifth and lowest (LWC) consists mainly of unskilled workers.

2.5   *Anniston, Alabama*

Feagin (1979) used her knowledge as a native of Anniston, Alabama, to select upper-class and working-class informants, using an informal Evaluated

Participation procedure. She is exceptional among sociolinguistic researchers in that she checked her class assignments by calculating Warner's Index of Status Characteristics (Warner et al. 1960) for all the speakers in her primary sample, using the scale that Warner established for Jonesville to define the social classes. The exercise is as much a confirmation of Warner's method as of Feagin's, since, as Warner says, the points of demarcation of the social classes properly should be established for each individual community by the methods of Evaluated Participation. Even so, there is very good agreement between Feagin's classification of her speakers and Warner's categorization. Her 27 upper class speakers include four who would be rated only as strongly upper-middle-class on Warner's scale, and her 41 working-class speakers include five who would be classified as lower-middle-class by Warner, plus one who would be classified as lower-class by Warner.

2.6   *Sydney, Australia and Paris, France*

While most researchers do not seem to think that occupation by itself is a sufficient determiner of social class, Horvath (1985) used it alone effectively in her study of variation and change in Sydney. She categorized speakers on the basis of occupation, following Congalton (1962, 1969), in which a random sample of 303 Sydney citizens ranked 135 occupations, and the rankings were later confirmed in a follow-up study of university students. Horvath conflated Congalton's four classes to three, which she termed Middle Class, Upper Working Class, and Lower Working Class. The Middle Class consists of professionals and skilled workers who are professional-like, including, for example, accountants, real estate agents, and pharmacists. The Upper Working Class consists of less skilled workers, e.g. flight attendants, arc welders, builders, chefs, and salesmen; and the Lower Working Class consists of unskilled workers such as truck drivers, metal workers, and factory workers.

Like Horvath, Lennig (1978) also used occupation alone as a measure of social class in his study of variation and change in the vowel system in Paris, and he too divided his sample into three categories:

1   Working Class: Manual workers who are not self-employed
2   Lower Middle Class: Office employees, secretaries, service personnel, self-employed manual workers, and artisans
3   Upper Middle Class: Corporation managers, professionals, and students in academic high schools

The main difference between the two is that Horvath has one middle-class and two levels of working-class, while Lennig has one working-class and two levels of middle-class. Horvath's upper-working-class seems to be the same as Lennig's lower-middle-class.

2.7 *Panama City, Panama*

Cedergren reports that Biesanz and Biesanz's (1955) sociological study of Panama City established a three-class system in Panama, consisting of an upper-class, a middle-class, and a lower-class, comprising 2 percent, 23 percent, and 75 percent of the population, respectively. Upper-class membership requires having the proper family background as well as occupation; middle-class membership is achieved through education and includes white collar workers; and the large lower-class consists of semi-skilled and unskilled workers. Cedergren's study did not attempt to follow this division, but rather derived a finer ranking of speakers by an index calculated without weighting based on education, occupation, and barrio of residence. Education ranges from less than junior high school to at least some college. Occupation is a simple four-point scale of managers, professionals, and proprietors; white collar workers; skilled workers; and unskilled laborers and domestic workers. The ranking of the barrio differs the most from the criteria that are encountered in North America and Europe: each barrio was ranked on the basis of the average number of persons per room in each household, the proportion of households with a private toilet, and the proportion of households with a refrigerator. With an index calculated for each speaker, Cedergren divided her sample of 79 subjects into four groups. As it happens, these groups map onto the distribution of population laid out by Biesanz and Biesanz rather well, with the subdivision of the lowest group into two; the top group consists of less than 10 percent of the sample, the next two groups are each about a quarter of the sample, and the lowest group is just under half the sample.

2.8 *Cairo, Egypt*

In studying linguistic variation and change in the diglossic setting of Cairene Arabic, Haeri (1997) used a weighted index of social factors which was then translated into a small set of social classes. In this case, the factors are father's or mother's occupation, with a weight of 0.5; whether the speaker attended a private language school, a private Arabic school, or a public school, with a weight of 0.25; the speaker's neighborhood, with a weight of 0.15; and the speaker's occupation, with a weight of 0.1. The weighted factors are summed, and the resulting index values are grouped into social classes designated Lower Middle Class, Middle Middle Class, Upper Middle Class, and Upper Class.

Thus there are many different ways to stratify a society, both in number of strata and in criteria for stratification. The researcher should try to employ an approach that has validity for the goal of the particular project and type of community. Most researchers, however, are not in a position to measure the validity of any approach. As Warner demonstrated, that is a study in itself. In practice, researchers typically formulate an index of social class, usually based on a combination of measures, which are likely to include both objective and subjective indices. The index is divided into larger categories, and correlations are calculated between the dependent variable and both the index, with its finer scale, and the larger categories, with its grosser scale.

3 The Linguistic Market

Sankoff and Laberge (1978) took a new approach to the ranking of speakers on the basis of their place in society, one which was geared to be specific to language use in a way that social class itself may not be. They adapted the notion of "linguistic market" from Bourdieu and Boltanski (1975) to construct an index intended to measure the extent to which a speaker's situation in life requires the use of the standard language. While the 1989 recalculation of occupational prestige in the United States (Nakao and Treas 1990) employed 1,250 lay judges, Sankoff and Laberge based their index on ratings by just eight judges. However, these were not lay judges; they were practicing sociolinguists who were intimately familiar with the sociolinguistic relationships within the Montreal francophone community. They were each asked to rank the 120 speakers of the Montreal corpus on the basis of "the relative importance of the legitimized language in the socioeconomic life of the speaker." As a basis for making their decisions, they were provided with a description of the socioeconomic life history of each speaker. This included all the information available to provide as full a picture of each individual's economic context as possible, including occupation, job description, details about parents or spouses, and occupation of the head of the household. The agreement among judges on the ranking of individuals was strikingly high, with a rate of disagreement ranging from less than 2 percent to less than 10 percent for all pairwise comparisons of judges. This finding echoes the observation by researchers on occupational prestige that such rankings are highly reliable.

From the rankings, Sankoff and Laberge (1978) calculated a linguistic market index for each speaker, and then they examined the correspondence between the index and a parameter indicating the tendency to use the standard variant for each of three linguistic variables. An extension of this method would be to use the same kind of ranking technique to develop a linguistic market index and match it to occupation, just as the NORC socioeconomic index is matched to the occupations listed by the US Census Bureau. This would respond to the objection many linguists have raised that indices of social class do not adequately relate to linguistic behavior. Like virtually every measure of social class, it would be strongly tied to an individual's occupation, but it would embody other dimensions as well.

The goal of studies of linguistic change and variation is to determine what can be learned about language from the differences in linguistic behavior of people of different social positions. Therefore, the determinants of social position that a linguist considers must be ones that are actually relevant to linguistic variation. This problem is akin to that of dividing the age continuum into linguistically relevant groups. Where age is concerned, the linguist can (usually) easily determine exactly what the chronological age of a speaker is. However, Eckert (1997) argues convincingly that a composite of factors relating to the life stage and social identity of an individual are more significant to the determination of linguistic behavior than simple chronological age. Such turning points as the formation of peer groups and joining the workforce, which can demonstrably be shown to affect linguistic behavior, should be taken into account in dividing the age continuum into linguistically relevant categories. Likewise, social factors that can realistically be judged – or better, can positively be demonstrated – to affect linguistic behavior are ones that should be included in a measure of social class. These might include an index of the linguistic market, as discussed above. Social mobility is another factor that would plausibly have a strong effect on a person's speech and could be incorporated into a linguist's conception of social class. The same holds for orientation towards or away from the local community, which was found to play a major role in Labov's (1972) study of Martha' Vineyard and has been shown to carry weight elsewhere as well (Wolfram et al. 1999, Feagin 1998). In the spirit of Warner's work on Evaluated Participation, another possible component of "sociolinguistic class" might be judgments by peers of who is an "effective speaker." In Labov's search (2001) for the innovators in sound change, where all indications point to people who are central figures in their local neighborhoods, the ranking by individuals of their peers as "good", "average", or "poor" speakers could be a promising avenue for investigation.

4   Subcommunities

Milroy (1980) objects that the large groupings derived from calculation of an index or other means "do not necessarily have any kind of objective, or even intersubjective, reality" (1980: 14) and that membership in a particular group, while serving as an expedient for the researcher, does not necessarily form an important part of the speaker's own definition of his social identity. She introduces the notion of community in a specific, technical sense, as a cohesive group to which people have a sense of belonging, that is rooted to a particular locale. Indeed, there are numerous studies of such small, closely knit, territorially based communities or subpopulations within larger speech communities. They are on a different scale from the survey-type studies of entire urban areas, and they clearly call for different methods, as she amply demonstrates in her own work in Belfast.

In one such case, Dayton (1996) studied a network of African-American Vernacular English speakers in Philadelphia. She observes that in the broad perspective, her speakers would be classified as urban working-class. A more detailed view would note distinctions that are significant to the speakers themselves. For one, the women were more upwardly mobile than the men. The women had high school diplomas, some of them had some college education, and they expected their children to go to college. Among the men, on the other hand, only half had high school diplomas, and none had completed any years of college. Most of the speakers had full-time jobs, and the women's jobs tended to be of higher status. They held administrative, secretarial, and clerical jobs, while the men were factory workers, janitors, restaurant workers, and maintenance men. The locally meaningful perspective relates to the African-American definition of class, which differentiates between those who hold a job (and are therefore working-class) and those who do not. The men in her sample described the women as "middle class", recognizing their upward mobility.

Eckert (1989, 2000) provides another example of a case in which the circumscription of the community under investigation compels a focus on local values. Her study of a high school cohort in suburban Detroit reveals the self-defined social groups of Jocks and Burnouts to be fundamentally opposed to each other in multiple ways. The Jocks are oriented toward the corporate structure of the school and stand to gain rights, privileges, and power by cooperating with the middle class, adult-oriented institutions around them. The Burnouts see little advantage in what the school offers them, as they will not go on to the college and professional training that the Jocks look forward to. The Burnouts are connected rather to the world outside the school, which is where they will work and find entertainment and social life after graduation, and in the meantime the school offers them only restrictions. This opposition of relationship to the school and all the structure it embodies sets the stage for a permanent state of conflict between the two groups, which is expressed in all the symbolic behavior the students have at their command, including language.

Rickford's (1979, 1986) fieldwork in Cane Walk, Guyana, provides a final example of a small community of speakers that must be understood on its own terms. In the context of an East Indian sugar estate community, the social class divisions that are appropriate to an industrialized economy were not applicable. Instead, Rickford found that there were two groups, which could be called social classes, except that they were motivated by such opposed ideologies that they could be taken for different universes. On the one hand, there was the Estate Class, composed of fieldworkers on the sugar estate who performed unskilled, labor-intensive jobs and occupied the lower stratum of the local society. The opposite group was the Non-estate Class, consisting of drivers and foremen on the sugar estate, as well as clerks, shopowners, and skilled tradesmen.

Like the Jocks and Burnouts in Eckert's study, the two groups differ dramatically in their opportunities for advancement. Members of the Non-estate Class are able to gain increments in income and power, while the efforts of the Estate Class to better their situations are rarely successful. At the same time, the speech of the Estate Class members is overwhelmingly creole, while the speech of the Non-estate Class members is much closer to standard English. Rickford proposes that members of the Estate Class use creole by choice, "as a revolutionary act" (1986: 218), to express solidarity with their class and opposition to the system that deprives them of upward mobility.

5   Social Class and Linguistic Variation

In determining the relationship between social class and variable language use, there are three cases to consider: stable variation, change from above (that is, from above the level of consciousness or social awareness), and change from below the level of social awareness. The linguistic variants that may be involved in stable variation or change from above may be prestige forms or stigmatized forms. In change from below, "there is no important distinction between stigmatized and prestige forms: the speech form assumed by each group may be taken as an unconscious mark of self-identification" (Labov 1966: 331).

Stratification by social class is not enough to diagnose linguistic change in progress. Since "change" means increasing use with the passage of time, the distribution of variants in apparent time is essential in determining whether a linguistic variable is undergoing change. The distribution of variants across contextual styles also provides strong evidence for the processes that are at work. Labov (1966) schematizes the expected distribution of linguistic variants for the possible cases:

1   A stigmatized feature (from Labov 1966: 325)

    (a)   Stable variation – e.g. the [ən] variant of (ing); see below.

	Lower class	Working class	Lower middle class	Upper middle class
Younger	*high*	*higher*	*higher*	*low*
Older	*high*	*lower*	*lower*	*low*

    (b)   Change from above the level of social awareness

	Lower class	Working class	Lower middle class	Upper middle class
Younger	[*lower*]	*lower*	*lower*	*low*
Older	[*higher*]	*higher*	*higher*	*low*

An example of this case is centralized, upgliding variants of the nucleus in *bird*, *curl*, and *verse* in New York City, realized as [ʌɪ], registered in the shibboleth "Toity-Toid Street." This scenario also holds for the relic forms examined by Trudgill (1974), the backing of (ir) in *bird*, *hurt*, *fern*; the shortening to [ʊ] of (ō) which had been raised to [uː] in *comb*, *alone*, *boat*; and the shortening to [ʊ] of the (ū) in *boot*, *spoon*, *roof*.

It is evident that without distinguishing age groups, the difference between stable variation and change from above for a stigmatized feature would likely be lost. The lowest class could demonstrate a difference between the two types, but only a slight one.

2   A prestige feature (from Labov 1966: 327)

(a)   Stable variation

	Lower class	Working class	Lower middle class	Upper middle class
Younger	*low*	*lower*	*lower*	*high*
Older	*low*	*higher*	*higher*	*high*

This case is simply the inverse of stable variation involving a stigmatized feature, schematized above in (1a). It holds for the standard or prestige members of a pair of variants in a state of stable variation: the [ɪŋ] variant of (ing), the interdental variants in the alternation of [θ] and [t], [ð] and [d] in *think* and *this*, and so on.

(b)   Change from above the level of social awareness – e.g. NYC postvocalic /r/

	Lower class	Working class	Lower middle class	Upper middle class
Younger	*low*	*lower*	*lower*	*high*
Older	*higher*	*higher*	*higher*	*low*

This process is also suggested by the pattern of stratification by contextual style. In what is probably the most-reprinted diagram in the history of linguistics, Labov presented the crossover pattern by which the lower middle class exceeds the upper middle class in the production of constricted (r) in wordlists and minimal pairs (Figure 11: Re-defined class stratification of (r): Six class groups, 1966, p. 240). It also displays fine stratification, in contrast to the finding of sharp stratification that is typical of stable linguistic variables.

3   Change from below the level of social awareness – early stage (from Labov 1966: 330)

	Lower class	Working class	Lower middle class	Upper middle class
Youngest	*high*	*high*	*high*	*medium*
Young adults	*medium*	*high*	*medium*	*low*
Middle aged	*low*	*medium*	*low*	*low*
Oldest	*low*	*low*	*low*	*low*

The predominant characteristic of linguistic changes from below is the curvilinear pattern of social distribution. Early observations of this pattern were Labov's study (1966) of the raising of (oh) in New York City, Cedergren's (1973) description of the lenition of (ch) in Panamanian Spanish, and Trudgill's (1974) investigation of the backing of (e) and the centralization and backing of (i) in *right, ride, rye* in Norwich. Labov's studies of the Philadelphia speech community show further evidence of innovation by the interior social classes for the fronting and raising of (aw) in *house, south*; the raising and backing of (ay) preceding voiceless segments, as in *right, bike*; the raising and fronting of checked (ey) in *made, take*; and the fronting of (uw) and (ow) in *move, boo* and *phone, go* (Labov 1980).

Over time, a change from below may become subject to social stigmatization, as is the case, for example, with the tensing and raising of short *a* in Philadelphia and New York City. This development complicates the picture of social class and age, as the middle social and age groups are caught between longer duration of exposure to the advancing change on one hand and the inclination to produce more prestigious forms on the other. The evidence of style shifting across the social spectrum is a considerable aid in untangling the picture of the processes at work. Evidence from the distribution of the variants with respect to other social factors, such as ethnicity and gender, is also called into play.

Stable variation shows sharp stratification, with monotonically increasing or decreasing use of the marked variant with ascending social class. (Of course, if you increase the number of designated social classes, you necessarily decrease the distances between them. The designations of sharp and fine stratification depend in part on the number of social classes.) This relation holds across social contexts (styles) as well: in more formal styles, speakers use less (or more, for a prestige feature) of the marked variant. The alternation of the velar and apical variants of the variable (ing) is a well-known example. These generalizations were found by Fischer (1958) in his study of New England schoolchildren, and they have been repeated in many successive studies of this variable. Labov (1966) presents the same findings for the adult white New York City speakers (Figure 3: Class stratification of (ing), p. 398). At every point, the ordering of social classes shows that lower classes use the [ɪn] variant more than higher classes. The finding is reinforced by being repeated three times, in the three contextual styles that are presented on the graph. Trudgill (1974) arrived at the same picture, with sharp stratification between the middle class and the working class in spontaneous speech (Figure 14: Variable (ng) by class and style, p. 92). It is also notable that the social class lines are quite widely and regularly separated. (The meeting at the zero point of the two highest classes in the most formal style does not disturb the regularity of the picture.) For a stable prestige feature, one would expect the social distribution to follow the same principles, except the slope of the lines is reversed.

When linguistic variation is part of a change in progress, the greatest use of the incoming variant is expected to be found in the innovating social group, with levels of use falling off progressively in adjacent social groups of increasing distance. However, beyond this, the levels of use of a variant for different age groups must be taken into account. In change from above, a simple plot of overall use of the incoming variant would not distinguish it from stable variation involving a prestige feature. Change from below is characterized by the curvilinear pattern of social distribution.

6 Understanding Social Class

Researchers interested in linguistic variation and change have been wrestling with the problems of defining and implementing the notion of social class as long as they have been studying the social embedding of language. Regrettably, there is as yet very little contact between sociolinguists and sociologists, nor has there been systematic study of social class itself within the field of sociolinguistics, and the use of the variable of social class is still quite mechanical and naive in the hands of many researchers.

That said, it cannot be denied that the dimension of social class is not only important, but it is also highly productive in sociolinguistic research. One might only imagine that it could be more so if it were used more systematically, applied in comparable ways by researchers working in different communities.

If social class is determined by a combination of features, the single indicator that accounts for by far the greatest portion of the variance is occupation. Some researchers use occupation alone as a determiner of social class, and it is hard to imagine a composite index that excludes occupation. Even the cross-cultural applicability of occupation as an indicator of social class may be greater than researchers are inclined to expect. Inkeles and Rossi (1956) found the ranking of occupations to be approximately the same in a cross-section of industrialized nations, including the United States, the United Kingdom, Germany, New Zealand, Japan, and the Soviet Union. Further, judgments of occupational prestige seem to be fairly stable over time, at least in the short run. Hodge et al. (1964) report a correlation of 0.99 between scores from the original North–Hatt study ranking occupational prestige in 1947 and a replication in 1963. The systematic small changes that were found include an increase in the prestige of scientific occupations, a decrease for culturally oriented occupations, and an upward trend for artisans. This stability is explained as a consequence of presumed stability in the prestige associated with the criteria on which the ratings are likely to be based, such as education, income, and functional importance. Nakao et al. (1990: 7) go so far as to state that "Occupational evaluations are clearly part of the core value system of American society." This is based on the findings that assessments of occupational prestige are consistent from one subgroup to another, are learned at a relatively early age, are relatively stable over time, and "are close to immutable in the short run."

Still, it is usually the case that occupation is not allowed to stand as the sole indicator of social class. When additional factors are included, they should be used in a motivated way, with an awareness of the distinction between objective factors of economic power and ownership as opposed to matters of status and prestige.

A second issue that comes from sociological theory is the distinction between a conflict model of class structure and a functional, or consensus model. As Rickford (1986) shows, both conflict and consensus can occur within one speech community. Linguists frequently express concern over the importance of tailoring the notion of social class to the particular community under study, and such customization extends to deciding whether a conflict or a consensus model applies to a community. In practice, though, a researcher working intensively in a community almost always does take the norms, values, and special characteristics of the community into account, though the understanding of local dynamics may take time to acquire. If the researcher is truly engaged in the community, if he or she has talked and listened to its members enough to visit in their homes, to ask about their families, to know what topics are of burning local interest and concern, then he or she will learn how the members of the community regard each other and will tailor the formulation of all social variables to describe the community in its own terms.

NOTE

1   Much of the material in this section is drawn from Edgell (1993) and Tumin (1967).

REFERENCES

Biesanz, J. and M. Biesanz (1955). *The People of Panama*. New York: Columbia University Press.

Bourdieu, P. and L. Boltanski (1975). Le fétichisme de la langue. *Actes de la recherche en sciences sociales* 4: 2–32.

Cedergren, Henrietta (1973). The interplay of social and linguistic factors in Panama. Ph.D. dissertation, Cornell University.

Cheshire, Jennifer (1982). *Variation in an English Dialect: A Sociolinguistic Study*. Cambridge: Cambridge University Press.

Congalton, A. A. (1962). *Social Standings of Occupations in Sydney*. Sydney:

School of Sociology, University of New South Wales.

Congalton, A. A. (1969). *Status and Prestige in Australia*. Melbourne: Cheshire.

Dayton, Elizabeth (1996). Grammatical categories of the verb in African American Vernacular English. Ph.D. dissertation, University of Pennsylvania.

Duncan, Otis Dudley (1961). A socioeconomic index for all occupations. In Albert Reiss, with O. D. Duncan, P. K. Hatt and C. C. North, *Occupations and Social Status*. New York: Free Press. 109–38.

Eckert, Penelope (1989). *Jocks and Burnouts: Social Categories and Identity in the High School*. New York: Teacher's College, Columbia University.

Eckert, Penelope (1997). Age as a sociolinguistic variable. In F. Coulmas (ed.), *The Handbook of Sociolinguistics*. Oxford: Blackwell. 151–67.

Eckert, Penelope (2000). *Language Variation as Social Practice: The Linguistic Construction of Identity in Belten High*. Oxford: Blackwell.

Edgell, Stephen (1993). *Class*. London: Routledge.

Feagin, Crawford (1979). *Variation and Change in Alabama English: A Sociolinguistic Study of the White Community*. Washington, DC: Georgetown University Press.

Feagin, Crawford (1998). Real time change in Alabama English: When speakers leave the community. Paper presented at NWAVE 27, Athens, GA.

Fischer, John (1958). Social influences on the choice of a linguistic variant. *Word* 14: 47–56.

Haeri, Niloofar (1997). *The Sociolinguistic Market of Cairo: Gender, Class, and Education*. London and New York: Kegan Paul International.

Hodge, R. W., P. M. Siegel and P. M. Rossi (1964). Occupational prestige in the United States, 1925–1963. *American Journal of Sociology* 70: 286–302.

Horvath, Barbara (1985). *Variation in Australian English: The Sociolects of Sydney*. Cambridge: Cambridge University Press.

Inkeles, Alex and Peter Rossi (1956). National comparisons of occupational prestige. *American Journal of Sociology* 61, 4: 329–39.

Labov, William (1966). *The Social Stratification of English in New York City*. Washington, DC: Center for Applied Linguistics.

Labov, William (1972). *Sociolinguistic Patterns*. Philadelphia: University of Pennsylvania Press.

Labov, William (1980). The social origins of sound change. In W. Labov (ed.), *Locating Language in Time and Space*. New York: Academic Press. 251–65.

Labov, William (1996). The leaders of linguistic change. Paper presented at NWAVE 25, Las Vegas, NV.

Labov, William (2001). *Principles of Linguistic Change*, vol. 2: *Social Factors*. Oxford: Blackwell Publishers.

Lennig, Matthew (1978). Acoustic measurement of linguistic change: The modern Paris vowel system. Ph.D. dissertation, University of Pennsylvania.

Michael, John (1962). The construction of the social class index. *Codebook for the Mobilization for Youth*. Appendix A. Mimeo. New York: Mobilization for Youth.

Milroy, Lesley (1980). *Language and Social Networks*. Oxford: Basil Blackwell.

Nakao, Keiko and Judith Treas (1990). Computing 1989 Occupational Prestige Scores. GSS Methodological Report No. 70. Chicago: National Opinion Research Council.

Nakao, Keiko and Judith Treas (1992). The 1989 Socioeconomic Index of Occupations: Construction from the 1989 Occupational Prestige Scores. GSS Methodological Report No. 74. Chicago: National Opinion Research Council.

Nakao, Keiko, Robert W. Hodge and Judith Treas (1990). On revising prestige scores for all occupations. GSS Methodological report No. 69. Chicago: National Opinion Research Council.

Rickford, John (1979). Variation in a creole continuum: Quantitative and implicational approaches. Ph.D.

dissertation, University of Pennsylvania.

Rickford, John (1986). The need for new approaches to social class analysis in sociolinguistics. *Language & Communication* 6, 3: 215–21.

Sankoff, David and Suzanne Laberge (1978). The linguistic market and the statistical explanation of variability. In D. Sankoff (ed.), *Linguistic Variation: Models and Methods*. New York: Academic Press.

Trudgill, Peter (1974). *The Social Differentiation of English in Norwich*. Cambridge: Cambridge University Press.

Tumin, Melvin M. (1967). *Social Stratification: The Forms and Functions of Inequality*. Englewood Cliffs, NJ: Prentice-Hall.

Warner, W. Lloyd and Paul S. Lunt (1941). *The Social Life of a Modern Community*. New Haven, CT: Yale University Press.

Warner, W. Lloyd, with Marchia Meeker and Kenneth Eells (1960). *Social Class in America: A Manual of Procedure for the Measurement of Social Status*. New York: Harper.

Wolfram, Walt, Kirk Hazen, and Natalie Schilling-Estes (1999). Dialect change and maintenance on the Outer Banks. *Publication of the American Dialect Society*, No. 81. Tuscaloosa: University of Alabama Press.

Wright, Erik Olin (1979). *Class Structure and Income Determination*. New York: Academic Press.

17 Sex and Gender in Variationist Research

JENNY CHESHIRE

Sex, together with social class, age, and ethnicity, is one of the most widely used social demographic categories, and so categorizing individuals into "females" and "males" has long been standard practice in the social sciences. In most variationist research carried out during the 1960s and 1970s the demographic categories were taken for granted, as they were in the social sciences generally. All these categories are now recognized as more complex than their labels would suggest, and as more complex than many sociolinguistic analyses give them credit for (Eckert 1989: 265). None, however, has become so highly charged, politicized, and problematized as sex.

To a large extent this reflects the impact of feminism and feminist theory in virtually all the humanities and social science disciplines. Research on language and gender has tended to follow the general development of feminist thought, moving from an essentialist paradigm where speakers were categorized in terms of their biological sex through a period where the significance of the cultural concept of gender was recognized, together with social psychological dimensions, to a more dynamic social constructionist approach (Holmes 1997: 195–6). In variationist research, ideas about sex and gender have also tended to follow this development, although what could be termed a modified essentialist approach remains dominant in much work. Indeed, for some researchers the only concession to the general heightened awareness of the complexity of the concept has been a simple change in terminology, so that what was once referred to as "sex" is now termed "gender."

The term "sex" has often been used to refer to the physiological distinction between females and males, with "gender" referring to the social and cultural elaboration of the sex difference – a process that restricts our social roles, opportunities, and expectations. Since the process begins at birth, it could be argued that "gender" is the more appropriate term to use for the category than "sex." Both terms are found in the variationist literature, sometimes used in an apparently indiscriminate way, but at other times used to distinguish between biological characteristics and social factors (see, for example, Chambers 1992,

1995). In this chapter I have tried to use "sex" when discussing research that relies on a simplistic classification of speakers into males and females, and "gender" when describing research that takes at least some account of relevant social and cultural factors. Like many writers, however, I have sometimes found myself slipping from one term to the other. It is difficult to keep the two concepts apart, especially when discussing studies that were designed with a gross categorization of individuals by their sex but that are then interpreted in terms of the lifestyles of women and men, or the interaction of sex with other social factors – which means, of course, that the focus has shifted to gender. Current thinking in the humanities accepts, in any case, that the dichotomy between sex and gender cannot be maintained, seeing the body and biological processes as part of cultural histories.

Both sex and gender have been treated as binary categories in sociolinguistic research. Gender differences need not map directly onto the physiological sex differences (see Milroy et al. 1994: 334), but in practice our social lives are organized around the physiological dichotomy to such an extent that a cultural connection has been forged between sex and virtually every other aspect of human experience (Bem 1993: 2). In fact it is difficult to see how it could be otherwise, given the importance of the binary physiological distinction for the procreation of human life. Yet neither sex nor gender are "naturally" binary. Bing and Bergvall (1996: 8–11) describe how in most cultures medical intervention polices the boundaries, to ensure that newborn babies fit neatly into the "female" or "male" physiological categories. They also draw attention to cultures where more than two gender groups, or an ambiguous gender group, are given explicit social recognition.

A current tendency in feminist research is to look for ways to move beyond theorizing in terms of two separate categories. At a time of social change, when the conventional gender roles are being challenged in many western societies, it no longer seems appropriate to work with polarized categories of either "sex" or "gender." As Bergvall and Bing point out (1996: 18): "it would be ironic if feminists interested in language and gender inadvertently reinforced gender polarization and the myths of essential female–male difference." On the other hand, since the binary distinction appears to be a fundamental organizing principle in all societies, we can expect this to guide our evaluations of our own and other's speech and, therefore, to constrain patterns of social and stylistic variation. (Bell's model of the derivation of style from inter-speaker variation can apply to inter-speaker variation in terms of sex just as well as to inter-speaker variation in terms of social class.) This seems a valid argument for continuing to analyze the speech of males on the one hand and females on the other hand. Milroy and Milroy (1997: 53) point out that speaker sex is intended to be a methodological, exploratory variable: in other words, it is a purposely broad, unrefined social variable that can be easily taken into account at the data-collection stage of research. If all researchers categorize speakers in the same, albeit simplistic way, we can ensure replicability and can draw useful comparisons between studies carried out in a range of

communities. Most researchers seem to agree that this methodological procedure will not lead to an explanation of the relation between gender and language variation, and that for this we need to investigate the everyday language
use of individual women and men in the local communities where the social
construction of gender and other identities takes place. Bergvall (1999) adds
that we must also look at forces larger than local communities: at the broadly
held social and cultural values, invoked and reified in the national and international media (1999: 289). It is against this backdrop of social stereotypes that
any performance of gender is constructed, accommodated to, or resisted (1999:
282). As with any research question, the fullest understanding will come from
a combination of methods and approaches.

In this chapter, I will first discuss work that has used "female" and "male"
as unanalysed speaker variables. I will then briefly discuss some small-scale
investigations that have focused on the way that language and gender interact
in specific communities. Finally I will briefly mention the role of sex and
gender in the quantitative analysis of pragmatic and syntactic features. This
format is intended to give a broad overview of the different ways that
researchers have approached the question of sex and gender in the study of
language variation and change, and of the advances that have been achieved
in our understanding of both sex and gender, and language variation and
change.

1   Variation with Speaker Sex

There are a few reports in the research literature of the exclusive use of one
phonological variant by women and another by men, for example, Jabeur
(1987), Keddad (1989), Mansfield and Trudgill (1994), but it is far more frequent to find sex-preferential variation, where women in a community, say,
use one variant more frequently than the men. For example, a large number of
sociolinguistic surveys carried out in the English-speaking world have shown
that for the (ing) variable (in words such as *running* or *laughing*) men use a
higher proportion of the alveolar /n/ variant than women in their social class
and, conversely, women use a higher proportion of the velar plosive. It is
usual for researchers to see one of the variants as "standard" or overtly prestigious, usually on the grounds that this variant is used with an increased
frequency in more formal speech styles. Within this perspective, Labov (1990:
205) finds that the clearest and most consistent results of more than 30 years of
sociolinguistic research in the speech community concern the linguistic differentiation of women and men. He summarizes these results in the principles
below (1990: 210, 213, 215):

> **Principle I**   In stable sociolinguistic stratification, men use a higher frequency of
> nonstandard forms than women.

Principle Ia   In change from above, women favour the incoming prestige forms more than men.

Principle II   In change from below, women are most often the innovators.

Dubois and Horvath (1999) point out that Principle I and its corollary, Principle Ia, concern language spread, whereas Principle II concerns innovation – a change that begins within a speech community. In most cases, they maintain, Principles I and Ia represent the tug-of-war between standard and nonstandard variants: "Principle I is like a lull in the tug-of-war game; for some reason the process has halted. Principle Ia captures the game becoming active once again" (Labov 1999: 309). It is Principles Ia and II that directly relate to language change, then, whereas Principle I represents a more stable state of affairs, albeit possibly a temporary one.

2   Stable Sociolinguistic Variables

The finding that women tend to use a higher proportion of the standard variants than men in the same social class (Labov's Principle I) has been of very wide general interest, so much so that it is presented in some textbooks as a fundamental tenet of sociolinguistics. Fasold (1990: 92), for example, refers to this as "the sociolinguistic gender pattern," and Chambers (1995) as "a sociolinguistic verity."

A wide range of explanations have been offered for this distributional pattern, most of which have some element of plausibility. They all, however, necessarily involve a move beyond using speaker sex as a simple exploratory variable, to thinking about the social and cultural behavior of women and men: in other words, to shifting from thinking in terms of speaker sex to thinking about gender. Eckert (1989: 265) has argued strongly that most variationist analyses have fallen short in confusing social meaning with the analyst's demographic abstractions. Further, most writers have offered a single explanation for what must surely be a multifaceted, complex phenomenon (Eckert 1989, James 1996, Cheshire and Gardner-Chloros 1998). For example, Fasold (1990) suggests that women use a higher proportion of standard variants than men because this allows them to sound less local and to have a voice, therefore, with which to protest against the traditional norms that place them in an inferior social position to men. Gordon (1997) presents experimental evidence for a symbolic association between local accents, nonstandard syntax and promiscuity, arguing that middle-class women may avoid using nonstandard forms in order to avoid being associated with this social stereotype. Deuchar (1988) develops an interpretation based on politeness theory, in which women's higher use of standard forms can be seen as a strategy for maintaining face in interactions where women are powerless. Trudgill's (1972) explanation has been very influential: based on evidence from subjective evaluation tests, he argues that women have to acquire social status vicariously, whereas men can acquire it through their occupational status and earning power. Women are more likely, therefore, to secure and signal their social status through their use of the standard, overtly prestigious variants. The higher proportion of nonstandard variants used by men can then be explained as an orientation not to the overt norms of the community but to the covert prestige of working-class forms, which symbolize the roughness and toughness that is associated both with working-class life and with masculinity.

These are just a few selections from the wide range of interpretations that have been proposed. These, and other suggestions, are discussed and critically assessed by James (1996), Cheshire and Gardner-Chloros (1998) and Romaine (1999). Clearly, the fact that so many different factors can be convincingly argued for indicates that no single interpretation can be possible. James' (1996) review concludes that there is far too much variation across and within different communities for any simple analysis to be viable. As she says, local economic conditions, the employment and educational opportunities available to each sex, social conditions affecting network strengths, the amount of status and respect accorded to women in particular communities and the extent to which they can participate in public life are just some of the factors that may account for the choices that women and men make in the speech forms that they use (1996: 119). The main relevant underlying sociological factor seems to be the relative access to power of women and men (James 1996: 119, Eckert 1989: 256); as James points out, however, the fact that women appear to be universally granted less power than men will certainly not cause all women and men to act alike, given all the other factors that are involved.

The empirical basis of the generalization presented as Labov's Principle I can also be challenged. The generalization is tightly bound to Labov's early definition of the speech community, which in turn depends on a stratificational model of social class. The model is implicit in early work (Milroy 1987), but is explicit in Labov's later writings and is typical of most quantitative research on language in the community, although the actual indicators used to assign social class may vary from one investigation to another (Labov 1990: 209). The concepts of "standard" and "nonstandard" tend to be taken for granted in social dialectology, with "standard" forms corresponding to those used with the greatest frequency by the highest social class in the hierarchy and, as mentioned earlier, used more frequently by all speakers in their more formal speech styles. These "standard" forms are taken as synonymous with the overtly prestigious forms of the speech community: since all members of the speech community are assumed to share a common set of norms and values, they are also assumed to agree on the social evaluation of the standard, or prestige, variants. Indeed, Labov's original definition of the speech community (Labov 1966) was in terms of participation in a set of shared norms. Although early surveys used subjective evaluation tests to determine the forms carrying overt or covert prestige (for example, Labov 1966, Trudgill 1972), such tests have rarely been performed in subsequent work. This is unfortunate, because it is notoriously difficult for researchers to be objective about concepts of "standard" and "nonstandard" (see, for discussion, Cheshire and Stein 1997) and the related notion of prestige is not uniform in all communities (Milroy 1991). Furthermore the concepts can have different social meanings not only in different communities but also for different groups within what we might think of as the "same" community, as well as within the lives of different individuals (Cheshire and Gardner-Chloros 1998: 28–9).

The criteria used to assign women to the different social classes on the hierarchy have also been challenged (see, for example, Cameron and Coates 1989, Romaine 1999). Romaine (1999: 174) discusses the problems associated with the "patriarchal concept of social class, where the family is the basic unit of analysis, the man is regarded as the head of the household, and his occupation determines the family's social class." Although in more recent work women are classified in terms of their own occupations, several problems remain, especially when individuals do not have occupations outside the home. It can be argued, in fact, that comparisons drawn between women and men in what the analyst assumes to be the same social class will always be false, since women and men do not have equal status with men either inside the home or outside it (Eckert 1989: 255). The power dimension of the relations between the sexes, therefore, means that we can never compare like with like when we try to compare men and women.

These criticisms suggest that the empirical basis for the "sociolinguistic gender pattern" is questionable, to say the least. It is unfortunate that the generalization seems to be passing into the accepted sociolinguistic wisdom, without explicit recognition of the fact that statements involving class, prestige or "standardness" are less objective than has been supposed. What does appear to be uncontroversial is that there are likely to be gross differences between the linguistic behavior of men in a community on the one hand, and women on the other. Given the social and cultural significance of the male–female dichotomy, these differences are likely to be socially evaluated and to have an important role in the relation between social and stylistic variation, as I said earlier (see, again, Bell 1984) and in the social construction of a range of identities. As it stands, this stark generalization does not tell us much, if anything, about the relation between language and gender in social life: but this is not the aim of research carried out in this framework. Rather, the intention is to make replication possible between one study and another and, in this way, to gain the largest possible understanding of the general nature of the language faculty and of the general nature of language change Labov (1990: 11).

3   The Role of Women in the Social Mechanism of Language Change

A stratificational model of social class is also typical of much of the research on language change, as is a reliance on notions of prestige and "standardness."

Discussions of Labov's Principle Ia usually point to women leading both in the acquisition of new prestige forms from outside the speech community, and in the elimination of forms that have become stigmatized (Labov 1990: 213, Dubois and Horvath 1999: 299). In fact, the literature contains few examples of the spread of incoming prestige forms. (One relevant instance is Labov's (1966) account of the adoption of the (r)-pronouncing norm in New York City.) Principle Ia, then, is mainly a corollary of Principle I, describing the social redistribution of variants that have become stigmatized. Thus although Principles Ia and II appear contradictory, portraying women as simultaneously conformist (in preferring more overtly prestigious forms) and progressive (in adopting new forms more quickly), they can be reconciled by considering the way in which sound changes typically spread through the speech community.

For cities in the USA at least, a characteristic development of a sound change that begins from below is a curvilinear pattern, with younger speakers in the "interior" social classes (that is, the lower middle and upper working classes) using the new variants most frequently. In the early stages of a change, sex differentiation is relatively small, but it increases as the change becomes older and more established in the community. At this point sex differentiation interacts with other types of social differentiation relevant to the community. As the new forms become more widespread and speakers become consciously aware of them, sex differentiation becomes more marked, most notably in the speech of the second highest status group. There is some disagreement about whether the increasing sex differentiation is due primarily to the linguistic behavior of men or of women: for example, it could be argued that men take the more active role, recognizing that a given variant has become characteristic of female speech and so refraining from using it. However, Labov insists that the empirical evidence from the Philadelphia survey shows that as a rule women are the active agents, and lower-class women in particular. He concludes that "the interaction of sex and social class leave us no choice but to focus on women's behavior, and to assess its effect on linguistic change" (1990: 240).

This marks a change from the focus in early work in social dialectology, where social class was seen as the primary variable, and speaker sex was treated very much as a side issue. This did not always, in fact, produce the best fit with the data, as Coates (1986) has shown. Coates regraphed data from several classic sociolinguistic surveys, demonstrating that the linguistic variation patterned with the sex of speakers at least as well as, and sometimes better than, their social class. Class was still a determining factor, but women from the working classes and the middle classes behaved more similarly to each other than to men from the same social class as themselves (see also Horvath 1985).

The Milroys have long argued that sex differentiation may be prior to social class differentiation in driving language change (see, for example, Milroy 1992, Milroy and Milroy 1993, 1997, Milroy et al. 1994). In particular they maintain that it is misleading to say that women favor prestige forms: rather, women create the prestige forms in the sense that the forms they use become overtly prestigious in the community. Persuasive evidence for this comes from Milroy et al.'s (1994) review of a number of investigations into the spread of the glottal stop as a variant of word final and medial /t/ (in words such as *but* and *butter*) in urban British English. T-glottaling has been a socially stigmatized pronunciation, but a number of recent, separate, studies in different parts of the country show that its spread is associated particularly with the speech of middle-class women. In some phonetic environments – notably intervocalically in word final position (as in *not enough*) – the glottal stop is becoming established as characteristic of Received Pronunciation (Milroy et al. 1994: 329). This sociolinguistic pattern, then, goes against Labov's Principle II, because women are leading in the use of what is – or was – a socially stigmatized form. Milroy et al. argue that the geographically widespread glottal variant is a supra-local form, and that if any generalizations are to be made, it is that women are instrumental in the spread of forms of this kind. Male speakers, on the other hand, are associated with more localized patterns of variation and change. This can be seen from the male preference in Tyneside for glottalized variants of (p), (t) and (k), or in Coleraine for a flapped variant of (t).

"Standard" or "prestige" forms are often supra-local forms, so this generalization can include Labov's Principle I. It can also incorporate research findings from cultures where the standard variety and the prestige variety are not identical. In diglossic Arabic-speaking cultures, for example, the high prestige of classical Arabic means that non-classical forms are generally considered "nonstandard." However Haeri (1994) shows that variation in the Arabic spoken in Cairo can be analyzed without recourse to classical Arabic, and that women can then be seen as orienting to a supra-local "standard" Cairene Arabic in the same way that women in urban centers in the West orient to a standard variety. Milroy et al. (1994: 352) conclude that "the partial identity of supra-local and prestige norms in Western industrialized countries may have led us to the wrong generalization."

A generalization in terms of supra-local forms can also cover a difference noted by Labov (1990) between changes led by women, such as the chain shifts occurring in several northern cities in the USA, and the relatively small number of changes that have been found to be led by men, such as the centralization of /ay/ and /aw/ in Martha's Vineyard (Labov 1963) or the rounding of /o/ in Norwich (Trudgill 1974). The changes led by men are linguistically isolated, in that they do not rotate the vowel system, like the chain shifts; but they are also geographically isolated, occurring in one locality only. Chambers (1992) has proposed a generalization along similar lines. He explains the fact that in many studies women have been found to have a wider range of style-shifting than men by noting that the women in these studies frequently have a greater range of social contacts, extending over a wider geographical range. He formulates a "gender-based variability hypothesis" to account for this, and presents this alongside a "sex-based variability hypothesis" which claims that females have a neurological verbal advantage over males (1992: 204).

Woods (1997) adds a further dimension to a generalization in terms of supra-local forms. She notes that women's behavior in face-to-face communication has been shown to be more cooperative and listener-oriented than men's, and that women construct interaction around the objectives of providing support and solidarity. These preferred discourse strategies make them more likely, then, to accommodate to speakers of other dialects and to subsequently introduce new phonological features into their own speech communities.

Formulating generalizations that incorporate the results of an increasing number of empirical investigations is the mark of a mature discipline. Indeed, Kuiper (1998) has argued that it is time to go still further, producing hypotheses that can be put to the test in future studies. The central place given to sex differentiation in these generalizations shows the importance that this social variable has assumed in our attempts to understand the social mechanism of sound change. It is important to recall, however, that no single factor can account for variation in the linguistic behavior of men and women in all communities. This is the case both for stable sociolinguistic variables and for features involved in ongoing language change. Eckert (1989: 206) has made this point strongly, arguing that generalizations about the relation between sound change and gender are best deferred until more communities have been examined in a way that takes account of the sociocultural contexts in which women and men live (though in her 1999 paper with McConnell-Ginet she suggests that work carried out within a Community of Practice perspective – see below – may suggest new generalizations and more adequate explanations; see 1999: 200). Eckert and McConnell-Ginet (1992: 468) argue for a view of language and gender that sees each as jointly constructed in the everyday social practices of particular local communities: this type of explanation, they say, "will require a significant leap beyond the correlational and class-based modes of explanation used so far" (1992: 469). Others, however, take a more moderate view. Holmes (1998: 106), for example, argues that the fact that there are limits on the applicability of generalizations should not blind us to their immense value: "We should be concerned with refining generalisations, rigorously confining the area to which they apply, but we should not regard them as useless when exceptions are identified".

Their value is perhaps best shown in studies carried out in communities that differ from the large urban centers that have tended to dominate the literature. For example, Cravens and Giannelli (1995) tested Labov's Principles against data from Bibbiena, a small town in central Italy where the socioeconomic differentiation takes a different form from the urban centers of the USA. They find that previous findings from the US concerning gender- and class-based parameters of change are borne out in essence, but only once sufficient detail has been teased out (Cravens and Giannelli 1995: 282). Dubois and Horvath (1999), on the other hand, find the Principles are not confirmed by their analysis of changes in Cajun English in rural areas of Louisiana. This leads them to examine in detail the different sociolinguistic settings in which language change takes place for different generations in the community, as we will see in the following section.

4   Variation with Gender

Operationalizing the category of speaker sex in a simple undifferentiated way, then, has allowed quantitative studies to be replicated across a range of communities. It has also allowed increasingly general statements to be formulated about the nature of the sex differentiation that has been observed. Of equal importance, however, are careful, detailed ethnographic studies within specific communities, which can look beyond the conventional social categories of class, sex, age, and ethnic group, and take into account other social categories that may be more meaningful to speakers themselves.

For example, for the young Latino adults that Fought (1999) investigated in a western suburb of Los Angeles, the social category that was most relevant was gang-membership. All the young people she interviewed had been obliged to make a choice at some point about whether or not they would be a gang member (1999: 9). Fought found significant patterns of /u/-fronting which did not fit the curvilinear pattern of social class variation that Labov (1990, 1994) predicts for a change from below. Instead, there was a complex interaction between social class, gender, and gang membership. Social class did not correlate with /u/-fronting for non-gang women, who all showed some degree of fronting. For gang-affiliated women, however, (which included women who had some connection with the gang, even if they did not participate in gang activities) social class was crucial in predicting variation, with the middle-class women fronting most. For men, the social class factor correlated with the degree of /u/-fronting, whether or not they were gang-affiliated; and the effect of gang affiliation overall was stronger for them than it was for women.

Fought explains that /u/-fronting is associated more with the middle classes and with non-gang speakers; conversely, a lack of /u/-fronting is associated with the lower classes and with gang-affiliated speakers. For women, societal pressures to be "good" dovetail well with non-gang status and with the conservative norms of middle-class membership. For men, on the other hand, the societal pressures are to be tough rather than to be good, and these pressures are maximally strong in the Latino community. Gang membership emphasizes exactly these qualities, so it may be more difficult for men to express their dissociation from the gang linguistically, even if they have chosen not to be gang members. The correlation with social class for men reflects the greater association with toughness for working-class males: a point made by Trudgill (1972).

Eckert (1988) also correlated linguistic variation with the social categories that were relevant to the adolescents themselves, rather than using only the conventional social demographic categories. Through long-term participant observation she studied adolescent speech in a high school in suburban Detroit. There were three adolescent categories: Jocks, who were more oriented to the school and school-based activities, Burnouts, who were more oriented to the values perceived as associated with the more exciting life of the city center, and the self-styled In-betweens. These categories were better predictors of variation in the realization of certain vowels than was the social class to which individual speakers could be assigned on the basis of their parents' socioeconomic characteristics (Eckert 1988).

Eckert and McConnell-Ginet's (1992) paper has been extremely influential in language and gender research. They argue for a more dynamic view of gender. Instead of seeing gender as something static that speakers "have", that can be analyzed either in isolation from other aspects of social identity, or in interaction with them, it is something that we "do" or "perform" in a complex array of social practices. Following Wenger (1988), they use the concept of a Community of Practice to refer to an "aggregate of people who come together and mutually engage in an endeavour" (Eckert and McConnell-Ginet 1992: 464). In the course of this engagement shared ways of doing things, shared values, beliefs, and ways of talking emerge. Eckert (2000) and Eckert and McConnell-Ginet (1999) see the Jocks and the Burnouts as Communities of Practice, and use the concept to analyze the spread of sound changes from the Burnout group to the Jocks. By looking in detail at the Burnout individuals who used the newer changes most frequently, Eckert was able to observe the early stages of extensions to the ongoing Northern Cities vowel shift. Eckert also showed that sex differentiation did not take the same form for all variables involved in ongoing sound changes: overall, variation correlated better with group membership for girls than for boys, but more so for some variables and in different ways for different variables. This clearly demonstrates that the sex of speakers is not directly related to linguistic behavior, but reflects complex social practice. The fact that the girls were exploiting the variation in the system to display their category identities through language more than the boys were is "the adolescent manifestation of the broader generalization that women, deprived of real power, must claim status through the symbols of social membership" (Eckert 2000: 265). This is reminiscent of the point made by Trudgill (1972) to explain the "sociolinguistic gender pattern", as Eckert points out; in her view, however, Trudgill's argument did not go far enough.

The research of both Eckert and Fought, then, takes up points made by Trudgill (1972) in his suggested explanation for the greater use by women of the prestige forms in the speech community. But the ethnographic methods adopted by Eckert and Fought allow them to investigate different aspects of the complexities of the relation between linguistic variation and gender, and to consider the implications for the spread of the changes in progress. In each case relevant social categories were identified for the speakers which differed between the communities, and which had more significance for some speakers than others; and Eckert was able to operationalize the concept of "performing" gender through social practice, and to relate this to patterns of variation and change.

A number of correlational studies suggest that gender has more relevance for individuals at some stages of their lives than others. Habbick's (1991) analysis of /u/-fronting and other vowel changes in Farmer City, Illinois, shows that although adolescent social categories (here, Burnouts and Rednecks) correlated better than gender with the frequency of /u/-fronting for younger speakers, gender was a more significant factor for older speakers in the community, for whom the adolescent categories were no longer relevant. Nichols' (1983) analysis of the use of features of Gullah Creole in parts of the southeastern USA showed that older women were the heaviest users of Gullah whereas younger speakers, both male and female, used a higher proportion of standard English variants. Nichols linked this distribution to occupation: younger people tended to work in white collar jobs and service occupations, where they came into contact with speakers of standard English, whereas older women held domestic or agricultural positions. Older men, who also used a relatively high proportion of Gullah forms, tended to work in the construction industry. This time, then, a detailed small-scale study provides a balance to generalizations appealing to geographical mobility and the use of supra-local forms: here it is the younger generation, both female and male, who use the supra-local forms.

Dubois and Horvath (1999) showed how the significance of gender varied across three generations of Cajun individuals. Sociohistorical changes in the community affected the social and economic roles of Cajun men and women at specific historical moments. Thus the mandate of English as the language of education was an important determinant of the linguistic behavior of the older generation; local industrialization affected the language of middle-aged speakers; and the so-called Cajun Renaissance influenced the younger generation. As a result, the interaction of gender and social network varied at different points in historical time, with different effects on linguistic variation for different generations.

Studies such as these make it possible to gain some understanding of the way that gender is constructed in specific communities, and of some of the relevant interactions between gender and other social factors. We can therefore begin to gain a better idea of the role of gender in the social mechanism of language change in these communities. Clearly, however, detailed investigations of this kind cannot be used to draw cross-community comparisons (see Labov 1990). Dubois and Horvath (1999), whilst acknowledging the importance of Eckert's "landmark study" (1989: 289), point out that the disadvantages of an ethnographic approach undermine the original goal of the study of language change in progress. If a range of social classes is not studied, there is no way of knowing how locally specified social groups fit in with the rest of the speech community. Without a range of age groups, it is impossible to investigate what should be the focus of investigation – the origin and spread of a linguistic change through a speech community. This will not matter for research that is less concerned with language change than with, say, the expression of a range of social identities through language, or with the "performance" and construction of gender in social practice. But for research that shares the original aims set out for the study of language in its social context, what is needed, Dubois and Horvath argue (1999: 291), are alternative approaches which do not give up the benefits of large-scale studies but that are "more sensitive to Eckert's call for a deeper understanding of the social categories that we work with" (1999: 310). They see the ethnographic approach as an important adjunct for urban surveys rather than as a replacement for them: urban survey methods need to be supplemented by detailed social analysis. Their solution for their own research was to refer to the general social science research literature on Cajun communities and to ensure that their sociolinguistic interviews elicited relevant aspects of the speakers' life histories. They observed the community during the data collection process; and they were able to consult the replies given to an extensive questionnaire that had been used in a previous sociological survey.

Few researchers are fortunate enough to be able to access a pre-existing sociological survey in this way, though it may be possible to elicit individual life histories during recorded interview sessions. Other types of compromise are also possible. For example, Cheshire et al. (1999) used an "ethnographic interview" with groups of adolescents in three English towns to obtain information not only on life histories but also about the adolescents' lifestyles and their orientation to different kinds of youth culture. Although our explorations of the social variables in this study are necessarily more limited than would be possible with a full ethnographic study, the structured approach does allow some comparisons to be drawn between the three towns.

Small-scale studies, then, have shown that the complexity of the relation between linguistic variation and gender cannot be captured by a single generalization based on a division into "females" and "males." Yet despite the apparent incompatibility between small studies and large-scale urban surveys, and despite Cameron's assertion that the category of gender does not lend itself well to the conventional models of the speech community (Cameron 1996: 34), recent research is trying to find compromise positions, as we have seen.

5 Gender from a Social Psychological Perspective

Whereas variationist research has, until recently, treated social categories as if they were static, correlating them with a speaker's overall frequency of use of a specific variant, the approach of social psychologists fits better with a view of gender as a dynamic construct, with individuals "performing" or creating different aspects of their social identities in different situations, or at different moments within a single interaction. This approach is more difficult to marry with quantitative analysis, but some researchers have attempted to do so.

For example, Takano (1998) analyzed variation in ellipsis of the postpositional particles *-wa* and *-ga* in informal spoken Japanese. Previous research had found that these particles were ellipted more frequently by women than by men, but Takano's research design allowed her to show that the frequency of ellipsis depended on whether conversations took place in mixed-sex groups, cross-sex dyads or same-sex dyads. Sex differentiation was greatest in the

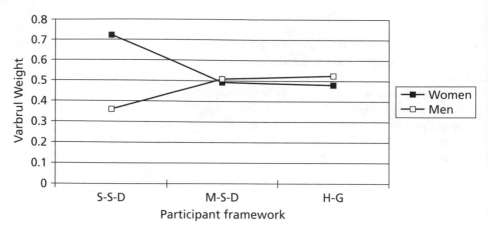

Figure 17.1 Mutual convergence in particle ellipsis across three participant frameworks

same-sex dyads: women talking to women ellipted the particles significantly more frequently than men talking to men. As figure 17.1 shows, in cross-sex interactions the rate of ellipsis amongst men increased, whereas the rate of ellipsis amongst women decreased, with the result that in this conversational context there was virtually no difference between their frequencies of ellipsis.

Takano argues that gender as a social division is most evident in single-sex interactions, where speakers use gender-linked linguistic differentiation to maintain in-group norms. In mixed-sex interactions the speakers' gender identity becomes less salient, and mutual accommodation occurs. This has been a recurrent finding in experimental research from social psychologists working within the framework of communicative accommodation theory (see, for example, Hogg 1985, Mulac et al. 1988), although other social factors may affect the salience of gender identity rather than other social identities in a specific interaction (see, for discussion, Meyerhoff 1996: 207–11, Cheshire and Gardner-Chloros 1998: 10–11, Takano 1998: 296–7). Takano argues that integrating intra-speaker variability into the quantitative paradigm will result in a more adequate sociolinguistic theory (1998: 317). It can also inform methodology: for example, this could usefully be taken into account when designing sociolinguistic interviews. These are typical situations where Communicative Accommodation Theory predicts communicative divergence, because interviewer and interviewee share a complementary relationship where their social roles are discrepant (Thakerar et al. 1982). In these situations individuals can gain communicative confidence by diverging stylistically from the "outgroup" represented by their interlocutor and by emphasizing the prototypical linguistic behavior of the group with which they identify (Giles and Coupland 1991: 83).

Meyerhoff (1996) also discusses the potential of a social psychological framework for incorporating a more dynamic concept of gender into variationist analyses. Individuals can be seen as possessing many different identities, some personal and some social, whose salience in different communicative events varies depending on a range of non-linguistic variables. As Meyerhoff points out (1996: 207), the kinds of variables that social psychology research has found to influence the salience of gender identity in an interaction are precisely those that sociolinguists have found to be important; and she discusses a range of variationist studies that can be interpreted within a dynamic social psychological framework.

6   Gender from a Discourse Analysis Approach

A social constructionist approach based on discourse analysis can also incorporate a dynamic conception of gender into the quantitative paradigm. The approach depends on the idea that although sounds are inherently meaningless, they can derive social significance from their distributional patterns, becoming associated with the culturally-recognized attributes of the social groups who use them most frequently. Thus, if a particular variant is used more often by women, it may become associated with the expression of femininity and be used to construct a stereotypically "female" identity in discourse contexts where this aspect of the speaker's identity is salient (Holmes 1997: 216). Similarly, if a variant is associated with the working classes, it may index various culturally-recognized attributes of working-class culture (Kiesling 1998: 94).

Holmes (1997) shows how one woman constructs a stereotypical gender identity for herself on one occasion in a conversational narrative, presenting herself through her story as a good mother and dutiful daughter. She does this partly through the content of her story, but she also expresses this conservative gender identity through her use of phonological variants which are more frequent in New Zealand women's speech than men's. For example, she uses the standard realization of the (ing) variable and the conservative aspirated variant of intervocalic /t/. She also uses pragmatic particles and attenuators such as *you know* and *sort of* with affective meaning, a use which is also favoured by women (Holmes 1995). Thus the speaker constructs a conservative feminine gender identity in this instance through a combination of phonological choices, lexical selections and her use of pragmatic devices, as well as through the topic and structure of the narrative she chooses to recount (1995: 217). Holmes also shows how a range of different masculine identities is constructed through the linguistic choices made in the dialogue of an advertisement. Some of these identities are stereotypically masculine, but one is a more "feminine" powerless, polite identity.

Kiesling (1998) also combines a quantitative analysis of the (ing) variable with a qualitative discourse analysis, this time of individual fraternity men speaking at a weekly meeting. Again, the men construct a range of identities through their discourse. Kiesling assumes that because (ing) is an old and stable sociolinguistic marker, its possible meanings are varied and complexly inter-related (1998: 93). The /n/ variant can therefore have a range of social meanings, though all are culturally-recognized attributes of the working-class group with which the variant is associated. They include, for example, "rebellious," "hardworking," "casual," and "confrontational." Like Holmes, Kiesling sees these identities as constructed not only through the realization of (ing) – in this case, as the alveolar variant rather than the velar variant on which Holmes focuses – but through the co-occurrence of this feature with other sociolinguistic variables, such as multiple negation, as well as other aspects of discourse form and structure. Kiesling stresses that the variable alone has no "meaning" as such: "meaning" comes about "only when an identity takes shape through the tension between text and content and the negotiation between speaker and hearer" (1998: 94).

Investigating how individuals express or construct their gender identities in specific interactions in particular social contexts, then, is a way of going beyond a simple binary classification; and it makes it possible to integrate qualitative and quantitative approaches within a single analysis.

7   Beyond Phonological Variation

As we have seen, although sounds are inherently meaningless they can acquire social significance through their habitual associations with specific social groups. But features that have an intrinsic meaning can also acquire social significance. Tag questions or pragmatic particles have a "core" meaning related to their lexical content or discourse function, but they also express different social meanings such as assertiveness, rapport, or tentativeness, which emerge in the discourse context. These social meanings may be sex differentiated, with men in English-speaking societies using the forms mainly with referential meaning and women using them mainly with affective meaning (Holmes 1995). In cultures where the expression of solidarity is culturally valued, such as Indonesian cultures (Wouk 1999) there may be little or no sex differentiation in the use of such forms. For English speakers, however, they may become "gendered" through their association with male or female speakers, and they can then be used to construct different identities, as Holmes and Kiesling have shown.

A wide range of forms can acquire social significance in this way, if they occur frequently enough to become associated with certain groups. High Rising Terminal contours, for example, have a positive politeness function as an important part of their interactional meaning, and are used more frequently by Pakeha women than by men in Porirua, New Zealand (Britain 1992) and in Sydney (Guy et al. 1986). (In the New Zealand research they were also used more frequently by Maori speakers, another social group that values the expression of solidarity and rapport.)

It is important to remember, however, that not all women prefer affective meanings, or speak in a cooperative speech style; and that those who do, do not always do so. The same applies to men and their apparent preference for referential meanings, and to the patterns of sex differentiation discussed earlier. Situations where there is no sex differentiation can be very revealing: Freed and Greenwood (1996), for example, found no differences in the use of *you know* and questions between women and men participating in the same type of conversational activity in a controlled experimental setting. They conclude that it is the specific requirements of the type of talk in which speakers are engaged that motivate the use of these features, not the sex or gender of the individual speaker: a conclusion that points to an interpretation in terms of Community of Practice. Thus the points made above about generalizations concerning the sociolinguistic gender pattern and the role of women and men in sound change apply equally to generalizations about conversational style. In both cases it is important to take account of the overlap between women's and men's behavior as well as the differentiation.

There has been relatively little research to date on syntactic variation and its relation to sex and gender. However, when a sex difference in the use of a specific construction is identified, it can point to further ways in which speakers construct a gendered identity in discourse. For example, lone *wh*-clauses with no accompanying main clause (such as *when we went to the Isle of Wight*) were used almost exclusively by male speakers in adolescent conversations that I recorded in Reading, England. Further analysis revealed that these clauses were used as attempted story openers, to introduce narratives whose function was to initiate "joint remembering" among groups of male friends and thereby to create a sense of group identity. The girls constructed more individual friendship identities through their narratives, and their narrative styles differed from the boys'. The syntactic constructions used as story openers were a preliminary indication of these friendship patterns though, again, there were overlaps in the usage of the girls and the boys (Cheshire 1999, 2000).

Syntactic constructions, of course, are likely to have many different discourse functions, only some of which may be used in the construction or performance of gender. There is no reason to suppose that syntactic features will follow similar patterns of variation to phonological variables, because they are unlikely to occur frequently enough to become habitually associated with the speech of either women or men.

8   Conclusion

We have seen that the place of sex and gender in variationist research has moved from a position where it was hardly taken into account at all, to a position where many consider it the main social factor driving variation and change. Approaches to the analysis of sex and gender have tended to mirror those adopted in neighboring disciplines, and have been influenced by the development of feminist theory. Although there has been controversy and disagreement between scholars, on the whole this has been productive. It has led to a respect for diverse approaches and to a realization that there is much to be learned from attempting to integrate them. Not only has this led to a richer understanding of the relation between sex and gender, and language variation and change; it has also shown how other social dimensions might be similarly explored, and how aspects of social theory might be profitably incorporated into the variationist enterprise.

REFERENCES

Bell, Allan (1984). Language style as audience design. *Language in Society* 13: 145–204.

Bem, Sandra (1993). *The Lenses of Gender: Transforming the Debate on Sexual Inequality*. New Haven, CT: Yale University Press.

Bergvall, Victoria L. (1999). Toward a comprehensive theory of language and gender. *Language in Society* 28: 273–93.

Bing, Janet M. and Victoria L. Bergvall (1996). The question of questions. In V. L. Bergvall, J. M. Bing and A. F. Freed (eds.), *Rethinking Language and Gender Research: Theory and Practice*. London: Longman. 1–30.

Britain, David (1992). Linguistic change in intonation: The use of high rising terminals in New Zealand English. *Language Variation and Change* 4: 77–104.

Cameron, Deborah (1996). The language-gender interface: challenging co-optation. In V. L. Bergvall, J. M. Bing and A. F. Freed (eds.), *Rethinking Language and Gender Research: Theory and Practice*. London: Longman. 31–53.

Cameron, Deborah and Jennifer Coates (1989). Some problems in the sociolinguistic explanation of sex differences. In J. Coates and D. Cameron (eds.), *Women in their Speech Communities*. London: Longman. 13–26.

Chambers, J. K. (1992). Linguistic correlates of gender and sex. *English Worldwide* 13: 173–218.

Chambers, J. K. (1995). *Sociolinguistic Theory*. Oxford: Blackwell.

Cheshire, Jenny (1999). Spoken standard English. In A. R. Bex and R. J. Watts (eds.), *Standard English: The Continuing Debate*. London: Routledge. 129–45.

Cheshire, Jenny (2000). The telling or the tale? Narratives and gender in adolescent friendship networks. *Journal of Sociolinguistics* 4: 234–62.

Cheshire, Jenny and Penelope Gardner-Chloros (1998). Codeswitching and the sociolinguistic gender pattern. *International Journal of the Sociology of Language* 129: 5–34.

Cheshire, Jenny and Dieter Stein (1997). The syntax of spoken language. In J. Cheshire and D. Stein (eds.), *Taming the Vernacular: From Dialect to Written Standard Language*. London: Longman. 1–12.

Cheshire, Jenny, Paul Kerswill and Ann Williams (1999). *Adolescents in Dialect Levelling*. Final Report to the Economic and Social Research Council.

Coates, Jennifer (1986). *Women, Men and Language*. London: Longman.

Cravens, Thomas D. and Luciano Giannelli (1995). Relative salience of gender and class in a situation of competing norms. *Language Variation and Change* 7: 261–85.

Deuchar, M. (1988). A pragmatic account of women's use of standard speech. In J. Coates and D. Cameron (eds.), *Women in their Speech Communities*. London: Longman. 27–32.

Dubois, Sylvie and Barbara Horvath (1999). When the music changes, you change too: Gender and language change in Cajun English. *Language Variation and Change* 11: 287–314.

Eckert, Penelope (1988). Adolescent social structure and the spread of linguistic change. *Language in Society* 17: 183–207.

Eckert, Penelope (1989). The whole woman: Sex and gender differences in variation. *Language Variation and Change* 1: 245–68.

Eckert, Penelope (2000). *Variation and Social Practice: The Linguistic Construction of Social Meaning in Belton High*. Oxford: Blackwell.

Eckert, Penelope and Sally McConnell-Ginet (1992). Think practically and look locally: Language and gender as community-based practice. *Annual Review of Anthropology* 21: 461–90.

Eckert, Penelope and Sally McConnell-Ginet (1999). New generalizations and explanations in language and gender research. *Language in Society* 28: 185–201.

Fasold, Ralph (1990). *The Sociolinguistics of Language*. Oxford: Blackwell.

Fought, Carmen (1999). A majority sound change in a minority community: /u/-fronting in Chicano English. *Journal of Sociolinguistics* 3: 5–23.

Freed, Alice F. and Alice Greenwood (1996). Women, men and type of talk: What makes the difference? *Language in Society* 25: 1–26.

Giles, Howard and Nikolas Coupland (1991). *Language: Contexts and Consequences*. Pacific Grove, CA: Brooks/Cole.

Gordon, E. M. (1997). Sex, speech and stereotypes: why women's speech is closer to the standard. *Language in Society* 26: 47–63.

Guy, G., B. Horvath, J. Vonwiller, E. Daisley and I. Rogers (1986). An intonation change in progress in Australian English. *Language in Society* 15: 23–52.

Habbick, Timothy (1991). Burnouts versus rednecks: effects of group membership on the phonemic system. In P. Eckert (ed.), *New Ways of Analysing Sound Change*. San Diego, CA: Academic Press. 185–212.

Haeri, Niloofar (1994). A linguistic innovation of women in Cairo. *Language Variation and Change* 6: 87–112.

Hogg, Michael (1985). Masculine and feminine speech in dyads and groups: a study of speech style and gender salience. *Journal of Language and Social Psychology* 4: 99–112.

Holmes, Janet (1995). *Women, Men and Language*. London: Longman.

Holmes, Janet (1997). Women, language and identity. *Journal of Sociolinguistics* 1: 195–224.

Holmes, Janet (1998). Response to Koenraad Kuiper. *Journal of Sociolinguistics* 2: 104–6.

Horvath, Barbara (1985). *Variation in Australian English: The Sociolects of Sydney*. Cambridge: Cambridge University Press.

Jabeur, M. (1987). A Sociolinguistic Study in Rades, Tunisia. Ph.D. dissertation, University of Reading, UK.

James, Deborah (1996). Women, men and prestige speech forms: a critical review. In V. L. Bergvall, J. M. Bing and A. F. Freed (eds.), *Rethinking Language and Gender Research: Theory and Practice*. London: Longman. 98–125.

Keddad, Sadika (1989). Codeswitching patterns in an Algerian Community. Ph.D. dissertation, University of London.

Kiesling, Scott Fabius (1998). Men's identities and sociolinguistic variation: The case of fraternity men. *Journal of Sociolinguistics* 2: 69–99.

Kuiper, Koenraad (1998). Thinking about gender, power and speech. *Journal of Sociolinguistics* 2: 101–4.

Labov, William (1963). The social motivation of a sound change. *Word* 19: 273–309.

Labov, William (1966). *The Social Stratification of English in New York City*. Washington, DC: Center for Applied Linguistics.

Labov, William (1990). The intersection of sex and social class in the course of linguistic change. *Language Variation and Change* 2: 205–54.

Labov, William (1994). *Principles of Linguistic Change*, vol. 1: *Internal Factors*. Oxford: Blackwell.

Mansfield, Peter and Peter Trudgill (1994) A sex-specific linguistic feature in a European dialect. *Multilingua* 13: 381–6.

Meyerhoff, Miriam (1996). Dealing with gender identity as a sociolinguistic variable. In V. L. Bergvall, J. M. Bing and A. F. Freed (eds.), *Rethinking Language and Gender Research: Theory and Practice*. London: Longman. 202–27.

Milroy, James (1991). The interpretation of social constraints on variation in Belfast English. In J. Cheshire (ed.), *English around the World: Sociolinguistic Perspectives*. Cambridge: Cambridge University Press. 75–85.

Milroy, Lesley (1987). *Observing and Analysing Natural Language*. Oxford: Blackwell.

Milroy, Lesley (1992). New perspectives in the analysis of sex differentiation in language. In K. Bolton and H. Kwok (eds.), *Sociolinguistics Today: International Perspectives*. London: Routledge. 163–79.

Milroy, James and Lesley Milroy (1993). Mechanisms of change in urban dialects: the role of class, social network and gender. *International Journal of Applied Linguistics* 3: 57–77.

Milroy, James and Lesley Milroy (1997). Varieties and variation. In F. Coulmas (ed.), *The Handbook of Sociolinguistics*. Oxford: Blackwell. 47–64.

Milroy, James, Lesley Milroy, Sue Hartley and David Walshaw (1994). Glottal stops and Tyneside glottalization: Competing patterns of variation and change in British English. *Language Variation and Change* 6: 327–58.

Mulac, A., J. M. Wiemann, S. Widenmann and T. W. Gibson (1988). Male/female language differences and effects in same-sex and mixed-sex dyads: the gender-linked language effect. *Communication Monographs* 55: 315–35.

Nichols, P. C. (1983). Linguistic options and choices for black women in the rural South. In B. Thorne, C. Kramerae and N. Henley (eds.), *Language, Gender and Society*. Cambridge, MA: Newbury House. 54–68.

Romaine, Suzanne (1999). *Communicating Gender*. Mahwah, NJ: Lawrence Erlbaum.

Takano, Shoji (1998). A quantitative study of gender differences in the ellipsis of the Japanese post-positional particles -*wa* and -*ga*:

Gender composition as a constraint on variability. *Language Variation and Change* 10: 289–323.

Thakerar, J. N., H. Giles and J. Cheshire (1982). Psychological and linguistic parameters of speech accommodation theory. In C. Fraser and K. R. Scherer (eds.), *Advances in the Social Psychology of Language*. Cambridge: Cambridge University Press. 205–55.

Trudgill, Peter (1972). Sex, covert prestige and linguistic change in the urban British English of Norwich. *Language in Society* 1: 179–95.

Trudgill, Peter (1974). *The Social Differentiation of English in Norwich*. Cambridge: Cambridge University Press.

Wenger, Etienne (1998). *Communities of Practice*. Cambridge: Cambridge University Press.

Woods, Nicola (1997). The formation and development of New Zealand English: Interaction of gender-related variation and linguistic change. *Journal of Sociolinguistics* 1: 95–126.

Wouk, Fay (1999). Gender and the use of pragmatic particles in Indonesian. *Journal of Sociolinguistics* 3: 194–219.

18　Ethnicity

CARMEN FOUGHT

What is *ethnicity*, and how is it reflected in language variation and change? Just as labeling by sex (i.e. assigning a speaker to the category "male" or "female") cannot substitute for a careful study of the social practices that constitute gender in a particular community (cf. Eckert and McConnell-Ginet 1992), race as a category is useless to us without an understanding of the construction of ethnicity by individuals and communities. As has been shown for gender, ethnicity is not about what one *is*, but rather about what one *does*. Unlike sex, however, where individuals can be grouped biologically into one of two basic categories, and those who cannot are relatively easy to identify, the category of race itself has historically been socially constructed, and is extremely difficult to delimit scientifically (as Zack 1993 and Healey 1997, among others, show).

Moreover, the population of "mixed-race" individuals is increasing dramatically in a number of countries, affecting the functions and definition of ethnicity. In the USA, individuals whose parents represent two different ethnic groups, for example, might choose to identify themselves as belonging to one of these ethnicities only, to both of them, or to neither, with resulting effects on language (Azoulay 1997, Harriman 2000). There is also the case of immigrants of African descent from Spanish-speaking countries such as Panama, who may bring with them a "combined" cultural ethnicity, e.g. "Black Latina" (Thomas 2000). Le-Page and Tabouret-Keller (1985) found that a main feature of the construction of ethnicity in Belize was the unusually high number of individuals who would describe themselves as "Mixed" (1985: 244). Despite these intriguing facts, the use of sociolinguistic variables in the speech of mixed-race individuals has not been systematically investigated, as far as I know, yet it no doubt contains crucial insights for the study of language and ethnic identity.

Note that I have biased my discussion of this topic in such a way that the speaker's self-selection of an ethnicity (or of several) is given priority. For the purposes of this chapter, I will use Giles' definition of *ethnic group* as "those individuals who perceive themselves to belong to the same ethnic category" (Giles 1979: 253).[1] Because this distinction is often relevant, I will use the term *minority ethnic group* to refer to groups that are not the politically dominant group in a particular country or region. Following Le Page and Tabouret-Keller (1985), I will examine the uses of linguistic variables by members of different ethnic communities for their value as "acts of identity", related in complex ways to ethnicity. Phenomena such as *crossing*, to which I will return later, where speakers deliberately use styles associated with ethnic groups other than their own, particularly highlight the complex interaction between race and ethnicity, since an individual may, for example, "look white" but "sound black" (cf. Jacobs-Huey 1997). In studying the relationship of ethnicity to language, linguists would be well served by making more use of materials from fields such as anthropology, sociology, African-American studies, etc., where the social category of ethnicity has been the object of study in its own right (see the short annotated bibliography in the Appendix).

This chapter will explore some of the theoretical contributions of the study of language variation and change in minority ethnic communities to the field of sociolinguistics. Though there will be brief discussion of the role of European-American ethnic groups (such as Italian or Irish) in language change, the chapter deals predominantly with the language of non-white groups. (See Waters 1990 for a discussion of European-Americans "choices" about claiming ethnicity.) And while there exists a vast body of literature on the role of ethnicity in such processes as language maintenance, loss, and revitalization, and on the role of language choice in national identity, these topics will not be covered here. In addition, the chapter will not address attitudes toward minority ethnic dialects, or the ways in which linguistic research in this area might be applied to education. (See Rickford 1999 for discussion of these topics.) I have chosen to focus mainly on studies that feature sociolinguistic variables of some type, usually grammatical or phonological, and on communities within the USA, where a majority of the studies in the variationist tradition have been done. So many significant works have been produced on language and ethnicity that it will not be possible to discuss all of them; in many places I have selected illustrative examples, rather than trying to list everything that has been done on a particular theme.

1 Research on Ethnicity and Variation in Language

The majority of sociolinguistic studies of language and ethnicity have focused on variation, which I will discuss below, rather than on change, the topic of the next section.

1.1   Relationship between minority ethnic and matrix dialects

One of the first issues to be raised in studying language in minority ethnic groups is the relation of dialects from these communities to other dialects of the same region, particularly those spoken by European-Americans. Much of this research has focused on African-American Vernacular English (AAVE). Although there is not room in this chapter to do it justice, the debate over whether AAVE and various European-American dialects in the United States are diverging or converging has been a central focus of recent research (as in Fasold et al. 1987, Bailey and Maynor 1989). Rickford's contribution notes that different components of the various dialects must be looked at separately, since it is possible to have, for example, convergence in the phonology, and divergence in the grammar (1987: 57). Both Rickford and Wolfram (1987) provide diagrams illustrating the many permutations of convergence and divergence patterns that are possible between European-American and African-American dialects. They stress the importance of looking at the direction of changes in the relationship, determining whether dialects are becoming more alike (or more different), and whether one dialect is responsible for this increase (or decrease). Interestingly, the diagrams do not include the possibility of some varieties of AAVE converging with local European-American varieties, while others are diverging. There will be more discussion of these issues later in the chapter.

Even among those linguistic variables that are shared by both a minority ethnic variety and a European-American variety, the specifics of a variable's realization may be different. Santa Ana (1991, 1996), for example, found that final consonant cluster simplification in Chicano English, as spoken by Mexican-American speakers in the southwestern United States, was governed by slightly different constraints from those found in many European-American dialects. There have been numerous studies of this process in AAVE (e.g. Labov 1972a), which also show different orderings of constraints. Sometimes the differences between minority ethnic and other dialects for particular sociolinguistic variables involve a wider range of contexts for the feature. For example, with respect to multiple negation, African-American speakers in some communities use constructions that are not found in European-American dialects which permit multiple negation, e.g. negative inversion (*Didn't nobody play in the sandbox*) and transfer of negation to a lower clause (*Ain't no cat can't get in no coop*) (Labov 1972a, Wolfram 1969). The latter type of construction is also found in Chicano English (Fought 1999b), although apparently not in the Puerto Rican English of New York City (Wolfram 1974a).

In some cases, a variety associated with a minority ethnic group may integrate features of a separate language associated with that group, as is the case with many dialects of English spoken in Latino communities. Wald (1984), for example, refers to Chicano English as a "phonological creole" (1984: 21), whose sound system originated in numerous non-native English systems of immig-rants, which were later inherited by their children and developed into a stable dialect with phonological norms of its own. Chicano English also has unique semantic, intonational, and other features, some of which can be traced to the influence of Spanish, while others represent independent innovations (cf. Penfield and Ornstein-Galicia 1985, Peñalosa 1980, García 1984, Wald 1984). Though historically more remote, the influences of African languages and patterns on AAVE are another example. Similarly, Leap (1993) provides an analysis of the role of ancestral languages in a number of dialects spoken by Native-Americans in different parts of the United States.

Finally, there exists the possibility of influence from the minority ethnic variety onto the surrounding mainstream version of the regional dialect. Of course such influence is clearly acknowledged in the realm of the lexicon (see Smitherman 1998), but less investigation of possible phonological and gram-matical influences in this direction has been done. Wolfram (1974b) found evidence of African-American influence on European-Americans in the South with respect to copula absence (as in, e.g., *He my friend* instead of *He is my friend*). Moreover, Feagin (1997) concludes that non-rhoticity (lack of post-vocalic /r/) in European-American dialects of the South was influenced by the speech of African-Americans as well.

1.2 What it means to be a member of a speech community

In general, sociolinguists have relied on the notion of the "speech community" as the focus for the study of linguistic variation and change, although recently there has been some increase in approaches that focus on other units, such as social networks or the family (Milroy 1980, Hazen, this volume). But there has not always been agreement on how to define the community for purposes of situating individuals within a larger context. Studies of variation among minority group speakers have helped to enlighten us about what it means to be a "member" of a particular community, and have revealed some interesting facets of the role of language in signaling group identity.

In one of the early studies of variation in a minority community, Labov (1972a) found that among African-American adolescents in New York, being a "lame" (an individual who is not a member of a local vernacular peer group) correlated with less use of AAVE phonological and grammatical features. This result has serious implications for the sociolinguistic researcher because lames "are the typical informants made available to investigators who study non-standard language in schools, recreation centers, and homes" (Labov 1972a: 255). The study also shows that two speakers of the same ethnicity may not have the same relationship to the ethnic speech community, and that the notion of community itself must be constructed.

While the above study was concerned with the degree of membership of an individual *within* an ethnic community, there are also interesting issues revolving around the degree to which individuals of various ethnicities identify with dominant European-American communities in their region. Studies of variation can illuminate how speakers might choose to highlight their membership in a minority ethnic community as well as in the local, mainstream community, either in alternation or simultaneously.

If a particular ethnic group has a language other than the socially-dominant one at its disposal, individuals can use it in the construction and signaling of ethnic identity. This includes the selection of different languages for different symbolic purposes, as well as code-switching, which can be a quite dramatic illustration of moving back and forth linguistically between ingroup and outgroup cultures. There are numerous studies of variation in language choice. A particularly comprehensive work is Zentella (1997), which also contains a detailed analysis of code switching and its role in the construction of Puerto-Rican American identity.

While many code switching studies have focused, like Zentella's study, on Hispanic-American groups, there are also some interesting studies of the role of code switching in the construction of Asian ethnic identities. The work of Lesley Milroy and Li Wei (Milroy and Wei 1995, Wei et al. 1992) on a Chinese community in Britain (Tyneside) seeks to provide an integrated model of language choice and code switching. The researchers constructed an "ethnic index" of the strength of ties that a particular individual had to others of the same ethnic group. They found that this ethnic index helped to explain patterns of language choice that could not be predicted by a model based on age and generation, and that the use of certain code switching strategies was also related to ethnic network. An interesting study done in the USA is Lo (1999), one of the few studies addressing the linguistic construction of Asian-American identities. Lo analyzes a conversation in which code switching is used as a way of "crossing" by one of the participants, while another participant "rejects" the code switching and refuses to acknowledge the speaker's appropriation of Korean-American ethnicity. This study also raises issues about the role of others within a community in validating an individual's ethnicity (Azoulay 1997; also see Wieder and Pratt 1990 for a discussion of the role of the community in determining whether or not one is a "real Indian").

Even if a group does not have an additional language as a resource, there are ways for individuals to signal membership in the minority ethnic community as well as the surrounding regional communities. For ethnic minority speakers, the question of "membership" in the wider regional community is a particularly tricky one. The dialect of the dominant European-American ethnic group for an area is privileged as being representative of "regional speech" in that area. The stereotype of New York City, whether one sees it as positive or negative, involves *white* New Yorkers. Individuals who grow up in a minority ethnic community find themselves in a position where the linguistic signals of local (e.g. New York) identity are tied to European-American ethnicities. The option of rejecting this local identity and signaling only their ethnic affiliation is technically open to them. However, there is usually pressure from outside (and sometimes from within) the community to assimilate, including the exhortation to learn "Standard English" in order to "get ahead" (Lippi-Green 1997). The borrowing of features from a neighboring minority ethnic group, which will be discussed below, is one of the ways in which speakers might signal affiliation with a local region beyond their specific community while avoiding "sounding white," which is often viewed negatively (Jacobs-Huey 1997, Rickford 1992, Wolfram 2000).

2   The Role of Interethnic Contacts

2.1   *Contacts in large urban settings*

Interethnic contacts between a minority ethnic group and the local European-American majority group play an important role in language variation. From a historical perspective, for example, Rickford (1986b) examines the possible origins of AAVE habitual *be*, as in *He be at the playground* with the meaning "He is usually/often at the playground", in contact with Irish English speakers, ultimately concluding that the feature comes from an earlier creole, with the Irish influence indirect rather than direct. Ash and Myhill (1986) looked in detail at contact between African-American and European-American speakers in Philadelphia, focusing particularly on those individuals who have a large number of contacts in the other ethnic group. They found that the effects of contact were asymmetrical across different components of the linguistic system. For European-American speakers with African-American contacts, phonological features seemed much more permeable than grammatical ones. The effects of contact were also asymmetrical for blacks and whites; numerous contacts outside the ethnic group affected the dialects of African-American individuals to a greater degree than those of European-American speakers, although both groups showed evidence of the contact. Labov and Harris (1986) also found linguistic asymmetry. African-Americans who had contacts in the Philadelphia white community showed shifts away from AAVE variables in their grammar, but did not adopt the phonological variables characteristic of Philadelphia European-Americans.

These findings are interesting in relation to the various patterns of divergence and convergence of dialects discussed earlier, where a number of possible patterns for the direction of convergence were proposed (Wolfram 1987, Rickford 1987). Edwards (1992) also found contact with European-Americans to be a significant factor which correlated with a relatively lower use of AAVE variables by young African-American speakers in Detroit. Generally, it would seem that in contact between European-American and other ethnic groups, the uneven power relationship and the pressure to assimilate would lead to more, if not all, of the convergence coming from the minority ethnic group, as Ash and Myhill's (1986) study suggests. However, the recent phenomenon of crossing, typical particularly of members of the dominant European-American group, represents a small countercurrent in this respect.

A further possibility within the framework of using language to signal ethnic identity is that of a minority ethnic group borrowing linguistic features from another local minority community. This phenomenon has been well documented for Puerto Rican-American groups, where adolescents in particular have been found to use certain features of AAVE in their English. Wolfram (1974a), for example, found that Puerto Rican speakers in New York who had many African-American contacts used habitual *be*, or had surface realizations of /θ/ as [f] (cf. also Poplack 1978, Labov et al. 1968, Zentella 1997). Not surprisingly, the strongest use of AAVE features tends to occur among those who have the most extensive contacts in local African-American communities. However, as Wolfram (1974: 200) points out, even those with very few outgroup contacts may assimilate AAVE features from Latino speakers in their social circle who *do* have such contacts. Cutler (1999) highlights a similar function for white speakers with black contacts in the transmission of hip-hop culture, the urban teen subculture based on African-American styles including rap music. The role of such "dialect brokers" in dialect contact would be an interesting subject for future study.

2.2   *Contacts in rural settings*

A large number of the studies of language variation and ethnicity, including most of those mentioned above, involve speakers in urban settings. However, there are special insights about this topic to be gained by looking at smaller, rural, and somewhat isolated communities. Wolfram and Dannenberg (1999) discuss research on the Lumbee Indians of North Carolina. Their situation is of interest because it involves a particularly long period (almost 300 years) of tri-ethnic contact among Lumbee, African-American, and European-American groups. Wolfram and Dannenberg explore various aspects of the Lumbee Indians' construction of ethnic identity, including the legal classification of the Lumbee as "free people of color" or "mulattos" in 1835, and the many ways in which the Lumbee have worked towards an identity which goes beyond the white/non-white dichotomy that is the focus of the surrounding culture. Wolfram and Dannenberg's research on current Lumbee speakers found specific grammatical markers of Lumbee ethnicity (such as regularization of *was* to *were*) that the other varieties in the region do not share. The Lumbee also use features from the local variety of AAVE, but with a slightly different distribution, such as the extension of habitual *be* into non-habitual contexts. Similarly, Hazen (1997) discusses another Native-American group in North Carolina which adopts copula absence from AAVE but with a different pattern of distribution. This pattern of some shared and some distinct forms was found in the Lumbee phonological system and lexicon as well. As with other cases of variables borrowed in a slightly different form, the use of variables from outside the community by the Lumbee Vernacular English speakers may serve to reinforce both local ties and a specific and separate ethnic identity.

Rickford (1985) looked at two older speakers, one white and one black, on one of the South Carolina Sea Islands. This study is interesting because it focuses on two individuals and how their life histories affect their use of language, an approach which has been disfavored by the variationist tradition (in which looking at large numbers of speakers is treated as crucial), but which has now begun to find favor again (e.g. Wolfram and Beckett 1999). Both speakers' histories involve a fair amount of contact with members of the other group. Rickford's hypothesis was that they would show the effects of this contact in their linguistic systems, and this was true at the phonological level. However, in terms of morphology and syntax, they were quite different despite their history of interethnic contact, which parallels the findings of Ash and Myhill discussed above. In particular, the European-American speaker showed a complete absence of the creole grammatical features used by the African-American speaker. Rickford's interpretation is that "non-standard phonological features are part of a regional Sea Island identity in which both Blacks and Whites participate, but non-standard morpho-syntactic features are more heavily marked as creole and serve as ethnic markers" (1985: 107). Here again we see the interplay of local vs. specifically ethnic identity. Despite their phonological similarities, the morpho-syntactic differences that have been preserved between the European-American and African-American speakers reflect the social distance between these groups that is characteristic of life on the island.

Wolfram et al. (1999) report on a similar case, that of Muzel Bryant, who grew up as a member of the single African-American family on Ocracoke, a North Carolina island populated by European-Americans. One might expect that without a separate minority ethnic community to "compete" with the European-American community, she would simply have assimilated to European-American language norms. However, Muzel's phonological system is basically typical of what Wolfram et al. call "a basilectal AAVE variety" (1999: 156). She shows relatively few phonological features of the local island dialect; particularly noticeable is her almost complete lack of use of the [ɔi] variant of /ai/, as in the pronunciation of "high" as [hɔi], which is a crucial marker of Ocracoke speech. In the areas of morphology and syntax, however, Muzel's speech is more mixed, and the researchers found both AAVE features (many occurring less frequently than in most AAVE varieties) and features of the local Outer Banks English. She also revealed a lack of familiarity with local terms such as *O'cocker* for "Ocracoker."

These cross-currents in Muzel Bryant's speech reflect the fact that though she had frequent contact with European-Americans, her ethnicity served as a significant barrier to integration in the island community. While Wolfram et al. (1999) report that the islanders now care for Muzel and speak fondly of her, they also note the historical evidence that this family was not fully accepted into the social life of the community by the other islanders, and that this social distance is reflected in Muzel's speech. It is particularly interesting that the relative lack of assimilation in phonology coupled with more convergence in the area of morpho-syntactic features is an exact reversal of the findings from Rickford's Sea Islands study.

Wolfram et al. (1999) suggest that the phonology and lexicon are the components of the Ocracoke brogue that are most often identified as unique, and thus it makes sense that the social distance experienced by Muzel's family would be reflected more in these components, rather than in the morphology or syntax. This analysis coincides well with Rickford's discussion, in a footnote to the Sea Islands study, of the difference between *local* and *generalized* prestige. Rickford disagrees with the analysis by Labov (1984), in which sound changes are treated as associated with local identity and prestige while grammatical variables are associated with more generalized resources (Rickford 1985: 111). He accepts the distinction itself, but rejects the association of phonology with "local" and syntax or morphology with "general," and gives a number of examples of grammatical variables strongly associated with local communities, and phonological ones that seem to have a generalized prestige. This analysis can encompass both the speech of Muzel Bryant, which lacks the phonological features so symbolic of Ocracokers, and the speech of Mr. King which lacks the grammatical features most characteristic of Creole/black identity on the Sea Islands.

It is also clear from both these studies that the boundaries of ethnicity can be very strong indeed, rooted in prejudice and a deep sense of the "other", even in small isolated communities where a more complete integration than among large urban populations might have been expected. This returns us to the question of what it means to be a member of a community. Even where, on the surface, extensive inter-ethnic contact and integration might seem to be the norm, the study of linguistic variation reveals the underlying preservation and expression of identities divided along the lines of ethnicity. For example, Henderson (1996) discusses racial isolation in Philadelphia among African-Americans who seem completely integrated into European-American communities.

3   Intra-ethnic Variation and the Expression of Ethnicity

3.1   *Interaction with other social factors: socio-economic status, gender and age*

Numerous studies show the importance of social categories in analyzing the use of particular features within the dialect of minority ethnic groups. I have selected only a few as examples, though many others are mentioned elsewhere in the chapter. One of the first and most comprehensive studies of socioeconomic status and linguistic variation in a minority community is Wolfram's (1969) Detroit study of AAVE. He reports strong correlations of social class with all the phonological and grammatical variables that he analyzed, although the differences were more marked for some of the variables than for others. Many of the variables showed effects of gender as well. More recently, Edwards (1990) looked at a number of AAVE phonological features, also in Detroit, and found that social class and gender interacted in their correlation with these features. Interestingly, Edwards found no gender differences in his later study of four linguistic variables within a working class African-American neighborhood (Edwards 1997). Edwards attributes this finding to the very similar social roles filled by men and women in this community.

A good example of the importance of age as a social category is Fasold's (1972) study of African-American speakers in Washington, DC. Fasold made a three way distinction between children, adolescents, and adults, and found that children had the highest use of each of the AAVE variables studied (and adults had the lowest). More recently, Edwards' (1992) study of African-Americans in Detroit found marked generational differences in the use of AAVE variables. Younger speakers, and particularly those whose networks included more contacts with Anglos, tended to use the AAVE variants of these features less frequently. Of course, in any case where age is a factor there exists the possibility of a change in progress. Though most of the variables in the studies I have mentioned so far are considered to be stable, cases of shifts toward or away from the "standard" norm will be discussed below in the section on change.

3.2   Categories relevant to the particular community

In addition to these broad social categories, there may be more localized distinctions, which must be accounted for if our study of the relation of language to community is to be complete. A typical example is the distinction between *jocks* and *burnouts* discussed by Eckert (1989). "Jock" students in the US high school where Eckert did fieldwork were oriented toward the activities and culture of the school, whereas "burnout" students were oriented toward the working-class urban culture outside the school, with corresponding differences in their use of local sociolinguistic variables. Another example is the categories related to gang membership, which were first studied in Labov (1972a). More recently, in Fought (1997), I found that the distinction between gang members and non-gang members sometimes overrode other categories such as social class or gender in its correlations with certain variables among adolescents of Mexican-American background in Los Angeles. This study also revealed an additional category of people who "know gangsters" which was crucial to an understanding of the social structure of this young adult group. Mendoza-Denton (1997) explored the complex construction of identity among

Latinas in Northern California. In her study, the distinction between two different gang groups (Norteñas and Sureñas), was of primary importance with respect to the linguistic variable she was studying – -in/-ing alternation. She also discusses a number of other distinctions with local significance.

Outside the USA, Meyerhoff (1997) found that among the Bislama speakers of northern Vanuatu, membership in a family clan was a crucial element of the social structure. Clan affiliation affected the variable use of inclusive vs. exclusive first person plural pronouns (*yumi* and *mifala*). Although many studies have uncovered such local categories in their ethnographic research on particular communities, there is still a tendency among variationists to focus on age, gender, and social class, and then consider the sociological part of the study complete. These general categories are certainly important. Nonetheless, it is crucial to do the ethnographic fieldwork, particularly when minority ethnic communities are studied by a linguist from outside the ethnic group, who may not have, a priori, enough information about culturally-relevant distinctions.

3.3   The effect of interlocutors

The field of sociolinguistics in general has begun to give more attention to the role of interlocutors as part of the context of speaking. For years, the sociolinguistic interview as a methodology has dominated the field, particularly in the variationist tradition. Though this method has numerous advantages, it also has the marked disadvantage of inserting someone who is usually to some degree an outsider into the speech situation, and this is of particular concern for those studying ethnicity and language, in light of the observations of ethnicity as a sociolinguistic boundary discussed above. Recently, some sociolinguists have shifted their focus to other methods of data collection (e.g. Bailey 1993, Cukor-Avila 1997), while others have initiated systematic research on the role of other interactants.

Two recent studies of interlocutor effects are of particular interest to the topic of ethnicity and language. Rickford and McNair-Knox (1994) compared two interviews with the same young female African-American speaker: one where the interviewer was a 25-year-old European-American woman, and one where the interviewer was a 41-year-old African-American woman. As might be expected, the speaker used significantly higher levels of AAVE features with the African-American interviewer. That ethnicity is the key factor in such shifting, rather than some form of accommodation (cf. Giles and St. Clair 1979) specifically related to the interviewer's usage of the same forms, is suggested by an earlier study that Rickford and McNair-Knox cite, Fasold (1972). In Fasold's study, African-American speakers used vernacular variants more with African-American than with European-American interviewers, even though the African-American interviewers were generally middle-class speakers of "Standard English" (Fasold 1972: 214).

Another very relevant study is Bell and Johnson (1997), conducted in New Zealand. The authors selected four speakers as research subjects: a Maori ethnicity male, a Maori female, a Pakeha (Anglo ethnicity) male, and a Pakeha female. Each of these people was interviewed three times: once by a person who shared their gender and ethnicity, once by a person of the same sex but the other ethnicity, and once by a person from their same ethnic group, but of the opposite sex. Bell and Johnson were able to trace quite specific rises and falls in the levels of linguistic variables as the characteristics of the interviewer were varied. For example, the use of *eh* functioned primarily as a marker of ethnicity (Maori), but also secondarily as a gender marker associated with Maori men. Once again, this underscores the importance of looking at ethnicity in the context of other factors such as gender, rather than in isolation, and confirms that differences between intraethnic and interethnic discourse can have a tremendous effect on the realization of linguistic variables by a particular speaker. We must not forget that the identity of the interviewer will influence the type of data collected, and that such data may or may not be representative of that speaker's use of variables, particularly those related to ethnicity and identity, when the interviewer is not present (Rickford 1987).

3.4   Crossing: "borrowing" someone else's ethnicity

The phenomenon of "crossing", where speakers deliberately use styles associated with other ethnic groups (Rampton 1995), represents one of the most interesting current trends in research on language and ethnicity. Rampton (1995) looks at the use of several language varieties associated with particular ethnic groups in London (including Jamaican Creole, Asian-accented English, and Punjabi) by young people outside the particular ethnic group, such as Anglo Londoners using "creole". There was also a study of the same topic by Hewitt (1982), which focused on the role of creole use in black British identity, as well as at its symbolic use by white adolescents. Both of these studies explore the complex attitudes of the in-group users of a variety toward crossing by outsiders. Hewitt, for example, points out that while black youngsters in London often talk negatively about Anglos' use of the creole, even to the point of saying "they are stealing our language" (1982: 226), these same adolescents may have Anglo friends among whom they freely encourage creole use. Rampton (1995) discovered that an emblematic use of Punjabi (e.g. swearing terms and stock phrases) by out-group individuals seemed to reflect a sense of interethnic unity among Asians and their non-Asian friends.

Cutler (1999) is particularly revealing in the context of issues relating to language use and integration into the community. She focuses on a European-American speaker who used AAVE features, but clearly was not attempting to construct a black identity for himself, or to be integrated into an African-American peer group. Instead, he seemed to be "borrowing" elements of the African-American experience, through hip-hop culture, while maintaining an identity that is "in opposition to the black community" (Cutler 1999: 435). Bucholtz (1999) also argues that crossing does not necessarily represent the breaking down of boundaries between ethnic groups, and that it can in fact be used to perpetuate racial stereotypes.

Hall (1995) shows that workers in the telephone sex industry sometimes use stereotypes of race in creating "characters" for their clients. In her interviews, Hall found that some European-American women were more successful at performing a stereotyped "Black identity" on the phone than African-American women (successful in the sense that clients were more likely to believe that they were black). Conversely, one of the managers told Hall that "the best white woman we ever had here was Black" (1995: 202). It is important to keep in mind that an individual speaker's repertoire may include linguistic elements characteristic of his or her own ethnic group, of other groups, or of stereotypes of other groups.

4   Research on Ethnicity and Language Change

4.1   *The focus of research on language in minority ethnic groups*

The sociolinguistic research on which current theories of language change are based, particularly in the area of sound change, has focused on majority communities, often on speakers of European-American ethnicity in large urban settings. Almost all the variationist studies of dialects associated with minority ethnic groups have focused on the following areas:

- grammatical variables that are unique to the community in question, such as habitual *be* in AAVE (e.g. Rickford 1992, Bailey and Maynor 1987, etc.)
- stable variables found also in a number of European-American dialects, such as variation between [ɪn] and [ɪŋ], or simplification of consonant clusters (e.g. Labov 1972a, Gilbert 1986, Mendoza-Denton 1997, Santa Ana 1996, etc.)
- variation between standard and non-standard variants, whether grammatical or phonological, including changes that involve either more use of a prestige variant (such as post-vocalic /r/), or less use of a nonstandard variant (such as Ø for 3rd person singular –s, as in Wolfram 1969, Edwards 1992, Rickford 1992, etc.).

Surprisingly little has been done on internally-motivated sound changes in minority ethnic communities, despite the crucial role that changes in progress have played in sociolinguistic theory. Possible reasons for this will be discussed below.

4.2   Minority ethnic group participation in European-American sound changes

One factor that may have contributed to the inadequate research on phonological change among minority ethnic groups is the finding in a number of studies that members of these groups were not participating in the local sound changes affecting European-American speakers (e.g. Labov 1966, Labov and Harris 1986, Bailey and Maynor 1987). Taken as a group, these studies have been interpreted as illustrating a general fact about the role (or lack thereof) of non-European-American speakers in sound change. Labov (1994), for example, comments on the non-participation of minority speakers in regional vowel shifts by suggesting that they "are instead oriented to a national pattern of koine formation within the nonwhite groups" (1994: 157). The sociolinguistic literature shows a fairly uniform acceptance of these ideas.

There is clear evidence that African-Americans in *some* communities do not show evidence of *some* local European-American sound changes, and that ethnicity can act as a strong sociolinguistic boundary. This pattern, however, has been generalized into claims that go beyond what can be supported by the research that has been done so far on various minority ethnic groups in the United States. It is worth emphasizing the danger inherent in generalizing about "nonwhite" ethnic groups, e.g. taking the language behavior of African-Americans in Philadelphia as possibly indicative of what one might find among Chinese-Americans in Berkeley. In fact, Hinton et al. (1987) and Luthin (1986) found that the Asian speakers in their sample were participating in the sound changes characteristic of European-Americans in the Bay Area. Many minority ethnic communities in the United States have been under-researched by variationists: numerous Asian groups, Native-Americans, even African-Americans in places like Ohio or Oregon. It is risky to guess whether *specific* ethnic speakers in *specific* regions will participate in any local European-American sound changes without studying them.

This is particularly true in light of the fact that there *are* actually some studies which show members of minority communities participating in sound changes characteristic of local European-American speakers. Labov's (1963) classic study of Martha's Vineyard is a case in point. Both the Portuguese and the Native-American groups on the island were participating in the centralization of (aw) and (ay). In fact, in the youngest generation, these groups often showed more of the local variables than their European-American counterparts. Similarly, Poplack (1978) found that among Puerto Rican children in Philadelphia there was evidence of phonological influences from the European-American local community. Most notably, the children were participating in several Philadelphia vowel shifts, including the fronting of /ow/ and the raising and backing of the nucleus of /ay/ before voiceless consonants. In Fought (1997), I looked at young Chicano speakers in Los Angeles and found that they were participating in the fronting of /u/ and in the backing of /æ/, both known to be sound changes in progress in California (Hinton et al. 1987).

Although it is tempting to conclude from these studies that speakers from various other groups participate in sound changes, while African-Americans do not, there are studies which suggest that even this statement is too global. Wolfram et al. (1997) looked at language change in the Outer Banks region of North Carolina, and found that some sound changes were in progress in both the black and white communities, including ungliding of /ai/ and the loss of front-glided /au/. Anderson (1997) found the ungliding of /ai/ among a group of Native Americans in North Carolina as well. However, other changes originating among European-Americans were not picked up by African-American speakers. In general, older speakers showed more influence from the local European-American dialect than younger ones, who seemed to be mostly shifting away (see also Wolfram 2000).

Also relevant is Bailey (1993), which reports on a large-scale phone survey of the state of Texas. A number of features known to represent current changes in European-American Texan dialect varieties (including /ai/-ungliding, as in Wolfram et al. 1997) were analyzed, focusing particularly on African-Americans. Bailey found that "blacks and whites participate equally in changes that became robust before World War II but not in those that have become robust since the war" (1993: 310). Note that as Bailey says, the groups do not participate *equally* in recent changes; the figures he gives for the (recent) /ai/-ungliding, for example, are 27 percent among white Texans, and 10 percent among black Texans. However, these figures do not tell us whether some segments of the African-American population are using as much monophthongal /ai/ as European-Americans, while others use none, or if African-Americans are simply progressing through the same changes but at a slower rate. It would be worthwhile to track such patterns in other populations, particularly in areas of the north and west which have more recent histories of settlement, in order to learn more about when African-Americans do and do not take part in local sound changes.

We must be on our guard against overgeneralizing the findings from a particular type of community to all others. Unfortunately, and this is of course true in fields other than linguistics, when a finding has been replicated several times, it becomes part of the canon, and subsequent studies tend to take it as a given, the point from which they begin. It is particularly important not to discourage younger scholars from pursuing the many unexplored areas of variation and change in minority ethnic communities by suggesting that there is nothing of interest to find. With luck, future research on the many communities that have not yet been studied will resolve some of the questions raised here.

5   Research on Changes in Progress in Ethnic Minority Communities

There are a few studies which explore the role of different European-American ethnic groups in sound changes. Labov (1966) showed in detail how Jewish,

Italian, and Irish groups were involved in the various vowel shifts characteristic of New York City. Laferriere (1979) looked at phonological change among these same groups in Boston, and found that [ɒ] was associated with Italian and Irish ethnicities, but stigmatized by Jewish speakers. These studies and some others (Knack 1991) show that ethnicity among European-American groups can be an important factor.

As mentioned in the first part of this section, the studies of changes in progress within non-European-American ethnic communities in the USA have overwhelmingly focused on areas other than internally-motivated sound changes. We do, however, have in-depth research on grammatical variables unique to particular minority ethnic varieties, such as increased use of habitual *be* in AAVE (e.g. Rickford 1992, Bailey and Maynor 1987). Overall, many of the same social factors that affected stable variation like consonant cluster deletion, are also relevant to these types of changes in progress: e.g. gender, age, social class. In addition, Cukor-Avila and Bailey (1996) investigate a social factor that I have not discussed yet: the urban/rural distinction. Their study not only examines some of the differences between urban and rural varieties of AAVE, but also documents, through a longitudinal study of one individual, how the urban variety (including features like copula deletion and habitual *be*) is spreading into rural areas.

Several studies have also looked at shifts toward more use of standard forms – in other words "change from above" (Labov 1972b: 178). Some of these focus mainly on grammatical variables. One very interesting study in this group is Nichols 1983. Her fieldwork with African-American speakers in a rural area of coastal South Carolina revealed complex correlations of gender with the use of creole-like vs. standard forms. In particular, while there was little difference between the oldest groups of men and women, young and middle-aged women led in the use of standard forms. Nichols shows how this pattern is related to different economic and employment opportunities for men and women of the younger generation. In a similar vein, Rickford (1992) looks at six different morphological and syntactic variables among African-Americans in East Palo Alto. Rickford's results are intriguing in that the younger speakers in the study showed decreasing use of some nonstandard forms, but increasing use of others.

Other studies of change in the use of nonstandard features focus on phonological variables, although there are fewer of this type. Bailey and Thomas (1998), for example, report on the increased use of post-vocalic /r/ among African-American speakers in Texas. Denning (1989) looks at the tendency toward realizations of final /i/ (as in *happy*) among young AAVE speakers in East Palo Alto that are higher and fronter than those of older speakers. This represents a change away from the southern origins of the dialect and toward the surrounding European-American dialects of California. He also raises the possibility of some further phonological similarities between young African-American and European-American speakers in California, but as far as I know these have not been investigated further. Butters (1986) looks at phonological, morphological, and syntactic features in Wilmington, NC, and finds a shift toward standard forms among younger speakers.

There are only a handful of studies that focus on "changes from below" (Labov 1972b: 179) in minority communities, and most of these do so in relation to changes taking place in the matrix dialect. As was mentioned earlier, my research on Mexican-American speakers in Los Angeles (Fought 1997, 1999a) revealed that these speakers are taking part in sound changes characteristic of the local European-American community, namely /u/-fronting, /æ/-backing, and /ɑ/-raising. The social factors that correlated with the use of these variables included gender, social class, and gang status, and the three factors interacted with one another in complicated ways.

Interestingly, the "curvilinear pattern" (Labov 1980) of interior social classes leading changes from below did not apply among these speakers. The effects of gang status and gender were more powerful than those of social class with respect to the variables in this community. This serves as a good reminder that until more research is done on change in minority ethnic communities, we cannot be certain which patterns associated with change among European-Americans will apply. There is no reason to expect that categories such as "working class," for example, would have the same significance in majority European-American and other ethnic communities. The relationship of such categories to linguistic variables must be determined for each community (cf. Rickford 1986a, Edwards 1996).

Some studies of change among African-Americans in the South, discussed earlier, are also relevant here. Wolfram et al.'s (1997) study of an African-American family in the Outer Banks region found that the AAVE dialect of older speakers was strongly influenced by the local European-American dialect, but that younger speakers seemed to use fewer local dialect features and more "general" AAVE features. Bailey's (1993) Texas phone survey data showed a difference for the participation of African-Americans in sound changes that became robust before and after World War II. It would be interesting to see if a detailed study of migration patterns to and from these areas revealed any correlations with the linguistic changes. Another report on the same Texas survey data is found in Bailey and Thomas (1998), which looks more broadly at the vowel systems for several African-American speakers, and tracks a number of changes across speakers representing different generations. The results confirmed the findings of Bailey (1993): the African-American speakers were more likely to show evidence of older changes from the European-American dialect. Like Wolfram et al. (1997), they found that older speakers' systems were more similar to those of their European-American counterparts. Interestingly, where there were differences in this older group, Bailey and Thomas were often able to trace creole sources for the AAVE variants.

Each of these studies is motivated by questions about how the minority ethnic dialects, AAVE or Chicano English, fit in with the local European-American vernaculars. To my knowledge, *there has not been a single large-scale study of sound change internal to an ethnic minority community.* That is, nobody has looked for sociolinguistic patterns of vowel shift within, say, an African-American community, in the same way that such shifts have been studied for European-American speakers in Philadelphia, Detroit, etc., focusing on the internal phonological system of the dialect without reference to European-American varieties. Bailey and Thomas' study is perhaps the one that comes closest to this idea, in that it looks at entire vowel systems and discusses, at least briefly, some features (e.g. lack of glide with /e/ and /o/) outside the context of comparisons with European-Americans. Nonetheless, it focuses on individuals, without investigating any correlation with other social factors, such as gender, social class, etc., and it ultimately emphasizes the question of convergence or divergence from European-American dialects. I do not mean to detract from what is in fact a fine and much needed study. However, the field lacks a comprehensive investigation of sound change "from below" and of the social factors with which it correlates within a community of speakers other than European-Americans.

Sound changes are a universal feature of languages over time, and as such must be present in AAVE, Chicano English, etc. Research on this topic could make great contributions to sociolinguistic theory. First, some minority ethnic communities might have a very different social organization from European-American communities in terms of class structure, local categories, etc. Also, with dialects such as Chicano English, the presence of a second language in the community (Spanish), with its historical influence on the phonological system, presents some intriguing possibilities. For example, do sound changes in Chicano English tend to move toward or away from Spanish phonology (or neither)?

Why has so little been done on this topic? It is easy to fall into a pattern of treating minority ethnic groups as marked, as the "other," even for those who come from non-European-American ethnic backgrounds themselves. The debate about divergence and convergence, the study of inter-ethnic contacts, the findings about when ethnic minority speakers do or do not participate in European-American sound changes, all have contributed to the field of socio-linguistics as a whole. Yet all of them can be seen as lenses for viewing the dialects of ethnic minority groups relative to a European-American standard. Even research on features such as habitual *be* is based in part on the fact that such features are perceptually salient due to their absence in other dialects. Here again, there is a parallel with sociolinguistic studies of gender, which have often focused on how women are different from men. In contrast with this earlier research, Coates (1996) focuses only on women's language, even though the study had collected data on men also. Researchers on ethnic minority communities and language should be similarly confident in taking an "internal" approach to this topic, and moving beyond comparisons with European-Americans. Wolfram (2000) takes a step in this direction in his discussion of the development and maintenance of vernacular language norms in two ethnic minority speech communities.

5.1   Sound change and regional differences in minority ethnic dialects

Very little systematic study of regional pronunciation differences within the dialects of ethnic minority groups, e.g. AAVE, has been done. In this section I will address the following questions, related to regional variation in AAVE (since it is the ethnic minority dialect that has been most studied to date):

- To what extent is there regional variation in AAVE?
- Is AAVE strikingly more homogeneous across the USA than European-American vernacular varieties? and if so, is this surprising?
- Is the degree of cross-regional similarity different for different components of the grammar (e.g. syntax vs. phonology)?
- What are the possible explanations for similarities and differences across AAVE dialects?

Despite the fact that much more cross-regional research on AAVE is needed, certain assumptions about regional variation (or lack thereof) in AAVE have become accepted within the field of sociolinguistics.

First of all, primary importance has been given to the grammatical similarities in the dialect that have been found across the country. Rickford (1992), in discussing real-time evidence of change, comments:

> Implicit in Labov and Harris's [1986] original claims about divergence . . . was the assumption that *urban Vernacular Black English was pretty similar from one city to the next*, so that comparisons with earlier studies in other cites could serve as evidence of change in real time. This is by no means an ideal strategy, since the assumption of uniformity might be invalid for specific variables, and the social dynamics of change might be quite different from one city to the next. However, since no major grammatical differences have emerged from the study of Vernacular Black English in Detroit, New York City, Philadelphia, Washington DC, Atlanta, Wilmington, Berkeley, and Los Angeles, it seems reasonable to accept comparisons with earlier studies in other cities as preliminary real-time evidence.
>
> (Rickford 1992: 262, italics added)

In a similar vein, Wolfram and Schilling-Estes (1999) give the following summary of regional variation in AAVE in their textbook *American English*, which, though not completely evident from its title, is a comprehensive, up-to-date survey of sociolinguistic topics.

> Up to this point we have discussed AAVE as if it were a unitary variety in different regions of the United States. We must, however, admit regional variation within AAVE, just as we have to admit regional variation within vernacular Anglo American varieties. Certainly, some of the Northern metropolitan versions of AAVE are distinguishable from some of the Southern rural versions, and South Atlantic coastal varieties are different from those found in the Gulf region.

> While admitting some of these regional variations, we hasten to point out that one of the most noteworthy aspects of AAVE is the common core of features shared across different regions. Features such as habitual *be*, copula absence, inflectional –s absence, among a number of other grammatical and phonological structures, are found in locations as distant as Los Angeles, California; New Haven, Connecticut; Meadville, Mississippi; Austin, Texas; and Wilmington, North Carolina, as well as in both urban and rural settings. Thus we recognize regional variation in AAVE while concluding, at the same time, that the regional differences do not come close to the magnitude of regional differences that exist across Anglo varieties.   (Wolfram and Schilling-Estes 1999: 174–5)

This passage summarizes accurately the prevailing stance of sociolinguists toward the issue of regional variation in AAVE. It is known that there are some regional differences, but generally this is taken to be minor, relative to differences among European-American populations. A northern/southern dichotomy is often acknowledged, as in the citation above (and also Labov 1998: 147), but otherwise dialect variation within AAVE is rarely discussed.

There is a tremendous need for more research on the question of AAVE and regional variation. The major studies of AAVE grammar (e.g. Wolfram 1969, Fasold 1972, Labov 1972a, Baugh 1983, Rickford 1992) do not necessarily overlap completely in terms of the grammatical features on which they report. It might be worth exploring more carefully whether there are certain AAVE grammatical features that appear in some parts of the country and not others. With respect to the phonological component, as Bailey and Thomas put it "phonology is the neglected stepchild of research on . . . AAVE" (1998: 85). Even in what has been done, when researchers say that there are phonological similarities across AAVE dialects, they may be referring to anything from nonstandard features (e.g. [θ]/[f] alternation), which may themselves be variable within the dialect, to consonant cluster simplification, found in most other dialects of English but quantitatively different in AAVE. Again, we should find out more about exactly which subsets of these features are definitely characteristic of which regions, as well as exploring the phonological features which are *not* common across regional variants of AAVE. There can be no doubt, as Wolfram and Schilling-Estes (1999) point out above, that there are distinguishable regional varieties of AAVE[2], but these have not been systematically explored.

A crucial question is whether the degree of similarity across AAVE dialects is noticeably greater than the regional variation found among European-American varieties, and if so, whether this is surprising. One explanation which has been proposed for similarities that have been found across AAVE dialects in different regions is that African-Americans all speak more or less the same way because they are oriented to a sense of ethnic solidarity and nation-wide cohesiveness. This is suggested, for example, in the citation from Labov (1994) above; Wolfram and Schilling-Estes (1999: 181) and Wolfram (2000) give similar explanations for the shift of younger speakers away from the local dialect in South Carolina. As far as I know, sociolinguists have not explored independently the validity of the social orientation implied in this interpretation.

Do African-Americans in Atlanta feel a strong sense of kinship with those in San Francisco, and at what level? Does this override their sense of local pride in being Atlantans (or Southerners)? These questions go back to the issue of how ethnicity is defined and constructed. If we believe that African-Americans are somehow involved in a process of keeping their dialects very similar across the country because of some sense of national black identity we must investigate how the social process of a shared identity works, quite apart from linguistic issues. (See Marable 1995 for a sociological discussion of divisions within African-American groups.) An additional, and in my opinion more promising, explanation is provided by Wolfram (2000), who suggests that patterns of expanded and regular contact among African-Americans in different regions, such as "homecoming" events and family reunions, may also play a role in the transmission of vernacular features across regions.

The only research that I know of which shows some evidence of increased use of "general" AAVE phonological features (as opposed to just a lack of local European-American features) is that of Wolfram and his associates (Wolfram et al. 1997, Wolfram 2000) done in the south. Wolfram (2000) found that the dialect of older AAVE speakers in Hyde County was associated with "sounding country" by the younger generation of African-Americans, which provides an explanation for their increased use of features associated with urban AAVE. Of course, this urban/rural distinction is not equally relevant in all areas of the country. It would be tremendously interesting to see whether phonological studies in other areas, particularly the west, north, etc., show evidence of this tendency toward "general AAVE" features among young speakers. Denning (1989) suggests that AAVE speakers in California, for example, may be moving away from these general norms.

It is possible that once the cross-regional research on AAVE phonology is undertaken, focusing not on specific stigmatized variants but on entire vowel systems, we may find some clear phonological differences in the AAVE of geographically distant regions. This pattern of strong grammatical similarities with significant phonological differences exactly parallels that of European-American dialects across the USA. The total number of grammatical differences in the English of different regions (and even different countries) is small compared with the vast and varied body of phonological differences, as discussed by Wald (1984: 17), and as is evident from the chapters on grammatical versus phonological differences in Wolfram and Schilling-Estes (1999). In sum, we may not need to treat regional variation (or lack thereof) in AAVE as a special or noteworthy case, qualitatively different from variation across European-American communities.

6   Future Directions

The most crucial direction for future research, in my view, is the study of sound change within ethnic minority communities, as discussed above. Sound change has had a central role in sociolinguistic theory, and yet the vast majority of our data on this phenomenon comes from European-American communities. More research on communities outside the USA, particularly in areas where ethnic differences are an important part of the social structure, is also needed. Along with these projects, an in-depth study of regional dialect differences within AAVE and other dialects across the USA would be extremely interesting. In particular, the area of intonation in studies of AAVE, Chicano English and other dialects has been fairly sparse, although the few studies that exist suggest that this would be a very fruitful area (e.g. Thomas 1999, Penfield and Ornstein-Galicia 1985).

In addition, more research on US communities that are neither African-American nor Latino is badly needed. There has been some work on Native-American communities (e.g. Leap 1993, Anderson 1997, Wolfram and Dannenberg 1999, etc.) but much less than for other groups, and there is very little study of Asian-American groups at all. There is no nationally recognized dialect associated with an Asian group, although there are occasional references in the literature to Vietnamese English (Wolfram and Schilling-Estes 1999: 167). The difficulties of an outsider doing fieldwork within, for example, the "Chinatown" areas found in many large urban centers may have contributed to the lack of research on these communities. With luck, linguistic researchers from inside the communities will be available in the future, since these ethnographically complex social settings could make great contributions to the field of sociolinguistics.

Finally, an area that has received very little attention from linguists is, as mentioned above, the construction of ethnicity by people of mixed race. Not everyone belongs unequivocally to a single ethnic group. Investigation of the speech of such individuals, along with an in-depth study of their construction of identity, both personally and within a community, could provide an exciting new area for sociolinguistic research on language and ethnicity.

Appendix: Sociological References on Ethnicity with Annotations

General theory of race/ethnicity

Anthias, F. and N. Yuval-Davis (1992). *Racialized Boundaries*. New York: Routledge.
  Discusses race in the context of theories of nationalism, class, gender, and identity, focusing particularly on the situation in the UK.

Davis, F. J. (1991). *Who is Black? One nation's definition*. University Park, PA: Pennsylvania State University Press.
    Very broad. Discusses laws about race, effects of skin tone, construction of race in other countries (Brazil, Korea, Haiti, etc.), trans-racial adoptions.

Gandy, O. (1998). The social construction of race. In O. Gandy, *Communication and Race: A Structural Perspective*. New York: Oxford University Press. 35–92.
    Various sociological theories of race, race (not just ethnicity) as constructed, identity and reference groups.

Healey, J. (1997). *Race, Ethnicity and Gender in the United States: Inequality, Group Conflict and Power*. Thousand Oaks, CA: Pine Forge Press.
    Statistics on economic status, education, attitudes; also discusses interaction of race with gender, specific issues related to African-American, Native-American, Hispanic-American and Asian-American groups.

Omi, M. and H. Winant (1994). *Racial Formation in the United States: From the 1960s to the 1990s*. New York and London: Routledge.
    Political history of "race," class-based and other theoretical approaches.

Yinger, J. M. (1985). Ethnicity. *Annual Review of Sociology* 11: 151–80.
    Review of sociological work on the definition and analysis of ethnicity, including a large bibliography.

Studies of ethnicity among African-Americans

Hecht, M., M. J. Collier and S. Ribeu (1993). *African American Communication: Ethnic Identity and Cultural Interpretation*. Newbury Park, CA: Sage.
    Detailed information on theories of construction of identity, interactions of race/sex/class, communication patterns.

Marable, M. (1995). *Beyond Black and White: Rethinking Race in American Politics and Society*. London: Verso.
    Links race and culture to power structures, history of the concept of "multiculturalism," effects of class within African-American communities.

Miscellaneous

Azoulay, K. (1997). *Black, Jewish and Interracial: It's Not the Color of Your Skin but the Race of your Kin, and other Myths of Identity*. Durham, NC: Duke University Press.
    Interethnic (i.e. mixed race) identities, role of perception of others in identity, history of the concept of "biracial."

Waters, M. (1990). *Ethnic Options: Choosing Identities in America*. Berkeley, CA: University of Cahfornia Press.
   The concept of ethnicity among European-Americans, "choice" of ethnicity, views on topics such as interracial marriage.

Zack, N. (1993). *Race and Mixed Race*. Philadelphia: Temple University Press.
   Social history of the concept of mixed race, "racial theory," laws about mixed race people.

ACKNOWLEDGMENT

I am grateful to John Fought, Ronald Macaulay, Peter Trudgill, and Walt Wolfram for providing comments on an earlier version of this chapter.

NOTES

1   Of course, this is not the only possible perspective. Anulkah Thomas (p.c.) reports the experience of a Panamanian girl of African descent who was told by a teacher to check "Black" on the census form because "that's what people see when they look at you."

2   An anecdote told to me by John Fought (personal communication) confirms that these differences can be significant even at a relatively short geographical distance. While standing in line in Philadelphia, he overheard an exchange in AAVE between the person in front of him and the clerk who was assisting customers. The clerk was a local African-American man, and the customer was a young African-American woman. After the two had conversed very briefly about the transaction at hand, the clerk said, "You're not from around here, are you?" and the woman responded, "No, I'm from New York."

REFERENCES

Anderson, Bridget (1997). Adaptive sociophonetic strategies and dialect accommodation: /ay/ monophthongization in Cherokee English. *University of Pennsylvania working papers in linguistics* 4, 1: 185–202.

Ash, Sharon and John Myhill (1986). Linguistic correlates of inter-ethnic contact. In D. Sankoff (ed.), *Diversity and Diachrony*. Amsterdam: John Benjamins. 33–44.

Bailey, Guy (1993). A Perspective on African-American English. In D. Preston (ed.), *American Dialect Research*. Amsterdam: John Benjamins. 287–318.

Bailey, Guy and Natalie Maynor (1987). Decreolization? *Language in Society* 16: 449–73.

Bailey, Guy and Natalie Maynor (1989). The divergence controversy. *American Speech* 64, 1: 12–39.

Bailey, Guy and Erik Thomas (1998). Some aspects of African-American Vernacular English phonology. In S. Mufwene, J. Rickford, G. Bailey and J. Baugh (eds.), *African-American English: Structure, History, and Use.* New York: Routledge. 85–109.

Baugh, John (1983). *Black Street Speech: Its History, Structure, and Survival.* Austin, TX: University of Texas Press.

Bell, Allan and Gary Johnson (1997). Towards a sociolinguistics of style. *University of Pennsylvania working papers in linguistics* 4, 1: 1–21.

Bucholtz, Mary (1999). You da man: Narrating the racial other in the production of white masculinity. *Journal of Sociolinguistics* 3, 4: 443–60.

Butters, Ronald (1986). Linguistic convergence in a North Carolina community. In K. Denning et al. (eds.), *Variation in Language: NWAV-XV at Stanford.* Stanford: Department of Linguistics. 52–60.

Butters, Ronald and Ruth Nix (1986). The English of Blacks in Wilmington, North Carolina. In M. Montgomery and G. Bailey (eds.), *Language Variety in the South.* Tuscaloosa: University of Alabama Press. 254–63.

Coates, Jennifer (1996). *Women Talk.* Cambridge: Blackwell.

Cukor-Avila, Patricia (1997). An ethnolinguistic approach to the study of rural Southern AAVE. In C. Bernstein et al. (eds.), *Language Variety in the South Revisited.* Tuscaloosa: University of Alabama Press. 447–62.

Cukor-Avila, Patricia and Guy Bailey (1996). The spread of urban AAVE: A case study. In J. Arnold et al. (eds.), *Sociolinguistic Variation: Data, Theory, and Analysis.* Stanford, CA: CSLI. 469–85.

Cutler, Cecilia (1999). Yorkville Crossing: White teens, hip hop, and African American English. *Journal of Sociolinguistics* 3, 4: 428–42.

Denning, Keith (1989). Convergence with divergence: A sound change in Vernacular Black English. *Language Variation and Change.* 1, 2: 145–67.

Eckert, Penelope (1989). *Jocks and Burnouts.* New York: Teachers' College Press.

Eckert, Penelope and Sally McConnell-Ginet (1992). Think practically and look locally: language and gender as community-based practice. *Annual Review of Anthropology* 21: 461–90.

Edwards, Walter (1990). Phonetic differentiation between Black and White speech in East-Side Detroit. *Word–Journal of the International Linguistic Association* 41, 2: 203–18.

Edwards, Walter (1992). Sociolinguistic behavior in a Detroit inner-city black neighborhood. *Language in Society* 21: 93–115.

Edwards, Walter (1996). Sex-based differences in language choice in an African-American neighborhood in Detroit. In E. Schneider (ed.), *Focus on the USA.* Amsterdam: John Benjamins. 183–94.

Edwards, Walter (1997). The variable persistence of Southern Vernacular sounds in the speech of inner-city black Detroiters. In C. Bernstein et al. (eds.), *Language Variety in the South Revisited.* Tuscaloosa: University of Alabama Press. 76–86.

Fasold, Ralph (1972). *Tense Marking in Black English: A Linguistic and Social Analysis.* Arlington, VA: Center for Applied Linguistics.

Fasold, Ralph W., William Labov, Fay Vaughn-Cooke, Guy Bailey, Walt

Wolfram, Arthur Spears and John Rickford (1987). *Are Black and White Vernacular Diverging? Papers from the NWAVE XIV Panel Discussion.* American Speech 62, 1: 3–80.

Feagin, Crawford (1997). The African contribution to Southern states English. In C. Bernstein et al. (eds.), *Language Variety in the South Revisited*. Tuscaloosa: University of Alabama Press. 123–39.

Fought, Carmen (1997). A majority sound change in a minority community: /u/-fronting in Chicano English. *Journal of Sociolinguistics* 3, 1: 5–23.

Fought, Carmen (1999a). *The English and Spanish of young adult Chicanos.* IRCS report 97–09.

Fought, Carmen (1999b). I'm not from nowhere: Negative concord in Chicano English. Paper presented at NWAVE-28, University of Toronto.

García, Maryellen (1984). Parameters of the East Los Angeles speech community. In Jacob Ornstein-Galicia and Allan Metcalf (eds.), *Form and Function in Chicano English.* Rowley, MA: Newbury House. 85–98.

Gilbert, Glenn (1986). Phonological variation among Blacks, Brandywines, and Whites in Charles County, Maryland. In K. Denning et al. (eds.), *Variation in Language: NWAV-XV at Stanford.* Stanford, CA: Department of Linguistics. 160–72.

Giles, Howard (1979). Ethnicity markers in speech. In K. Scherer and H. Giles (eds.), *Social Markers in Speech.* London: Cambridge University Press. 251–89.

Giles, Howard and Robert St. Clair (1979). *Language and Social Psychology.* Baltimore, MD: University Park Press.

Hall, Kira (1995). Lip service on the fantasy lines. In K. Hall and M. Bucholtz (eds.), *Gender Articulated: Language and the Socially Constructed Self.* New York: Routledge. 183–216.

Harriman, Aya (2000). Biracial identity and language choice. Unpublished MS.

Hazen, Kirk (1997). Ethnolinguistic boundaries and social change. Paper presented at the American Dialect Society Annual Meeting, Chicago, IL.

Henderson, A. (1996). The short *a* pattern of Philadelphia among African American speakers. *University of Pennsylvania working papers in linguistics* 3, 1: 127–40.

Hewitt, Roger (1982). White adolescent creole users and the politics of friendship. *Journal of Multilingual and Multicultural Development* 3, 3: 217–32.

Hinton, Leanne, Birch Moonwomon, Sue Bremner, Herb Luthin, Mary Van Clay, Jean Lerner and Hazel Corcoran (1987). It's not just the Valley Girls: A study of California English. In Jon Aske, Natasha Beery, Laura Michaels and Hana Filip (eds.), *Proceedings of the Thirteenth Annual Meeting of the Berkeley Linguistics Society.* Berkeley, California. 117–27.

Jacobs-Huey, Lanita (1997). Is there an authentic African-American speech community: Carla revisited. *University of Pennsylvania working papers in linguistics* 4, 1: 331–70.

Knack, Rebecca (1991). Ethnic boundaries in linguistic variation. In P. Eckert (ed.), *New Ways of Analyzing Sound Change.* San Diego, CA: Academic Press. 251–72.

Labov, William (1963). The social motivation of a sound change. Reprinted in William Labov, *Sociolinguistic Patterns.* Philadelphia: University of Pennsylvania Press. 1–42.

Labov, William (1966). *The Social Stratification of English in New York*

City. Washington, DC: Center for Applied Linguistics.

Labov, William (1972a). *Language in the Inner City: Studies in the Black English Vernacular*. Philadelphia: University of Pennsylvania Press.

Labov, William (1972b). *Sociolinguistic Patterns*. Philadelphia: University of Pennsylvania Press.

Labov, William (1980). The social origins of a sound change. In W. Labov (ed.), *Locating Language in Time and Space*. New York: Academic Press.

Labov, William (1984). The transmission of linguistic traits across and within communities. Paper presented at the Symposium on Language Transmission and Change, Centre for Advanced Study in the Behavioural Sciences, Stanford, CA.

Labov, William (1991). The three dialects of English. In P. Eckert (ed.), *New Ways of Analyzing Sound Change*. San Diego, CA: Academic Press. 1–44.

Labov, William (1994). *Principles of Linguistic Change*, vol. 1: *Internal Factors*. Cambridge, MA: Blackwell Publishers.

Labov, William (1998). Co-existent systems in African-American vernacular English. In S. Mufwene, J. Rickford, G. Bailey and J. Baugh (eds.), *African-American English: Structure, History, and Use*. New York: Routledge. 110–53.

Labov, William and Wendell Harris (1986). De facto segregation of black and white vernaculars. In David Sankoff (ed.), *Diversity and Diachrony*. Amsterdam: John Benjamins. 1–24.

Labov, William, Paul Cohen, Clarence Robins, and John Lewis (1968). A Study of the Non-standard English of Negro and Puerto Rican Speakers in New York City. Cooperative Research Report 3288. New York, New York: Columbia University.

Laferriere, Martha (1979). Ethnicity in phonological variation and change. *Language* 55: 603–17.

Leap, William (1993). *American Indian English*. Salt Lake City: University of Utah Press.

Le Page, Robert and Andrée Tabouret-Keller (1985). *Acts of Identity: Creole-Based Approaches to Language and Ethnicity*. Cambridge: Cambridge University Press.

Lippi-Green, Rosina (1997). *English with an Accent*. New York: Routledge.

Lo, Adrienne (1999). Codeswitching, speech community membership, and the construction of ethnic identity. *Journal of Sociolinguistics* 3, 4: 461–79.

Luthin, Herbert (1986). The story of California (ow): The coming-of-age of English in California. In K. Denning et al. (eds.), *Variation in Language: NWAV-XV at Stanford*. Stanford, CA: Department of Linguistics. 312–24.

Mendoza-Denton, N. (1995). Gang affiliation and linguistic variation among high school Latina girls. Paper presented at NWAVE XXIV in Philadelphia.

Mendoza-Denton (1997). Chicana/ Mexicana identity and linguistic variation: an ethnographic and sociolinguistic study of gang affiliation in an urban high school. Ph.D. dissertation, Stanford University.

Meyerhoff, Miriam (1997). Engendering identities: Pronoun selection as an indicator of salient intergroup identites. *University of Pennsylvania working papers in linguistics* 4, 1: 23–38.

Milroy, Lesley (1980). *Language and Social Networks*. Oxford: Blackwell.

Milroy, Lesley and Li Wei (1995). A social network approach to code-switching: The example of a bilingual community in Britain. In Lesley Milroy and Pieter Muysken (eds.), *One Speaker, Two Languages: Cross-Disciplinary Perspectives on Code-switching.* 136–57.

Nichols, Patricia (1983). Linguistic options and choices for black women in the rural south. In B. Thorne et al. (eds.), *Language, Gender and Society.* Rowley, MA: Newbury House. 54–68.

Ornstein-Galicia, Jacob and Allan Metcalf (1984). *Form and Function in Chicano English.* Rowley, MA: Newbury House.

Peñalosa, Fernando (1980). *Chicano Sociolinguistics: A Brief Introduction.* Rowley, MA: Newbury House.

Penfield, Joyce and Jacob Ornstein-Galicia (1985). *Chicano English: An Ethnic Contact Dialect.* Varieties of English around the world, Series G7. Amsterdam: John Benjamins.

Poplack, Shana (1978). Dialect acquisition among Puerto Rican bilinguals. *Language in Society* 7: 89–103.

Rampton, Ben (1995). *Crossing: Language and ethnicity among adolescents.* New York: Longman.

Rickford, John (1985). Ethnicity as a sociolinguistic boundary. Reprinted in John Rickford, *African American Vernacular English.* Malden, MA: Blackwell. 90–111.

Rickford, John (1986a). The need for new approaches to social class analysis in sociolinguistics. *Language & Communication* 6: 215–21.

Rickford, John (1986b). Social contact and linguistic diffusion: Hiberno-English and New World Black English. Reprinted in John Rickford *African American Vernacular English.* Malden, MA: Blackwell. 174–218.

Rickford, John (1987). Are black and white vernaculars diverging? In Ralph W. Fasold et al. (eds.), *Are Black and White Vernacular Diverging? American Speech* 62: 55–62.

Rickford, John (1992). Grammatical variation and divergence in Vernacular Black English. Reprinted in John Rickford, *African American Vernacular English.* Malden, MA: Blackwell. 261–80.

Rickford, John (1999). *African American Vernacular English: Features, Evolution, Educational Implications.* Malden, MA: Blackwell. 174–218.

Rickford, John and Faye McNair-Knox (1994). Addressee- and topic-influenced style shift: A quantitative sociolinguistic study. Reprinted in John Rickford, *African American Vernacular English.* Malden, MA: Blackwell. 112–54.

Rickford, John, Arnetha Ball, Renee Blake, Raina Jackson, and Nomi Martin (1991). Rappin on the Copula Coffin: Theoretical and Methodological Issues in the Analysis of Copula Variation in African-American Vernacular English. Reprinted in John Rickford, *African American Vernacular English.* Malden, MA: Blackwell. 61–89.

Santa Ana, Otto (1991). Phonetic simplification processes in the English of the barrio: A cross-generational sociolinguistic study of the Chicanos of Los Angeles. University of Pennsylvania. Ph.D. dissertation.

Santa Ana, Otto (1996). Sonority and syllable structure in Chicano English. *Language Variation and Change* 8: 1–11.

Smitherman, Geneva (1998). Word from the hood: The lexicon of African-American vernacular English. In S. Mufwene, J. Rickford, G. Bailey and J. Baugh (eds.), *African-American English: Structure, History, and Use.* New York: Routledge. 203–25.

Thomas, Anulkah (2000). The connection between racial–ethnic identity and language among youths of Afro-Caribbean Panamanian descent. Unpublished MS.

Thomas, Erik (1999). A first look at AAVE intonation. Paper presented at NWAVE-28, University of Toronto.

Wald, Benji (1984). The status of Chicano English as a dialect of American English. In Jacob Ornstein-Galicia and Allan Metcalf (eds.), *Form and Function in Chicano English*. Rowley, MA: Newbury House. 14–31.

Wei, Li, Lesley Milroy and Pong Sin Ching (1992). A two-step sociolinguistic analysis of code-switching and language choice: The example of a bilingual Chinese community in Britain. *International Journal of Applied Linguistics* 2, 1: 63–86.

Wieder, D. Lawrence and S. Pratt (1990). On being a recognizable Indian among Indians. In D. Carbaugh (ed.), *Cultural Communication and Intercultural Contact*. 45–64.

Wolfram, W. (1969). *A Sociolinguistic Description of Detroit Negro Speech*. Washington, DC: Center for Applied Linguistics.

Wolfram, Walt (1974a). *Sociolinguistic Aspects of Assimilation: Puerto Rican English in New York City*. Arlington, VA: Center for Applied Linguistics.

Wolfram, Walt (1974b). The relationship of White Southern Speech to Vernacular Black English. *Language* 50: 498–527.

Wolfram, Walt (1987). Are black and white vernaculars diverging? In Ralph W. Fasold et al. (eds.), *Are Black and White Vernacular Diverging?* *American Speech* 62: 40–8.

Wolfram, Walt (2000). On the construction of vernacular dialect norms. Paper presented at the Chicago Linguistic Society, Chicago, IL.

Wolfram, Walt and Daniel Beckett (1999). The role of individual differences in Earlier African American Vernacular English. Paper presented at NWAVE-28, University of Toronto.

Wolfram, Walt and Clare Dannenberg (1999). Dialect identity in a tri-ethnic context: The case of Lumbee American Indian English. *English World-Wide* 20: 79–116.

Wolfram, Walt and Natalie Schilling-Estes (1999). *American English*. Malden, MA: Blackwell.

Wolfram, Walt, Kirk Hazen and Natalie Schilling-Estes (1999). *Dialect Change and Maintenance on the Outer Banks*. Tuscaloosa: University of Alabama Press, for American Dialect Society.

Wolfram, Walt, Erik Thomas and Elaine Green (1997). Dynamic boundaries in African American Vernacular English: The role of local dialects in the history of AAVE. Paper presented to the American Dialect Society, New York.

Zentella, Ana Celia (1997). Growing up Bilingual. Malden, MA: Blackwell.

Domains

In the previous section we looked at forms of social differentiation which, although they have come to be recognized even by linguists to be to a certain extent constructs rather than givens, are nevertheless conceptually reasonably straightforward. In this section we turn to aspects of human societies, and ways of considering human societies, relationships and behaviors, which are inherently more complex and interactional. Everyone knows what a family is, it is true, but how exactly can it affect linguistic behavior? And how are we as linguists to come to grips with the notion of identity? The term *domain* in sociolinguistics is most usually associated with the work of Joshua Fishman in the sociology of language. Here we are using it in a related sense but one which is more applicable to work in linguistic variation and change: we take it to refer here to, as it were, relational arenas within which variable linguistic behavior takes place.

Norma Mendoza-Denton, in her chapter "Personal and Interpersonal Identity", characterizes the concept of identity as having to do with the negotiation of a speaker's relationships with the social groups to which they belong. The point of this for our science is that such relationships, because they are negotiated, are variable, changing, and complex, and thus are highly suitable for consideration in quantitative variationist linguistic studies.

One of the social groups relative to which speakers presumably have to negotiate their identities is the family. Kirk Hazen, in his chapter on "The Family", suggests that we, as linguists, should be able to describe and account for the effects of the family on linguistic variation. The family has not figured very largely in sociolinguistic work, but Hazen seeks out a number of revealing studies which have yielded information on language variation as this relates to families. It will be no surprise, in the context of this section generally, that the relationship between linguistic variation and the family emerges as a complex one.

Miriam Meyerhoff in "Communities of Practice" introduces a relatively new domain to sociolinguistics which, however, is clearly related in different ways to the other domains covered in this section. She explains that a Community of Practice has to do with speakers' subjective experiences of the boundaries between their community and others, and the activities that speakers carry out which lead to the formation of such boundaries. The potential of this domain for sociolinguistics lies in the fact that it can provide an overall framework within which social and linguistic aspects of sociolinguistic variation can be viewed.

In her chapter on "Social Networks", Lesley Milroy indicates that speakers' social networks are the "aggregate of relationships contracted with others". A particular strength of the social network approach lies in its recognition that these interpersonal relationships can be of different strengths, something which turns out to be very important for the diffusion (at least) of linguistic changes. Milroy's presentation of work employing this concept shows that it has much in common with the approaches of scholars cited in the chapters by Mendoza-Denton and Meyerhoff, in particular: they all have a focus on the dynamic nature of social interactions and relationships. Social networks are not fixed categories but, like identities, are changeable and variable.

In contrast, the term "Speech Community", the subject of Peter Patrick's chapter, appears to be much more static in its conception for most sociolinguists. As with many of the concepts discussed in this section, the term has typically been used as if it were unproblematic. It is a concept which has been used, as Patrick shows, very frequently indeed in sociolinguistics, but it is also one which has not been well-defined, and about which there has been very little consensus in the field. Patrick's very interesting conclusion is that Speech Communities, unlike many of the other categories dealt with here, are constructs not of speakers or communities but of sociolinguists themselves.

PETER TRUDGILL

19   Language and Identity

NORMA MENDOZA-DENTON

This chapter will sketch some current findings, questions, and trends in approaches to the study of language variation and identity. The term "identity" functions outside of linguistics to cover a variety of concepts; for our purposes, we will understand identity to mean the active negotiation of an individual's relationship with larger social constructs, in so far as this negotiation is signaled through language and other semiotic means. Identity, then, is neither attribute nor possession, but an individual and collective-level process of semiosis. We shall be concerned with its emblematic sites, its codes and its channels (Silverstein 1998), and, crucially for variation theory, with its richly patterned, multivariate nature. The scope of this particular review will be limited to works that are broadly representative of or that stand in dialogue with the Labovian quantitative sociolinguistic tradition, and will of necessity exclude significant qualitative research on linguistic identity that falls under the rubric of sociology of language and discourse analysis. (For a review of the literature within this field, see Tabouret-Keller 1998.) Though much-debated in identity theory, psychological processes internal to the individual, such as (Freudian prelinguistic) identification, sublimation, fantasy and desire, and their role in identity formation (Zizek 1993, Salecl 1994, Lacan 1977) are, to say the least, difficult to study under the standard empiricist lens of variationist inquiry unless they are overtly signaled in interaction (but see Kulick 2000 for an exhortation to undertake exactly such studies in the area of language and sexuality).

Although this review will incorporate selected developments in anthropology, psychology, social theory, and literary theory, for more in-depth analysis in these areas I refer the reader to other works dealing with field-specific perspectives on identity and identity politics (Appiah and Gates 1995, Butler 1990, Hale 1997, Cerulo 1997, Said 1993, Michaels 1992, 1994, Williams 1994, Bhabha 1990).

1   Identities as multivalent

One of the great challenges in the variationist study of identity over the past 15 years arises in conjunction with related developments in social construction-ist approaches in anthropology and social theory: it is the challenge against essentialism in analytic explanation (Cameron 1990, Romaine 1984, Fuss 1989, Potter 1996, Janicki 1990, 1999). Essentialism as conceptualized by these re-searchers refers to the (Aristotelian) reductive tendency by analysts to designate a particular aspect of a person or group as explanations for their behavior: the "essence" of what it means, for instance, to be Asian, or Indian, or female, etc. (Said 1993), despite the recognition that agents stand in complex relationships to a variety of larger social constructs. Can we think about identity in a way that does not reduce or simplify individuals to a single dimension? Collins (1990), argues for a "fundamental paradigmatic shift that rejects additive approaches. . . . Instead of starting with gender and then adding in other variables such as age, sexual orientation, social class, . . . these distinctive systems . . . [interlock and are] part of one overarching structure" (1990: 347). Janicki argues that the proliferation of definitions is useless, and similarly, Butler (1995: 440–1) proffers: "We know that identities, however they are defined, do not belong to a horizontal sequence, separated and joined by a kind of conceptual neigh-borliness. But the problem of interrelation is almost impossible to think outside the frame of sequence and multiplication once we begin with "identity" as the necessary presupposition." (In all fairness, Butler later advocates throwing out the investigation of identity altogether.)

The growing awareness in philosophy and postcolonial studies that identi-ties are not univalent has resulted in their conceptualization as historically-situated (Said 1993, Tsitsipis 1998), fractured and strategic (Spivak 1992), intersecting (Williams 1994) pluralities. Nonetheless, there still reigns confusion as to how one should model these multiple identities. Anxious substitution of the plural for the singular (note the number of recent volumes that purport to uncover "identities", "masculinities", etc.) does not solve the problem of modeling identity at all (Butler 1995), since the wages of essentialism continue to apply, only now compounded.

By theorizing the inextricability of race/gender/class and the necessity to view them holistically and simultaneously, Collins is in fact partially aligned with prevailing sociolinguistic practice. It would appear that sociolinguistic variation is enviably poised to contribute to this debate, equipped with (1) many studies solely devoted to disentangling the intricacies of linguistic and social relationships within and among groups and individuals (Payne 1980, Guy 1981, Lane 1999); and (2) copious speech archives and replicable methodo-logies for the diachronic testing of putative relationships. Multivariate studies of linguistic phenomena that recognize and track the complex influence and interaction of various social (external) factors as well as linguistic (internal) factors have been the gold standard since the inception of the field. Statistical techniques allow researchers to calculate the probability weights of gender versus class in the prediction of speakers' linguistic behavior, and to debate issues such as whether our model for social and linguistic variables should be additive, multiplicative, or logarithmic – surely exceeding the wildest dreams of philosophers like Collins or Butler. So what then, can a charge of essentialism mean in the realm of sociolinguistics, with its tradition of multivariate coding and holistic thinking?

Essentialism in sociolinguistics includes the analytic practice of using categories to divide up subjects and sort their linguistic behavior, and then linking the quantitative differences in linguistic production to explanations based on those very same categories provided by the analyst.

We will define the problem of essentialism as roughly coextensive with the difference between analysts' categories and participants' categories, between "etic" and "emic" categorizations of the social world. Consider a simple example: if we were to study the stratification of the laxing of high vowels in a randomly sampled population in Mexico City, utilizing age categories divided in 5-year intervals, we might find that there is an apparent-time effect: a relative increase in the use of laxed variants among those subjects in their teenage years, ages 15–20. One possible interpretation would be that Mexican teenagers are using vowel laxing to index their youthful identity, rejecting older adult norms (they are teenagers, after all), and that younger children are not participating in this change because they are under greater adult supervision and influence. The problem with this type of explanation, as Cameron (1990) and Romaine (1984) argue, is that it is in fact not an explanation at all, but a statistically motivated observation-cum-speculative-description that does not rely on any principled social theory. It is not possible, for instance, to know whether the statistical spike in that age group is due to other factors (we might find interactions if we were wise enough to code them), or whether the explanation that we gave is one that is *oriented to* by speakers of the group in question. Is it the case, for instance, that Mexico City teenagers recognize a boundary that the researcher has introduced between children of age 10–15 and those of age 15–20? Does this analyst's boundary correspond to the structuring of local speech communities? It may well be that local children and teens follow a ternary division between *primaria, secundaria,* and *preparatoria* school cohorts, but then how could the analyst explain the complicated age-mixing this introduces? Moreover, how could we then compare this study with that of "equivalent" age-groups in other societies? Frighteningly, what if there were no equivalencies to be found at all? And what if there were little social evidence for the "teenage rebellion" assumed in our explanation, and the teens interviewed did not intend to express rejection of adult norms? How can we factor into our analysis their subject positioning, their intentions, and their agency? (For similar concerns, see Cameron 1990, Janicki 1990, 1999, Le Page and Tabouret-Keller 1985.)

The problem of agency in variation is intimately woven into that of analysts' vs. participants' distinctions, and is aggravated as we take Euro/American folk analyses of identity categories in the domains of age, class, gender, ethnicity, sexuality, etc. (social constructions such as "teenager," "woman," "working class," or "gay") and apply them to invoke identity in disparate contexts (Haeri 1998, Rickford 1986, Gaudio 2001).

Potter (2000: 22) concurs with Schegloff (1997) in the opinion that "Given that the relevant contextual particulars of some text or interaction can be variably and flexibly formulated, who is to judge what is actually relevant?" They offer the suggestion that the analyst look to participants' own explicitly signaled orientations and formulations, and their relevance in the sequencing of interaction. That is, they exhort us to look to situated practices rather than analysts' formal categories for explication.

This critique has not only great impact on what the study of linguistic variation might have to say about identity, but in fact poses a theoretical and methodological challenge, one that may potentially lead to a deep reworking of the frameworks and strategies through which variationist sociolinguists conceptualize and investigate identity. The gauntlet has been thrown down, as certain strands of scholarship doubt that quantitative study is up to this task: a recent proposal by Carter and Sealy (2000) for a unified social theory of sociolinguistics states that a large-scale, quantitative sociolinguistic study would "fail to identify" evidence that "competent social actors . . . reveal creative, inventive uses of language in pursuit of their own interests" (2000: 18). Sociolinguistics in this view can only be infused with social theory by setting aside the project of understanding quantitative aspects of variation.

One of the ways in which variation scholars have chosen to resolve the conflict between analysts' and participants' categories can be seen in a strengthening trend toward ethnographic studies which look at situated practices and at participants' explicit interactional orientations. Ethnography, a methodology that involves the researcher in the community for extended periods as a participant-observer, has allowed variation studies a focus at the level of participant-defined activity systems, and has given rise to research that orients to *local* categories of practice, whether they be poker playing on the Outer Banks of North Carolina (Wolfram and Schilling-Estes 1994), cruising in a car on a Saturday night in Detroit (Eckert 1999), signifying gay identity in Chinese magazines (Wong and Zhang 2001), or participating in street gang activities in New York or California (Labov 1972c, Mendoza-Denton 1997).

A caveat: trading in one methodology for another (ethnography for sociological survey or psycholinguistic experiment) does not allow the object of investigation to remain constant, especially when dealing with a process such as identity which is fluid and multidimensional, and most especially when one works in a field such as sociolinguistics with its well-known observer's paradox (Labov 1972a: 69, Wolfram and Fasold 1974). Ethnographies are understood in anthropology to be the unique products of the personal histories of the ethnographers themselves and of their interactions within particular communities (Agar 1996). This throws into question the notion of replicability of an ethnography by another researcher, or even by the same researcher at another time. This awareness of research product as radically affected by the researcher (simultaneous agent and instrument) is inherent in the foundational notion of the observer's paradox, and has been observed to hold the potential for circularity in sociolinguistic research: for instance, the researcher may linguistically accommodate perceived social class characteristics of the interlocutor who in turn accommodates to the researcher (Giles 1973). Jahr (1979) (cited in Trudgill 1986) carried out a self-analysis of his interview data from Oslo, and noted that his syntax was influenced not only by informants' sex but also by their syntactic usage. Trudgill (1986), however, observes that in an analysis of his own speech and that of his informants in the Norwich study (Trudgill 1974), interviewer usage is stylistically stratified in the general direction of informants' usage but does not actually match or overshoot it.

The full implications of accommodation studies are only beginning to take hold with regard to data collected in the sociolinguistic interview (Briggs 1989, Rickford and McNair-Knox 1994). The idea that the *researcher's* identity and ideological positioning vis-à-vis the interviewee crucially contribute to the patterning of data deserves more systematic exploration. In their study, Rickford and McNair-Knox (1994) found that two radically different data sets with quantitative and qualitative disparities at multiple levels of the grammar were elicited from the same African-American participant in two separate controlled-topic interviews, with the crucial difference being that one interview was conducted by a Euro-American researcher and the other by an African-American researcher. As might be predicted from prior research in the frameworks of speech accommodation (Giles 1980), audience design (Bell 1984), and acts of identity (Le Page and Tabouret-Keller 1985), the African-American participant used African-American English variables more frequently when speaking to the African-American interviewer. The mutual co-construction of participants' and researchers' identities has profound implications, as variationist scholars widely accept the notion of replicability and re-study, and routinely compare data gathered by different interviewers to build on prior results and to investigate issues of performance that could be strongly affected by differences in the interviewers. One interesting line of study that would carry the insights of accommodation theorists further might be to measure the degree of style shifting or convergence over time in the speech of an ethnographer. It is possible that long-term convergence on the part of the researcher might lead to a reinforcement of norms, and limit our ability to compare data gathered ethnographically with data gathered in stratified rapid-survey samples.

In this introduction I have outlined some of the issues facing variationist research on identity, including questions of essentialism, of analysts' vs. participants' categories, of individual agency, and of replicability of research. The rest of this chapter organizes some research exemplars into three broad types: studies based on: (1) sociological category-based identity, (2) practice-based identity, and (3) practice-based variation, headings that range along a continuum of the use of analysts' categories vs. participants', and that are as much about their attendant methodologies as they are about their findings. Note that not all studies fit easily into a type, and some may use mixed methodologies that place them in more than one type. Further, there may appear to be a chronological organization to the research, since the bulk of practice-based identity studies generally started appearing in the 1980s, yet in reality all three approaches have been pursued since the inception of the field, sometimes concurrently and sometimes complementarily. Most variationist research on identity today engages at least the first two approaches to some degree. In the conclusion I will argue for a multiplicity of approaches to maintain both the breadth of the survey method, the controlled quality of psycholinguistic experiments, and the depth of the ethnographic approach in variation studies.

2 Type I: Sociodemographic Category-based Identity

Studies of linguistic identity that are based on the stratification of a population according to sociological/demographic categories (such as region, age, sex, occupation, social class, ethnicity) were the first explorations of the systematicity of the relation of social and linguistic constructs. Were it not for the pioneering studies of Labov (1972a, 1972c, 1972d) in New York City, we would not know which variants are innovative, which conservative, and which newly introduced; without Wolfram (1969) we would lack a compass to investigate the linguistic expression of a speaker's ethnicity in Detroit today; similarly, the reference point for a study of Spanish in Panama is Cedegren (1973). Much work in the discipline of sociolinguistic variation has its roots in the sociological study of urban areas beginning in the 1960s and 1970s, and to date hundreds of city-studies in the United States and around the world have applied this kind of methodology, creating stratified models of the speech of urban populations. (Just a few recent examples: Silva-Corvalán 1989 for Santiago, Chile; Thibault and Daveluy 1989, Thibault and Sankoff 1993 for Montreal, Canada; Tagliamonte 1999 for York, UK; Kontra and Váradi 1997 for Budapest, Hungary; Lennig 1978 for Paris, France; Trudgill 1974, 1986 for Norwich, UK; Horvath 1985 for Sydney, Australia; Labov et al. 2000 for 145 central cities in the United States alone).

Although it is in theory possible to achieve comparable coverage with practice-based, ethnographic approaches, the investment of time and resources for groups of ethnographers to cover an entire city would be astronomical and highly impractical. Studies of Type I, with their findings of the systematicity of linguistic variation, their broad coverage and emphasis on statistical representativeness, orient us to the linguistic variables and social issues at play. In complement with the experimental studies of psycholinguistics, they provide the basis and background for the practice of ethnography. These studies are of necessity a synchronic snapshot from which we can infer processes of change by observing differential distributions of variables, through real-time and apparent-time studies (cf. Bailey, this volume).

Labov's early work provided a blueprint for the study of large-scale patterns of variation, where the objective was to discover statistically significant correlations, and later to create multivariate models of the covariation of individual tokens of a single linguistic type (the dependent variable) and social categories (the independent variables). As with any discipline that prides itself on being scientific, the emphasis is on objectivity and replicability (Labov 1994).

And yet if identity would be studied by the correlation of these stratified social categories to various quantifiable linguistic variables, then the most important questions to be asked are how and why particular categories are chosen. Were they observed to be important by the researchers? Are the categories themselves traditional classifications in sociology and demography? In most instances, it was a combination of these criteria that determined the categories chosen for investigation. Wolfram and Fasold (1974: 96–7) explicitly caution against applying the same criteria for social status to situations that the researcher knows to differ, yet at the same time acknowledge the limitations of researchers who do not possess extensive ethnographic knowledge of a community.

For example, the project on language change and variation (LCV) in Philadelphia has the following independent variables available to the analyst (Labov 1994: 58):

1 Age
2 Education (in years)
3 Occupation
4 Residence value
5 Socioeconomic class (based on indicators 2–4)
6 A five-point measure of house upkeep
7 The neighborhood
8 A classification of social mobility
9 Four indices of participation in communication networks
10 Foreign language background
11 Generational status in the United States
12 Whether or not the person's telephone is listed.

This array of variables ranges from easily accessible "objective" public information about the participants (telephone listing; residence value, often available from census statistics) to highly "subjective" (yet quantified) measures such as analyst judgments of participants' house upkeep. The latter are to be used especially cautiously in correlational investigations, as they rely on analysts' categories par excellence: it is doubtful that participants in this study would orient to that type of outsider-observed behavior.

Researchers typically approach the investigation of a speech community with an eye to the broadest possible coverage and to the representativeness of the sample, beginning usually with census tracts, carefully constructing random samples that will be statistically balanced with respect to some predetermined demographic categories in the population, plus other categories that the researcher considers as having potential to elucidate social processes in the population in question – for example, urban orientation in Jamaica (Patrick 1999) and in Yucatan, Mexico (Solomon 1998). Many indices are composites, and notable among these is social class, often based on a composition of several different factors, such as occupation, educational rank, income, and residency, as above. Critiques of this way of modeling social class have surfaced in Pidgin and Creole studies, in language and gender, and in studies of endangered languages, as researchers have challenged these ways of typologizing social class on grounds of presuppositions that were untenable in different societies where gender-specific labor, education, or capital holdings were differently structured (Nichols 1983, Rickford 1986, Sidnell 1999, Nagy 2000).

Nevertheless, the contributions of Type I studies to what we know about identity have been remarkable, not only for their theoretical advances but for their public impact. In the United States, these are arguably some of the most socially useful contributions the discipline of variation has made, speaking to communities beyond the scholarly and often having an impact on public policy. Studies on African American English have served to debunk deficit models of African-American language and identity (for critical reviews, see Rickford 1997, 1999, Morgan 1994); similarly, studies of Spanish/English bilinguals have served to combat common myths of bilingual speakers as linguistically confused, or worse, "alingual." Research on Puerto Rican English and Spanish (Poplack 1979, Urciuoli 1996, Zentella 1997), and Chicano English and Spanish (Valdés 1981, García 1984) still enriches debates on bilingual education today (for a review on the sociolinguistics of US Latinos see Mendoza-Denton 1999a).

A related area in the study of identity in variation has been that of shifting and multiple identities that are indexed in the act of speaking different linguistic varieties, whether they be different languages (code switching) or different varieties of a single language (style-shifting). In the area of code switching, Myers-Scotton (1993) has applied rational choice theory to understanding how a change in code might signal a different identity by theorizing that a switch indexes a different set of social rights and obligations (a particular RO set) that the speaker proposes to apply in that particular interaction. A speaker switching from Modern Standard Arabic to Tunisian Arabic in Tunisia, for instance (Walters 1996) would be indexing the specific rights and obligations that derive from being a member of a local community, rather than the supra-local RO set that is indexed by Modern Standard Arabic. And yet, as Walters and Woolard point out, these indexicalities are not so straightforward, since a particular utterance can be bivalent (Woolard 1998), that is to say, fitting both varieties ambiguously, or even more complex, having the syntax of one variety and the phonology of another (Walters 1996: 551).

Much work on identity in sociolinguistics works under the assumption of relatively stable identities, with researchers assigning identities based on social category membership (cf. critique in Eckert 1999) or using emergent participant self-identification categories (Mendoza-Denton 1997). Dubois and Melançon (2000) carried out an investigation of Creole identity in Louisiana, showing that self-identification as "Creole" by African-Americans given a questionnaire task is historically contingent and involves shifting relationships between skin color, ethnicity, material capital, language patterning, and ancestry. As in Baugh (1999), Modan (forthcoming), Johnstone and Bean (1997), and Michaels (1992) the various overlapping and contradictory meanings of identity-designators over time, space and within a single community are highlighted, showing that sociohistorical and ideological factors should be carefully considered in studies of identity and identity attribution.

In variation studies, another arena for the study of attribution of identity has been the psycholinguistic study of speech perception. Significant findings from experimental work in the area of perceptual phonetics have had profound implications for our basic understanding of topics ranging from the nature of the phoneme, to gender categorization, to the operationalization of discrimination.

Strand (1999) has carried out a series of striking experiments showing the influence of gender identity and gendered expectations on processes of phonological perception that are ordinarily thought to be impervious to higher-level (social) information. Variations of the well-known McGurk audio-visual integration effect, these experiments set up conflicts between simultaneous aural and visual inputs, forcing a resolution at the perceptual level. In the original experiment, McGurk found that upon being presented with an aural [ba] and a visual [ga], subjects would automatically "integrate" the information and perceive [da] (McGurk and MacDonald 1976; for a demonstration go to http://www.psych.ucr.edu/faculty/rosenblum/McGurk Effect Demo). In Strand's experiments subjects are presented with synthesized consonantal continua: ten synthetic steps from [s] to [ʃ], embedded in the carrier words "sod" and "shod." Given either the lip-synched video of a man or a woman uttering a carrier phrase with the synthesized segment, subjects routinely assign a different phonological category to the same acoustic signal (see figure 19.1). This is because the [s] and [ʃ], homorganic and largely similar save for the lower frequency of the latter, lead to anticipatory normalization following from listener's expectations regarding the size of the speaker's vocal tract. In other words, given an ambiguous auditory stimulus, seeing a male subject who might be expected to have a longer vocal tract would lead a listener to believe that the stimulus lay in the higher frequency [s] range of the s/sh continuum for that speaker. Presentation of the same stimulus with a female speaker's face would lead to the perceptual ambiguity resolution that the stimulus lay in the lower-frequency range of the s/sh continuum for the speaker (and thus the listener would perceive [ʃ]).

This perceptual resolution based on higher-level information may seem unsurprising to the reader and easily subsumed under the well-known processes of speaker normalization (Peterson and Barney 1952). However, depending on

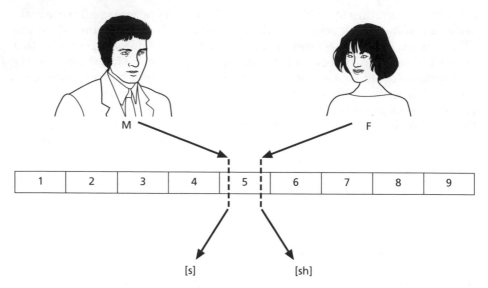

Figure 19.1 Gender of face determines the final precept in a fricative continuum

whether the video shows a "prototypical" or "non-prototypical" man or woman (as determined by prior subject ratings), the phonological boundary itself shifts in frequency. Physical characteristics that are plainly subject to social construction – such as big and elaborately coiffed hair, rated by Ohio State undergraduates as more prototypically feminine – have an effect on the baseline level perception of a phoneme. Johnson et al. (1999) have tested this effect further on vowels and prompted the shifting of phonological boundaries on the mere *suggestion* to the listener of male or female identity of the speaker. These studies have tremendous implications in (1) gender theory, showing gradiency rather than categoriality of gender attribution, and (2) in phonology because they imply that the identification of a phonological category does not depend merely on the system of oppositions within the sounds of a language, but also on the moment-to-moment processing of social information about the speaker. Social stereotypes affect even our basic categorization of the speech signal.

Purnell et al. (1999) have conducted experimental phonetic studies of housing discrimination based on speech. Using controlled speech samples of a tridialectal speaker from Los Angeles (Baugh himself) who commands African-American English (AAE), Chicano English (ChE), and Standard Euro-American English (SEAE), they set up a three-way matched-guise experiment (cf. Lambert 1967), where the same speaker's voice (albeit in a different dialect guise) serves as stimulus. The experiment consisted of telephoning rental agencies about vacancies in San Francisco and leaving a recorded message in one of the three dialects. From the responses, they were able to show that apartments that had been described as unavailable to the AAE and ChE voices were later offered as vacant to the SEAE voice. Although accent discrimination and its transmission is well-documented in sociolinguistic studies (Lippi-Green 1997), the fact that Baugh and associates are working with the US government in these studies might well lead to federal reform designed to prevent housing discrimination on the basis of accent.

Next I will describe some research that links sociodemographic identity studies with the next category, that of practice-based identity. The following studies extend the assumptions of demographic correlation to show that the deployment of speech varieties is crucially involved in political economy and represents differently valued local symbolic capital (Bourdieu 1977, 1991).

Gal's (1978) classic study of the village of Oberwart in Austria showed the effect of sex role differences on language change. Her focus was the shifting linguistic repertoire in a Hungarian–German bilingual community, where German was symbolic of the newly available social status of worker, while Hungarian was symbolic of the traditional social status of peasant, and "young women's language choices [favoring German could be understood] as part of their expression of preference for [the] newer social identity" (1978: 2). Gal created a language choice questionnaire for this study on the basis of native categories, uncovering subtle implicational hierarchies of language usage. At the extreme ends of the continuum, bilingual speakers talked to God (the most intimate, private situation) primarily in Hungarian and to doctors (the most formal, public situation) primarily in German. Her findings showed that because young women had more to gain in the transition from a peasant economy to an industrialized economy, their symbolic and actual choice of German-speaking men as husbands was resulting in both language change within the village, and exogamous marriage patterns for young peasant men. Significantly, this study relies on ethnographic information to give texture to correlational phenomena and to more fully articulate the mechanisms which might account for earlier findings of women's selection of prestige variants.

Sidnell (1999) similarly seeks to go beyond prior generalizations about the effect of gender in Caribbean creole-speaking societies. Noting that research had failed to find significant correlations between gender and linguistic patterning in creole pronominal syntax, Sidnell shows that a separation within the categories of pronominal usage indeed turns up dramatic gender differences. Men in his ethnographic study were more likely to use a greater range of the creole continuum, whereas women used a more focused range, leading mesolectal marking in certain categories (3sg. obj.), but avoiding others (1sg. subj.). Sidnell shows from overt orientations to the phenomenon in his data that the mesolectal 1sg. subj. was evaluated as arrogant and overly urban/streetwise when used by women vs. playful and cosmopolitan for men, showing how the indexical marking of mesolectal variants differ in their evaluation depending on the speaker. He states, "women must be careful in both how they move through a community (who they interact with, etc.) and in how they talk – both concerns that emanate from a community construction of gender roles" (Sidnell 1999: 394). In this way, Sidnell goes beyond the agglutination of speakers into "sex" categories that may be masking overall practices of gender: how we *do* being-a-woman.

3   Type II: Practice-based Identity

Studies that I include under the heading of practice-based identity are centrally concerned with the identities that speakers accrue not because they claim or are assigned category membership, but rather because identities are accomplished in the joint practice of particular activities (for fundamental contributions to practice-based theories of social action see Bourdieu 1978, 1991, Certau 1984, Wenger 1998, Eckert and McConnell-Ginet 1992). Some examples of types of practice are participation in common social projects, or in voluntary affiliation groups that are defined around activities or enterprises.

In the research exemplars that follow I aim to clarify what is gained in variationist inquiry by engaging in practice-based identity research, and how practice-based identity might differ from other situationally relevant linguistic or sociodemographic groupings such as speech community, regional dialect, or age.

By placing the focus of variationist study at the level of the construction of social relationships, practice-based studies often display a dramatically different orientation and an implicit challenge to sociodemographic definitions of identity. One example of this challenge can be found in Linde et al. (1987), who shows how the local relevance of a hierarchy can emerge within ongoing practice.

Drawing a distinction between rank hierarchy (who is more highly ranked) and task hierarchy (who is more expert in a particular task), Linde et al. (1987) examined linguistic behaviors in cockpit interactions, using videotape of full mission simulated commercial flights where either the captain or the first officer was the pilot. Different patterns of mitigation and address were shown to emerge according to local, moment-to-moment fluctuations in the relevance of rank hierarchy vs. task hierarchy within the interaction. By focusing on participants' orientations in the practice of flying a plane, Linde et al. go beyond the sociodemographic factors that might otherwise describe the pilots and co-pilots.

The reworking of variationist understandings of class and hierarchical stratification has also attracted much attention in the study of Pidgins and Creoles, where Rickford (1986), Winford (1984), and Le Page and Tabouret-Keller (1985), among others, have argued that definitions of a stratified speech community that assume a widely agreed-upon focus of prestige do not apply in the Creole-speaking Caribbean, where complicated ethnohistorical dynamics are at play in defining not only class but other types of social constructs (cf. Sidnell, above).

The complexity of the definition of ethnicity in Belize involves relationships among language, class, provenance, nationality, and physical appearance, all of which are symbolically linked to language, and explored in the influential work of Le Page. *Acts of Identity: Creole-Based Approaches to Language and Ethnicity* (Le Page and Tabouret-Keller 1985) locates variation in the agentive activity of individuals with respect to larger groups. Le Page's framework of acts of identity holds that individual users of language strategically deploy varieties and variation to affiliate themselves with groups with which they may from time to time wish to be associated, or conversely, to be distinguished from groups with which they wish no such association. To this hypothesis, Le Page adds four riders:

> We can only behave according to the behavioural patterns of groups we find it desirable to identify with to the extent that:
> 1 we can identify the groups
> 2 we have both adequate access to the groups and ability to analyze their behavioural patterns
> 3 the motivation to join the groups is sufficiently powerful, and is either reinforced or reversed by feedback from the groups
> 4 we have the ability to modify our behaviour.
> (Le Page and Tabouret-Keller 1985: 182)

The acts of identity framework has inspired researchers investigating what Bell (1984) calls "initiative design" (see Schilling-Estes, this volume, on contextual styles), that is to say, speakers' implementation of variation that goes beyond a speaker's desire to match the speech of an audience. Trudgill (1983), for instance, investigates the variation through time in the musical lyric phonology of various British pop music groups. Trudgill shows how in the beginning of their careers (1963, *Please Please Me*), the Beatles consistently used some phonetic variants that are closely identified in Britain with American English phonology (such as /æ/ in *can't*, vs. the British /aː/), even engaging in some hypercorrection with non-prevocalic /r/. By the time of their 1967 *Sergeant Pepper*, /æ/ was in alternation with the British variant /aː/, with the progression completed by 1969's *Abbey Road*, where /aː/ was as established as the Beatles' singing success. It was in the *practice* of trying to anchor themselves in a market dominated by American rock musicians that British singers modified their speech, and their success itself changed the industry (making it acceptable and even desirable to sound British) so that later groups enjoyed commercial success without necessarily deploying American-oriented musico-phonological acts of identity.

Crucially, the explanatory power of (Type II) practice-based accounts of identity lies in their ability to identify evolving conditions that are reified in changed practices which in turn have linguistic consequences. It is precisely in detailed understandings of practice-shaping *processes* that comparison across different settings becomes possible, comparisons not of the statistical properties of the variables themselves but rather at the next level of abstraction: the processes that give rise to their use. For instance, results paralleling those reported for the early Beatles by Trudgill are identified in an ongoing ethnography of Australian country music singers by Snider et al. (2000). Australian country is a genre where globalization, perceptions of "authenticity" and the pressures of music marketing interact to create overt, metalinguistic conflict between American and Australian phonological variants.

Walters (1996) makes use of the acts of identity framework and of the communities of practice framework (Lave and Wenger 1991, Eckert and McConnell-Ginet 1992, Meyerhoff, this volume) in explaining language choice among the community of native anglophone wives of Tunisian husbands living in Tunisia. Here Walters provides one of the clearest examples of how radically different a community of practice can be from a speech community. Given our understanding of a speech community (cf. Patrick, this volume), the native anglophone wives of Tunisian husbands could not be considered one, since they come from varied dialect, geographic, and socioeconomic backgrounds, and in fact define themselves not through their similarity to each other but through their collective difference from an external norm. What they do have in common, however, is practice, since they are similarly situated with respect to their husbands and with respect to Tunisian society, and it is this similarity of practices that allows them to think of themselves as a community and allows Walters to find commonalties in their negotiation of the various linguistic codes at their disposal (English, Standard Arabic, Tunisian Arabic and French) vis-à-vis their husbands, children, in-laws, and adopted country of Tunisia.

Wenger defines a community of practice as requiring mutual engagement, a joint negotiated enterprise, and a shared repertoire of negotiable resources accumulated over time (1998: 76). All of these factors are exemplified in the school-based work of Eckert (1993, 1999), the most influential sociolinguistic theorist of communities of practice. Eckert examines a great range of practices among the Jocks and Burnouts in her ethnography of Belten High, an American high school in the suburbs near Detroit. These practices, ranging from student council participation, to smoking, to bell-bottom jeans-wearing, and the attainment of popularity or particular grades, give fine-pen texture to linguistic variation that might otherwise be incompletely described by broad-brush correlations with socioeconomic status differences among the students. One enlightening example of praxis in this study is cruising (traveling by car to participate in leisurely activities in Detroit unmediated by institutions), a pursuit that positively correlates and indexically connects the greater use of urban space to the greater use of urban variables. We might surmise that cruising represents a literal vehicle for the transmission of urban change from the city to the suburbs, and yet in this setting there is a complication: cruising is "a constraining issue among girls [. . .] often forbidden" (Eckert 1999: 152). The practice of cruising may adversely affect a girl's reputation, and thus the correlations between cruising, gender, and urban variables are delicately patterned, with urban variable use among girls indexing a threat to standard gender norms that is lacking among the boys. Studies of practice such as Eckert's allow us to trace variation beyond abstractions such as gender or class, and extend our understanding to socially controlled uses of broader semiotic resources, such as space, the body, and material artefacts (Mendoza-Denton 1997).

Sociolinguistic research under various theoretical frameworks (accommodation theory, acts of identity, social networks, and communities of practice, among others) has delineated the link between indexical language variation and social practice. It is these studies that provide the strongest and most productive link between variationist sociolinguistics with its emphasis on linguistic variables, and linguistic anthropology, with its focus on speech settings and their social consequences. Some of the research that does focus on linguistic variables includes Labov's study of islanders' orientations in Martha's Vineyard (1972b); Halliday (1976) on "anti-languages," where structural variation is motivated by an ideology of opposition to the establishment; Irvine (forthcoming) on Senegalese Wolof linguistic registers linked to a system of rank and nobility; Errington (1988) on pronominal variation in Javanese speech styles; Wolfram and Schilling-Estes (1994) on vocalic variation among poker-playing men on the Outer Banks of North Carolina; Bucholtz (1998) on hyper-standard speech among California Euro-American nerd girls; Woolard (1997) on gender and children's peer-group structure in bilingual Catalonia; Meyerhoff (1999) on apology routines in Vanuatu Bislama; Blake (1996) on ethnic identity in Barbados; Okamoto (1995) on masculine speech forms among young Japanese women; Lane (1999) on social networks and their symbolic effects on Thyborønsk Danish; Tsitsipis (1998) on poetic performances in Arvanitika Greek, and Chambers (1993) on the Canadian/American linguistic border.

The Type II studies of practice-based identity discussed above are a springboard for studies that I will group under Type III: practice-based variation. The starting point in these two types of studies is similar, in that they derive from identifiable practices of speakers.

4 Type III: Practice-based Variation

Rather than aggregating behavior and comparing variation across either sociological categories or practice groups, Type III studies seek to focus on variation as practices unfold, identifying the use of symbolic variants in the moment-to-moment dynamics of interaction. Almost always ethnographic and discourse-/conversation-analytic in perspective, studies of Type III track the shifting identities of speakers as interaction progresses, affording researchers a closer look at the microdynamics of indexicality in variation as well processes of performance, achievement, and construction of identity. In these studies speakers' identities are not a determinate given, but open to transformation, contextually derived, and emergent in interaction. This type of qualitative re-search focusing at the level of discourse and discourse strategies is nowadays relatively common in various areas of study such as language and gender (i.e. Tannen (1990) in her influential *You Just Don't Understand!*); language and ethnicity (Labov (1969) on the logic of Black English, Bailey 1997 on the (mis)communication of respect in service interactions between immigrant Korean merchants and African-American customers in Los Angeles); language socialization (Schieffelin (1990) on socializing practices in Papua New Guinea), language and power (Reisigl and Wodak (1990) on anti-semitic discourse in Austria); language and racism (Van Dijk (1993) on institutional discourse in Holland, Hill (1993) on mock uses of Spanish in the United States), etc. The fact that it is relatively rare for discourse studies of identity to have an expli-citly *variationist* focus points to a lacuna, with great potential for future re-search. Below I will examine a few representative studies exemplifying some theoretical perspectives, and conclude with one note of caution and one of encouragement in the integration of all three types of studies.

Johnstone and Bean (1997) argue that self-expression and individuality have been under-explored in studies of linguistic variation. Taking as their corpus the speech and writings of two prominent Texas women (Barbara Jordan and Molly Ivins), they aim to show that speakers choose how they sound; that they may be making speech choices to identify with large groups (i.e. African-Americans) or individuals (the way one's teacher speaks, for instance); that their speech choices occur at all levels of language; and that speakers' linguistic choices express one or more self-images (1997: 222–3). Johnstone and Bean show how self-conscious dialect stereotypes, unconventional figurative language, poetic repetition (see also Tannen 1989), and alliteration are among the devices recruited by these speakers in the creation of their personal styles. Special emphasis is placed on public-speech case studies to argue for the study of variation beyond the levels of sound and syntax to rhetorical discourse.

Schiffrin (1996) on the other hand, looks carefully at everyday narratives among Jewish-Americans to track speakers' portrayal of agentive selves and epistemic stances, both indexical of ongoing relationships within the family. Mothers' portrayals of their daughters "pivot between solidarity and distance, between the provision of autonomy and the exercise of power," conveying a range of identities for the speaker within a single stretch of discourse (1996: 197). Schiffrin stresses that just as Labov (1972d) argued that there are no single-style speakers, similarly, there are no single-identity speakers. Such re-conceptualizations of identity as multiple and emergent-in-interaction, closely related to the postmodern theoretical developments reviewed in the introduc-tion, leads researchers to modify the representation of identity in coding ma-trices commonly employed in variation.

In the legal arena, Matoesian (1999) examines the role of grammar, sequential action, and footing in the construction of expert identity by the defendant in the 1991 William Kennedy Smith (WS) rape trial. WS, a physician by training, takes the stand during his trial, where the prosecutor attempts to impeach his testimony on the nature and provenance of the victim's injuries. By shifting from defendant to expert footing, WS shifts from answering questions about his actions to providing medical opinion and raising the possibility of alternative diagnoses for the victim's injuries. Exploiting a variety of grammatical devices that strip his testimony of personal agency and his actions of transitivity, he uses expert medical terminology to evaluate the epistemological status of the prosecution's claims, and casts rhetorical doubt on the prosecution's case. This blurring between the status of defendant and expert provides a window into the workings of spontaneous identity negotiation and the resources that can be mobilized by speakers at different levels.

In my own research, Mendoza-Denton (1997, 1999a), I examine the speech patterns of Latina (Americans of Mexican descent) gang girls in California and trace their use of grammatically innovative discourse markers and constructions as carriers of vocalic and consonantal variation, linking the statistical patterns of phonetic variation among the subgroups (core gang girls vs. wannabes) to innovative discourse uses of the carrier constructions by specific members of the community. The coordination of discourse- and segmental-level strategies with other performative modes (such as makeup, dress, and intonation) is crucial to a semiotic conception of these gang-based identities as complex homologies of signs, operating simultaneously on various communicative channels.

Milroy (1999) also seeks to explain wider phonological patterning by looking at discourse-level constraints on variation. The analysis focuses on exceptions to the Pre-Pausal Constraint (glottalized realizations of /t/ in prepausal contexts) in Tyneside, England. Milroy finds that exceptions to the PPC are primarily found in utterance-final grammatical tags, and that an understanding of the discourse-management functions of such tags can shed light on the spread of sound change through the dynamics of conversation (see also Local et al. (1986)). Indeed, some researchers are turning to discourse markers as cross-linguistic (Fleischman and Yaguello, forthcoming) sites for the production of epistemically stanceful elements that can signal speaker identities. Discourse markers bear several important properties such as phonological reduction, relative syntactic freedom, and semantic bleaching that are the outcomes of processes of grammaticalization. All of these elements may encourage flexibility of implementation (see Schwenter (1996) on Castilian Spanish; Matsumoto (1985) on Japanese; Traugott (1997) on historical developments in discourse marking).

5 Automaticity and Intentionality

Constant transformation is an essential feature of the political structures and social circumstances that bring identities into existence. Given this instability, and our power as agents to vary the meaning and the configuration of identities, the very notion of identity may seem untenable (as indeed, Butler 1995 and Michaels 1992, 1994 argue). What this suggests for variation theory is that identities and their linguistic reflexes are the product of continuous axes of difference (race/ethnicity, class, sexuality, age, status, profession, momentary stance), none of which is solely determinate. At any given moment, symbolic actors may self- and other-mark in specific ways, only to shift footing in the midst of an interaction.

Some of the literature cited above draws inspiration from performative (Grice 1975, Searle 1969, Butler 1990, Tsitsipis 1998) theories of meaning and action in explaining particular linguistic acts as strategic and intentional. Consider the contrapuntal viewpoint of Moerman (1988) and Heritage (1991) in problematizing pervasively intentionalist analyses of action. To quote Moerman in his discussion of overlapping talk:

> all of these meaningful, consequential, structurally complex, and densely cultural overlaps were certainly undeliberate, unanticipated, unconscious, and unremembered. No individual human actor is their author. We build our experienced, lived in, significant social reality out of a mesh of interactive processes too tiny and too quick for the thinking, planning "I" to handle.   (Moerman 1988: 30)

Such perspectives stressing automaticity are echoed in functionalist and psycholinguistic perspectives on phonology (Bybee 1999, Hammond 1999), morphology (Hay 2000), and language acquisition (MacWhinney 1999). So far the implications for the theory of identity remain to be worked out. It is perhaps this dissonance between automaticity and intentionality that will lead us to new insights.

REFERENCES

Agar, M. (1996). *The Professional Stranger*. 2nd edn. New York: Academic Press.

Appiah, A. K. and H. L. Gates (eds.) (1995). *Identities*. Chicago: The University of Chicago Press.

Bailey, B. (1997). Communication of respect in interethnic service encounters. *Language in Society* 26, 3: 327–56.

Baugh, J. (1999). Changing terms of self-reference among American slave descendants. *American Speech* 66, 2: 133–46.

Bell, A. (1984). Language style as audience design. *Language in Society* 13: 145–204.

Bhabha, H. (1990). *Nation and Narration*. London: Routledge.

Blake, R. (1996). Notions of Identity: Social and Linguistic Variation in Barbadian Communities. Ph.D. dissertation, Stanford University.

Bourdieu, P. (1977). *Outline of a Theory of Practice*. Cambridge: Cambridge University Press.

Bourdieu, P. (1991). *Language and Symbolic Power*. Cambridge, MA: Harvard University Press.

Bucholtz, M. (1998). Geek the girl: Language, femininity, and female nerds. In N. Warner et al. (eds.), *Gender and Belief Systems: Proceedings of the Fourth Berkeley Women and*

Language Conference. Berkeley: Women and Language Group. 119–31.

Butler, J. (1990). *Gender Trouble.* London: Routledge.

Butler, J. (1995). Collected and fractured: Response to identities. In A. K. Appiah and H. L. Gates (eds.), *Identities.* Chicago: The University of Chicago Press. 439–47.

Briggs, C. (1989). *Learning How to Ask.* Cambridge: Cambridge University Press.

Bybee, J. (1999). Usage-based phonology. In M. Darnell et al. (eds.), *Functionalism and Formalism in Linguistics.* Amsterdam: John Benjamins. 211–42.

Cameron, D. (1990). De-mythologizing sociolinguistics: Why language does not reflect society. In J. Joseph and T. Taylor (eds.), *Ideologies of Language.* London: Routledge. 79–93.

Carter, B. and A. Sealy (2000). Language, structure, and agency: What can a realist social theory offer to sociolinguistics? *Journal of Sociolinguistics* 4, 1: 3–20.

Cedegren, H. (1973). The interplay of social and linguistic factors in Panama. Ph.D. dissertation, University of Pennsylvania.

Certau, M. D. (1984). *The Practice of Everyday Life.* Berkeley: University of California Press.

Cerulo, K. (1997). Identity construction: new issues, new directions. *Annual Review of Sociology* 23: 385–409.

Chambers, J. K. (1993). Sociolinguistic dialectology. In D. Preston (ed.), *American Dialect Research.* Amsterdam: John Benjamins. 133–64.

Collins, P. H. (1990). *Black Feminist Thought.* New York: Routledge.

Dubois, S. and M. Melançon (2000). Creole is, Creole ain't: Diachronic and synchronic attitudes toward Creole identity in Southern

Louisiana. *Language in Society* 29, 2: 237–58.

Eckert, P. (1993). Cooperative competition in adolescent girl talk. In Deborah Tannen (ed.), *Gender and Conversational Interaction.* New York: Oxford University Press. 32–61.

Eckert, P. (1999). *Linguistic Variation as Social Practice.* London: Blackwell.

Eckert, P. and S. McConnell-Ginet (1992). Think practically and look locally. *Annual Review of Anthropology* 21: 461–90.

Errington, J. (1988). *Structure and Style in Javanese.* Philadelphia: University of Pennsylvania Press.

Fleischman, S. and M. Yaguello (forthcoming). Discourse markers across languages? Evidence from English and French. In C. L. Moder and A. Martinovic-Zic. (eds.), *Discourse across Languages and Cultures.* Amsterdam: John Benjamins.

Fought, C. R. (1997). The English and Spanish of young adult Chicanos. Ph.D. thesis, University of Pennsylvania, Philadelphia.

Fuss, D. (1989). *Essentially Speaking: Feminism, Nature and Difference.* New York: Routledge.

Gal, S. (1978). Peasant men can't get wives: Language change and sex roles in a bilingual community. *Language in Society* 7: 1–16.

García, M. (1984). Parameters of the East Los Angeles speech community. In J. Ornstein (ed.), *Form and Function in Chicano English.* Rowley, MA: Newbury House. 85–98.

Gaudio, R. (2001). White men do it too: Racialized (homo)sexualities in postcolonial Hausaland. *Journal of Linguistic Anthropology* 11, 1.

Giles, H. (1973). Accent mobility: A model and some data. *Anthropological Linguistics* 15: 87–105.

Giles, H. (1980). Accommodation theory: Some new directions. *York Papers in Linguistics* 9: 105–36.

Grice, H. P. (1975). Logic and conversation. *Syntax and Semantics* 3: 41–58.

Guy, G. R. (1981). Variation in the group and the individual. In W. Labov (ed.), *Locating Language in Time and Space*. New York: Academic Press. 1–36.

Haeri, N. (1998). *The Sociolinguistic Market of Cairo: Gender, Class and Education*. London: Kegan Paul.

Hale, Ken (1997). Cultural politics of identity in Latin America. *Annual Review of Anthropology* 26: 567–90.

Halliday, M. A. K. (1976). Anti-languages. *American Anthropologist* 78: 570–84.

Hammond, M. (1999). The embarrassment of lexical frequency. In M. Darnell et al. (eds.), *Functionalism and Formalism in Linguistics*, Amsterdam: John Benjamins. 329–58.

Hay, J. B. (2000). Causes and consequences of word structure. Ph.D. dissertation, Northwestern University.

Heritage, J. (1991). Intention, meaning, and strategy: Observations on constraints in conversation analysis. *Research on Language and Social Interaction* 24: 311–32.

Hill, J. H. (1993). "Hasta la vista, baby:" Anglo-Spanish in the American Southwest. *Critique of Anthropology* 13: 145–76.

Hill, J. H. (1995). Mock Spanish: A site for the indexical reproduction of racism in American English. http://www.language-culture.org/colloquia/symposia/hill-jane

Horvath, B. (1985). Variation in Australian English: the sociolects of Sydney. New York: Cambridge University Press.

Hymes, D. (1974). *Foundations in Sociolinguistics: An Ethnographic Approach*. Philadelphia: University of Pennsylvania Press.

Irvine, J. (2001). "Style" as distinctiveness: The culture and ideology of linguistic differentiation. In P. Eckert and J. R. Rickford (eds.), *Style and Sociolinguistic Variation*. Cambridge: Cambridge University Press. 21–43.

Jahr, E. H. (1979). Er det sånn jeg snakker? In J. Kleiven (ed.), *Språk og Samfunn*. Oslo: Pax. 122–37.

Janicki, K. (1990). *Toward non-Essentialist Sociolinguistics*. Berlin: Mouton de Gruyter.

Janicki, K. (1999). *Against Essentialism: Toward Language Awareness*. Munich: Lincom Europa.

Johnson, K., E. Strand and M. D'Imperio (1999). Auditory-visual integration of talker gender in vowel perception. *Journal of Phonetics* 24, 4: 359–84.

Johnstone, B. and J. M. Bean (1997). Self expression and linguistic variation. *Language in Society* 26, 2: 221–46.

Keane, W. (2000). Voice. *Journal of Linguistic Anthropology* 9, 1–2: 271–3.

Kiesling, S. (1998). Variation and men's identity in a fraternity. *Journal of Sociolinguistics* 2, 1: 69–100.

Kontra, M. and T. Váradi (1997). The Budapest sociolinguistic interview: Version 3. *Working Papers in Hungarian Sociolinguistics* 2.

Kroskrity, P. (2000). Identity. *Journal of Linguistic Anthropology* 9, 1–2: 111–13.

Kulick, D. (2000). Language and Sexuality. *Annual Review of Anthropology* 29. Palo Alto: Annual Reviews, Inc.

Labov, W. (1969). The logic of non-standard English. In J. Alatis (ed.), *Georgetown Monographs on Language and Linguistics* 22: 1–44.

Labov, W. (1972a). Hypercorrection by the lower middle class as a factor in linguistic change. In *Sociolinguistic Patterns*. Philadelphia: University of Pennsylvania Press.

Labov, W. (1972b). The social motivation of a sound change. In *Sociolinguistic Patterns*. Philadelphia: University of Pennsylvania Press.

Labov, W. (1972c). Contraction, deletion, and inherent variability of the English copula. In *Language in the Inner City*. Philadelphia: University of Pennsylvania Press.

Labov, W. (1972d). The Isolation of Contextual Styles. In *Sociolinguistic Patterns*. Philadelphia: University of Pennsylvania Press.

Labov, W. (1994). *Principles of Linguistic Change: Internal Factors*. London: Blackwell.

Labov, W., S. Ash and C. Boberg (2000). *The Phonological Atlas of North America Project*. http://babel.ling.upenn.edu/phono_atlas/home.html

Lacan, J. (1977). The agency of the letter in the unconscious or reason since Freud. In *Écrits: A Selection*. New York and London: W. W. Norton. 146–78.

Lambert, W. (1967). A social psychology of bilingualism. *Journal of Social Issues* 23: 91–189.

Lane, L. A. (1999). "We just don't do that anymore": Patterning dialect change through social networks and social transformation. *Proceedings of the Symposium for Language and Society Austin (SALSA IV)*.

Lave, J. and E. Wenger (1991). *Situated Learning: Legitimate Peripheral Participation*. Cambridge and New York: Cambridge University Press.

Lennig, M. (1978). Acoustic measurement of linguistic change: the modern Paris vowel system. Ph.D. dissertation, University of Pennsylvania.

Le Page, R. B. and A. Tabouret-Keller (1985). *Acts of Identity: Creole-Based Approaches to Language and Ethnicity*. Cambridge: Cambridge University Press.

Linde, C., J. Gougen, E. Finnie, S. Mackay and M. Wescoat (1987). Rank and status in the cockpit: Some linguistic consequences of crossed hierarchies. In K. Dennig (ed.), *Variation in Language: Proceedings of the NWAV-XV Conference at Stanford University*. Stanford: Stanford Linguistics. 300–11.

Lippi-Green, R. (1997). Teaching children to discriminate: What we learn from the Big Bad Wolf. In *English with an Accent: Language, Ideology and Discrimination in the United States*. New York: Routledge. 79–103.

Local, J., W. Kelly and W. G. H. Wells (1986). Towards a phonology of conversation: Turn-taking in Tyneside. *Journal of Linguistics* 22: 411–37.

Matoesian, G. M. (1999). The grammaticalization of participant roles in the constitution of expert identity. *Language in Society* 28, 4: 491–521.

Matsumoto, Y. (1985). A sort of speech act qualification in Japanese: Chotto. *Journal of Asian Culture* IX: 143–59.

McGurk, H. and J. W. MacDonald (1976). Hearing lips and seeing voices. *Nature* 264: 746–8.

MacWhinney, B. (1999). Emergent language. In M. Darnell et al. (eds.), *Functionalism and Formalism in Linguistics*. Amsterdam: John Benjamins. 361–86.

Meyerhoff, M. (1999). *Sorry* in the Pacific: Defining communities, defining practices. *Language in Society* 28, 2: 225–38.

Mendoza-Denton, N. (1997). Chicana/Mexicana identity and linguistic variation: An ethnographic and sociolinguistic study of gang affiliation in an urban high school. Ph.D. dissertation, Stanford University.

Mendoza-Denton, N. (1999a). Sociolinguistic and linguistic anthropological studies of US Latinos. *Annual Review of Anthropology* 28: 375–95.

Mendoza-Denton, N. (1999b). Turn-initial "No": Collaborative Opposition among Latina Adolescents. In Bucholtz, Liang and Sutton (eds.), *Reinventing Identities: From Category to Practice in Language and Gender*. New York: Oxford University Press. 273–92

Michaels, W. B. (1992). Race into culture: A critical genalogy of cultural identity. *Critical Inquiry* 18: 655–85.

Michaels, W. B. (1994). American modernism and the poetics of identity. *Modernism/Modernity* 1, 1: 38–56.

Milroy, L. (1999). The prepausal constraint in Tyneside English: a discourse level mechanism of linguistic change. In *Proceedings of the Symposium for Language and Society Austin (SALSA IV)*.

Modan, G. (forthcoming). White, whole wheat, rye: Jews and ethnic categorization in Washington, DC. *Journal of Linguistic Anthropology*.

Moerman, M. (1988). *Talking Culture: Ethnography and Conversation Analysis*. Philadelphia: University of Pennsylvania Press.

Morgan, M. (1994). Theories and politics in African American English. *Annual Review of Anthropology* 23: 325–45.

Myers-Scotton, C. (1993). *Social Motivations for Codeswitching: Evidence from Africa*. Oxford: Oxford University Press.

Nagy, N. (2000). What I didn't know about working in an endangered language community: Some fieldwork issues. *International*

Journal of the Sociology of Language 144: 143–60.

Nichols, P. (1983). Linguistic options and choices for black women in the rural South. In B. Thorne et al. (eds.), *Language, Gender and Society*. Cambridge, MA: Newbury House. 54–68.

Okamoto, S. (1995). "Tasteless" Japanese: Less "feminine" speech among young Japanese women. In K. Hall and M. Bucholtz (eds.), *Gender Articulated: Language and the Socially Constructed Self*. New York: Routledge. 297–325.

Patrick, P. (1999). *Urban Jamaican Creole: Variation in the Mesolect*. Amsterdam and Philadelphia: John Benjamins.

Payne, A. (1980). Factors controlling the acquisition of the Philadelphia dialect by out-of-state children. In W. Labov and D. Sankoff (eds.), *Locating Language in Time and Space*. New York: Academic Press. 143–78.

Peterson, G. E. and H. L. Barney (1952). Control methods used in a study of vowels. *Journal of the Acoustical Society of America* 24: 174–84.

Pierrehumbert, J. (1999). Formalizing functionalism. In M. Darnell et al. (eds.), *Functionalism and Formalism in Linguistics*. Amsterdam: John Benjamins. 385–400.

Poplack, S. (1979). Function and process in a variable phonology. Ph.D. thesis, University of Pennsylvania, Philadelphia.

Potter, J. (1996). *Representing Reality: Discourse, Rhetoric, and Social Construction*. London: Sage.

Potter, J. (2000). Realism and sociolinguistics. *Journal of Sociolinguistics* 4, 1: 21–4.

Purnell, T., W. Idsardi and J. Baugh (1999). Perceptual and phonetic experiments on American English dialect identification. *Journal of Social Psychology* 18, 1: 10–30.

Reisigl, M. and Wodak, R. (2001). *Discourse and Discrimination: Rhetorics of Racism and Anti Semitism*. London: Blackwell.

Rickford, J. R. (1986). The need for new approaches to social class analysis in sociolinguistics. *Language and Communication* 6, 3: 215–21.

Rickford, J. R. (1997). Unequal partnership: Sociolinguistics and the African American speech community. *Language in Society* 26, 2: 161–97.

Rickford, J. R. (1999). *African American Vernacular English*. London: Blackwell.

Rickford, J. R. and F. McNair-Knox (1994). Addressee- and topic-influenced style shift: A Quantitative and Sociolinguistic Study. In D. Biber and E. Finegan (eds.), *Sociolinguistic Perspectives on Register*. Oxford: Oxford University Press. 235–76.

Romaine, S. (1984). The status of sociological models and categories in explaining linguistic variation. *Linguistische Berichte* 90: 25–38.

Said, E. (1993). *Culture and Imperialism: The T.S. Eliot lectures at the University of Kent 1985*. New York: Knopf.

Salecl, R. (1994). *The Spoils of Freedom: Psychoanalysis and Feminism after Socialism*. New York: Routledge.

Schegloff, E. (1997). Whose text? Whose context? *Discourse and Society* 8: 165–87.

Schieffelin, B. (1990). *The Give and Take of Everyday Life: Language Socialization of Kaluli Children*. New York: Cambridge University Press.

Schiffrin, D. (1996). Narrative as self portrait: Sociolinguistic constructions of identity. *Language in Society* 25, 2: 167–203.

Schilling-Estes, N. (1998). Investigating self-conscious speech: The performance register in Ocracoke English. *Language in Society* 27, 1: 53–83.

Schwenter, S. (1996). Some reflections on the sea: a discourse marker in Spanish. *Journal of Pragmatics* 25: 855–74.

Searle, J. R. (1969). *Speech Acts: An Essay in the Philosophy of Language*. Cambridge: Cambridge University Press.

Sidnell, J. (1999). Gender and pronominal variation in an Indo-Guyanese creole speaking community. *Language in Society* 28, 3: 367–399.

Silva-Corvalán, C. (1989). *Sociolingüística: Teoría y análisis*. Madrid: Alhambra.

Silverstein, M. (1998). Contemporary transformations of local linguistic communities. *Annual Review of Anthropology* 27: 401–26.

Silverstein, M. (1976). Shifters, linguistic categories, and cultural description. In K. Basso and H. Shelby (eds.), *Meaning in Anthropology*. Albuquerque, NM: SAR. 13–55.

Snider, S., K. Mauro and A. Neuzil (2000). I [ay] can't talk to myself [masehlf] when I'm[a:m] drinkin': Realization of /ay/ in the Australian Country music scene. Unpublished manuscript, University of Arizona.

Solomon, J. (1998). External constraints and subject expression in Yucatec Spanish. Ph.D. dissertation, Stanford University.

Spivak, G. (1992). Acting bits/identity talk. *Critical Inquiry* 18, 4: 770–803.

Strand, E. A. (1999). Uncovering the role of gender stereotypes in speech perception. *Journal of Social Psychology* 18, 1: 86–99.

Tabouret-Keller, A. (1998). Language and identity. In F. Coulmas (ed.), *Handbook of Sociolinguistics*. Oxford: Blackwell. 315–26.

Tagliamonte, S. (1999). Was-were variation across the generations:

View from the city of York. *Language Variation and Change* 10, 2: 153–91.

Tannen, Deborah (1989). *Talking Voices: Repetition, Dialogue, and Imagery in Conversational Discourse*. New York: Cambridge University Press.

Tannen, Deborah (1990). *You Just Don't Understand: Talk between the Sexes* (New York: Morrow).

Thibault, P. and M. Daveluy (1989). Quelques traces du passage du temps dans le parler des Montrealais, 1971–1984. *Language Variation and Change* 1, 1: 19–45.

Thibault, P. and G. Sankoff (1993). Diverses facettes de l'insecurite linguistique: Vers une analyse comparative des attitudes et du francais parle par des Franco- et des Anglo-montrealais. *Cahiers de l'Institut de Linguistique de Louvain* 19, 3–4: 209–18.

Traugott, E. (1997). The Role of the Development of Discourse Markers in a Theory of Grammaticalization. Paper presented at ICHL XII, Manchester 1995; Version of 11/97, http://www.stanford.edu/ ~traugott/ect-papersonline.html

Trudgill, P. (1974). *The Social Differentiation of English in Norwich*. Cambridge: Cambridge University Press.

Trudgill, P. (1983). Acts of conflicting identity: The sociolinguistics of British pop-song pronunciation. In P. Trudgill (ed.), *On Dialect: Social and Geographical Perspectives*. Oxford and New York: Basil Blackwell and NYU Press. 141–60.

Trudgill, P. (1986). *Dialects in Contact*. London: Blackwell.

Tsitsipis, L. (1998). *A Linguistic Anthropology of Praxis and Language Shift: Arvanítika and Greek in Contact*. Oxford: Clarendon Press.

Urciuoli, B. (1996). *Exposing Prejudice: Puerto Rican Experiences of Language, Race, and Class*. Boulder, CO: Westview Press.

Valdés, G. (1981). Codeswitching as deliberate verbal strategy: A microanalysis of direct and indirect requests among bilingual Chicano speakers. In R. P. Duran (ed.), *Latino Language and Behaviour*. Norwood, NJ: Ablex. 95–107.

Walters, K. (1996). Gender, identity, and the political economy of language: Anglophone wives in Tunisia. *Language in Society* 25, 4: 515–55.

Wenger, E. (1998). *Communities of Practice*. Cambridge: Cambridge University Press.

Williams, K. C. (1994). Mapping the margins: Intersectionality, identity politics, and violence against women of color. In M. Fineman and R. Mykitiuk (eds.), *The Public Nature of Private Violence*. New York: Routledge.

Winford, D. (1984). The linguistic variable and syntactic variation in Creole continua. *Lingua: International Review of General Linguistics* 62, 4: 267–88.

Wolfram, W. (1969). *A Sociolinguistic Description of Detroit Negro Speech*. Washington, DC: Center for Applied Linguistics.

Wolfram, W. and R. Fasold (1974). Field methods in the study of social dialects. *The Study of Social Dialects in American English*. Englewood Cliffs, NJ: Prentice-Hall.

Wolfram, W. and N. Schilling-Estes (1994). On the social basis of phonetic resistance: The shifting status of Outer Banks /ay/. In Arnold et al. (eds.), *Sociolinguistic Variation*. Stanford: CSLI.

Wong, A. and Q. Zhang (2001). The linguistic construction of the Tongzhi community. *Journal of Linguistic Anthropology*. 10, 2: 1–31.

Woolard, K. (1997). Gender, peer group structure, and bilingualism in urban Catalonia. *Language in Society* 26, 4: 533–60.

Woolard, K. (1998). Simultaneity and bivalency as strategies in bilingualism. *Journal of Linguistic Anthropology* 8, 1: 3–29.

Zentella, A. C. (1997). *Growing up Bilingual: Puerto Rican Children in New York*. Oxford: Blackwell.

Zizek, S. (1993). Enjoy your nation as yourself! In *Tarrying with the Negative: Kant, Hegel and the Critique of Ideology*. Durham, NC: Duke University Press.

20   The Family

KIRK HAZEN

Parents were invented to make children happy by giving them something to ignore.

Ogden Nash (quoted in Simpson 1988)

... parental models must count for something in the acquisition stages and perhaps exert discernible effects not yet understood or appreciated.

Chambers (1995: 160)

Both psychology and sociology have specific subfields designed to investigate the family,[1] one of the most basic units in society (Benson and Deal 1995). Although sociolinguistics has at least some of its roots in sociology (Chambers 1995), the field has never thoroughly investigated the family. While we certainly do not have to rigorously subscribe to all the methods of other fields, we should have the capacity to detail and explain the effects of the family on linguistic variation. Does the family need to be a distinct subset of the speech community; does its inclusion in a sociolinguistic analysis make an appreciable difference? How does the study of the family help our understanding of language variation for the individual? Can our analysis of language variation in the family help sociological and psychological fields better understand the processes and properties of families? Although a study of familial influence could be wide ranging in sociolinguistics, this chapter focuses primarily on the family's effects on language variation.[2]

As is well recognized by most variationists, children do not retain their parents' language variation patterns as complete sets through their adolescent years. When given two models of transmission, the parents' and the peer group's, children normally follow the peer group. As Chambers (1995: 159) notes, "when Scots school-teachers settle and work in London, England, they retain most features of their native Scottish accents, but their London-born offspring do not retain their parents' Scottishness in their own accents."

However, exceptions to this rule do exist and can inform our understanding of language variation. Chambers (1995: 160) argues, "the children of the Scots parents should have Scots dialect features – at least some – up to around age five, and should lose them – probably rapidly – thereafter." Whether children lose all features, and those beyond just phonology, has yet to be thoroughly investigated.

Perhaps the best approach to language variation in the family is through analysis of language transmission (Labov 2001).[3] Generativists in formal fields traditionally view language transfer between generations as between parents and children (Halle 1962, McMahon 1994). Sociolinguists view language transfer as between older and younger members of the same speech community with the main point of transfer as the peer group. Neither group has put the family into the model of language transfer.

The study of language variation in the family is also at the intersection of the study of language acquisition and language change: Within the family we have children, in part instigators of language change (Roberts and Labov 1995, Romaine 1984), and we have parents who may act as a foil to adolescent peer groups (Kerswill and Williams 2000, Payne 1980).[4] Often, these details about language variation in the family come as a side product of the study of child language or discourse analysis of families. This chapter draws together studies that have produced data on language variation in the family and suggests questions for future study. I first offer some related assumptions and approaches for family language variation study, then review several relevant studies, and third, present case studies to note the complexity of language variation in the family. In concluding, I outline potential research questions.

1. Theoretical Issues and Questions

1.1 The individual, the family, and the speech community

Since the family may be seen as an intermediate grouping between the individual and the speech community, the study of the family from a variationist perspective investigates the language variation patterns of individuals and compares them to subgroups of the speech community (i.e. families). For some researchers, the language variation patterns of individuals are idiolects. But according to traditional variationist analysis, specifically Weinreich et al. (1968) and Labov (1989b), idiolects are not a theoretical reality. Labov (1999) has called this foregrounding of the speech community "the central dogma" of variationist analysis. In this view, the language variation grammar exists at the level of the speech community but not at the level of the individual. These assumptions prohibit a nested view of language variation whereby dialects are collections of similar idiolects, and languages are collections of similar dialects. What then would language variation in the family be? Is the family a unit of society in the same way as a social division like ethnicity? Are there family dialects? These are appropriate research questions, but it is not clear that we have appropriate answers at this point in variationist research.

In language change, what role does the family play? Could the children in a family have exactly the same language variation patterns as the parents? Roberts (1999) and Roberts and Labov (1995) note that children actively participate in language change by extending the parameters of variation as a natural part of their acquisition process. Given that children and parents do not acquire language at the same time and that parental language acquisition modules are no longer operational, children should always have some differences in their language variation patterns from their parents. While peer groups may play a large role in shaping socially significant language variation patterns, some of the differences between family members may result from the natural structure and processes of the human language faculty which lead to the constant flow of language change (Labov 2001).

For any given speaker, how is a researcher to determine which language variation patterns come from the rest of the speech community and which come from the family? The easiest scenario would be if the language variation patterns of the family were different from those of the speech community either qualitatively or quantitatively but within the same language. For example, if a family from the Southern US with features such as /ai/ ungliding (e.g. [baːd] for *bide*), the /ɪ/~/ɛ/ merger before nasals (e.g. *pin~pen* [pɪn]), and syllable-initial stress in words like *pecan* ['pikan] and *cement* ['simɪnt] moved to Canada, the family language variation patterns the children preserve after their teenage years would be much easier to detect. If the family unit has an influence on language variation independent from other social factors (e.g. gender or age), then we would expect the children in these families to align, in terms of dialect features, with their parents to some extent and not necessarily with their social categories or the larger speech community. If the family has an influence on the children, the children would demonstrate language variation that would be unexplainable through any influence other than the family unit (cf. Chambers 1995: 168).

1.2   Types of influences of the family on language variation patterns

What does it mean to study language variation in the family? For language variation analysis, ontogeny and phylogeny need to be distinguished. Specifically, two questions arise: (1) What is the effect of the family on the language variation patterns of a speaker within that family and (2) what is the effect of families on variation in the speech community? The second question grapples with a system of compounded complexity, but it moves towards providing answers for how language variation becomes embedded in a speech community and becomes language change. Most studies reviewed here focus on the first question since a large-scale study of a collection of families has not been attempted.[5]

In focusing on variation effects within the family, two possible influences could be demonstrated with family language variation patterns: transfer of patterns from child to parent or transfer of patterns from parent to child. Either of these may result in family markers distinguishing one family from others in the speech community. Although not formally documented, there is no a priori reason to restrict language transmission to simply the realm of child language acquisition. At future stages of investigation, researchers should assess other social relationships associated with family: accommodation between parents; accommodation between extended family; different cultural constructions of family; influences, both accommodating and distancing, between siblings.

Parents' norms may be modified through contact with their children. Since teenagers in the western world focus intensely on what is popular in their culture, some parents may try to win back the affections of their children by identifying with them. This situation would foster accommodation on the part of the parent. Of research interest would be which of the teenager's language variation patterns are attempted – lexical, phonological, morphological – and how accurately can the parent produce them. In a nonwestern context, parental accommodation may also be possible. Meyerhoff (2000) investigates a situation of language change in Bislama involving subject deletion. Although it is clear that deletion of subject pronouns is a relatively recent innovation in Bislama and is more widespread among younger speakers, an examination of the community-wide patterns showed no monotonic relationship between rates of subject deletion and speaker age. Based on more detailed data from one extended family, she hypothesizes that the reason there is an absence of clear age-grading in the community at large is because, even though the children in these families learn the general trend of the change from the wider speech community, the parents adjust their norms to fit those of their children. Dubois and Horvath (1999: 303) also report a context for sociolinguistic acquisition where children may influence their parents in Cajun English.

The most frequent transfer of language variation patterns is the language acquisition process itself. Most often, parents provide the stimulus triggering language acquisition, helping the child form their grammar(s). What is obviously not determined by this process is the exact language variation patterns of the child. Given our current understanding of language variation and change and the stances on principles and parameters (Chomsky 1995, Henry 1995, Roberts and Labov 1995, Wilson and Henry 1998), a safe hypothesis is that no child copies exactly the language variation patterns of the parents. Neither is there a radical break from the parents: no child creates a separate language from the language(s) of the parents. Given these extremes, the questions for variationists are not clear. If we ask what socially significant language variation patterns children acquire and maintain in the face of competing patterns from peer groups, then we have a dilemma because most often the socially significant patterns are the ones linked to the peer groups. Except in cultures where kinship families are a predominant part of the social structure (Rogles et al. 1989), the socially significant patterns will be the peer-group patterns.

If variationists ask what parts of the child's overall language resemble those of the parents, there will of course be a great deal of overlap: within the same language, the child and the parent will share the majority of lexical items and grammatical processes. The foundering point is that the child also shares the majority of lexical items and grammatical processes with most speakers of the same language. The most revealing question might be which language variation patterns, including lexical items, are shared by family members but not by the community at large. Although family language patterns may occur in every family, the effects may be masked by overlap between the parents and the community if the parents are originally members of the community. As Chambers (1995: 159) notes, "In the most common social situations, the disparity between family and friends as linguistic influences is inconsequential because family and friends are natives of the same speech community. It is when we look at the situations in which the parents belong to a different speech community from the one in which the children are being raised that the primacy of age-mates over elders becomes very obvious."

If differences between the family and the speech community exist, members of a family could be unified in some language variation pattern if they use it as a sociolinguistic marker for the family (Fasold 1990). For example, one quantitatively variable feature of a rural North Carolina community is the negative, past *be* (e.g. *We wont going to the store* – Hazen 1998, 2000). Although in most English speaking communities the negative past *be* paradigm bifurcated into *wasn't* and *weren't*, in Warren County and other areas of North Carolina there is a tripartite paradigm: *wasn't*, *weren't*, and *wont* (spelled without the apostrophe to distinguish it from the future auxiliary, *won't*, as in Hazen 1998). *Wont* is a separate linguistic variant, and in Warren County is a highly diagnostic social variant. In one particular family, this feature is highly variable for the three adult children, but is frequent and stable for the parents. For the children, in more formal, nonfamily contexts, the rates of *wont* are most often nil, but in family contexts, the children often demonstrate rates of *wont* at 100 percent (see Hazen 2000: ch 5). In nonfamily, less formal contexts, *wont* varies with both *wasn't* and *weren't* for the children. Essentially, the children's rates are lower than those of the parents in most contexts except family gatherings, where they exceed or match those of the parents. Considering the close ties of the children with the parents in this family, their variable rates of *wont* may be the children's attempt for family unity and identity.[6]

The transfer from parent to child may be considered an inheritance model. There are four family-pattern types by which the children may vary in relation to the parents and the community.

1   Children may pattern with the parents.
2   Children may pattern with the community.
3   Children's patterns may be in between the parents and the community, possibly moving towards one or the other as they grow older.
4   Children in a family may be split. In other words, one child may fit Family Pattern 1 and another in the same family may fit Family Pattern 2. However, children in a family may also be split with systematic variation. In other words, one child may align as in 3, but another child in the same family may align as in 3 but in a different manner.

For family pattern type three, this midpoint may mean having both parental and community norms, or it may be that their language variation patterns fall between parents and community quantitatively (e.g. the parents' rates of certain variants are high, the community's rates are low, but the children's rates fall in the middle).[7] In family pattern type four, some children lean towards the parents' patterns while their siblings lean towards the community's for reasons of identity (or nonidentity) with other members of the family.

2   Related Studies

Large-scale sociolinguistic studies have most often focused on the speech community as the place where sociolinguistic variation happens, in contrast to the individual or smaller social units being the locus of language variation. Labov (1972) in New York City, Wolfram (1969) in Detroit, Fasold (1972) in Washington, DC and Trudgill (1974) in Norwich, England, all focused on how independent social variables affected the dependent linguistic variables. Individuals were categorized as subdivisions of social groups (e.g. 18-year-old, Native-American female). This methodology was taken to its logical extension by Wolfram et al. (1997) and Wolfram et al. (1999) in the study of the speech of Muzel Bryant, an older, African-American woman living in Ocracoke, NC. Although recognized as an individual, she was also cast as the last representative of her speech community, that of African-Americans socially isolated on a historically isolated island.

The borrowing of social network theory into sociolinguistic analysis (Milroy 1987) redirected analytical attention to the individual within the speech community and to the interactions between individuals. With the study of social networks in Belfast (Milroy and Milroy 1997: 59), "the main methodological difference between network . . . and other variables that have been examined is that it is based, not on comparisons between groups of speakers, but on relationships contracted by individual speakers with other individuals." Social network ties may act as norm-enforcing mechanisms if strong enough to constrain individuals in the maintenance of their vernacular. Families certainly played a role in the social network analysis of Belfast speakers, but the family relations were treated no differently than those of other social connections, such as having the same employer.

In discourse studies, the family is seen as a context for interactions between speakers, and discourse analysis has been the most productive field for studies of language in the family (e.g. Attanucci 1993, Beaumont 1995, Blum-Kulka 1993, Burrell 1995, Connidis 1989, Daly 1983, Haviland 1979, Mathews et al. 1989, Varenne 1987). In language and gender studies the family is seen as a context for power relations and social organization (Hartmann 1981, Ochs and Taylor 1995). The fields of discourse analysis and language and gender studies illustrate that the family is an influential context for construction of social identities.

Innovative scholarship bearing on the sociolinguistics of the family has come about from Community of Practice (CofP) theorists (Holmes 1999, Meyerhoff this volume). A CofP is defined as "An aggregate of people who come together around mutual engagement in an endeavor" (Eckert and McConnell-Ginet 1992: 464), and Holmes and Meyerhoff (1999: 174) label the family as a type of CofP. One working assumption of the CofP model is that becoming a "core member" of a CofP involves the acquisition of sociolinguistic competence (Ochs and Schieffelin 1983, Romaine 1984); the implication is that family members do follow the sociolinguistic patterns of their families (cf. Daly 1983). But family members are also going to be members of other CofPs – groups of friends, clubs, sports teams – and the sociolinguistic norms of the family may compete with those other CofPs.

Turning to work in the variationist tradition, Weinreich et al. (1968: 145) criticize Halle's (1962) model of language acquisition for relying on the "unexamined assumption that the children's grammars are formed upon the data provided by their parents' speech." Weinreich et al. emphasize the role of the peer group in restructuring the grammars of children. They comment that "there are two situations where parents' language may indeed be taken as the definitive model for children's language. One is in the isolated household – rural or urban – where the child cannot or may not play with other children. The other is in the direct transfer of a prestige feature from parent to child in the variety of careful speech used for scolding or correcting." Almost all variationist research since this work confirms that the peer group is the predominant model, but whether it is the only model is still a question.

In an article challenging some of the claims of Weinreich et al., Kazazis (1970) argues that occasionally "the linguistic model provided by the parents may sometimes resist successfully the model provided by the peers even in the absence of . . . the isolated households or the direct transfer of prestige features from the parents to the children." He focuses on the retention of Istanbul features among children born and raised in Athens but with parents from Istanbul. These children mixed with children of native-born Athens parents, but Kazazis identifies lexical, morphological, and syntactic differences between the children of Istanbul parents and those of native Athenian parents. For example, Istanbul Greek does not make a distinction for the accusative pronoun in an indirect or direct object context whereas Athenian Greek does; although this does not detract from the functional load of a phrase, Kazazis notes that it does function as a social marker. He notes the strong place of the family in Greek society, but in harmony with Kerswill and William's (2000) findings below, the children with strong allegiance to their families often come from nonlocal families. Like the CofP model, Kazazis construes membership in the family in Greek society as allegiance to an "in-group."

In an often-cited study, Payne (1980) looked at 24 families from a middle-class suburb of Philadelphia. Half of the families were originally from out of state and half were native to the neighborhood, giving precisely the context necessary to distinguish parental from community influence. Payne showed that both parental and peer influences were active in the language acquisition of the children, noting that the peer influence affects the active and completed language acquisition from the parents' influence. Payne focuses on the complex short *a* pattern: The constraints on this language variation pattern make a fine-grained diagnostic instrument to help determine the language acquisition abilities of the children. Specifically, Payne (1980: 143) investigates, "first, whether a child freely reorganizes and/or restructures his grammar up to the age of 14; and second, whether a child will learn to speak like his peers or retain the system learned from his parents." She concludes that even if the child is born and raised in this neighborhood, unless the parents were also natives of the area, then the child has a slim chance of fully acquiring this short *a* pattern with native competence. Here is direct evidence for the impact of parent to child transmission on language variation patterns.

Results like these lead to the assumption that there is an early window of opportunity for children learning more complex patterns which is usually filled by parental input, or perhaps that the more complex patterns take longer periods of input than do simpler processes. Of those children who did not fully acquire the short *a* pattern, there were two general approaches to language learning: focusing on lexical items and focusing on phonetic classes. Although children of nonnative parents did not fully acquire the pattern, they did learn it to some extent, demonstrating the influence of the peer group. Payne also concludes that the most important factor for acquiring the pattern was the age of arrival in the community, with age 8 being the cut-off point. This finding demonstrates that children do not have the ability to restructure their grammars, but may add low level rules to them.

The implication for the study of language variation in the family is that if patterns are set by the family from a young age, later peer groups may only be able to modify what is already established. However, a new study of Payne's data forces a modified view. Labov (2001) revises Payne's finding that the major social variable was the age of arrival in Philadelphia. His multiple regression reanalysis reveals that the most significant independent variable was the number of times the speaker was mentioned by peers in their interviews. Labov relates this factor to the density of the speaker's social network.

As with Payne's analysis of acquisition success of a complex phonological feature, Trudgill (1986: 35) indicates that although they may otherwise have perfect local accents, speakers born and raised in Norwich who do not have native parents cannot acquire a vowel distinction between /ʊu/ (e.g. *moan, nose, rose, sole*) and /ou/ (e.g. *mown, knows, rows, soul*). A good complement to the complex phonological features of Payne (1980) and Trudgill (1986) is Local (1983), which investigates fine phonetic variations of stressed /i/ for a Tyneside boy over different interviews covering a year of development. Local (1983: 452) finds that at age 5–6, "this child is still engaged in gaining control of the relevant localized phonological patterning of the variants of this vowel." This case again exemplifies that some phonological dialect features are so complex that they require either early acquisition or extensive time for acquisition for the child to fully adopt them.

In another vowel comparison of parents and children, Roberts (1997b) reports findings of a study of vowel changes in progress. The three Philadelphia changes – the fronting of the nucleus of (aw), the raising of the nucleus of (ey) in checked position, and the backing of (ay) before voiceless final obstruents – offered the opportunity to study if children could acquire changes in progress which their parents themselves may not have, as compared with the almost-completed short *a* pattern of Roberts and Labov (1995). Roberts (1997b) finds that, as with the other studies, all the children were making at least some progress in learning their local vowel system. All of Roberts's subjects had mastered the fronting of the (aw) nucleus, but the raising of the (ey) nucleus created a division of those with parents native to the area and those with at least one nonlocal parent. Roberts (1999) explores the role of children (and their parents) in language change through acoustic vowel analysis in the same set of children. In her subject pool, she has children of native Philadelphian parents and children of parents with mixed dialect background. Except for one child's production of (aw), the children of native Philadelphian parents are qualitatively similar. When considering the other children, more heterogeneity arises. Roberts finds that the simpler vowel changes (e.g. fronting of (uw), (aw), and (ow)) were similar amongst all of the children, but the more complex changes revealed possible parental influence in the children's acquisition of the Philadelphia changes in progress. The children with nonnative parents did not have the advanced tokens of a more complex change, the raising of (ey) in checked environments. With an even more complex change, that of the Phila-delphia short *a*, the children of nonnative parents again show the least advanced tokens of the change. Roberts emphasizes that even the children of nonnative parents are not out of "community range" but are not leading the pack in terms of language change. This distinction between children with two native parents versus those with parents of any other orientation is a recurrent theme.

Chambers (1992) also employs methodology useful to the study of family language variation in the investigation of Canadian children's success at acquiring British features after several years in England. This study of dialect acquisition also allows us to see that the influence of peer groups is in part limited by the biological ability of the learner, since one finding was that the older the child, the less thoroughly the child was able to acquire the new dialect. Chambers' methodology consisted of a longitudinal study of multiple phonological and lexical variables. By focusing on a net of both simple and complex processes, there were many possible points of linguistic variation. When analyzing families, subtle influences may be the only influences from the family members and such cautious searching for language variation patterns should be the norm for family studies.

Surek-Clark (2000) discusses the relative importance of parental influence and of the prestige of the dialect features acquired. In Brazilian Portuguese, the standard dialect has a rule of raising /e/ to [i] which partly feeds a rule of palatalization of /t,d/ before [i]. The Curitiba dialect Surek-Clark investigates does not have this feeding relationship. In her study of 41 informants, a child needed both parents to be from Curitiba for that child to acquire the Curitiba pattern. If either parent had the more prestigious dialect (that from Rio de Janeiro), then the child's patterns would more closely follow the standard version. Surek-Clark (2000: 266) finds that, "These results seem to indicate that pressure from within a family with regard to accommodating to the most prestigious dialect present within the home has a stronger effect than outside [i.e. Curitiba] peer pressure." Her findings demonstrate that the sociolinguistic competence as well as the linguistic competence of the child influences the language variation patterns acquired.

In another study of the acquisition of socially constrained variable patterns, Roberts (1997a) examined the pattern of (-t, -d) deletion in word final consonant clusters for 16 three- and four-year-old children. These patterns were then compared with eight of their mothers. Roberts found that these young children had successfully acquired the phonological constraints of (-t,-d) deletion, including the phonological and morphological distinctions.[8] She notes that the children acquired not a general process of deletion but the specific geographically-restricted constraints of their parents. In addition, the children do show social differentiation, for example by gender, but they do not demonstrate the same sociolinguistic patterns as their parents.

Internal constraints of the children's grammar may also direct how closely they follow their parents. Guy and Boyd (1990) and Labov (1989a) both consider (-t/-d) deletion in semiweak verbs (e.g. *keep ~ kept*). A relatively small class of verbs, semi-weak verbs fall between the dental-preterite weak verbs and the ablaut strong verbs. For both studies, the younger children who have consonant clusters follow a pattern of a high deletion rate, whereas their parents have either a medium or low deletion rate depending on their age. Guy and Boyd (1990: 11) argue that the child's lexicon is restricted to only two types of verbs, weak and strong, and does not have a category of semi-weak verbs. The children in these situations cannot match the patterns of the parents because their language faculties are not at the same point of development.

Labov (1989a) makes an additional important point about the influence of parents and the wider community on sociolinguistic norms. Although the children in his study had not acquired, at ages 6 and 7, the grammatical constraints on alveolarization of *–ing* pertaining to its morphological category, the children showed the parental patterning of stylistic constraints: (1989a: 96) "Children first show the social and stylistic constraints on variation, then the language-specific grammatical and articulatory constraints." This finding indicates that children acquire sociolinguistic competence from parents before strictly linguistic patterns are set, which helps to explain Surek-Clark's findings (cf. Chambers 1995: 151–9).

Andersen (1990) also investigates the sociolinguistic skills of children, specifically the ability of the children to acquire registers. The children investigated – four, five, and six year-olds – had the best understanding of different registers in the context of the family and were best able to maintain a certain social role when play acting in that context. But the children did not learn all of the register variation for the family roles at home, and Andersen (1990: 164) notes media influence on the children's concepts of the family registers. Apparently, even a child's understanding of the sociolinguistics of the family does not come exclusively from the family.

Working with an assumption of language variation resulting from continuous dialect contact, Kerswill (1996) examines the speech of younger children and adolescents during their acquisition of a new dialect in Milton Keynes, Great Britain. Although some younger children mirrored the productions of their older peers, one child more closely followed his father, and another appeared to have a compromise variety between his parents (family pattern type I). Kerswill cites Howe (1981) and Newport et al. (1977) to demonstrate that individual differences between parents (speaking the same language) have an impact on the acquisition of language features. Kerswill concludes that children learn most of their phonological features of the local variety by age 6. He also claims that for more salient variables, the children move away from the parents towards peer groups possibly from age 7 on. Kerswill proposes a language change difficulty hierarchy whereby some types of language change (e.g. lexically unpredictable phonological rules) are more complex, requiring input from the earliest age; others (e.g. lexical borrowings) are learnable at any age. Obviously, if certain language variation patterns require early input, the parental influence will be greater.

Kerswill and Williams (2000) details a comprehensive, in-progress view of koineization in Milton Keynes through a study of 48 children and the principal caregiver of each child. They document the ability of children to restructure their phonologies rapidly: within 18 months one child had transformed himself from a Scots speaker to a southern English speaker, essentially moving from his parents' variety to that of his classmates. Kerswill and Williams also found that the language variation patterns of the parents do make a difference in the production of the children. In an analysis of one phonological variable, Kerswill and Williams (2000: 100) illustrate that having both parents of London extraction gives a greater likelihood of having the London variant than does having only one parent of London heritage, which in turn gives a greater likelihood than having neither parent from London. It appears that the input variation from the home does have an influence on what quantitative rates of variation are attainable for some variables. Perhaps the family has a more predominant influence on the rates of variation rather than the establishment of language variation patterns not found in the wider community. They also conclude that younger children are more oriented to the parental norms of variation than are older children. They justify this progression of moving away from parental norms by noting that as children approach adolescence, they become more fully integrated into peer networks.

In an observation of the family and the speech community, Kerswill and Williams (2000) note that when children are more family oriented, they are oriented to a family-language variety originating from somewhere besides the local community, holding on to an outsider identity. As they (2000: 102) write, "when children are for some reason more parent- or family-oriented, they are inevitably oriented toward language varieties that originate elsewhere." Perhaps social isolation from the community is a self-reinforcing process whereby some social distance of the children, marked by nonnative language variation patterns, feeds a closer association to the family, which in turn heightens a distinction between the family oriented dialects of the children and the local dialects of the wider community.

Different, though not necessarily contradictory, results come from Wolfram, Thomas, and Green's demonstration that families sometimes have little molding influence on socially significant language variation patterns (Wolfram et al., forthcoming). In their study of Hyde County, North Carolina, they focus on four generations of one African-American family. Whereas the grandfather shares most of the phonological features of the local European-American community, each younger generation adopts progressively more AAVE features. Although parental influence persisted in adjacent generations, with the youngest family members, there is no differentiation from the rural AAVE found in other areas of North Carolina.

Along the same line, in his study of Hebrew speaking communities, Bentolila (2000) writes, "One cannot help noticing that the linguistic behaviour of children is often very dissimilar to their parents', mostly as the result of different social routes, at adult ages, and of ties with peer groups, in the adolescent phase of life (Eckert 1988; Peleg 1992)." Given that Oriental Hebrew is the more socially marked variety perhaps it is little wonder that children speak the more general variety even if their parents speak the Oriental variety. However, he notes that of the exceptional cases, those that maintain some linguistic patterns of their Oriental Hebrew parents, "only very few may keep their parents' way of speaking, in most cases because they married Oriental spouses outside the village and went to live in heavy Oriental social environment." In this context, reinforcement of the parental norms by the speech community is necessary to maintain those norms in the face of sociolinguistic stigmatization.

Trudgill (1986) makes a comprehensive study of dialect accommodation and new dialect formation resulting from contact. In a discussion on irregularity in accommodation (1986: 29), Trudgill provides exemplary methods for the study of children in a family by surveying a wide variety of variables over a range of time. Trudgill focuses on twins raised in Britain till age seven who then were relocated and recorded in Australia over a six month period.[9] Fifteen variables are assessed for each month's recording to determine if and to what extent the twins had acquired the Australian variants. One would expect that their acquisition of the Australian patterns would be similar, but they are not, perhaps from their different friends, activities, and personalities. Both children, however, accommodated to a large number of Australian features, and although it is not documented, one would assume that their parents would not have been so rapidly able to accommodate such a cornucopia of features.

Labov (2001) reports a revised study by Sankoff of Tok Pisin verb structure and its quantitative distribution amongst parent–child dyads. Sankoff found both a shift by children away from parents and a child–parent alignment. For the morphophonemic reduction of the future *bai* (e.g. /em bai igo/ "he will go") either secondary stress or full vocalic reduction is applied. In a group comparison, children assign this future secondary stress 30 percent of the time compared with 50 percent for the parents; with complete reduction, the adults only had a rate of 1 percent but the children had 10 percent. For the group comparison, the children are distancing themselves from the parents. When parent–child dyads are compared, a striking pattern results. The percent differences between the children correlate with those between the parents so that the child with the lowest rate has the parent with the lowest rate and the child with the highest rate has the parent with the highest rate. The relationships indicate the primary influence of the peer group while highlighting the molding influence of the family. As Labov (2001) notes, "Their [the children's] system is a regular projection from the language of their parents."

Henry (1995) explores through a study of overt imperatives (e.g. *Go you away*) how children handle the syntactic input from both parents and the wider speech community. The parents of Henry's young subjects had this construction, but some of their children were learning the more standard forms. Henry asks how a child comes to view such constructions as ungrammatical considering its occurrence in their parent's dialect, leading her to conclude: "What is clear from this [situation] is that language learning does not involve selecting a grammar which fits all the data. Rather, it must involve selecting, from the options provided by UG, the grammar which best fits the majority of the data" (1995: 79). Even with syntactic variation, parents input is not a hegemonic influence.

Mæhlum (1992) promotes a model of dialect socialization built around the family; besides the dialect varieties of North-Norwegian and Standardized East-Norwegian, Mæhlum runs the poles of the model as a continuum between family-internal and family-external norms. In her study of Longyearbyen, a stable, local dialect has not formed as a result of continuous intervals of population movement. With a lack of a "indigenous and genuine basic dialect" Mæhlum (1992: 121) finds that, "the dialects of the parents here seem to influence the spoken language of the children to a greater extent than is usually the case in mainland Norway." This unusual circumstance results from the prominence of the family in comparison with other social groups available to the children of Longyearbyen. Mæhlum (1992: 121) claims the "social and dialectal conditions are so unstable that the parents are precisely the ones who normally represent the most, or even the only, really stable social unit over some period of time." Clearly the influence of the family on the language variation patterns of the children must take into account the relative importance of the wider speech community.

In a lexical study, Hart and Risley (1995) report findings from an amazingly comprehensive study of lexical frequency in 42 families over a two year and a half-year span. They (1995: 176) find that for the three-year-olds, between 86 to 98 percent of the children's words were also recorded in their parents' speech. The finding they focus on most is that families speaking less often had children who spoke less often and who used fewer different words per hour. By their one significant social factor, socioeconomic status, the children of professional families averaged 297 different words per hour compared to 216 for the working class and 149 for the welfare children; these rates directly correspond to those of the parents.[10] The different families also speak to the children at different rates, which Hart and Risley (1995) interpret as the cause for the greater diversity in the professional children's vocabulary. What is clear is that for young children, the family has a dramatic influence on aspects of their lexical usage.

3   Case Studies of Language Variation in the Family

Deser (1989, 1990) studied six African-American families in Detroit, Michigan, analyzing vowels to determine parental influence on children's language variation patterns. The Detroit families were recorded in the 1960s as part of an urban language study (Shuy et al. 1968), and the interviews were conducted with one parent and two children, all of whom were born in Detroit. Deser conducts two different studies on these data. First is an impressionistic judgment by three speech pathologists as to the dialect orientation of the 18 people studied: subjects were judged as Northern (Detroit) or Southern.[11] If speakers got equal numbers of votes for Northern or Southern, then they were deemed mixed. The six families are shown in table 20.1. All of the Northern families are upper-middle-class and all of the Southern families are lower-working-class.

Table 20.1, although based on impressionistic judgments, allows for a simple comparison of dialects.[12] For the Harper family, the interviewed parent is Northern, as is the first child, but the other child is more Southern, apparently following the other parent. For the other Northern–Southern parent set, the Sanders, the interviewed parent is mixed, but both children are Southern. From these two families, it appears that children of parents from different dialect regions can go either way in terms of their own development. The

Table 20.1   Impressionistic dialect judgments of children and parents

Families		Parent's dialect	Parent	Child 1	Child 2
Northern	Harper	Louisiana, NY	N	N	S
	James	Detroit, Detroit	mixed	N	N
	Shawn	Detroit, Indiana	N	mixed	N
Southern	Atkinson	Georgia, Georgia	S	S	N
	Sanders	Detroit, Alabama	mixed	S	S
	Jones	Kentucky, Illinois	S	mixed	S

Source: Deser (1989: 116, tables 1 and 2)

James and Shawn families demonstrate mostly mixed or Northern orientation which is in line with the parents' dialect origins. Of interest, when the one interviewed parent is mixed, as in the James and Sanders families, the children had no restrictions as to which dialect variety to follow. In the James family, both parents had Detroit dialects but the Sanders family had one Northern and one Southern parent. The Jones children have followed the parents for the most part in their Southern traits. What is missing in this family comparison is the social situations of the children and the parents: are the children fully integrated into the Detroit community? Do they or their parents associate with mostly Detroiters from the North or the South?

The main focus of Deser's study is the acoustic analysis and comparison of /ai/ and /æ/ vowel qualities between parents and children. The unglided /ai/ vowel is a sociolinguistic stereotype of Southern speakers. From these comparisons, she concludes that at least for the more Northern families, the older children deviate from the parents while the younger children adhere more to the parental model. For the more Southern families, the opposite seems to be true: the older children follow the parents' more extreme /ai/ ungliding while the younger children deviate more. Overall, the older children are more Southern and the younger children are more Northern. This pattern seems to fit the general assimilation of speakers of different dialects to a new region. The /æ/ vowel plays a crucial role in language change in the Detroit area (Eckert 1999, Labov 1994, Labov et al. 1972). For the children, the Northern speakers have slightly raised /æ/ tokens as compared to their Southern counterparts. Here the younger children more closely approach the raised Northern norm than do their older siblings, who follow their parents' patterns more closely. In an expanded report of the study, Deser (1990: vii) finds that, "contrary to the Neogrammarians [sic] error-in-transmission theory as well as Labov's theory of adolescent rebellion, children do continue to show the influence of their parents' dialect model even through the teen years."

Hazen and Hall (1999) investigated two West Virginia families involved in dialect contact. West Virginia is bifurcated by a northern–southern dialect boundary, although some features bleed over the entire state: a semi-accurate generalization is that the northern half follows more of the norms of western Pennsylvania and eastern Ohio while the southern half has more in common with the southern Appalachian region. Family 1 has one parent from Michigan, the mother, but the father is from northern West Virginia and the children were born and raised in suburban, southern West Virginia. The mother is a lawyer, the father an iron worker, and both children have graduated from college. Family 2's parents are from rural, southern West Virginia, but the son was born and raised in northern West Virginia. The daughter was born in the southern half of the state but has lived most of her life at the northern edge of the state, although the family did move often when she was younger. Neither parent is college educated but both children are. The father retired as a civil servant and is now a computer specialist, the mother is a transcriptionist, the daughter has a graduate degree, and the son is in college. Family 1 presents a situation of children receiving input from parents of two different dialect regions; Family 2 presents a situation of children being raised in a different dialect area than the parents.

The children of Family 1 do not demonstrate socially diagnostic phonological patterns that would identify them as Southerners[13] (e.g. they have extremely restricted /ai/ ungliding). This may be explained by both of them having some high school friends who were not Southerners, but mere contact is not enough. Perhaps more compellingly, both strongly reject a Southern identity. Here the children align with their family. The parents also were quite direct in their rejection of a Southern identity, and in their interviews this sociocultural orientation seemed to be one of the few unifying points for the family.

For Family 2, the son, the younger of the two children, patterns like his peers in the urban north and does not show any influence from his parents, having no instance of a sociolinguistically Southern feature. In the interview, the daughter does have predominantly two Southern traits: /ai/ ungliding and the /i/ ~ /ɪ/ merger preceding /l/ (e.g. *heel* ~ *hill* [hil]).[14] She also commented on numerous encounters where she was identified as being Southern. For the daughter, peer influence may have either contributed or been a reinforcer of family language patterns. This daughter associated with what would be the rednecks of this Northern speech community, and she claims that they "sound more Southern." However, it is plausible that she acquired her /ai/ ungliding and her high front vowel merger at home, and then chose her peer group based on who she identified with as marked by their dialect features. The Family 2 son associated with an altogether different peer group. The key difference in the upbringing of the daughter and the son is stability of their young peer groups. Whereas the family moved often during the first seven years of the daughter's life, they did not move again after the son was born. The mother commented in the interview that since they moved so often, her daughter was her constant companion and her little buddy. Clearly, the daughter had more extended contact with the parents and relied on them more for social interaction (and vice versa) than did the son.

Despite the son's different language variation patterns, he does not hear anything unusual in his parents' speech. When asked directly, he said that everybody in his family sounded the same to him. In contrast, he does notice the Southern accent of his parents' relatives when visiting them in West Virginia. Perhaps children think their parents sound normal, even if they differ from the surrounding community, which leads to a wider question: under what circumstances do children remark that the parents' language seems other than normal?[15]

These differences between the older and younger siblings of Family 2 may point out the fluid and complex nature of language variation in families originally from other speech communities.

In most communities, the children who most closely follow the language variation patterns of their parents are those in families more recently immigrated (Deser 1989, Kerswill and Williams 2000). How local the family is – how dense and complex their social network ties may be or how many CofPs they may be a part of – will usually increase over time if they harmoniously live in the community. As the social integration of the family changes, the effects on older and younger siblings will differ. Whereas an older sibling may be more connected to the family when the family is recently immigrated, a younger sibling a few years later may have more opportunity for peer group interaction. For both, the family guides their language variation patterns: the older child by the lack of social integration of the family and the younger by its higher degree of social integration. For the younger child, this stability from the family in the community then allows wider social exploration outside the family.

What may also be transpiring in these situations of older/younger sibling differences is what many researchers found for more complex phonological processes. They require early and extended exposure for children to fully acquire them. The older sibling may have been exposed to more norms of the original speech community than the younger sibling and the more complex processes would not have been acquired by the younger child.

Contributing to the lessening or complete absence of the original speech community's language variation patterns in the younger sibling may also be the parents' accommodation to the new speech community. As Henry (1995) points out, children do not fit their emerging grammars to all the observed data in their environment but just most of it, which makes the variable frequency of the input a crucial factor for the acquisition of a linguistic feature. For the father of Family 2, his /ai/ ungliding patterning is erratic by the normal phonetic constraints. His constraint ordering is voiced obstruents > nasals > liquids > voiceless obstruents as compared to the traditional liquids > nasals > voiced obstruents > voiceless obstruents (following the sonorancy hierarchy). His rates also vary depending on his interlocutor, providing lower rates for a non-/ai/ ungliding interlocutor (57 percent) as compared to an/ai/-ungliding interlocutor (88 percent). After 20 years of living in a non-ungliding environment, this father's rates may have been different during the language acquisition period of his youngest child. Most likely the scenario is more complex than even this analysis, probably involving gender (e.g. the daughter patterns more like the mother, who has traditional /ai/ ungliding patterns) and peer group reinforcement of family-learned norms.

Hazen (1999) extends this intrafamily comparison with data from Warren County, NC; Family 3 has both parents and the father's mother, since she also raised the children (a daughter and a son). Except for the mother, who is from the Outer Banks of North Carolina, the family is from Warren County. The mother graduated from college and the father went to two years of college but earned a professional license instead of finishing school. Given that both children were raised in the same small, rural community as their father, next door to their grandmother, one would expect the children to have the language variation patterns of Warren County. For the older child, the son, this expectation plays out: for example, he has traditional features of the area such as /ai/ -ungliding, /r/- and /l/-vocalization, consonant cluster reduction, and negative concord. For the daughter, she patterns like no other native in the community. Except for the /ɪ/ ~ /ɛ/ merger before nasals, the daughter has not a single Southern feature. She does, however, follow to some extent the language variation patterns of her mother.[16] An important sociocultural connection is that the daughter identifies in part with the mother's family on the Outer Banks, but she is in the local public schools, has never lived anywhere but Warren County, and also strongly identifies with her Warren County, born-and-bred grandmother who lives next door.[17]

The daughter's adherence to the mother's patterns may seem to be an identity alignment by gender, especially since the son more closely adheres to the patterns of his father and the rest of the speech community. But this daughter's language variation patterns are not strictly motivated by gender per se; she does not follow the patterns of her grandmother, who lived next door and spent considerable time raising her.[18] She also does not follow the patterns of her European-American peers, most of whom consider her speech a bit bizarre.[19]

4 Family and Language Variation

To date, most relevant research touches upon the transfer of language variation patterns from parent to child. Other effects of the family, such as the influence of the children on the parents and sociolinguistic marking of the family as a group have not been as widely explored.

Language transfer between parent and child, as a point of departure for future research, definitely occurs. How strongly the parental patterns emerge probably depends on the child's degree of identification with the family. How noticeable the effects of the family are probably depends on how different the parents' patterns are from that of the surrounding speech community. If the norms of the parents and the speech community are similar, influences may be impossible to tease apart.

Current research results in five general findings relating to the family's influence on language variation:

1   Children first acquire the language variation patterns of their immediate caregivers; these patterns will survive if reinforced by the language variation patterns of the children's peer groups.
2   Family variation patterns will be noticeable to the extent that they differ from community norms. If family traits, be they lexical items or phonological patterns, are not social markers, there is no reason to assume that peer group influence will necessarily counteract those traits.
3   Complex phonological patterns require early and extended input to be fully acquired by the child.
4   Language-variation-pattern differences between older and younger siblings of the same family is not unusual. They may be the result of different parental input or different social connections in the community, and thereby different opportunities for identification with and participation in CofPs.
5   Amongst families, the children of families recently immigrated to a community may demonstrate more family-oriented language variation patterns. The effects on the children may vary by age and the relative prestige of the family's variety versus that of the community.

For the study of language variation of the individual, the family provides another point of social connection to the speech community. Instead of viewing individuals as directly linked to the speech community, individuals may be seen as connected through small groups, and that normally includes the family (Holmes 1999, Meyerhoff this volume). The concept of the speech community may be expanded and modified so that it includes families. As a basic component of every community, families and their linguistic influence (or lack of it) should be integrated into the description of the speech community.

In the future, language researchers should be capable of detailing the influence the family has both in a speech community and on an individual. At this point, however, some questions have yet to be asked and others remain unexplored. Future studies on language variation in the family may include the following:

1   Which level of language is most effected by the family? Do families make their mark most in the realm of the lexicon or perhaps phonology?
2   What role does the family have on the child's acquisition of communicative competence, not just the language variation patterns (Ochs and Schieffelin 1983, Romaine 1984)?
3   When is the family least influential on a child's language and when is the family most influential (both in terms of stage of development and sociocultural context)?

4 Are family factors such as birth order an influence on sociolinguistic variation? Are there differences between types of families (e.g. single-parent vs. extended families)?
5 Do families use sociolinguistic patterns to mark in-group/out-group status? For example, could blood relatives in a family adhere to a certain language variation pattern which married relatives do not?
6 Does the effect of families on sociolinguistic patterns of the speech community vary between different cultures (Collins 1998)? Furbee and Stanley (1996) describe a time (1880–1920) in the language attrition of the Chiwere Siouan language where the original tribes were so fragmented by European settlement that the Chiwere language was restricted to home usage. This situation allowed each family to view their language as the acrolect, in essence creating family dialects. Dorian (p.c.) finds similar trends in her study of Gaelic. Romaine (1984: 158) notes that in some societies, the older siblings are responsible for raising younger children: would this situation dampen the effect of the peer group or possibly distance further the language variation patterns of the younger children from that of the parents?
7 What role does the family play in the child's identification with the peer group? When the child begins to identify more with the peer group and less with the family, how do the language variation patterns alter. Does diminishing identification with the family push the child away from their language patterns and towards those of the peer group?
8 Are the choices of a child's peer group influenced by the language variation patterns of the family? Might some children feel more comfortable with peer groups whose language variation patterns match those of their family?
9 How do highly mobile families, such as military families in the USA, differ from geographically stable families? Do families in rural areas differ from those in urban areas?
10 What is the effect of the entire family, and not just parent–child transfer, on language variation patterns of every member of the family? Could an older daughter influence the language variation patterns of a younger brother, who in turn influences the language variation patterns of the parents? Such complex loops of accommodation may be the reality in families, and until we investigate the possibilities of such interactions, we have no evidence that bears on the questions (cf. Dubois and Horvath 1999: 303).
11 If families play a minimal role in the language(s) of the speech community, why? Why would the family be the focus of so much social interaction but its influence on sociolinguistic variation be negligible?

The system of how children acquire and then modify their language variation patterns is complex. As with any complex system (Zimmer 1999), multiple factors not only affect language variation, but most likely interact with each other, producing effects not predictable by independent application of factors. This property of emergence (Mayr 1982) may be a necessary part of the study of language variation in the family in that we necessarily have a social system, the family, embedded in another social system, the speech community, and properties may emerge which are unpredictable when analyzing each system in theoretical isolation. In the end, describing how the family affects language variation patterns will require rigorous investigation of the identities of family members, integration of the family into models of the speech community, and comprehensive quantitative analysis of family language variation patterns.

ACKNOWLEDGMENTS

Many people have helped me with this focus on the family. I would like to especially thank Miriam Meyerhoff, Walt Wolfram, William Labov, Julie Roberts, Nancy Dorian, Laine Hall, Erdogan Gunel, Kathleen Frich, Natalie Schilling-Estes, Peter Trudgill, Jack Chambers, Naomi Nagy, Janet Fuller, N. Louanna Furbee, and Deborah Tannen.

NOTES

1   The term *family* will be used to refer to any modern instantiation of the family. There may very well be differences in sociolinguistic variation as factors of types of families (e.g. single parent vs. two parent families; gay parents vs. straight), but discovering this first requires general assessments about the influence of any family on sociolinguistic variation.

2   Other comprehensive work focusing on how sociolinguistics can help fields such as sociology better understand the family is undertaken by Daly (1983).

3   Labov (2001: ch 13) states that the core of the transmission problem is that children must learn to speak differently from their mothers, the primary caregivers, and these differences must be in the same direction in each succeeding generation. This is the general condition for language change.

4   There are also many fine studies of language acquisition based on quantitative studies of parent–child interactions (e.g. Rondal 1985, Snow and Ferguson 1977).

5   In the sociology of the family, statistical analysis of mean differences between families first requires that interactional processes within families be accounted for:

> In a research context, within-group differences should be examined first, before between-group analyses are examined. Any between-group differences should then be interpreted in the context of the within-group findings. Testing for differential processes within groups, then, coincides with conceptual and analytical underpinnings for advancing science.   (Benson and Deal 1995)

6 Interestingly, the married spouses in the family, the non-blood relatives of the same community, do not have different rates of *wont* between the family and nonfamily contexts.

7 This midpoint (of whatever type) may constitute the basis of the range of their style shifting. This tension between language variation pattern norms may be their initiation to style shifting.

8 The children's pattern disfavored deletion when in the environment of a following pause and also made a distinction between monomorphemic and weak past tense.

9 The children were recorded by Inge Rogers of Macquarie University (Rogers 1981).

10 Parents: professional (382); working-class (251); welfare (167). The average utterances per hour were professional (parents 487; children 310), working class (parents 301; children 223), Welfare (parents 176, children 168). Hart and Risley assume that vocabulary is a direct reflection of cognitive ability (1995: 6): "the vocabulary that individuals can command reflects so well their intellectual resources." There is no linguistic evidence suggesting that vocabulary reflects a person's cognitive ability.

11 The obvious drawback which Deser notes (1989: 116) is that only one parent is interviewed. An additional drawback is that we do not know the background or experience of the speech pathologists with Detroit or Southern dialects.

12 The column "parents' dialect" is given in Deser (1989) without any comment as to whether these were the home areas of these parents, if these are of both parents (I suspect they are), or if in some method it was determined that these are the *dialects* of the parents.

13 The possible exception is the /ɪ/~/ɛ/ merger before nasals (e.g. *pin~pen* [pɪn]). Although traditionally a Southern US feature, I have found that most people under the age of 30 in West Virginia have this feature regardless of sociocultural identity.

14 Although this merger is a feature of some sociolects of Pittsburgh, PA, an hour to the north of this speech community (McElhinny 1999), few speakers in this area have this feature, and all of those who do have strong ties to the Southern USA.

15 Teenagers may remark how their parents use out-of-date words or how they sound old fashioned. This dissonance may be an indication of their alliance with Communities of Practice other than the family.

16 The mother herself has engaged in long-term accommodation (Trudgill 1986) by lowering the Outer Banks backed and raised /ai/ (Wolfram et al. 1999) and occasionally ungliding it.

17 The daughter's language variation patterns do not match those of her mother exactly. Unlike her daughter, the mother has occasional /ai/ ungliding and diphthongization with /ɛ/ as in *bed* [bɛjd].

18 The daughter of Family 3 also thinks highly of her grandmother, but does not have her language variation patterns.

19 Knowing that I am a linguist, others in the community have asked me on numerous occasions, "Where did she get that accent?" in reference to the daughter of Family 3.

REFERENCES

Andersen, Elaine Slosberg (1990). *Speaking with Style*. New York: Routledge.

Attanucci, Jane (1993). Timely characterization of mother–daughter and family–school relations: Narrative understandings of adolescence. *Journal of Narrative and Life History* 3,1: 99–116.

Beaumont, Sherry (1995). Adolescent girls' conversations with their mothers and friends. *Discourse Processes* 20: 109–132.

Benson, Mark J. and James E. Deal (1995). Bridging the individual and the family. *Journal of Marriage & the Family* 57,3: 561–7.

Bentolila, Yaakov (2000). Spoken modern Hebrew across generations. Paper presented at Corpus Linguistics and the Study of Modern Hebrew. Emory University, Atlanta, February 4, 2000.

Blum-Kulka, Shoshana (1993). "You gotta know how to tell a story": Telling, tales, and tellers in American and Israeli narrative events at dinner. *Language in Society* 22: 361–402.

Burrell, Nancy (1995). Communication patterns in stepfamilies: Redefining family roles, themes, and conflict styles. In Mary Anne Fitzpatrick and Anita L. Vangelisti (eds.), *Explaining Family Interaction*. Sage. 290–309.

Chambers, J. K. (1992). Dialect acquisition. *Language* 68,4: 673–705.

Chambers, J. K. (1995). *Sociolinguistic Theory*. Cambridge, MA: Blackwell.

Chomsky, Noam (1995). *The Minimalist Program*. Cambridge, MA: MIT Press.

Connidis, Ingrid (1989). Siblings as friends in later life. *American Behavioral Scientist* 33: 81–93.

Collins, James (1998). Our ideologies and theirs. In Bambi B. Schieffelin,

Kathryn Ann Woolard, Paul Kroskrity (eds.), *Language Ideologies: Practice and Theory*. Oxford Studies in Anthropological Linguistics, 16. New York: Oxford University Press.

Daly, Lou Ann (1983). Family communication: A sociolinguistic perspective. Ph.D. dissertation, Georgetown University, Washington.

Deser, Toni (1989). Dialect transmission and variation: An acoustic analysis of vowels in six urban Detroit families. *York Papers in Linguistics* 13: 115–28.

Deser, Toni (1990). Dialect transmission and variation: An acoustic analysis of vowels in six urban Detroit families. Ph.D. dissertation, Boston University.

Dubois, Sylvie and Barbara Horvath (1999). When the music changes, you change too: Gender and language change in Cajun English. *Language Variation and Change* 11: 287–313.

Eckert, Penelope (1988). Adolescent and social structure and the spread of linguistic change. *Language in Society* 17: 183–207.

Eckert, Penelope (1999). *Linguistic Variation as Social Practice: The Linguistic Construction of Identity in Belten High*. Cambridge, MA: Blackwell.

Eckert, Penelope and Sally McConnell-Ginet (1992). Think practically and look locally: Language and gender as community-based practice. *Annual Review of Anthropology* 21: 461–90.

Fasold, Ralph W. (1972). *Tense Marking in Black English*. Washington, DC: Center for Applied Linguistics.

Fasold, Ralph W. (1990). *Sociolinguistics of Language*. Oxford: Blackwell.

Furbee, N. Louanna and Lori A. Stanley (1996). Language attrition and language planning in accommodation perspective. *Southwest Journal of Linguistics* 15: 46–62.

Guy, Gregory and Sally Boyd (1990). The development of a morphological class. *Language Variation and Change* 2: 1–18.

Halle, Morris (1962). Phonology in generative grammar. *Word* 18: 54–72.

Hartmann, Heidi I. (1981). The family as the locus of gender, class, and political struggle: The example of housework. *Signs* 6, 3: 366–94.

Hart, Betty and Todd R. Risley (1995). *Meaningful Differences in the Everyday Experience of Young American Children.* York, PA: Brookes Publishing.

Haviland, John B. (1979). Guugu Yimidhirr: brother-in-law language. *Language in Society* 8: 365–93.

Hazen, Kirk (1998). The birth of a variant: Evidence for a tripartite negative past *be* paradigm. *Language Variation and Change* 10: 221–44.

Hazen, Kirk (1999). The family as a sociolinguistic unit. Paper presented at NWAV 28. Toronto, Canada.

Hazen, Kirk (2000). *Identity and Ethnicity in the Rural South: A Sociolinguistic View Through Past and Present* Be. Publications of the American Dialect Society No. 83. Durham, NC: Duke University Press.

Hazen, Kirk and Laine Hall (1999). Dialect Shift in West Virginia Families. A paper presented at SECOL 60. Norfolk, VA.

Henry, Alison (1995). *Belfast English and Standard English.* New York: Oxford University Press.

Holmes, Janet (1999). Preface. *Language in Society* 28: 171–3.

Holmes, Janet and Miriam Meyerhoff (1999). The Community of Practice:

Theories and methodologies in language and gender research. *Language in Society* 28: 173–84.

Howe, C. (1981). *Acquiring Language in a Conversational Context.* London: Academic.

Kazazis, Kostas (1970). The relative importance of parents and peers in first-language acquisition: The case of some Constantinopolitan families in Athens. *General Linguistics* 10, 2: 111–20.

Kerswill, Paul (1996). Children, adolescents, and language change. *Language Variation and Change* 8: 177–202.

Kerswill, Paul and Ann Williams (2000). Creating a new town koine: children and language change in Milton Keynes. *Language in Society* 29: 65–116.

Labov, William (1972). *Language in the Inner City: Studies in the Black English Vernacular.* Philadelphia: University of Pennsylvania Press.

Labov, William (1989a). The child as linguistic historian. *Language Variation and Change* 1: 85–97.

Labov, William (1989b). Exact description of the speech community: Short *a* in Philadelphia. In Ralph W. Fasold and Deborah Schiffrin (eds.), *Language Change and Variation.* Washington, DC: Georgetown University Press. 1–57.

Labov, William (1994). *Principles of Linguistic Change: Internal Factors.* Cambridge, MA: Basil Blackwell.

Labov, William (1999). The inexplicable homogeneity of North American regional dialects. Plenary delivered at NWAVE 28. Toronto, Canada. October.

Labov, William (2001). *Principles of Linguistic Change: External Factors.* Cambridge, MA: Basil Blackwell.

Labov, William, Malcah Yaeger and Richard Steiner (1972). *A Quantitative Study of Sound Change in Progress*. Philadelphia, PA: The US Regional Survey.

Local, John (1983). How many vowels in a vowel? *Child Language* 10: 449–53.

Mathews, Sarah H., Paula J. Delaney and Margaret E. Adamek (1989). Male kinship ties: Bonds between adult brothers. *American Behavioral Scientist*.

Mæhlum, Brit (1992). Dialect socialization in Longyearbyen, Svalbard (Spitsbergen): a fruitful chaos. In Ernst Håkon Jahr (ed.), *Language Contact and Language Change*. Berlin: Mouton de Gruyter. 117–30.

Mayr, Ernst (1982). *The Growth of Biological Thought*. Cambridge, MA: Belknap.

McElhinny, Bonnie (1999). More on the third dialect of English: Linguistic constraints on the use of three phonological variables in Pittsburgh. *Language Variation and Change* 11: 171–96.

McMahon, April M. S. (1994). *Understanding Language Change*. New York: Cambridge University Press.

Meyerhoff, Miriam (2000). *Constraints on Null Subjects in Bislama (Vanuatu): Social and Linguistic Factors*. Pacific Linguistics, series-B. Canberra: The Australian National University.

Milroy, Lesley (1987). *Language and Social Networks*. 2nd edn. Oxford: Blackwell.

Milroy, James and Lesley Milroy (1997). Varieties and Variation. In Florian Coulmas (ed.), *The Handbook of Sociolinguistics*. Oxford: Blackwell. 47–64.

Newport, E. L., H. Gleitman and L. R. Gleitman (1977). Mother, I'd rather do it myself: Some effects and noneffects of maternal speech. In C. E. Snow and C. Ferguson (ed.), *Talking to Children*. Cambridge: Cambridge University Press. 109–49.

Ochs, Elinor and Bambi B. Schieffelin (1983). *Acquiring Conversational Competence*. London: Routledge & Kegan Paul.

Ochs, Elinor and Carolyn Taylor (1995). The "father knows best" dynamic in dinnertime narratives. In Kira Hall and Mary Bucholtz (eds.), *Gender Articulated*. New York: Routledge. 97–120.

Payne, Arvilla (1980). Factors controlling the acquisition of the Philadelphia dialect by out-of-state children. In William Labov (ed.), *Locating Language in Time and Space*. New York: Academic. 143–78.

Peleg, E. (1992). Simplification of the [εi] diphthong in Israeli Hebrew: Social processes as reflected in a phonological change in progress (Hebrew). In U. Ornan, R. Ben-Shahar and G. Turi (eds.), *Hebrew: A Living Language*, Haifa University Press, Haifa. 141–52.

Roberts, Julie (1997a). Acquisition of variable rules: a study of (-t, d) deletion in preschool children. *Journal of Child Language* 24: 351–72.

Roberts, Julie (1997b). Hitting a moving target: Acquisition of sound change in progress by Philadelphia children. *Language Variation and Change* 9: 249–66.

Roberts, Julie (1999). Going younger to do difference: The role of children in language change. *University of Pennsylvania Working Papers in Linguistics* 6, 121–36.

Roberts, Julie and William Labov (1995). Learning to talk Philadelphian: Acquisition of short *a* by preschool children. *Language Variation and Change* 7: 101–12.

Rogers, Inge (1981). The influence of Australian English intonation on the speech of two British children. *Working Papers of the Speech and Language Research Centre, Macquarie University* 3: 25–42.

Rogles, David, Lori A. Stanley and Louanna Furbee (1989). Lack of accommodation in a dying language. Paper presented at the 88th annual meeting of the American Anthropological Association. Denver, November.

Romaine, Suzanne (1984). *The Acquisition of Communicative Competence.* New York: Blackwell.

Rondal, Jean A. (1985). *Adult-Child Interaction and the Process of Language Acquisition.* New York: Praeger.

Shuy, Roger, Walt Wolfram and William Riley (1968). *Field Techniques in an Urban Language Study.* Washington, DC: Center for Applied Linguistics.

Simpson, James B. (1988). *Simpson's Contemporary Quotations.* New York: Houghton Mifflin.

Snow, Catherine E. and Charles Ferguson (1977). *Talking to Children.* Cambridge: Cambridge University Press.

Surek-Clark (2000). Dialect acquisition and prestige. *University of Pennsylvania Working Papers in Linguistics* 63: 259–67.

Trudgill, Peter (1974). *The Social Differentiation of English in Norwich.* Cambridge: Cambridge University Press.

Trudgill, Peter (1986). *Dialects in Contact.* Oxford: Blackwell.

Varenne, Herve (1987). Talk and real talk: The voices of silence and the voices of power in American family life. *Cultural Anthropology* 2: 369–94.

Weinreich, Uriel, William Labov and Marvin Herzog (1968). Empirical foundations for a theory of language change. In W. P. Lehmann and Yakov Malkiel (eds.), *Directions in Historical Linguistics.* Austin, TX: University of Texas Press. 95–188.

Wilson, John and Alison Henry (1998). Parameter setting within a socially realistic linguistics. *Language in Society* 27: 1–21.

Wolfram, Walt (1969). *A Sociolinguistic Description of Detroit Negro Speech.* Washington, DC: Center for Applied Linguistics.

Wolfram, Walt, Erik R. Thomas and Elaine W. Green. (2000) The regional context of earlier African-American speech; evidence for reconstructuring the development of AAVE. *Language in Society* 29: 315–45.

Wolfram, Walt, Kirk Hazen and Jennifer Ruff Tamburro (1997). Isolation within isolation: A solitary century of African-American Vernacular English. *Journal of Sociolinguistics* 1: 7–38.

Wolfram, Walt, Kirk Hazen and Natalie Schilling-Estes (1999). *Dialect Change and Maintenance on the Outer Banks.* Publications of the American Dialect Society No. 81. Tuscaloosa, AL: University of Alabama Press.

Zimmer, Carl (1999). Life after Chaos. *Science* 284, 5411: 1–212.

21 Communities of Practice

MIRIAM MEYERHOFF

The notion of the community of practice (CofP) is a comparatively recent addition to the sociolinguistic toolbox, though as we will see in this chapter aspects of its underlying philosophy can be traced to early work in sociolinguistics. The CofP describes an analytical domain, and its use invokes certain principles for, or assumptions about, the proper analysis of variation. The goals associated with the CofP framework require a serious investigation of both the social and the linguistic aspects of sociolinguistics. This chapter will describe the domain, explain its use in terms of its basic associated principles, and show how it has been used to satisfy those goals.

The CofP domain is rather smaller than that usually circumscribed by the term "speech community" (though see Santa Ana and Parodi 1998); crucially, a CofP is defined in terms of the members' subjective experience of the boundaries between their community and other communities. Especially important are the range of activities that members participate in and that contribute to the construction of these boundaries. Analyses of variation based on the CofP emphasize the role of language use and linguistic variation as pre-eminently social practices, and they link the analysis of linguistic variables to speakers' entire range of social practices. In this way, language is understood as but one vehicle by which speakers construct, maintain, or contest the boundaries of social categories and their membership in or exclusion from those categories. The CofP is not a different way of talking about social categories analogous to groups like the middle class. Social categories will certainly have significance at a very local level but they may also have broader significance, recognized by society at large. By focusing on speakers' engagement in a matrix of inter-related social practices, the CofP can provide a framework for understanding both the social and the linguistic facets of sociolinguistic variation.

This chapter is structured as follows. In section 1, I provide an overview of what the CofP is and how it is defined. In order to provide a meaningful context for evaluating what motivates researchers to use the CofP as the basis for analyzing variation, I will show how the CofP functions as an alternative to other frameworks for the analysis of variation. This shows both the extent to which the CofP provides a novel perspective for understanding the social significance of linguistic variation and change, and the extent to which it codifies existing practices within sociolinguistics, re-emphasizing earlier theoretical and analytical concerns of the field. In section 2, the heart of the chapter, I outline the use of the CofP in the analysis of language variation. The CofP has been applied infrequently to the analysis of language change, but some researchers see it as having potential in this domain too. The case studies selected reveal both the explanatory potential and the explanatory limits of the construct. Finally in section 3, I conclude with some brief remarks on how the goals and results of linguists working with the CofP tie in with theoretical traditions beyond linguistics, such as the fields of anthropology, social psychology and philosophy.

1   Defining the Community of Practice

A concise definition of the CofP is provided by Eckert and McConnell-Ginet (1992a): "A community of practice is an aggregate of people who come together around mutual engagement in an endeavor. . . . practices emerge in the course of this mutual endeavor" (1992a: 464).

In a more detailed exposition, Wenger (1998) uses the CofP to study the duality of participation and reification. Wenger spells out the three criteria (summarized by Eckert and McConnell-Ginet) which must be met in order to talk of a CofP. In the spirit of the CofP itself, they are to an extent mutually dependent, inseparable from one another when it comes to their detailed explication. I will first go over the basic criteria and then discuss in more detail some case studies that illustrate how they are significant.

First, there must be *mutual engagement* of the members. That is, the members of a CofP need to get together in order to engage in their shared practices. Wenger points out (1998: 77, 85) that mutual engagement may be harmonious or conflictual, so a CofP is not necessarily a group of friends or allies. An example of a CofP based on harmonious engagement might be a group of women from different workplaces who regularly get together on Friday evenings, sharing drinks and giving each other a fresh perspective on issues that may have arisen at their respective workplaces. The routines and practices that this CofP converges on might primarily be positive and constructive. You can imagine that such a CofP would be sustained over time because this mutual engagement is so useful to the members' emotional and practical needs.

But less harmonious engagement might also hold. Imagine a group of divisional heads (say, department chairs) who regularly meet in order to discuss their organization's shrinking budget and the allocation of funds in the organization as a whole. This group might be characterized by the continual re-enactment of personal feuds, or repetitions of complaints about undue favoritism of one group over another. Perhaps some divisional heads constantly stonewall any actions that might advance one of the other divisions. The practices that may evolve in a situation like this might be called unhelpful and may simply perpetuate the existing conflicts, but we could still talk of the group as a CofP as it satisfies the requirement for mutual engagement (and, indeed, the next two criteria to be discussed).

The second criterion for a CofP is that members share some *jointly negotiated enterprise*. Because the enterprise is negotiated, there is some circularity involved in its identification: members get together for some purpose and this purpose is defined through their pursuit of it. It is the pursuit of this enterprise that creates relationships of mutual accountability among the participants (Wenger 1998: 77–8). It is important that this shared enterprise be reasonably specific and not very general or abstract, a position I will motivate more fully below. I have argued (Meyerhoff 1999) that however the enterprise is defined (and Wenger (1998: 84) points out that the members of a CofP themselves may not be able to articulate their shared enterprise) it ought to contribute something meaningful to an understanding of the dynamics of the group involved. Sociolinguists who wish to use the notion of CofP in their analyses have to exercise caution and ensure that as researchers they are not attempting to constitute "CofPs" for which a shared enterprise is explanatorily vacant.

Third, a CofP is characterized by the members' *shared repertoire*. These resources (linguistic or otherwise) are the cumulative result of internal negotiations. An analysis can focus on the variables that members of a CofP are actively negotiating as currency in their CofP. Bucholtz's (1999) discussion of teenage girls does this. Alternatively, an analysis may focus on the outcome of such negotiations, as for example Holmes et al. (1999) do in discussing differences in the practices that have been established as normative for the repertoire of several different workplace CofPs.

In short, the CofP is a domain defined by a process of social learning. Lave and Wenger (1991) originally developed the CofP as a means of describing and understanding how professional communities (tailors or insurance company employees) induct and train new members, and perpetuate set routines for accomplishing specific tasks. It has been suggested that because the CofP is so crucially tied up with the notion of learned social behavior it may be inherently better suited to the study of certain groups or certain periods in peoples' lives than it is for others. As we will see, the CofP framework has frequently and very successfully been employed for the analysis of variation in adolescent groups. Bergvall (1999) wonders whether this represents an intrinsic constraint or limitation on the CofP. She notes that American culture expects adolescents to expend a good deal of time and effort working on their self-image (both through identification with and differentiation from others). She suggests that because of this, the framework of the CofP might transpose more readily into the analysis of variation among this age cohort than it does for variation among other age groups. I think the pattern she has observed is an accident rather than a genuine limitation on the framework, and an alternative explanation for why the variation found in adolescent groups seems to be particularly amenable to analysis under the CofP framework is discussed below.

We can illustrate the importance of these criteria with some case studies. Castellano (1996) studied the narratives told by women learning or working in skilled trades such as plumbing and carpentry and her work simultaneously shows the significance of mutual engagement and of a shared repertoire. Castellano compared the themes in the narratives that were told by journey-women in the trades and by trainees. She found that they differed quite mark-edly: journeywomen told stories that illustrated the perceived importance of forming a community at work, of finding ways to deal with adversity, and of achieving a high level of technical competence. The trainees' stories overlapped with the journeywomen's only on the last topic. This fundamental difference was of more than just descriptive interest. It meant that not only did the groups talk about work issues differently, but this difference affected the journey-women's ability to successfully induct the trainees into their professions.

Without using the CofP terminology, Castellano traces the difference to the women's membership in very different CofPs, separated by a fundamental lack of mutual engagement. Although the trainees and journeywomen shared some qualities, such as sex and profession (which, we might note, is often taken as an indication of class), other factors set them apart from each other. The journeywomen were generally older, white, and came from middle-class backgrounds. By contrast, the trainees were African-American or Latina, and many were learning their profession after having been enrolled in some form of federal aid program. It was hoped that the training program would be successful because it could build on the qualities that the two groups shared. But Castellano points out that its success was compromised by the fact that before they enrolled in the training program, most of the trainees would sel-dom have had cause to engage with women like the journeywomen. Their social worlds were sufficiently different that this kept them apart even in the context of their working world. Their membership in quite different CofPs manifested itself in very different linguistic repertoires, as shown by the limited overlap in their workplace narratives. Castellano notes that the journeywomen's narrative themes focused on the need to form communities and fight adversity at work. But these narrative themes can be construed as constructing an identity of self based on victimization or oppression. She suggested that the trainees avoided practices that construct such identities, since one of the focuses of the trainees' mutual engagement was on defining themselves as successes.

The importance of a jointly negotiated enterprise can be illustrated by a case study from Vanuatu (a nation in the southwest Pacific). I examined the distri-bution of an apology routine in Bislama in northern Vanuatu (Meyerhoff 1999), and noted that there was marked variability in terms of who used the apology routine *sore* "sorry" and for what purpose. Both men and women used it to express regret for a transgression and to say they missed someone, but only women were observed using it to express empathy with another person. Here then we had a clear difference in practice, but I argued against calling women and men separate CofPs. Although women shared a practice (use of *sore* to show empathy) the criterion of mutual engagement was satisfied only weakly. But even more problematic was the fact that it was impossible to specify what kind of enterprise all the women who were observed using *sore* to express empathy might share. The most one could say is that the women observed using it were engaged in an enterprise of constructing an association between being female and being empathetic. But this would fail to elucidate the relationship between language and its users any further than a simple description of the variation does. To claim that women engage in empathetic practices in order to define themselves as members of the category of women might be a faithful description of the way in which language and society are mutually constitutive, but it brings us no closer to explaining and understanding what it actually means to be a woman in this community nor to understanding the social significance of empathy there. Moreover, defining the enterprise in this way would also ignore the fact that the association between empathy and femaleness (which certainly is part of larger local ideologies about sex roles) is partly constructed by men through their avoidance of the use of *sore* to express empathy.

Since one goal of analysing variation in the CofP framework is to better understand the social meaning of language, I would argue that we need to avoid situations where the closest we can get to defining a shared enterprise is to say that speakers are engaged in "constituting a social category". If the so-called enterprise is specified at such a high level of abstraction we begin to (1) be divorced from the sensitive social goals of the CofP; (2) lose a good deal of the explanatory power of the CofP; and (3) be left with something very little different from established notions such as groups (in intergroup theory) or social strata in the speech community. Consequently, it seems to me that the criterion of a shared, negotiated, and fairly specific enterprise is absolutely crucial.

So we have established that the CofP is about an aggregate of individuals negotiating and learning practices that contribute to the satisfaction of a common goal. These fundamental criteria are associated with even more specific characteristics. Wenger's (1998) lengthy list of such typical features not only helps explain the concept more fully, but it has the added bonus of providing analysts interested in examining variation and change from the CofP perspective with a useful basis for formulating research questions. Wenger (1998: 125–6) suggests that a CofP will be characterized by (among other things):

- the rapid flow of information and propagation of innovation;
- absence of introductory preambles and very quick setup of a problem to be discussed;
- substantial overlap in participants' descriptions of who belongs and mutually defining identities;
- specific tools, representations, and other artefacts, shared stories and inside jokes;
- jargon and shortcuts to communication;
- a shared discourse that reflects a certain perspective on the world.

1.1   Distinguishing the Community of Practice from other Frameworks

The CofP shares a good deal with the notion of social networks in sociolinguistics (e.g. L. Milroy 1987, J. Milroy 1992, also L. Milroy, this volume). However, Eckert points out (2000: 35) that although variation acquires meaning within dense social networks, the CofP also captures the fact that linguistic variants acquire their meaning beyond dense networks. In addition, members of dense networks and CofPs are characterized by different degrees of agency: one can be a member of a dense network by chance or circumstance, while membership in a CofP is conscious (cf. the characteristic of mutual identification, above). Of course, the notion of simplex vs. multiplex ties in a network does introduce the kind of qualitative measures of relationships that are important to defining a CofP. Milroy (this volume) discusses networks in great detail and readers are encouraged to consult that chapter as a complement to the discussion here.

The CofP differs in more fundamental ways from some pre-existing concepts which have been widely used for analyzing linguistic variation, e.g. the speech community, social networks, and intergroup theory (intergroup theory provides part of the theoretical backdrop for Giles' communicative accommodation theory (e.g. Giles 1973, Gallois et al. 1995) which is perhaps more widely known in sociolinguistics). A sketch of what seem to be the most salient aspects of the CofP setting it apart from the speech community and intergroup theory might focus on the following five features (see also Patrick, this volume, and Kerswill, this volume). Due to space constraints, this will necessarily be brief. The outline that follows builds on the discussion in Holmes and Meyerhoff (1999).

Relationship between an individual's multiplicity of identities

Individuals may belong to or participate in a number of different communities of practice and their memberships are mutually constitutive. The kind of role that they play in a CofP will partly reflect their own personal history and goals, and also the goals of the group that is jointly engaged in those practices.

At different points in time, intergroup theory has postulated different relationships between individuals' group (or social) and personal identities. Tajfel (1978) saw group and personal identities as being part of a single continuum; the continuum expressed his intuition (similar to the stance within the CofP framework) that it is unlikely that any identity is defined wholly in interpersonal or intergroup terms. Subsequent work has expressed this interdependence in other ways. Giles and Coupland (1991) represent group and personal identities as orthogonal to one another; Tajfel's basic intuition about the relationship of the interpersonal and the intergroup is shared, but their fundamental distinctiveness is asserted. Turner, too, sees the personal and the group as distinct bases of self-categorization (Turner 1999).

However, a major difference between the CofP and the other constructs lies in how individual style is conceptualized. The CofP framework sees the larger styling of the self as involving the interplay and resolution of an individual's participation in multiple CofPs (Eckert and McConnell-Ginet 1999: 189), while intergroup theory does not see membership in a group to be necessarily part of a broader enterprise of self-styling. The classic definition of a speech community, of course, says little about the relationship between an individual's personal and group identities. Labov's observation that in New York City it may be difficult "to distinguish . . . a casual salesman from a careful pipefitter" (1972: 240) makes some connection between personal, stylistic variation and social or class-based variation, but there is no onus to explain how the dimensions casual–careful and blue collar–white collar are defined by members of the speech community and how these dimensions might become linked in this way.[1]

Boundaries

Although most of the case studies that follow involve groups in which participation is voluntary, a CofP may not always have members that are actively in control of their membership. For example, the family unit may constitute a CofP (see Hazen, this volume), yet while children are young, the possibilities for opting in and out of membership as parent or child are extremely limited.

The way in which boundaries are maintained can also provide a salient basis for discriminating between the constructs. For instance, competitive opposition to others is a feature of intergroup theory (and critical discourse analysis, discussed further in section 3), but it is not necessarily a feature of the constitution of a CofP. There are some clear examples showing that opposition to other groups is not central to the process of constituting a CofP.

Hall (1996) provides an interesting discussion of how Hindi kinship terms are co-opted by the hijra community in Banaras (northeast India) and are used to denote relationships particular to the hijras' community (hijras are people who were born biologically male but in various ways construct female identites for themselves). So, for example, it is the practice among the hijras to use Hindi /beï/ "daughter" to denote a hijra's disciple. Hijras' practice of metaphorically using these terms is not technically in opposition to the practices of the larger Hindi-speaking community; rather, this practice of lexical appropriation involves mapping from the domain of Hindi usage to a domain constructed by the hijras. (Besnier (1994) makes similar points about lexical appropriation by fakaleitī in Tonga. Fakaleitī are a traditional transgendered category of individuals; comparable categories are found in much of Polynesia.)

Kiesling (2000) also points out that the relationship between language and identity is often an extremely indirect form of indexing (cf. Ochs 1992) through metaphor and irony. Kiesling shows that the value of a heterosexual masculinity is often subtly reified through mocking and allusion in a group of fraternity members.

Nonetheless, it is often through practices that stand in opposition to those of other groups that the boundaries of a CofP are revealed most clearly. Bucholtz (2000) examines the way women strive to define themselves as competent members of the hacker community among computer users using evidence from the discourses these women employ as a way of presenting themselves in the virtual world on-line. Through these practices, the feminist identities they construct for themselves are placed in (sometimes sharp and explicit) contrast to other discourses of feminism and other feminist identities that the hackers wish to set themselves apart from.

Basis for defining membership in the salient group

The membership and boundaries of a CofP, including whether an individual is a core or peripheral member, are defined on the basis of criteria that are subjectively salient to the members themselves and membership is reciprocally recognized. Membership in a speech community can be defined on externally salient criteria, such as whether or not one lives in a particular region or town. However, it is worth noting that Labov (1972) gave a prominent place to subjective factors too, defining membership in a speech community by shared evaluations of norms. Others' uses of the term have sometimes relied more on externally defined or objective criteria (see Hudson 1980: 25–6 for examples).

Experimental exploration of intergroup principles often arbitrarily assigns participants to a group (e.g. Billig and Tajfel 1973) or highlights characteristics of the participants in the hope that subjects will share the exprimenters' intuition about the salience of those characteristics. Some work on intergroup theory attempts to blend participants' subjective group membership with externally salient criteria (e.g. Noels et al. 1999).

Member's shared goals

A fundamental difference between the CofP, the speech community and intergroup theory lies in the nature of goals shared by co-members. By definition, participants in a CofP are engaged in the satisfaction of some jointly negotiated enterprise. No such requirement exists for defining members of a speech community or of groups in the framework of intergroup theory.

A decision to use the CofP as the basis for analyzing variation does not mean that it is inevitably to be preferred over other frameworks. Eckert (2000) makes it clear that its introduction constitutes an addition to the tool chest, not an attempt to throw out the old tools. The value of the CofP lies in the social information which it highlights and which other constructs may, by virtue of the features just discussed, miss. It explicitly focuses on (1) individuals' social mobility and (2) the negotiated nature of social identities, thereby elucidating ties between abstract social categories and the social groups that people are members of on an everyday basis (Eckert 2000: 40–1). Insightful generalizations involving a social category like gender "are most likely to emerge when gender is examined . . . in interaction with other social variables" (Eckert and McConnell-Ginet 1999: 191).

In the next section, I look at how an analysis of variation that integrates social and linguistic practice helps shape a more textured analysis of abstract categories like gender that we might be interested in.

2   The Community of Practice in the Analysis of Variation and Change

Undoubtedly, the most exemplary exponent and user of the CofP in sociolinguistics has been Penelope Eckert. Not only did Eckert co-author (with Sally McConnell-Ginet) the paper that introduced the term "community of practice" to most sociolinguists (Eckert and McConnell-Ginet 1992a, 1992b; see also the developments in Eckert and McConnell-Ginet 1999) but in addition she has done more than any one other linguist to show how contextualizing linguistic variation within a larger picture of individuals' social behavior enriches the overall analysis. What makes Eckert's body of work particularly valuable is the fact that she so comprehensively satisfies two important goals for any sociolinguist.

First, she demonstrates how analyzing variation within speakers' CofPs advances the sociolinguist's goal of better understanding the social significance of linguistic variation. Eckert shows how linguistic variation fits coherently into the picture of speakers' broader social patterns. The analysis of variation does not occur independently of the analysis of other social facts, because the sociolinguistic variants themselves do not exist independently of other behavioral variants. An important corollary of this is that linguistic style shifting is neither a function of the attention speakers pay to their speech (cf. Labov 1972), nor of their attention to social characteristics of the addressee or audience (cf. Giles' 1973; Gallois et al.'s 1995 accommodation theory, and Bell 1984). Instead, linguistic style is part and parcel of speakers' work to construct a social identity (or identities), which is meaningful to themselves and to others.

The second task that Eckert tackles is answering the question: how best to understand the relation between variation at the level of the individual and variation across large and heterogeneous groups? Her work on variation neatly illustrates how macro-level categories like social class emerge, are sometimes contested and sometimes maintained, through the actions of individuals (see Bucholtz 2000, discussed above, for a good example of such contestation). Variation "has to do with concrete places, people, styles, and issues. At the same time, these concrete local things are what constitute broad cultural categories such as gender, class, ethnicity, region" (Eckert 2000: 4). The meanings associated with variants at the most local level do not, Eckert points out, emerge "with no relation to larger social patterns" (2000: 24).

One hazard of focusing on practices in highly local groups like CofPs is that it potentially leads to positions of extreme relativism, for instance, as Dubois and Horvath (1999) suggest, generating results that cannot be used for further generalization. However, by grounding the use of the CofP in the broader goals of sociolinguistics, Eckert shows that the CofP framework is not necessarily a Trojan Horse for extreme relativism.

Eckert conducted her research in four high schools in the suburbs of Detroit. Because she wanted to avoid being caught up in the institution of school and the power hierarchies associated with being an adult in the adolescent world of high school, she chose not go into classrooms and not to use teachers as intermediaries in her research. (Recognizing that this left her out of a lot of the important social practices in which kids participate, Eckert has negotiated ways to observe students in class as well as out in her current research in California; see Eckert 1996, Eckert and McConnell-Ginet 1999).

Instead, she wandered the corridors and the courtyards of the school, watching who talked to whom, who wore what and who avoided or congregated in different spaces. In other words, she observed patterns of mutual engagement and shared repertoires and practices (both verbal and non-verbal). Gradually, she got to know the students and started out by asking them if they would agree to chat about themselves and who their friends were while she tape-recorded the conversation. The taped conversations were supplemented by observations and note-taking about practices as diverse as what kinds of jeans the students wore, how they carried their cigarettes (if they smoked), whether they walked across or around the school's central courtyard and what other school activities (academic, athletic, social) they participated in. With some of the students she had further follow-up conversations, so the amount of speech, and to a large extent the topics covered, were not controlled by Eckert.

In some other studies of variation an attempt is made to control the topics covered; when researchers make this effort it is usually because they believe it will enable them to isolate the effects of specific, objectively identified social variables. That is, they hope that by controlling variation in the topics speakers discuss, they will strengthen any subsequent claims about the effects attributable to differences in, for example, speakers' class or sex. Controlling content and amount of speech is not a concern for the analyst working with CofPs. The CofP is not intended to be treated as an independent variable, like class or ethnicity in other studies. Rather, by studying the ways in which the students participated in a variety of social practices, the CofPs that Eckert identified ultimately help to shed light on the meaning of more objectively identifiable social categories like class and gender. In this way, she shows that the use of CofPs in the analysis of variation and change is not "to dispense with global categories, but to attach them to personal and community experience in such a way that the structure of variation makes everyday sense" (Eckert 2000: 222).

In one respect, what Eckert is saying here is that this approach to data collection and analysis is a constructive response to the feeling that the way social dialectologists often divide up a "speech community", masks salient aspects of individual variation. Horvath (1985), for example, reanalyzed some of Labov's (1972) data from the New York City survey and showed that generalizations about style based on speaker sex masked some men's adherence to more standard-like norms. She noted that this meant that some salient information about the social factors defining the notion of a "standard" was missed. Similarly, in a study of the English spoken in Porirua (New Zealand), it was found that grouping all women together on the basis of sex (or even separating them on the basis of ethnicity) obscured the influence of social contact between some young Pakeha (European) women with Maori or Polynesian men. Linguistic practices (variables) generally found more often in the speech of Maori men were more likely to be a part of the young Pakeha women's repertoire than of older Pakeha women's speaking styles (Holmes 1997; Meyerhoff 1994).

In the course of her investigations (interviews with 200 students, eventually culled to 69 for detailed analysis) Eckert found, for instance, that in the Detroit suburbs, adolescents formed three major groups while in high school: jocks, who identified with school values and participated most actively in the activities sponsored by the high school; and burnouts, whose most significant social ties and aspirations were often shared with the urban and more working-class culture of Detroit city, and who chose not to participate in the activities that generally measure success in school. Finally, there were a large number of students who defined themselves negatively in terms of these polarized groups. The so-called "in-betweens" participated to a greater or lesser extent in the school-based activities associated with the jocks, and the external activities (such as cruising certain areas between their home suburb and Detroit) associated with burnouts. The heart of Eckert's most recent work (Eckert 2000) lies in elucidating the complex relationship between individuals' participation in practices associated with these groups – their shared repertoire of social practices defining them as more or less prototypical or core members of those groups – and their linguistic practices. The links she establishes shed light on the process by which other, larger social categories such as gender are understood and maintained or contested.

The high schools Eckert studied were located in an area in which a major vowel shift is taking place (for information on the Northern Cities Chain Shift, see Gordon, this volume). She examined both the relative frequency with which the teenagers she interviewed used innovative and conservative variants of the vowels undergoing the shift, and also the same teenagers' participation in practices that serve as other indices of social innovation or conservatism. By employing this bifurcated approach, Eckert could show that the high school students who used the most innovative forms of newer variables in the vowel shift (backing of the vowels in *cut* and *bet* and raising of the nucleus in *bite*) were also the speakers who participated in other social practices that positioned them beyond the pale of conservative norms of the school (and sometimes the wider community too). These were, in many cases, the so-called "burned out burnout" girls, that is, girls who were identified as extreme exemplars of the social category of burnouts. Eckert found that their linguistic flamboyance (i.e. their more frequent use of innovative variants of the newer variables) was accompanied by other flamboyant displays. In addition to the way they talked, their makeup, clothes and ways of finding fun outside of school also indicated their distance from, or rejection of, conservative norms. In other words, having a cutting edge personal style was linked to being the kind of person who defines and leads in the diffusion of linguistic innovations.

Similarly, Eckert (1996) discusses the social significance of emphatic, low, back tokens of short *a* before nasals. Use of this variant before nasals sets Latina girls in northern California apart from the non-Latino tendency to raise short *a* in this environment. But Eckert noted that the girl who produced the most extreme forms of this variant also tended to engage in other behaviors which established her as a leader in other domains, particularly as being savvy and forward with boys. In this case, you could say that the shared enterprise of the CofP lies in defining the social roles of trend-setter, follower or those who opt out and the hierarchy attendant on that social structure.

Of course, these indicators are not equally salient or meaningful to all observers. But within the larger community of practice of the Detroit high school or the California elementary school their significance was clear. There, both the fact that some speakers actively participate in even the incipient changes of a vowel shift, and that others choose not to participate in the shifts until they have acquired significance in the community/ies outside the school, are understood as part of a more general pattern of participation in practices that confer status or prestige in the school or the society in which the school is located.

Use of the CofP framework allows this nexus to be highlighted. It also enables us to focus on the way an innovation is coined, crystallized and begins to spread because it focuses on the negotiation of meaning based on individual praxis.

In the same spirit, Mendoza-Denton (1997) and Bucholtz (1999) have found the CofP framework useful for studying how linguistic variation relates to other practices in which adolescents participate, shaping their personal and group identity in school and beyond. Mendoza-Denton showed that the extent to which speakers participate in vowel shifts taking place in California is but one way of demonstrating their social position in wider social networks. Selection of linguistic variants correlates with speakers' dress and fashion sensibilities and their decision to be involved in different local gangs.

Bucholtz (1999) shows how a small group of determinedly uncool girls differentiate themselves from the other kids in their high school through a range of social practices. These girls fail to participate quite so actively in the ongoing California vowel shifts (especially fronting of the vowels in *boot* and *boat*). This sets them off from cool students, who use fronted variants much more frequently, and the girls she studied bolstered their distance from whatever defines coolness by developing a repertoire of other practices that cool students seldom participate in, e.g. demonstrating a taste for reading and verbal play.

Studies of the phenomenon known as "crossing" (after Rampton 1995) have frequently been conducted with a sensibility close to that underlying the CofP even if the researchers do not themselves invoke the term CofP. Cutler (1996), for instance, is a case study of Mike, a white New York teenager who (with a group of friends, who are also white) consciously adopts the vocabulary and (with more limited success) the phonology and syntax associated with black hip-hop culture. Cutler places Mike's linguistic behavior in the context of other practices that indicate an affiliation with or desire to be identified with hip-hop culture, such as the clothes the group members wear, the music they listen to, and some of the ways they occupy themselves as a group in their spare time.

Fought (1999a, 1999b) examines variation in the English of Hispanic high school students in Los Angeles. She presents her study in a classic quantitative paradigm, yet when she analyzes patterns of variation she locates frequent use of, e.g., a fronted *boot* vowel (1999a) or negative concord (1999b), in the context of other social information. She shows that the teenagers who form groups solely based on their linguistic behavior also group together through their participation in other practices. These practices cohere more meaningfully among the teenagers themselves than they do in the wider community. Amongst these teenagers, Fought found that their regular mutual engagement led to a focus on distinctions that depended on the extent to which individuals participated in gang-related activities or were members of graffiti tagging crews. Fought also found that another salient group in the high school was teenagers who were parents. This group, largely invisible beyond the high school CofP, worked actively to construct an identity distinct from other groups in the school. They succeeded in this by negotiating distinct patterns of social behavior and by actively highlighting their special interests and concerns (which they discussed openly with Fought) but they also, less consciously, patterned together in their use of the linguistic variables examined. That is, their shared repertoire helped satisfy a (conscious or unconscious) goal of setting themselves apart from the other groups in the high school.

Although the CofP may seem to apply most productively to the analysis of variation among adolescents (we noted earlier Bergvall's (1999) suggestion that this related to the importance of developing self-image for this group), there is no inherent reason why its usefulness should be limited to this age group. It may prove to be true, as Eckert and McConnell-Ginet suggest (1999: 189), that some of the CofPs we belong to in our youth have especially strong and perseverative effects on our verbal styling, but the business of constructing a social identity for ourselves hardly finishes after adolescence. Throughout adulthood, we continue to participate in a variety of CofPs (both as expert, core members and peripheral, neophyte members). These present the possibility of strengthening existing identifications and redefining ourselves with new ones as Wenger's (1998) and Holmes' (1998, 2000) workplace studies so clearly demonstrate.

A major benefit of the recent interest in the notion of the CofP is that it restores an emphasis on relating large-scale, quantitative analyses to the micro-level practices of the groups of speakers being studied, very much in the spirit of Labov's analysis of variation on Martha's Vineyard (1972). Dubois and Horvath's (1998, 1999) discussion of language variation among Louisiana Cajuns is particularly compelling because of the way they approach this synthesis. They link speakers' use of variants of the (th) and (dh) variables and voiceless stops with their participation in other social practices. Users of variants that are strongly indexed as Cajun also engage in other practices marked as Cajun, such as learning and playing Cajun music, or maintaining a household where tasks and roles are divided along traditional Cajun lines (Dubois and Horvath 1999).

Their work also reminds us that practices pursued within a CofP may be reinforced by external factors such as others' expectations. They point out that being identified as "Cajun" in Lousisiana nowadays sometimes translates into important economic opportunities in an otherwise depressed region. So using variants that are strong markers of Cajun-ness and playing Cajun music help define a speaker as authentically Cajun, but ironically the significance of these practices as *ingroup* markers has been ratcheted up by *external* factors such as the rewards of catering to tourists' expectations or demands (Dubois and Horvath 1998).

To date, the CofP as a domain of analysis has been adopted most wholeheartedly by researchers working on language and gender, and a survey of the proceedings from the Berkeley Women and Language Group conferences shows that the CofP has broad currency in the study of gender (a number of the studies in these collections explore the cultural construction of gender via practices that are not linguistic; see also *Language in Society*, vol. 28, no. 2, and Bucholtz et al. 1999). I think there are a number of reasons for the apparent specialization of the CofP in language and gender studies. As is often the case, the reasons have perhaps as much to do with the history of the science as the philosophical underpinnings of the theory. Historically, the CofP was first introduced to sociolinguists in the context of language and gender research (Eckert and McConnell-Ginet 1992a, 1992b). Presented to this audience, the CofP gained a sympathetic ear; the CofP was attractive to gender researchers because it provides a useful framework for exploring gender as a learned (and consequently, mutable) social category, rather than a categorial primitive. This perspective is enticing for gender theorists for several reasons. First, it immediately foregrounds the likelihood of there being considerable differences in how the notion of "being a woman" or "being a man" is constructed among any aggregate of individuals. Second, it makes clear the possibility or even inevitability of these notions being constructed differently across a person's life span, through participation in different practices.[2] Third, cross-cultural variability in what constitutes gendered practices is also highlighted.

In theory, there is no reason why these advantages should not be as attractive to researchers on the linguistic construction of age and aging, or ethnicity, but in fact, less research has focused on these constructs within the CofP framework (though some studies investigating the linguistic construction of ethnicity were mentioned above; cf. also Foster 1995). Of course, since a tenet of the CofP approach is that categories like "Japanese," "woman" or "grand-parent" cannot be handled atomistically, even a study focusing principally on gendered practices inevitably tells you something about what it might mean to be, e.g., a Hispanic teenage mother with former gang affiliations (as Fought's work does).

Again, it is perhaps a historical accident that relatively little work within the CofP framework has studied the social construction of age and how this relates to agism. There is a vigorous and extremely productive program among social psychologists examining these topics but the focus of these studies is rather different to the focus you would expect to find if CofPs were taken as the starting point for analysis. The social psychology research has focused on how people talk to the elderly, and how they interpret the utterances of older speakers (or apparently older speakers, in the case of matched guise experiments). A number of studies (e.g. Ryan et al. 1995, Giles et al. 1994, Harwood and Giles 1996, Harwood 2000) have examined patronizing modes of talk directed at elders, younger people's interpretations of such patronizing talk, and younger people's attitudes towards talk produced by elders. This research strongly suggests that what these patronizing speech patterns do is construct an identity for the elderly that associates age with qualities such as confusion, incompetence, enfeeblement, and asexuality.

In other words, this research takes the reverse perspective of the CofP. Instead of foregrounding speaker agency and the relationship between the social construction of *self* through speech (and other) behaviors, this research scrutinizes on how *others* construct identities for us.

Even though the CofP highlights speaker agency (by contrast with, e.g., the speech community), some interesting work has been done within the CofP framework exploring how individuals' identities interact with and may be shaped by other CofPs. Freed (1999) looks at how pregnant women (who do not constitute a CofP themselves by all three criteria), struggle to develop individual identities for themselves and their pregnancies in the face of contact with the practices of members of other CofPs, such as doctors and midwives. Their practices attempt to impose certain standards or reify norms related to more general ideologies about pregnancy and pregnant women on the trajectory of individual women's experiences. Freed's study draws attention to the fact that practices engaged in by members of a CofP may be contentious and externally problematized (as the individual women she interviewed attempted to problematize and oppose practices they encountered by the people caring for them). I think the resistance Freed documents shows how important the work of maintaining boundaries is for a strong and vital CofP like doctors.

In a similar vein, Ehrlich (1999) looks at how the communicative practices, or shared repertoire, which members of a sexual harassment tribunal engage in, manage to compete with the way two female university students represent experiences in which they were the victims of date rape. The tribunal members' discursive practices constructed an alternative view of the women's roles.

Because the tribunal members shared certain assumptions (cf. Wenger's characteristic features of a CofP, above) about what constitutes reasonable behavior under the circumstances of the complaints, and because the tribunal members shared questioning practices that reified these assumptions, they managed to effectively recast the salient identity of the women complainants as architects of their own misfortune, not as victims of fear and assault.

Up to this point, this part of the chapter has principally dwelt on how the CofP informs the analysis of variation. I turn briefly now to discuss its usefulness in the longitudinal analysis of language change.

As has already been intimated, Eckert (2000) provides perhaps the clearest exposition of how the CofP framework can inform the study of language change. She proposes that synchronic, individual variation is transformed, or mapped, into community-wide, diachronic processes of change. Eckert hypothesizes that as the fact that these linguistic variables have social significance crystallizes, they become available to be transformed into indices of categories that are salient in the wider communities affected by the NCCS. So, for example, because use of backed variants of the vowel in *bet* comes to be associated with burnouts in the high school CofP, and because the jocks' reaction to this is to begin to use lowered variants of the *bet* vowel (Eckert 2000: 120–1), the variable becomes marked as one whose variants are socially salient. Ultimately, as this significance becomes more widely recognized, or as the high school students mature and disperse into other CofPs as adults, the variants may map onto social categories that are more salient in the larger speceh community, such as regional origin, class, or ethnicity. This is how Eckert shows that the description of micro-level stylistic innovations is essential for an understanding of the macro-level phenomena of linguistic change.

Riley (1996), too, looks at language change, and her analysis is sympathetic with the CofP. She outlines a situation of language simplification and incipient language loss in the Marquesas (southeast Pacific). Her work there shows that shifts in social practices are having an effect on the linguistic landscape. Marquesan is increasingly being marginalized as a language of the home, instead acquiring status as a men's argot.[3] In the Marquesas, Riley reports that women are using Marquesan in an increasingly restricted set of interactional domains. More and more, they use French, which they see as giving their children a head start in future competition for socially and economically rewarding occupations. Younger girls are also actively contributing to the shift towards French, because they tend to be oriented more towards school (which is conducted in French) than boys are (though the outcome is a somewhat creolized form of the language. See Sankoff, this volume, for more on creolization and language change). Boys, on the other hand, continue to have to participate in some of the practices and routines that traditionally defined a masculine identity, and these activities also give them greater exposure to Marquesan. Since the language continues to be used more generally as a means of communication by men, and because it has also acquired an association with gendered exclusion, this means that girls and boys have quite different competency in Marquesan. This, in turn, has social effects. Most older members of the community have limited or no French. With girls choosing to target French and being excluded from practices that foster competency in Marquesan, this means that girls' interactions with older members of the community are increasingly problematic and subject to miscommunication.

Simon (2000) has also begun to explore the use of the CofP construct in a historical case of language loss. She examines the shift to English by several immigrant communities who moved to Michigan in the late nineteenth and early twentieth centuries seeking work in the copper mines. It remains to be seen whether the CofP contributes much insight into the interaction of social and linguistic processes when researchers are restricted to using archival materials.

3   The Community of Practice in Broader Perspective

In the previous sections, I canvassed some aspects of the speech community, social networks, and intergroup theory that the CofP stands as an alternative to. In this final section, I attempt to place the CofP in a somewhat broader perspective, showing how the concerns and research questions of the CofP are a link in a much longer chain of humanist theory and discourse. I hope that by explaining the origins and current uses of the CofP, I can also indicate the potential that the construct might have for the future.

Similarities with a number of theories and methodologies in the social sciences are immediately apparent. Clearly, the CofP approach is much influenced by the methods and sensibilities of (linguistic) anthropology. In addition, the centrality it places on the notion of shared experience and negotiated social meaning shares a good deal with theories of language in some other fields, for example, some of the theories of intercultural communication such as Cronen's Co-ordinated Management of Meaning (Cronen et al. 1988) or Gudykunst's (1995) Uncertainty Reduction Theory. Latour and Woolgar (1979) also emphasizes the manner in which meaning is derived through practices, with the provocative addendum that inanimate objects centrally involved in social practices might also be considered participants. But the CofP has even deeper roots in the history of the humanities.

In some respects, the emphasis on analyzing language within a very local, practice-based framework as an alternative to large-scale, quantitative studies of the speech community is the daughter of a tension between positivism and relativism that goes back to at least the seventeenth century. Berlin (1997a) discusses a number of features of the Counter-Enlightenment movement that took hold in Europe in the late seventeenth and early eighteenth centuries. There are some remarkable similarities between the discourse emerging out of the tension between the Enlightenment and Counter-Enlightenment philosophers and some of the discussion born of the tension between the more positivist (quantitative) approaches to sociolinguistics and the more relativistic (qualitative) approaches. Tensions between the Enlightenment ideal of establishing an objective and universal means of expressing human experience and the Counter-Enlightenment's rejection of this as a goal – its emphasis instead on the situated and particular nature of human behavior – seem similar to discussions among sociolinguists about what kind of information is forfeited by different approaches to the study of variation. The challenge for sociolinguistics is the one that the Counter-Enlightenment movement chose not to accept: how to specify the manner in which the particular becomes or relates to the general or universal. As Eckert and Dubois and Horvath have shown, we can begin to meet the task if we employ a catholic enough approach.

Berlin credits the Italian philosopher Giambattista Vico (1688–1744) with having been the first to seriously explore these differences and it was Vico too who appears to have first perceived the long-term significance of them. Vico held that knowledge of what happened, to what, and in what order, may constitute a sufficient and necessary method for understanding the natural sciences, but he claimed that when you come to try and understand things that relate to humans, individuals, and societies, such disembodied knowledge is no longer sufficient. Vico argued that in order to understand events that occur at the human level, the researcher must foster a degree of empathy with the subject of her or his investigation. This methodological distinction may have been original to Vico, and Vico's observation of this distinction may date the start of separate empirical paths of development for the sciences and the humanities (Berlin 1997b: 357). Vico clearly saw the study of language as falling into the latter category, which he called New Science. "Language . . . [is a form] of self-expression, of wishing to convey what one is and strives for", according to Vico (Berlin 1997a: 246–7). Consequently, no matter how superficially similar cultures might appear, or how similar groups' practices within a culture might appear, Vico believed that cross-comparison was not possible.[4]

Each culture or set of practices was the unique product of the unique circumstances in which it arose. In order to understand a culture or a set of practices, Vico believed it was first and foremost necessary to gain a full understanding of the historical and contemporary setting in which the object of study played itself out. One might say, it is necessary to gain a full understanding of the community in which any given practice acquires meaning.

So by way of conclusion, let me suggest that the CofP, as an attempt to inform the general through the study of the particular, is not only an attempt to theorize the social as fully as the linguistic; it is also an attempt to achieve something more fundamental and more ambitious. To the extent that it successfully provides a model for satisfying all goals for the study of variation and change, it offers the hope of successfully bridging a rift between western scientific approaches that, arguably, has yawned for several hundred years.

ACKNOWLEDGMENTS

I thank Sally McConnell-Ginet, Marisol Del Tesso, and Janet Holmes for insightful and challenging discussion of the use of and theory behind the community of practice construct. Their comments have very much informed my thoughts on this topic, though they are not to be held responsible for the manner in which I formulate them in this chapter. This chapter is dedicated to Mary Cresswell and Ruth-Mary Beach who so lovingly held Sam in order that it could be written.

NOTES

1 Santa Ana and Parodi's (1998) notion of nested speech communities attempts to marry speakers' multiplicity of identities with the basic notion of the speech community, thereby bringing the intent (if not the terminology) of speech community theory and the praxis-based theory of the CofP closer together (see Patrick, this volume).

2 The possibility or even likelihood of such change across the life span presents a potential challenge to the notion of studying change through the apparent-time construct. However, the validity of the apparent-time construct for some variables does not mean all variables are necessarily amenable to this form of analysis (see Bailey, this volume).

3 Riley's work is reminiscent of Nichols' (1983) on women's shift away from Gullah and toward English on a Georgia island community and Gal's (1979) on the community-wide shift from Hungarian to German in an Austrian village.

4 A major implication of Vico's position for linguists is that he rejected entirely the notion that one could describe the world in some purely logical form – language for Vico was quintessentially a product of the users and their environment (Berlin 1997a: 248). Gottfried Herder made similar arguments. Like Vico, Herder stressed that in order to truly understand something we have to understand the basis of its uniqueness and singularity. To do so, requires a degree of empathy (or *Einfühlung*) that is generally excluded or marginalized from positivist modes of inquiry (Berlin 1997a: 253).

REFERENCES

Bell, Allan (1984). Language style as audience design. *Language in Society* 13: 145–204.

Bergvall, Victoria L. (1999). Toward a comprehensive theory of language and gender. *Language in Society* 28: 273–93.

Berlin, Isaiah (1997a [1979]). The Counter-Enlightenment. In *The Proper Study of Mankind: An*

Anthology of Essays. New York: Farrar, Straus and Giroux. 243–68.

Berlin, Isaiah (1997b [1979]). The divorce between the sciences and the humanities. In *The Proper Study of Mankind: An Anthology of Essays*. New York: Farrar, Straus and Giroux. 326–58.

Besnier, Niko (1994). Polynesian gender liminality in time and space. In Gilbert Herdt (ed.), *Third Sex, Third Gender: Beyond Sexual Dimorphism in Culture and History*. New York: Zone Books. 285–328.

Billig, Michael and Henri Tajfel (1973). Social categorization and similarity in intergroup behaviour. *European Journal of Social Psychology* 3: 27–52.

Bucholtz, Mary (1999). "Why be normal?" Language and identity practices in a community of nerd girls. *Language in Society* 28: 203–23.

Bucholtz, Mary (2000). Geek feminism. Paper presented at the first International Gender and Language Association conference, Stanford University, May.

Bucholtz, Mary, A. C. Liang and Laurel A. Sutton (1999). *Reinventing Identities: The Gendered Self in Discourse*. Oxford: Oxford University Press.

Castellano, Marisa (1996). Building community across different belief systems: An ethnographically informed perspective on the role of narrative and dialogue. In Natasha Warner, Jocelyn Ahlers, Leela Bilmes, Monica Oliver, Suzanne Wertheim and Melinda Chen (eds.), *Gender and Belief Systems: Proceedings of the Third Berkeley Women and Language Conference*. Berkeley, CA: Berkeley Women and Language Group. 133–43.

Cronen, Vernon E., Victoria Chen and W. Barnett Pearce (1988). Coordinated management of meaning: A critical theory. In Yun Kim Young and William B. Gudykunst (eds.), *International and Intercultural Communication Annual*, vol. 12: *Theories in Intercultural Communication*. Newbury Park, CA: Sage. 66–98.

Cutler, Cecilia (1996). Yorkville Crossing: A case study of the influence of Hip Hop culture on the speech of a white middle class adolescent. *University of Pennsylvania Working Papers in Linguistics* 4, 1: 371–97.

Dubois, Sylvia and Barbara Horvath (1998). Let's tink about dat: Interdental fricatives in Cajun English. *Language Variation and Change* 10: 246–61.

Dubois, Sylvie and Barbara Horvath (1999). When the music changes, you change too: Gender and language change in Cajun English. *Language Variation and Change* 11: 287–313.

Eckert, Penelope (1996). Vowels and nail polish: The emergence of linguistic style in the preadolescent heterosexual marketplace. In Natasha Warner, Jocelyn Ahlers, Leela Bilmes, Monica Oliver, Suzanne Wertheim, and Melinda Chen (eds.), *Gender and Belief Systems: Proceedings of the Third Berkeley Women and Language Conference*. Berkeley, CA: Berkeley Women and Language Group. 183–90.

Eckert, Penelope (2000). *Linguistic Variation as Social Practice*. Oxford: Blackwell Publishers.

Eckert, Penelope and Sally McConnell-Ginet (1992a). Think practically and look locally: Language and gender as community-based practice. *Annual Review of Anthropology* 21: 461–90.

Eckert, Penelope and Sally McConnell-Ginet (1992b). Communities of practice: Where language, gender, and power all live. In Kira Hall, Mary Bucholtz and Birch

Moonwomon (eds.), *Locating Power: Proceedings of the Second Berkeley Women and Language Conference.* Berkeley, CA: Berkeley Women and Language Group. 89–99.

Eckert, Penelope and Sally McConnell-Ginet (1999). New generalizations and explanations in language and gender research. *Language in Society* 28: 185–201.

Ehrlich, Susan (1999). Communities of practice, gender, and the representation of sexual assault. *Language in Society* 28: 239–56.

Foster, Michèle (1995). "Are you with me?" Power and solidarity in the discourse of African American women. In Kira Hall and Mary Bucholtz (eds.), *Gender Articulated: Language and the socially constructed self.* New York/London: Routledge. 329–50.

Fought, Carmen (1999a). A majority sound change in a minority community: /u/-fronting in Chicano English. *Journal of Sociolinguistics* 3: 5–23.

Fought, Carmen (1999b). "I'm not from nowhere": Negative concord in Chicano English. Paper presented at NWAV 28, Toronto, Canada.

Freed, Alice F. (1999). Communities of practice and pregnant women: Is there a connection? *Language and Society* 28: 257–71.

Gal, Susan (1979). *Language Shift: Social Determinants of Linguistic Change in Bilingual Austria.* New York: Academic Press.

Gallois, Cynthia, Howard Giles, Elizabeth Jones, Aaron C. Cargile and Hiroshi Ota (1995). Accommodating intercultural encounters: Elaborations and extensions. In Richard L. Wiseman (ed.), *International and Intercultural Communication Annual*, vol. 19: *Intercultural Communication Theory.* Thousand Oaks, CA: Sage. 115–47.

Giles, Howard (1973). Accent mobility: A model and some data. *Linguistic Anthropology.* 15: 87–105.

Giles, Howard and Nikolas Coupland (1991). *Language: Contexts and Consequences.* Pacific Grove, CA: Brooks/Cole.

Giles, Howard, Susan Fox, Jake Harwood, and Angie Williams (1994). Talking age and aging talk: Communicating through the life-span. In Mary Lee Hummert, John M. Wiemann and Jon F. Nussbaum (eds.), *Interpersonal Communication and Older Adulthood: Interdisciplinary Theory and Research.* Newbury Park, CA: Sage. 130–61.

Gudykunst, William B. (1995). Anxiety/uncertainty management (AUM) theory. In Richard L. Wiseman (ed.), *International and Intercultural Communication Annual*, vol. 19: *Intercultural Communication Theory.* Thousand Oaks, CA: Sage. 8–58.

Hall, Kira (1996). Lexical subversion in the *hijra* community. In Natasha Warner, Jocelyn Ahlers, Leela Bilmes, Monica Oliver, Suzanne Wertheim and Melinda Chen (eds.), *Gender and Belief Systems: Proceedings of the Third Berkeley Women and Language Conference.* Berkeley, CA: Berkeley Women and Language Group. 279–91.

Harwood, Jake (2000). "SHARP!" Lurking incoherence in a television portrayal of an older adult. *Journal of Language and Social Psychology* 19: 110–40.

Harwood, Jake and Howard Giles (1996). Reactions to older people being patronized: The roles of response strategies and attributed thoughts. *Journal of Language and Social Psychology* 15: 395–421.

Holmes, Janet (1997). Setting new standards: Sound changes and gender in New Zealand English. *English Wolrd-Wide* 18: 107–42.

Holmes, Janet (1998). Analysing power at work: an analytical framework. Paper presented at the Sixth International Conference on Language and Social Psychology. University of Ottawa. Ottawa, Ontario. [Published as an ERIC Clearinghouse on Languages and Linguistics document. ED 414 733, FL 024 823.]

Holmes, Janet (2000). Having a laugh at work: how humour contributes to workplace culture. Paper presented at the Seventh International Conference on Language and Social Psychology. Cardiff University, Wales.

Holmes, Janet and Miriam Meyerhoff (1999). The Community of Practice: Theories and methodologies in language and gender research. *Language in Society* 28: 173–83.

Holmes, Janet, Maria Stubbe, and Bernadette Vine (1999). Constructing professional identity: "Doing power" in policy units. In Srikant Sarangi and Celia Roberts (eds.), *Talk, Work and Institutional Order: Discourse in Medical, Mediation and Management Settings*. Berlin and NewYork: Mouton de Gruyter. 351–85.

Horvath, Barbara (1985). *Variation in Australian English*. Cambridge: Cambridge University Press.

Hudson, R. A. (1980). *Sociolinguistics*. Cambridge: Cambridge University Press.

Kiesling, Scott F. (2000). Playing the straight man: Displaying and maintaining male heterosexuality in discourse. Paper presented at the first International Gender and Language Association conference, Stanford University, May 2000.

Labov, William (1972). *Sociolinguistic Patterns*. Philadelphia: University of Pennsylvania Press.

Latour, Bruno and Steve Woolgar (1979). *Laboratory Life: The Social Construction of Scientific Facts*. Beverly Hills, CA: Sage.

Lave, Jean and Etienne Wenger (1991). *Situated Learning: Legitimate Peripheral Participation*. Cambridge: Cambridge University Press.

Mendoza-Denton, Norma (1997). Chicana/Mexicana Identity and Linguistic Variation: An Ethnographic and Sociolinguistic Study of Gang Affiliation in an Urban High School. Ph.D. dissertation. Department of Linguistics, Stanford University.

Meyerhoff, Miriam (1994). "Sounds pretty ethnic eh?" – a pragmatic particle in New Zealand English. *Language in Society* 23: 367–88.

Meyerhoff, Miriam (1999). *Sorry* in the Pacific: Defining communities, defining practices. *Language in Society* 28: 225–38.

Milroy, James (1992). Social network and prestige arguments in sociolinguistics. In Kingsley Bolton and Helen Kwok (eds.), *Sociolinguistics Today: International perspectives*. London and New York: Routledge. 146–62.

Milroy, Lesley (1987). *Language and Social Networks*. 2nd edn. Oxford: Blackwell Publishers.

Nichols, Patricia C. (1983). Linguistic options and choices for Black women in the Rural South. In Barrie Thorne, Cheris Kramarae and Nancy Henley (eds.), *Language, Gender and Society*. Cambridge, MA: Newbury House. 54–68.

Noels, Kimberly, Richard Clement and Luc G. Pelletier (1999). Perceptions of teachers' communicative style and students' intrinsic and extrinsic motivation. *The Modern Language Journal* 83: 23–34.

Ochs, Elinor (1992). Indexing gender. In Alessandro Duranti and Charles

Goodwin (eds.), *Rethinking Context: Language as an Interactive Phenomenon*. Cambridge: Cambridge University Press. 335–58.

Rampton, Ben (1995). *Crossing: Language and Ethnicity Among Adolescents*. Harlow, UK: Longman.

Riley, Kathleen C. (1996). Engendering miscommunication in the Marquesas, French Polynesia. In Natasha Warner, Jocelyn Ahlers, Leela Bilmes, Monica Oliver, Suzanne Wertheim and Melinda Chen (eds.), *Gender and Belief Systems: Proceedings of the Third Berkeley Women and Language Conference*. Berkeley, CA: Berkeley Women and Language Group. 623–32.

Ryan, Ellen Bouchard, Mary Lee Hummert and L. H. Boich (1995). Communication predicaments of aging: Patronizing behavior towards older adults. *Journal of Language and Social Psychology* 14: 144–66.

Santa Ana, Otto and Claudia Parodi (1998). Modeling the speech community: Configurations and variable types in the Mexican Spanish setting. *Language in Society* 27: 23–51.

Simon, Beth Lee (2000). The practices of gender in the acquisition of literacy. Paper presented at the first International Gender and Language Association conference, Stanford University, May.

Tajfel, Henri (1978). Interindividual behaviour and intergroup behaviour. In Henri Tajfel (ed.), *Differentiation between Social Groups: Studies in the Social Psychology of Intergroup Relations*. London and New York: Academic Press. 27–60.

Turner, John C. (1999). Some current issues in research on social identity and self-categorization theories. In Naomi Ellemers, Russell Spears and Bertjan Doosje (eds.), *Social Identity: Context, Commitment, Content*. Oxford: Blackwell. 6–34.

Wenger, Etienne (1998). *Communities of Practice: Learning, Meaning, and Identity*. Cambridge: Cambridge University Press.

22 Social Networks

LESLEY MILROY

An individual's social network is straightforwardly the aggregate of relationships contracted with others, and social network analysis examines the differing structures and properties of these relationships. Such analysis has been applied by variationists fairly extensively over the last two decades or so to explicate informal social mechanisms supporting language varieties specific to particular social groups. Researchers have also addressed the question of how some social groups maintain nonstandard dialects or minority languages, often over centuries, despite pressures (of the kind described by Lippi-Green 1997) to adopt publicly legitimized national languages or varieties.

Social network is better treated as a means of capturing the dynamics underlying speakers' interactional behaviors than as a fixed social category (see Eckert 2000: 1–33 for a discussion of different concepts of "speaker variables" in sociolinguistics). Given that the ties contracted by individuals within and between speech communities may change for many reasons, analysis of change in the operation of the same social network mechanisms which support localized linguistic codes can illuminate the phenomenon of linguistic change. Network-oriented accounts of linguistic change have emerged both in variationist studies of contemporary speech communities, and as post hoc sociohistorical studies of changes completed at earlier stages of the language (Lippi-Green 1989, Milroy 1992, Milroy and Milroy 1985, Nevalainen 2000).

1 The Concept of Social Network

Social network analysis of the kind generally adopted by variationists was developed by social anthropologists mainly during the 1960s and 1970s (see Milroy 1987a, Li 1996, Johnson 1994). Contrary to the assertions of Murray (1993: 162), it is clear from even a cursory reading of the literature that no canonical "real" procedure for analyzing social networks can be identified;

scholars from many different disciplines employ the concept for a range of theoretical and practical reasons. For example, Johnson's (1994) survey alludes to a wide range of approaches within anthropology which hardly overlap with the largely quantitative modes of analysis described by Cochran et al. (1990). This international and interdisciplinary team of scholars is interested in the role of networks in providing support for urban families. Accordingly, their methods are to a great extent driven by a concern with social policy and practice.

Personal social networks are always seen as contextualized within a macro-level social framework, which is "bracketed off" for purely methodological reasons – i.e. to focus on less abstract modes of analysis capable of accounting more immediately for the variable behavior of individuals. Since no one claims that personal network structure is independent of broader social, economic, or political frameworks constraining individual behavior, a social network analysis of language variation does not compete with an analysis in terms of a macro-level concept such as social class.

A fundamental postulate of network analysis is that individuals create personal communities which provide a meaningful framework for solving the problems of daily life (Mitchell 1986: 74). These personal communities are constituted by interpersonal ties of different types and strengths, and structural relationships between links can vary. Particularly, the persons to whom ego is linked may also be tied to each other to varying degrees – ego being the person who, for analytic reasons, forms the "anchor" of the network. A further postulate with particular relevance to language maintenance or change is that structural and content differences between networks impinge critically on the way they directly affect ego. Particularly, if a network consists chiefly of strong ties, and those ties are multiplex or many-stranded, and if the network is also relatively dense – i.e. many of ego's ties are linked to each other – then such a network has the capacity to support its members in both practical and symbolic ways. More negatively, such a network type can impose unwanted and stressful constraints on its members. Thus, we come to the basic point of using network analysis in variationist research. Networks constituted chiefly of strong (dense and multiplex) ties support localized linguistic norms, resisting pressures to adopt competing external norms. By the same token, if these ties weaken conditions favorable to language change are produced. The idealized maximally dense and multiplex network is shown in figure 22.1 in contrast with a loose-knit, uniplex type of network shown in (figure 22.2).

A social network may be seen as a boundless web of ties which reaches out through a whole society, linking people to one another, however remotely. However, interest generally focuses on first-order network ties, constituted by those persons with whom an individual directly interacts. Second-order ties are those to whom the link is indirect, as shown also in figure 22.1. Within the first order zone, it is important for the reasons noted above to distinguish between "strong" and "weak" ties of everyday life – roughly ties which connect friends or kin as opposed to those which connect acquaintances. To supplement the notions of multiplexity and density, Milardo distinguishes "exchange"

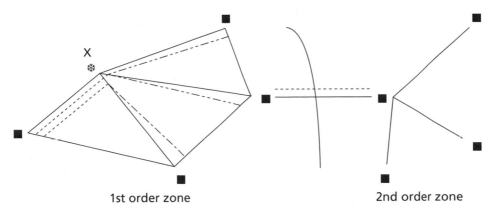

Figure 22.1 High density, multiplex personal network structure, showing first and second order zones

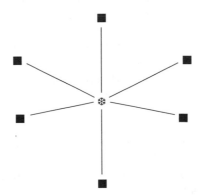

Figure 22.2 Low density, uniplex personal network structure

from "interactive" networks (1988: 26–36). Exchange networks consist of persons such as kin and close friends with whom ego not only interacts regularly, but also exchanges direct aid, advice, criticism, and support. Interactive networks on the other hand consist of persons with whom ego interacts frequently and perhaps over prolonged periods of time, but on whom he or she does not rely for material or symbolic resources. An example of an interactive tie would be that between a store owner and customer. In addition to exchange and interactive ties, Li (1994) distinguishes a "passive" tie, which seems particularly important to migrant or mobile individuals. Passive ties entail an absence of regular contact, but are valued by ego as a source of influence and moral support. Examples are physically distant relatives or friends.

Eckert notes that the people who comprise an individual's personal communities change, as indeed do the everyday problems which such personal communities help to solve (2000: 34). Furthermore, individuals engage on a daily basis in a variety of endeavors in multiple personal communities. Eckert employs the concept of *community of practice*, which is closely related to that of social network, to locate the interactional sites where social meaning is indexed by linguistic elements, and linguistic change and social meaning are co-constructed. A community of practice may be defined as an aggregate of people coming together around a particular enterprise (Eckert 2000: 35), and in her analysis of the social dynamics of language change among Detroit adolescents, Eckert focuses on intersecting clusters of individuals engaged in such enterprises, (2000: 171–212). Such clusters constitute gendered subgroups instantiating the adolescent social categories which participants themselves construct. Network analysis typically does not attend to the identification of such clusters or the enterprises undertaken by members, but deals primarily with the structural and content properties of the ties which constitute egocentric personal networks.

While close-knit networks vary in their degree of approximation to the idealized representation shown in figure 22.1, networks of this type are the interactional site where localized styles and norms of all kinds are constructed. Thus, for example, Eckert (2000: 210) comments that for the high school students she studied, the construction of local styles was "a function of integration into local networks and access to information. The importance of information is clear at the level of clothing style." She goes on to note that "[c]ertain aspects of linguistic style are also negotiated consciously. I can recall explicit discussions in my own high school crowd of 'cool' ways to say things, generally in the form of imitations of cool people. . . . But in general, linguistic influence takes place without explicit comment and all the more requires direct access to speakers. The adoption of a way of speaking, like a way of dressing, no doubt requires both access and entitlement to adopt the style of a particular group" (Eckert 2000: 211). Eckert is here describing very general social mechanisms by which local conventions and norms – of dress, religion, and general behavior, for example – are negotiated and created, and linguistic norms are no exception. Close-knit networks of the kind where this activity takes place are commonly contracted in adolescence. These are the linguistically influential peer groups which are of such interest to sociolinguists attempting to understand the kinds of language change associated with different points in the life span (see Kerswill 1996). However, such networks also flourish in low-status communities (both rural and urban) in the absence of social and geographical mobility and are important in fostering the solidarity ethos associated with the long-term survival of socially disfavored languages and dialects.

2   Social Networks and Language Variation: Methods and Findings

This section reviews some variationist studies which have employed the network concept, and begins by noting that the effect of interpersonal relationships on language choices has been explored for a long time in sociolinguistics; witness Gauchat's (1905) account of variation in the vernacular of the tiny Swiss village of Charmey. Much later, Labov's (1972) sociometric analysis of the relationship between language use and the individual's position in the group resembles in important respects Eckert's account of communities of practice as the sites where linguistic norms and social meaning are co-constructed (see also Cheshire 1982 for a comparable account of language variation in adolescent peer groups). Following an ethnographic, non-quantitative tradition of research which has strongly influenced variationist methods, Gumperz's *Discourse Strategies* (1982) provides an extensive discussion of the effects of changing network structures on language choice in bilingual communities. Chambers (1995) identifies a study carried out in Belfast, Northern Ireland, in the mid-1970s (Milroy and Milroy 1978, Milroy 1987a) as the first systematic account of the relationship between language variation and social network structure in the variationist literature. In this section, I discuss some of the major methods and findings of this research, before reviewing three later studies which take it as a point of departure.

An ethnographically-oriented data-collection procedure, influenced by the work of John Gumperz mentioned above, was used in Belfast whereby the researcher introduced herself to initial contacts as a "friend of a friend" – i.e. a second order network contact of the people participating in the study. These initial contacts passed her on to others, and observation and recording continued until sufficient speakers with the desired characteristics (e.g. of age and gender) were sampled. Crucially, the unit of study was the pre-existing social group, rather than a series of isolated individuals as representatives of particular social categories. By attaching herself to this group and retreating to its fringes as interactions between members progressed, she was able to obtain large amounts of spontaneous speech as well as relevant social and demographic information, and the effect of the observer on the data was lessened. Fieldwork procedures of this general type have been used extensively in both bilingual and monolingual communities (as described by Milroy et al. 1995), and problems of access are rarely reported. Kerswill (1994) describes their implementation in western Norway.

Data recorded in the Belfast study were examined to compare the language patterns of 46 speakers from three low status urban working-class communities – Ballymacarrett, Hammer, and Clonard. Eight phonological variables, all of which were clearly indexical of the Belfast urban speech community, were analyzed in relation to the network structure of individual speakers. In all three communities networks were relatively dense, multiplex, and often kin-based, corresponding to those described by many investigators as characteristic of traditional, long-established communities minimally impacted by social or geographical mobility (see, e.g., Young and Wilmott 1962, Cohen 1982).

Although a social class index of the kind used in the early days of socio-linguistics could not discriminate between these speakers, the extent of individuals' use of vernacular variants was found to be strongly influenced by level of integration into neighborhood networks. For example, some people worked outside the neighborhood and had no local kin and few local ties of friendship, while others were locally linked in all these capacities. Such differences in personal network structure clearly spring from many complex social and psychological factors, and so interact with a number of other variables; examples are generation cohort, the recent history of the neighborhood, and gender. Since the gender/network relationship has proved to be suggestive of a general explanation of gendered patterns of language variation and change, I shall comment on it here.

Men in the Belfast neighborhoods generally contracted denser and more multiplex localized network ties than women, and network structure correlated with language use patterns differently for men and women. A similar disjunction between the effect of male and female networks is reported in Dubois and Horvath's (1998) variationist account of Cajun English. Eckert confirms and elaborates the strongly gendered character both of network clusters and of the network/language relationship (2000: 120–4). Noting a tendency for women to contract ties across a wider social spectrum, Chambers (1995: 124–8) attributes the frequently observed tendency of men to approximate more closely than women to vernacular norms to this difference in network structure. In broader investigations of the social trajectory of language change in two different urban locations, Milroy and Milroy (1993) and Docherty et al. (1997) explore the interaction between gender and network; male norms are associated with localized variants, and female norms with supra-local (but not necessarily standardized) variants. Milroy (1999) attributes the relative conservative, localized character of male speech behavior to the particularly constraining effect of male peer networks. The interacting effect of network and gender on patterns of language variation and change remains an extremely important research topic which will be alluded to again in this chapter.

2.1   *Measuring social network structure*

Given the ethnographic orientation of social network analysis, a major challenge for variationist researchers is to devise a procedure for characterizing differences in network structure which reflects the everyday social practices of speakers. The Belfast study developed a Network Strength Scale to assess speakers' network characteristics on five indicators of multiplexity and density. Milroy (1987a: 141f) describes in detail both the rationale for selecting the indicators and procedures for operationalizing the Network Strength Scale. Briefly, a score of one or zero was assigned to each indicator, and a total network strength score calculated for each individual which was the sum of individual indicator scores. The indicators focused on various relationships *within the neighborhood* of kin, work, and friendship which had emerged in the course of the fieldwork as significant to participants. They were

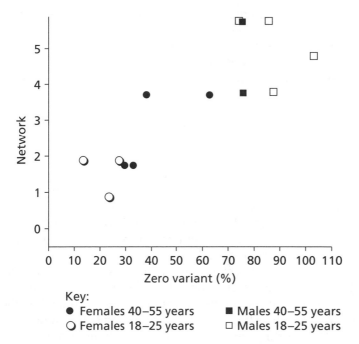

Figure 22.3 Ballymacarrett men's and women's scores for (th), plotted against network scores

- membership of a high density, territorially based group (e.g. a bingo or card-playing group, a gang, or a football team or football supporters' club);
- having kinship ties with more than two households in the neighborhood;
- same workplace as at least two others from the neighborhood;
- same workplace as at least two others of the same gender from the neighborhood;
- voluntary association with workmates in leisure hours.

A series of statistical analyses revealed a clear relationship between personal network structure and phonological variation, usually complicated by the interaction of other social variables such as the age and gender of the speaker. The strongest vernacular speakers were generally those whose neighborhood network ties were the strongest. Figure 22.3 illustrates this tendency in Ballymacarrett, where patterns of use for the variable (th) are plotted against network structure. The variable pattern represented here is the presence vs. absence of the voiced interdental fricative [ð] in intervocalic contexts in such words as *mother* and *brother*; deletion scores for each speaker, whose age group and gender are also specified, are plotted as percentages against individual network strength scores. The interacting effects of gender and network noted above are also evident; not only are women's network scores lower than men's, but the woman with the highest (th) index scores a full 10 percent lower than the man who scores the lowest.

It is on the basis of language/network relationships such as these across several linguistic variables and many more speakers that the close-knit network is interpreted as an important mechanism of dialect maintenance.

2.2   Network concept in small-scale communities: some examples

The attractions for variationists of a network approach can be stated quite briefly. First, it provides a set of procedures for studying small groups where speakers are not discriminable in terms of any kind of social class index – as for example the eastern US island communities investigated by Wolfram et al. (1999). Other examples are minority ethnic groups, migrants, rural populations, or populations in nonindustrialized societies.

A second advantage of a social network approach is that it is intrinsically a participant rather than an analyst concept, and so has the potential to elucidate the social dynamics driving language variation and change. Finally, network analysis offers a procedure for dealing with variation between individual speakers, rather than between groups constructed with reference to predetermined social categories. Eckert (2000: 1–33) discusses in some detail the very different concepts of a social variable implied here. These methodological issues are exemplified in many studies carried out in the 1980s and 1990s, such as that by Russell (1982) in Mombasa, Kenya; Schmidt (1985) of Australian Aboriginal adolescents; Bortoni-Ricardo (1985) of changes in the language of rural migrants to a Brazilian city; V. Edwards (1986) of the language of British black adolescents; Schooling (1990) of language differences among Melanesians in New Caledonia; Lippi-Green (1989) on dynamics of change in the rural alpine village of Grossdorf, Austria; W. Edwards (1992) of variation in an African-American community in inner-city Detroit; and Maher (1996) of the persistence of language differences in the isolated island community of St. Barthélemy, French West Indies. Lippi-Green (1989), Edwards (1992) and Bortoni-Ricardo (1985) are briefly reviewed below, to illustrate a range of different applications of the network idea.

The relative socioeconomic homogeneity of the inner-city Detroit neighborhood studied by Walter Edwards (1992) made social network analysis an attractive procedure for dealing with intra-community linguistic variation. While the principal factor associated with choice of variant was age, the most important factor which distinguished age-peers of a comparable social and educational background was participation in neighborhood culture. Edwards interpreted such participation as indicative of relative integration into local networks, and measured this integration by means of a Vernacular Culture Index. This was constructed from responses to 10 statements which could range from Strongly Disagree (1 point) to Strongly Agree (4 points). Five statements were designed as indicators of the individual's physical integration into the neighborhood, and, like the Network Strength Scale used in Belfast, focused on localized interactions with kin, workmates, and friends (e.g. "Most of my relatives live in this neighborhood or with me"; "Most of my friends live in this neighborhood"). Convinced of the importance of attitude in accounting for variation, Edwards designed the other five statements to indicate evaluations of the neighborhood and of black/white friendship ties (e.g. "I would like to remain living in this neighborhood"; "I do not have white friends with whom I interact frequently").

Yet another set of indicators was relevant to Lippi-Green's (1989) study of language change in progress in Grossdorf, an isolated Austrian Alpine village with 800 inhabitants. Noting the unhelpfulness of macro-level concepts such as class in uncovering the relationship between language variation and social structure, Lippi-Green examined in considerable detail the personal network structures of individuals, constructing a scale which used 16 differentially weighted indicators. Some of these were associated with the familiar domains of work, kin, and friendship, while others dealt more specifically with local conditions – such as the number of grandparents familiar to the speaker who was a core member of the village, or the involvement of the speaker's employment with the tourism industry. Particularly important were indicators which linked speakers to major village family networks. Overall, the best correlate of linguistic behavior (conservative vs. innovatory) was integration into three important networks, including those which involved workplace and exposure to non-local language varieties. However, the subtlety of Lippi-Green's network measurement scale allowed her to examine correlations both with all of it and some parts of it, revealing for example gender-specific social trajectories of language change and variation.

In addressing the changing language behavior of mobile individuals, Bortoni-Ricardo's (1985) account of the sociolinguistic adjustment of rural migrants to Brazlandia, a satellite city of Brasilia exemplifies a very different application of the network concept from those discussed above. Again, the social class concept is not particularly useful in this context, since it does not discriminate between the individuals studied by Bortoni-Ricardo, all of whom were relatively poor. Taking the group's own linguistic norms as a starting point, Bortoni-Ricardo examined the extent to which speakers had moved away from their stigmatized Caipira dialect, rather than attempting to identify a linguistic standard "target".

Bortoni-Ricardo's main hypothesis is that the change in social structure associated with rural to urban migration involves a move from an "insulated" network consisting largely of kinsfolk and neighbors to an "integrated' urban network where links are less multiplex but contracted in a wider range of social contexts. The linguistic counterpart of this change is increasing dialect diffuseness – a movement away from the relatively focused norms of the Caipira dialect (see further Le Page and Tabouret-Keller 1985). Two separate network indices are constructed to measure the changing patterns of the migrants' social relationships; the *integration index* and the *urbanization index*. The integration index assesses relevant characteristics of the three persons with whom each migrant most frequently interacts – for example, whether they are kin or non-kin, whether ties were contracted prior to migration. The final score measures progress in the transition from an insulated to an integrated type of network – effectively the gradual loosening of close-knit network ties. These changes are correlated with a linguistic movement away from the norms of the Caipira dialect.

The urbanization index focuses not on the migrant, but the characteristics of members of his or her personal network, such as educational level and mobility; indicators are selected to assess the extent to which the migrant's contacts are integrated into urban life. In developing these two quite different types of index Bortoni-Ricardo extends the application of the network concept beyond an analysis of small, close-knit groups of the kind described so far to consider the extent to which individuals have detached themselves from such groups and the linguistic consequences of that detachment.

In an extended discussion of sociolinguists' use of the network concept, Murray (1993) is particularly critical of the quantitative analysis employed by Labov (1972) and Milroy (1987a) on grounds which are more controversial than he claims, and are moreover not always entirely clear. Murray's strongly stated claims of what constitutes an appropriate approach to social network analysis and an appropriate statistical method are disputable. Moreover, a subsequent clarification in *American Speech* (Butters 1995: 20) points out that specific criticisms of Milroy's statistical procedures and results rest on a misreading of her text.

3   Language Maintenance and Shift in Bilingual Communities

Although the discussion so far has concentrated on the language/network relationship in monolingual communities, researchers investigating the social mechanisms of language maintenance and shift in bilingual communities have employed a variant of the same general principle: networks constituted chiefly of strong ties function as a mechanism to support minority languages, resisting institutional pressures to language shift, but when these networks weaken, language shift is likely to take place. This section reviews some of this work, starting with a consideration of the network structure characteristic of immigrant communities.

It has sometimes been suggested that close-knit networks such as those studied in Belfast and Detroit are marginal to contemporary urban life; for example, there is a large sociological literature on "the stranger", the mobile, marginal individual who is often seen as typical of a modern city dweller (Harman 1988). While this perception certainly reflects important aspects of contemporary urban life (we shall later discuss the linguistic consequences of social and geographical mobility) it does not tell the whole story. Certainly traditional working-class communities like the Italian American "urban villagers" described by Gans (1962) or the close-knit Yorkshire mining communities described by Dennis et al. (1957) have all but disappeared. However, Giddens (1989) points out that neighborhoods involving close kinship and personal ties seem still to be created rather than discouraged by city life, since those who form part of urban ethnic communities gravitate to form ties with, and often to live with, others from similar linguistic or ethnic backgrounds. Hence, the older style of close-knit working class community is apparently being replaced in industrialized countries by similar types of community created by newer immigrants. Dabène and Moore (1995) describe the supportive function of such migrant networks during the period when immigrants are developing resources to integrate more fully into urban life.

The type of close-knit network structure which seems to help maintain community languages is therefore by no means a residue of an earlier type of social organization; not only immigrants, but also long-term stigmatized and marginalized minorities, like the New York Puerto Ricans studied by Zentella (1997), construct personal communities which function as powerful support systems in a hostile environment. Gal (1978) and Li (1994), whose work is discussed in more detail below, have correlated observed patterns of language use with specific network patterns in much the same way as researchers working in monolingual communities. Indeed, Gal explicitly compares her model of language shift to a variationist model of language change, in being both gradual and rooted in synchronic patterns of variation in language use. Zentella also adopts a broad variationist perspective, but like Gumperz (1982), uses the concept of network informally and non-quantitatively.

Gumperz's (1982) account of the Slovenian/German bilingual community in a remote part of Austria's Gail Valley associates the move towards monolingualism with economic changes. Members of this poor and socially stigmatized farming community had traditionally been embedded in classic close-knit networks of mutual support which linked them in many capacities – as co-workers, neighbors, and friends who socialized together within the boundaries of their community. However, such behaviors changed as the economy shifted from a dependence on subsistence farming to a primarily service economy. Improvements in the road system gave rise to a host of other changes which affected network structure and, ultimately, language behavior followed. Farmers sold produce to incomers and to factories rather than dealing with other local farmers; farm buildings were converted into tourist accommodation for the many visitors entering the area; work and leisure activities were no longer confined to the immediate locality. As many day to day interactions came to be with urban outsiders, villagers lost their reliance on the local support network. Although of course local conditions give rise to variations, the pattern Gumperz describes here appears to be a very general one in much of western Europe (and probably elsewhere in the developed and developing world). Ó'Riagáin's (1997) description of a series of studies carried out in Ireland between 1973 and 1993 suggests a situation broadly similar to that in the Gail Valley where change to a service economy triggers associated change in personal social network structures. Consequent changes in the categories of individual involved in face-to-face encounters shifted the balance from bilingual Irish-speaking insiders to monolingual English-speaking outsiders, inevitably resulting in the further decline of Irish.

Gal's (1978) analysis of language shift in the bilingual German/Hungarian community in Oberwart, Austria, identifies similar triggers. Individuals are measured in terms of the relative "peasantness" (a local social category) of their networks. This variable operates differently for men and women (recall this pattern in other network studies) but is found to correlate more closely than individual peasant status with patterns of language choice. Like the Gail Valley and the Irish Gaeltacht, Oberwart had been bilingual for several centuries, and again, changes in network structure are associated with higher-level economic changes. We now turn to Li's (1994) and Zentella's (1997) work in immigrant communities where typically pressure to assimilate to the monolingual norm of the host country is intense and, in contrast to the communities discussed above, a pattern of language shift over three generations is common. Grosjean (1982) and Jørgensen (1998) describe these pressures in the United States and Europe respectively.

Despite a general sense that Spanish in the United States is resistant to shift (Bourhis and Marshall 1999) Zentella provides evidence of this three-generational shift pattern in a Puerto Rican community in New York City (*el bloque*). In an account which is compiled from long-term participant oservation, she notes some characteristic sociolinguistic patterns. First, while choice of code is heavily network-dependent, several distinguishable varieties of both Spanish and English give rise to multiple-code repertoires (Zentella 1997: 48). For example, while youngsters and young mothers have access to a range of Spanish and English codes, they favor a Puerto Rican variety of English. Older men and women however prefer Puerto Rican Spanish, while "young dudes" favor African-American Vernacular English but also have access to varieties of Spanish and English. Many of the children speak very little Spanish, mixing Spanish into their English to produce the code popularly described as *Nuyorican*; interestingly, only one child in Zentella's sample is monolingual in English. Patterns of code choice from this multidimensional repertoire are thus systematically associated with a range of distinctive gender- and age-related networks.

Zentella comments on the significance of what she describes as "the Puerto Rico language learning connection" in offering an explanation of the strength and persistence of Spanish in New York City and elsewhere in the United States. She cites the combined effect of continuing network ties of immigrants to individuals in adjacent Spanish-speaking countries of Latin America, and cyclic patterns of immigration (see again Bourhis and Marshall 1999). This Puerto Rican connection (and its counterpart in other Spanish-speaking communities in the United States) may explain why young people use a mixed

Spanish-English code; in accordance with the expected pattern of language shift in immigrant communities, they have shifted substantially to English mono-lingualism but still need to communicate with Spanish monolingual speakers.

Li (1994) and Milroy and Li (1995) report an investigation of social trajec-tories of language shift which associates different network types with vari-able patterns of language use. However, they describe a much less complex community repertoire than Zentella, providing a quantitative analysis of both network types and language patterns. Three migrant groups are distinguished, overlapping with (but not exactly corresponding to) a grandparent, parent, and child generation. Each group contracts characteristically different types of network ties, the first associating mainly with kin, the second chiefly with other British Chinese, and the third more extensively with non-Chinese peers. Variable network patterns were in turn correlated with seven different patterns of language choice, where English and Chinese were used either monolingually or in different combinations. Following Milardo (1988), interactive and exchange networks were distinguished, corresponding roughly to "weak" and "strong" types of tie.

Since the Chinese in Tyneside did not live within a specificable neighborhood, assessments of network strength could not be based on the territorially restricted strong ties as in several of the studies reviewed in the previous section. Instead comparative analysis of individual exchange networks was based on a list of up to 20 persons who constituted significant and regular contacts for each individual, adapting the procedure described by Mitchell (1986). These sets of 20 could then be compared on relevant dimensions – for example, different ethnic compositions. Not surprisingly, the strongest ethnic networks were associated both with the oldest generation and with the most extensive use of Chinese, and the weakest with the British-born generation and with the most extensive use of English. There were, however, many subtleties associated with different network patterns within each group; particularly interesting is the role of the True Jesus Church, one of the community's institutions.

Li (1995) suggests the raison d'être of this church to be a support mechanism for cultural and socialization activities rather than a religious institution, noting that member families were distinctive in having contracted pre-migration net-work ties on the island of Ap Chau, close to Hong Kong. He further documents a very much stronger pattern of Chinese language maintenance amongst the young British-born members of the True Jesus Church than amongst the young community as a whole, a pattern attributed to the strong ties maintained by True Jesus youngsters with church members monolingual in Cantonese. Inter-estingly, Li also notes a pattern of fluent Cantonese/English code mixing as characteristic of the True Jesus teenagers, which he explains in much the same way as Zentella (1997) explains widespread Spanish/English mixing by New York City Puerto Rican youngsters. In both cases the young people have come up with a similar solution to a similar problem; proficiency in the community language is limited, but they maintain network ties which require them to communicate with non-English speakers. Thus, a network analysis can help explain not only the social trajectory of language shift, but specific patterns of code switching (see also Labrie's (1988) network-based account of code switching by Italians in Montreal).

4   Weak Ties and Theories of Language Change

Social network analysis has most commonly been employed in communities where ties between speakers are generally strong. While studies such as those reviewed above show that it is relatively straightforward to operationalize the network concept in this way, how to handle socially and geographically mobile speakers whose personal network ties are not predominantly dense or multiplex is much less obvious. In fact, network-based accounts of such speakers are rare, and the only study examined so far which has attempted anything like this is Bortoni-Ricardo's (1985) account of the progressive urbanization patterns of Brazilian rural migrants. Geographical and social mobility is, however, the rule rather than the exception in contemporary cities, and an increasing amount of work carried out by variationists within dialect contact frameworks focuses on such speakers (see for example Trudgill 1986, Trudgill and Britain forthcoming, Chambers 1995: 52–65, Kerswill and Williams 2000). Chambers (1992) points out that sociolinguistics as well as dialectology is quite generally oriented to non-mobile speakers in isolated communities; the focus of network studies over two decades has reflected this orientation.

At a purely operational level, loose-knit networks are hard to work with. Analysis of close-knit networks involves comparing speakers who differ from each other in certain respects (for example, multiplexity of ties contracted at the workplace) but are still similar enough in other relevant ways for a comparison to be meaningful. But it is difficult to see how the loose-knit network structures of individuals who differ from each other in many different respects (educational level, occupation, region of origin, mobility inter alia) might meaningfully be compared with each other. This problem was noted in the Belfast suburbs of Andersonstown and Braniel (Milroy 1987b: 108) and was encountered also in an attempt to apply social network analysis in the prosperous Berlin suburb of Zehlendorf (Dittmar and Schlobinski 1988). However, from the perspective of a person who has changed employment and place of residence several times, the networks of speakers studied in Belfast, Detroit, and Grossdorf are all close-knit, and might be compared in a general way with those of more mobile speakers (see Kerswill and Williams 1999).

To identify these operational difficulties is not to suggest that loose-knit networks are uninteresting to the variationist: quite the contrary. For if a close-knit network structure supports localized linguistic norms and resists change originating from outside the network, the corollary, that communities composed of weak ties will be susceptible to such change, is also likely to hold. Following Granovetter's (1973) argument that "weak" and apparently insignificant interpersonal ties (of "acquaintance" as opposed to "friend", for example) are important channels through which innovation and influence flow from one close-knit group to another Milroy and Milroy (1985) have proposed that linguistic innovators are likely to be individuals who are in a position to contract many weak ties. Since such weak ties link close-knit groups to each other and to the larger regional or national speech community, they are likely to figure prominently in a socially accountable theory of linguistic diffusion and change.

Milroy and Milroy (1985) argue that a "weak tie" model of change can account rather generally for the tendency of some languages to be more resistant to change than others (Icelandic vs. English, or Sardinian vs. Sicilian, for example). They suggest that a type of social organization based on overlapping close-knit networks will inhibit change, while one characterized by mobility (for whatever reason), with a concomitant weakening of close ties, will facilitate it. Grace (1992) explains in a similar way some puzzling developments among the Austronesian languages, which show widely differing patterns of susceptibility to change inexplicable in terms of traditional assumptions (see also Grace 1990). As well as explaining different large-scale linguistic outcomes by comparing different types of social organization, the weak tie model can account for specific problematic examples of change, of which two are considered below.

Innovations have been widely observed to skip from city to city, bypassing intervening territory. This appears to be the pattern of the Northern Cities Shift, a vigorous change in vowel systems affecting cities of the northern USA from western New England to an unspecified point westward (Labov 1991, Wolfram and Schilling-Estes 1998: 138). On the other side of the Atlantic, Trudgill (1988) notes the relatively recent adoption by young speakers in Norwich of a merger between /f/ ~ /θ/ and /v/ ~ /ð/ (as in *fin ~ thin; lava ~ lather*). Milroy (1996) subsequently documents this merger by young working-class speakers in the northern English cities of Sheffield and Derby, and Stuart-Smith (1999) reports its recent appearance yet further north in Glasgow. As it saliently indexes working-class London speech, this change, in the British context, appears to be contact-induced rather than to originate from within communities. While attributing its rapid spread to Norwich to greater mobility and contact between speakers, Trudgill points out that the teenagers who use the merged variants are less mobile than their seniors and tend to contract close ties locally. For this reason, it is hard to explain the precise mechanisms of diffusion in terms of close contact between London and Norwich speakers. The same objection can be made even more tellingly since this very vigorous change has extended across large areas of urban Britain in the years since Trudgill's observations of its spread to Norwich. A weak tie model would however predict its diffusion from one community to another through multiple weak ties; in fact, Trudgill suggests tourists and football supporters as individuals who might be implicated in the diffusion process (1986: 54).

A second problematic case of change to which a weak-tie model offers a principled solution involves the alternating phonolexical variable (u), as in

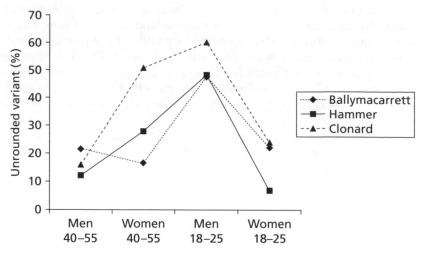

Figure 22.4   The distribution of (u) by age, gender, and neighborhood in Belfast

pull, push, foot, discussed in detail by, for example, Milroy (1987a) and Milroy (1992). A rounded and an unrounded vowel variant appear in a lexically limited set, the unrounded variant strongly indexing working-class identity.

Figure 22.4 provides clear evidence of cross-community consensus between young (but not middle-aged) speakers on the use of these alternative realizations to index gender also in the three working-class communities of Ballymacarrett, Hammer, and Clonard. However, the fact that middle-aged Ballymacarrett speakers use (u) to index gender in much the same way as younger speakers in all three communities suggests that the change is diffusing from Ballymacarrett. The problem is this: how has this change crossed the notorious sectarian lines of demarcation in the Belfast of the 1970s, since the civil disturbances which began during the childhood years of these young speakers prevented them from contracting close ties across the sectarian divide? Older speakers, who report having contracted many cross-community ties prior to the civil disturbances, display no cross-community consensus on the use of (u). The age-related pattern of this change is puzzling if we adopt the commonsense assumption that innovations are transmitted via strong ties (for such a model, see Labov 1980: 261; Labov and Harris 1986), but not if we assume that the conduits of innovation are the multiple weak ties of everyday urban interaction in the neutral areas outside close-knit community territories (for further discussion of this issue, see Milroy and Milroy 1985).

Although it may at first seem counter-intuitive, a "weak tie" model of change is plausible for several reasons, as suggested by Granovetter (1973). First, persons central to a close-knit, norm-enforcing group are likely to find innovation of any kind socially risky, but the adoption of an innovation already on the fringes of the group less so. Second (in the networks of mobile individuals at least), weak ties are more numerous than strong ties, providing links to many more individuals; consider, for example, the ties set up by participants at academic or business conferences, which link cohesive groups associated with each institution and provide conduits for new ideas and information. Conversely, information relayed through strong ties tends not to be innovatory, since strong tie contacts are likely to be shared (that is to belong to overlapping networks). Thus, mobile individuals who have contracted many weak ties, but occupy a position marginal to any given cohesive group, are in a favorable position to diffuse innovation. Interestingly, this argument is consistent with the traditional assumption of historians of language that the emergent, mobile merchant class were largely responsible for the appearance of northern (and other) dialectal innovations in Early Modern London English (see, for example, Baugh and Cable 1978: 194). Using standard variationist methods, historical sociolinguists have begun to examine systematically the social trajectories of such earlier changes with attention to the effects not only of social network, but of gender and social status, with promising results (Nevalainen 1999, Nevalainen and Raumolin-Brunberg 1996, Tieken-Boon van Ostade et al. in press). Sociohistorial linguistics continues to develop as a significant subfield of variationist theory.

5 Social Network, Social Class and Mobility

The weak tie model of change discussed above can illuminate the dynamics of dialect leveling – that is the eradication of socially or locally marked variants (both within and between linguistic systems) in conditions of social or geographical mobility and resultant dialect contact. Leveling might reasonably be viewed as a linguistic reflex of the large-scale disruption endemic in the modern world of close-knit, localized networks which have historically maintained highly systematic and complex sets of socially structured linguistic norms. Such disruption arises from (for example) internal and transnational migration, war, industrialization, and urbanization. While these dynamics have operated earlier and more intensively in colonial contexts, as discussed by Chambers within a broad social network framework (1995: 57–66), they continue to affect geographically or socially mobile populations. In any event, leveling gives rise to homogenization and a tendency for the localized norms of the kind supported by a close-knit network structure to become obliterated (Chambers 1995, Trudgill et al. 2000, Kerswill and Williams 2000, Britain 1997, Watt and Milroy 1999). This process raises interesting psycholinguistic as well as sociolinguistic issues concerning the functions of close-knit networks, which are briefly explored below.

On the basis of evidence from language attitudes research, sociolinguists generally assume an ideological motivation to underlie the long-term maintenance of often stigmatized norms in the face of pressures from numerically or socially more powerful speech communities; speakers want to sound (for example) Welsh, Irish, Northern English, New Zealandish, Canadian, African-American, American Southern and unlike whatever social group they perceive themselves as contrasting with. The dialect loyalty of such speakers and their resistance to change originating from outside the group is usually said to be motivated by their desire to index group identity. Yet, motivations alone are insufficient to maintain nonstandard varieties reliably (see Wolfram et al. 1999 for a discussion of this issue in an American context). Relevant here is Payne's (1980) demonstration of the social conditions needed for children to learn the highly localized phonolexical complexities of the Philadelphia system; particularly, their parents needed to be locally born for such learning to take place. What this amounts to is that if a close-knit community network structure loosens and members become mobile, the social prerequisites for supporting highly localized norms disappear, and dialect leveling takes place. Thus, not only does a community's sense of distinctiveness become redundant as network ties loosen (a social and ideological issue), but from a psycholinguistic perspective speakers lack the extensive and regular input needed to maintain localized norms.

Such norms are sometimes complex; for example, Belfast speakers whose networks are relatively loose-knit reduce the number of linguistically conditioned allophones of /a/ by eliminating the extreme back and front variants characteristic of the vernacular system, often converging on a very narrow area of vowel around the centre of the vernacular range (Milroy 1982, Milroy 1999). Thus, close-knit networks may be viewed not only as social and sociolinguistic support mechanisms which facilitate the construction and maintenance of local distinctiveness; from the point of view of the language learner, they also provide the intensive input required to master complex, localized linguistic structures which lack the support of institutional models. Leveling, which from this cognitive perspective can be viewed as a simplification strategy, takes place when such input is no longer present. Trudgill (1989, 1992) and Schilling-Estes (2000) provide relevant discussions of the social conditions in which both simplification and structural complexity flourish.

We turn now to consider more specifically the links between mobility, social network structure, and social class. Following Giddens (1989: 205–73), class is viewed here as one of four systems of stratification which promote inequality in society. While the other three (slavery, caste, and estates) depend on institutionally sanctioned inequalities, class divisions are not officially recognized, and since an individual's class position is to some extent achieved, class stratification is accompanied by varying degrees of mobility. Issues of power inequalities between groups and individuals are raised in this discussion, which so far have only been touched upon.

Different types of network structure seem to be broadly associated with different social classes: loose-knit networks with the socially and geographically mobile mainly middle classes, and close-knit ties with very low status and very high status speakers. In terms of the predictions of the weak tie model of change discussed above, this association is consistent with Labov's principle that innovating groups are located centrally in the social hierarchy, characterized as lower-middle or upper-working class (1980: 254). The question then arises of how an integrated model of change and variation might be constructed which takes account of the relationship between social class and social network structures. Such an integration is desirable, since the association of different network types with different social class groups is not arbitrary, but springs from the operation of large scale social, political and economic factors (*contra* Guy 1988, who views network and class as unrelated, but pertaining respectively to a micro- and macro-level of analysis).

Traditionally, sociolinguistics has assumed a consensus model of class, where the community is said to be fundamentally cohesive and self-regulating. Yet, the vitality and persistence of nonstandard vernacular communities highlighted by network studies is more readily interpreted as evidence of conflict and division than of consensus. Accordingly, Milroy and Milroy (1992) argue that a dynamic model of class as a process which splits the community into subgroups (characterized by different orientations to work, leisure and family) is helpful in constructing an integrated theory of variation and change. Højrup's (1983) analysis of these subgroups as characterized by different lifemodes with different network structures "falling out" from those lifemodes is proposed as an approach which links the variables of class and network in an illuminating way.

With the link between social class and network structure as their point of departure, Kerswill and Williams (1999) have recently investigated the relationship between social class, mobility, and susceptibility to change by comparing the language behavior of low and high mobility speakers of different social statuses in the English towns of Reading and Milton Keynes. They conclude that network structure has the predicted effect – that is, close-knit networks maintain localized norms, while loose-knit networks facilitate change. However, they argue that the variables of class and network need to be considered independently, given the different language behaviors of mobile high status and mobile low status groups.

While the relationship between class, network, and mobility is evident, its precise character is as yet unclear as are the linguistic outcomes associated with interactions between these social variables. However, since they are constructed at different levels of abstraction, it is likely that a two-level sociolinguistic theory would be helpful. Such a theory should link the small-scale networks where individuals are embedded and act purposively in their daily lives with larger-scale social structures which determine relationships of power at the institutional level. The different sociolinguistic patterns associated with both strong and weak ties would need to be considered, with attention to recent work on the sociolinguistics of mobility. For, while strong ties give rise to a local cohesion of the kind described by network studies of close-knit neighborhoods such as those in Belfast or Detroit, they lead also to overall fragmentation in the wider community. Conversely, it is weak ties which give rise to the linguistic uniformity across large territorries such as that described by Chambers in Canada, Labov in the United States, and Trudgill et al. (2000) in New Zealand. The social dynamics underlying both diversity and uniformity lie at the core of an accountable theory of language variation and change.

ACKNOWLEDGMENTS

The support of the US National Endowment for the Humanities in providing me with time to carry out this work is gratefully acknowledged.

REFERENCES

Auer, P. (1998). *Code-switching in Conversation: Language, Interaction and Identity*. London: Routledge.

Baugh A. C. and T. Cable (1978). *History of the English Language*, 3rd edn. London: Routledge and Kegan Paul.

Bortoni-Ricardo, S. M. (1985). *The Urbanisation of Rural Dialect Speakers: A Sociolinguistic Study in Brazil*. Cambridge: Cambridge University Press.

Bourhis, R. Y. and D. F. Marshall (1999). Language and ethnic identity in the United States and Canada. In J. Fishman (ed.), *Language and Ethnic Identify*. Oxford and New York. Oxford University Press.

Britain, D. (1997). Dialect contact and phonological reallocation: "Canadian Raising" in the English Fens. *Language in Society* 26, 1: 15–46.

Butters, Ronald R. (1995). Important clarification. *American Speech* 70, 1: 20.

Chambers, J. K. (1992). Dialect acquisition. In *Language* 68, 3: 673–705.

Chambers, J. K. (1995). *Sociolinguistic Theory*. Oxford: Blackwell.

Cheshire, J. (1982). *Variation in an English Dialect: A Sociolinguistic Study*. Cambridge: Cambridge University Press.

Cochran, M., M. Larner, D. Riley, L. Gunnarsson and C. R. Henderson (1990). *Extending Families: The Social Networks of Parents and their Children*. Cambridge: Cambridge University Press.

Cohen, A. (ed.) (1982). *Belonging*. Manchester: Manchester University Press.

Dabène, L. and A. Moore. (1995). Bilingual speech of migrant people. In L. Milroy and P. Muysken (eds.), *One Speaker, Two Languages*. Cambridge: Cambridge University Press. 17–44.

Dennis, N., F. M. Henriques and C. Slaughter (1957). *Coal is our life*. London: Eyre and Spottiswoode.

Ditmarr, N. and P. Schlobinski (1988). *The Sociolinguistics of Urban Vernaculars*. Berlin: de Gruyter.

Docherty, G. P., J. Foulkes, J. Milroy, L. Milroy and D. Walshaw (1997). Descriptive adequacy in phonology: a variationist perspective. *Journal of Linguistics* 33: 1–36.

Dubois, S. and B. M. Horvath (1998). Let's tink about dat: interdental fricatives in Cajun English. *Language Variation and Change* 10, 3: 245–61.

Eckert, P. (2000). *Linguistic Variation as Social Practice*. Oxford: Blackwell.

Edwards, V. (1986). *Language in a Black Community*. Clevedon, Avon: Multilingual Matters.

Edwards, W. (1992). Sociolinguistic behaviour in a Detroit inner city black neighbourhood. *Language in Society* 21: 93–115.

Fishman, J. (1999). *Language and Ethnic Identity: Before and After the Ethnic Revival*. Oxford and New York: Oxford University Press.

Fridland, Valerie (1999). The Southern Shift in Memphis, TN. *Language Variation and Change* 11, 3: 267–85.

Gal, S. (1978). Variation and change in patterns of speaking: language shift in Austria. In D. Sankoff (ed.), *Linguistic Variation: Models and Methods*. New York: Academic Press. 227–38.

Gans, H. J. (1962). *The Urban Villagers: Group and Class in the Life of Italian-Americans*, 2nd edn. New York: Free Press.

Gauchat, L. (1905). L'unité phonétique dans le patois d'une commune. *Festschrift Heinrich Morf: aus Romanischen Sprachen und Literaturen*. Halle: M. Niemeyer. 175–232.

Giddens, A. (1989). *Sociology*. Cambridge: Polity.

Grace, G. (1990). The "aberrant" (vs. "exemplary") Melanesian languages. In P. Baldi (ed.), *Linguistic Change and Reconstruction Methodology*. Berlin: Mouton de Gruyter. 155–73.

Grace, W. (1992). How do languages change? (more on "aberrant" languages). *Oceanic Linguistics* 31, 1: 115–30.

Granovetter, M. (1973). The strength of weak ties. *American Journal of Sociology* 78: 1360–80.

Grosjean, F. (1982). *Life with Two Languages*. Cambridge, MA: Harvard University Press.

Gumperz, J. J. (1982). Social network and language shift. In J. J. Gumperz (ed.), *Discourse Strategies*. Cambridge and New York: Cambridge University Press. 38–58.

Guy, Gregory, R. (1988). Language and social class. In F. Newmeyer (ed.), *Linguistics: The Cambridge Survey*, IV: 37–63.

Harman, L. D. (1988). *The Modern Stranger: On Language and Membership*. Berlin: Mouton de Gruyter.

Højrup, T. (1983). The concept of lifemode: a form-specifying mode of analysis applied to contemporary western Europe. *Ethnologia Scandinavica* 1–50.

Horvath B. (1985). *Variation in Australian English*. Cambridge University Press, Cambridge.

Johnson, J. C. (1994). Anthropological contributions to the study of social networks: a review. In S. Wasserman and J. Galaskiewicz (eds.), *Advances in Social Network Analysis: research in the social and behavioral sciences*. Thousand Oaks CA: Sage Publications. 113–51.

Jørgensen, J. N. (1998). Children's acquisition of code-switching for power wielding. In P. Auer (ed.), *Code-switching in Conversation*. London: Routledge. 237–60.

Kerswill, P. (1994). *Dialects Converging: Rural Speech in Urban Norway*. Oxford: Oxford University Press.

Kerswill, P. (1996). Children, adolescents and language change. *Language Variation and Change* 8, 2: 177–202.

Kerswill, Paul and A. Williams (1999). Mobility versus social class in dialect levelling: evidence from new and old towns in England. *Cuadernos de Filologia Inglesa* 8: 47–57. Departamento de Filologia Inglesa de la Universidad de Murcia.

Kerswill, Paul and A. Williams (2000). Creating a new town koine: children and language change in Milton Keynes. *Language in Society* 29, 1: 65–115.

Labov, W. (1972). The linguistic consequences of being a lame. In W. Labov (ed.), *Language in the Inner City*. Philadelphia: University of Pennsylvania Press. 255–92.

Labov, W. (ed.) (1980). *Locating Language in Time and Space*. New York: Academic Press.

Labov, W. (1991). The three dialects of English. In P. Eckert (ed.), *New Ways of Analyzing Sound Change*. New York: Academic Press. 1–44.

Labov, W. and Wendell A. Harris (1986). De facto segregation of black and white vernaculars. In D. Sankoff (ed.), *Diversity and Diachrony*. Philadelphia: John Benjamins. 1–24.

Labrie, Normand (1988). Social networks and code-switching: a sociolinguistic investigation of Italians in Montreal. In N. Ditmarr and P. Schlobinski (eds.), *The Sociolinguistics of Urban Vernaculars*. Berlin: de Gruyter. 217–232.

Le Page, R. B. and A. Tabouret-Keller (1985). *Acts of Identity*. Cambridge: Cambridge University Press.

Li Wei (1994). *Three Generations, Two Languages, One Family*. Clevedon, Avon: Multilingual Matters.

Li Wei (1995). Variations in patterns of language choice and codeswitching by three groups of Chinese/English speakers in Newcastle upon Tyne. *Multilinga* 14, 3: 297–323.

Li Wei (1996). Network analysis. In H. Goebl, P. Nelde, S. Zdenek and W. Woelck (eds.), *Contact Linguistics: A Handbook of Contemporary Research*. Berlin: de Gruyter. 805–12.

Lippi-Green, R. (1989). Social network integration and language change in progress in an alpine rural village. *Language in Society* 18: 213–34.

Lippi-Green, R. (1997). *English with an Accent: Language, Ideology and Discrimination in the United States*. London: Routledge.

Maher, J. (1996). Fishermen, farmers, traders: language and economic history on St. Barthélemy, French West Indies. *Language in Society* 25, 3: 373–406.

Milardo, R. M. (1988). Families and social networks: an overview of theory and methodology. In R. M. Milardo (ed.), *Families and Social Networks*. Newbury Park, CA: Sage. 13–47.

Milroy, J. (1982). Probing under the tip of the ice-berg: phonological normalization and the shape of speech communities. In S. Romaine (ed.), *Sociolinguistic Variation in Speech Communities*. London: Arnold. 35–47.

Milroy, J. (1992). *Linguistic Variation and Change*. Oxford: Blackwell.

Milroy J. (1996). A current change in British English: variation in (th) in Derby. *Newcastle and Durham Papers in Linguistics* 4: 213–22.

Milroy, J. and L. Milroy (1978). Belfast: Change and variation in an urban vernacular. In P. Trudgill (ed.), *Sociolinguistic Patterns in British English*. London: Arnold. 19–36.

Milroy, J. and L. Milroy (1985) Linguistic change, social network and speaker innovation. *Journal of Linguistics* 21: 339–84.

Milroy, J. and L. Milroy (1993) Mechanisms of change in urban dialects: the role of class, social network and gender. *International Journal of Applied Linguistics*, 3, 1: 57–78.

Milroy L. (1987a). *Language and Social Networks*, 2nd edn. Blackwell, Oxford.

Milroy, L. (1987b). *Observing and Analyzing Natural Language*. Oxford: Blackwell.

Milroy, L. (1999). Women as innovators and norm-creators: The sociolinguistics of dialect leveling in a northern English city. In S. Wertheim, A. C. Bailey and M. Corston-Oliver (eds.), *Engendering Communication*, Proceedings of the Fifth Berkeley Women and Language Conference. 361–76.

Milroy, L. and Li Wei (1995). A social network approach to code-switching. In L. Milroy and P. Muysken (eds.), *One Speaker, Two Languages*. Cambridge: Cambridge University Press. 136–57.

Milroy, L. and J. Milroy (1992). Social network and social class: towards an integrated sociolinguistic model. *Language in Society* 21: 1–26.

Milroy, L. and P. Muysken (eds.) (1995). *One Speaker, Two Languages*. Cambridge: Cambridge University Press.

Milroy, L., W. Li and S. Moffatt (1995). Discourse patterns and fieldwork strategies in urban settings: some methodological problems for fieldworkers in urban communities. In Iwar Werlen (ed.), *Verbale Kommunikation in der Stadt*. Narr: Tubingen. 277–94.

Mitchell, J. C. (1986). Network procedures. In D. Frick et al. (eds.), *The Quality of Urban Life*. Berlin: de Gruyter. 73–92.

Murray, S. O. (1993). Network determination of linguistic variables. *American Speech* 68, 2: 161–77. (See also subsequent clarification, *American Speech* 1996, 70, 1: 20.)

Nevalainen, T. (1999). Making the best use of "bad" data: evidence for sociolinguistic variation in Early modern English. *Neophilologische Mitteilungen* 4, C: 499–533.

Nevalainen, T. (2000). Mobility, social networks and language change in Early Modern England. *European*

Journal of English Studies 4, 3: 253–64.

Nevalainen, T. and H. Raumolin-Brunberg (1996). *Sociolinguistics and Language History*. Amsterdam and Atlanta: Rodopi.

Ó'Riagáin, P. (1997). *Language Policy and Social Reproduction: Ireland, 1893–1993*. Oxford: Oxford University Press.

Payne, A. (1980). Factors controlling the acquisition of the Philadelphia dialect by out of state children. In W. Labov (ed.), *Locating Language in Time and Space*. New York: Academic Press. 143–58.

Russell, J. (1982). Networks and sociolinguistic variation in an African urban setting. In S. Romaine (ed.), *Sociolinguistic Variation in Speech Communities*. London: Arnold. 125–40.

Schilling-Estes, N. (2000). On the nature of insular and post-insular dialects: innovation, variation and differentiation. Paper presented at Bristol, Sociolinguistics Symposium 2000 at colloquium on the theme of dialect contact research in sociolinguistics.

Schmidt, A. (1985). *Young Peoples' Djirbal*. Cambridge: Cambridge University Press.

Schooling, S. (1990). *Language Maintenance in Melanesia*. Dallas: Summer Institute of Linguistics.

Stuart-Smith, J. (1999). Glasgow: accent and voice quality In P. Foulkes and G. J. Docherty (eds.), *Urban Voices*. London: Arnold. 203–22.

Tieken-Boon van Ostade, I., T. Nevalainen and L. Caon (2000). *European Journal of English Studies*: special issue on Social network analysis and the history of English.

Trudgill, P. (1986). *Dialects in Contact*. Oxford: Blackwell.

Trudgill, P. (1988). Norwich revisited: recent linguistic changes in an

English urban dialect. *English World-Wide* 9, 1: 33–49.

Trudgill, P. (1989). Contact and isolation in linguistic change. In Leiv Egil Breivik and Ernst Håkon Jahr (eds.), *Language Change: Contributions to the Study of its Causes*. Trends in Linguistics: Studies and Monographs 43. Berlin: Mouton de Gruyter. 227–37.

Trudgill, P. (1992). Dialect typology and social structure. In Ernst Håkon Jahr (ed.), *Language Contact: Theoretical and Empirical Studies*, Trends in Linguistics: Studies and Monographs 60. Berlin: Mouton de Gruyter. 195–212.

Trudgill, P. and D. Britain (2001). *Dialects in Contact*. 2nd edn. Oxford: Blackwell.

Trudgill, P., E. Gordon, G. Lewis and M. Maclagan (forthcoming). Determinism in new-dialect formation and the genesis of New Zealand English. *Journal of Linguisitcs* 36(2): 299–318.

Watt, D. J. L. and L. Milroy (1999). Patterns of variation and change in three Tyneside vowels: is this dialect levelling? In P. Foulkes and G. J. Docherty (eds.), *Urban Voices*. London: Arnold. 25–46.

Wolfram, W., K. Hazan, and N. Schilling-Estes (1999). *Dialect Change and Maintenance on the Outer Banks*, Publication of the American Dialect Society. Tuscaloosa and London: University of Alabama Press.

Wolfram, W. and N. Schilling-Estes (1998). *American English*. Oxford: Blackwell.

Young, M. and P. Wilmott (1962). *Family and Kinship in East London*. Harmondsworth: Penguin.

Zentella, Ana Celia (1997). *Growing up Bilingual*. Oxford: Blackwell.

23 The Speech Community

PETER L. PATRICK

The speech community (SpCom), a core concept in empirical linguistics, is the intersection of many principal problems in sociolinguistic theory and method. I trace its history of development and divergence, survey general problems with contemporary notions, and discuss links to key issues in investigating language variation and change. I neither offer a new and correct definition nor reject the concept (both misguided efforts), nor exhaustively survey its applications in the field (an impossibly large task).

1 General Problems with Speech Community as a Concept

Every branch of linguistics that is concerned with representative samples of a population; that takes individual speakers or experimental subjects as typical members of a group; that studies *langue* as attributable to a socially coherent body (whether or not it professes interest in the social nature of that body); or that takes as primitive such notions as "native speaker," "competence/ performance," "acceptability," etc., which manifestly refer to collective behavior, rests partially on a concept equivalent to the SpCom. Linguistic systems are exercised by speakers, in social space: there they are acquired, change, are manipulated for expressive or communicative purposes, undergo attrition, etc. Whether linguists prefer to focus on speakers, varieties or grammars, the problem of relating a linguistic system to its speakers is not trivial.

In studying language change and variation (geographical or social), reference to the SpCom is inescapable, yet there is remarkably little agreement or theoretical discussion of the concept in sociolinguistics, though it has often been defined. Some examples from research reports suggest the degree of its (over-)extension (Williams 1992: 71).

The term "SpCom" has been used for geographically bounded urban communities, both large (Philadelphia; Labov 1989) and small (Anniston, Alabama; Feagin 1996); for urban neighborhoods ("Veeton" in Kingston, Jamaica; Patrick 1999) and subgroups – Belfast vernacular speakers (Milroy and Margrain 1980, but see Macaulay 1997: 15) and "the French-speaking minority of Ontario, Canada" (Mougeon and Beniak 1996: 69). It has been denied for other cities (London; Wardhaugh 1998: 123) but used for Anglo-Saxon England (Labov 1982: 35), for urban immigrants, as distinct from both their source and target groups (Kerswill 1994), and for the "national unity of a people" (Dittmar 1976: 106). Cutting across geographic and class lines, it has been used of very general assemblages such as children (Romaine 1982: 7) and women (Coates 1993: 140), as well as specific and temporary ones such as members of a jury (Durant 1999).

For rural populations, it has been used to pick out named settlements of Warlpiri speakers (Bavin 1989), but also for a discontinuous, larger region – the Gaeltacht – in Ireland (Watson 1989) where speakers do not define their communities in linguistic terms. Joly (1981) calls the Afro-Hispanic population of Panama's Costa Abajo both a SpCom and a "ritual community." Dimmendaal (1989) uses SpCom for the Turkana in Kenya, who have absorbed a variety of ethnic and linguistic groups (with consequent language loss) and undergone significant dialect differentiation. The famously complex case of Eastern Tukanoan language speakers in the Vaupés region of Amazonia, where each patrilineal exogamic group is ideally identified by language but "one does not marry someone who speaks one's own language" (Gomez-Imbert 1996: 442), is analyzed as a SpCom by Jackson (1974: 55) but not by Gomez-Imbert.

In textbooks the SpCom is ignored surprisingly often (Chambers and Trudgill 1980, Chambers 1995, Downes 1998, Wolfram and Schilling-Estes 1998, Trudgill 2000). Elsewhere it is considered too difficult to explore (Fasold 1984: 44), or treated narrowly within a single paradigm, usually ethnographic (Fasold 1990, Romaine 1994, Salzmann 1998), with contrasting approaches briefly outlined but not pursued.

Occasionally the SpCom is seriously treated, but with no positive resolution of difficulties. Hudson (1996) compares several major definitions but, starting from the premise that language is an individual possession, takes a radical subjectivist view that ends by entirely dismissing the utility of the concept. Wardhaugh (1998) similarly develops the idea from idealized homogeneity to fragmented individualism, with community dependent upon the impulse to identify oneself with others. Instead of rejection he prefers a vague, one-size-fits-all approach: "some kind of social group whose speech characteristics are of interest and can be described in a coherent manner" (1998: 116). More helpfully, but equally radically, Duranti (1997) recommends abandoning the SpCom as "an already constituted object of inquiry," instead taking it as an analytical perspective: "the product of the communicative activities engaged in by a given group of people" (1997: 82). Despite this trend towards rejection, the SpCom is still referred to by most researchers as though it were either unproblematic or, at any rate, necessary.

This partial review suggests a general lack of analysis and synthesis concerning the SpCom; the next section considers more thoughtful treatments. Reading the history of this concept, one is struck by the programmatic character of the chief sociolinguistic definitions. Many influential ones were advanced early in the field's development – formulated in the 1960s and refined in the 1970s – perhaps as signposts staking out territories their proponents wished to pursue. Based on a few early studies (e.g. Labov in NYC, Gumperz in India), they reflect the concerns of each researcher – multilingualism for Gumperz, linguistic evaluation and style-shifting for Labov, ways of speaking and communicative competence for Hymes – to the relative exclusion of other emphases. As practitioners developing an idea for use in their own projects, each created a contingent concept, later retooled for general use.

This retrospective view exaggerates: convergences did occur, notably between Hymes and Gumperz. Yet when each new conception is introduced, one finds little or no reference to existing ones: Gumperz is not concerned with stratification, or Labov with shared communicative patterns across language areas, while Hymes discusses interactional criteria only with reference to Bloomfield, not Gumperz. Clearly, definitions were not developed on the basis of any taxonomy of case studies or survey of existing work.

Despite general early concern for the classification of sociolinguistic situations (Weinreich 1953, Ferguson 1959, 1966, Stewart 1962, Hymes 1972) and Hymes's statement that "The natural unit for sociolinguistic taxonomy . . . is not the language but the speech community" (1972: 43), apparently no such enterprise has formed the basis for examination and empirical development of the speech community concept. Indeed, the taxonomic enterprise itself has languished or perhaps been abandoned: we have nothing equivalent to anthropology's cross-cultural Human Relations Area Files. Though comparative studies flourish in specific areas (urban dialectology, dialect contact, language attrition), overall profiles and general models are lacking, such as attempts to analyze speech communities holistically as sociolinguistic systems and then typologize them (Trudgill, this volume).

A good deal of theorizing in a young, expanding field is polemical in nature. Common external targets have been structuralists' reduction of the speech community to a mere extension of a linguistic system (Hymes 1972: 54), and Chomsky's famous "ideal speaker-listener, in a completely homogeneous speech community" (1965: 3). Within the field, Labov's (1966) definition has been repeatedly attacked, often by researchers with similar methodological and analytical predilections.

Such efforts typically identify overly broad claims or narrow restrictions in the original by introducing new data, and sometimes innovative methods. Often they over- or misinterpret earlier ideas, maximizing their unfashionability in the light of recent changes in direction, anchoring a predecessor's general insight implausibly to specific associated elements as if to threaten the whole enterprise, which can then be saved by adopting their innovation. The historical account below attempts to sever spurious attachments, in order to enhance our vision both backwards and forwards.

Another polemical tactic is to claim that sociolinguistic research paradigms are efficiently encapsulated by their definitions of the SpCom, which serve as proximate targets. If the view sketched here of the concept's development is correct, these brief statements make only partial, often early or shifting, statements of their associated approaches' basic principles. To this extent, radical attacks (or, equally, promotions) miss their mark unless they look to practice as well as prose.

As the sociolinguistic research base massively expands, and the oppositional influence of theory groups and founders' ideas (Murray 1996, Figueroa 1994) perhaps begins to recede, discussion of the SpCom shifts away from the polemics of paradigm wars towards cooler engagement with relatively abstract major issues (but see Bucholtz 1999, a recent attempt to supplant SpCom with "community of practice"). One that has received considerable attention is the problem of appropriate social models: the consensus-vs.-conflict debate, stratification, and social class. Two others are not always carefully distinguished and are sometimes misguidedly opposed: the problems of correlation (linking linguistic behavior to social position/structure) and indexicality (explaining how linguistic forms index social meaning). These are related to an emphasis on linguistic and normative uniformity vs. subjective identification, and a choice of focus on institutional power vs. individual agency – and thus to another issue: scale, the size of the group studied and its influence on assumptions, methods, and interpretation. These are not new problems for sociolinguistics, but their interrelationship and connection to the SpCom needs clarification.

On ground more familiar to general linguists, if equally uncertain, two claims critically underlie classic definitions: the uniformity of speech by different speakers, on distinct occasions; and the possibility of identifying a group of speakers who share a single language (or conversely, identifying the boundaries of a language, as spoken by individuals). Notions of competence, nativeness, and language boundaries are too basic and problematic to address here, but the SpCom represents no escape from them.

Yet more fundamental issues loom. What precisely is the status of the equation between shared linguistic knowledge and social membership, which most definitions raise? In referring to the SpCom, are (socio-)linguists assuming that speakers united by linguistic criteria form a social group? Is this axiomatic? Are we instead hypothesizing, nominating this as a research question which empirical studies will eventually answer? Is it below awareness, an equation made primarily in method, with unexplored consequences for analysis and interpretation? Confusion on this point is rampant, with the same author sometimes implying different positions.

The SpCom is evidently fraught with difficulties. In mixing social and linguistic issues, matters of fact and philosophy, it brings us to the brink of issues many practicing sociolinguists feel uncomfortable with, perhaps even unprepared to answer. For example, it is unclear whether the SpCom is primarily a social or linguistic object (or inhabits a ground where this distinction is unmotivated). Is it appropriate to build a model using linguistic matter, and then treat it on a par with concepts like social group, network, community of practice – purely social notions, in the definition of which language plays no role? Bucholtz portrays the SpCom as "a language-based unit of social analysis" (1999: 203) and complains of the centrality of language, contending that "all non-linguistic aspects of social activity are marginalized or ignored" (1999: 207). For Hymes, however, the SpCom is not a naive attempt to use language to compass a social unit, but rather "an object defined for purposes of linguistic inquiry", not to be confused with "attributes of the counterpart of that object in social life . . . It postulates the unit of description as a social, rather than linguistic, entity" (1974: 48, 47).

Ultimately I adopt a similar view, turning around Bucholtz's phrasing to see the SpCom as "a socially-based unit of linguistic analysis", and advocate an approach which addresses the issues implied in current SpCom definitions as questions in formulating methodology and interpretations.

2 History of the Speech Community: Principal Theorists

The roots of the concept lie in the general sources of sociolinguistics: historical linguistics, philosophy of language, dialectology, anthropology, early structuralism. Tracing "the Humboldtian (and Herderian) sources of [American] structural linguistics" (Hymes and Fought 1981: 98) through Boas, Sapir and Whorf reveals a persistent link between community and language form. Hymes characterizes a "Herderian model of one language, one people, one culture, one community – the Hopi and their language, etc." (1974: 123), and describes what

> "Cartesian" and "Herderian" approaches . . . have fundamentally in common: isolation of a language as the object of linguistic description; equation of a language with a speech community (or culture); taking of the social functions of language as external, given, and universally equivalent. (Hymes 1974: 120)

Von Humboldt thought we must "seek the basic explanation of our present-day cultural level in . . . national intellectual individualities . . . Since they [languages] always have a national form, nations as such are really and directly creative" (1971: 20; see Aarsleff 1982 against the Herder-via-Humboldt lineage).

Boas and his students more cautiously represent the bond as complex and note merely that "all languages reflect the history and culture . . . of the community of which they have been a part" (Hymes and Fought 1981: 81). Likewise Sapir, whose Master's thesis investigated Herder's influence on von Humboldt, claimed that "Speech . . . is a purely historical heritage of the group, the product of long-continued social usage" (1921: 4). After Boas, he argues early on and influentially against biological determinism, the linkage of language change and origins with the progress and genius of nations and races:

"Language, race and culture are not necessarily correlated . . . The coincidences of cleavage point merely to a readily intelligible historical association" (Sapir 1921: 215–16). He grants no simple corporate identity to the speakers of a language variety, and appears not to use a specific term like SpCom.

Hymes embraces a basic idea of the "Herderian" approach: "emphasis on language as constituting cultural identity . . . a methodology of sympathetic interpretation of cultural diversity sui generis – Herder coined the German verb *einfühlen* – if within a larger universal framework" (1974: 120). (See Meyerhoff, this volume; the last phrase affirms the possibility of taxonomy and comparison, contra Vico.) Hymes cautions that "the focus, however, must be changed from a language as a correlate of a people, to persons and their ways of speaking" (1974: 123).

Other nineteenth century historical linguists give the community's role short shrift. Saussure speaks only in passing of a "community of speakers" in the context of explanations for language change. For Whitney (1979), individuals innovate but communities actually change languages by selecting among innovations: "Language is not an individual possession, but a social . . . The community . . . [is the] final tribunal which decides whether anything shall be language or not" (1979: 149–50). This position is held by Gauchat (1905, Weinreich et al. 1968) and Sapir, in his discussion of drift (1921, Ferguson 1996). Further elaboration by historical linguists is slow arriving. Even in 1960 Martinet, observing that "We must first of all attempt to define the notion of a linguistic community, if such a thing is possible" (1964: 136), does so minimally. He notes variation within varieties, and alternation between them, but affirms straightforward extension of a language to a set of speakers: "Human beings who belong to one or more linguistic communities . . . use one or the other language according to the person addressed" (1964: 139).

This extension is the classic position, first explicitly adopted by Bloomfield (1926) (though Fishman thinks SpCom is "probably translated from the German *Sprachgemeinschaft*," 1971a: 232, Raith 1987). He locates it within the theoretical framework of his postulates:

> 1. Definition. An act of speech is an utterance. 2. Assumption. Within certain communities successive utterances are alike or partly alike . . . 3. Definition. Any such community is a speech community.   (Bloomfield 1926: 153–4)

This formulation highlights the problem of linguistic uniformity (how alike must utterances be, and in what ways, to constitute their speakers as sharing a speech community?), smuggling in "community" as an unquestioned prime – two problems that remain with us. A later, widely-read version emphasizes that intelligibility governs the boundaries of SpComs – though since this is a continuum, "the term speech-community has only a relative value" (Bloomfield 1933: 54). By this criterion, "speech-communities differ greatly in size" (1933: 43), while bilinguals belong to disparate communities. Bloomfield also notes variation within single communities on geographic and social axes. He thus touches on problems of scale, overlapping communities, and normative heterogeneity.

Crucially, he explains both internal variation and external boundaries by interactional networks: "a speech-community is a group of people who interact by means of speech" (Bloomfield 1933: 42). Gumperz attributes this to structuralist awareness of dialect geography findings: "By the mid 1930s . . . language change could thus be explained as a direct function of the amount and intensity of verbal interaction among speakers" (1972: 23; but see Milroy and Milroy 1998). In this view, "differences of speech within a community are due to differences in density of communication" (Bloomfield 1933: 46), while "sub-groups are separated by lines of weakness in this net of oral communication" (1933: 47). He includes social classes, age-groups, and occupations; indeed the chapter, entitled "Speech-Communities," is essentially a survey of extra-linguistic correlations. The discussion is primitive compared to later sociolinguists' use of social network theory (beginning perhaps with Fishman 1971a); and social features are largely discounted as influences on linguistic structure, as issues of linguistic relativity are subsequently suppressed by universalists (Gumperz and Levinson 1996). Yet Bloomfield's emphasis on interaction, and his suggestion that its impact might be quantified, importantly prefigure work by Gumperz and the Milroys. The idea that networks are neutral and mechanical in effect remains critical.

In the early 1960s, sociolinguists elaborated the SpCom. Classic definitions were still being offered – "all the people who use a given language (or dialect)" (Lyons 1970: 326) – but Gumperz in 1962 located the problem: "While the anthropologist's description refers to specific communities, the universe of linguistic analysis is a single language or dialect, a body of verbal signs abstracted from the totality of communicative behavior" (1972: 460). From the latter position many problems of language use are inaccessible; Gumperz was interested, among others, in language choice and code switching in multilingual settings. Weinreich (1953), bridging the gap between structural and functional approaches, introduced the notion of "bilingual speech community" in opposition to extensions of the classic position, such as Mackey's

> An individual's use of two languages supposes the existence of two different language communities; it does not suppose the existence of a bilingual community. The bilingual community can only be regarded as a dependent collection of individuals who have reasons for being bilingual. (Mackey 1972: 554)

Gumperz, reformulating the SpCom "as a social group which may be either monolingual or multilingual," adopts "the term 'linguistic community' by analogy with Emeneau's term 'linguistic area'" (1972: 463) – pointing to work which demonstrated that social contact leads to extensive structural parallels across the boundaries not only of individual languages, but of language families (Emeneau 1956). However, Gumperz clearly did not intend to imply the traditional concept was adequate; in 1968 he revised the notion but returned to the term SpCom.

His approach is explicitly functional: "The criterion for inclusion of a code in a study of a linguistic community is that its exclusion will produce a gap in the communication matrix" (1972: 464). In this spirit he facilitates the taxonomic enterprise, recommending a typology of relationships "between the overall characteristics of the code matrix and certain features of social structure" (1972: 465), and developing a terminology (largely abandoned) to allow more general formulations.

Gumperz' initial version of SpCom closely follows Bloomfield (1933) in its focus on the frequency of social interaction. Interestingly, Hymes later insists that frequency is not enough. Rather, he claims (citing Gumperz' own findings), the "definition of situations in which, and identities through which, interaction occurs is decisive" (1974: 47). Initially Gumperz, like Bloomfield, leaves open questions of scale: linguistic communities "may consist of small groups bound together by face-to-face contact or may cover large regions, depending on the level of abstraction we wish to achieve" (Gumperz 1972: 463). Note his implication that social cohesion is optional; Hymes will not allow that "identity, or commonality, of linguistic knowledge" is sufficient to unify members of a community (1974: 47).

In the 1968 revision, Gumperz introduces two elements absent from the previous definition (which depended entirely on social criteria). Both are shared with Labov and Hymes, and enormously influential in subsequent conceptions. He defines the SpCom as "any human aggregate characterized by regular and frequent interaction by means of a shared body of verbal signs and set off from similar aggregates by significant differences in language usage" (1968: 381). This "shared body" reintroduces common linguistic knowledge as a necessary criterion. He adds that "speech varieties employed within a speech community form a system because they are related to a shared set of social norms" (1968: 382); such normative regulation is also at the heart of Labov's conception.

This pair of criteria alone satisfies many sociolinguists as an all-purpose definition. For Fishman (1971b: 28), a SpCom is a subtype of community "all of whose members share at least a single speech variety and the norms for its appropriate use." Eckert and McConnell-Ginet (1998: 490) claim that though lip-service is usually paid to a Rules+Norms model (ironically credited to Gumperz 1982), sociolinguists "seldom recognize explicitly the crucial role of practice in delineating speech communities". In such characterizations the interactional criterion is omitted. Fishman and many others reduce the Rules component to a minimum collective competence in grammatical knowledge. Kerswill (1994), viewing Gumperz' larger body of work, proposes a more complex interpretation of this "shared body." He believes it refers not only to "linguistic similarities among the various codes in use", but also to "agreement on the social meaning of various linguistic parameters" (1994: 24), including sociolinguistic variables, code switching, and contextualization cues; such parameters can only be fully understood by members of the same SpCom. However, I separate shared grammatical competence as a criterion from organization and interpretation of sociolinguistic norms.

Gumperz' revision (1982) expresses ideas shared with Hymes and Labov:

> A SpCom is defined in functionalist terms as a system of organized diversity held together by common norms and aspirations . . . Members of such a community typically vary with respect to certain beliefs and other aspects of behavior. Such variation, which seems irregular when observed at the level of the individual, nonetheless shows systematic regularities at the statistical level of social facts.   (Gumperz 1982: 24)

This definition sympathetically assimilates Labov's work into a broader social framework. Yet Gumperz makes clear that he is more interested in exploring how interaction, including language, constitutes social reality. From this perspective he seriously questions the applicability of the SpCom concept (1982: 26).

Classic definitions conceived of it as a "linguistic distribution within a social or geographical space" (Gumperz 1972: 463); some current models require "a geographical area delimited by non-linguistic criteria, such as demography or socio-political boundaries" (Kerswill 1994: 23). Dialect geography and anthropology, too, have often assumed that the most local and insular units are somehow the purest and strongest, thus the canonical community. But Gumperz cites a worldwide weakening of social boundaries and deference to group norms, drawing attention to the processes by which individuals index identity. This requires a renewed focus on face-to-face interaction, ethnographic observation, and a consequent restriction to small-scale studies. In effect he first confines the speech community to quantitative, correlational work – rejecting the broad conception sought in earlier approaches – and then abandons (though does not dismiss) it as a research focus. This move is influential in current debates, where the divorce of the correlational and indexing enterprises assumes an appearance of historical inevitability.

That, however, is not Gumperz' current perspective. As part of a rejuvenated linguistic anthropological interest in social indexicality, he maintains his interest in face-to-face interaction:

> If meaning resides in interpretive practices . . . located in the social networks one is socialized in, then the "culture-" and "language-" bearing units are not nations, ethnic groups or the like . . . but rather networks of interacting individuals. (Gumperz and Levinson 1996: 11)

Such networks may "cross-cut linguistic and social boundaries of all sorts, creating regional and even global patterns of shared, similar communicative strategies in specialist networks" (1996: 12). In order to locate both local and extended networks, and to grapple with supra-local problems such as standard language ideologies, a familiar larger entity is required: "Speech communities, broadly conceived, can be regarded as collectivities of social networks" (Gumperz 1996: 362). In this view, the rehabilitated SpCom is not an abstract nexus of category lines, but instead is composed of network building-blocks in

which "interpretive strategies are embedded . . . and passed on as shared communicative traditions." The difficulty with studying social meaning above the
network level is that "indexicality reflect[s] network-specific practices" while
SpComs "tend towards diversification and this restricts the extent to which
linguistic forms, conceptual structures, and culture are shared" (1996: 363).
Thus a notion of SpCom persists, but not one which presumes or requires
unity of norms and ways of speaking. This notion inhabits an upper region of
the scale, and must allow for nesting and interlocking network patterns.

This extended discussion of Gumperz' approaches to the SpCom has served
to introduce many themes still current and problematic. One might have done
the same via other theorists; Gumperz is convenient because his definitions
are clear and easily dated in their progress, not subsumed early on into a
theoretical or methodological apparatus which promotes other concepts as
more basic – as with Hymes and Labov. Consideration of their competing and
complementary approaches will be contrastive as much as historical, but the
progressive focusing of Gumperz' views raises a key question: has the SpCom
become restricted to certain (possibly incompatible) paradigms of sociolinguistics, or is a broad conception still viable? (Though indeed the idea began
in particular contexts, early efforts all tended towards generalization.)

Dell Hymes has always maintained a broad notion of the SpCom, rooted in
his understanding of the sociolinguistic enterprise:

> Speech community is a necessary, primary concept . . . It postulates the unit of
> description as a social, rather than linguistic, entity. One starts with a social
> group and considers the entire organization of linguistic means within it.
>
> (Hymes 1974: 47)

In many respects Hymes and Gumperz agree: in shifting the classical focus from
varieties to the relations among speakers, discarding on functional grounds the
restriction to monolingual situations, promoting sociolinguistic taxonomy, and
insisting on both shared grammar and shared norms. Where Gumperz' descriptions start from individuals (like social network theory and the community of
practice approach), emphasizing speaker agency, boundary shifting and emergent meaning, ethnography of communication began with a concern for collective resources, bounded events, and ritual performance, privileging community
and structure – it focused on social meaning, but was not speaker-based.

In Hymes's theorizing, the nature of the SpCom is inferred from more
basic terms: "The starting point of description is . . . a repertoire of ways
of speaking . . . a speech community defined through the concurrence of rules
of grammar and rules of use" (Hymes 1974: 120). It is not a methodological
prime: one cannot know what practices are critical, or who shares in them,
before a study has been carried out. *Communicative competence, ways of speaking*
(especially) and *verbal repertoire* are principal terms. (Privileging contexts and
institutions as a vantage point yields an alternative, more abstract approach,
"the study of the speech economy of a community" (1974: 46), pursued by Gal

1989, Irvine 1989, Silverstein 1996, among others.) An ideal ethnographer of speaking identifies a verbal repertoire, catalogues speech events and rules of communicative practice, and describes what communicative competence consists of: the SpCom can then be defined as the set of speakers who appropriately exploit these resources. As in the classic definition, SpCom members are an identifiable existing group located and bounded by shared knowledge – though Hymes stresses social knowledge of language functions and norms.

Knowledge of ways of speaking, and ability, are unequally distributed within a community, however, raising the problem of how much knowledge is required (Dorian 1982), while knowledge alone is not sufficient to distinguish members from mere participants (e.g. experienced fieldworkers), as Hymes acknowledges (1974: 50–1). He allows wholly non-linguistic criteria here, such as birthright, reminding us that his conception presumes a cohesive entity, not just a set of interacting speakers – a stricter requirement than Gumperz' loose interactional collectivity. Thus Hymes's "socially constituted linguistics" (1974: 196) looks to social material to constrain the ways in which language is encountered empirically. His SpCom is a socially-based unit of linguistic analysis, and he explicitly warns that sociolinguistics "requires the contribution of social science in characterising the notions of community, and of membership". Pending this solution, however, he follows early Gumperz in specifying "a local unit, characterised for its members by common locality and primary interaction" (1974: 51).

Yet from the start, Hymes's approach emphasizes shared norms over interaction. He restates Bloomfield's fundamental principle of linguistic theory: "in a speech community some utterances are the same," in terms of normative information derived from speech events: "in a speech community, some *ways of speaking* are the same" (1974: 201). Ways of speaking imply knowledge not only of forms and their co-occurrence, but also their social distribution and appropriacy for social function. The uniformity problem thus shifts its focus from linguistic production to community-based interpretation.

There are obvious links to Labov's (1966) conception, perhaps the first to couple productive and evaluative norms. Both place value on describing normative behavior, as displayed consciously and unconsciously by speakers. It has proven more difficult to grasp how norms develop and change, are acquired and understood – but this is a question which interaction-based analysis must also answer. Language socialization theory (Ochs 1996) addresses this, and practice theorists (Eckert 2000, Meyerhoff, this volume) have begun to explore it, both from anthropological traditions. More sociologically-inclined adherents of network theory, such as the Milroys, say little about local norms at this level, despite crucial contributions to modeling networks as channels for linguistic change (often styled "mechanisms" for norm enforcement) and "prerequisite[s] for a focused set of distinctive vernacular norms" (Milroy and Milroy 1998: 188). Their point that networks are a neutral, relative structural concept (1998: 193) indicates the need for companion studies of linguistic ideology to explore the values being transmitted across weak or strong ties.

Hymes's model supports multiple varieties, like Gumperz', and insists on shared form in addition to shared ways of speaking, unlike many later definitions privileging the latter (Romaine 1994: 22, Fasold 1990: 41, Trask 1997: 204). That the two may diverge is usefully captured in the *Sprachbund/Sprechbund* distinction (Neustupny 1978) – areal terms defined on just these grounds – but a SpCom must be located in the union of the two (Hymes 1974: 50 gives a more precise account). Orientation to linguistic uniformity is often a dividing line for theorists: where later Gumperz downplays it, radical subjectivists deny it (Corder 1973, Hudson 1996) and variationists privilege it (Labov's "uniform structural base" 1989: 2, Kerswill 1994, Kroch 1996). Hymes, like Labov, holds a nuanced view, interpreting uniformity as an abstract regularity, not equivalent to identity of forms. Recognizing that language use may constitute social relationships, he suggests that a scale of distinctiveness be left open: "Part of the creativity of users of language lies in the freedom to determine what and how much linguistic difference matters" (Hymes 1974: 123) to boundary maintenance.

William Labov's SpCom conception has been enormously influential. It is more empirically-rooted, less generalized, than Hymes's or Gumperz'. It emerges in the course of a well-defined program of research on language structure and change, rather than in the context of sociolinguistic theorizing. Consider three aspects.

1   It is closely based on results from a series of urban studies which established goals for later researchers; its outlines emerge from a particular set of questions and answers, and may be inappropriate for others.
2   More than other theorists, Labov makes explicit and testable his conceptions of linguistic uniformity and normative sociolinguistic structure, which have been widely adopted and debated.
3   It is allied to a rich array of methods, also commonly used – often by researchers with diverging assumptions and objectives.

Labov's definition was the first to posit both shared norms and linguistic uniformity (as structured variation), in that order, as criteria for identifying a SpCom. While Romaine and others incorrectly charged that in Labov's conception of uniformity, SpCom members "share rules of grammar in the form of variable rules" (Romaine 1982: 19), the variable rule (Labov 1969) is not his solution to the problem. (Romaine herself admits it is peripheral to the SpCom: "the thrust of my argument is against the specific descriptive device, the variable rule," (1982: 23); but the misunderstanding persists, e.g. Kerswill 1994: 137.) Instead this is handled through the earlier invention of the linguistic variable (Labov 1966: 32ff), a set of variants which is specifiable independent of any predictability by linguistic conditioning, and capable of crossing phonemic or morphemic lines. The normal heterogeneity characteristic of speech production is expressed as differential use of variants, but the SpCom is "defined on the level of interpretation; the obverse of heterogeneous speech production is homogeneity in the interpretation of the variants" (Romaine 1982: 18). Thus uniformity and interpretation are inseparable.

Subsequently, the importance of linguistic uniformity for Labov is highlighted: matching the complex distribution of short-*a* in Philadelphia (Labov 1989) is prima facie evidence for membership. But it is the normative criterion that has vexed critics. Since many later considerations focus on the 1963–4 New York City study as though representative of current Labovian practice, discussion of his contribution to the SpCom is also concentrated here. It must be borne in mind, however, that what Labov prescribed were analytical and interpretive practices – not outcomes in the sense that subsequent speech communities should resemble New York's.

Labov's SpCom model is the direct product of his survey of the Lower East Side (LES) neighborhood of New York City. Here the SpCom definition was developed; from here it was generalized, by Labov and others. This study's goal was "to investigate the structure of NYC English" (Labov 1966: 110). Understanding the social distribution of linguistic forms, and exploring their social meaning – the correlation and indexicality problems which constitute dominant interests in sociolinguistics today – proved necessary, but subsidiary. Many later criticisms of the SpCom come from researchers primarily concerned with these issues, especially indexing (e.g. Eckert), or even with no interest in linguistic structure (e.g. Bucholtz).

For Labov, the constituency of a SpCom must be discovered through the research process. It is an outcome, not an assumption; a matter for observation, not theory (Labov 1994: 4–5). He breaks cleanly with classic definitions that endow a group of speakers with social coherence, warning sociolinguists to "avoid any error which would arise in assuming that a group of people who speak alike is a fundamental unit of social behavior" on the grounds that "asking about the language characteristics of a social group . . . seems more fundamental and more closely tied to the genesis of linguistic differentiation" (Labov 1966: 136–7). This approach avoids circularity on the assumption, shared with Hymes, that social units can be clearly identified on non-linguistic criteria – a point challenged explicitly by Gumperz, who considered that both social and linguistic categories are "signalled and subject to change in response to similar forces", asking "How can one set of categories be used to establish an objective basis against which to evaluate the other?" (Labov 1982: 29). It is therefore critical that Labov not focus (as he does not) on how language as a semiotic resource is manipulated to constitute social identity.

Labov's method in New York was to delimit a sample first by applying social criteria, then by raising issues of competence via acquisition patterns (excluding non-native speakers of English, and of NYC English), and finally by analysis of linguistic structure (e.g. the ultimate separation of African-American speakers on phonological grounds). The notion of community guiding the LES survey was primarily defined not by interaction, shared norms, or social stratification, but residence. The LES was selected because (1) the city's main social classes and ethnic groups were well represented; (2) it was a focus for both social mobility and local loyalty; (3) as a former port of entry, the influence of immigrant groups could be tested; and (4) residential structure was typical of the city and allowed for interaction between social groups. There was no requirement of strong social bonds or coherence (even his 1989 definition begins "an aggregate of speakers": Labov 1989: 2). No linguistic criteria were applied.

As the emphasis was on results of dialect acquisition, convergence, focusing, and transmission, interaction was important for the resulting system's nature. Yet Labov's interest was not in the diversity of ways of speech produced by interaction within particular networks (like Gumperz), but rather the consequent uniformity across a larger collectivity. New York City turned out to show a surprising degree of convergent behavior, reflected in Labov's statement: "NYC is a single speech community, united by a common set of evaluative norms, though divergent in the application of these norms" (Labov 1966: 355; note, however, the last clause).

This normative regularity is an empirical finding. The claim rests primarily on the evidence of synchronic style-shifting patterns, supported by covert and overt measures of evaluative norms (subjective reaction, self-evaluation, and linguistic-insecurity tests, plus language-attitude interviews). Results recurred strikingly across social classes, the sexes, age, and ethnic groups; irregularities were minor, largely mirroring changes in progress or contrasting changes of a different age. The tests were conceived and interpreted in the light of a model of social stratification which has been much criticized (discussed below). Only the subjective-reaction test implicated such a model in its administration, however, and the overall convergence of Labov's findings has never been challenged (Santa Ana and Parodí 1998). The character of this specific case undergirds the general definition of the SpCom in his later synthesis:

> The speech community is not defined by any marked agreement in the use of language elements, so much as by participation in a set of shared norms. These norms may be observed in overt types of evaluative behavior, and by the uniformity of abstract patterns of variation which are invariant in respect to particular levels of usage.   (Labov 1972: 120–1)

Several points require emphasis because of frequent misinterpretations. The norms are not limited to evaluation or ideology (contra Fasold 1984: 148, Bucholtz 1999: 208) but include quantitative patterns of production showing structured variation. Generalizations about such norms are thus not merely interpretive statements filtered through the analyst's preferred model of society. Labov's first assertion that "New York forms a single speech community" occurs (1966: 202) before evaluative data have even been introduced. Crucially, Labov's conception requires *reference* to a set of shared norms – not deference or uniform adherence. He repeatedly describes departures from the overall patterns, by individuals and subgroups, which do not falsify the existence of these norms. This is consistent with the definition given above, allowing for "divergence in application."

It has been charged that Labov's model specifies rigid allegiance to sociolinguistic norms. Milroy wonders, "Why should we suppose that individuals at different social levels make the same social evaluations?" (1982: 46). Kerswill suggests that "Labov's model . . . seems blindly consensus-based and does not allow for multiple norms" (1994: 27). Bucholtz refers to "the expectation of consensus in speech community norms" as "the problem of homogeneity in the speech community model" (1999: 209), brashly conflating Labov's conception with that of Bloomfield and Hymes. Milroy and Milroy attribute to Labov the claim that "every speaker agrees on the evaluation of the varying norms of language" (1997: 53). Milroy even argues that given "the doctrine of common evaluation . . . it is difficult to see how socially motivated linguistic change can take place" (Milroy 1982: 38). The word "consensus" reverberates across these analyses, which unconsciously echo the variationist critique of categorical structuralist linguistics (Weinreich et al. 1968).

These criticisms, however, fail to distinguish the analyst's view of social structure from generalizations about dominant sociolinguistic patterns of production and evaluation. (Labov (1966) clearly separates them, and noncircularly orders the two.) Though framed as objections to the SpCom model, they are actually objections to the "consensus" view of society the LES study adopted. They also appear to suggest that surveys following Labovian methods lead, through expectations and prejudgments, to predetermined results. Thus they not only make a mild, plausible claim – that the consensual sociolinguistic patterns found in 1960's NYC are a narrow basis for a general SpCom model – but a more serious one: that Labov's social-theory assumptions led to wrong conclusions about NYC speech and generally render his model inadequate.

Yet no evidence for exceptionless norms exists in the LES survey itself. Labov repeatedly noted divergence, both in production and evaluation. A striking individual example is Steve K, who "consciously tried to reverse his college-trained tendency towards formal speech, and . . . deliberately rejected the pattern of values reflected" in the speech of other LES individuals (Labov 1966: 80). Despite this rejection, Steve K was unable to significantly differentiate himself in test speech. The method clearly does not *preclude* opposing values, then; in NYC they simply appeared to be exceptional, or to have insignificant consequences for speech production. This underlies Labov's dual stress on evaluative behavior and patterns of variation: attitude differences unaccompanied by speech differences are epiphenomena.

When a significant group of speakers differs on both levels, however, the model treats them as a distinct speech community. This is the case of the African-Americans examined separately: "Negro speakers share the white attitudes towards correctness . . . [but] reverse white attitudes towards the cultural values of NYC speech" (Labov 1966: 352). "The use of (eh), (oh), (ay) and (aw) by Negro speakers is quite different than for whites" (1966: 370). Differences of class and age among black speakers are noted, too, but overall they are consistently distinguished on many grounds from the white ethnic groups, who pattern together. Again, Labov noted "the resistance of children to the middle-class norm" (1966: 348), and argued that "many lower class subjects fall outside the influence of the unifying norms . . . many seem to lack the cultural values which maintain the working class pattern of speech in opposition to massive pressure from above" (Labov 1966: 351).

On close examination, it is clear that this seminal study, like many subsequent ones influenced by it, recognized rather than suppressed diverse patterns of evaluation and production in the community examined. The thrust of Labov's "unifying norm" was not to paint, or prescribe, uniformity, but to stress the pressure of standard linguistic norms that were accepted more than resisted. It is true that Labov does not formally raise the resistance observed to the level of competing norms and reify it in a "conflict" model; neither is it obvious that this would be a correct analysis of his data. Finally, the study identified several levels of generalization – local unity, patterns of divergence that nevertheless refer to local norms, and shared acceptance of external norms by members of different SpComs (black and white New Yorkers) – pointing to the need for a "nested" SpCom model.

3   The Speech Community and Models of Society

To the extent that the normative organization of a SpCom is discovered through empirical research, it can clearly be distinguished from the socioeconomic structure of the society to which that SpCom belongs. Standard procedure in sociolinguistic surveys requires consulting existing social science and historical research to understand the makeup of a community and inform the use of social variables as explanatory factors for language variation and change.

In this approach, analyses of social structure and linguistic behavior must be kept separate so the former may have explanatory value for the latter: "The nature of these [speech] norms, especially whether they relate to standard, legitimized, and literate forms of language, is determined by larger socio-economic structures, in particular those based on power" (Kerswill 1994: 27). As noted, Gumperz' challenge to this results in an opposed set of research concerns, called "interpretive sociolinguistics" by LePage (1997): "work which starts from the observation of linguistic behavior and interprets it in terms of social meaning, rather than starting from social structure and looking for linguistic correlates" (1997: 31).

Recently it has been argued within the correlational paradigm, as well, that the two levels cannot be separated. To the Milroys, "Labov's key sociolinguistic notion of speech community seems to assume a consensus model of social class whereby the community is fundamentally cohesive", while applying such a model to the speakers they studied requires analyzing the Belfast vernacular "as an unsuccessful approximation to educated . . . or standard English varieties" (Milroy and Milroy 1998: 180–1). Yet if "vernacular maintenance can result in conflict between two opposing norms," one standard and one low-prestige, then vernacular speakers do not share a common set of (evaluative) norms with standard speakers: "The pattern arising is . . . one of conflict rather than consensus" (Milroy and Milroy 1997: 53). (Here they follow Rickford 1986, who describes a Guyanese Creole-speaking community where opposed sets of attitudes aligned with distinct patterns of variation.) They argue that "a social class model based on conflict, division and inequality can account better than one based on consensus for many patterns of language variation" (Milroy and Milroy 1998: 181).

The latter point is persuasive; but the isomorphy proposed for the two levels of social organization is not. The type of evidence cited from Belfast to support the Milroy's view is also found in NYC, as shown above, if to a different degree. Yet neither conflict nor consensus models can be preferred in the abstract; as social analyses they are more or less applicable in specific situations. Choice is related to scale factors: higher points on the population scale may be more heterogeneous and divided. Delimitation of SpCom boundaries is also critical. In Dorian (1981), focus on the competence of Gaelic-speaking fisherfolk alone lends itself to a consensus model, while including the attitudes of English monolinguals in the same villages might be better handled in a conflict approach. In NYC, Labov's exclusion of certain native and immigrant groups is related to his concentration on the linguistic system. The legitimacy of analytical choices thus depends upon selection of the research question, in addition to the site.

If such models are intended to help elucidate sociolinguistic patterns, they must be defined independently. An approach should be adopted not based on the results of subjective evaluation or matched-guise tests, but because broader patterns of social, economic, historical, and cultural organization make it compelling. To contend that conflict models are generally preferable because of sociolinguistic findings, and then use the former to interpret the latter, is circular. Further, the claim that a social model binds the linguist to a particular view of the varieties under study – that under a consensus model, New Yorkers must fail in speaking Standard English, while in a conflict model they success-fully maintain a low-prestige variety – is simply false. It does not reflect usual practice among sociolinguists, which is to recognize the hegemonic character of standard languages while considering structurally distinct varieties to have their own integrity.

The introduction of conflict models has benefited correlational studies in several ways. It draws attention to the choices open to analysts and their impact. It raises the question: does recognition of competing norms within a SpCom invalidate emphasis on overarching norms as a definitional criterion? Undoubtedly, conflict models suit some social situations better (e.g. post-plantation Caribbean societies with characteristically strong racial and class antagonisms). They are not panaceas, however, to be universally preferred. They carry no explanations with them – but there are caveats. It is easily over-looked that in the absence of a broad societal consensus on values, stratification may still be powerful. Conflict analysts (Rickford 1986, Milroy and Milroy 1998) typically assign opposed groups each to a set of normative values, so that discord occurs between relatively homogeneous factions. Reality is often more complicated, with individuals holding conflicting values, each ratified by society (Patrick 1999); but individual agency is not easily captured in theories derived from Marx.

Finally, the connection between models of society and characterizations of the SpCom is not transparent, despite claims in the literature. Interpreting SpCom models primarily through the lens of social class is unnecessarily restrictive. Whether one privileges structural uniformity and stresses the institutionalization of power in shared attitudes towards a standard (regarding dissent as minimal and covert) – or privileges acts of identity and focuses on speaker agency in social positioning through linguistic choice, celebrating diverse attitudes – are to some extent predilections of the analyst that do not invalidate competent description and theorizing.

4   Other Developments in the Speech Community Concept

The principal concepts of SpCom have received reactions and modifications of two broad types: variations on a theme, intended to refine (usually broaden) a SpCom model; and general rejection of their applicability, on various grounds. An important trend among the latter is the rise of radical subjectivist approaches, influenced by the work of Robert LePage, especially his "acts of identity" model (LePage and Tabouret-Keller 1985). LePage's principal theoretical concern is to reject the privileging of language as an abstract object of investigation and substitute a speaker-based model, building up both notions of linguistic system and sociolinguistic patterns from individual data – especially perceptions and motivations. LePage's emphasis on diversity of speaker orientations and fluidity of linguistic boundaries is driven by the challenges of "Caribbean sociolinguistic complexes" (Carrington 1993, Winford 1988). LePage and Tabouret-Keller are interested in understanding how "individuals . . . can be considered members of linguistic communities" (1985: 158), but fall short of modeling this.

Subjectivist positions postdate Labov's and Gumperz' introduction of shared social norms as a criterion but stress individual perception of norms to the exclusion of other elements. Corder, considering second language learners, defines a SpCom as "made up of individuals who regard themselves as speaking the same language; it need have no other defining attributes" (1973: 53). Hudson carries this emphasis on individual perception to a logical extreme, claiming that "Our sociolinguistic world is not organised in terms of objective 'speech communities'" (1996: 29), and that sociolinguistics should stick to "the micro level of the individual person and the individual linguistic item" (1996:

229). Such radical positions are in sympathy with "interpretive sociolinguistics" but problematic for efforts to describe linguistic systems – or language change, where many structural developments are "quite removed from social affect or recognition" (Labov 1982: 84).

The issue of determining membership versus lesser degrees of participation is highlighted by Dorian's (1982) study of Gaelic "semi-speakers." Here it is not extension beyond traditional bounds (see works by LePage; cf. Rampton 1995) but contraction within them that is problematic. Low-proficiency Gaelic semi-speakers do not adequately possess productive competence in the variety; may not be significantly differentiated from monolingual English-speakers in terms of their language use; and are insensitive to normative judgments of usage. On the other hand, they display strong receptive competence and knowledge of norms of appropriateness, and may be self- and other-identified as Gaelic bilinguals. Gaelic speakers are strikingly aware of regional, and unaware of social, variation, so that the latter Labovian criterion is irrelevant. While Dorian thus finds Labov's definition unsuitable for including semi-speakers and prefers Hymes', Labov (1982: 50) himself notes that this situation carries heterogeneity of production and homogeneity of norms to a logical extreme.

The notion of simultaneous membership in multiple overlapping SpComs – alongside membership in distinct ones – is first posed in a Hymesian framework (Saville-Troike 1982). It leads directly to the conclusion that "there is no limit to the number and variety of SpComs that are to be found in a society" (Bolinger 1975: 333). But this same position may be reached without loosening the notion of SpCom to "personal network," simply by taking seriously the requirement for explicitly multi-variety situations, since there is no principled limit to language/dialect contact and creation. As this conclusion appears unavoidable, what is needed is not a wholesale retreat from the notion of coherent communities, but a conception which makes possible the integration of complex patterns of membership. Whether the top-down approach of Labov or the bottom-up one of Gumperz and LePage is selected as a starting-point, a comprehensive SpCom model must allow intermediate structures: in the first case, nesting, and in the second, overlapping. Since the latter seem to be untheorized – speaker- and interaction-based theories have yet to reach above the level of networks – I consider only nested models below.

Scale, interpreted demographically, has been little investigated in linguistics (on diffusion see Trudgill 1974, Callary 1975, Labov 1982). Romaine gives five levels of abstraction in linguistic analysis: "individual – network – social group – speech community – language" (1982: 8). Considering a different list (individual speakers, dyads, multi-party face-to-face interactions, communities of practice, and large communities), Hanks concludes that

> No single metalanguage for participant roles will be adequate at all levels . . . We can hope to cast our descriptions of face-to-face participation and larger-scale discursive formations in such a way that they intersect – or if not, that the points of divergence are made visible. (Hanks 1996: 223)

Such scales are not unidimensional – networks, as asynchronous assemblages, involve interaction at several levels – but concentric mappings occur. In practice, applications of the SpCom are scattered across higher levels and cannot be restricted to one point. It has a lower bound (it has been used for a single longhouse of two nuclear families, Jackson 1974), but cannot be distinguished in principle from networks, which are themselves potentially unbounded upwards. SpCom is a multi-leveled concept cutting across the ecology of nested contexts.

Kerswill's (1994) study of rural migrants to Bergen requires a focus on the integration of nested contexts. He spells out the monolingual character of Labov's SpCom model, arguing that as urban natives and migrants are groups at the same level of social organization, a higher level is required to understand the social evaluation and symbolic functions of locally competing varieties. In this model, groups exhibiting internally coherent patterns of production and evaluation, but contrasting with their neighbors, can still be united in a "larger" SpCom if they can be systematically related. Stril migrants form a linguistically heterogeneous group speaking regionally differentiated varieties (Kerswill 1994: 37). They acquire a low-prestige Bergen feature, schwa-lowering, but accord it high prestige among themselves, which Kerswill explains in terms of distinct symbolic functions in migrant and dominant communities. Building on this line, simultaneous membership of distinct SpComs can be modeled so long as they are systematically relatable (though, Kerswill admits, non-nested overlapping memberships remain problematic).

Santa Ana and Parodí (1998) also work to expand Labov's concept into a general typology. In a study of Spanish dialect contact in Mexico, they discovered that a subset of community members speaking a regional vernacular – not distinguishable linguistically by separate features or socially by age, region, family, or similar descriptors – appear unaware of the social evaluation of locally stigmatized markers. Other degrees of awareness of regional and national/ standard linguistic variables are distinguished. Recognition, evaluation and production of socially marked features form the basis of a four-field typology of SpCom configurations; fields are analytically distinct, but (like Kerswill) systematically relatable. Membership in a field is a measure of social influence from the wider society on an individual speaker and appears to correspond to "the extent of the effective social network . . . [and] the size of the economic market in which they actively participate" (Santa Ana and Parodí 1998: 38).

In preserving the primacy of shared evaluation, but also common patterns of linguistic variation, as criteria – and not utilizing self-identification or social functions of language – this is an explicitly Labovian model. It is at present monolingual, though a bilingual extension is contemplated; it is empirically derived but intended for taxonomy and predicated on a careful review of existing work. It is not interactional in its definition, but its explanation is linked to social network theory; it is aimed at the correlation problem but is a bottom-up process identifying units of the size and type required for studying indexicality as well. As with Kerswill, issues of scale are implied, and it appears to account well for the nested, non-overlapping relations described. It has not yet been applied to more complex situations involving dual membership or individual responses to conflicting norms.

This review of the SpCom suggests several generalizations. The work required of the concept ideally includes, at least: application to the correlation problem and appropriate interfacing with indexicality; handling multivariety situations; allowing for nested communities and articulating with issues of scale; realistically addressing linguistic uniformity in the light of structured variation; specifying relevant types of sociolinguistic evaluation and the minimum degree to which they must be shared; systematic relation of communities in contact on the latter two criteria; application to a wide range of competences; recognition of conflicting norms held by individuals or within groups; and attention to processes of conventionalization, as well as their normative results. In some cases, work must be shared with concepts like social network (Milroy, this volume) or community of practice (Meyerhoff, this volume).

The SpCom ought to abjure certain kinds of work, too. Users should not presume social cohesion or accept it to be an inevitable result of interaction; size and its effects should not be taken for granted; social theories, including class analyses, must be explicitly invoked, not accepted as givens; the SpCom should not be taken for a unit of social analysis; and we ought not to assume SpComs exist as predefined entities waiting to be researched or identify them with folk notions, but see them as objects constituted anew by the researcher's gaze and the questions we ask. Finally, the job of proper SpCom taxonomy, fitting case studies to typology and refining the latter, awaits.

REFERENCES

Aarsleff, H. (1982). *From Locke to Saussure: Essays on the Study of Language and Intellectual History.* Minneapolis: University of Minnesota Press.

Bavin, E. L. (1989). Some lexical and morphological changes in Warlpiri. In N. C. Dorian (ed.), *Investigating obsolescence: Studies in Language Contraction and Death.* Cambridge: Cambridge University Press. 267–86.

Bloomfield, L. (1926). A set of postulates for the science of language. *Language*, 2, 153–4.

Bloomfield, L. (1933). *Language.* New York: Holt.

Bolinger, D. (1975). *Aspects of Language.* 2nd edn. New York: Harcourt Brace.

Bucholtz, M. (1999). "Why be normal?" Language and identity practices in a community of nerd girls. *Language in Society*, 28, 2: 203–23.

Callary, R. E. (1975). Phonological change and the development of an urban dialect in Illinois. *Language in Society* 4: 155–70.

Carrington, L. D. (1993). Creole space – a rich sample of competence? *Journal of Pidgin and Creole Linguistics*, 8, 2: 227–36.

Chambers, J. K. (1995). *Sociolinguistic Theory.* Oxford: Blackwell.

Chambers, J. K. and P. Trudgill (1980). *Dialectology*. Cambridge: Cambridge University Press.

Chomsky, N. A. (1965). *Aspects of the Theory of Syntax*. Cambridge, MA: MIT Press.

Coates, J. (1993). *Women, Men, and Language*. London: Longman.

Corder, S. P. (1973). *Introducing Applied Linguistics*. Harmondsworth: Penguin.

Dimmendaal, G. J. (1989). On language death in eastern Africa. In N. C. Dorian (ed.), *Investigating Obsolescence: Studies in Language Contraction and Death*. Cambridge: Cambridge University Press. 13–31.

Dittmar, N. (1976). *Sociolinguistics: A Critical Survey of Theory and Application*. London: Arnold.

Dorian, N. C. (1981). *Language Death: The Life Cycle of a Scottish Gaelic Dialect*. Philadelphia: University of Pennsylvania Press.

Dorian, N. C. (1982). Defining the speech community in terms of its working margins. In S. Romaine (ed.), *Sociolinguistic Variation in Speech Communities* London: Edward Arnold. 25–33.

Dorian, N. C. (ed.), (1989). *Investigating Obsolescence: Studies in Language Contraction and Death*. Cambridge: Cambridge University Press.

Downes, W. (1998). *Language and Society*, 2nd edn. Cambridge: Cambridge University Press.

Durant, A. (1999). Clarifying notions of "meaning" at stake in linguistic evidence as to meaning: libel as an illustration. Paper to the International Association of Forensic Linguists' 4th Biennial Conference, Birmingham, UK.

Duranti, A. (1997). *Linguistic Anthropology*. Cambridge: Cambridge University Press.

Eckert, P. (2000). *Language Variation as Social Practice*. Oxford: Blackwell.

Eckert, P. and McConnell-Ginet, S. (1998). Communities of practice: where language, gender and power all live. In J. Coates (ed.), *Language and Gender: A Reader*. Oxford: Blackwell. 484–94.

Emeneau, M. B. (1956). India as a linguistic area. *Language* 32: 3–16.

Fasold, R. F. (1984). *The Sociolinguistics of Society*. Oxford: Blackwell.

Fasold, R. F. (1990). *The Sociolinguistics of Language*. Oxford: Blackwell.

Feagin, C. (1996). Peaks and glides in Southern States short-a. In G. R. Guy, C. Feagin, D. Schiffrin and J. Baugh (eds.), *Towards a Social Science of Language: Papers in Honor of William Labov*, vol. 1: *Variation and Change in Language and Society*. Amsterdam: Benjamins. 135–60.

Ferguson, C. A. (1959). Diglossia. *Word* 15: 325–40.

Ferguson, C. A. (1966). National sociolinguistic profile formulas. In W. Bright (ed.), *Sociolinguistics*. The Hague: Mouton. 309–15.

Ferguson, C. A. (1996). Variation and drift: Loss of agreement in Germanic. In G. R. Guy, C. Feagin, D. Schiffrin and J. Baugh (eds.), *Towards a Social Science of Language: Papers in Honor of William Labov*, vol. 1: *Variation and Change in Language and Society*. Amsterdam: Benjamins. 173–98.

Figueroa, E. (1994). *Sociolinguistic Metatheory*. Oxford: Pergamon.

Fishman, J. A. (1971a). The sociology of language: An interdisciplinary social science approach to language in society. In J. A. Fishman (ed.), *Advances in the Sociology of Language*. The Hague: Mouton. 217–404.

Fishman, J. A. (1971b). *Sociolinguistics*. Rowley, MA: Newbury House.

Gal, S. (1989). Language and political economy. *Annual Review of Anthropology* 18: 345–67.

Gauchat, L. (1905). L'unité phonétique dans le patois d'une commune. In *Aus Romanischen Sprachen und Literaturen: Festschrift Heinrich Morf.* Halle: M. Niemeyer. 175–232.

Gomez-Imbert, Elsa (1996). When animals become "rounded" and "feminine": Conceptual categories and linguistic classification in a multilingual setting. In J. J. Gumperz and S. C. Levinson (eds.), *Rethinking Linguistic Relativity.* Cambridge: Cambridge University Press. 438–69.

Gumperz, J. J (1968). The speech community. In D. L. Sills (ed.), *International Encyclopedia of the Social Sciences.* New York: Macmillan. 381–6.

Gumperz, J. J. (1972). Types of linguistic communities. *Anthropological Linguistics*, 4 (1962): 28–40. (Reprinted 1972 in J. A. Fishman (ed.), *Readings in the Sociology of Language*, The Hague: Mouton. 460–72.)

Gumperz, J. J. (1982). *Discourse Strategies.* Cambridge: Cambridge University Press.

Gumperz, J. J. (1996). Introduction to part IV of J. J. Gumperz and S. C. Levinson (eds.), *Rethinking Linguistic Relativity.* Cambridge: Cambridge University Press. 359–73.

Gumperz, J. J. and S. C. Levinson (1996). Introduction: Linguistic relativity re-examined. In J. J. Gumperz and S. C. Levinson (eds.), *Rethinking Linguistic Relativity.* Cambridge: Cambridge University Press. 1–18.

Hanks, W. F. (1996). *Language and Communicative Practices.* Boulder CO: Westview.

Hudson, R. (1996). *Sociolinguistics,* 2nd edn. Cambridge: Cambridge University Press.

Humboldt, W. von. (1971). *Linguistic Variability and Intellectual Development,* trans. G. C. Buck and F. A. Raven, Philadelphia: University of Pennsylvania Press. (Original work published 1836.)

Hymes, D. H. (1972). Models of the interaction of language and social life. In J. J. Gumperz and D. H. Hymes (eds.), *Directions in Sociolinguistics.* New York: Holt, Rinehart and Winston. 35–71.

Hymes, D. H. (1974). *Foundations of Sociolinguistics.* Philadelphia: University of Pennsylvania Press.

Hymes, D. H. and J. Fought (1981). *American Structuralism.* The Hague: Mouton.

Irvine, J. T. (1989). When talk isn't cheap: Language and political economy. *American Ethnologist* 16, 2.

Jackson, J. (1974). Language identity of the Colombian Vaupés Indians. In R. Bauman and J. Sherzer (eds.), *Explorations in the Ethnography of Speaking.* Cambridge: Cambridge University Press. 50–64.

Joly, L. G. (1981). The ritual "play of the Congos" of north-central Panama: Its sociolinguistic implications. *Sociolinguistic Working Paper* No. 85. Austin, TX: Southwest Educational Development Laboratory.

Kerswill, P. (1994). *Dialects Converging: Rural Speech in Urban Norway.* Oxford: Oxford University Press.

Kroch, A. (1996). Dialect and style in the speech of upper class Philadelphia. In G. R. Guy, C. Feagin, D. Schiffrin and J. Baugh (eds.), *Towards a Social Science of Language: Papers in Honor of William Labov,* vol. 1: *Variation and Change in Language and Society.* Amsterdam: Benjamins. 23–45.

Labov, W. (1966, reprinted 1982). *The Social Stratification of English in New York City.* Washington, DC: Center for Applied Linguistics.

Labov, W. (1969). Contraction, deletion and inherent variability of the English copula. *Language* 45: 715–62.

Labov, W. (1972). *Sociolinguistic Patterns*. Philadelphia: University of Pennsylvania Press.

Labov, W. (1982). Building on empirical foundations. In W. P. Lehmann and Y. Malkiel (eds.), *Perspectives on Historical Linguistics*. Amsterdam: Benjamins. 17–92.

Labov, W. (1989). The exact description of the speech community: Short-a in Philadelphia. In R. Fasold and D. Schiffrin (eds.), *Language Change and Variation*. Amsterdam: Benjamins. 1–57.

Labov, W. (1994). *Principles of Linguistic Change*, vol. 1: *Internal factors*. Oxford: Blackwell.

LePage, R. B. (1997). The evolution of a sociolinguistics theory of language. In F. Coulmas (ed.), *Handbook of Sociolinguistics*. Oxford: Blackwell. 15–32.

LePage, R. B. and A. Tabouret-Keller (1985). *Acts of Identity: Creole-Based Approaches to Language and Ethnicity*. Cambridge: Cambridge University Press.

Lyons, J. (ed.) (1970). *New Directions in Linguistics*. London: Penguin.

Macaulay, R. K. S. (1997). *Standards and Variation in Urban Speech: Examples from Lowland Scots*. Amsterdam: Benjamins.

Mackey, W. F. (1972). The description of bilingualism. In J. A. Fishman (ed.), *Readings in the Sociology of Language*. The Hague: Mouton. 554–84. (Originally published 1962 in *Canadian Journal of Linguistics* 7: 51–85.)

Martinet, A. (1964). *Elements of General Linguistics*, trans. E. Palmer. Chicago: University of Chicago Press. (Originally published Paris, 1960, as *Éléments de linguistique générale*.)

Milroy, J. (1982). Probing under the tip of the iceberg: Phonological "normalization" and the shape of speech communities. In S. Romaine (ed.), *Sociolinguistic Variation in Speech Communities*. London: Arnold. 35–47.

Milroy, J. and L. Milroy (1997). Varieties and variation. In F. Coulmas (ed.), *The Handbook of Sociolinguistics*. Oxford: Blackwell.

Milroy, J. and L. Milroy. (1998). Mechanisms of change in urban dialects: The role of class, social network and gender. In P. Trudgill and J. Cheshire (eds.), *The Sociolinguistics Reader*, vol. I: *Multilingualism and Variation*. London: Arnold. 179–95. (Originally published 1993 in *International Journal of Applied Linguistics* 3, 1.)

Milroy, L. and S. Margrain (1980). Vernacular language loyalty and social network. *Language in Society* 9: 43–70.

Mougeon, R. and E. Beniak (1996). Social class and language variation in bilingual speech communities. In G. R. Guy, C. Feagin, D. Schiffrin and J. Baugh (eds.), *Towards a Social Science of Language: Papers in Honor of William Labov*, vol. 1: *Variation and Change in Language and Society*. Amsterdam: Benjamins. 69–99.

Murray, S. O. (1996). *Theory Groups and the Study of Language in North America*. Amsterdam: Benjamins.

Neustupny, J. V. (1978). *Post-structural Approaches to Linguistics*. Tokyo: University of Tokyo Press.

Ochs, E. (1996). Linguistic resources for socializing humanity. In J. J. Gumperz and S. C. Levinson (eds.), *Rethinking Linguistic Relativity*. Cambridge: Cambridge University Press. 407–37.

Patrick, P. L. (1999). *Urban Jamaican Creole: Variation in the Mesolect*. Amsterdam: Benjamins.

Raith, J. (1987). Sprachgemeinschaft (speech community). In U. Ammon, N. Dittmar and K. J. Mattheier (eds.), *Sociolinguistics: An*

International Handbook of the Science of Language and Society. Berlin: de Gruyter. 200–07.

Rampton, B. (1995). *Crossing: Language and Ethnicity among Adolescents*. London: Longman.

Rickford, J. R. (1986). The need for new approaches to social class analysis in sociolinguistics. *Language and Communication* 6: 215–21.

Romaine, S. (ed.), (1982). *Sociolinguistic Variation in Speech Communities*. London: Arnold.

Romaine, S. (1994). *Language in Society: An Introduction to Sociolinguistics*. Oxford: Oxford University Press.

Salzmann, Z. (1998). *Language, Culture and Society: An Introduction to Linguistic Anthropology*, 2nd edn. Boulder CO: Westview.

Santa Ana, O. and C. Parodí (1998). Modeling the speech community: Configuration and variable types in the Mexican Spanish setting. *Language in Society* 27: 23–51.

Sapir, E. (1921). *Language: An Introduction to the Study of Speech*. New York: Harcourt, Brace.

Saussure, F. de (1916). *Course in General Linguistics*. (C. Bally and A. Sechehaye (eds.), with A. Riedlinger; trans. W. Baskin, published 1966.) New York: McGraw-Hill.

Saville-Troike, M. (1982). *The Ethnography of Communication: An Introduction*. Oxford: Blackwell.

Silverstein, M. (1996). Monoglot "standard" in America: Standardization and metaphors of linguistic hegemony. In D. Brenneis and R. K. S. Macaulay (eds.), *The Matrix of Language: Contemporary Linguistic Anthropology*. Oxford: Westview Press. 284–306.

Stewart, W. A. (1962). An outline of linguistic typology for studying multilingualism. In F. Rice (ed.), *Study of the Role of Second Languages in Asia, Africa and Latin America*. Washington, DC: Center for Applied Linguistics. 15–25.

Trask, R. L. (1997). *A Student's Dictionary of Language and Linguistics*. London: Arnold.

Trudgill, P. (1974). Linguistic change and diffusion: Description and explanation in sociolinguistic dialect geography. *Language in Society* 3: 215–46.

Trudgill, P. (2000). *Sociolinguistics*, 4th edn. London: Penguin.

Wardhaugh, R. (1998). *An Introduction to Sociolinguistics*, 3rd edn. Oxford: Blackwell.

Watson, S. (1989). Scottish and Irish Gaelic: The giant's bed-fellows. In N. C. Dorian (ed.), *Investigating Obsolescence: Studies in Language Contraction and Death*. Cambridge: Cambridge University Press. 41–59.

Weinreich, U. (1953). *Languages in Contact: Findings and Problems*. Publications of the Linguistic Circle of New York, No. 1.

Weinreich, U., W. Labov and M. I. Herzog (1968). Empirical foundations for a theory of language change. In W. P. Lehmann and Y. Malkiel (eds.), *Directions for Historical Linguistics: A Symposium*. Austin: University of Texas Press. 95–188.

Whitney, W. D. (1979). *The Life and Growth of Language: An Outline of Linguistic Science*. (Original work published 1875.)

Williams, G. (1992). *Sociolinguistics: A Sociological Critique*. London: Routledge.

Winford, D. (1988). The creole continuum and the notion of the community as locus of language. *International Journal of the Sociology of Language* 71: 91–105.

Wolfram, W. and N. Schilling-Estes (1998). *American English: Dialects and Variation*. Oxford: Blackwell.

Part IV
Contact

Contact

The purpose of this section is to review work in sociolinguistics which has been devoted to the study of language varieties in contact. It deals with both languages in contact and dialects in contact, the difference between the two being typically defined as involving contact between non-mutually intelligible as opposed to mutually intelligible varieties, although it is of course acknowledged that mutual intelligibility is not an absolute criterion. Although there are quite naturally differences between the two types of contact, it is also the case that some of the same linguistic processes appear to be involved in both cases – and it is precisely linguistic processes and outcomes which are of interest to workers in linguistic variation and change. It is important to point this out since language contact is a subject which has been studied by many non-variationist linguists who have a number of different goals and foci. These include sociologists of language; social psychologists of language; bilingual acquisition specialists; and applied linguists. Dialect contact, on the other hand, is an area of study in which variationists have always been very much at the forefront, doubtless as a consequence of their following in the dialectological tradition, which was always aware of the importance of the geographical diffusion of linguistic innovations and the development of transition zones and linguistically intermediate forms.

David Britain in his chapter "Space and Spatial Diffusion" argues that it is ironic, given that dialect geography was in this way undoubtedly one of the most important antecedents of our form of sociolinguistics, that geographical space is one social category that has received very little attention in variationist linguistics. Britain says that, like many other categories dealt with in this *Handbook*, but to a much greater degree, space has remained unproblematized and untheorized in sociolinguistics – a simple given which variationists have taken for granted. Britain turns to the field of human geography, and shows that geographically informed variationist linguistics can benefit from the insights and methodologies of this science.

In her chapter on the "Linguistic Outcomes of Language Contact", Gillian Sankoff looks at the way in which languages spoken by bilinguals influence each other. Although she describes the growing rapprochement between Second Language Acquisition studies and variationist sociolinguistics, she takes the speech community, a notion extensively discussed earlier in this handbook, as her focus, as is typical in sociolinguistic rather than psycholinguistic research. The main objective of variationist work in language contact is to achieve an understanding of the linguistic consequences of this contact. The same is equally true of work in dialect contact.

In "Koineization and Accommodation", Paul Kerswill examines the linguistic consequences of koineization, whereby new varieties of a language come into existence as a result of contact between speakers of varieties which are mutually intelligible. As Kerswill points out, one of the major questions we want to ask about varieties such as New Zealand English which are the relatively recent result of dialect contact, dialect mixture, and new-dialect formation is why they are like they are.

Peter Trudgill

24 Space and Spatial Diffusion

DAVID BRITAIN

Space was treated as the dead, the fixed, the undialectical, the immobile. Time, on the contrary, was richness, fecundity, life, dialectic.

Foucault (1980: 70)

Given the historical origins of variationism in traditional dialectology, and given the advances the discipline has made over the past decades in unpacking the initially rather crude attempts at understanding the social embedding of variation and change (see, for example, Rickford 1986, L. Milroy 1980, Milroy 1992, for social class, Eckert and McConnell-Ginet 1992 for gender, Eckert 1997 for age, Bell 1984 for style, and so on), it is paradoxical that one of the social categories that has received least attention of all is *space*. Almost without exception, space has been treated as a blank stage on which sociolinguistic processes are enacted. It has been unexamined, untheorized, and its role in shaping and being shaped by variation and change untested. One function of this chapter, therefore, is to strongly assert that space makes a difference, and to begin, in a very hesitant way, to map out what a geographically informed variation analysis might need to address.

It might be reasonable to think that human geography would provide some of the answers. I will draw on some influential work of human geographers in this chapter, but they, too, have engaged in a great deal of soul searching about the goals of their discipline and its very existence as a separate field of enquiry. As we will see, there are remarkable parallels between the recent history of human geographic thought, and the ongoing interest in language variation across space. Although space has been undertheorized in variation studies, a number of researchers, from the traditional dialectologists through to those interested in the dialectology of mobility and contact, have, of course, been actively engaged in research on geographical variation and language use. Their work will be contextualized here to highlight the parallels with human geographic theory, and some of the criticisms of earlier approaches which have fed through to human geography, but remain largely unquestioned in variationist practice.

The second half of the chapter will present an overview of the current state of play in the spatial realization of linguistic performance. Two topics will be considered most prominently: the spatial diffusion of linguistic innovations, and the (related) spatial configuration of linguistic boundaries (i.e. isoglosses and transitions).

1   Where is Space?: Putting the Geo- into Variationist Sociolinguistics

> Space is not an empty dimension along which social groupings become struc-
> tured, but has to be considered in terms of its involvement in the construction of
> systems of interaction.   (Giddens 1984: 368)

Three types of space can be distinguished which are relevant to the discussion here:

1   Euclidean space – the objective, geometric, socially divorced space of math-
    ematics and physics.
2   Social space – the space shaped by social organization and human agency,
    by the human manipulation of the landscape, by the contextualization of
    face-to-face interaction, by the creation of a built environment, and by the
    relationship of these to the way the state spatially organizes and controls at
    a political level.
3   Perceived space – how civil society perceives its immediate and not so
    immediate environments – important given the way people's environ-
    mental perceptions and attitudes construct and are constructed by everyday
    practice.

Together these three combine to create *spatiality*, a key human geographic dimension. None of these three can exist independently of one another. Geometric space is appropriated and thus made social through human settlement, but social space can never be entirely free of the physical friction of distance. And our perceptions and value systems associated with our surroundings, although deeply affected by both social and Euclidean space, can in them- selves affect the way space is later appropriated and colonized. Importantly, spatiality is not fixed and concrete but, as Pred puts it, always in a state of "becoming" (1985: 338).

A sociolinguistic example, here, illustrates the interdependency and evolution of the three forms of space. The low-lying Fens of eastern England separate the counties of East Anglia – Norfolk and Suffolk – from the Midlands and the north – Lincolnshire, Northamptonshire and Leicestershire. The area has a rather unique geomorphological and demographic history. Before the early seventeenth century, the Fens were mostly poorly navigable undrained marshland, and most of the population lived on a few islands of higher ground and in small communities on the northern coastline. The southern two-thirds of the Fenland was particularly subject to tidal flooding in summer, more continuous flooding in winter and was, therefore, too unstable in most places for permanent settlement. Darby, for example, notes that "even those portions that escaped winter flooding were subject to an annual heaving motion, the mud absorbing water and swelling" (1931: 18). The overall livelihood of many small Fenland communities was directly related to the success of efforts to hold the water back.

Until the seventeenth century, the Fens were seen as a miserable place, where its inhabitants eked out a meagre living in the most difficult of circumstances. White (1865: 264) claims, for example, that "on these [Fenland] banks, the inhabitants for their better security erect their miserable dwellings, at a great distance sometimes from each other and very remote from their parish churches to which they rarely resort . . . so that they seem to be cut off from the community and are deprived of almost every advantage of social life". The geographical boundary that the area created between east and west, and the perceptions of the Fens and Fenlanders, engendered a strongly negative reaction to the area. Darby (1931: 61) claims that there arose "a mythical fear of a land inhabited by demons and dragons, ogres and werewolves", and he quotes Felix who claimed the Fens were "especially obscure, which ofttimes many men had attempted to inhabit, but no man could endure it on account of manifold horrors and fears and the loneliness of the wide wilderness – so that no man could endure it, but everyone on this account had fled from it".

Reclamation from the mid-seventeenth century onward proved to be a major turning point in the history of the Fens. A previously barely passable marshland evolved into fertile arable land. The impact of the reclamation on the Fenland's demographic structure was considerable. Subsequent to drainage, the Fens saw quite rapid demographic growth, particularly in those central Fenland areas which had previously been less accessible (see Britain 1997a: 19–20 for more detail about demographic growth and settler origins).

Despite this, the Fens remains an important boundary to east–west communication. Politically, the area is still very much a peripheral one. It sits at the northwestern edge of East Anglia, and at the eastern and southern edges of the Midlands and north. Road and rail links crossing the area remain relatively poor, and, functionally, the absence of a large urban centre in the Fens means its inhabitants look beyond the area for the provision of major products, services, and leisure facilities (see further below). Perceptions of the area today are still rather negative, fueled by high profile media coverage of crime and ethnic tension. The physical impenetrability of the Fens to outsiders before reclamation, the concentration of socio-political spheres of influence to the East and West, and the almost demonic external perception of the area and its inhabitants led to the Fens becoming seen as a major boundary between two important and economically powerful regions, East Anglia and the Midlands. The historically evolving spatiality of physical, social, and perceptual space in the Fens have created not just a geographical boundary, but a linguistic one too – the site of one of the largest clusters of dialect transitions in the country (see Britain 1991, 1997a, 1997b, 1998, 2000), including:

- the realization of (u) in "cup", "butter", etc. [ʊ] to the west-northwest, [ʌ] to the east-southeast;
- the realization of (a) in "castle", "last", etc. [a] to the west-northwest, [aː] to the east-southeast;
- the presence or absence of /h/: absent to the west, present to the east;
- the realization of /au/: [ɛː] to the west, [ɛu] to the east;
- the realization of vowels in unstressed syllables: e.g. past tense "-ed" forms and "-ing" forms are realized with [ɪ] to the west, but [ə] to the east;
- the preservation (to the east) or not (to the west) of a "nose" [nʊuz]/ "knows" [nʌuz] distinction;
- third person present tense –s absence (to the east) or presence (to the west);
- the realization of (ai): [ɑi] to the west, [əi] to the east (and "Canadian Raising" in between).

Doreen Massey (1984, 1985; see also Curry (1996) and Johnston (1991) for similar overviews) has charted three distinct periods in the theoretical development of spatiality in social scientific thought. These three stages are mirrored in quite direct ways in the investigation of spatial variation in language use. Before the 1960s, she claims, human geography was about "regions," the focus of study being on place, difference, and distinctiveness. Rather than focusing on spatial processes or structures, individual areas were analyzed for individual unique characteristics. "Too often," she states (Massey 1984: 2), however, "it degenerated into an essentially descriptive and untheorized collection of facts." This period coincides most obviously with that of traditional dialectology. It, too, focused on regions, on focal areas and their boundaries, on the local dialectal variability, and differentiation from place to place which fueled its opposition to the neogrammarian hypothesis of regular exceptionless sound change. Making few demands on social theory of any kind, it treated space, at least in its initial forms, as little more than a container, a background setting against which dialectological findings could be mapped. The introduction of the *Linguistic Atlas of England* (Orton et al. 1978) is extremely revealing in this respect:

> Wright had observed that in the current state of knowledge only an approximate classification of M[iddle] E[nglish] dialects could be made because it was impossible . . . to fix the exact boundaries where one dialect ends and another begins . . . Wright was taking an even longer historical view than Kurath in suggesting that regional dialect boundaries in the past could be reconstructed on the basis of modern evidence . . . they decided to set as their objective the oldest kind of traditional vernacular . . . which would demonstrate the continuity and historical development of the language.   (Orton et al. 1978: i)

So although traditional dialectology is often (always?) portrayed as one of the earliest forms of geographical linguistics, in fact there is virtually no *geographical* contribution to the work at all. The role of space is reduced to that of data presentation on a map. In fact, the historicist agenda of traditional dialectology is one which has pervaded variation studies throughout its brief life – consider the primacy for many variationists of the apparent-time model. Soja (1989) is probably the most prominent human geographer to question this obsession with time over space:

> An essentially historical epistemology continues to pervade the critical conscious-
> ness of modern social theory. It still comprehends the world primarily through
> the dynamics arising from the emplacement of social being and becoming in the
> interpretive contexts of time. . . . This historicism . . . has tended to occlude a com-
> parable critical sensibility to the spatiality of social life, a practical theoretical
> consciousness that sees the life-world of being creatively located not only in the
> making of history, but also in the construction of human geographies, the social
> production of space and the restless formation and reformation of geographical
> landscapes.   (Soja 1989: 10–11)

In the 1960s the whole situation changed, in human geography, dialectology, and the social sciences in general. The quantitative revolution broke out. The consequences of this revolution had different effects on sociology and sociolinguistic dialectology on the one hand, and human geography and geographical dialectology on the other. Within the former, spatiality was largely ignored. Social relations and social structures were quantified and correlated with other social structures, or in the case of sociolinguistic dialectology, with linguistic variables (Labov 1966). The scientific empiricism of the time meant that the regular, the general, and the neutral took precedence over the specific, the individual, and the unique.

The introduction to Sociolinguistic Patterns (Labov 1972) makes it quite clear that Labov considered his work as a reaction to Chomskyan linguistics first and foremost, rather than an attempt to radically shift dialectological practice. His initial work in Martha's Vineyard (Labov 1963), a largely rural community, contrasted with later work carried out in New York (Labov 1966), then one of the largest urban centers in the world. It is interesting, therefore, that most of the major studies carried out within the same framework for many years after looked at *urban* communities: Wolfram (1969) in Detroit; Sankoff and Cedergren (1971) in Montreal; Trudgill (1974a) in Norwich, etc, and very few focused on rural locations. This point appears rarely to have been questioned. On the surface, it appears an obvious reaction to the largely rural focus of traditional dialectology. Researching in the city was most probably seen as the way to gain access to the most fluid and heterogeneous communities, and therefore to tackle the issue of the social embedding of change "where it's all happening." In some senses, though, it could be seen as throwing the rural baby out with the traditional dialectological bathwater. The outmoded methods of traditional dialectology possibly stigmatized research in rural communities and so they became avoided as a focus of analysis. This urbanism still pervades much of the discipline, however: the rural is still portrayed as the insular, the isolated, the static, as an idyll of peace and tranquility rather than as composed of heterogeneous communities, of contact, of change and progress, and of conflict (See, for example, Cloke and Little 1997, Macnaghten and Urry 1998, Cloke 1999, Shucksmith 2000.) But language varies and changes in rural as well as urban communities.

Sociologists had society to quantify, sociolinguistic dialectologists had linguistic variables to quantify, but what about human geographers? All they had was space, a dimension. So they set about the task of establishing a quantified human geography, drawing up spatial laws, spatial relationships, and spatial processes all of which could be explained by spatial factors, without reference to social content. It was at this time that such concepts as "the friction of distance" and, hence, gravity models, were drawn upon to explain empirically discovered spatial regularities. Euclidean space came into its own.

Just as social theory despatialized itself as a result of the quantitative revolution, and human geography became concerned solely with space, Labov (1982), in his review of the first 20 years of variationism, firmly separated "spatial" contributions to language change from the "social," and treated the study of linguistic heterogeneity in space, society, and time as a "natural alliance" (1982: 20) but of separate disciplines. Dialect geographers study language in space and, he says, sociolinguists study heterogeneity in society. Labov (1982: 42) went on to state that "the study of heterogeneity in space has not advanced at the same tempo as research in single communities." Interestingly, the division implies that heterogeneity in both time and society are somehow not in space, that spatiality has not shaped the communities (or their evolution) under investigation. But this view was typical of the time. Massey (1984) notes that "in terms of the relation between the social and the spatial, this was the period of perhaps the greatest conceptual separation. . . . For their part, the other [nongeographic – DB] disciplines forgot about space altogether" (1984: 3) and that "the other disciplines continued to function, by and large, as though the world operated, and society existed, on the head of a pin, in a spaceless, geographically undifferentiated world" (1984: 4).

The human geographic focus on spatial causes and motivations stimulated much of the early sociolinguistic work in dialect geography, perhaps most notably in the analysis of the spatial diffusion of innovations and, in particular, the adoption and adaptation of gravity models (e.g. Trudgill 1974b, 1983, Callary 1975, Larmouth 1981, Hernández Campoy 1999, 2000a, 2000b), but was also evident, earlier, in the neolinguistic tradition (see, e.g., Bartoli 1945, Bonfante 1947, Weinhold 1985). Early sociolinguistic work on the geographical diffusion of innovations was triggered by the highly influential models of diffusion proposed by the Swedish human geographer Torsten Hägerstrand (e.g. 1952). His work began a whole sub-discipline of human geography – time geography – which investigated the creation of spaces through the bundling of people's "time-space biographies" (see also Pred 1981, Carlstein 1981, etc). It was his modeling of spatial diffusion, however (rather a small part of the project of time-geography), which had the most impact on dialectology (and geography), however, since it provided a methodological framework that could be readily adopted to visually display geographical distributions of the frequencies of linguistic innovations, "the spatial diffusion of ratios" (Trudgill 1983: 61). Examples from the dialectological literature will follow in the next section. But its purely spatial, asocial approach was criticized by a number of human geographers.

In a detailed critique, Gregory (1985) underlined the fact that the model Hägerstrand proposed failed to "cut through the connective tissue of the world in such a way that its fundamental integrities are retained. Obvious examples include the detachment of 'potential adopters' from their social moorings and the displacement of subjects from social struggles" (Gregory 1985: 328) and presented the world as "squashed into a flat surface, pockmarked only by the space-time incidence of events" (1985: 328). Furthermore, as highlighted by Yapa (1977: 359) and Gregory (1985: 319), the model treats the non-adoption of an innovation as "a passive state where the 'friction of distance applies a brake to innovation . . . rather [than] an active state arising out of the structural arrangements of society." In addition, Gregory suggested that the model provided no attempt to account either for the relationship between social structure and human agency, or for the *consequences* of innovation diffusion, which, in the time-geographic model are merely "a sequence of distributional changes" (Gregory 1985: 304). If feature A diffuses from place X to place Y, will feature A (1) be unchanged at Y from its state at place X and (2) carry the same social connotations, the same values, in the two places? We will return to this point later.

Gravity models, too, depend on a Euclidean, geometric view of space where physical distance and total population count as the sole determinants of the influence one community is likely to have on another. First, however, although gravity models predict influence of place X on place Y (and perhaps more importantly *rank* the influences of place X on a number of places, W, Y, Z), based on the distance between place X and the other locations, we know little about the spatiality of that distance. Physical, social, and perceptual factors (mountains, marshes, motorways, lack of roads or public transport, employment blackspots, shopping malls, xenophobia, or external negative perceptions of place) can all minimize or maximize that distance in the eyes (and mouths) of speakers, and, thereby, the actual effect place X will have on others. Second, innovations travel in different ways. The desire to purchase a new brand of washing powder or chocolate bar could be provoked by a range of different media – TV adverts, promotional material through the mail, as well as recommendations from neighbors and school friends. It is widely acknowledged now that most linguistic innovations (especially non-lexical ones) are transmitted through face-to-face interaction (Trudgill 1986), and not through exposure on TV. Therefore the spatiality of face-to-face communication, and the nature of what Hägerstrand called "coupling constraints" will additionally interact with that distance. Third, and related to the previous points somewhat, is the problem that the gravity model assumes everyone in place X has an equal and likely chance of coming into contact with any resident of the other location. But some groups are more mobile than others, and are more likely therefore to meet non-locals than more territorially circumscribed groups. As the Milroys have shown (L. Milroy 1980, J. Milroy and L. Milroy 1985, J. Milroy 1992), it is the central classes of society who have weaker social networks, and who tend to be more mobile (in the hunt for job stability and socioeconomic advancement) whilst at the extremes are those who cannot move or do not need to. I have shown in previous work (Britain 1991, see also, in preparation; cf. Urry 1985) that the degree to which class experiences are both heterogeneous and spatially concentrated can have a particular effect on language variation and change. Some communities, therefore, may be in a better position to influence than others. Specific examples of gravity model analyses will be considered in the next section.

In admitting some of the problems, Trudgill, one of the pioneers of the application of gravity models to dialectology, adapted the gravity model to include a calculation of prior-existing linguistic similarity, given that "it appears to be psychologically and linguistically easiest to adopt linguistic features from those dialects or accents that most closely resemble one's own, largely . . . because the adjustments that have to be made are smaller" (1983: 74–5; see also below, and Britain 1999).

More generally, Massey criticizes the quantificational approach to space as being insensitive to the local and the unique: "The 'old regional geography' may have had its disadvantages but at least it did retain within its meaning of 'the spatial' a notion of 'place', attention to the 'natural' world, and an appreciation of richness and specificity. One of the worst results of the schools of quantification and spatial analysis was their reduction of all this to the simple (but quantifiable) notion of distance" (Massey 1984: 5).

The difference, then, in terms of spatiality between this "sociolinguistic dialect geography" (Trudgill 1974b) and the largely urban speech community sociolinguistics of the late 1960s and 1970s cannot be clearer, the former asocially quantifying space, and the latter aspatially quantifying society. Dialect geographers were busy quantifying geometric space, devoid of its social content, whilst urban sociolinguists studied their speech communities with little regard for their integration into a larger socio-*spatial* framework.

Since the mid-1970s, a radical shift has taken place away from the spatial fetish in human geography Massey (1984, 1985). The initial move was to deny the spatial altogether, with a view, diametrically opposed to that of its philosophical predecessors, that the spatial was purely social, a construct of practice and social structure. The role of human geographers in this initial stage descended into "a position at the end of the transmission belt of the social sciences, dutifully mapping the outcomes of processes which it was the role of others to study" (Massey 1985: 12). It is important to note at this point, therefore, that the tremendous and valuable progress that has been made of late in mapping techniques in dialectology (see further below) still largely represents the *portrayal*, the *display* – sophisticated and eyecatching, admittedly – of data, rather than an *explanation* of the patterns found. The response to this rejection of the spatial in the 1970s was that "'geography' was underestimated . . . Space *is* a social construct – yes. But social relations are also constructed over space, and that makes a difference" (Massey 1985: 12).

"The difference that space makes" (Massey 1984, Sayer 1985, Cochrane 1987, Johnston 1991) became a dominant theme of mainstream human geography in the 1980s. Rather than space being seen as having no effect whatsoever on social process or it having, in itself, causal powers, geographers argued for the need to consider spatiality as a contingent effect which contributes to the contextual conditions which can affect how or if causal powers act (see Duncan, for example, 1989: 133). Johnston (1991) expands on this view, suggesting that cultural geography (dialectology, therefore, included?) provides strong evidence for this position:

> Places differ culturally, in terms of . . . the "collective memory". For a variety of reasons, some associated with the local physical environment, people's responses to the problems of surviving collectively vary from place to place, at a whole range of scales. How they respond becomes part of the local culture, the store of knowledge on which they draw. . . . That store . . . becomes the inheritance of those who succeed, being transmitted intergenerationally to others who will modify it as they in turn tackle problems old and new. Thus cultures develop in places and are passed on in places . . . people learn what they are and what they should do at particular times and in particular places.   (Johnston 1991: 50–1)

Here I will tentatively introduce a few linguistic issues or contexts which highlight how dialectology could be sensitized to these issues: the spatiality of sociolinguistic processes; the role of the perpetual "becoming" of place; the analysis of the unique; and the question of *whose* geographies we should be interested in (see Britain, in preparation, for a more fully worked out application of one socio-spatially oriented model of the structure of civil society to sociolinguistic concerns).

2   The Spatiality of Sociolinguistics: Functional Zones and Dialect Boundary Formation

The social networks that people tie in their everyday lives are partly constrained by space and spatiality and contribute to creating and maintaining spatiality in their neighborhoods, villages or towns. Network strength – a measure of the time, emotional intensity, intimacy, function, and reciprocity of relationships – as is now well-established (Milroy 1980, Milroy and Milroy 1985, Milroy 1992), restricts or encourages the adoption of innovations from outside. "Linguistic change is slow to the extent that the relevant populations are well established and bound by strong ties, whereas it is rapid to the extent that weak ties exist in populations" (Milroy and Milroy 1985: 375). In Britain (1997a), I drew on the work of Giddens whose structuration model of society relies heavily on concerns for time-investment and interpersonal trust and intimacy in explaining social reproduction and change. His theory puts particular emphasis on the role of routinization – "the habitual taken-for-granted character of the vast bulk of activities of day-to-day social life, the prevalence of familiar styles and forms of conduct" (Giddens 1984: 376) – in the perpetuation of social structure. One function of routinization, according to Giddens, is the "material grounding of the recursive nature of social life" (1984: xxiii). Our routinized daily activities are reproduced by their very performance. In this sense, routines, like strong social networks, often lead to system preservation. Second, claims Giddens, it is through routines that norm-enforcement is achieved: "the routinised character of . . . daily life does not just 'happen'. It is made to happen by the reflexive monitoring of action which individuals sustain in circumstances of co-presence" (1984: 64). So routines lead to system preservation and enforcement. If we investigate the geographies of routines and of social networks, we can see how spatiality (space in its physical, social, and perceptual guises) helps construct functional zones, and, in a very real sense, communities of practice (Holmes and Meyerhoff 1999, Meyerhoff, this volume).

A linguistic example will come again from the Fens (Britain 1991). Figures 24.1a, 24.1b and 24.1c show an area of the eastern Fens. In the east is the urban centre of King's Lynn, and 14 miles (22 km) to the southwest lies Wisbech, a smaller town. Between the two lies a cluster of dialect boundaries, including those of: the realization of /au/: [ɛː] in Wisbech, [ɛu] in King's Lynn; the preservation (in King's Lynn) or not (in Wisbech) of a "nose" [nʊuz] /"knows" [nʌuz] distinction (except in the word "go" where the realization of [gʊu] is used variably in Wisbech); and third person present tense –s absence (in King's Lynn) or presence (in Wisbech). This boundary has emerged partly due to the distance between the settlements (a distance that once felt much greater due to the Fenland marshes) and a relatively sparse population in the intervening rural areas, partly as a result of relatively poor infrastructural connections between the two towns (they sit in different counties, separated by a number of substantial rivers and drainage channels which have only been bridged in a few places), partly as a result of local rivalries and negative stereotyping of each other's residents, and partly as a result of the routinized geographies of everyday interactions and behaviors which residents in the intervening areas have mapped out for themselves, *given these spatiality constraints*. Villages to the west of the dialect boundary orient themselves to Wisbech for the provision of employment, services, entertainment, and so on, and villages to the east to King's Lynn. Note how in figure 24.1c these geographies are recreated by public transport provision. This boundary cannot be understood simply as motivated by physical spatial factors, nor by solely social ones – a whole host

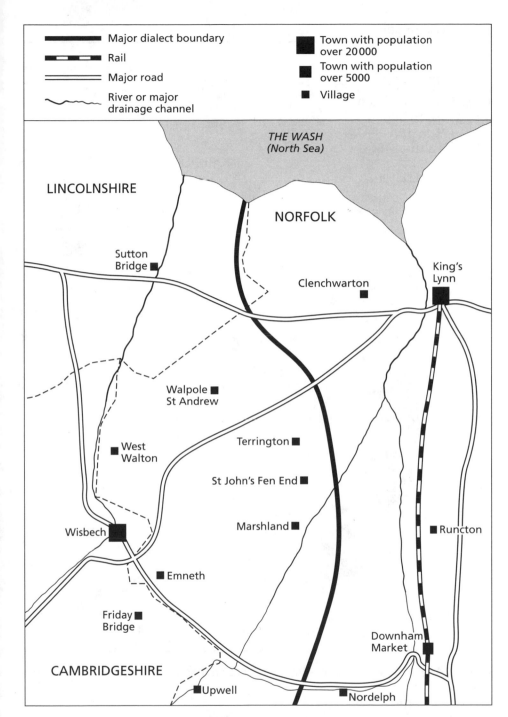

Figure 24.1a The King's Lynn–Wisbech functional zone in the Fens: the dialect boundary and the major roads, rail and waterways

Source: Britain (1991: 134)

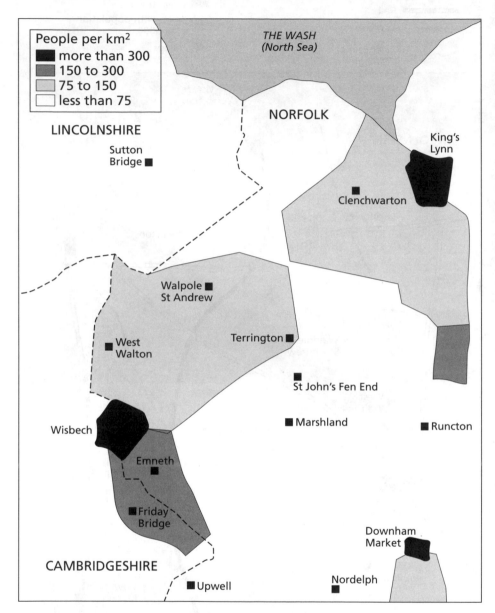

Figure 24.1b The King's Lynn–Wisbech functional zone in the Fens: population density

Source: Britain (1991: 134)

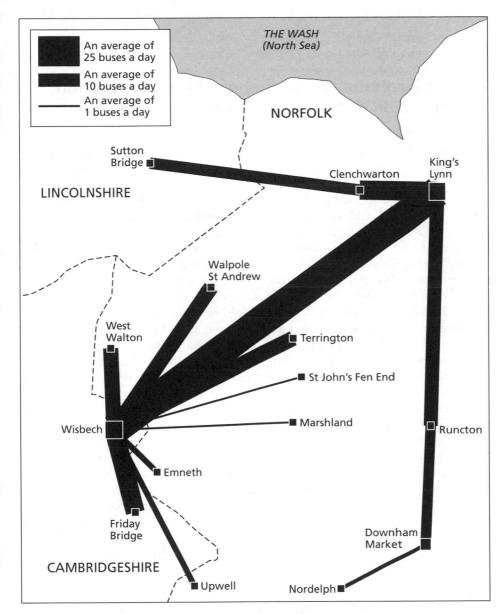

Figure 24.1c The King's Lynn–Wisbech functional zone in the Fens: the density of bus routes

Source: Britain (1991: 134)

of factors combine (and are recreated by their routinization by locals) to account for the (rather narrow) transition zone for these variables.

3   The Perpetual Becoming of Place: Contact and Migration as Catalysts of Change

The applicability to dialectology of the idea that "place is an ongoing process" (Pred 1985: 361) cannot be clearer than in the work of those interested in dialect contact (Trudgill 1986, Trudgill and Britain forthcoming, Siegel 1987, Milroy forthcoming), new dialect formation (Trudgill et al. forthcoming, Britain 1991, Kerswill and Williams 2000, Simpson and Britain in preparation), and second dialect acquisition (Payne 1980, Trudgill 1986, Chambers 1992, Amastae and Satcher 1993, Al-Dashti 1998, Watts 2000). The very basis for this research are the linguistic consequences of changes in space and place as a result of migration, labor indentation, colonization, suburbanization, gentrification, New Town formation, land reclamation, and so on. All these processes cause breaks both in social networks and socialized routines, always for the migrants, and often for those in settlements receiving newcomers too. Giddens has claimed that routines psychologically instill in humans what he calls "ontological security" – "a sense of trust in the continuity of the object world and in the fabric of social activity" (1984: 60), or, in Gregory's words, "a mode of self-reassurance brought about by the agent's involvement in the conduct of everyday life" (1989: 197). When routines are broken, as they are in the situations which lead to dialect contact, people seek to reroutinize their lives to some degree, as a natural development of their need for ontological security (Johnson 1990: 127). The linguistic consequences of reroutinization are twofold. First it leads to the gradual development of stonger social network ties. Second, it leads to the (re)establishment and subsequent social enforcement of a more focused koineized linguistic system (Le Page and Tabouret-Keller 1985, Britain 1997a, forthcoming, Kerswill, this volume). In virtually every human settlement this process is ongoing as the place evolves, as routines are formed and broken and reformed, as routines create, break down, and recreate new spatialities.

4   The Analysis of the Unique and the Local: The Onward March of "Estuary English"?

Over the past 500 years at least, London and the southeast of England have been an influential focus of linguistic innovation, and many new forms appear to have had their origins there. In the latter decades of the twentieth century, however, interest in the apparent leveling of traditional dialects in Britain has grown, particularly in the media, who have created a beast known as "Estuary English" ("Estuary" here relating to the Estuary of the Thames, the principal river flowing through London and southern England) which is, apparently, eating up dialects as it marches across the dialect landscape of southern England and beyond. And, it is fair to say, a number of researchers have found evidence of apparently southeastern English features – particularly consonants – appearing in northern England and Scotland (see, for example, Foulkes and Docherty 2000, Llamas 1998, and many of the papers in Foulkes and Docherty 1999). These researchers and others have been careful to try and dampen the media's enthusiasm for the appetite of the beast, but point out, quite rightly, that, as in other places (e.g. the northeast of England (Watt and Milroy 1999, Watt, forthcoming)) leveling tendencies are afoot in the southeast which are reducing some of the marked minority forms of local dialects in the London– southeast functional zone, and that the leveling is a result of contact between various London, RP, and local southeastern varieties. Features spreading include labiodental [ʋ] variants of prevocalic /r/, the fronting of /θ/ and /ð/ to /f/ and /v/, the glottalization of /t/, and the vocalization of /l/. So what role is there for the local dialects in the face of this influence? As we saw earlier, the mainstream models of diffusion in the 1960s paid little attention to the *consequences* of diffusion, assuming that the process involved "a sequence of distributional changes" (Gregory 1985: 304) rather than a process which had locally specific outcomes, and which may be resisted by local identity practices.

A number of dialectological studies have found such locally specific outcomes and practices. In the Fens, for example, I found that whilst the changes listed above, plus others such as the fronting of /uː/ and /ʊ/, were advancing rapidly in the speech of the young, other reported changes were not. In the eastern Fens, where a /uː/–/ʌʊ/ distinction between *moan* and *mown* is retained, /ʌʊ/ fronting was mostly only affecting the *mown* lexical set: hence "rows of roses" /rɐuzərʊuzəz/. Similarly for /ai/, the backing, rounding, and monophthongizing process ongoing elsewhere (Tollfree 1999: 168) is only affecting the diphthong before voiced consonants in the central Fens: "night time" being realized as [nəiʔtɑːm] (Britain 1997a, 1997b). In each case the local structures *interact* with the incoming ones and produce new but local not universal outcomes. The classic Martha's Vineyard study by Labov (1963) provides a superb example of how local solutions are found in the face of external threats: in this case, the use of raised onsets of /ai/ and /au/ as a reaction to the influx of summer visitors. Trudgill's work in Norwich demonstrates other possible reactions to threats from outside: hyperdialectisms (1986: 66–78). In Norwich, which traditionally preserved the Middle English distinction between **aː** and **ai**, (daze = /deːz/; days = /dæiz/), some youngsters, during the latter period of the attrition of this phonological split in the city, were found to be using /eː/ in *both* lexical sets. Similarly Vivian, in the still quite consistently rhotic town of Accrington in Lancashire, found young people using hyperdialectal /r/ in words such as "sauce" and "lager" (Vivian 2000).

It should be remembered that the diffusion of innovations leads to contact between dialects. In contact situations, linguistic accommodation is the norm, and since accommodation among adults is less than perfect, and is driven by a whole host of social psychological factors, it may not be complete or accurate, often deliberately so (Trudgill 1986, Giles and Coupland 1991). Where an innovation comes into contact with a traditional local form, therefore, a number of potential outcomes emerge: adoption of the innovation; the emergence of interdialect forms between the local form and the innovation; the rejection of the innovation, including the use of hyperdialectisms. In each case, there will be local outcomes determined by local circumstances, including the structure of the local varieties under attack, and the socio-spatial structures of the community vis-à-vis that of the innovation. The supposed rampant advance of Estuary English is a case in point – some of its features seem to be eradicating traditional forms (leveling), others are "renegotiated" during the koineization process at a local level (interdialectalization) (see Trudgill and Britain, forthcoming; Kerswill chapter 26 of this volume; Britain, forthcoming), others are rejected, reacted against, or at least slowed down, by local social, spatial, linguistic, attitudinal, and other factors.

5   Whose Geographies? Mapping Children and Gender

Maps are superb visual devices. An instant picture of the spread of an innovation is possible, and comparisons can be drawn with earlier periods (particularly using the apparent-time model). But whose maps should we be drawing? When we discuss the interactions between spatiality and linguistic structure, as in the diffusion of innovations, for example, whose geographies should we write to help us understand the patterns we find? Perhaps, given recent advances (Eckert 2000), we should be looking at the geographies of *adolescents* as keenly as we do the geographies of other age groups. Very often our explanations of the spread of change rely on the ease of mobility, social structures, networks, gender and ethnic relations, and so forth of the (often middle-class) adult population, rather than the differently constrained spatialities of the young among whom innovations are generated, socialized, and diffused. Commenting on the tendency of variationism to choose *adult* variables and then study their use in children, Eckert comments that: "one might want to begin a . . . study of variation with a focus on children's linguistic resources, social identities and strategies, asking how these patterns are transformed into adult strategies" (2000: 11); "the focus on adult social practice in the study of variation may well obscure age-specific use and interpretation among children" (2000: 10). The spatiality constraints discussed above (mountains and marshes . . .) need to be comprehended as much as possible from the viewpoints of adolescents.

The existence of a motorway from A to B may help relatively little in the diffusion of a change if the diffusers cannot drive. Hence, what for adults may be highly accelerating or restricting constraints, are necessarily differently experienced by adolescents and the young. (And the adult constraints need to be understood alongside contexts of the poorer accommodative ability discussed above.) This issue was faced by Trudgill (1986: 53–7) when trying to explain how the form most rapidly spreading from London to Norwich was found most precisely in the group that had least contact with Londoners – children. His explanation relied both on attitudinal factors, and on an understanding of the geographies of members of local peer groups. In the Fens, potential contact with linguistic innovation often took place in the clubs, skating rinks and other leisure facilities offered by the New Town of Peterborough, a city with many migrants from London (and elsewhere). This contact was restricted not just by the distance, and by poor transport facilities, but also by reactions by parents and local authorities, and the adolescents of Peterborough themselves: "They don't wanna talk to us anyway – they call us 'carrot crunchers'," one youngster from the Fenland town of March reported.

Research on dialect leveling and dialect supralocalization (Milroy et al. 1994, Watt and Milroy 1999, Milroy 1999, Watt, forthcoming) has also hinted, though rather indirectly, that there may be a role for an analysis of the geographies of gender in the diffusion of supra-local forms. Their research, largely looking at the abandonment of traditional local forms of Newcastle English in favor of more regionally widespread (but nevertheless non-standard) forms, such as the shift from glottalized [t?] to glottalled [?], has found without exception that it is women who lead the change to the supra-local forms. An understanding of women's and men's (and boys' and girls') geographies could help account for such findings, which, Milroy claims (1999), is not just restricted to the northeast of England.

The aim of this section has not been to criticize or undermine much of the tremendous work which has been carried out in traditional dialectology, dialectological cartography, or variationist sociolinguistics. As much as anything, it has shown that, perhaps without really being aware of it, the work produced was symptomatic of its time, and of the changing philosophical underpinnings of human geography itself. What is clear, I hope, is a recognition that space is important, that space matters in variationist research. But space is not (just) about maps and the archiving of data analyses, not about space as a causal effect, not about "settling for a position at the end of the transmission belt of sociolinguistics, dutifully mapping the outcomes of processes which it is the role of sociolinguists to study" to alter Massey's phrasing somewhat. It is about the role of physical, social, and perceptual space in "time-deep clusters of network biographies," places. The examples given above of what a geographically informed variationism might look like and may need to address come from the existing literature, rather than provide a map of the way forward. Much more interdisciplinary research is needed at the local level of face-to-face interaction (see, for examples, the social geographies of the Jocks and Burnouts in

Eckert 2000: ch 2), and of language use in what Giddens called "locales", as well as at the regional level of innovation diffusion.

6   The Spatial Reflection of Linguistic Performance

Having discussed the evolution of geolinguistic practice, this concluding section charts some of the findings of research on the geographical distribution of linguistic forms. It begins with a mention of cartography, followed by an exemplified discussion of the two most studied geolinguistic phenomena – patterns of spatial diffusion, and linguistic boundaries.

6.1   Dialect cartography

As mentioned above, the display of dialectological data on maps has both a long painstakingly detailed historical past and a recent, more technologically driven present. Chambers and Trudgill indeed talk of a renaissance in dialect geography in the late twentieth century (1998: 19), following a lull after the demise of traditional dialectology during which time "dialect geography all but disappeared as an international discipline" (1998: 20; see discussion above). They put this down first to technology (see also Kretzschmar and Schneider 1996): the ability to readily create and display, on computer, large numbers of maps containing complex data sets for many linguistic variables, and make them readily available both in publication and on interactive websites, such as that maintained by Bill Kretzschmar at the University of Georgia, and the *Atlas of North American English* (Labov et al. 2001). Dialect atlases were huge, often cartographically dull, and expensive; the newer work is more interactive, freely available at the end of an ethernet connection and visually more appealing. The second reason for the revival is, ironically, the reason for the obsolescence of traditional dialectology in the first place: the advent of variationist method in the 1960s. The new cartographic dialectology has begun to sensitize itself to questions of inter-speaker variability, to change across the generations, to the social embedding of variation, and so forth – the very factors which saw dialect geography wither in the mid-twentieth century.

We now have a variationist dialect geography. It is also noteworthy that in many cases the data that are being described using the new techniques are the very same data collected half a century previously: large-scale national survey corpora (see, for example, Kretzschmar and Schneider 1996, Upton and Widdowson 1996), rather than freshly collected data sets, which supports the claim by Trudgill (1983: 31–51) that traditional dialectological data are useful if handled with care. The whole range of levels of variation have been mapped: lexical, most predominantly, but also phonological, morphological, and grammatical. The example below is interesting in that, unlike the mostly lexically and phonologically oriented cartographic work in the field, it deals with the grammatical constraints on syntactic variation and change. It is based on Heap's (1999) analysis of pro-drop variation in the Romance varieties of central France, southern Switzerland and northern Italy. Figures 24.2a, 24.2b and 24.2c show, respectively, the areas with 100 percent, 80–99 percent or 0–20 percent

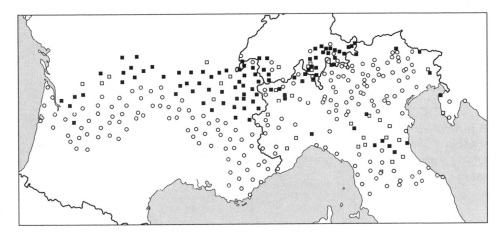

Figure 24.2a Pronoun presence in first person contexts in central France, southern Switzerland, and northern Italy (filled squares = categorical presence; empty squares = 80–100% presence; circles = 0–20% presence)

Source: Heap (1999: 93)

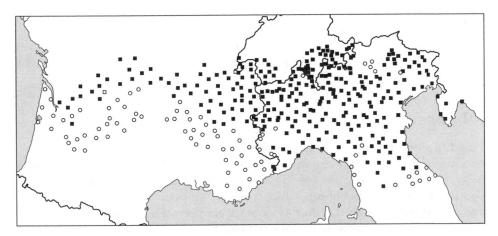

Figure 24.2b Pronoun presence in second person contexts in central France, southern Switzerland, and northern Italy (filled squares = categorical presence; empty squares = 80–100% presence; circles = 0–20% presence)

Source: Heap (1999: 95)

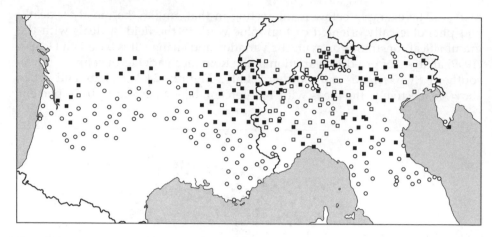

Figure 24.2c Pronoun presence in third person contexts in central France, southern Switzerland, and northern Italy (filled squares = categorical presence; empty squares = 80–100% presence; circles = 0–20% presence)
Source: Heap (1999: 97)

pro-retention in 1st, 2nd, and 3rd persons respectively, as found in Gilliéron and Edmont's (1902–10) *Atlas Linguistique de la France*, and Jaberg and Jud's (1928–40) *Sprach- und Sachatlas Italiens und der Südschweiz*. Figure 24.2a shows a relatively small area of consistent pro-retention across central France, the far northwest of Italy and southeast Swizerland, whereas figure 24.2b shows that all of southern Switzerland, most of northern Italy and a good part of central France retain the pronoun in second person contexts. Interestingly, here, there are very few speakers between 20 percent and 100 percent pro-retention. Figure 24.2c, for 3rd person contexts shows a pattern mid-way between figures 24.2a and 24.2b – a greater distribution of locations with a high frequency of pro-retention than in 1st person, but less categorically than for 2nd person.

6.2 Spatial diffusion

The diffusion of innovations across space is sometimes divided into two types: *relocation diffusion*, where the innovations are carried by individuals or groups migrating to new locations (see Trudgill 1986, Chambers 1992, Britain, forthcoming, Kerswill, this volume) and *expansion diffusion* where the innovations are passed on through day-to-day contact between those who have acquired the innovation and those who have not (see Gerritsen 1987 for a discussion of the contrast). There appears to me at least to be no serious reason why this division is made. As discussed above, expansion diffusion involves contact and accommodation in the same way as the more extreme examples of the "collision," following relocation, of radically distinct dialects, outlined, for example, in Trudgill (1986) and Siegel (1987), and it is often the case in less extreme situations that it is difficult to tease apart expansion effects from relocation effects (see, for example, Kingston, forthcoming; Bailey et al. 1993). But a division is made in the literature. Expansion diffusion will be exemplified below, and relocation diffusion by Paul Kerswill later in this volume.

The earliest suggested model of the spatial diffusion of innovation, and the simplest since it relies solely on the friction of distance, is the "wave model" (sometimes referred to as "contagion diffusion" – Bailey et al. 1993), whereby innovations, over time, radiate out from a central focal area, reaching physically nearby locations before those at ever greater distances. Relatively few examples of such diffusion have been found in the literature, however, perhaps reflecting its status as an iconic representation of diffusion – with diagrams ressembling the ripples created by raindrops falling in a puddle of water – rather than one representing some empirically discovered pattern. Bailey et al. (1993: 379–80), however, do suggest that contagion diffusion is at work in the spread of lax nuclei of /i/ in "field" across Oklahoma. Trudgill's (1986: 51–3) discussion of the diffusion of changes from London to East Anglia suggests also that the slow, unsalient, and phonetically gradual diffusion of fronter realizations of /ʌ/ (so "cup" [kɐp–kap] is spreading in a wave-like way.

A more common finding is a hierarchical effect, with innovations descending down an urban hierarchy of large city to city, to large town, to town, village and country. Bailey et al. (1993: 368–72) convincingly demonstrate this hierarchy in action in their investigations of the diffusion of the unrounding of /ɔ/ to [ɑ] (in words such as "hawk") in Oklahoma. Before 1945, the unrounding was found predominantly only in the urban centres of Tulsa, Oklahoma City, and Enid (see figure 24.3a below). Among respondents born after 1945 (figure 24.3b) the change has spread rapidly, and has been resisted "only in four sparsely populated areas . . . each of the conservative areas is far removed from metropolitan centres, and all but one lie some distance from major interstate highways. The infrequency of innovative forms in these areas points to the major path of diffusion for this feature" (Bailey et al. 1993: 370).

Hierarchical effects have also been found: by Trudgill investigating the diffusion both of /æ/ lowering (Trudgill 1983: 66–72) and [sj] to [ʂ] (Chambers and Trudgill 1998: 178) in Brunlanes peninsular in southern Norway; and the diffusion of /h/-dropping in East Anglia (Trudgill 1983: 76–8); in Callary's (1975) study of the raising and diphthongization of /æ/ in northern Illinois; by Gerritsen and Jansen (1980) investigating the spread of open monophthongised variants of /ɛi/ in the Netherlands; by Hernández Campoy (2000a, 2000b) studying the standardization of Spanish in the region of Murcia, in addition to my own findings that /l/ vocalization had arrived in the Fens following an urban hierarchical path (see Radford et al. 1999: 82). The usual explanation for this finding is that whilst distance plays some role, interaction between urban centers in modern societies is likely to be greater, and therefore a more frequent and effective conduit for accommodation and transmission of innovations, than between urban and rural. Transportation networks tend to

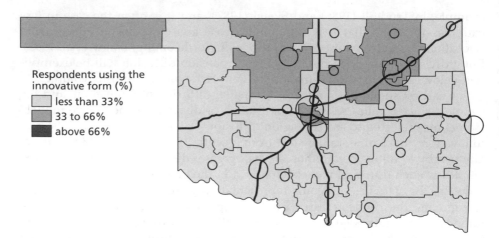

Figure 24.3a   The geographical distribution of /ɑ/ in *hawk* among respondents born in or before 1945

Source: Bailey et al. (1993: 369)

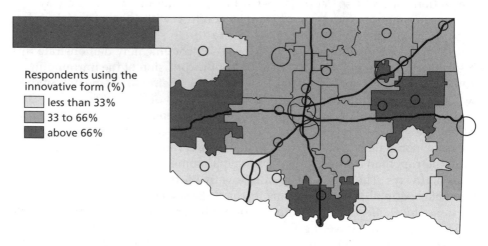

Figure 24.3b   The geographical distribution of /ɑ/ in *hawk* among respondents born in or after 1946

Source: Bailey et al. (1993: 369)

link urban with urban, the socioeconomic and consumer infrastructure tends to be based in and oriented towards urban centers, with the ensuing consequences for employment and commuting patterns, and these obviously feed the hierarchical nature of diffusion.

In some of the earliest work in sociolinguistic dialect geography, Trudgill (1974b) adopted from the human geography of the time *gravity models* which suggested both that a combination of distance and population interacted in the likely influence two places would have on each other, and that they could be used to predict the routes of change an innovation may take. (The standard calculation of the interaction of places A and B involves multiplying the populations of the two places, and then dividing that total by the square of the distance between the two places.) Many of the urban hierarchy studies listed above (Trudgill's both in Norway and England, Callary, and Hernández Campoy) adopted this technique in their own research. Hernández Campoy's discussions (1999, 2000a, 2000b) of the urban hierarchical flow of standardization in southeastern Spain provide a very detailed outline both of the theory and methodology of gravity models. He shows how, in the region of Murcia, the local deletion of intervocalic /d/ (especially in past participles "–ado", e.g. "terminado" "finished") is being eroded by standardization. Using an adaptation of the gravity model formula, he calculates an "interaction potential index" (IPI) and shows how the use of the standard form of (d) in past participles has diffused hierarchically through the region, first to places with high IPIs, trickling down to smaller urban centers with lower scores (see figure 24.4 and table 24.1 below).

The model predicts that the larger urban centers of Murcia City and Cartagena, with higher IPIs should receive the innovation most vigorously, and smaller centres such as Yecla and Caravaca less so. The predictions are borne out by the variation analysis of (d).

Horvath and Horvath (1997) show, in research on the vocalization of /l/ in Australian English, that perhaps a combination of contagion and hierarchy can help explain some changes. Quite unexpectedly, they found that vocalization was at its greatest not in the first order cities of Sydney and Melbourne, but in "the most slowly growing parts of the older core" (1997: 120) of the country, the South Australian centers of Adelaide and Mount Gambier. They propose a "cultural hearth model" whereby the feature gains a foothold in both town and country in one particular region before diffusing to other regions. In later work (Horvath and Horvath 2000), and adding investigations of New Zealand cities into the equation, they make important inroads into the

Table 24.1 The interaction potential indices and use of standard [d] realizations of intervocalic (d) in five urban centers of the Region of Murcia, Spain

Urban center	Interaction Potential Index	% use of standard [-d-]
Murcia City	28.35	41
Cartagena	5.67	32
Lorca	1.39	14
Caravaca	0.76	5
Yecla	0.23	4

Source: Hernández Campoy (2000a, 2000b)

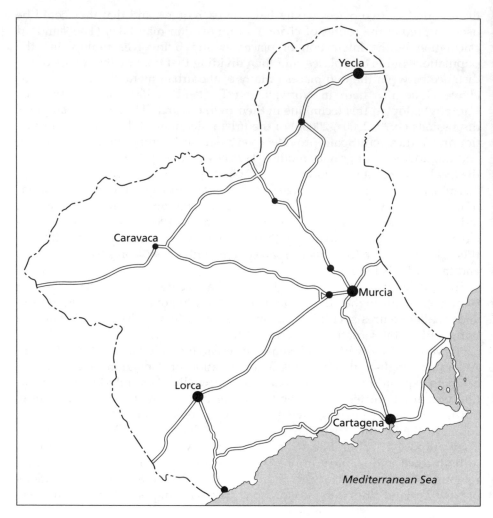

Figure 24.4   The region of Murcia in southeastern Spain, showing the main urban centers

cartography of diffusion, by using Varbrul analyses to visually display statistically significant *interactions* between place and social and linguistic constraints.

Sometimes, and possibly for reasons of identity-marking and the rejection of incoming forms and the values they represent, innovations diffuse against the urban hierarchy. Bailey et al. (1993: 371–3), who found a case in point with the diffusion of the quasi-modal "fixing to" in Oklahoma from rural to urban, label these cases *contrahierarchical* diffusion (1993: 374). Another, rarely cited example comes from Trudgill's (1986) East Anglian research. He found that a number of smoothing processes found in rural north Norfolk were

Figure 24.5 The contrahierarchical diffusion of smoothing in East Anglia
Source: Trudgill (1986: 50)

diffusing southwards to urban centres in the county of Suffolk. These processes include:

Tower	/tɑuə/ → /tɑː/
Fire	/faiə/ → /faː/
Do it	/dʉːəʔ/ → /dɜːʔ/
Player	/plæiə/ → /plæː/
Pure	/pʉːə/ → /pɜː/, etc.

The southward progress of this smoothing can be seen in figure 24.5.

7   Boundaries

Paradoxically, linguistic boundaries can be signs either of contact and change
– the "beachheads" (Chambers and Trudgill 1998: 112) of diffusing innovations
– or of relative isolation and conservatism – the mountain barrier, the break in

Figure 24.6a   Two major isoglosses of England, marking the southern limit both
of [ʊ] in *some* (solid line) and [a] in *chaff* [dotted line]
Source: Chambers and Trudgill (1998: 107)

interaction networks. The concentration on regions and focal areas in traditional dialectology (and, as we saw earlier in human geography generally) led to the need to describe and explain the boundaries between regions. These *isoglosses* were usually portrayed as abrupt, discrete, and invariable. Form *x* was used consistently on one side and form *y* on the other. Chambers and Trudgill's (1980) discussion and reanalysis of two of the most widely cited isoglosses in the English dialect literature – the ʊ/ʌ (in the STRUT lexical set) and a/ɑː (in the BATH set) divisions between the northern and southern dialects of England – provided a damning critique of this key concept of traditional dialectology. These isoglosses, shown in figure 24.6a, came from publications based on

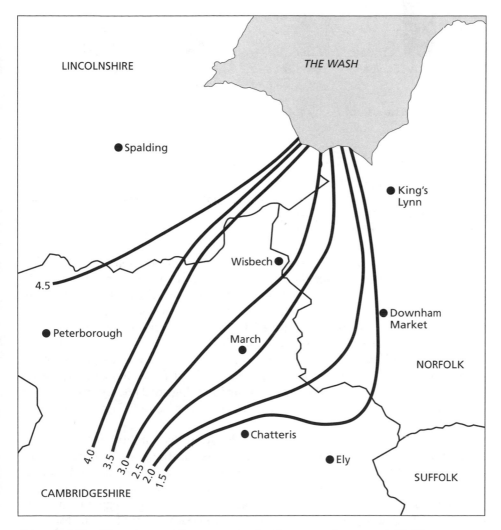

Figure 24.6b   The ʊ/ʌ transition zone in the Fens: speakers aged 15–30 (index score 5 = [ʊ], 4 = [o̝], 3 = [ɤ], 2 = [ʌ̝], 1 = [ʌ])

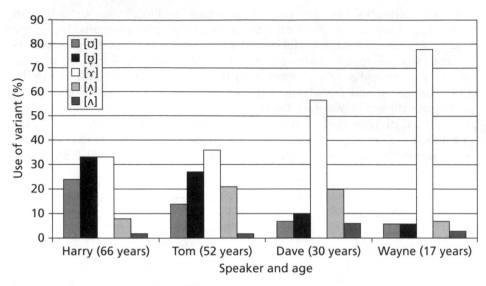

Figure 24.6c   The use of /ʌ/ by four central Fenland speakers from Wisbech

the Survey of English Dialects (e.g. Wakelin 1972). Chambers and Trudgill reanalyzed the very same data (this time from the SED's Basic Materials (Orton and Tilling 1969–71)) and found that these isoglosses were in fact *transition zones*, broad areas of linguistic variability dividing regions of categoricity. My own variationist analyses of part of this transition zone (Britain 1991, 1997b, 2000), based on informal conversational data, showed an area of variability in which a wide range of interdialectal forms [ʊ̈–ɤ–ʌ̈] were found between the northern and western [ʊ] and southern and eastern [ʌ] extremes. Whilst the overall index scores for the region showed a more or less gentle progression from northwest to southeast (figure 24.6b), an analysis of the lects of individual speakers, as Chambers and Trudgill had conducted on the SED data, was very revealing: within the transition zone, there was considerable evidence of a gradual focusing on an interdialectal [ɤ] form, indicative perhaps of a stabilization or fossilization of the transition. Figure 24.6c shows the range of variants used by four male speakers from the central Fenland town of Wisbech.

Chambers and Trudgill (1998: 113–18) also found variability in the SED data in the transition from /a/ to /ɑː/ in the same location. My analyses of conversational data (Britain 2000), however, unearthed a rather different pattern, one quite unlike the ʊ/ʌ variability, and one which perhaps begs us to forgive the isogloss somewhat. Figures 24.7a and 24.7b show the regional distribution of short [a] and long [ɑː] forms in the *bath* lexical set in the Fens for older and younger speakers respectively. Both maps show that those speakers who

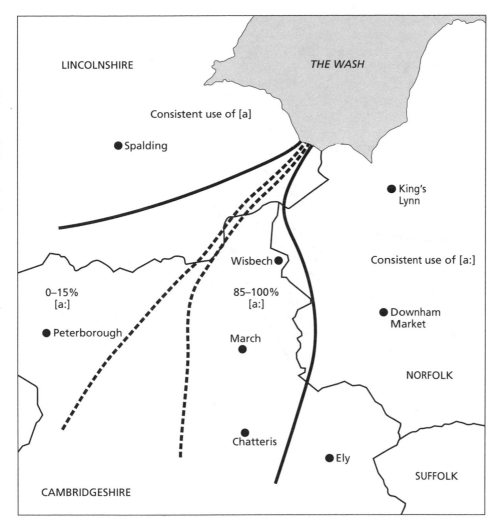

LINCOLNSHIRE

THE WASH

Consistent use of [a]

● Spalding

● King's
Lynn

Consistent use of [a:]

Wisbech ●

0–15%
[a:]

85–100%
[a:]

● Peterborough

● Downham
Market

March
●

NORFOLK

Chatteris
●

● Ely

SUFFOLK

CAMBRIDGESHIRE

Figure 24.7a   The a/a: transition zone in the Fens: speakers aged 45–65

are variable have nevertheless a very dominant tendency indeed to prefer one or other of the variants. The area between the zones of near-categoricity on either side is very sparsely populated, and marks a socioeconomic functional zone boundary between the west and the central Fens. Two older speakers living in that area, however, demonstrated robust variability. Among the young, the area between near-categorical zones on either side was narrower, and the near-categorical speakers on each side were more categorical than the older generations – an emerging *isoglossization* of a former transition, perhaps?

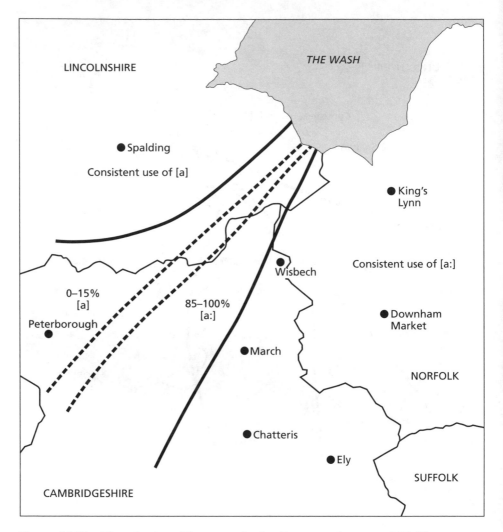

Figure 24.7b   The a/a: transition zone in the Fens: speakers aged 15–30

8   Space as an Independent Variable

The chapter has attempted to put geolinguistic practice into context and to highlight some of its principal findings. Possibly not surprisingly, the sub-discipline has evolved along similar paths to human geography itself, but the direct interaction between the two has been extremely limited (Trudgill 1974b, Britain 1991, Hernández Campoy 1999). It was suggested here that rather than abandoning space altogether as a variable, or fetishising it, endowing it with causal powers in its own right, sociolinguistics should take account of the role space in its physical, social, and attitudinal guises *contingently* plays in the construction, maintenance, and change of speech communities of practice. We must find a place for space if we are to fully understand the geographical differentiation of language.

Advances in mapping technology have revolutionized access to and dissemination of dialectological survey work, and have contributed, along with the vigor of the variationist enterprise, to a resurgence of interest in dialect geography. The spatial distribution of variability that maps portray enable us to examine with more sophistication the diffusion of linguistic innovations and the transitional zones this diffusion creates. But maps display, they do not explain. Closer attention to the spatiality of interaction, however, may lead us nearer to that explanatory goal.

REFERENCES

Al-Dashti, A. (1998). Language choice in the State of Kuwait: a sociolinguistic investigation. Ph.D. dissertation, Essex University, Colchester.

Amastae, J. and D. Satcher (1993). Linguistic assimilation in two variables. *Language Variation and Change* 5: 77–90.

Bailey, G., T. Wikle, J. Tillery and L. Sand (1993). Some patterns of linguistic diffusion. *Language Variation and Change* 5: 359–90.

Bartoli, M. (1945). *Saggi di linguistica spaziale*. Turin: Bona.

Bell, A. (1984). Language style as audience design. *Language in Society* 13: 145–204.

Bonfante, G. (1947). The neolinguistic position. *Language* 23: 344–75.

Britain, D. (1991). Dialect and space: a geolinguistic study of speech variables in the Fens. Ph.D. dissertation, Essex University, Colchester.

Britain, D. (1997a). Dialect contact and phonological reallocation: "Canadian Raising" in the English Fens. *Language in Society* 26: 15–46.

Britain, D. (1997b). Dialect contact, focusing and phonological rule complexity: the koineisation of Fenland English. In C. Boberg, M. Meyerhoff and S. Strassel (eds.), *A Selection of Papers from NWAVE 25. Special issue of University of Pennsylvania Working Papers in Linguistics* 4: 141–70.

Britain, D. (1998). Accounting for the growing diversity of North American English dialects: a reply. Response paper presented at the Nijmegen Lecture Series "William Labov: Linguistic Change: Some Solved & Unsolved Problems," Max Planck Institute, Nijmegen, Netherlands, December 14–16.

Britain, D. (1999). Local and supra-local dialect contact: the "estuaryisation" of the Fens? Paper presented at the Research Seminar Series, Department of Linguistic Science, University of Reading.

Britain, D. (2000). Welcome to East Anglia! two major dialect "boundaries" in the Fens. In J. Fisiak and P. Trudgill (eds.), *East Anglian English*. Woodbridge: Boydell and Brewer. 217–42.

Britain, D. (forthcoming).
Geolinguistics and linguistic
diffusion. In U. Ammon, N. Dittmar,
K. Mattheier and P. Trudgill (eds.),
*Sociolinguistics: International
Handbook of the Science of Language
and Society*, 2nd edn. Berlin:
Mouton De Gruyter.

Britain, D. (in preparation). Space:
the final frontier? the application
of human geographic theory to
language variation and change.
Manuscript.

Callary, R. (1975). Phonological change
and the development of an urban
dialect in Illinois. *Language in Society*
4: 155–70.

Carlstein, T. (1981). *Time Resources,
Society and Ecology: On the Capacity
for Human Interaction in Time and
Space*. London: Arnold.

Chambers, J. (1992). Dialect acquisition.
Language 68: 673–705.

Chambers, J. and P. Trudgill (1980).
Dialectology. Cambridge: Cambridge
University Press.

Chambers, J. and P. Trudgill (1998).
Dialectology, 2nd edn. Cambridge:
Cambridge University Press.

Cloke, P. (1999). The country.
In P. Cloke, P. Crang and
M. Goodwin (eds.), *Introducing
Human Geographies*. London:
Arnold. 256–67.

Cloke, P. and J. Little (1997). *Contested
Countryside Cultures*. London:
Routledge.

Cochrane, A. (1987). What a difference
the place makes: the new
structuralism of locality. *Antipode* 19:
354–63.

Curry, M. (1996). On space and spatial
practice in contemporary geography.
In C. Earle, K. Mathewson and
M. Kenzer (eds.), *Concepts in Human
Geography*. Lanham: Rowman &
Littlefield. 3–32.

Darby, H. (1931). The role of the
Fenland in English history. Ph.D.

dissertation, St Catherine's College,
Cambridge University, Cambridge.

Duncan, S. (1989). Uneven development
and the difference that space makes.
Geoforum 20: 131–9.

Eckert, P. (1997). Age as a sociolinguistic
variable. In F. Coulmas (ed.), *The
Handbook of Sociolinguistics*. Oxford:
Blackwell. 151–67.

Eckert, P. (2000). *Linguistic Variation as
Social Practice*. Oxford: Blackwell.

Eckert, P. and S. McConnell-Ginet (1992).
Think practically and look locally:
language and gender as community-
based practice. *Annual Review of
Anthropology* 21: 461–90.

Foucault, M. (1980). Questions on
geography. In C. Gordon (ed.),
*Power/Knowledge: Selected Interviews
and other Writings, 1972–77*. New
York: Pantheon. 63–77.

Foulkes, P. and G. Docherty (1999).
Urban Voices. London: Arnold.

Foulkes, P. and G. Docherty (2000).
Another chapter in the story of /r/:
"labiodental" variants in British
English. *Journal of Sociolinguistics* 4:
30–59.

Gerritsen, M. (1987). Sociolinguistic
developments as a diffusion process.
In U. Ammon, N. Dittmar and
K. Mattheier (eds.), *Sociolinguistics:
An International Handbook of the
Science of Language and Society*.
Berlin: De Gruyter. 1574–91.

Gerritsen, M. and F. Jansen (1980).
The interplay of dialectology
and historical linguistics: some
refinements of Trudgill's formula.
In P. Maher (ed.), *Proceedings of the
Third International Congress of
Historical Linguistics*. Amsterdam:
Benjamins. 11–38.

Giddens, A. (1984). *The Constitution of
Society: Outline of the Theory of
Structuration*. Cambridge: Polity
Press.

Giles, H. and N. Coupland (1991).
Language: Contexts and Consequences.

Milton Keynes: Open University Press.

Gilliéron, J. and E. Edmont (1902–1910). *Atlas linguistique de la France*. Paris: Champion.

Gregory, D. (1985). Suspended animation: the stasis of diffusion theory. In D. Gregory and J. Urry (eds.), *Social Relations and Spatial Structures*. 296–336.

Gregory, D. (1989). Presences and absences: time-space relations and structuration theory. In D. Held and J. Thompson (eds.), *The Social Theory of Modern Societies: Anthony Giddens and his Critics*. Cambridge: Cambridge University Press. 185–214.

Hägerstrand, T. (1952). *The Propagation of Innovation Waves*. Lund: Gleerup.

Heap, D. (1999). *La variation grammaticale en geolinguistique*. Munich: Lincom Europa.

Hernández Campoy, J. (1999). *Geolingüística: modelos de interpretación geográfica para lingüistas*. Murcia: Universidad de Murcia.

Hernández Campoy, J. (2000a). Requisitos teórico-metodológicos para el estudio geolingüístico del dialecto murciano. In J. M. Jiménez Cano (ed.), *Estudios sociolingüísticos del dialecto Murciano*. Murcia: Universidad de Murcia.

Hernández Campoy, J. (2000b). Geolinguistic patterns of diffusion in a Spanish region: the case of the dialect of Murcia. MS.

Holmes, J. and M. Meyerhoff (1999). The community of practice: theories and methodologies in language and gender research. *Language in Society* 28: 173–83.

Horvath, B. and R. Horvath (1997). The geolinguistics of a sound change in progress: /l/ vocalisation in Australia. In C. Boberg, M. Meyerhoff and S. Strassel (eds.),

A Selection of Papers from NWAVE 25. Special Issue of University of Pennsylvania Working Papers in Linguistics 4: 109–124.

Horvath, B. and R. Horvath (2000). A multilocality study of a sound change in progress: the case of /l/ vocalisation in New Zealand and Australian English. MS.

Jaberg, K. and J. Jud (1928–40). *Sprach- und Sachatlas Italiens und der Südschweiz*. Zofingen: Ringier.

Johnson, D. (1990). Security versus autonomy motivation in Anthony Giddens' concept of agency. *Journal for the Theory of Social Behaviour* 20: 111–30.

Johnston, R. (1991). *A Question of Place: Exploring the Practice of Human Geography*. Oxford: Blackwell.

Kerswill, P. and A. Williams (2000). Creating a new town koine: children and language change in Milton Keynes. *Language in Society* 29: 65–115.

Kingston, M. (forthcoming). Geolinguistic diffusion and rural dialect attrition: Is London taking over? Ph.D. dissertation, Essex University, Colchester.

Kretzschmar, W. and E. Schneider, (1996). *Introduction to Quantitative Analysis of Linguistic Survey Data: An Atlas by the Numbers*. London: Sage.

Labov, W. (1963). The social motivation of a sound change. *Word* 19: 273–309.

Labov, W. (1966). *The Social Stratification of English in New York City*. Washington, DC: Center for Applied Linguistics.

Labov, W. (1972). *Sociolinguistic Patterns*. Oxford: Blackwell.

Labov, W. (1982). Building on empirical foundations. In W. Lehmann and Y. Malkiel (eds.), *Perspectives in Historical Linguistics*. Amsterdam: John Benjamins. 79–92.

Labov, W., S. Ash and C. Boberg (2001). *Atlas of North American English*. Berlin: Mouton de Gruyter.

Larmouth, D. (1981). Gravity models, wave theory and low-structure regions. In H. Warkentyne (ed.), *Methods IV: Papers from the 4th International Conference on Methods in Dialectology*. Victoria: University of Victoria. 199–219.

Le Page, R. and A. Tabouret-Keller (1985). *Acts of Identity: Creole-based Approaches to Language and Ethnicity*. Cambridge: Cambridge University Press.

Llamas, C. (1998). Language variation and innovation in Middlesbrough. *Leeds Working Papers in Linguistics and Phonetics* 6: 98–115.

Macnaghten, P. and J. Urry (1998). *Contested Natures*. London: Sage.

Massey, D. (1984). Introduction: Geography matters. In D. Massey and J. Allen (eds.), *Geography Matters!* Cambridge: Cambridge University Press. 1–11.

Massey, D. (1985). New directions in space. In D. Gregory and J. Urry (eds.), *Social Relations and Spatial Structures*. London: Macmillan. 9–19.

Milroy, J. (1992). *Linguistic Variation and Change*. Oxford: Blackwell.

Milroy, J. and L. Milroy (1985). Linguistic change, social network and speaker innovation. *Journal of Linguistics* 21: 339–84.

Milroy, J., L. Milroy and S. Hartley (1994). Local and supra-local change in British English: the case of glottalisation. *English World-Wide* 15: 1–33.

Milroy, L. (1980). *Language and Social Networks*. Oxford: Blackwell.

Milroy, L. (1999). Women as innovators and norm-creators: The sociolinguistics of dialect leveling in a northern English city. In S. Wertheim, A. C. Bailey and M. Corston-Oliver (eds.), *Engendering Communication: Proceedings of the 5th Berkeley Women and Language Conference*. 361–76.

Milroy, L. (ed.) (forthcoming). Contact approaches to language variation and change. Special issue of *Journal of Sociolinguistics* 6(1).

Orton, H. and P. Tilling (eds.) (1969–71). *Survey of English Dialects: The Basic Material*, vol. 3: *The East Midland Counties and East Anglia*. Leeds: Arnold.

Orton, H., S. Sanderson and J. Widdowson (eds.), (1978). *The Linguistic Atlas of England*. London: Croom Helm.

Payne, A. (1980). Factors controlling the acquisition of the Philadelphia dialect by out-of-state children. In W. Labov (ed.), *Locating Language in Time and Space*. New York: Academic Press. 143–78.

Pred, A. (1981). Social reproduction and the time-geography of everyday life. *Geografiska Annaler* 63B: 5–22.

Pred, A. (1985). The social becomes the spatial, the spatial becomes the social: enclosures, social change and the becoming of places in the Swedish province of Skåne. In D. Gregory and J. Urry (eds.), *Social Relations and Spatial Structures*. London: Macmillan. 337–65.

Radford, A., M. Atkinson, D. Britain, H. Clahsen and A. Spencer (1999). *Linguistics: An introduction*. Cambridge: Cambridge University Press.

Rickford, J. (1986). The need for new approaches to social class analysis in linguistics. *Language and Communication* 6, 3: 215–21.

Sankoff, G. and H. Cedergren (1971). Some results of a sociolinguistic study of Montreal French. In R. Darnell (ed.), *Linguistic Diversity in Canadian Society*. Edmonton: Linguistic Research Inc. 61–87.

Sayer, A. (1985). The difference that space makes. In D. Gregory and J. Urry (eds.), *Social Relations and Spatial Structures*. London: Macmillan. 49–66.

Shucksmith, M. (2000). *Exclusive Countryside? Social Inclusion and Regeneration in Rural Britain.* York: Joseph Rowntree Foundation.

Siegel, J. (1987). *Language Contact in a Plantation Environment: A sociolinguistic history of Fiji.* Cambridge: Cambridge University Press.

Simpson, S. and D. Britain (in preparation). Dialect levelling in Telford new town. MS.

Soja, E. (1989). *Postmodern Geographies: The Reassertion of Space in Critical Social Theory.* London: Verso.

Tollfree, L. (1999). South East London English: discrete versus continuous modelling of consonantal reduction. In P. Foulkes and G. Docherty (eds.), *Urban Voices*. London: Arnold. 163–84.

Trudgill, P. (1974a). *The Social Differentiation of English in Norwich.* Cambridge: Cambridge University Press.

Trudgill, P. (1974b). Linguistic change and diffusion: description and explanation in sociolinguistic dialect geography. *Language in Society* 3: 215–46.

Trudgill, P. (1983). *On Dialect: Social and Geographical Perspectives.* Oxford: Blackwell.

Trudgill, P. (1986). *Dialects in Contact.* Oxford: Blackwell.

Trudgill, P. and D. Britain (forthcoming). *Dialects in Contact*, 2nd edn. Oxford: Blackwell.

Trudgill, P., E. Gordon, G. Lewis and M. Maclagan (2000). Determinism in new-dialect formation and the genesis of

New Zealand English. *Journal of Linguistics* 36: 299–318.

Upton, C. and J. Widdowson (1996). *An Atlas of English Dialects.* Oxford: Oxford University Press.

Urry, J. (1985). Social relations, space and time. In D. Gregory and J. Urry (eds.), *Social Relations and Spatial Structures*. 20–48.

Vivian, L. (2000). /r/ in Accrington: an analysis of rhoticity and hyperdialectal /r/ in East Lancashire. Undergraduate dissertation, Essex University, Colchester.

Wakelin, M. (1972). *English Dialects: An Introduction.* Edinburgh: Athlone Press.

Watt, D. (forthcoming). "I don't speak Geordie, I speak Northern": contact-induced levelling in two Tyneside vowels. *Journal of Sociolinguistics*.

Watt, D. and L. Milroy (1999). Patterns of variation and change in three Newcastle vowels: is this dialect levelling? In P. Foulkes and G. Docherty (eds.), *Urban Voices*. London: Arnold. 25–46.

Watts, E. (2000). The acquisition of Cheshire English by American immigrants. MA dissertation, Essex University, Colchester.

Weinhold, N. (1985). *Sprachgeographische Distribution und chronologische Schichtung: Untersuchungen zu M. Bartoli und neueren geographischen Theorien.* Hamburg: Helmut Buske Verlag.

White, W. (1865). *Eastern England.* London: Chapman and Hall.

Wolfram, W. (1969). *A Sociolinguistic Description of Detroit Negro Speech.* Washington, DC: Center for Applied Linguistics.

Yapa, L. (1977). The green revolution: a diffusion model. *Annals of the Association of American Geographers* 67: 350–9.

25 Linguistic Outcomes of Language Contact

GILLIAN SANKOFF

In virtually every country in the world at the inception of the twenty-first century, linguistic minorities can be found. These have arisen both through immigration and through the adoption – or often, but not always, the imposition – of languages not previously spoken by local populations. Though this has led in hundreds of cases to language loss and to a reduction of linguistic diversity (as documented in the Wolfram chapter in this volume), language contact is part of the social fabric of everyday life for hundreds of millions of people the world over.

To what extent have these different historical and contemporary social processes produced different linguistic outcomes? The crucial point here, almost too obvious perhaps to merit stating, is that languages spoken by bilinguals are often altered such that ensuing changes differ from the results of internal processes of change within monolingual speech communities. In other words, languages spoken by bilinguals influence each other in various ways. The goal of this chapter is to review work in sociolinguistics devoted to understanding what has happened to languages "in contact", i.e. spoken by bilinguals (Weinreich 1968). The other chapters in this section (by Britain on diffusion and Kerswill on koineization) deal with contact among speech varieties that are more closely related. However, some of the same processes involved in these cases will also be seen to operate across language boundaries – the diffusion of uvular (r) in a number of European languages is one well-known example (Trudgill 1974b; see also Tristram 1995).

In this review, I will concentrate on research that, following Weinreich, (1) takes the speech community, rather than the individual, as its angle of vision; (2) focuses on the linguistic results of contact; and (3) and seeks to elucidate the social structuring of diversity internal to the speech community. This last criterion stems from the demonstration of Weinreich et al. (1968) that synchronic and diachronic linguistics can be reconciled within a perspective that recognizes the relationship between synchronic variation and ongoing change.[1]

1   Sociolinguistics and Second Language Acquisition

The working title of this chapter was "interlanguage," a term that emerged in the early 1970s in studies of second language acquisition (henceforth, SLA), in work by, e.g., Selinker (1972), Richards (1972), and Schumann (1974). Earlier, *interference* was introduced by Weinreich as a neutral term: "those instances of deviation from the norms of either language which occur in the speech of bilinguals as a result of their familiarity with more than one language, i.e. as a result of language contact" (1968: 1). However, SLA researchers had come to feel that *interference* reflected critically on the bilingual individual, in that individuals' inability to keep their languages entirely separate could be seen as a flaw or a failure. The concept of *transfer* began to replace *interference* in this work, and the term *interlanguage* was also introduced in an effort to conceptualize the linguistic system of the second language learner as rule-governed and orderly, rather than an error-ridden version of the target language.[2] In this respect, the concept of *interlanguage* in SLA parallels to some extent the notion of the *vernacular* in sociolinguistics. Pointing out this and other parallels between the two fields, a number of sociolinguists worked towards a rapprochement with SLA, and have been successful in establishing a tradition of "variationist" or "sociolinguistic" work within SLA (Dickerson 1975, Adamson 1988, Tarone 1988, Young 1988, Preston 1989, Bayley and Preston 1996, Major 1998).

The variationist current aside, most research in SLA is markedly distinct from an approach to language contact grounded in sociolinguistics. SLA as a field has its roots in psycholinguistics, where different themes tend to dominate. First, there is a focus on the individual, rather than on the speech community. Second is a methodological practice that stems from this focus: subjects tend to be sampled according to their characteristics as individual learners, rather than as community members. Many studies are geared to evaluating instructional methods in the classroom, and subjects are drawn from the student population in academic settings. Third, the idea of acquisition is central: the learners studied are generally regarded as instantiating way-stations in a process that is incomplete (this despite some classic cases of individuals whose progress toward acquisition has been somehow arrested, e.g. Schumann 1975). Fourth, there seems to be an overarching, dominant concern with model- and theory-building as the higher goals of the enterprise, rather than on establishing the nature of the linguistic systems that have emerged from language contact.[3]

In contrast, sociolinguistics, as developed over the past four decades, is anchored in a research paradigm that has had great success in the study of majority language speech communities. Many of the classic studies (e.g. Labov 1966, Cedergren 1973, Trudgill 1974a, Milroy 1980) were devoted to investigating, if not entirely monolingual speech communities, at least the majority language spoken by natives of the city in question, usually defined as either native-born or having arrived prior to school age. Our own study of Montreal French, for example, set aside the question of language contact in Montreal (Sankoff and Sankoff 1973). We dealt explicitly with the 65 percent of Montrealers who were native speakers of French as reported in the 1971 census, and who unquestionably form a speech community. Like the Philadelphians described in Labov (1989), these Montreal French speakers share an invariant structural base that anchors the sociolinguistic variability we observe.

And yet, from the beginning of modern sociolinguistics, a major goal has also been the study of speech communities characterized by language contact (Weinreich 1951, Ferguson and Gumperz 1960, Gumperz 1964). Far from conceiving of language contact as an individual enterprise, these authors recognized that language contact is always the historical product of social forces. Their goal, as ours remains today, was to understand the linguistic outcomes. Although the dominant trend in language contact studies has been SLA, and the dominant trend in sociolinguistics has been the study of monolingual speech communities, sociolinguists have continued to study language contact, and it is this community- and historically-oriented body of work that will be reviewed here. This research has been difficult to assimilate into the mainstream of sociolinguistics partly because the variability found in bi- and multilingual speech communities is more extensive than that found in monolingual and majority-language communities (Mougeon and Nadasdi 1998). Members do not share the invariant structural base typical of the communities described above, and speakers vary across continua of proficiency. Thus description of a bilingual community involves more social parameters, more daunting inter-individual variation and major sampling and other methodological problems.

The linguistic outcomes of language contact are determined in large part by the history of social relations among populations, including economic, political, and demographic factors. Although a more extensive discussion of the speech community is to be found in the "Speech Community" chapter by Patrick, it is important to situate any discussion of the results of language contact within a sociohistorical perspective that considers the historical forces that have led to language contact. Such a perspective is central to the important and influential work of Thomason and Kaufman (1988) (henceforward, T&K), who attribute to these sociohistorical factors a unique causal weight in determining language contact outcomes. Lacking a quantitative perspective, however, T&K are forced to deny the importance of internal linguistic factors. Devoting a major chapter to "The failure of linguistic constraints on interference," they argue that: "linguistic constraints on linguistic interference . . . are based ultimately on the premise that the structure of a language determines what can happen to it as a result of outside influence. And they all fail" (1988: 14–15).

The burden of T&K's argument is that, given enough social pressure, *anything* can happen language-internally, and they adduce examples in which suggested internal, structural constraints have been overridden. Sociolinguists have, understandably, been largely approving of the pride of place T&K attribute to social constraints. However, in rejecting the contribution of internal linguistic structure, T&K have thrown out the baby with the bathwater. The cumulative weight of sociolinguistic research on language contact suggests that although it may be true that "anything can happen" given enough social pressure, T&K are very far from the truth in their blanket rejection of internal constraints. In this chapter, I will review literature from a quantitative sociolinguistic perspective, in which internal constraints have been shown to act jointly with external constraints in shaping language contact outcomes.

2   The Sociohistorical Context

Language contacts have, historically, taken place in large part under conditions of social inequality resulting from wars, conquests, colonialism, slavery, and migrations – forced and otherwise. Relatively benign contacts involving urbanization or trade as a contact motivation are also documented, as are some situations of relative equality (Sorensen 1967, Sankoff 1980). Language contacts have in some times and places been short-lived, with language loss and assimilation a relatively short-term result, whereas other historical situations have produced relative long-term stability and acceptance by the bi- or multilingual population.

The question for the linguist interested in understanding the relationship between social forces and linguistic outcomes is, to what extent do these kinds of social differences result in different linguistic outcomes? T&K distill out from the potential morass of social parameters only two dimensions: the first is the directionality of the influence, characterized in terms of speakers' native language. They envision two alternative directions in which language contact can go, resulting in two distinct linguistic processes: *borrowing* and *substratum interference*. T&K reserve the term *borrowing* to refer only to "the incorporation of foreign elements into the speakers' native language" (1988: 21). When the influence goes the other way, and native language structures influence the second language, they speak of *substratum interference*. Having made this distinction, their second dimension brings back the social factors by setting up a scale of *relative pressure* of one group (one language) on the other. This schema neatly brings together the macro-level of the language and the micro-level of the individual speaker. Its tacit assumptions are that (a) individual speakers can be characterized in terms of native and second languages, and (b) that groups or communities, as collectivities of such individual speakers, are relatively homogeneous in this regard – or at least, that one can abstract away from differences internal to the speech community. Although there are situations in which these conditions hold perhaps only tenuously – individuals whose life experience leads them to feel that, psychologically, their two languages are on an equal footing, and communities in which subgroups vary in terms of language dominance – T&K's distinction between substratum influence and borrowing is a useful heuristic in reviewing the individual cases.

From a sociolinguistic perspective, I believe that we can go farther than T&K in exploring types of sociohistorical situations that have given rise to different linguistic outcomes. Moreover, a good deal of light can be shed on the nature of linguistic outcomes in language contact by systematically considering internal variability, both inter-individual within bilingual communities, and by the quantitative analysis of linguistic constraints on language contact outcomes.

Broadly speaking, two major social processes have given rise to contact situations of interest to linguists: conquest and immigration. The imposition of a language of wider communication has occurred both as a result of conquest per se,[4] and in the establishment of standard languages via institutions like universal elementary education, where local populations have been transformed into linguistic minorities in a broader political unit. In the case of a local linguistic group that has been conquered or surrounded by a larger group, slow language shift may mean many generations of bilinguals, providing ample opportunity for substratum influence to become established in the language towards which the community is shifting. Historically, many conquered or colonized peoples, or those who have found themselves newly incorporated into a nationstate, have felt the linguistic effects of these social changes only very slowly, giving rise to language contacts that have endured over decades, generations, or even centuries. These situations of stable bilingualism are perhaps the most likely of all to lead to what Weinreich called "integration": the acceptance of structures due to interference as part of the receiving language, and even to structural convergence and the Sprachbund phenomenon recognized in many parts of the world (Gumperz and Wilson 1971, Trudgill 1976, Sridhar 1978, Moral 1997).

On the other hand, the kind of population movements usually described as immigration, where newcomers fit themselves into an existing polity rather than establishing a new one, has often led to rapid linguistic assimilation of newcomers. Although there are exceptions (cases where immigrants have populated previously unsettled, relatively isolated territories, and have thus consituted new language isolates or relatively stable bilingual communities), immigration has usually resulted in rapid linguistic assimilation. Short duration of contact has often led to borrowing into the immigrant languages (Haugen 1955, 1970), and more extensive structural changes have been documented in those that have survived for several generations (cf. Clausing 1986 on German and Icelandic in the USA). However, in so far as such immigrant varieties have been relatively short-lived, the long-term effects have been modest. On the other hand, the influence of immigrant languages on the language to which immigrants have shifted has also tended to be rather restricted, unless descendants of particular immigrant groups have been numerically dominant, or in a position such that their speech patterns influence those of the wider community rather than the reverse. A major variable here would seem to be the duration of contact: whether linguistic assimilation is relatively rapid (often only one generation) or relatively slow, possibly over many generations.

In dealing with the particular linguistic phenomena that students of languages in contact have described, we will see many cases that lead us to nuance the broad characterization of social differences in the preceding paragraphs. Though scholars may differ as to whether or to what extent different aspects of linguistic structure are affected by language contact, there is broad agreement, following Weinreich, that the locus of language contact is the bilingual speaker, and that the process of "interlingual identification" is at the heart of ensuing language change.

3   Linguistic Outcomes of Contact

This section, which consitutes the heart of the chapter, discusses the linguistic outcomes of language contact in terms of four major domains. The first two of these constitute a privileged window of linguistic inter-influence: the phonetic/phonological level (section 3.1), and the lexical level (section 3.2). These are the two corridors which, in my view, constitute the major "gateways" to all of the other aspects of contact-influenced change. When a common second language is learned and used by a group of people – whether immigrants or by virtue of the introduction of a new language to a resident population – they often find themselves introducing second-language lexical items into conversation with fellow bilinguals in their original first language. Such items, referred to by Weinreich as nonce borrowings (Weinreich 1968: 47) seem to constitute the thin end of the wedge in various types of subsequent linguistic change. First, nonce borrowings are clearly the route for the later adoption or integration of these lexical items as loan-words in the immigrant or minority language (Poplack and Sankoff 1984). Along with numerous lexical borrowings there usually ensue phonological changes in the recipient language: almost all the studies reviewed in section 3.1 indicate *both* alterations in the phonology of the borrowed words, *and* subsequent adjustments in the phonology of the recipient language. Such alterations may include processes that apply only to the foreign-origin vocabulary, but may also spread to native vocabulary. Phonological change is also almost universally characteristic of adult L2 speakers, but for social reasons, the "substratum potential" such speakers have is usually very limited. When they do constitute an important segment of the speech community, they may have a very strong influence in bringing about phonological changes that can have far-reaching influences in morphology and syntax as well. The introduction of foreign lexical material carries not only phonological baggage, but often may carry morphological and syntactic baggage as well. As we shall see, the case frames and other morphological trappings from the foreign languages may also be the source of syntactic change (section 3.3) in the recipient language. Pragmatics and discourse will be dealt with in the same section, because of the intimate relations between interlingual identification at the discourse level in bilingual linguistic usage, and subsequent developments in syntax. Finally, section 3.4 will deal with morphological and semantic consequences of language contact. Semantics is included in this latter section because most of the work with a semantic focus in the languages-in-contact literature has dealt with the question of grammatical categories, a topic intimately related to morphology.

3.1   *Phonology*

What happens when a group of speakers begins learning another language is well documented in the SLA literature. Phonological interference or transfer is overwhelmingly observed (Major 1988, Ioup and Weinberger 1987, Nagy et al. 1996, Archibald 1998). It would appear likely, then, that farther along in the contact history, in the process of acquiring bilingual competence, the version of the second language spoken by such people would still contain many phonological features derivable from their native language, i.e. substratum phonological influence. However, such a development constitutes a long-term linguistic influence only in so far as the descendants of these people have acquired and carried forward the substratum-influenced version of their parents, perhaps even transmitting it, or some of its features, to descendants of the native speakers.

In an independent development, Van Coetsem (1988) enunciated a general theory of loan phonology based on a binary distinction consonant with the one proposed in the same year by T&K. Like T&K, Van Coetsem distinguishes between the "source language" and the "recipient language," and regards the factor of agency as primary. His term "phonological borrowing" is quite parallel to "borrowing" in T&K, as he restricts this process to "recipient language agentivity" (1988: 10), i.e. native speakers of the recipient language import into their language something from another, source language. The obverse of this, analogous to T&K's notion of substratum interference, is called "imposition" (1988: 11) – which occurs when foreign language speakers *impose* their own first language phonological habits on their own use of the second language. Van Coetsem notes that "in our usage the term imposition does not carry negative connotations; it simply denotes an agent other than the recipient language speaker" (1988: 11). He carefully distinguishes these acts of individual speakers from the acceptance, spread, or integration of such innovations (whether "phonological borrowings" or "phonological impositions") by the recipient language as a whole. Because few subsequent authors seem to have adopted the term "imposition" (Guy 1990 and Ross 1991 being the two exceptions known to me), I have not used this term in what follows. However, the general distinction between recipient and source language agency seems crucial in the study of language contact, and Van Coetsem's thoughtful discussion of several interesting cases (including Afrikaans–English contact) has informed our thinking on phonological issues.

3.1.1   Substratum influence

3.1.1.1   Immigration

Sociolinguistic studies that have examined the transition between the first contact generation and subsequent generations have tended to find the expected phonological interference among adults acquiring the second language. For example, Lee (2000) found only partial acquisition of the American English flapping rule among Korean immigrants to Philadelphia who had arrived as adults. McDonald's (1996) data from two groups of Cuban American high school students living in Miami's "Little Havana" revealed that "the degree and nature of Spanish-influenced phonology correlated with the age at which English acquisition began." Adamson and Regan (1991) found that in the Vietnamese and Cambodian immigrant community in Philadelphia, variation in the unstressed (-ing) suffix of English showed partial acquisition of majority community stylistic variation, as well as nonnative patterns.

If rapid language shift occurs, the contact situation obviously does not continue and thus there is no long-term substratum effect of immigrant language phonology. Both Lee's and McDonald's studies indicated that immigrant language influences tended to disappear in subsequent generations, as immigrant languages were lost and immigrants' descendants became monolingual speakers of the majority language. Lee's research showed that even immigrants who arrived as children were indistinguishable in terms of flapping from the native-born.

Two studies of contemporary immigrant groups, however, document some continuing substrate influence of original immigrant languages on the speech of their monolingual (or "new country language"-dominant) descendants. Santa Ana's (1996) quantitative study of (t,d) deletion among 45 English-speaking Chicanos in Los Angeles indicated that this population differs from other English speakers in several ways. He found sonority effects of adjacent preceding and following syllables, and also established that syllable stress does not influence deletion. Fought (1999), also working in Los Angeles, found that only some of the second-generation adolescents from the Mexican American community participate in the u-fronting typical of the Anglo community.[5] Those with strong Mexican American peer group ties were likely to prefer the more backed [u] that is more readily identified with the Spanish high back vowel. Sociolinguistic studies of third and fourth generation descendants of immigrants have shown remarkably few effects in any way attributable to the history of language shift among their parents and grandparents. Labov (1994), however, reported that Philadelphians of Italian ethnicity showed a strong conservative tendency with respect to the /o/-fronting that is typical of the city as a whole, a result that parallels Fought's report on Mexican American Angelenos. Lastly, Laferriere (1979) showed differences among Boston Irish, Jewish, and Italian ethnic groups in the treatment of the low back vowels. (On ethnicity, see the chapter by Fought.)

With such substrate-influenced phonological features so rare even among direct descendants of immigrants, it is even more exceptional to find regional features where language shift constitues a putative source for difference. The exceptions tend to be cases in which the immigrant group and its descendants have become a local majority population, often geographically isolated.[6] Lance (1993) suggests that the northern dialect phonology found in a 10-county area of eastern Missouri that is otherwise in the South Midland dialect region is a result of heavy German settlement. He corroborates the influence of German phonology through interviews with elderly speakers who are assumed to represent the last generation of bilinguals in the area. Herold (1997) attributes the emergence of the *cot/caught* merger in the former coal mining towns of eastern Pennsylvania to the large numbers of Polish and other non-German immigrants to the area at the beginning of the twentieth century. A final case documented on the basis of the historical record concerns five sound changes in Czech that occurred in the fourteenth century, subsequent to a significant immigration of German speakers to urban and peripheral Bohemia (Boretzky 1991).

3.1.1.2   *Local groups bilingual in languages imported from outside*

Sociolinguistically, these situations are the obverse of those just discussed. Here a later-arriving group, rather than assimilating to the language already spoken in the area, imports a new language that is subsequently spoken by those already living there. In so far as ensuing bilingualism (and possibly, language shift) is often a very slow process, substratum influence may flourish under such conditions. To mention a few well-known historical examples, Latin displaced the languages in the western part of the Roman Empire (though it did not displace Koine Greek in the east); Anglo-Saxon largely displaced the preexisting Celtic languages in the British Isles (although the Danes and then the Norman French, conquerors whose languages survived for long periods of time, did not in the end impose their languages).

In modern times, standard languages have made incursions into areas where they were not previously spoken. The Cajun French population of Louisiana has been in contact with English since the mid-nineteenth century, and bilingualism there is longstanding, with massive language shift over the past several decades. Dubois and Horvath (1998) document stops (attributable to the French substrate) as frequent phonetic variants of interdental fricatives in Cajun English. Native speakers of Québec French, also with a long history of English contact, are described as hypercorrecting in their use of initial-h words in English (Auger and Janda 1992). In contrast, Bayley's (1994) study of t/d deletion in Tejano English in San Antonio, Texas, showed no effect attributable to Spanish among adult speakers (for example, as with speakers of mainstream English dialects, retention was categorical after r). However, his sample of 25 young people aged 14–21 was similar to the Los Angeles population of Santa Ana's study in the absence of a stress effect.[7]

A similar result has occurred in postcolonial situations where many speakers of local languages also speak languages of wider communication. One example is Muthwii (1994), who documents a case of trilingual Kenyans transferring vowel harmony, stress and pitch patterns from their native Kalenjin into Kiswahili and English.

3.1.2   Borrowing

Adhering to both Van Coetsem's and T&K's concept of borrowing as, by definition, involving speakers' importing features from other languages into their native language, it is not surprising to find many studies that document the influence of native phonological patterns on foreign lexical items borrowed into the language. One example is Pereira (1977), who discusses numerous such processes in a study of the phonological adaptation of 300 English loan words into Brazilian Portuguese.

Sometimes phonological changes appear to be introduced despite the existence of more similar segments across donor and borrowing languages. Naim (1998) reports that although non-pharyngealized consonants occur in Beirut Arabic, consonants in Italian and French loan words are pharyngealized when they occur preceding long low vowels, apparently due to an identification speakers make between the vowels in these foreign words and the local allophone of Arabic /a/ that occurs after pharyngeals.

If it were the case that no speakers from the borrowing language ever became fluent in the language being borrowed from, this pattern might be more universal.[8] Nevertheless, most studies report that phonological adaptation of loan words is not total. Some foreign pronunciations are retained, and indeed have often been a source of phonological innovation in the receiving language. This is recently documented in the case of 1,500 English loan words in Italian (Socanac 1996). Davidson and Noyer (1997) discuss borrowings from Spanish into the Penutian language Huave that violate Huave stress rules, arguing that optimality theory can account for the nativization process by a re-ranking of the constraints that operate in native Huave phonology. Tsuchida (1995), also working in an optimality framework, notes similar results for English loan words in Japanese: native Japanese well-formedness conditions must be modified to account for the phonology of English loans. Penalosa (1990) documents partial phonological assimilation of Spanish loan words in four Mayan languages.

Paradis and Lacharité (1997) studied 545 French loanwords in Fula, spoken in Mauritania and Senegal, both countries that have been influenced by French for more than a century since initial French colonization. They found that the loan words were introduced by bilinguals of varying degrees of bilingualism, who adapted the foreign phonological sequences according to what they call "repair strategies." In Fula, these include breaking up French consonant clusters by either cluster simplification or vowel insertion, and the denasalization of French nasal vowels. Paradis (1995) found similar patterns in French loans in Moroccan Arabic and Kinyarwanda, and English loans in Quebec French. Other studies of English loans into Quebec French (Walker 1982, Picard 1983, Patry 1986, and McLaughlin 1986) show similar results: influence of the receiving language (French) coupled with change imported to that language via the borrowings). Coetser (1996) reports that Afrikaans names borrowed into Xhosa during several centuries of contact have only been partially assimilated phonologically. Another example of mixed influences, also from the Pacific, concerns English loan words in Hawaiian. Schutz (1976) argues that in addition to the influence of Hawaiian phonetics on the borrowed words, missionaries were successful in "imposing" (in a sense quite different from that of Van Coetsem) a series of English consonants into Hawaiian in order to "preserve the identity" of English loan words. Finally, Stenson (1993), in a study of borrowings from English into Irish, also found only partial adaptation of foreign phonological features. In examining English interdental fricatives, alveolar stops, affricates, voiced sibilants, glides, and velar nasals, she found variability for all features except for the interdental fricatives in which there is overlap between Irish and Hiberno-English pronunciations. Stenson attributed the overall preference for adoption of foreign phonological features (rather than assimilation to Irish patterns) to universal bilingualism in English.

Boberg (1997, 1999) has studied the process of phonological assimilation historically in thousands of English words containing "foreign a." He points out that when English borrows words like *llama, Mazda, pasta, spa,* and *tobacco,* the "foreign a" must be assimilated either to the regular short-a class (like *cat* and *bag*), or to the "broad a" class (like *father* and *calm*). The longer a word has been in English, the more likely it is to have migrated into the "short a" class – a process that is also subject to phonological and dialect influences.

Of the many studies consulted on the phonological assimilation of loanwords, only one was devoted specifically to the lack of assimilation. Oswalt (1985) reports that English words are often used in Kashaya, a Native American language of California. However, they are unassimilated to Kashaya phonology, leading speakers to deny that they are borrowings (in contrast with the phonologically assimilated borrowings from Spanish). Two further studies (Ndiaye 1996, on the assimilation of French words into Wolof, and Shinohara 1996 on French loan phonology in Japanese) did not mention the retention of aspects of source language phonology. Although it is not clear whether such phenomena do not exist in these contact situations, or whether the authors simply chose not to discuss them, two other papers explicitly deny the existence of phonologically unassimilated loans in borrowing. Bergsland (1992) attributes the phonological assimilation of Scandinavian borrowings into Southern Sami (or Lapp), a Finno-Ugric language, to active resistance to outside influences by community members. Yip (1993) argues that Cantonese speakers do not perceive all the distinctions that English speakers do, and subject the nonnative input (English loanwords) to Cantonese well-formedness rules.

3.1.3 Borrowings or substratum influence? Cases of long-term coterritoriality

Studies of populations that have shared a territory for a long time, and where long term bilingualism has been the norm, may be more difficult to categorize.

All the cases discussed in this section appear to fall on the "borrowing" side, but the processes involved are less clearly determinable than in the studies reviewed so far.

Nagy's (1994, 1996) research on Faetar, an isolated dialect of Francoprovençal spoken in an isolated mountain area of southern Italy where its speakers have lived for several centuries, presents such a case. Faetar's geminate consonants, a feature atypical of Francoprovençal, would seem to have been borrowed from Italian by generations of Faetar's bilinguals. The geminates are found in native Faetar words as well as in borrowings from Italian, attesting to a thorough nativization of the phonological process.

In the Semitic language Maltese, the long contact with Sicilian and Italian has resulted in complete phonological integration of the approximately 25 percent of vocabulary from those languages (Krier 1980). However, English loans, numerous though not reaching 25 percent, are reported not to be phonologically assimilated, due to the shorter duration of contact and to lesser knowledge of English among the Maltese population. Nurse (1985) attributes the unusual feature (worldwide and in Bantu languages in general) of a dental, rather than alveolar, obstruent series in three Bantu languages of northeastern Kenya to historic, long-term contact with Cushitic languages.

In parts of the Western Pacific, groups speaking Polynesian languages migrated west from central Polynesia after the original great migrations eastward across the Pacific. Such languages, referred to as "Polynesian outliers" have been in contact for many generations with the Melanesian languages spoken in these islands. Ozanne-Rivierre (1994) reports that the Polynesian Outlier language Fagauvea, spoken on the island of Uvea, has evolved a 9-vowel, 27-consonant system due to contact with the Melanesian language Iaai. She reports that the influence has gone almost uniquely from Iaai (the pre-existing language) to Fagauvea (the immigrant language). The reverse process seems to have occurred in the Philippine language Sama Abaknon which, under the influence of several centuries of domination by Visayan, has reduced its vowel inventory from 6 to 3 (Jakobson and Jakobson 1980).

3.2   Lexicon

In discussing lexical aspects of languages in contact, it is overwhelmingly clear that the major process involved is borrowing. In the majority of contact situations, borrowing occurs most extensively on the part of minority language speakers from the language of wider communication into the minority language. On the other hand, one can readily identify words that have become accepted within majority language communities that derive from language shift by various immigrant groups and would thus clearly fall under the definition of "substratum influence." For example, a sampling of words from Yiddish that are known to a majority of the non-Jewish students in classes I teach at the University of Pennsylvania include *shmuck* and *shtick* (whereas familiarity with other Yiddish-origin words like *meshuggeh*, *goniff*, and *tochas* tend to be known only to students with a Yiddish family background). However, as my search of the literature did not turn up any studies of this phenomenon, only borrowing will be dealt with in this section.

3.2.1   Borrowing

One of the most carefully researched areas in the entire field of languages in contact concerns the status of foreign lexical elements that appear in the everyday discourse of bilinguals. Research into nonce borrowings began as part of the larger study of code switching, in which the grammatical conditioning of switches – both single lexical items and longer strings – have been the focus of attention. It is not possible in this review to do justice to the massive topic of code switching. However, it is necessary to use code switching behavior as a point of departure, since the well-documented ability of bilinguals to draw on lexical items from both their languages can reasonably be considered as the beginning point of lexical borrowing.

Much of the work on the grammatical constraints on code switching for the past 20 years (beginning with Pfaff 1979, Poplack 1980) was devoted to grappling with the problem of how to distinguish single word code switches from borrowings. This seemed all the more pressing in light of two facts. The first is that "[i]n virtually all bilingual corpora empirically studied, mixed discourse is overwhelmingly constituted of lone elements, usually major-class content words, of one language embedded in the syntax of another" (Poplack and Meechan 1998: 127). There has been much debate about the formal linguistic constraints that condition or regulate switching, which grammatical sites accept or constitute barriers to switching, and indeed whether in the formal model of code switching it is useful to postulate a matrix language (Woolford 1983, Joshi 1985, di Sciullo et al. 1986, Myers-Scotton 1993, Mahootian 1994). However, there is a very broad consensus among researchers on the empirical generalization as stated above by Poplack (1980).

The second important fact is that it is clear (from, e.g., Haugen 1950, Poplack et al. 1988, and van Hout and Muysken 1994) that "major-class content words such as nouns, verbs, and adjectives are the most likely to be borrowed" (Poplack and Meechan 1998: 127). This consonance between switching and borrowing made it abundantly clear that switching was the royal road to borrowing, pointed out in Poplack and Sankoff (1984) as well as in work by other scholars (e.g. Heath 1990). However, most researchers were reluctant to go to the extreme of labeling every single-word "switch" they observed as a borrowing, especially in the absence of community-wide ratification or legitimation. Various criteria were invoked in an attempt to separate the legitimate, or legitimated loan words, from the nonce borrowings or switches. These included phonological or morphological integration, as well as attestations of use by a wider community of speakers. All of these criteria were applied in an attempt to identify individual cases or tokens of these single-word elements as to whether or not they should individually constitute borrowings, and all were unsatisfactory given the variability in the data (e.g., many such words are found to be *partially* phonologically integrated, so that phonological integration cannot constitute a litmus test).

A significant breakthrough in resolving the question of single-word tokens as "code switches" vs. "borrowings" was made in 1998 via the application of quantitative sociolinguistic methodology, crucially including the criterion of accountability, to numerous corpora of spontaneous bilingual discourse. Poplack and her colleagues outline a quantitative methodology that renders operational the clear conceptual distinction between code switching and borrowing (Poplack and Meechan 1998). According to their method, bilingual discourse was analyzed as having five major observable components: (1) unmixed L1; (2) unmixed L2; (3) multiword alternations (readily understood as code switches); (4) attested loanwords; and (5) ambiguous lone items. Of these, only the last, the ambiguous lone items, are problematic. The methodological innovation was to statistically compare the patterning of these items with analogous, identified items in the same corpus. As explained by Adalar and Tagliamonte (1998) with respect to the Turkish Cypriots known as "Londrali" (who have lived for significant periods in England), this consists of comparing the lone noun, in Turkish or in English, "in contexts in which it is surrounded by the other language" (1998: 139) vs. when it appears in a multiword fragment of English or Turkish. In five different language pairs, this technique was applied successfully to resolve the code switching/borrowing question. The clear progression that exists between individual, nonce-borrowed items which testify to the productivity of other-language access for the individual bilingual speaker, and the social ratification of borrowings at the community level, can thus be studied independently of the muddy waters of code switching. In my opinion, this development has for the first time put the study of lexical borrowing on a sound methodological and theoretical footing.

Noteworthy in the sociolinguistic study of lexical borrowing are two other corpus-based studies by authors not employing the Poplack et al. methodology as such. The first is Mougeon and Beniak's (1987) demonstration of the social parameters associated with "core" lexical borrowing from English in the Francophone community of Ontario. Though "non-core" or "cultural" borrowing has long been accepted as a usual concomitant of language contact, the replacement of core L1 vocabulary by other-language lexical items, usually in situations where most minority group members make extensive use of the majority language, has been poorly understood, and the work by Mougeon, Beniak, and associates goes a long way towards filling that gap. The second corpus-based study (Boyd 1993) is important because it compares two groups of bilingual immigrants in the same host speech community: American English speakers and Finns living in and around Göteborg, Sweden. While different patterns of code switching behavior had previously been contrasted across different communities (Poplack 1985), Boyd's is the first to explicitly compare two different minorities in the same community, finding that Swedish incorporations into Finnish were more readily identifiable as borrowings, whereas those into English more closely resembled code switching.

3.3   Syntax and discourse/pragmatics

Whether or not "grammar" or "syntax" can be borrowed at all is still very much in question. Although the T&K view has its proponents (e.g. Campbell 1993),[9] many students of language contact are convinced that grammatical or syntactic borrowing is impossible or close to it (e.g. Lefebvre 1985, Prince 1988, King 2000). These authors generally see grammatical change subsequent to contact as a consequence of lexical or pragmatic interinfluence, that may then lead to internal syntactic change. It is for this reason that I have chosen to combine syntax and discourse/pragmatics into one section of this review.

Among the varied proposals regarding the chains of events that can lead to contact-induced syntactic change, four lines of explanation have been proposed. The first derives from the type of phonological changes widely attested (and reviewed in section 3.3.1), attributable in the first instance to substratum influence and thus classified in the "substratum influence" section below. The second derives from lexical borrowing (section 3.3.2). The third, variously described as "camouflage" (Spears 1982); "covert interference" (Mougeon and Beniak 1991), and "normative assimilation" (Wald 1996) and also, I believe, related to the equivalence constraint in code switching (Poplack 1980) appears to be a syntax-internal contact process related more to substratum than to borrowing, and thus it will also be discussed in section 3.3.2. Fourth, in a related line of work, several studies have traced a discourse-to-syntax path in bilingual inter-influence, also apparently more characteristic, though not perhaps uniquely so, of substratum influence.

3.3.1   Substratum influence

As in phonology, the study of second-language acquisition in syntax may be of considerable potential interest in helping us to locate potential areas of influence from speakers' L1. Perhaps more than in phonology, however, scholars who have examined L2 acquisition have been less willing to attribute non-target like language to an L1 source, and have also given considerable weight to the influence of universals. Papers on the acquisition of French as a second language (e.g. Hulk 1991, Hawkins 1989, Hawkins et al. 1993) have considered both lines of explanation. One reason that authors may be more cautious in adducing contact sources for syntactic change is that markedness is often less clear in syntax than in phonology, and internally motivated change is often as likely, and more parsimonious, an explanation.

3.3.1.1   Immigration
The consequences of contact-induced phonological change may indeed be far reaching, and extend to morphological and even syntactic domains. As

described in section 3.2.1.1 above, language shift on the part of large numbers of Scandinavian invaders was a major influence in the development of the Northern and East-Midland dialects of Old English. Kroch and Taylor (1997) postulate a train of events beginning with contact-induced phonological change that resulted in the "impoverishment of agreement morphology." This in turn prevented V-to-I movement and led in these dialects to the development of the CP V2 structure typical of the modern Scandinavian languages.

The immigration of large numbers of L1 speakers of Yiddish to the United States in the early years of the twentieth century resulted in language shift that has in turn produced substratum effects in the English of their descendants. Prince (1988) has analyzed the "Yiddish movement" construction[10] not as a syntactic but as a discourse level example of Yiddish influence on English. The syntax of Y-movement is identical to the focus-movement constructions that exist already in English; the change involves a widening of the pragmatic domain in which these constructions can be used to a context in which the moved NP is not previously salient in the discourse (as opposed to the standard English case in which the moved NP must already be salient). Though Prince dubs this process "borrowing," she includes in a prescient footnote: "Intuitively, one may thus call the Yiddish-Movement case an instance of 'interference' rather than borrowing, but I am at a loss to find a principled basis for such a distinction" (Prince 1988: 516). This is exactly the type of case that both van Coetsem and T&K would understand as interference, for the principled social reason that it is a concomitant of language shift, but these arguments were unavailable to Prince since they were published in the same year as her paper.

Sociolinguistic research on contemporary language contact situations has been able to carefully trace the differential usage patterns among bilinguals that apparently provide a path for often subtle contact effects. Mesthrie and Dunne (1990) document a continuum of varieties in English relative clause types in the English of Indians in South Africa, with major influence on second-language speakers but some continuing influences of substratum on English-dominant speakers as well. In a study of reported speech in East Los Angeles English, Wald (1987) observes that when a large, ethnically homogeneous community shifts from one language (L1) to another (L2 for those in the initial stages of the contact), the opportunity arises for substratal influences to survive. He analyzes this process as one in which interlingual identification skews the pattern of grammatical variation to maximize matching with L2 of L1 grammatical structures, as well as resulting in lexical reinterpretation that may then lead to the creation of novel grammatical patterns. Following this line of research, Wald (1996) formulates two principles that govern bilingual usage: (1) "normative assimilation," i.e. not violating the grammatical norms of the socially dominant language (English in this case) and (2) "shortest path", i.e. selecting the norms of the socially dominant language that most closely correspond to those of the prior language, in studying the use of English *would* among Mexican Americans in east Los Angeles. That the general English modal/stative verb interaction operates in this dialect is attributed to the principle of normative assimilation, but in hypothetical contexts, this interaction is weaker, which Wald attributes to the fact that Spanish provides no basis for the interaction.

3.3.1.2   *Local groups bilingual in externally imposed languages*

As pointed out earlier, local groups bilingual in externally imposed languages, or who have a history of language shift that has taken place over a long period of time, provide perhaps the most fertile ground for features of substratum origin to become established in the speech community as a whole. However, careful studies of such situations have often cautioned against jumping to conclusions about substratum influence, first, because sources other than substratum may turn out to be historically correct, and second, because descriptions of contact varieties may be descriptions of L2 speakers, not of stable bilingual or L1 speech. In a study of eight characteristics that have been widely described as characteristic of "Andean Spanish," i.e. the Spanish of speakers from Quechua and Aymara backgrounds, Escobar (1995) states that many of the features in fact only hold for L1 speakers of Quechua and Aymara who have limited proficiency in Spanish. Distinguishing between these speakers and the truly bilingual, her detailed study of possessive constructions parallels the work of Harris in attributing some construction types common to Andean Spanish as a whole to "older varieties of Spanish" (1995: 62), and, like him, cautions against jumping to conclusions about substratum influence in contact varieties.

In the case of Irish English, Harris (1984) concludes that, with the exception of the "after +Ving" construction, "the nonstandard Hiberno-English 'perfect' forms, far from being Hiberno English innovations with an exclusive background in substratum interference, are actually retentions of older English patterns" (1984: 320).[11] In a follow-up study, however, Harris (1991) cites data from an unpublished 1982 thesis by Markku Filppula that he regards as a convincing demonstration of an Irish Gaelic substrate source for the "informative-presupposition" *it*-clefts[12] in Irish English. Harris notes that "quantitative differences confirm the existence of a post-contact continuum with the most markedly nonstandard varieties displaying a greater degree of substratal input than intermediate varieties which have undergone varying degrees of convergence towards the superstrate"(1991: 201).

Mithun (1992) traces a discourse-to-syntax path in documenting the often subtle influence of Eastern Pomo on several syntactic patterns in the English spoken by members of several communities in northern California, including the use of pronouns and of the definite article, as well as clause-linking strategies.

3.3.2   *Borrowing*

What about the immigrant or minority languages themselves? What are the effects of borrowings brought back into the erstwhile L1 by its speakers who have become bilingual in the dominant or majority language? Here we must come face to face with the question of "structural borrowing." This notion has been criticized by, e.g., King (2000) for vagueness, lack of precision and/or lack of detailed evidence or analysis in oft-cited but scantily documented cases frequently referred to in the languages-in-contact literature. There is, however, a growing body of research that goes farther than hand-waving or invoking isolated surface parallels.

A detailed study of Prince Edward Island French has documented a variety of French that shows numerous morphological and syntactic differences from other French varieties, including the incorporation of many borrowings from English, the dominant language with which it has been in contact for centuries (King 2000). Based on her analyses of the introduction of English *back* in identification with the French *re-* morpheme, of preposition stranding, and of the borrowing of English wh-words with ensuing changes in relative clauses, King concludes that "the influence of English on PEI French . . . has been essentially lexical," and that these lexical innovations "have triggered particular language-internal changes, resulting in the emergence of a number of structural changes in PEI French" (King 2000: 173). Our own study of French–English contact in Montreal is difficult to categorize because although Anglophones are the minority, English has been in many ways the socially and politically dominant language. Substrate-related linguistic influence could be argued for the dramatically increased use of *comme* "like" as a discourse marker for Anglophone speakers of French, but this appears to be the case for young native speakers as well (Sankoff et al. 1997).

Prince (1988), in a study of the influence of the Slavic focus-presupposition construction on Yiddish, examines the apparent modeling of the Yiddish *dos-*initial sentences on the Slavic *eto-*initial sentences of, e.g., Russian. She concludes that sentences of the type: *Dos shlogst du di puter* (lit. "it beats you the butter" or "It's you who's churning the butter!") constitute a pragmatic, not a syntactic borrowing from Slavic. Prince shows that (1) there was already a syntactic model in the language: the Yiddish *es-*sentences, and (2) the Yiddish V2 syntax was not altered via this language-contact innovation, because in contrast to Slavic, Yiddish can front only subjects, and must have the verb in the second position. This case is of particular interest not only because of Prince's clear and persuasive exposition, but also because it is a case of speakers clearly importing something other than a lexical item into their native language from a second language: but still, according to Prince, not a structural borrowing. As she states, "While the syntax of *dos-*sentences was native to Yiddish, the discourse function associated with them was clearly a Slavic borrowing" (1988: 511).

A final study that links discourse and syntax is Matras (1998), who explains the frequent borrowing of "utterance modifiers" from the pragmatically dominant language by minority group members as being related to the "cognitive pressure" they experience to "use the dominant language's resources for situative discourse regulation."

Although stable, long-term bilingualism is well-documented in many minority language communities all over the world, it is also the case that language shift and language loss has occurred with linguistic minorities as well as in the case of immigrant communities. The linguistic concomitants of language attrition or obsolescence is not a topic that can be taken up in this review (cf. Dorian 1989). However, some of the literature that documents heavy influence of the majority language in such situations may be reflecting diminished competence in the minority language by younger, majority-language dominant speakers. Kroskrity (1978) on complex syntax in Tewa, and Fortescue (1993) on word-order changes in West Greenlandic Eskimo, both under the influence of English, appear to be examples of minority languages in situations of language shift.

3.4   Morphology/grammatical categories

The adoption of bound morphemes has been stated by many authors to be the among the most resistant features of language to contact-induced change. After reviewing the literature, I am more convinced than ever that this is true. Only a few cases came to light, and almost all involved morphemes that are, if not entirely free, not really bound either. The other type of case to be reviewed here concerns grammatical categories.

3.4.1   Substratum influence

3.4.1.1   Immigration
The Norse invasion of England provides a case in which language shift by newcomers led to morphological change in the receiving language – a rare type of change that seems only to have been possible because of the massive numbers of Scandinavians involved, and the intimacy of their contacts with the pre-existing population. The third person plural pronouns with initial th-forms were borrowed into English at that time, though during the thirteenth century they were in competition with the English h-initial forms (Morse-Gagne 1988).

The massive migration of foreign workers into northern European countries, where most languages have relatively rich inflectional morphology, has led to a fertile field of investigation into the new varieties of these languages as spoken by immigrants and their children. However, it has been less easy to document substrate influences on morphological regularization given that similar results can be explained by, e.g., universal processes of simplification.

3.4.1.2   Local groups bilingual in externally imposed languages
Studies of morphological change attributable to language shift or substratum influence seem to be almost nonexistent, prompting this author at least to assume that such changes are also very rare in language contact. A recent paper by Dede (1999) documents the use of an ablative postposition in the Xining dialect of Chinese, which he attributes to the fact that the original inhabitants of the region were speakers of Monguor, a Mongolian language, who shifted to Chinese.

Two further studies would also be potential candidates for a "borrowing" explanation, since they concern changes in minority languages in which L1 minority speakers may have made changes in their usage patterns modeled in some way on the majority language. Both concern reduced use of the subjunctive in Romance languages in contact with English: Silva-Corvalán (1994) on Los Angeles Spanish; and Poplack (1997) on Ontario French. Silva-Corvalán comes to the conclusion that internal tendencies toward a reduction of the use of the subjunctive are strengthened in the language contact situation. Poplack, however, finds that higher levels of bilingual ability, which were associated with upper class speakers, in fact favored the use of the subjunctive. She concludes that when community members regularly use both languages, language loss, language shift, and convergence are not necessary consequences in a minority language situation.

3.4.2   Borrowing

By the definitions we have adopted, any change to the immigrant language that is brought about through the bilingualism of its speakers in the language of their new country is technically a borrowing. However, this is a less obvious process in the case of morphology, said by many authors to be much more resistant to contact-induced change in general, a generalization supported by the relative paucity of documented cases of contact-induced morphological change.

More common, though still a very small number, are situations in which lexical borrowings must be adapted to the morphological categories of the receiving language. The borrowing of nouns into languages with a gender or noun-class system is one type of example in which the borrowing process involves a reconfiguration of the borrowed material into new categories. Barkin (1980) studied the gender assignment of borrowed nouns from English into Spanish, finding that the assimilation of borrowed words requires gender assignment. In Swahili, borrowed words from German were studied by Pasch and Strauch (1998), who discovered animacy to be a major factor in class assignment. Bokamba (1993) shows that in multilingual language contact situations, the transformation of a pre-existing language into a lingua franca may result in morphological simplification even when the participants already have very similar category systems in their native languages. Thus KiTuba, Kinshasa LiNgala, and Shaba KiSwahili deviate from KiKongo, Standard LiNgala, and Standard KiSwahili, respectively, in terms of a simplification of the noun class morphology.

4   The State of the Art

This review has sampled recent work on languages in contact, largely from a sociolinguistic and quantitative perspective, in an attempt to deal with the major outstanding issues regarding the linguistic consequences of language contact. (I might add that this reviewer has been considerably daunted by the sheer amount of new research on these questions, and considerably impressed by its quality.)

The three major questions I have tried to address are as follows. First, to what extent do social distinctions of the kind made by van Coetsem and by T&K, and elaborated on in this review, constitute a useful angle of vision in differentiating the linguistic phenomena? Second, does the idea of a cline of "borrowability" stand up to scrutiny? Third, what is the relationship between the individual bilingual speaker (central to the concerns of SLA) and the speech community (of primary importance in sociolinguistics)?

4.1   The social embedding of language contact

When we look at the varying social circumstances of language contact separately according to the various domains of linguistic structure, it is clear that these circumstances have a differential effect. The distinction between borrowing and substratum interference with language shift, made so forcefully both by van Coetsem and by T&K, holds up very well in general, as does the additional distinction between immigrant communities and linguistic minorities created by political developments in the areas where they have lived for many years. These different social circumstances do not, of course, have a direct effect on language; rather, they lead groups of individuals involved to differentially deploy their linguistic resources, and thus in turn affect developments at the level of linguistic structure.

4.2   A cline of borrowability?

Though most language contact situations lead to unidirectional, rather than bidirectional linguistic results, conditioned by the social circumstances, it is also the case that linguistic structure overwhelmingly conditions the linguistic outcomes. Morphology and syntax are clearly the domains of linguistic structure least susceptible to the influence of contact, and this statistical generalization is not vitiated by a few exceptional cases. On the other hand, lexicon is clearly the most readily borrowable element, and borrowing lexicon can lead to structural changes at every level of linguistic structure (cf. Muysken 1985, 1999 in addition to the individual studies discussed above). And phonology is very susceptible to change, both on the part of the individual L2 speakers (see section 4.3 below), and as a result of word borrowing, where most studies document the influence of recipient-language structure on foreign borrowings, as well as long-term influence on the phonology of the recipient language.

4.3   *The individual and the community in language contact*

Language change presupposes diffusion from individuals or smaller groups to the speech community as a whole, and this applies to language contact every bit as much as to internal linguistic change. This review has not focused directly on this question as regards language contact, but it is clear that individual strategies, individual practices in bilingual discourse, add up to community-level change.[13] To cite Benveniste's dictum: *Nihil est in lingua quod non prius fuerit in oratione* (1966: 131). Thus the massive SLA literature, the question of the critical period (Harley 1986, Scovel 2000), the question of linguistic change across individual life spans and how it interacts with language change in general (Hyltenstam and Obler 1989) – all are relevant to the linguistic outcomes of language contact. To my way of thinking, the reintegration of the individual into the overall matrix of the speech community and the evolving languages, represents the greatest challenge and the greatest scope for advancement in the research of the next decade.

NOTES

1   Given the enormous literature on languages in contact, it was not possible in this review to do justice to the more extreme results of contact in generating new languages or radically different language varieties. Regrettably, I have had to omit consideration of pidgins and creoles (cf. Mufwene 2001), mixed languages (cf. Bakker and Mous 1994), or contact languages per se (cf. Wurm et al. 1996).

2   Tarone (1988), reviewing the history of the development of the concept of interlanguage, sees Richards' critique of the error-analysis paradigm in SLA, as well as the influence of the Chomskian focus on universal grammar, as pivotal in the formulation and early popularity of "interlanguage" as a new way of conceptualizing second-language grammars.

3   A further property of the SLA literature is the idea that acquiring second languages is difficult. Since it focuses on SLA mainly in the educational context, a major goal is to measure relative success in SLA, much the way educators evaluate relative success in other school subjects. It would be foolish to deny that learning second languages has been experienced by millions of people worldwide as a difficult task in which success is often only partial. However, the dominance of this perspective obscures the normalcy of bilingualism elsewhere, and the fact that it can be seen by the bilinguals themselves as relatively unproblematic (Gumperz and Wilson 1971, Sorensen 1967).

4   It is certainly not historically the case that all political conquests have resulted in a shift to the language of the conquerors, and the number of

attested instance of conquerors or their descendants eventually shifting to the language of the conquered is also very numerous. Whichever the *direction* of shift, however, history has generally documented a relatively slow shift that has led in general to similar types of substratum influence.

5   One other surprising result is the study by Flege et al. (1995) that shows that the pronunciation of English consonants by Italian immigrants who arrived in Canada in early childhood can still be reliably distinguished, many decades later, from that of native-born native speakers. This result distinguished those immigrants who speak Italian on a regular basis from those who do not.

6   Such a demographic effect was identified in creole studies by Baker and Corne (1982) in their historical study of the evolution of Mauritian Creole, and later adopted as a key diagnostic in Bickerton's (1984) "bioprogram" theory of creole genesis. Mufwene (1996, 2001) has more recently given great weight to the relative proportions of speakers of languages in contact situations over time, in his articulation of the "founder principle" in creole genesis.

7   In treating the Mexican American young people in Los Angeles who were studied by Santa Ana and by Fought as the descendants of immigrants (section 3.1.1.1), I followed details in their descriptions of their speakers in terms of their families' (almost all very recent) immigration history. Bayley, in contrast, makes the point that a high proportion of the Mexican Americans in the San Antonio area are the descendants of people who were there prior to English speakers,

and so is treated in this, the "contact with languages imported from outside" section of the current paper. I realize that in neither geographical area is the socio-historical distinction hard and fast.

8   It is generally accepted that the longer it has been since a foreign word was introduced into the borrowing language, the more likely the pronunciation is to have been nativized. The idea that it is in initial contact that foreign phonological patterns might seem most foreign may seem to introduce a paradox here. If so, one might expect the converse: words pronounced via native (borrowing language) phonology earlier on, with later familiarization leading to an acceptance of the foreign features. However, the normal path of introduction is for bilinguals (who can pronounce the foreign sounds) to introduce the words to the wider community in which the later-adopting monolinguals progressively impose native phonological patterns.

9   It should be noted that Campbell (1993) nuances his support for this position as follows: "Thus I conclude with Thomason & Kaufman (1988: 14) that 'as far as the strictly linguistic possibilities go, any linguistic feature can be transferred from any language to any other language.' This being the case, it is safer to think of these proposed universals and principles of borrowing as general tendencies, and not as absolute constraints" (1993: 104).

10   An example of Yiddish-Movement from Philip Roth's *Portnoy's Complaint* (Y-moved constituent underlined): "In less than a week it's Rosh Hashana and he thinks I should take a vacation. *Ten people*

I'm having" (cited in Prince 1988: 512).

11 Harris (1984) does attribute an Irish Gaelic substratum source to two other syntactic features of Hiberno-English: the failure of negative attraction (sentences like "anyone wasn't at home," where other English dialects would have "no-one was at home"); and "subordinating *and* with subject pronoun and *ing*-participle" (1984: 305), such as "He fell and him crossing the bridge".

12 Harris (1991) cites the following example from Filppula: "In God's name, what happened to you?" asked the father. "It was Micheal Rua who gave me a beating", said the son (1991: 199).

13 That individual difference in orientation to other language groups are relevant here is evident from Poplack's (1978) early study of how Puerto Rican immigrant children in Philadelphia differentially deploy phonological variants typical of White vs. Black Philadelphians.

REFERENCES

Adalar, Nevin, and Sali Tagliamonte (1998). Borrowed nouns, bilingual people: the case of the "Londrali" in Northern Cyprus. *International Journal of Bilingualism* 2: 139–59.

Adamson, H. Douglas (1988). *Variation Theory and Second Language Acquisition*. Washington, DC: Georgetown University Press.

Adamson, H. D. and Vera M. Regan (1991). The acquisition of community speech norms by Asian immigrants learning English as a second language: a preliminary study. *Studies in Second Language Acquisition* 13: 1–22.

Archibald, John (1998). *Second Language Phonology*. Amsterdam and Philadelphia: John Benjamins.

Auger, Julie and Richard Janda (1992). Quantitative evidence that qualitative hypercorrection involves a sociolinguistic variable: On French-speakers' 'eadhaches with the English h/Ø contrast. *Language and Communication* 12: 195–236.

Baker, Philip and Chris Corne (1982). *Isle de France Creole: Affinities and Origins*. Ann Arbor: Karoma.

Bakker, Peter and Maarten Mous (eds.) (1994). *Mixed Languages*. Amsterdam: Dordrecht.

Barkin, Florence (1980). The role of loanword assimilation in gender assignment. *Bilingual Review/Revista bilingue* 7: 105–12.

Bayley, Richard and Dennis Preston (eds.) (1996). *Second Language Acquisition and Linguistic Variation*. Amsterdam and Philadelphia: John Benjamins.

Bayley, Robert (1994). Consonant cluster reduction in Tejano English. *Language Variation and Change* 6: 303–26.

Benveniste, Émile (1966). *Problèmes de linguistique générale*, vol. 1. Paris: Gallimard.

Bergsland, Knut (1992). Language Contacts between Southern Sami and Scandinavian. In Ernst Håkon Jahr (ed.), *Language Contact: Theoretical and Empirical Studies*. Berlin: Mouton de Gruyter. 5–15.

Bickerton, Derek (1984). The language bioprogram hypothesis. *The Behavioral and Brain Sciences* 7: 173–221.

Boberg, Charles (1997). Variation and change in the nativization of Foreign (a) in English. Ph.D. dissertation, University of Pennsylvania, Philadelphia.

Boberg, Charles (1999). The Attitudinal Component of Variation in American English Foreign (a) Nativization. *Journal of Language and Social Psychology* 18, 1: 49–61.

Bokamba, Eyamba G. (1993). Language variation and change in pervasively multilingual societies: Bantu languages. In Salikoko S. Mufwene and Moshi Lioba (eds.), *Topics in African Linguistics*. Amsterdam and Philadelphia: John Benjamins. 207–52.

Boretzky, Norbert (1991). Contact-induced sound change. *Diachronica* 8: 1–16.

Boyd, Sally (1993). Attrition or expansion? Changes in the lexicon of Finnish and American adult bilinguals in Sweden. In Kenneth Hyltenstam and Åke Viberg (eds.), *Progression and Regression in Language: Sociocultural, Neuropsychological, and Linguistic Perspectives*. Cambridge: Cambridge University Press. 386–411.

Campbell, Lyle (1993). On proposed universals of grammatical borrowing. In Henk Aertsen and Robert J. Jeffers (eds.), *Historical Linguistics 1989: Papers from the 9th International Conference on Historical Linguistics 1989*. Rutgers University, 14–18 August 1989. Amsterdam: John Benjamins. 91–109.

Cedergren, Henrietta (1973). The interplay of social and linguistic factors in Panama. Unpublished dissertation Cornell University, New York.

Clausing, Stephen (1986). *English influence of American German and American Icelandic*. New York, NY: Peter Lang.

Coetser, A. (1996). Afrikaans Influences in Xhosa family names: Afrikaans se Bydrae tot Familiename in Xhosa. *Nomina-Africana* 10, 1–2: 43–53.

Davidson, Lisa and Rolf Noyer (1997). Loan phonology in Huave: Nativization and the ranking of faithfulness constraints. In Brian Agbayani and Sze-Wing Tang (eds.), *The Proceedings of the Fifteenth West Coast Conference on Formal Linguistics*. Stanford, CA: Center Study Language and Information. 65–79.

Dede, Keith (1999). An ablative postposition in the Xining Dialect. *Language Variation and Change* 11: 1–17.

Dickerson, Lonna J. (1975). The learner's interlanguage as a system of variable rules. *TESOL Quarterly* 9: 401–7.

Di Sciullo, A.-M., P. Muysken and R. Singh (1986). Government and code-mixing. *Journal of Linguistics* 22: 1–24.

Dorian, Nancy (ed.) (1989). *Investigating Obsolescence: Studies in Language Contraction and Death*. Cambridge: Cambridge University Press.

Dubois, Sylvie and Barbara M. Horvath (1998). Let's tink about dat: interdental fricatives in Cajun English. *Language Variation and Change* 10: 245–61.

Escobar, Anna María (1995). Andean Spanish and bilingual Spanish: linguistic characteristics. In Peter Cole and Gabriela Harmon (eds.), *Language in the Andes*, 51–73.

Ferguson, C. and J. J. Gumperz (1960). Introduction in Linguistic diversity in South Asia. *Anthropology, Folklore & Linguistics*, Publication 13, Indiana University Publications.

Flege, James Emil, Murray J. Munro and Ian R. A. MacKay (1995). Effects of age of second-language learning on the production of English consonants. *Speech Communication* 16: 1–26.

Fortescue, Michaell (1993). Eskimo word order variation and its contact-induced perturbation. *Journal of Linguistics* 29: 267–89.

Fought, Carmen (1999). A majority sound change in a minority community: /u/-fronting in Chicano English. *Journal of Sociolinguistics* 1999: 5–23.

Gumperz, John (1964). Linguistic and social interaction in two communities. In J. Gumperz and D. Hymes (eds.), *The Ethnography of Communication* 66, 6: 137–53.

Gumperz, John and Robert Wilson (1971). Convergence and creolization: A case from the Indo-Aryan/Dravidian border. In D. Hymes (ed.), *Pidginization and Creolization of Languages*. Cambridge: Cambridge University Press. 151–68.

Guy, Gregory (1990). The sociolinguistic types of language change. *Diachronica* 7: 47–67.

Harley, Birgit (1986). *Age in Second Language Acquisition*. Clevedon, Avon: Multilingual Matters.

Harris, John (1984). Syntactic variation and dialect divergence. *Journal of Linguistics* 20: 303–27.

Harris, John (1991). Conservatism versus substratal transfer in Irish English. In Peter Trudgill and J. K. Chambers (eds.), *Dialects of English: Studies in Grammatical Variation*. London and New York: Longman. 191–212.

Haugen, Elinar (1950). The analysis of linguistic borrowing. *Language* 26: 210–31.

Haugen, Einar (1955). *Bilingualism in the Americas: A Bibliography and Research Guide*. Tuscaloosa: University of Alabama Press.

Haugen, Einar (1970). Bilingualism, language contact, and immigrant languages in the United States: a

research report 1956–1970. *Current Trends in Linguistics* 10: 505–91.

Hawkins, Roger (1989). Do second language learners acquire restrictive relative clauses on the basis of relational or configurational information? *Second Language Research* 5(2): 156–88.

Hawkins, Roger, Richard Towell, and Nives Bazergui (1993). Universal grammar and the acquisition of French verb movement by native speakers of English. *Second Language Research* 9: 189–233.

Heath, Jeffrey (1990). *From Code Switching to Borrowing: Foreign and Diglossic Mixing in Moroccan Arabic* (Library of Arabic Linguistics).

Herold, Ruth (1997). Solving the actuation problem: Merger and immigration in eastern Pennsylvania. *Language Variation and Change* 9: 149–64.

Hulk, Aafke (1991). Parameter setting and the acquisition of word order in L2 French. *Second Language Research* 7, 1: 1–34.

Hyltenstam, Kenneth, and Loraine K. Obler (eds.) (1989). *Bilingualism across the Lifespan: Aspects of Acquisition, Maturity, and Loss*. Cambridge: Cambridge University Press.

Ioup, Georgette, and Steven Weinberger (1987). *Interlanguage Phonology: The Acquisition of a Second Language Sound System*. Cambridge, MA: Newbury House Publishers.

Jakobson, Marc R. and Suzanne M. Jakobson (1980). Sama Abaknon Phonology Philippine. *Journal of Linguistics* 11: 32–44.

Joshi, A. K. (1985). Processing of sentences with intrasentential code-switching. In D. Dowty et al. (eds.), *Natural Language Processing: Psychological, computational, and theoretical perspectives*. Cambridge:

Cambridge University Press. 190–205.

King, Ruth (2000). *The Lexical Basis of Grammatical Borrowing: A Prince Edward Island French Case Study.* Amsterdam and Philadelphia: John Benjmains.

Krier, Fernande (1980). Lehnwort und Fremdwort im Maltesischen. *Folia Linguistica* 14: 179–84.

Kroch, Anthony and Ann Taylor (1997). Verb movement in Old and Middle English: Dialect variation and language contact. In Ans Van Kemenade and Nigel Vincent (eds.), *Parameters of Morphosyntactic Change.* Cambridge: Cambridge University Press. 297–325.

Kroskrity, Paul V. (1978). Aspects of syntactic and semantic variation within the Arizona Tewa speech community. *Anthropological Linguistics* 20: 235–57.

Labov, William (1966). *The Social Stratification of English in New York City.* Washington, DC: Center for Applied Linguistics.

Labov, William (1989). The exact description of the speech community: short a in Philadelphia. In R. Fasold and D. Schiffrin (eds.), *Language Change and Variation.* Washington, DC: Georgetown University Press. 1–57.

Labov, William (1994). *Principles of Linguistic Change,* vol. 1: *Internal Factors.* Oxford: Blackwell Publishers.

Laferriere, Martha (1979). Ethnicity in phonological variation and change. *Language* 55: 603–17.

Lance, Donald M. (1993). Some dialect features in the speech of Missouri Germans. In Timothy C. Frazer (ed.), *"Heartland" English: Variation and Transition in the American Midwest.* Tuscaloosa: University of Alabama Press. 187–97.

Lee, Hikyoung (2000). Korean Americans as speakers of English: the acquisition of general and regional features. Ph.D. dissertation, University of Pennsylvania.

Lefebvre, Claire (1985). Grammaires en contact: définition et perspectives de recherche. *Revue québécoise de Linguistique* 14: 11–47.

Mahootian, Shahrzad (1994). A null theory of codeswitching. Ph.D. dissertation, Northwestern University.

Major, Roy C. (1998). Interlanguage phonetics and phonology: An introduction. *Studies in Second Language Acquisition* 20: 131–7.

Matras, Yaron (1998). Utterance modifiers and universals of grammatical borrowing. *Linguistics* 36: 281–331.

McDonald (1996). Bilinguals in Little Havana: The phonology of a new generation. In Ana Roca and John B. Jensen (eds.), Somerville, MA: Cascadilla. 143–50.

McLaughlin, Anne (1986). Les Emprunts a l'anglais et la phonologie des voyelles hautes en francais montrealais. *Revue québécoise de linguistique théorique et appliquée* 5: 179–214.

Mesthrie, Rajend and Timothy T. Dunne (1990). Syntactic variation in language shift: the relative clause in South African Indian English. *Language Variation and Change* 2: 31–56.

Milroy, Leslie (1980). *Language and Social Networks.* Oxford: Basil Blackwell.

Mithun, Marianne (1992). The substratum in grammar and discourse. In Ernst H. Jahr (ed.), *Language Contact: Theoretical and Empirical Studies.* Trends in Linguistics Studies and Monographs 60. Berlin: Mouton de Gruyter. 103–15.

Moral, Dipankar (1997). North-East India as a Linguistic Area. *Mon-Khmer-Studies* 27: 43–53.

Morse-Gagne, Elise (1988). Adoption of Scandinavian pronouns into English. *Proceedings of the Eastern States Conference on Linguistics* (ESCOL) 5: 361–70.

Mougeon, Raymond and Edouard Beniak (1987). The extralinguistic correlates of core lexical borrowing. In Keith M. Denning et al. (eds.), *Variation in Language: NWAV-XV at Stanford*. Stanford, CA: Department of Linguistics, Stanford University. 337–47.

Mougeon, Raymond and Edouard Beniak (1991). *Linguistic Consequences of Language Contact and Restriction: The Case of French in Ontario, Canada*. Oxford: Clarendon Press.

Mougeon, Raymond and Terry Nadasdi (1998). Sociolinguistic discontinuity in minority language communities. *Language* 74: 40–55.

Mufwene, Salikoko (1996). The founder principle in creole genesis. *Diachronica* 13: 83–134.

Mufwene, Salikoko (2001). *The Ecology of Language Evolution*. Cambridge: Cambridge University Press.

Muthwii, Margaret J. (1994). Kalenjin in Kenya: the socio-phonological interaction of an ethnic language with English and Kiswahili. *Language Forum* 2(1): 1–48.

Muysken, Pieter (1985). Linguistic dimensions of language contact: the state of the art in interlinguistics. *Revue québécoise de Linguistique* 14: 49–76.

Muysken, Pieter (1999). Three processes of borrowing: borrowability revisited. In Guus Extra and Ludo Verhoeven (eds.), *Bilingualism and Migration*. Berlin: Mouton de Gruyter. 229–46.

Myers-Scotton, Carol (1993). *Duelling Languages: Grammatical structure in codeswitching*. Oxford: Oxford University Press.

Nagy, N. (1994). Language contact and change: Italian geminates in Faetar. *Belgian Journal of Linguistics* 9: 111–28. (Also appeared in *University of Pennsylvania Working Papers in Linguistics* 1: 87–101.)

Nagy, N. (1996). Language contact and language change in the Faetar speech community. Ph.D. dissertation, University of Pennsylvania, Philadelphia: Institute for Research in Cognitive Science.

Nagy, Naomi, Christine Moisset, and Gillian Sankoff (1996). On the acquisition of variable phonology in L2. *University of Pennsylvania Working Papers in Linguistics* 3, 1: 111–26.

Naim, Samia (1998). L'Aventure des mots arabes venus d'ailleurs: emprunts et pharyngalisation. *Linguistique* 34: 91–102.

Ndiaye, Moussa D. (1996). Quelques faits de contact linguistique franco-wolof. *Revue québécoise de linguistique théorique et appliquée* 13: 107–19.

Nurse, Derek (1985). Dentality, areal features, and phonological change in Northeastern Bantu. *Studies in African Linguistics* 16: 243–79.

Oswalt, Robert L. (1985). The infiltration of English into Indian. *International Journal of American Linguistics* 51: 527–9.

Ozanne-Rivierre, Francoise (1994). Iaai loanwords and phonemic changes in Fagauvea. In Tom Dutton and Darrell Tryon (eds.), *Language Contact and Change in the Austronesian World*. Berlin: Mouton de Gruyter. 523–49.

Paradis, Carole (1995). Derivational constraints in phonology: Evidence from loanwords and implications. Papers from the Regional Meetings, Chicago Linguistic Society 31: 360–74.

Paradis, Carole and Darlène Lacharité (1997). Preservation and minimality in loanword adaptation. *Journal of Linguistics* 33: 379–430.

Pasch, Helma and Christiane Strauch (1998). Ist das Klassenpaar 5/6 des Swahili ein Zwischenlager fur Lehnworter? *Afrikanistische Arbeitspapiere* 55: 145–54.

Patry, Richard (1986). Le Traitement de la duree vocalique dans l'evolution des emprunts lexicaux a l'anglais en francais quebecois historique. *Revue québécoise de linguistique théorique et appliquée* 4: 145–77.

Penalosa, Fernando (1990). Los prestamos en las narraciones en las lenguas q'anjob'alanas. *Winak: Boletin Intercultural* 5: 176–95.

Pereira, Vera Regina Araujo (1977). Adaptações fonológicas dos emprestimos ingleses. *Letras de Hoje* 27: 53–71.

Pfaff, Carol (1979). Constraints on language-mixing. *Language* 55: 291–318.

Picard, Marc (1983). La Productivité des règles phonologiques et les emprunts de l'anglais en québécois. *Revue de l'Association québécoise de linguistique* 3: 97–108.

Poplack, Shana (1978). On dialect acquisition and communicative competence: the case of Puerto Rican Bilinguals. *Language in Society* 7: 89–104.

Poplack, Shana (1980). "Sometimes I'll start a sentence in Spanish y termino en Espanol": toward a typology of code-switching. *Linguistics* 18: 581–618.

Poplack, S. (1985). Contrasting patterns of code-switching in two communities. In H. Warkentyne (ed.), *Methods – V: Papers from the Fifth International Conference on Methods in Dialectology*. Victoria: University of Victoria Press. 363–86.

Poplack, Shana (1997). The sociolinguistic dynamics of apparent convergence. In Gregory R. Guy,

Crawford Feagin, Deborah Schiffrin and John Baugh (eds.), *Towards a Social Science of Language: Papers in Honor of William Labov*, vol. 2: *Social Interaction and Discourse Structures*. Amsterdam: John Benjamins. 285–309.

Poplack, Shana and Marjory Meechan (eds.) (1998). Instant loans, easy conditions: the productivity of bilingual borrowing. Special Issue, *International Journal of Bilingualism* 2, 2: 127–234.

Poplack, S. and D. Sankoff (1984). Borrowing: The synchrony of integration. *Linguistics* 22: 99–135.

Poplack, S., D. Sankoff and C. Miller (1988). The social correlates and linguistic processes of lexical borrowing and assimilation. *Linguistics* 26: 47–104.

Preston, Dennis (1989). *Sociolinguistics and Second Language Acquisition*. Oxford: Blackwell Publishers.

Prince, Ellen (1988). On pragmatic change: the borrowing of discourse functions. *Journal of Pragmatics* 12: 505–18.

Richards, Jack C. (1972). Social factors, interlanguage, and language learning. *Language Learning* 22: 159–88.

Ross, Malcolm (1991). Refining Guy's sociolinguistic types of language change. *Diachronica* 8: 119–29.

Sankoff, David and Gillian Sankoff (1973). Sample survey methods and computer-assisted analysis in the study of grammatical variation. In R. Darnell (ed.), *Canadian Languages in their Social Context*. Edmonton, Alberta: Linguistic Research. 7–64.

Sankoff, Gillian (1980). Multilingualism in Papua New Guinea. In G. Sankoff, *The Social Life of Language*. Philadelphia: University of Pennsylvania Press. 95–132.

Sankoff, G., P. Thibault, N. Nagy, H. Blondeau, M.-O. Fonollosa and L. Gagnon (1997). Variation in the use of discourse markers in a language contact situation. *Language Variation and Change* 9: 191–217.

Santa Ana, Otto (1996). Sonority and Syllable Structure in Chicano English. *Language Variation and Change* 8: 63–89.

Schumann, John H. (1974). The implications of interlanguage, pidginization and creolization for the study of adult second language acquisition. *TESOL Quarterly* 8: 145–52.

Schumann, John H. (1975) Second Language Acquisition: the Pidginization Hypothesis. Ph.D. thesis, Harvard University.

Schutz, Albert J. (1976). "Take My Word for It": missionary influence on borrowings in Hawaii. *Oceanic Linguistics* 15: 75–92.

Scovel, Thomas (2000). A critical review of the critical period research. *Annual Review of Applied Linguistics* 20: 213–23.

Selinker, Larry (1972). Interlanguage. *IRAL* 10: 209–31.

Shinohara, Shigeko (1996). The roles of the syllable and the mora in Japanese: Adaptation of French words. *Cahiers de Linguistique Asie Orientale* 87–112.

Silva-Corvalán, Carmen (1994). The gradual loss of mood distinctions in Los Angeles Spanish. *Language Variation and Change* 6: 255–72.

Socanac, Lelija (1996). Phonological Adaptation of Anglicisms in Italian: Phoneme Redistribution; Fonoloska adaptacija anglicizama u talijanskom jeziku: fonemska redistribucija SO. *Suvremena-Lingvistika* 22, 1–2(41–42): 571–81.

Sorensen, Arthur (1967). Multilingualism in the North West Amazon. *American Anthropologist* 69: 670–84.

Spears, Arthur (1982). The Black English semi-auxiliary *come*. *Language* 58: 850–72.

Sridhar, S. N. (1978). Linguistic convergence: Indo-Aryanization of Dravidian languages. *Studies in the Linguistic Sciences* 8: 197–215.

Stenson, Nancy (1993). Variation in phonological assimilation of Irish loanwords. In Mushira Eid and Gregory Iverson (eds.), *Principles and Prediction: The Analysis of Natural Language: Papers in Honor of Gerald Sanders*. Amsterdam: John Benjamins. 351–66.

Tarone, Elaine (1988). *Variation in Interlanguage*. London: Edward Arnold.

Thomason, Sarah and Terrence Kaufman (1988). *Language Contact, Creolization, and Genetic Linguistics*. Berkeley: University of California Press.

Tristram, Hildegard L. C. (1995). Linguistic contacts across the English Channel: the case of the Breton retroflex <r>. In Jacek Fisiak (ed.), *Linguistic Change under Contact Conditions*. Berlin: Mouton de Gruyter. 291–313.

Trudgill, Peter (1974a). *The Social Differentiation of English in Norwich*. Cambridge: Cambridge University Press.

Trudgill, Peter (1974b). Linguistic change and diffusion: description and explanation in sociolinguistic dialect geography. *Language in Society* 3: 215–46. Reprinted as ch. 3 of *On Dialect*, 1984.

Trudgill, Peter (1976). Creolization in reverse: reduction and simplification in the Albanian dialects of Greece. *Transactions of the Philological Society* 7: 32–50.

Tsuchida, Ayako (1995). English loans in Japanese: constraints in loanword phonology. *Working Papers of the Cornell Phonetics Laboratory* 10: 145–64.

Van Coetsem, Frans (1988). *Loan Phonology and the Two Transfer Types in Language Contact*. Dordrecht: Foris, Publications in Language Sciences, 27.

Van Hout, Roland and Pieter Muysken (1994). Modeling lexical borrowability. *Language Variation and Change* 6, 1: 39–62.

Wald, Benji (1987). Spanish–English grammatical contact in Los Angeles: the grammar of reported speech in the East Los Angeles English contact vernacular. *Linguistics* 25: 53–80.

Wald, Benji (1996). Substratal effects on the evolution of modals in East Los Angeles. In Jennifer Arnold, Renee Blake, Brad Davidson, Scott Schwenter and Julie Solomon (eds.), *Sociolinguistic Variation: Data, Theory, and Analysis: Selected Papers from NWAV 23 at Stanford*. Stanford, CA: Center Study Language & Information. 515–30.

Walker, Douglas C. (1982). On a phonological innovation in French. *Journal of the International Phonetic Association* 12: 72–7.

Weinreich, Uriel (1951). Research problems in bilingualism, with special reference to Switzerland. Ph.D dissertation, Columbia University, New York.

Weinreich, Uriel (1968). *Languages in Contact: Findings and Problems*. The Hague: Mouton. (Originally published as Publications of the Linguistic Circle of New York, no. 1, 1953.)

Weinreich, Uriel, William Labov and Marvin Herzog (1968). Empirical foundations for a theory of language change. In W. Lehmann and Y. Malkiel (eds.), *Directions for Historical Linguistics*. Austin, TX: University of Texas Press. 97–195.

Woolford, Ellen (1983). Bilingual code-switching and syntactic theory. *Linguistic Inquiry* 14: 520–36.

Wurm, Stephen A., Peter Mühlhäusler and Darrell Tryon (eds.) (1996). *Atlas of Languages of Intercultural Communication in the Pacific, Asia, and the Americas*. Berlin: Mouton DeGruyter, Trends in Linguistics, Documentation 13, vol. I, Maps; vol. II1 and II2, Texts.

Yip, Moira (1993). Cantonese loanword phonology and optimality theory. *Journal of East Asian Lingustics* 2: 261–91.

Young, Richard (1988). Variation and the interlanguage hypothesis. *Studies in Second Language Acquisition* 10: 281–302.

26 Koineization and Accommodation

PAUL KERSWILL

In this chapter, I discuss *koineization*, a contact-induced process that leads to quite rapid, and occasionally dramatic, change. Through koineization, new varieties of a language are brought about as a result of contact between speakers of mutually intelligible varieties of that language. Koineization is a particular case of what Trudgill (1986) calls "dialect contact." Typically, it occurs in new settlements to which people, for whatever reason, have migrated from different parts of a single language area. Examples of *koines* (the outcomes of koineization) include the Hindi/Bhojpuri varieties spoken in Fiji and South Africa, and the speech of "new towns" such as Høyanger in Norway and Milton Keynes in England. Dialect contact, and with it koineization, is one of the main external causes of language change – "external" here referring to social factors, in this case migration, which can reasonably be expected to promote change. Contrasted with this are "internal" factors, which have to do with aspects of the structure of a particular language (its phonology and its grammar) which, perhaps because of structural imbalances, are predisposed to change.

1 Koineization as language change

Because koineization can take place relatively swiftly (though probably more gradually than pidginization – see Siegel forthcoming), a central theme of this chapter will be the immediate mechanisms of change rather than the description of longer-term trends that take place over a century or more (like the English Great Vowel Shift or the rise of the auxiliary "do"). I will be posing a number of questions: Are permanent language changes prefigured in the utterances of the people whose speech communities are undergoing change? Is it children, adolescents, or adults who are the main agents of change? Do the social network characteristics of the migrants have an effect? Does it matter whether the contributing dialects are very different or very similar? How long does it take for a koine to emerge? Are there circumstances in which dialect contact does not lead to the formation of a koine? On the more "linguistic" side, I shall be asking: Which features found in the melting pot of the early stages of koineization survive in the koine, and which are lost? Are there particular characteristics of these features that leads to one outcome or another?

Koineization, as we shall see, typically takes two or three generations to complete, though it is achievable within one. It is in principle possible for us to observe specific cases, though this has (to my knowledge) not been achieved for the complete process. Thus, the literature contains detailed descriptions of koines from a number of parts of the world, together with conjectural reconstructions of the social and linguistic history of the speakers who contributed to the koine. In the literature, we can also find a very small number of descriptions of the inception of koines, with direct observations of the first generation of speakers in new locations. For one established koine, the English of New Zealand, we even have recordings of the offspring of the original English-speaking immigrants (albeit as elderly people) to compare with the modern form of the language.

Labov (1972) shows that language variation is systematic, in that it can be related to social divisions within a community, such as class and gender. Change can be shown to originate with particular social groups based on these divisions. However, a number of linguists have recently argued that language change lies with the individual (Milroy 1992, Croft 2000). Thus, the only circumstance under which language change may result is when the collective use of a new linguistic feature by individual speakers is sufficiently frequent to be taken up as a new norm. This position need not conflict with that of Labov, since these individual-speaker behaviors take place against the backdrop of larger social structures. As we shall see, the individual-as-agent-of-change approach is particularly relevant in the case of koineization, because this is a process which starts with the first generation of incomers adapting their speech to the other speakers they encounter. This adaptation is an example of *speech accommodation*, a research area to which we will return.

2   Mixing, leveling, simplification, and reallocation in established koines

The term "koine" (whose Greek meaning is "common") was first used to refer to the form of Greek used as a lingua franca during the Hellenistic and Roman periods (Siegel 1985: 358, Bubenik 1993). It arose as a mixed vernacular among ordinary people in the Peiraieus, the seaport of Athens, which was inhabited by Greeks from different parts of the Mediterranean (Thomson 1960: 34, quoted in Siegel 1985: 358). This kind of "koine" is, of course, rather different from the examples given in the previous section, in that it is not a new variety used as a vernacular, but rather a compromise dialect used for communication between speakers of other Greek varieties. This Koine later became the language of the Macedonian empire, and was widely used as a second language, though it did acquire some native speakers (Thomson 1960). According to Siegel (1985: 358), the Koine was characterized by *reduction* and *simplification*. "Reduction" refers to "those processes that lead to a decrease in the referential or non-referential potential of a language" (Mühlhäusler 1980: 21), involving, for example, a reduced vocabulary or fewer stylistic devices. To judge from the recent literature, reduction is not pervasive in koines, though, as we shall see, it may be present. However, it is a defining feature of pidgins, whose genesis is very different from that of most koines. (Similarities and differences between these two kinds of contact varieties will be explored in the final section.) "Simplification," which is a notion we will return to repeatedly, refers to "either an increase in regularity or a decrease in markedness" (Siegel 1985: 358, quoting Mühlhäusler). In practice, this means a decrease in irregularity in morphology and an increase in invariable word forms (Mühlhäusler 1974, cited in Trudgill 1986: 103), to which can be added the loss of categories such as gender, the loss of morphologically marked cases, simplified morphophonemics, and a decrease in the number of phonemes. Siegel's recent definition is a useful, very general, reference point:

> A koine is a stabilized contact variety which results from the mixing and subsequent levelling of features of varieties which are similar enough to be mutually intelligible, such as regional or social dialects. This occurs in the context of increased interaction or integration among speakers of these varieties.
>
> (Siegel forthcoming)

As Siegel (1985) points out, the term "koine" has been variously used to refer to different aspects of mixed, compromise languages – their form, their function, and their origin – and there has been disagreement as to what should or should not be included in the definition. Two categories stand out, already alluded to above: *regional koine* and *immigrant koine*. The original Koine was at first a regional koine, which did not replace the contributing dialects. By contrast, a new dialect in a new settlement is an immigrant koine, which, once established, becomes the vernacular of the new community, replacing the regional dialects of the original migrants – though not, of course, having any effect on the dialects in their place of origin.

Between these two categories we find *regional dialect leveling*, which, as we shall see, shares certain important properties with koineization. "Regional dialect leveling" refers to the decrease in the number of variants of a particular phonological, morphological, or lexical unit in a given dialect area, and should be distinguished from *diffusion*, which is the spread of linguistic features across a dialect area. Leveling leads to a reduction in differences between dialects and hence a gradual homogenization of the vernacular speech of a region. For example, in many parts of Italy new regional varieties have emerged, usually centered on a city. Linguistically, they are a compromise between a number of local dialects and the standard language. Some scholars, such as Sobrero (1996: 106), actually refer to these as "koines," a use of the term which has some justification since there is evidence that Italian "koines" do not necessarily supplant the local dialects, with speakers regularly switching between dialect and koine (Trumper and Maddalon 1988). By far the more usual case is dialect leveling entailing the loss, or at least attrition, of dialects. This is widespread in modern Europe (Auer and Hinskens 1996, Hinskens 1996, 1998, Sandøy 1998, Thelander 1980, 1982, Williams and Kerswill 1999) as well as elsewhere (see Inoue 1986, on recent changes in Tokyo). Regional dialect leveling may lead to varieties that resemble any koines that may be spoken in the same region, particularly with respect to simplification – a point I shall return to.

I will be concerned mainly with immigrant koines, or, to use Trudgill's term, *new dialects* (Trudgill 1986: 83). In this section, I outline some of the key features of established koines, before, in the remaining sections, tracing the stages through which a potential koine must pass if it is to reach stability. According to Trudgill (1986: 127), koineization is composed of three processes: *mixing*, *leveling*, and *simplification*. (Elsewhere in his book, he refers just to leveling and simplification – a fact that is unproblematic since leveling can only take place if, in the new speech community, there has been prior dialect mixing leading to the presence of more than one form for a particular linguistic category, such as a vowel, a pronoun, or a suffix.) In koines, we also find what Trudgill has called *reallocation*, which is defined thus: "Reallocation occurs where two or more variants in the dialect mix survive the levelling process but are refunctionalised, evolving new social or linguistic functions in the new dialect" (Britain and Trudgill 1999: 245; cf. Trudgill 1986: 110). We turn now to the first of our examples.

One of the major population movements of the late nineteenth and early twentieth centuries was the shipment of people from the Indian subcontinent to work as indentured laborers in the European colonies (Mesthrie 1993). This resulted in new varieties of Indian languages, particularly Bhojpuri (a Hindi variety of northeast India), being established across a wide region ranging from the West Indies and the Caribbean to South Africa (Mesthrie 1992) and Fiji (Siegel 1987, Moag 1977).

Table 26.1 illustrates the mixed nature of the koine known as Fiji Hindi in one area of its grammar. The form *egā* clearly comes from Braj; in fact, it appears to be a compromise between the various forms available in Braj – an example of what Trudgill (1986: 62) calls an *interdialect* form. The form ī presumably comes from Bhojpuri or Avadhi. The manner in which variants have been selected from the range of possibilities provided by the input dialects is an example of leveling. At the same time, the table shows extensive simplification, involving the loss of distinct suffixes for the first and second persons singular and plural, the third person singular and plural, and, predictably perhaps, a failure to adopt the gender distinction in the second person found in one of the contributing dialects (Bhojpuri). A gender distinction in verb

Table 26.1 Indian Hindi dialects and Fiji Hindi definite future suffixes

	Bhojpuri	Avadhi	Braj	Fiji Hindi
1sg	bō, ab	b~ū̃, ab	ihaū, ū̃gau	egā
1pl	ab, bī, iha	ab	ihaī, aīgai	egā
2sg (masc.)	bē, ba	bē, ihai	(a)ihai, (a)igau	egā
(fem.)	bī, bis			
2pl (masc.)	bâ(h)	bō, bau	(a)ihau, augau	egā
(fem.)	bū			
3sg	ī	ī, ihai, ē	(a)ihau, agau	ī
3pl	ih, ē, ihen	ihaī, aī	(a)ihaī, aīgai	ī

Source: Siegel (1997: 115)

morphology is functionally redundant, and it is not surprising that it is lost from overseas Hindi/Bhojpuri varieties generally, including South African Bhojpuri (Mesthrie 1993: 40), Fiji Hindi (Siegel 1997: 113), and in Mauritian Bhojpuri except in the past-tense second person singular (Domingue 1980, 1981, cited in Trudgill 1986: 109).

While this simplification can be related to the special conditions of language acquisition in a mixed, or "unfocused" speech community (Le Page 1980; a topic to be explored in a later section), there is one example of simplification (or, arguably, reduction) that seems to stem directly from the threatening situation the indentured laborers found themselves in. Mesthrie explains:

> The same [i.e. reduction – PK] is true of the feature "respect," which is manifested systematically in Indic languages in verbal and pronominal paradigms. It seems this feature did not survive the koineization process in Natal, for there is no systematic morphological way of signaling respect in SB [South African Bhojpuri]. Power relations between interlocutors once indexed by pronoun usage must have given way to the expression of solidarity on the plantations.   (Mesthrie 1993: 40)

This is a very clear indication that, for a koine to form, the speakers must waive their previous allegiances and social divisions to show mutual solidarity. Where they do not, koineization is slowed, or may not result at all, and we will return to this point in the next-to-final section. The absence of solidarity is also a factor in pidginization, where social divisions and restricted communication directly contribute to the reduced nature of pidgins. However, when dialects (and not languages) are in contact as in koineization, speakers can continue to use their own vernaculars for all informal interaction within a newly-formed community (Siegel, forthcoming). When this is coupled with solidarity, mutual accommodation on the part of the speakers results. (See Trudgill 1994, for a discussion of the different outcomes of language contact

Table 26.2   Origins of factory workers in Odda and Tyssedal shortly after establishment

Western Norway	Eastern Norway	Norway (other)	Other countries
Origin of people working at Odda Smelteverk in 1916 (from Sandve 1976: 19)			
81%	5%	7%	7%
Origin of people working at Tyssedal Smelteverk in 1916–18 (from Sandve 1976: 23)			
36%	35%	16%	12%

Source: Information on Odda and Tyssedal derived from Sandve (1976)

and dialect contact. (For a further discussion of overseas Bhojpuri/Hindi, see Trudgill 1986: 99–102, 108–10.)

Our second example is the development of not one, but two separate koines in Odda and Tyssedal, small towns just 5 kilometers apart in southwestern Norway. Both grew up at the beginning of the twentieth century around smelting works located at the head of the Sørfjord in Hardanger to exploit the plentiful supply of hydroelectric power. People moved to these new towns from other parts of the country, with the result that each now has a dialect distinct from surrounding rural varieties. Interestingly, the dialects are radically different, in a way that reflects the regional origin of the majority of the in-migrants. At the same time, they share features which do not have their origins either in the contributing dialects or in the existing speech of the area before industrialization. Sandve (1976) describes the differences between the two new dialects mainly in terms of morpho-lexical variables (the variant forms taken by morphological categories, such as the Norwegian suffixed definite article, and closed-class words, such as pronouns). He finds that the distribution to a considerable extent reflects the dialects spoken by the original migrants. Table 26.2 shows the origins of the workers at the two factories, while table 26.3 illustrates some of the morpho-lexical and phonological features.

It is clear from Table 26.3 that the Odda koine closely resembles the majority, mainly rural dialects of western (strictly speaking, southwestern) Norway, from where the vast majority of migrants arrived. The infinitive suffix is /a/, and the indefinite and definite suffixes of "weak" feminine nouns are /a/ and /u/, respectively, as exemplified by /jɛnta/ and /jɛntu/. The pronoun "I" is /eːg/, and words such as *kvit* "white" and *kval* "whale" have /kv/. Nonetheless, this koine contains forms such as /viː/ for western /meː/ "we", as well as the loss of the southwestern cluster /dl/ in favor of /l/ in words such as *alle* "all." At first sight, this could be interpreted as straightforward mixing; however, another factor clearly plays a part. One of the characteristics of leveling is the removal of *marked* forms (Trudgill 1986: 98), where "marked" describes

Table 26.3   Morpho-lexical features in Odda and Tyssedal and in majority West and East Norwegian dialects

<table>
<tr><td>(i)</td><td colspan="5">Odda has West Norwegian, Tyssedal East Norwegian variant:</td></tr>
<tr><td></td><td>Odda</td><td>Tyssedal</td><td>W Norwegian</td><td>E Norwegian</td><td></td></tr>
<tr><td></td><td>kasta</td><td>kastə</td><td>kasta</td><td>kastə</td><td>"throw" (infinitive)</td></tr>
<tr><td></td><td>jɛnta</td><td>jɛntə</td><td>jɛntu</td><td>jɛntə</td><td>"girl"</td></tr>
<tr><td></td><td>jɛntu</td><td>jɛnta</td><td>jɛnta</td><td>jɛnta</td><td>"the girl"</td></tr>
<tr><td></td><td>eːg</td><td>jɛi</td><td>eːg</td><td>jɛi</td><td>"I" (pronoun)</td></tr>
<tr><td></td><td>kviːt</td><td>viːt</td><td>kviːt</td><td>viːt</td><td>"white"</td></tr>
<tr><td></td><td>hɛima</td><td>jɛmə</td><td>hɛima</td><td>jɛmə</td><td>"at home"</td></tr>
<tr><td>(ii)</td><td colspan="5">Both Odda and Tyssedal have leveled towards the East Norwegian variant:</td></tr>
<tr><td></td><td>viː</td><td>viː</td><td>meː</td><td>viː</td><td>"we"</td></tr>
<tr><td></td><td>alə</td><td>alə</td><td>adlə</td><td>alə</td><td>"all"</td></tr>
<tr><td></td><td>çøt, gʉt</td><td>çøt, gʉt</td><td>çøːt, gʉːt</td><td>çøt, gʉt</td><td>"meat", "boy"</td></tr>
<tr><td>(iii)</td><td colspan="5">Simplified and/or interdialect forms:</td></tr>
<tr><td></td><td>taːk, taːkə</td><td>taːk, taːkə</td><td>taːk, taːçə</td><td>taːk, taːkə</td><td>"roof", "the roof"</td></tr>
<tr><td></td><td>kɔmə</td><td>kɔməʁ</td><td>çeːmə</td><td>kɔmər</td><td>"come" (present tense)</td></tr>
<tr><td></td><td>sɔːvə</td><td>sɔːvəʁ</td><td>søːvə</td><td>sɔːvə</td><td>"sleep" (present tense)</td></tr>
<tr><td></td><td>vɛgaʁ</td><td>vɛgəʁ</td><td>vɛjjər</td><td>vɛgər</td><td>"walls" (masc. noun)</td></tr>
<tr><td></td><td>ɛlvaʁ/ɛlvaʁ</td><td>ɛlvaʁ</td><td>ɛlvar</td><td>ɛlvər</td><td>"rivers" (fem. noun)</td></tr>
</table>

Source: Information on Odda and Tyssedal derived from Sandve (1976)

features that are in a minority in the mix, in terms of the number of speakers who use them, or have a restricted regional currency. The latter is clearly the case here: /meː/ is restricted to the southwest, while /viː/ is found in the rest of Norway, including the regional center, Bergen, as well as in most forms of written Norwegian. The cluster /dl/ has practically the same geographical distribution as /meː/, and is therefore used by a small minority of Norwegian speakers. It is in any case gradually being lost in the rural dialects. By contrast, the maintenance of the pronoun form /eːg/ and the /kv/ cluster is no doubt supported by the fact that both are widespread in western and northern Norway, and are also found in the working-class urban vernaculars in the west, including Bergen.

Markedness (in Trudgill's sense) cannot, however, be a factor in the widespread substitution of a short vowel in items such as /çøːt/ and /gʉːt/, since the long vowel is found in almost all western and many southern dialects. However, the short vowel is found in Bergen and in the east, and (like the loss of /dl/) is beginning to spread throughout the west as part of regional dialect leveling.

Tyssedal has a mainly eastern dialect, the morpho-lexis being eastern in form. This is surprising, given that the proportion of east Norwegians among the incomers was only 35 percent. Part of the explanation may lie in the fact that other parts of Norway were well represented, as well the presence of a substantial foreign, mainly Swedish workforce, whose speech would have been partly mutually intelligible with that of the Norwegians. The mixing situation in Tyssedal was clearly more complex than in Odda, with greater linguistic differences involved and no one group predominating. Tyssedal must have been a linguistically highly *diffuse* community, and this may go some way to explaining the eastern character of its koine. "Diffusion" is the opposite of *focusing* in Le Page's (1980) terminology: it refers to great linguistic hetero-geneity among the population, with variability both between and within individuals. There is also likely to be an absence of stable norms of any kind, and hence a lack of adult norms for children to converge on – again, a point we will return to. Unmarked forms are more likely to survive here than in koineizing communities which have a dominant group. In this context, it should be noted that, nationally, speakers of various east Norwegian varieties form by far the largest group. Moroeover, many of the eastern forms coincide with the majority Bokmål standard. Thus, the eastern and/or standard forms had a better chance of surviving in Tyssedal than they did in Odda. Standard forms may also have been adopted as a "strategy of neutrality" in a highly diffuse situation (Mæhlum 1992).

Yet in one respect the two koines show continuity with the region in which they were established: both have the uvular [ʁ] for /r/, a pronunciation that has been diffusing out from the towns throughout the west and south of Norway for the past 100 years, replacing an alveolar articulation (see Chambers and Trudgill 1998). The pre-new town Odda/Tyssedal area already used the uvular [ʁ] (Gjørv 1986: 28). What is surprising is its adoption in Tyssedal, whose dialect in almost all other respects has a strongly eastern character. A possible explanation for this is that it is an early example of the leveling between the two towns which, according to Sandve (1976), mainly involves the adoption of Odda features by younger people in Tyssedal.

Finally in our discussion of these Norwegian koines, we look for cases of simplification and interdialect forms. First, we note the absence in both dialects of the velar-palatal alternation in nouns whose stems end in /k/, /g/ or /ŋ/. In western and central dialects, the definite form substitutes a palatal for the velar, giving /taːçə/ for "the roof;" cf. the indefinite /taːk/. Both koines have the form /taːkə/. However, this apparent simplification may be the selection of a "simple" feature from among the possibilities offered by the input dialects. Second, we observe that, in Odda, the forms /kɔmə/ and /sɔːvə̆/ are used for the present tense of "come" and "sleep." These are simple in that they do not show the present-tense stem change found in some "strong" verbs in parts of the southwest (as in /çeːmə/ and /søːvə/, cf. infinitives /kɔmɑ/ and /sɔːvɑ/). It is likely that these are genuine interdialect forms – it is unlikely that they existed in any of the input dialects, since they combine the simplified, eastern stem with the western strong-verb suffix /ə/. Interestingly, similar forms are increasingly found more generally in western dialects through leveling (Sandøy

1987: 234), an indication that, in all dialect contact situations, the same processes are found. The third feature does seem to have arisen in the koine itself, since there is only recent evidence of it in the rural dialects (Helge Sandøy, pc): this is the Odda noun plural system represented by the forms /vɛgaʁ/ and /ɛlvəʁ/, which (as table 26.3 shows) differ from the majority western variants. These show an increase in morphological regularity, the reasoning being as follows. In west Norwegian dialects, masculine and feminine nouns fall into two classes, depending on whether the plural ending is /ar/ or /ər/. Most, but not all, masculine nouns, like *hest* "horse", take /ar/, while feminine nouns, like *seng* "bed", tend to take /ər/. What has happened in Odda is that this pattern has been generalized to *all* masculine and feminine nouns, leading to the new, interdialect forms /vɛgaʁ/ and /ɛlvəʁ/.

All the features mentioned in the paragraph above are identical to developments in another western Norwegian koine: that of Høyanger, a new town which grew up under very similar conditions to Odda and Tyssedal (Omdal 1977, Trudgill 1986, 95–106). The Høyanger dialect is strikingly similar to that of Odda, a fact which reflects the mainly western origin of the incomers. However, it contains features characteristic of its somewhat more northern location in Sogn (from where many of the migrants came), especially an alveolar /r/ and the infinitive ending /ə/. The results from the three towns taken together demonstrate that the features that survive the leveling prior to koine formation reflect not only the role of simplification but also the importance of the geographical origins of the original migrants. The latter has been explored by Trudgill and his co-researchers in an investigation of the origins of New Zealand English, to be discussed later (Trudgill 1998, Trudgill et al. 2000).

Our final example of a koine is, in fact, often not regarded as one at all: the variety of spoken Hebrew that has emerged in Palestine/Israel since about 1900. The crucial difference is that the first modern speakers of Hebrew spoke it as a *second* language. This meant that, in the Hebrew input to the modern spoken variety, there were substrates reflecting a number of different languages. What leads Siegel (1997: 129–30) to accept it as a koine is that all the features of koineization can be found. Modern Hebrew is a revived classical language which now performs all the functions of a community vernacular. In its premodern form, it ceased to be a vernacular around AD 200, but it continued to be used both as a liturgical language and as a written and spoken lingua franca among Jews in Europe. The decisive phase in its modern revival as a spoken language came with the establishment by Eliezer Ben-Yehuda of the Hebrew Language Council in 1890. Throughout the first half of the twentieth century, Hebrew was promoted by the occupying forces, including the British Mandate of 1922–48. By 1948, there were Hebrew-using institutions, including a Hebrew radio station (see Blanc 1968, and Ravid 1995, for further details).

Today, practically all the Israeli-born population are speakers of Modern Hebrew, which preserves much of the lexis, morphology, and syntax of the old language. Ravid points to the rather slow stabilization of the contemporary language (we return to this issue later in this chapter), and states that, even today, it has "a number of parallel constructions, none of which has been rendered obsolete by the others" (Ravid 1995: 5). She gives the following examples, which all translate as "the king's clothes":

1   bigdey ha-mélex
    clothes-of the-king

2   ha-bgadim ʃel ha-mélex
    the-clothes of the-king

3   bgadav ʃel ha-mélex
    clothes-his of the-king

Ravid states that "they complement each other and are used in distinct semantic, syntactic and pragmatic contexts, constituting part of the linguistic competence of the Modern Hebrew speaker" (1995: 5). We can say that the variability in the input to modern Hebrew has not been leveled in this case, but has been *reallocated* to new functions.

As already pointed out, a defining feature of Israeli Hebrew is the fact that the input was a series of second-language varieties with European and other substrates, particularly Yiddish and Arabic. We must also assume that the first speakers' proficiency in Hebrew varied a great deal, showing varying degrees of interlanguage (Selinker 1992). All of this took place in a situation where there was no established native spoken norm. A look at the consonant system shows the effect of these substrate languages. Glinert (1989: 10) points out that there has been considerable reduction in the phonological inventory when compared to the liturgical language. Like many other Semitic languages, Biblical Hebrew had a distinction between the pharyngeal consonants /ħ/ and /ʕ/ and the velar /x/. Neither /ħ/ nor /ʕ/ was acquired by most of the (adult) Ashkenazi immigrants, whose first languages were European. Instead, they merged /ħ/ with /x/ – a phone widely found in European languages – and deleted /ʕ/ altogether. The Sephardic Jews, who had an Arabic substrate, used the pharyngeals in their Hebrew vernacular. In the majority, high-status Ashkenazi-based vernacular, the pharyngeals have been leveled out (or never acquired) despite being widely considered to be correct. This leads to an unusual sociolinguistic situation. According to Blanc (1968: 245), when "General" (or majority Ashkenazi) speakers want to "improve" their speech for whatever reason, they use /ʕ/ when the orthography demands it, without changing other aspects of their speech. On the other hand, /ħ/ is not adopted by these speakers, because it is apparently too closely associated with Oriental speech (in Trudgill's 1986 terms, it has "extra-strong salience" – a notion to be discussed below). This treatment of the two pharyngeals – their social evaluation and their sociolinguistic patterning – is a complex case of *reallocation*.

Just as with regular sound change, the leveling and simplification of the Hebrew consonant system has led to complications in the morphology. (See

Aitchison 1991, on the effect of phonological change on morphology.) Unlike the koines discussed so far, Modern Hebrew is morphologically more opaque (irregular) than its antecedent. Ravid (1995: 133) argues that this is because of the "phonological erosion" due to its being "revived as a spoken medium using a new phonological system only loosely related to that of Classical Hebrew, with entire phonological classes being obliterated." This is, of course, the point at which Modern Hebrew is radically different from other koines, whose speakers are first-language users of the input varieties. Not surprisingly, she finds among child learners the development of nonstandard reanalyses of morphological classes promoted by the principles of "Transparency, Simplicity and Consistency." The ability of these reanalyses to persist into adult usage and then to become mainstream is, however, constrained by literacy and the "literate propensity towards marked structures" (Ravid 1995: 162). Israeli Hebrew was relatively slow to stabilize; we will return to reasons for this in a later section.

3   The Pre-koine: Linguistic Accommodation by the First Migrants in a New Settlement

We now deal with koineization itself, viewed as a process with distinct but overlapping stages and a variable but finite time span. If and when it reaches completion, a koine, or a "new dialect," results. Trudgill identifies the following three stages of new-dialect formation, in his opinion roughly corresponding to the first three generations of speakers (Trudgill 1998, Trudgill et al. 2000):

Stage	*Speakers involved*	*Linguistic characteristics*
I	adult migrants	rudimentary leveling
II	first native-born speakers	extreme variability and further leveling
III	subsequent generations	focusing, leveling, and reallocation

As we shall see, there is a great deal of variability in the time-depth of koineization, with focusing being possible already by Stage II, and the absence of focusing sometimes persisting over several generations of Stage III. In this section, we deal with Stage I, what Siegel calls the "pre-koine". Siegel states:

> This is the unstabilized stage at the beginning of koineization. A continuum exists in which various forms of the varieties in contact are used concurrently and inconsistently. Levelling and some mixing has begun to occur, and there may be various degrees of reduction, but few forms have emerged as the accepted compromise. (Siegel 1985: 373)

The question we address in this section is the following: How does this rudimentary mixing and leveling eventually find its way into the everyday speech of the first generation of koine speakers? Given that definable changes have occurred as a result of koineization, it follows that these changes must be foreshadowed *in some way* in the speech of the pre-koine generation. Trudgill proposes an extension of *speech accommodation theory* to account for this process (Giles and Powesland 1997/1975, Giles and Smith 1979, Giles and Coupland 1991, Giles et al. 1991, Trudgill 1986: 1–4). Simply put, accommodation theory assumes that interlocutors converge linguistically (and on other behavioral dimensions) when they want to gain each other's approval, show solidarity, etc., and that they diverge when they do not. Accommodation can be mutual, or one-sided. It can be "downward" (as when a higher-status person uses lower-status forms, or what he or she believes to be lower-status forms), or it can be "upward" (the inverse pattern). Accommodation is therefore a response to a conversational context (though it can also be used to define the context). When people speak different varieties, as in a new settlement, the dialect differences are likely to be exploited – consciously or passively – as part of accommodation. This can explain the mechanism behind the survival of majority forms in a koine: there will be more "acts of accommodation" involving the adoption of majority rather than minority variants simply because there are more conversational contexts in which this can take place.

The link between these individual acts and the new dialect, according to Trudgill, is *long-term accommodation* (Trudgill 1986: 11–38), which can be defined as semi-permanent changes in a person's habitual speech after a period of contact with speakers using different varieties. Long-term accommodation results from the cumulative effect of countless acts of *short-term accommodation* in particular conversational interactions. These changes are then picked up by the next generation, who will begin the process of focusing. Trudgill discusses a number of cases of long-term accommodation in the context of the linguistic and social constraints that promote or inhibit the acquisition of particular features. Before we consider these below, we must examine two questions: (1) What is the evidence that the features found in dialect leveling and koines really are foreshadowed in short-term accommodation? (2) What is the evidence that these features are found in the long-term accommodation of the original adult migrants?

3.1   Evidence that short-term accommodation foreshadows leveling and koine formation

The link from individual behavior in specific contexts (short-term accommodation) to a future koine could involve the following mechanisms. First, the features of the future varieties are adopted by adult and child migrants in individual acts of accommodation to other speakers who happen to use them already. This has been called a "behavioral-frequency model" (Auer 1998, Hinskens and Auer forthcoming). Second, accommodation may not be in response to a particular interlocutor, but to images, or stereotypes, of the group the interlocutor belongs to, or of a socially attractive group not actually represented in the immediate context (cf. Bell 1997, on the role of different kinds of audience). This can be labeled an "identity projection model" (Auer 1998). Third, in the case of interdialect forms, we cannot be dealing with accommodation at all, since such forms are not in the dialect mix; therefore, they must be created by these speakers. There is clear evidence of the "behavioral-frequency model" in Trudgill's account of his own accommodation to his Norwich interviewees (Trudgill 1986: 7–10), though the changes only took place in the case of markers (see below, on "salience"). Coupland's (1984) study of speech accommodation by a travel agent to her customers is another case in point. However, as Auer points out, even though there is demonstrable accommodation, Coupland interprets this more in line with the "identity projection model":

> Sue [the travel agent] is not attempting to reproduce the actual levels of standardness for particular variables that she detects in the speech of her interlocutors; rather, she is attempting to convey via her pronunciation and presumably other behaviors, verbal and non-verbal, a persona which is similar to that conveyed by her interlocutors.   (Coupland 1984: 65)

Taking this non-interactional approach to accommodation may also help us understand the spread of dialect features by geographical diffusion where face-to-face contact with users of the diffusing features is rare, if it is present at all. An example is the rapid and recent spread of the merger of /f/ and /θ/ in British English (Williams and Kerswill 1999, Trudgill 1986: 53–7).

However, studies which concentrate on dialect leveling and koineization provide only marginal evidence of the use of the new, leveled features in short-term accommodation between speakers of different dialects. In an investigation of dialect leveling in the Limburg region of the Netherlands, Hinskens (1996: 447–52) finds that short-term accommodation on the part of speakers interacting with speakers of other varieties does not follow the predictions of accommodation theory. The theory predicts that speakers should reduce dialect features that are not shared with the interlocutor, and preserve features that are. This turns out not to be the case, accommodation being much less differentiated and more "across the board," regardless of the interlocutor's variety. More striking still are the results of a study of ongoing dialect leveling in *Lëtzebuergesch*, the Germanic language of Luxembourg, by Gilles (1996, 1997). He discusses Luxembourg speakers' belief that they accommodate each other's speech in inter-dialect communication, but finds that this is not the case (see discussion in Auer 1998, and Hinskens and Auer, forthcoming). An extremely telling micro-example of non-accommodation is the following excerpt from a conversation between two strangers, FA from the north of the Grand Duchy and AN from the south (Gilles 1996: 7):

FA	Bas du och nach am zweete Jor?	"Are you also in the second year?"
AN	Nä am ischte [iʃtə] Jor.	"No, in the first year."
FA (echoing)	Am éischten [eɪʃtən].	"In the first (year)"

Both speakers use their own variant, a pattern which is general in Gilles's data. Despite this, leveling is present in the language.

In summary, it appears that short-term accommodation as a precursor to dialect leveling follows the same patterns as speech accommodation generally: a speaker may well converge with another's dialect, but we should not expect this to be the only pattern. Accommodation theory and conversation analysis show that interactions are highly complex, with a number of agendas on the part of the speakers – and the creation of a new dialect is not one of them. The need to distinguish between actual speech accommodation and other factors was already recognized by Thakerar et al. (1982) when they posited a "psychological dimension" to accommodation. This refers to "individuals' *beliefs* that they are integrating with and differentiating from others respectively" [emphasis in original] (Thakerar et al. 1982: 222). We need to accept this complexity if we are to understand the nature of the input to koineization.

3.2   Evidence that the features found in dialect leveling and in koines are foreshadowed in the long-term accommodation of the original adult migrants

While the information on short-term accommodation is complex and rather unclear, the same cannot be said for the relationship between long-term accommodation and the outcomes of dialect leveling and koineization. Our example is the speech of adult rural migrants in the city of Bergen in western Norway (Kerswill 1994a). Because they are a linguistic minority in a city, they are not potential "koineizers." However, as we shall see, their accommodation to Bergen urban vernacular involves the adoption of some of the features found in Odda and Høyanger as well as in the increasingly leveled dialects of rural southwest Norway. We start with a transcript of portions of a recorded conversation between Mr. BS, a 41-year-old industrial worker who moved to Bergen at the age of 24, and another rural migrant.

The most striking facet of this extract is its extreme variability. Not only are features from the two dialects mixed within an utterance, but they also appear within a single word, as in ['frɛmtiːɛ], which is ['frɑmtiːɛ] in the rural dialect, and ['fʁɛmtiːdn̩] in Bergen dialect. The mixing among this group of speakers is relatively unrestricted, with great variation both between and within individuals. As we shall see in the next section, this is also characteristic of the first native-born generations in many koines (Trudgill 1998, Trudgill et al. 2000, Omdal 1977).

While this variability is, of course, not characteristic of established koines, some of the features involved include those which appear in the west

Table 26.4 Extracts from conversational data for Mr. BS, a rural migrant in Bergen

Example	Comment
(i) [ɪ fr̩ɔ 'moːløɪnɛ] i frå Måløya "from Måløya"	Rural dialect
(ii) [fɔˌəʉ 'sɛ̞ːvɑ] får ikkje du sova? "Can't you get to sleep?"	Rural dialect

(iii)   [fɛr̩ 'flɑskəklɪr̩ĩjɛ̞ 'dɛn jɪk 'r̩ɛt 'ɪn soṇ vɑ
     'heɛlt . . .]
for flaskeklirringa den gjekk rett inn så han
     var heilt . . .
"because the rattling of the bottles, it went
     straight in so it was completely . . ."
	Mixture of rural and Bergen dialect

(iv)   [bjœɪgɛn]
Bjørg-the "Bjørg"
(female personal name + Bergen idiomatic
     addition of article in Bergen common
     gender form)
	Mixture of rural and Bergen dialect

(v) [o jɑ 'hʊn jɑ] og ja ho ja "oh yes, her"	Bergen dialect
(vi) [ɛɪn gɔ̞ŋ ɪ 'fr̩ɛmtiːɛ] ein gang i framtida "some time in the future"	Rural and Bergen dialect, with within-word mixing
(vii) 'sɑːkɛn 'ʊptɑː dɛg] saka opptar deg "the matter at hand keeps you busy"	Bergen dialect

Key: Bergen features: <u>single underlining</u>
       Rural dialect features: <u><u>double underlining</u></u>
       Unmarked forms (i.e. both rural and Bergen): normal type
       Except for /r/, the features marked are morpho-lexical.

Source: Kerswill (1994a: 148)

Table 26.5   Simplificatory processes found in southwestern Norwegian varieties

Process		Presence in the long-term accommodation of rural migrants in Bergen?	Presence in West Norwegian dialect leveling?	Presence in West Norwegian koines?
(i)	Simplification of /dn/, /dl/, and /bm/ to /n/, /l/, and /m/ in e.g. /fidnɑ/, /ɑdlə/, /kobmɑ/	yes	yes	Odda, Tyssedal (Høyanger did not have clusters)
(ii)	Reduction in vowel inventory	yes (specifically, avoidance of /ɐ/ and /ɐː/: /gɐlv/ > /gɔlv/ "floor", /vɐːrə/ > /vɔːrə/ "been" (part.)	yes (general reduction; Sandøy 1987: 238–9)	yes (general reduction)
(iii)	Loss of the morphophonemic velar-palatal alternation in e.g. /tɑːk/ – /tɑːçə/	yes	yes (Sandøy 1987: 234)	yes
(iv)	Loss of vowel change in present tense of some strong verbs, e.g. /tɛːk/ > /tɑːɾ/, "take" (present)	yes	yes (Sandøy 1987: 236)	yes

Norwegian koines and in west Norwegian dialect leveling. Table 26.5 lists simplificatory features noted in the speech of the rural migrants recorded for the study (Kerswill 1994a), along with information as to whether they occur in koines and dialect leveling in the region.

It is in fact likely that some of these ostensible simplifications represent the straightforward borrowing of a Bergen item, since in most cases the Bergen form is identical to the simpler variant. However, for process (ii) – the loss of /ɐ/ and /ɐː/ – this cannot be the case. In almost all the relevant words, these vowels are replaced by /ɔ/ or /ɔː/ – a simple, predictable substitution. However, this does not always represent a convergence with Bergen dialect, which has a range of vowels, and often differing lexical forms, for these words. For example, rural /hɐːvə/ "head" is replaced by /hɔːvə/, not by Bergen /hɔvə/ or either of the standard forms *hode* or *hovud*. Similarly, /skɔːtə/ "shot" (past participle) appears as /skɔːtə/, rarely as Bergen /skʉt/ (Kerswill 1994a: 157, 159–61). Of course, we cannot claim that any of these simplifications have been arrived at individually by the particular speakers who were recorded, because there remains the possibility that these simplifications form part of a "norm" of migrant speech (Kerswill 1994a: 145–7) – and are therefore spread to new individuals by borrowing. Yet, the processes are natural, and it is likely that some of the speakers do respond to the contact situation with simplification. Moreover, the rural migrants do *not* acquire complex features of the Bergen dialect (Kerswill 1994a: 161–2).

We return now to the factors that inhibit or promote the adoption of linguistic features in long-term accommodation. Trudgill discusses a number of cases, including British people living in the USA, Americans in Britain, and Swedes in Norway. Dealing mainly with phonological changes, he finds that accommodation follows similar patterns, the basic order being as follows.

1   "Natural" and phonologically predictable phonetic changes. An example is the early adoption of the tap [ɾ] for intervocalic /t/ by British people in the USA, as in *letter* – in this case a feature already present to some extent in many British people's speech (Trudgill 1986: 19).
2   Substitutions of phonemes in clearly defined lexical sets. An example is the substitution of /æ/ for /ɑː/ in items like *dance*, *last*, *half*, by the same group (Trudgill 1986: 18).
3   "Complex" changes, some of which may never be acquired. These include:

   (i)   the reversal of a merger, as when older Canadian children living in Britain generally fail to separate the sets of *cot* and *caught*, which are merged in Canadian English (Chambers 1992: 687–8);
   (ii)   the use of phonemes in what are phonotactically impermissible positions in the speaker's own dialect, exemplified by the failure of English migrants in the USA to realize /r/ non-prevocalically, e.g., in *cart* (Trudgill 1986: 15–16);
   (iii) the acquisition of lexically unpredictable phonological processes. An example is the Philadelphia "short a" pattern. This refers to the tensing and raising of the vowel in words like *man* and *bad*, which is both phonologically and lexically determined – that is to say, tensing/raising only takes place before certain consonants, and there are lexical exceptions; this feature is rarely learned even by young child incomers to Philadelphia (Payne 1980, Roberts and Labov 1995, Trudgill 1986: 36–7, Kerswill 1996: 186–7).

This ordering is in effect a difficulty hierarchy, with features higher up being psycholinguistically "easier" and, other things being equal, more likely to be involved in accommodation. (See Kerswill 1996: 200, for a more elaborated hierarchy which adds lexical, grammatical, and prosodic features.) The order predicted by this hierarchy interacts, however, with the factor of *salience*, invoked by Trudgill to explain why some features are adopted earlier, or later, than others. Trudgill states that the following factors (adapted from Trudgill 1986: 11) lead to greater awareness of a linguistic feature, so that it becomes a *marker*, in Labov's sense, and therefore has the potential to become salient:

1   the variable has at least one variant which is overtly stigmatized;
2   the variable has a high-status variant reflected in the orthography;
3   the variable is undergoing linguistic change;
4   variants are phonetically radically different;
5   variants are involved in the maintenance of phonological contrasts in the accommodating speaker's variety.

Trudgill states (1986: 37): "During accommodation, it is indeed salient features of the target variety that are adjusted to, except that, in the case of adults at least, a number of factors combine to delay this modification to different extents." These factors include those that come under (ii) and (iii) in the difficulty hierarchy. To complete the model, Trudgill adds a further inhibitory factor: that of *extra-strong salience*. One of the conditions leading to salience is the involvement of a phonological contrast. However, in some cases this can lead to a heightened awareness on the speakers' part, so that the feature becomes a stereotype and therefore something to be avoided. This, in Trudgill's view, explains why northern English speakers tend not to acquire the southern vowel /ɑː/ in *dance* for their own /æ/, while they may acquire southern /ʌ/ in *butter*. In the *dance* case, they are aware that southern speakers use a different phoneme from themselves, while with *butter* they are less aware of it, because /ʌ/ is not a phoneme for them (Trudgill 1986: 155).

Trudgill's account is intended as a comprehensive model of long-term accommodation. However, there are certain problems with it. Most particularly, these concern the role of extra-strong salience. It seems that the same criterion, that of the presence of a contrast in the speaker's dialect, can lead either to a feature's adoption or to its rejection (Hinskens 1996: 10–13). One solution to the problem is to look at a feature within the linguistic system of both dialects, as well as viewing it from a dialect geography and social perspective. The *dance* case involves a number of common lexical items, including *grass*, *bath*, *chance*, *last*, and *past*. Because of this, and because it involves a phonemic contrast, it is easily stereotyped and easily labeled: southerners talk of the northern "flat" *a*, while northerners hear the southern variant as "posh," doubtless because it also occurs in Received Pronunciation. A second example comes from the dialects in the rural hinterland of Bergen in southwest Norway. As we saw, these dialects have two vowels, /ɐ/ and /ɐː/, which are not found in the city. They are widely considered "ugly;" speakers, both rural and urban, comment on them spontaneously. It therefore comes as no surprise that they

are being leveled out, as well as being removed in the long-term accommodation of rural people moving to the city. Reasons for their extra-strong salience
probably lie in the fact that they are both regionally restricted and phonetically distant from other vowels, typically /ɔ/ and /ɔ:/, which are used in the
same words in other dialects (Kerswill 1994a: 157).

Even with explanations such as these, we come up against difficulties. In a
study of long-term accommodation among eastern German (former GDR)
migrants to western Germany, Auer et al. (1998) apply criteria for salience that
are broadly similar to Trudgill's, with some additions; in particular, they draw
a more explicit distinction than he does between "objective" (linguistic) and
"subjective" (social and social psychological) parameters. The principal additional linguistic criterion is whether or not a feature is *lexicalized* – that is, it is
not possible to predict on phonological grounds which lexical items are involved. We have already seen an example of lexicalization in the Philadelphia
"short *a*" pattern. Of the 12 phonological variables they investigated in the
Upper Saxon Vernacular (USV) of the migrants, three will serve to illustrate
their point.

1 (A:) – USV velarized (rounded, back) low vowel: standard [ɑ:], USV [ɔ̈:], as
   in *wahr* "true".
2 (AI) – USV monophthong for the standard diphthong: standard [aə], USV
   [ë:], as in *kein* "no" (determiner). It is lexicalized in that it is restricted to
   those standard German words which contain /ai/ derived from MHG
   (Middle High German) /ei/, not MHG /i:/. USV [ë:] merges with /ɛ:/,
   which occurs in another lexical set, e.g., in [lë:bm̩] *leben* "to live"; hence, in
   accommodation to standard German, a merger must be undone.
3 (P,T) – USV syllable-initial voiceless lenis stops instead of fortis stops: standard [p], [t], Saxon [b̥], [d̥], as in *paar* "some", *Tante* "aunt". The USV feature
   involves a merger between standard German /p, t/ and /b, d/. Accommodation entails the undoing of a merger.

Table 26.6 shows that, by their criteria, (A:) is non-salient, while (P,T) and (AI)
are rather more salient. In the table, a "yes" entry is evidence of salience. Auer
et al. (1998) then compare this classification with the percentage loss of the
USV features between the first interview and the last, two years later. These
percentage changes (a positive score represents a loss), shown in table 26.7,
do not match expectations at all.

The authors' predictions that (A:) would shift the least, and (AI) the most,
were patently not borne out. They argue (Auer et al. 1998: 182) that the fact
that (AI), along with a similar variable, (AU), is lexicalized shelters it from
loss; however, they admit that this is not an explanation for the "relatively
positive prestige of the vernacular realizations" of (AI) and (AU), and refer to
the fact that the Berlin vernacular has similar monophthongs. In the case of
(P,T), expectations are met: a salient, stigmatized pronunciation is rapidly
dropped. However, (A:) is subject to massive attrition as well, even though

Table 26.6 Salience of three Upper Saxon variables in contact with standard German – "strong" vernacular realizations

Criterion	(A:)	Variable (P,T)	(AI)
Merger to be split?	no	yes	yes
Discrete variable?	no	no	yes
Lexicalization?	no	no	yes
Style differences?	yes	yes	—
Represented in writing?	no	yes	yes
Stereotyping?	no	yes	yes

— data not available
Source: Auer et al. (1998: 177, table 2a)

Table 26.7 Percentage loss of "strong" Upper Saxon realizations of three variables over a two-year period

	(A:)	(P,T)	(AI)
Percentage loss	65%	72%	−3%

Source: Auer et al. (1998: 180)

this feature only fulfils one of the criteria for salience (style shifting, which as an explanation of salience is circular). While (A:) does not involve phoneme replacement, it can be argued that USV [ɔː] could be taken by some listeners for standard German /oː/ as in *Chor* "choir" – a possibility not mentioned by the authors – in which case its behavior is less surprising. The authors conclude that, for this variable at least, the subjective factors (represented by style shifting) outweigh the objective ones.

Auer and his colleagues find that there is little match between the objective and subjective criteria. However, for the lexicalized variables "objective" criteria do play a part; for the remainder, different "subjective" ones seem to take precedence. Moreover, salience "does not indicate the attitudinal polarity (positive or negative) of this [social and interactional] significance, let alone its precise 'ideological value'" (Auer et al. 1998: 184).

Yet, salience of either kind is clearly an extremely significant factor in dialect accommodation, as a related case study of an individual migrant showed (Auer et al. 1997). In this study, a man who had accommodated during the first year restored most of the USV features by the end of the second, as a result of a drastic change in his social network, attitudes, and degree of integration following an industrial accident. The authors show that the features which changed, first to standard, then back to USV, were mostly the ones the main study had already identified as "salient" by the six criteria given in table 26.6. The non-salient variables mainly had a "flat" graph rather than the "zig-zag" pattern of the salient ones.

The problem with salience is that it may consist of a far more disparate range of effects than research has hitherto been able to uncover, both linguistic and non-linguistic (Kerswill and Williams, forthcoming). The fairly wide range of factors discussed in this section goes some way to address this point.

4 Focusing: The Language of the Koineizing Generation(s)

Trudgill's second stage of new-dialect formation involves the first generation of children born in the new community. As we saw above, he states that this stage is characterized by "extreme variability" and "further leveling." We will examine five cases to see the extent to which this characterization is true: New Zealand English; Høyanger; the speech of children in the English new town, Milton Keynes; Modern Hebrew; and, finally, children's speech in the Norwegian Arctic territory of Spitsbergen. To anticipate: we find broad similarities among speakers of this generation, and conclude that focusing usually belongs to the following generation (the migrants' grandchildren). Particular conditions may mean that focusing takes place earlier, later, or not at all. Moreover, variations we observe are ascribable to a small set of social and linguistic factors.

The data for Trudgill's New Zealand study come from recordings made by the National Broadcasting Corporation of New Zealand in 1946–8. As Trudgill (1998) explains, "[t]he recordings were oral history pioneer reminiscences, mostly from people who were the children of the first European settlers in New Zealand. . . . About 325 speakers born between 1850 and 1900 were recorded." This generation of people represents the first native-born speakers of English in New Zealand – though of course they were elderly by the time they were recorded. The most striking fact about this data archive is its tremendous variability, both between and within individuals. Trudgill (1998) argues that, in situations where there is no single, stable adult model, children are able to choose from a wider variety of adult models than otherwise. Also, in the absence of a stable peer-group variety, adults, especially parents and other caregivers, will have a greater than usual influence on children's speech (Trudgill et al. 2000). In such a situation, one can expect individuals to make novel selections of features from the available choice. This turns out to be the case. Thus, Mr. Malcolm Ritchie has the following features:

1 /θ/ and /ð/ are realized as dental stops, [t̪] and [d̪], as in Irish English;
2 Syllable-final /l/ may be clear (i.e. non-velarized), as in Irish English;
3 He has h-dropping in words like *home*, an English feature absent in Ireland;
4 He has a distinction between /ʍ/ and /w/, thus distinguishing *which* and *witch*. This feature is never combined with h-dropping in the British Isles.

Not surprisingly, there is great inter-individual variation even between people with near-identical backgrounds. For example, Mr. Ritchie's sister-in-law, Mrs. H. Ritchie, attended the same school at the same time as he did, yet has some quite different features in her speech. Unlike Mr. Ritchie, she has close realizations of /æ/ as [ɛ] and /e/ as [e], while he typically has more open variants.

Despite this variability, there is evidence of leveling in this group of speakers. For example, there is an almost complete absence of the use of the vowel /ʊ/, as in FOOT, in the STRUT set – a feature of the northern half of England. In terms of the demography of the settlers, northern speakers were certainly in a minority, and it had clearly been leveled out already in the first generation of native-born speakers.

Trudgill does not provide any information about the transition from Stage II to the fully-fledged, focused Stage III of present-day New Zealand English. However, he comments on the relationship between the apparently random speech of the earlier generations and present day speech, as follows:

> The "original" [i.e. highly individual] mixtures demonstrated by *individual* informants such as Mr. Riddle are the result of random selection. But the proportions of variants present in the accents of groups of second-stage speakers in a particular location, *taken as a whole*, derive in a probabilistic manner from, and will therefore reflect at least approximately, the proportions of the same variants present in the different varieties spoken by their parents' generation *taken as a whole*.

Trudgill examines some of the features of Stage III in the light of the proportions of those features found in his Stage II corpus. Thus, 75 percent of the speakers (and, to judge from available statistics, a majority of the earliest immigrants from the British Isles) did not use h-dropping in words like *house*, despite the fact that this is the norm in much of England today; h-dropping has almost completely disappeared from modern New Zealand English. A similar explanation can be put forward for the maintenance of the distinction between /ʍ/ as in *which* and /w/ as in *witch*, despite its being rapidly lost in England.

Trudgill's findings on the early speech of New Zealand match Omdal's comments on the Norwegian town of Høyanger very closely indeed. Høyanger was founded in 1916 and received in-migrants from various parts of Norway. Omdal writes:

> As it turned out, the first generation to be born and raised in Høyanger, i.e., people who today [=1977] are in their fifties, do not have a uniform dialect, but have a spoken language that to a great extent bears the imprint of their parents' dialect. There is a good deal of variation between individuals.   (Omdal 1977: 7; my translation)

We can presume that the reasons for the lack of early focusing in Høyanger are similar to those adduced for New Zealand: but are there any specific, local circumstances that gave this result? It turns out that, in the early years of

Høyanger's existence, there was considerable social segregation between the families of managers and professionals and those of the workers, with housing in different parts of the town. Crucially, while the workers mainly came from the same county as Høyanger, the managers and professionals came from the east of the country. This meant that linguistic convergence between the two groups could only take place later, as social and geographical allegiances became more oriented toward the new community. A second factor is the relatively large linguistic differences between dialects in Norway, particularly at that time; the factor of dialect differences would have played a similar part in New Zealand. (See Kerswill and Williams 2000: 73–4, for a more detailed discussion of Høyanger.)

Koineization did, however, ensue in the next generation: "To find a uniform spoken variety, we must move a generation on, to people who are in their 20s or younger. The speech of these people gives the impression that it is just as 'firm' as in other similar places with a more stable population growth" (Omdal 1977: 7; my translation).

We now have a clearer picture of the relationship between Trudgill's three stages. The observations from New Zealand are entirely consistent with what we have seen of the relationship between the speech of the Bergen rural migrants (who can be taken to represent Stage I of a west Norwegian leveling/koine formation process), the speech of the first native-born generation in Høyanger (Stage II), and the features found in the koines which subsequently developed there and in Odda and Tyssedal (Stage III).

Our next example is the southeast English new town of Milton Keynes, designated in 1967 in a location roughly 80 kilometers from London, Oxford, and Cambridge. From that date to 1991, the population of the area rose from 44,000 to 176,000. Recordings were made of children and adults in 1991–2, some 24 years, or one generation, after its foundation. Further recordings of a different sample were made in 1996 (Kerswill and Williams 2000, Kerswill 1994b, Cheshire et al. 1999). Thus, almost all the child speakers in the samples were the offspring of adult migrants to the town. We consider first the degree to which this first native generation has focused its speech, in comparison with that of the caregivers. The variable (ou) refers to the realization of the offset of the vowel /əʊ/ as in *goat*, which is currently being fronted in southeast England. The parents of the children originate from various parts of Great Britain, and would therefore be expected to show a range of pronunciations for this vowel, from both the southeast and elsewhere. In order to see whether any focusing among the children has occurred, we can compare the fronting scores for the parents (only the mothers were recorded in the study) with those of their children. The variable has the following values:

(ou) – 0: [oː], [oʊ]	score: 0	(Northern and Scottish realization)
(ou) – 1: [əʊ], [əʉ̟]	score: 1	(older Buckinghamshire and London)
(ou) – 2: [əʏ]	score: 2	(fronting)
(ou) – 3: [əɪ]	score: 3	(fronting and unrounding)

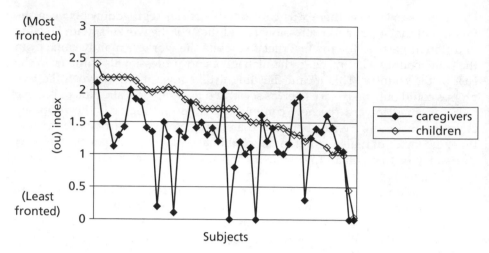

Figure 26.1   Association of Milton Keynes children's (ou) scores with those of their caregivers

Source: Kerswill & Williams (2000, p. 102)

Figure 26.1 shows the association of the children's scores (ranked from highest to lowest) with those of their caregivers. Two points should be noted. First, with two notable exceptions (at bottom right on the graph), the overall range of the children is much smaller than that of their caregivers, suggesting a high degree of focusing. The caregivers' scores reflect their regional origins, with the six very low scorers coming from outside the southeast. Thus, the caregivers' vowel realizations are not reflected at all in their children's scores. On the evidence of this and other variables (Kerswill and Williams 2000), Milton Keynes children seem not to be much influenced by their parents' speech – in distinct contrast to the first generation native speakers in New Zealand and Høyanger. The fact that the two exceptions just mentioned turn out to be 4 year olds suggests that it is the older, not the younger children who are engaged in the focusing – a point to which we will return. Moreover, the fact that the children's scores are significantly higher also suggests that they are orienting their focusing towards the new, fronted norm for this vowel (Kerswill and Williams 2000: 101).

The Milton Keynes study also allows us to examine which age group is most involved in the formation of the koine. We saw in the previous section an example of adult migrants' speech, characterized by a high degree of mixing and instability, yet also anticipating the forms that will appear in a later koine. In Milton Keynes, most of the adults speak linguistic varieties that are far more similar to each other than do their Norwegian counterparts. This, we must assume, is because of the extensively leveled nature of British English, especially in southern England; in any case, it means that investigating their long-term accommodation is difficult.

However, the Milton Keynes child data allows us further insights into the early stages of koine formation. It has recently been argued that language

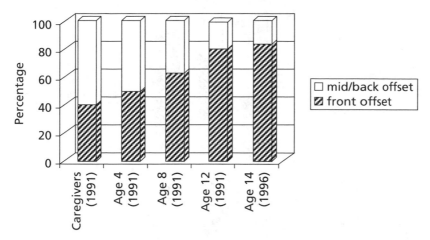

Figure 26.2   Percent front/non-front offset of (ou) (*goat*), Milton Keynes women and girls

Source: Cheshire et al. (1999), Kerswill and Williams (2000)

change is unlikely to be mainly due to misanalyses of adult grammars on the part of young children during their acquisition phase, for two main reasons. First, developmental forms that appear in child language are rarely the same as those which appear in change (Croft 2000: 47). Second, young children, for sociolinguistic reasons, are not able to be part of the diffusion of changes (Aitchison 1981: 180). Instead, it seems likely that older children and adolescents are the main "agents of change", because of their willingness to innovate and their orientation towards their peer groups and older adolescents (Eckert 2000; Kerswill 1996). Careful examination of the Milton Keynes children's and adolescents' data allows us to draw conclusions about their contribution to any new dialect that may develop there. Figure 26.2 recodes the data from Figure 26.1 into two categories: mid/back offset and front offset, and adds information from the adolescents recorded in 1996.

As can be seen, the amount of fronting increases with the age of the subjects from 1991 (the 4, 8, and 12 year olds), while the adults have the lowest score. Interestingly, the 14 year olds recorded in 1996 show a further small increase. Bearing in mind that the 14 year olds would have been 9 in 1991, these results strongly suggest that the children themselves actually increase their fronting as they reach adolescence. Figure 26.3 shows a rather similar result for another vowel that is currently being fronted, /uː/ as in *goose*, with the process remaining vigorous into the teens.

On the face of it, focusing has been fully achieved in the speech of Milton Keynes children. However, there are characteristics of this new speech community which are not typical of long-established settlements. We return to this point in the final section.

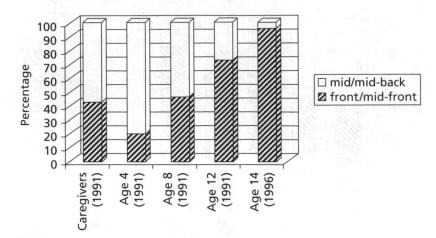

Figure 26.3   Percent front/non-fronted variants of (uː) (*goose*), Milton Keynes working-class women and girls

Source: Cheshire et al. (1999), Kerswill and Williams (2000)

The koines we have looked at in this chapter have generally become focused by the time of the third generation (the grandchildren of the migrants) – though for Milton Keynes it is too early to say. As we saw earlier, Modern Hebrew arose under somewhat different conditions, with second-language speakers forming the input. Despite this, it seems that a measure of stability was reached by that generation, too, despite the continued massive immigration to Israel and the fact that most, even Israeli-born, people continued not to be native speakers. Blanc (1968) sets out the stages of stabilization in terms of "typical" 45-year-old speakers and their communities at different points in time. They are as follows, with Trudgill's stages given in parentheses (adapted from Blanc 1968: 239–40):

1   1900: Eliezer Ben-Yehuda's contemporary. East European, a Yiddish native speaker. He refers to written sources to guide him in his speech. (Stage I)
2   1930: Still likely to be of East European birth or background, and not a native speaker. (Stage II) The children of this group start to diverge, and level their speech, especially in their informal style (incipient Stage III).
3   1960: A 50–50 chance of being a native speaker. By now, there is considerable leveling of "communal differentiation" (that is, it is no longer possible to tell people's language background from their speech). His informal speech is imitated as a matter of course by many new speakers. (Stage III)

It is clear from this that new, leveled norms began to be established 30–40 years after the first migrations (that is, Blanc's stage 3 speakers when they were children), in other words, in the speech of the second native-born generation.

Finally, we briefly look at a new community which, despite having existed for over 90 years, has never developed a koine. This is the Norwegian Arctic territory of Spitsbergen (Svalbard) (Mæhlum 1992), where, because families stay on average only for ten years, there is no possibility of a stable adult norm. Children there have an "unclear dialect identity" (Mæhlum 1992: 123), expressing identification both with the "home" town or village on the mainland and with Spitsbergen. Very much in line with findings from New Zealand and Høyanger, these children apparently retain more influence from their parents' speech than children do in established communities. Consequently, they are much more heterogeneous, as well as internally inconsistent. Mæhlum argues that they use code switching, dialect mixing, and a version of standard East (Oslo) Norwegian as "strategies of neutrality."

Three main points emerge. First, the *kind and level of social integration* of the new community affects the speed of koineization. Thus, a socially homogeneous community is likely to koineize faster than one with considerable social divisions. Perhaps surprisingly, continued massive immigration seems to have only a minor inhibitory effect on koineization – as long as, crucially, there is a stable "core" of speakers who remain after the initial settlement who can act as a focus for new incomers (cf. Mufwene's "founder principle" 1996); this factor differentiates Israel from Spitsbergen. Second, *children's access to peer groups* is crucial. Child speakers must be able to interact freely with other, perhaps older, children for them to be able to establish norms in the absence of a stable adult model. The development of adolescent norms is likely to be accelerated by compulsory schooling – a point made by Britain (1997a: 165), in the context of slow dialect leveling in the Fens of eastern England following seventeenth-century migrations (on this, see Britain 1997b). Schooling in early New Zealand was sporadic and not centralized, because many of the settlements were remote and communications were poor; this is obviously not true of Milton Keynes. (See Eckert 2000, on the role of the adolescent years in socialization and language change, and the importance of the school.) Third, the *degree of difference between the input varieties* will affect the amount of accommodation that individuals have to engage in. In Milton Keynes (unlike all the other cases considered in this chapter), the dialect differences are for the most part subtle, being restricted to minor subphonemic variations. As a result, most of the usual heterogeneity found among first-generation children is simply bypassed, given sufficient opportunities for contact among children and adolescents, and focusing toward a new variety is accelerated.

5   Koineization and Continuity

In this final section, we compare koineization with other forms of contact-induced language change. The reason for doing so is to answer the question, "Are there any characteristics which distinguish a speech community with a koine as its everyday vernacular from one which uses a language variety which is the result of 'normal' transmission across the generations?" It seems clear that, although koine formation shares some features with pidgin and creole development, especially in the crucial role of face-to-fact contacts between speakers of different language varieties, it is very distinct from these. Siegel (forthcoming: 6–7) sets out criteria differentiating koine formation from pidgin and creole genesis, as follows:

1   Koine formation involves continuity, in that speakers do not need to abandon their own linguistic varieties. This is not so for pidgin and creole development.
2   In koine formation, there is no "target variety." In pidgin and creole development, there is a target variety.
3   Koine formation requires intimate and prolonged social interaction between speakers. We must assume that this is not so in pidgin and creole development, where contact is restricted.
4   Koine formation can be a long process; pidgins and creoles are thought to develop rapidly from an immediate need for communication.

We can take issue with the first of these points. Continuity is not clear-cut, in that a community using a koine is likely not to have the "normal" contact with earlier generations' speech. This places a koine between a pidgin or creole, where transmission is interrupted, and a dialect that is the result of "normal" transmission. Normal transmission is defined by Thomason and Kaufman (1988: 9–10) as taking place when "a language is passed on from parent generation to child generation and/or via peer group from immediately older to immediately younger." Our final example will illustrate this intermediate status of a koine.

As we have already noted, Milton Keynes children use features that are characteristic of general dialect leveling the southeastern area, including the fronting of /əʊ/ as in *goat* and /uː/ as in *goose*. How can we be sure that the developments are the result of koineization, and not regional dialect leveling by geographical diffusion? We now look at evidence showing that, even if the outcome of the two processes is similar, the mechanism is different, because of the discontinuity that exists across the generations in Milton Keynes. We examine the vowel /aʊ/ as in *mouth*, which appears to be converging on an Received Pronunciation-like /aʊ/, moving away from local pronunciations such as [ɛɪ] and [ɛʊ+]. Table 26.8 shows how this change appears in apparent time in Reading, a town roughly the same size, and distance from London, as Milton Keynes, but with a long-established local population (Cheshire et al. 1999). There has clearly been a substantial shift away from the older forms to a leveled [aʊ].

Table 26.9 shows the corresponding data from Milton Keynes. With the inclusion of data from the "young adult" generation, this gives an apparent-time snapshot of four generations of the area, with the new town being

Table 26.8   Percentage use of variants of /aʊ/ (*mouth*), Reading Working Class, interview style

	[ɛʊ̞]	[ɛɪ]	[ɛː]	[aːᵊ]	[æʊ]	[aʊ]
Survey of English Dialects informants, 1950–60s	100	–	–	–	–	–
Elderly (2f, 2m)	53.5	38.1	3.3	0.0	4.1	0.7
Girls age 14 (n = 8)	0.0	2.3	0.0	8.0	0.0	90.4
Boys age 14 (n = 8)	3.8	3.2	0.0	5.7	0.0	87.1

Source: Orton et al. (1968)

Table 26.9   Percentage use of variants of /aʊ/ (*mouth*), Milton Keynes Working Class, interview style

	[ɛʊ̞]	[ɛɪ]	[ɛː]	[aːᵊ]	[æʊ]	[aʊ]
Survey of English Dialects informants, 1950–60s	100	–	–	–	–	–
Elderly (2f, 2m)	63.2	25.6	9.8	0.0	1.2	0.0
Women age 25–40 (1991 data; n = 48)	0.0	0.0	11.7	17.2	38.6	31.5
Girls age 14 (n = 8)	0.0	0.0	0.0	5.9	4.7	88.8
Boys age 14 (n = 8)	0.0	0.0	0.0	12.3	3.8	83.1

Source: SED informants, Orton et al. (1968)

established between the "elderly" and "women's" generations. Despite the similarities, there are differences between the two towns. In Milton Keynes, there appear to be three stages in the development of this vowel: first, a period of stability in which [ɛʊ̞] and [ɛɪ] predominated, followed at the height of the Milton Keynes settlement in the 1970s by a period of greater heterogeneity in which [æʊ], the form favored by the majority of the in-migrants (represented here by the women aged 25–40), was dominant. A "re-focusing" finally began with the second-generation migrants (today's children), who are settling on [aʊ]. Starting with the "elderly", there is a marked discontinuity in the scores between each succeeding generation, shown particularly by the total absence of the older forms in the speech of the women and children. This reflects the lack of social continuity in this town, where most children have parents as well as grandparents originating elsewhere. In Reading, young WC speakers are similarly rejecting the regionally marked forms in favor of [aʊ]. However, it is significant that some young speakers retain the old forms of their grandparents in a way that is indicative of the strong social continuity in this working-class part of Reading. It is this distinction between the absence and presence of continuity that marks a koine from a "normal" regional variety: the outcomes may, in the end, be the same, but the mechanism is quite different.

ACKNOWLEDGMENTS

I would like to thank Peter Auer, Arne Kjell Foldvik, Frans Hinskens, and Helge Sandøy for so willingly providing me with last-minute information during the writing of this article, and Peter Trudgill for answering my queries so promptly.

REFERENCES

Aitchison, J. (1981). *Language Change: Progress or Decay?* London: Fontana.

Aitchison, J. (1991). *Language Change: Progress or Decay?* 2nd edn Cambridge: Cambridge University Press.

Auer, P. (1998). Structural convergence and interpersonal accommodation in a theory of language change. Plenary paper given at the final open conference of the European Science Foundation Network on "The convergence and divergence of dialects in a changing Europe," University of Reading, September.

Auer, P. and F. Hinskens (1996). The convergence and divergence of dialects in Europe. New and not so new developments in an old area. *Sociolinguistica* 10: 1–30.

Auer, P., B. Barden and B. Grosskopf (1997). Long-term accommodation: A single case analysis of inner-German West-East migration and its wider implications. Paper given at the workshop "Migration as a factor in connection with convergence and divergence processes of dialects in Europe," Heidelberg, October. (European Science Foundation

Network on "The convergence and divergence of dialects in a changing Europe.")

Auer, P., B. Barden and B. Grosskopf (1998). Subjective and objective parameters determining "salience" in long-term dialect accommodation. *Journal of Sociolinguistics* 2: 163–87.

Bell, A. (1997). Language style as audience design. In N. Coupland and A. Jaworski (eds.), *Sociolinguistics: A Reader.* Basingstoke: Macmillan. 240–50.

Blanc, H. (1968). The Israeli koine as an emergent national standard. In Joshua Fishman, C. Ferguson and J. Das Gupta (eds.), *Language Problems of Developing Nations.* New York: John Wiley. 237–51.

Britain, D. (1997a). Dialect contact, focusing and phonological rule complexity: the koineisation of Fenland English. In C. Boberg, M. Meyerhoff and S. Strassel (eds.), *A Selection of Papers from NWAVE 25. University of Pennsylvania Working Papers in Linguistics* 4: 141–70.

Britain, D. (1997b). Dialect contact and phonological reallocation: "Canadian

Raising" in the English Fens. *Language in Society* 26: 15–46.

Britain, D. and P. J. Trudgill (1999). Migration, new-dialect formation and sociolinguistic refunctionalisation: *reallocation as an outcome of dialect contact. Transactions of the Philological Society* 97: 245–56.

Bubenik, V. (1993). Dialect contact and koineization: the case of Hellenistic Greek. *International Journal of the Sociology of Language* 99: 9–23.

Chambers, J. K. (1992). Dialect acquisition. *Language* 68: 673–705.

Chambers, J. K. and P. J. Trudgill (1998). *Dialectology*, 2nd edn. Cambridge: Cambridge University Press.

Cheshire, J., A. Gillett, P. E. Kerswill and A. Williams (1999). The role of adolescents in dialect levelling. Final report submitted to the Economic and Social Research Council of Great Britain, ref. R000236180.

Coupland, N. (1984). Accommodation at work. *International Journal of the Sociology of Language* 46: 49–70.

Croft, W. (2000). *Explaining Language Change: An Evolutionary Approach.* Harlow: Longman.

Domingue, N. (1980). Syntactic innovations in Mauritian Bhojpuri. Unpublished MS.

Domingue, N. (1981). Internal change in a transplanted language. *Studies in the Linguistic Sciences* 4: 151–9.

Eckert, P. (2000). *Linguistic Variation as Social Practice.* Oxford: Blackwell.

Giles, H. and N. Coupland (1991). *Language: Contexts and Consequences.* Milton Keynes: Open University Press.

Giles, H. and P. Powesland (1997/1975). Accommodation theory. In N. Coupland and A. Jaworski (eds.), *Sociolinguistics: A Reader.* Basingstoke: Macmillan. 232–9. (Reprinted from H. Giles and P. Powesland (1975), *Speech Style and Social Evaluation.* London: Academic Press. 154–70.

Giles, H. and P. M. Smith (1979). Accommodation theory: optimal levels of convergence. In H. Giles and R. St Clair (eds.), *Language and Social Psychology.* Oxford: Blackwell. 45–65.

Giles, H., N. Coupland and J. Coupland (1991). Accommodation theory: communication, context and consequences. In H. Giles, N. Coupland and J. Coupland (eds.), *Contexts of Accommodation: Developments in Applied Linguistics.* Cambridge: Cambridge University Press. 1–68.

Gilles, P. (1996). Virtual convergence and dialect levelling in Luxemburgish. Paper given at the workshop "The role of standard varieties in the convergence and divergence of dialects", University of Nijmegen, July. (European Science Foundation Network on "The convergence and divergence of dialects in a changing Europe".)

Gilles, P. (1997). Heidelberg. Ph.D. on Luxemburgish.

Gjørv, S. (1986). Mål og samfunn i utvikling. Unpublished Ph.D. thesis, Department of Nordic Languages and Literature, University of Bergen.

Glinert, L. (1989). *The Grammar of Modern Hebrew.* Cambridge: Cambridge University Press.

Hinskens, F. (1996). *Dialect Levelling in Limburg: Structural and Sociolinguistic Aspects.* Tübingen: Niemeyer.

Hinskens, F. (1998). Dialect levelling: a two-dimensional process. *Folia Linguistica* 32: 35–51.

Hinskens, F. and P. Auer (forthcoming). Inter-personal convergence and divergence: implications for language change. In P. Auer, F. Hinskens and P. E. Kerswill (eds.), *Dialect Change: The Convergence and Divergence of Dialects in Contemporary*

Societies. Cambridge: Cambridge University Press.

Inoue, F. (1986). Sociolinguistic aspects of new dialect forms: language change in progress in Tokyo. *International Journal of the Sociology of Language* 58: 73–89.

Kerswill, P. E. (1994a). *Dialects Converging: Rural Speech in Urban Norway*. Oxford: Clarendon Press.

Kerswill, P. E. (1994b). Babel in Buckinghamshire? Pre-school children acquiring accent features in the New Town of Milton Keynes. In G. Melchers and N.-L. Johannessen (eds.), *Nonstandard Varieties of Language: Papers from the Stockholm symposium*. Stockholm: Almqvist & Wiksell. 64–84.

Kerswill, P. E. (1996). Children, adolescents, and language change. *Language Variation and Change* 8: 177–202.

Kerswill, P. E. and A. Williams (2000). Creating a new town koine: children and language change in Milton Keynes. *Language in Society* 29: 65–115.

Kerswill, P. E. and Williams, A. (forthcoming). "Salience" as a factor in language change: evidence from dialect levelling in urban England. In M. C. Jones and E. Esch (eds.), *Language Change: The Interplay of Internal, External and Extra-Linguistic Factors*. Berlin: Mouton de Gruyter.

Labov, W. (1966). *The Social Stratification of English in New York City*. Washington, DC: Center for Applied Linguistics.

Labov, W. (1972). *Sociolinguistic Patterns*. Philadelphia: Pennsylvania University Press.

Le Page, R. B. (1980). Projection, focusing, diffusion, or, steps towards a sociolinguistic theory of language, illustrated from the Sociolinguistic Survey of Multilingual

Communities. *York Papers in Linguistics* 9: 9–32. Department of Language and Linguistic Science, University of York.

Mæhlum, B. (1992). Dialect socialization in Longyearbyen, Svalbard (Spitsbergen): A fruitful chaos. In E. H. Jahr (ed.), *Language Contact and Language Change*. Berlin: Mouton de Gruyter. 117–30.

Mesthrie, R. (1992). *Language in Indenture: A sociolinguistic history of Bhojpuri–Hindi in South Africa*. London: Routledge.

Mesthrie, R. (1993). Koineization in the Bhojpuri–Hindi diaspora – with special reference to South Africa. *International Journal of the Sociology of Language* 99: 25–44.

Milroy, J. (1992). *Linguistic Variation and Change*. Oxford: Blackwell.

Moag, R. (1977). *Fiji Hindi*. Canberra: Australian National University Press.

Mufwene, S. (1996). The founder principle in creole genesis. *Diachronica* 13: 83–134.

Mühlhäusler, P. (1974). *Pidginization and Simplification of Language*. Pacific Linguistics B-26. Canberra: Australian National University.

Mühlhäusler, P. (1980). Structural expansion and the process of creolization. In A. Valdman and A. Highfield (eds.), *Theoretical Orientations in Creole Studies*. New York: Academic Press. 19–55.

Omdal, H. (1977). Høyangermålet – en ny dialekt. *Språklig Samling* 18: 7–9.

Orton, H., E. Dieth and M. Wakelyn (1968). *The Survey of English Dialects*, vol. 4: *The Southern Counties*. Leeds: E. J. Arnold.

Payne, A. (1980). Factors controlling the acquisition of the Philadelphia dialect by out-of-state children. In W. Labov (ed.), *Locating Language in Time and Space*. New York: Academic Press. 143–78.

Ravid, D. D. (1995). *Language Change in Child and Adult Hebrew: A Psycholinguistic Perspective.* New York: Oxford University Press.

Roberts, J. and W. Labov (1995). Learning to talk Philadelphian; Acquisition of short a by preschool children. *Language Variation and Change* 7: 101–12.

Sandøy, H. (1987). *Norsk dialektkunnskap.* Oslo: Novus.

Sandøy, H. (1998). The diffusion of a new morphology in Norwegian dialects. *Folia Linguistica* 32: 83–100.

Sandve, B. H. (1976). Om talemålet i industristadene Odda og Tyssedal. Generasjonsskilnad og tilnærming mellom dei to målføra [On the spoken language in the industrial towns Odda and Tyssedal. Generational differences and convergence between the two dialects]. Ph.D. thesis, Department of Nordic Languages and Literature, University of Bergen.

Selinker, L. (1992). *Rediscovering Interlanguage.* London: Longman.

Siegel, J. (1985). Koines and koineization. *Language in Society* 14: 357–78.

Siegel, J. (1987). *Language Contact in a Plantation Environment.* Cambridge: Cambridge University Press.

Siegel, J. (1993). Introduction: controversies in the study of koines and koineization. *International Journal of the Sociology of Language* 99: 5–8.

Siegel, J. (1997). Mixing, leveling, and pidgin/creole development. In A. K. Spears and D. Winford (eds.), *The Structure and Status of Pidgins and Creoles.* Amsterdam/: John Benjamins. 111–49.

Siegel, J. (forthcoming). Koine formation and creole genesis. In N. Smith and T. Veenstra (eds.), *Contact and Creolization.* Amsterdam: John Benjamins. 175–97.

Sobrero, A. A. (1996). Italianization and variations in the repertoire: the Koiné. *Sociolinguistica* 10: 105–11.

Thakerar, J. N., H. Giles and J. Cheshire (1982). Psychological and linguistic parameters of speech accommodation theory. In C. Fraser and K. R. Scherer (eds.), *Advances in the Social Psychology of Language.* Cambridge: Cambridge University Press. 205–55.

Thelander, M. (1980) De-dialectalisation in Sweden. FUMS Rapport No. 86. Uppsala: Uppsala University.

Thelander, M. (1982). A qualitative approach to the quantitative data of speech variation. In S. Romaine (ed.), *Sociolinguistic Variation in Speech Communities* London: Edward Arnold. 65–83.

Thomason, S. G. and T. Kaufman (1988). *Language Contact, Creolization and Genetic Linguistics.* Berkeley: University of California Press.

Thomson, G. (1960). *The Greek Language.* Cambridge: W. Heffer & Sons.

Trudgill, P. J. (1986). *Dialects in Contact.* Oxford: Blackwell.

Trudgill, P. J. (1994). Language contact and dialect contact in linguistic change. In U.-B. Kotsinas and J. Helgander (eds.), *Dialektkontakt, språkkontakt och språkförändring i Norden. Föredrag från ett forskarsymposium.* Series: MINS, No. 40. Stockholm: Institutionen för nordiska språk, Stockholms Universitet. 13–22.

Trudgill, P. J. (1998). The chaos before the order: New Zealand English and the second stage of new-dialect formation. In E. H. Jahr (ed.), *Advances in Historical Sociolinguistics.* Berlin: Mouton de Gruyter. 1–11.

Trudgill, P. J., E. Gordon, G. Lewis and M. Maclagan (2000). Determinism in new-dialect formation and the genesis of New Zealand English. *Journal of Linguistics* 36: 299–318.

Trumper, J. and M. Maddalon (1988).
Converging divergence and
diverging convergence: the dialect-
language conflict and contrasting
evolutionary trends in modern Italy.
In P. Auer and A. di Luzio (eds.),
Variation and Convergence. Berlin:
de Gruyter. 216–58.

Williams, A. and P. E. Kerswill (1999).
Dialect levelling: change and
continuity in Milton Keynes,
Reading and Hull. In P. Foulkes
and G. Docherty (eds.), *Urban
Voices*. London: Arnold.
141–162.

Part V
Language and Societies

Language and Societies

We talk about language and society as if they are interdependent, but in fact the relationship is implicational. Societies can obviously exist without language, as witness the social organizations of carpenter ants and honey bees and great apes. But languages cannot exist without societies. Language ⊃ Society.

The difference between societies with language and those without it is not, however, a matter of degree but of kind. Quite rightly, when we learn about the lower animals coordinating their labors and distributing their duties, we marvel at them. We recognize these levels of social organization as crucial for their propagation and survival, but our admiration increases because we know that they manage to do what they do without language. Indeed, there is a venerable tradition in science fiction that imagines sub-human species gifted with language, often accompanied by the conceit that it accords them not just a human advantage but a superhuman one. Some ethologists indulge the same fantasies with scientific trappings instead of science fiction.

Before language existed, our hominoid ancestors organized bands for food-gathering and habitats for sheltering for their young. And probably, by analogy with the great apes, not much more. In the absence of language, finding daily sustenance and protecting yourself and your young from becoming sustenance for others are pretty much full-time preoccupations.

Since survival and propagation can be achieved in the absence of language, it was obviously not survival or propagation that called language into being. "Poetry is the mother tongue of humankind," said Johann Georg Hamann in 1762, reminding us by the power of his aphorism that language is the tool for virtually every human aspiration beyond plain survival and propagation.

We are just beginning to understand how language shapes societies and how societies shape languages. Discovering the roots of those relations stands as an ultimate goal for sociolinguistics. In this final section, we include three chapters that provide different perspectives on the relation between society and language.

Peter Trudgill's "Linguistic and Social Typology" takes a macro-sociolinguistic view, with typological characteristics such as phoneme inventories and paradigm complexity as points of departure. He suggests that certain types of linguistic features tend to accrue to languages in proportion to the amount of social traffic and linguistic mixing they are exposed to, with cosmopolitan societies susceptible to phonological complexity, among other features, in contrast to isolated societies, which tend toward small phonemic inventories, and, between them, societies sharing linguistic traits of both poles of the continuum. Trudgill takes a cautious tone (he uses the words "possible/perhaps/may/might" 78 times), a persistent reminder that his proposal is intended as a source of hypothesis-formulation and that it awaits variationist testing.

Sali Tagliamonte, in "Comparative Sociolinguistics," discusses methods for comparing linguistic processes from one community to another. She shows that quantitative methods, especially finely calibrated rule constraints, can establish probabilities of typological similarity and grammatical relatedness. Her case studies draw on evidence for African-American Vernacular English origins, perhaps the earliest major debate in sociolinguistics, and on British sources of North American English dialect features. Her discussion judiciously emphasizes the importance of accountability in comparative sampling.

In "Language Death and Dying," Walt Wolfram discusses the complex sociolinguistic process of obsolescence. Though the most frequent pattern involves "dissipation," defined as the constriction of social uses for the dying language and consequently of its grammatical forms, Wolfram describes five other attested patterns as well. He shows, moreover, that dissipation does not affect structural levels equally or synchronously. Variationists, for better or worse, have a special stake in the investigation of the death of languages and dialects because accelerated variation is its most conspicuous symptom.

Though linguistic obsolescence is rampant in our time, it is (in Wolfram's words) "part of the life cycle of language." Until a century or so ago, it went unnoticed, or nearly so, but increased mobility, urbanization, migration, and education, among other factors, are destroying enclaves and, with them, the languages (and dialects) that served them. Our sense of loss is tempered by the inevitability of it, but even more by the certain knowledge that language will continue to fill every vital social function, including new ones that might arise from radically changing conditions. Human speech is nothing if not adaptable. That was never as clearly appreciated before the advent of sociolinguistics.

J. K. Chambers

27 Linguistic and Social Typology

PETER TRUDGILL

A number of scholars have attempted to explore links between aspects of societies and aspects of the languages spoken by those societies. Much research of this type has focused on culture: one obvious site for the study of such links is in the reflection of aspects of a community's material and physical culture in its lexicon, such as large numbers of words for different types of reindeer in Sami; or in its deictic system, such as the Tenejapa Tzeltal uphill/downhill spatial orientation system (Levinson 1996). Another site lies in links between cultural values and some relatively peripheral aspects of grammar: Wierzbicka (e.g. 1986) has investigated links of this latter type, and points out that some aspects of grammar are more likely to have some connection with culture than others. She argues that optional grammatical categories are more likely to be connected to a society's culture than obligatory ones, as are "those parts of language, including grammar in the narrow sense of the word, which have to do with the relationship between the speaker and the addressee". She then produces a convincing sociocultural account of why Australian English favors "antidiminutives" such as Shaz (for Sharon) and Tez (for Terry) as terms of address. The explanation lies in the high value attached in Australian culture to solidarity, and anti-intellectualism. She contrasts the way in which "cultural ideas such as 'mateship', 'toughness', 'antisentimentality,' and 'congenial fellowship' have found their way into the grammatical system of the language" in Australia with the rich system of affectionate diminutives found in Polish.

In the present chapter, I want to suggest that, in the study of linguistic variation and change, there is a challenging and similar issue for us to focus on which has to do, however, with non-cultural attributes of societies. This involves the relationships which might exist between societal type generally, on the one hand, and non-lexical, core aspects of linguistic structure, on the other. There are good reasons to explore these issues. Linguistic-typological studies have provided us with a series of insights into the range of structures available in human languages; into what the constraints on these structures might be; and into relationships between different typological characteristics. But we do not yet have explanations for why, of all the possible structures available to human languages, particular languages select particular structures and not others. A legitimate sociolinguistic viewpoint would be that some such explanations may nevertheless be available, and that some of these might be social in nature; that is, the distribution of linguistic features over languages may not be totally random when viewed from a social perspective. One challenge in the study of linguistic variation and change, therefore, has to do with whether there are indeed any social determinants of linguistic patterning, and, if so, what these determinants might be (Trudgill 1989a, 1989b, 1989c, 1992, 1996a). The issue at hand is whether it is possible to suggest that certain linguistic features are more commonly associated with certain types of society or social structure than others.

In examining this issue, we need to decide what societal features it might initially be promising to look at. Here, it seems to me, we may be able to learn from what we already know about differences in the speed of linguistic change in different types of society, because it is very clear that social factors do impinge on language at this point; and it has been very clear since the work carried out by J. Milroy and L. Milroy (see below) what at least some of these social factors are. Linguistic change affects all living language varieties, but we know that the rate of linguistic change is not constant chronologically. In a remarkable claim, for instance, Jackson (1953) argues that nearly all the sound changes which converted Brittonic into Welsh, Cornish, and Breton took place between the middle of the fifth and the end of the sixth century, and that evolution was so rapid that "we can be fairly sure that Vortigern around 450 could not have understood Aneirin around 600" (1953: 690). Nor is rate of change constant across communities. In an often cited example, in the last thousand years Danish, Swedish, Norwegian, Faroese, and Icelandic have diverged from a common source, Old Norse. This divergence obviously has taken place because different linguistic changes have occurred in the different places. It is clear, however, that many more of these changes have occurred in the continental languages, especially Danish, than in Faroese and Icelandic which have undergone fewer changes and thus preserved more of the structure of Old Norse than their continental counterparts.

This contrast between conservative and innovating periods (see Dixon 1997), and between conservative and innovating varieties, is very well-known, but it has not been a simple matter to come up with clear analytical, as opposed to intuitive, explanations for why it should exist. Happily, we now have explanations arising out of the pioneering work of Milroy and Milroy (1985), and Milroy (1992). The answers lie in social network structure; the point is that dense network ties lead to closer maintenance of community norms, and loose ones to lack of maintenance. The Milroys' brilliant and surely correct claim is that "linguistic change is slow to the extent that the relevant populations are well established and bound by strong ties whereas it is rapid to the extent that weak ties exist in populations".

We see now how this works. Ties have to do with contact, which is why lack of contact favors lack of change: Icelandic and Faroese have been much more geographically isolated than the continental languages. Weak ties have to do with lack of social stability: societal breakdown, such as that caused by the Anglo-Saxon invasions of Britain – sixth-century Britain was a socially very unstable place indeed – accelerates change. Strong ties, which inhibit change, are more typical of dense social networks, which are in turn more common in small, stable communities: Faroese and Icelandic have always been spoken by small communities of speakers (there are today approximately 45,000 Faroese speakers and 250,000 Icelandic-speakers as opposed to 4.5 million Norwegians, 5 million Danes and 8.5 million Swedes).

In what follows, I explore these two features of human societies – contact, and social network structure and stability – in the expectation that what has proved relevant for an understanding of the speed of linguistic change may also prove relevant to the study of the type of linguistic change, and thus type of linguistic structure, also. First, I will consider that the degree of contact one language community has with another may have two different types of implication for linguistic structure. One is the increased complexification that may occur in languages as a result of borrowing, in situations of long-term contact involving child-language bilingualism. The other is the reverse type of process in which increased simplification may occur in languages as a result of pidginization, in those situations involving adult and therefore imperfect language acquisition on the part of speakers who have passed the critical threshold (Lenneberg 1967).

Second, I will consider that society size, network structure, and stability may also have two different types of implication for linguistic structure. One is that members of small, stable, tightly-knit societies are likely to share more information than members of larger, more dynamic loosely-knit communities. The other is that dense multiplex networks may lead to greater conformity in linguistic behavior, and to the stricter maintenance of group norms, since tightly-knit communities are more able to enforce continued adherence to such norms.

1   Contact, Complexification and Redundancy

1.1   *Phonological inventories*

Haudricourt (1961) addresses the issue of the relationship between societal type and size of phonological inventories (see Trudgill, 1998). He points out that the languages of the Caucasus are famous for their enormous phoneme inventories (citing Ubykh, which had 78 consonants). He argues that this language was spoken by a smaller population in a smaller area than related languages with smaller inventories. He also points to North America, where East Coast Amerindian languages have fewer than 20 consonants (e.g. Oneida with 10), while the further west one goes, the bigger the inventories get, *and* the more languages there were per square mile. Is this, he asks, just a coincidence? Given that languages generally both lose and develop new phonemes, how do we explain this relationship between geographical language density and phoneme inventories?

Nichols has an answer. She writes (1992: 193): "It can be concluded that contact among languages fosters complexity, or, put differently, diversity among neighbouring languages fosters complexity in each of the languages." The contact of course will have to be of a very particular type, namely long-term contact situations involving childhood – and therefore proficient – bilingualism. Large inventories will be favored by stable contact situations because the long-term presence of many neighboring languages means that segments can readily be borrowed from one language to another, thus leading to increased inventories, such as the well-known borrowing of velaric-ingressive stops by some Bantu languages from the Khoi-San languages in southern Africa.

1.2   *Syntagmatic redundancy*

Since languages can operate with very much smaller phoneme inventories than Ubykh, we have to suppose that such large inventories represent a considerable degree of paradigmatic redundancy. Another example of long-term contact leading to increased redundancy, though of a different sort, is suggested by Joseph (1983). One of the well-known features of the Balkan linguistic area is the loss of the infinitive in Greek, Macedonian, Bulgarian, Albanian, Rumanian, and certain dialects of Serbian. It is widely agreed that it was language contact which led to the spread of this feature; indeed, linguistic areas of the well-known Balkan *Sprachraum* type are obviously the result of contact-driven diffusion from one language to another of large numbers of features over a long period of time. However, more interestingly for our purposes, Joseph argues that contact is not only the cause of the spread of this feature but also of its origin. He points out that the use of forms such as Greek

thelo na grapso "I want that I write"

where the first-person singular present is marked on both verbs in the construction is easier for non-native hearers to process than forms such as English

I want to write

where the same information is given only once. He argues that the Balkan-wide loss of the infinitive arose and spread in part because of sensitivity on the part of native speakers in contact situations to the comprehension difficulties of nonnative listeners. We will see below how the learning difficulties of adult speakers in contact situations can lead to simplification (including loss of redundancy). Here we observe that, in the other type of contact situation, involving long-term, stable contact and child bilingualism, the needs of the nonnative as listener may also have the opposite effect, namely the growth of syntagmatic redundancy.

2 Contact and Simplification

2.1 *Morphological simplification*

We have compared Faroese to the continental Scandinavian languages and seen that Faroese can quite legitimately be called more "conservative" than the continental languages in that it has undergone fewer changes than Norwegian, Danish, or Swedish. It is also of interest, however, that changes in the different Scandinavian languages over the last thousand years have led to a clear typological split between the insular and the continental languages at the level of morphology. Consider the contrast between the verbal morphology of Faroese and Norwegian Bokmål. Two examples will suffice:

"to throw"			
Norwegian		Faroese	
kaster	pres.	*kasti*	pres. sing. 1
kastet	past; past part.	*kastar*	pres. sing. 2,3
		kasta	pres. pl.
		kastaði	past sing.
		kastaðu	past pl.

There are five forms in Faroese (Lockwood 1955) corresponding to the two of Norwegian. More dramatic is the contrast in adjectival morphology:

"narrow"			
Norwegian		Faroese	
smal	sing. masc./fem.	*smalan*	masc. acc. sing.
smale	pl./weak	*smalar*	acc. pl.
smalt	neut. sing.	*smalt*	neut. nom./acc. sing.
		smala	fem. acc., weak masc. acc./dat. sing., weak fem. nom. sing., neut. nom/acc. sing.
		smalari	fem. dat. sing.
		smali	weak masc. nom. sing.
		smalir	masc. nom. pl.
		smalur	masc. nom. sing.
		smøl	fem. nom. sing., neut. nom./acc. pl.
		smølu	weak fem. acc. sing., weak fem. acc./dat. pl.
		smølum	masc./neut. dat. sing., dat. pl.

The contrast is very striking. This adjective has three forms in Norwegian, but two stems and eleven different forms in Faroese. Compared to Faroese, we can surely say that Norwegian has undergone considerable loss of morphological complexity.

If we acknowledge that Faroese has been a relatively isolated language over the last millennium, we can hypothesize that contact has played an important role in the developments in continental Scandinavian. Adult language and dialect contact, because of the diminished language-learning abilities of speakers who have passed the critical threshold, favor pidginization. (Notice that pidginization is a process which occurs wherever adult language acquisition takes place, and only in very exceptional circumstances leads to the development of a pidgin language.) One of the major components of pidginization (see Trudgill 1996b) is simplification; and loss of complexity on this scale can surely be described as simplification. Another of the major features of pidginization, seen at its most extreme of course in pidgin languages themselves, is the favoring of analytic over synthetic structures. Loss of morphology, as illustrated above in the case of Norwegian, often entails replacement of synthetic by analytical constructions involving, for example, pronouns to indicate person on verbs, and prepositions to indicate nominal case. (Note, however, that unlike the case of the Balkan infinitive, the growth of analyticity in pidginization is not accompanied by any growth in syntagmatic redundancy.) Many other examples could be given from the history of European and other languages. Analyticity is undoubtedly a feature which facilitates processing on the part of imperfect adult learners. It also of course has the effect of reducing memory load on the acquiring adult, a factor we shall have cause to return to shortly.

2.2 Fast speech processes (1)

It has not been very usual in linguistics to discuss in print whether some languages or dialects employ more fast speech phenomena than others, but it is at least possible that this is so (see further below). If so, then contact may play a role in this differential availability of fast speech processes. These processes of course make speech easier for the native speaker; the same message can be communicated more quickly and with less articulatory effort. However, they also make the task of the nonnative speaker in decoding and comprehending more difficult by reducing the amount of phonetic material available for processing. I would further suggest that, perhaps more surprisingly, they may also make the task of the nonnative more difficult *as a speaker*. Consider a low-level phonetic rule of lower-working-class Norwich English (Trudgill 1974), illustrated below converting /nð/ to /l/ in the pronunciation of *there* as [lɛ]:

[nʌ̈ ə ɪʔ bdæ lɛ læiʔlɪi]   *No, I in't been down there lately*

The rule /Vn/##/ð/ → /V/##/l/ is not obviously motivated by universal or natural factors. It is variety-specific. Such rules constitute extra material for the adult learner in contact situations to acquire, remember, and implement (see Trudgill 1996a). It is therefore quite possible that low-contact varieties are likely to demonstrate more fast-speech phenomena than high-contact varieties with a history of adult second-dialect or second-language acquisition. In so far as these processes may become generalized (see below) to slower forms of speech through linguistic change, then we would expect this to occur more often in low-contact than in high-contact varieties. This is certainly true of high-contact pidgins, which have little or no stylistic variation in phonology.

2.3   Phonological inventories (2)

We saw above that large phonological inventories may be the result of borrowing. But what of small inventories? These might also result from relatively mechanical factors associated with language contact. In this case, however, it would have to involve, once again, adult language contact and acquisition. The point is, as we have just seen, that simplification, both in language contact and in dialect contact situations (see Chambers 1995: 160), is brought about by the imperfect language learning of adults and post-adolescents. Simplification may very well lead to loss of phonological contrast: the smaller the inventory, the easier it is to learn, which is why the most extreme products of pidginization, pidgin languages themselves, tend to have small phoneme inventories. Labov (1994) has also maintained that in dialect contact situations mergers tend to spread at the expense of contrasts. Isolated dialects are thus those which are likely to resist mergers most strongly (and thus have larger phonological inventories). Many examples of this could be given. For example, ME o: and ou which have for centuries been merged in most varieties of English, including RP and the central dialects of England, remain distinct as in moan and mown in peripheral East Anglia and South Wales. Similarly, the distinction between /ʍ/ and /w/ has been lost in nearly all of England, and in the RP accent, but still survives as in witch versus which on the periphery in northeastern England and in Scotland. Obviously, other things being equal, mergers also lead to smaller inventories.

2.4   Word length

One would suppose on mathematical grounds that there might be a connection between phonological inventories and word length. Surely, the smaller the number of available syllables, the longer words will have to be? Maddieson (1984) has shown in fact that there is, perhaps surprisingly, no necessary connection at all between phoneme inventory size and word length. Languages nevertheless do differ enormously in the average length of even monomorphemic words. In Trudgill (1996a), for instance, I showed that in the first 50 items on the Swadesh word list, Modern Greek basic vocabulary items are much longer than the corresponding English items. This cannot altogether be explained by phonotactic restrictions on syllable-final consonants in Greek, and not at all by case-endings or the like. Standard Modern Greek, in these 50 words, has an average of 2.06 syllables per word, 81 percent more syllables than the same items in English, which have 1.14 syllables, as exemplified in, for instance, *knee* versus *ghonato; big* versus *meghalo*; and *head* versus *kefali*. In terms of segments, too, there is a remarkable difference: English has 3.06 vowels and consonants per word, while Greek has 4.58, an increase of around 50 percent.

I have already referred to the imperfect language-learning of adults as an important factor in certain sorts of developments typical of contact situations. One of the biggest problems for adult language learners is surely memory load. The less there is to remember, the easier language acquisition is. This is particularly true of the acquisition of lexis, which is one of the reasons why pidgins have small vocabularies. Memory-load, though it is much less likely to be a factor in most aspects of the acquisition of phonology, is relevant, at the interface of phonology and lexis, to the quasi-phonological feature of word-length, in terms of syllables and/or segments. The longer a word is, the more difficult it will be, other things being equal, to remember. It is interesting to note, therefore, that there are dialects of Greek in which word length is greatly reduced in comparison to Standard Modern Greek. In the north of mainland Greece, the same 50 words have an average length much closer to English, namely 1.76 syllables. This is accounted for by a phonological change in these dialects in which unstressed /i/ and /u/ have been lost. We may observe, moreover, that northern Greece is precisely the area of the country which has been most exposed to language contact with Albanian, Slavic, Arumanian, and Turkish.

2.5   Allophonic invariance

Jim Milroy (1982) showed that in Belfast English there is a remarkable difference between middle-class and working-class accents in terms of allophonic complexity. In just one example, the TRAP vowel is consistently realized as [a] in middle-class speech, whereas in working-class speech it has a wide range of allophones (see below). Milroy suggests that lack of variance in the middle-class variety is typical of standardized varieties; standardization imposes invariance and standard varieties of languages are therefore more likely to show allophonic invariance than vernacular varieties (see also Chambers 1995: 241). I would like to look at middle-class Belfast English from a different perspective, however. I want to argue that it may not be standardization itself which imposes allophonic invariance but rather contact, in the form of koineization (see Trudgill 1986). Contact between adult speakers of different languages – speakers who have passed the critical threshold – is well-known to lead to pidginization, and one essential component of pidginization is simplification (see Trudgill 1996b). The point is that simplification, which occurs both in language contact and in dialect contact situations, is brought about by the imperfect language learning of adults and post-adolescents. Two of the most important components of simplification are regularization and loss of redundancy, and loss of allophonic complexity can be regarded as simplification on both counts. It may not, therefore, be the "standardization" of the Belfast middle-class norm that has led to its invariance but its status as a koine – a city-wide variety which has arisen out of dialect leveling between various forms of northern Irish and British English. This also fits in with observations by other writers. For instance, Jakobson (1929) suggested that the geographically more widely used varieties of a language, particularly prestige varieties which, I would argue, tend to be most heavily koineized, tend to have simpler phonological systems than dialects with a more restricted function.

3   Community Size and Information

3.1   *Fast speech processes (2)*

There is some reason, as we have noted, to believe that fast speech phenomena might be more common in some types of society than others. Contact may not be the only explanation for this. Martinet (1962) argued that in spoken communication a dynamic equilibrium exists between the needs of the speaker to speak quickly and easily, on the one hand, and the needs of the listener to comprehend what is being said, on the other. This equilibrium, in other words, is usually conceived of as balancing the hearer's need to understand as effortlessly as possible against the speaker's need or desire to speak as effortlessly as possible. Dressler (1984) has similarly pointed out that phonological processes are concerned with pronounceability and perceptibility but that "the goals of better perception and better articulation often conflict with one another."

Anecdotal evidence supports the view that some, often nonstandard, varieties are harder to learn to understand than others for precisely this sort of reason. In the context of this dynamic equilibrium, an insight of Bernstein's suggests why this might be so. Bernstein, in his work in the 1970s, made a crucial and interesting observation: that people who spend most of their lives in relatively small social circles, who are part of relatively tight social networks, and who are used to communicating mainly with people with whom they share considerable amounts of background information, will tend to talk in what he (1971) called "restricted code," this term implying, amongst other more controversial things, that they would take shared information for granted, even, perhaps, when this was not appropriate. On the other hand, those who moved in wider social circles and were more used to communicating with people they did not know well would be more likely to talk in "elaborated code," a term which implies the surely accurate observation that they would be more likely to supply background information to those without it.

It is interesting to suppose that this insight concerning background information could be extended to other linguistic levels. Just as less information, generally, needs to be imparted in small non-fluid communities with large amounts of shared background information than in larger, more fluid ones, I would argue that less phonetic information, in particular, is also necessary for successful communication in these small communities. Fast speech processes, obviously, reduce the amount of phonetic information available. In smaller communities, therefore, the dynamic equilibrium might be weighted somewhat in favour of the needs of the speaker, since the listener more often than in other communities may already have a good idea of what is going to be said, and fast speech phenomena might therefore as a consequence be more common.

Dressler and Wodak (1982), on the subject of the dynamic equilibrium, have further argued that formal speech situations are typically those where the needs of the speaker are subordinated to the needs of the hearer, while in casual situations the balance is tipped in the other direction. I would suggest (and Dressler, personal communication, agrees) that it is very probable that some societies and some social groups are more characterized by the occurrence of formal situations than others. If this is true, then we can suppose that the balance between the needs of the speaker and hearer will not necessarily be constant between one society and another. The balance may be swayed in one direction or another by the extent to which a society favors or disfavors formal situations, and fast speech phenomena are more likely to be prevalent in communities which do not favor formal situations.

In support of this thesis, we can cite the fact that Trudgill (1974) showed that the speech of the Norwich lower-working-class, a relatively isolated social group, was characterized by more phonetic reduction processes – one of them illustrated above – than upper-working-class speech. The Norwich research revealed examples of extreme phonological reduction in lower-working-class speech which were simply not found amongst other social groups.

3.2   Fast speech and linguistic change

The differential availability of fast speech phenomena in different types of speech community may also have implications, as mentioned briefly above, for linguistic change. One of the developments that occurs in linguistic change is that fast-speech phenomena become institutionalized; they may eventually become slow speech phenomena as well. According to Dressler (1984: 34): "a typical scenario of diachronic change consists in the generalisation of assimilatory processes which are first limited to casual speech into more and more formal speech situations until they become obligatory processes." The community size and network factor will undoubtedly also be relevant. That is, following our argumentation above, the institutionalization of fast speech phenomena into slow speech phenomena might be more typical of small tightly-knit communities where everybody knows everybody else and where there is a large fund of shared information – and fewer formal situations.

It is not impossible, for example, that the enormously greater degree of phonetic erosion that has taken place in French as opposed to, say, Italian, can at least partly be explained in this way. It may well be that the contrast between Latin /hominem/ > Italian /uomo/, > French *homme* /om/; Latin /augustum/ > Italian /agosto/, > French *août* /u/; Latin /unum/ > Italian /uno/, > French *un* /œ̃/ can be ascribed partly to the degree to which French had no formal role, under a Germanic-speaking Frankish aristocracy, until relatively late in its development.

3.3 *Grammaticalization*

The relative prevalence or absence of fast speech phenomena might have repercussions at other linguistic levels also. In Trudgill (1995) I argued that certain types of grammaticalization process might be more common in some types of community than others. The degree to which grammaticalization is the result of pragmatic, cognitive, discourse, semantic, syntactic, and/or phonological processes is very much an open question. To the extent that phonetics and phonology may be involved, however, I would suggest that grammaticalization may be a more frequent process in those communities which favor fast speech phenomena than in those which do not. I suggest, for example, that the rather remarkable development in East Anglian traditional dialects of a whole series of nouns, verbs, adverbs, and adjuncts into conjunctions represents a more widespread and rapid process than might be expected in more widely-spoken varieties. This is precisely because grammaticalization has occurred as a result of – or at least accompanied by – the phonological reduction involved in fast speech processes, with eventual deletion of lexical material.

For example, *more* is used in traditional East Anglian rural dialects as a conjunction equivalent to Standard English *neither* as a result of contraction from an original *no more:*

> *The fruit and vegetables weren't as big as last year, more weren't the taters and onions*

Similarly, *time* has become a conjunction equivalent to Standard English *while* as a result of the phonological deletion of lexical material such as *during the*:

> *Go you and have a good wash and a change, time I get tea ready*

Similarly, *do* has become a conjunction equivalent to *otherwise* as a result of the deletion of material such as *because if* [Pronoun]:

Don't you sleep there, do you'll be laughing on the wrong side of your face

The argument here is not, obviously, that such processes occur only in village dialects. Rather, the proposal is that the large number of (in this case) conjunctions which have developed in this way in rural East Anglia suggests that grammaticalization processes which are due ultimately to phonological reduction and deletion may be more common in small, tightly-knit communities with relatively few outside contacts, i.e. the same sorts of communities which particularly favor fast speech phenomena.

3.4   *Phonological inventories (2)*

We have seen that long-term contact involving child bilingualism may produce large inventories through borrowing; and adult language contact produces smaller inventories through simplification. Unfortunately, however, this cannot be the only explanation for small inventories, because we also find some well-known cases of small isolated languages with small inventories. One example which is often cited is that of Hawai'ian. It is worth looking at the history of the Hawai'ian consonantal inventory, in particular, in some historical depth, since it does seem to show an inexorable movement over the centuries in a minimalist direction. Hawai'ian is a member of the Polynesian sub-family of the Oceanic sub-family of the Malayo-Polynesian sub-family of the Austronesian language family. Proto-Austronesian (see Dutton 1992), which was spoken around 4000 BC and perhaps on the mainland of southeast Asia, had a phoneme inventory including 23 consonants:

```
m    n                         ŋ
p    t                         k      q      ʔ
b    d        ɖ      ɟ         g
     ts
     dz
     s               ʃ                        h
     z
     l        ɭ
     r                                ʁ
```

Proto-Oceanic, which was spoken about 2500 BC and probably in the area of the western Pacific, had a consonant system with 18 members:

```
m    n    ɲ    ŋ
p    t    c    k    q
b    d    ɟ    g
     s
w    r    j              ʁ
```

In Proto-Polynesian, whose separate identity has to postdate the settlement of Tonga and Samoa at around 1000 BC, the consonant system was already rather reduced as compared to that of Proto-Austronesian and Proto-Oceanic. It had (see Clark 1976) a consonant inventory of 13 consonants:

```
m    n    ŋ
p    t    k    ʔ
f    s         h
v
     l
     r
```

This was somewhat reduced in Proto-Nuclear Polynesian (the ancestor of all modern Polynesian language groups except Tongic) by the loss of /h/, and the merger of /r/ with /l/, giving a system of 11 consonants. In Proto-Central Eastern Polynesian, which postdates the eastward expansion of the Polynesian peoples into the more remote areas of the Pacific, which in latest research is now believed to have begun around 200 BC, this was further reduced to 10 consonants, as a result of the loss of /ʔ/. This is already a very minimal consonant system, especially bearing in mind that there were only five vowels. Then, however, and remarkably, Hawai'ian, whose separation from the other eastern Polynesian languages obviously postdates the settlement of Hawaii from the Society Islands around 500 AD or later (see Sutton 1994), reduced the consonant system even further by merging /f/ and /s/ as /h/, and merging /ŋ/ with /n/. In addition to this, /k/ became /ʔ/ and /t/ changed to /k/:

```
m    n
p         k    ʔ
               h
v
     l
```

Hawai'ian thus has only eight consonants and, according to Maddieson (1984), a total of only 162 possible different syllables. The question we can then ask is this: is it just a coincidence that the gradual centuries-long but dramatic and pioneering dispersal of the ancestors of the modern Polynesian Hawai'ians from mainland Asia into more and more remote areas of the hitherto uninhabited Pacific Ocean was accompanied by an equally gradual but no less dramatic reduction in the size of the phonological inventories of the languages spoken by these people?

Haudricourt (1961) attempts an explanation. Small inventories, he says, are the result of:

> "impoverishment," which occurs in situations characterized by monolingualism and isolation (the opposite of the situation obtaining in the Caucasus) – and/or by "non-egalitarian bilingualism." Haudricourt suggests that in certain situations

the superiority of a dominant group in a diglossic bilingual environment may be "so obvious they no longer have any need to articulate well to be understood – they may confuse two different phonemes or no longer pronounce one – no one will dare to mock them. This is why we find fewer consonants in the language of the Iroquois who terrorised their neighbours, or in the languages of the people of Tahiti and Hawai'i who combine island isolation with significant demographic development as compared to other less favoured archipelagos." (Haudricourt 1961: 10, my translation).

This is not an especially happy thesis, but it does perhaps contain the germs of an explanation. Maddieson (1984) argues that there is no actual evidence that languages such as Hawai'ian show signs that they "suffer from problems due to lack of contrastive possibilities". Let us suppose, however, that a small number of available syllables, and therefore a relatively small amount of re-dundancy may, other things being equal, lead to greater communicative difficulty. If this is so, then we should probably turn away in this case from high vs. low contact as explanatory factors. (In fact, it is actually important to point out that Eastern Polynesian cultures are not now thought to have been so isolated from one another as ethnocentric Europeans unused to immensely long ocean canoe voyages might suppose (see Sutton 1994).) We should probably turn instead to our other major factor, community size and structure, as being the most important. My argument here is identical to one used above in connection with fast speech phenomena. The chain of inference in the development of the Hawai'ian phonological system, whose small size might in other types of society have led to communicative difficulties, is as follows: initial small community size (the number of people who could arrive on a relatively small number of relatively small boats) would have led in turn to tight social networks, which would have implied large amounts of shared background information – a situation in which communication with a relatively low level of phonological redundancy would have been relatively tolerable.

3.5   Deixis

Nearly all European languages have lost the dual number in the last 2,000 years or so. Some, like English, lost it long ago. Others, like Polish, lost it much more recently. Yet others still retain it. One striking thing about this development is that this loss has gone hand in hand with demographic expansion. This may be just a coincidence, but it is noticeable that those European languages which have retained the dual number are spoken by relatively small numbers of speakers, such as Slovenian, or by very small numbers of speakers, such as Sami. There are grounds for at least considering the proposition that the larger the community, the less likely dual number is to be retained. Why this might be is not easy to say, but some clues may become available from a consideration of "cultural complexity."

Linguists are naturally sceptical about relating linguistic and cultural complexity. As Bickerton (1996) says, "if there were any link between cultural complexity and linguistic complexity, we would expect to find that the most complex societies had the most complex languages while simpler societies had simpler languages . . . We do not find any such thing." It does depend, of course, on what exactly we mean by complexity. Interestingly, though, I would like to point out that there is some information in the literature which could be interpreted as suggesting that there *is* a relationship but that it is the other way round: some aspects of linguistic complexity, or at least irregularity, may be more evident in simpler than in more complex societies.

Some suggestive work which bears on this point has been carried out by Perkins (1980). He investigates certain aspects of linguistic complexity, concentrating on deixis generally. He takes as the starting point for his research a suggestion by Keenan (1976) that deictic systems are better developed in non-literate communities with fewer than 4,000 speakers. In this work we can witness observations being made by linguists which remind us of the points made by Bernstein, cited above, and which also seem to be in agreement with my own suggestions concerning, for example, fast-speech phenomena. Kay (1976), for instance, says that "in small, homogeneous speech communities there is a maximum of shared background between speakers, which is the stuff on which deixis depends. As society evolves toward complexity and the speech community becomes less homogeneous, speakers share less background information, and so one would need to build more of the message into what was actually said." Givón (1979), too, observes that people in more complex cultures are more frequently required to interact with other people who they do not know.

Perkins' (1980) argument is that "deictics identify referents by connecting them to the spatial–temporal axis of speech events". Deictics in his terms include persons, tenses, demonstratives, directionals (*here, there*), inclusive vs. exclusive etc. The point about deictics, he argues, is that they "involve the requirement that the spatio-temporal context of their use be available for the interpretation of the intended referents." Perkins thus conjectures that deictics will be more salient in less complex than in more complex cultures, and are therefore more likely to appear in the central inflectional systems of the languages concerned than more peripherally in the lexis or periphrastically. This is in turn because the more frequently free deictic morphemes occur, the more likely they are to be subject to grammaticalization processes which turn them into bound morphemes through coalescence and morphologization.

Perkins investigated 50 languages and their usage of seven deictic affixes: tense, person on verb, person on nouns, spatial demonstratives on verbs, spatial demonstratives on nouns, inclusive vs. exclusive on person markers, and dual in person markers. Communities are ranged for cultural complexity from 1 (e.g. Andamanese) to 5 (e.g. Vietnamese). The measurement of cultural complexity that Perkins uses is based on the work of anthropologists such as Carneiro (1973) and computed in terms of factors such as type of agriculture, settlement size in terms of population, craft specialization, and numbers of levels in political and social hierarchies.

Perkins shows statistically that there is a correlation between complexity and the presence of deictic affixes. For example, languages associated with the most complex cultures – those scoring 5 – have on average 1.22 deictic affixes, while those scoring 1, the lowest, have on average 3.28. Perkins concludes "deictic affixes . . . are lost as cultures become complex." Our guess about the loss of the dual number, above, is confirmed.

Most linguists are likely to feel a little uncomfortable about the notion of cultural complexity. I am therefore happy, at least for the time being, to leave this issue to the anthropologists, and to point out that we probably do not need to look any further, for our own linguistic purposes, than actual community size. As I suggested above in connection with fast speech processes, what is probably crucial here is simply how many individuals are involved in a particular speech community, and how much shared information is available.

4   Social Networks and Conformity

4.1   Allophonic complexity

We noted above Milroy's (1982) observation that in Belfast English there is a difference between middle-class and working-class accents in allophonic complexity. As we saw, the TRAP vowel is realized only as [a] in middle-class speech. In working-class speech, however, this vowel has allophones in different phonological contexts which cover an astonishing range from [ɛ] through [æ], [a] and [ɑ] to [ɒ]. Interestingly and crucially, moreover, front [ɛ] occurs before back (velar) consonants, while back [ɒ] occurs before front (alveolar) nasals, so that we are clearly once again, as with the Norwich fast speech rule, dealing with dialect-specific rather than universal assimilatory processes.

I would argue that it is not absence of standardization, as Milroy suggests, which has led to this allophonic complexity. Andersen (1988) has argued that socially peripheral communities in general are more likely to favor the proliferation of low-level pronunciation rules. We now have an explanation for this. It is the tightly-networked working-class Belfast community structure described by Milroy (1980) which sustains the allophonic complexity of the vernacular as opposed to the standard. As Grace (1990) has written:

> A language exists in the people who speak it, but people do not live very long, and the language goes on much longer. This continuity is achieved by the recruitment of new speakers, but it is not a perfect continuity. Children (or adults) learning a language learn it from people who already speak it, but these teachers exercise considerably less than total control over the learning process.
>
> (Grace 1990: 126)

There will always be limits on how far an individual can diverge linguistically from the group (Chambers 1995: 100). But my thesis is that in some communities the "teachers" may have more control over individuals than in others. Small, tightly-knit communities are more able, it seems, to encourage continued adherence to norms from one generation to another, however complex they may be, and it is therefore not unreasonable to suppose that the maintenance of allophonic complexity, just like the acquisition of non-natural fast speech rules, will be favored precisely in such communities (see Chambers 1995: 67).

4.2 Fast speech phenomena (3)

Tightly-knit networks may also be a factor in the proliferation of fast speech processes, already discussed. We saw above that some of the reduction processes investigated in lower-working-class Norwich English are not universal. Neither are they haphazard. They are the product of rules which are peculiar to the local speech community. The particular /nð/ > /l/ rule cited above, once acquired, does make production easier for speakers – there is only one segment to pronounce instead of two – but the point I would wish to make here is that its acquisition will also constitute a difficulty of learning during the child language acquisition process. The rule is complex, even if it simplifies speech production. A reasonable hypothesis, arising from the observations of Milroy and Grace, would be that the learning of complex and non-natural rules for such reduction processes is facilitated by membership of more tightly-knit social groups demonstrating close inter-generational contacts, and therefore more likely to be found in such social settings.

4.3 Non-natural sound change

Andersen (1988) discusses a series of sound changes – fortitions – which he regards as at least "slightly unusual." He points to the development of parasitic velar consonants after high or mid vowels in a number of isolated European varieties, including dialects of Provençal, Danish, German, and Flemish. In Romansch, he points out that three non-contiguous isolated high Alpine dialects of the already rather isolated Romansch language share, presumably as separate and independent developments, fortitions such as /vos/ > /voks/ 'you', and /kreʃta/ > /krekʃta/ 'crest'.

I have suggested that small isolated communities might be more able, because of their network structures, to sustain complex norms such as allophonic complexity and complex fast speech rules from one generation to another, than more loosely networked societies. This kind of consequence of tight social network structure might also have implications for aspects of linguistic change. For example, small, tightly networked communities might be able to push through, enforce, and sustain phonological changes which would have a much smaller chance of success in larger, more fluid communities. These would be phonological changes of a relatively non-natural or at least unusual type, and/ or changes that are relatively complex in some way.

There is some evidence to support this speculation (Trudgill 1996a). Faroese, as we saw above, has clearly undergone fewer changes in general than the continental Scandinavian languages. A number of the sound changes it has undergone, however, do seem to be good candidates for the labels "complex" and/or "unusual." First, it is clear from reading the works of experts in the phonological history of Faroese that they feel perplexed by its complexity. Küspert (1988: 197) writes (my translation) that "the development of vowels in stressed syllables from Old Norse to modern Faroese is clearly a complex and opaque one." Arnason (1980: 81) shares this view: "to give a simple and reliable picture of the history of Faroese vocalism is difficult, partly because the development seems to have been so complicated." Secondly, Faroese does demonstrate a series of changes involving fortitions, which many historical linguists seem to feel are perhaps less to be expected than lenitions: thus /kigv/ has developed out of earlier /kuː/ cf. modern Danish /kuː/, and /nʊdʒ/ has developed out of earlier /nyː/, cf. modern Danish /nyː/. Many other examples could be given: for instance, while mainland Greek dialects, as we saw above, are characterized by the consequences of diachronic segment deletion, fortitions are a feature of the more remote southeastern island dialects of Greek. For example, in Cypriot, the plural *matia* of *mati* "eye" is pronounced /matka/. And amongst the Polynesian languages, a number of fortitions such as the remarkable Marquesan change of /l/ to /ʔ/ (Harlow 1982) tend to arouse attention.

5   Caveat: Time Lag

5.1   *Gender*

One problematic category not dealt with by Perkins in his discussion of deixis is grammatical gender. Corbett (1991) posits a likely origin for grammatical gender in "nouns with classificatory possibilities such as 'woman', 'man', 'animal'", followed by diachronic processes involving the grammaticalization of such nouns as classifiers (see also Lee 1988). Classifiers can then in turn either come to be used anaphorically and turn into demonstratives – and subsequently pronouns and other gender markers – or they can be repeated within the noun phrase and give rise to gender agreement in that way (see also Harris and Campbell 1995: 341–2).

If grammaticalization is more common in some types of community than others, as we argued in the case of East Anglian conjunction-formation, then we might suppose that grammatical gender would be more common in smaller societies than larger. Similarly, given that deixis plays a bigger role, as we saw, in smaller communities than larger, this would give us another reason to expect to find grammatical gender more frequently in smaller than in larger languages. Obviously this is not the case. The reason for this must be that gender marking occurs with a very high degree of frequency in languages which have it, and is thus a feature with a high degree of *entrenchment* (Langacker 1987: 59). It is thus very readily maintained in the speech of individuals; and because of the language learning abilities of the human infant, even languages spoken in large communities readily maintain this complex historical baggage across generations (see Trudgill 1999). Having perhaps arisen in small tightly-knit communities, it can therefore persist for many centuries even if community size increases enormously. No doubt this will not be the only feature of which this may be true.

The correct generalization in fact seems to be that gender marking reduces or disappears only in high-contact adult-learning situations. The standard koineized forms of Swedish and Danish, for instance, have only two genders, while many non-standard dialects of these languages still have three. English and Afrikaans, the Germanic languages with the greatest history of contact, have lost grammatical gender altogether. It is also typical of creoles that they do not have it: French creoles, for example, having lost gender during pidginization, have never redeveloped it, unlike other categories, during creolization.

6 Conclusion

We have discussed three different types of community:

1 High-contact language communities where contact is stable, long-term and involves child bilingualism. In languages spoken in such communities, there may be a tendency to develop large phonological inventories through borrowing, and to develop other types of complexity and syntagmatic redundancy.
2 High-contact language communities where contact is short-term and/or involves imperfect language learning by adults. Languages spoken in such societies may tend to develop small phonological inventories through mergers, and to manifest other aspects of pidginization such as loss of morphological complexity, loss of redundancy including grammatical gender, and regularization. Linguistic change will tend to be relatively rapid.
3 Isolated low-contact language communities. Languages spoken in such communities may develop small phonological inventories as a result of the balance of the dynamic equilibrium of communication being swung heavily in favor of the speaker as opposed to the hearer. Such communities will also favor the retention of deictic and allophonic complexity. Linguistic change will be slow but will involve greater institutionalization of fast speech phenomena, a relatively high level of grammaticalization, and the greater likelihood of marked changes.

This brief survey of a small range of linguistic phenomena of different types points to the conclusion that it may well be profitable for students of linguistic variation and change to attempt to explain the distribution of at least some typological linguistic characteristics across languages sociolinguistically, that is to say in terms of certain of the social characteristics of the societies in which they are spoken, of which community size, social network structure, and amount of shared information available may turn out to be only some of the most important.

ACKNOWLEDGMENTS

I am very grateful for their comments and information to Sasha Aikhenvald, Kurt Braunmüller, George Grace, Jan Terje Faarlund, Malgorzata Fabiszak, Stephane Goyette, Robert Orr, Andy Pawley, and Natalie Schilling-Estes.

REFERENCES

Andersen, Henning (1988). Center and periphery: adoption, diffusion and spread. In Jacek Fisiak (ed.), *Historical Dialectology: Regional and Social*. Berlin: Mouton de Gruyter. 39–84.

Arnason, Kristjan (1980). *Quantity in historical phonology*. Cambridge: Cambridge University Press.

Bernstein, Basil (1971). *Class, Codes and Control*. London: Routledge.

Bickerton, Derek (1996). *Language and Human Behaviour*. London: UCL Press.

Carneiro, R. (1973). Scale analysis, evolutionary sequences, and the range of cultures. In: R. Naroll and R. Cohen (eds.), *A Handbook of Method in Cultural Anthropology*. New York: Columbia University Press. 834–71.

Chambers, J. K. (1995). *Sociolinguistic Theory*. Oxford: Blackwell.

Clark, Ross (1976). *Aspects of Proto-Polynesian Syntax*. Auckland: Linguistic Society of New Zealand.

Corbett, Greville (1991). *Gender*. Cambridge: Cambridge University Press.

Dixon, R. M. W. (1997). *The Rise and Fall of Languages*. Cambridge: Cambridge University Press.

Dressler, Wolfgang U. (1984). Explaining natural phonology. *Phonology Yearbook* 1: 29–51.

Dressler, Wolfgang, and Ruth Wodak (1982). Sociophonological methods in the study of sociolinguistic variation in Viennese German. *Language in Society* 11: 339–70.

Dutton, Tom (1992). *Proto-Austronesian Dictionary*.

Givón, Talmy (1979). *On Understanding Grammar*. New York: Academic Press.

Grace, George (1990). The 'aberrant' (vs. 'exemplary') Melanesian languages. In P. Baldi (ed.), *Linguistic Change and Reconstruction Methodology*. Berlin: Mouton de Gruyter. 155–73.

Harlow, Ray (1982). Some phonological changes in Polynesian languages. In

A. Ahlqvist (ed.), *Papers from the 5th International Conference on Historical Linguistics*. Amsterdam: John Benjamins. 98–109.

Harnard, S. R. et al. (eds.) (1976). *Origins and Evolution of Language and Speech*. New York: Academy of Sciences.

Harris, Alice and Lyle Campbell (1995). *Historical Syntax in a Cross-linguistic Perspective*. Cambridge: Cambridge University Press.

Haudricourt, André (1961). Richesse en phonèmes et richesse en locateurs. *L'Homme* 1: 5–10.

Jackson, Kenneth (1953). *Language and History in Early Britain*. Edinburgh: Edinburgh University Press.

Jakobson, Roman (1929). *Remarques sur l'évolution phonologique du Russe comparée à celle des autres langues Slaves*. Travaux du Cercle Linguistique de Prague 2.

Joseph, Brian (1983). *The Synchrony and Diachrony of the Balkan Infinitive*. Cambridge: Cambridge University Press.

Kay, Paul (1976). Discussion of papers by Kiparsky and Wescott. In Harnard et al. (eds.), *Origins and Evolution of Language and Speech*. New York: Academy of Sciences. 17–19.

Keenan, E. (1976). Discussion. In Harnard et al. (eds.), *Origins of Language and Speech*. New York: Academy of Sciences. 92–6.

Küspert, Klaus-Christian (1988). *Vokalsystem in Westnordischen*. Tübingen: Niemeyer.

Labov, W. (1994). *Principles of Linguistic Change*. Oxford: Blackwell.

Langacker, Ronald W. (1987). *Foundations of Cognitive Grammar: Theoretical Prerequisites*. Stanford, CA: Stanford University Press.

Lee, Michael (1988). Language, perception and the world. In John A. Hawkins (ed.), *Explaining Language Universals*. Oxford: Blackwell. 211–46.

Lenneberg, Eric (1967). *Biological Foundations of Language*. New York: Wiley.

Levinson, Stephen (1996). Relativity in spatial orientation and description. In J. Gumperz and S. Levinson (eds.), *Rethinking Linguistic Relativity*. Cambridge: Cambridge University Press. 133–44.

Lockwood, W. B. (1955). *An Introduction to Modern Faroese*. Tórshavn: Munksgaard.

Maddieson, Ian (1984). *Patterns of Sounds*. Cambridge: Cambridge University Press.

Martinet, André (1962). *A Functional View of Language*. Oxford: Oxford University Press.

Milroy, James (1982). Probing under the tip of the iceberg: phonological normalisation and the shape of speech communities. In S. Romaine (ed.), *Sociolinguistic Variation in Speech Communities*. London: Arnold. 32–48.

Milroy, James (1992). *Linguistic Variation and Change*. Oxford: Blackwell.

Milroy, James and Lesley Milroy (1985). Linguistic change, social network and speaker innovation, *Journal of Linguistics* 21: 339–84.

Milroy, Lesley (1980). *Language and Social Networks*. Oxford: Blackwell.

Nichols, Johanna (1992). *Linguistic Diversity in Space and Time*. Chicago: University of Chicago Press.

Perkins, Revere (1980). The Covariation of Culture and Grammar. Ph.D. thesis, University of Michigan, Ann Arbor.

Sutton, D. (ed.) (1994). *The Origins of the First New Zealanders*. Auckland: Auckland University Press.

Trudgill, Peter (1974). *The Social Differentiation of English in Norwich*. Cambridge: Cambridge University Press.

Trudgill, Peter (1986). *Dialects in Contact*. Oxford: Blackwell.

Trudgill, Peter (1989a). Language contact and simplification. *Nordlyd* 15: 113–21.

Trudgill, Peter (1989b). Contact and isolation in linguistic change. In L. E. Breivik and E. H. Jahr (eds.), *Language Change: Contributions to the Study of its Causes*. Berlin: Mouton de Gruyter. 227–37.

Trudgill, Peter (1989c). Interlanguage, interdialect and typological change. In S. Gass et al. (eds.), *Variation in Second Language Acquisition: Psycholinguistic Issues*. Clevedon, Avon: Multilingual Matters. 243–53.

Trudgill, Peter (1992). Dialect typology and social structure. In E.-H. Jahr (ed.), *Language Contact and Language Change*. Berlin: Mouton de Gruyter. 195–212.

Trudgill, Peter (1995). Grammaticalisation and social structure: nonstandard conjunction-formation in East Anglian English. In F. R. Palmer (ed.), *Grammar and Meaning: Papers in Honour of Sir John Lyons*. Cambridge: Cambridge University Press. 136–47.

Trudgill, Peter (1996a). Dialect typology: isolation, social network and phonological structure. In G. Guy et al. (eds.), *Towards a Social Science of Language,* vol. 1. Amsterdam: John Benjamins. 3–21.

Trudgill, Peter (1996b). Dual-source pidgins and reverse creoloids: northern perspectives on language contact. In E.-H. Jahr and I. Broch (eds.), *Language Contact in the Arctic: Northern Pidgins and Contact Languages*. Berlin: Mouton de Gruyter. 5–14.

Trudgill, Peter (1998). Typology and sociolinguistics: linguistic structure, social structure and explanatory comparative dialectology. *Folia Linguistica* 31(3/4): 349–60.

Trudgill, Peter (1999). Language contact and the function of linguistic gender. *Poznan Studies in Contemporary Linguistics* 35: 9–28.

Wierzbicka, Anna (1986). Does language reflect culture? Evidence from Australian English. *Language in Society* 15: 349–74.

Wierzbicka, Anna (1992). *Semantics, Culture and Cognition: Universal Human Concepts in Culture-Specific Configurations*. Oxford: Oxford University Press.

28 Comparative Sociolinguistics

SALI TAGLIAMONTE

Comparison has always been at the root of sociolinguistics. The study of language behavior from a comparative perspective – comparative sociolinguistics – concerns the connection (relationship) of linguistic variation in one body of materials to another. This requires a methodology that, first, enables the many different influences on linguistic features to be disentangled through systematic examination of their behavior, and, second, that situates and explains the linguistic features through comparison with like features in related varieties. This methodology builds directly from two strands of linguistics – historical linguistics and quantitative sociolinguistics.

The comparative method in historical linguistics is based on comparative reconstruction, which has as its basis shared correspondences of linguistics features (e.g. Hoenigswald 1960, Meillet 1967). The application of these methods in sociolinguistics began with Weinreich et al.'s (1968) introduction of the notion of "structured heterogeneity" in the speech community which was later developed further by Labov (1982). This work laid the foundations of the quantitative variationist approach (Labov 1966, 1970, 1972, Labov et al. 1968) which elaborated a method of analysis founded on assumptions of accountability, testing hypotheses systematically against data, and building generalizations on well-formed comparative studies. Further, constraints on linguistic features were brought into the picture and were held to be a reflection of diachronic patterns even after centuries of geographic separation (Labov 1980: xvii).

A comparative approach had been, at least implicitly, adopted for tracking historical connections between related varieties since the turn of the century (Kurath 1928, 1964). Subsequently, it has been implicitly or explicitly adopted by numerous scholars in a wide range of applications: for making trans-Atlantic connections (Montgomery 1989a, 1989b, 1997); for contrasting data sets in real- and apparent-time (Bailey and Maynor 1985, Bailey et al. 1989, Cukor-Avila 1997, 1999); for tracing the roots of extraterritorial varieties of English (Clarke 1997a, 1997b, 1997c, Hickey forthcoming); and for isolating systems in language contact (Poplack and Meechan 1995, 1998a). More recently, a comparative element has become increasingly prevalent in dialect studies (Wolfram 1999, 2000, Wolfram and Schilling-Estes to appear, Wolfram and Sellers forthcoming, Wolfram et al. 1997).

Comparative sociolinguistic research developed initially from issues surrounding the origins and development of African-American Vernacular English (AAVE) (Holm 1975, Rickford 1986, 1991, Rickford and Blake 1990, Singler 1991). This long-term debate provides a conundrum for the comparative sociolinguistic endeavor as researchers from all areas of the field attempt to reconstruct the likely characteristics of the ancestor of AAVE.

In this chapter my goal is to demonstrate, using case studies, comparative sociolinguistic methodology as it has developed in two research programs. The first involves tracking the origins and development of African-American Vernacular English (Poplack and Tagliamonte 1999, Poplack 2000, Poplack and Tagliamonte 2001). The second involves tracking the origins of nonstandard linguistic features of North American dialects in comparable British dialects (Godfrey and Tagliamonte 1999, Jones and Tagliamonte 2000, Tagliamonte and Smith 2000, Tagliamonte 1999).

I begin by describing the methods of the comparative sociolinguistic approach to language variation and change.

1   Variationist Sociolinguistics

Quantitative variationist methodology falls within the framework of empirical linguistics known as variation theory and employs multivariate analysis to model the linguistic phenomena under investigation, a type of analysis which forms part of the "descriptive-interpretative" strand of modern linguistic research (Sankoff 1988: 142–3). Studies employing this methodology are based on the premise that the features of a given speech community, whether morphosyntactic, phonological, lexical or discursive, may vary in a systematic way, and that this behavior can be quantitatively modeled (Young and Bayley 1996: 254). The approach rests on the assumption that whenever a choice exists among two (or more) alternatives in the course of linguistic performance, and where that choice may have been influenced by any number of factors, then it is appropriate to invoke statistical techniques (Sankoff 1988: 2).

The relationship between linguistic variables and external factors such as class and gender has often been criticized because social identities are not categorical or fixed notions, but are locally situated and constructed (Schiffrin 1996: 199). However, when the goal of research is to gauge and model the individual and combinatory effects of multidimensional internal linguistic factors alongside broadly defined external factors, a quantitative approach is particularly useful. The advantage of this type of analysis lies in its ability to model subtle grammatical tendencies and regularities in the data and assess their relative strength and significance when all possible factors operating on them are treated simultaneously. The combination of factors exerting an influence on a given linguistic feature will often be extremely complex. The task for the analyst is to identify those factors which are the most meaningful for analysis and interpretation.

One of the foundations of variationist analysis is its attempt to discover not individual occurrences or overall rates of occurrence, but *patterns* of variability in the body (or bodies) of material under investigation.[1]

Practically speaking, we take the following steps.

1   Select an appropriate linguistic feature, ideally a diagnostic area of grammar:

   (i)   circumscribe the variable context;
   (ii)   code the data into factors which test hypotheses, claims and observations in the literature.

2   Examine the patterns of use of the linguistic feature according to the principle of accountability using the lines of evidence provided by statistical modeling techniques of multivariate analysis:

   (i)   Which factors are statistically significant?
   (ii)   What is the relative contribution of the linguistic features selected, i.e. which factor group is most significant (largest range) or least? (smallest range)
   (iii) What is the order (from more to less) of factors within a linguistic feature? (constraint hierarchy)
   (iv)   Does this order reflect the direction predicted by one or the other of the hypotheses being tested?

Since linguistic change proceeds as "an ordered set of shifts in the frequency of application of the rule in each environment" (Labov 1982: 75) we can expect that not only rates, but especially the conditioning of linguistic variability will be language specific. Thus, the environmental constraints (i.e. the "factors" in item 1(ii)) on variation are the fundamental units of linguistic change (Labov 1982: 75), while the constraint ranking (i.e. 2(ii)) of factors provides a critical diagnostic for comparison. In this way, similarities and differences in the significance, strength, and ordering of constraints provide a microscopic view of the grammar from which we can infer the structure (and possible interaction) of different grammars. Thus, it is through the evidence provided by the various statistical techniques outlined in B above that we can "trace the path of linguistic development through a multidimensional space." These measures enable us to infer whether the data sets under comparison share an underlying grammar, and to what extent. For example, if the constraint ranking of one (or more) factor groups is shared by a set of varieties, we infer that they have inherited it from a common source. If the constraint ranking of factors is parallel, but operates at varying strengths or patterns in different varieties this can be explained by the stage of development of the system of grammar under investigation as represented by each data set.

How are these procedures used to make comparisons and reconstruct origins? According to Poplack and Tagliamonte (1991: 318) determining the precise historical origins of a linguistic feature requires not only the existence of an apparently similar or identical feature in a putative source dialect, but also the same distribution in the language, as determined by the hierarchy of constraints conditioning its appearance. Thus, in order to determine the status of a form, it is not its current *existence* in a variety which is decisive, nor even its rates of occurrence. This is because overall rates of presence of absence of the variants under investigation will likely vary according to features of the situation (Poplack and Tagliamonte 1991: 318). However, the *distribution*, i.e. precisely where it occurs in the language, as determined by the relative frequency of the feature across its different contexts of use, is taken to represent the underlying grammatical structure.

The approach I describe here involves consistent comparison of each of the lines of evidence above but with the added triangularization of two or more relevant bodies of material to compare and/or contrast. This is where the comparative method comes in.

2 The Comparative Method

In historical linguistics it is widely held that earlier stages in the history of a language can be observed through comparative analysis of cognate forms (sets of reflexes) in later, sister varieties (e.g. Hoenigswald 1960: 119, Meillet 1967). The comparative method is "the procedure whereby morphs of two or more sister languages are matched in order to reconstruct the ancestor language" (Hoenigswald 1960: 119). In comparative sociolinguistics, the means by which the sister varieties are compared is the set of correspondences provided by the results of the statistical techniques of multivariate analysis, what Labov referred to as "finely articulated structures" (1982: 75). In fact, the quantitative paradigm provides the kind of "precise information on the states of the language" called for by Meillet (1967: 138).

We approach this by comparing the patterning of variability in each possible source. If the conditioning effects on the variable linguistic features show patterns approximating those found in a putative source, we can conclude that they represent structures drawn from that source (e.g. Poplack and Tagliamonte 1999, 2001). On the other hand, where there are dissimilarities, we have grounds for concluding that the phenomena in question belong to different linguistic systems (e.g. Tagliamonte 1998a, Tagliamonte et al. 1997).

A key notion in a comparative sociolinguistic approach is the notion "conflict site". This is defined as a form or class of forms which differs functionally and/or structurally and/or quantitatively across the varieties in question

(Poplack and Meechan 1998b: 132). By quantitatively analyzing patterns of distribution at grammatical sites where varieties are held to be distinct, the precise nature of similarities and differences across data sets can be pinpointed. If the results match the observations made in the literature for the putative source varieties, then we appeal to this similarity to posit a link between the two. On the other hand, where there are dissimilarities, we must contextualize and evaluate the differences in the context of linguistic developments in all the varieties under investigation. If the variability in the data is part of ongoing linguistic change, then it must be analyzed in terms of where it came from, consistent with Jespersen (1924) that "to understand a linguistic system, we must know how it came to be".

Thus, by utilizing the lines of evidence made available by variationist statistical techniques, we then proceed according to the following procedure:

3 Compare and contrast conditioning factors across sets of data which can be related (at least putatively) across some external set of criteria according to:

(i) statistical significance;
(ii) relative strength;
(iii) constraint hierarchy.

I now illustrate this comparative sociolinguistic approach in practice and show how it can elucidate the nature of variability through an examination of similarities and differences across varieties.

3 Target of Investigation – Sisters under the Skin?

In the analyses that follow I will examine a number of different linguistic variables (diagnostics) in up to six different data sets. These data sets represent varieties which can be differentiated on a number of broad extralinguistic characteristics, as summarized in table 28.1.[2]

The data, which consist of hundreds of hours of tape-recorded conversations, include discussions about local traditions, narratives of personal experience, group interactions, and local gossip. Moreover, the interviews in BCK, GUY, NPE, and DVN were conducted by community members. All of these materials are highly informal and as far as possible represent the typical discourse found in each community.

Aside from the samples from OTT and YRK, the speakers in each of the corpora have relatively homogeneous socioeconomic characteristics. They were born and raised in the community in question and in each case they represent the oldest living generation at the time of the fieldwork. They are usually employed in traditional or service industries. Level of education among the

Table 28.1   Extralinguistic characteristics of varieties under investigation

Locale	Abbreviation	Geographic location	Separation from mainstream	Ethnic affiliation
Buckie	BCK	Northeast Scotland	yes	British
Guysborough Enclave	GYE	Nova Scotia, Canada	yes	African
North Preston	NPR	Nova Scotia, Canada	yes	African
Ex-Slave recordings	ESR	Southern United States	yes	African
Samaná	SAM	Dominican Republic	yes	African
Devon	DVN	Southwest England	yes	British
Guysborough village	GYV	Nova Scotia, Canada	intermediate	British
Ottawa	OTT	Ontario, Canada	no	British
York	YRK	York, England	no	British

informants ranges from none to 12 years, with most speakers falling into the lower range. The speakers are similar in that they are members of "dense" networks (Milroy 1980) in that their social circles were generally confined to the community in question.

The communities are also differentiated by the ethnic ancestry of their inhabitants. In four data sets the speakers are of African descent (SAM, ESR, NPR, GYE); in the other four, the speakers are of British ancestry (GYV, BCK, DVN, OTT). Although all the African speakers represented in these data sets live in relatively isolated circumstances, the speakers of British ancestry represent a range of different backgrounds ranging from highly isolated (BCK) to mainstream/standard (OTT). Thus, we are provided with an unprecedented opportunity to conduct a cross-variety comparison in which linguistic features may be viewed across these two extralinguistic dimensions relatively independently.

Moreover, these contrasting extralinguistic characteristics along with standard accounts of the effects of language contact (Pousada and Poplack 1982, Thomason and Kaufman 1988), would lead us to expect that the more separate from mainstream culture, the higher the degree of impermeability to influence from surrounding mainstream vernaculars (see Poplack and Tagliamonte 2001). In the case of the Nova Scotian communities, these considerations, in conjunction with a standard diffusionist hypothesis, would lead us to expect that NPR should retain more local vernacular features; while GYE may show similarities with neighboring GYV. In the case of the British varieties which are situated at two extremes of dialect regions in Britain, one in the northeast (BCK) and the other in the southwest (DVN) we would expect both locales to retain local vernacular features, but that those features might be highly differentiated.

Each community differs with respect to the relative degree of exposure of residents to mainstream culture and language. OTT and YRK are clearly situated in the mainstream, while GYV, a rural village in Nova Scotia, stands in an intermediary position (see for discussion Poplack and Tagliamonte 1999). The remaining areas are rural and, in addition to geographic separation, they have all have had relatively limited contact with mainstream culture and outsiders.[3] In each, the speakers live in a remote fringe area, where they are also separated from large urban populations on additional sociocultural grounds. In these cases, each data set represents a variety which has evolved in a context of relative isolation.

These data bear many, if not all, of the characteristics of "peripheral" areas, which in historical linguistics are widely-known to provide choice evidence about earlier stages of a language (e.g. Anttila 1989: 294, Hock 1986: 442). Indeed, the two varieties from Britain can be characterized as highly conservative. Each retains features recorded in historical English, which have since become obsolescent or moribund. For example, BCK retains [f] in *wh-* words, velar fricatives, *-en* participles and adverb placement between verb and complement, while DVN retains initial voiced fricatives, pronoun exchange and *thee* as 2nd person pronoun. Many of these can be traced back to at least the Early Modern English period, with some having arisen in Old English and early Middle English supporting an interpretation of their status as peripheral.

Preservation of features from earlier stages in the history of English in these and other comparable communities are reported extensively in the sociolinguistic literature (e.g. Hazen 1996, Poplack and Tagliamonte 1989, Poplack and Tagliamonte 1994, Schilling-Estes and Wolfram 1994, Tagliamonte 1997b, Tagliamonte and Poplack 1988, Wolfram and Sellers forthcoming). Thus, these peripheral varieties can provide an interesting test site for models of language change and a critical window on the past.

In the remainder of this chapter, I present a series of analyses which consistently compare different combinations of these data sets, depending on the linguistic feature under investigation.

4 The Importance of Proportional Analysis

One of the most widely-studied areas of grammar to receive comparative investigation is variation between marked and unmarked past temporal reference weak verbs, as illustrated by variable marking on the verb *look* in (1):

(1) (a) Bunch of us walked up the stairs and sat down and Caroline *looked* up. (NPR/039/735–6) (Poplack and Tagliamonte 2001)

    (b) When I *look*Ø in like that, and I *look*Ø in that door, and I *look*Ø back in the corner, I seen them great big eye. (NPR/030/884–6) (Poplack and Tagliamonte 2001)

Table 28.2   Simple count: number of bare verbs with past temporal reference

	NPR	GYE	SAM	ESR
Number of bare verbs	127	159	518	100

Source: Meechan et al. (1996)

Table 28.3   Total verbs in past contexts

	NPR	GYE	SAM	ESR
Number of bare verbs	127	159	518	100
Total verbs in past contexts	362	534	1234	283
Percent of bare verbs (%)	35	30	42	35

Source: Meechan et al. (1996)

This is an area of the grammar which is widely-agreed to differentiate Standard English, English-based creoles, indigenized Englishes and contact vernaculars (e.g. Patrick 1999, Winford 1992, Wolfram and Hatfield 1984).

Let us examine this feature in four of the varieties whose origins can be traced to a common geographic area (the United States), but which have been separated for 150 years in widely-separated contexts in Canada (NPR and GYE), the Dominican Republic (SAM), and the Southern United States (ESR).

First, let us simply count the number of unmarked (bare stem) verbs with past temporal reference in each body of materials, as in table 28.2.

This count of the data makes it look like one variety, SAM, has considerably more zero forms than the other corpora ($n = 518$). This is, in fact, precisely what would be expected of creoles since these varieties are widely-known to have considerably less verbal affixation than other languages (e.g. Bickerton 1975). SAM is located in the Caribbean where many creoles are spoken and further, Samaná English is spoken by people of African descent. Since most creoles are spoken by people of the same ethnic affiliation, then one might be led to hypothesize that the reason SAM has many more bare verbs is because it has a more creole-like grammar than the other varieties.

However, bare numbers do not take into account the *proportion* of these verbs that occur of all relevant verbal constructions in each data set. Table 28.3 displays a distributional analysis according to the "principle of accountability" (Labov 1972: 72), in which the number of bare verbs is reported as a proportion of the total number of relevant constructions (either inflected or not).

It is now clear that the apparent differences between varieties observable in table 28.2 comes from the fact that there is a disproportionate number of bare verbs in the data. The SAM data simply had more past temporal reference contexts. The percentages show that the overall rate of bare verbs across varieties is quite similar. The exact opposite of the result indicated by table 28.2.

This illustrates a fundamental component of the comparative sociolinguistic approach. It is necessary to deal with proportions in order to compare rates consistently and accountably across data sets.

However, as we shall see, even such a calculation provides only a first step in demonstrating that the varieties in table 28.3 are patterning in the same way. In fact, this view of the data reveals very little about the mechanism, i.e. internal organization, of the variability. Thus, it provides insufficient evidence which would enable us to distinguish between contrasting grammatical systems.

5 Contrasting Constraints across Varieties

As it happens, this linguistic variable, i.e. variation in marked and unmarked verbs in past temporal reference contexts, is a good conflict site to compare varieties because the environmental constraints on its application can be expected to differentiate grammatical systems. In creole vernaculars widespread and frequent absence of inflection on past reference verbs is said to be the result of an underlying stative/nonstative distinction combined with a tense/aspect system that is relative, rather than absolute. When past time is marked, the marker is there as an *anterior* marker, to mark the relationship of states and events in the discourse to each other. Even a variety at an advanced stage of decreolization (approximating Standard English norms) may still reflect this underlying grammatical organization of past markers. In Standard English, however, all events prior to speech time are required to mark past tense. The device most frequently employed for this is the preterite, where weak verbs take a suffix, i.e. *–t,d*. However, quantitative analyses of this feature in English dialects have revealed regular phonological conditioning on these word final suffixes, such that *–t,d* may be deleted by surface level (consonant cluster) reduction processes (e.g. Guy 1980, 1991, Guy and Boyd 1990, Neu 1980, Santa Ana 1996).

Exactly which constraints are in operation in the varieties depicted in tables 28.3 and 28.4? Is it consonant cluster simplification or a distinct grammatical system involving anterior marking coupled with a stative/nonstative distinction? Whichever ones they are will have a major bearing on making a decision about the underlying system (or grammar) in a given data set. Such a decision cannot be based on frequency or proportion alone. How can we decide on the nature of variability across varieties?

Let us now employ the techniques of variable rule analysis and the lines of evidence offered by statistical significance, relative strength of factors and constraint ranking of factors to consider the variation between marked and

Table 28.4   Five independent variable rule analyses of the contribution of selected factors selected as significant to the probability that weak verbs will surface as *stems*

	SAM	ESR	NPR	GYE	GYV
Corrected mean:	0.45	0.29	0.31	0.59	0.14
Total *n*:	1,236	281	360	503	282
Preceding phonological segment					
Consonant cluster	0.81	0.73	0.73	0.62	0.76
Single consonant	0.60	0.51	0.55	0.55	0.70
Vowel	0.26	0.32	0.35	0.35	0.11
Following phonological segment					
Consonant	0.58	0.65	0.68	0.72	0.81
Vowel	0.38	0.32	0.31	0.29	0.30
Factors not selected:					
Stativity/anteriority	X	X	X	X	X

Source: Adapted from Poplack and Tagliamonte (2001)

unmarked verbs in table 28.4. Further to the comparison in tables 28.2 and 28.3, a critical comparative component is added – data from GYV, the variety of English spoken by the descendants of British loyalists in Guysborough, Nova Scotia (GYV), the closest village to GYE. This provides a sample which can be expected to embody conservative English patterns, a critical control for the other four varieties which involve isolated conditions and speakers of African descent.

Table 28.4 (and all tables in ensuing sections) presents all the information necessary for interpreting the variable rule analyses that have been performed on each data set. The *corrected mean* at the top of the tables indicates the overall tendency of the dependent variable (in this case the verb stem) to surface in the data. The *total n* records the denominator of the total number of contexts treated in the analysis. Each of the factor groups that have been considered in the analysis are listed with the results for each factor. Point-form numbers are *factor weights*. These indicate the probability of the dependent variable to occur in that context. The closer these numbers are to 1, the more highly favoring the effect is; the closer they are to zero the more disfavoring the effect is. The *range* indicates the relative strength of the factor. The higher this number is, the greater the contribution of that factor to the probability of the form.

We can now see that all five varieties behave near identically. Despite the varying corrected mean values which range from .14 in GYV, to .59 in GYE, the same phonological factors are chosen as significant and condition the variability in the same way. In each case the ranking of more to less is parallel. *Preceding phonological segment* consonant clusters are the most highly favorable environment for stem verbs, then single consonants, while vowels disfavor. *Following phonological segment* consonants favor stem verbs but vowels disfavor. On the other hand the major factor relevant to creoles (stativity/anteriority) was not even selected as significant.

These results provide substantial evidence to conclude that the zero-forms on weak past temporal reference verbs in all these communities are the result of surface level phonological reduction processes, rather than the underlying functional distinctions of stativity and anteriority. Is this enough evidence to give a decisive answer to the question of the underlying system, i.e. what grammar underlies these varieties and what their source may have been?

The problem is that phonological constraints such as these which involve consonant cluster simplification of *–t/d* may be the result of universal phonotactic principles of grammar. If so, they can tell us little about the origin of these varieties. This highlights the fact that all linguistic features do not provide the same calibre of evidence for cross-variety comparison. Many so-called conflict sites are actually not *conflict* sites at all, since the same surface forms may appear across varieties that have no filial relationship. In other words, the constraints operating on the variation may be irrelevant to the issues of origins and system identification.

Let us now consider a linguistic feature whose variable *forms* appear globally, but for which examination of the historical record reveals distinctive patterning which can be traced to different source dialects in Britain. This obviates the possibility that the patterns in the data would have arisen independently.

6 Using Constraint Hierarchies to Disentangle Source Dialects

"Vernacular features" which appear robustly in dialects of English all over the world (Chambers 1995: 242–9), such as *was/were* variation in example (2), are particularly useful for the comparative sociolinguistic endeavor. The inter-variety parallelism in form permits consistent analysis of variable constraints which operate on their distribution and conditioning.

(2) (a) We *were* all thegither ... I think we *was* all thegither. (BCK/h:72.44)
         (Smith and Tagliamonte 1998)
    (b) He *was* lost all night once, and when he come back he *were* covered in dung. (DVN/001/56,43) (Jones and Tagliamonte 2000)
    (c) There *was* a lot of us that *were* sort of seventeen. (004/180,27)
         (Tagliamonte 1998b: 155)
    (d) It *weren't* us with the funny accent; it *was* them. (Schilling-Estes and Wolfram 1994: 298)

One explanation for *was/were* variation is that it is the result of "regularization" processes in language (Fries 1940). This is based on the idea that the verb *to be* is gradually becoming more like the other more regular verbs in English in having the same form, i.e. *was*, throughout the verbal paradigm, rather than the more complex distinction between 1st and 3rd person singular *was*, and 2nd person singular and 1st, 2nd, and 3rd person plural *were*.

However, the question that arises is where did the synchronic variation illustrated in (2) come from in the first place? One hypothesis is the standard diffusionist explanation, in which *was/were* was carried to these locations by people speaking varieties which contained the same features (Weinreich et al. 1968). Another hypothesis suggests that it is the result of a more general tendency in all nonstandard varieties of English to gravitate toward more primitive (i.e. not learned) linguistic patterns (Chambers 1995: 247). Still other hypotheses argue that *was/were* variation in some varieties is the result of innovative restructuring. For example in some dialects in the United States it has become differentiated according to polarity, with *was* used for positive contexts and *weren't* used for negative contexts, as in (2d) (Schilling-Estes and Wolfram 1994, Wolfram and Sellers forthcoming).

What is a viable way to evaluate these explanations? First, early research on this variability revealed that *was/were* variation occurred robustly in English vernaculars all over the world. However, as demonstrated in tables 28.2 and 28.3, overall distributions alone do not provide sufficient evidence to evaluate the mechanism that produces the variation from the underlying grammar. Second, *was/were* variation is the result of longitundinal linguistic variation and change in the English language as well. Thus, examination of the historical background is imperative in order to contextualize the synchronic situation. Moreover, detailed analysis modeling the internal grammatical constraints operating on the variation can reveal the extent and nature of the spread through linguistic structure (Labov 1982: 75). Again, comparative sociolinguistic analysis provides a means to disentangle these different hypotheses as well as, and perhaps more importantly, a means to constrain explanations.

7   Contextualizing Variation in Diachrony

At earlier stages in the history of English in Britain, variation in the forms of preterit indicative *be* was rampant (Curme 1977, Forsström 1948, Jespersen 1954, Pyles 1964, Visser 1963–73).

Use of *was* in 1st and 3rd person contexts was uniform across regions, but in 2nd person singular it varied according to geographic location. The southern regions of England mirrored contemporary standard English norms – the preterit indicative was *were* with all the plural personal pronouns (*we, you, they*) as well as 2nd person singular (*thou*). In the north and northeast, however, *was* was employed almost exclusively with 2nd person singular, as in (3) (Forsström 1948). And this pattern continued into Early Modern English, as in (4).[4]

(3) Caym, Caym, thou *was* wode.   (The Towneley Plays c.1450: 350)
(4) For in your last ye shew me that ye *was* troubled with ane swelling of the spleen.   (Memorials of the family of Wemyss of Wemyss 1659)

Perhaps the most famous linguistic constraint on this variation, known as the Northern Subject Rule, involves a combination of the type of subject and the adjacency of the subject and verb to each other. According to Murray (1873: 211–12), "when the subject is a noun, adjective, interrogative or relative pronoun, or when the verb and subject are separated by a clause, the verb takes the termination -*s* in all persons." (see also Montgomery 1994, Tagliamonte 1999). Thus, *was* appeared after Full NPs as in (5), as opposed to plural pronouns, as in (6):

(5) The bernis both *wes* basit of the sicht.   ("King Hart", Douglas, 1475–1522)
(6) They *wer* informed that my brother William his soun, should be a ward.   (Letters on Duntreath, 1627)

While the association of *was* with 2nd person singular remained a northern feature, the tendency for plural NPs to have -*s* appears to have spread southward in the sixteenth and seventeenth centuries (see Godfrey and Tagliamonte 1999, Jones and Tagliamonte 2000).

A further constraint may be inferred from more recent studies. *Was/were* variation is sensitive to negation, but in contrasting ways depending on the dialect. Tagliamonte and Smith (2000) report a tendency for *was* to appear in negative, as opposed to affirmative, constructions in BCK, GYE, and NPR. Yet in contemporary non-mainstream varieties, both American (Schilling-Estes and Wolfram 1994) and British (Britain, forthcoming), a near categorical distinction between affirmative *was*, and negative *weren't* is reported. Indeed nonstandard use of *were* in negative contexts is reported in many British dialects (Hughes and Trudgill 1979: 63–5, Milroy and Milroy 1993).

Thus, three internal factors may be extrapolated from the literature.

1 *Was* was used almost exclusively in 2nd person singular in northern British dialects, while southern dialects used *were* (Brunner 1963, Forsström 1948, Mossé 1952).
2 *Was* occurred more often with plural NPs than pronouns. While originally a northern feature (Murray 1873), by the Early Modern English period it had spread throughout Britain (Visser 1963–73).
3 *Was* occurs in affirmative contexts; and *were* occurs in negative contexts, regardless of grammatical person in some dialects in the United States and Britain (Britain forthcoming, Schilling-Estes and Wolfram 1994).

Let us now test the data, once again using the comparative method in order to address broader questions regarding the nature of linguistic change, as well as processes of diffusion and/or innovation in time and space. The data sets available enable us to compare a number of dimensions: first, I compare two different geographic locations, North America and Britain. Second, I compare different varieties in North America according to their relative degree of participation in mainstream norms. Third, I compare according to African vs. British ancestry. Fourth, I contrast different dialect regions in Britain, north vs. south. Finally, I attempt to interpret these findings according to the putative origins of the major founding populations of the ancestors of the North American varieties, and thus in broad terms the composition of the original dialect input.

In the latter enterprise, I am abstracting away from the tremendous language and dialect contact of the early colonization period in the United States (e.g. Kurath 1928, 1949, 1964, Montgomery 1989a: 236) as well as the dialect mixture in Britain pre-dating the large scale migrations to North America in the 1700s. These, and other extralinguistic factors surely influenced the shaping of the varieties which emerged in North America in the early colonization period. However, to date there is no precise information about the nature of these factors as well as (and perhaps more importantly) any principled method for factoring their impact on linguistic structure into a quantitative analysis. Therefore, I focus on broad trends that can be inferred from migration patterns and population proportions from the historical record (e.g. Bailyn 1986, Bailyn and DeWolfe 1986) and rely on the details of the linguistic evidence for corroboration.[5]

8   Operationalizing Constraints on *was/were* Variation

First, consider the overall distribution of *was* in 2nd person singular and 1st, 2nd, and 3rd person plural in the five varieties targeted for investigation, figure 28.1. This view of the data reveals that *was/were* variation is robust across all the varieties under investigation. The relevant observation however is that the frequency of nonstandard use of *was* is not differentiated by broad geographic locale, i.e. North American vs. British, or even national locale, i.e. northern vs. southern Britain. Instead, the rates of nonstandard *was* are high everywhere, except in GYV, the variety which has evolved much more closely in tandem with mainstream developments in English than the other locales. This result suggests that the use of nonstandard *was* may be the result of differential contact with prescriptive norms. The overarching fact that use of nonstandard *was* is a pan-variety effect supports the hypothesis that *was/were* variation may be the result of vernacular primitives.

As with the analysis of *past temporal reference*, however, the overall distribution of forms tells us that all the varieties make extensive use of this nonstand-

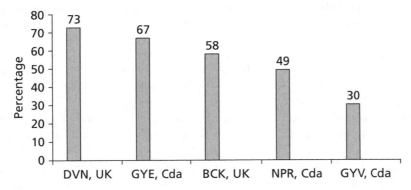

Figure 28.1 Overall distribution of *was* in 2nd person singular, 1st, 2nd, and 3rd person plural

ard feature, but tell us little about possible internal constraints that differentiate the communities.

As discussed earlier, at least three linguistic features can be extrapolated from the historical and synchronic record. This presents three diagnostic constraints with which to compare and contrast varieties. First, consider the use of *was/were* according to grammatical person and number of the subject.

8.1 Grammatical person

Figure 28.2 shows the distribution of *was*, but now separates the data into each of the grammatical persons for each of the communities. Where are the

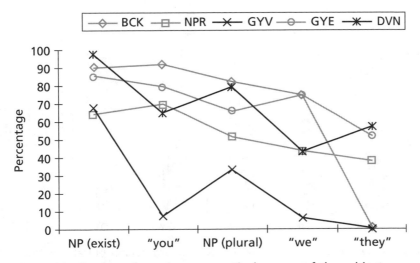

Figure 28.2 Distribution of *was* by *grammatical person* of the subject

similarities and differences? These results reveal that some communities favor the use of *was* in certain contexts. First, consider plural existential constructions. This context favors the use of *was* across all communities, a correlation which has been traced back to the Old English period (Visser 1970), and which is widely reported in all contemporary varieties of English (Britain forthcoming, Britain and Sudbury 1999, Eisikovits 1991, Meechan and Foley 1994, Schilling-Estes and Wolfram 1994, Tagliamonte 1998b).

More importantly however, consider *non*-existential use of *was*. In three varieties, BCK, NPR, and GYE, this feature patterns according to a very similar hierarchy – 2nd person singular tends to have the highest rates, then 3rd person plural NPs, then 1st person plural, and finally 3rd person pronouns.[6] Most notably, *was* is highly favored in 2nd person singular. Moreover, it is this tendency which clearly sets these three communities off from GYV and DVN where 2nd person singular has one of the lowest rates of *was*. These results separate the varieties according to the differences between northern vs. southern British patterns, which in turn correspond to what we know about the general historical dialect roots of the ancestor populations of these communities.

Nevertheless, a single diagnostic provides only one piece of evidence. Consider another.

8.2   Type of subject

Figure 28.3 displays the results for the distinction between full noun phrases and pronouns.

This historically-attested "Northern Subject Rule" is visible across all the communities. In every case, plural NP subjects exhibit a high, or relatively higher, frequency of use of *was* than with *they*.

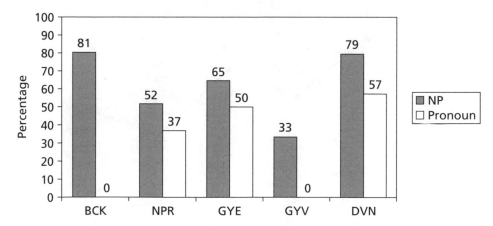

Figure 28.3   Distribution of *was* by *full* NPs vs. 3rd person plural *pronouns*

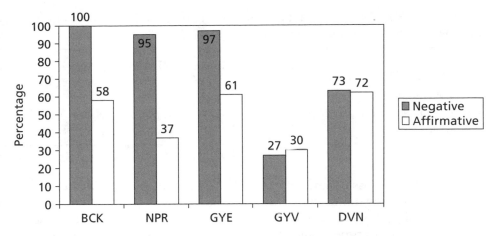

Figure 28.4   Distribution of *was* by *negative* vs. *affirmative* contexts

BCK and GYV appear very similar in this feature in that they have categorical *were* with pronouns. However, plural NPs are the *only* location where *was* occurs in GYV (see figure 28.2). Whereas in BCK *was* is robust in every other context – a pattern that it shares with NPR and GYE. Thus, the relevant finding here is the *relative* high rates of *was* with NPs as opposed to *pronouns* precisely the same *direction* of effect attested in the historical record.[7]

8.3   The effect of negation

Figure 28.4 displays the result for the distinction between negative and affirmative contexts. Once again, we observe a parallel pattern with BCK, NPR, and GYE: *was* is more frequent in negative, as opposed to affirmative contexts. In contrast, in GYV and DVN there is little to differentiate either affirmative or negative. None of the varieties exhibits the polarity effect found in Ocracoke or in southeast England.

9   Interpreting Similarities and Differences

The comparison of constraints on the use of *was* in all the varieties reveals that *was/were* variation is the result of systematic internal linguistic conditioning. It cannot be explained as the result of across-the-board regularization processes. The only pan-community effect is the strong propensity for *was* in existential contexts. Whether this is the result of diffusion, drift, or primitives remains an open question. However, in the rest of the verbal paradigm *was* exhibits a distinct and quite consistent set of constraints, and there are two sets of patterns

Table 28.5   Variable *was*: Comparison of similarities and differences in internal linguistic features across communities

	BCK	NPR	GYE	GYV	DVN
NP > Pronoun	✓	✓	✓	✓	✓
2nd person singular	✓	✓	✓	✗	✗
Negation	✓	✓	✓	✗	✗

which *contrast* across communities. Table 28.5 provides a checklist of which varieties share constraints and which do not.

Based on the parallel constraint rankings in NPR, GYE, and BCK Tagliamonte and Smith (2000) argued that the use of *was* in these varieties reflects the synchronic retention of linguistic patterns from northern varieties of British English, which would have embodied both the favoring effect of 2nd person singular *and* the favoring effect of plural NPs. The fact these communities also share the negation effect suggest that this too may have been one of the set of conditioning factors on *was/were* variation in these varieties, despite the fact that it had not been mentioned in the historical dialect literature.

However, such inter-variety parallelism does not unambiguously rule out the possibility that they represent universal constraints on variability (Wolfram 2000) or are the result of the strong vernacular tendencies discussed by Chambers (1995). Moreover, parallel constraints across one set of varieties is not conclusive proof of a common origin unless contrastive corroborating evidence can be found elsewhere. Thus, the additional data from Devon in the southwest bring crucial evidence to the comparative arena of *was/were* variation. How do the explanations offered by Tagliamonte and Smith (2000) fare with the Devon data added to the comparison?

First, figure 28.1 showed that this variety has extremely high rates of nonstandard *was* (73 percent), a rate which is on a par with the other non-mainstream varieties (BCK, NPR, and GYE), as well as many nonstandard North American dialects. However, the internal linguistic factors in figures 28.2 and 28.3 revealed that the ranking of constraints are not the same as the patterning reported for BCK, nor the African-American isolates in Nova Scotia (NPR and GYE).

All the varieties share the NP/PRO distinction, but with respect to the other two constraints, there is a clear demarcation between varieties. BCK, NPR, and GYE pattern together; while GYV and DVN pattern together. The question is why?

One way to interpret these linguistic results is to consider the history from which the varieties in these communities arose. While two (BCK and DVN) have remained in situ in Britain, the remainder are transported varieties whose original source may be traced back, at least in the first instance, to the United

States. The precise nature and proportion of the dialect features in contact in the colonial United States during the early formative period of American dialects is, at best, uncertain. Relevant to the present discussion, however, is the general fact that a disproportionate number of British northerners went to the early American backcountry or interior south (e.g. Bailyn 1986, Bailyn and DeWolfe 1986). As detailed in Poplack and Tagliamonte (2001), the original input settlers to NPR and GYE can be traced to the southern states. GYV, on the other hand, represents a variety which can be traced to the northern United States, an area which had a large proportion of input settlers from southern England.

The patterning of checks and crosses in table 28.5 reflects this. The three varieties which can be traced back to northern dialects of Britain or their input share the same three constraints, while GYV and DVN share a different set. This provides *linguistic* corroboration of the general sociohistorical facts and suggests a plausible interpretation of *was/were* variation in the North American context as being a retention of earlier dialect patterns traceable to the British Isles.

Thus, when internal linguistic constraints are consistently compared in data of appropriate size, character, and nature and if they also differentiate source varieties and/or regions, then they may hold the key to disentangling the thorny issue of dialect origins. Moreover, the convergence of evidence from three independent internal constraints which exhibit both parallel *and* constrastive patterns in a way which differentiates geographic dialects regions, diminishes the possibility that they have arisen by chance or are entirely the result of universals. Finally, such findings highlight how vital it is to consider linguistic features of English in terms of the highly differentiated regional dialects at earlier stages of the development of the language, back at its British source.

10   Using Factor Weights to Measure Grammatical Change

Up to this point we have been considering evidence from distributional analyses and constraints on morphosyntactic variation. Yet a great deal of variability in language comes from the fact that at any given point in the history of a language there are a tremendous number of linguistic features which are undergoing grammatical change. Such processes provide an invaluable area for cross-variety comparison.

Indeed, grammaticalization – a longitudinal process which may go on for centuries – necessarily produces variability in the grammar and this variability reflects the varying layers of grammaticalization attained by different forms (Hopper 1991: 23). Moreover, in the process of change, linguistic forms gradually shift from one function to another. This trajectory can be viewed in the varying strength and distribution of independent linguistic features associated with one of the evolving grammatical morphemes. Indeed, such environmental correlations are held to be the keys to viewing the mechanism of diachronic grammaticalization in synchronic data (Traugott and Heine 1991). Moreover, because this process is gradual, sometimes lasting for centuries, the tracks of language change can be preserved across great distance and time. Practically speaking, such changes should be visible in an ordered series of shifts in factor weights (Labov 1982: 76). Thus, multivariate analysis which can model complex constraints and relative weights of numerous factors that operate simultaneously on linguistic features, provides an invaluable tool for actually tracking a grammaticalizing linguistic feature (see Labov 1972: 323).

11   Contextualizing Variation in Grammatical Change

Perhaps one of the best examples of ongoing linguistic change in English grammar is the *future reference* system. A number of different forms compete to mark contexts in which the speaker is making a prediction about an event which is yet to occur (Bybee and Pagliuca 1987), as in (7) (Poplack and Tagliamonte 1999, Tagliamonte 1997a).

(7)   (a)   She say, "if you looking for good you*'ll find* good . . . you looking for bad, you *gon find* bad. Ain't it true?   (SAM/003/1282)
      (b)   It's like everything else. Some*'ll work*, and some *is* not *gonna* work. (NPR/074/1308–10)
      (c)   I think it*'s gonna get* worse before it*'ll get* better.   (OTT/117/224B/17–20)
      (d)   I knew he *wasn't gonna be* any better, and he'd be an invalid all his life because I knew he *would never be* any- I thought I *was gonna be* sick right away.   (GYV/101/B2A/7.07)
      (e)   I think she*'s gonna be* pretty cheeky. I think she*'ll be* cheeky.   (YRK/O/04–23)

Although *will* and *shall* shared the *future temporal* reference system in English for centuries, the construction *going to* has more recently begun to encroach steadily on their functions. Interestingly enough, this change is not only well-documented, but a multitude of internal linguistic factors are implicated in its increasing frequency and gradual grammaticalization.

First, consider the diachronic picture. In early Old English future time was expressed by the simple non-past, with appropriate adverbial specification, for example:

(8)   The ship sails *tomorrow*.

In this early period, two verbs *sceal* (shall) and *wille* (will) expressed present obligation and volition/willingness respectively. Gradually they both began to lose their intrinsic meaning (Traugott 1972, Visser 1963–73: 677) and entered into a long phase of variabililily. The two markers alternated according to the illocutionary act performed and the grammatical person of the subject noun (Lowth 1762/1967, Taglicht 1970, Zandvoort 1969).

   This picture was complicated by the emergence of *going to*. First attested in the late 1400s, in future-in-the-past contexts, it became well-established with a wide array of lexical verbs by the seventeenth century while still retaining strong associations with its literal meaning of "intention" and "movement" (Danchev and Kytö 1994). However, *going to* as a future reference has been gaining ground ever since, particularly in the last century (Mair 1997).

12   Operationalizing Constraints on Grammaticalization

But precisely how *going to, shall*, and *will* compete as exponents of future expression has never quite been agreed upon. Factors contributing to different readings include: connotations of modality, degree of volition, certainty or prediction, intentionality, point of view, speaker attitude, probabilty or imminence of the event taking place, etc. Fortunately, at least some of these gradient semantic distinctions may also be observed in more mechanical subsystems of the grammar. I now demonstrate how such factors can be operationalized by focusing on syntactic and lexical features attested and/or claimed to have affected *future* expression (in general) throughout the history of English (see further detail Poplack and Tagliamonte 1999).

   At least six constraints can be extracted from the literature. As mentioned earlier, the original association of *going to* with future-in-the-past is reflected in more contemporary observations. These suggest that *going to* used more frequently from the perspective of time passed than from the point of view of the present (Royster and Steadman 1923/1968), as in example (9a). Similarly, subordinate clauses are often discussed as being a favorable location for *going to*, perhaps in part due to the fact that many of the early attestations occurred in subordinate clauses, example (9b). As its meaning generalized from movement/ intention to prediction, *going to* began to appear with non-human subjects, example (9c). This kind of lapse in restriction, here, on type of subject collocated with *going to*, is a common feature of grammaticalization, and shows up as the item is generalizing in meaning – subjects are no longer confined to animates capable of movement. Thus a propensity for *going to* to be favored with non-human subjects is a sign of further grammaticalization. Another factor heavily implicated in this grammatical change is the person and number of the subject.

Factors reflecting volition, or control, a reading said to be associated with *will*. First person subjects, as in example (9d), exercise it more, and so are predicted to occur more with *will*. Lexical content is another factor implicated in the grammaticalization of a form. Increased use of *going to*, originally a verb of motion, with another verb of motion, particularly *go* as in example (9e), implies bleaching or desemanticization of the original lexical meaning. Thus, a tendency toward such collocations is consistent with further grammaticalization. Finally, *going to* has long been associated with immediacy, example (9f).

(9) (a) They told him in the conference that uh, they *was going to give* him the bishop crown.   (SAM/011/9014)
     (b) I don't know whether she's *gointa teach* the sheep yoga or what! (YRK/t/20–04)
     (c) They said his barn *was gonna burn* down.   (/NPR/074/1244)
     (d) I'm goin' up now and split now and I'*ll come* back and I'*ll get* a cup of tea or something or other and then I'*ll go back* up for another hour or so.   (GYV/107/15.45)
     (e) He's *gonna go* over there.   (YRK/™/436,16)
     (f) Now she's *gonna* make sandwiches and bologna.   (GYE/048/404)

These detailed observations from the literature provide hypotheses about the development of *going to* which in turn provide critical diagnostics for the purpose of inter-variety comparison.

13   Language Change across Varieties

Given the linguistic pathways of this grammatical change described above, consistent comparison of the forms used for *future reference* in varieties which are distinguished by their relative degree of participation in mainstream norms may provide a view of this development. Such information can then be used to situate varieties vis-à-vis each other as well as to reveal important insights into the details of the mechanism of linguistic change.

Let us now consider the results when these factors are operationalized in a multivariate analysis. Once again, we compare across some of the same communities in table 28.1, this time the three enclaves: SAM in the Dominican Republic, and African Nova Scotian English as spoken in NPR, and GYE. These three varieties are expected to contrast with the rural variety spoken in GYV. Moreover, this time, we add to the comparison a control sample of Standard Canadian English as represented by a sample of elderly residents of Ottawa, Canada. This variety should reflect the most advanced stage of development of *going to*. The results are shown in table 28.6 (abstracted from Poplack and Tagliamonte 1999). In this table significant factors are in bold.

Table 28.6 Five independent variable rule analyses of the contribution of factors selected as significant to the probability of *going to* in five North American varieties (factor groups selected as significant in bold)

	Enclaves			Rural	Urban
	SAM	NPR	GYE	GYV	OTT
Overall tendency:	**0.59**	**0.55**	**0.50**	**0.31**	**0.48**
Total N:	**396**	**723**	**994**	**199**	**302**
Point of reference					
Past	**0.85**	**0.86**	**0.86**	**0.67**	**0.92**
Speech time	**0.44**	**0.40**	**0.43**	**0.45**	**0.40**
Range	*41*	*46*	*43*	*22*	*52*
Type of clause					
Subordinate	0.58	**0.68**	**0.69**	0.59	0.55
Main	0.48	**0.46**	**0.45**	0.47	0.48
Range	*10*	*22*	*24*	*12*	*7*
Animacy of subject					
Human	0.50	0.50	0.50	0.50	0.48
Non-human	0.49	0.52	0.53	0.48	0.59
Range	*1*	*2*	*3*	*2*	*11*
Grammatical person					
Non-first person	0.50	0.51	**0.57**	0.54	**0.61**
First person	0.50	0.49	**0.42**	0.46	**0.38**
Range	*0*	*2*	*15*	*8*	*23*
Lexical content					
Verb of motion	**0.34**	**0.33**	**0.35**	**0.32**	0.51
Other verb	**0.56**	**0.54**	**0.54**	**0.61**	0.50
Range	*22*	*21*	*19*	*29*	*1*
Proximity in the future					
Immediate	0.47	0.49	0.53	**0.66**	0.59
Non-immediate	0.51	0.52	0.48	**0.35**	0.43
Range	*4*	*3*	*5*	*21*	*16*

Source: Poplack and Tagliamonte (1999)

I focus here on: (1) the constraint hierarchies of each of these effects, that is the ordering of factors within a linguistic factor group and (2) how this order reflects the direction predicted by the hypotheses in the literature. There are the noteworthy correspondences across varieties. Looking across the rows for each of the features under investigation, the relation of more to less in each factor (the constraint hierarchy), for each variety is virtually identical across the board.

There are only two places where these six varieties can be differentiated. The first is the effect of proximity in the future. Here, the five varieties partition into two groups, with the dividing line being between the three enclave varieties and the others. *Going to* is clearly favored for immediate future reference (consistent with prescriptive characterizations) in GYV and OTT; but there is no effect of temporal specialization in any of the enclaves. The second feature distinguishing the varieties is the effect of animacy. Only in OTT is *going to* favored for inanimate subjects, a context which is claimed to represent the most generalized and hence the most grammaticalized for *going to* (Bybee et al. 1994: 5).

The strength of these effects differs across varieties, as measured by the numbers for the *range*. *Point of reference* is one of the strongest constraints operating on the variation across all the varieties, while the effects of other factors shift in systematic ways. *Going to* rarely occurs with a (main) verb of motion. This avoidance of "redundancy," dating back to the time that *going to* was itself mainly perceived as a motion verb, is evidenced only in the enclave/rural communities. It has been neutralized in OTT. In contrast, an OTT innovation favoring *going to* with non-human subjects (.59) cannot be detected in any of the other varieties. These differences can be interpreted as a result of the fact that the different varieties are located at different points on the continuum of the grammaticalization of *going to*.

The position of GYV is pivotal. It shares its remoteness and relative isolation with the neighboring GYE (as well as with the other enclaves), but shares ethnic, racial, and other attendant characteristics with urban OTT. Interestingly, however, in its progress along the cline of grammaticalization, as measured by the range, Nova Scotian Vernacular English spoken in GYV appears to be more closely aligned with the African-origin enclaves: the effects of clause type and lexical content remain greater in these varieties when compared with OTT, while the effects of animacy and grammatical person of the subject have neutralized or are in the process thereof. On a fifth measure, point of reference, GYV has a much lower range than any of the others. Only on one measure, proximity in the future, is GYV aligned with urban OTT, i.e. along racial and ethnic lines.

These findings suggest that the language spoken by isolated speakers, whether of African or British origin, instantiates constraints that were operative at an earlier stage of the English language, and which are now receding from mainstream varieties.

Once again, we may ask if the comparative method provides conclusive evidence? As convincing as these inter-variety correspondences are, further exploitation of the comparative method can bolster the evidence even more.

The fact of the matter is that these findings are based on *separate* varieties of English spoken in different communities. These were in turn taken to reflect different points along the trajectory of grammaticalization of *going to* as a marker of *future reference* in the history of the English language. But how do we know that these inter-variety differences are actually the result of language change happening at different rates? Could they instead be the result of spontaneous parallel developments? Another interesting question is to what extent such claims can be corroborated by evidence from change in *apparent time* in *one* variety? As Bybee and Pagliuca (1987: 297) suggest, it is necessary to conduct an analysis of the use of grammaticalizing morphemes "as these changes are taking place." A further question is to what extent the conditioning factors reported in a North American context can be replicated on varieties of English elsewhere – particularly in the geographic context where the grammatical change originated.

14 Language Change in Apparent-time

In this section, I illustrate a quantitative analysis of the *future reference* system in a British variety of English (YRK, see table 28.1). Further, the data sample in table 28.7 was designed to include three broad age groups in order to examine the grammaticalization of *going to* in apparent-time in a single speech community.

In this demonstration the data set was coded, analyzed, and then configured for variable rule analysis to replicate the analyses in table 28.6. For the cross-generational comparison I focus on the relative *importance* of each factor (as indicated by its range), and above all, the extent to which its constraint hierarchy is shared by the other age groups. These findings will be interpreted in terms of the progress of each generation along the cline of grammaticalization of *going to* as a marker of *future reference*. The results are shown in table 28.8.

There are not only consistent parallels in the constraint ranking of factors across age groups, they are nearly identical to the hierarchy of constraints for the North American varieties in table 28.6. Moreover, these results are consistent with the known trajectory of *going to*. The same path is visible, in the

Table 28.7 Distribution of sub-sample members

	Male	Female	Total
20–35	9	8	17
35–65	7	10	17
65+	10	10	20
Total	26	28	54

Table 28.8   Three independent variable rule analyses of the contribution of factors selected as significant to the probability of *going to* in three age groups in the city of York (factor groups selected as significant in bold)

	Britain (northern England)		
	Young	Middle	Old
Overall tendency:	**0.36**	**0.32**	**0.25**
Total *N*:	**534**	**387**	**409**
Point of reference			
Past	**0.85**	**0.65**	**0.80**
Speech time	**0.45**	**0.48**	**0.44**
Range	*40*	*17*	*36*
Type of clause			
Subordinate	0.56	0.55	0.52
Main	0.49	0.49	0.50
Range	*7*	*6*	*2*
Animacy of subject			
Human	0.50	0.56	0.51
Non-human	0.50	0.49	0.39
Range	*0*	*7*	*12*
Grammatical person			
Non-first person	**0.58**	**0.58**	0.52
First person	**0.41**	**0.40**	0.48
Range	*17*	*18*	*4*
Lexical content			
Verb of motion	0.53	**0.29**	0.47
Other verb	0.50	**0.52**	0.50
Range	*3*	*23*	*3*
Proximity in the future			
Immediate	**0.61**	0.48	0.46
Non-immediate	**0.45**	0.51	0.53
Range	*16*	*3*	*7*

Source: Tagliamonte (1997a)

behavior of each measure of grammaticalization in apparent-time just as it was visible across varieties.

Point of reference is one of the strongest effects on the choice of *going to*. The constraint ranking of type of clause is the same for all three age groups. However, it is the factors that are shifting in strength and significance that are most revealing. First, allocation of *going to* to proximate future reference is exhibited in the statistically significant effect amongst the youngest speakers only. Second, the neutrality between 1st vs. other grammatical subjects in the oldest generation shifts to a statistically significant, favoring effect of *going to* with 1st person subjects in the two younger generations. Third, the tendency for use of *going to* with animate nouns, apparent in the lower factor weights for non-human subjects in the oldest generations, is neutralized in the youngest generation. Such incremental alternations in apparent-time are consistent with the gradualness of grammatical change and reflect an ordered series of shifts in factor weights of the type noted by Labov (1982: 76). Moreover, each of the trends is comparable to the findings from the North American varieties studied previously. This provides additional corroboration that the effects are typical of English and part of the broader grammatical changes underway in the *future reference* system of the language.

Let us now compare the results from the British data and the North American data and focus on the factors most heavily implicated in grammatical change. Consider the factor weights for grammatical person. The patterning for the middle and youngest generations in YRK is similar to the elderly speakers in OTT, GYV, and GYE. Next, consider the oldest age group in York. Their patterning of constraints is quite distinct from the middle and younger age groups in the same community in that there is no effect. But notice how similar the overall pattern here is to SAM and NPR – two African-American isolates. Now, consider the proximity in the future results. Here, the youngest speakers in York are also not patterning with their elders. There is a distinct favoring effect of proximate future reference in the youngest generations, but not in the middle or oldest generation. Once again, the youngest generation in York are patterning like the elderly speakers from GYV and OTT, the two varieties representing a further advanced step along the grammaticalization cline for *going to*.

Thus, with respect to these two constraints which are highly implicated in the ongoing grammaticaliztion of *going to*, we can now make the observation that the *youngest* generation in Britain looks like the *oldest* generation in Canada. Perhaps even more surprisingly, however, is that the *oldest* generation in Britain looks much like the African-American enclaves in North America.

The two analyses in conjunction with one another provide corroborating evidence for a number of hypotheses. They suggest that grammatical change can be viewed in synchronic data. Further, the details of the lexical history of a grammaticalizing form appear to be reflected in variable constraints on its grammatical distribution. This may be viewed across sister varieties, as well as across different generations of the same community. The differences and similarities across the generations in York *and* across varieties in both Britain and North America can be attributed to the fact that they reflect different points on the pathway of change of *going to* as a marker of *future reference* in English. This also lends support to the hypothesis that the relative *degree* of grammaticalization across *communities* may be related to the different ecological circumstances of their sociocultural history (Poplack and Tagliamonte 1999, Tagliamonte and Smith 2000). Finally, the multidimensional comparative perspective has revealed an additional and broader dimension. Grammaticalization of *going to* has progressed more quickly in North America than in Britain, and there appears to have been an acceleration of that change in the last 50–60 years. Further comparative research will undoubtedly fill in more of this emerging picture.

16   Conclusions

The studies I have summarized in this chapter apply a specific set of methodological principles to the study of language variation and change from a comparative cross-variety perspective. In any empirical discipline, hidden assumptions and details of method need to be laid out in an explicit way (see Lass 1993). The procedures discussed here are not new, but provide a detailed "unpacking" of the importance of accountability and proportional analysis and demonstrate the critical information provided by constraint ranking, the relative strength of effects and statistical significance. At the same time none of these lines of evidence is conclusive without additional procedures. Checking individual vs. group patterns, lexical effects, statistical fluctuation from small cells, interaction between constraints, and other problems are all a part of the method illustrated here, but I have not had enough space to elaborate on these details (see e.g. Poplack and Tagliamonte 2001). Any of these can mitigate confidence in the conclusions that can be drawn from a given data set. Thus, while a quantitative statistical method provides a powerful tool, any comparison is only as good as the accountability of the analysis that underlies it.

As language variation and change research develops further the application of quantitative methodology and a consistent comparative dimension will undoubtedly become more important, and techniques will become more refined. Such developments will increase the need for detailed linguistic criteria for determining the provenance or system membership of linguistic features. Moreover, as more data sets are discovered, collected and added to the body of materials available for analysis it will become even more critical to maintain rigorous and replicable standards in method. Although comparative reconstruction can be complicated by numerous factors, appropriate data exploited within a methodological framework such as described here can go a long way toward fulfilling the challenges of this continually evolving field.

NOTES

1   The target of investigation will typically be varieties of a language, e.g. a dialect, but the comparison might also involve different age groups in a single community, different speakers interviewed at different points in time (e.g. Cukor-Avila 1997), or even different stages of acquisition (Hudson 1998).

2   Further information on the sociohistorical and linguistic characteristics of these varieties can be found in: Poplack and Sankoff 1987, Poplack and Tagliamonte 1989, 1991, 1994, 1999, 2001; Godfrey and Tagliamonte 1999, Jones and Tagliamonte 2000, Smith and Tagliamonte 1998, Tagliamonte 1998a, Tagliamonte and Smith 2000.

3   The issue of degree of isolation of SAM, NPR, and GYE is discussed more fully elsewhere (Poplack and Sankoff 1987, Poplack and Tagliamonte 1991, Poplack and Tagliamonte forthcoming). For further discussion of isolation in relation to BCK and DVN see (Godfrey and Tagliamonte 1999, Smith and Tagliamonte 1998) respectively.

4   Differentiation of 2nd person singular *was,* and 2nd person plural *were* is reported in a number of southern writers, but here its use was restricted and primarily stylistic (Petyt 1985, Pyles and Algeo 1993).

5   Support for a primary focus on linguistic evidence comes from a large-scale research project tracking the emergence of New Zealand English from diverse dialects which were in contact during the formative period. Trudgill et al. (2000) report that the mechanisms of dialect formation in the New Zealand context appear to have proceeded in a primarily deterministic fashion, regardless of external factors.

6   The exception is 1st person plural in GYE which has a heightened factor weight for *was* in comparison to BCK and NPR (for further discussion see Tagliamonte and Smith 2000)

7   Murray's (1873) observations acknowledge that the NP/Pro distinction is variable. His qualification is that *was* is present in NPs "though only as an alternative form."

REFERENCES

Anttila, R. (1989). *An Introduction to Historical and Comparative Linguistics.* Amsterdam and New York: John Benjamins.

Bailey, G. and N. Maynor (1985). The present tense of *be* in Southern Black Folk Speech. *American Speech* 60, 3: 195–213.

Bailey, G., N. Maynor and P. Cukor-Avila (1989). Variation in subject-verb concord in Early Modern English. *Language Variation and Change.* 1, 3: 285–300.

Bailyn, B. (1986). *The Peopling of British North America.* New York: Alfred A. Knopf.

Bailyn, B. and B. DeWolfe (1986). *Voyagers to the West: A Passage in the Peopling of America on the Eve of the*

Revolution. New York: Alfred A. Knopf.

Bickerton, D. (1975). *Dynamics of a Creole System.* New York: Cambridge University Press.

Britain, D. (forthcoming). *Was/weren't* levelling in Fenland English. *Essex Research Reports in Linguistics.*

Britain, D. and A. Sudbury (1999). There's tapestries, there's photos and there's penguins: Variation in the verb BE in existential clauses in conversational New Zealand and Falkland Island English. Paper presented at Methods X. St John's, Newfoundland, Canada.

Brunner, K. (1963). *An Outline of Middle English Grammar.* Oxford: Basil Blackwell.

Bybee, J. L. and W. Pagliuca (1987). The evolution of future meaning. In A. G. Ramat, O. Carruba and G. Bernini (eds.), *Papers from the 7th International Conference on Historical Linguistics.* Amsterdam and Philadelphia: John Benjamins. 107–22.

Bybee, J. L., R. D. Perkins and W. Pagliuca (1994). *The Evolution of Grammar: Tense, Aspect, and Modality in the Languages of the World.* Chicago: University of Chicago Press.

Chambers, J. K. (1995). *Sociolinguistic Theory: Linguistic Variation and its Social Significance.* Oxford: Blackwell Publishers.

Clarke, S. (1997a). English verbal -*s* revisited: The evidence from Newfoundland. *American Speech* 72, 3: 227–59.

Clarke, S. (1997b). On establishing historical relationships between New World and Old World varieties: Habitual aspect and Newfoundland Vernacular English. In E. W. Schneider (ed.), *Englishes around the World I.* Amsterdam: John Benjamins. 277–93.

Clarke, S. (1997c). The search for origins: Habitual aspect and Newfoundland Vernacular English. Paper presented at NWAVE 26. Laval University, Quebec City, Canada.

Cukor-Avila, P. (1997). Change and stability in the use of verbal -*s* over time in AAVE. In E. W. Schneider (ed.), *Englishes around the World I.* Amsterdam: John Benjamins. 295–306.

Cukor-Avila, P. (1999). Reordering the constraints on copula absence in African American Vernacular English. Paper presented at Aix-en-Provence, France.

Curme, G. O. (1977). *A Grammar of the English Language.* Essex, Connecticut: Verbatim.

Danchev, A. and M. Kytö (1994). The construnction *be going to* + infinitive in Early Modern English. In D. Kastovsky (ed.), *Studies in Early Modern English.* Berlin: Mouton de Gruyter. 59–77.

Eisikovits, E. (1991). Variation in subject-verb agreement in Inner Sydney English. In J. Cheshire (ed.), *English around the World: Sociolinguistic Perspectives.* Cambridge: Cambridge University Press. 235–56.

Forsström, G. (1948). *The Verb "to be" in Middle English: A Survey of the Forms.* Lund: C. W. K. Gleerup.

Fries, C. C. (1940). *American English Grammar.* New York: Appleton, Century, Crofts.

Godfrey, E. and Tagliamonte, S. (1999). Another piece for the verbal -*s* story: Evidence from Devon in Southwest England. *Language Variation and Change.* 11, 1: 87–121.

Guy, G. (1980). Variation in the group and the individual: The case of final stop deletion. In W. Labov (ed.), *Locating Language in Time and Space.* New York: Academic Press. 1–36.

Guy, G. (1991). Explanation in variable phonology: An exponential model of morphological constraints. *Language Variation and Change* 3, 1: 1–22.

Guy, G. and S. Boyd (1990). The development of a morphological class. *Language Variation and Change* 2, 1: 1–18.

Hazen, K. (1996). Dialect affinity and subject-verb concord: the Appalachian Outer Banks. *SECOL Review* 20, 1: 25–53.

Hickey, R. (ed.) (forthcoming). *The Legacy of English Dialects*. Cambridge: Cambridge University Press.

Hock, H. H. (1986). *Principles of Historical Linguistics*. Amsterdam: Mouton de Gruyter.

Hoenigswald, H. M. (1960). *Language Change and Linguistic Reconstruction*. Chicago: University of Chicago Press.

Holm, J. (1975). Variability of the copula in Black English and its creole kin. *American Speech* 59, 4: 291–309.

Hopper, P. J. (1991). On some principles of grammaticization. In E. C. Traugott and B. Heine (eds.), *Approaches to Grammaticalization*, vol. 1: *Focus on Theoretical and Methodological Issues*. Amsterdam: John Benjamins. 17–35.

Hudson, R. (1998). Looking to the future: a study of the acquisition of Future Temporal Reference. MA Research Dissertation, University of York.

Hughes, A. and P. Trudgill (1979). *English Accents and Dialects: An Introduction to Social and Regional Varieties of British English*. London: Edward Arnold.

Jespersen, O. H. (1924). *The Philosophy of Grammar*. London: George Allen and Unwin.

Jespersen, O. H. (1954). *A Modern English Grammar on Historical Principles*, vol. 6: *Morphology*. London: George Allen and Unwin.

Jones, M. and S. Tagliamonte (2000). Comparative deconstruction: Disentangling the diagnostics of

continuity and change. Paper presented at New Ways of Analyzing Variation (NWAV) 29, East Lansing, Michigan, USA. October 5–7.

Kurath, H. (1928). The origin of the dialect differences in spoken American English. *Modern Philology* 25: 385–95.

Kurath, H. (1949). *A Word Geography of the Eastern United States*. Ann Arbor: University of Michigan Press.

Kurath, H. (1964). British sources of selected features of American pronunciation: problems and methods. In D. Abercrombie and et al. (eds.), *In Honour of Daniel Jones: Papers Contributed on the Occasion of his Eightieth Birthday, 12 September 1961*. London: Longmans. 146–55.

Labov, W. (1966). *The Social Stratification of English in New York City*. Washington, DC: Center for Applied Linguistics.

Labov, W. (1970). The study of language in its social context. *Studium Generale* 23, 1: 30–87.

Labov, W. (1972). *Sociolinguistic Patterns*. Philadelphia: University of Pennsylvania Press.

Labov, W. (ed.) (1980). *Locating Language in Time and Space*. New York: Academic Press.

Labov, W. (1982). Building on empirical foundations. In W. Lehmann and Y. Malkiel (eds.), *Perspectives on Historical Linguistics*. Amsterdam: John Benjamins. 17–92.

Labov, W., P. Cohen, C. Robins, et al. (1968). *A Study of the Non-standard English of Negro and Puerto Rican Speakers in New York City*. Final report, Co-operative Research Report 3288, Vol I. U.S. Regional Survey.

Lass, R. (1993). Projection: Procedures and constraints. In C. Jones (ed.), *Historical Linguistics: Problems and*

Perspectives. London and New York: Longman. 156–89.

Lowth, R. (1762/1967). *A Short Introduction to English Grammar*, no. 18. Menston, England: The Scholar Press.

Mair, C. (1997). The spread of the *going-to*-future in written English: A corpus-based investigation into language change in progress. In R. Hickey and S. Puppel (eds.), *Language History and Linguistic Modelling*. Berlin: Walter de Gruyter. 1537–43.

Meechan, M. and M. Foley (1994). On resolving disagreement: Linguistic theory and variation – *There's bridges*. *Language Variation and Change* 6, 1: 63–85.

Meechan, M., S. Tagliamonte and S. Poplack (1996). Isolating systems in language contact: A variationist method. Paper presented at Methods IX. Bangor, Wales.

Meillet, A. (1967). *The Comparative Method in Historical Linguistics*. Paris: Librairie Honoré Champion.

Milroy, J. and L. Milroy (1993). *Real English: The Grammar of English Dialects in the British Isles*. New York: Longman.

Milroy, L. (1980). *Language and Social Networks*. Baltimore: University Park Press.

Montgomery, M. B. (1989a). Exploring the roots of Appalachian English. *English World-Wide* 10: 227–78.

Montgomery, M. B. (1989b). The pace of change in Appalachian English. *English World-Wide* 10: 227–8.

Montgomery, M. B. (1994). The evolution of verbal concord in Scots. In A. Fenton and D. A. MacDonald (eds.), *Proceedings of the Third International Conference on the Languages of Scotland*. Edinburgh: Canongate Academic Press. 81–95.

Montgomery, M. B. (1997). Making transatlantic connections between varieties of English. *Journal of English Linguistics*. 25, 2: 122–41.

Mossé, F. (1952). *A Handbook of Middle English*. Baltimore: Johns Hopkins University Press.

Murray, J. A. H. (1873). *The Dialect of the Southern Counties of Scotland: Its Pronunciation, Grammar and Historical Relations*. London: Philological Society.

Neu, H. (1980). Ranking of constraints on /t,d/ deletion in American English: A statistical analysis. In W. Labov (ed.), *Locating Language in Time and Space*. New York: Academic Press. 37–54.

Patrick, P. L. (1999). *Urban Jamaican Creole: Variation in the Mesolect*. Amsterdam: John Benjamins.

Petyt, K. M. (1985). *Dialect and Accent in Industrial West Yorkshire*. Amsterdam: John Benjamins.

Poplack, S. (ed.) (2000). *The English History of African American English*. Oxford: Blackwell Publishers.

Poplack, S. and M. Meechan (1995). Patterns of language mixture: Nominal structure in Wolof-French and Fongbe-French bilingual discourse. In L. Milroy and P. Muysken (eds.), *One Speaker, Two Languages*. Cambridge: Cambridge University Press. 199–232.

Poplack, S. and M. Meechan (eds.) (1998a). *Instant Loans, Easy Conditions: The Productivity of Bilingual Borrowing*, Special issue, *International Journal of Bilingualism*. London: Kingston Press.

Poplack, S. and M. Meechan (1998b). Introduction. How languages fit together in codemixing. Instant loans, easy conditions: The productivity of bilingual borrowing. *Journal of Bilingualism* 2, 2: 127–38.

Poplack, S. and D. Sankoff (1987). The Philadelphia story in the Spanish Caribbean. *American Speech* 62, 4: 291–314.

Poplack, S. and S. Tagliamonte (1989). There's no tense like the present: Verbal *-s* inflection in Early Black English. *Language Variation and Change* 1, 1: 47–84.

Poplack, S. and S. Tagliamonte (1991). African American English in the diaspora: The case of old-line Nova Scotians. *Language Variation and Change* 3, 3: 301–39.

Poplack, S. and S. Tagliamonte (1994). *-S* or nothing: Marking the plural in the African American diaspora. *American Speech* 69, 3: 227–59.

Poplack, S. and S. Tagliamonte (1999). The grammaticalization of *going to* in (African American) English. *Language Variation and Change* 11, 3: 315–42.

Poplack, S. and S. Tagliamonte (2001). *African American English in the Diaspora: Tense and Aspect*. Oxford: Blackwell Publishers.

Pousada, A. and S. Poplack (1982). No case for convergence: The Puerto Rican Spanish verb system in a language-contact situation. In J. A. Fishman and G. D. Keller (eds.), *Bilingual Education for Hispanic Students in the United States*. New York: Teachers' College, Columbia University. 207–37.

Pyles, T. (1964). *The Origins and Development of the English Language*. New York: Harcourt, Brace and World.

Pyles, T. and J. Algeo (1993). *The Origins and Development of the English Language*. Orlando: Harcourt Brace.

Rickford, J. (1986). Some principles for the study of Black and White speech in the south. In M. B. Montgomery and G. Bailey (eds.), *Language Variety in the South*. Alabama: University of Alabama Press. 38–62.

Rickford, J. R. (1991). Contemporary source of comparison as a critical window on the Afro-American linguistic past. In W. F. Edwards and D. Winford (eds.), *Verb Phrase Patterns in Black English and Creole*. Detroit: Wayne State University Press. 302–23.

Rickford, J. R. and R. Blake (1990). Copula contraction and absence in Barbadian English, Samaná English and Vernacular Black English. In K. Hall, J.-P. Koenig, M. Meecham, S. Reinman and L. A. Sutton (eds.), *Proceedings of the Sixteenth Annual Meeting of the Berkeley Linguistic Society*. Berkeley: Berkeley Linguistics Society. 257–68.

Royster, J. F. and J. M. Steadman (1923/1968). The "going-to" future. In *Manly Anniversary Studies in Languages and Literature*. Freeport, NY: Books for Libraries Press. 394–403.

Sankoff, D. (1988). Sociolinguistics and syntactic variation. In F. J. Newmeyer (ed.), *Linguistics: The Cambridge Survey*. Cambridge: Cambridge University Press. 140–61.

Santa Ana, Otto (1996). Sonority and syllable structure in Chicano English. *Language Variation and Change*. 8, 1: 63–90.

Schiffrin, D. (1996). Narrative as self-portrait: Sociolinguistic constructions of identity. *Language in Society* 25: 167–203.

Schilling-Estes, N. and W. Wolfram (1994). Convergent explanation and alternative regularization patterns: *Were/weren't* leveling in a vernacular English variety. *Language Variation and Change* 6, 3: 273–302.

Singler, J. V. (1991). Copula variation in Liberian Settler English and American Black English. In W. F. Edwards and D. Winford (eds.), *Verb Phrase Patterns in Black English and Creole*. Detroit: Wayne State University Press. 129–64.

Smith, J. and S. Tagliamonte (1998). "We were all thegither . . . I think we was all thegither": *was* regularization in

Buckie English. *World Englishes* 17: 105–26.

Tagliamonte, S. (1997a). Grammaticalization in apparent time: Tracing the Pathways of "gonna" in the city of York. Paper presented at Québec City, Canada.

Tagliamonte, S. (1997b). Obsolescence in the English Perfect? Evidence from Samaná English. *American Speech* 72(1): 33–68.

Tagliamonte, S. (1998a). Modelling an emergent grammar: Past temporal reference in St Kitts Creole in the 1780's. In P. Baker, A. Bruyn and N. Shrimpton (eds.), *St Kitts and the Atlantic Creoles*. Westminster: Westminster University Press. 201–36.

Tagliamonte, S. (1998b). *Was/were* variation across the generations: View from the city of York. *Language Variation and Change* 10(2): 153–91.

Tagliamonte, S. (1999). Back to the roots: What British dialects reveal about North American English. Paper presented at Methods X, St John's, Newfoundland, Canada. August 1–6, 1999.

Tagliamonte, S. and S. Poplack (1988). How Black English *past* got to the present: Evidence from Samaná. *Language in Society* 17(4): 513–533.

Tagliamonte, S., S. Poplack and E. Eze (1997). Pluralization patterns in Nigerian Pidgin English. *Journal of Pidgin and Creole Languages* 12(1): 103–29.

Tagliamonte, S. and J. Smith (2000). Old *was*; new ecology: Viewing English through the sociolinguistic filter. In S. Poplack (ed.), *The English History of African American English*. Oxford: Blackwell Publishers. 141–71.

Taglicht, J. (1970). The genesis of the conventional rules of "shall" and "will". *English Studies* 51(3): 193–213.

Thomason, S. G. and T. Kaufman (1988). *Language Contact, Creolization and*

Genetic Linguistics. Berkeley and Los Angeles, California: University of California Press.

Traugott, E. C. (1972). *A History of English Syntax: A Transformational Approach to the History of English Sentence Structures*. New York: Holt, Rinehart and Winston.

Traugott, E. C. and B. Heine (1991). Introduction. In E. C. Traugott and B. Heine (eds.), *Approaches to Grammaticalization*. Amsterdam: John Benjamins. 2–14.

Trudgill, P., E. Gordon, G. Lewis et al. (2000). Determinism in new-dialect formation and the genesis of New Zealand English. *Journal of Linguistics* 36: 299–318.

Visser, F. (1963–73). *An Historical Syntax of the English Language*. Leiden: E. J. Brill.

Weinreich, U., W. Labov and M. Herzog (1968). Empirical foundations for a theory of language change. In W. P. Lehmann and Y. Malkiel (eds.), *Directions for Historical Linguistics*. Austin, TX: University of Texas Press.

Winford, D. (1992). Back to the past: The BEV/Creole connection revisited. *Language Variation and Change* 4: 311–57.

Wolfram, W. (1999). Principles of donor dialect attribution. Paper presented at Methods X, Memorial University of Newfoundland, St. John's, Newfoundland, Canada.

Wolfram, W. (2000). Issues in reconstructing earlier African-American English. *World Englishes* 19(1): 39–58.

Wolfram, W. and D. Hatfield (1984). *Tense Marking in Second Language Learning: Patterns of Spoken and Written English in a Vietnamese Community*. Washington, DC: Center for Applied Linguistics.

Wolfram, W. and N. Schilling-Estes (to appear). Remnant dialects in the coastal United States. In R. Hickey (ed.), *The Legacy of Colonial English: A Study of Transported Dialects*. Cambridge: Cambridge University Press.

Wolfram, W. and J. Sellers (1999). Ethnolinguistic marking of past be in Lumbee Vernacular English. *Journal of English Linguistics* 27: 94–114.

Wolfram, W., E. Thomas and E. Green (1997). Reconsidering the development of AAVE: Insights from isolated African American speakers. Paper presented at NWAVE 26, Québec City.

Young, R. and R. Bayley (1996). VARBRUL analysis for second language acquisition research. In R. Bayley and D. R. Preston (eds.), *Second Language Acquisition and Linguistic Variation*. Amsterdam: John Benjamins. 253–306.

Zandvoort, R. W. (1969). *A Handbook of English Grammar*. London: Longman, Green.

29 Language Death and Dying

WALT WOLFRAM

For as long as humans have used language to communicate, particular languages have been dying. In an important sense, obsolescence is simply part of the natural life cycle of language. At the same time, language death has taken on heightened significance in recent decades because it is occurring in epidemic proportions.[1] According to Krauss (1992), up to 90 percent of the world's estimated 6,000 languages face possible extinction in this century, including 80 percent of the languages of North America. By comparison with endangered biological species, language endangerment is astronomical; biologists estimate that less than 8 percent of all mammals and less than 3 percent of all birds are imperiled. Nonetheless there is little public concern over the state of the world's languages while concern for endangered biological species is considered an international crisis.

The proliferation of symposia, special interest groups, and publications (e.g. Dorian 1989, Hale et al. 1992, Robins and Uhlenbeck 1991, Wolfram 1997, Grenoble and Whaley 1998a) dedicated to obsolescing language varieties in the last couple of decades points to the escalating severity of language endangerment. On a theoretical level, the loss of a language variety without adequate documentation deprives language scientists of an essential database for inquiry into the general knowledge of human language; on a social level, it deprives people of one of the most integral components of diverse cultural behavior (Hale 1998). Both the theoretical and humanistic issues underscore the concern for language death here, but our focus is on describing and understanding the process of language death as a sociolinguistic phenomenon rather than the theoretical and/or practical implications of the situation.

Although the traditional treatment of language death limits this designation to whole languages typically existing in bilingual contexts, our treatment extends this focus to include obsolescing varieties of a language in monolingual contexts as well, following the argument offered in Wolfram and Schilling-Estes (1995) and Schilling-Estes and Wolfram (1999). In fact, the empirical study of dialect death in a monolingual context informs our understanding of the linguistic process and the sociolinguistic context of language obsolescence in significant ways.

1 Types of Language Death

Campbell and Muntzel (1989) identify four primary types of language death, each of which has linguistic and sociolinguistic consequences.

1.1 Sudden language death

Sudden language death occurs when a language abruptly disappears because its speakers die or are killed. In such cases (e.g. Tasmanian; Nicoleño, a Native American Indian language in California), the transitional phase is so abrupt that there are few if any structural consequences as the language dies. It is, of course, possible for an already-dying language to suddenly become extinct, so that this type of death is not necessarily mutually exclusive with other types, but it is also possible for sudden language death to affect a monolingual group of speakers.

1.2 Radical language death

This process resembles sudden language death in terms of the abruptness of the process, but is distinguished by the shift to another language rather than the complete disappearance of the speakers of a language. In radical language death, speakers simply stop speaking the language as a matter of survival in the face of political repression and genocide. Campbell and Muntzel (1989) cite radical language death for several Native American languages in El Salvador after an Indian uprising in the 1930s. Those thought to be Indian by appearance, including language use, were rounded up and killed in wanton acts of genocide. Many speakers of indigenous languages simply abandoned their native languages to avoid recognition as Indians. In such cases of language abandonment, there are still speakers who were once productively competent in the language, so there may be linguistic consequences on speakers' use of the language after long-term non-use or covert use (Holloway 1997). For example Bereznak and Campbell (1996) note that speakers in this situation may retain good command of the phonology while losing productive use of some of the lexicon over years of non-productive language use. There are also reports of a "recovery process" as speakers may start to use the language productively again after a period of disuse (Torres 1989: 66) or even a type of recovery as native speakers consult intensively about their language with linguists (Hill 1979).

1.3   Gradual language death

The most common type of language death, and the one most critical for our examination of language variation here, is the case of language loss due to "the gradual shift to the dominant language in a contact situation" (Sasse 1992: 22). In such cases, there is often a continuum of language proficiency that correlates with different generations of speakers. For example, fewer younger speakers use the dying language variety and with less proficiency in more restricted contexts than their older cohorts within the community; speakers who do not have a full range of functional or structural competency in the language have often been labeled *semi-speakers* (Dorian 1977), though the label obviously covers a wide range of proficiency levels.

1.4   Bottom-to-top language death

The distinguishing feature of bottom-to-top language death is the way in which the situational contraction of language use takes place. In many cases, a dying language will be retained in more casual and informal contexts while it is not used in more formal settings. In the case of bottom-to-top language death, the language loss takes place in everyday conversation and casual settings while the language is retained in more formal, ritualistic contexts. This contraction follows the Latinate pattern where the language was used in formal ecclesiastical contexts long after it died in everyday conversation.

1.5   Discussion

A couple of qualifications should be made about Campbell and Muntzel's (1989) taxonomy of language death. First, the various types of processes are not mutually exclusive so that, for example, a language undergoing gradual language death may suddenly disappear due to changes in social and political circumstances, or going through radical language death may actually be maintained covertly while it is not used in public interaction. It should also be noted that the process of dying is often much more complex than models of death that presume a unidimensional recession continuum in terms of language form and function. For example, Schilling-Estes's (1998) study of the performance register in the moribund Ocracoke dialect spoken on the Outer Banks of North Carolina does not show a simple top-to-bottom or a bottom-to-top stylistic recession in the use of a traditional dialect icon. Instead, there is a complex array of factors that come into play, ranging from a variety of situational contexts to the proactive personal initiative of speakers in the construction of a linguistic self. Detailed analyses of obsolescing forms suggest that their decline cannot be reduced neatly to a universally predictable regression slope. In fact, as we shall see, it cannot even be assumed that the reduction of language forms is the only path to obsolescence.

2 Causes of Language Death

The factors leading to language death are non-linguistic rather than linguistic, and may involve a wide array of variables. For example, Campbell (1994) includes the following factors responsible for language death:

> Discrimination, repression, rapid population collapse, lack of economic opportunities, on-going industrialization, rapid economic transformation, work patterns, migrant labor, communication with outside regions, resettlement, dispersion, migration, literacy, compulsory education, official language policies, military service, marriage patterns, acculturation, cultural destruction, war, slavery, famine, epidemics, religious proselytizing, resource depletion and forced changes in subsistence patterns, lack of social cohesion, lack of physical proximity among speakers, symbolism of the dominant language . . . , stigmatization, low prestige of the dying variety, absence of institutions that establish norms (schools, academics, texts), particular historical events, etc.   (Campbell 1994: 1963)

Taxonomies of the causes for language endangerment and death (e.g. Grenoble and Whaley 1998b, based on a typology of minority languages by Edwards 1992) generally include both *macro-variables* referring to broader situations external to the community and *micro-variables* relating to specific factors affecting a particular speech community. On a macro-level, for example, general economic conditions and the emergence of telecommunications technology may affect different language groups in varied situations, whereas on a micro-level, the specific local economy and particular patterns of telecommunicative access impact the everyday life of the speech community in a distinctive way.

Most inventories of language endangerment include economic, political, ideological, ecological, and cultural factors. One of the most prominent factors is economics; in fact, Grenoble and Whaley (1998b: 31) point out that "for endangered languages one must take into account the potential of economic issues to outweigh all others combined." They note that over and over again, relinquishing a native language variety is tied to the belief that success in another language is crucial for economic survival and advantage. Furthermore, economics may impact a minority community's ability to maintain its indigenous language due to the cost of published materials, schools, and minority language media.

Political factors involve asymmetrical relations of power between different ethnic and social groups. Languages representing politically subordinate groups are more likely to undergo shift than those associated with dominant groups, although there are well-known exceptions where the language of the politically oppressed group has been retained while the language of the dominant group is lost (Fasold 1984: 217). Most notable is the shift to English by the Norman conquerors of England in the eleventh century (Kahane and Kahane 1979). Political power is also typically related to other important variables accounting for language loss, including economic advantage, cultural ethnocentrism, and ideological indoctrination.

Ideological factors include assumed belief systems and underlying values about language use and diversity. For example, one of the reasons that there is so little public concern for endangered languages in the USA is the widespread belief that language diversity only impedes communication and that world understanding would actually increase significantly if everyone spoke the same language – English. This ideology underscores the "unifying" function of a standard language (Garvin and Mathiot 1956) and justifies an attitude of monolingual ethnocentrism in the USA. In the process, it promotes general disregard for maintaining minority languages.

Ecological factors include geographical location and physical environment, as well as population demographics. The numbers and concentrations of speakers and their physical proximity to other groups are important factors in language maintenance and death (Thomason forthcoming). On a micro-level, the kinds of social networks within the community and the interactions of community members with outsiders are essential variables in the maintenance and recession of a language variety.

At the same time, cultural values have to be considered along with patterns of contact. Henning Andersen (1988) observes that it is not uncommon for communities that are becoming more open in terms of increasing contacts with the outside world to remain psychologically closed; nor is it unheard of for relatively closed communities to be psychologically open, wholeheartedly embracing the cultural and linguistic innovations they happen to encounter. Thus, Andersen urges that a distinction be drawn between *open* vs. *closed* communities and *endocentric* vs. *exocentric* ones (1988: 74–5), with the former distinction referring to levels of contact with the outside world and the latter referring to the degree to which the community is focused on its own internal norms or is more outwardly focused. Andersen maintains that community attitudes often play a far greater role in guiding the directionality of change in contact situations than levels of contact itself. Grenoble and Whaley (1998b: 24) state that "subjective attitudes of a speech community towards its own and other languages are paramount for predicting language shift" and Grinevald (1998: 142) observes that "Language loss is . . . mostly a matter of shift in language loyalty."

Both broad-based macro- and micro-variables are involved in language death, and socio-political, sociocultural, sociopsychological, and sociodemographic variables must be factored into understanding the social context of language demise. Some of these factors may take precedence over others in a particular language contact situations, but most cases of language loss are framed by an interrelated, multidimensional set of social conditions.

3 Models of Language Loss

According to Cook (1989: 235), the most consistently reported phenomena for dying languages are "(a) structural (and stylistic) simplifications and (b) dramatic increases of variability due to incongruent and idiosyncratic 'change'." In fact, in some instances, language "decay" and language loss are simply assumed to be inextricably linked (e.g. Dressler 1988). Although there is ample support for a *dissipation model* of language death (Schilling-Estes and Wolfram 1999) in which language structures and functions are reduced, it cannot simply be assumed that this is the only alternative for language loss. Thus, Swadesh (1948: 235) observes that the last speaker of Yahi, a Native American language, had "a flawless command of his own language" and Dorian (1982: 31) cites Hill's (1973) observation of Native American languages in which the last speakers "either speak fairly well or not at all."

Our own research (Schilling-Estes and Wolfram 1999) on moribund varieties of English indicates that the dissipation model is not the only path for change in obsolescing language varieties. The investigation of Smith Island English (Schilling-Estes 1997, 2000; Schilling-Estes and Wolfram 1999) in the Chesapeake Bay region of Maryland shows that, as Smith Islanders come into increasing contact with the outside world, they are *not* losing the features of their dialect that serve to distinguish their speech variety from surrounding varieties and from mainstream varieties of English. Rather, their dialect is actually becoming more rather than less distinctive – and doing so rather rapidly. Nonetheless, the Smith Island dialect is classified as a moribund language variety, since it is rapidly losing speakers as more and more islanders move off the island in search of employment in the face of the declining maritime industry. The Smith Island dialect is actually characterized by a *concentration model*, in which structural distinctiveness is intensified among a reduced number of speakers.

In figures 29.1 and 29.2 we compare the change for two dialectally distinctive diphthongs, /au/ and /ai/, for three generations of speakers in Ocracoke and Smith Island. For quite different reasons, we consider both of these language varieties to be moribund. Ocracoke is being inundated by outsiders as its economy changes from a marine-based to a tourist-based service industry; as noted above, Smith Island, a traditional fishing community, is rapidly losing its population as islanders move away from the island in search of economic opportunity. On each island, speakers may realize /ai/ in *tide* or *time* with a raised nucleus, such as [ʌ¹] or [ə¹], and /au/ with a raised and/or fronted nucleus and a fronted glide, as in [hæ¹s] for *house* or [bræ¹n] for *brown*. In examining three generations of speakers in these communities, we assume the apparent-time construct (Bailey et al. 1991) with respect to language change.

Figures 29.1 and 29.2 show that the patterning of these diphthongs is changing in each community in significant but different ways. Younger speakers in Ocracoke are losing the traditional raised nucleus of the /ai/ diphthong and the fronted glide of the /au/ diphthong, whereas the younger generation on

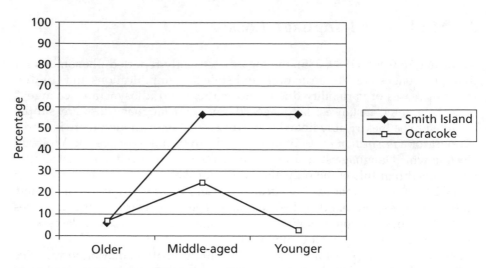

Figure 29.1 The incidence of front-gliding /au/ in Ocracoke and Smith Island for three generations of speakers

Source: Schilling-Estes and Wolfram (1999)

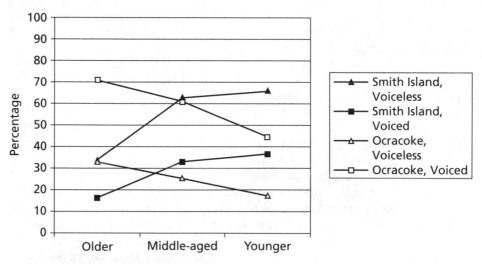

Figure 29.2 The incidence of back/raised nucleus for /ai/ in Ocracoke and Smith Island for three generations of speakers in two linguistic environments

Source: Schilling-Estes and Wolfram (1999)

Smith Island is greatly increasing these distinctive dialect traits. We thus see that the death of these language varieties is proceeding quite differently in the two communities; in the one case by receding and in the other case by heightening the use of distinctive dialect traits.

Although the concentration model is not generally discussed with respect to situations in which entire languages are lost, the survey of the structural consequences in the next section clearly presents some cases where it is implied. For example, Campbell and Muntzel (1989) indicate that some dying languages are characterized by a type of intensification in which marked features are "overused" when compared with healthy varieties of the language. However, the intensification we find on Smith Island is not simply the erratic overgeneralization or hypercorrection of a few scattered language features. Rather, it seems to represent the orderly progression of ordinary language change, if at a heightened pace. Furthermore, it seems to affect the language variety as a whole rather than just a few marked features (Schilling-Estes 1997). A similar case of genuine concentration of an entire language may be that of Copper Island Aleut. According to Vakhtin (1998), Copper Island Aleut originated as a pidgin Aleut with a Russian substrate. Through contact with Russian, it quickly became increasingly Russianized, so rapidly in fact that the youngest generation could barely communicate with the oldest. At this point, young speakers began reintroducing Aleut stems into the language – in effect rendering the language more distinct from the Russian that surrounded it. It can also be argued that cases in which the progress of language death has been halted or reversed via the implementation of revitalization programs (e.g. Mohawk; see Jacobs 1998) are instances of linguistic concentration, although the process can clearly take place apart from direct intervention.

The kinds of grammatical and lexical processes found in some instances of language loss have sometimes led researchers to regard language death and pidginization as different aspects of the same phenomenon, thus leading researchers to hypothesize a *pidginization model* of language recession in language death. Dressler and Wodak-Leodolter (1977) conclude that "language death therefore can be looked at as a sort of pidginization" and Samarin (1971: 132) observes that "pidginization should be seen as any consistent reduction of the function of language both in its grammar and its use." Whereas some kinds of reduction in obsolescing languages are analogous to the processes found in pidginization, such as the reduction of vocabulary, reduced clause subordination, emergence of simpler, more transparent surface structures, and so forth, Dorian (1978) and Schmidt (1985), among others, argue that it is simplistic and erroneous to equate a dying language with a pidgin or the pidginization process. Dorian (1978: 606–7), for example, points out that "radical morphological simplification, as found in many pidgins, is not characteristic of ESG [East Sutherland Gaelic], even among its most halting speakers, and even very near the point of extinction." She notes further that the quantity of morphological complexity and variety of allomorphs is hardly typical of that found in pidgins. Schmidt (1985) shows that Dyirbal, a moribund Australian language, shows resistance to some kinds of morphological simplification while engaging in others, which is also not typical of pidginization. Certainly, the cases of concentration we noted above offer strong counterevidence to the pidginization hypothesis.

There are also functional differences between pidgins and dying languages. Schmidt (1985: 394) notes that pidgins typically begin in more formal contact situations between strangers for purposes that often relate to commerce and trade whereas dying languages serve quite different functions and may contract differently; for example, obsolescing language varieties may be used in informal situations among people sharing close personal ties. Pidgins often serve a primary instrumental function whereas dying languages often serve an integrative function. Such evidence supports the contention that there are fundamental formal and functional differences in pidgins and the pidginization process and language death.

We should also mention the *deacquisition model* of language loss in which language death is viewed as the mirror image of language acquisition. Based on the examination of phonological change in the two moribund Athapaskan languages, Cook (1989: 241) suggests that "the degenerative process of language death produces a mirror image of the orderly developmental process of child language." As noted in the previous paragraphs, however, there is ample counterevidence to reject this hypothesis. The degeneration of language structures, for example, is not a necessary condition of death and dying. Even in cases of structural reduction, there is ample counterevidence to conclude that the order of recession is a mirror image of the hierarchical order of language acquisition.

Finally, we should mention the *matrix language turnover model* proposed by Myers-Scotton (1998; Myers-Scotton and Jake, forthcoming) to explain the morphosyntactic dimensions of language attrition. The model was proposed to account for all kinds of bilingual speech, including the kind of language attrition that may take place in language death. Briefly put, this model proposes that many instances of language death involve a shift from one dominant, or matrix language, to another, and that not all morphemes have the same freedom of appearance in either monolingual or bilingual production. Accordingly, it is proposed (Myers Scotton 1998; Myers-Scotton and Jake forthcoming) that "content morphemes" carrying thematic roles are more likely to resist loss than "system morphemes," which do not carry thematic roles. Although many cases of language attrition may follow this pattern, other factors, including focused socio-symbolic meaning associated with selective obsolescing forms (Schilling-Estes and Wolfram 1994; Schilling-Estes 2000) may inhibit (or enhance) the operation of internal linguistic principles.

As we document further in the next section, there may be quite different structural and functional paths that characterize language obsolescence. Language loss is a sociolinguistic phenomenon that is subject both to the internal cognitive principles of language organization and external social factors; therefore, no single model or explanation exclusively can account for the process of obsolescence in a given speech community.

4   Structural Levels in Language Death

Language death may affect all levels of language organization, from the formal structural properties of phonology and syntax to the contextual domains of language use. In the following sections, we discuss the consequences of language death on specific levels of language structure and use. While there are obviously shared characteristics, there are also peculiar manifestations associated with different levels of structure and function.

4.1   Phonology

Several phonological traits of dying languages have been highlighted in the research literature on language death. Among the prominent traits are (1) the reduction in inventorial and syllable structure distinctions (Dressler 1972, Andersen 1982, Cook 1989, Holloway 1997); (2) the loss of marked phonological features (Dressler 1972, Campbell and Muntzel 1989, Cook 1989, Holloway 1997, Bereznak and Campbell 1996); and (3) the increased variability of phonetic and phonemic variants (Cook 1989, Campbell 1985). None of these attributes, however, is without some important qualifications. For example, some marked features may be quite persistent and maintained during language loss under particular linguistic and sociolinguistic conditions. Thus, a marked phonological feature typologically shared by both the dying language and the replacement language tends to persist during the obsolescing process (Thomason and Kaufman 1988, Holloway 1997: 56). By the same token, the social saliency of marked phonological features during the dying process may support their maintenance (Schilling-Estes and Wolfram 1999) apart from typological congruency with the replacement language variety. Campbell and Muntzel (1989: 187), for example, cite the case of a Xinca speaker who would "sometimes go hog-wild" in the use of glottalized consonants as the speaker extended the phonetic context and frequency of glottalization well beyond the parameters of use in the healthy version of the language.

There is also evidence that so-called "peripheral language varieties" (Andersen 1988), which may include many moribund varieties, actually gives rise to an increase in exorbitant phonetic variants. We thus cannot unilaterally conclude that phonological reduction is the only alternative for receding language varieties, although it is certainly a dominant pattern. Furthermore, there is no singular hierarchical path when languages do reduce their phonological distinctions, since the reduction is affected by both independent linguistic factors and external social and psychological variables.

4.2   Morphology

Several alternatives are available to obsolescing language varieties in their morphological change. Again, the most commonly cited pattern is a reduction in the number of morphologically marked categories and in the number of allomorphs (Elmendorf 1981, Schmidt 1985, Campbell and Muntzel 1989, Dressler 1988, Huffines 1989, Holloway 1997), along with increased variability in morphological marking. The number of morphologically marked grammatical categories is often reduced, and there may be a concomitant tendency to move from polysynthetic to analytic structures in the process (Schmidt 1985, Holloway 1997). For example, Holloway (1997: 197) reports that the dying Brule dialect of Spanish spoken in Louisiana in the USA "parallels many other dying languages in its preference for the analytical future construction *ir a +* *infinitive*" as compared with a verbal suffix; Silva-Corvalán (1989: 59) observes the same pattern for Puerto Rican Spanish in New York City. Factors that affect morphological change in language death include frequency, functional load, and markedness (Andersen 1982: 97), although it is difficult to determine the interactive effect of these factors and a precise definition for variables such as "functional load."

Some researchers have also suggested that there is a predictable ordering in the decline of morphemes during language death (Markey 1980, Dressler 1981, Myers-Scotton 1998) based on language-systemic factors. However, other factors, including focused socio-symbolic meaning associated with selective obsolescing forms (Schilling-Estes and Wolfram 1994, Schilling-Estes 2000) argue against concluding that there is an irrevocable ordering hierarchy in the reduction of morphemes.

As with phonology, reduction is not the only alternative for obsolescing language varieties (Dorian 1973, Trudgill 1977, 1986, Voegelin and Voegelin 1977). Dorian (1978: 608) concluded that East Sutherland Gaelic is "dying with its morphological boots on" after observing that there is very little morphological reduction in this obsolescing variety. It is even possible for morphological restructuring in obsolescing varieties to augment and restructure the morphology as a language dies. For example, Schilling-Estes (2000) notes that on Smith Island in the Chesapeake, the system of past tense *be* marking is remorphologizing among younger speakers of this obsolescing variety of English so that leveling to *was* is used primarily for positive constructions (e.g. *I was there, you was there*, etc.) and leveling to *were* for negative constructions (e.g. *I weren't there, you weren't there*). In Smith Island, the morphological restructuring is part of a more widespread pattern of dialect intensification in a dying dialect, but it is also quite possible for morphological restructuring to take place on a selective level in language varieties that are otherwise in line with the dissipation model (cf. Schilling-Estes and Wolfram 1994).

4.3   Syntax

The syntax of dying languages may reveal several different strategies that contract the number of syntactic devices available to speakers of a dying language, resulting in what Andersen (1982: 99) refers to as the tendency to "preserve and overuse syntactic constructions that more transparently reflect the underlying semantic and syntactic relations." One manifestation is the reduction of subordinate clauses (Voegelin and Voegelin 1977, Dorian 1981, Tsitsipis 1984,

Schmidt 1985). Hill's (1989) quantitative study of language death in two Uto-Aztecan languages of Southern California over a 40-year time span shows a significant reduction in the use of relative clauses and gerunds and concomitantly, the number of verbs per sentence. As noted under the discussion of morphology, there is also an increased preference for analytic constructions in the obsolescing process (Dorian 1977, 1978, Trudgill 1977, 1986). For example, Campbell (1985) documents a change from morphological future marking to a periphrastic future in Pipil, a moribund Native American language of El Salvador, while Dorian (1983) documents the change from prepositional and pronominal affixes to free morphemes in East Sutherland Gaelic. This change toward more analytic structures is, of course, a modification that works in tandem with the loss of morphological marking. The reduction of case systems often found in dying languages may also give rise to a more fixed word order (Campbell and Muntzel 1989), as this change typically does when polysynthetic languages become more analytic in non-moribund situations.

It is possible for languages to introduce new structures as well. Thus, Campbell and Muntzel (1989) cite a case in which American Finnish adds a new syntactic structure as it recedes, namely non-co-referential gerundial clauses. In this case, however, the new structure is attributable to English, the dominant language, a fairly common phenomenon of language shift, including language loss. Many innovative cases in the syntax may be attributable to a kind of syntactic calquing from the dominant language, but it is also possible that language varieties might independently add new structures as a by-product of other changes taking place in the syntax. Schmidt (1985), for example, documents the creation of a new purposive clause conjunction as it loses some morphosyntactic categories.

4.4 Lexicon

The decline in the lexicon is one of the most prominent traits noted with reference to language death. Both linguists (Miller 1971, Dorian 1973, Andersen 1982) and native speakers comment on the reduction in the lexicon in moribund language varieties. Dorian (1973: 119) notes that "explicit comment on the decline of Gaelic focuses almost entirely on the lexicon" for speakers of East Sutherland Gaelic who regularly observe that older speakers had more words for items than younger speakers. Although it is sometimes assumed that the lexicon is "the first thing to go" in a dying language, Thomason and Kaufman (1988: 38) dispute this assumption by noting cases where other levels of language organization are affected before the lexicon.

Despite the focus on lexical decline in language death, the processes affecting the lexicon are no different from those found in language contact situations existing in healthy languages. The asymmetries found in borrowing are also typical of asymmetrical social relations in other language contact situations. Thus, massive lexical loans from the dominant language may come into the obsolescing language whereas the converse never happens. At the same time, it cannot simply be assumed that extensive lexical borrowing typifies all cases of language moribundity. Thomason (forthcoming) cites a case where speakers of Montana Salish are quite purist in resisting lexical borrowing from the dominant language in spite of overall lexical attrition, and Craig (1992) cites a similar case in Rama, a Nicaraguan language.

For the most part, the lexical inventories of speakers of moribund varieties will depend on their experience in different situational domains, with frequently used vocabulary in common domains the most persistent as the language dies. Mithun (1989: 284), for example, notes that in Oklahoma Cayuga "words for objects no longer discussed have been forgotten." The strategies for dealing with the recession of the lexicon in a moribund variety are no different from those found in other contact situations (Weinreich 1953, Thomason forthcoming). Words may be borrowed from the dominant language intact or they may be restricted or extended in their semantic reference; calques or loan translations may also take place to compensate for limited knowledge of the obsolescing language, along with circumlocution and topical avoidance. Craig (1992) cites the case of a speaker with limited knowledge of Rama who avoided topics such as fishing due a lack of appropriate vocabulary.

Although most of the focus in the literature is on the process of lexical reduction, it is important to recognize the possibility for lexical innovation as well. Gal (1989) shows that younger speakers with more limited proficiency in Hungarian in an Austrian German-Hungarian bilingual community rely on lexical innovations where more fluent speakers of Hungarian use well-established items. Once again, we cannot rule out the role of creativity and innovation as an adaptive strategy in a dying language.

4.5   *Language use*

One of the most often cited traits of obsolescing language varieties is their contraction in the contexts or domains of use, often referred to as *stylistic shrinkage.* Mougeon and Beniak (1989: 299) note that the process of dying "usually involves the decline of stylistic options which are tied to those societal domains where use of the minority language is excluded." Stylistic shrinkage in the process of language death is amply documented in the literature on language death (Campbell 1985, Gal 1984, 1989, Hill 1973, Hill and Hill 1977, Holloway 1997), with the predominant pattern restricting language use to the more casual styles as opposed to the more formal. However, as noted previously, the bottom-up model (Bereznak and Campbell 1996) is also a viable pattern for contracting language use; communities may restrict the dying language to more formal, ceremonial functions as language use in everyday situations ceases.

It is also quite possible to combine different registers in obsolescing varieties in ways that expose the dichotomy between formal and informal domains as vastly oversimplified (see Schilling-Estes in the current volume). For example, particular registers found in more formal settings of language may be retained selectively along with casual speech styles. Campbell (1985), for example, reports that traditional narratives and storytelling are no longer used in Pipil whereas Tsitsipis (1983) reports that this tradition is preserved as other dimensions of communicative competence recede in Arvanítika.

It must also be recognized that particular language functions related to the moribund status of the language may evolve during the obsolescing process. Tsitsipis (1989) notes that a moribund language may become an *object language*, attracting conscious attention and specialized language behavior. We noted the creative use of neologism exhibited by younger Hungarian speakers (Gal 1989) in conversational interactions with older, more fluent Hungarian speakers. Schilling-Estes (1998) also shows that conscious attention to a dialect icon of a moribund language variety in Ocracoke may evoke a "performance style" in which obsolescing forms are offered in rote phrases. This performance style may be used in response to situational factors of various types, but it may also be proactive in the sense that the speaker chooses to initiate the style in the presentation of self. Such cases of stylistic manipulation suggest that the use of different speech styles in moribund language varieties is much more varied and complex than the simple unidimensional casual-to-formal axis on which it is sometimes situated.

5   Variability in Language Obsolesence

Sociolinguistic study over the past three decades has indicated time and time again that there is a great deal of variability inherent in all language varieties (e.g. Labov 1966, 1969, 1972, 1994). Furthermore, this variation often reflects language change in progress. All language change implies variation although the converse does not necessarily hold (Bailey 1973). Variation between fluctuating forms should be expected in language death as well. The real question about this variation is whether it is, in the words of Cook (1989: 235) one of the "most conspicuous phenomena reported on dying languages" and whether there are "dramatic increases in variability due to incongruent and idiosyncratic change" (1989: 235). Dressler (1972) also notes that "fluctuations and uncertainties" are notable traits of dying languages, while Campbell and Muntzel (1989: 187) observe that one of the major characteristics of dying languages is the fact that "obligatory rules may come to apply optionally." Such observations suggest that the variation is unconstrained by the kinds of independent linguistic and external social constraints that have become the benchmark of variation analysis over the past several decades (Labov 1969; Cedergren and Sankoff 1974; Sankoff and Labov 1979).

Although variability is certainly one of the traits that typifies change in moribund language varieties, there exist a limited number of studies that have empirically examined the quantitative dimensions of variability in obsolescing forms (King 1989, Dorian 1994, Mougeon and Beniak 1989, Bavin 1989), and even fewer studies that frame this variation in terms of systematic constraints on variability (King 1989, Wolfram and Schilling-Estes 1995, Schilling-Estes and Wolfram 1999). Based on her study of moribund Newfoundland French variety, King (1989) concludes that variation is strongly correlated with age but that it "does not carry the weight of social meaning which variation carries in healthy speech communities"; this conclusion is also confirmed in studies by Mougeon and Beniak (1989: 309) and Bavin (1989: 283–84). The correlation with age is no doubt a function of the change in progress reflected in different generations of speakers. At the same time, King (1989) finds that "it would appear to be change without the classic social motivation, since no particular social group stands out as linguistically different" (1989: 144–5). Holloway (1997: 71) suggests that a primary reason for the lack of social correlation has to do with the fact that this variation "is not salient to its speakers." However, social saliency is not a necessary condition for establishing social and linguistic co-variance; there are many cases of correlation that exist below a conscious level (Labov 1972).

Dorian (1994), like King (1989) and Mougeon and Beniak (1989), finds that the variants examined in her detailed study of the East Sutherland Gaelic community over three decades do not appear to carry social meaning or stylistic significance; in fact, different variants of the same variable are found to be used at different points in the discourse of one speaker without any evidence of a stylistic shift. Dorian (1994: 633) thus concludes that "a profusion of variant forms can be tolerated within a small community over a long period without a discernible movement toward reduction of variants and also without the development of differences in the social evaluation of most variants." Accordingly, she proposes that *personal-pattern variation* is separate from stylistic, geographic, and proficiency-related variation. While personal pattern variation must be recognized in both healthy and moribund language varieties (Wolfram and Beckett 2000), it is possible that it may be a much more prominent trait in moribund language varieties.

With respect to independent linguistic constraints on variability, King (1989) finds that variation in obsolescing forms is quite sensitive to linguistic environment. For example, her analysis of variation in clitic pronoun usage in Newfoundland French suggests a systematic correlation with linguistic environment in much the same way that variation in healthy languages is constrained by independent linguistic constraints (Labov 1969, Cedergren and Sankoff 1974, Guy 1993). Quantitative studies of variation in interlanguage (Dickerson 1976, Tarone 1980, Wolfram 1978, 1985) add further support for the conclusion that independent linguistic constraints systematically affect the relative incidence of obsolescing variants in ways that are quite analogous to inherent variability within a self-contained language variety.

Our empirical examination of obsolescing language forms in Ocracoke (Wolfram and Schilling-Estes 1995) also indicates that the fluctuation of the variants

Table 29.1   Systematic variability for /ai/ backing and raising in Smith Island and Ocracoke

Ocracoke raising Input probability = 0.37	Smith Island raising Input probability = 0.26
Age/gender group: Older women = 0.56 Older men = 0.63 Middle-aged women = 0.52 Middle-aged men (poker group) = 0.67 Middle-aged men (Non-poker) = 0.36 Younger women = 0.32 Younger men = 0.37 *Following segment:* Vl. Obs. = 0.36 Vd. Obs. = 0.72	*Age/gender group:* Older women = 0.14 Older men = 0.42 Middle-aged women = 0.62 Middle-aged men = 0.51 Younger women = 0.55 Younger men = 0.69 *Following segment:* Vl. Obs. = 0.77 Vd. Obs. = 0.51 Nasal = 0.40 Liquid = 0.06
Chi-square per cell = 1.708 Total Chi-square = 23.911	Chi-square per cell = 0.719 Total Chi-square = 17.262

Source: Schilling-Estes and Wolfram (1999)

may be systematically constrained in ways that are no different from other types of inherent variability. That is, both independent linguistic and social constraints may affect variability. For example, consider the results of the Varbrul statistical analysis for the raising/backing of the nucleus in the diphthong /ai/ in Ocracoke and Smith Island in table 29.1. At least in Ocracoke, the backing/raising of /ai/ is clearly an obsolescing variant.

Table 29.1 shows patterned variation of the obsolescing form is quite analogous to the kind of systematic variation typical of others kinds of linguistic change. For example, following voicing affects variability in a systematic way: as shown in figure 29.2, following voicelessness favors the incidence of raising to [əɪ] and following voicing favors the incidence of backing and raising to [ʌɪ]. This constraint pattern follows that found in non-moribund varieties of English that show variation in these variants (Chambers 1973, 1995). Table 29.1 also shows that there are orderly patterns of systematic variation constrained by social factors as well, although they are not necessarily straightforward. For example, cross-sex patterning of variants is different for different generations of speaker, with women sometimes showing higher levels of raising and backing than men and sometimes lower (Schilling-Estes 1999). We also see that there is a correlation of the backing/raising for /ai/ with a particular social group of men we have designated the "poker game network," a middle-aged group of men known for their espousal of traditional ways of island life (Wolfram and Schilling-Estes 1995, 1997).

While there may be a profusion of variability in language death because of the number of linguistic structures undergoing language change simultaneously, our investigation suggests that some receding structures may, in fact, take on social meaning. This is not to say that all variability in obsolescing language varieties is socially meaningful, but it is certainly possible for some receding features to take on social significance. It may well be that a kind of *sociolinguistic focusing* takes place in language death in some speech communities, where variation in selective structures carries social meaning while variation in many other features does not.

The investigation of obsolescing forms in Ocracoke and Smith Island also lends further insight into the nature of the "increased variability" that is said to characterize dying languages. For example, in the Smith Island case, increased variability appears to be a by-product of the rapid change the dialect is undergoing rather than a product of moribundity per se. Such evidence lends support to Hill's (1989) contention that language change in language death is distinguished only by its rapidity.

It may be argued that much of the variability typifying obsolescing forms is orderly rather than "incongruent" or "idiosyncratic" and is therefore no different from the variability that characterizes healthy languages and language varieties. This is not to deny cases in which variation may overextend the use of features, as in the case of extended use of glottalized consonants by some Xinca speakers as reported by Campbell (1992: 5); he notes that the speaker "glottalized nearly every possible consonant, having failed to learn the rule." Such cases may, however, be restricted to socially noticeable language features (Schilling-Estes and Wolfram 1999). In the case of *overgeneralization*, or *hyperdialectalism* (Trudgill 1986: 66–78), forms are extended to environments where they are not linguistically expected. Cases of hyperdialectalism may parallel the "overuse" of "exotic" features that sometimes accompanies overall structural recession in language death situations (Campbell and Muntzel 1989: 188–9). There may be a linguistic and sociopsychological basis for such cases, linguistic in the sense that there are extended linguistic environments for the use of such forms and sociopsychological in the sense that these forms have become socially obtrusive or "object forms." These cases in language death do not, however, seem to be appreciably different from well-attested cases of structural and statistical hypercorrection cited in the sociolinguistic literature (Wolfram and Schilling-Estes 1998). In cases where the variability does seem to be somewhat disorderly from a linguistic point of view, we can often point to the strong social meaning attached to the variable features to explain the unusual linguistic patterning (Wolfram and Schilling-Estes 1995).

Although a number of researchers seem to hold the view that variability in language death is different from that found in ordinary language change, there is little empirical evidence to support this contention. The profusion of variation may simply be a product of the extent and rapidity of language change. In a situation where change is simultaneously affecting many different structures within the system in a compressed time frame, there will be many more items undergoing variation, thus giving the appearance that change is chaotic and incongruent. Given the rapidity of change in many cases of language death, it may well be the case that different speakers are simply more widely dispersed for more variables along the S-curve of language change (Bailey 1973), in which variation starts slowly in a limited linguistic environment, goes through a rapid mid-point of variation as it extends its structural boundaries, and ends slowly in restricted environments. Importantly, when variation is examined for specific structures undergoing change, the change cycle appears to show the kind of systematic variability found in more stable language situations as well as language variation in interlanguage (Dickerson 1976, Wolfram 1978, 1985). The variation is at least constrained by independent linguistic variables and, in some cases, may be constrained by social constraints as well.

While the empirical examination of the quantitative dimensions of language variation in moribund language situations is still in its infancy, there is no reason to suspect that such variation will turn out to be radically different from the systematic variation found in other kinds of language variation.

6   Complexity in Obsolesence

Our profile reveals that language death is a complex sociolinguistic process involving alternative paths to obsolescence. Unfortunately, the metaphor of death and decay so often used to describe language loss has tended to obscure an understanding of the varied responses to obsolescing language varieties. On all levels of languages organization we have examined, for example, innovative options are available to speakers of moribund language varieties, arguing against a simplistic, unidimensional reduction-based model of language obsolescence. Furthermore, there is a range of cultural and individual responses that may be manifested in the process of language shift, making it a dynamic sociolinguistic phenomenon. As Gal (1989) notes:

> we should examine the linguistic changes occurring during language shift not only through the metaphor of death and decay that the "pastoral" tradition provides, but also through an image of conflict and competition between differing forces – cognitive, interactional, symbolic – whose effects on the details of linguistic practice are sometimes contradictory.   (Gal 1989: 330)

The circumstances framing obsolescing language varieties are as multidimensional and complex as any other sociolinguistic situation. Obsolescing language varieties are affected by the same linguistic-cognitive principles and the same patterns of variation as those found in other language contact situations; they are also affected by an interactive array of macro- and micro-social and sociopsychological variables. Responses to the loss of a language variety are at once both collective and individualistic, and they may be reactive and/or proactive. In this respect, language death resembles the loss of human life itself: there are many paths that lead to the same ultimate destiny and a wide array of responses that affect the journey in significant ways.

NOTE

1   The term *language death* has been used in two different senses in the research literature. It has been used both for cases in which an entire language becomes extinct as well as for cases of *language shift* (Fasold 1984: 213), where a language variety is lost in one community but continues to be used in another setting. For example, even though a Hungarian dialect may be lost in a German-Hungarian community in Austria, there are still plenty of speakers of Hungarian. The sociolinguistic dynamics of language attrition discussed here seem to apply to both types of situations though it may be necessary to recognize differences in these situations for other reasons.

REFERENCES

Andersen, Henning (1988). Center and periphery: Adoption, diffusion, and spread. In J. Fisiak (ed.), *Historical Dialectology*. Berlin: Mouton de Gruyter. 39–83.

Andersen, Roger W. (1982). Determining the linguistic attributes of language attrition. In R. D. Lambert and B. F. Freed (eds.), *The Loss of Language Skills*. Rowley, MA: Newbury House. 83–118.

Bailey, Charles-James N. (1973). *Variation and Linguistic Theory*. Arlington, VA: Center for Applied Linguistics.

Bailey, Guy, Tom Wikle, Jan Tillery, and Lori Sand (1991). The apparent time construct. *Language Variation and Change* 5: 359–90.

Bavin, Edith L. (1989). Some lexical and morphological changes in Walpiri.

In Nancy C. Dorian (ed.), *Investigating Obsolescence*. Cambridge: Cambridge University Press. 267–86.

Bereznak, Catherine and Lyle Campbell (1996). Defense strategies for endangered languages. In H. Goebl, P. H. Nelde, Z. Star and W. Wölck (eds.), *Contact Linguistics: An International Handbook of Contemporary Research*. Berlin: Walter de Gruyter. 659–66.

Campbell, Lyle (1985). *The Pipil Language of El Salvador*. Berlin: Mouton de Gruyter.

Campbell, Lyle (1992). Language death. In Keith Brown and Nigel Vincent (eds.), *The Encyclopedia of Linguistics*. London: Aberdeen University Press.

Campbell, Lyle (1994). Language death. In R. E. Asher and J. M. Y. Simpson (eds.), *The Encyclopedia of Language and Linguistics*, vol. 4. Oxford/New York: Pergamon. 1960–8.

Campbell, Lyle and Martha Muntzel (1989). The structural consequences of language death. In Nancy C. Dorian (ed.), *Investigating Obsolescence*. Cambridge: Cambridge University Press. 181–96.

Cedergren, Henrietta J. and David Sankoff (1974). Variable rules: Performance as a statistical reflection of competence. *Language* 50: 333–55.

Chambers, J. K. (1973). Canadian raising. *Canadian Journal of Linguistics* 18: 113–35.

Chambers, J. K. (1995). *Sociolinguistic Theory*. Oxford: Blackwell.

Cook, Eung-Do (1989). Is phonology going haywire in dying languages? Phonological variations in Chipewyan and Sarcee. *Language in Society* 18: 235–55.

Craig, Colette (1992). Language shift and language death: The case of Rama in Nicaragua. *International Journal of the Sociology of Language* 93: 11–26.

Dickerson, Wayne B. (1976). The psycholinguistic unity of language learning and language change. *Language Learning* 26: 215–32.

Dorian, Nancy C. (1973). Grammatical change in a dying dialect. *Language* 49: 414–38.

Dorian, Nancy C. (1977). The problem of the semi-speaker in language death. *International Journal of the Sociology of Language* 12: 23–32.

Dorian, Nancy C. (1978). The fate of morphological complexity in language death: Evidence from East Sutherland Gaelic. *Language* 54: 590–609.

Dorian, Nancy C. (1981). *Language death: The Life Cycle of a Scottish Gaelic Dialect*. Philadelphia, PA: University of Pennsylvania Press.

Dorian, Nancy C. (1982). Linguistic models and language death evidence. In L. Obler and L. Menn (eds.), *Exceptional Language and Linguistics*. New York: Academic Press. 31–48.

Dorian, Nancy C. (1983). Natural and second language acquisition from the perspective of the study of language death. In R. Andersen (ed.), *Pidginization and Creolization of Language Acquisition*. Rowley, MA: Newbury House. 158–67.

Dorian, Nancy C. (1986). Abrupt transmission failure in obsolescing languages: How sudden the "tip" to the dominant language communities and families. In V. Nikiforidu, M. Van Clay, M. Niepokuj and D. Feder (eds.), *Proceedings of the Twelfth Annual Meeting of the Berkeley Linguistics Society*. Berkeley: Berkeley Linguistics Society. 72–83.

Dorian, Nancy C. (ed.) (1989). *Investigating Obsolescence: Studies in Language Contraction and Obsolescence*. Cambridge: Cambridge University Press.

Dorian, Nancy C. (1994). Varieties of variation in a very small place: Social homogeneity, prestige norms, and linguistic variation. *Language* 70: 631–96.

Dorian, Nancy C. (1998). Western language ideologies and small-language prospects. In L. A. Grenoble and L. J. Whaley (eds.), *Endangered Languages*. Cambridge: Cambridge University Press. 3–21.

Dressler, Wolfgang (1972). On the phonology of language death. *Chicago Linguistic Society* 12: 448–57.

Dressler, Wolfgang (1981). Language shift and language death – a protean challenge for the linguist. *Folia Linguistica* 12: 448–57.

Dressler, Wolfgang (1988). Language death: linguistics. In F. J. Newmeyer (ed.), *The Cambridge Survey*, vol. 4:

Language: The Socio-cultural Context. Cambridge: Cambridge University Press. 184–92.

Dressler, Wolfgang and Ruth Wodak-Leodolter (1977). Language preservation and language death in Brittany. *International Journal of the Sociology of Language* 12: 33–44.

Edwards, John (1992). Sociopolitical aspects of language maintenance and loss: Towards a typology of language minority situations. In W. Fase, K. Jaspaert, and S. Kroon (eds.), *Maintenance and Loss of Minority Languages*. Philadelphia: John Benjamins. 37–54.

Elmendorf, William (1981). Last speakers and language change: Two California cases. *Anthropological Linguistics* 23: 36–49.

Fasold, Ralph W. (1984). *The Sociolinguistics of Society*. Oxford: Blackwell Publishers.

Gal, Susan (1984). Peasant men can't get wives. In J. Baugh and J. Sherzer (eds.), *Readings in Sociolinguistics*. Englewood Cliffs, NJ: Prentice Hall. 292–304.

Gal, Susan (1989). Lexical innovation: The use and value of restricted Hungarian. In Nancy C. Dorian (ed.), *Investigating Obsolescence*. Cambridge: Cambridge University Press. 313–31.

Garvin, Paul and Madeline Mathiot (1956). The urbanization of the Guaraní language. In A. F. C. Wallace (ed.), *Men and Cultures: Selected Papers from the Fifth International Congress of Anthropological and Ethnological Sciences*. Philadelphia: University of Pennsylvania Press. 365–74.

Grenoble, Lenora A. and Lindsay J. Whaley (eds.) (1998a). *Endangered Languages: Current Issues and Future Prospects*. Cambridge: Cambridge University Press.

Grenoble, Lenora A. and Lindsay J. Whaley (1998b). Toward a typology of language endangerment. In L. A. Grenoble and L. J. Whaley (eds.), *Endangered Languages*. Cambridge: Cambridge University Press. 22–54.

Grinevald, Colette (1998). Language endangerment in South America: A programmatic approach. In L. A. Grenoble and L. J. Whaley (eds.), *Endangered Languages*. Cambridge: Cambridge University Press. 124–59.

Guy, Gregory (1993). The quantitative analysis of linguistic variation. In D. R. Preston (ed.), *American Dialect Research*. Amsterdam: John Benjamins. 223–49.

Hale, Ken (1998). On endangered languages and the importance of linguistic diversity. In L. A. Grenoble and L. J. Whaley (eds.), *Endangered Languages*. Cambridge: Cambridge University Press. 192–216.

Hale, Ken, Michael Krauss, Lucile Watahomigie, Akiri Amamoto, Colette Craig, Laverne Masayesva and Nora England (1992). Endangered languages. *Language* 68: 1–42.

Hill, Jane H. (1973). Subordinate clause density and language function. In C. Corum, T. Smith-Stark and A. Weiser (eds.), *You Take the High Node and I'll Take the Low Node: Papers from the Comparative Syntax Festival*. Chicago: Chicago Linguistic Society. 33–52.

Hill, Jane H. (1979). Language death, language contact, and language evolution. In W. McCormack and S. Wurm (eds.), *Approaches to Language: Anthropological Issues*. Mouton: The Hague. 47–78.

Hill, Jane H. (1989). The social functions of relativization in obsolescent and non-obsolescent languages. In

Nancy C. Dorian (ed.), *Investigating Obsolescence*. Cambridge: Cambridge University Press. 347–54.

Hill, Jane H. and Ken Hill (1977). Language death and relexification in Tlaxcalan Nahuatl. *International Journal of the Sociology of Language* 12: 55–69.

Huffines, Marion Lois (1989). Case usage among the Pennsylvania German sectarians and nonsectarians. In Nancy C. Dorian (ed.), *Investigating Obsolescence*. Cambridge: Cambridge University Press. 211–41.

Holloway, Charles E. (1997). *Dialect Death: The Case of Brule Spanish*. Amsterdam: John Benjamins.

Jacobs, Annette. (1998). A chronology of Mohawk language instruction at Kahnawàke. In L. A. Grenoble and L. J. Whaley (eds.), *Endangered Languages*. Cambridge: Cambridge University Press. 117–23.

Kahane, Henry and Renée Kahane (1979). Decline and survival of Western prestige languages. *Language* 55: 183–98.

King, Ruth (1989). On the social meaning of linguistic variability in language death situations: Variation in Newfoundland French. In Nancy C. Dorian (ed.), *Investigating Obsolescence*. Cambridge: Cambridge University Press. 139–48.

Krauss, Michael (1992). The world's languages in crisis. *Language* 68: 4–10.

Labov, William (1963). The social motivation of a sound change. *Word* 19: 273–307.

Labov, William (1966). *The Social Stratification of English in New York City*. Washington, DC: Center for Applied Linguistics.

Labov, William (1969). Contraction, deletion, and inherent variability of the English copula. *Language* 45: 715–62.

Labov, William (1972). *Sociolinguistic Patterns*. Philadelphia: University of Pennsylvania Press.

Labov, William (1994). *Principles of Linguistic Change: Internal Factors*. Cambridge, MA: Blackwell Publishers.

Markey, Thomas (1980). *Diffusion, Fusion, and Creolization: A Fieldguide to Developmental Linguistics*. Papiere zur Linguistik.

Miller, Wick (1971). The death of language or serendipity among Shoshoni. *Anthropological Linguistics* 13: 114–20.

Mithun, Marianne (1989). The incipient obsolescence of polysynthesis: Cayuga. In Nancy C. Dorian (ed.), *Investigating Obsolescence*. Cambridge: Cambridge University Press. 243–58.

Mougeon, Raymond and Edouard Beniak (1989). Language contraction and linguistic change: The case of Welland French. In Nancy C. Dorian (ed.), *Investigating Obsolescence*. Cambridge: Cambridge University Press. 287–312.

Myers-Scotton, Carol (1998) A way to dusty death: The matrix language turnover hypothesis. In L. A. Grenoble and L. J. Whaley (eds.), *Endangered Languages*. Cambridge: Cambridge University Press. 289–316.

Myers-Scotton, Carol and Janice L. Jake (forthcoming). Explaining aspects of codeswiching and their implications. In J. Nicol and T. Langendoen (eds.), *Bilingualism*. Oxford: Blackwell Publishers.

Robins, Robert H. and Eugenius M. Uhlenbeck (eds.) (1991). *Endangered Languages*. Oxford: Berg.

Samarin, William A. (1971). Salient and substantive pidginization. In D. Hymes (ed.), *Pidginization and Creolization of Languages*. London:

Cambridge University Press. 188–213.

Sankoff, David and William Labov (1979). On the uses of variable rules. *Language in Society* 8: 189–222.

Sasse, Hans-Jürgen (1992). Theory of language death, language decay, and contact-induced change: Similarities and differences. In M. Brenzinger (ed.), *Language Death: Factual and Theoretical Explorations with Special Reference to East Africa*. Berlin: Mouton de Gruyter. 59–80.

Schmidt, Annette (1985). The fate of ergativity in dying Dyirbal. *Language* 61: 378–96.

Schilling-Estes, Natalie (1997). Accommodation vs. concentration: Dialect death in two post-insular island communities. *American Speech* 72: 12–32.

Schilling-Estes, Natalie (1998). Investigating "self-conscious" speech: The performance register in Ocracoke English. *Language in Society* 27: 53–83.

Schilling-Estes, Natalie (1999). Reshaping economies, reshaping identities: Gender-based patterns of language variation in Ocracoke English. *Proceedings of the Fifth Berkeley Women and Language Conference*. Berkeley: Berkeley Women and Language Group. 509–20.

Schilling-Estes, Natalie (2000). Exploring morphological change: The *was/ weren't* pattern in Smith Island. Unpublished manuscript.

Schilling-Estes, Natalie and Walt Wolfram (1994). Convergent explanation and alternative regularization: *Were/weren't* leveling in a vernacular English variety. *Language Variation and Change* 6: 273–302.

Silva-Corvalán, Carmen (1989). Past and present perspectives on language change in US Spanish. *International*

Journal of the Sociology of Language 79: 53–66.

Swadesh, Morris (1948). Sociologic notes on language loss. *International Journal of American Linguistics* 14: 226–35.

Tarone, Elaine (1980). Some influences on the syllable structure of interlanguage phonology. *International Review of Applied Linguistics* 18: 139–52.

Thomason, Sarah G. (forthcoming). *Language Contact*. Edinburgh: Edinburgh University Press.

Thomason, Sarah G. and Terrence Kaufman (1988). *Language Contact, Creolization, and Genetic Linguistics*. Berkeley, CA: University of California Press.

Torres, Lourdes (1989). Mood selection among New York Puerto Ricans. *International Journal of the Sociology of Language* 79: 67–77.

Trudgill, Peter (1977). Creolization in reverse: Reduction and simplification in the Albanian dialects of Greece. *Transactions of the Philological Society 1976–1977*: 32–50.

Trudgill, Peter (1986). *Dialects in Contact*. Oxford: Blackwell Publishers.

Tsitsipis, Lukas D. (1983). Narrative performance in a dying language: Evidence from Albanian in Greece. *Word* 34: 25–36.

Tsitsipis, Lukas D. (1984). Functional restriction and grammatical reduction in Albanian language in Greece. *Zeitschrift für Balkanologie* 20: 122–31.

Tsitsipis, Lukas D. (1989). Skewed performance and full performance in language obsolescence: The case of an Albanian variety. In Nancy C. Dorian (ed.), *Investigating Obsolescence*. Cambridge: Cambridge University Press. 139–48.

Vakhtin, Nikolai (1998). Copper Island Aleut: A case of language "resurrection." In L. A. Grenoble and L. J. Whaley (eds.), *Endangered Languages*. Cambridge/New York: Cambridge University Press. 317–27.

Voegelin, Carl and Francis Voegelin (1977). Is Tübatulabal deacquisition relevant to theories of language acquisition? *International Journal of American Linguistics* 43: 333–6.

Weinreich, Uriel (1953) *Languages in Contact*. New York: Linguistic Circle of New York.

Wolfram, Walt (1978). Contrastive linguistics and social lectology. *Language Learning* 28: 1–28.

Wolfram, Walt (1985). Variability in tense marking: A case for the obvious. *Language Learning* 35: 229–53.

Wolfram, Walt (1997). Issues in dialect obsolescence: An introduction. *American Speech* 73: 1–12.

Wolfram, Walt and Dan Beckett (2000). The role of individual differences in Earlier African American Vernacular English. *American Speech* 75: 1–30.

Wolfram, Walt and Natalie Schilling-Estes (1995). Moribund dialects and the language endangerment canon: The case of the Ocracoke Brogue. *Language* 71: 696–721.

Wolfram, Walt and Natalie Schilling-Estes (1997). *Hoi toide on the Outer Banks: The story of the Ocracoke Brogue*. Chapel Hill, NC: University of North Carolina Press.

Wolfram, Walt and Natalie Schilling-Estes (1998). *American English: Dialects and Variation*. Oxford: Blackwell Publishers.

Index